TEACHER'S EDITION

PRENTICE HALL WRITING AND GRAMMAR

GRADE TWELVE

Boston, Massachusetts
Upper Saddle River, New Jersey

ISBN 0-13-200976-5

1 2 3 4 5 6 7 8 9 10   10 09 08 07 06

Program Authors

The program authors guided the direction and philosophy of *Prentice Hall Writing and Grammar: Communication in Action.* Working with the development team, they contributed to the pedagogical integrity of the program and to its relevance to today's teachers and students.

Joyce Armstrong Carroll

In her forty-year career, Joyce Armstrong Carroll, Ed.D., has taught on every grade level from primary to graduate school. In the past twenty years, she has trained teachers in the teaching of writing. A nationally known consultant, she has served as president of TCTE and on NCTE's Commission on Composition. More than fifty of her articles have appeared in journals such as *Curriculum Review, English Journal, Media & Methods, Southwest Philosophical Studies, Ohio English Journal, English in Texas,* and the *Florida English Journal.* With Edward E. Wilson, Dr. Carroll co-authored *Acts of Teaching: How to Teach Writing* and co-edited *Poetry After Lunch: Poems to Read Aloud.* Beyond her direct involvement with the writing pedagogy presented in this series, Dr. Carroll guided the development of the Hands-on Grammar feature. She co-directs the New Jersey Writing Project in Texas.

Edward E. Wilson

A former editor of *English in Texas,* Edward E. Wilson has served as a high-school English teacher and a writing consultant in school districts nationwide. Wilson has served on the Texas Teacher Professional Practices Commission and on NCTE's Commission on Composition. With Dr. Carroll, he co-wrote *Acts of Teaching: How to Teach Writing* and co-edited the award-winning *Poetry After Lunch: Poems to Read Aloud.* In addition to his direct involvement with the writing pedagogy presented in this series, Wilson provided inspiration for the Spotlight on Humanities feature. Wilson's poetry appears in Paul Janeczko's anthology *The Music of What Happens.* Wilson co-directs the New Jersey Writing Project in Texas.

Gary Forlini

Gary Forlini, a nationally known education consultant, developed the grammar, usage, and mechanics instruction and exercises in this series. After teaching in the Pelham, New York, schools for many years, he established Research in Media, an educational research agency that provides information for product developers, school staff developers, media companies, and arts organizations, as well as private-sector corporations and foundations. Mr. Forlini was co-author of the *S.A.T. Home Study* program and has written numerous industry reports on elementary, secondary, and post-secondary education markets.

National Advisory Panel

The teachers and administrators serving on the National Advisory Panel provided ongoing input into the development of *Prentice Hall Writing and Grammar: Communication in Action.* Their valuable insights ensure that the perspectives of teachers and students throughout the country are represented within the instruction in this series.

Dr. Pauline Bigby-Jenkins
Coordinator for Secondary English
  Language Arts
Ann Arbor Public Schools
Ann Arbor, Michigan

Lee Bromberger
English Department Chairperson
Mukwonago High School
Mukwonago, Wisconsin

Mary Chapman
Teacher of English
Free State High School
Lawrence, Kansas

Jim Deatherage
Language Arts Department
  Chairperson
Richland High School
Richland, Washington

Luis Dovalina
Teacher of English
La Joya High School
La Joya, Texas

JoAnn Giardino
Teacher of English
Centennial High School
Columbus, Ohio

Susan Goldberg
Teacher of English
Westlake Middle School
Thornwood, New York

Jean Hicks
Director, Louisville Writing Project
University of Louisville
Louisville, Kentucky

Karen Hurley
Teacher of Language Arts
Perry Meridian Middle School
Indianapolis, Indiana

Karen Lopez
Teacher of English
Hart High School
Newhall, California

Marianne Minshall
Teacher of Reading and Language Arts
Westmore Middle School
Columbus, Ohio

Nancy Monroe
English Department Chairperson
Bolton High School
Alexandria, Louisiana

Ken Spurlock
Assistant Principal
Boone County High School
Florence, Kentucky

Cynthia Katz Tyroff
Staff Development Specialist
  and Teacher of English
Northside Independent School District
San Antonio, Texas

Holly Ward
Teacher of Language Arts
Campbell Middle School
Daytona Beach, Florida

Grammar Review Team

The following teachers reviewed the grammar instruction in this series to ensure accuracy, clarity, and pedagogy.

Kathy Hamilton
Paul Hertzog
Daren Hoisington
Beverly Ladd

Karen Lopez
Dianna Louise Lund
Sean O'Brien

v H • T3

CONTENTS IN BRIEF

Chapters 1–16

Part 1: Writing 1

Note: Some features of the *Writing and Grammar* Student Edition do not appear in the Handbook Edition. Please consult the Handbook table of contents for more information.

CONTENTS
PART 1: WRITING

Chapter 1

The Writer in You 2

Chapter 2

A Walk Through the Writing Process 12

Chapter 3

Sentences, Paragraphs, and Compositions
Structure and Style. 28

INTEGRATED SKILLS

INTEGRATED SKILLS

INTEGRATED SKILLS

Chapters begin on the following pages in the Handbook Edition🄷:

Chapter 4 32

Chapter

4 Narration
Autobiographical Writing 48

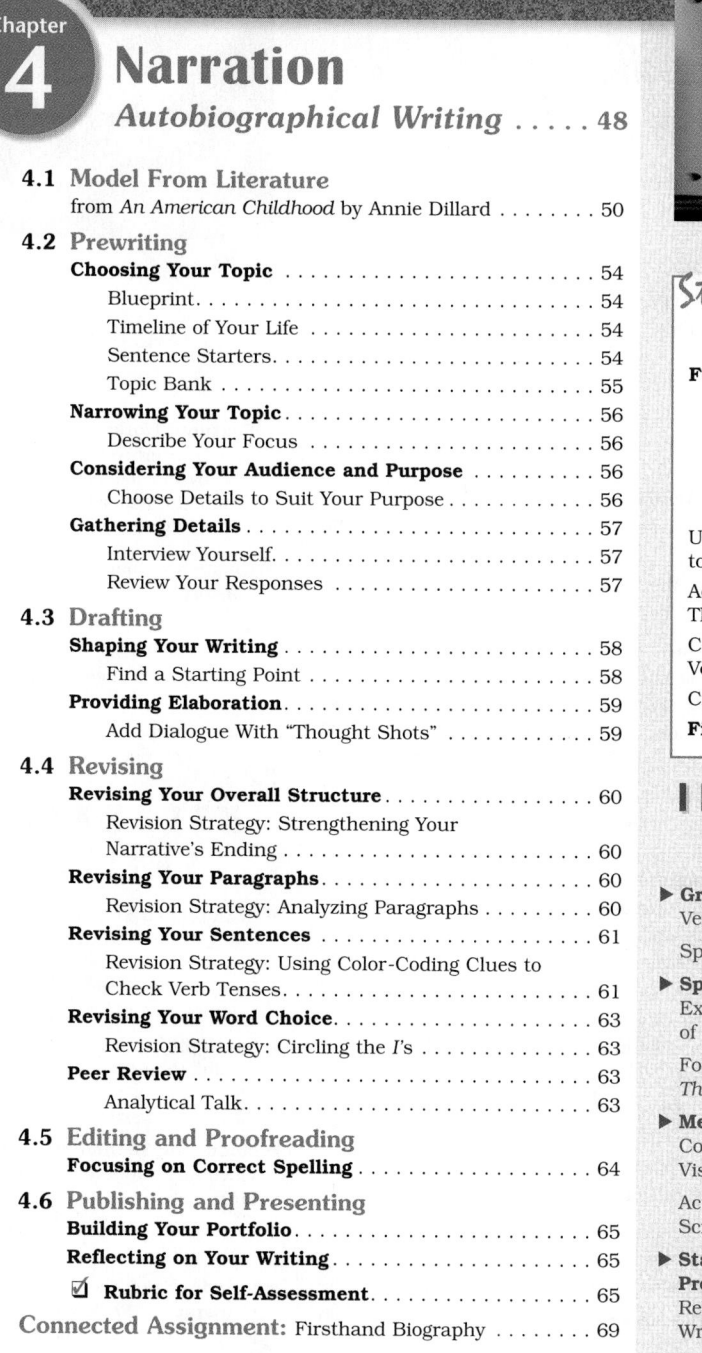

Student Work
IN PROGRESS

Featured Work:
  "Where Are You When the
    Dandelions Bloom?"
  by Melissa Sanborn
  Seneca High School
  Louisville, Kentucky

INTEGRATED SKILLS

Contents • **ix**

Chapter 5 Narration
Short Story 74

x • Contents

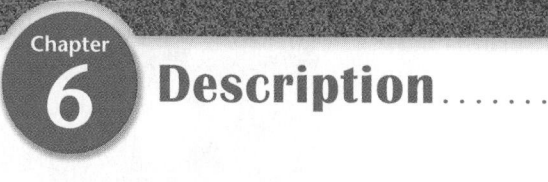

Chapter 6 Description 98

Chapters begin on the following pages in the Handbook Edition 🖽:

Chapter 6 60

Student Work
IN PROGRESS

Featured Work:
   "Final Night"
by Laura Emily Goldblatt
Princeton High School
Princeton, NJ

INTEGRATED SKILLS

Contents • **xi**

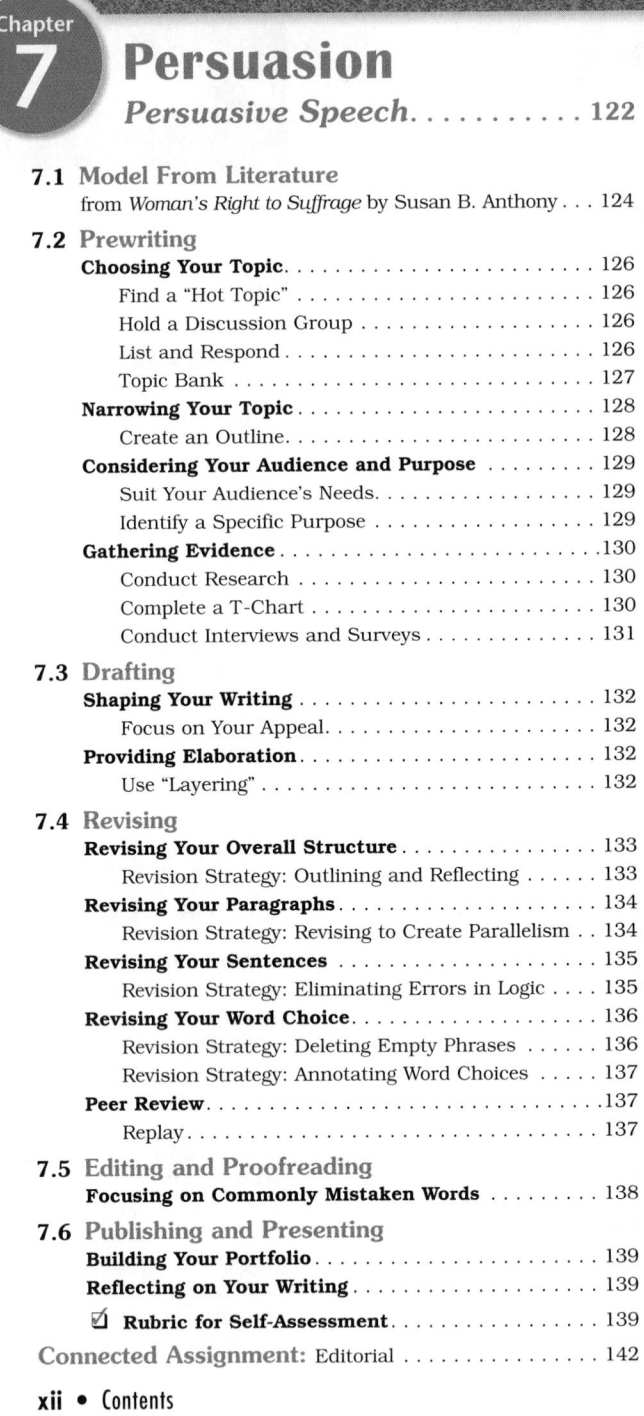

xii • Contents

Chapters begin on the following pages in the Handbook Edition :

Chapter 8 92

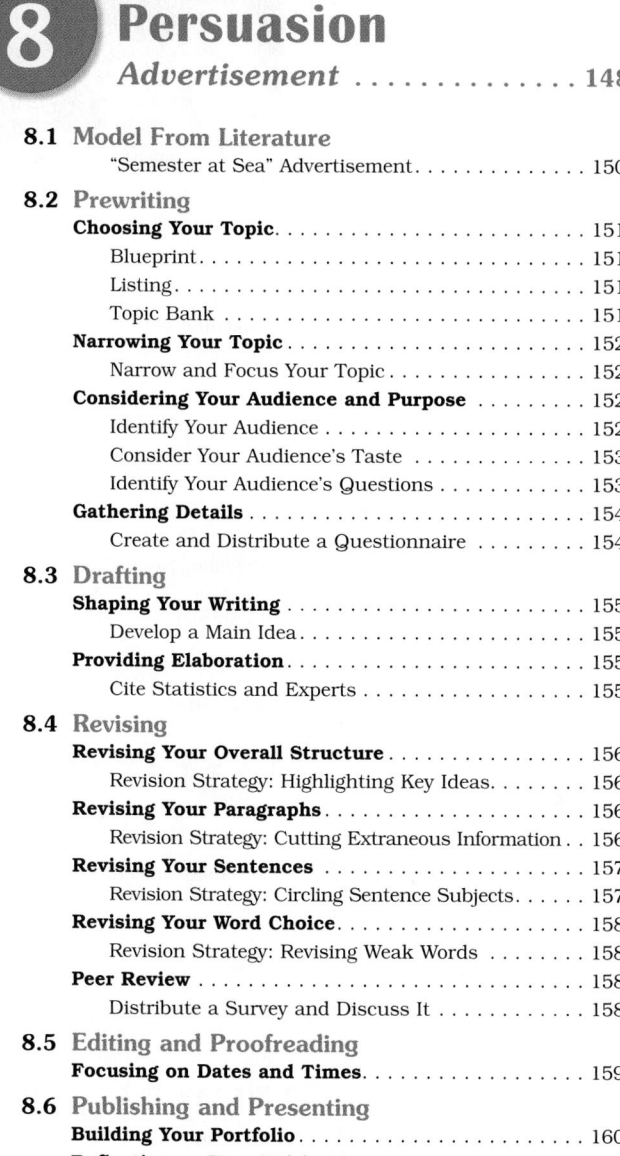

Student Work
IN PROGRESS

Featured Work:
"Not Your Everyday Yard Sale"
by Matt Bezerman
General Douglas MacArthur
High School
Seaford, New York

Creating and Distributing
a Questionnaire 154
Circling to Identify
Run-on Sentences 157
Final Draft **161**

INTEGRATED SKILLS

▶ **Grammar in Your Writing**
Abbreviating Dates and
Ordinals 159

▶ **Spotlight on the Humanities**
Recognizing Connections
Focus on Film: *Camille* . . . 164

▶ **Media and Technology Skills**
Using Technology to Extend
Meaning
Activity: Enhance a Video . . 165

▶ **Standardized Test
Preparation Workshop**
Reading Critically 166

Chapters begin on the following
pages in the Handbook Edition🄷:

Chapter 9 106

Student Work
IN PROGRESS

INTEGRATED SKILLS

Chapters begin on the following
pages in the Handbook Edition H:

Chapter 10 122

Chapter 10 Exposition
Cause-and-Effect Essay 194

Student Work
IN PROGRESS

Featured Work:
"Why Swing Is Here to Stay"
by Carl Byers
Muncie Central High School
Muncie, Indiana

INTEGRATED SKILLS

Contents • **xv**

Chapter 11 Exposition
Problem-and-Solution Essay . . 218

xvi • Contents

Student Work
IN PROGRESS

Featured Work:
    "Fear of the Speech"
    by Gabrielle Frame
    Northeast High School
    Omaha, Nebraska

INTEGRATED SKILLS

Chapters begin on the following
pages in the Handbook Edition 🄷:

Chapter 12 154

Chapter 12 Research

Documented Essay 246

Student Work
IN PROGRESS

Featured Work:
"Youths Offer a Helping Hand"
by Tameeka Mitchem
Satellite Academy
New York City, NY

INTEGRATED SKILLS

Contents • **xvii**

Chapter
13 Research

Research Paper 274

xviii • Contents

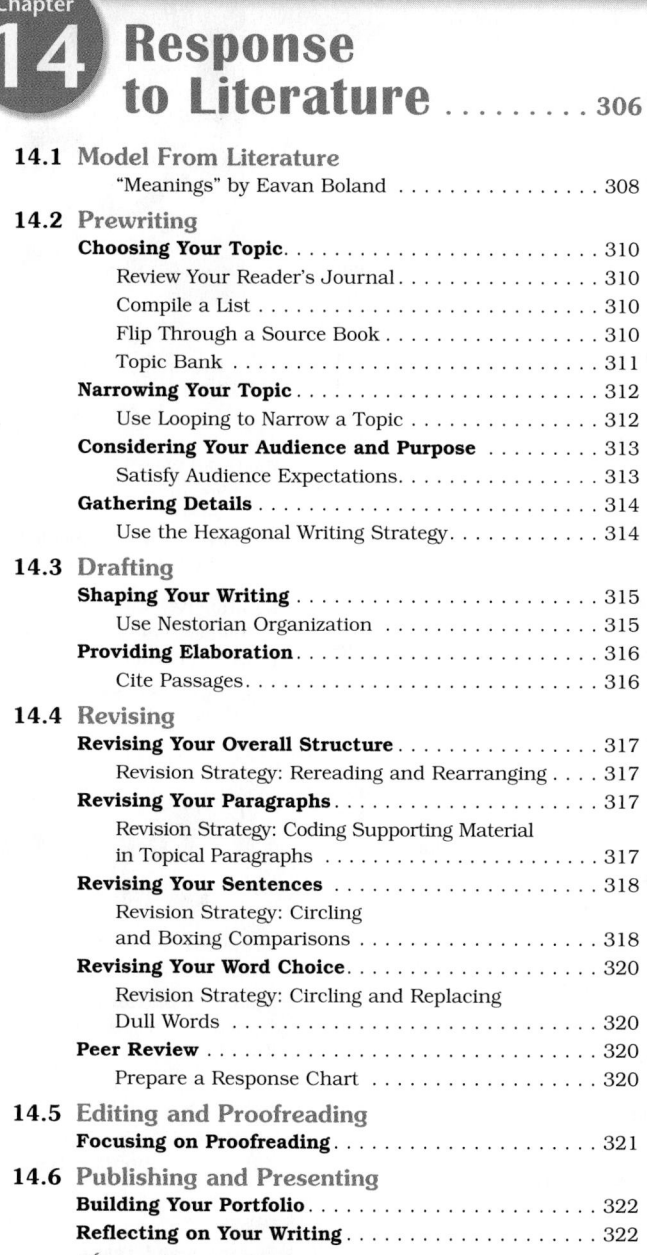

Chapter 14 Response to Literature 306

Student Work
IN PROGRESS

Featured Work:
"'Kubla Khan': A Response"
by Emily Elstad
Tupelo High School
Tupelo, Mississippi

INTEGRATED
SKILLS

Chapter 15 Writing for Assessment 330

Student Work IN PROGRESS

Featured Work:
  "Dream and Dreamer"
  by Scott Sang-Hyun Lee
  Duncanville High School
  Duncanville, Texas

INTEGRATED SKILLS

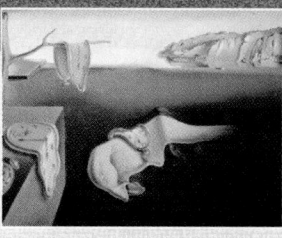

Chapter 16 Workplace Writing 348

INTEGRATED SKILLS

PART 2: GRAMMAR, USAGE, AND MECHANICS

Contents • **xxiii**

xxiv • Contents

Chapters begin on the following
pages in the Handbook Edition:

Chapter 25 470
Chapter 26 492
Chapter 27 508

Contents • **xxv**

xxvi • Contents

Contents • **xxvii**

What's new

Prentice Hall Writing and Grammar now includes:

- **Online Essay Scorer – see page T29**
  Save time while helping your students become better writers. The Prentice Hall Online Essay Scorer provides instant holistic essay scoring along with analytical feedback and multiple opportunities for revision.

- **Test Preparation Handbook – see page T34**
  Prepare your students for success on high-stakes standardized tests with the new Test Preparation Handbook in the Student Edition—**a Prentice Hall exclusive!**

- **TeacherEXPRESS™ – see page T36**
  Everything you need to teach your class! TeacherEXPRESS™ includes a robust lesson planner that automatically adds lessons to your calendar with links to every printable resource you need!

- **Exam***View*® **Test Bank – see page T36**
  From customized, multi-version tests in minutes to LAN-based assessment and reporting, the new **Exam***View*® Test Bank does it all!

Clear, consistent organization

Prentice Hall Writing and Grammar develops and reinforces skills through easy-to-follow chapter organization

Writing
Guided writing instruction walks students through each step of the writing process.

Correlated to the Six Traits Model

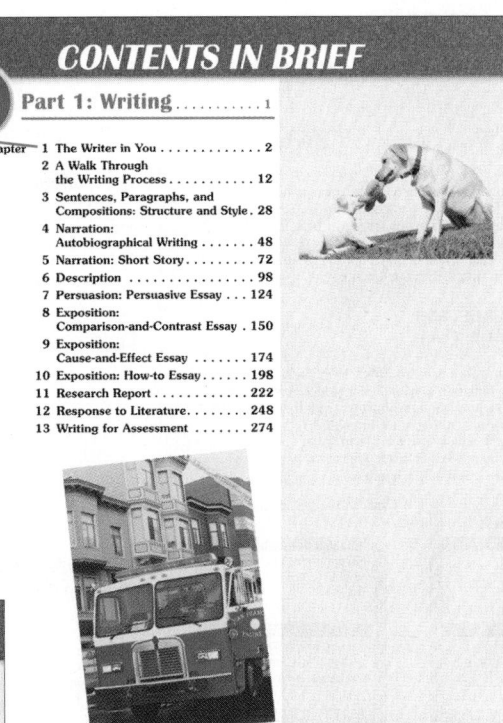

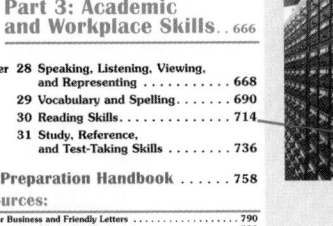

Grammar, Usage, and Mechanics
Comprehensive grammar instruction, practice, and ongoing diagnostics ensure skills mastery.

Academic and Workplace Skills
Help students develop real-world skills for success in school and beyond.

Complete writing support

Guide students through every step of the writing process

7.4 Revising

Once you've written your first draft, look for ways to make it better. Start by reviewing the overall structure of your essay and paragraphs.

Revising Your Overall Structure

Analyze the Organization

As you reread your draft, look at the arrangement of your main points. Is it logical? Is it effective? Do your main points build toward a climax, with your strongest point last? Each point in your essay is like a rung in a ladder leading readers to your viewpoint—each must be in the proper position. To check your organization, highlight your main points.

▶ **REVISION STRATEGY**
Highlighting Main Points

Highlight the main points you have used to convince your readers. Then, number each in order. Next, look at the connections between your main points. For instance, will readers understand main point 3 if you haven't explained main point 4? If not, you should probably move point 4 before point 3. Write down any changes you need to make to the order of your points in the margin of your draft. Refer to this chart for more ideas about how points might connect.

Relation Between Main Points	Possible Revision
This main point is stronger than the others.	Save this main point until the very end of the essay.
This main point means the same thing as another.	If found in different paragraphs, combine the paragraphs.
This main point is related to, but different from, another.	Make sure that the paragraphs in which you discuss the two are next to each other.
The reader needs to know this main point before he or she can understand a second one.	Make sure the first main point comes before the second.

Technology Tip

If you are using a word processor, highlight or use boldface type for your main ideas so that you can more easily review your organization and supporting arguments.

134 • Persuasive Essay

Hands-on Strategies

Writing and Grammar provides systematic, hands-on strategies for every step of the writing process and comprehensive support in areas where students struggle most.

7.2 Prewriting

Choosing Your Topic

To create a powerful persuasive essay, write on an issue about which you care. Use the following strategies to choose a good topic. (Remember, your issue must have more than one side.)

Strategies for Generating a Topic

1. **Round Table** With a group of classmates, hold a round-table discussion of problems in your school and community. Raise as many different issues as possible. Jot down topics on which you have strong feelings. Choose among these subjects for your essay topic.

2. **Media Flip-Through** Your city government announces a budget crisis. A slumping basketball team trades its key forward. Every day, controversies blare from newspapers and television sets. Over the course of a few days, flip through newspapers, watch TV, and listen to the radio for possible topics. Choose one that interests you.

3. **Quicklist** Fold a piece of paper lengthwise in three. In the first column, write a list of issues and ideas that interest you. In the second, write a descriptive word for each. In the third, give an example supporting that description. Review your list, and decide which topic interests you most.

Interactive Textbook

Try it out! Use the interactive Quicklist in **Section 7.2**, online or on CD-ROM.

Authentic Student Models

Authentic student models in every chapter track the development of one student's writing through a specific writing mode, illustrating writing techniques in action.

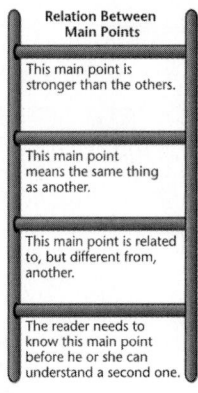

Student Work IN PROGRESS

Name: Josh McWhirter
College Station Junior High
College Station, TX

Using a Quicklist

Here's the quicklist Josh McWhirter used to choose his topic:

Topic	Descriptive Word	Examples
After-school clubs	helpful	Mr. Heisen's Math Club
Sports on TV	action-packed	table-tennis championships
Television comedies	stupid	Honey, I'm Home!
Mountain climbing	thrilling	weekend backpack trip with Dad
Computers	neat	program I wrote in Basic
Homelessness	sad	high rents
Global warming	scary	hole in the ozone over Australia

128 • Persuasive Essay

T28

Prentice Hall Online Essay Scorer

Help your students become better writers while providing valuable practice in writing on demand! Our Online Essay Scorer provides:

- Instant essay scoring and analytical feedback

- Summaries of misspelled words, grammatical errors, and redundant sentences

- Scoring rubrics

- Sample scored essays

- Interactive model essays and graphic organizers

- Writing and grammar tips along with frequently asked questions

Comprehensive grammar instruction

Ensure mastery of grammar skills

Section 15.2 Linking Verbs

Some verbs do not show action. Instead, they link two parts of a sentence. These *linking verbs* thus show a relationship between words in a sentence.

KEY CONCEPT A **linking verb** connects a noun or pronoun with a word that identifies or describes it. ■

EXAMPLES: New York *is* a city.

The best swimmers *were* Margie and Pia.

Lucy *seems* unhappy.

Linking verbs act almost as equal signs. *City* identifies *New York; Margie* and *Pia* identify the *swimmers; unhappy* describes *Lucy*.

The Most Common Linking Verb

In English, the most common linking verb is *be*. This verb has many forms.

FORMS OF *BE*		
am	can be	have been
are	could be	has been
is	may be	had been
was	might be	could have been
were	must be	may have been
am being	shall be	might have been
are being	should be	must have been
is being	will be	shall have been
was being	would be	should have been
were being	.	will have been
		would have been

Exercise 10 Writing Sentences With Linking Verbs Write a sentence using each form of *be* listed below.
1. might have been
2. should have been
3. could be
4. were being
5. will be
6. has been
7. shall be
8. is being
9. would be
10. had been

320 • Verbs

Theme: Immigration
In this section, you will learn about linking verbs. The examples and exercises in this section are about immigration.
Cross-Curricular Connection: Social Studies

Step-by-step Teaching Guides
Key concepts are introduced, modeled, and practiced.

Hands-on Grammar

Subject-Verb Agreement Color Match

Cut three strips of paper of equal length. Draw a blue line across the center of one. Draw a red line across the center of the other. Fold the strip into thirds, as shown in the illustration. Then, write a sentence with a singular subject, a singular verb form, and a phrase across the blue line. Write the subject in the first fold, the verb in the second, and the remaining words in the third fold. Write the same sentence on the strip with the red line, but use a plural subject and plural verb form. Next, cut each strip on the folds. Finally, try to line up the parts of the sentence. You will find that you can't create a color match between a singular subject and a plural verb form.

The Minister	attends	every session

The Ministers	attend	every session

The Ministers	attends	every session

Find It in Your Reading Do this activity with a sentence from the Grammar in Literature passage from "Glory and Hope," on page 578. If the sentence has too many phrases, just use the subject and verb.

Find It in Your Writing Review a recent piece of writing in your portfolio. Use this activity with several sentences from the piece.

Exclusive Hands-on Grammar Exercises
Our unique interactive exercises encourage active learning and reinforce grammar concepts.

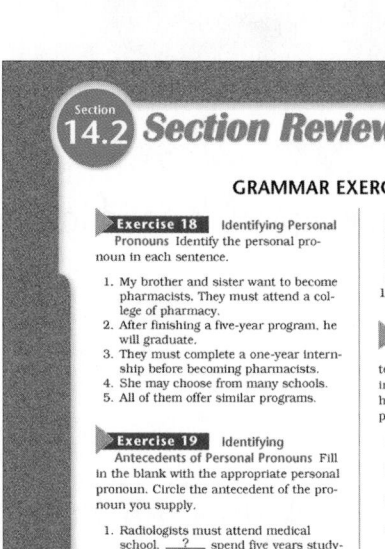

Section 14.2 *Section Review*

GRAMMAR EXERCISES 18–24

▶ **Exercise 18** Identifying Personal Pronouns Identify the personal pronoun in each sentence.

1. My brother and sister want to become pharmacists. They must attend a college of pharmacy.
2. After finishing a five-year program, he will graduate.
3. They must complete a one-year internship before becoming pharmacists.
4. She may choose from many schools.
5. All of them offer similar programs.

▶ **Exercise 19** Identifying Antecedents of Personal Pronouns Fill in the blank with the appropriate personal pronoun. Circle the antecedent of the pronoun you supply.

1. Radiologists must attend medical school. ___?___ spend five years studying radiology.
2. If my brother studies radiology, ___?___ will have to complete a residency program.
3. My aunt is a radiologist. ___?___ has her own practice.
4. After completing ___?___ residency, radiologists may decide to specialize.
5. ___?___ may choose to teach instead.

▶ **Exercise 20** Recognizing Types of Pronouns Identify each of the pronouns in the sentences below as *personal, demonstrative, interrogative,* or *indefinite.*

1. My brother is in high school. He wants to study forensic medicine.
2. That is the study of medical evidence.
3. It helps police officers solve crimes.
4. You may have seen popular shows about "crime doctors."

5. Who wants to know more?
6. These are copies of fingerprints.
7. Each is unique.
8. Whose is this fingerprint?
9. What can we learn from fingerprints?
10. Few can identify a fingerprint.

▶ **Exercise 21** Revision Practice Replace each italicized noun in the sentences below with the type of pronoun indicated in brackets. Som[...] have to be rewritten as qu[...] punctuation as needed.

1. *Family practitioners* [p[...] primary medical care.
2. Family doctors know [...] [personal] patients.
3. *Dedication* [demonstra[...] son they enter the fie[...]
4. *Family practitioners* [i[...] refer patients to a spe[...]
5. *General practitioners* [...] had many years of m[...]

▶ **Exercise 22** Find[...] Reading Identify three [...] nouns in the excerpt from [...] Thought She Was a Dog .[...]

▶ **Exercise 23** Find[...] Writing In your own w[...] least one example of each [...]

▶ **Exercise 24** Writ[...] Write a brief descriptio[...] in a job that interests you[...] kinds of pronouns you us[...]

Se[...]

Chapter 14 *Chapter Review*

GRAMMAR EXERCISES 25–36

▶ **Exercise 25** Identifying Nouns in Sentences Identify the nouns in each sentence below.

1. The pack of wolves chased the rabbit.
2. The rabbit, filled with fear, ran away.
3. Because of their hunger, the wolves continued to hunt.
4. They found no more prey in the forest.
5. The howls of the hungry animals showed their frustration.

▶ **Exercise 26** Identifying Nouns in Paragraphs Identify the nouns in the paragraph below.

Wolves are wild animals that look similar to dogs. A wolf has fur that can be white, black, or gray. Wolves travel in packs, using their speed and strength to hunt as a group. They live in most climates, but rarely in deserts or tropical forests.

▶ **Exercise 27** Identifying Common and Proper Nouns Identify the nouns in each sentence below. Then, tell whether each noun is *common* or *proper.*

1. My sister Lucy, my mother, and I took our cat to the animal hospital.
2. The hospital is in Philadelphia.
3. We took the cat on the train.
4. The train passed through cities in New York and New Jersey.
5. Our cat Trudy needed special surgery.
6. Dr. Kim, the veterinarian, was very kind.
7. While we waited, my mother and I read a magazine.
8. We saw a dog that looked like a character from the movie *Benji.*
9. A poodle sat on a chair next to us.
10. Before we returned home, we stopped to see the Liberty Bell.

▶ **Exercise 28** Identifying Collective Nouns Identify the collective noun in each sentence below.

1. My class went on a trip to the animal hospital last week.
2. The team of veterinarians sees many types of patients.
3. Yesterday, they treated a group of monkeys from the zoo.
4. Sometimes, they go to farms to check a herd of cattle.
5. My family brought our cat to this animal hospital.

▶ **Exercise 29** Identifying Compound Nouns Identify the compound noun in each sentence below.

1. My sister-in-law brought a new cat home from the pound.
2. They told her that a police officer had found the cat.
3. It does not get along with the sheepdog in the house.
4. She brought it to the middle school where she teaches.
5. On the way home, they crossed the George Washington Bridge.

▶ **Exercise 30** Identifying Personal Pronouns Identify each personal pronoun below as *first person, second person,* or *third person.* Then, tell whether the pronoun is *singular* or *plural.*

1. you
2. she
3. their
4. our
5. them
6. I
7. his
8. yours
9. mine
10. we

Develop Skills through Meaningful Practice

Provide the practice your students need to improve their grammar skills and apply them in both writing and speaking.

And for even more practice:

- **Interactive Textbook** features thousands of interactive grammar exercises with instant feedback.

- The **Grammar Exercise Workbook** provides hundreds of grammar exercises for your students

- **Extra Grammar and Writing** give students additional practice in both grammar and writing.

- The **Daily Language Practice Book** offers brief, daily activities that sharpen students' proofreading skills.

- The **Hands-on Grammar Activity Book** offers easy-to-use templates for every Hands-on Grammar Activity in the Student Edition.

Grammar Exercise Workbook

PRENTICE HALL
WRITING AND GRAMMAR

Academic and workplace skills

Prepare students for the world beyond school!

Writing and Grammar's Academic and Workplace Skills chapters provide solid instruction in and hands-on practice with real-world skills.

28.2 VIEWING AND REPRESENTING SKILLS

Developing a Multimedia Presentation

In most multimedia presentations, the presenter gives an oral report, illustrating the main points with media selections. This type of presentation can be effective and memorable if it is well planned and executed.

KEY CONCEPT Multimedia presentations supply information through a variety of media, including text, slides, videos, music, maps, charts, and art. ■

Tips for Preparing a Multimedia Presentation

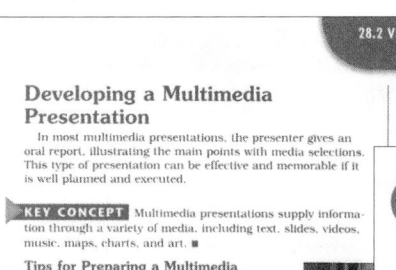

• Create an outline of your report first, and then decide which parts to illustrate through the use of media.

• Choose a medium that is suited to your topic. For example, if you were discussing the art of Leonardo da Vinci, reproductions of his artwork and music selections from his time would enhance your presentation.

• Evenly space the media within your presentation. Don't bunch them up at the beginning or end of your presentation.

• Check to ensure that the media you've selected will be able to be seen or heard by everyone. A postage stamp, for example, is too small to be held up in front of a large audience. It would be better to photocopy it and enlarge the image.

• Before the presentation, check your equipment—slide projectors, overhead projectors, microphones, cassette players—to be sure that they are in working condition.

• Always have a backup plan in case anything goes wrong with the equipment.

• Plan to rehearse with the equipment the day before the presentation. Be sure you know the location of all controls—for focus or for volume, for example—and understand their use.

Exercise 13 Preparing a Multimedia Presentation Read through the saved writings in your portfolio. Select one that could be made into a multimedia presentation. Then, using an outline, select the media you'd like to include, and decide on the sequence of your presentation.

Viewin

Section 28.2 *Viewing and Representing Skills*

Visual representation is an important way to communicate. Television programs, textbooks, and works of art are common types of media that use images to expand your view of the world. Graphic organizers, multimedia presentations, and performances are ways in which you can express yourself to the world. In this section, you will learn how to receive—and provide—information through visual representations.

Interpreting Maps, Graphs, and Photographs

Any map, graph, or photograph can provide a wealth of information. The key to the information these representations hold is your ability to interpret them.

KEY CONCEPT Use your knowledge of the features of maps, graphs, and photographs to get information visually. ■

Follow these general guidelines when reading a visual aid:

• **Determine Your Purpose** Knowing your purpose helps you focus on the information you need.

• **Read the Title, Caption, and Labels** The title or caption tells you what kind of information to expect.

• **Decode Symbols** Symbols are sometimes used to give information. Find out what they represent.

• **Look for Notable Features** Areas that stand out usually contain important information.

• **Link Information to Text** Determining the relationship between the visual elements and the text allows you to use the text to understand the visual elements better and vice versa.

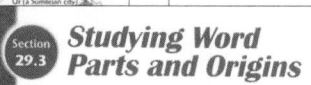

Maps A map can do more than simply indicate the location of a state capital. For example, maps can identify population clusters, clarify wartime battle activities, and report weather forecasts.

Use these steps when interpreting maps:
1. Familiarize yourself with the map.
2. Find out which way is north on the map.
3. Look at the distance scale (usually found at the bottom of the map).

Graphs There will be times when you have to get information from graphs. Graphs provide a quick and easy way to compare several pieces of related information.

Viewing an

Speaking, Listening, Viewing, and Representing

Develop effective communication skills with a wide variety of exercises and activities.

Section 29.3 *Studying Word Parts and Origins*

Using Roots

Learning roots, the most basic parts of words, will help you learn the meanings of groups of words. For example, if you know that the root *-gress* means "to step or move forward," you have a key to the meaning of the following words: *regress, progress, retrogress, transgress, egress,* and *digress.*

KEY CONCEPT A **root** is a word part that determines an important part of the meaning of a word. ■

FIVE COMMON ROOTS		
Root	**Meaning**	**Example**
-mit- (-mis-)	to send	*dismiss* (to *send* away)
-mov- (-mot-)	to move	*motion, movement*
-ven- (-vent-)	to come	*convene* (to *come* together)
-vert- (-vers-)	to turn	*reversal* (*turning* around)
-vid- (-vis-)	to see	*vision* (ability to *see*)

Exercise 7 Learning Word Roots Match the words in the first column with the words in the second column that appear to have the same root. Look up each pair of words in a dictionary. Identify the root they share, and write its meaning.

1. reflect   a. manuscript
2. motivate   b. deflect
3. dimension   c. centipede
4. pedal   d. immense
5. hapless   e. modify
6. model   f. happiness
7. manufacture   g. motion
8. picture   h. circumstance
9. distance   i. assent
10. sentence   j. depict

Exercise 8 Using Roots to Determine the Meaning of Words Match each word in the first column with its definition in the second column. Explain how the roots you learned in the previous exercise helped you to determine each answer.

1. motility   a. person walking
2. pedestrian   b. by hand
3. manual   c. one of a set of units
4. module   d. unfortunate accident
5. mishap   e. ability to move on one's own

More Practice

Academic and Workplace Skills Activity Book
• pp. 22–23

Vocabulary and Spelling

Expand students' vocabulary and improve their spelling with exercises using context, word structure and origins, reference tools, and spelling tips.

Reading Skills

Teach students how to use reading skills to improve their comprehension of materials they read in or out of school.

Section 30.2 Reading Nonfiction Critically

Nonfiction is writing that is based on fact. When you read nonfiction critically, you examine and question the ideas the author presents. You learn to distinguish between fact and opinion, to identify the author's purpose, and to recognize when language is being used to distort your understanding of the text. This section will guide you through a number of reading strategies that you can use to become a critical reader.

Comprehending Nonfiction

Before you begin to read a text critically, you need to have a general understanding of it. This process involves finding and interpreting important information, identifying the author's purpose, and understanding the relationship the material has to what you are studying.

KEY CONCEPT Comprehending nonfiction involves understanding the author's purpose as well as the information presented in the writing. ■

Locate Main Ideas and Major Details The main ideas are the key points an author wishes to convey. The major details explain and support these main points.

Interpret What You Are Reading Paraphrase, or state in your own words, the information in the text, starting with the main ideas and major details. This technique will help you to remember ideas and their relationship to each other.

Identify the Author's Purpose for Writing After you have a general idea of the content, examine the writer's choice of words and details to determine the author's purpose. As you continue to read, look for additional information that supports this purpose.

Reflect on What You Have Read After you have finished reading, take a moment to think about what the author has written. Consider the following questions: How does the information relate to what you are studying? How does this information relate to your life?

Exercise 6 Comprehending Nonfiction Use the strategies mentioned above to read a chapter from one of your textbooks. Then, answer these questions: What main points and major details did you locate? What was the author's purpose? What details did you use to identify it? What is the importance of the information you read?

📖 Learn More

These critical reading skills are also helpful when revising the ideas in your own writing. See Chapters 1, 2, and 3.

▶ More Practice

Academic and Workplace Skills Activity Book
• pp. 38-39

Reading Nonfiction Critically • 721

Taking Notes

Taking good notes is an important and useful study skill. Taking notes in class helps you remember what you heard, and taking notes while reading helps you remember what you read. Later, you can use your notes to study for a test or just to review the information you have learned.

TIPS FOR TAKING NOTES

• Don't record every word; focus on capturing main ideas.
• Label your notes with the topic and date.
• Keep notes for different subjects in separate notebooks or in separate sections of a general notebook.

Modified Outlines One note-taking device that you can use to sort out main ideas and major details is a *modified outline*. List each main idea, and underline it. Place major details below the main idea, and number them. Jot down supporting details under each major detail.

SAMPLE MODIFIED OUTLINE

Solar System ⟩——— Main idea
1. Sun ⟩——— Major detail
    A star ⟩——— Supporting details
    Center of the solar system
2. Planets
    Nine planets
    Orbit the sun in west to east direction
    Most have moons or satellites
3. Asteroids, Meteoroids, and Comets
    Asteroids—fragments of rock
    Meteoroids—the result of asteroid collisions
    Comets—solid nucleus surrounded by
        frozen gases and dust particles

Summaries Writing a *summary* is another way of organizing information you've learned. After reading a chapter or attending a class, write one or more paragraphs stating the key points covered and explaining how the ideas are connected.

Exercise 4 Making a Modified Outline and a Summary Create a modified outline and a summary of a chapter in your science or social studies textbook.

31.3

Answering Different Types of Questions

If you are familiar with the different kinds of questions that are frequently asked on tests, you may improve your performance. It is also important to know various strategies for answering the different kinds of questions.

Answering Multiple-Choice Questions This kind of question asks you to choose from several possible responses.

EXAMPLE:
What is a URL?
a. an Internet service provider   c. a universal reference
b. an Internet Web site address   d. a periodical index

In the preceding example, the answer is b.

ANSWERING MULTIPLE-CHOICE QUESTIONS

1. Try answering the question before looking at the choices. If your answer is one of the choices, select that choice.
2. Eliminate the obviously incorrect answers, crossing them out if you are allowed to write on the test paper.
3. Change a question into a statement by inserting your answer to see whether the statement makes sense.

Answering Matching Questions Matching questions ask that you match items in one group with items in another.

EXAMPLE:
___ 1. negligible   a. causing fear or dread
___ 2. formidable   b. difficult to understand
___ 3. inscrutable   c. small or unimportant

In the preceding example, the answers are c, a, and b.

ANSWERING MATCHING QUESTIONS

1. Count each group to see whether items will be left over. Check the directions to see whether items can be used more than once.
2. Read all the items before you start matching.
3. Match the items you know first. If you can write on the paper, cross out the items when you use them.
4. Match remaining items about which you are less certain.

💻 Internet Tip

You can find additional information, strategies, and practice on test-taking on the Internet.

▶ More Practice

Academic and Workplace Skills Activity Book
• p. 59-60

752 • Study, Reference, and Test-Taking Skills

Study, Reference, and Test-taking Skills

Help students make the most of their study time with study and note taking tips, research skills, and test-taking strategies.

Help your students succeed on high-stakes assessments

Prentice Hall's exclusive Test Preparation Handbook features detailed instruction—along with ample practice questions and essays in standardized test format—in reading comprehension, grammar, and writing on demand.

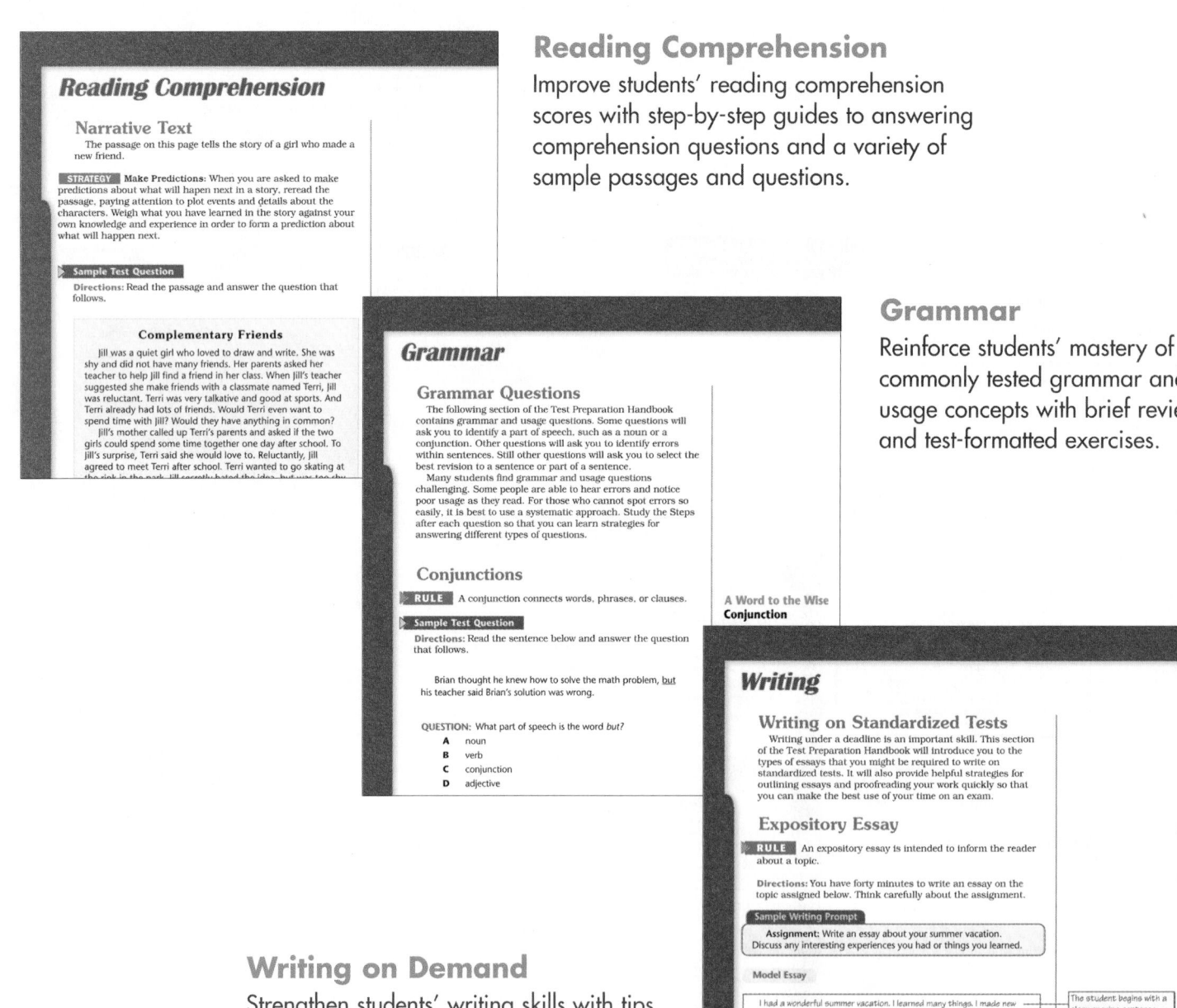

Reading Comprehension

Improve students' reading comprehension scores with step-by-step guides to answering comprehension questions and a variety of sample passages and questions.

Grammar

Reinforce students' mastery of commonly tested grammar and usage concepts with brief review and test-formatted exercises.

Writing on Demand

Strengthen students' writing skills with tips, sample prompts, annotated student essays, and writing exercises in test format.

Reading Comprehension

Narrative Text

The passage on this page tells the story of a girl who made a new friend.

STRATEGY Make Predictions: When you are asked to make predictions about what will happen next in a story, reread the passage, paying attention to plot events and details about the characters. Weigh what you have learned in the story against your own knowledge and experience in order to form a prediction about what will happen next.

Sample Test Question

Directions: Read the passage and answer the question that follows.

Complementary Friends

Jill was a quiet girl who loved to draw and write. She was shy and did not have many friends. Her parents asked her teacher to help Jill find a friend in her class. When Jill's teacher suggested she make friends with a classmate named Terri, Jill was reluctant. Terri was very talkative and good at sports. And Terri already had lots of friends. Would Terri even want to spend time with Jill? Would they have anything in common?

Jill's mother called up Terri's parents and asked if the two girls could spend some time together one day after school. To Jill's surprise, Terri said she would love to. Reluctantly, Jill agreed to meet Terri after school. Terri wanted to go skating at the rink in the park. Jill secretly hated the idea, but was too shy

Grammar

Grammar Questions

The following section of the Test Preparation Handbook contains grammar and usage questions. Some questions will ask you to identify a part of speech, such as a noun or a conjunction. Other questions will ask you to identify errors within sentences. Still other questions will ask you to select the best revision to a sentence or part of a sentence.

Many students find grammar and usage questions challenging. Some people are able to hear errors and notice poor usage as they read. For those who cannot spot errors so easily, it is best to use a systematic approach. Study the Steps after each question so that you can learn strategies for answering different types of questions.

Conjunctions

RULE A conjunction connects words, phrases, or clauses.

Sample Test Question

Directions: Read the sentence below and answer the question that follows.

Brian thought he knew how to solve the math problem, <u>but</u> his teacher said Brian's solution was wrong.

QUESTION: What part of speech is the word *but*?

A noun
B verb
C conjunction
D adjective

A Word to the Wise
Conjunction

Writing

Writing on Standardized Tests

Writing under a deadline is an important skill. This section of the Test Preparation Handbook will introduce you to the types of essays that you might be required to write on standardized tests. It will also provide helpful strategies for outlining essays and proofreading your work quickly so that you can make the best use of your time on an exam.

Expository Essay

RULE An expository essay is intended to inform the reader about a topic.

Directions: You have forty minutes to write an essay on the topic assigned below. Think carefully about the assignment.

Sample Writing Prompt

Assignment: Write an essay about your summer vacation. Discuss any interesting experiences you had or things you learned.

Model Essay

I had a wonderful summer vacation. I learned many things. I made new friends. I went to a few places I had never visited before. I relaxed and enjoyed being out of school. Most of all, I realized how much I love to go swimming.

My summer started in late June. My parents drove me to camp. My camp, Camp Friendship Lake, was the same camp my Dad went to when he was my age. I had never been to camp before and wasn't sure I'd like it. But before I knew it, I

The student begins with a clear opening sentence.

Additional support throughout the Student Edition

Standardized Test Preparation Workshops

Standardized Test Preparation Workshops after each chapter provide comprehensive preparation for the PSAT, SAT, ACT, AP*, state, and local standardized tests.

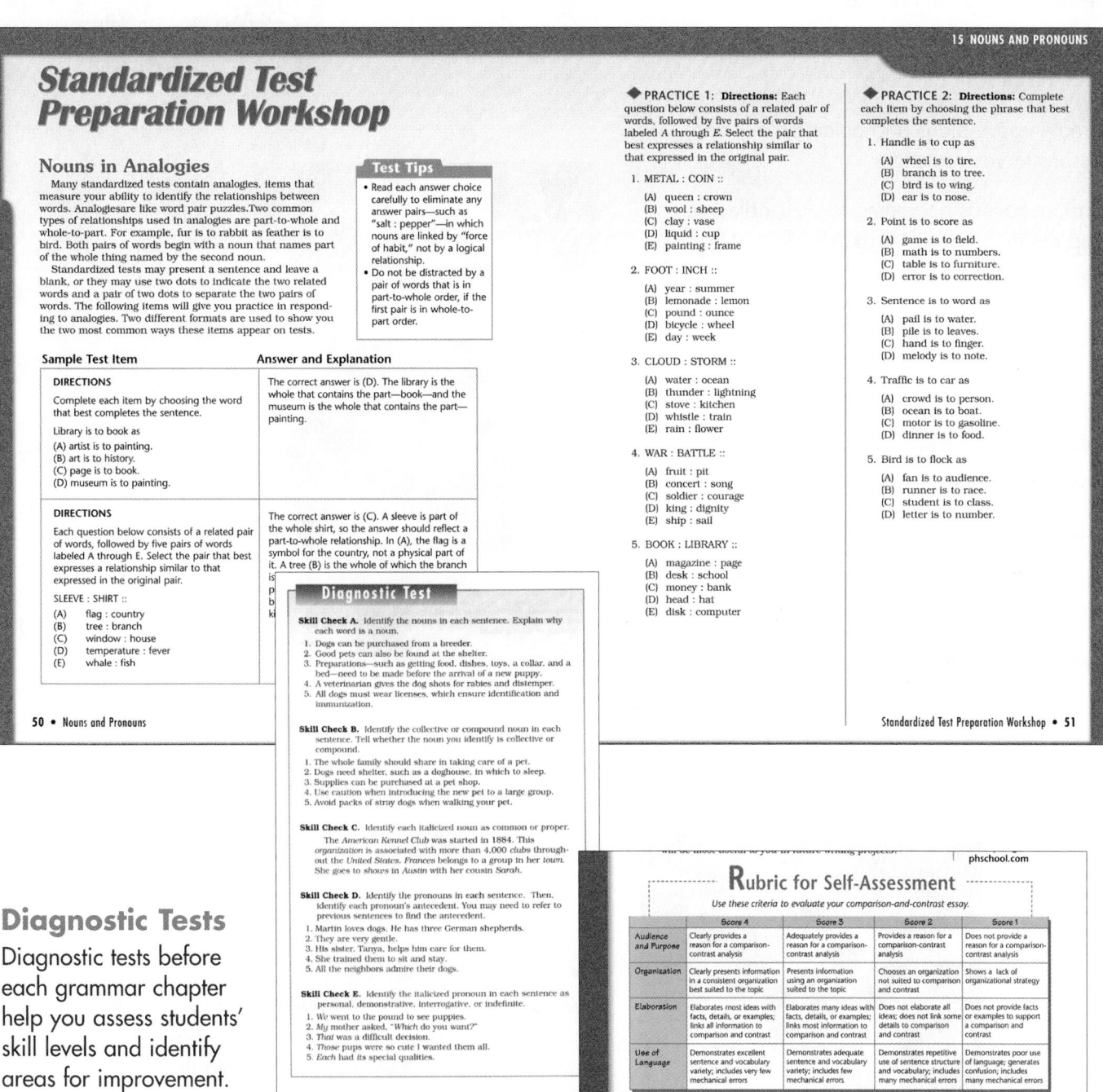

Standardized Test Preparation Workshop

Nouns in Analogies

Many standardized tests contain analogies, items that measure your ability to identify the relationships between words. Analogies are like word pair puzzles. Two common types of relationships used in analogies are part-to-whole and whole-to-part. For example, fur is to rabbit as feather is to bird. Both pairs of words begin with a noun that names part of the whole thing named by the second noun.

Standardized tests may present a sentence and leave a blank, or they may use two dots to indicate the two related words and a pair of two dots to separate the two pairs of words. The following items will give you practice in responding to analogies. Two different formats are used to show you the two most common ways these items appear on tests.

Test Tips

- Read each answer choice carefully to eliminate any answer pairs—such as "salt : pepper"—in which nouns are linked by "force of habit," not by a logical relationship.
- Do not be distracted by a pair of words that is in part-to-whole order, if the first pair is in whole-to-part order.

Sample Test Item	Answer and Explanation
DIRECTIONS Complete each item by choosing the word that best completes the sentence. Library is to book as (A) artist is to painting. (B) art is to history. (C) page is to book. (D) museum is to painting.	The correct answer is (D). The library is the whole that contains the part—book—and the museum is the whole that contains the part—painting.
DIRECTIONS Each question below consists of a related pair of words, followed by five pairs of words labeled A through E. Select the pair that best expresses a relationship similar to that expressed in the original pair. SLEEVE : SHIRT :: (A) flag : country (B) tree : branch (C) window : house (D) temperature : fever (E) whale : fish	The correct answer is (C). A sleeve is part of the whole shirt, so the answer should reflect a part-to-whole relationship. In (A), the flag is a symbol for the country, not a physical part of it. A tree (B) is the whole of which the branch is...

50 • Nouns and Pronouns

◆ **PRACTICE 1: Directions:** Each question below consists of a related pair of words, followed by five pairs of words labeled A through E. Select the pair that best expresses a relationship similar to that expressed in the original pair.

1. METAL : COIN ::
   (A) queen : crown
   (B) wool : sheep
   (C) clay : vase
   (D) liquid : cup
   (E) painting : frame

2. FOOT : INCH ::
   (A) year : summer
   (B) lemonade : lemon
   (C) pound : ounce
   (D) bicycle : wheel
   (E) day : week

3. CLOUD : STORM ::
   (A) water : ocean
   (B) thunder : lightning
   (C) stove : kitchen
   (D) whistle : train
   (E) rain : flower

4. WAR : BATTLE ::
   (A) fruit : pit
   (B) concert : song
   (C) soldier : courage
   (D) king : dignity
   (E) ship : sail

5. BOOK : LIBRARY ::
   (A) magazine : page
   (B) desk : school
   (C) money : bank
   (D) head : hat
   (E) disk : computer

◆ **PRACTICE 2: Directions:** Complete each item by choosing the phrase that best completes the sentence.

1. Handle is to cup as
   (A) wheel is to tire.
   (B) branch is to tree.
   (C) bird is to wing.
   (D) ear is to nose.

2. Point is to score as
   (A) game is to field.
   (B) math is to numbers.
   (C) table is to furniture.
   (D) error is to correction.

3. Sentence is to word as
   (A) pail is to water.
   (B) pile is to leaves.
   (C) hand is to finger.
   (D) melody is to note.

4. Traffic is to car as
   (A) crowd is to person.
   (B) ocean is to boat.
   (C) motor is to gasoline.
   (D) dinner is to food.

5. Bird is to flock as
   (A) fan is to audience.
   (B) runner is to race.
   (C) student is to class.
   (D) letter is to number.

Standardized Test Preparation Workshop • 51

Diagnostic Test

Skill Check A. Identify the nouns in each sentence. Explain why each word is a noun.

1. Dogs can be purchased from a breeder.
2. Good pets can also be found at the shelter.
3. Preparations—such as getting food, dishes, toys, a collar, and a bed—need to be made before the arrival of a new puppy.
4. A veterinarian gives the dog shots for rabies and distemper.
5. All dogs must wear licenses, which ensure identification and immunization.

Skill Check B. Identify the collective or compound noun in each sentence. Tell whether the noun you identify is collective or compound.

1. The whole family should share in taking care of a pet.
2. Dogs need shelter, such as a doghouse, in which to sleep.
3. Supplies can be purchased at a pet shop.
4. Use caution when introducing the new pet to a large group.
5. Avoid packs of stray dogs when walking your pet.

Skill Check C. Identify each italicized noun as common or proper.

The *American Kennel Club* was started in 1884. This *organization* is associated with more than 4,000 *clubs* throughout the *United States*. *Frances* belongs to a group in her *town*. She goes to *shows* in *Austin* with her cousin *Sarah*.

Skill Check D. Identify the pronouns in each sentence. Then, identify each pronoun's antecedent. You may need to refer to previous sentences to find the antecedent.

1. Martin loves dogs. He has three German shepherds.
2. They are very gentle.
3. His sister, Tanya, helps him care for them.
4. She trained them to sit and stay.
5. All the neighbors admire their dogs.

Skill Check E. Identify the italicized pronoun in each sentence as personal, demonstrative, interrogative, or indefinite.

1. *We* went to the pound to see puppies.
2. *My* mother asked, "*Which* do you want?"
3. *That* was a difficult decision.
4. *Those* pups were so cute I wanted them all.
5. *Each* had *its* special qualities.

Diagnostic Tests

Diagnostic tests before each grammar chapter help you assess students' skill levels and identify areas for improvement.

phschool.com

Rubric for Self-Assessment

Use these criteria to evaluate your comparison-and-contrast essay.

	Score 4	Score 3	Score 2	Score 1
Audience and Purpose	Clearly provides a reason for a comparison-contrast analysis	Adequately provides a reason for a comparison-contrast analysis	Provides a reason for a comparison-contrast analysis	Does not provide a reason for a comparison-contrast analysis
Organization	Clearly presents information in a consistent organization best suited to the topic	Presents information using an organization suited to the topic	Chooses an organization not suited to comparison and contrast	Shows a lack of organizational strategy
Elaboration	Elaborates most ideas with facts, details, or examples; links all information to comparison and contrast	Elaborates many ideas with facts, details, or examples; links most information to comparison and contrast	Does not elaborate all ideas; does not link some details to comparison and contrast	Does not provide facts or examples to support a comparison and contrast
Use of Language	Demonstrates excellent sentence and vocabulary variety; includes very few mechanical errors	Demonstrates adequate sentence and vocabulary variety; includes few mechanical errors	Demonstrates repetitive use of sentence structure and vocabulary; includes many mechanical errors	Demonstrates poor use of language; generates confusion; includes many mechanical errors

2 • Comparison-and-Contrast Essay

Rubrics for Self-Assessment

Rubrics for Self-Assessment with each writing lesson help build critical thinking skills as students evaluate their own work.

Teaching resources

Powerful tools for powerful results

TeacherEXPRESS™
One-stop classroom management!

- Access, search, and print any teaching resource with the click of a mouse

- Create lesson plans and automatically add lessons to your calendar

- Customize tests according to skills objectives and ability level with **Exam**View® Test Bank

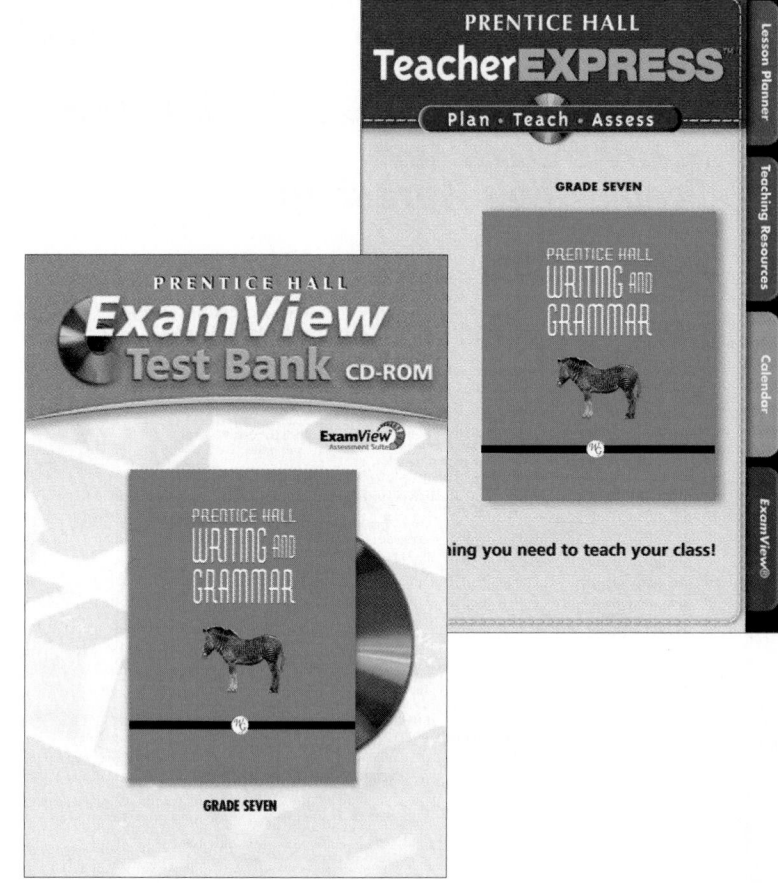

ExamView® Test Bank CD-ROM
Powered by **Exam**View® test generator!

- Easy to use and teacher–friendly

- Easily create and customize tests, worksheets, and study guides in minutes

- Create paper, LAN–based, and Internet tests

Writers at Work DVD
Demonstrate the real-world relevance of the writing process as professionals explain how they incorporate the writing process into their daily lives.

Interactive Textbook—Available online or on CD-ROM

Take the weight off their shoulders! The Interactive Textbook provides the same trusted content as your textbook without the weight in the backpack, and includes:

- **Online Essay Scorer**—The Prentice Hall Online Essay Scorer provides instant holistic essay scoring along with analytical feedback and multiple opportunities for revision.

- **Interactive writing and grammar exercises**—Web codes throughout the Student Edition allow students to quickly access interactive online grammar exercises, reviews, writing tools, and tutorials—all with instant feedback.

- **Diagnostic tests**—Instantly assess student readiness to learn new skills.

- **Scoring rubrics and scored student models**—Reliable, scored essays use a 4- or 6-point rubric with specific suggestions for improved writing.

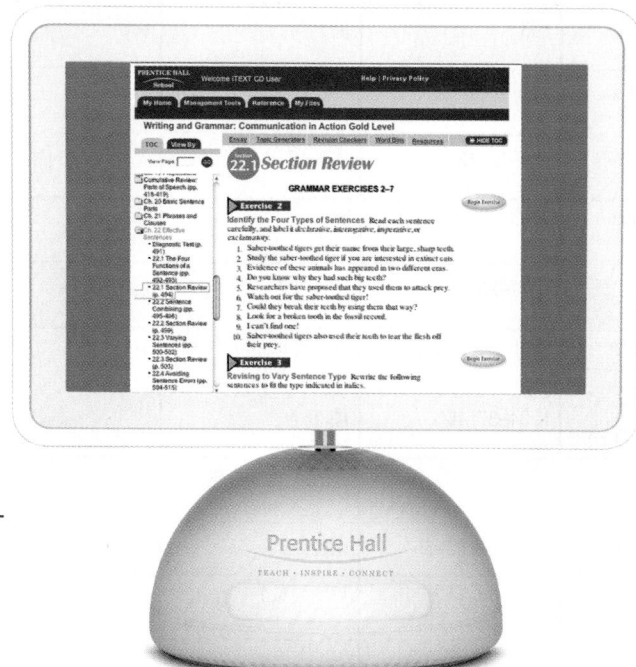

Writing and Grammar Components

Student Edition
Interactive Textbook
Student Handbook Edition
Teacher's Edition
Spanish Speakers' Handbook

Teaching Resources
Teaching Resources:
  Writing Support Activity Book
  Topic Bank for Heterogeneous Classes
  Grammar Exercise Workbook Teacher's Edition
  Daily Language Practice
  Hands-on Grammar Activity Book
  Academic and Workplace Skills Activity Book Teacher's Edition
  Vocabulary and Spelling Workbook Teacher's Edition
  Reading Support Practice Book Teacher's Edition
  Standardized Test Preparation Workbook Teacher's Edition
  Writing Assessment and Portfolio Management
  Formal Assessment Book
SuccessNet Teacher Access Pack
Scoring Rubrics on Transparency

Assessment
Formal Assessment Book
Standardized Test Preparation Workbook
Standardized Test Preparation Workbook Teacher's Edition
Writing Assessment and Portfolio Management

Grammar, Usage, and Mechanics
Grammar Exercise Workbook
Grammar Exercise Workbook Teacher's Edition
Extra Grammar and Writing Exercises
Grammar Exercises Answers on Transparencies
Hands-on Grammar Activity Book
Hands-on Grammar Activity Book Teacher's Edition
Daily Language Practice
Daily Language Practice Transparencies

Writing
Writing Support Activity Book
Writing Support Activity Book Teacher's Edition
Writing Support Transparencies
Topic Bank for Heterogeneous Classes

Academic and Workplace Skills
Academic and Workplace Skills Activity Book
Academic and Workplace Skills Activity Book Teacher's Edition

Reading, Vocabulary, and Spelling
Reading Support Activity Book
Reading Support Activity Book Teacher's Edition
Vocabulary and Spelling Workbook
Vocabulary and Spelling Workbook Teacher's Edition

Technology
TeacherEXPRESS™
Exam*View*® Test Bank CD-ROM
StudentEXPRESS™
Writers at Work DVD

Correlation to the Six Traits Analytic Model

Chapter	Ideas	Organization	Voice	Word Choice	Sentence Fluency	Conventions
1 The Writer in You	7	7	7	7	7	7
	H3	H3	H3	H3	H3	H3
2 A Walk Through the Writing Process	14–18; 20; 24	17–18		21	20	22
	H6–10; 12	H9–10		H13	H12	H14
3 Sentences, Paragraphs, and Compositions: Structure and Style	33–37; 41; 44	38–39	42	42	29–31; 42	31; 43
	H21–25; 29	H26–27	H30	H30	H17–19; 30	H19; 31
4 Narration: Autobiographical Writing	50–57; 60; 66–70	50–53; 58; 60; 66–69		61; 63		62; 64
	H34–37; 40	H38; 40		H41; 43		H42; 44
5 Narration: Short Story	76–81; 83–85; 91–94	76–77; 82; 84; 90–93		87	85	86; 88
	H48–51; 53–55	H52; 54		H57	H55	H56; 58
6 Description	100–109; 115–118	115–116		100–101; 104–105; 110; 112; 115–117	110	111; 113
	H62–69; 75			H64–65; 70; 72; 75	H70	H71; 73
7 Persuasion: Persuasive Speech	124–131; 133; 135; 140–142; 144	124–125; 132; 143		134; 136–137; 143	134	135; 138; 143
	H78–83; 85; 87	H84		H86; 88–89	H86	H87; 90
8 Persuasion: Advertisement	150–156; 161–164	161–163	152–153	153; 158; 161–163		157; 159
	H94–100; 105	H105	H96–97	H97; 102; 105		H101; 103
9 Exposition: Comparison-and-Contrast Essay	170–177; 179–181; 187–189; 190	170–173; 178; 180–181; 187–189	170–173	170–173; 184; 187–189	182; 187–189	183; 185
	H108–111; 113–115; 121	H112; 114–115; 121		H118; 121	H116; 121	H117; 119
10 Exposition: Cause-and-Effect Essay	196–201; 203; 210–214	196–197; 202; 204; 210–213		207; 213		205–206; 208
	H124–127; 129	H128; 130		H133		H131–132; 134
11 Exposition: Problem-and-Solution Essay	196–201; 203; 210–214	228; 230–233; 237–241	237–241	234	233	232; 235
	H138–141; 143–147; 151–153	H142; 144–147; 151–153	H151–153	H148	H147	H146; 149
12 Research: Documented Essay	248–256; 258; 260; 267–270	248–251; 257; 259; 267–269		263–264	261	252–255; 262; 265
	H156–160; 162; 164; 171	H161; 163; 171		H167–168	H165	H156–159; 166; 169
13 Research: Research Paper	276–290; 297–302	276–279; 286–287; 289–290; 297–301		293	291	292; 295
	H174–184; 191–193	H180–181; 183–184; 191–193		H187	H185	H186; 189

Correlation to the Six Traits Analytic Model

Chapter	Ideas	Organization	Voice	Word Choice	Sentence Fluency	Conventions
14 Response to Literature	308–314; 316; 318; 323–326	308–309; 315; 317; 323–325	308–309	310–311; 320	318	319; 321
	[H]196–200; 202; 204; 209	[H]201; 203; 209		[H]196–197; 206	[H]204	[H]205; 207
15 Writing for Assessment	332–333; 335; 336; 340–344	334; 336–337; 340–343		337		338
	[H]212–213; 215–216	[H]214; 216–217		[H]217		[H]218
16 Workplace Writing	350–355; 360	350–355				
	[H]222–227	[H]222–227				
17 The Parts of Speech				379		368–409
				[H]245		[H]234–271
18 Basic Sentence Parts						412–435
						[H]274–295
19 Phrases and Clauses					469	440–473
					[H]327	[H]298–329
20 Effective Sentences					483–491; 501–515	480–515
					[H]335–343; 353–365	[H]332–365
21 Verb Usage						520–559
						[H]368–405
22 Pronoun Usage						564–581
						[H]408–423
23 Agreement						586–617
						[H]426–455
24 Using Modifiers						622–635
						[H]458–469
25 Miscellaneous Problems in Usage						640–661
						[H]472–491
26 Capitalization						668–683
						[H]494–507

Correlation to the Six Traits Analytic Model

Chapter	Ideas	Organization	Voice	Word Choice	Sentence Fluency	Conventions
27 Punctuation						688–759
						H510–577
Sentence Diagraming Workshop						764–775
						H698–699
28 Speaking, Listening, Viewing, and Representing	780–781	781		781		
	H582–583	H583		H583		
29 Vocabulary and Spelling	804			801–811		812–821
	H604			H601–611		H612–621
30 Reading Skills	831–841	841	835; 838; 841	835; 841	841	
	H629–639	H639	H633; 636; 639	H633; 639	H639	
31 Study, Reference, and Test-Taking Skills						
32 Workplace Skills and Competencies						

PRENTICE HALL
WRITING AND
GRAMMAR

Grade Twelve

PEARSON

Prentice
Hall

Upper Saddle River, New Jersey
Boston, Massachusetts

WRITING AND GRAMMAR

Grade Twelve

ISBN 0-13-200967-6

1 2 3 4 5 6 7 8 9 10   10 09 08 07 06

Go Online
PHSchool.com

Use  *Writing and Grammar,* your textbook online!

> Includes every grammar exercise in this book!

- instant feedback on interactive grammar exercises
- interactive writing tools and writing tutorials
- access to the *Prentice Hall Online Essay Scorer*

Interactive Textbook is also available on CD-ROM.

Go on-line to get instant help on the Writing and Grammar Web site!

- additional grammar practice opportunities
- scoring rubrics with scored student models for different modes of writing

Here's how to use the Writing and Grammar Web site:

Look for these Web Codes in your book:

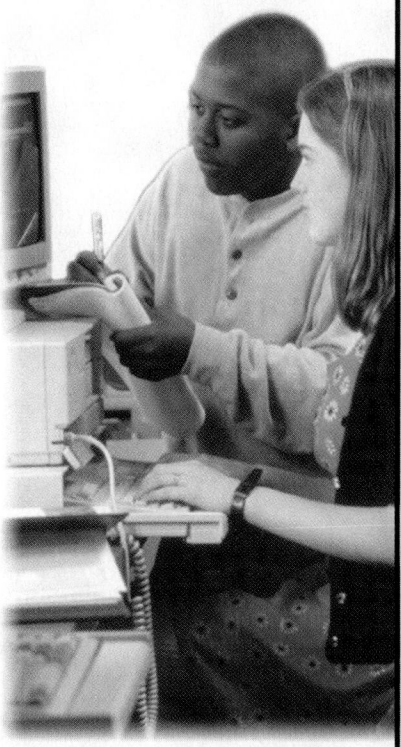

> egk-1201
> egk-1202

Here's how to use Web Codes:

1. Go on-line. Enter URL: PHSchool.com

2. If you want instant feedback on interactive grammar exercises, enter Web Code: egk-1202

   Choose the appropriate chapter from the menu that appears.

3. If you want to review writing rubrics and scored student models, enter Web Code: egk-1201

   Choose the appropriate chapter from the menu that appears.

iii

▶ Lesson Objectives

1. To understand writing as a recursive process and to develop ownership of one's own writing process

2. To write in a variety of forms, including narrative, descriptive, persuasive, expository, and literary texts, and to develop skills in writing for assessment

3. To analyze works of literature and student drafts as models and examples of specific writing strategies

4. To develop voice and adjust one's writing to various audiences and purposes

5. To develop research skills and to use writing as a tool for learning

6. To apply specific prewriting strategies for generating and narrowing writing topics

7. To use graphic organizers and other methods for organizing and supporting ideas in drafting

8. To approach revision in a systematic way in terms of overall structure, paragraphs, sentences, and word choice

9. To edit and proofread drafts to ensure appropriate usage and accuracy in spelling and the conventions and mechanics of written English

10. To understand rubrics and to use them to evaluate one's own writing and the writing of others

Josephine and Mercie. Edmund Tarbell, The Corcoran Museum of Art, Washington, DC

PART

1

Writing

Responding to Fine Art

Josephine and Mercie (1908)
by Edmund Tarbell

Use this artwork to start a discussion about the process of writing.

1. Have students examine the painting. You might use the following questions to prompt discussion:

   How would you describe the setting of this painting? What mood does the painting project?

   What is each woman doing? In what ways has the artist drawn the viewer's attention to the woman writing? (One woman is reading; one is writing. The writer is prominently placed in the foreground, and her white dress is set off by the darkness of the writing desk.)

2. Point out the open door of the secretary, or writing desk.

   What geometrical forms are seen? What might have been the artist's intent of having this door open? (Possible response: The geometric shapes form an interesting contrast to the rounded shapes of lamp and lampshade, chairs, and carving atop the secretary. The open door, giving access to books, might symbolize an invitation to reading.)

3. Each woman seems oblivious to the presence of the other. Ask students to suggest why reading or writing can be such an absorbing activity.

About the Artist

In 1898, Massachuetts-born Edmund Tarbell (1862–1938) joined a group of artists based in Boston and New York whose artistic credo was "poetic gentility"—the depiction of elegance and harmony with soft light. Tarbell became famous for his portraits of intimate family groupings. He usually painted curtained interiors and often used his own family members as subjects (as he did here with Josephine and Mercie, two of his daughters). Tarbell's canvases often display the patterns, informality, and free-brushstroke features of Impressionism.

1H • 1

In-Depth Lesson Plan

	LESSON FOCUS	PRINT AND MEDIA RESOURCES
DAY 1	**Writing in Everyday Life** Students discuss the value of writing in everyday life. (p. 2/H2)	*Writers at Work* **DVD,** selected segments *Writing and Grammar* **Interactive Text,** Ch. 1
DAY 2	**Developing Your Writing Life** Students identify strategies for generating and organizing ideas for writing. They learn strategies for working with others. (pp. 3–6)	**Teaching Resources** *Writing Support Transparencies,* 1-A–B; *Writing Support Activity Book,* 1-1–2
DAY 3	**Qualities of Good Writing; Reflecting on Your Writing** Students identify the qualities of good writing and write a reflective response on their own writing practices. (p. 7/H3)	**Teaching Resources** *Formal Assessment,* Ch. 1

Accelerated Lesson Plan

	LESSON FOCUS	PRINT AND MEDIA RESOURCES
DAY 1	**Writing in Everyday Life; Developing Your Writing Life** Students discuss the value of writing in everyday life. Students identify strategies for generating and organizing ideas, for working with others, and for publishing their work. (pp. 2–6/H2)	*Writers at Work* **DVD,** selected segments **Teaching Resources** *Writing Support Transparencies,* 1-A–B; *Writing Support Activity Book,* 1-1–2
DAY 2	**Qualities of Good Writing; Reflecting on Your Writing** Students identify the qualities of good writing and reflect on their own writing practices. (p. 7/H3)	**Teaching Resources** *Formal Assessment,* Ch. 1

Options for Adapting Lesson Plans

HOMEWORK

Have students complete any of the exercises for homework.

FEATURES

Extend coverage with Spotlight on the Humanities (p. 8), Media and Technology Skills (p. 9), and the Standardized Test Preparation Workshop (p. 10).

Writing and Grammar Handbook Alignment

Page numbers in Step-by-Step Teaching Guides in this Teacher's Edition refer to pages from the full student text. Handbook page references, indicated with this icon ⊞, are provided in Time and Resource Manager boxes and at the bottom of each Teacher's Edition page.

INTEGRATED SKILLS COVERAGE

Viewing and Representing Skills
Critical Viewing, SE pp. 2, 5, 6, 8/⊞2
Analyzing How Meaning Is Communicated Through the Arts, SE/ATE p. 8

Real-World Connection
ATE p. 4

Technology Skills
SE pp. 4, 9

Speaking and Listening Skills
ATE p. 7

Time-Management Skills
ATE p. 5

ASSESSMENT SUPPORT

Standardized Test Preparation Workshop, SE p. 10

Standardized Test Preparation Workbook, pp. 1–2

Formal Assessment, Ch. 1

Writing Assessment and Portfolio Management

MEETING INDIVIDUAL NEEDS

Less Advanced Students ATE p. 11. See also Ongoing Assessment, ATE p. 5.

AP Students ATE pp. 4, 11

ESL Students ATE p. 6

BLOCK SCHEDULING

Pacing Suggestions
For 90-minute Blocks
• Cover the content of Chapter 1 in a single period.

• You may wish to use part of a second period to administer the sample prompt from the Standardized Test Preparation Workshop and the assessment for Chapter 1 from *Formal Assessment.*

Resources for Varying Instruction
• *Writing and Grammar* Interactive Text A 90-minute block provides an ideal opportunity for students to work on the computer.

• *Writers at Work* DVD Show selected segments in class to introduce several professional writers.

Professional Development Support
• *How to Manage Instruction in the Block* This teaching resource provides management and activity suggestions.

MEDIA AND TECHNOLOGY

For the Teacher
• *Writers at Work* DVD, selected segments

• TeacherEXPRESS™ CD-ROM

WRITING AND GRAMMAR ON-LINE

Interactive Text (On-line or on CD-ROM)
• Easily navigable instruction with interactive Revision Checkers
• Full use of e-rater™, the essay-scoring system (on-line only)

Companion Web Site PHSchool.com
• Scoring rubrics with models (use Web Code egk-1201)

See the Go On-line! feature, SE p. iii.

LITERATURE CONNECTIONS

Related selections from *Prentice Hall Literature, Penguin Edition,* The British Tradition:
from *Midsummer* and from *Omeros,* Derek Walcott, ATE p. 3
"In Memory of W. B. Yeats" and "Musée des Beaux Arts," W. H. Auden, ATE p. 6

The Writer in You

Lesson Objectives

1. To identify a variety of writing forms, including business, personal, literary, and persuasive texts, for various audiences and purposes

2. To recognize the qualities of good writing, including ideas, organization, voice, word choice, sentence fluency and variety, and appropriate usage

3. To use writing as a study tool to collect, clarify, and recall ideas

4. To appreciate writing as a means to formulate questions, refine topics, and convey ideas

5. To explore working with others to develop ideas, to evaluate one's own and others' writing, and to write collaboratively

6. To recognize strategies used by writers in different fields

Critical Viewing

Speculate Students may imagine the girl is writing in a journal or diary because of her surroundings and look of contemplation.

▲ Critical Viewing
What type of writing do you imagine that this student is doing? Why?
[Speculate]

Writing is an activity like any other. You improve through practice and reflection. Just as you can't run a marathon if you haven't been training, your writing won't be effective if you haven't devoted time and energy to honing your writing skills. As Samuel Johnson said, "What is written without effort is in general read without pleasure."

Writing in Everyday Life

Writing is probably already an integral part of your daily routine. Consider everything you might write in one day: messages or reminders at home, e-mail at the computer, notes in school, and ideas in a journal. Your school life also includes many different forms of writing—from creative short stories and poems to well-researched reports and presentations. Short-answer quizzes and essay tests are also a familiar challenge.

2 • The Writer in You

⏱ TIME AND RESOURCE MANAGER

Resources
Print: *Writing Support Transparencies*, 1-A–B
Technology: *Writers at Work* DVD, selected segments

Using the Full Student Edition	Using the Handbook Ⓗ
• Cover pp. 2–7 in class. • Bring in samples of a clipping file or a reader's journal for students to peruse. • Have students track their ideas using one or more of these strategies for at least a week.	• Cover pp. 2–3 in class.

Why Write?

There is nothing you will ever learn in school that is more important than learning to be a good writer. That is because you will be called on to use your writing skills throughout your life—both in work situations and in your life outside of work. In addition to helping you achieve success in your life, writing can enable you to express your feelings and observations to others. As you go through life, you'll discover that the opportunities that writing can provide for you are almost limitless.

Developing Your Writing Life

You will communicate with writing throughout your life. Long after you finish your last school essay, you will be applying the writing skills you are developing now. You will write in your future career to prepare clear reports, notes, and correspondence. Writing will help you organize your personal life, too.

Keep Track of Your Ideas

A writer cannot write without ideas any more than a mason can build a brick wall without bricks. You need to collect, select, and develop ideas throughout any writing project. Here are some methods you can use to keep track of your inspirations:

Writer's Notebook You need to be ready for inspiration when it strikes. Carry a small notebook to record writing ideas or thoughts wherever you go. You might use it to record thoughts that pique your interest, subjects for further research, or snippets of overheard conversation. You can include quotations from the media or the Internet. Some writers prefer to carry a small audio recorder to dictate their thoughts. When you transcribe them into writing, new connections and relationships may jump out at you.

Clipping File You can store a wide variety of materials in a clipping file. Include anything from a newspaper article to a printout from a Web page. Look in unusual sources like daily calendars, "junk" mail, and travel brochures, too.

Personal Journal Write regularly in a personal journal. You can write about anything you observe or feel or anything that captures your interest. The act of writing regularly will help you improve as a writer.

Style Journal Keep a Style Journal in which you experiment with different writing forms and ways of writing. For example, you might try writing the opening sentence for three different kinds of novels. You might take an idea and write it in three or four different poetic forms.

Writers in ACTION

For many writers, the process of creation is a journey of discovery. Through writing, you can explore new ideas and new approaches. Poet Derek Walcott says that writing is "a process not of knowing, but of unknowing, of learning again. The next word or phrase that's written has to feel as if it's being written for the first time, that you are discovering the meaning of the word as you put it down."

The Writer in You • 3

More About the Writer

Derek Walcott won the Nobel Prize for Literature in 1992. Possibly as a result of his mixed cultural heritage, his writing explores the theme of the "opposites" that make up his life. For example, having grown up in St. Lucia, he feels both British and Caribbean. His writing explores the boundaries of race and nationality. Excerpts from Walcott's *Midsummer* and *Omeros* may be found in *Prentice Hall Literature, Penguin Edition, The British Tradition.*

Keep Track of Your Writing and Reading

1. Bring in some samples of writing completed at the beginning and the end of a school year. Demonstrate how a student's writing can develop over a year.

2. Bring in a reader's journal and discuss how each quote means something to the reader. Suggest that students begin keeping reader's journals.

3. Encourage students to critique the entries in their reader's journals and share them with friends. This will allow others an opportunity to consider their peers' recommendations.

Customize for
AP Students

Encourage students to bring in two samples of their writing from the beginning and end of the last school year. Encourage students to assess their writing development.

Experiment With Different Approaches

1. Emphasize that different writers use different strategies, depending on the nature of the writing.

2. Display some visual outlines or graphic organizers such as idea webs or flowcharts.

3. Show on an overhead projector a Student Work in Progress at the revision stage. (You can find these in Chapters 4–16.) The more crossouts and major changes the better. Discuss how the changes affect the writing.

Real-World Connection

In the past, writers left a trail of evidence in the form of revised drafts sprinkled with the author's notes. With the advent of computers, most writers' works are now viewed only in their final format. Discuss with students the value of unpublished drafts. Why do they think people are anxious to see unpublished work by well-known writers?

Keep Track of Your Writing and Reading

Writing Portfolio The best way to track your progress as a writer is to keep a writing portfolio—a file box in which you store past writing projects. Keeping a portfolio gives you an opportunity to review your work to see areas of improvement and to identify areas in which you still need work. Reviewing the works in your portfolio may also give you ideas for new pieces of writing. Your portfolio should include a wide range of different types of writing, and, ideally, it should include not only final drafts but also samples of earlier drafts, prewriting notes, and graphic organizers.

Reader's Journal Reading other writers' works can stimulate your own writing. Keeping a reader's journal can help you stay aware of what you have read and what has made an impact on you. Jot down memorable quotations and observations about characters and themes.

Experiment With Different Approaches

An approach to writing that works well for one writer may not work well for another writer. As a writer, you have to find the approach that is best suited for you. Experiment with different writing strategies and approaches. Note what is most and least effective. Continue using the techniques that work well, and avoid using those that do not.

Prewriting Prewriting refers to all of the work you do before you actually sit down to write. It includes generating ideas, collecting information, and organizing your material. You may find it helpful to devote much of your time to prewriting. Doing so may make it a lot easier to sit down and assemble a piece of writing.

Drafting Some writers find it most effective to write an entire first draft in one sitting. They write in a single burst, without making revisions as they go along. Other writers break up the production of a first draft into stages, pausing every now and then to read over what they've written and make revisions.

Refining Your Work Revising is perhaps the most important part of the process of writing. However, there are many different ways of revising. You might, for example, want to approach the revision process in stages, focusing on individual aspects of your writing one at a time.

Being Flexible Regardless of how you approach each stage of writing, it is important to be flexible. Writing is not a linear process. It is a recursive process, which means that if you find that something isn't working for you, go back to an earlier stage of the process. For instance, if you begin writing and you discover that you don't have enough material to work with, go back and gather more information.

⊚ Technology Tip

You can keep an electronic writing portfolio on a computer or on a disk. Use a separate folder for each piece of writing. Make sure that you also save a print copy.

Plan Where and When to Write

Developing a successful approach to writing involves not only the stages you go through to complete a piece of writing, but also where and when you choose to write.

Choose an Effective Location

Experiment with writing in different places until you find one that works for you. You may find that you are most successful working on a computer at your desk, or you may like working in a comfortable chair with music playing and a notebook and pen in your hands. Whatever place you choose should be free of outside distractions, should be well lit, and should have all of the implements you need to write. Keep your writing portfolio close at hand, along with a dictionary and a thesaurus, and post any writing schedules that you are currently following.

Follow a Schedule
In order to complete a long project, you need to break your long-term goal into smaller, intermediate goals. Devise a schedule that includes each step you must achieve in order to complete the project. As you decide on deadlines, estimate the time each step will require, allowing extra time to accommodate stages that take longer than expected. You may want to include group conferences or peer-review meetings in your schedule, remembering to notify others about any changes. Post your schedule in your writing area, and refer to it regularly to make sure that you are still on track. If you find that a particular step takes longer than anticipated, make modifications in your schedule.

Take Writing Breaks
Put your writing aside every so often, and move on to another activity. You can then return to your writing with a fresh eye. Doing so will help you look at your writing more objectively and may also enable you to find outside inspiration that will help move your work along.

▲ **Critical Viewing**
What are the pros and cons of drafting on a computer? [**Analyze**]

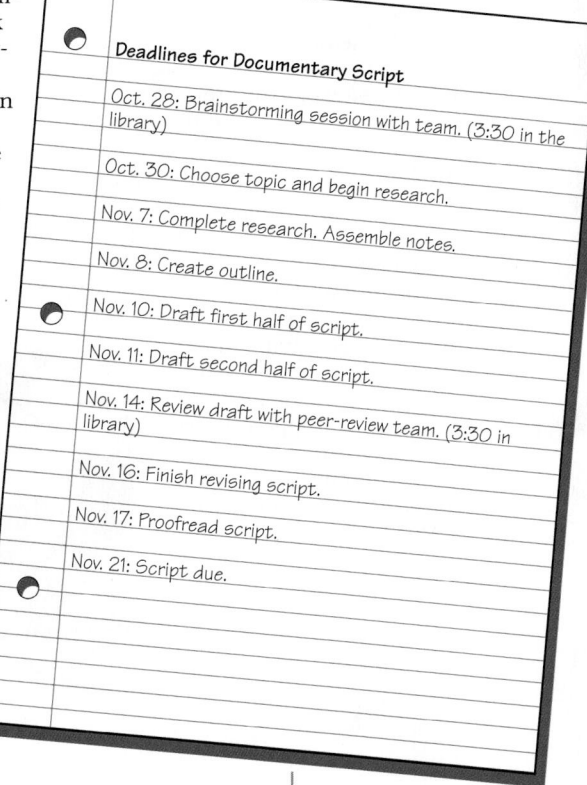

Deadlines for Documentary Script

Oct. 28: Brainstorming session with team. (3:30 in the library)

Oct. 30: Choose topic and begin research.

Nov. 7: Complete research. Assemble notes.

Nov. 8: Create outline.

Nov. 10: Draft first half of script.

Nov. 11: Draft second half of script.

Nov. 14: Review draft with peer-review team. (3:30 in library)

Nov. 16: Finish revising script.

Nov. 17: Proofread script.

Nov. 21: Script due.

The Writer in You • 5

For the first writing assignment of the school year, require students to turn in notes and drafts before the final due date. Review their work and return it promptly so they can incorporate your feedback into their final product. For subsequent writing assignments, set fewer and fewer short-term deadlines. Eventually, students should be able to set these goals on their own.

Plan Where and When to Write

Teaching Resources: Writing Support Transparencies 1-B; Writing Support Activity Book, 1-2

1. Ask students to consider their ideal writing location. Discuss the effect of having the TV or radio on versus having a quiet room. Do students thrive in the "white noise" of the lunchroom, or do they prefer the quiet early morning hours?

2. Remind students that deadlines can affect the quality of a writer's work. Encourage students to plan their time carefully and avoid the stress of looming deadlines.

3. Emphasize that setting smaller deadlines prior to the due date of a project will make the workload more manageable and improve a work's quality.

4. Ask students to make a chart in which they break a writing assignment into tasks according to the writing process steps. Then, ask them to estimate how long each step would take. Point out that students often underestimate small writing tasks and overestimate large writing tasks, such as cause-and-effect or research papers.

Integrating Time-Management Skills

Encourage students to use a calendar or planner to plot out each week in advance. Linking dates to deadlines allows students to plan and prepare for assignments. Remind students that taking breaks from writing is also part of time management.

Critical Viewing

Analyze Students' responses should note that one advantage is that a computer is quick, assuming the student is a quick typist. Creating a first draft on computer also has the advantage of allowing a writer to more easily "cut and paste" elements in the draft during the writing process. However, first drafts may be "lost" if they are not saved correctly or printed out.

Work With Others

1. Remind students that publishing a piece of writing requires the effort and expertise of many people. Literary agents and editors suggest and make changes to an author's work. Proofreaders check manuscripts for accuracy.

2. Assign, or allow students to choose, editorial groups.

3. Ask each editorial group to use the round-robin technique of having each student contribute a segment at a time to compose a group story, poem, or article.

4. Students might exchange their projects with another group. Allow groups to apply the editorial process to the writing. Provide guidelines for peer review.

5. Encourage students to present completed work to the class.

Publishing

1. Have students make a class list of places students might publish their writing (local newspapers, school newspaper, school literary magazine, etc.).

2. Have students explore Internet opportunities for publishing.

Customize for
ESL Students

For the group brainstorming activity, pair students with more-fluent English speakers. The partners can help those learning English if they have trouble phrasing their ideas.

Critical Viewing

Analyze The peer-review session looks successful because all of the students are focused on the topic. One student is giving feedback, and the others are listening closely to his ideas.

1

Work With Others

Working with others can help you come up with ideas, discover ways of improving your work that you have missed, and find new strategies for approaching your work.

Group Brainstorming A group brainstorming session is a free-flowing discussion on a broad topic. Encourage participants to share any ideas that come to mind. Don't critically evaluate the ideas that are expressed. Instead, let the discussion flow. Let one idea lead to the next. Take notes as the discussion progresses. Use your notes as a source of writing topics.

Collaborative Writing In collaborative writing, a group works together to complete a writing project. Every team develops its own dynamics. Some teams divide the work into tasks, such as researching, drafting, and revising. Others divide a large topic into subtopics, with each member responsible for writing about one subtopic.

Peer Reviewers Even if you are writing independently, you might decide to ask a partner to read a draft to help you catch mistakes and identify ideas that need further elaboration. Listen carefully to your reviewer's advice. Discuss comments you don't agree with, and then make your own final decisions.

Publishing

For sheer satisfaction, few experiences can match reaching an audience with your writing. Seeing your work in print can boost your self-confidence as a writer and inspire you to set and achieve even more challenging writing goals. Look for opportunities to publish your writing, whether through a student Web site or by submission to a magazine contest.

Writers in
ACTION

Writing doesn't begin with a pen—it begins with a mental spark. Poet W. H. Auden said that the first act of writing is "noticing." Novelist John Irving agrees that inspiration comes from a "vision—not so much what we make up but what we witness."

▼ **Critical Viewing** Does this look like an effective peer-review session? Why or why not? **[Analyze]**

More About the Writers

W. H. Auden's poetry often deals with a quest or journey. Auden's poems "In Memory of W. B. Yeats" and "Musée des Beaux Arts" can be found in *Prentice Hall Literature, Penguin Edition,* The British Tradition.

John Irving is an unlikely writer given his difficulties reading and writing—he is dyslexic. Irving says he has learned a lot from his disability. Reading slowly has taught him to "pay more particular attention to the way a sentence works and the way a word sounds than people for whom the act comes naturally."

What Are the Qualities of Good Writing?

Ideas Think about the most captivating pieces of writing you've read. Most interesting writing begins with a good idea—an unusual perspective or viewpoint. The first step toward making your own writing captivating is coming up with interesting ideas. Think about the topics that fascinate you most. Then, decide how you can present topics in unique ways.

Organization It is essential to present your ideas in a logical, organized way. Think about your topic and the type of writing that you are doing, and choose the organization that makes the most sense to you. For example, if you are comparing and contrasting two items, you may want to present all of the similarities first and then present all of the differences.

Voice Voice refers to all of the qualities that set your writing apart. The qualities include the words you use, the way you put your words together, the topics you explore, and more. Focus on developing your voice to give your writing a personal touch.

Word Choice Words are the most essential components of writing. Choosing the right word can make a difference in whether a reader understands what you are trying to convey or is willing to accept your viewpoint. Take care in choosing your words so that they convey the exact meaning you intend and stir up the types of emotions you desire from your audience.

Sentence Fluency Use transitions and sentence variety to produce a rhythm in your writing and to ensure that one sentence flows smoothly into the next.

Conventions Follow the conventions of English grammar, usage, mechanics, and spelling in your writing.

Reflecting on Your Writing

You can foster your own growth as a writer by asking yourself questions about your writing successes and the obstacles that you have encountered. Here are some questions to begin your reflection:

- Which of your writing projects makes you feel most proud? Why did you connect so well with this project?
- What specific challenges have you faced when writing? How did you overcome these challenges?
- What writers do you admire? How does reading their work suggest ideas you can apply to your own writing?
- What was the most valuable writing "mistake" you ever made?

Share your responses with a partner, and then note your ideas in your writer's journal.

What Are the Qualities of Good Writing?

1. Discuss with the class the six aspects of writing listed on page 7. Point out that even those categories that concern basic communication, such as organization, can involve distinctive effects, as when a writer organizes information in a story to create a surprise ending.

2. Have students name favorite writers and describe distinctive features of their work, relating each feature to one of the six categories.

Reflecting on Your Writing

1. Ask students to add questions to the list. (Examples: What do you do about writer's block?)

2. Ask students to imagine that they are famous writers. Have students write short essays detailing their writing careers, discussing the genre in which they write and their characteristic themes and style.

Integrating Speaking and Listening Skills

Remind students of the importance of active listening in group discussion. Students should focus their attention as they interpret and respond to a speaker's message.

ASSESS AND CLOSE

Teaching Resources: Formal Assessment, Ch. 1

1. Ask students to write a response to one of the reflecting questions on page 7 for inclusion in their portfolios. The response will serve as a benchmark of their current abilities and perspectives on writing.

2. Review the Standardized Test Preparation Workshop on pages 10–11 and have students respond to the writing prompt.

3. Administer the Chapter 1 assessment from *Formal Assessment* in the Teaching Resources to measure students' grasp of concepts.

✓ ONGOING ASSESSMENT: Assess Mastery

Use one of the following options to assess students' learning.

Option 1 Ask students to answer each of the questions in Reflecting on Your Writing. Then, have them write a single paragraph describing what type of writing they look forward to most in the coming school year.

Option 2 Students may choose a writer—such as Walcott, Auden, or Irving—and do research in the library or on the Internet to add to their knowledge about his or her career. Suggest that students share their findings with the class.

Step-by-Step Teaching Guide

Analyzing How Meaning Is Communicated Through the Arts

1. Discuss with students a definition of *humanities* (the branches of learning concerned with human thought and relations, as distinguished from the sciences).

2. Go over the specific characteristics of each art form described on this page. Then, ask students to share specific examples of fine art, photography, theater, film, music, and dance they have participated in or seen.

3. Compare and contrast the various art forms in terms of setting, location and role of the audience, and the different ways each form evokes audience response.

4. Help students come up with a topic to write about. You might bring in books of fine art and photography, as well as musical recordings. Brainstorm for titles of films, plays, and dance performances. Remind students to support their opinions with specific details about the artwork.

Viewing and Representing

Activity Give students an opportunity to present their essays to the class. Encourage students to visually display some aspect of the work of art as part of their presentation.

Critical Viewing

Analyze Students might note that an exhibit allows viewers to compare and contrast artists and their works. It also gives them an overall sense of the art of a specific time period.

Spotlight on the Humanities

Analyzing How Meaning Is Communicated Through the Arts
Introducing Spotlight on the Humanities

Whether woven in the moving notes of a great composer, in the storyline of a classic drama, or in the brilliant colors of a painted masterpiece, self-expression can be exhibited through several different media. As artists experiment and challenge boundaries, definitions of various art forms grow and change. However, to give you a framework for a study of the humanities, consider these broad categories:

- **Fine Art** fashions meaning through color, line, texture, and subject. It includes paintings, sketches, sculpture, and collage.

- **Photography** captures still images of people, places, and events. Photographers can express ideas through their choice of subjects and their use of composition and lighting.

- **Theater** is designed to be performed by actors on a stage. Using props, scenery, sound effects, and lighting, drama brings a story to life.

- **Film** records sound and motion. Like dramatic theater, most films tell a story and use setting and characterization to develop it. A filmmaker can also portray a unique point of view using camera angles and lighting and sound techniques.

- **Music** creates meaning through pitch and rhythm. Whether presented as an oboe solo, an operatic aria, or a symphony, music can create moods or present variations on a theme.

- **Dance** generates meaning through organized movement. It can be performed by a single person, a pair, or larger groups.

Writing Activity
Think about a classic work of art that you like from any of the categories in the above list. Write an explanation of why you believe this work of art has stood the test of time and still inspires audiences today.

▲ Critical Viewing
What are the benefits of attending a museum exhibit such as this one? **[Analyze]**

Media and Technology Skills

Making Technology Work for You

Activity: Experiment With a Variety of Tools

Writers use tools that range from a simple pencil to a complex computer network. Experimenting with a wide variety of technologies will help you develop many useful writing strategies. Spend some time learning how these tools work.

Word-Processing Software Many writers prefer to draft and revise their work using a word processor because this software includes many powerful writing functions. For example, using cut-and-paste tools, a writer can easily try different arrangements of sentences or paragraphs.

Desktop-Publishing Software Use desktop-publishing software to produce newsletters, brochures, or other forms that incorporate text and art. You might add art using graphics software or digital photos. Interesting and bold fonts can also heighten the appeal of your final document. This software allows you to plan and change the layout of a document easily.

The Internet Writers need access to information. The Internet provides millions of ideas, facts, data, images, and sounds. When you sign on, you connect your computer to this network and can collect information stored throughout the world.

E-mail Sending electronic mail, called e-mail, from your computer to another computer, is a great way to swap ideas with friends or students in other areas. You can also share early or final drafts of your current writing projects.

Tracking Your Use of Technology Over the course of the year, keep a log of the different types of technology that you use in writing, and note whether they are effective and why.

Media and Technology Skills • 9

Lesson Objectives

1. To use technology for aspects of creating, revising, editing, and publishing texts
2. To compile written ideas and representations into reports, summaries, or other formats and draw conclusions

Step-by-Step Teaching Guide

Making Technology Work for You

1. Have students summarize the basic uses of each writing tool described on this page. Discuss specific ways in which these tools are used for business, education, entertainment, and everyday communication.

2. Point out the example of a history textbook layout. Discuss the advantages of desktop-publishing software. Have students bring in examples of newsletters, pamphlets, brochures, or other items they have generated with computer software.

3. Review the word-processing tips listed in the sidebar box. Allow students to add any additional suggestions or observations they may have.

4. If your school has computer facilities, you might give the class an opportunity to use various writing tools. For example, they might use word-processing tools to create a chart for logging the different types of technology they use for writing.

Lesson Objectives

1. To write an essay in response to a writing prompt
2. To write in a voice and style appropriate to audience and purpose
3. To use prewriting strategies to generate ideas, develop voice, and plan
4. To produce error-free writing in the final draft

Step-by-Step Teaching Guide

Responding to Writing Prompts

Teaching Resources: Standardized Test Preparation Workbook, pp. 1–2

1. Review with students the elements of writing that will be assessed on a standardized test. Emphasize the importance of understanding the prompt. Have students read the sample prompt and then explain what their essay should include.

2. Tell students that once they are sure about the directions, they should quickly choose a topic. Tell them that it is essential to choose a topic about which they can recall and describe specific details.

3. Suggest that students use a graphic organizer such as a chart, web, or outline in which to organize the details that support their topic.

4. Remind students to keep in mind their intended purpose and audience. Explain that some prompts mention a specific audience, such as the local school board or the student body. If the audience is not mentioned, students should assume they are writing for well-educated adults.

5. Point out the clocks in the student text, and discuss the suggested time frames for each segment of the writing process.

Standardized Test Preparation Workshop

Responding to Writing Prompts

As you must have already discovered in your experience as a student, writing plays a critical role in assessment. For example, writing is often a major component of both national and local standardized tests.

When you are asked to write on standardized tests, you will most often have to work within a limited amount of time. As a result, it is important to budget your time among gathering ideas, drafting your essay, and revising it.

To do well on standardized test essays, it is essential to do the following:

- Respond directly to the prompt.
- Make your writing thoughtful and interesting.
- Make sure your essay has a clear main idea that is supported by facts, examples, and other types of details.
- Make sure that your essay has a clear, logical, and consistent organization.
- Include only ideas or materials that relate directly to the prompt.
- Take care to avoid errors in grammar, usage, mechanics, spelling, and sentence structure.

Following is an example of one type of writing prompt that you might find on a standardized test. Use the suggestions on the following page to help you respond. The clocks next to each stage show a suggested plan for organizing your time.

Sample Writing Situation

Certain books can have a major influence on our lives. Some books are so important that they may even change the way we think. Write an essay about a book you've read that made you change the way you thought about something. Explain your viewpoint on the issue before you read the book. Then, tell how your point of view changed and why it changed.

Test Tip

Because there are many ways of responding to this type of prompt, you need to set a specific topical goal. The more specific you are, the easier it will be to get your point across.

TEST-TAKING TIP

Draw students' attention to the Test Tip on this page. After they have a specific topic for their essay, students should jot down a number of examples they might use to support it. Discuss various ways a writer can be specific. These might include details from a book, quotations from an expert, or examples or statistics from a study.

Explain that even though the prompt asks for the writer's opinion, it still must be backed up by examples and facts. If they cannot think of at least three examples to support their ideas, students might consider choosing a different topic.

Prewriting

Allow about one quarter of your time for prewriting.

Choose Your Topic Begin by searching your memory for books you have read that had a major influence on you. Choose one of these books. Then, jot down some notes about how the book affected you and why it affected you.

Gather Specific Details The success of your essay will depend on how well you explain how the book brought about the changes in your thinking. To make your explanation effective, you need to provide as much detail as possible. Jot down details from the book that support your points about the book's impact. Then, arrange the details in an order that makes sense.

Drafting

Allow almost half of your time for drafting.

Write Your Introduction Begin with an introductory paragraph in which you state your main point about how the book affected you. If possible, begin your introduction with a question or a quotation that will grab your reader's interest.

Use a Personal Tone Because you are writing about your own experiences, it is appropriate to use a personal, somewhat conversational, tone in your writing.

Provide Examples to Support Your Points Back up your points with details from the book. Describe characters, settings, and events that affected you, and tell why they affected you. Be as specific as possible.

Revising, Editing, and Proofreading

Allow the remainder of your time for this part of the process.

Make Sure Your Point Comes Across Check carefully to see that you have presented your main points clearly and directly and that you have thoroughly backed them up with details from the book.

Proofread Your Work Errors in grammar, usage, mechanics, and spelling can detract from the impact of your essay and hurt your score. Allow time to proofread your work carefully. Place a line through text that you want to delete. Add words or phrases neatly in the space above the text, using a caret [^] to indicate the exact placement.

Customize for
Less Advanced Students

Give students several opportunities in class to practice writing in a timed situation. Help them learn to estimate time by calling out ten-minute intervals and having them note which stage in the writing process they have reached.

Customize for
AP Students

Help students practice monitoring time by giving them short, in-class writing assignments. Tell them to check the clock after completing each stage of the writing process to determine how well they are budgeting their time.

In-Depth Lesson Plan

	LESSON FOCUS	PRINT AND MEDIA RESOURCES
DAY 1	**Introduction to the Writing Process** Students become familiar with the modes of writing and the five stages of the writing process. (pp. 12–13/H4–5)	*Writing and Grammar* Interactive Text, Ch. 2 **Teaching Resources** *Writing Support Transparencies*, 2-A
DAY 2	**Prewriting** Students learn strategies for choosing and narrowing a topic, considering audience and purpose, and gathering details. (pp. 14–17/H6–9)	**Teaching Resources** *Writing Support Transparencies*, 2-B–E; *Writing Support Activity Book*, 2-1–3
DAY 3	**Drafting** Students learn strategies for shaping their writing and providing elaboration. (p. 18/H10)	**Teaching Resources** *Writing Support Transparencies*, 2-G–H
DAY 4	**Revising** Students learn strategies for revising sentences, paragraphs, and overall structure. (pp. 19–21/H11–13)	**Teaching Resources** *Writing Support Transparencies*, 2-I–L
DAY 5	**Editing and Proofreading; Publishing and Presenting** Students learn strategies for checking their work and presenting their final drafts. (pp. 22–23/H14–15)	**Teaching Resources** *Formal Assessment*, Ch. 2

Accelerated Lesson Plan

	LESSON FOCUS	PRINT AND MEDIA RESOURCES
DAY 1	**Introduction to the Writing Process; Prewriting** Students become familiar with the five stages of the writing process and learn strategies for prewriting. (pp. 12–17/H4–9)	*Writing and Grammar* Interactive Text, Ch. 2 **Teaching Resources** *Writing Support Transparencies*, 2-A–E; *Writing Support Activity Book*, 2-1–3
DAY 2	**Drafting Through Presenting** Students learn strategies for drafting, revising, editing, and presenting their writing. (pp. 18–23/H10–15)	**Teaching Resources** *Writing Support Transparencies*, 2-G–L; *Formal Assessment*, Ch. 2

Options for Adapting Lesson Plans

HOMEWORK

Have students complete any stage of the lesson for homework.

FEATURES

Extend coverage with Spotlight on the Humanities (p. 24), Media and Technology Skills (p. 25), and the Standardized Test Preparation Workshop (p. 26).

TECHNOLOGY

Students can complete any stage of the lesson on the computer, using *Writing and Grammar* Interactive Text or a word-processing program. Have them print out their completed work.

Writing and Grammar Handbook Alignment

Page numbers in Step-by-Step Teaching Guides in this Teacher's Edition refer to pages from the full student text. Handbook page references, indicated with this icon 🄷, are provided in Time and Resource Manager boxes and at the bottom of each Teacher's Edition page.

INTEGRATED SKILLS COVERAGE

Viewing and Representing
Critical Viewing, SE pp. 12, 24/🄷4
Evaluating Photographic Techniques, SE p. 24, ATE p. 24

Speaking and Listening
ATE p. 16

Technology
SE p. 25, ATE p. 25

Vocabulary Skills
ATE p. 21

Real-World Connection
ATE p. 22

BLOCK SCHEDULING

Pacing Suggestions
For 90-minute Blocks
• Have students complete the Introduction and the Prewriting and Drafting strategies in a single period.
• Focus one class period on Revising, Editing and Proofreading, and Presenting strategies.

Resources for Varying Instruction
• *Writing and Grammar* Interactive Text A 90-minute block provides an ideal opportunity for students to work on the computer.

Professional Development Support
• *How to Manage Instruction in the Block* This teaching resource provides management and activity suggestions.

ASSESSMENT SUPPORT

Standardized Test Preparation Workshop SE p. 26; ATE pp. 21, 26
Standardized Test Preparation Workbook, pp. 3–4
Formal Assessment, Ch. 2
Writing Assessment and Portfolio Management

MEDIA AND TECHNOLOGY

For the Student
• *Writing and Grammar* Interactive Text, Ch. 2

For the Teacher
• TeacherEXPRESS CD-ROM

MEETING INDIVIDUAL NEEDS

Less Advanced Students ATE pp. 19, 27. See also Ongoing Assessments, ATE pp. 16, 20.
AP Students ATE p. 27
ESL Students ATE pp. 14, 22
Spatial Learners ATE pp. 15, 23

WRITING AND GRAMMAR ON-LINE

Interactive Text (On-line or on CD-ROM)
• Easily navigable instruction with interactive Revision Checkers
• Full use of e-rater™, the essay-scoring system (on-line only)

Companion Web Site PHSchool.com
• Scoring rubrics with models (use Web Code egk-1201)

See the Go On-line! feature, SE p. iii.

A Walk Through the Writing Process

Lesson Objectives

1. To write in a variety of forms appropriate for various audiences and purposes
2. To read to appreciate a writer's craft and to discover models for writing
3. To use prewriting strategies to generate ideas, develop voice, and plan
4. To develop and revise drafts in terms of structure, paragraphs, sentences, and word choice
5. To organize and record information in systematic ways such as notes, charts, and graphic organizers
6. To produce error-free writing in the final draft
7. To refine a selected piece to publish for general and specific audiences
8. To accumulate and review one's own written work to determine its strengths and weaknesses

Critical Viewing

Connect Student responses will vary. Ask volunteers to explain why one particular part of the process appeals to them most.

From prewriting through publishing and presenting, knowing and using the stages of the writing process will help you produce better writing.

Types of Writing

Writing can be categorized by **mode**—the form or shape that it takes. Each type has characteristics that are unique and qualities it shares with other types. For example, narration tells a story, but it may also incorporate elements of description. This chart shows several common modes you'll encounter in this book.

As you work on any piece of writing, you should consider its audience and purpose as well as its form. **Reflexive writing** is from yourself and for yourself. When you write reflexively, you choose what to write, what format to use, and whether to share your writing with others. Because it is for yourself, this type of writing can be tentative and exploratory.

In contrast to reflexive writing, the ideas of **extensive writing** are generated by others and intended for others. With extensive writing, you purposely write something for someone else to read. Therefore, you pay closer attention to conventions, and your writing is less exploratory and more definitive.

▲ **Critical Viewing**
What is your favorite part of writing—the planning shown here, the drafting, or the polishing? Explain. **[Connect]**

Modes of Writing

Narration
Description
Persuasion
Exposition
Research
Response to Literature
Poems and Plays
Writing for Assessment
Workplace Writing

⏱ TIME AND RESOURCE MANAGER

Resources
Print: *Writing Support Transparencies,* 2-A

Using the Full Student Edition	Using the Handbook🄷
• Read pp. 12–13 in class.	• Read pp. 4–5 in class.
• Discuss the definitions of extensive and reflexive writing, and ask students to give examples of each.	• Discuss the definitions of extensive and reflexive writing, and ask students to give examples of each.
• Discuss the stages of the writing process to ensure that students understand each stage.	• Discuss the stages of the writing process to ensure that students understand each stage.

The Process of Writing

These are the stages of the writing process:

• **Prewriting** Freely exploring topics, choosing your topic, and beginning to gather and organize details before you write

• **Drafting** Getting your ideas down on paper in roughly the format you intend

• **Revising** Correcting any major errors and improving the writing's form and content

• **Editing and Proofreading** Polishing the writing; fixing errors in grammar, spelling, and mechanics

• **Publishing and Presenting** Sharing your writing

While these steps may seem sequential, writers may jump back to earlier stages as they work. For example, as you draft, you may realize you want to learn more about your topic. Similarly, during revision, you may need to conduct additional prewriting to refine or elaborate upon an idea. You may even leave a piece of writing in the prewriting stage, save it in your portfolio, and come back to it several weeks later.

A Guided Tour

This chapter introduces you to skills and strategies that you may find useful at each stage of the writing process. As you complete the guided tour the chapter offers, consider the ways each step and each suggested technique could enhance your writing process and, ultimately, your writing.

A Walk Through the Writing Process • 13

PREPARE and ENGAGE

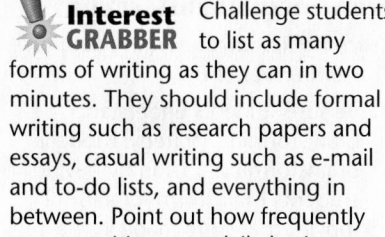 **Interest GRABBER** Challenge students to list as many forms of writing as they can in two minutes. They should include formal writing such as research papers and essays, casual writing such as e-mail and to-do lists, and everything in between. Point out how frequently we use writing on a daily basis.

Activate Prior Knowledge

Draw students' attention to the graphic labeled "Modes of Writing" on page 12. See how many of these modes they can clearly define. If they have trouble defining any of the modes, encourage them to offer examples instead.

TEACH

Step-by-Step Teaching Guide

The Process of Writing

Teaching Resources: Writing Support Transparencies, 2-A

1. Ask students to define the word *process* (a method of doing something, usually involving many steps).

2. Ask students why it is helpful to think of writing as a process rather than as an action involving a single step. (Students should note that the process form allows the writer to divide writing into separate steps and give full attention to each.)

3. Display Transparency 2-A and discuss each step in the writing process. Make sure students understand the purpose of each step.

☑ **ONGOING ASSESSMENT: Diagnose**

Use one of the following options to diagnose students' current level of proficiency in using the writing process.

Option 1 Ask students to bring in their strongest writing sample from last year. Review the samples and determine the step with which each student seems to need the most support.	**Option 2** Ask students to write a paragraph that describes how they go about writing an essay for class. Students who are not familiar with the steps of the writing process will need extra support.

Prewriting: Brainstorming

Teaching Resources: Writing Support Transparencies, 2-B

1. Be sure students understand the brainstorming strategy. Model a brainstorming session by having students brainstorm for a list of movies that were made in the past five years. Write their answers on the board.

2. Next, have students brainstorm in small groups. Tell them to imagine they have to write a how-to essay. They should brainstorm for a list of things they are good at and could explain clearly.

3. Have students look over their lists and circle the topics they find most interesting.

Customize for
ESL Students

Because the goal of brainstorming is to get students' ideas flowing and to create a list of ideas, students might want to brainstorm in their first languages. This way, they can focus on ideas rather than on language and vocabulary. They can go back later and translate their lists into English.

2.1 *What Is Prewriting?*

Just as competitive swimmers need to warm up by stretching before a major race, writers prepare for writing with their own techniques. Before you dive into a first draft, take the time to test the waters by considering the topic you'll address, gathering the details you'll include, and identifying the main idea you'll convey. In this book, each writing chapter will offer several strategies for getting started.

Choosing Your Topic

Before you can write the great American novel, argue persuasively, or respond to a work of literature, you need a topic. Each chapter begins with strategies to help you choose a topic that interests you. Try the sample strategies here to explore the process of choosing your topic.

SAMPLE STRATEGY

Brainstorming Whenever you answer the question, "What should we do today?" you are using the technique of brainstorming. Using a formalized version of this strategy can help you find a writing topic. Make a list of potential ideas that a category suggests, allowing each idea to prompt another. By freeing your mind to make quick connections between ideas for several minutes, you generate a wide list of topics from which to choose. In this sample, a group brainstormed for ideas related to the word *history*, and then, chose to pursue "Winston Churchill" as a writing topic.

BRAINSTORMING TOPICS ABOUT HISTORY		
elections	fortresses	yesterday
wars	Tower of London	historians
castles	stories	-textbooks
ancient:	leaders:	-questions
-Egypt	-Churchill	-interpretations
-Rome	-FDR	-argument
-pyramid	-Lincoln	
technology	followers	
	law	

14 • A Walk Through the Writing Process

🔍 Learn More

For additional prewriting strategies suited to specific writing tasks, see Chapters 4–16.

🔦 Challenge

When you brainstorm with classmates, you get the benefit of their ideas and the connections they see among responses. This is why brainstorming is most effective in a group.

⏲ TIME AND RESOURCE MANAGER

Resources
Print: *Writing Support Transparencies, 2-B–E; Writing Support Activity Book, 2-1–3*

Using the Full Student Edition	Using the Handbook🄷
• Read and discuss pp. 14–17 in class.	• Read and discuss pp. 6–9 in class.
• Work through the four sample strategies in class.	• Work through the four sample strategies in class.
• Have students complete the Applying the Prewriting Strategies assignments on p. 17.	• Have students complete the Applying the Prewriting Strategies assignments on p. 9.

Narrowing Your Topic

The scope of your topic will dictate the amount of detail and explanation you'll need to provide. For example, if your topic is food, you could write a 300-page book comparing the cuisines of the world, a 10-page paper on the unique features of French cuisine, or a 3-page essay explaining the process of making crepes. To identify the topic you'll want to develop, narrow your general topic to one you can address adequately in the time and space you anticipate. You will find a topic-narrowing activity in each lesson.

SAMPLE STRATEGY

Using a Pentad To examine your topic as if it were a drama, use the pentad. This strategy lets you analyze your subject by identifying these five key elements:

- **Actors:** *Who* did the action?
- **Acts:** *What* was done?
- **Scenes:** *When* or *where* was it done?
- **Agencies:** *How* was it done?
- **Purposes:** *Why* was it done?

In the model pentad below, the writer analyzed a summer job as a tour guide to narrow the focus of an autobiographical essay.

PENTAD

Broad Topic: My job as a tour guide

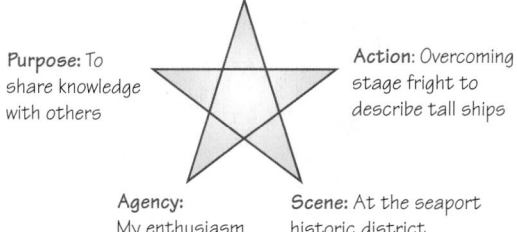

Actors: Me, the tour guides, the tourists

Purpose: To share knowledge with others

Action: Overcoming stage fright to describe tall ships

Agency: My enthusiasm

Scene: At the seaport historic district

Narrow Topic: How my job helped me overcome stage fright and gain self-confidence

Narrowing Your Topic

Teaching Resources: Writing Support Transparencies, 2-C; Writing Support Activity Book, 2-1

1. Work through a sample pentad with the class using the topic "the first lunar landing." Challenge students to identify the five key elements in this topic. (Sample response: Actors—the three astronauts; their spacecraft; Mission Control. Action—escaping Earth's atmosphere, landing on the moon, redocking with the space capsule, and returning safely to Earth. Scene—the launch pad, outer space, the moon. Agency—the spirit of adventure and inquiry; the government. Purpose—to gather knowledge; to establish United States supremacy in the conquest of space.)

2. Encourage students to choose one part of the sample pentad, such as the astronauts involved, that might make for an interesting and narrow essay topic.

3. Ask students to write out their topic in a sentence below the pentad. Example: *"I will examine the background and training of Neil Armstrong."*

Customize for
Spatial Learners

Have students create posterboard diagrams of the pentad strategy. They should label each of the five points of the pentad with one of the five questions. Display it in the room as a reference source.

⏱ **TIME SAVERS!**

Writing Support Transparencies
Use the transparencies for Chapter 2 to facilitate teaching of strategies.

Writing Support Activity Book
Use the blackline masters for Chapter 2 to facilitate student planning.

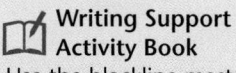

Prewriting: Considering Your Audience and Purpose

Teaching Resources: Writing Support Transparencies, 2-D; Writing Support Activity Book, 2-2

1. Help students get a better understanding of their audience by having them answer the following questions:

   What does my audience already know about this topic?

   What else do I want them to know about the topic?

   Will the audience be a hostile one? A receptive one? Why?

2. Have students think of examples of pieces of writing for each of the following purposes: to entertain (a stand-up comedy act); to persuade (a print ad); to inform (a campaign speech); to reflect (a childhood memoir).

3. Point out to students that purpose and intended audience determine the tone and type of language that are appropriate for any writing assignment.

Integrating Speaking and Listening Skills

Have students choose a topic and discuss it with an actual member of their intended audience. They should ask questions that help them decide what tone and language to use. This exchange can take place in person, over the phone, or on e-mail.

2.1

Considering Your Audience and Purpose

To make your writing more effective, take time to consider your audience or the people you intend to address. Then, focus on a purpose, or your specific reason for writing.

Analyzing Your Audience The knowledge level, background, and interest your audience has will affect their ability to understand and respond to the points you make. For example, if you are writing to show young children how to train a pet, you would choose a specific level of vocabulary and detail. In contrast, if you are addressing the same topic for an audience of adults, your word choice and sophistication would be different.

Refining Your Purpose The reason you are writing will influence the kinds of information you include about your subject. For example, you may want to entertain, persuade, inform, or reflect on an experience. Look at this example.

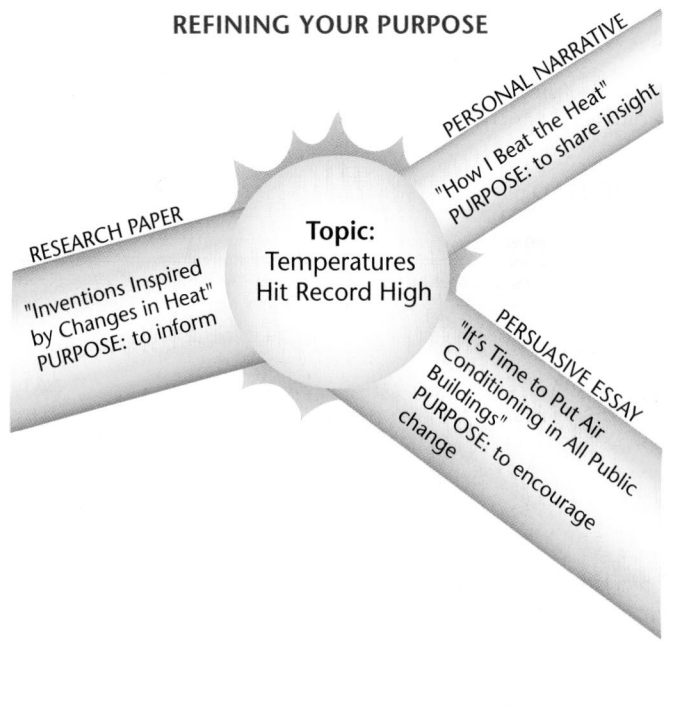

REFINING YOUR PURPOSE

PERSONAL NARRATIVE
"How I Beat the Heat"
PURPOSE: to share insight

Topic:
Temperatures
Hit Record High

RESEARCH PAPER
"Inventions Inspired by Changes in Heat"
PURPOSE: to inform

PERSUASIVE ESSAY
"It's Time to Put Air Conditioning in All Public Buildings"
PURPOSE: to encourage change

☑ ONGOING ASSESSMENT: Monitor and Reinforce

If students have difficulty writing for an audience other than the teacher, try one of the following options.

Option 1 Suggest they write to a specific person, such as a parent or neighbor. Ask students to brainstorm for the type of vocabulary this person would readily understand.	**Option 2** Have them write down a brief profile of their intended audience, including their level of education, background knowledge of the topic, and interest in the topic.

Gathering Details

If you collect the information you need before you begin to write, you'll make the writing task easier. Gather facts, details, examples, or any other information that will help you prove the point you want to make in your draft. Each writing chapter offers a strategy for gathering details for the specific mode of writing.

SAMPLE STRATEGY

Analyzing by Cubing Use cubing to study your subject from many angles, following these steps:

- **Describe it.**
- **Associate it:** List ideas your subject suggests.
- **Apply it:** Tell how your subject can be used or what it does.
- **Analyze it:** Break your subject into smaller elements.
- **Compare and contrast it.**
- **Argue for or against it.**

SAMPLE STRATEGY

Using Hexagonal Writing When writing about literature, use hexagonal writing to gather the details you'll need for a thoughtful, thorough analysis. The instructions in the illustration at right show you how to complete a hexagon. Use your responses as a springboard for collecting more of the information you'll need to support your ideas.

▶ **APPLYING THE PREWRITING STRATEGIES**

1. Using the word *movies* as a prompt, brainstorm for ideas with classmates. Review your ideas for a writing topic.
2. Complete a pentad on a topic like "my favorite sport." Then, identify a focused idea you could develop in a paper.
3. Develop two different audience profiles for an essay on courage. Complete one for newsmagazine readers. Make a second profile for a group of sixth-grade students.
4. Identify a purpose in writing about spelling bees in each of these modes: (a) narration, (b) persuasion, (c) research.
5. Complete a hexagon for a short story you have read.

PLOT — Summarize or paraphrase the work.
EVALUATION — Decide whether you liked the work.
PERSONAL ALLUSION — Note ideas or experiences the selection suggests to you.
LITERARY ALLUSION — Name other literature with a similar theme.
ANALYSIS — Cite evidence to support the theme.
THEME — State the message the work conveys.

Prewriting: Analyzing by Cubing

1. Set six small containers in the front of the classroom labeled as follows: Describe It, Associate It, Apply It, Analyze It, Compare and Contrast It, and Argue For or Against It.
2. With the class, choose an interesting multisensory experience to describe, such as a Thanksgiving dinner.
3. Challenge students to jot down brief descriptions of the topic for each category. Their notes may be written on note cards and placed in the containers.
4. Once the bins are filled, share the results that the class generated. Point out the large number of angles from which almost any topic can be explored.

Prewriting: Using Hexagonal Writing

Teaching Resources: Writing Support Transparencies, 2-E; Writing Support Activity Book, 2-3

1. Read and discuss the hexagonal writing strategy with students. Display Transparency 2-E as you analyze the diagram in detail.
2. With the students, fill in a hexagon for a novel, short story, or poem they read this year. Point out that the hexagonal writing strategy ensures that students examine many different elements of the selection.
3. Then, have students work in pairs to fill in a hexagonal chart based on another selection they read this year.

Drafting: Focusing on the Form

1. Discuss examples of the different forms of writing listed in the text. Have students generate a list of characteristics that define each.

2. Give students a list of topic ideas and have them decide which form would best suit each topic. Make sure they defend their answers with reasons.

Drafting: Grabbing Readers' Interest With a Powerful Lead

Teaching Resources: Writing Support Transparencies, 2-G

1. Display the quotes on Transparency 2-G. Discuss the ways these leads serve to capture readers' interest.

2. Explain that Clarke provokes the reader by using absolutes such as *never* and *always*. This quickly grabs readers' interest because they will likely feel an urge to disprove Clarke's ideas.

3. Discuss the way Orwell captures the readers' curiosity by admitting that he was hated. This gets attention because it is unusual for people to admit openly that they are hated.

4. Ask students to discuss the effect of Dickens's list of contrasting statements.

Drafting: Using the SEE Method

Teaching Resources: Writing Support Transparencies, 2-H

1. Display Transparency 2-H to demonstrate the SEE Strategy: make a statement, extend the statement, then elaborate with additional details.

2. Remind students that, when elaborating, they should choose only details that are relevant. Some details may be interesting, but they may not relate to the purpose of the essay.

3. Give students a sample topic, such as "Deciding Where to Apply to College." Ask them to use the SEE method to write about the topic. Have them share their results with the class.

2.2 What Is Drafting?

Shaping Your Writing

Focusing on the Form Each type of writing follows a set of expectations and conventions. For example, persuasion provides details to convince, exposition provides elaboration to explain, and narration tells a story. Identify the expectations for the form you've chosen, and maintain this focus as you draft.

Grabbing Readers' Interest With a Powerful Lead The opening sentences of your writing present you with an opportunity to grab your readers' attention and invite them to keep reading. Consider a quotation, a compelling fact, or an intriguing description, and then link the lead to your topic.

Providing Elaboration

Elaboration of your ideas will help your writing succeed. The SEE method can help you add details, facts, and examples. You will find an elaboration strategy in each writing chapter.

SAMPLE STRATEGY

Using the SEE Method The SEE method of Statement, Extension, and Elaboration can strengthen your writing by encouraging you to provide a greater depth of information. Begin with a statement that conveys a main idea. Write an extension by restating or explaining the first sentence. Elaborate further by providing even more details about the main idea.

STATEMENT: We decorated the room for a surprise party.

EXTENSION: The balloons and streamers we draped across the room transformed it.

ELABORATION: When Belinda walked in, we tossed confetti, showering her with sparkles to complete the effect.

▶ **APPLYING THE DRAFTING STRATEGIES**

1. Write an interest-grabbing lead for an essay developing one of the following topics: (a) the importance of a varied diet; (b) a valuable lesson you've learned; (c) your response to a favorite piece of literature; (d) a description of a beach.

2. Complete each of the sentences below. Then, using the SEE method, elaborate on each one.
   a. Every student should know how to ___?___.
   b. ___?___ is my favorite television show.

Learn More

Each writing chapter presents and elaborates the conventions for a specific mode of writing. For more information, see Chapters 4–16.

⏱ TIME AND RESOURCE MANAGER

Resources
Print: *Writing Support Transparencies, 2-G–H*

Using the Full Student Edition	Using the Handbook H
• Read and discuss p. 18 in class. • Using the board or overhead projector, demonstrate the SEE method. • Assign the writing tasks in Applying the Drafting Strategies on p. 18 to be completed in class.	• Read and discuss p. 10 in class. • Using the board or overhead projector, demonstrate the SEE method. • Assign the writing tasks in Applying the Drafting Strategies on p. 10 to be completed in class.

2.3 *What Is Revising?*

Color-Coding Clues to Revision

To give your writing the best chance to succeed, devote attention to the revision stage of the writing process. **Ratiocination** (rash´ ē äs ə nā´shen) is a word that means "to think logically." Apply this approach to your writing by marking your draft with color-coded clues that will help you focus on one element of your writing at a time. When segments are highlighted, bracketed, or circled for your review, you can evaluate your draft and make informed revisions. As you work through the revision sections of the writing chapters, you will find ratiocination strategies to help you revise structure, paragraphs, sentences, and word choice.

Revising Your Overall Structure

Whether you are revising a business letter, a research paper, or a short story, a logical first step of the revision process is to look at the overall structure of your draft. Before you begin analyzing word choice and polishing punctuation, make sure that the structure of your writing is sound.

SAMPLE STRATEGY

▶ **REVISION STRATEGY**
Color-Coding to Compare the Draft to Purpose

To be sure your draft achieves the effects you planned, return to your prewriting work. Write your purpose on a self-sticking note, and attach it to your draft for easy reference. Then, review your draft to highlight sentences, words, or phrases that address your purpose. If you can't identify at least one sentence in each paragraph, consider adding or revising a sentence to clarify how the paragraph supports your purposes. In this example, the writer added more details to make the writing achieve its intended purpose.

Writers in **ACTION**

"Writing is hard work. A clear sentence is no accident. Very few sentences come out right the first time, or the third. Keep thinking and rewriting until you say what you want to say."

—William Zinsser

COMPARING DRAFT TO PURPOSE

When you arrive in a city for the first time, you notice its unique energy. Some cities, like Chicago and New York, are exciting, hectic, and fast-paced. You can pick up the energy as soon as you step off the train. Others are a little sleepier, and depending on the time of day you arrive, you can measure that as well. Don't lose hope; even a sleepy town has its charm.

Purpose: to encourage people to travel

What Is Revising? • 19

Step-by-Step Teaching Guide

Revising: Color-Coding to Compare the Draft to Purpose

Teaching Resources: Writing Support Transparencies, 2-I

1. Display Transparency 2-I. Explain that the additions made by the writer add appeal to the descriptions of both big cities and small towns.

2. Remind students that sticking to the purpose of the writing will strengthen their drafts. It will help them avoid distracting and unnecessary details.

More About the Writer

Journalist William Zinsser is the author of what may be the most widely read reference on nonfiction writing, the classic book *On Writing Well,* an inspiring work that every aspiring nonfiction writer should own. A former writer and editor for the *New York Herald Tribune,* Zinsser believes that writing should exhibit clarity, simplicity, economy, and humanity. Other books by Zinsser include *Writing to Learn* and *Extraordinary Lives: The Art and Craft of the American Biography.*

Customize for
Less Advanced Students

Students may be somewhat stolid and narrowly focused in the first draft. Challenge students to work in pairs on this color-coding exercise to discover a fresh perspective.

⏱ TIME AND RESOURCE MANAGER

Resources
Print: *Writing Support Transparencies, 2-I–L*

Using the Full Student Edition	Using the Handbook🄷
• Read and discuss pp. 19–21 in class. • Work through the sample strategies using the transparencies or the examples in the student text. • Assign the writing tasks in Applying the Revision Strategies on p. 21 to be completed in class.	• Read and discuss pp. 11–13 in class. • Work through the sample strategies using the transparencies or the examples in the student text. • Assign the writing tasks in Applying the Revision Strategies on p. 13 to be completed in class.

⏱ TIME SAVERS!

Writing Support Transparencies
Use the transparencies for Chapter 2 to facilitate teaching of strategies.

Writing Support Activity Book
Use the blackline masters for Chapter 2 to facilitate student planning.

Revising: Circling Contradictory Information

1. Discuss the strategy of circling contradictory information with students. Tell them that they will occasionally encounter a paragraph that has no clear main idea. In this case, the whole paragraph must be either revised or eliminated.

2. Have students review their drafts and apply the circling strategy.

3. Remind students that details that do not support the main idea of the essay are distracting, no matter how interesting they may be. In an effective essay, every detail of every sentence somehow relates to the main point.

Revising: Identifying Sentence Beginnings

Teaching Resources: Writing Support Transparencies, 2-J

1. Display Transparency 2-J and ask students to devise a way to change the beginning of one more of the sentences in the model. Have them share their ideas.

2. Remind students that one option is to begin sentences with subordinate clauses. Some words that frequently introduce subordinate clauses are the following: *after, although, before, since, unless, until, whenever, wherever, while.*

3. Explain that adding variety to sentence beginnings is an easy way to make their writing livelier.

2.3

Revising Your Paragraphs

To begin another layer of revision, look at each paragraph in your draft. Topical paragraphs that develop an idea should present information without introducing contradictions or distractions. To ensure unity, eliminate this type of information.

SAMPLE STRATEGY

▶ **REVISION STRATEGY**
Circling Contradictory Information

For each topical paragraph in a draft, identify the main idea the paragraph develops. Read the paragraph, confirming that each sentence supports that idea. If you notice words, sentences, or phrases that distract from your main idea, circle these elements. When you have reviewed each paragraph, evaluate the circled information. Consider these revision options:

- If the circled items are important to your essay, write a new paragraph to address the information, revise the topic sentence, or introduce transitions to make the information fit.

- Eliminate items you cannot link to your essay's main idea.

Revising Your Sentences

Generate energy in your writing by analyzing and revising your sentence beginnings.

SAMPLE STRATEGY

▶ **REVISION STRATEGY**
Identifying Sentence Beginnings

To evaluate the variety of your sentence beginnings, list the first word of each sentence in your draft. Review your list to identify any pattern your draft includes. For example, you may have begun many sentences with the word *I* or *The*. To improve your draft, insert phrases or clauses that break the pattern. Look at this example:

LISTING SENTENCE BEGINNINGS

My baby brother has an adorable habit of saying "yesh" to almost anything we ask him. He says "yesh" when we ask if he wants to go to bed. *Even if he was up all night,* He says "yesh" if we ask him if he slept well. He says "yesh" if we ask him if he signed the Declaration of Independence. *Sam* He doesn't understand the content of the questions, but he knows he is being asked. It keeps the family laughing.

My
He
He *Even*
He
He *Sam*
It

☑ **ONGOING ASSESSMENT: Prerequisite Skills**

If students have difficulty understanding how to begin sentences with phrases and clauses, you may find it helpful to refer them to the following materials to ensure coverage of prerequisite knowledge.

In the Textbook	Print Resources	Technology
Phrases, Sections 19.1–19.2; Clauses, Sections 19.3–19.4	*Grammar Exercise Workbook,* pp. 33–40, 41–46	*On-Line Exercise Bank,* Sections 19.1–4

Revising Your Word Choice

As you revise your writing, check to see whether each word is the best one for your purpose. In the writing chapters, you will learn about refining your word choice.

SAMPLE STRATEGY

▶ **REVISION STRATEGY**
Generating a Synonym Bank

When you write about a specific topic, you may find that you use the same words to name it each time. For example, if you write an editorial to state your position about school taxes, you may use the words *student* or *funding* frequently.

Identify the key words in your writing, and circle examples of them in your draft. Using a thesaurus, generate a synonym bank, and revise your draft as appropriate. Look at the examples shown on the cards at right.

students
young people
adolescents
teenagers

funding
financing
subsidizing
stocking

voters
citizens
taxpayers
community members

Peer Review

You may be your best editor; however, tapping the reactions of your peers can give you useful suggestions. Peer reviewers can help you see things from a distance, noticing strengths or weaknesses that you may not have seen. Each writing chapter offers specific suggestions for inviting a peer review.

Ask for Specific Feedback Instead of asking whether your paper was effective, focus your questions to get more specific feedback. This chart offers some suggestions:

Focusing Peer Review	
Purpose	**Ask**
Evaluate characterization	What kind of person was the main character?
Test your argument	Which reason was most convincing?
	Which point was least compelling?

▶ **APPLYING THE REVISION STRATEGIES**

Choose an early draft of an essay you have recently written. Experiment with each of the revision strategies presented in this chapter. Discuss your experiences with a partner.

What Is Revising? • 21

Revising: Generating a Synonym Bank

Teaching Resources: Writing Support Transparencies, 2-K

1. Remind students that a *synonym* is a word that has the same or similar meaning to another word. Using a variety of words adds flavor to writing and avoids unnecessary repetition.

2. Point out that words that are listed as synonyms often have slightly different meanings or connotations. Students might need to consult a dictionary before substituting a word.

3. Encourage students to create a synonym bank for frequently used words in a selection from their portfolios. They might use a print or electronic thesaurus for assistance.

4. Have students substitute overused words in their essays with words from their synonym banks.

Integrating Vocabulary Skills

Have students compile a class list of frequently overused words. Then, have them create a synonym list for each of the words. Ask students to turn this synonym bank into a poster or booklet to keep in the classroom for students to use as a reference source when they write.

Revising: Peer Review

Teaching Resources: Writing Support Transparencies, 2-L

1. Display Transparency 2-L and discuss the advantages of peer editing.

2. Have students brainstorm for questions they think should be added to the peer-editing checklist.

3. Encourage students to begin peer edits by focusing on the selection's strengths. Every piece of writing has some strength, whether it is a logical organization, an interesting theme, or just a memorable image.

🎸 **STANDARDIZED TEST PREPARATION WORKSHOP**

Synonyms Standardized tests may require students to recognize synonyms and antonyms of words.

Read the sentence and choose the word whose meaning is most similar to the underlined word.

The sad woman found <u>solace</u> in reading her favorite novel, Great Expectations.

A depression   **C** grief

B comfort   **D** rapture

Students should note that the answer is **B**. Reading one's favorite novel is a positive experience, so the answer cannot be A or C. Answer choice D is too strong.

Editing and Proofreading

1. Work with students to create a proofreading checklist for the class. You might divide the list into three categories: grammar, usage, and mechanics. Come up with at least three specific things to check in each category.

2. Emphasize the importance of checking spelling, especially for words that are less familiar to students or that are easily confused.

3. Point out that students should not only check outside sources, but should also check things they think they know, to make sure the facts are complete and precise.

4. Give students a copy of an article from a local newspaper and have them use the checklist to proofread it. Discuss their answers.

5. Have students repeat the exercise with a selection from their own portfolios.

Real-World Connection

Point out that professional writers have many different types of relationships with their editors. Some writers prefer editors to be collaborators, helping them to revise their work. Others want them to be more like advisors, offering suggestions but staying out of the revising process. With what type of editor do students feel most comfortable?

Customize for
ESL Students

Some students may need additional guidance during the proofreading stage. Work with them to revise the checklist so it covers issues that relate to the challenges of learning a second language, such as word choice and syntax.

2.4 What Are Editing and Proofreading?

Once you have revised your draft for content, edit and proofread it to correct any errors. Each writing chapter offers a proofreading focus and a brief lesson on a related grammar, usage, or mechanics topic to help you hone your proofreading skills.

Focusing on Proofreading

Whether you work in an office and develop professional publications or you share your writing with others using a less formal technique, the care you take to identify and correct errors will show the pride you take in your work.

To help you develop strong editing and proofreading skills, each writing chapter offers a specific focus. Look at your draft with this specific element in mind. However, always review your work to correct any errors you see. These are the categories you should address as you revise your work:

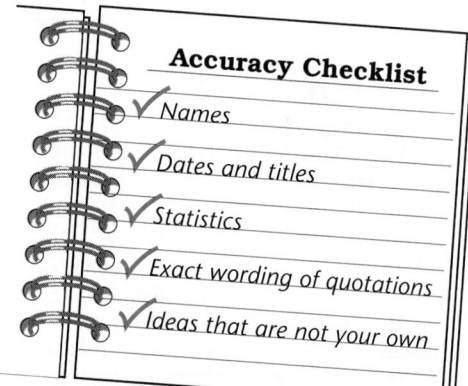

Accuracy Checklist
- ✓ Names
- ✓ Dates and titles
- ✓ Statistics
- ✓ Exact wording of quotations
- ✓ Ideas that are not your own

Scrutinize Spelling Take a look at every word in your draft, consulting a dictionary to check words that raise doubt. Confirm the spelling of any proper nouns, such as the names of people and places.

Follow Grammar, Usage, and Mechanics Rules Apply the conventions of grammar, usage, and mechanics to everything you write. For example, analyze your writing for its use of complete sentences, subject-verb agreement, and correct punctuation.

Fact Check When you include information from outside sources, confirm the accuracy of your work. Consult your research notes or double-check by using encyclopedias, the Internet, or other sources.

▶ **APPLYING THE EDITING AND PROOFREADING STRATEGIES**

Take a moment to consider the types of grammar, usage, and mechanics errors you frequently make. Add this list to your portfolio, revise it as you improve as a writer, and refer to it as you review the writing assignments you complete this year.

2.5 What Are Publishing and Presenting?

Moving Forward

This guided tour of the writing process has presented you with an overview of strategies and techniques that can enhance your writing. Each of the writing chapters in this section will extend your choices, introducing new strategies for each of the stages of the writing process. Here are the features you'll find in the Publishing and Presenting sections of each chapter:

Building Your Portfolio A writing portfolio captures the successes and experiences of your life as a writer. Keep your finished writing products in a folder, box, or other organized container. Use it to record your progress and growth as a writer. In addition to providing a showcase of your finished work, your portfolio can also serve as a place for works in progress, records of peer conferences, documentation of presentations, and inspirations for future writing.

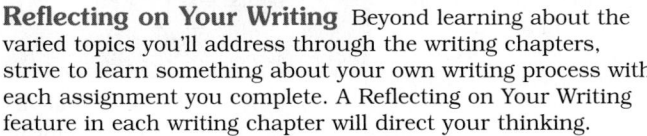

PORTFOLIO

Reflecting on Your Writing Beyond learning about the varied topics you'll address through the writing chapters, strive to learn something about your own writing process with each assignment you complete. A Reflecting on Your Writing feature in each writing chapter will direct your thinking.

Assessing Your Writing While all writing should meet certain criteria for clarity, each type of writing must also meet requirements unique to its form. For example, a test response must answer a given question, but persuasive writing must present a fair and logical argument to convince readers. Use the Rubric for Self-Assessment in each writing chapter to be sure you are addressing the key features of each type of writing.

▶ **APPLYING THE PUBLISHING AND PRESENTING STRATEGIES**

1. Review the prewriting activities you used in this introductory walk-through. Choose one to put in your portfolio as an inspiration for a later piece of writing. Talk with a partner about the activity you selected.
2. To begin reflecting on your writing process, jot down a response to one of these questions. Save your writing in your portfolio.
   - What is your greatest strength as a writer?
   - Which writing experience in your life have you enjoyed most? Why?

What Are Publishing and Presenting? • 23

1. To analyze relationships, ideas, and cultures as represented in various media

2. To describe how meanings are communicated through elements of design

3. To investigate the source of a media presentation or production such as who made it and why it was made

Evaluating Photographic Techniques

1. Choose one of the Spotlight elements for class discussion, or have students work individually or in groups to research the element of their choice.

2. Encourage students to find images that illustrate the topic they select.

3. Interested students might wish to research the history of photography, including the contributions of Southworth and Hawes to the development of the form.

4. Point out that Daguerre's life offers two possible areas of study: the development of photography and the development of panoramas.

5. Some students might like to read a few of Longfellow's famous poems. They could then present images that illustrate the poems. Alternatively, they could research the poems' subjects.

Viewing and Representing

Activity Ask students to display, if possible, the photos that fire their imaginations and to attach their writing topic ideas.

Critical Viewing

Respond Students may point out that the rough black-and-white image emphasizes the poet's dark eyes and intense expression.

Spotlight on the Humanities

Evaluating Photographic Techniques

Focus on Photography: Southworth and Hawes

Every step—from choosing and researching your topic to revising and editing—is crucial to a finished writing product. Similarly in photography, the developing process is critical to the quality of the final image. Two American photographers who pioneered in their field during the nineteenth century were pharmacist Albert Sands Southworth (1811–1894) and painter Josiah Johnson Hawes (1808–1901). Through their partnership, they refined an already existing process for creating daguerreotypes, early photographs in which images were captured on plates covered with silver iodide. In addition to their scientific advances with developing techniques, Southworth and Hawes also created exceptional portraits.

Art Connection Albert Sands Southworth learned about daguerreotypes through an agent of Louis Daguerre (1789–1851), the man whose name inspired the word. Daguerre was a French painter who invented the photographic technique of the daguerreotype. Working first as a painter of scenery for the opera, he later painted expansive panoramas that inspired the diorama form, a technique for three-dimensional scenes with figures.

Literature Connection One of the eminent individuals that Southworth and Hawes photographed was American author and poet Henry Wadsworth Longfellow (1807–1882). Longfellow brought poetry back to popularity with his clear, simple language and technically proficient style of writing. Among his most famous works are *The Song of Hiawatha* (1855), *Evangeline* (1847), and "Paul Revere's Ride" (1863).

Writing Process Activity: Using Photographs to Choose a Topic

Review photographs you have taken or flip through magazines to find images that inspire you. For each photograph you select, brainstorm to list several writing topic ideas. Keep this list in your portfolio for later development.

▲ Critical Viewing
How do the quality and texture of this daguerreotype influence your response to its subject, Henry Wadsworth Longfellow?
[Respond]

Media and Technology Skills

Using Technology for All Aspects of the Writing Process

Activity: Building an Electronic Portfolio

If you have ever saved a file on a computer and then were unable to find it again, you know how frustrating a disorganized computer drive can be. Setting up and maintaining an effective portfolio structure can help you access files more easily.

Think About It The structure you choose for your portfolio will depend on the types of writing you plan to do. Think about the classes for which you will complete writing assignments and the writing projects you will complete on your own.

Structure It Computer platforms differ, but your portfolio will be best organized using folders and files. You can nest subfolders within folders to create narrower topic groups. In the sample below, a folder for each work in progress and folders for finished projects and a writing journal makes the organization orderly.

```
📂—Works in Progress:  College Essay
    ├──Prewriting
    ├──Drafting
    ├──Revising
    └──Final Draft

📁  Works in Progress:  Research Report

📁  Works in Progress:  Letter to the Editor

📁  Finished Reports

📁  Writing Journal
```

Use It When creating a document, make sure to place it in the correct folder. To keep a trail of your revision work, consider renaming files as you revise them. You might use a point system to show the progress of one essay. For example, you could name the first draft "camp.1" and subsequent revisions "camp.2" and "camp.3."

Maintain It Your electronic portfolio is a flexible project. Take time at least once a month to evaluate and amend the structure. This can help you see your progress and preferences as a writer. After you've used the electronic portfolio long enough to become comfortable with it, decide what works for you and what does not.

Media and Technology Skills • **25**

Step-by-Step Teaching Guide

Building an Electronic Portfolio

Teaching Resources: Writing Support Transparencies, 2-M

1. Have students go through their portfolios and make a list of the title and genre of each selection.
2. Then, have them categorize the selections into groups based on genre, subject, date, or some other logical system.
3. Explain that in an electronic portfolio, they could create a folder for each of these categories (expository, persuasive, research) and place the selections in the appropriate folders. This is a simple way to keep all of their work organized and accessible. Display Transparency 2-M to illustrate how this would look on a computer screen.
4. Remind students that, although computers can be helpful aids at all stages of the writing process, malfunctions do occur. The best way to prevent problems is to print a hard copy at the end of each writing session or to save files in more than one place (on the hard drive and on a disk, for instance).

Integrating Technology Skills

There are many types of computer word-processing programs. If students do the majority of their work at home in a program that is incompatible with the school's program, encourage them to bring in hard copies of their drafts and make pencil revisions at school. They can then keyboard in their revisions at home.

25

1. To develop drafts by organizing content and by refining style to suit audience and purpose

2. To use effective sequences and transitions to achieve coherence and meaning

3. To produce legible work that shows accurate spelling and correct use of the conventions of punctuation and capitalization

4. To demonstrate control over grammatical elements

Step-by-Step Teaching Guide

Using the Writing Process to Respond to Prompts

Teaching Resources: Standardized Test Preparation Workbook, pp. 3–4

1. Emphasize that students should follow the writing process when responding to a test prompt that calls for an essay or editorial.

2. Go over the sample prompt, and define FCC if necessary (Federal Communications Commission).

3. Ask students to recall newspaper editorials they have read. Point out that editorial writers do not use the pronoun *I*, unlike columnists, and seldom use the plural pronoun *we*. Be sure students understand the audience for their writing.

4. Have students read through page 27, and then assign the writing prompt for completion within a class period.

Standardized Test Preparation Workshop

Using the Writing Process to Respond to Prompts

Using the writing process helps writers create well-organized, interesting, and coherent works. When responding to a test prompt for a standardized test, you can use the steps of the writing process to construct an effective response. Your response will be evaluated on your ability to do the following:

- Choose a logical, consistent organization.

- Elaborate with the appropriate amount of detail for your specific audience and purpose.

- Use appropriate transitions to show the connections among ideas.

- Use complete sentences and follow the rules of grammar.

- Use correct spelling and punctuation.

The process of writing for a test, or any kind of writing, can be divided into stages. As you write an essay for a standardized test, plan to spend a specific amount of time prewriting, drafting, revising, and proofreading.

Following is an example of a writing prompt that you might find on a standardized test. Use the suggestions on the following page to help you respond. The clocks next to each stage show a suggested plan for organizing your time.

Sample Writing Situation

The Internet was originally used as a research tool for the U.S. Department of Defense and educational institutions. Now anybody with a home computer and a modem can access the Internet. Regardless of age, background, or experience, anyone can have access to virtually any type of information easily. Should the Internet be monitored, or policed? If so, by whom—the FCC, parents, or Internet users themselves? Choose a position, and prepare a newspaper editorial presenting your point of view.

Test Tip

When you want to be persuasive, create the proper *tone* for your argument by expressing your attitude toward your subject. For example, your tone may be humorous, angry, or sympathetic. Use a tone you think is best suited to your topic.

 TEST-TAKING TIP

Since the purpose of an editorial is to persuade, tell students to take a few minutes before they begin drafting to jot down their views about the Internet. They may decide that various opinions about the issue of control are almost equally valid. If so, they should decide which view they favor, but they may admit the validity of other points of view.

Although the general tone among newspapers varies, depending on the nature of their audiences, tell students that in their test responses, they should aim for reasonably formal language. Remind them that formal language does not preclude humor, and writers may express a sympathetic tone to a view that opposes their own even though they may not agree with it.

Prewriting

Allow one quarter of your time for prewriting.

Consider Both Sides Brainstorm to jot down facts or opinions that will help you clarify where you stand on the issue, Note any ideas that come to mind, both pro and con. Then, review your list, and decide which points reflect your position. Circle these ideas for full development. Then, identify one or two points that support the opposing argument. You may address and refute these in your writing, too.

Gather Examples Prepare to support your ideas by citing specific examples from your own personal experience or knowledge.

Drafting

Allow almost half of your time for drafting.

Remember Your Readers Since you are writing an editorial to be read by a wide audience, keep your ideas simple and concise. Explain the subject without assuming your readers even know what the Internet is, and be sure to provide information about the controversy.

Introduce Your Topic Start your editorial with a strong introduction. Make sure your opinion is included in the first paragraph. Then, summarize the points you'll cover in the editorial.

Use Evidence for Support In the following paragraphs, use the best examples you have collected in prewriting to support your position. Show how these examples back up your ideas.

Conclude Write a conclusion that effectively summarizes the points you have made and leaves your readers with something to consider long after they have finished reading.

Revising, Editing, and Proofreading

Allow about one quarter of your time for revising, editing, and proofreading your work.

Review the Clarity of Your Writing Read your draft to evaluate your ability to convey ideas clearly. Add transitional phrases and more persuasive language to communicate your ideas to readers.

Check for Errors Review your editorial for any mistakes you may have made in spelling, punctuation, and sentence structure. Finally, make sure your writing is neat and readable. Make deletions with a single line, and add corrected words or phrases neatly in the space above the text. Use a caret [^] to indicate the exact placement of inserts.

Customize for
Less Advanced Students

Some students may have difficulty supporting their views. Go over the points that students have jotted down during the prewriting stage, and talk through their supporting ideas to make certain they are specific.

Customize for
AP Students

Ask students to review their editorials and to mark places where they could have used more persuasive language. You may want to have them revise their work, inserting stronger verbs, for example.

In-Depth Lesson Plan

	LESSON FOCUS	PRINT AND MEDIA RESOURCES
DAY 1	**Sentence Combining; Main Idea and Topic Sentence** Students practice sentence combining, review samples from literature, and learn how to identify and write topic sentences. (pp. 28–34/🅗16–22)	*Writing and Grammar* Interactive Text, Ch. 3; Section 20.2
DAY 2	**Supporting Details; Paragraph Organization** Students examine strategies for supporting the main idea of a paragraph and learn a basic pattern of organization. (pp. 35–36/🅗23–24)	**Teaching Resources** *Writing Support Transparencies,* 3-A
DAY 3	**Unity and Coherence in Compositions** Students learn the importance of unity in a composition and study organizational strategies and transitions that create coherence. (pp. 37–38/🅗25–26)	**Teaching Resources** *Writing Support Transparencies,* 3-B
DAY 4	**Parts of a Composition; Types of Paragraphs** Students plan a composition, examine functional and block paragraphs, and review an example of functional paragraphs in literature. (pp. 39–41/🅗27–29)	**Teaching Resources** *Writing Support Transparencies,* 3-C; *Writing Support Activity Book,* 3-1
DAY 5	**Writing Style** Students learn how sentence variety, diction, and tone contribute to style and when to use formal and informal English. (pp. 42–43/🅗30–31)	**Teaching Resources** *Formal Assessment,* Ch. 3

Accelerated Lesson Plan

	LESSON FOCUS	PRINT AND MEDIA RESOURCES
DAY 1	**Sentence Combining; Paragraph Organization** Students practice sentence combining, review paragraph purpose and structure, and learn the TRI pattern. (pp. 28–36/🅗16–24)	*Writing and Grammar* Interactive Text, Ch. 3 **Teaching Resources** *Writing Support Transparencies,* 3-A
DAY 2	**Unity and Coherence; Types of Paragraphs** Students review unity and coherence and paragraph types. (pp. 37–41/🅗25–29)	**Teaching Resources** *Writing Support Transparencies,* 3-B–C; *Writing Support Activity Book,* 3-1
DAY 3	**Writing Style** Students review diction, tone, and the appropriate use of formal and informal English. (pp. 42–43/🅗30–31)	**Teaching Resources** *Formal Assessment,* Ch. 3

Options for Adapting Lesson Plans

HOMEWORK

Have students complete any stage of the lesson for homework.

FEATURES

Extend coverage with Spotlight on the Humanities (p. 44), Media and Technology Skills (p. 45), and the Standardized Test Preparation Workshop (p. 46).

TECHNOLOGY

Students can complete any stage of the lesson on the computer, using *Writing and Grammar* Interactive Text or a word-processing program. Have them print out their completed work.

Writing and Grammar Handbook Alignment

Page numbers in Step-by-Step Teaching Guides in this Teacher's Edition refer to pages from the full student text. Handbook page references, indicated with this icon 🅗, are provided in Time and Resource Manager boxes and at the bottom of each Teacher's Edition page.

INTEGRATED SKILLS COVERAGE

Integrating Grammar Skills
SE p. 36/🅗24
ATE pp. 36, 38

Viewing and Representing
Critical Viewing, SE pp. 28, 30, 35, 37, 39, 43, 44/🅗16, 18, 23, 25, 27, 31
Exploring Cultural History Through the Arts, SE p. 44; ATE p. 44

Vocabulary Skills
ATE p. 35

Real-World Connection
ATE p. 37

ASSESSMENT SUPPORT

Standardized Test Preparation Workshop SE p. 46; ATE pp. 35, 46

Standardized Test Preparation Workbook, pp. 5–6

Formal Assessment, Ch. 3

MEETING INDIVIDUAL NEEDS

Less Advanced Students ATE pp. 34, 36, 41, 47. See also Ongoing Assessments, ATE pp. 32, 36, 38, 43.

Visual/Spatial Learners ATE p. 30

AP Students ATE pp. 39, 47

Gifted and Talented Students ATE p. 38

ESL Students ATE p. 35

BLOCK SCHEDULING

Pacing Suggestions
For 90-minute Blocks
• Follow the Accelerated Lesson Plan, and cover topic and support sentences and paragraph organization in one class period and compositions and writing style in a second class period.
• Allow class time for students to complete and discuss all exercises.

Resources for Varying Instruction
• *Writing and Grammar* Interactive Text A 90-minute block provides an ideal opportunity for students to work on the computer.

Professional Development Support
• *How to Manage Instruction in the Block* This teaching resource provides management and activity suggestions.

MEDIA AND TECHNOLOGY

For the Student
• *Writing and Grammar* Interactive Text, Ch. 3

For the Teacher
• Teacher EXPRESS CD-ROM

WRITING AND GRAMMAR ON-LINE

Interactive Text (On-line or on CD-ROM)
• Easily navigable instruction with interactive Revision Checkers
• Full use of e-rater™, the essay-scoring system (on-line only)

Companion Web Site PHSchool.com
• Scoring rubrics with models (use Web Code egk-1201)

See the Go On-line! feature, SE p. iii.

LITERATURE CONNECTIONS

Related selections from *Prentice Hall Literature, Penguin Edition,* The British Tradition:
from "We'll Never Conquer Space," Arthur C. Clarke, SE p. 33/🅗21
from "Shooting an Elephant," George Orwell, SE p. 33/🅗21
from "The Rocking-Horse Winner," D. H. Lawrence, SE p. 40/🅗28

▶ Lesson Objectives

1. To practice sentence-combining skills to improve sentence style and fluidity
2. To analyze and discuss published paragraphs as writing models and apply criteria developed by self and others to evaluate writing
3. To organize ideas in writing to ensure coherence, logical progression, and support for ideas
4 To employ precise language to communicate ideas clearly and concisely
5. To use effective sequences and transitions to achieve coherence and meaning
6. To employ literary devices to enhance style and voice
7. To use varied sentence structure to express meanings and achieve desired effect
8. To evaluate how well writing achieves its purpose

Critical Viewing

Connect Students might say that in both a painting and a paragraph, many details and strategies work together to communicate one main idea.

Chapter

3 Sentences, Paragraphs, and Compositions
Structure and Style

▲ **Critical Viewing**
Explain how painting a picture is like producing an effective paragraph or composition. **[Connect]**

What Are Sentences, Paragraphs, and Compositions?

The **sentence** is the basic unit of writing: It expresses a complete thought. To fully develop your ideas, however, you may need to connect several sentences in a paragraph.

A **paragraph** is one of the building blocks of writing. It presents a single main idea. Paragraphs may be as short as one sentence or contain several dozen sentences. Paragraphs are either indented or set off by extra space above and below.

When you put together a series of related paragraphs, you are constructing a **composition.** Like a good paragraph, an effective composition should focus on a single main idea. All of the sentences within a composition work together to introduce, develop, and support that main idea.

28 • Sentences, Paragraphs, and Compositions

⏱ TIME AND RESOURCE MANAGER

Resources
Print: *Grammar Exercise Workbook,* pp. 51–52; *Extra Writing and Grammar Exercises,* pp. 22, 28–30
Technology: *Writing and Grammar* Interactive Text, Section 20.2

Using the Full Student Edition	Using the Handbook ⊞
• Read and discuss pp. 28–32 in class. • Have students work through Exercises 1–4 in class. Discuss their responses.	• Read and discuss pp. 16–20 in class. • Have students work through Exercises 1–4 in class. Discuss their responses.

3.1

Sentence Combining

Writing Effective Sentences

Sentences are the basic building blocks of paragraphs. A series of short sentences can produce a choppy, repetitive effect. By combining two or more short sentences, you can show connections between events, stress important information, and create a smooth flow of ideas. Your use of varied and sophisticated sentence structure will improve your writing, making it more appealing and more effective in conveying meaning.

Inserting Words and Phrases

Two sentences can often be combined by taking key information from one and inserting it into the other. The information to be inserted may be a word or a phrase. To combine sentences successfully, you may have to change the form of the words and use additional punctuation.

EXAMPLE:	The Lake District is known for its lovely mountain scenery. The Lake District is located in the northwestern part of England.
INSERTING A PHRASE:	The Lake District, located in the northwestern part of England, is known for its lovely mountain scenery.
EXAMPLE:	She enjoyed the view from the top of Scafell Pike. The view from the top was stunning.
INSERTING A WORD:	She enjoyed the stunning view from the top of Scafell Pike.

▶ **Exercise 1** Combining With Words and Phrases Combine each pair of sentences by inserting key information from one sentence into the other. Add commas as necessary.
1. The Thames is the longest river entirely in England. It flows east to the North Sea.
2. The Scilly Islands are located beyond Land's End in southwestern England. The islands are filled with color.
3. London is the capital of England. It is the largest city in England.
4. The Isle of Man is not part of England. It is located in the Irish Sea.
5. The white cliffs of Dover tower over the English Channel on England's southeast coast. These cliffs are famous.

Sentence Combining • 29

Using Compound Elements

1. Using the first two examples on page 30, have students discuss how compound elements can help writers avoid repetition.

2. Help students recognize the compound direct objects and prepositional phrases in the third and fourth sets of examples.

Customize for
Visual/Spatial Learners

To help clarify compound sentence elements for visual learners, write the following sentence on the chalkboard, labeling elements as shown.

```
       S           S
    Mark (and) Theresa

       V
    bought a new

      DO          DO
    television (and) a DVD

                  V
    player (but) kept their

    old television for the

    guest room.
```

As students complete Exercise 2, have them label elements in the same way.

Answer Key

> **Exercise 2**

Possible answers:
1. The River Lagan runs through Belfast and flows into the North Channel between Ireland and Scotland.
2. The columns of Giant's Causeway are made of basalt and form a natural stairway between the cliffs and the sea.
3. The North Atlantic Current causes the winters in Ireland and England to be relatively mild.
4. Londonderry and Belfast are cities in Northern Ireland.
5. When I visit Belfast, I want to visit the Ulster Museum and Belfast Castle.

Critical Viewing
Possible response: A combination of long and short sentences will give a paragraph interest in the same way that short and tall formations add to the interest of the Giant's Causeway.

3.1

Using Compound Elements

Ideas from two sentences can be combined by joining elements from each to form compound subjects, verbs, or objects.

EXAMPLE:	Captain Matthew Webb swam the English Channel. Gertrude Ederle also swam the English Channel
COMPOUND SUBJECT:	Captain Matthew Webb and Gertrude Ederle both swam the English Channel.
EXAMPLE:	We visited the white cliffs of Dover. Then, we toured Leeds Castle.
COMPOUND VERB:	We visited the white cliffs of Dover and toured Leeds Castle.
EXAMPLE:	The Romans built roads in England. They also built forts and military supply bases.
COMPOUND OBJECT :	The Romans built roads, forts, and military supply bases in England.
EXAMPLE:	Before touring England, you should read about the Roman ruins. You should also read about the ancient circle of stones called Stonehenge.
COMPOUND PREPOSITIONAL PHRASE:	Before touring England, you should read about the Roman ruins and the ancient circle of stones called Stonehenge.

▶ **Exercise 2** Using Compound Sentence Elements Combine each pair of sentences using compound elements.
1. The River Lagan runs through Belfast. It flows into the North Channel between Ireland and Scotland.
2. The columns of Giant's Causeway are made of basalt. They form a natural stairway between the cliffs and the sea.
3. The North Atlantic Current causes the winters in Ireland to be relatively warm. It keeps the winters mild in England, too.
4. Londonderry is a city in Northern Ireland. Belfast is another city in Northern Ireland.
5. When I visit Belfast, I want to visit the Ulster Museum. I would also like to see Belfast Castle.

30 • Structure and Style

Ⓛ Learn More

For additional information about direct objects, see Section 18.3; for additional information about prepositional phrases, see Section 19.1.

▼ **Critical Viewing** These columns of the Giant's Causeway appear as if they were put there by design; however, they are naturally occurring volcanic rock formations. In what way does a strong paragraph resemble these formations? **[Connect]**

☑ ONGOING ASSESSMENT: Diagnose

Use one of the following options to diagnose students' current level of proficiency in combining sentences.

Option 1 Have students review recent written work and identify any passages that are flawed by repetition or lack of sentence variety. Have them revise these passages, and then hold conferences with individual students, reviewing their revisions. Prepare to give extra help to students who have difficulty with the assignment.

Option 2 Ask students to write a brief paragraph about a figure in English and American literature whom they find inspiring or intriguing. Have them review their paragraph and combine sentences for smoother style and clear connections between ideas. Plan extra help for students whose revised paragraphs are repetitive, unclear, or lacking in sentence variety.

3.3 Paragraphs in Essays and Other Compositions

Unity and Coherence

Maintain Unity

A paragraph has unity, or singleness of effect, when all of its sentences relate to the main idea. All of the sentences should either support, explain, or develop the topic sentence. When you revise, strengthen a paragraph's unity by deleting those details or sentences that do not support, develop, or explain the main idea. Look at this example.

EXAMPLE: If we were to choose a single symbol to evoke the image of the modern American city, it would have to be the skyscraper. From San Francisco's Transamerica Pyramid building to Chicago's Sears Tower to the Empire State Building in New York, skyscraper means "city." ~~Other symbols for American cities include Gateway Arch in St. Louis and the Astrodome in Houston.~~ If we accept the idea that skyscraper means "city," then we can be very precise about the place and time that the modern city was born, because the first skyscraper was built in Chicago in 1885.

For a composition to have unity, all of the paragraphs should develop the thesis statement. The **thesis statement** of a composition is a sentence or two that sums up the main idea you are trying to express.

▶ **Exercise 10** Revising for Unity On a separate sheet of paper, copy the following paragraph. Mark for deletion any sentences that detract from the unity of the paragraph.

In the United States, cities have grown dramatically since the late nineteenth century. Over the same period, the general population has increased, making the population growth in the cities even more dramatic. The percentage of the population living in urban areas has continually increased, while the percentage of people living in rural areas has declined. A person's choice to live in an urban or a rural area may be voluntary or it may depend on employment opportunities or other controlling factors. In 1890, about 35 percent of the population lived in cities; but by 1990, more than 75 percent of the population was urban. The population figures for Chicago illustrate how dramatic the growth of cities has been: Chicago's population, increased through annexation, surpassed 1 million for the first time in 1890; by 1990, it had surpassed 2.7 million. Urban life may offer cultural advantages that rural life does not, while rural life may proceed at a more relaxed pace.

▼ Critical Viewing
Come up with a topic for a paragraph based on this photograph. **[Connect]**

Paragraphs in Essays and Other Compositions • 37

Step-by-Step Teaching Guide

Maintain Unity

1. Ask students to define the word *unity* in their own words. Have students share their definitions. If they cannot think of definitions, they can offer examples of things that display unity, such as the voices in a choir.

2. Tell students that even though some details are very interesting, they must be eliminated from a paragraph if they are irrelevant.

3. Have students check a paragraph in their portfolios for unity.

Critical Viewing

Connect Student answers will vary but might include topics related to architecture or urban planning.

Real-World Connection

In many businesses, employees communicate with each other through memos. Whether in print or on e-mail, people in an office sometimes receive dozens of memos each day. As a result, memos need to be unified and coherent in order to receive full attention. The writer should make his or her memo clear and concise.

Answer Key

▶ **Exercise 10**

Tell students they can mark a sentence for deletion simply by drawing a line through it. Students should mark the fourth sentence ("A person's choice . . .") and the last sentence ("Urban life may . . .") as detracting from the unity of the paragraph.

⏱ **TIME SAVERS!**

 Writing Support Transparencies
Use the transparencies for Chapter 3 to facilitate the teaching of strategies.

Organize for Coherence

Teaching Resources: Writing Support Transparencies, 3-B

1. Explain that transition words and phrases help a paragraph's coherence by connecting ideas and clarifying relationships. Display Transparency 3-B, and ask students to review the exercises they have done. Ask them to identify examples of transition words and phrases and share these with the class.

2. Ask students to compare the list on this page to the one they compiled when examining the exercises. Are there words and phrases on one list that are not on the other? What do all the words and phrases have in common? (They are connecting words.)

Customize for
Gifted and Talented Students

Have students rewrite the paragraph in different ways to create different effects. For example, they may want the paragraph to be forceful, lighthearted, or humorous. Allow them to rearrange and add words and sentences to the paragraph.

Integrating Grammar Skills

Transitions Have students write a description of something routine in their lives. (Examples: what they do to get ready for school, what they do after school.) Then, have them circle all of the transition words they used. Have them try it again without using the words *next* or *then*. Encourage them to try new words and phrases from the transition word bin.

Answer Key

▶ **Exercise 11**

Answers will vary, but revisions should make use of transitional words and phrases.

3.3

Organize for Coherence

In a paragraph or a composition that has **coherence**, the supporting ideas are logically connected and the reader is able to see how one idea is related to another. Order the sentences in a paragraph so that one leads logically to the next, and organize the paragraphs in a composition in a logical order. Following are some methods for organizing your ideas:

- **Chronological Order** Details are arranged in time order.
- **Spatial Order** Details are presented according to their physical relationship to one another.
- **Order of Importance** Details are arranged from least to most important or vice versa.
- **Comparison and Contrast** Details are grouped according to corresponding points of comparison.

Use transitional words and phrases appropriate to your organization to help readers follow the flow of information.

🔄 Learn More

In the chapters that follow, you will learn more about each of these types of organizations, along with other possible organizations.

COMMON TRANSITIONS

Comparison and Contrast	Chronological Order	Spatial Order	Logical Relationships	Order of Importance
along with	first	alongside	whether or not	first of all
also	second	above	unless	most of all
as well as	third	beneath	in fact	more
similarly	next	in front of	in essence	importantly
although	then	behind	therefore	less
in spite of	finally	on the right	to conclude	significantly
yet	before	on the left	as proof	primarily
nevertheless	afterward	in the northeast	for example	secondarily
unless	simultaneously	in the west	as you can see	best of all
on the other hand	soon	on top of		worst of all
in contrast	later	inside		the main reason
except for	recently	outside		more outstanding
				the most vital

▶ **Exercise 11** Revising for Coherence Revise this paragraph to make it more coherent.

Practice your scales and chord changes every day so you'll develop the necessary technical skills. If you keep practicing, you'll find that persistence pays off. Take lessons with an experienced guitar player so that you can avoid a lot of the mistakes beginners tend to make. Remember, Rome wasn't built in a day, and you won't become a good musician overnight. If you start practicing the guitar now and keep working at it for the next ten years, someday you'll become an accomplished musician.

38 • Structure and Style

☑ ONGOING ASSESSMENT: Monitor and Reinforce

If students are having trouble creating unity and coherence in their paragraphs, try these strategies.

Option 1 Have students work with a paragraph they have written recently. Ask them to add a concluding sentence that summarizes the information in the paragraph. If they find this difficult, it is possible that the information is too varied. Some of it might belong in a different paragraph.	**Option 2** Have students analyze stories from the newspaper to find examples of how paragraphs are organized. Ask them to find examples of paragraphs whose details are organized in chronological order, cause-and-effect order, or order of importance. Have them try one of these methods of organization in their own writing.

The Parts of a Composition

A composition is a series of related paragraphs that focus on a single topic and develop a single **thesis**, or main idea. Compositions can assume a wide variety of different forms and can have a range of purposes. However, most compositions have the following common features.

Introduction

The **introduction** usually consists of a single paragraph, although a long composition may have two or more. The introduction presents opening remarks on the topic, establishes the writer's attitude toward the topic, presents the thesis statement, and previews the subtopics to be covered in the paragraphs that follow. The **thesis statement** is the most important sentence in the introduction because it presents the controlling idea or main point of the composition.

Body

The **body** consists of a series of paragraphs that support, explain, and elaborate on the thesis. The number of body paragraphs in a composition depends on the complexity of the thesis statement, the number of subtopics into which the writer divides the main topic, and the quantity of available supporting information.

Conclusion

The **conclusion** wraps up the composition with a reminder of the main point and closing remarks. It leaves the reader satisfied that the topic has been fully covered.

> **Exercise 12** Planning a Composition Outline the parts of a composition on a topic related to something you are studying in one of your other classes.

▼ Critical Viewing
At what stage of the writing process might these students be? **[Speculate]**

Paragraphs in Essays and Other Compositions • 39

The Parts of a Composition

1. To review the parts of a composition and reinforce students' familiarity with the concepts in this lesson, you may wish to have students bring in writing they have done for other classes. Ask students to review their writing for the characteristics defined in this section.

2. To illustrate the variety of techniques employed by writers of compositions, you may wish to provide students with examples of the work of well-known newspaper or magazine essayists. Have them identify the introduction, body, and conclusion of each piece, and compare and contrast them.

Customize for

AP Students

Encourage students to bring in two samples of their writing from the beginning and end of the previous school year. Ask students to assess their writing development, either individually or in pairs.

Critical Viewing

Speculate Students may speculate that the students are in the prewriting stage, brainstorming for possible writing topics.

Answer Key

> Exercise 12

Make sure students' outlines reflect their knowledge of the features of a composition.

⏱ **TIME AND RESOURCE MANAGER**

Resources
Print: *Writing Support Transparencies*, 3-C; *Writing Support Activity Book*, 3-1

Using the Full Student Edition	Using the Handbook🄷
• Read and discuss p. 39. • Use the Model From Literature on p. 40 to demonstrate one purpose of a functional paragraph. • Read and discuss p. 41. • Have students work on Exercises 12–14 in class.	• Read and discuss p. 27. • Use the Model From Literature on p. 28 to demonstrate one purpose of a functional paragraph. • Read and discuss p. 29. • Have students work on Exercises 12–14 in class.

Types of Paragraphs

1. Discuss the differences between topical and functional paragraphs. Explain to students that a topical paragraph explores a certain topic, while a functional paragraph exists to serve a purpose, such as to grab the reader's attention or signal a change in speaker.

2. Draw students' attention to the Writing Model on this page. Ask students to explain why, in dialogue, a new paragraph begins with each new speaker. (It shows the reader which character is speaking. If dialogue is run together without paragraph indentations, it is difficult or impossible to discern who said what.)

Teaching From the Model

In this short passage, D. H. Lawrence's dialogue contrasts sharply with the omniscient third-person narration that precedes and follows it. Point out to students how such a technique accentuates the building tension in a narrative. Encourage students to include passages of dialogue in a writing assignment.

More About the Writer

During his lifetime, much of the work of D. H. Lawrence was overshadowed by his controversial views on politics and morality. Today, his work is admired for its fine craftsmanship and psychological insight. Two of his best-known novels are *Sons and Lovers* and *The Rainbow*. The complete text of "The Rocking-Horse Winner" can be found in *Prentice Hall Literature, Penguin Edition,* The British Tradition.

3.3

Types of Paragraphs

There are a number of different types of paragraphs you can use in your compositions and creative writing:

Topical Paragraphs

A topical paragraph consists of a group of sentences containing one main idea and several sentences that support or illustrate that main idea.

Functional Paragraphs

Functional paragraphs serve a specific purpose within a piece of writing. Though they may not contain a topic sentence, they have unity and coherence because the sentences are clearly connected and logically ordered. Functional paragraphs can be used for the following purposes:

To arouse or sustain interest A few vivid sentences can work together to capture the reader's attention.

To create emphasis A short paragraph of one or two sentences can be an effective way of restating or reinforcing one of your key points.

To make a transition A short paragraph can help readers move between the main ideas in two topical paragraphs.

To indicate dialogue In written dialogue, a new paragraph begins each time the speaker changes.

WRITING MODEL

from The Rocking-Horse Winner
D. H. Lawrence

"But what are you going to do with your money?" asked the uncle.

"Of course," said the boy, "I started it for mother. She said she had no luck, because father is unlucky, so I thought if *I* was lucky, it might stop whispering."

"What might stop whispering?"

"Our house! I *hate* our house for whispering."

"What does it whisper?"

"Why—why"—the boy fidgeted—"why, I don't know! But it's always short of money, you know, uncle."

"I know it, son, I know it."

In this excerpt, a young boy explains to his uncle why he has wanted to make money. Each time the speaker changes, a new paragraph begins.

Paragraph Blocks

Sometimes, you have more information about a single idea than you can include in one manageable paragraph. When this occurs, you may develop that idea over several paragraphs. These "blocks" of paragraphs all support the same main idea or topic sentence. By separating the contributing ideas into blocks, you make your ideas clearer and more accessible.

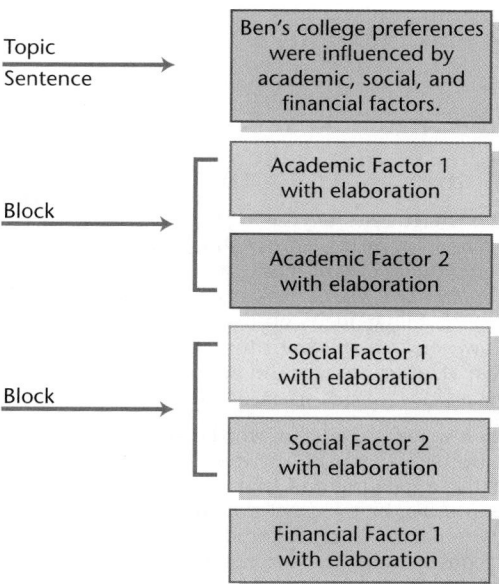

Exercise 13 Identifying Functional Paragraphs Skim a short story, persuasive essay, or review. Find one example of a functional paragraph that sustains interest or creates emphasis and one example of a functional paragraph that either indicates dialogue or makes a transition. Explain how these paragraphs work in the context of the complete piece of writing.

Exercise 14 Creating Paragraph Blocks Write a "block" of three to five paragraphs in which you explain one of your favorite hobbies.

Paragraph Blocks

Teaching Resources: Writing Support Transparencies, 3-C; Writing Support Activity Book, 3-1

1. Explain that sometimes an author wants to convey so much information that he or she needs to write several paragraphs to express one main idea.

2. Display Transparency 3-C and ask students to identify the main idea of the paragraph block. Then, ask them to consider the main idea of each paragraph within the block. Students should find that the main idea of each paragraph is one small part of the main idea of the block as a whole. Have students use the blank organizer (3-1) to break down the topic sentence of their choosing into smaller "blocks."

Answer Key

Exercise 13

When they finish, have students repeat the exercise with a selection from their portfolios. It is likely that they have used functional paragraphs without realizing it.

Exercise 14

Make sure students understand the difference between a paragraph block and an essay. A paragraph block explores one main idea. An essay not only explores a main idea, it also makes some sort of statement or argument about it.

Customize for
Less Advanced Students

Make Exercise 13 more structured by giving students a story that contains examples of all three types of functional paragraphs. Have them look for one type at a time.

 TIME SAVERS!

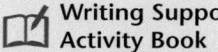 **Writing Support Transparencies**
Use the transparencies for Chapter 3 to facilitate the teaching of strategies.

Writing Support Activity Book
Use the graphic organizers for Chapter 3 to facilitate student planning.

Writing Style

1. Remind students that too many short sentences can make writing sound choppy and can make it hard for readers to connect ideas. On the other hand, too many long sentences can make a selection difficult to follow.

2. To explore diction, give students a list of adjectives and have them come up with synonyms for each. One synonym should be mild in connotation and one should be forceful or extreme. For example, synonyms for *happy* could be *content* or *ecstatic*. Remind students to be aware of the purpose of the essay and the connotations of words when writing.

3. To illustrate tone, have students reflect on the Models from Literature in this chapter and choose one word that describes the tone of each. Make sure they can defend their answers with evidence from the text.

Answer Key

> **Exercise 15**

In addition to evaluating tone and diction, have partners check the paragraphs to make sure the main idea is clear.

3.4 Writing Style

Just as no two people are exactly alike, no two writers are exactly alike. Every writer has his or her unique style. **Style** refers to the way a writer puts his or her ideas into writing. It includes everything about the writing, except for the ideas on which the writing focuses. It includes such features as the way the writer uses sentences, the types of words that a writer uses, and the attitude that a writer conveys toward his or her subject and audience.

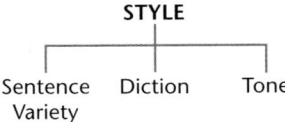

STYLE

Sentence Variety · Diction · Tone

Sentence Variety One of the key elements of your style is the types of sentences you use. When you want your writing to come across as scholarly or sophisticated, you might rely mainly on longer, more complex sentences. When you want your writing to be simple and easy to follow, focus on using shorter sentences. Most often, however, you will want to use a blend of long and short sentences; also, try to vary the sentence structures you use.

Diction Diction, which refers to a writer's choice of words, is one of the most immediately noticeable aspects of a writer's style. Choose language that you find appealing and that conveys the exact meaning you intend. Also, be aware of the connotations, or associations, that your words bring to mind. Some words, for example, might convey a positive impression of a topic, while others convey a negative impression.

Tone Your attitude toward your subject is conveyed in the tone of your writing. You may approach your subject in many ways: with delight, reverence, or understatement. A note to a friend or relative will probably have a casual and lighthearted tone, while a warning about the need to drive safely will be stern and cautionary.

> **Exercise 15** Read the two Writing Models on page 33. Study the sentence lengths and structures, the word choice, and the tone of each. Discuss with a partner how the styles of the two paragraphs are similar and different. Then, write a paragraph of your own, modeled on the style of one of them. See if your partner can tell which style you used as a model.

Learn More

For more on sentence variety, see Chapter 20, "Effective Sentences."

⏱ TIME AND RESOURCE MANAGER

Resources
Technology: Technology: *Writing and Grammar* Interactive Text, Section 3.3

Using the Full Student Edition	Using the Handbook 🔠
• Read and discuss pp. 42–43. • Have students complete Exercises 15–16 in class. • Have students repeat Exercise 15 by emulating the style of an author they read and enjoyed this year in class.	• Read and discuss pp. 30–31. • Have students complete Exercises 15–16 in class. • Have students repeat Exercise 15 by emulating the style of an author they read and enjoyed this year in class.

Formal and Informal English

Standard English may be either formal or informal. Formal English is appropriate for serious and academic purposes. Informal English is appropriate for casual writing or when you want your writing to resemble conversation.

Use the Conventions of Formal English

You will use formal English for business communications, college-application essays, newspaper editorials, and most school assignments. When writing in formal English, you should observe these conventions:

• Avoid contractions.
• Do not use slang.
• Use standard English and grammar.

Use Informal English

Informal English is the language of everyday speech. You can use informal English in friendly letters, in journal entries, and—to create realistic dialogue—in personal narratives. In informal English, you can:

• Use contractions.
• Use slang and popular expressions, especially to capture the natural sounds of speech.

FORMAL ENGLISH:	Key West, Florida, boasts beautiful beaches, exciting water sports, and international shopping with a local flair. Tourists can stroll the grounds at Ernest Hemingway's house or visit a monument marking the southernmost tip of the continental United States. Visitors and natives alike gather to watch Key West's famous sunsets.
INFORMAL ENGLISH:	I had a super weekend in Key West, Florida. We spent a lot of time on the beach, soaking up the amazing rays. While I was chilling-out on the sand, I saw lots of brave souls parasailing! No way would you ever get me to try that! I did other cool stuff, too. We bought these tacky souvenirs, ate conch fritters, and checked out the sunset.

> **Exercise 16** **Using Formal and Informal English** Find a paragraph written in formal English and rewrite it in informal English. Then, find a paragraph written in informal English and rewrite it in formal English.

▲ Critical Viewing
Write two descriptions of this photograph: one in formal English and one in informal English. **[Connect]**

Writing Style • 43

Step-by-Step Teaching Guide

Formal and Informal English

1. Ask students to discuss the use of formal and informal English while speaking. Are there certain situations in which they try to speak more formally than in others?

2. Have students write a paragraph about their plans for the future. One paragraph should be written as if it were part of a school assignment, and another as if it were part of a letter to a friend.

Critical Viewing

Connect Sample responses: A beautiful sunset inspires awe. A cool sunset always gives me goosebumps.

Answer Key

> **Exercise 16**

Suggest that students rewrite passages from newspaper articles in informal English and paragraphs from teen magazines in formal English.

ASSESS and CLOSE

Step-by-Step Teaching Guide

Assessment

Teaching Resources: Formal Assessment, Chapter 3

1. Review the chapter by asking students to restate its key points.

2. You may wish to use the following assessment options:

   • review the Standardized Test Preparation Workshop on pages 46–47 and have students complete the practice items.

   • administer the Chapter 3 assessment from *Formal Assessment* in Teaching Resources to measure students' grasp of concepts presented.

☑ **ONGOING ASSESSMENT: Monitor and Reinforce**

If students have difficulty distinguishing between formal and informal English, use the following strategies.

Option 1 Present a list of situations such as a job interview, a first date, a student government meeting, and a college interview. Ask students to describe the appropriate language for each situation. Chances are, their instincts will tell them what type of language is formal and what is not.

Option 2 Ask students to research the definitions of *slang, jargon,* and *dialect.* Have them write a paragraph that explains the differences among these terms. Make sure they include at least two examples of each.

Exploring Cultural History Through the Arts

1. Focus on one of the Spotlight features for discussion, or have students select a feature to research.

2. Let students know that a key element of Greek tragedy was the idea of the *protagonist*, or hero of the story, and the *antagonist*, or villain.

3. Students will find that Greek tragedy often focused on the individual, on the tragic flaw in the character of an otherwise heroic protagonist such as Oedipus. Greek comedy, in contrast, often focused satirically on the foibles of the many, as in *Lysistrata*. Ask students whether they think this kind of distinction is still made in the modern television, film, or stage dramas they see.

Viewing and Representing

Activity Allow class time for willing students to present their acceptance speeches. As an alternative activity, suggest that interested students prepare and deliver a scene from a Greek tragedy or comedy. Encourage them to prepare a short talk on the history and background of the play before they begin the performance.

Critical Viewing

Compare Students may point out that contemporary American drama does not commonly feature masks or robes such as those in the photograph.

Spotlight on the Humanities

Exploring Cultural History Through the Arts

Focus on Theater: Greek Drama

If you were to write a brief overview of Greek drama, your overview would contain at least one paragraph on tragedies and at least one paragraph on comedies. A Greek tragedy involved an individual who was above average, like a king or a god. Comedy centered on average or below-average individuals. In tragedy, language was elevated; and in comedy, the language was like that spoken in everyday life. A central part of all Greek drama was the chorus who, under a leader, sang to the audience and imparted important facts about the plot and action of the play.

Literature Connection In 1872, the German author and philosopher Friedrich Nietzsche (1844–1900) had his first book published, entitled *The Birth of Tragedy*. His study of the components of Greek tragedy led him to assert that two types of cultures existed: the Apollonian and the Dionysian. He believed that true creativity grew from Dionysian cultures, which emphasized emotion and instinct, rather than Apollonian cultures, which accentuated reason and logical thought.

Theater Connection The Greek chorus evolved into the singers and dancers in American musical theater who comprise the chorus behind the lead performers. An examination of the musical chorus appeared in the 1976 Pulitzer Prize-winning musical *A Chorus Line*. For many years, *A Chorus Line* was the longest-running show on Broadway, playing to audiences for fifteen years.

Writing Activity: Acceptance Speech

Imagine that you are a dramatic actor who has just won an award. Write an acceptance speech for the award to read to the audience. Break down your speech into several paragraphs, first discussing your part and your inspiration, next discussing the significance of the award, and finally thanking all of the people who helped strengthen your performance.

▲ **Critical Viewing** How does the production of this Greek drama look different from what you know about performances in today's American theater? [**Compare**]

Media and Technology Skills

Recognizing the Varieties of Media Sources of Information

Activity: Conduct a Media Survey

Everyone uses technology differently. Some people rely heavily on traditional sources of information, such as books, newspapers, and magazines. Others depend mostly on newer technologies, such as the Internet, e-mail, and CD-ROMs. Conducting a media survey will help you evaluate your classmates' research patterns.

Think About It You will survey your class or school to identify how your peers use different media sources of information. Devise an action plan for your survey, including these features:

- **Sample group:** Decide whether you will survey all students or a representative sample.
- **Survey scope:** Choose a specific focus for your survey, such as what source students use when researching history or science topics.
- **Question format:** The results of your survey need to be tabulated and analyzed. Choose a format that produces measurable data, such as multiple-choice questions, a ratings scale, or a checklist.

Design It Write enough survey questions to get a significant amount of information, but don't make your survey too long. Participants may lose interest and rush through a long survey, giving careless or inaccurate responses.

Collect Data and Analyze It Collect data from your chosen survey sample. Make sure you give respondents enough time to answer each question on your survey. Then, tabulate and analyze the results. Look for trends, and make generalizations based on your findings.

Report It Write a short paragraph summarizing your survey results. Include a graph showing the most significant or interesting data you collected. Publish your report in a classroom, school, or community bulletin.

Types of Media

Print
- Books
- Magazines
- Newspapers
- Photography

Broadcast
- Film
- Radio
- Television
- Internet Broadcasts

Which of the following sources provided you with information

yesterday?	within the last week?
___ book	___ book
___ catalog	___ catalog
___ CD-ROM	___ CD-ROM
___ e-mail	✓ e-mail
___ Internet	___ Internet
___ magazine	___ magazine
✓ newspaper	___ newspaper
___ radio	___ radio
___ telephone call	___ telephone call
___ television	___ television

▶ Lesson Objectives

1. To create, present, test, and revise a project and analyze a response using data-gathering techniques such as questionnaires, group discussions, and feedback forms

2. To distinguish the purposes of various media forms such as informative texts, entertaining texts, and advertisements

3. To recognize genres such as nightly news, newsmagazines, and documentaries and identify the unique properties of each

Step-by-Step Teaching Guide

Recognizing the Varieties of Media Sources of Information

Teaching Resources: Writing Support Transparencies, 3-D; Writing Support Activity Book, 3-2

1. Discuss in class the degree to which technological sources of information are or are not replacing print sources such as books, magazines, and newspapers.

2. Ask students how much they depend on sources such as the Internet and e-mail for information and communication. Encourage them to give examples.

3. Display Transparency 3-D to show that the range of communication technology is wider than the telephone and e-mail.

4. Give students a blank copy of the Media Information Checklist (3-2) or have them devise their own form to track their survey data. Review survey results in class.

TIME SAVERS!

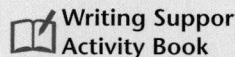

Writing Support Transparencies
Use the transparencies for Chapter 3 to facilitate the teaching of strategies.

Writing Support Activity Book
Use the graphic organizers for Chapter 3 to facilitate student planning.

1. To analyze aspects of texts such as patterns of organization and choice of language for their effect on audiences

2. To analyze text structures such as compare/contrast, cause/effect, and chronological order for how they influence understanding

3. To analyze strategies that writers in different fields use to compose

4. To analyze the characteristics of clear text such as conciseness, correctness, and completeness

Step-by-Step Teaching Guide

Analyzing Strategy, Organization, and Style

Teaching Resources: Standardized Test Preparation Workbook, pp. 5–6

1. Go over the bulleted points with students.

2. Have students read the passage and answer the sample question. Then check to see that students have answered correctly.

3. Have students continue with the four questions about the passage.

4. Go over students' answers, and ask students to explain what is wrong with the incorrect choices.

Standardized Test Preparation Workshop

Analyzing Strategy, Organization, and Style

Questions on standardized tests frequently measure your knowledge of writing skills. In these tests, items may include a passage in which part of a sentence is marked for your analysis. You will be asked to analyze strategy, organization, sequence of sentences, and style within a passage. The following are three types of questions you may encounter:

- **Strategy questions** ask whether a given revision is appropriate in the context of the passage.

- **Organization questions** ask you to choose the most logical sequence of ideas or to decide whether a sentence should be added, deleted, or moved.

- **Style questions** focus on your ability to identify the writer's point of view or evaluate the use of language for an intended audience.

The sample test item that follows will give you practice in answering these types of questions.

Test Tips

- Read the passage through at least once, and then go back and mark places where you think a transitional phrase or sentence is needed.

- If you become confused as you read a passage, think about rearranging sentences to make it more logical.

Sample Test Item	Answer and Explanation

Directions: Read the passage, and then answer the question that follows.
 	
[1]Relieved and surprised, Andrea found that the noise was actually her two cats chasing each other around the couch. [2]After leaving her room, she decided to grab the phone in case she needed to call for help. [3]Frightened by a noise in her living room, Andrea tiptoed out of her bedroom.
 	
1 Choose the sequence that will make the passage the most logical.
 	
  A 1, 2, 3
  B 2, 3, 1
  C 3, 2, 1
  D 2, 1, 3
	The correct answer is C. This sequence begins with Andrea being frightened by a noise and ends with her discovering the source of the noise.

46 • Structure and Style

✏ TEST-TAKING TIP

Encourage students to jot down the numbers of sentences that seem incorrect or confusing as they read the test passage. This will give them a head start on answering questions about how to improve it.

Students should note that on a test of this type, they are asked to analyze the best choices for revising organization and style. Sometimes making the best choice may require an analysis of the writing form the author is using. For example, answering the question about organization (as in the sample test item) requires the reader to make a judgement about author's purpose in order to choose the correct answer.

Answer Key

1. C
2. A
3. A
4. C
5. D

▶ **Practice 1** **Directions:** Read the passage, and then answer the questions that follow. Choose the letter of the best answer.

¹Born in Ireland in 1900, my grandmother boarded a ship to the United States when she was just twenty-three years old. ²Her family in Ireland needed financial help, and since she was the oldest child, she felt that it was her responsibility to help her family.

³After a short time in New York, she found work as a nanny and cook for a family in Manhattan. ⁴In return, she received room and board and a small paycheck. ⁵Each month, she mailed a majority of her pay back to her family.

⁶Born and raised on a farm, my grandmother endured some culture shock while living in a big city. ⁷The crowded streets, the apartment buildings, and the noise were overwhelming at times. ⁸In addition to the cultural changes, she felt homesick. ⁹Ireland was very far away, and the only communication she had with her family was through letters. ¹⁰She looked forward to the day she could return to Ireland.

¹¹After seven years in New York, she packed up her bags for her return to Ireland. ¹²It was a rainy and windy day. ¹³She had worked hard and supported her family well, but by then, her younger siblings were older and more capable of supporting her family. ¹⁴In 1930, she returned to her homeland as an even stronger, more independent woman, with a much wider knowledge of the world.

1 Which of the following would be the best order of the first sentences?

  A 1, 3, 2, 4

  B 2, 3, 1, 4

  C 1, 2, 3, 4

  D 4, 3, 2, 1

2 Which would be the best sentence to add at the beginning of the third paragraph to show a transition from the previous paragraph?

  A Although she knew that she needed to be in New York to support her family, it was a difficult time for many reasons.

  B She became great friends with the family she worked for in New York.

  C She wrote letters to her family twice a week.

  D My grandmother was a courageous woman.

3 If the author wanted to include more information about the culture shock experienced by the grandmother, which of the following would be an appropriate addition?

  A The variety of food available in New York was very surprising to my grandmother, who had never even heard of a pizza pie.

  B The journey by ship to the United States was fun but also filled with anxiety.

  C The family was kind to my grandmother and treated her like part of the family.

  D She kept a journal every day because she knew that one day she would want to share her experiences with her children.

4 Which best identifies the author's purpose?

  A To evaluate

  B To entertain

  C To inform

  D To persuade

5 Which of the following draws attention away from the main focus?

  A Part 3

  B Part 8

  C Part 10

  D Part 12

Customize for

Less Advanced Students

If students have difficulty choosing the best answers, you may wish to review organizational strategies tested, such as chronological order and transitional phrases.

Customize for

AP Students

After students have completed the assignment within the allotted time, ask them to go back and review the test passage. How could it be improved? What other parts of the passage could be strengthened?

In-Depth Lesson Plan

	LESSON FOCUS	PRINT AND MEDIA RESOURCES
DAY 1	**Introduction to Autobiographical Writing** Students learn key elements of autobiographical writing and analyze the Model From Literature. (pp. 48–53/H32–33)	*Writers at Work* **DVD**, Narration *Writing and Grammar* **Interactive Text**, Ch. 4, Introduction
DAY 2	**Prewriting** Students choose and narrow a topic, consider their audience and purpose, and gather information. (pp. 54–57/H34–37)	*Writing and Grammar* **Interactive Text**, Section 4.2 **Teaching Resources** *Writing Support Transparencies*, 4-A–D; *Writing Support Activity Book*, 4-1–2; *Topic Bank for Heterogeneous Classes*, Ch. 4
DAY 3	**Drafting** Students organize their ideas and write their first drafts. (pp. 58–59/H38–39)	*Writing and Grammar* **Interactive Text**, Section 4.3 **Teaching Resources** *Writing Support Transparencies*, 4-E
DAY 4	**Revising** Students revise their drafts in terms of overall structure, paragraphs, sentences, and word choice. (pp. 60–63/H40–43)	*Writing and Grammar* **Interactive Text**, Section 4.4 **Teaching Resources** *Writing Support Transparencies*, 4-F–G
DAY 5	**Editing and Proofreading; Publishing and Presenting** Students check their work for accuracy and correctness and present their final drafts. (pp. 64–65/H44–45)	*Writing and Grammar* **Interactive Text**, Sections 4.5–6 **Teaching Resources** *Scoring Rubrics on Transparency*, Ch. 4; *Writing Assessment and Portfolio Management*; *Formal Assessment*, Ch. 4

Accelerated Lesson Plan

	LESSON FOCUS	PRINT AND MEDIA RESOURCES
DAY 1	**Introduction Through Drafting** Students review characteristics of autobiographical writing, select topics, and write drafts. (pp. 48–59/H32–39)	*Writers at Work* **DVD**, Narration *Writing and Grammar* **Interactive Text**, Ch. 4, Introduction through Section 4.3 **Teaching Resources** *Writing Support Transparencies*, 4-A–E; *Writing Support Activity Book*, 4-1–2
DAY 2	**Revising Through Presenting** Students work individually or with peers to revise, edit, and proofread their work for presentation. (pp. 60–65/H40–45)	*Writing and Grammar* **Interactive Text**, Sections 4.4–6 **Teaching Resources** *Writing Support Transparencies*, 4-F–G; *Scoring Rubrics on Transparency*, Ch. 4; *Writing Assessment and Portfolio Management*; *Formal Assessment*, Ch. 4

Options for Adapting Lesson Plans

HOMEWORK
Have students complete any stage of the lesson for homework.

FEATURES
Extend coverage with Connected Assignment (p. 69), Spotlight on the Humanities (p. 70), Media and Technology Skills (p. 71), and the Standardized Test Preparation Workshop (pp. 71–72).

TECHNOLOGY
Students can complete any stage of the lesson on the computer, using *Writing and Grammar* Interactive Text or a word-processing program. Have them print out their completed work.

Writing and Grammar Handbook Alignment

Page numbers in Step-by-Step Teaching Guides in this Teacher's Edition refer to pages from the full student text. Handbook page references, indicated with this icon **H**, are provided in Time and Resource Manager boxes and at the bottom of each Teacher's Edition page.

INTEGRATED SKILLS COVERAGE

Integrating Grammar
Verb Tenses, SE p. 62/**H**42
Spelling Homophones, SE p. 64/**H**44
ATE p. 59

Reading/Writing Connection
Use Context Clues, SE p. 50
Writing Application, SE p. 53

Viewing and Representing
Critical Viewing, SE pp. 48, 50, 51, 52, 53, 55, 58, 66, 67, 68, 70/**H**32, 35, 38
Examining Media Portrayals of Characters, SE p. 70
Conveying Messages Using Visuals, SE p. 71

Speaking and Listening
ATE p. 64

Real-World Connection
ATE p. 51

Technology
SE p. 65/**H**45

Workplace Skills
ATE pp. 52, 57

Vocabulary
ATE p. 52

ASSESSMENT SUPPORT

Standardized Test Preparation Workshop SE p. 71; ATE pp. 50, 56
Standardized Test Preparation Workbook, pp. 7–8
Scoring Rubrics on Transparency, Ch. 4
Formal Assessment, Ch. 4
Writing Assessment and Portfolio Management

MEETING INDIVIDUAL NEEDS

Less Advanced Students ATE pp. 56, 68, 73. See also Ongoing Assessments ATE pp. 55, 57, 62.
AP Students ATE pp. 61, 73
ESL Students ATE pp. 57, 61
Linguistic Learners ATE p. 58

BLOCK SCHEDULING

Pacing Suggestions
For 90-minute Blocks
• Have students complete the Prewriting and Drafting stages in a single period.
• Focus one class period on Revising and Editing and Publishing and Presenting. Allow at least 30 minutes for peer revision.

Resources for Varying Instruction
• *Writing and Grammar* **Interactive Text** A 90-minute block provides an ideal opportunity for students to work on the computer.
• *Writers at Work* **DVD** Show the Narration segment in class.

Professional Development Support
• *How to Manage Instruction in the Block* This teaching resource provides management and activity suggestions.

MEDIA AND TECHNOLOGY

For the Student
• *Writing and Grammar* **Interactive Text,** Ch. 4
• *On-line Exercise Bank,* Section 21.1, Verb Tenses

For the Teacher
• *Writers at Work* **DVD,** Narration
• **Teacher**EXPRESS™ **CD-ROM**

WRITING AND GRAMMAR ON-LINE

Interactive Text (On-line or on CD-ROM)
• Easily navigable instruction with interactive Revision Checkers
• Full use of e-rater™, the essay-scoring system (on-line only)

Companion Web Site PHSchool.com
• Scoring rubrics with models (use Web Code egk-1201)

See the Go On-line! **feature, SE p. iii.**

LITERATURE CONNECTIONS

Related selections from *Prentice Hall Literature, Penguin Edition,* The British Tradition:
Professional Model "Shooting an Elephant," George Orwell, SE p. 53
Topic Bank Option "Follower," Seamus Heaney, SE p. 55

Lesson Objectives

1. To write an autobiographical narrative appropriate to audience and purpose

2. To understand literary forms and terms such as *autobiography* as appropriate to the selection being read

3. To read to appreciate a writer's craft and to discover models for writing

4. To use writing as a tool for reflection, learning, and personal growth

5. To use prewriting strategies to generate ideas, develop voice, and plan

6. To use writing to refine an autobiographical topic and clarify ideas

7. To develop and revise drafts in terms of structure, paragraphs, sentences, and word choice

8. To edit and proofread to ensure standard English usage and grammar

9. To evaluate how well writing achieves its purposes and to engage in conversations with peers and the teacher

10. To refine selected work for publication

Critical Viewing

Analyze Student responses should focus on the kinds of information the character might choose to include in an autobiographical narrative.

Chapter 4 Narration
Autobiographical Writing

In Front of the Mirror, K. N. Istomin

▲ Critical Viewing
If the character in this painting were to write an autobiographical narrative, how might she describe herself? **[Analyze]**

Autobiographical Writing in Everyday Life

"What did you do on your vacation?" "What happened in school today?" "How was work?" Whether you realize it or not, everyday questions like these are an invitation to tell an **autobiographical narrative**—a true story from your life. In response to these questions, you would explain what you did or experienced and tell the story from your own point of view, using *I* and *my*. The unique experiences and perspectives of a person's own life form the essence of autobiography.

Autobiographical writing comes in many forms, ranging in formality and length. For example, you might write a humorous letter to a friend, telling about your experiences on your vacation; or you might describe your past job experiences in a cover letter to an employer; or you could relate an incident from your past in a college-application essay.

48 • Narration

⏱ TIME AND RESOURCE MANAGER	
Resources **Technology:** *Writers at Work* DVD, Narration; *Writing and Grammar* Interactive Text, Ch. 4	
Using the Full Student Edition	**Using the Handbook⊞**
• Cover pp. 48–49 in class. • Show the Narration section of the *Writers at Work* DVD. • Read the Model From Literature (pp. 50–53) in class, and use it to brainstorm for autobiographical narrative ideas with students.	• Cover pp. 32–33 in class. • Show the Narration section of the *Writers at Work* DVD.

What Is Autobiographical Writing?

The telling of stories—whether real or imagined—is called **narration. Autobiographical stories** are stories we tell about ourselves or our experiences. In most autobiographical writing, you'll find

- characters, including the writer as a character.
- settings, drawn from real life.
- a series of events that form a plot.
- conflict or tension between characters or between a character and another force.
- insights that the writer gained from the experience.

To preview the criteria on which your autobiographical writing may be evaluated, see the Rubric for Self-Assessment on page 65.

Types of Autobiographical Writing

You may be familiar with full-length autobiographies that are often featured in bookstore windows. Following are other types of autobiographical writing:

- **Personal narratives** tell a true story about an important experience, relationship, or period in the writer's life.
- **Autobiographical incidents** capture and explore in detail a short episode or moment in time from the writer's life.
- **Memoirs** are written records of people and events as experienced and remembered by the writer.
- **Anecdotes** are episodes in the writer's life that usually are amusing and end with a punch line or general insight.

PREVIEW
Student Work
IN PROGRESS

In this chapter, you'll read the autobiographical writing of Melissa Sanborn, a student at Seneca High School in Louisville, Kentucky. You'll see how Melissa used prewriting, drafting, and revising techniques to shape her memoir "Where Are You When the Dandelions Bloom?"

Writers in ACTION

It is the rare writer who does not draw from his or her life in some form. Acclaimed writer Isaac Bashevis Singer often drew upon his own life as inspiration for his stories. He believed that one's life experience would find its way into one's writing:

"Writers always go back to their young days, to their young lives. If a writer writes about his life, and he is serious, he will go back there. . . ."

Autobiographical Writing • 49

PREPARE and ENGAGE

Interest GRABBER Ask students to brainstorm for the most interesting things that happened to them in the last week, and jot down notes about their experiences. Do any of these events seem to be promising as topics?

Activate Prior Knowledge

Ask students to recall the last time they read or heard a good autobiographical narrative. Such a narrative might have been in a magazine, heard around the lunchroom table, or presented on a television talk show. What made the narrative interesting? How did the writer or speaker maintain interest? After discussing these techniques, refer students to the characteristics of autobiographical writing in the text.

More About the Writer

Nobel Laureate Isaac Bashevis Singer became known as the world's foremost writer of Yiddish literature. Although Yiddish uses the Hebrew alphabet, it incorporates words and phrases from Hebrew, German, Aramaic, French, and Italian. Singer did all of his writing in Yiddish, which was then translated into English. Many of his beautiful tales about the vanished world of his youth in Poland have been made into films and plays. Singer was awarded the Nobel Prize for Literature in 1978.

☑ ONGOING ASSESSMENT: Diagnose

Use one of the following options to diagnose students' current level of proficiency in autobiographical writing.

Option 1 Ask students to select their strongest example of autobiographical writing from last year. Have them read over their work and make a list of at least two skills they'd like to improve (writing introductions, adding details, creating dialogue). Meet with students to discuss their work and their goals.

Option 2 Ask students to write down examples of autobiographical writing they've read lately. Read over their lists. You might suggest that students who are unfamiliar with this genre do some reading to familiarize themselves with it. Recommend specific articles or essays for them to read.

Reading\Writing Connection

Reading: Use Context Clues

Context clues can unlock the meaning of an unfamiliar word. Model this process for students using the word segments from the second paragraph of the selection on page 50. The surrounding text tells the reader that the segments of tissue are thin, made with "an ingenious cutting device," and would probably go on a microscope slide. Segments may therefore be small pieces, parts, or sections of something. Have students check this hypothesis in a dictionary.

Step-by-Step Teaching Guide

Engage Students Through Literature

1. Use questions like these to prompt discussion:

   How did Dillard feel when she found the amoeba?

   Why did she want to share her find with her parents?

   How did her parents' attitude affect Dillard?

2. Ask students to brainstorm for other autobiographical topics that Dillard might have written about. Some possibilities:

   The author's drawings and poems

   The author as an athlete

   The author's many collections

3. Students may add these topics to their own autobiographical ideas in their topic banks.

Critical Viewing

Apply Students will observe that microscopes help us to see and analyze structures and processes too small to be observed by unaided eyes.

Model From Literature

Pulitzer Prize-winning author Annie Dillard often draws upon her own life in her writing. In the following memoir, Dillard describes a turning point in her life during which she came to realize her full potential.

Reading Strategy: Use Context Clues The personal narrative that follows is full of scientific terminology. When you come across unfamiliar terms, look for **context clues**—definitions, restatements, or descriptions in the surrounding text—to help you figure out their meanings.

▲ **Critical Viewing** In what way do microscopes, such as the one pictured, help us understand our world? **[Apply]**

from

An American Childhood

Annie Dillard

After I read *The Field Book of Ponds and Streams* several times, I longed for a microscope. Everybody needed a microscope. Detectives used microscopes, both for the FBI and at Scotland Yard. Although usually I had to save my tiny allowance for things I wanted, that year for Christmas my parents gave me a microscope kit.

In a dark basement corner, on a white enamel table, I set up the microscope kit. I supplied a chair, a lamp, a batch of jars, a candle, and a pile of library books. The microscope kit supplied a blunt black three-speed microscope, a booklet, a scalpel, a dropper, an ingenious device for cutting thin segments of fragile tissue, a pile of clean slides and cover slips, and a dandy array of corked test tubes.

One of the test tubes contained "hay infusion." Hay infusion was a wee brown chip of grass blade. You added water to it, and after a week it became a jungle in a drop, full of one-celled

Because this is a piece of autobiographical writing, the writer uses the first-person "I" to tell the story.

50 • Autobiographical Writing

---

animals. This did not work for me. All I saw in the microscope after a week was a wet chip of dried grass, much enlarged.

Another test tube contained "diatomaceous earth." This was, I believed, an actual pinch of the white cliffs of Dover. On my palm it was an airy, friable chalk. The booklet said it was composed of the silicaceous bodies of diatoms—one-celled creatures that lived in, as it were, small glass jewelry boxes with fitted lids. Diatoms, I read, come in a variety of transparent geometrical shapes. Broken and dead and dug out of geological deposits, they made chalk, and a fine abrasive used in silver polish and toothpaste. What I saw in the microscope must have been the fine abrasive—grit enlarged. It was years before I saw a recognizable, whole diatom. The kit's diatomaceous earth was a bust.

All that winter I played with the microscope. I prepared slides from things at hand, as the books suggested. I looked at the transparent membrane inside an onion's skin and saw the cells. I looked at a section of cork and saw the cells, and at scrapings from the inside of my cheek, ditto. . . .

All this was very well, but I wanted to see the wildlife I had read about. I wanted especially to see the famous amoeba, who had eluded me. He was supposed to live in the hay infusion, but I hadn't found him there. He lived outside in warm ponds and streams, too, but I lived in Pittsburgh, and it had been a cold winter.

Finally late that spring I saw an amoeba. The week before, I had gathered puddle water from Frick Park; it had been festering in a jar in the basement. This June night after dinner I figured I had waited long enough. In the basement at my microscope table I spread a scummy drop of Frick Park puddle water on a slide, peeked in, and lo, there was the famous amoeba. He was as blobby and grainy as his picture; I would have known him anywhere.

Before I had watched him at all, I ran upstairs. My parents were still at table, drinking coffee. They, too, could see the famous amoeba. I told them, bursting, that he was all set up, that they should hurry before his water dried. It was the chance of a lifetime.

▲ **Critical Viewing**
Judging from this photograph, why might some people find amoebas interesting to study? **[Connect]**

Dillard uses vivid details to bring to life both the setting and the event she is describing.

Teaching From the Model

You can use this Model From Literature to show students how to find a topic for an autobiographical narrative. Help students see that Dillard's childhood interest in microscopic life made a good topic because it fascinated her and influenced her to study and write about the natural world. Have students think about possible topics that interest them. Which topics say something about the author and also suggest details that would interest a reader?

More About the Writer

When Annie Dillard was only twenty-nine, she won the Pulitzer Prize for general nonfiction for *Pilgrim at Tinker Creek*, an account of a period in her life spent in communion with nature. She says of the writer's effort to uncover experience and describe it: " . . . we have been as usual asking the wrong question. It does not matter a hoot what the mockingbird on the chimney is singing. The real and proper question is: Why is it beautiful?"

Real-World Connection

When starting research on a new project, scientists write a grant proposal to ask for funding. The grant proposal is a narrative detailing what they want to study, how they expect to find out what they want to know, and describing their qualifications. The grant proposal must also tell why the research is important. Ask students what they would look for in a grant proposal if they were reviewing it for possible funding. Which elements of the proposal's narrative would be most important in determining whether or not to fund the project? (Funds for the study would not be granted if key elements were missing from the proposal. Key elements include establishing the importance of the project and the credibility of the researchers.)

Critical Viewing

Connect Students may note that the amoeba looks complex despite its microscopic size.

Integrating Workplace Skills

Science Encourage students to brainstorm for personal attributes and skills needed to work in the physical sciences, as biologists and chemists do. (*Attributes:* determination, perseverance, curiosity, and organization. *Skills:* well-developed math and science skills, observation skills, fine motor skills, problem-solving skills, the ability to concentrate and to retain information, and patience.)

Integrating Vocabulary Skills

The author states, "I had *essentially* been handed my own life. In *subsequent* years, my parents would praise my drawings and poems, and supply me with books, art supplies, and sports equipment, and listen to my troubles and *enthusiasms* . . . "

Have students guess at the meanings of the italicized words based on the context clues. Then have students look in the dictionary to determine whether their guesses were accurate.

Critical Viewing

Analyze Answers will depend on students' familiarity with biology. Descriptions may range from *grainy blob* to *single-celled protozoan propelled by the cilia that run the length of the organism.*

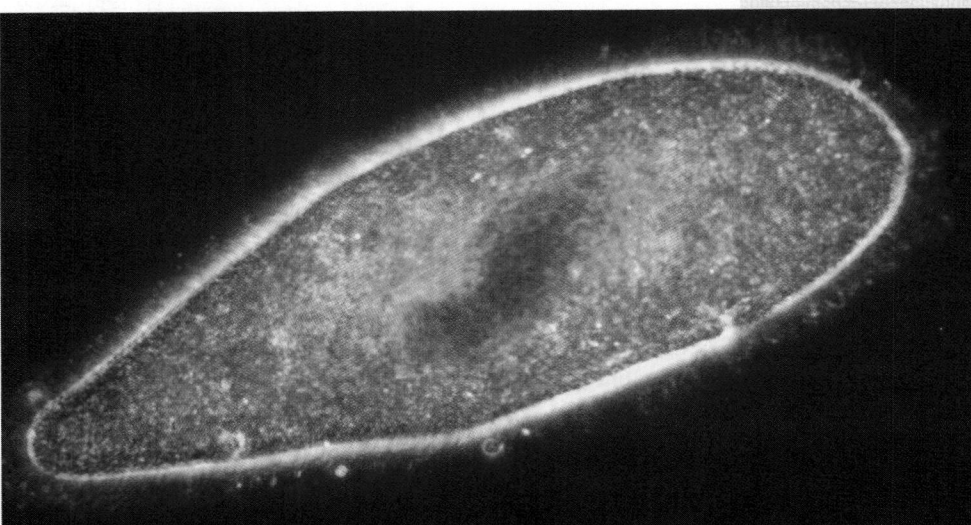

▲ **Critical Viewing** How would you describe a paramecium to someone who had never seen one before? [**Analyze**]

Father had stretched out his long legs and was tilting back in his chair. Mother sat with her knees crossed, in blue slacks. . . . The dessert dishes were still on the table. My sisters were nowhere in evidence. It was a warm evening; the big dining-room windows gave onto blooming rhododendrons.

Mother regarded me warmly. She gave me to understand that she was glad I had found what I had been looking for, but that she and Father were happy to sit with their coffee, and would not be coming down.

She did not say, but I understood at once, that they had their pursuits (coffee?) and I had mine. She did not say, but I began to understand then, that you do what you do out of your private passion for the thing itself.

I had essentially been handed my own life. In subsequent years my parents would praise my drawings and poems, and supply me with books, art supplies, and sports equipment, and listen to my troubles and enthusiasms, and supervise my hours, and discuss and inform, but they would not get involved with my detective work, nor hear about my reading, nor inquire about my home-work or term papers or exams, nor visit the salamanders I caught, nor listen to me play the piano, nor attend my field

This is the climax, or high point of interest, in the story.

hockey games, nor fuss over my insect collection with me, or my poetry collection or stamp collection or rock collection. My days and nights were my own to plan and fill.

When I left the dining room that evening and started down the dark basement stairs, I had a life. I sat next to my wonderful amoeba, and there he was, rolling his grains more slowly now, extending an arc of his edge for a foot and drawing himself along by that foot, and absorbing it again and rolling on. I gave him some more pond water.

I had hit pay dirt. For all I knew, there were paramecia, too, in that pond water, or daphniae, or stentors, or any of the many other creatures I had read about and never seen: volvox, the spherical algal colony; euglena with its one red eye; the elusive, glassy diatom; hydra, rotifers, water bears, worms. Anything was possible. The sky was the limit.

This is the insight offered in the memoir: Annie Dillard's young world had opened up.

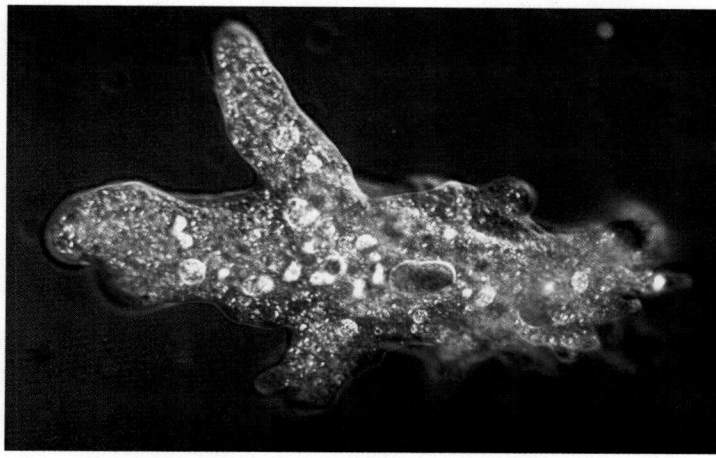

◀ **Critical Viewing**
Why are one-celled animals so fascinating to many students? **[Relate]**

Reading Writing Connection

Writing Application: Give Context Clues If you were writing an autobiographical narrative about a special interest of yours, what terms might you use that readers would need to have defined in context?

To read another autobiographical account, read George Orwell's "Shooting an Elephant" in *Prentice Hall Literature, Penguin Edition,* The British Tradition.

Critical Viewing

Relate Students may say that the idea of an entire organism consisting of a single cell is interesting or cite the fact that single-celled organisms have such a huge impact on life, from breaking down dead leaves, to aiding digestion, to causing many diseases.

Connections With Literature

If students read the selection, ask them to think about what they learn from "Shooting an Elephant." Besides details about Orwell as a young man, what can they learn about the period in which the piece was written? Ask them to apply the same question to Dillard's writing. Does Dillard's home life as a child seem to have taken place in another era, or is it very like students' own experience with families?

Reading\Writing Connection

Writing Application: Give Context Clues

Ask students to list all the unfamiliar terms they encounter in the excerpt from Dillard's book, *An American Childhood,* and try to determine their meanings from the context. Then, have students check the words' definitions in a dictionary and write them in their readers' journals. Encourage students to make sure that challenging vocabulary in their own writing is defined, restated, or described in the text so that readers have enough context clues to determine the words' meanings.

Step-by-Step Teaching Guide

Prewriting: Blueprint

1. If you wish to have students do this activity in class, you might supply graph paper. Give each student a piece of graph paper and have him or her plan the diagram so that it is large enough to fill the page. This will ensure that students have enough room for notes.

2. Encourage students to explain which of their ideas might make more effective autobiographical narratives.

Step-by-Step Teaching Guide

Prewriting: Timeline of Your Life

1. You may wish to provide students with oversized sheets of paper. On the paper, have students begin to list the important events in their lives along a timeline.

2. As students review their timelines, have them circle any topics they may want to consider further for their narrative writing.

3. On another sheet of paper, have students list the topics they circled. Under each topic, they should list the events and people they associate with each topic.

Step-by-Step Teaching Guide

Prewriting: Sentence Starters

Teaching Resources: Writing Support Transparencies, 4-A

1. Have students copy the sentence starters onto a piece of paper. You may wish to suggest other sentence starters. Then, have them finish each of the sentences.

2. Encourage students to take their time and allow their memories to flow freely when finishing the sentences. Students may well have more than one answer for each sentence.

3. Display Transparency 4-A to draw students' attention to the student sample and discuss the writer's sentence endings.

Choosing Your Topic

Sift through your memories to come up with a topic for your autobiographical narrative, or try one of these strategies for choosing a topic:

Strategies for Generating Topics

1. **Blueprint** Draw a diagram of your home or school. Label each room. Then, jot down memories or associations that come to mind when you recall each place. Choose one of these ideas as the basis for an autobiographical narrative.

2. **Timeline of Your Life** Beginning with your earliest memory, write important events and dates in chronological order on a timeline. Include significant people and places. Review the timeline for possible ideas, and choose one as your topic.

3. **Sentence Starters** Finishing an unfinished sentence helps generate writing ideas. Complete these sentence starters. Then, choose one as the starting point for your narrative.

The funniest thing happened when ____?____ .

My favorite holiday was ____?____ .

The strongest memory from childhood ____?____ .

interactive Textbook

Try it out! Use the interactive Timeline of Your Life in **Section 4.2**, on-line or on CD-ROM.

Student Work IN PROGRESS

Name: Melissa Sanborn
Seneca High School
Louisville, KY

Using Sentence Starters to Find a Topic

Melissa Sanborn used sentence starters to generate a topic for her memoir. She reviewed her responses and decided to write about her grandfather.

The funniest thing happened when I fell off the stage during a ballet recital.

My favorite holiday is Independence Day.

The strongest memory from childhood involves my grandfather.

54 • Autobiographical Writing

⏱ TIME AND RESOURCE MANAGER

Resources
Print: *Writing Support Transparencies*, 4-A–D; *Writing Support Activity Book*, 4-1–2
Technology: *Writing and Grammar* Interactive Text, Section 4.2

Using the Full Student Edition	Using the Handbook🄷
• Cover pp. 54–57 in class. • Work through Strategies for Generating Topics. • Use the Responding to Fine Art transparency (4-B) to generate additional topics. • Allow class time and offer guidance for writing questions for the Interview Yourself exercise.	• Cover pp. 34–37 in class. • Work through Strategies for Generating Topics. • Use the Responding to Fine Art transparency (4-B) to generate additional topics. • Allow class time and offer guidance for writing questions for the Interview Yourself exercise.

TOPIC BANK

For more specific topic ideas, consider the following suggestions:

1. **Narrative About a Discovery** Think about a time in your life when you discovered something wonderful in nature. For example, maybe you discovered a family of chipmunks in your yard or spotted a hawk roosting on top of your apartment building. In your narrative, tell of the events leading up to and following your discovery.

2. **Memoir of a Person or an Event** Write a memoir that captures a special time or person in your life. Include details about why that time or person was so memorable.

Responding to Fine Art

3. What reaction does *Highway Patrol* by James Doolin evoke in you? Write a narrative about an exciting car trip or getting your driver's license. Bring your experience to life through description and dialogue.

Responding to Literature

4. Read "Follower" by Seamus Heaney, in which the poet describes following the plow as his father tilled the fields. Then, write a memoir describing someone you, as a young child, followed around and wanted to be like. You can find "Follower" in *Prentice Hall Literature, Penguin Edition*, The British Tradition.

🕐 Timed Writing Prompt

5. Think about a moment in your life when you felt inspired. It may have been after hearing a moving speech, witnessing an athletic feat performed in the Olympics, or realizing something for the first time. Moments of inspiration enliven us with new energy and ideas. Write a memoir about an inspiring moment that you experienced. Explain what prompted you to feel inspired and what actions you took as a result. **(30 minutes)**

Highway Patrol, James Doolin, Courtesy of Koplin Gallery, Los Angeles, CA

▲ **Critical Viewing**
What words would you use to bring to life the color and movement depicted in this image? **[Analyze]**

Prewriting • 55

Step-by-Step Teaching Guide

Responding to Fine Art

Highway Patrol **by James Doolin**

Teaching Resources: Writing Support Transparencies, 4-B

1. Explain that the artist, James Doolin, has done several paintings that highlight aspects of life in Los Angeles, California. Ask students whether they have been to California. If so, ask what images they would have highlighted. If not, ask them to consider what they would highlight about where they live. Remind them that, since this is for an autobiographical account, their impressions and experiences of places are what is important here.

2. Point out that this is the view from the seat of an officer in the California Highway Patrol. Ask whether students know any police officers, or have ever needed to turn to the police for assistance. If so, these might be interesting topics for an autobiographical narrative.

3. Tell students that many American writers have written autobiographical narratives of road trips, such as John Steinbeck's *Travels with Charlie* or William Least Heat Moon's *Blue Highways*. Ask students why they think road trips are popular. Ask whether they have been on any road trips that they might want to write about.

4. Students may include these topic ideas along with their own suggestions in their topic banks.

Critical Viewing

Analyze Students may suggest words such as *speed*, *downhill*, *lights*, or *traffic*.

🕐 Timed Writing Prompt

• To help students refine their ideas, ask them to think about types of art work, sports figures, news figures, or personal relationships that inspire them in their everyday lives.

• Have them define the term *awe-inspiring*.

• Suggest that students allow five minutes for prewriting, twenty minutes for writing, and five minutes for reviewing and proofreading.

☑ **ONGOING ASSESSMENT: Monitor and Reinforce**

If you observe that some students are having difficulty choosing a topic, use one of the following options.

Option 1 Suggest that students choose an idea from the Topic Bank. If many students have difficulty, the whole class may work on a single idea selected from the Topic Bank or from ideas selected by students.	**Option 2** If Topic Bank ideas seem too challenging, suggest that students try one of the assignments from the *Topic Bank for Heterogeneous Classes* in the Teaching Resources.

Prewriting: Choose Details to Suit Your Purpose

Teaching Resources: Writing Support Transparencies, 4-C; Writing Support Activity Book, 4-1

1. Have students make three rows on a sheet of paper. Have students head the paper *Writing Purposes*. Rows may be labeled *to inform, to entertain*, and *to re-create*.

2. Draw students' attention to the chart on the bottom of page 56, or display Transparency 4-C.

3. Model brainstorming for details according to writing purpose, possibly using your own experiences. Write the following sentences on the board.

   To Inform:

   How I became a teacher

   Types of details:

   I decided to become a teacher when ___.

   I studied at ___.

   On my first day I ___.

Customize for
Less Advanced Students

Divide students into three groups and assign one writing purpose per group. Then, have students share their responses.

4.2

Narrowing Your Topic
Describe Your Focus

If the topic you have chosen is very specific—for example, the time a cake you baked exploded in the oven—you may not need to narrow it further. On the other hand, if your topic is fairly general—such as your first year in high school—you'll need to narrow it down. You can do this by writing a sentence in which you describe the highlight or main focus you want your narrative to reveal. Refer to this focus as you gather details for and revise your writing.

Considering Your Audience and Purpose

Decide who your audience is and how you want them to respond to your writing. For example, if you plan to share your autobiographical writing with your family, you may want to include lots of "inside information" that they will understand and appreciate. If, on the other hand, you plan to share your narrative with a general audience, you may have to more fully explain the characters and situations you describe.

Choose Details to Suit Your Purpose

In real life, you automatically adjust your word choice depending on your purpose. If, for example, you were telling someone about getting a terrible case of the flu and wanted to get sympathy from that person, you'd choose dramatic words and emphasize details about your illness; if, however, you wanted to reassure your audience, you'd choose more neutral language and de-emphasize details about your illness.

Following is a chart that shows how your purpose affects the types of details you'll gather for your writing.

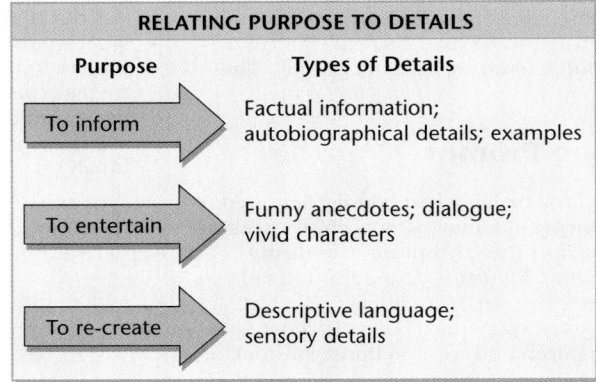

RELATING PURPOSE TO DETAILS

Purpose	Types of Details
To inform	Factual information; autobiographical details; examples
To entertain	Funny anecdotes; dialogue; vivid characters
To re-create	Descriptive language; sensory details

56 • Autobiographical Writing

⏱ Timed Writing Hint

Read the prompt carefully to determine the specific audience and purpose it calls for in your essay.

⏱ **TIME SAVERS!**

 **Writing Support Transparencies**
Use the transparencies for Chapter 4 to facilitate the teaching of strategies.

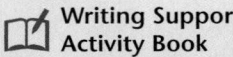 **Writing Support Activity Book**
Use the graphic organizers for Chapter 4 to facilitate student planning.

✏ **STANDARDIZED TEST PREPARATION WORKSHOP**

Organize and Plan Standardized tests may require students to answer questions about how to organize prewriting notes. Read the following scenario.

Before writing her report, Lisa wrote an outline of her school life from her first experience to her last. The major headings in the outline are shown below.

My Life at School

I. Grade School Years	*III. Preschool Years*
II. High School Years	*IV. College Years*

Which item is out of order in this outline?

A I

B III

C II

D IV

Students should recognize that **B** is the item out of order, since Preschool Years should not be the third point; it should be the first. Items A, C, and D are in the correct chronological order.

Gathering Details

As the writer of an autobiographical narrative, you have an advantage: an intimate knowledge of your subject. This can help you create a compelling story, but only if your writing is vivid and detailed. Consider the following strategy for gathering specific details that will bring your writing to life.

Interview Yourself

On talk shows, guests often relate stories from their lives. If you were being interviewed about the topic of your narrative, what would you have to say about it? Make a list of interview questions, and answer them in writing in as much detail as you can recall. Below is an example of a self-interview you could use to generate details for your narrative:

Self-Interview

1. What makes this experience/event/person special to you?_____
_____

2. What is the one word you would choose to describe this experience/event/person?_____
_____

3. Who else shared in this experience or event, or who else knew the person about whom you are writing? Does he or she share your feelings? Why or why not?_____
_____

4. Did you change in any way because of this experience/event/person? Explain. _____
_____

5. What did you learn from this experience/event/person?_____
_____
_____

Review Your Responses

Read through your responses to the Self-Interview. Note where there are gaps of information. Fill those gaps by using the following strategies:

• Look through photo albums and memorabilia that relate to your pick. Jot down details that relate to your topic.

• Interview someone who was also present during the time and place of your autobiographical narrative. If you like, base your questions on the Self-Interview form.

Interactive Textbook

Try it out! To list your interview questions, use the Essay Builder, accessible from the menu bar, on-line or on CD-ROM.

Prewriting: Interview Yourself

Teaching Resources: Writing Support Transparencies, 4-D; Writing Support Activity Book, 4-2

1. Encourage each student to imagine that he or she is being interviewed about his or her life. What kinds of questions, other than those listed, do they think the interviewer would ask? How can an interviewer make sure that he or she learns the most important things about someone's life experience?

2. Display the Self-Interview transparency (4-D). Ask students to write down any further questions that the interviewer might ask.

3. Allow students time to answer the questions, listing all necessary details.

Customize for
ESL Students

Suggest that students write their questions and do their interviews in their first language. This may help them with the flow of ideas and with coming up with vivid details, especially if the topics they have chosen predate their coming to the United States or learning English. They can then work on translating the details later.

Integrating Workplace Skills

Point out to students that a number of careers involve being able to write and ask good interview questions. Skill and care are involved in the crafting of questions that will elicit interesting or important details. Some of the people who need to hone these skills are newspaper reporters, police investigators, and nonfiction writers. As important as writing good questions is listening carefully to the responses.

✓ ONGOING ASSESSMENT: Monitor and Reinforce

If students are having difficulty gathering relevant details to include in their narratives, try the following strategy.

Have students meet and briefly discuss their topics with partners. Then, have the partner write three or four questions that will generate more information about the topic. The questions should elicit important information	that the writer omitted in the initial discussion. As the writers answer the questions, they will probably find that their answers contain details that they can use in their narratives.

Drafting: Find a Starting Point

1. Point out to students that an interesting beginning is vital to an autobiographical narrative—an effective beginning grabs the reader's interest from the start.

2. Have students experiment with writing an opening sentence. Students can write sample opening sentences using each of the techniques listed in the text. Ask students whether one technique seems more natural to them or more suited to their narratives.

3. Have students write a draft using the technique they chose. Make sure students have explored more than one technique to find the most effective one. Reassure them that they can change the opening if another seems better as the draft develops.

Customize for
Linguistic Learners

Some students may find it easier to talk about a starting point than write it. Suggest that students discuss with others ways to begin their narratives. They might use a tape recorder to record starting point ideas. Replaying their ideas should facilitate the beginning of the writing process.

Critical Viewing

Analyze Most students will realize that photographs of past events can bring back a flood of memories.

4.3 Drafting

Shaping Your Writing

Using the notes and ideas you have gathered, begin drafting your narrative. Consider the following approaches to help you identify the starting point for your story.

Find a Starting Point

Because your narrative is autobiographical, its organization can be at least partially determined by the order of actual events. The starting point, however, is up to you. Here are some ideas for beginning your narrative:

- **Start With a Character** If your personal narrative centers around a relationship, begin with a vivid description or revealing anecdote about the dominant character.

EXAMPLE: My Aunt Estelle wrapped her arms around my life, sheltering me from a world she believed was too harsh for her beloved niece.

- **Start With Dialogue** Opening with dialogue immediately captures your readers' interest while, at the same time, provides insight into a key character or situation.

EXAMPLE: "Hold on to the reins, honey!" shouted my father as he angled to get a snapshot of me and my sister on our first pony ride.

- **Start With the Setting** If the setting—the time and place in which your narrative takes place—is a critical element of your personal narrative, begin with a colorful description that evokes the time and place.

EXAMPLE: Sunlight blistered the walls of the shed in back of our little cottage by the seashore.

- **Start With Your Theme** Beginning your narrative with a statement of your theme—the story's main message—can focus your readers' attention as well as whet their curiosity about what's to come.

EXAMPLE: Don't count your chickens until they've hatched. On the morning of my tenth birthday, I woke to the sound of party preparations. . . .

▲ Critical Viewing Why might photographs such as this one inspire autobiographical writing? [Analyze]

58 • Autobiographical Writing

⏱ TIME AND RESOURCE MANAGER

Resources
Print: *Writing Support Transparencies,* 4-E
Technology: *Writing and Grammar* Interactive Text, Section 4.3

Using the Full Student Edition	Using the Handbook🄷
• Cover pp. 58–59 in class. • Work through the Find a Starting Point strategies. • Have students begin drafting their narratives in class.	• Cover pp. 38–39 in class. • Work through the Find a Starting Point strategies. • Have students begin drafting their narratives in class.

Providing Elaboration

As you write your draft, flesh out your narrative by incorporating the details you gathered earlier as well as new details that come to mind as you write. Another way to give your narrative depth is to include dialogue through "thought shots."

Add Dialogue With "Thought Shots"

A "thought shot" is a passage that reveals the inner workings of a character's mind. One of the most effective ways to bring forth a character's thoughts is through dialogue. Dialogue enables you as the writer to show, not tell about, interesting aspects of characters.

To create a thought shot, write lines of dialogue that reveal a character's inner thoughts, motivations for his or her actions, or personal reactions to what is happening in the narrative. If you finish a paragraph and then decide to add a thought shot, write the dialogue on a self-sticking tag and place it according to where it will go.

Grammar and Style Tip

When writing dialogue, keep in mind that people often speak in incomplete sentences and use contractions and slang.

Student Work IN PROGRESS

Name: *Melissa Sanborn*
Seneca High School
Louisville, KY

Adding Dialogue With Thought Shots

As she drafted, Melissa provided insight into her grandfather's character with a thought shot. She then added another one to further show his personality.

By that time we were hungry and went out to eat. After we stuffed our bellies completely full, we would return to the camper and, once again, admire our site. "Best site in the park, huh, Squirt?" he would comment proudly. I always agreed, because it was, and because it was the only one that was ours. . . . After rest time, Poppop would watch me swim for a couple of hours.

> This line of dialogue provides insight into Poppop's personality through a "thought shot."

> "Leave some water in the pool for everyone else," he'd say with a slight grin and a chuckle.

Drafting • 59

Drafting: Add Dialogue with "Thought Shots"

Teaching Resources: Writing Support Transparencies, 4-E

1. Use Transparency 4-E to show students how "thought shots" might look in practice. Point out that the author added the thought shot to help the reader understand the relationship between the author and her grandfather.

2. Explain that using thought shots makes writing more interesting by providing vivid insights into the characters. This is especially important in autobiographical narratives, since understanding the characters is crucial to the success of the story.

3. Suggest that students look at the characters in each paragraph they have written. Are the characters' thoughts and motives clear? If not, encourage them to insert "thought shots."

4. Students can create "thought shots" with self-sticking notes, which are easy to attach to their drafts.

Integrating Grammar Skills

Dialogue Punctuation After students have added "thought shots" to their narratives, review punctuation rules for written dialogue. Have students proofread their stories, checking their writing for proper punctuation and capitalization for written dialogue. Point out to students that actual thoughts are written without using dialogue punctuation. Suggest that they consider using italics to indicate characters' thoughts.

⏱ TIME SAVERS!

Writing Support Transparencies
Use the transparencies for Chapter 4 to facilitate the teaching of strategies.

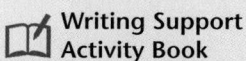
Writing Support Activity Book
Use the graphic organizers for Chapter 4 to facilitate student planning.

Revising: Strengthening Your Narrative's Ending

1. Explain to students that autobiographical narratives need to sustain interest and close memorably. Good writers always try to end their stories with a satisfying conclusion.

2. After reviewing the three strategies on page 60 for strengthening a narrative's ending, have students review their drafts. Ask whether anyone used one of these strategies. If so, how did it work for them?

3. Let students reread the ends of their narratives to re-evaluate whether they need to strengthen their endings.

4. Point out that the strategies in the text are not the only ways to close a narrative. Ask students whether they have used other techniques. Encourage them to share their ideas with the class.

Revising: Analyzing Paragraphs

1. Using the paragraphs on page 60, let students explain in their own words why the text is more effective when broken into functional paragraphs.

2. Challenge students to review their own writing and look for places to restructure their paragraphs.

4.4 Revising

Revising Your Overall Structure

Review your narrative to be sure that it has a definite beginning, middle, and end. Its beginning should capture the readers' interest, its middle should develop the story, and its end should leave the readers satisfied with the story's conclusion.

▶ **REVISION STRATEGY**
Strengthening Your Narrative's Ending

Does your narrative end on a strong note or does it trail off? Give your narrative an effective and memorable ending. Below are some ideas for ending your narrative:

- **Write an Epilogue** Tell what ended up happening to you or another character since the events of the story took place. This can be a satisfying conclusion to an autobiographical narrative.

- **Sum Up** Another way to end a personal narrative is to sum up your feelings or insights about your experience or state what you learned from your experience.

- **Pose a Question** It is sometimes effective to leave the readers with a question, especially when your narrative explores the conflict in a situation or relationship.

Revising Your Paragraphs
Create Functional Paragraphs

In contrast to topical paragraphs that develop the point of a topic sentence, functional paragraphs serve another purpose. They may arouse or sustain interest; present a special effect; emphasize a point; indicate dialogue; or make a transition.

▶ **REVISION STRATEGY**
Analyzing Paragraphs

As you revise, analyze your paragraph structure. Look for places where material from a longer paragraph may be more effective as a functional paragraph. Restructure your paragraphs accordingly.

Evaluate

"This storm is especially fierce, Brian," Stacey said in a wavery voice. That's when the lights went out.

Revise

"This storm is especially fierce, Brian," Stacey said in a wavery voice.

That's when the lights went out.

⏱ Timed Writing Hint

When revising your writing under timed conditions, read your essay silently to yourself. Check that your conclusion sums up your main point.

⟳ Learn More

To learn more about writing effective paragraphs, see Chapter 3.

⏱ TIME AND RESOURCE MANAGER	
Resources	
Print: *Writing Support Transparencies*, 4-F–G	
Technology: *Writing and Grammar* Interactive Text, Section 4.4	
Using the Full Student Edition	**Using the Handbook**🄷
• Cover pp. 60–63 in class.	• Cover pp. 40–43 in class.
• Work through the Revision Strategies.	• Work through the Revision Strategies.
• Have students begin to revise their paragraphs in class.	• Have students begin to revise their paragraphs in class.
• Address individual revision concerns as they arise.	• Address individual revision concerns as they arise.

Revising Your Sentences

Review the sentences in your draft to be sure you have no unintentional fragments or run-on sentences. Add transitions where necessary to connect the ideas in your narrative, and check to be sure that you've chosen correct verb tenses.

▶ **REVISION STRATEGY**
Using Color-Coding Clues to Check Verb Tenses

Writing about your past can be tricky, especially if your narrative moves back and forth in time. Use differently colored highlighters to call out verb tenses in your draft. For example, use pink for present tense, yellow for past tense, and green for future tense. Then, review your draft to be sure that if you've switched tenses, you've done so intentionally. Avoid switching verb tenses in mid-sentence unless you mean to show that the events in the sentence did not occur at the same time.

Student Work
IN PROGRESS

Name: *Melissa Sanborn*
Seneca High School
Louisville, KY

Color-Coding to Identify Verb Tenses
Upon reviewing her narrative, Melissa discovered that she had unintentionally switched verb tenses in the middle of a sentence. Notice how she fixed the error.

Our days were filled with adventure and excitement. We woke
                                          went
up early, ate big bowls of cereal, and go to the playground for a
while. Then, we went to see a show and visited the flea market
in town.

> Melissa realized that she unintentionally switched tenses in this sentence.

We always came back to camp for lunch, and then I would
listen to Poppop read *The Little Rascals* or *The Counting Book*
for the thousandth time. No matter how many times I had
heard the stories, they always made me laugh.

> Because this change in tense was intentional, Melissa did not have to revise the sentence.

Revising • 61

Step-by-Step Teaching Guide

Revising: Color-Coding to Identify Verb Tenses

Teaching Resources: Writing Support Transparencies, 4-F

1. Allow students time to check their narratives for fragments and run-on sentences as well as for the presence of smooth transitions.

2. Use the transparency (4-F) to show how Melissa's revision is color-coded for verb tense. Discuss with students the reason for Melissa's change in verb tense in the first paragraph. Ask students to explain why Melissa did not change her use of the same verb tense in the second paragraph.

3. After students have highlighted their verbs with markers to show verb tense, let them exchange papers and have their partners check their work, marking any verbs they feel should be changed.

Customize for
ESL Students

If students are having difficulty identifying verb tense or using tense properly, have them work with partners who can help them choose the correct tenses.

Customize for
AP Students

Encourage students to go beyond basic tense forms to employ progressive and emphatic forms. Also, suggest that they utilize verbals as well, including gerunds, infinitives, and participial phrases.

Verb Tenses

1. Point out that using different tenses is how a writer creates a sense of time within a narrative.

2. Explain that there is a logic in the sequencing of tenses. For example, if two things happened in the past, but one happened before the other, one would use the past perfect to describe the event that happened first, and past to describe the event that happened next. For example: *Yesterday, I had left for school before he called.*

3. Ask students why they think it's important to use verb tense carefully (so the reader knows when things happened).

4. Review the progressive and emphatic forms of the six tenses. Have students suggest examples (past progressive: *I was working;* emphatic: *I did work*).

Find It in Your Reading

Many verbs are in the past tense *(read, contained)*. There are examples of past perfect *(had eluded, hadn't found)*. There are a few verbs in present tense *(come, see*—often in verb phrases, such as *would praise, could see)* and the present perfect tense, again in a verb phrase *(What I saw must have been)*. In addition, students might identify past progressive *(was rolling, was extending)*, past emphatic *(did not work, did not say)*, and past in the passive voice *(was composed)*. You may want to discuss verb phrases *(had been handed)*, participles used as adjectives (He *was supposed)*, and infinitives (I *wanted to see*—infinitive as direct object).

Find It in Your Writing

If students do not find any place in their drafts that would benefit from changed tenses, ask them to write sample sentences that use more than one tense.

4.4

Grammar in Your Writing
Verb Tenses

As the narrator of an autobiographical story, you need to be able to move between the past and present with clarity. Proper use of verb tenses will enable you to do this. The **tenses** of verbs are the forms that show time. There are six main tenses:

THE BASIC FORMS OF THE SIX TENSES		
Tense	**Explanation**	**Example**
Present	This tense tells of an action or a condition that exists at the present time.	I *look* for the old camper.
Past	This tense tells of an action or a condition that began and ended at a given time in the past.	I *looked* for the old camper yesterday.
Future	This tense tells of an action or a condition that has not yet occurred.	I *will look* for the old camper tomorrow.
Present Perfect	This tense tells of an action or a condition that occurred at an indefinite time in the past or that began in the past and has continued into the present.	I *have looked* for the old camper wherever I go.
Past Perfect	This tense tells of a past action or condition that ended before another past action began.	I *had looked* for the old camper before leaving.
Future Perfect	This tense tells of a future action or condition that will have ended before another begins.	By nightfall I *will have looked* for the old camper.

Find It in Your Reading Review the excerpt from Annie Dillard's *An American Childhood* on pages 50–53. Identify five different examples of verb tenses. Describe when the action or condition in each example took place.

Find It in Your Writing Review the verb tenses in your writing. If you find that you've relied too much on a particular tense, add depth and sophistication to your story by using another tense to show time relationships between events.

To learn more about verb tenses, see Chapter 21.

62 • Autobiographical Writing

☑ **ONGOING ASSESSMENT: Prerequisite Skills**

If students have difficulty with the correct use of verb tenses, you may wish to refer them to the following materials to ensure coverage of prerequisite knowledge.

In the Textbook	Print Resources	Technology
Verb Usage, Section 21.1	*Grammar Exercise Workbook,* pp. 71–78	*On-Line Exercise Bank,* Section 21.1

Revising Your Word Choice

▶**REVISION STRATEGY**
Circling the *I*'s

Go through your draft, and circle every use of the pronoun *I*. As a general rule, avoid beginning more than two sentences in a row with *I*. Use the same strategy to evaluate your use of *we* and *my*.

Student Work
IN PROGRESS

Name: *Melissa Sanborn*
Seneca High School
Louisville, KY

Circling the *I*'s

Melissa circled the I's in her draft and found that she had overused that pronoun. Here is how she fixed her draft:

(I) loved the stories of his adventures out West ~~because they~~ were exciting, but (I) loved them for another reason, too: With these tales, my summer vacation began. (I) knew that soon Poppop would load up again and take me with him.

Peer Review

Work with a group of peer reviewers to get different perspectives on your writing. Peer reviewers may spot weaknesses or confusing jumps in your narrative that you missed. Use the following idea to get feedback from your peers:

Analytical Talk

In a group, read your narrative twice, pausing between readings. Direct the other members of the group to simply listen the first time. The second time, tell them to listen and jot down words, phrases, images—whatever catches their interest. Then, ask your group to respond to the following questions:

1. Which parts of the narrative do you find most interesting?
2. Which parts of the narrative, if any, need improvement?

Revising • 63

Step-by-Step Teaching Guide

Revising: Circling the *I*'s

Teaching Resources: Writing Support Transparencies, 4-G

1. Before beginning the activity, ask students to quickly scan their drafts looking only at pronouns. Do they notice any patterns?

2. Show the transparency and discuss with students how the paragraph has been improved. Let students know that the overuse of *I* may signal that the narrative focuses too exclusively on the narrator. Point out that the changes allow other figures and events in the story to appear more clearly. In addition, the overuse of *any* word can become tedious and make the reader lose interest.

3. Let students revise a sentence in their narratives to avoid the overuse of *I* or *my*. Invite students to read aloud their original sentences and the revised versions.

Step-by-Step Teaching Guide

Revising: Peer Review

1. Encourage students to identify a draft's strengths before zeroing in on its drawbacks.

2. Remind students that some errors will be corrected at the proofreading stage and that the focus here should be on content, dialogue, and character.

3. If students feel that some narratives are confusing or uneventful, suggest that students elicit further details about the story from the author being reviewed. Is information missing that could help clarify events?

4. Point out that many comments made during peer review will be helpful to all students. Suggest that students jot down important ideas raised in discussion, and consult them later.

Spelling Homophones

1. Remind students that homophone errors must be spotted in proofreading. They cannot be picked up when a work is read aloud because homophones sound the same as other words with different meanings. Also, computer spell-checkers will not catch homophones (though some now challenge such words) since the word may be spelled correctly but still be the wrong word.

2. Write the following sentence on the board.

> *Whenever I look for the test tubes in there holder, I find that their still they're.*

3. Challenge students to spot the three homophones, *there, their, they're.* Have a student write the sentence correctly on the board. *(Whenever I look for the test tubes in their holder, I find that they're still there.)*

Find It in Your Reading

Ask students to identify the homophones for *weak* and *here (week, hear).* You may want to ask students to identify any other words with homophones that appear in the story *(read, too, there, see).*

Find It in Your Writing

Have students search their narratives for homophones. List the homophones students have found on the board. Have students define their homophones or use them in a sentence.

Integrating Speaking and Listening Skills

It is not only in writing that we communicate autobiographical information. When students talk to friends, to new acquaintances, or to small groups, it is important to be able to relate autobiographical experience in an interesting, concise, and easy-to-follow manner. Challenge students to pick a topic related to their narratives and tell it in the form of a short anecdote.

4.5 Editing and Proofreading

You want your readers to become completely absorbed in your narrative. Don't let them become distracted by a glaring error in spelling, mechanics, grammar, or usage. Check for errors before you create your final draft.

Focusing on Correct Spelling

Proofread your narrative carefully to locate mistakes in spelling. Because this narrative is autobiographical, be especially careful to spell the names of people and places correctly.

💡 **Spelling Tip**

Keep in mind that the spell-check feature on a word-processing program is a great tool, but it is not a substitute for careful proofreading.

Grammar in Your Writing
Spelling Homophones

Homophones are words that sound alike but have different spellings and meanings. They are a common source of spelling errors and need careful proofreading. While you are probably aware of the differences in spelling and meaning among most homophones, it is easy to make a mistake when you are writing quickly. The following homophones are frequently misspelled:

COMMONLY USED HOMOPHONES

there	to	its	accept	affect
their	too	it's	except	effect
they're	two			

Find It in Your Reading Look through the excerpt from *An American Childhood* to find the sentences containing the homophones *weak* and *here.* Think about how the meaning of those sentences would change if Dillard had chosen the wrong homophone.

Find It in Your Writing As you proofread your autobiographical narrative, double-check the spelling of homophones. If you are unsure whether you have spelled a homophone correctly, look it up in a dictionary.

To learn more about homophones, see Chapter 29.

64 • Autobiographical Writing

⏱ TIME AND RESOURCE MANAGER

Resources
Print: *Scoring Rubrics on Transparency,* Ch. 4; *Writing Assessment and Portfolio Management; Formal Assessment,* Ch. 4
Technology: *Writing and Grammar* Interactive Text, Section 4.5

Using the Full Student Edition	Using the Handbook🅗
• Review p. 64 in class, including Grammar in Your Writing. • Give step-by-step coverage to Publishing and Presenting (p. 65). • Have students edit and proofread their narratives in class.	• Review p. 44 in class, including Grammar in Your Writing. • Give step-by-step coverage to Publishing and Presenting (p. 45). • Have students edit and proofread their narratives in class.

4.6 Publishing and Presenting

The story of your life is unique. Share it with others. Consider these possibilities for publishing or presenting your work:

Building Your Portfolio

1. **Share With People Who Were There** Send your personal narrative to people who played a part in the story you told. Possible recipients might include family members, relatives, old friends, teachers, or employers.

2. **Send to a Student Publication** Submit your work to a student magazine for publication. This might be a school publication or a literary magazine for young people.

Reflecting on Your Writing

Take a moment to reflect on the experience of writing your autobiographical narrative. Then, answer the following questions. Save your answers in your portfolio.

- How did writing the narrative affect your attitude toward the topic you chose?

- Which part of the writing process—prewriting, drafting, revising, or editing—did you find most challenging? Why?

🖥 Internet Tip

To see an autobiographical narrative scored according to this rubric, go on-line:
PHSchool.com
Enter Web Code:
egk-1201

Rubric for Self-Assessment

Use these criteria to evaluate your autobiographical narrative.

	Score 4	Score 3	Score 2	Score 1
Audience and Purpose	Contains details that engage the audience	Contains details appropriate for an audience	Contains few details that appeal to an audience	Is not written for a specific audience
Organization	Presents events that create an interesting narrative; told from a consistent point of view	Presents sequence of events; told from a specific point of view	Presents a confusing sequence of events; contains a point of view that is inconsistent	Presents no logical order; is told from no consistent point of view
Elaboration	Contains details that create vivid characters; contains dialogue that develops characters and plot	Contains details that develop character and describe setting; contains dialogue	Contains characters and setting; contains some dialogue	Contains few or no details to develop characters or setting; no dialogue provided
Use of Language	Uses language to create a tone; contains no errors in grammar, punctuation, or spelling	Uses vivid words; contains few errors in grammar, punctuation, and spelling	Uses clichés and trite expressions; contains some errors in grammar, punctuation, and spelling	Uses uninspired words; has many errors in grammar, punctuation, and spelling

Publishing and Presenting • 65

✓ ONGOING ASSESSMENT: Assess Mastery

Use one of the following options to assess final drafts of students' autobiographical narratives.

Self-Assessment Ask students to score their essays using the rubric provided. Then, have students write a single paragraph reflecting on the most valuable thing they learned in completing this narrative.

Teacher Assessment You may wish to use the rubric and the scoring models provided in *Writing Assessment and Portfolio Management* to score the autobiographical narratives.

Publishing and Presenting

1. Remind students that the publishing phase is a time for sharing what they've done. Encourage students to consider finding more places to share their work, for example, on related Web sites, in the school library, or with a writers' group.

2. In preparing their narratives for publication, students may wish to add illustrations, diagrams, or photos to their narratives. Ask them to extend the process of composition by considering which of these items would help a reader most.

ASSESS and CLOSE

Assessment

Teaching Resources: Scoring Rubrics on Transparency, Ch. 4; Writing Assessment and Portfolio Management; Formal Assessment, Ch. 4

1. Display the Scoring Rubric Transparency and review the criteria in class.

2. Before students proceed with self-assessment, you may wish to review the Final Draft of the Student Work in Progress on pages 66–68.

3. In addition to student self-assessment, you may wish to use the following options:

   - score student narratives yourself, using the rubric and scoring models in *Writing Assessment and Portfolio Management*.

   - review the Standardized Test Preparation Workshop on pages 72–73 and administer a timed writing assessment.

   - administer the Chapter 4 assessment in *Formal Assessment* to measure students' grasp of concepts presented.

Final Draft

1. Help students see that "Where Are You When the Dandelions Bloom?" incorporates key elements of the autobiographical narrative.

   • The topic has been well-chosen, and the incidents are high-interest and manageable in scope.

   • Audience and purpose have been considered carefully. The narrative is addressed to general readers and offers a touching personal memoir.

   • The introduction is engaging and gives the reader a good idea of what is to come.

   • The body of the narrative tells the reader what summers with Poppop were like. Dialogue and vivid description provide an engrossing narration.

   • Finally, a short conclusion brings the reader up to date and explains how the author feels about her memories.

2. Ask students whether there are any changes they would recommend to make the narrative flow better or to fine-tune the language. How might students apply these suggestions to their own writing?

3. Students should know that a writer may have characters use informal language in a story. Have students reread the paragraph beginning "Let's see, I know . . ." Let students identify the informal language ("real close to the store," "swimmin' pool"). Ask students to explain why the author purposely used this language in the narrative. (The informal language reflects the way Poppop actually spoke; it gives the reader insight into his character.)

Critical Viewing

Connect Student responses should include the fact that Melissa begins and ends the narrative with a reference to dandelions—the flower associated in her mind with her grandfather.

4.7 Student Work IN PROGRESS

FINAL DRAFT

Where Are You When the Dandelions Bloom?

Melissa Sanborn
Seneca High School
Louisville, Kentucky

▲ **Critical Viewing** Why might Melissa have chosen to mention dandelions in the title of her autobiographical narrative? **[Connect]**

"I'll be home when the dandelions bloom." Those were my grandfather's words as he loaded up the camper to head out on his annual trip. Sure enough, every spring, as soon as I caught sight of the first dandelion, I'd see the trusty old camper pushing down the lane. My "Poppop" was home, and right on time.

We sat and talked for hours about the exciting places he had traveled, tracing his journey on the brightly colored map tacked to the inside of the camper door. "See, Squirt, it's right here. . . . This is Kentucky—where we are—the green state. I went over this way, across the blue, that's Illinois, to the red, Iowa, then through

This opening line of dialogue makes an interesting beginning to Melissa's narrative.

Melissa is the writer as well as the main character in her narrative.

66 • Autobiographical Writing

the purple, South Dakota, and over to the big yellow state, Montana. Follow it with your finger."

The stories of his adventures out West were exciting, but I loved them for another reason, too: With these tales, my summer vacation began. I knew that soon Poppop would load up again and take me with him. Every vacation I can remember was spent with Poppop in the blue-and-beige camper. Whether we were headed up north, down south, or to the Horse Park down the street, I was thrilled to spend time with my grandfather.

Making our way into a campground on the first day, my heartbeat seemed to race. Poppop was anxious to find our site.

"Let's see, I know that number twenty-two is a good one. It's real close to the store, so it will be easy for us to go get ice cream sandwiches after dinner. . . . Oh, it's taken. What else is there? Ohhh, I forgot about number twenty-seven. It's right across from the swimmin' pool and game rooms. There it is, and there's even a big shade tree for the really hot days."

It was perfect, as were all the sites he picked out. Poppop always knew the best lots in the park.

He backed the camper slowly into the space, making sure we were far enough from the tree to set up the awning. He got out to make sure the trailer was straight and to chock the tires. Then, we set up. Out came the brightly striped blue awning. We pulled the picnic table over into the shade and strung the old lantern lights—green, red, and yellow—along the edge of the awning. The finishing touch was the old blue duck, wooden with propellers for wings, which spun around when the wind blew. It had our last name on it. We always marked our spot this way.

By that time, we were hungry and went out to eat. After we had stuffed our bellies completely full, we returned to the camper and, once again, admired our site.

Long passages of dialogue give the reader a sense of Poppop's personality.

Vivid description helps the reader visualize the campsite setting.

◀ **Critical Viewing** Why does camping appeal to many vacationers? Use details from the photograph to support your response. **[Analyze]**

Teaching From the Final Draft

Point out the many details the narrator includes about her experiences with her grandfather. Point out that such details help the reader understand why these experiences were so important to Melissa. Remind students that changing the details in an autobiographical narrative can change the import of the narrative as a whole. Ask students how this piece would have been different if it had described Poppop's regular help with Melissa's homework during the school year. (Students may suggest that the tone of the narrative would have been more serious.)

Critical Viewing

Analyze Student responses may include the adventure, the "getting back to basics" aspect of camping, that it is economical, or other elements from conjecture or personal experience. The details in the story seem best to support the adventure aspect of camping, as Melissa relates that her grandfather speaks of "exciting places he had traveled," "his adventures out West," and "our adventures and summers together."

4.7

"Best site in the park, huh, Squirt?" he would comment proudly. I always agreed, because it was, and because it was the only one that was ours.

Our days were filled with adventure and excitement. We woke up early, ate big bowls of cereal, and went to the playground for a while. Then, we went to see a show and visited the flea market in town.

We always came back to camp for lunch, and then I would listen to Poppop read *The Little Rascals* or *The Counting Book* for the thousandth time. No matter how many times I had heard the stories, they always made me laugh.

After rest time, Poppop would watch me swim for a couple of hours. "Leave some water in the pool for everyone else," he'd say with a slight grin and a chuckle.

By the time we got back to the motor home, it was dinner time. We had the best dinners, too: pot roast, corn on the cob, green beans, mashed potatoes, and spaghetti (my favorite). After dinner, we'd stay up late, laughing and playing Yahtzee or Dominoes.

This was our routine, every day for the rest of the summer. Then, September came, and it was time for me to go back home. That was the worst part, but I always knew we would do it again the next year.

Every spring, as the dandelions begin to bloom, I still look for Poppop's old camper coming down the lane, but it never comes. Our adventures and summers together have gone, but the memories remain. The summertime camping trips with Poppop were the highlight of my childhood. They brought me sunshine, fun times, and a whole bunch of laughs.

▲ **Critical Viewing**
If you were to use a dandelion as a symbol, what would it symbolize? Explain. **[Apply]**

This detail vividly captures the personality of Poppop.

Melissa concludes her narrative by sharing this insight with readers.

68 • Autobiographical Writing

Connected Assignment Firsthand Biography

Chances are, you often tell stories from your life. In school, you've been taught how to use research to tell the life stories of notable people. There is, however, another kind of storytelling, in which you combine your own firsthand knowledge with research. This is called a **firsthand biography.** In this type of writing, you blend firsthand observations and experiences with researched information to recount the life of someone you know well. For example, subjects for a firsthand biography may include your neighbor or a coach at your school.

Write your own short firsthand biography with the writing process steps suggested below:

Prewriting Because a firsthand biography depends on first-hand observations, it's important to choose a person you know well. Consider writing about a close friend, a person with whom you have worked, or a member of your family.

Once you choose your subject, create a K-W-L chart like the one below. This will help you identify what you already know about your subject as well as things you will need to research to find out.

What I Know	What I Want to Know	What I've Learned
Grandma's birthday	Where she was born	Grandma was born in Poland during WWII

Drafting Use the first-person point of view to include your-self in the story. Start with your first experience or memory of your subject. Refer to your prewriting notes to organize additional events in chronological sequence and to check facts.

Revising and Editing Have a classmate read your firsthand biography. Discuss passages of the paper in which the subject's actions or words seem unrealistic or don't make sense. Insert transitions or modifiers to clear up these confusing passages. Also, check to be sure that you have consistently used the first-person point of view.

Publishing and Presenting Make a cover for your firsthand biography and give it as a gift to the person about whom you wrote.

Connected Assignment: Firsthand Biography • 69

Lesson Objectives

1. To write a firsthand biography appropriate to audience and purpose
2. To use prewriting strategies to generate ideas and develop voice
3. To use effective sequences and transitions
4. To evaluate how well writing achieves its purposes

Step-by-Step Teaching Guide

Firsthand Biography

Teaching Resources: Writing Support Transparencies, 4-H; Writing Support Activity Book, 4-3

1. Discuss biographies students have read. Were any firsthand biographies?
2. Suggest that students review strategies from Chapter 4. The chart below identifies resources that may be especially helpful.
3. Have students give examples of possible subjects. They should choose someone they know well, and preferably someone who will be available to interview.
4. Display Transparency 4-H and demonstrate how students might fill out the columns, using a student volunteer as the subject.
5. Give students copies of the K-W-L chart from the activity book (4-3), or have them create their own charts for organizing information.
6. Have students read each other's first drafts. Did readers get a clear picture of the subject? Did they want to know more about particular incidents?
7. Students might want to include in their biographies a photograph of the subject about whom they are writing.

☑ **ONGOING ASSESSMENT: Prerequisite Skills**

Students may find the following resources from Chapter 4 particularly helpful in completing their firsthand biographies.

In the Textbook	Print Resources	Technology
Choosing Your Topic, Section 4.2 Interview Yourself, Section 4.2	*Writing Support Transparencies,* 4-C–D *Writing Support Activity Book,* 4-1–2	*Writing and Grammar* Interactive Text, Section 4.2

1. To investigate the source of a media presentation or production such as who made it and why it was made

2. To deconstruct media to get the main idea of the message's content

3. To recognize how visual and sound techniques or design convey messages in media, such as special effects, editing, camera angles, reaction shots, sequencing, and music

4. To use a range of techniques to plan and create a media text and reflect critically on the work produced

5. To write in a variety of forms

Step-by-Step Teaching Guide

Examining Media Portrayals of a Character

1. Choose one of the Spotlight elements for class discussion, or have students discuss the elements of their choice individually or in groups.

2. Students may be interested to know that most of the characters in *The Tragedy of Macbeth* really existed. In real life, Macbeth was not the villain he was in Shakespeare's play. Interested students may wish to research the historical Macbeth.

3. You might help interested students find Kurosawa's film, Fuseli's artwork, and Verdi's music. Encourage these students to find a way to share these works with the class.

Viewing and Representing

Activity Give interested students an opportunity to share their "autobiographies" with the class. Encourage students to use photographs, film clips, or their own artwork to show their villains in action.

Spotlight on the Humanities

Examining Media Portrayals of a Character

Focus on Film: *Throne of Blood*

The life stories of historical figures, whether autobiographical or told by others, are often fascinating. In 1957, Akira Kurosawa directed his classic film *Throne of Blood*, an adaptation of Shakespeare's historical play *Macbeth*. This powerful film moves the story of Macbeth to medieval Japan. After a great military victory, lords Washizu and Miki are lost in the dense Cobweb Forest, where they meet a mysterious old woman who predicts great things for Washizu and even greater things for Miki's descendants. Once out of the forest, Washizu and Miki are immediately promoted by the emperor. Washizu, encouraged by his ambitious wife, plots to make even more of the prophecy come true, even if it means killing the emperor.

Art Connection Considered one of the precursors of Symbolism and Surrealism in painting, Swiss artist Henry Fuseli often used Shakespearean subjects in his work. His 1784 painting of Lady Macbeth is one example. The work now hangs in the Louvre in Paris, France.

Music Connection In 1847, Italian composer Giuseppe Verdi wrote his famous opera *Macbeth* based upon the Shakespearean play. The musical work premiered in Florence, Italy, and is known for its complex orchestral themes that challenge its principal performers.

Narrative Writing Activity: Autobiography of a Famous Villain Choose a film that you've watched recently or a book you have read that had a memorable villain. Imagine that you are that person. Based on what you saw or read, write an autobiography in his or her voice. In your autobiography, be sure to explain your motivation for your actions, as well as your inner feelings about your actions. Share your autobiography with your classmates.

▲ Critical Viewing
Study these photographs of two portrayals of Lady Macbeth. In what ways do the actresses' costumes help to convey Lady Macbeth's personality? **[Distinguish]**

Critical Viewing

Distinguish Students may observe that each actress is dressed richly and regally as befits a proud and ambitious queen.

Media and Technology Skills

Lesson Objectives

1. To create a video scrapbook
2. To use video to communicate specific messages
3. To use a range of techniques to plan and create a media text

Conveying Messages Using Visuals

Activity: Create a Video Scrapbook

Scrapbooks, which may contain photographs, report cards, playbills, or awards, are a popular way to capture and revisit your special memories and experiences. Technology tools may help you effectively capture your memories and, if you choose, share them with others. Choose a memorable event, and create a video scrapbook or capture a current experience in your scrapbook.

Think About It Choose a focused topic for your video. Rather than try to capture your whole summer vacation, for example, capture the side trip you took to a folk festival.

Gather It Gather artifacts, mementos, and photographs related to your topic. These items will be used in filming your video scrapbook. Also, choose shooting locations and obtain permission to film there. Once you have gathered items and located filming sites, create a storyboard or chart that shows the order in which you will videotape the items. Also on your storyboard, jot down ideas for the way you will use the camera. You might, for example, use a soft focus for some scenes or a kaleidoscope special effect for another.

STORYBOARD

Series of pictures → Soft focus on postcard → Funny Music as I show swim gear photos

Shoot It Follow your storyboard plan, and shoot your film. Set up each shot individually. Film it until you are satisfied with the results. Then, refer to your storyboard and complete the next shot.

When you have completed filming, use a double-deck videocassette recorder, or hook up your video camera to a single-deck recorder and edit your video. To do this, record the scenes you like best in the order you like onto a fresh tape. Select appropriate music to help create a mood or atmosphere for your video.

What You'll Need

- Video recorder
- Single-deck or double-deck videocassette recorder
- CD or audiocassette player

Special Techniques

Use special lighting:

- Use a desklamp as a spotlight.

Use camera angles:

- Pan across a series of objects arranged on a piece of fabric.
- Shoot a scene through a window.

Use camera effects:

- Fade in and out as you go through a series of snapshots.
- Use special framing devices, as provided by your video recorder.

Step-by-Step Teaching Guide

Conveying Messages Using Visuals

1. Brainstorm with students for focused topics, perhaps a special family gathering, a memorable weekend, a personal achievement, or an exciting competition. It need not be recent.

2. Using a topic of your own, model the use of a storyboard on a flip chart or the chalkboard.

3. Point out the list of necessary materials and lighting suggestions for camera angles. Students may offer additional ideas for special visual effects.

4. Let students know that it might take longer to plan a shot than to actually film it.

5. When they have finished their video scrapbooks, students may enjoy exchanging ideas about which special techniques worked well.

6. If students do not have access to a video recorder or other equipment, you may want to try to set up a photo-shoot day during class time, making school equipment available for on-site use.

Lesson Objectives

1. To write a narrative appropriate to audience and purpose
2. To organize ideas and details to ensure coherence
3. To use effective sequences and transitions
4. To demonstrate control over grammatical elements

Step-by-Step Teaching Guide

Responding to Narrative Writing Prompts

Teaching Resources: Standardized Test Preparation Workbook, pp. 7–8

1. Students taking a writing test must first identify the type of writing they are being asked to do. Remind students that narrative has a story-like structure, and that this piece will be a narrative. Introductory and concluding paragraphs should explain the purpose for telling these stories or anecdotes.

2. Students should spend part of their prewriting time jotting down ideas and focusing their topics.

3. Emphasize the importance of having a clear purpose and a specific audience in mind. These will help students identify which events to highlight, what language to use, and what terms might need to be defined.

4. Discuss how a narrative essay intended as a speech would differ from a narrative essay intended as a job application. Who is the audience for each?

5. Review the basic drafting procedure. Emphasize the importance of leaving time to proofread and edit.

Standardized Test Preparation Workshop

Responding to Narrative Writing Prompts

Standardized tests often measure your ability to use the elements of narrative writing when responding to a prompt. The following are the criteria upon which your narrative writing will be evaluated:

- Words and constructed sentences that are appropriate for the purpose and audience named in the response
- Details of your narrative that are organized in a meaningful and coherent way
- Appropriate transitions that enable ideas to flow and that unify your narrative
- Elaboration that makes effective use of description, characterization, and other details
- Correct grammar, spelling, and punctuation

When writing for a timed test, devote a specified amount of time to prewriting, drafting, revising, and proofreading.

Following are examples of narrative writing prompts. Use the suggestions on the following page to help you respond. The clocks next to each stage show a suggested percentage of time to devote to each stage.

Sample Writing Situation

As a senior, you are eligible to take part in a mentor program for freshmen at your school. The program includes sharing your experiences: what you have learned from them about being a successful high-school student and how to prepare for the future. You may also offer advice based on your experiences on how to make the most of the high-school experience. Think about the ways you could positively influence these students and then respond to one of the following prompts.

Prepare an application essay to be submitted to your school principal. In the essay, outline your achievements, the lessons you have learned, and how your experiences could influence students in a positive way.

Write a speech that you would give to incoming high-school students, in which you describe what you have learned from your experiences in high school and offer advice to others that will help them meet the challenges of high school.

72 • Autobiographical Writing

✍ TEST-TAKING TIP

A clear understanding of the writing prompt is the first step to success on a written test. Tell students to make sure to identify the exact words in the prompt that specify audience, purpose, topic, and form. They might find it useful to mark these words in the prompt before they begin to plan their responses.

Ask students to pick out the key words in the Sample Writing Situations on this page.

Situation 1: application essay, school principal, outline achievements, influence students, positive

Situation 2: speech, incoming students, describe what you've learned, offer advice that will help

Prewriting

Allow close to one fourth of your allotted time for prewriting.

Focus Your Topic Don't try to cover four years of high school in your essay or speech. Narrow your topic by using a timeline to plot significant events. Then, choose to write about those events that taught you the most and would most likely have a positive impact on your audience.

Consider Your Audience As you gather details for your narrative, keep in mind the audience indicated in the prompt you have chosen. For example, if you were writing to the principal, you would use more formal language than if you were writing to incoming high-school students.

Identify Your Purpose Decide on your purpose for writing, and choose words and details that will help you to achieve that purpose. For example, if your purpose is to encourage, you might choose to write many imperative sentences that contain words with positive connotations.
For a sample purpose planner, see page 56.

Drafting

Allow almost half of your time for drafting.

Choose a Structure and Organization Write an introduction, body, and conclusion in which you state and develop your main idea. In this type of writing, you will most likely organize the body of your essay or speech chronologically, listing events in time order.

Elaborate To convey the significance of your experience, give examples, comparing your experience to another, providing a telling quotation, or describing your sensory experience.

Put It on Paper Neatly write your response on your test paper. Begin with a statement of your opinion. Pause occasionally to review your outline or list, and make sure you continue to follow the logical sequence you have chosen.

Revising, Editing, and Proofreading

Allow almost one fourth of your time to revise and edit. Use the last few minutes to proofread your work.

Add Transitions As you review your work, mark places where the connections between ideas is not obvious. Then, use appropriate transitions to make ideas flow.

Make Corrections Review your response for errors. Change language that is inappropriate for your audience, and correct errors in spelling, grammar, and punctuation.

Customize for
Less Advanced Students

Have students choose one high-school experience to write about, in order to practice the logical sequence of a narrative. They should focus, too, on revising and proofreading in a timed situation.

Customize for
AP Students

Have students identify at least ten words in their narratives that could be replaced by more descriptive words. They could use a dictionary or a thesaurus to locate synonyms.

In-Depth Lesson Plan

	LESSON FOCUS	PRINT AND MEDIA RESOURCES
DAY 1	**Introduction to Short Stories** Students learn key elements of a short story and analyze the Model From Literature. (pp. 74–77/H46–47)	*Writers at Work* **DVD**, Narration *Writing and Grammar* **Interactive Text,** Ch. 5, Introduction
DAY 2	**Prewriting** Students choose and narrow a topic, consider their audience and purpose, and gather information. (pp. 78–81/H48–51)	*Writing and Grammar* **Interactive Text,** Section 5.2 **Teaching Resources** *Writing Support Transparencies,* 5-A–E; *Writing Support Activity Book,* 5-1–2 *Topic Bank for Heterogeneous Classes,* Ch. 5
DAY 3	**Drafting** Students organize their ideas and write their first drafts. (pp. 82–83/H52–53)	*Writing and Grammar* **Interactive Text,** Section 5.3 **Teaching Resources** *Writing Support Transparencies,* 5-F–G; *Writing Support Activity Book,* 5-3
DAY 4	**Revising** Students revise their drafts in terms of overall structure, paragraphs, sentences, and word choice. (pp. 84–87/H54–57)	*Writing and Grammar* **Interactive Text,** Section 5.4 **Teaching Resources** *Writing Support Transparencies,* 5-H–I
DAY 5	**Editing and Proofreading; Publishing and Presenting** Students check their work for accuracy and correctness and present their final drafts. (pp. 88–91/H58–59)	*Writing and Grammar* **Interactive Text,** Sections 5.5–6 **Teaching Resources** *Scoring Rubrics on Transparency,* Ch. 5; *Writing Assessment and Portfolio Management; Formal Assessment,* Ch. 5

Accelerated Lesson Plan

	LESSON FOCUS	PRINT AND MEDIA RESOURCES
DAY 1	**Introduction Through Drafting** Students review characteristics of a short story, select topics, and write drafts. (pp. 74–83/H46–53)	*Writing and Grammar* **Interactive Text,** Ch. 5, Introduction through Section 5.3 **Teaching Resources** *Writing Support Transparencies,* 5-A–G; *Writing Support Activity Book,* 5-1–3
DAY 2	**Revising Through Presenting** Students work individually or with peers to revise, edit, and proofread their work for presentation. (pp. 84–91/H54–59)	*Writing and Grammar* **Interactive Text,** Sections 5.4–6 **Teaching Resources** *Writing Support Transparencies,* 5-H–I; *Scoring Rubrics on Transparency,* Ch. 5; *Writing Assessment and Portfolio Management; Formal Assessment,* Ch. 5

Options for Adapting Lesson Plans

HOMEWORK

Have students complete any stage of the lesson for homework.

FEATURES

Extend coverage with Connected Assignment (p. 92), Spotlight on the Humanities (p. 94), Media and Technology Skills (p. 95), and the Standardized Test Preparation Workshop (pp. 96–97).

TECHNOLOGY

Students can complete any stage of the lesson on the computer, using *Writing and Grammar* Interactive Text or a word-processing program. Have them print out their completed work.

Writing and Grammar Handbook Alignment

Page numbers in Step-by-Step Teaching Guides in this Teacher's Edition refer to pages from the full student text. Handbook page references, indicated with this icon 🄷, are provided in Time and Resource Manager boxes and at the bottom of each Teacher's Edition page.

INTEGRATED SKILLS COVERAGE

Integrating Grammar
Using Phrases to Create Sentence Variety, SE p. 86/🄷56
Punctuating Direct Quotations and Dialogue, SE p. 88/🄷58

Reading/Writing Connection
Identify With a Character, SE p. 76
Writing Application, SE p. 77

Viewing and Representing
Critical Viewing, SE pp. 74, 76, 82, 90, 91, 92, 94/🄷46, 52
Making Connections in the Arts, SE p. 94
Video Adaptation of a Short Story, SE p. 95

Speaking and Listening
ATE pp. 83, 93

Real-World Connection
ATE p. 77

Critical Thinking Skills
ATE p. 77

Technology Skills
SE p. 85/🄷55

ASSESSMENT SUPPORT

Standardized Test Preparation Workshop, SE p. 96; ATE p. 87
Standardized Test Preparation Workbook, pp. 9–10
Scoring Rubrics on Transparency, Ch. 5
Formal Assessment, Ch. 5
Writing Assessment and Portfolio Management

MEETING INDIVIDUAL NEEDS

Less Advanced Students ATE pp. 82, 84, 97. See also Ongoing Assessments ATE pp. 76, 79, 80, 83, 85.
AP Students ATE pp. 82, 97
ESL Students ATE pp. 81, 87
Spatial Learners ATE pp. 80, 93
Linguistic Learners ATE p. 90

BLOCK SCHEDULING

Pacing Suggestions
For 90-minute Blocks
• Have students complete the Prewriting and Drafting stages in a single period.
• Focus one class period on Revising and Editing and Publishing and Presenting. Allow at least 30 minutes for peer revision.

Resources for Varying Instruction
• *Writing and Grammar* Interactive Text A 90-minute block provides an ideal opportunity for students to work on the computer.
• *Writers at Work* DVD Show the Narration segment in class.

Professional Development Support
• *How to Manage Instruction in the Block* This teaching resource provides management and activity suggestions.

MEDIA AND TECHNOLOGY

For the Student
• *Writing and Grammar* Interactive Text, Ch. 5
• *On-line Exercise Bank,* Sections 19.1–2

For the Teacher
• *Writers at Work* DVD, Narration
• Teacher**EXPRESS** CD-ROM

WRITING AND GRAMMAR ON-LINE

Interactive Text (On-line or on CD-ROM)
• Easily navigable instruction with interactive Revision Checkers
• Full use of e-rater™, the essay-scoring system (on-line only)

Companion Web Site PHSchool.com
• Scoring rubrics with models (use Web Code egk-1201)

See the Go On-line! **feature, SE p. iii.**

LITERATURE CONNECTIONS

Related selections from *Prentice Hall Literature, Penguin Edition,* The British Tradition:
Professional Model "A Shocking Accident," Graham Greene, SE p. 77
Topic Bank Option "The Rocking-Horse Winner," D. H. Lawrence, SE p. 79/🄷49

▶ *Lesson Objectives*

1. To write a short story appropriate to audience and purpose

2. To analyze and discuss published pieces as writing models and apply criteria developed by self and others to evaluate writing

3. To develop drafts independently by organizing content such as paragraphing and outlining and by refining style to suit occasion, audience, and purpose

4. To compose increasingly more involved sentences that contain gerunds, participles, and infinitives in their various functions

5. To develop and revise drafts in terms of structure, paragraphs, sentences, and word choice

6. To produce legible works that show accurate spelling and correct use of the conventions of punctuation and capitalization such as ellipses and direct quotations

7. To evaluate how well writing achieves its purposes

8. To refine a short story for publication

Critical Viewing

Analyze Students might respond that the photograph suggests a story about outdoor adventure or exploration.

▲ **Critical Viewing**
What sort of story might this photograph inspire? Explain. **[Analyze]**

Storytelling in Everyday Life

What would your world be like without stories? Think for a moment about the stories you hear and tell each day. For example, did you read an adventure story before going to sleep last night? On your way to school, did your friend tell you about his exciting weekend?

Stories can thrill, teach, and inspire their readers. Some stories are true, some are based on truth, and some are completely fictional. Some contain a single character, and some contain casts of hundreds. Some stories revolve around a single plot, whereas others contain intricately intertwined plots and subplots.

Despite the wide variety of stories around us, however, they often teach us something about ourselves and our world.

74 • Narration

🕐 **TIME AND RESOURCE MANAGER**

Resources
Technology: *Writers at Work* DVD, Narration; *Writing and Grammar* Interactive Text, Ch. 5

Using the Full Student Edition	Using the Handbook🄗
• Cover pp. 74–75 in class.	• Cover pp. 46–47 in class.
• Show the Narration section of the *Writers at Work* DVD.	• Show the Narration section of the *Writers at Work* DVD.
• Read the Model From Literature (pp. 76–77) and use it to brainstorm for short story ideas with students.	

What Is a Short Story?

A **short story** is a short piece of fiction that has a simple plot and few settings. Short stories often revolve around a key incident that reveals insights about its main character. Short stories frequently contain

- a narrator—either a character or an impersonal voice—who tells the story from a particular point of view.
- characters—fictional people who participate in the events—whose personalities may be revealed through dialogue.
- plot—a sequence of events that creates tension or suspense and that usually centers on one particular struggle or conflict.
- setting—the time and place in which the plot unfolds.

To preview the criteria on which your short story may be evaluated, see the Self-Assessment Rubric on page 89.

Types of Short Stories

Short stories can take many forms, from realistic tales to fantastic ones. Following are descriptions of types of short stories you may encounter:

- **Adventure stories** tell about a character who faces a huge challenge—either from nature or from other people.
- **Fantasies** are set in a time and place that is invented by the writer.
- **Science-fiction stories** often take place in the future, in outer space, or in some other environment that helps us see how science affects our lives.

Writers in ACTION

Author James Berry bases the elements of his narratives on his life experiences. His Caribbean childhood and life in England provide rich inspirations for colorful settings, interesting characters, and compelling plots. To gather and develop his ideas, Berry jots down his thoughts in a notebook:

"I have over the years had dozens and dozens and dozens of notebooks. . . . When I read something, when I see something, [when] somebody has said something to me or I overhear a conversation, [or] I see something in the newspaper or on television—I want to write my own story about that particular thing."

PREVIEW Student Work IN PROGRESS

In this chapter, you'll follow the work of Cormac Levenson, a student at Palmetto Senior High School in Pinecrest, Florida. Cormac used prewriting, drafting, and revising techniques to develop his story "Butterbee the Wise," which appears in its entirety at the end of the chapter.

Short Story • 75

Reading\Writing
Connection

**Reading: Identify With a
Character**

After they read the story, have students
discuss which character they most
identified with. Was it the main
character or one of the characters
who join him in shouting "Teresa"?
What makes them identify with one
character as opposed to another?

Step-by-Step Teaching Guide

Engage Students Through
Literature

1. Have prepared students take turns
   reading the story aloud.

2. After the reading, ask students to
   discuss the story. You can use
   questions such as these to prompt
   discussion:

   *Why does the main character call
   out the name "Teresa"?*

   *This story has been called a
   "modern fable." A fable is a short
   story that teaches a lesson. What
   lesson do students think this story
   teaches? Why?* (Answers will
   vary, but students may point out
   that people act on assumptions
   about things they see that may
   not be true.)

3. Allow students to make other
   observations about the story.
   Then, have them brainstorm for
   other short-story topics. Here are
   some possibilities:

   *the same story told from the
   perspective of a different
   character*

   other experiences with strangers

   *another day in the life of the man
   who shouts "Teresa"*

Students may add these to their own
short-story ideas in their Topic Banks.

Critical Viewing

Analyze The style of architecture is
a clue to its setting, apparently in
Europe and very likely Italy.

5.1 Model From Literature

*Writer Italo Calvino was born in Cuba but moved with
his parents to Italy when he was young. His works have
been called "modern fables" because they use elements
of the fable form to comment on modern life.*

Reading\Writing Connection

**Reading Strategy: Identify With a
Character** When you identify with
a character from fiction, you use
your own experiences to imagine
how you would think, feel, or act in the character's
situation. This strategy allows you to understand and
participate more fully in the story. As you read this
story, identify with its main character.

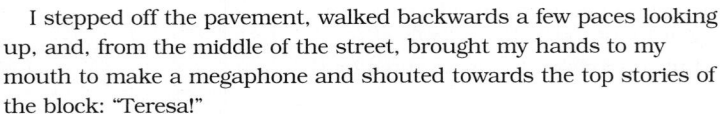

The Man Who Shouted Teresa

Italo Calvino

I stepped off the pavement, walked backwards a few paces looking
up, and, from the middle of the street, brought my hands to my
mouth to make a megaphone and shouted towards the top stories of
the block: "Teresa!"

My shadow took fright at the moon and huddled between my feet.

Someone walked by. Again I shouted: "Teresa!" The man came up
to me and said: "If you don't shout louder she won't hear you. Let's
both try. So: count to three, on three we shout together." And he
said: "One, two, three." And we both yelled, "Tereeeesaaa!"

A small group of friends passing by on their way back from the
theater or the cafe saw us calling out. They said: "Come on, we'll
give you a shout too." And they joined us in the middle of the street
and the first man said one two three and then everybody together
shouted, "Te-reee-saaa!"

Somebody else came by and joined us; a quarter of an hour later
there were a whole bunch of us, twenty almost. And every now and
then somebody new came along.

Organizing ourselves to give a good shout, all at the same time,

76 • **Short Story**

*The story's main
character, who is
unnamed, is also the
narrator, the voice
telling the story.*

*In the story's second
paragraph, Calvino
uses personification
to help create a
mood.*

*This story's plot is
simple and has few
events: The main
character is joined
by others as he calls
out for Teresa.*

▲ **Critical Viewing**
What clues in the
photograph above
help reveal where it
was taken? **[Analyze]**

☑ ONGOING ASSESSMENT: Monitor and Reinforce

After previewing the Model From Literature, you may anticipate that some students will have
difficulty in understanding the main character's motivation. If so, use one of the following options.

Option 1 If students read the model independently, have them write a paragraph about the main character and whether or not they would like to have him as a friend. Then, have students discuss their answers.	**Option 2** If you or a prepared student reads the model aloud in class, take time to discuss the main character's personality and whether or not he would make a good friend.

wasn't easy. There was always someone who began before three or who went on too long, but in the end we were managing something fairly efficient. We agreed that the "Te" should be shouted low and long, the "re" high and long, the "sa" low and short. It sounded great. Just a squabble every now and then when someone was out.

We were beginning to get it right, when somebody, who, if his voice was anything to go by, must have had a very freckly face, asked: "But are you sure she's at home?"

"No," I said.

"That's bad," another said. "Forgotten your key, have you?"

"Actually," I said, "I have my key."

"So," they asked, "why don't you go on up?"

"Oh, but I don't live here," I answered. "I live on the other side of town."

"Well then, excuse my curiosity," the one with the freckly voice asked carefully, "but who does live here?"

"I really wouldn't know," I said.

People were a bit upset about this.

"So could you please explain," somebody with a very toothy voice asked, "why you are standing down here calling out Teresa?"

"As far as I'm concerned," I said, "we can call another name, or try somewhere else. It's no big deal."

The others were a bit annoyed.

"I hope you weren't playing a trick on us?" the freckly one asked suspiciously.

"What?" I said, resentfully, and I turned to the others for confirmation of my good faith. The others said nothing, indicating they hadn't picked up the insinuation.

There was a moment's embarrassment.

"Look," someone said good-naturedly, "why don't we call Teresa one last time, then we'll go home."

So we did it again. "One two three Teresa!" but it didn't come out very well. Then people headed off home, some one way, some the other.

I'd already turned into the square, when I thought I heard a voice still calling: "Tee-reee-sa!"

Someone must have stayed on to shout. Someone stubborn.

Writing Application: Give Readers Characters With Whom They Can Identify As you prepare to write your short story, think of ways in which the story's characters will be understood or appreciated by your readers.

To read another short story that has an unusual twist, read "A Shocking Accident," by Graham Greene. You can find the story in *Prentice Hall Literature, Penguin Edition,* The British Tradition.

Through dialogue, Calvino "shows," rather than tells, about the characters.

Here, the conflict develops as the characters begin to suspect the motives of the main character.

Calvino uses a series of functional paragraphs to indicate speakers of dialogue and to make transitions.

The resolution, which begins here, provides a finish to the story.

Model From Literature • 77

Teaching From the Model

You can use this Model From Literature to show students how to find a relevant topic for a short story. The author, Italo Calvino, uses the streets of a city, such as the one where he grew up, as the setting for his story. Why is the setting important to this story? What kind of story can students envision taking place on the streets of their own city?

More About the Writer

Born in Cuba but raised in Italy, Italo Calvino (1923–1985) is famous for his short stories, many of which are actually Italian fables like "The Man Who Shouted Teresa." Much of his writing displays his "talent for transforming the mundane into the marvelous."

Real-World Connection

Explain to students that a surprising amount of what we think and do every day results from someone else's ideas. We listen to and sing along with popular songs, donate clothes and food to the needy when asked, and support or work for others' political ideals. Have students discuss the good and bad effects of behaving as others want us to.

Integrating Critical Thinking Skills

Conclusions Students may find it peculiar that the joiners don't get upset when they realize the capriciousness of the man shouting the name of someone merely at random. Explain that the story was written in Italy in 1943, during the collapse of Fascism. This is one of Calvino's fables that mark his social and political observations at the time—"the unpracticed exercise of authority by ordinary men."

Reading\Writing Connection

Writing Application: Characters

Tell students to resist creating characters that are outlandish or cartoonish. While it may be fun for a writer to imagine the adventures of "wild and crazy" characters, it takes very proficient writing to get readers to respond to such characters.

Prewriting: Choosing a Story Type

1. Have students fold a sheet of paper vertically into four parts to make a chart. At the top of the first column, have them write *Type of Story*. Write *Where It Takes Place*, *Who Is Involved*, and *What Happens* as headings for the other columns. Have them repeat the headings on the reverse side.

2. Students' completed sheets may suggest a type of story to them. Refer students to the *Writing Lab* CD-ROM side note on this page for more topic ideas.

Prewriting: Naming Characters

1. Suggest that students jot down names of intriguing people they've encountered in their lives. This will help them write the character descriptions. (The names should be altered to fictionalize the story.)

2. After writing several names and character descriptions, have students circle their favorites to help them narrow their choices.

Prewriting: Using Real Life

Teaching Resources: Writing Support Transparencies, 5-A; Writing Support Activity Book, 5-1

1. After students have finished drawing their settings, display Transparency 5-A and encourage them to discuss the importance of reality to fiction. Remind them that not all elements of a piece of fiction need come solely from the imagination of the writer.

2. Give students a blank copy of the chart (5-1) to apply to their work. Allow them time to discuss and develop ideas in small groups.

5.2 Prewriting

Choosing Your Topic

Choose a topic for your short story. Select a topic that will reach your audience, making them laugh, think, feel, or see things in a new way.

Strategies for Generating Topics

1. **Choosing a Story Type** Select a type of story to tell. For example, you may want to write a mystery, a western, or a fable or folk tale. Then, write a sentence or two telling about the story: where it takes place, who is involved, what the conflict is, and what happens at the story's end. Use these ideas as the basis for your short story.

2. **Naming Characters** Jot down the names of characters that you might like to write about. These might be ordinary names or fantastic names, such as Winky McPluto and Parsep IV. Then, write a few phrases about each character you've named. Choose the character that most interests you as the central character of your short story.

3. **Drawing a Setting** Interesting settings can sometimes trigger story ideas. Start by sketching a setting. It can be an actual setting, like a schoolroom; a historical setting, like a mining camp in the Old West; or a fantasy setting, like an undiscovered planet. Then, look at your drawing, and think of a conflict that may occur in the scene and the characters who might be in the conflict. Use these ideas to build your short story.

4. **Using Real Life** Some short stories are loosely based on real life. Think of a real-life incident that had an impact on you, and adapt it into a short story. Make a chart like the one below to help you adapt elements from real life into fiction.

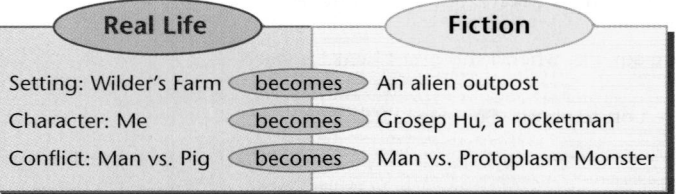

Real Life		Fiction
Setting: Wilder's Farm	becomes	An alien outpost
Character: Me	becomes	Grosep Hu, a rocketman
Conflict: Man vs. Pig	becomes	Man vs. Protoplasm Monster

⏰ Timed Writing Hint

If you are given a prompt, read it carefully to determine the audience for your writing.

Interactive Textbook

Try it out! Use the interactive Using Real Life chart in **Section 5.2**, on-line or on CD-ROM.

⏱ TIME AND RESOURCE MANAGER

Resources
Print: *Writing Support Transparencies*, 5-A–E; *Writing Support Activity Book*, 5-1–3
Technology: *Writing and Grammar* Interactive Text, Section 5.2

Using the Full Student Edition	Using the Handbook 🄷
• Work through Prewriting strategies in class to help students choose and narrow their topics.	• Work through Prewriting strategies in class to help students choose and narrow their topics.
• Use the Responding to Fine Art transparency to generate additional interest.	• Use the Responding to Fine Art transparency to generate additional interest.
• Discuss the importance of considering audience and purpose, and help students fill out a character history like the one on p. 81.	• Discuss the importance of considering audience and purpose, and help students fill out a character history like the one on p. 51.

TOPIC BANK

For help coming up with a topic for your story, consider these ideas:

1. **Story Set in the Past** Choose a past time period and place that interests you, and write a short story that takes place then and there. Develop a main character with a problem to solve, and tell how he or she solves it.

2. **Continuation of a Story or Movie** Think of an interesting story, movie, TV show, or play that you've read or seen. Then, in a short story, tell what happened *after* the ending.

Responding to Fine Art

3. Use the image in *Informal Evening* by Milton Avery to spark a short-story idea. Who are these people? What has just happened? Focus your storytelling by identifying a conflict among the characters in which one person wants something that the other two oppose, and let your imagination run free as you imagine what happens next.

Responding to Literature

Informal Evening, Milton Avery, D C Moore Gallery

4. Read "The Rocking-Horse Winner" by D. H. Lawrence. Then, write your own modern-day version of the story, set in familiar surroundings. You can read "The Rocking Horse Winner" in *Prentice Hall Literature, Penguin Edition,* The British Tradition.

Timed Writing Prompt

5. Write a short story about a main character whose strongest characteristic is ambition. Tell his or her story. Give your reader a sense of why your main character is so ambitious and what he or she is prepared to do to achieve his or her goal. Include details such as the time and place where your short story happens. **(30 minutes)**

Prewriting • 79

Step-by-Step Teaching Guide

Responding to Fine Art
Informal Evening by Milton Avery

Teaching Resources: Writing Support Transparencies, 5-B

1. Display Transparency 5-B and involve students in discussion about *Informal Evening*.

2. Ask students to brainstorm for short-story ideas suggested by this piece of art. Students may include these topic ideas along with their own suggestions in their topic banks.

Timed Writing Prompt

• To help students generate plot and character ideas for their stories about ambition, ask them to create scenarios where plot and character development are based on the attainment of a specific goal.

• Ask students to consider more than one scenario for each goal. For example, consider a character whose goal is to increase his or her wealth. This person may be a wealthy individual behaving ruthlessly to get ahead or a poor person working diligently to escape poverty.

• Suggest that students allow five minutes for prewriting, twenty minutes for writing, and five minutes for reviewing and proofreading.

☑ ONGOING ASSESSMENT: Monitor and Reinforce

If you observe that some students are having difficulty coming up with a topic, use one of the following options.

Option 1 Suggest that students choose an idea from the Topic Bank. If many students have difficulty, work with the whole class on one idea selected from the Topic Bank or from an idea suggested by a student.	**Option 2** If the Topic Bank ideas seem too difficult, suggest that students try one of the assignments from the *Topic Bank for Heterogeneous Classes* in the Teaching Resources.

⏱ TIME SAVERS!

Writing Support Transparencies
Use the transparencies for Chapter 5 to facilitate teaching of strategies.

Writing Support Activity Book
Use the graphic organizers for Chapter 5 to facilitate student planning.

Prewriting: Narrowing Your Topic

Teaching Resources: Writing Support Transparencies, 5-C; Writing Support Activity Book, 5-2

1. Draw students' attention to the CASPAR chart on this page and display Transparency 5-C. Briefly discuss each component of the chart.

2. Give students copies of the blank chart (5-2), or have them make their own charts by writing their topics at the top and listing the components down the side.

3. Encourage students to examine their answers to the second question. Does the personality of the character match his or her actions during the story?

Prewriting: Identify Your Purpose and Create a Plan

Teaching Resources: Writing Support Transparencies, 5-D

1. Start this activity by discussing the purpose and plan chart on this page. Display Transparency 5-D and have students extend the chart in their notebooks by offering other purposes and the methods for achieving them.

2. On the board, make a list of some of the stories the class has read so far this year. Have students determine the purpose of each and support their answers with specific examples.

3. Have students determine the purpose of their own stories. Encourage them to come up with at least three specific details they will include to make the purpose evident.

Customize for
Spatial Learners

Encourage students to sketch quick storyboards of their short story to identify its important elements. Then, have them make notes under each scene about details they want to include.

5.2

Narrowing Your Topic

Once you've chosen a topic, focus your story. Use the technique known as CASPAR to help you identify important elements you'll need for your story.

Character	Who is your main character? What does he or she want?
Adjectives to describe character	What type of person is your main character?
Setting	When and where does your story take place?
Problem (conflict)	What does your character want? What is preventing him or her from getting it?
Actions (plot)	What does your character do to get what he or she wants? What happens as a result?
Resolution	How do things finally turn out?

Considering Your Audience and Purpose

How do you want your short story to affect your audience? For example, do you want them to laugh, cry, or learn something important? First, identify your purpose, and then choose details that will help you to accomplish it.

Identify Your Purpose and Create a Plan

To help you craft an effective story, identify your purpose for writing and create a plan to achieve that purpose. The chart below shows different plans to help you fulfill your purpose:

If You Want Your Audience to . . .	Then You Might . . .
. . . laugh	. . . have your characters say witty things . . . put your characters into absurd situations . . . give the narrator a dry, humorous tone
. . . cry	. . . show your characters' pain so that the audience can feel it, too . . . make your characters likeable and understandable
. . . see things in a new way	. . . create a character who learns an important lesson . . . set up events so that your audience expects one thing, and then show why something quite different must happen

80 • Short Story

☑ ONGOING ASSESSMENT: Monitor and Reinforce

If you observe that students develop a habit of always writing for the teacher, try one of the following options.

Option 1 Suggest that students pick a very specific audience of one—a family member, a friend, or a much older person. It might be easier to tailor writing to a specific person than to a vaguely defined or broad group.	**Option 2** Have students write a brief profile of their audience, including their level of education, skills, and background knowledge of the topic.

Gathering Details

Choose details to make your short story come alive. Vivid, specific details help make plot events more believable and characters more interesting.

Capture Details About Characters and Setting

The more thought you put into your characters and settings, the better you'll be able to capture them on paper when it comes time to draft your short story. Following are some strategies for gathering details about character and setting:

- **Tape-Record Your Ideas** Talk about the story's characters and its settings. You could base your ideas on reality or let your imagination run free. Just talking aloud about your story will help you identify important details.

- **Sketch Your Characters and Settings** Sometimes, you can crystallize your ideas about characters and settings by sketching them. As you work, let one idea lead to another, until you have a completed vision to draw from as you draft.

- **Fill in a Character "History"** Create a history for your main character(s). Start by giving details about his or her family and background. Then, get more creative, and jot down your character's likes, dislikes, habits, and eccentricities. Refer to this "history" as you draft your short story.

Research Tip

If you've set your story in an unfamiliar time or place, do some research so that you can provide authentic details within the story.

Student Work IN PROGRESS

Name: *Cormac Levenson*
Palmetto Senior High School
Pinecrest, FL

Creating a Character "History"
Cormac created a character history to help make the character Butterbee come alive for his readers.

Character name: George Butterbee
Age: Young man through 70's
Family: Only child of Doris and Alvin Butterbee of
　　Breekenwood, Massachusetts
Background: Public-school education; Rossiter College,
　　B.A. degree
Likes: Pistachio ice cream, rugby, and science fiction . . .

Prewriting • 81

Prewriting: Sketch Your Characters and Settings

1. If you are doing this activity in class you may want to supply colored pencils and blank paper.

2. Encourage students to visualize their short stories as if they were paintings, planning how the characters would look and what they would do. Also, have students visualize the specific details of the setting.

3. Students might find it helpful to scan books or magazines for photographs that resemble the way they imagine their characters and setting. Tell them to look closely at the photographs—they might notice interesting details to include in their stories.

Prewriting: Fill in a Character "History"

Teaching Resources: Writing Support Transparencies, 5-E

1. Start this activity by having the class brainstorm for a list of questions to list about their main character, such as name, age, schooling, hobbies, family members, likes, and dislikes. Have them try to come up with at least twenty different questions.

2. Draw students' attention to the Student Work in Progress on this page, or display Transparency 5-E for an example of a character "history."

3. Give students time in class to answer the questions. Have students meet in small groups and share their answers. Sometimes, listening to the ideas of classmates will spark more ideas for students.

Customize for
ESL Students

Have students do the tape-recording activity in their native language and then translate it into English later. This way, they can concentrate on letting their ideas flow rather than on finding the right words in English.

Drafting: Make a Plot Diagram

Teaching Resources: Writing Support Transparencies, 5-F; Writing Support Activity Book, 5-3

1. Point out to students that pacing for each part of a short story is important to keep the reader's interest high from the beginning of the narrative to its end.

2. Display Transparency 5-F and write the terms *exposition, rising action, climax, falling action,* and *resolution* on the board or overhead projector. Discuss with students the meaning of each term.

3. Give students copies of the blank diagram (5-3) and have them make a plot diagram for their own short stories.

Customize for
Less Advanced Students

Using a plot diagram or word web to generate details for the short-story topic is beneficial if students do not labor over each point. These diagrams and webs are used as part of the brainstorming and organizing process while drafting. Encourage students to write their points and words as they think of them and then go back and "flesh out" the details later.

Customize for
AP Students

Have a group of students make a chart listing the five elements in the plot diagram. Then, have them analyze the plots of a current movie, a television show, a novel, a fairy tale, and a Shakespearean play. Point out that all stories, regardless of length, contain all five elements in order to be complete.

Critical Viewing

Analyze Students will probably settle on names that imply gentleness and obedience.

5.3 Drafting

Shaping Your Writing

Stories can take various shapes—they sometimes begin in the middle of the action, they sometimes contain stories within stories, and they sometimes contain flashbacks that interrupt the narrative to tell of events that happened earlier in time. Most stories, however, conform to a traditional plot structure, which never grows stale and enables the writer to fulfill and satisfy the expectations of the reader. Following is an example of how to use a plot diagram to shape your narrative:

Make a Plot Diagram

Making a plot diagram can help you shape your plot. A plot diagram contains the following elements: an **exposition,** which introduces the characters and setting; **rising action,** which introduces the conflict and builds gradually in intensity; and the **climax,** during which the **conflict** reaches its peak. The **falling action** refers to the events that immediately follow the climax and lead to the **resolution,** in which any unfinished issues within the story are resolved.

▲ **Critical Viewing** If this dog were a character in a short story, what would you name him, and why? **[Analyze]**

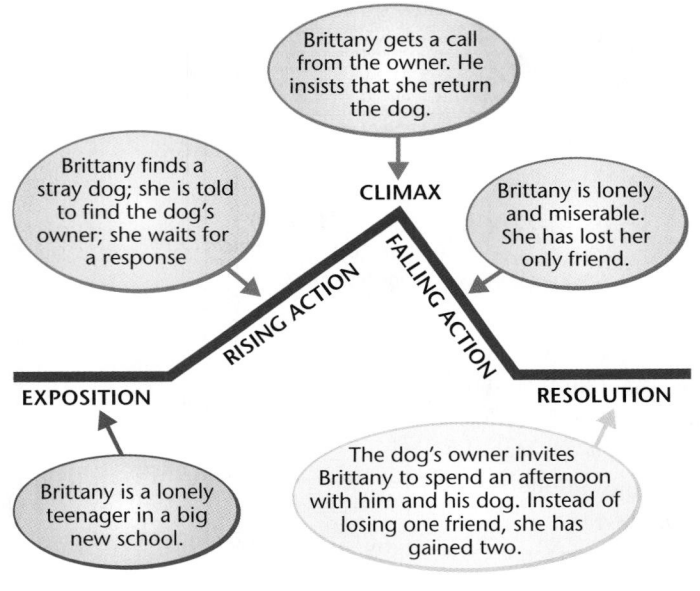

Brittany gets a call from the owner. He insists that she return the dog.

Brittany finds a stray dog; she is told to find the dog's owner; she waits for a response

CLIMAX

Brittany is lonely and miserable. She has lost her only friend.

RISING ACTION

FALLING ACTION

EXPOSITION

RESOLUTION

Brittany is a lonely teenager in a big new school.

The dog's owner invites Brittany to spend an afternoon with him and his dog. Instead of losing one friend, she has gained two.

Try it out! Use the interactive Plot Diagram in **Section 5.3,** on-line or on CD-ROM.

82 • Short Story

⏱ TIME AND RESOURCE MANAGER

Resources
Print: *Writing Support Transparencies,* 5-F–G; *Writing Support Activity Book,* 5-3
Technology: *Writing and Grammar* Interactive Text, Section 5.3

Using the Full Student Edition	Using the Handbook🄷
• Use Transparencies 5-F–G to demonstrate the Plot Diagram and the SEE method of elaboration.	• Use Transparencies 5-F–G to demonstrate the Plot Diagram and the SEE method of elaboration.
• Have students complete the drafting exercises in class.	• Have students complete the drafting exercises in class.

Providing Elaboration

As you draft, use the SEE structure to help you develop incidents in your plot or to flesh out descriptions of characters, events, and settings.

Use SEE: Statement, Extension, Elaboration

This technique, also known as "layering," can help you add depth to your writing. Each layer should help you understand more about the subject of your original statement.

S: Write a **statement** that conveys a basic idea.

E: Next, write an **extension** of that statement. An extension should take the basic thought and "go a little further" toward explaining it or defining it.

E: Finally, **elaborate** on your original statement by giving more information about it.

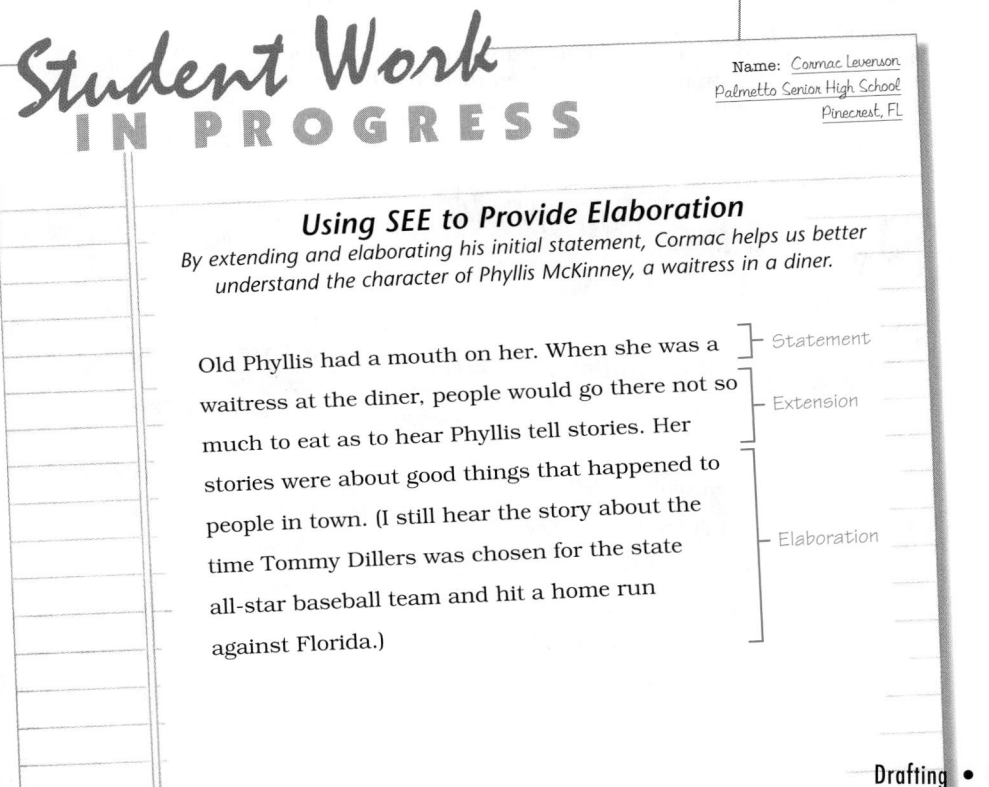

Student Work IN PROGRESS

Name: Cormac Leverson
Palmetto Senior High School
Pinecrest, FL

Using SEE to Provide Elaboration

By extending and elaborating his initial statement, Cormac helps us better understand the character of Phyllis McKinney, a waitress in a diner.

Old Phyllis had a mouth on her. When she was a — Statement

waitress at the diner, people would go there not so — Extension
much to eat as to hear Phyllis tell stories. Her

stories were about good things that happened to — Elaboration
people in town. (I still hear the story about the
time Tommy Dillers was chosen for the state
all-star baseball team and hit a home run
against Florida.)

Drafting • 83

Teaching Resources: Writing Support Transparencies, 5-G

1. Have students explain why the SEE technique is also called "layering." (More information is layered on with each additional sentence.)

2. Explain that layering makes writing much more interesting because it provides more information about the characters and setting in the narrative. This elaboration is especially important in short stories, since understanding the characters and setting is integral to the success of the story.

3. Guide students' attention to the Student Work in Progress with Transparency 5-G. Show students how using SEE might look in practice. Ask students why the writer may have decided to use elaboration (to explain the character, to clarify the plot).

Integrating Speaking and Listening Skills

After students have written their drafts, have them choose one paragraph that they believe is a good example of the SEE technique and read it to a partner. After listening carefully to the paragraph, the partner writes the main idea statement and then retells in his or her own words the elaboration used in the paragraph. Also, have the partner mention any important information he or she feels is missing.

☑ ONGOING ASSESSMENT: Monitor and Reinforce

If your students have a hard time developing the plots of their short stories, try the following strategy.

Have students work in pairs. Have each student write the details of his or her plot, including exposition, rising action, and so on. Then, have each student explain the plot to the partner in his or her own words. Let the partner ask questions, make suggestions, and point out gaps in the plot. Have students write down their new ideas.

⏱ TIME SAVERS!

 Writing Support Transparencies
Use the transparencies for Chapter 5 to facilitate teaching of strategies.

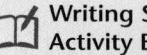 **Writing Support Activity Book**
Use the graphic organizers for Chapter 5 to facilitate student planning.

Revising: Adding Details to Create Foreshadowing

Teaching Resources: Writing Support Transparencies, 5-H

1. Explain to students that short stories need to build suspense to sustain interest. Short stories should also be carefully paced so that one part of the story leads quickly to the next to hold the reader's interest.

2. To demonstrate the use of foreshadowing in building suspense, have students read the Student Work in Progress in the text or on Transparency 5-H, which can be displayed.

3. Discuss how Cormac's addition of his personal doubts about seeing Butterbee adds to the suspense about what will happen.

4. If students seem to need more examples, help them identify foreshadowing in recent movies or in stories the class has read so far this year.

Customize for
Less Advanced Students

Tell students that sentences containing foreshadowing are often added after the first draft. Have students reread their drafts to see whether they can include foreshadowing in their short stories. Remind them that the foreshadowing should not be so blatant that it removes the suspense by revealing too much of the plot.

5.4 Revising

Once you have drafted your short story, revise it to make it more effective. Start by looking at its overall structure. Then, make sure that each paragraph and every sentence works the way you want it to. Finally, reread your story carefully to see whether your word choices support your purpose.

Revising Your Overall Structure

Build Suspense

Consider altering the structure of your short story to build suspense. For example, if your story has a very long exposition in which the setting and characters are introduced, you could eliminate some descriptive detail to more fully develop the story's conflict. Following is another strategy for making your short story interesting and suspenseful:

▶ **REVISION STRATEGY**
Adding Details to Create Foreshadowing

One way to create reader interest is to add details to create **foreshadowing**, a writer's use of clues to hint at story events that might happen next. These clues cause readers to think about what might happen next and keep them involved and interested in the story.

Student Work
IN PROGRESS

Name: *Cormac Levenson*
Palmetto Senior High School
Pinecrest, FL

Building Audience Interest Through Foreshadowing

Cormac decided to increase tension in his story by adding foreshadowing. The use of foreshadowing helps build the readers' interest in upcoming plot events.

Eventually, it was my turn to go see Butterbee, but I
What if he gave me advice that I didn't want to take—advice that ruined my
didn't really want to go. ∧ I was supposed to see *whole life?*
What if he
George Butterbee the same day as a Greg Brown *turned out to*
be a phony?
concert that I had eagerly anticipated for almost a

year. My mother didn't care; she felt you weren't

really an adult until you went to see what Mr.

Butterbee had to teach.

⏱ TIME AND RESOURCE MANAGER

Resources
Print: *Writing Support Transparencies, 5-H–I*
Technology: *Writing and Grammar* Interactive Text, Section 5.4

Using the Full Student Edition	Using the Handbook🅗
• Work through the Revision Strategies. • Use Transparency 5-H to demonstrate the addition of foreshadowing. • Work through the use of phrases to create sentence variety. • Use Transparency 5-I on revising dialogue.	• Work through the Revision Strategies. • Use Transparency 5-H to demonstrate the addition of foreshadowing. • Work through the use of phrases to create sentence variety. • Use Transparency 5-I on revising dialogue.

Revising Your Paragraphs

Create Functional Paragraphs

Functional paragraphs are short paragraphs written for effect. They can arouse or sustain interest, emphasize a point, indicate dialogue, and make transitions.

▶ **REVISION STRATEGY**

Creating Functional Paragraphs to Set Off Dialogue

Review your draft, and begin a new paragraph each time a new character begins speaking. You could give just the words of the dialogue or add a description about how the character felt, behaved, or spoke.

"Well, I guess you'll be taking your dog home now," Brittany said.
    This functional paragraph reveals a character's words.

"Sure. I guess I will."
    When the speaker changes, start a new paragraph.

"Goodbye, Goldie." Brittany's voice was very small. "Be good."
    The paragraph does not break after the description of Brittany's voice because she continues speaking.

"Actually, his name is Max."

Revising Your Sentences

Work with the sentences in your story to be sure they flow together and convey your intended meaning.

▶ **REVISION STRATEGY**

Varying Sentences

If many sentences in your story begin the same way and are of the same approximate length, vary them to liven up your story. To do this, you might throw in a long question or a short exclamation. Start a few sentences with an introductory word or phrase, or add emphasis by inverting the word order.

REPETITIVE SENTENCES: Tryson walked into the room. He looked around. He saw his long-lost baseball glove. It was on the shelf, next to the trophy.

VARIED SENTENCES: As soon as Tryson walked into the room, he looked around for his long-lost baseball glove. Would it be there? Yes! There it was, on the shelf, next to the trophy.

🖴 Technology Tip

Select the Show Invisibles option in your word-processing program to allow you to readily see paragraph breaks within your story.

Interactive Textbook

Get instant help! Use the Revision Checker for Sentence Length, accessible from the menu bar, on-line or on CD-ROM.

Revising • 85

Step-by-Step Teaching Guide

Revising: Creating Functional Paragraphs to Set Off Dialogue

1. Review how functional paragraphs tell who is speaking and give additional information about the character.

2. Distribute copies of a story from your local newspaper. Explain that journalists often use functional paragraphs to draw attention to important details in a story. Have students try to identify the reasoning behind some of the functional paragraphs in the handout.

3. Have students reread their stories and determine whether there are any sections that would be more clear if they were divided into shorter paragraphs.

Step-by-Step Teaching Guide

Revising: Varying Sentences

1. Use the student example to discuss with students the advantages of using varied sentence structures.

2. Have students read through their short stories, underlining adjoining sentences that begin in the same way.

3. Have a volunteer write some of his or her repetitive sentences on the board. Allow the class to find ways to vary the structure of these sentences.

4. Encourage students to vary sentence structures in their own short stories.

✓ **ONGOING ASSESSMENT: Monitor and Reinforce**

Students sometimes have trouble knowing what to revise in their short stories. If this is the case with your students, try the following strategy.

Let students work in pairs to prepare a "report card" for each other. Have students list the following topics for the report card: Suspense, Foreshadowing, Dialogue, and Sentence Variation. Let students read each other's drafts and then "grade" each other on each component from 1 to 3, with 1 meaning "excellent," and 3 meaning "needs to be reworked." Have them discuss ways of improving any component that receives a grade lower than a 1.

Using Phrases to Create Sentence Variety

1. Point out that creating sentence variety by using various types of phrases brings vitality and interest to a short story.

2. Give students a copy of a short story from an anthology or current magazine. Have students copy sentences with prepositional phrases, gerund phrases, and infinitive phrases, identifying each sentence according to the type of phrase it contains.

3. Have students choose a paragraph to rewrite in sentences that all contain the same structure. Then, have them compare the two versions. Which is more interesting to read, and why?

4. Students will readily find examples of a variety of sentence structures in the Student Work in Progress. Have them share these examples and the examples from their own narratives. Write some of these examples on the board for students to refer to while revising.

Find It in Your Reading

Have students write a paragraph that follows the same sentence structure as Calvino's paragraph. They may write about any subject; the goal is to get comfortable with various sentence structures by using them.

Find It in Your Writing

Let students trade papers with a partner to check variety in sentence phrasing. If students find sentences that require corrections, let them write the suggested change on another piece of paper so that the author can consider it.

5.4

Grammar in Your Writing
Using Phrases to Create Sentence Variety

When sentences fall into a pattern, such as subject-verb-object, it can have a dulling effect on writing. One way to inject variety into your writing is to use a variety of sentence patterns. Following are ways to begin sentences with phrases, rather than with subjects:

Prepositional Phrases: When you begin a sentence with a prepositional phrase, it stirs interest in what follows. Adjective phrases modify nouns or pronouns. Adverb phrases modify a verb, an adjective, or another adverb by pointing out *where, when, in what way,* or *to what extent.*

Adjective Phrase: With her head held high, Lana glowed as she was presented to the audience.

Adverb Phrase: Before the end of school, several students were already headed for the soccer field.

Gerund Phrases: A gerund is a form of a verb that acts as a noun. For example, in the sentence "Running is my favorite sport," *running* is a gerund. A gerund with modifiers or a complement is called a gerund phrase. Gerund phrases may contain a variety of modifiers and complements.

Gerund Phrase With Adjective: Loud hammering broke the quiet of the dawn.

Gerund Phrase With Direct Object: Delivering mail has its rewards.

Infinitive Phrases: An infinitive is a form of a verb that generally appears with the word *to* and acts as a noun, an adjective, or an adverb. An infinitive phrase is an infinitive with modifiers, a complement, or a subject, all acting together as a single part of speech.

Infinitive Phrase With an Adverb: To succeed quickly, Ned had to drop his initial plans.

Infinitive Phrase With Direct Object and Prepositional Phrase: To warn others of the danger, the group posted fliers.

Find It in Your Reading Choose a long paragraph from Italo Calvino's "The Man Who Shouted Teresa," on pages 76–77. Write out the paragraph on a sheet of paper, and identify its sentence patterns. Then, analyze the variety of sentences. Are they varied or similar in length and pattern? Why might Calvino have made the choices he made?

Find It in Your Writing Review your draft to find at least three different sentence patterns. If you can't find three different patterns, challenge yourself to add at least two more sentence patterns to your writing. You might like your story better once you've added a bit more variety!

For more on phrases, see Chapter 19.

☑ ONGOING ASSESSMENT: Prerequisite Skills

If students have difficulty recognizing and using various types of phrases, you may find it helpful to refer them to the following materials to ensure coverage of prerequisite knowledge.

In the Textbook	Print Resources	Technology
Prepositional Phrases, Section 19.1 Gerund Phrases, Section 19.2 Infinitive Phrases, Section 19.2	*Grammar Exercise Workbook,* pp. 33–40	*On-Line Exercise Bank,* Sections 19.1–2

Revising Your Word Choice

Revising Words to Suit the Characters

Not everyone speaks the same way. As you revise your characters' dialogue, make sure they use the words that fit their age, background, and personality, as well as the time and place in which they live and their relationships with the other characters. Below are three basic types of speech, which might help you identify your characters' distinct voices:

> **Formal:** People who are in business situations, unfamiliar situations, or simply proper in their manner tend to use formal speech. Their word choice is precise and carefully considered.
>
> "The short story you wrote is superb, Ms. Lopez."

> **Informal:** Many people use informal speech when they speak with acquaintances or peers.
>
> "Your short story is pretty amazing, Marisol."

> **Casual:** People may use nicknames and slang when they speak with family members and close friends.
>
> "Mari! That was a great story!"

▶ **REVISION STRATEGY**

Adding Partial Sentences, Contractions, and Slang

Most people—no matter their age, educational background, and circumstances—use some degree of informality when they speak. Review the passages of dialogue in your short story. Then, consider adding the following elements to any passages that seem stilted or overly formal.

- **Partial Sentences:** "Sure, enough . . ."
- **Contractions:** "I can't find the clicker."
- **Slang:** "You're kidding me, right?"

Peer Review

Read Aloud

Another way to evaluate the dialogue in your story is to hear it read aloud. Ask a small group of peers to read your story aloud, assigning each character to a different reader. Listen closely as your characters speak, to make sure they're using the words that suit their personalities. Ask your readers for feedback, too. When you've finished working with your peers, revise your dialogue based on their responses.

 Timed Writing Hint

When writing for an exam, use formal, academic language unless a prompt asks for a conversational style.

Revising • 87

Revising Words to Suit the Characters

Teaching Resources: Writing Support Transparencies, 5-I

1. Using examples on Transparency 5-I, point out how formal, informal, and casual types of speech vary and how the choice of language reflects both the character and the situation the character is in.

2. Have students go over their own writing, highlighting dialogue.

3. Let students identify the basic type of speech used in each case and evaluate it to see whether it adequately fits the character and setting.

4. Have students modify their dialogue as necessary.

Revising: Peer Review

1. Begin the peer review process by inviting students to identify a draft's strengths before focusing on its drawbacks.

2. Remind students that some errors will be corrected at the proofreading stage and that the focus here should be on content.

3. Suggest that students who will be reading their drafts aloud take notes when the listeners offer comments about their narratives.

4. Point out that many comments made during peer review will be helpful to all students. Suggest that students note helpful suggestions and share them with the class later.

Customize for
ESL Students

Students might have trouble matching a character's vocabulary with his or her personality. This skill requires an extensive knowledge of word connotations, which might be difficult for English-language learners. Have them discuss the personalities of their characters with a fluent English speaker. That student can then help them make sure the dialogue fits the character.

 STANDARDIZED TEST PREPARATION WORKSHOP

Prepositional Phrases Standardized test questions may require students to identify various types of phrases. Provide students with opportunities to practice identifying prepositional phrases.

Which sentence below contains a prepositional phrase?

A The young girl walked *down*.

B The ball rolled *down* the hill.

C He quickly ran *ahead*.

D The tired girl sat *up*.

Students should recognize that **B** is the correct answer because *down* is a preposition and its object is *hill*. In the other sentences, the italicized words are acting as adverbs.

Editing and Proofreading

1. Point out to students that editing and proofreading may be viewed as an extension of the paragraphing process.

2. Check that students proofread carefully for spelling errors. Have all questionable spellings been checked with a dictionary or computer spell-checker?

Punctuating Direct Quotations and Dialogue

1. Tell students to do a separate reading to check for correct placement of punctuation marks in direct quotations and dialogue.

2. Write this sentence on the board:

   I just got a job announced Mia at the movie theater.

   Point out that as it is written, the sentence is hard to understand because it lacks punctuation.

3. Then, challenge students to punctuate the sentence in two ways to give it two different meanings. In the first, Mia gets a job at the movie theater. In the second, she makes her announcement at the movie theater:

   "I just got a job," announced Mia, "at the movie theater."

   "I just got a job," announced Mia at the movie theater.

4. This will demonstrate the importance of punctuating direct quotations and dialogue correctly.

Find It in Your Reading

Students may cite the group's agreeing on a method for shouting "Te," "re," and "sa" as an example of indirect quotation. The story contains many examples of direct quotations, including the first line.

Find It in Your Writing

Let students work as partners to check punctuation in quotations found in each other's work.

5.5 Editing and Proofreading

Errors in your short story can distract your audience and reduce the impact of your story. To make your writing error-free, fix all errors in spelling, punctuation, and grammar.

Focusing on Punctuation

Carefully review the punctuation in your story. Be especially sure you have punctuated your dialogue correctly. Review the rules for punctuating direct quotations, paying particular attention to which punctuation marks go inside quotation marks and which appear outside them.

Grammar in Your Writing
Punctuating Direct Quotations and Dialogue

Use the following guidelines to help you punctuate your dialogue correctly:

1. Only direct quotations are enclosed in quotation marks.

   Direct Quotation: "Please help me clean up," said Brian.

   Indirect Quotation: Brian said that he wanted his friend to help him clean up.

2. Enclose the actual words spoken by a character in quotation marks. Note, however, that only the beginning of each sentence is capitalized, not the beginning of every quotation.
   "Give me the keys," said Stella, "and I'll lock up."

3. Use a comma or colon after an introductory expression.
   The boy said slowly, "I hate to see you so upset."

4. Use a comma, question mark, or exclamation point after a quotation followed by a concluding expression.
   "I'll never be happy again!" shouted Brittany.
   "That's too bad," said her mother. "What if we got you another dog?"

Find It in Your Reading Find an instance of a direct quotation and an indirect quotation within Italo Calvino's "The Man Who Shouted Teresa" on pages 76–77. Explain the difference between them.

Find It in Your Writing As you proofread your short story, double-check your punctuation of dialogue.

For more on punctuating dialogue, see Chapter 27.

⏱ TIME AND RESOURCE MANAGER

Resources
Print: *Scoring Rubrics on Transparency,* Ch. 5; *Writing Assessment and Portfolio Management; Formal Assessment,* Ch. 5
Technology: *Writing and Grammar* Interactive Text, Sections 5.5–6

Using the Full Student Edition	Using the Handbook 🄷
• Review p. 88 in class, including Grammar in Your Writing. • Give step-by-step coverage to Publishing and Presenting (p. 89). • Analyze the Final Draft (pp. 90–91). • Have students proofread their stories in class.	• Review p. 58 in class, including Grammar in Your Writing. • Give step-by-step coverage to Publishing and Presenting (p. 59). • Have students proofread their stories in class.

5.6 Publishing and Presenting

Part of the fun of writing a short story is sharing it with others. Consider these ideas for publishing and presenting:

Building Your Portfolio

1. **Record Your Story** Alone or with a group of classmates, read your story aloud, speaking the dialogue as your characters might speak it. Tape-record your reading, and make the recording available for others to borrow.

2. **Enter a Literary Contest** Many magazines for young people or adults sponsor short-story contests. Find out the rules, submit your work, and see what happens!

Reflecting on Your Writing

Think about your experience writing a story. Then answer these questions and record your responses in your portfolio.

- As you created your story, what did you learn about yourself?
- If a friend were writing a story and wanted your advice, what would you suggest?

🖥 Internet Tip

To see a story scored according to this rubric, go on-line:
PHSchool.com
Enter Web Code:
egk-1201

Rubric for Self-Assessment

Use the following criteria to evaluate your short story.

	Score 4	Score 3	Score 2	Score 1
Audience and Purpose	Contains details that create a tone to engage the audience	Contains details and language that appeal to an audience	Contains few details that contribute to its purpose or appeal to an audience	Contains no purpose; is not written for a specific audience
Organization	Presents events that create an interesting, clear narrative; told from a consistent point of view	Presents sequence of events; told from a specific point of view	Presents a confusing sequence of events; contains inconsistent points of view	Presents no logical order; is told from no consistent point of view
Elaboration	Contains details that provide insight into character; contains dialogue that reveals characters and furthers the plot	Contains details and dialogue that develop character	Contains characters and setting; contains some dialogue	Contains few or no details to develop characters or setting; no dialogue provided
Use of Language	Uses word choice and tone to reveal story's theme; contains no errors in grammar, punctuation, or spelling	Uses interesting and fresh word choices; contains few errors in grammar, punctuation, and spelling	Uses clichés and trite expressions; contains some errors in grammar, punctuation, and spelling	Uses uninspired word choices; has many errors in grammar, punctuation, and spelling

Publishing and Presenting • 89

Publishing and Presenting

1. Remind students that the publishing phase is the writer's reward, the opportunity to share his or her work with an audience. Encourage students to consider finding more places to share their work (examples: on related Web sites, with family members, with young children if appropriate).

2. In preparing to record their short stories, students may want to rehearse several times, practicing authentic dialogue.

ASSESS and CLOSE

Assessment

Teaching Resources: Scoring Rubrics on Transparency, Ch. 5; Writing Assessment and Portfolio Management; Formal Assessment, Ch. 5

1. Display the Scoring Rubric transparency and review the criteria in class.

2. Before students proceed with self-assessment, you may wish to review the Final Draft of the Student Work in Progress on pages 90–91.

3. In addition to student self-assessment, you may wish to use the following options:
   - score student essays yourself, using the rubric and scoring models in *Writing Assessment and Portfolio Management*.
   - review the Standardized Test Preparation Workshop on pages 96–97 and administer a timed writing assessment.
   - administer the Chapter 5 assessment in *Formal Assessment* to measure students' grasp of the concepts presented.

☑ ONGOING ASSESSMENT: Assess Mastery

Use one the following options to assess final drafts of students' short stories.

Self-Assessment Ask students to score their stories using the rubric provided. Then, have students write a single paragraph reflecting on the most valuable thing they learned in completing this assignment.

Teacher Assessment You may wish to use the rubric and the scoring models provided in *Writing Assessment and Portfolio Management* to score the short stories.

Final Draft

1. Help students see that "Butterbee the Wise" incorporates key elements of the short story.

   • The topic has been well chosen.

   • The author's experience is easy to relate to and interesting.

   • Audience and purpose have been carefully considered.

   • The story is written for anyone familiar with a small town or an eccentric person.

   • The purpose is to entertain.

   • The introduction establishes the identity of the main character and engages the reader in what is happening.

   • The body of the narrative describes George Butterbee and the legend created around him.

   • Dialogue is used to reveal characters' motivations.

   • Finally, there is a short conclusion, giving an unexpected ending that makes us smile.

2. Ask students whether there are any changes they would recommend for this short story to fine-tune it or make it better. How might they apply these suggestions to their own writing?

Customize for
Linguistic Learners

Let students write a short poem that captures the spirit of this short story or of the character of Butterbee the Wise. Ask volunteers to read their poems to the class.

Critical Viewing

Make a Judgment Students should feel that with scraggly hair and sunken eyes, the man in the photograph resembles what Butterbee probably looked like.

FINAL DRAFT

Butterbee the Wise

Cormac Levenson
Palmetto Senior High School
Pinecrest, Florida

I live in the small town of Breckenwood, Massachusetts, population 248. Anyway, in the town we have a legend, the legend of George Butterbee.

As the story goes, at the age of twenty-five, George Butterbee simply decided to stop talking. No one knows why, but he just stopped. At first, everyone thought he was crazy. He even tried to keep his job as a teacher. Some people think that he was so smart that they should have let him stay on anyway. But everyone at the diner was always talking about how much of a loon he was.

Luckily for all of us, old Phyllis McKinney had a crush on him, and old Phyllis had a mouth on her. When she was a waitress at the diner, people would go there not so much to eat as to hear Phyllis tell stories. Her stories were about good things that happened to people in town. (I still hear the story about the time Tommy Dillers was chosen for the state all-star baseball team and hit a home run against Florida.) Anyway, old Phyllis didn't like people talking badly about her George, so she would always stick into any conversation, whenever she could, stories about all of the smart things Butterbee had done.

Finally, after two years of telling everyone how great George was, Phyllis finally persuaded her mother's best friend, Mary Lou, to send her Mikey to get a little bit of wisdom from Butterbee. No one knew what Mr. Butterbee did, but Mikey insisted that it was the most enlightening experience he ever had. It wasn't long before everyone called him Butterbee the Wise, and all the

◄ **Critical Viewing**
Does the man in the photograph look like a "Butterbee"? Explain why or why not. **[Make a Judgment]**

Because the story's narrator is a character in the story, the story is told from the first-person point of view.

Cormac uses elaboration to provide an in-depth look at Phyllis, one of the story's characters.

parents began waiting impatiently for their children to come of age so they, too, could go learn from Butterbee the Wise.

Eventually, it was my turn to go see Butterbee, but I didn't really want to go. What if he gave me some advice that I really didn't want to take—advice that I followed and that then ruined my whole life? What if I believed everything he said and he turned out to be a big phony?

I was supposed to see George Butterbee the same day as a Greg Brown concert that I had eagerly anticipated for almost a year. My mother didn't care; she felt you weren't really an adult until you went to see what Mr. Butterbee had to teach.

My mother eventually did make me go and see him. He was exactly what I expected, all long gray hair and sunken eyes, with leathery skin folding over itself. He smelled horrible. He waved me in hastily, making me feel very unwanted. He took me into the bathroom, grabbing four paper cups, a notepad, and a pen on the way. He turned the nozzle on his bathtub and on his bathroom sink. Then, he simply put a cup under both of them and ushered me into the kitchen.

I was confused: I had noticed there wasn't any water coming out of either tap. In the kitchen, he put a third cup under the faucet and turned the nozzle. The water came out with such force that both of us and everything else in the kitchen became very, very wet. He wrote on his notepad, "This is not what I want." Then, he took a pitcher and poured water from it slowly into the fourth cup.

He was trying to teach me about moderation. I was very disappointed, more so than I thought I would be. He wrote on his pad, "This is what I want."

I frowned deeply and said, "I already know about that."

He smiled deeply and took me into the bathroom, where it seemed the bathroom sink was working, just barely, so that the cup was only half full of water. The bathtub wasn't working at all, and its cup was, of course, empty. Butterbee took a long, satisfied sip of the half-full cup and wrote, "It's better than nothing."

I left, very disappointed. But with every day and every drop, I became less and less disappointed with his teachings. That was, of course, until I found out the truth about them. Two years later, Butterbee the Wise became very sick. Finally, when rumor was that he had only a day or two left, a large group of friends and I went to see him. He died looking into my eyes, asking me a question that left me forever disenchanted with his teachings. I often think back to those words and smile a sad smile. He had simply asked, "Why didn't you fix my plumbing?"

Here, Cormac uses foreshadowing, dropping hints about the story's ending, to build suspense.

At this point, the plot takes an important turn: The main character is to visit Butterbee.

▲ **Critical Viewing**
If you were to capture the essence of water in a photograph, would your photo resemble this one? Explain. **[Compare and Contrast]**

This functional paragraph contains dialogue.

The story's final sentence serves two purposes: It provides a humorous surprise ending as well as reveals the story's theme.

Integrating Reading Skills

Predict Have students predict what will happen when the narrator meets Butterbee. Make sure they support their predictions with clues from the text. When they finish reading, have them compare their predictions to the actual ending. How accurate were their predictions?

Integrating Literary Skills

Foreshadowing After they finish reading, have students return to the beginning of the story and look for instances where the author seems to be foreshadowing the ending. How is Butterbee described? What specific words are used to describe him? Does this reveal anything about the ending?

Critical Viewing

Compare and Contrast Students might say they would be drawn to photograph the more dramatic aspects of water, as found in a huge wave or a long waterfall.

Lesson Objectives

1. To write a dramatic scene
2. To use prewriting strategies to develop characters
3. To employ precise language to generate ideas, develop voice, and plan

Step-by-Step Teaching Guide

Drama

Teaching Resources: Writing Support Transparencies, 5-J; Writing Support Activity Book, 5-4

1. Read through the excerpt from *Pygmalion* with students. Discuss the large amount of information that is provided by stage directions. Have students describe the location, season, weather, and characters' actions. Remind them that stage directions can also describe a character's mood, appearance, and tone.

2. Suggest that students review strategies from Chapter 5. See the chart below for resources.

3. Display Transparency 5-J. Use a familiar short story, book, or film to illustrate how to break it into specific elements. Point out the similarities between a short story and a play in terms of their basic elements. Give students copies of the blank organizer (5-4) so they can analyze the short story they will use for their dramatic scenes.

4. As students work on developing characters, return to the *Pygmalion* excerpt. Have them describe the differences in speech patterns between the mother/daughter pair and the bystander. Suggest that students listen carefully to speech patterns and tones of voice as they go through the day. Their observations may become models for the characters in their scenes.

Critical Viewing

Interpret Students might mention, "Wherefore art thou Romeo?"

Connected Assignment
Drama

When you tell a story through dialogue for a live audience, you are performing **drama**. Stories and dramas have a lot in common. What distinguishes the two is that drama is written to be performed, whereas stories are meant to be read. Actors in a drama get directions from a script, which tells them what to say—their dialogue. Stage directions tell actors how and where to move and what the setting looks like.

Below is an excerpt from a drama. Notice how the dialogue and stage directions are formatted.

Bring a story to life by writing a dramatic scene. Use the strategies on the following page to guide you as you write.

▲ **Critical Viewing**
This still photo is of the character Juliet from the movie *Romeo and Juliet.* What lines of dialogue do most people associate with this character? **[Interpret]**

MODEL

Pygmalion
George Bernard Shaw

ACT I

London at 11:15 P.M. Torrents of heavy summer rain. Cab whistles blowing frantically in all directions. Pedestrians running for shelter into the portico of St. Paul's Church (not Wren's cathedral but Inigo Jones's church in Covent Garden vegetable market), among them a lady and her daughter in evening dress. All are peering out gloomily at the rain, except one man with his back turned to the rest, wholly pre-occupied with a notebook in which he is writing. The church clock strikes the first quarter.

The Daughter (*in the space between the central pillars, close to the one on her left*) I'm getting chilled to the bone. What can Freddy be doing all this time? He's been gone twenty minutes.

The Mother (*on her daughter's right*) Not so long. But he ought to have got us a cab by this time.

A Bystander (*on the lady's right*) He won't get no cab, not until half-past eleven, missus, when they come back after dropping their theater fares.

92 • Short Story

☑ ONGOING ASSESSMENT: Prerequisite Skills

Students may find the following resources from Chapter 5 particularly helpful in preparing their dramatic scenes.

In the Textbook	Print Resources	Technology
Choosing Your Topic, Section 5.2 Make a Plot Diagram, Section 5.3	*Writing Support Transparencies,* 5-F *Writing Activity Book,* 5-3	*Writing and Grammar* Interactive Text, Sections 5.1–2

Prewriting

Find an Idea You may start with a setting, character, or plot idea. If you like, you can base your drama on another work and adapt it to suit the needs of the stage.

Plan a Plot Decide on the conflict your main character will face and how it will be resolved. Then, organize plot events in chronological order, and think about how you will tie up loose ends.

Story Map

Exposition:
Events: 1. 2. 3.
Climax:
Resolution:

Develop Characters Consider physical appearance, personality traits, likely skills, and speech style as you jot down ideas about each character. Before you begin writing, pause to listen in your head to the characters' dialogue. Try to hear the way each character speaks.

Drafting Look at the excerpt from *Pygmalion* on page 92 for clues to script formatting. Craft your story as much as possible through the actors' words and actions. To do this, experiment with dialects, slang, and informal speech. Say each line of dialogue aloud, and then transcribe it exactly as you spoke it. Once you establish a speech style for a character, keep it consistent throughout the drama, unless you have a particular reason for showing how a character has grown or changed over time.

Revising and Editing Reread your script, focusing first on what happens to whom. Make sure the plot events make sense, that they forward the action of the play, and that they are interesting. Then, revise dialogue to make it realistic and to help develop characters' personalities and reveal their motivations. Also, add or revise stage directions as necessary to provide actors and directors with information about sets, movements, lighting, sound effects, and so on.

Publishing and Presenting Make a clean copy of your script and photocopy it. Distribute copies to peers and hold a script reading for your class.

Connected Assignment: Drama • 93

Customize for *Spatial Learners*

Explain to students that being able to envision the movement of actors on stage is critical to a dramatic performance. The stage directions can be as necessary to the development and realism of the story as is the dialogue. Students should practice the movements they create for their dialogue and see whether everything seems logical.

Integrating Speaking and Listening Skills

Inform students that stage dialogue presents an opportunity for informal speech that would often seem stilted and artificial in prose. However, the actors delivering these lines need to catch the correct voice inflection, and the writer must be aware of the dangers of producing dialogue filled with dialects and slang, for fear that the actors will not be able to make it seem natural for their characters.

Lesson Objectives

1. To write a short story based on a song
2. To deconstruct media to get the main idea of the message's content
3. To recognize how visual and sound techniques or design convey messages in media

Step-by-Step Teaching Guide

Making Connections in the Arts

1. Describe briefly the Spotlight elements included in the text. Have students choose one of the elements to learn more about, either individually or in small groups.

2. Interested students might bring in recordings of songs by Noel Coward and by Gilbert and Sullivan. You might discuss ways in which students think Coward's work was influenced by the earlier artists.

3. Consider showing a video of the film *Brief Encounter* in class. Discuss how various elements of the film, such as plot, conflict, and characters, contribute to its lasting popularity.

Viewing and Representing

Activity Allow time for students to read their short stories to classmates. Students might enjoy figuring out the song on which each story is based.

Critical Viewing

Apply Students' responses should explain the relationship between the man and woman, where they are located, and what they are talking about.

Spotlight on the Humanities

Making Connections in the Arts

Focus on Theater: Sir Noel Coward

Short stories can be read in books, shared in the oral tradition, told through song, or acted out in plays and films. Sir Noel Coward was a master storyteller who wrote in several different media. Not only was Britain's Coward (1899–1973) a playwright, producer, composer, and singer, but he was also an actor. He starred in many of his own plays, which were known for their wit, sophistication, and charm. His first play was produced in 1917, when he was eighteen, and he published his first song at age twenty. Coward's most famous plays include *Private Lives*, *Blithe Spirit*, *Present Laughter*, and *Design for Living*.

Music Connection Noel Coward wrote more than three hundred songs in his career. Known for their ingenious story lines and plays upon words, Coward's songs were inspired by the work of Gilbert and Sullivan. William Gilbert (1836–1911) and Arthur Sullivan (1842–1900) wrote a series of comic operas called the Savoy Operas, which were originally produced at the Savoy Theatre in London during the late nineteenth century. Among their best-known operas are *H.M.S. Pinafore* (1878), *The Pirates of Penzance* 1879), and *The Mikado* (1885).

Film Connection Written by Noel Coward, the film *Brief Encounter* (1945) has become a cinematic classic. Starring Trevor Howard and Dame Celia Johnson, *Brief Encounter* was directed by the legendary David Lean. Dame Celia Johnson was awarded the Best Actress Oscar for her performance in the film as well as the New York Film Critics Circle Award for Best Actress. An accomplished actress on the British stage, Dame Johnson went on to become one of the most famous British actresses of the 1940's based upon her role in this popular, timeless film.

Narrative Writing Activity: Short Story Inspired by a Song

Noel Coward often said that the music of Gilbert and Sullivan inspired many of his songs and story lines. Choose a song that you find particularly inspirational, and write a short story based on it. When finished, read your short story aloud for your classmates.

▲ Critical Viewing Re-create this scene by writing a description of its characters and their costumes. **[Apply]**

94 • Short Story

Media and Technology Skills

Video Adaptation of a Short Story

Activity: Create a Short Film

Many film professionals agree that short stories are ideal source material for effective films. They often contain a clearly focused structure that can be enhanced and illuminated by a transfer to film. The writer, director, designers, and actors work together to bring words on the page to life on a screen.

Think About It Choose a short story of your own or by another writer. Beginning filmmakers should look for stories that are direct and uncomplicated. Even the simplest story will take on layers of complexity when adapted for video. Brainstorm for a list of possibilities. Narrow the list to three strong choices. Have each member of your production team read the stories, and then select one to adapt.

Script It Use these two techniques to build a script for your video adaptation:

• **Storyboard the Action** A storyboard is an illustrated sequence of sketches that shows each scene in your film. Directors use storyboards to plan a film's flow of scenes.

• **Improvise Dialogue** After you decide the flow of scenes, improvise the dialogue by acting out the events in the scene. Transcribe the best lines for use in your script. Improvise an important scene several times with different actors to generate a wealth of possible lines.

"B. Wordsworth" by V. S. Naipaul: Storyboard

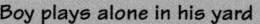
Boy plays alone in his yard

B. Wordsworth appears

Boy hears noise

Shoot It Follow your storyboard as you shoot your film. Make sure that you film each scene in your storyboard, but allow time and tape for unexpected "happy accidents." For example, if you are filming at sunset, think about how this atmospheric setting can enhance your film.

Media and Technology Skills • 95

What You'll Need

• video camera
• single-deck or double-deck videocassette recorder

Styles of Editing

• **In-Camera Editing** Film the scenes in the order of your storyboard. Use fade in/fade out features to form transitions.

• **Post-Shooting Editing** Shoot several versions of each scene. Then, use your recorder's editing features to copy the best takes onto a new tape.

Lesson Objectives

1. To create a video adaptation of a short story
2. To recognize how visual and sound techniques or design convey messages in media
3. To use a variety of forms and technologies to communicate specific messages

Step-by-Step Teaching Guide

Video Adaptation

Teaching Resources: Writing Support Transparencies, 5-K; Writing Support Activity Book, 5-5

1. Emphasize to students the importance of choosing a short story in which the setting, plot, and characters are fairly straightforward. They might consider using a favorite children's book as the basis for their video.

2. Display Transparency 5-K, and use a familiar story to demonstrate how to break down plot elements into scenes for a storyboard.

3. Using the sample scene you displayed on the transparency, have volunteers improvise dialogue between the characters. Tell students that realistic dialogue is the basis for convincing characters.

4. Give students copies of the blank storyboard graphic (5-5). They might benefit from working in pairs, so that partners can evaluate completed storyboards for coherence.

5. Point out in the student text the list of equipment needed and the styles of editing described. When students finish shooting their videos, they will enjoy sharing them with the class. Suggest that they keep a record of techniques that worked well, for future use.

Lesson Objectives

1. To draw upon the distinguishing characteristics of written forms and to write effectively

2. To organize ideas in writing to ensure coherence, logical progression, and support for ideas

3. To use prewriting strategies to generate ideas and plan

4. To compare and contrast elements of texts both within and across texts

Step-by-Step Teaching Guide

Teaching Resources: Standardized Test Preparation Workbook, pp. 9–10

1. Review the basic elements of a short story so that students will be familiar with language that may be used in test prompts, as well as to use in their responses.

2. Point out the importance of budgeting time in most standardized tests. Tell students to decide on a prompt quickly. In a test situation, students will have less time for drafting their responses than they would for a class assignment.

3. As they gather details, students should pay attention to ways details fit together or fall into certain categories. This will help them organize their thoughts as they begin to write a draft.

4. Students might benefit from working in small groups or in pairs on the sample prompts. When they have gathered and organized their details, have groups compare their work with that of other groups.

5. Remind students to leave time during the test to proofread their drafts for coherence and for mechanical errors.

Standardized Test Preparation Workshop

Responding to Questions About Short Stories

Understanding the basic elements of a short story helps you write about them. Some standardized tests will present you with questions evaluating your interpretation of and response to what you have read. Your answers may be in the form of a brief response or a longer essay.

To respond effectively, you should become familiar with the components of a short story. These include its plot—the story's sequence of events; characters—people, animals, or other beings performing the action in the story; setting—the time and place in which the story occurs; and theme—the subject or reoccurring message of the story. Your response will be measured by the following criteria:

- a clearly stated main idea that answers the response
- writing that is focused
- proper language and use of details that skillfully elaborate upon your focus
- correct spelling, grammar, punctuation, and sentence structure

Choose one of the prompts in the following sample writing situation for the short story "The Man Who Shouted Teresa," and write a brief response.

Test Tips

- If you are responding in a timed test, allow yourself enough time to prewrite, revise, and proofread your draft.
- Keep your focus while writing your response. Make sure that you specifically answer the question being asked.

Sample Writing Situations

> Italo Calvino's short stories are famous, in part, for their quirky humor and unique messages about life. "The Man Who Shouted Teresa" fits that mold: It conveys a message about life in a strangely humorous way.
>
> > Explain the ways in which Italo Calvino uses humor to get across the message of "The Man Who Shouted Teresa."
>
> > Would the impact of "The Man Who Shouted Teresa" be different if it were told from the third-person point of view? Why or why not?

96 • Short Story

 TEST-TAKING TIP

Tell students that before choosing a prompt, they should read each one carefully in order to understand fully what they are being asked to do. For example, after reading the first sample prompt, students might quickly try to come up with several examples of humor in the story. For the second prompt, students would need to have a clear understanding of differences between first- and third-person narration. Point out that in responding on tests to most questions about short stories, they will need to have a basic idea about the story's theme or message. Usually, prompts will include some reference to a story's main idea.

Prewriting

Allow about one quarter of your time for prewriting.

Gather Details Writing down details you know about the story will help you give shape to and support your response. The details can consist of character traits, personal observations on theme or setting, or any specific feature you notice in the story (style of writing, overlapping themes, and so on). Taking note of these details will help give shape to your response.

Organize Details Organize your details according to the kind of response you are writing. For example, if you are writing about plot events, you will want to organize details chronologically; if you are comparing and contrasting, you will want to use point-by-point or subject-by-subject organization. If you are making an evaluation, you may want to list your details in order of importance so that your argument builds in intensity.

Drafting

Allow approximately half of your time for drafting.

Use the Story as Support Use details you have from the story to support your opinions. If your topic is about the relationship between the central characters, your details may include examples of dialogue between them, other story characters' observations about the couple, and passages from the story that help indicate their relationship.

Conclude Effectively Write a concluding paragraph that summarizes your main idea. To make your conclusion memorable, you may want to end with a tantalizing question, an astute observation, or an appropriate quotation.

Revising, Editing, and Proofreading

Allow about one quarter of your time for the revising and editing of your paper.

Check Language and Details Carefully review the language in your response to be sure your usage is academic and precise. Keep only those details that are essential to your response; eliminate any unnecessary details you find.

Make Corrections Above all, be sure that your response precisely answers the prompted question. If it does not, fix your response as best you can by crossing out irrelevant details and adding details that answer the question. Then, edit your writing for errors. After fixing errors in grammar, critique the content and style of your response.

Customize for *Less Advanced Students*

Show students some examples of graphic organizers that may help them sort their supporting details visually. For example, if they are responding to a compare-and-contrast prompt, they could list similarities and differences in two columns, and draft each column as a paragraph.

Customize for *AP Students*

Have students practice organizing their supporting details into an outline or some other graphic organizer as they write them down. This helps highlight possibilities for a discussion of interrelationships among thematic ideas, characters, plot events, etc.

Time and Resource Manager

In-Depth Lesson Plan

	LESSON FOCUS	PRINT AND MEDIA RESOURCES
DAY 1	**Introduction to Description** Students learn key elements of descriptive writing and analyze the Model From Literature. (pp. 98–101/H60–61)	*Writers at Work* DVD, Description *Writing and Grammar* Interactive Text, Ch. 6, Introduction
DAY 2	**Prewriting** Students choose and narrow a topic, consider their audience and purpose, and gather information. (pp. 102–105/H62–65)	*Writing and Grammar* Interactive Text, Section 6.2 **Teaching Resources** *Writing Support Transparencies*, 6-A–D; *Writing Support Activity Book*, 6-1; *Topic Bank for Heterogeneous Classes*, Ch. 6
DAY 3	**Drafting** Students organize their ideas and write their first drafts. (pp. 106–107/H66–67)	*Writing and Grammar* Interactive Text, Section 6.3 **Teaching Resources** *Writing Support Transparencies*, 6-E
DAY 4	**Revising** Students revise their drafts in terms of overall structure, paragraphs, sentences, and word choice. (pp. 108–112/H68–72)	*Writing and Grammar* Interactive Text, Section 6.4 **Teaching Resources** *Writing Support Transparencies*, 6-F–G
DAY 5	**Editing and Proofreading; Publishing and Presenting** Students check their work for accuracy and correctness and present their final drafts. (pp. 113–116/H73–74)	*Writing and Grammar* Interactive Text, Sections 6.5–6 **Teaching Resources** *Scoring Rubrics on Transparency*, Ch. 6; *Writing Assessment and Portfolio Management*; *Formal Assessment*, Ch. 6

Accelerated Lesson Plan

	LESSON FOCUS	PRINT AND MEDIA RESOURCES
DAY 1	**Introduction Through Drafting** Students review characteristics of descriptive writing, select topics, and write drafts. (pp. 98–107/H60–67)	*Writing and Grammar* Interactive Text, Ch. 6, Introduction through Section 6.3 **Teaching Resources** *Writing Support Transparencies*, 6-A–E; *Writing Support Activity Book*, 6-1
DAY 2	**Revising Through Presenting** Students work individually or with peers to revise, edit, and proofread their work for presentation. (pp. 108–116/H68–74)	*Writing and Grammar* Interactive Text, Sections 6.4–5 **Teaching Resources** *Writing Support Transparencies*, 6-F–G; *Scoring Rubrics on Transparency*, Ch. 6; *Writing Assessment and Portfolio Management*; *Formal Assessment*, Ch. 6

Options for Adapting Lesson Plans

HOMEWORK

Have students complete any stage of the lesson for homework.

FEATURES

Extend coverage with Connected Assignment (p. 117/H75), Spotlight on the Humanities (p. 118), Media and Technology Skills (p. 119), and the Standardized Test Preparation Workshop (pp. 120–121).

TECHNOLOGY

Students can complete any stage of the lesson on the computer, using *Writing and Grammar* Interactive Text or a word-processing program. Have them print out their completed work.

Writing and Grammar Handbook Alignment

Page numbers in Step-by-Step Teaching Guides in this Teacher's Edition refer to pages from the full student text. Handbook page references, indicated with this icon 🖥, are provided in Time and Resource Manager boxes and at the bottom of each Teacher's Edition page.

INTEGRATED SKILLS COVERAGE

Integrating Grammar
Descriptive Phrases, SE p. 111/🖥71
Commas With Appositives, SE p. 113/🖥73
ATE p. 116

Reading/Writing Connection
Reading: Form Mental Images, SE p. 100
Writing Application, SE p. 101

Viewing and Representing
Critical Viewing, SE pp. 98, 100, 106, 112, 115, 117, 118/🖥60, 66, 72, 75
Appreciating Art, SE p. 118
Evaluating Images, SE p. 119

Speaking and Listening
ATE pp. 104, 110

Real-World Connection
ATE p. 101

Integrating Workplace Skills
ATE p. 101

ASSESSMENT SUPPORT

Standardized Test Preparation Workshop, SE p. 120; ATE p. 110
Standardized Test Preparation Workbook, pp. 11–12
Scoring Rubrics on Transparency, Ch. 6
Formal Assessment, Ch. 6
Writing Assessment and Portfolio Management

MEETING INDIVIDUAL NEEDS

Less Advanced Students ATE pp. 119, 121. See also Ongoing Assessments ATE pp. 103, 107.
AP Students ATE pp. 105, 116, 121
ESL Students ATE pp. 106, 107
Spatial Learners ATE p. 109

BLOCK SCHEDULING

Pacing Suggestions
For 90-minute Blocks
• Have students complete the Prewriting and Drafting stages in a single period.
• Focus one class period on Revising and Editing and Publishing and Presenting. Allow at least 30 minutes for peer revision.

Resources for Varying Instruction
• *Writing and Grammar* **Interactive Text** A 90-minute block provides an ideal opportunity for students to work on the computer.
• *Writers at Work* **DVD** Show the Description segment in class.

Professional Development Support
• *How to Manage Instruction in the Block* This teaching resource provides management and activity suggestions.

MEDIA AND TECHNOLOGY

For the Student
• *Writing and Grammar* **Interactive Text**, Ch. 6
• *On-line Exercise Bank,* Section 19.1

For the Teacher
• *Writers at Work* **DVD**, Description
• **Teacher**EXPRESS™ **CD-ROM**

WRITING AND GRAMMAR ON-LINE

Interactive Text (On-line or on CD-ROM)
• Easily navigable instruction with interactive Revision Checkers
• Full use of e-rater™, the essay-scoring system (on-line only)

Companion Web Site PHSchool.com
• Scoring rubrics with models (use Web Code egk-1201)

See the Go On-line! **feature, SE p. iii.**

LITERATURE CONNECTIONS

Related selections from *Prentice Hall Literature, Penguin Edition,* The British Tradition:
Professional Model Introduction to *Frankenstein,* Mary Wollstonecraft Shelley, SE p. 101
Topic Bank Option from *The Diary,* Samuel Pepys, SE p. 103/🖥63

Lesson Objectives

1. To write a description appropriate to audience and purpose
2. To read to appreciate the writer's craft and to discover models for writing
3. To use prewriting strategies to generate ideas, develop voice, and plan
4. To use writing to refine topics and clarify ideas
5. To develop and revise drafts in terms of structure, paragraphs, sentences, and word choice
6. To edit and proofread to ensure standard English usage and grammar
7. To evaluate how well writing achieves its purposes
8. To refine selected work for publication

Critical Viewing

Interpret Students might use words such as *mountainous, majestic, awe-inspiring, breathtaking, uninhabited, vast,* or *serene.*

Chapter 6 Description

Description in Everyday Life

Words can bring worlds to life. All around you, in day-to-day life, you use words to describe what you see, hear, smell, taste, touch, imagine, and remember. Through the power of description, you can amaze, horrify, or gladden your listeners. You may also use description as a tool, guiding others step by step through a process or in giving directions.

Descriptive writing is part of many other types of writing: You might use description to report on a scientific experiment; explain a historic event; or discuss a painting, story, or movie. Later in life, you might have to describe yourself in a college essay or job application; tell about a product you're trying to sell; write a progress report; or provide a job description.

▲ Critical Viewing
What descriptive words would you choose to describe this landscape? [Interpret]

⏱ TIME AND RESOURCE MANAGER

Resources
Technology: *Writers at Work* DVD, Description; *Writing and Grammar* Interactive Text, Ch. 6

Using the Full Student Edition	Using the Handbook Ⓗ
• Cover pp. 98–101 in class. • Show the Description section of the *Writers at Work* DVD. • Use the Model From Literature to brainstorm for topic ideas with students.	• Cover pp. 60–61 in class. • Show the Description section of the *Writers at Work* DVD.

What Is Description?

Description is writing that appeals to one or more of the five senses—sight, sound, smell, taste, and touch. It can make you smell the smoke from a dying campfire, hear the crickets sing, or see the face of the author's friend. Description can stand on its own or breathe life into other types of writing, such as poems or stories.

Many descriptions contain

- sensory language, appealing to the five senses, which helps create a dominant impression.
- figurative language, such as simile, metaphor, hyperbole, and personification.
- vivid verbs and precise nouns.
- a logical organization.

To preview the criteria on which your description may be evaluated, see the Rubric for Self-Assessment on page 114.

Types of Description

Following are some specific types of description:

- **Functional descriptions** include precise details that objectively describe basic physical characteristics of people, places, and things.
- **Character profiles** describe actual people—their appearance, thoughts, history, accomplishments, and goals.
- **Character sketches** are detailed descriptions of fictional characters. The writer reveals a character's personality and history through description and dialogue.
- **Observations** are firsthand, factual accounts of an event or experience the writer has personally witnessed.

PREVIEW Student Work IN PROGRESS

In this chapter, you'll follow the work of Laura Emily Goldblatt of Princeton High School, in Princeton, New Jersey. Laura's descriptive piece, "Final Night," uses sensory details to convey what a summer at camp meant to her.

Writers in ACTION

Almost all writers use the power of description in their writing. Travel writer Guy Garcia, for example, uses description to enable readers to envision the places, people, and sights he has encountered on his travels throughout the world:

"What I'm trying to convey is the actual experience of being in a new place, . . . of looking at what's around you with a very open appreciation for the sounds, the sights, the emotions that are being triggered by your environment. . . . And if I'm doing that with honesty and clarity, the reader will be drawn along on the journey that I experienced."

Description • 99

PREPARE and ENGAGE

Interest GRABBER Ask students to choose an object in the classroom and write a brief description of it without mentioning it by name. Encourage students to make their descriptions vivid and clear. Have volunteers read their descriptions aloud. Afterward, have the rest of the class try to guess what was being described.

Activate Prior Knowledge

A good description is visual information translated into words. Show students a scene without dialogue from an old film, perhaps a passage from *The Third Man* or from one of Alfred Hitchcock's mysteries. Invite students to imagine they are being interviewed as witnesses about the events in the scene. Can they describe the settings and people in the film in sufficient detail to help the police in their investigations?

More About the Writer

Guy Garcia was born in Los Angeles and attended the University of California at Berkeley. The author of the novel *Obsidian Sky*, he is a contributor to the fiction anthologies *Iguana Dreams* and *Pieces of the Heart*, and lives in New York City. Garcia is featured in the Description section of the *Writers at Work* DVD.

Reading\Writing Connection

Reading: Form Mental Images

The ability to visualize what a writer is describing is essential to effective reading. Borges describes his relationship with the color yellow as one might describe a relationship with a dear friend. He says that yellow has remained "faithful" and that he treasures his "friendship" with the color. What ideas or images do these terms conjure up? What does Borges mean when he says he has a "friendship" with the color yellow? Ask students as they read to note other ways Borges helps his readers "visualize" his experience of blindness.

Step-by-Step Teaching Guide

Engage Students Through Literature

1. Read the Model From Literature aloud or have a prepared student read it.

2. Use questions such as the following to prompt discussion:

   According to Borges, how do most people imagine blindness?

   According to Borges, how does the world really look to the blind?

   Which colors can Borges see? Which ones can't he see?

   Why is Borges so intrigued by the many names for the color scarlet?

3. Ask students which image in the excerpt they find most memorable. Do students think a writer can create images as vivid as those of a painter?

Critical Viewing

Reflect Students' color preferences will vary. Be sure to have students explore why they have a particular color preference.

6.1 Model From Literature

Argentinian Jorge Luis Borges's writings, both fiction and nonfiction, are renowned throughout the world. The following excerpt is from an autobiographical essay entitled "Blindness."

▲ **Critical Viewing**
Of the colors in the photographs above, which do you appreciate most? Why? **[Reflect]**

Reading Writing Connection

Reading Strategy: Form Mental Images
When you read descriptions, pause occasionally to form a mental image of what the author is describing. By doing so, you will be able to more fully understand and appreciate what the author is conveying.

from *Blindness*

Jorge Luis Borges

In the course of the many lectures—too many lectures—I have given, I've observed that people tend to prefer the personal to the general, the concrete to the abstract. I will begin, then, by referring to my own modest blindness. Modest, because it is total blindness in one eye, but only partial in the other. I can still make out certain colors; I can still see blue and green. And yellow, in particular, has remained faithful to me. I remember when I was young I used to linger in front of certain cages in the Palermo zoo: the cages of the tigers and leopards. I lingered before the tigers' gold and black. Yellow is still with me, even now. I have written a poem entitled "The Gold of the Tigers," in which I refer to this friendship.

People generally imagine the blind as enclosed in a black world.

In his opening paragraph, Borges tells readers what his descriptive essay will be about. The remaining paragraphs clearly describe what it is like to "see" through Borges's eyes.

100 • Description

✓ **ONGOING ASSESSMENT: Diagnose**

Use one of the following options to diagnose students' current level of proficiency in descriptive writing.

Option 1 Have each student select an example of his or her descriptive writing from the previous year's writing portfolio. You may wish to hold brief conferences with each student to review and assess these samples.

Option 2 Ask students to write a descriptive paragraph about the scene outside the classroom window. Students who do not include sufficient descriptive detail may need extra help.

There is, for example, Shakespeare's line: "Looking on darkness which the blind do see." If we understand *darkness* as *blackness*, then Shakespeare is wrong.

One of the colors that the blind—or at least this blind man—do *not* see is black; another is red. *Le rouge et le noir* are the colors denied us. I, who was accustomed to sleeping in total darkness, was bothered for a long time at having to sleep in this world of mist, in the greenish or bluish mist, vaguely luminous, which is the world of the blind. I wanted to lie down in darkness. The world of the blind is not the night that people imagine. (I should say that I am speaking for myself, and for my father and my grandmother, who both died blind—blind, laughing, and brave, as I also hope to die. They inherited many things—blindness, for example—but one does not inherit courage. I know that they were brave.)

The blind live in a world that is inconvenient, an undefined world from which certain colors emerge: for me, yellow, blue (except that the blue may be green), and green (except that the green may be blue). White has disappeared, or is confused with gray. As for red, it has vanished completely. But I hope some day—I am following a treatment—to improve and to be able to see that great color, that color which shines in poetry, and which has so many beautiful names in many languages. Think of *scharlach* in German, *scarlet* in English, *escarlata* in Spanish, *écarlate* in French. Words that are worthy of that great color.

Writing Application: Create Mental Images
Before you begin to write your description, think about the words you'll choose to help your readers create mental images.

Vivid words like "bluish mist" and "luminous" help Borges create a mental image for readers.

The use of repetition, such as the word "blind," throughout the essay creates a memorable, dominant impression.

For another nonfiction work containing vivid description, read Mary Wollstonecraft Shelley's introduction to *Frankenstein*. The introduction to *Frankenstein* appears in *Prentice Hall Literature, Penguin Edition*, The British Tradition.

Real-World Connection

Radio reporters, sports announcers, television journalists, and other media professionals are skilled at using words to create images in people's minds. Have students name other fields in which the ability to describe observations in either writing or speaking is an essential skill.

Integrating Workplace Skills

During job interviews, applicants frequently are asked to describe their relevant experiences and talents. Interviewers are more inclined to hire applicants who describe people and events clearly and with detail and precision. Why would the ability to describe things clearly when speaking be an asset in an employee?

More About the Writer

Poet, critic, and short-story writer Jorge Luis Borges was born in Argentina in 1899. Borges helped to found several literary and philosophical journals early in his career. He soon became one of the foremost figures in Latin American and world literature, known mostly for the fantastical dream worlds he created in his short stories.

Reading\Writing Connection

Writing Application: Create Mental Images

Encourage students to use vivid words that appeal to all five senses: sight, sound, smell, taste, and touch. This will help their readers create mental images and become more engaged in the description.

Prewriting: Choose an Unusual Point of View

1. Ask students how the following people might describe the classroom scene:

   an electrician on a ladder

   a journalist from another country

   their great-great-great grandparents

2. Ask students to generate and jot down observations from these points of view.

3. Encourage students to generate a list of additional points of view they might use in their writing.

Prewriting: Blueprint

1. Remind students that blueprints are meant to evoke memories. Students need not worry about accuracy and precision. You might model the process by blueprinting the school library or a local landmark.

2. After students have chosen subjects for their blueprints, encourage volunteers to share their ideas. This may help classmates approach an unfamiliar task with confidence.

Prewriting: Freewrite

Teaching Resources: Writing Support Transparencies, 6-A

1. Display Transparency 6-A and then model the freewriting technique on the board.

2. Assure students that authors often have doubts. Encourage students to be honest and uninhibited in their freewriting.

3. Remind students that they need not be concerned with grammar, spelling, or mechanics when freewriting.

6.2 Prewriting

Choosing Your Topic

The best topics for description are those that are especially vivid or those with which you have a personal connection. Use the following strategies to help you choose a topic:

Strategies for Generating Topics

1. **Choose an Unusual Point of View** Sometimes, it's fun to describe something from a new perspective. What would the ocean look like to a high-flying gull or to a crab burrowing in the sand? Make a list of familiar people, places, and experiences—and then, imagine two or three new perspectives from which you might view each one. Choose the most interesting one as the topic for your description.

2. **Blueprint** Memories associated with places can be especially strong and vivid. Sketch a building or place that holds a special meaning for you. Label each area, and then jot down ideas that spring to mind when you remember that place. Choose your topic from among your notes.

3. **Freewrite** A great way to find out what you want to write about is to just start writing. Write nonstop for five minutes. Then, review your writing, and look for repeated ideas or for interesting ideas. Choose one to use as the topic for your description.

Try it out! Freewrite using the Essay Builder, accessible from the menu bar, on-line or on CD-ROM.

Name: Laura Emily Goldblatt
Princeton High School
Princeton, NJ

Freewriting to Generate a Topic
Laura Emily Goldblatt used the freewriting strategy to help her come up with a descriptive writing topic.

What what what what to write about? I'm not sure nothing interesting ever happens around here. School bus, school fuss. I wish I was back at camp. Crickets, trees, clouds, campfire. Making new friends. Sharing, sharing, sharing. The way we all sat together, what it felt like to be part of a teem. I mean a team. The Red Team. My Team.

102 • Description

⏱ TIME AND RESOURCE MANAGER

Resources
Print: *Writing Support Transparencies, 6-A–D; Writing Support Activity Book, 6-1*
Technology: *Writing and Grammar* Interactive Text, Section 6.2

Using the Full Student Edition	Using the Handbook🅗
• Cover the Prewriting Strategies in class.	• Cover the Prewriting Strategies in class.
• Use the Responding to Fine Art transparency to generate additional topics.	• Use the Responding to Fine Art transparency to generate additional topics.
• Have students narrow their topics and gather details in class.	• Have students narrow their topics and gather details in class.

TOPIC BANK

If no topic for your description comes to mind, consider these topic suggestions:

1. **Description of an Exam Room** Think of a place where you recently took a test. What did you see, hear, and smell? Use specific sensory details in a description that helps your readers join you in that room.

2. **Character Profile of a Friend** Decide on a special friend to portray. Include descriptive details that bring your friend's personality to life. You also may want to include quotations from your friend to illustrate his or her personality and views on life.

Responding to Fine Art

3. Study *Fishing Boats on the Beach at Saintes-Maries* by Vincent van Gogh. Using descriptive details, first describe the painting itself and then describe its mood.

Responding to Literature

4. Samuel Pepys's *Diary* describes the Great Fire of London. Read the diary entry dated September 2, 1666, noting the ways in which Pepys brought that historic event to life. Then, think about an important or exciting event you've witnessed, and write a descriptive account of it. You can find Pepys's *Diary* in *Prentice Hall Literature, Penguin Edition*, The British Tradition.

Fishing Boats on the Beach at Saintes-Maries, Vincent van Gogh, Amsterdam, Van Gogh Museum

🕐 **Timed Writing Prompt**

5. Writers often write about their own experiences. Write a description of the first hour of the first day of twelfth grade. Try to capture the sights, sounds, and feelings that you experienced as you began your final year in high school.
(35 minutes)

Responding to Fine Art

Fishing Boats on the Beach at Saintes-Maries by Vincent van Gogh

Teaching Resources: Writing Support Transparencies, 6-B

1. Display Transparency 6-B and prompt discussion with questions such as these:

   How would someone standing on this beach feel?

   What would it be like to swim here?

   How would sailing these boats differ from being on a cruise ship?

2. Have students make a close examination of this piece of art and list any details they note.

3. Students may include these ideas for description topics along with other ideas in their topic banks.

🕐 **Timed Writing Prompt**

• Remind students that visual images, such as colors, people's faces, and their everyday surroundings, are very powerful and may help them recall specific experiences in their lives.

• To help students describe their experiences, have them come up with one modifier that sums up their first day of high school.

• Suggest that students allow five minutes for prewriting, twenty-five minutes for writing, and five minutes for reviewing and proofreading.

☑ ONGOING ASSESSMENT: Monitor and Reinforce

You may wish to explore the elements of descriptive writing in greater depth with students who have difficulty generating topics.

Option 1 Use *Fishing Boats on the Beach at Saintes-Maries* to prompt a student brainstorming session. Display Transparency 6-B, and ask students to generate lists of adjective-and-noun pairs suggested by the painting (examples: calm water, quiet beach). These may be expanded into topic ideas.	**Option 2** Supply students with real-world examples of descriptive writing to jog their imaginations, such as the travel writing of John McPhee in *Coming into the Country* or the clinical observations of Oliver Sacks in *The Man Who Mistook His Wife for a Hat*.

⏱ TIME SAVERS!

**Writing Support
Transparencies**
Use the transparencies for Chapter 6 to facilitate the teaching of strategies.

Step-by-Step Teaching Guide

Prewriting: Narrowing Your Topic

1. You may wish to distribute unlined drawing paper and materials such as colored pencils and thin-lined markers.

2. Encourage students to label their drawings and jot down thoughts directly on their drawings.

3. Invite students to share their drawings and thoughts with partners before using them to direct their own writing.

Step-by-Step Teaching Guide

Prewriting: Considering Your Audience and Purpose

Teaching Resources: Writing Support Transparencies, 6-C

1. Display the transparency (6-C) and ask students to note similarities and differences between the two versions.

2. Ask students to consider why someone might choose to write in one style rather than another. How might the needs and expectations of readers affect this choice?

3. Suggest that students reflect on the tone they adopt when writing a letter to a friend, a business letter, and a thank-you note to a relative. How do the purpose and audience affect the way each of these is written?

Integrating Speaking and Listening Skills

Read aloud from examples of speeches for different purposes and audiences, such as a news broadcast or an award-acceptance speech. Have students consider the nonverbal cues, such as gestures and facial expressions, that speakers use to convey their desired tone.

Narrowing Your Topic

Once you know the general topic you want to describe, take time to narrow your description. You might choose to describe just one moment of an event or experience, just one part of a place, or just one aspect of a person.

Drawing can also help you narrow your topic.

Draw to Narrow a Topic

Make a sketch of the person, place, or event you're describing to help you bring details into focus. Don't worry about how well you draw—you never have to show your sketch to anyone else. Just think about the details that you'd like to include when you paint a picture in words.

Refer to your completed drawing as you gather details, draft, and revise your description.

Considering Your Audience and Purpose

Think about who will read your description and your purpose for writing it. What do you want your audience to feel, think, or understand when they have finished reading your description? Choose words and details that will appeal to your audience and help you to achieve your purpose for writing.

In the examples below, notice how different word choices help to achieve different purposes.

Purpose:
To Attract
The air was clear and crisp, and leaves crunched beneath my feet. The scent of burning leaves hung faintly in the air. As I entered the woods, a sudden darkness fell, and even the leaves seemed to hush in response.

Purpose:
To Amuse
The crisp air assaulted my nose, and the roar of leaves underfoot nearly deafened me. The stench of burnt leaves overpowered me as I ran for the woods. Once inside the woods, a dark cloak mercifully drowned out the raucousness of the bright autumn day, and I was able to think.

104 • Description

⏱ Timed Writing Hint

Read the prompt carefully to determine how to narrow your topic for a descriptive essay.

Gathering Details

Details bring a description to life. Sensory details can help your readers see, hear, smell, taste, and touch—right along with you. Use the following strategy to generate sensory details:

Use All Five Senses

Sometimes, we rely so much on our eyes that we forget about our other senses. Think of what you're describing. Then, shut your eyes. What do you hear, smell, taste, and feel? Sit inside the experience for a few minutes. Next, list the other four senses, and jot down at least two details relating to each.

Writers in
ACTION

Famed writer Joseph Conrad says this about the power of description:

"My task . . . is, by the power of the written word, to make you hear, to make you feel—it is, before all, to make you see."

Student Work
IN PROGRESS

Name: Laura Emily Goldblatt
Princeton High School
Princeton, NJ

Using All Five Senses

Laura listed each of the five senses and challenged herself to come up with at least two details relating to each. Although Laura didn't use all of these images in her final draft, she liked having them there to choose from.

SIGHT	HEARING	SMELL	TASTE	TOUCH
clouds hang suspended like marionettes	crickets singing a duet with the wind	tang of smoke in the air	taste of smoke in your mouth as you smell it	crushed leaves between our fingers
red and white uniforms side by side	crackle of the campfire	the smell of rich earth	the clean, fresh air	cold autumn air
glancing across the schism to see a friend's face	wind whistling	burnt wood	mountain water	hard earth

---

Prewriting: Use All Five Senses

Teaching Resources: Writing Support Transparencies, 6-D; Writing Support Activity Book, 6-I

1. Begin this activity by having students read Laura's list of sensory images. Then ask students to close their books, and challenge them to reconstruct the list by category, from memory.

2. Give students copies of the blank sensory language chart. Invite students to observe their surroundings and list their impressions in the chart.

3. Have students make a similar chart for their topics. Suggest that they do the "Sight" column last to discourage them from relying too heavily on visual images.

More About the Writer

Joseph Conrad was born in Poland. At age sixteen, he went to sea, learned English, and became a sea captain. At age thirty-two, he began to write. Though his writing did not bring him fame in his lifetime, he is now regarded as one of the great writers of the English language. Conrad's story "The Lagoon" can be found in *Prentice Hall Literature, Penguin Edition,* The British Tradition.

Customize for
AP Students

Encourage students to explore the work of Joseph Conrad. They may appreciate *Lord Jim,* a novel about an Englishman in a remote land who attempts to atone for an act of desertion by making sacrifices for others.

⏱ TIME SAVERS!

Writing Support Transparencies
Use the transparencies for Chapter 6 to facilitate the teaching of strategies.

Writing Support Activity Book
Use the graphic organizers for Chapter 6 to facilitate student planning.

Drafting: Choose a Point of View

1. Make a three-column chart on the board, headed with each of the three points of view described on this page.

2. Have students list common characteristics of each point of view in the appropriate columns. (For example, first-person writing might be honest, intimate, or confessional. Third-person limited writing might be objective and impersonal.)

3. Have students share and discuss their answers. When they feel they have a clear understanding of each point of view, ask them to choose the one that best suits their topics.

Critical Viewing

Analyze Ask students to consider how descriptions of this scene would differ if written from the first-person, third-person limited, or third-person omniscient point of view.

Customize for
ESL Students

You may wish to have students review personal pronouns in Chapter 17. Suggest that they generate a list of pronouns that signal each of the three points of view presented. (First person: *I, mine, me*. Third person: *his, her, its, their, they, them*.)

6.3 Drafting

Shaping Your Writing
Choose a Point of View

Choose a point of view from which to write your description. Different points of view will give you access to different kinds of details and create different emotional effects. Choosing to write in the first person, using the pronoun *I*, may bring your readers closer to your experience. The third-person limited point of view gives your writing less of a personal feel. The third-person omniscient point of view allows you to show the same event or person from many different angles.

If you're describing a person—for example, your best friend—you might write from the *first-person point of view:*

> I was glad to be able to attend the concert, which was sure to be a record-breaking event. As I watched, thousands upon thousands of people streamed into the park, lugging hampers. . . .

If you were to write the same passage from the *third-person limited point of view,* you would adhere to a single point of view, but avoid the use of the pronoun *I*.

> The concert at the park was a record-breaking event. Thousands upon thousands of concert-goers streamed into the park at six o'clock, lugging hampers and chairs. . . .

Yet another choice is the *third-person omniscient point of view,* with a narrator who sees and knows everything. This point of view is usually used in fiction.

> The concert at the park was a record-breaking event. Stephanie Othaller and her children felt very lucky to have tickets. Her neighbor, however, was extremely envious, although she tried to hide her feelings from Stephanie.

▲ **Critical Viewing**
From what point of view would you choose to write a description of the scene in this photograph? Why?
[Analyze]

⏱ TIME AND RESOURCE MANAGER

Resources
Print: *Writing Support Transparencies,* 6-E
Technology: *Writing and Grammar* Interactive Text, Section 6.3

Using the Full Student Edition	Using the Handbook Ⓗ
• Explore the different points of view described on p. 106. • Use the photograph on p. 106 to have students practice writing from each point of view. • Have students draft their descriptions in class.	• Explore the different points of view described on p. 66. • Use the photograph on p. 66 to have students practice writing from each point of view. • Have students draft their descriptions in class.

Providing Elaboration

As you draft your description, help your readers feel that they know, have seen, or have experienced your topic for themselves. One way to provide such depth in your writing is to use a technique known as "depth charging."

Use Depth Charging

When you use depth charging, you provide explanations and examples that develop or support your observations or ideas. This strategy also helps ensure that your writing will be unified—that the details given all flow together in a logical way.

To use the depth charging strategy:
- Write a sentence about your topic.
- Identify a word or idea within that sentence to further develop, and write a sentence that does so.
- Identify a word or idea within the second sentence that you would like to further develop, and write a sentence that does so.
- Repeat the process until the paragraph is complete.

Student Work
IN PROGRESS

Name: _Laura Emily Goldblatt_
Princeton High School
Princeton, NJ

Using Depth Charging to Elaborate
Laura used depth charging as she began drafting her description.

Our (friends) are the reason we come back year after year. They have (shared) our joys, defeats, sorrows, and triumphs. There are few people who will ever know us with the same (intensity) as the friends we've formed bonds with here. We all fear that they will slip through our fingers like crushed leaves when the solitude of autumn sets in.

> When depth charging, Laura circled key words as she drafted, then wrote sentences that elaborated on those key ideas.

Drafting • 107

Drafting: Use Depth Charging

Teaching Resources: Writing Support Transparency, 6-E

1. Review the steps of the depth-charging strategy shown on page 107.
2. Display Transparency 6-E to show how Laura used depth charging to develop her description.
3. Model the strategy for the class by writing a sentence on the board or on the transparency. Ask students what word or idea should be further developed. Write a sentence about that idea. Repeat these steps for two or three more sentences.
4. Note to students that the depth-charging strategy, by strongly linking ideas from one sentence to the next, will keep students' descriptive paragraphs unified and focused.

Customize for
ESL Students

Attending to conventions of English grammar and usage while attempting to write descriptively can be challenging for those learning English. Encourage students to draft their descriptions in their original languages. They can translate their work into English later; it is important that they get their ideas down first.

☑ ONGOING ASSESSMENT: Monitor and Reinforce

If students have difficulty elaborating on their ideas, try one of the following options.

Option 1 Have students choose a sentence from their drafts and write it at the top of a piece of paper. Then, have them freewrite about it for five minutes. They can then review it and pull interesting details to use in their drafts.

Option 2 Some students might benefit from talking about their ideas. Give them five minutes to meet with partners and ask each other questions about their topics.

Revising: Creating a Dominant Impression

1. Make sure students understand the concept of "dominant impression" by having them define it in their own words. (Students might say *overall feeling* or *tone*.)

2. Refer students to the Student Work in Progress on this page. Point out that the details about the red and white teams help to illustrate Laura's main idea, the atmosphere of cooperation and unity among team members.

Revising: Circling Details to Identify Function

Teaching Resources: Writing Support Transparencies, 6-F

1. Students might have trouble determining which details are relevant and which are not.

2. Display Transparency 6-F and discuss how Laura made this determination. For example, she removed the word *stifling* because it suggests an atmosphere that is smothering rather than one that is close and nurturing.

3. Remind students to pay attention to word connotations and make sure they suggest the dominant impression of the piece.

6.4 Revising

Read your draft critically, and revise it where necessary. Check to be sure that your description's overall structure, paragraphs, sentences, and words work together to create a unified whole.

Revising Your Overall Structure

Create a Dominant Impression

The details in your description should work together to shape a dominant impression—the main idea or overall impact you want to form in the minds of your readers.

▶ **REVISION STRATEGY**
Circling Details to Identify the Function

Circle in red pencil the details in your draft that contribute to your description's dominant impression. Circle in blue pencil any details that do not directly convey that main impression. Consider replacing or deleting passages circled in blue to give your description a specific focus and to strengthen the dominant impression you'd like to make.

Timed Writing Hint

When revising your writing under timed conditions, delete details that do not add to the impression you are trying to create and insert details that do.

Student Work IN PROGRESS

Name: *Laura Emily Goldblatt*
Princeton High School
Princeton, NJ

Circling Details to Identify Function

Laura used circling to identify details that did not help create a dominant impression. Notice how she revised her description accordingly.

Laura wanted to create a harmonious dominant impression. She rewrote passages that did not add to the piece's sense of harmony.

The red team and white team sit (parallel) across from to each other, and yet there is such a sense of unity that is (stifling). For ten weeks, we have been a single unit. as one. No longer are we only for ourselves, (but for everyone) and thus we 've learned are (forced) to be unselfish. ness Leaders emerge and we accept their authority, (allowing) ourselves to follow their (command) lead The emphasis is placed on (spirit and sportsmanship,) not just winning.

⏱ TIME AND RESOURCE MANAGER

Resources
Print: *Writing Support Transparencies*, 6-F–G
Technology: *Writing and Grammar* Interactive Text, Section 6.4

Using the Full Student Edition	Using the Handbook🅷
• Work through Revision Strategies in class. Use Transparencies 6-F–G as examples of these strategies. • Give students time in class to revise their work.	• Work through Revision Strategies in class. Use Transparencies 6-F–G as examples of these strategies. • Give students time in class to revise their work.

Revising Your Paragraphs

Revise for Impact and Unity

Read through your description, and locate topical paragraphs—paragraphs that are organized around a topic sentence. Check to be sure that your topic sentence is placed effectively within the paragraph. Also, check to be sure that each sentence in your paragraph supports its topic sentence.

A topic sentence may appear anywhere in the paragraph: at the beginning, in the middle, or at the end. The topic sentence may create different effects on the reader, depending on its position within the paragraph.

Topic sentence as opener: *The twentieth century will be known as the Information Age.* The advent of the radio, television, fax machine, business and personal computers, and the Internet all serve to share information and speed its transmission. Via television satellites, we watch wars unfold before our eyes, and vast stores of knowledge are a mouse click away on the Internet.

Topic sentence as closer: The advent of the radio, television, fax machine, business and personal computers, and the Internet all serve to share information and speed its transmission. Via television satellites, we watch wars unfold before our eyes, and vast stores of knowledge are a mouse click away on the Internet. *In fact, the twentieth century will be known as the Information Age.*

▶ REVISION STRATEGY
Color-Coding Topic Sentences and Support

Read through your draft, and use a highlighter to call out topic sentences. Then, examine the placement of the topic sentences to be sure they are in the most logical, effective positions. Then, in another color, highlight the details that support the topic sentence. Delete or move to another paragraph any details that do not support the topic sentence.

I like Dale a lot, because she's someone I can count on. Once I was home sick for three weeks with pneumonia. Dale came by my house every single day to make sure I was all right, even when she wasn't allowed to see me. ~~My mother is sometimes overprotective.~~ When I started getting better, she brought me comic books and videotapes to help me pass the time. She even brought me my homework assignments—though I wished she hadn't!

⊙ Technology Tip

In a word-processing program, highlight and drag topic sentences to various positions within a paragraph. Then, examine how each position affects the impact of the topic sentence on your writing.

Revising: Revise for Impact and Unity

1. Ask students to explain the relationship between the topic sentence, "The twentieth century will be known as the Information Age," and the paragraph that follows it. (The other sentences give examples of developments that would lead to that conclusion.)

2. Ask students how the placement of the topic sentence at the beginning or the end of the example paragraphs changes the impression that each paragraph creates. (Having the topic sentence at the beginning alerts the reader to the information to come. Having the topic sentence at the end brings the previous details into a central focus.)

Revising: Color-Coding Topic Sentences and Support

1. Prompt discussion with questions such as these:

   Which is the topic sentence in this example? (The first.)

   What details help support the central idea of the topic sentence? (Dale was a devoted friend to the narrator when he or she was ill.)

2. Ask students to share topic sentences from their own drafts. Invite students to help give suggestions for revision to classmates who are having difficulty identifying the central ideas of their paragraphs.

Customize for
Spatial Learners

Encourage students to make cluster diagrams or other schematic outlines of their paragraphs to show the relationship between the topic sentence and the supporting details.

Revising: Adding Detail With Appositives

Teaching Resources: Writing Support Transparencies, 6-G

1. Ask students to compare the sample sentences on page 110. How does the addition of the words "my best friend" change the sentence? (It highlights the writer's relationship with the subject and involves him or her more closely with the action.)

2. Invite students to consider how using appositives to combine two short, choppy sentences can improve a piece of writing. (Longer sentences can prevent unnecessary interruptions.)

Integrate Speaking and Listening Skills

Encourage students to read their revised sentences aloud. Suggest that they listen to the rhythm to make sure they haven't used too may short and choppy or long and involved sentences.

6.4

Revising Your Sentences

Add Descriptive Details to Your Sentences

Read through the sentences in your description, and add descriptive details, where necessary, to further explain, identify, or describe your topic. Descriptive details may include vivid nouns and verbs, adjectives and adverbs, quotations, and figurative language. Use the following strategy to add a specific type of descriptive detail to your writing.

▶ **REVISION STRATEGY**
Adding Details With Appositives

Appositives—nouns or pronouns that identify or rename other nouns or pronouns—are a good way to offer more detail about the person, place, or object being described. Examine your draft, and add appositives where more detail is necessary.

Original Sentence:
Dale finally finished the climb.

Sentence With an Appositive Phrase:
Dale, *my best friend,* finally finished the climb.

Student Work
IN PROGRESS

Name: *Laura Emily Goldblatt*
Princeton High School
Princeton, NJ

Adding Details With Appositives
As she reread her work, Laura began to feel that she had not fully conveyed how deep the camp friendships ran or how profound her experience had been. She added some appositives to develop her ideas.

A phoenix rising from the ashes, we , the Red Team, emerge, reborn and fresh after each trial, prepared to face the world again with our friends beside us.

⬦ STANDARDIZED TEST PREPARATION WORKSHOP

Appositives Standardized test questions may require students to determine which words in a sentence are appositives. Provide students with opportunities to practice finding appositives in descriptive writing.

Identify the appositive in the sentence.

Although it was brand new, the car, a sedan, was slow and unreliable.

A the car	**C** new
B a sedan	**D** unreliable

Students should recognize that **B** is the correct answer because "a sedan" adds information to the noun "car" and it is set off by commas. Students should also recognize that A is the subject of the sentence, and that C and D are adjectives.

Grammar in Your Writing
Descriptive Phrases

There are many ways to add descriptive details to your writing. Adjective phrases are prepositional phrases that modify a noun or pronoun by telling *what kind* or *which one*. Appositives and appositive phrases rename, identify, or explain the nouns or pronouns they are near.

Below, you'll learn how to identify appositives and appositive phrases and use them in your writing.

Appositives The word *appositive* comes from a Latin verb that means "to put near or next to." An **appositive** is, literally, a noun or pronoun that is put next to another noun or pronoun in order to identify, rename, or explain it.

His best quality, honesty, had always served him well.

The writer Ursula LeGuin is known for her science fiction.

Appositive Phrases When an appositive is accompanied by its own modifiers, it forms an appositive phrase. An **appositive phrase** is a noun or pronoun with modifiers, placed next to another noun or pronoun, in order to add information and details. The modifiers can be adjectives, adjective phrases, or other groups of words that function as adjectives.

Wilma Rudolph, my favorite athlete, was a great runner.

Marc introduced us to The Half-Baked Band, a group of musicians who had just returned from their world tour.

Find It in Your Reading Like appositive phrases, which rename nouns and pronouns, adjective phrases also add descriptive details to writing. Read through the excerpt from "Blindness" by Jorge Luis Borges on pages 100–101, and locate two adjective phrases. Why might Borges have chosen to use adjective phrases rather than appositive phrases there? Explain.

Find It in Your Writing Review your draft to find at least two appositives. If you can't find two appositives, challenge yourself to add them. See whether adding appositives makes your description stronger.

For more on appositives and appositive phrases, see Chapter 19.

Descriptive Phrases

1. Point out to students that adjective phrases, appositives, and appositive phrases are all identifiers that tell the reader more about a person, place, or thing.

2. Illustrate how useful the additional information in an appositive phrase can be. Ask students to imagine they are being seated at a formal party. Write these two statements on the board and discuss how they differ.

   Juan Rodriguez will be at your table.

   Juan Rodriguez, the famous writer, will be at your table.

3. Encourage students to find appositives and appositive phrases in the Final Draft on pages 115–116. Have them share examples that they discover in their own writing.

Find It in Your Reading

Answers will vary. Sample answers: *in one eye; of the tigers and leopards. Borges may have wished to add descriptive detail about certain nouns without restating or renaming them. Adjective phrases accomplish this purpose.*

Find It in Your Writing

Encourage students to team up and locate appositives in each other's writing. This gives writers an opportunity to focus on meaning in others' writing rather than solely on structure and mechanics.

✓ ONGOING ASSESSMENT: Prerequisite Skills

If students have difficulty recognizing adjective and appositive phrases, you may find it helpful to refer them to the following materials to ensure coverage of prerequisite knowledge.

In the Textbook	Print Resources	Technology
Prepositional Phrases and Appositives, Section 19.1	*Grammar Exercise Workbook,* pp. 33–36	*On-Line Exercise Bank,* Section 19.1

Revising: Circling and Replacing Words to Create a Tone

1. Before they revise, discuss with students the definitions of *connotation* and *denotation*.

2. Ask students to focus on a current political conflict in the news and to characterize the incident from a sympathetic, an unsympathetic, and a neutral point of view. Record the key words they use in a three-column chart on the board.

3. Supply students with a word such as *happy* and encourage them to generate as many synonyms as possible. As examples, use the words *ecstatic* and *pleased*.

4. Ask students to consider the differences among these words. What, for example, is suggested by *ecstatic* that is absent from the more matter-of-fact *pleased*?

Revising: Peer Review

1. Have peers talk about the vivid impressions they got from the writing. This will tell the writers which descriptive details were most successful.

2. Have peers ask each other questions about the parts that were unclear to them. This will direct the writer to attend to places where the point of view or other details may have been confusing.

Critical Viewing

Compare and Contrast Students should note that regardless of the arrangement or number of people present, peer editing involves classmates working together to help one another.

Revising Your Word Choice

Revise Word Choice to Create a Tone

Different words evoke different moods and emotions, allowing writers to create various tones, or attitudes, toward their writing subjects. You may have heard this word joke:

> I am *strong-minded*. (admiring tone)
>
> You are *stubborn*. (neutral tone)
>
> He is *pig-headed*. (critical tone)

Although "strong-minded," "stubborn," and "pig-headed" all mean more or less the same thing, each word conveys a different tone, or attitude, the writer has toward "I," "you," and "he." Use the following strategy to give your description a definite tone:

▶ **REVISION STRATEGY**

Circling and Replacing Words to Create a Tone

Read through your description, and circle words or passages that don't adequately convey your attitude. Use a dictionary, thesaurus, or your own memory to locate two or three synonyms or equivalent phrases. Then, make the choice that best projects the tone you intend.

Peer Review

Share Responses

Show your revised work to a group of peers, asking them to read your description carefully with an open mind. Then, ask them the following:

- Did I use enough sensory language and descriptive details to describe my subject fully? Explain.

- Was my point of view consistent and appropriate? Explain.

- What dominant impression did the description leave?

If your classmates understood your work differently from the way you intended, consider revising your draft to better achieve your original purpose.

112 • Description

▼ Critical Viewing How does this peer conference compare to ones with which you've been involved? **[Compare and Contrast]**

6.5 Editing and Proofreading

Errors in your description might mean that your audience will pay more attention to your mistakes than to the topic about which you're writing. Fix errors in spelling, punctuation, and grammar before you create your final draft.

Focusing on Mechanics

As you proofread, check to be sure that you have used commas in sentences correctly. Pay particular attention to appositives and appositive phrases to be sure you've correctly punctuated them.

Grammar in Your Writing
Commas With Appositives

To punctuate appositives and appositive phrases correctly, refer to the following rules:

> 1. An **essential appositive** is one that is necessary to the meaning of the sentence. It does not need commas.
>
> **Example:** The movie star Cary Grant is one of my favorites.
>
> Since the sentence does not make sense without the words *Cary Grant*, you don't need commas around the appositive.

> 2. A **nonessential appositive** or **appositive phrase** is one that can be removed without changing the sentence's meaning. It must always be set off with commas.
>
> **Example:** The real name of Cary Grant, one of my favorite stars, was Archibald Leach.
>
> **Example:** After the movie, we ate at Mr. Louis's, the restaurant with the best fries in the city.

Find It in Your Writing As you proofread your descriptive essay, double-check your punctuation of appositives and appositive phrases.

For more on punctuating appositives, see Chapter 19.

Editing and Proofreading • 113

Editing and Proofreading

1. Point out that proofreading requires more than one review. Encourage students to read their work several times, looking for a different type of error each time.

2. Remind students that good writing is a reflection of the care that a writer has taken to be understood. Discuss the effect that careless errors have on the readers of an otherwise well thought out and deeply felt piece of writing.

Commas With Appositives

1. Write the following sentence on the board.

   Ronny Swift gives away baseball tickets to schoolchildren.

   Point out to students that it is not clear who Ronny Swift is. Therefore, it is also unclear why he gives away baseball tickets.

2. Ask students to add an appositive phrase to give this sentence a fuller meaning.

   Ronny Swift, the centerfielder for the Newark Eagles, gives away baseball tickets to schoolchildren.

3. Have students share some of the examples of appositives and appositive phrases they find in "Final Night" and in their own writing.

Find It in Your Writing

Remind students that essential appositives need not be set off by commas.

⏱ TIME AND RESOURCE MANAGER

Resources
Print: *Scoring Rubrics on Transparency,* Ch. 6; *Writing Assessment and Portfolio Management; Formal Assessment,* Ch. 6
Technology: *Writing and Grammar* Interactive Text, Section 6.5

Using the Full Student Edition	Using the Handbook 🄷
• Review p. 113 in class, including Grammar in Your Writing. • Read and discuss p. 114. • Analyze the Final Draft on pp. 115–116. • Have students edit and proofread their essays in class.	• Review p. 73 in class, including Grammar in Your Writing. • Read and discuss p. 74. • Have students edit and proofread their essays in class.

Publishing and Presenting

1. Suggest that students submit their essays to the school literary magazine or to a Web site that posts student writing.

2. Invite students to answer the reflective questions in small groups rather than individually or as a whole-class discussion. This allows students to share ideas in an informal, low-risk environment.

ASSESS and CLOSE

Assessment

Teaching Resources: Scoring Rubrics on Transparency, Ch. 6; Writing Assessment and Portfolio Management; Formal Assessment, Ch. 6

1. Display the Scoring Rubric transparency and review the criteria in class.

2. Before students proceed with self-assessment, you may wish to review the Final Draft of the Student Work in Progress on pp. 115–116.

3. In addition to student self-assessment, you may wish to use the following options:

   • score the essays yourself, using the rubric and scoring models in *Writing Assessment and Portfolio Management.*

   • review the Standardized Test Preparation Workshop on pp. 120–121 and have students complete the practice test.

   • administer the Chapter 6 assessment in *Formal Assessment* to measure students' grasp of concepts presented.

6.6 Publishing and Presenting

Share your finished description with others. Following are some ideas for publishing and presenting your work:

Building Your Portfolio

1. **Illustration of Your Description** Illustrate your description with a drawing, sketch, photograph, or painting. Then, protect your work with a binder, and display it in the class library.

2. **Local Publication** Look through local publications to see whether your profile of a resident or your description of the county fair might find a home. Call or write to the editor for information on how to submit your work.

Reflecting on Your Writing

Reflect on your experience of writing a description by answering these questions. Save your responses in your portfolio.

• What strategies for finding and narrowing a topic seem most useful to you? Explain.

• What advice would you give to someone who was going to write a description?

Internet Tip

To see a descriptive essay scored according to this rubric, go on-line:
PHSchool.com
Enter Web Code:
egk-1201

Rubric for Self-Assessment

Use the following criteria to evaluate your description.

	Score 4	Score 3	Score 2	Score 1
Audience and Purpose	Contains details that work together to create a single, dominant impression of the topic	Creates through use of details a dominant impression of the topic	Contains extraneous details that detract from the main impression	Contains details that are unfocused and create no dominant impression
Organization	Is organized consistently, logically, and effectively	Is organized consistently	Is organized, but not consistently	Is disorganized and confusing
Elaboration	Contains creative use of descriptive details	Contains many descriptive details	Contains some descriptive details	Contains no descriptive details
Use of Language	Contains sensory language that appeals to the five senses; contains no errors in grammar, punctuation, or spelling	Contains some sensory language; contains few errors in grammar, punctuation, and spelling	Contains some sensory language, but it appeals to only one or two of the senses; contains some errors in grammar, punctuation, and spelling	Contains no descriptive details; contains many errors in grammar, punctuation, and spelling

114 • Description

☑ ONGOING ASSESSMENT: Assess Mastery

Use one of the following options to assess students' descriptive writing.

In the Textbook	Technology
Self-Assessment Ask students to score their essays using the rubric provided. Then, have them write a paragraph that discusses the strategy they found most helpful in composing their essays.	**Teacher Assessment** Use the rubric and the scoring models provided in *Writing Assessment and Portfolio Management* to score students' work.

6.7 Student Work IN PROGRESS

FINAL DRAFT

Final Night

Laura Emily Goldblatt
Princeton High School
Princeton, New Jersey

Summer's end 1999

I look around the campfire at the friends I've made this summer, and I wonder how I'll ever be able to say goodbye to these people, this place. There is so much here that I love. At night you can hear the crickets singing a duet with the wind as it swirls past the trees, while the clouds hang suspended like marionettes. In fact, if you hold still a moment, you can smell the rich earth on which you sit.

▲ **Critical Viewing**
Why might an event like the one in the photograph provide lasting memories? **[Connect]**

Sensory details such as "crickets singing a duet with the wind," "clouds hang suspended like marionettes," and "smell the rich earth on which you sit" help to create a dominant impression.

Final Draft

1. Help students see that "Final Night" incorporates key elements of the descriptive essay:
   - Audience and purpose have been carefully considered, and word choice is suited to the writer's nostalgic tone.
   - The central ideas of the essay and of each paragraph are expressed in unifying topic sentences.
   - Description is conveyed by the use of a variety of sensory images.
   - The main impression is extended and elaborated with carefully chosen details.

2. Ask students to describe the impression that this piece of writing made on them. Did it remind them of any events in their own lives?

3. Ask students whether there are any changes they would make to this essay to make it more effective or powerful. How might they apply these suggestions to their own writing?

Critical Viewing

Connect Students might say that spending a joyful night with close friends is always a memorable event.

115

Integrating Grammar Skills

Semicolon Point out the use of the semicolon between the words *ourselves* and *we've* in the second paragraph on this page. Explain to students that a semicolon is one way to connect two independent clauses. Another way is to use a comma and a coordinating conjunction.

Teaching From the Final Draft

In the third paragraph, Laura describes a moment that makes her think, "This is perfection." Have students write a descriptive paragraph or essay about a moment in their own lives that made them feel the same way. They might start by brainstorming for a list of joyful events in their lives.

Customize for
AP Students

Laura refers to a phoenix that rises from the ashes. Challenge students to research the origin of this symbol. Suggest that they look in the library or on the Internet for a dictionary of mythology. Have them share their findings with the class. This might help them understand Laura's simile.

This past week, the red team and white team were challenged to the utmost, vying for "The Golden Branch," the camp's highest honor. Now, in the glow of firelight, the red team and white team sit opposite each other, yet there is a powerful sense of togetherness.

For ten weeks, the teams have shared triumph and failure. We no longer look out only for ourselves; we've learned unselfishness. Leaders emerge and we accept their authority, allowing ourselves to follow their lead. Emphasis is placed upon spirit and sportsmanship, not just upon winning. We take our losses with smiles and cheer for the winning team. Our pride expands infinitely until everything seems possible.

This camp is no ordinary place. The fields are alive; they move with us in silent cycles that only those of us willing to watch patiently can see. Each of us has had a moment that we felt the earth around us, closed our eyes, and thought, "This is perfection."

Unlike other competing groups, we are small, closely united. Everyone knows everyone, if not by name, by sight. Even now, divided as we are, people sneak glances at one another across the schism. Camp, this camp, teaches us more about who we are, where we're going, and who we're taking with us than an entire lifetime can. Soon, a single glance reveals exactly what a person is feeling. Words become unnecessary as we sit knowing that no matter how far we fall, there will always be someone there to catch us. Like a phoenix, we, the red and white teams, rise from the ashes, reborn and refreshed after each trial, prepared to face the world again with our friends beside us.

Our friends are the reason that we come back year after year. They have shared in our joys, defeats, sorrows, and triumphs. There are few people who will ever know us with the same intensity as the friends we've formed bonds with here. We all fear that they will slip through our fingers like crushed leaves when the solitude of autumn sets in. But even if not a word is exchanged between us after that final good-bye, the emotions we have shared will last a lifetime. And so, at night, as we lie alone in our rooms, barren without the presence of our friends, our memories will creep up from under our eyelids, fly to the heavens, kiss the distances between us away, and we will once again be here together at camp.

Laura has logically organized her description, presenting one main idea with its accompanying details in each paragraph.

This instance of personification—"the fields are alive"—creates a vivid image in readers' minds.

A vivid verb and a precise noun are provided in the phrase "sneak glances."

This simile, in which campers are compared to a phoenix, helps readers understand how this experience transformed the people who shared it.

The final sentence of Laura's description is powerful and memorable.

Connected Assignment Poem

Successful descriptive writing makes readers feel as if they are seeing, hearing, feeling, smelling, or tasting just what the writing describes. Poems can achieve a similar effect, with words carefully chosen to create a picture for readers. Poets, too, focus particularly on the form and sound of words, and because poetry is generally brief, each word really counts.

Let the writing process skills described below guide you in writing your own poem.

Prewriting Read over journal entries to recall experiences that generated strong emotions, or talk with a friend about what makes you especially optimistic or somber. Choose one of those ideas to be the subject of your poem.

Then, brainstorm for sensory images that will help you bring the subject of your poem to life. Push yourself to go beyond visual images by completing a sensory language chart like the one shown here.

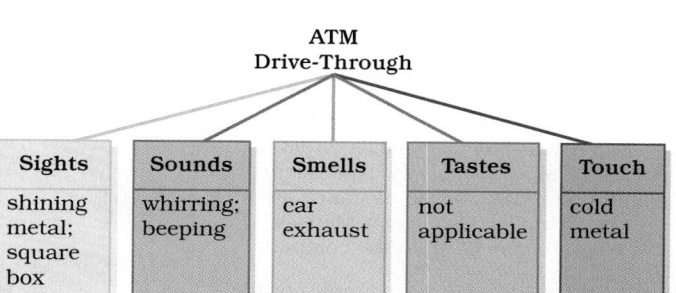

ATM Drive-Through

Sights	Sounds	Smells	Tastes	Touch
shining metal; square box	whirring; beeping	car exhaust	not applicable	cold metal

Drafting As you draft, string words together, listening to how the combinations sound. Experiment with various rhythms and sound combinations. Focus on expressing a specific mood, and choose descriptive modifiers, verbs, and nouns that support the mood.

Revising and Editing Test your poem by reading it to some peers and asking for feedback. Take notes as they give advice. If necessary, use a thesaurus to find words to replace weak or inappropriate words. A rhyming dictionary can help you to find alternative rhymes.

Publishing and Presenting With a few peers, hold a poetry reading for a group of friends or family. Ask for feedback, and answer questions when the reading is over.

▲ **Critical Viewing**
Why might this picture inspire a poem? **[Connect]**

Connected Assignment: Poem • 117

Lesson Objectives

1. To write a poem
2. To use prewriting strategies to generate ideas and develop voice
3. To employ literary devices to enhance style and voice
4. To employ precise language to communicate ideas clearly and concisely

Step-by-Step Teaching Guide

Poem

Teaching Resources: Writing Support Transparencies, 6-H; Writing Support Activity Book, 6-2

1. Help students brainstorm for topics. You might generate ideas by reading aloud various types of poems. Remind students to choose a topic they know and feel strongly about.

2. Review the writing strategies at the bottom of this page. Encourage students to refer to the strategies in the chapter for more instruction.

3. Review some literary devices that are frequently used in poetry, such as metaphor, simile, and personification.

4. Also, review some of the forms of poetry, such as haiku, sonnet, ballad, or free verse. Encourage students to choose a form that fits their topic.

5. Display Transparency 6-H to show students how the sensory language chart can stimulate new ways to describe familiar things. Give students copies of the blank chart (6-2) to use as they develop their poems.

Critical Viewing

Connect Students might say that images of a night sky and the sea often evoke strong feelings and have a lasting effect. As a result, observers are inspired to describe them in words.

☑ **ONGOING ASSESSMENT: Prerequisite Skills**

Students may find the following resources from Chapter 6 particularly helpful in composing their poems.

In the Textbook	Print Resources	Technology
Choosing your Topic, Section 6.2 Considering Your Audience and Purpose, Section 6.2 Using All Five Senses, Section 6.2	*Writing Support Transparencies, 6-C–D Writing Support Activity Book, 6-1*	*Writing and Grammar* Interactive Text, Section 6.2

Lesson Objectives

1. To discover how meanings are communicated through elements of design, including shape, line, color, and texture
2. To write a design review
3. To write in a voice and style appropriate to audience and purpose
4. To use writing to discover, record, review, and learn

Spotlight on the Humanities

Appreciating Art

Focus on Art: Art Deco

The style of Art Deco—with its emphasis on geometric shapes and sleek, slender lines—revealed itself in jewelry, furniture, and interior design in the 1920's and 1930's. The name *Art Deco* came from the title of a Paris design show in 1925: *Exposition Internationale des Arts Decoratifs et Industriels Modernes.* One of the early artists who created in the Art Deco style was glassmaker René Lalique. The style quickly became popular in the United States, and its characteristics were soon to be found not only in interior design but in roadside diners, skyscrapers, trains, and jukeboxes.

▲ Critical Viewing
What words would you choose to describe this theater? [Interpret]

Connection to Dance An important influence on the development of Art Deco was the ballet company Ballets Russes, founded by Russian director and art critic Sergei Diaghilev (1872–1929) in 1909. Centered in Paris, the Ballets Russes was noted for the magnificent Oriental designs in its stage decor as well as for its use of exotic colors in the production designs. Diaghilev experimented with music, costume design, and painting, as well as dance, and his work inspired such artists as Pablo Picasso, Henri Matisse, Anna Pavlova, and Vaslav Nijinsky to contribute to the company.

Connection to Architecture One of the great examples of the Art Deco style is Radio City Music Hall in New York City, pictured above. Opening its doors in 1932, Radio City Music Hall was known as "The Showplace of the Nation" with its lavish musical productions. A console organ sits on each side of the largest proscenium stage in the world. Each console weighs 2.5 tons and requires eleven rooms to house its pipes. The stage consists of four elevators that can be lowered twenty-seven feet into the basement. The hydraulic system that runs the elevators was considered so inventive that the U.S. Navy came to Radio City during World War II to study it for use on U.S. aircraft carriers.

Descriptive Writing Activity: Criticize a Design
Study the photograph above, which shows the interior of Radio City Music Hall in New York City. Then, write a review of the new theater, describing what it felt like to sit in such a massive Art Deco hall.

118 • Description

Media and Technology Skills

Evaluating Images

Activity: Analyzing Propaganda Images

Images in print and broadcast media are often used as propaganda to support or renounce a specific cause, institution, or person. Some propaganda is strictly political, such as the campaign advertisements in a presidential race. Other propaganda, such as public-service announcements, support a specific cause, such as smoking prevention or home safety.

Whether or not you agree with a piece of propaganda, you should always take time to evaluate the images being used. Because these issues are often highly emotional, the images used in propaganda are often loaded with positive or negative associations.

Think About It Choose a poster, magazine advertisement, or television commercial that you suspect contains propaganda. Select a piece that uses strong images to capture your attention. Your analysis will help you understand how these images work.

Describe It Begin by making a list of words that you associate with the images in the work. Your list can take the form of the list that follows, which was created in response to a political advertisement featuring workers on a construction site. Use the words in your list to create an overall description of the images used in the propaganda.

Image Shown	Inner Meaning
construction site	building and growth
	progress
	productivity
sunny day	prosperity
	comfort and warmth
	happiness

Analyze It After describing the images, analyze them to determine how effectively and fairly they persuade an audience. Consider whether or not some images are overly "weighted," or loaded with emotional appeals. Highly sentimental or sensational images can provoke a strong reaction, but one that might not be solidly supported by facts. Write a brief but complete assessment of the propaganda you have investigated.

Symbols and Propaganda

Symbols are potent images because viewers associate a wide range of meanings with common symbols. Think about what the following symbols might mean in various forms of propaganda:

- American flag
- rainbow
- babies or children
- Uncle Sam
- elephant
- donkey
- eagle
- Statue of Liberty
- dollar bill
- skull
- heart

Lesson Objectives

1. To describe how meanings are communicated through elements of design, including shape, line, color, and texture
2. To deconstruct media to get the main idea of the message's content
3. To evaluate and critique the persuasive techniques of media messages

Step-by-Step Teaching Guide

Evaluating Images

Teaching Resources: Writing Support Transparencies, 6-I; Writing Support Activity Book 6-3

1. Review the list of symbols in the sidebar box on page 119. Ask students to explain the symbolic meaning of each item. You may wish to have the class extend the list with at least five additional familiar symbols.
2. Display Transparency 6-I and use it to illustrate how images and their meanings might be charted.
3. Give students copies of the blank organizer (6-3) to use as they analyze the poster, advertisement, or television commercial they have selected for study. When they finish, have them discuss their results in small groups.

Customize for
Less Advanced Students

You may wish to have students work in small groups on this analysis activity. Provide each group with a different magazine advertisement to study.

Strategy, Organization, and Style

Teaching Resources: Standardized Test Preparation Workbook, pp. 11–12

1. Discuss the ideas of strategy, organization, and style as they are explained on this page. Remind students that style is determined by intended audience and purpose.

2. Remind students of the typical structure of a piece of writing: introduction, body, conclusion. Remind them also of the most common structure of a paragraph: topic sentence followed by supporting sentences.

3. Explain that in deciding how to revise words and phrases, students should keep the audience in mind. Students should choose words with which the audience will be familiar and that improve the logic and clarity of the passage.

Standardized Test Preparation Workshop

Strategy, Organization, and Style

Writing segments on standardized tests often measure your knowledge by asking you to evaluate a piece of writing. You may be asked to assess the writer's organizational strategy, the complexity of the language used, and the overall style of the passage. You will typically be given a descriptive passage to read in which each sentence is numbered. Following the passage will be several specific questions based on the reading.

Some of the types of questions you should expect follow:

- Style questions focus on the use of appropriate and effective language for the intended audience.

- Organization questions ask you to look at the order of sentences and paragraphs in the context of the overall organizational strategy of the passage.

- Strategy questions offer several options for revising words and phrases and ask you to select the best option within the context of the essay.

The sample test items that follow will give you practice answering questions on writing strategy, organization, and style.

Test Tip

If you are unsure of an answer, try eliminating one or more obviously incorrect answers and then choose between those remaining.

Sample Test Items

Directions: Read the passage, and then answer the questions that follow.

(1) It is a clear lake, devoid of the dangerous crocodiles and parasites found in many African lakes. (2) Lake Kivu, located on the border between Rwanda and the Democratic Republic of Congo in central Africa, is unique among African lakes. (3) Kivu is set among towering volcanoes. (4) It is a tragedy that political upheaval has led to widespread violence in Rwanda.

1. Which part does not support the main idea of the passage?
   A. part 1
   B. part 2
   C. part 3
   D. part 4

2. What revision would **best** improve the passage?
   A. Add a transition at the beginning of part 2.
   B. Change the present tense to the past tense.
   C. Delete part 4.
   D. Correct as is

Answers and Explanations

The correct answer for item 1 is *D.* It does not help describe Lake Kivu.

The correct answer for item 2 is *C* because part 4 does not support the topic sentence.

✏ TEST-TAKING TIP

Suggest that students underline the main idea when reading a passage. This will help them in a number of ways. First, it will aid their understanding of the passage. Second, it will serve as a reminder of the main idea and prevent them from getting bogged down in the details.

Third, knowing the location of the main idea will help them answer questions about organization. Suggest that students identify the audience and purpose of the piece. They might write it down in the margin of the test booklet and refer to it when answering questions about word choice.

Answer Key

▶ **Practice 1**

Practice 1 **Directions:** Carefully read the passage below. Select the letter that best answers each of the questions following the passage.

(1) Vehicles with advanced technologies are being designed now and will be available in the near future. (2) Several automobile manufacturers are already able to make <u>very advanced cars</u>. (3) Cars of all colors with on-board navigation, personal computers, infrared night-vision displays, and lane-sensing video cameras are the automotive wave of the future. (4) Some automobile makers are even researching collision-avoiding vehicles in which an on-board computer will be able to sense danger and automatically steer the car to safety.

(5) <u>The technological advances of the late twentieth century</u> surpass all of those in previous centuries combined. (6) The next ten years will make the accomplishments of the 1900's seem like child's play. (7) Researchers formerly dedicated only to military and space technologies are using their discoveries to enhance and even create new consumer products. (8) Advances in all areas, especially vehicle technology, will be exciting to watch and to use.

(9) Scientists and engineers are spending much of their time making the machines around us faster, safer, and easier to use. (10) Technology will guarantee an exciting twenty-first century. (11) More sophisticated automotive technology will mean decreased drive times and increased <u>performance</u> on the road.

1. Choose the **most logical** paragraph order.
   A. 1, 3, 2
   B. 3, 2, 1
   C. 2, 1, 3
   D. Correct as is

2. In which part should the underlined phrase be replaced by more precise language?
   A. part 2
   B. part 5
   C. part 11
   D. Correct as is

3. In part 3, which of the following should be deleted to eliminate irrelevant information?
   A. of all colors
   B. and lane-sensing video cameras
   C. automotive wave of the future
   D. personal computers

4. If the author wanted to rewrite part 4 for an audience of college engineering students, which of the following would be the **best** revision?
   A. A sophisticated on-board computer will be able to sense danger and automatically steer the car to safety.
   B. A computer will be able to sense danger. It will then automatically steer the car to safety.
   C. Collision-avoidance radar will improve safety statistics by sensing and correcting the vehicle's position relative to lane markings and other vehicles.
   D. Correct as is.

1. C
2. A
3. A
4. C

Customize for
Less Advanced Students

Tell students to read the first sentence of each paragraph in Practice 1. This should make it obvious that the second paragraph is meant to be the introductory paragraph. Knowing the topic sentence will make the passage easier to follow.

Customize for
AP Students

Ask students to explain how they knew that the first sentence of the second paragraph is meant to be the introduction to the passage. (They should note that it contains a broad idea—one that can easily be divided into smaller ideas, explored in depth, and supported.)

Chapter 7

Time and Resource Manager

In-Depth Lesson Plan

	LESSON FOCUS	PRINT AND MEDIA RESOURCES
DAY 1	**Introduction to Persuasive Speeches** Students learn key elements of persuasive speeches and analyze the Model From Literature. (pp. 122–125/Ⓗ76–77)	*Writers at Work* DVD, Persuasion *Writing and Grammar* Interactive Text, Ch. 7, Introduction
DAY 2	**Prewriting** Students choose and narrow a topic, consider their audience and purpose, and gather information. (pp. 126–131/Ⓗ78–83)	*Writing and Grammar* Interactive Text, Section 7.2 **Teaching Resources** *Writing Support Transparencies, 7-A–F; Writing Support Activity Book, 7-1–3; Topic Bank for Heterogeneous Classes,* Ch. 7
DAY 3	**Drafting** Students organize their ideas and write their first drafts. (p. 132/Ⓗ84)	*Writing and Grammar* Interactive Text, Section 7.3
DAY 4	**Revising** Students revise their drafts in terms of overall structure, paragraphs, sentences, and word choice. (pp. 133–137/Ⓗ85–89)	*Writing and Grammar* Interactive Text, Section 7.4 **Teaching Resources** *Writing Support Transparencies, 7-G–J; Writing Support Activity Book,* 7.4
DAY 5	**Editing and Proofreading; Publishing and Presenting** Students check their work for accuracy and correctness and deliver their speeches. (pp. 138–141/Ⓗ90–91)	*Writing and Grammar* Interactive Text, Sections 7.5–6 **Teaching Resources** *Scoring Rubrics on Transparency,* Ch. 7; *Writing Assessment and Portfolio Management; Formal Assessment,* Ch. 7

Accelerated Lesson Plan

	LESSON FOCUS	PRINT AND MEDIA RESOURCES
DAY 1	**Introduction Through Drafting** Students review characteristics of persuasive speeches, select topics, and write drafts. (pp. 122–132/Ⓗ76–84)	*Writers at Work* DVD, Persuasion *Writing and Grammar* Interactive Text, Ch. 7, Introduction through Section 7.3 **Teaching Resources** *Writing Support Transparencies, 7-A–F; Writing Support Activity Book,* 7-1–3
DAY 2	**Revising Through Presenting** Students work individually or with peers to revise, edit, and proofread their speeches for delivery. (pp. 133–141/Ⓗ85–91)	*Writing and Grammar* Interactive Text, Sections 7.4–6 **Teaching Resources** *Writing Support Transparencies, 7-G–J; Writing Support Activity Book, 7-4; Scoring Rubrics on Transparency,* Ch. 7; *Writing Assessment and Portfolio Management; Formal Assessment,* Ch. 7

Options for Adapting Lesson Plans

HOMEWORK
Have students complete any stage of the lesson for homework.

FEATURES
Extend coverage with Connected Assignment (p. 142), Spotlight on the Humanities (p. 144), Media and Technology Skills Workshop (p. 145), and the Standardized Test Preparation Workshop (pp. 146–147).

TECHNOLOGY
Students can complete any stage of the lesson on the computer, using *Writing and Grammar* Interactive Text or a word-processing program. Have them print out their completed work.

Writing and Grammar Handbook Alignment

Page numbers in Step-by-Step Teaching Guides in this Teacher's Edition refer to pages from the full student text. Handbook page references, indicated with this icon ⊞, are provided in Time and Resource Manager boxes and at the bottom of each Teacher's Edition page.

INTEGRATED SKILLS COVERAGE

Integrating Grammar
Parallelism, SE p. 135/⊞87
Commonly Mistaken Words, SE p. 138/⊞90
ATE p. 134

Reading/Writing Connection
Evaluate an Argument, SE p. 124
Writing Application, SE p. 125

Viewing and Representing
Critical Viewing, SE pp. 122, 124, 132, 140, 142, 144/⊞76, 84
Appreciating the Arts, SE p. 144
Recognizing Persuasion in Media, SE p. 145

Speaking and Listening Skills
ATE pp. 131, 141, 147

Current Events
ATE p. 143

ASSESSMENT SUPPORT

Standardized Test Preparation Workshop SE p. 146; ATE pp. 128, 136
Standardized Test Preparation Workbook, pp. 13–14
Scoring Rubrics on Transparency, Ch. 7
Formal Assessment, Ch. 7
Writing Assessment and Portfolio Management

MEETING INDIVIDUAL NEEDS

Less Advanced Students ATE pp. 130, 147. See also Ongoing Assessments ATE pp. 127, 129, 133.
AP Students ATE pp. 128, 147
ESL Students ATE pp. 132, 141
Bodily/Kinesthetic Learners ATE p. 129
Spatial Learners ATE p. 133
Linguistic Learners ATE p. 143

BLOCK SCHEDULING

Pacing Suggestions
For 90-minute Blocks
• Have students complete the Prewriting and Drafting stages in a single period.
• Focus one class period on Revising and Editing and Publishing and Presenting. Allow at least 30 minutes for peer revision.

Resources for Varying Instruction
• *Writing and Grammar* Interactive Text A 90-minute block provides an ideal opportunity for students to work on the computer.
• *Writers at Work* DVD Show the Persuasion segment in class.

Professional Development Support
• *How to Manage Instruction in the Block* This teaching resource provides management and activity suggestions.

MEDIA AND TECHNOLOGY

For the Student
• *Writing and Grammar* Interactive Text, Ch. 7
• *On-line Exercise Bank,* Section 20.6

For the Teacher
• *Writers at Work* DVD, Persuasion
• Teacher**EXPRESS** CD-ROM

WRITING AND GRAMMAR ON-LINE

Interactive Text (On-line or on CD-ROM)
• Easily navigable instruction with interactive Revision Checkers
• Full use of e-rater™, the essay-scoring system (on-line only)

Companion Web Site PHSchool.com
• Scoring rubrics with models (use Web Code egk-1201)

See the Go On-line! feature, SE p. iii.

LITERATURE CONNECTIONS

Related selections from *Prentice Hall Literature, Penguin Edition,* The British Tradition:
Professional Model "Wartime Speech," Winston Churchill, SE p. 124
Topic Bank Option "Defending Nonviolent Resistance," Mohandas K. Gandhi, SE p. 127/⊞79

Chapter
7

Persuasion
Persuasive Speech

Lesson Objectives

1. To write a persuasive speech appropriate to audience and purpose
2. To read to appreciate the writer's craft and to discover models for writing
3. To use prewriting strategies to generate ideas and plan
4. To research self-selected topics using texts and technical resources
5. To represent information in a variety of ways, including graphics
6. To develop and revise drafts in terms of structure, paragraphs, sentences, and word choice
7. To edit and proofread to ensure standard English usage and grammar
8. To evaluate writing for both mechanics and content
9. To refine selected work for publication

Critical Viewing

Analyze Answers will vary. Students may mention that the speaker seems focused, that she is looking at her audience, and that she appears to be confident.

Persuasion in Everyday Life

Persuasive communication is a powerful tool that is useful throughout life, in all types of situations. At home, for example, you might persuade your family to work together on a community project. At school, you might persuade classmates to vote for a student politician. Later, in the working world, you might convince an employer that you are the right person for a job. Once you have that job, you may need persuasion to convince buyers of the value of a product or to gain a raise or promotion.

▲ **Critical Viewing**
Presenting a persuasive speech successfully involves effective writing as well as presenting skills. What presenting skills does the woman pictured seem to be employing? **[Analyze]**

122 • Persuasion

⏱ **TIME AND RESOURCE MANAGER**

Resources
Technology: *Writers at Work* DVD, Persuasion; *Writing and Grammar* Interactive Text, Ch. 7

Using the Full Student Edition	Using the Handbook🄷
• Cover pp. 122–123 in class. • Show the Persuasion section of the *Writers at Work* DVD. • Read the Model From Literature (pp. 124–125) in class, and use it to brainstorm for persuasive speech ideas.	• Cover pp. 76–77 in class. • Show the Persuasion section of the *Writers at Work* DVD.

What Is a Persuasive Speech?

A **persuasive speech** is a spoken statement that presents a position and tries to convince an audience to accept that position or to take action. An effective persuasive speech

- addresses an issue of concern or importance to the speaker.
- clearly states the speaker's position and goal.
- supports the position with clearly organized facts, examples, and statistics.
- addresses the knowledge level, experiences, needs, and concerns of the intended audience.
- uses rhetorical, or speaking, devices to grab and hold the audience's attention.

To preview the criteria on which your persuasive speech may be evaluated, see the Rubric for Self-Assessment on page 139.

Types of Persuasive Speeches

There are many types of persuasive speeches. Following are some examples:

- **Campaign speeches** attempt to persuade voters in local, state, or national elections.
- **Public-service announcements** use advertising techniques to focus on important public issues such as wearing seat belts or getting an education.
- **Inspirational speeches** seek to persuade an audience to strive to reach specific goals.

PREVIEW
Student Work
IN PROGRESS

In this chapter, you'll follow the work of Marvin Astorga, a student at Bel Air High School in El Paso, Texas. Concerned about a proposal to adopt a four-day school week, Marvin prepared a speech to present at a school board meeting. A completed version of Marvin's speech appears at the end of the chapter.

Writers in ACTION

Many professionals, such as politicians and ad writers, use persuasion in work situations. Public defender Cary Bricker relies on persuasion to get the best possible results for her clients:

"To be persuasive in writing, I have to focus on word usage. I focus on issues. I have to be very clear in my writing. I have to tailor my writing toward the issues that I'm taking on. . . . The idea is to persuade, through my writing, through every step of the case."

Interest GRABBER Tell students that they will participate in an activity called "Take a Stand" to get a taste of how a persuasive speech can change people's minds. Draw an imaginary line at the front of the room. Label one end of the line "Totally Agree." Label the other end "Totally Disagree." State a controversial proposal facing your school, or use the four-day school week proposal discussed in the student work example in this chapter. Ask students to stand somewhere on the line to indicate how much they agree or disagree with the proposal. Then, have each student try to persuade the others that his or her stance is correct. After each student speaks, give students the opportunity to shift their positions on the line.

Activate Prior Knowledge

Ask students to remember the last time someone persuaded them to change their point of view. They may have heard this person speak on television or at a school assembly. They may have simply been listening to a friend, teacher, or parent. What did the speaker say or do to persuade them? After discussing the speaker's methods, refer students to the characteristics of persuasive speeches in the textbook.

More About the Writer

Cary Bricker is a federal defense attorney based in the New York City area. She has been practicing law since the early 1980's.

☑ ONGOING ASSESSMENT: Diagnose

Use one of the following options to diagnose students' current levels of proficiency in writing persuasive speeches.

Option 1 Ask students to select the strongest example of their persuasive writing from the previous year. Then, have them hold small-group conferences in which each one presents his or her work as if it were a speech. Use these conferences to determine which students need extra attention in developing a persuasive speech.	**Option 2** Ask students to write a sentence to persuade a school administrator to change a school policy for seniors. Then, have them list three reasons that support the sentence. If students have difficulty with this activity, you will need to spend more time on the evidence and elaboration phases of the process.

Reading\Writing Connection

Reading: Evaluate an Argument

Readers and listeners who consider the evidence presented in a speech are in a good position to judge the value of the speaker's ideas. As students read excerpts from Susan B. Anthony's speech (pages 124–125), ask them to weigh carefully the evidence that she presents and decide whether her argument is convincing, even if they don't agree with it.

Step-by-Step Teaching Guide

Engage Students Through Literature

1. Ask students to discuss the excerpt. You can use questions such as the following:

   Where and how does Anthony tell readers the topic of her speech? (She makes strong statements of her purpose in the first and last paragraphs.)

   What evidence does Anthony use to support her argument? (She reviews the ideas on which our country was founded, using quotations from both the Declaration of Independence and the Constitution.)

   After weighing Anthony's evidence, do you think she has made a convincing argument? What other evidence might she have included?

2. Allow students to make other observations about the passage. Ask students to brainstorm for other persuasive topics related to Anthony's ideas.

Critical Viewing

Analyze Students may infer that, like the restrictive, confining clothes pictured in the photograph, women's rights were also restricted at that time.

7.1 Model From Literature

In 1873, Susan B. Anthony was tried for breaking the law that forbade women to vote. Before her trial, she went on a speaking tour during which she delivered the following powerful persuasive speech.

Reading Strategy: Evaluate an Argument *When you read a piece of persuasion, evaluate the writer or speaker's argument by weighing the evidence that is presented and deciding whether you find the argument convincing.*

Woman's Right to Suffrage

Susan B. Anthony

Friends and Fellow-citizens: I stand before you to-night, under indictment for the alleged crime of having voted at the last Presidential election, without having a lawful right to vote. It shall be my work this evening to prove to you that in thus voting, I not only committed no crime, but, instead, simply exercised my citizen's right, guaranteed to me and all United States citizens by the national Constitution, beyond the power of any state to deny.

Our democratic-republican government is based on the idea of the natural right of every individual member thereof to a voice and a vote in making and executing the laws. We assert the province of government to be to secure the people in the enjoyment of their unalienable rights. We throw to the winds the old dogma that governments can give rights. Before governments were organized, no one denies that each individual possessed the right to protect his own life, liberty, and property. And when 100 or 1,000,000 people enter into a free government, they do not barter away their natural rights; they simply pledge themselves to protect each other in the enjoyment of them, through prescribed judicial and legislative tribunals. They agree to abandon the methods of brute force in the adjustment of their differences, and adopt those of civilization.

* * *

124 • Persuasive Speech

▲ **Critical Viewing** What can you learn about the time in which Anthony lived by looking at this photograph? **[Analyze]**

Anthony clearly states her purpose in her opening paragraph.

For another example of a persuasive speech, see Winston Churchill's stirring "Wartime Speech" in *Prentice Hall Literature, Penguin Edition,* The British Tradition.

"All men are created equal, and endowed by their Creator with certain unalienable rights. Among these are life, liberty, and the pursuit of happiness. That to secure these, governments are instituted among men, deriving their just powers from the consent of the governed."

Here is no shadow of government authority over rights, nor exclusion of any from their full and equal enjoyment. Here is pronounced the right of all men, and "consequently," as the Quaker preacher said, "of all women," to a voice in the government. And here, in this very first paragraph of the declaration, is the assertion of the natural right of all to the ballot; for, how can "the consent of the governed" be given, if the right to vote be denied?

* * *

The preamble of the federal constitution says:

"We, the people of the United States, in order to form a more perfect union, establish justice, insure domestic tranquillity, provide for the common defense, promote the general welfare and secure the blessings of liberty to ourselves and our posterity, do ordain and establish this constitution for the United States of America."

It was we, the people, not we, the white male citizens, nor yet we, the male citizens; but we, the whole people, who formed this Union. And we formed it, not to give the blessings of liberty, but to secure them; not to the half of ourselves and the half of our posterity, but to the whole people—women as well as men. And it is downright mockery to talk to women of their enjoyment of the blessings of liberty while they are denied the use of the only means of securing them provided by this democratic-republican government—the ballot.

* * *

For any State to make sex a qualification that must ever result in the disenfranchisement of one entire half of the people is to pass a bill of attainder, or an *ex post facto* law, and is therefore a violation of the supreme law of the land. By it, the blessings of liberty are forever withheld from women and their female posterity. To them, this government has no just powers derived from the consent of the governed. To them, this government is not a democracy. It is not a republic. It is an odious aristocracy; a hateful oligarchy of sex; the most hateful aristocracy ever established on the face of the globe.

Citing a familiar passage from the Declaration of Independence helps Anthony connect her ideas to the audience's background knowledge and experiences.

Repetition of the word we creates a stirring rhythm that supports Anthony's analysis of the Constitution.

Anthony ends this portion of her speech with a stirring restatement of her position.

Writing Application: Building an Argument
Build a strong argument in your speech by providing thorough supporting evidence.

Model From Literature • 125

Prewriting: Find a "Hot Topic"

Teaching Resources: Writing Support Transparencies, 7-A; Writing Support Activity Book, 7-1

1. Bring in newspapers or have students bring them in from home or the library. Ask students to scan, and then highlight or copy, the headlines for "hot topics" (controversial issues that elicit a strong response).

2. Ask students to fold their papers into thirds. Display Transparency 7-A and have them label their papers accordingly.

3. In groups, have students complete the chart for one of the topics.

Prewriting: Hold a Discussion Group

1. Have students identify a group with whom they could hold a discussion.

2. Students will ask this group to come up with a list of key issues that concern the members and then to talk about these issues.

3. Once students have their lists, ask them to highlight the topics that they find most compelling.

Prewriting: List and Respond

1. Have students note every time they hear a persuasive speech. Make sure they include all forms of speech: advertisements, pep rallies, public service announcements, and so on.

2. After noting each instance of persuasive speech, have students jot down their reaction to each one. (Were they excited, angry, bored?)

3. At the end of the allotted period, have students review their lists and highlight the topics to which they had the strongest reactions.

7.2 Prewriting

Choosing Your Topic

To write an effective persuasive speech, it helps to believe in the argument that you are making. Start with a topic that truly interests or concerns you, and develop it into a persuasive speech. Use the following strategies to find a topic that you can develop with honest commitment:

Strategies for Generating Topics

1. **Find a "Hot Topic"** When controversy flares up in the news, the debate usually centers on important political or social issues. Scan newspaper headlines, and listen to newscasts for controversial topics that evoke strong reactions in you. In a chart like the one below, note the specific conflict, the underlying issues, and your opinion about the topic. Review your chart to find a topic for your speech.

Topic	Underlying Issues	My Opinion
A student who missed four rehearsals is allowed to play in the winter concert.	◆ student responsibility ◆ appropriate punishments	It's not fair to let one student get away with breaking a rule, even if it seems minor.

2. **Hold a Discussion Group** Tap into school or community issues by holding a discussion with students, neighbors, or other local residents. Find out what key issues and concerns really get people talking. Note topics that generate the most controversy or disagreement. You may find that one topic is particularly interesting. If so, choose that as the topic for your persuasive speech.

3. **List and Respond** Make a list of the speeches you hear in one day or one week. You can include everything from advertisements and public-service announcements to campaign and pep-rally speeches. Briefly describe each speech, and note your response. Then, review your list of descriptions and responses, and choose the topic about which you have the strongest feelings.

126 • Persuasive Speech

Interactive Textbook

Try it out! Use the interactive Hot Topic Chart in **Section 7.2**, on-line or on CD-ROM.

Timed Writing Hint

If you are given thirty-five minutes to write a persuasive essay, you should spend five minutes revising.

⏱ TIME AND RESOURCE MANAGER

Resources
Print: *Writing Support Transparencies*, 7-A–F; *Writing Support Activity Book*, 7-1–3
Technology: *Writing and Grammar* Interactive Text, Section 7.2

Using the Full Student Edition	Using the Handbook🄗
• Cover pp. 126–131 in class. • Use Responding to Fine Art (p. 127) to generate more topic ideas. • Guide students as necessary as they narrow topics, analyze audience, and gather evidence.	• Cover pp. 78–83 in class. • Use Responding to Fine Art (p. 79) to generate more topic ideas. • Guide students as necessary as they narrow topics, analyze audience, and gather evidence.

TOPIC BANK

If you have trouble coming up with a topic on your own, try one of these:

1. **Address About Violence in Video Games** Plan a speech in which you present your opinions about the amount of violence in today's most popular video games. Choose a specific goal for your speech, such as regulating the games, instituting a stronger rating service, or eliminating current restrictions.

2. **Speech Concerning the Portrayal of Women on Television** When television became popular in the 1950's, women's roles were mostly restricted to housewives and entertainers. Give a speech in which you analyze how television portrays women today. In it, convince your audience that your analysis is accurate, and encourage them to take a specific action, such as writing letters or boycotting a network.

Responding to Fine Art

3. This painting of Christopher Columbus departing from Spain in 1492 suggests the artist's opinion of the explorer's achievements. Do you agree with the artist? Write a speech in which you argue for or against celebrating Columbus and his accomplishments with a national holiday.

Grand Voyages (Part Four, Plate VIII), DeBry, Courtesy of the John Carter Brown Library at Brown University

Responding to Literature

4. Read "Defending Nonviolent Resistance" by Mohandas K. Gandhi. Write a persuasive speech in which you respond to Gandhi's ideas, arguing for or against his philosophy. You can find this piece in *Prentice Hall Literature, Penguin Edition*, The British Tradition.

Timed Writing Prompt

5. Many towns and cities require teenagers to participate in community projects, such as tutoring or cleaning up parks. Write a persuasive essay about your position on this issue. Discuss why you agree or disagree with this practice. Support your point of view with examples. **(35 minutes)**

Prewriting • 127

Step-by-Step Teaching Guide

Responding to Fine Art
Grand Voyages by Theodor DeBry

Teaching Resources: Writing Support Transparencies, 7-B

1. Display the transparency and engage students in a discussion of DeBry's engraving. Ask them to identify the main figures in the picture (Columbus, King Ferdinand, Queen Isabella). Why is it significant that Columbus is moving from right to left? (He is moving "west" in the painting.)

2. Ask students for persuasive speech ideas that this piece of art suggests. Here are some possibilities:

   Arguing for or against acknowledging Columbus as the true "discoverer" of America

   Asking that other explorers from the past have a national holiday celebrated in their name

   Students may include these topic ideas in their Topic Banks.

Timed Writing Prompt

- Have students think about an issue they feel strongly about, such as the state driving age or global warming.

- To help students make strong arguments, ask them to write two short speeches arguing both sides of the issue. Have them prioritize the points of their arguments and counter-arguments from strongest to weakest.

- Suggest that students allow five minutes for prewriting, twenty-five minutes for writing, and five minutes for reviewing and proofreading.

✓ ONGOING ASSESSMENT: Monitor and Reinforce

If students have difficulty relating to the historical examples in Responding to Fine Art and Responding to Literature to the present day, try the following options.

Option 1 Have students halve a blank page vertically. Ask them to use one half of the page to list historical events referred to in the art or literature example. Ask them to list a present-day event on the other half of the page that is similar in some way to the historical event.	**Option 2** Ask students to imagine DeBry's or Gandhi's response to a modern conflict. Have students take turns role-playing the reactions of one of these historical figures.

TIME SAVERS!

📄 **Writing Support Transparencies**
Use the transparencies for Chapter 7 to facilitate the teaching of strategies.

Prewriting: Create an Outline

Teaching Resources: Writing Support Transparencies, 7-C

1. Ask students to select one topic from their topic bank. Have them look for something that interests them.

2. Display Transparency 7-C and discuss how Marvin used outlining to narrow his topic about school. Discuss how main ideas and supporting details are treated in an outline. Encourage students to suggest other ideas from Marvin's outline as persuasion topics.

3. Ask students to outline their topics, stating the topic as item "I" in their outlines. Have them use the Student Work in Progress as an example.

4. Have students review their outlines and make a list of the subtopics and supporting details that could serve as topics for persuasive speeches. Ask students to add these new items to their topic banks.

Customize for
AP Students

Students will benefit from the challenge of outlining each other's topics. Have them exchange the topic they have outlined with another student, and then outline each other's topics. When they are finished, have them compare outlines. They will find that the differences between their work and their partner's will help generate new ideas.

7.2

Narrowing Your Topic

After selecting a broad topic, focus on a specific element or aspect of it that you can fully and completely support. If, for example, you choose a topic such as "Health Care," you would need many hours to identify every important issue. A narrower related topic, such as "The Importance of Preventive Care," would be a more suitable topic for a short persuasive speech. Use the following strategy to help you narrow your topic.

Create an Outline

You may be familiar with outlining a topic as a way of organizing an essay, but you can also use this strategy to narrow your topic. Creating an outline helps to divide your topic into smaller parts. Begin by writing your broad topic as the main level of an outline. Divide the topic into lettered heads (A, B, C, and so on). Then, divide those headings into numbered subheads (1, 2, 3, and so on.) Review your outline, and choose a single subheading to be the narrowed topic for your persuasive speech.

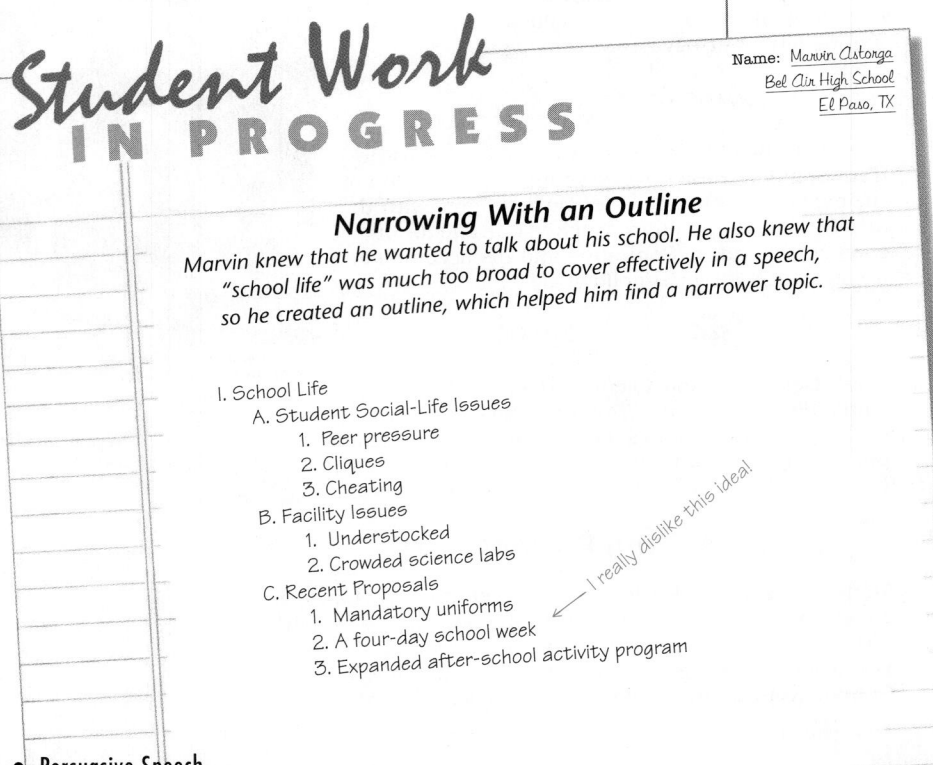

Student Work IN PROGRESS

Name: *Marvin Astorga*
Bel Air High School
El Paso, TX

Narrowing With an Outline

Marvin knew that he wanted to talk about his school. He also knew that "school life" was much too broad to cover effectively in a speech, so he created an outline, which helped him find a narrower topic.

I. School Life
    A. Student Social-Life Issues
        1. Peer pressure
        2. Cliques
        3. Cheating
    B. Facility Issues
        1. Understocked
        2. Crowded science labs
    C. Recent Proposals
        1. Mandatory uniforms   — I really dislike this idea!
        2. A four-day school week
        3. Expanded after-school activity program

128 • Persuasive Speech

✎ STANDARDIZED TEST PREPARATION WORKSHOP

Organize and Plan Standardized tests may require students to answer questions about how outlines are organized. Ask students to read the following outline and use it to answer the question.

  I. *Environmental Issues*
    A. *Land Destruction*
      1. *Overgrazing*
      2. *Landfills*
      3. *Lack of Public Parks*

    B. *Water Pollution*
      1. *Oil Spills*

      2. *Chemical Dumping*
      3. *Fish Farms*

According to this outline, which of the following supporting details is an example of land destruction, not water pollution?

A Oil spills   **C** Environmental issues

B Fish farms   **D** Lack of public parks

Students should note that the correct answer is **D**, "Lack of public parks." The first two, A and B, are examples of water pollution, while C is the main topic.

Considering Your Audience and Purpose

As you plan your speech, it is important that you consider both your audience and your purpose. Your audience might be one person, such as a friend, parent, or boss, or a large crowd, such as a school assembly or the readers of a newspaper. Your basic purpose is to persuade your audience, but you need to set a more specific goal to be able to assess the success of your speech.

Suit Your Audience's Needs

Putting yourself in your audience is a good way to make sure that you have gathered enough information about a topic. Imagine that you are an audience member, and make a list of the things you would like to find out when listening to a speech on your topic. As you gather ideas, use your list to help you make sure that you are tailoring your speech to your audience's specific concerns and expectations.

Identify a Specific Purpose

It's not enough to say that your purpose is to persuade. You need to state a specific purpose for your speech and then gather details that will help you to achieve that purpose. For example, do you want your listeners to sign a petition? To volunteer at a local recycling plant? Use a chart like the one below to state a general purpose, and then refine it into a definite action that you would like your audience to take.

General Purpose	Specific Purpose
Persuade people to support the school theater department.	Persuade parents to attend the opening-night benefit performance of the play.
Inspire students to achieve success at school.	Inspire every student in your class to set five specific school goals that they can achieve by the end of the month.
Convince people that animals have rights.	Convince students to support animal rights by writing letters to businesses discouraging testing on animals.

Try it out! To chart your specific purposes, use the Essay Builder, accessible from the menu bar, on-line or on CD-ROM.

Prewriting: Suit Your Audience's Needs

1. Have students choose a topic from their topic bank and list two or three possible audiences for this topic.

2. Ask students to choose one member of the audience and imagine his or her perspective on the subject. How much does this person know about the topic? How is this person likely to react to the topic initially?

3. Have students list questions about the topic from this audience member's point of view and tailor their writing to address his or her questions and concerns.

Customize for
Bodily/Kinesthetic Learners

Have students work in pairs. Ask one student to read the topic, and ask the other to react as if he or she were the audience member being addressed.

Prewriting: Identify a Specific Purpose

Teaching Resources: Writing Support Transparencies, 7-D; Writing Support Activity Book, 7-2

1. Use Transparency 7-D to show how to refine the purpose of a speech. Discuss how the purposes move from general to specific through the use of specific words and phrases.

2. Ask students to think of a specific purpose for each general one listed on the chart. (A general purpose might be trying to persuade an audience to support the school theater, while a specific one would be to convince classmates to volunteer to put up posters for the next performance.)

3. Have students create their own charts, choosing three topics from their topic banks.

4. Have students write the general purpose for making speeches on these topics. Then, have them write a specific purpose for each topic. They should be actions that they would like members of the audience to take.

☑ **ONGOING ASSESSMENT: Monitor and Reinforce**

If you observe students having difficulty identifying a broader audience, try one of the following options.

Option 1 Have students imagine that they could invite anyone they wanted to hear the speech. Whom would they invite? Have them write a profile of these people and include their age, education level, skills, and what they need to know about the topic.	**Option 2** Have students focus on one audience member in particular by drawing a sketch of that person and writing the person's distinguishing characteristics in a web around the drawing.

Prewriting: Conduct Research and Complete a T-Chart

Teaching Resources: Writing Support Transparencies, 7-E; Writing Support Activity Book, 7-3

1. Have students select a topic from their topic banks. Ask them to make a list of those parts of the topic that need to be supported by facts, statistics, and examples. Have students share their findings.

2. Explain to students that they can find supporting information by consulting both written texts and the Internet. To use their time effectively, they should only scan the material using indexes, tables of contents, and summaries. They will also need to keep track of both supporting and opposing information.

3. Show students the T-chart on Transparency 7-E. Discuss how it illustrates information for and against a controversial subject.

4. Have students each create a similar chart to track both supporting and opposing information. Have them refer to these charts when they draft their speeches.

Customize for
Less Advanced Students

Less advanced students may need to practice how to identify supporting and opposing information before they do their own research. If this is the case, do not show them the transparency chart right away. Instead, write the two opposing positions on the chalkboard in a T-chart. Read examples from the chart, ask students to identify which argument each example supports, and place the examples in the correct part of the chart.

7.2

Gathering Evidence

The strength of your persuasive speech will depend on the quality of your analysis and evidence. You won't persuade anyone unless you have facts, details, anecdotes, and personal experiences to support your statements. Use the following strategies to collect information you will use to support your claims.

Conduct Research

Unless you're already an expert on your topic, explore reliable sources to collect facts, statistics, and examples you can use to support your argument. The following are suggestions to guide your research:

- Consult books by experts, respected magazines, and influential periodicals.
- Visit Internet sites that are sponsored by well-known organizations or prominent individuals.
- Set specific goals and stay on track so your research time will be most effective.
- Scan indexes, tables of contents, and summaries for the information you need.
- Don't ignore facts that contradict your position. Keep track of them, and hunt down additional information that answers each assertion. You can use a T-chart to collect and categorize the details you uncover.

Complete a T-Chart

Use a two-sided T-chart to organize information for and against your position. This is particularly effective when you plan to talk about a controversial subject. It is important to collect information on both sides of an issue so that you can weigh the relative strengths of each position.

List your position in one column and the opposing position next to it. If you have more evidence against your position than for it, reconsider your position or find more evidence that supports your opinion.

Reasons to Vote for the Library Tax Levy	Reasons to Vote Against the Library Tax Levy
Library is understocked and overcrowded Reference sources are outdated The expansion will create a new multimedia center	Expensive The library is used by only 43% of the town

130 • Persuasive Speech

🔖 Research Tip

Make a research plan before you begin gathering evidence. Doing so will help you to stay focused on your topic. It will also help ensure that you gather evidence from a variety of sources.

Conduct Interviews and Surveys

In addition to conducting research, you may want to conduct live interviews—if appropriate for your topic. If you decide to conduct an interview, keep these tips in mind:

- Prepare a list of questions that will help you focus the interview.
- Always speak politely, and allow the subject enough time to respond.
- Use a tape recorder, if possible, or take accurate notes.

⚙ Grammar and Style Tip

Create survey questions that are unbiased. For example, instead of asking "Will you vote against the tax levy?" ask "How will you vote on the tax levy: for or against?"

Student Work IN PROGRESS

Name: *Marvin Astorga*
Bel Air High School
El Paso, TX

Interviewing to Assess Public Opinion
Marvin conducted a survey to find out how many students supported the four-day plan. Following is a portion of the survey he created.

Thank you for your help. Please circle your answers.

1) What grade are you in?

  9   10   11   12

2) Should we adopt the proposed four-day school week?

  yes   no

3) How do you think the plan will affect the amount of student stress?

  stress will decrease greatly

  stress will decrease a little

  stress will not change

  stress will increase a little

  stress will increase greatly

Prewriting • 131

Prewriting: Conduct Interviews and Surveys

Teaching Resources: Writing Support Transparencies, 7-F

1. Have students look through their topic banks to see which topics might be supported by interview and survey information.

2. After students have chosen their topics, have them brainstorm for a list of possible questions and a list of people or groups they will interview. Display Transparency 7-F to review Marvin's questions.

3. Ask students to exchange papers and check that their partner's questions are unbiased. Refer students to the Grammar and Style Tip on this page for more information about unbiased questions.

4. Have students conduct interviews with the people or groups they have targeted as audiences.

Integrating Speaking and Listening Skills

Have students do a practice interview or survey with a classmate. Have the classmate provide feedback about the interview, paying particular attention to whether the interviewer was polite and allowed enough time for the classmate to respond.

⏱ TIME SAVERS!

 Writing Support Transparencies
Use the transparencies for Chapter 7 to facilitate teaching of strategies.

 Writing Support Activity Book
Use the graphic organizers for Chapter 7 to facilitate student planning.

1. Ask students to identify the emphatic words and phrases in the samples ("adamantly oppose," "urge," and "clearly the strongest").

2. Have students draft their own appeals with these examples in mind. Encourage them to state their positions as clearly and strongly as possible.

3. Next, have students draft their speeches using all the evidence they have gathered.

4. Finally, make sure that students conclude their speeches with a restatement of their opening appeal.

Customize for
ESL Students

Students may not be aware of the connotations of the words in their appeal. They will benefit from creating a list of strong verbs. Have them work together to make a list of strong verbs (*urge, implore, oppose,* or *abandon*). Then, have them make a similar list for adverbs (*adamantly, emphatically, clearly,* or *undeniably*). They should choose appropriate words to create strong appeals as they begin writing their speeches.

Drafting: Use "Layering"

1. Have students write sample paragraphs using the SEE strategy. Have them exchange papers so a classmate can check their work.

2. Once students have practiced using the SEE strategy, have them continue their drafts.

Critical Viewing

Relate Students may mention appeals from candidates for student government.

7.3 Drafting

Shaping Your Writing

Once you've finished gathering evidence to include in your speech, write out a first draft. In preparing your draft, keep in mind that your argument will be presented orally. Pay attention to the sound of the language, as well as to its meaning.

Focus on Your Appeal

An effective persuasive speech presents a clear and specific appeal. Remember that your audience is listening to your ideas, not reading them. Begin with a precise and emphatic statement of your position.

SAMPLE APPEALS: I adamantly oppose the four-day school week proposal.

I urge you to vote for Vincent Hernandez, clearly the strongest candidate for Senior Class President.

After stating your appeal, present the facts and ideas that support your position. Finally, conclude your speech with a restatement of your original appeal. Because the final words of your speech will have a particularly strong effect on your audience, use this opportunity to present your most direct and attractive appeal.

Providing Elaboration

Use "Layering"

A unified paragraph, in which the ideas flow logically, is much easier for an audience to understand than a paragraph of disjointed ideas. As you draft, use layering to help you create unified, effective paragraphs.

The acronym SEE can help you remember the three parts of a successfully layered paragraph.

- **S** stands for **Statement.** Begin by stating the topic of the paragraph.
- **E** stands for **Extension.** Extend the topic by connecting it to the original statement.
- **E** stands for **Elaboration.** Provide the facts, statistics, and other elements that support your topic statement.

▲ **Critical Viewing**
What sorts of appeals have you seen on flyers like the one the student above is distributing? **[Relate]**

132 • Persuasive Speech

⏱ TIME AND RESOURCE MANAGER

Resources
Print: *Writing Support Transparencies,* 7-G–J; *Writing Support Activity Book,* 7-4
Technology: *Writing and Grammar* Interactive Text, Section 7.3

Using the Full Student Edition	Using the Handbook🄷
• Have students review p. 132 and write sample appeals in class.	• Have students review p. 84 and write sample appeals in class.
• Ask students to draft their speeches with the SEE strategy in mind during class.	• Ask students to draft their speeches with the SEE strategy in mind during class.
• Review Revision Strategies (pp. 133–137) in class.	• Review Revision Strategies (pp. 85–89) in class.
• Have students work with peer reviewers to revise their speeches.	• Have students work with peer reviewers to revise their speeches.

7.4 Revising

Once you've finished your first draft, revise it by focusing on its overall structure, paragraphs, sentences, and words.

Revising Your Overall Structure

Check for Unity

Your speech should leave listeners with a strong, lasting impression. To achieve this goal, you need to present a unified argument—one that focuses on a single important or main idea. Each paragraph in your speech should contribute to its main idea. Likewise, each sentence within each paragraph should support the main idea of the paragraph.

▶ **REVISION STRATEGY**
Outlining and Reflecting

Just as you can use outlining to narrow a topic, you can also use it to evaluate the structure of a first draft. First, summarize the main point of each paragraph. In the margin of your paper, write a heading that describes it. Then, organize the headings into an outline, and use this to review the unity of your overall structure. Eliminate paragraphs that are not directly related to your topic. Also, consider reordering your points to strengthen the flow of your ideas.

⏱ Timed Writing Hint

Make an outline after a first draft. This will help you revise your essay quickly under timed conditions.

Student Work IN PROGRESS

Name: _Marvin Astorga_
Bel Air High School
El Paso, TX

Outlining to Check Unity

After writing his first draft, Marvin created an outline and adjusted the order in which he presented his arguments.

I. Why I Am Against the Four-Day School Week Proposal
  A. Parents' schedules
  B. Hard for students to adjust
  C. Student fatigue
II. Survey Results

Revising • 133

✓ ONGOING ASSESSMENT: Monitor and Reinforce

If you observe students having difficulty reordering their drafts, try one of the following options.

Option 1 Have students cut their drafts into individual paragraphs. In this way, they can move the paragraphs around physically, trying different arrangements and assessing their value.	**Option 2** Have students work with partners. Reading the speech to others will help students to anticipate audience reactions.

Revising: Revising to Create Parallelism

Teaching Resources: Writing Support Transparencies, 7-H

1. Read aloud the examples of paragraphs with and without parallelism.

2. Ask students to evaluate the two paragraphs. Which has better rhythm? Which is more memorable? Which is more effective? Students should find that the paragraph with parallelism has better rhythm, which makes it more memorable and effective.

3. Display Transparency 7-H. Discuss how Marvin included a set of parallel ideas to establish an effective flow of ideas.

4. On the chalkboard, provide examples of sentences that do not have parallel construction:

   The most important aspects of education are to write well, learning to read, and math.

   The biggest drawback is that people don't like the plan, not having time to implement it, and money.

5. Have students work individually to revise the above statements so each has parallel structure, and then share their revisions with the class.

Integrating Grammar Skills

Parts of Speech Point out to students that sentences with parallel structure have words or phrases that are the same part of speech. ("To study, to learn, and to explore" are all infinitive phrases. "Reading, research, and technology" are all nouns. "In our daily lives, at school, and in an increasingly competitive marketplace" are all prepositional phrases.) Have students identify the parts of speech they used to create parallelism in the step-by-step Teaching Guide above.

7.4

Revising Your Paragraphs

▶ **REVISION STRATEGY**
Revising to Create Parallelism

Speakers use a variety of techniques to help them communicate effectively. One common strategy is to use parallelism, the repetition of words, phrases, or grammatical structures. Like repetition, parallelism helps speakers establish ear-catching rhythms that help listeners stay focused and attentive.

One of the most trusted strategies for effective speaking is the "rule of three." Look in your draft to find sets of three facts or elements. Then, place them in parallel structures.

Paragraph Without Parallelism
The new library will help our community in many ways. The media center will be a vital place to study and learn. Emphasizing the connection between reading and technology sends an important message to children growing up in our area. The improved library will help us all gain the skills we need every day.

Paragraph With Parallelism
The new library will help our community in many ways. The media center will be a vital place to study, to learn, and to explore. By emphasizing the connections among reading, research, and technology, we send an important message to children growing up in our area. The improved library will help us all gain the skills we need in our daily lives, at school, and in an increasingly competitive marketplace.

Student Work IN PROGRESS

Name: Marvin Astorga
Bel Air High School
El Paso, TX

Revising to Create Parallelism

Marvin revised the final sentence of his opening paragraph to include a set of parallel ideas that establish an effective flow of ideas.

I adamantly oppose the new proposal because it will increase student fatigue. The plan will also be disorienting, which could be dangerous. Parents' schedules will be disturbed, too.

, create potentially dangerous disorientation, and interfere with parents' schedules.

Revising Your Sentences

▶ **REVISION STRATEGY**
Eliminating Errors in Logic

Look for the following errors in logic as you review your draft. Correct any and all instances you find.

- **Circular reasoning** is an attempt to prove a statement by restating it in a new way. Example: *This recommendation is illegal because it is against the law.*

- An **either/or argument** allows for only two possibilities, when, in fact, there are many others. Example: *If we advertise on television, people will buy our magazine.*

- A **questionable cause-and-effect** statement gives a cause that did not necessarily result in the stated effect. Example: *Most offices today use computers instead of typewriters because typewriters are so noisy.*

- An **overgeneralization** is a broad statement that is all-inclusive but cannot be true. Example: *Everyone believes that this soup will cure the common cold.*

Grammar in Your Writing
Parallelism

Whenever you present a comparison or a series of ideas that are equal in importance, express them in parallel grammatical structures.

Parallel Words: The board reviewed three aspects of the plan: economic, social, and educational.

Parallel Phrases: Surveys were available at the library, in the cafeteria, and on the Internet.

Parallel Clauses: We learned who approved of the plan, who disapproved, and who had no opinion.

Avoid faulty parallelism, which results when ideas of equal importance are not expressed in equal grammatical structures. To correct faulty parallelism, make sure that each idea is expressed with the same grammatical structure.

Find It in Your Reading Review "Woman's Right to Suffrage" on pages 124–125. Identify three sentences that contain parallel words, phrases, or clauses.

Find It in Your Writing Review your draft, correcting faulty parallelism. Then, add parallel structure to emphasize key points.

For more on parallelism, see Chapter 20.

Revising • 135

Revising: Deleting Empty Phrases and Hedging Words

Teaching Resources: Writing Support Transparencies, 7-I

1. Explain that *empty phrases* and *hedging words* are unnecessary words that can make a speech boring and weaken the speaker's argument.

2. Display Transparency 7-I. Read Marvin's excerpt aloud, first as originally written, and then with the unnecessary words removed. Ask students to compare the two examples. Which speech is longer? Which captures the listener's attention better? Which sounds more confident? Which is more persuasive? Students should find that deleting qualifiers makes the speech shorter, more interesting, more assured and, thus, more convincing to the listener.

3. Ask students to read through their own speeches, drawing a single line through unnecessary words. Note that some hedging words are necessary to avoid over-generalization.

7.4

Revising Your Word Choice

Trim Unnecessary Words and Phrases

Few things are as tiring as listening to someone go on and on about a topic. Avoid boring your audience—trim unnecessary words and phrases from your persuasive speech. Doing so will ensure that your audience hears only the strong, important points in your speech.

▶ **REVISION STRATEGY**
Deleting Empty Phrases and Hedging Words

Empty phrases say nothing. Hedging words and phrases lessen the impact of what you say. Read through your draft, and, whenever you come across an empty or hedging word or phrase, delete it. Then, reread the surrounding text to be sure that it still makes sense.

Following are some examples of empty phrases and hedging words:

Empty Phrases: as I said before, needless to say, in my opinion, it is a fact that, it is also true that, there are, the reason was that, the thing is, what I mean is, given the fact that

Hedging Words and Phrases: almost, it seems, kind of, quite, rather, somewhat, sort of, tends, probably, fairly

Student Work IN PROGRESS

Name: Marvin Astorga
Bel Air High School
El Paso, TX

Deleting Unnecessary Words
Marvin revised these sentences to delete unnecessary qualifiers and to revise an overgeneralization.

Finally, ~~probably~~ one of the most important reasons for rejecting this proposal is that parents' schedules will be ~~fairly~~ drastically affected.

Working parents will have ~~no way of picking up their kids from school.~~ difficulty accommodating the new school hours.

✎ STANDARDIZED TEST PREPARATION WORKSHOP

Unnecessary Words Standardized test questions may require students to identify words or phrases that are unnecessary and can be eliminated from a draft. Read the following paragraph and have students answer the question below it.

On the whole, most high school students at our school do not like getting up for school at 8:00 A.M. Our survey shows that 80 percent would prefer to start school at 9:00 A.M This is a fairly large percentage of students.

Which words and phrases are unnecessary and can be eliminated from this paragraph?

A "On the whole" and "at our school"

B "At our school" and "fairly"

C "80 percent" and "8:00 A.M."

D "On the whole" and "fairly"

Students should recognize that **D** is the correct answer. In A and B, "at our school" is essential to knowing where the survey took place. In C, both "80 percent" and "8:00 A.M." are important details that should not be eliminated.

Consider Connotations

A word's dictionary definition is called its **denotation.** The feelings or associations the word suggests are its **connotations.** As you review your word choices, consider the positive or negative associations of each word.

Negative	Neutral	Positive
nosy	inquisitive	curious
relentless	unyielding	determined
trendy	in style	fashionable
bossy	firm	assertive

▶ **REVISION STRATEGY**
Annotating Word Choices

Use + or – signs to mark the positive or negative connotations of important words in your speech. You might use ++ or – – to indicate words with particularly strong connotations. After marking each important word, look at the overall pattern. If you have too many + or – symbols, consider changing some words to create a less emotional appeal.

Peer Review

Replay

Practicing your speech for a partner is one of the most valuable strategies you can use to review a persuasive speech. After practicing your speech, assess its impact by asking questions such as the following:

- What was your main impression of the speech?
- What do you think my goal was? Did I achieve it?
- Which connections confused or misled you?
- What arguments did I leave out?

You may want to make revisions in your speech based on your partner's suggestions. Then, practice delivering your speech once more before you make your formal presentation.

Writers in
ACTION

When it comes to persuading an audience, the words you choose are just as important as your argument or position. Joseph Conrad is acknowledged as a writer who used words brilliantly. Conrad emphasized the impact of words over meaning when he wrote,

"He who wants to persuade should put his trust not in the right argument, but in the right word."

More About the Writer

Joseph Conrad was a Polish-born writer who lived from 1857 to 1924. Although Conrad did not learn English until he was twenty-one, he became a major writer in the English language. Perhaps his most famous novels were *Heart of Darkness* and *Lord Jim*, works characterized by strong moral messages.

Revising: Consider Connotations

Teaching Resources: Writing Support Transparencies, 7-J; Writing Support Activity Book, 7-4

1. Give students an example of two synonyms with different connotations, such as *gabby* and *outgoing*. Ask them to identify which word their listeners would react to positively and which they would react to negatively. Explain that the associations that a listener makes with a word are the word's connotations.

2. Read to students the words on the chart without letting them look at their textbooks. Ask students to identify each word as "negative," "neutral," or "positive."

3. Have students look at the text and compare their answers to the chart. Note that some words have different connotations for different people, but that many words have strong connotations for most people.

Revising: Annotating Word Choices

1. Have students read through their drafts, making + signs above words with positive connotations and − signs above words with negative connotations. They can also use ++ or −− for words with extremely positive or negative connotations.

2. Then, ask students to check for variety in their use of positive and negative connotation. If they used only negative or positive language, have them revise the drafts to include more variety.

3. Have students also check to make sure they have not included too many words with strong connotations. Explain that this could lead to an overly emotional speech. Assign students to work in groups to find the average number of + and − marks used by students in the group. If any student varies greatly from the average, have the group help the student revise the speech.

Editing and Proofreading

1. Write the following sentence with several mistakes in it on the chalkboard:

   During the rain of Henry the Eaghth, they're where many be headings.

2. Ask a volunteer to read the sentence aloud. Discuss why this sentence would be difficult to read in the middle of a speech.

3. Explain that misspellings can throw a speaker off in the middle of a speech. Grammatical errors may make their listeners break their rhythm.

4. If students are using a word processor, have them use the spell-checker to double-check their work. Remind them that a spell-checker will not catch all mistakes.

Commonly Mistaken Words

1. Explain that some words are commonly confused because they share similar sounds, spellings, or meanings. These are the types of mistakes that spell-checkers cannot find.

2. Have students look at the example in Grammar in Your Writing. Challenge them to use the words "accept" and "except" correctly in a sentence.

3. Have students generate a list of other frequently confused words *(their/they're/there; to/too/two; your/you're)*.

Find It in Your Reading

Students may cite such words as *right* (write, rite), *their* (they're, there), *whole* (hole), *to* (two, too), and *through* (threw).

Find It in Your Writing

Have students make sure they correctly used the words *accept, except, affect, effect, than,* and *then*.

7.5 Editing and Proofreading

Before you present your speech aloud, check your grammar, usage, and spelling carefully.

Focusing on Proofreading

As you proofread your draft, look for words that are commonly mistaken for one another. Check for words that have similar sounds, such as *adapt* and *adopt*. Then, consult a dictionary to make sure you are using the correct word.

Grammar in Your Writing
Commonly Mistaken Words

The following words are commonly confused because of similar sounds, spellings, or meanings. When you use these words, make sure that you have chosen the correct one.

accept, except
Accept is a verb meaning "to receive." *Except* is a preposition meaning "other than" or "leaving out."

affect, effect
Affect is almost always a verb and means "to influence."
Effect may be used as a noun meaning "result."

than, then
Use *than* in comparisons. *Then,* an adverb, usually refers to time.

Find It in Your Reading Find three words in the "Woman's Right to Suffrage" on pages 124–125 that might be confused with other terms. Explain why each chosen word is correct.

Find It in Your Writing As you proofread, check that you have used each of these words correctly: *accept, except, affect, effect, than, then.*

For more on choosing the correct words, see Chapter 29.

138 • Persuasive Speech

⏱ TIME AND RESOURCE MANAGER

Resources
Print: *Scoring Rubrics on Transparency*, Ch. 7; *Writing Assessment and Portfolio Management; Formal Assessments*, Ch. 7
Technology: *Writing and Grammar* Interactive Text, Section 7.5

Using the Full Student Edition	Using the Handbook🄷
• Review p. 138 in class, including Grammar in Your Writing. • Ask students to edit and proofread their narratives in class. • Read and discuss the Final Draft, pp. 140–141.	• Review p. 90 in class, including Grammar in Your Writing. • Ask students to edit and proofread their narratives in class.

7.6 Publishing and Presenting

Building Your Portfolio

1. **Speech** Deliver your speech to your classmates or to another audience. While making your presentation, make frequent eye contact with your audience and use hand gestures to emphasize your key points. Speak slowly and clearly, and vary the tone and volume of your voice to match the content of your speech. If possible, record your delivery so that you can evaluate your own presentation.

2. **School Paper** Reformat your speech into a persuasive essay. Send it to your school newspaper to be published as an article.

Reflecting on Your Writing

After you have completed your persuasive speech, take some time to think about the experiences you had while writing and presenting it. Use these questions to direct your reflection, and record your responses in your portfolio:

- What aspects of the topic did you discover while collecting evidence for your speech?

- What specific techniques did you learn for persuading an audience?

 Internet Tip

To see a persuasive speech scored according to this rubric, go on-line:
PHSchool.com
Enter Web Code:
egk-1201

Rubric for Self-Assessment

Use the following criteria to evaluate your persuasive speech:

	Score 4	Score 3	Score 2	Score 1
Audience and Purpose	Chooses highly effective words; clearly focuses on persuasive task	Chooses effective words; focuses on persuasive task	Occasionally uses effective words; is minimally focused on persuasive task	Poor word choice shows lack of attention to persuasive task
Organization	Uses clear, consistent organizational strategy	Uses clear organizational strategy with occasional inconsistencies	Uses inconsistent organizational strategy and illogical presentation	Lacks organizational strategy; gives confusing presentation
Elaboration	Contains specific, well-elaborated reasons that provide convincing support for the writer's position	Contains two or more moderately elaborated reasons in support of the writer's position	Contains several reasons, but few are elaborated	Contains no specific reasons
Use of Language	Contains no empty or hedging words; makes no errors in grammar, spelling, and punctuation	Contains few empty or hedging words; makes few errors in grammar, spelling, and punctuation	Contains some empty and hedging words; makes errors in grammar, spelling, and punctuation	Contains many empty or hedging words; makes many errors in grammar, spelling, and punctuation

Publishing and Presenting • **139**

Step-by-Step Teaching Guide

Publishing and Presenting

1. Remind students that this is the learning phase in which they "take a stand" and deliver their persuasive speeches. Encourage students to find more places to give their speeches: school assemblies, club meetings, town forums, open-mike events, and so on.

2. Have students reassess their audience while preparing their speeches, if the audience will differ from the one to whom they initially targeted the speech.

3. Have students be sure to include eye contact and hand gestures to emphasize certain aspects of their speeches.

4. If students decide to reformat their speech into a persuasive essay, provide examples of persuasive essays previously published in the school newspaper.

ASSESS AND CLOSE

Step-by-Step Teaching Guide

Assessment

Teaching Resources: Scoring Rubrics on Transparency, 7; Writing Assessment and Portfolio Management; Formal Assessment, Ch. 7

1. Display the Scoring Rubric transparency and review the criteria in class.

2. In addition to student self-assessment, you may wish to use one of the following assessment options:

   - score student essays yourself, using the rubric and scoring models in *Writing Assessment and Portfolio Management.*

   - review the Standardized Test Preparation Workshop on pages 146–147 and have students respond to a persuasive writing prompt.

   - administer the assessment from *Formal Assessment* in the Teaching Resources to measure students' mastery of concepts.

☑ ONGOING ASSESSMENT: Assess Mastery

Use one of the following options to assess final drafts of students' persuasive speeches.

Self-Assessment Ask students to score their speeches using the rubric provided. Then, have students jot down notes and write a paragraph detailing the most valuable thing they learned in preparing their speeches.	**Teacher Assessment** You might use the rubric and scoring models provided in *Writing Assessment and Portfolio Management* to score students' persuasive speeches.

Final Draft

1. Help students see that "Four-Day School Week" incorporates key elements of the persuasive speech.

   • The topic is well chosen, and the incidents are high interest and manageable in scope.

   • Audience and purpose were considered carefully. The speech targets members of the school board and is respectful of their work.

   • The introduction tells the school board exactly what Marvin's position is. The body of the speech provides well-researched facts that support his position.

   • The use of parallel structures, logical progressions, and words with appropriate connotations contribute to Marvin's argument.

   • Marvin restates his initial appeal at the end of the speech.

2. Ask students to imagine how school board members will react to the speech. Explain that carefully crafted persuasive speeches can help convince listeners of the speaker's position and make them respect his or her work and opinions.

3. Ask students whether there are any changes they would recommend to make the speech more persuasive or to fine-tune the language. How might they apply these suggestions to their own writing?

Critical Viewing

Interpret Students may say that the student is deep in concentration. The biggest clue is body language.

7.7 *Student Work*
IN PROGRESS

FINAL DRAFT

◀ **Critical Viewing** How would you describe the emotional state of the student pictured? What clues helped you decide? **[Interpret]**

Four-Day School Week

Marvin Astorga
Bel Air High School
El Paso, Texas

Before I begin, I would like to compliment you and the entire school board on the wonderful job you are doing. I am a sophomore at Bel-Air High School, and it has recently come to my attention that the school board is considering a plan that would have students attend a four-day school week instead of the current five-day schedule. Each school day would be lengthened so that students would spend the same total amount of time in school each week. This may seem like a good idea at first, but a little reflection will reveal serious drawbacks. I adamantly oppose the new proposal because it will increase student fatigue, create potentially dangerous disorientation, and interfere with parents' schedules.

In the opening paragraph, Marvin respectfully and clearly states his opposition to the proposal.

Although it sounds like less time in school, this plan will actually exhaust even the best of students. The new plan calls for approximately two more hours per school day, which will leave students less time at home for homework and rest. If students are not given time to meet these needs, they will come to school tired and without their homework. The current five-day week is already as crammed with work as a stray dog is with fleas. Why burden kids with a heavier load to carry? In fact, a recent survey in the September 27, 1997, issue of *Newsweek* sternly states that 78 percent of students with two or more hours of homework a night fail not one, not two, but all of their core classes, which includes math, English, social studies, and science. Add a sleepy disposition to this calculation and students are even more likely to fail. Subtracting a day from the work week and adding the time to the other days is an aberration that will have students working toward failure. I doubt that even the mighty Hercules could handle this four-day proposition.

Another reason for not adopting this plan is that adjusting to the new schedule will be disorienting and possibly dangerous. Students will be confused by the new hours, as well as distracted by plans they will be making for their newly acquired free day. Disrupting the sequence of a person's biological clock can be harmful, especially to young people like ourselves; such disruption can be the catalyst for a breakdown. Dr. Robert Heely of the National Institute for Physiological Observation illustrates my point. In the April 1997 issue of *Parenting Magazine*, he writes, "When there is an abrupt change in a child's biological clock, it can often lead to migraine headaches, stomachaches, weakness, irregular eating habits and sleep patterns." Why create a situation that can contribute to such a wide range of potential health problems?

Finally, one of the most important reasons for rejecting this proposal is that parents' schedules will be drastically affected. Working parents will have difficulty accommodating the new school hours. Since their schedules revolve around their kids, a new schedule will disorient them as much as it will us. Confusion leads to frustration, and frustration to anger. I am sure that the school board does not want to create a band of angry parents.

For these reasons, I am totally against accepting the four-day plan. My research also indicates that I am not alone. I surveyed 80 of my fellow students and found that 79 percent were against the plan. An even greater percentage thought the plan would increase student stress. I urge you to consider their responses and reject this proposal. I know the school board is very busy, and I thank you for your time.

Marvin gains the audience's attention by using a light-hearted and humorous analogy when he compares the five-day week to a dog with fleas.

Marvin uses statistics to support the main idea of this paragraph.

At the end of his speech, Marvin widens the perspective from his own opinion to the collective opinion of his school.

Marvin concludes with a strong restatement of his position and a polite ending sentence.

Student Work in Progress • **141**

Customize for
ESL Students

Some students may be unfamiliar with the decision-making structure of most U.S. public school systems. To help them understand the potential impact of Marvin's speech, sketch out for them the reporting system of a school system before they read the speech. You might also want to describe a typical school board meeting, including who would be present and how the event would be recorded.

Integrating Speaking and Listening Skills

Have students take turns reading a paragraph from Marvin's speech as if they were actually giving the speech to the school board. Make sure that they use appropriate body language and eye contact. Ask them to vary the tone and volume of their voices. The student audience should listen as if they were school board members responding to both the content of the speech and the presentation. After the readings, ask students to discuss how body language, eye contact, and voice influence the listeners.

Connected Assignment
Editorial

Like persuasive speeches, editorials seek to influence readers or listeners about a particular issue. They appear in newspapers or magazines and on television or radio. Editorials may present the opinions of the media's management or those of guest writers or speakers. Writers construct a persuasive argument and then support it with facts, details, and examples.

An effective editorial contains

- a clearly stated position on a subject.
- details such as facts, statistics, and other examples to help support the opinion.
- a respectful yet persuasive tone.
- a clear and effective method of organization.

Write an editorial presenting your views on an issue. Use the writing process skills to guide your work.

Prewriting

Choosing Your Topic Because effective persuasion stems from conviction, choose an issue that is important to you. Then, chat with a group of friends about controversies in your school or community and in the nation as a whole. Note any issues that spark your interest, and choose one as your topic.

Narrowing Your Topic Narrow your topic to a manageable size to increase the persuasive impact. You cannot address everything about global pollution, for example, in an editorial, but you can respond to a specific law about pollution. Choose an aspect of your topic that you can adequately discuss in a brief paper. Keep narrowing your topic until you can hit all your main points quickly.

Gathering Your Details

Before you begin drafting your editorial, take time to gather details that will support your argument and help you achieve your purpose. Gather details from a variety of sources. The details themselves should also vary.

Types of details may include

- factual details or statistical details.
- quotations.
- personal opinions.

▲ **Critical Viewing**
Besides editorials, what types of persuasive writing might you find in a newspaper? **[Generalize]**

☑ **ONGOING ASSESSMENT: Prerequisite Skills**

Students may find the following resources from Chapter 7 particularly helpful in completing their editorials.

In the Textbook	Print Resources	Technology
Create an Outline, Section 7.2 Complete a T-Chart, Section 7.2	*Writing Support Transparencies,* 7-C–E *Writing Support Activity Book,* 7-2–3	*Writing and Grammar* Interactive Text, Section 7.2

Drafting

Choosing an Organizational Strategy Present your ideas effectively and logically. When writing persuasively, you may find order-of-importance organization particularly effective. Following is a sample outline that shows how to build an argument or build to a point using order-of-importance organization.

I. Introductory paragraph

II. Least important point

III. Points that build in importance

IV. Most important point

V. Concluding paragraph

Creating a Tone Use engaging and enthusiastic language to convey your idea's appeal. While it is appropriate to argue against specific aspects of the opposing viewpoint, keep a respectful tone and avoid name-calling. To do this, choose your words carefully, and address the opposition's views with respect.

Revising and Editing

Carefully check your editorial to be sure that it is free of faulty logic. Look for examples of overgeneralization, bandwagon appeals, begging the question, and circular reasoning within your editorial, and rewrite or delete them.

Then, reread your editorial, and evaluate its language. Make sure that you've chosen words that your audience will understand—especially if your topic is technical or is unfamiliar to the audience.

Confirm that you've provided sufficient supporting detail. Add details where lacking, and delete details that are unnecessary. Also, check to be sure that the details you've chosen help to create a tone.

Proofread your editorial carefully to be sure that it is free of errors in grammar, spelling, and punctuation.

Publishing and Presenting

Neatly print out a copy of your editorial and sign it. Then, mail it to your school paper or to a local newspaper. If you like, you can post a copy of your editorial on a bulletin board if you obtain permission to do so.

 **Spelling Tip**

Use a spell-check feature if you are working in a word-processing program. Then, reread the printout to be sure that you haven't left out any words and to catch errors that the spell check does not find, such as incorrect word usage.

Integrating Current Events

Have students look through newspapers for current events editorials they disagree with. Encourage them to write an editorial in response to one of them, addressing that writer's opinions and respectfully explaining why they are incorrect. Students must be able to defend their opinions with facts, which they can find in the news section of the newspaper.

Customize for
Linguistic Learners

Students might find it easier to detect the tone of words by hearing them, rather than seeing them. Have students circle words in their drafts whose tone they are unsure of. Then, have them meet with partners, say the words aloud, and work together to identify their tone.

Lesson Objectives

1. To describe how meanings are communicated through elements of design
2. To analyze relationships and ideas as presented in various media
3. To write a persuasive essay

Appreciating the Arts

1. Bring in illustrated art books or check them out from your school library.

2. Bring copies of *The American*, *Daisy Miller*, *The Bostonians*, and *The Turn of the Screw* to class. Read the first sentence of each book aloud, or have a student read it. Discuss the sentences. What is unusual about them? Which do they like best and why?

3. Use the art books to look for Sargent paintings. Have students work in small groups to find them, and then share them with the class. Ask students to discuss Sargent's use of light. Identify the source of light in each painting. What emotional effect does the light have on the viewer?

4. Most people agree that the preservation of art and artifacts is important to history and culture. However, not everyone agrees about how much money should be spent on such preservation. Have students brainstorm for a list of why museums are important. Using these reasons, ask students to draft a persuasive essay supporting an increase in state and public funding for museums in their area.

Viewing and Representing

Activity Have willing students present their essays to the class. Encourage them to use the works of art as part of their visual presentation.

Critical Viewing

Interpret Students might say that Gardner appears stately and cultured.

Spotlight on the Humanities

Appreciating the Arts

Focus on Art: Patron of the Arts, Isabella Gardner

Persuasion—getting others to agree with your opinion—is an essential skill for those who believe that the preservation of art and artifacts is important to history and culture. One of the nineteenth and twentieth centuries' most influential patrons of the arts was Bostonian Isabella Stewart Gardner (1840–1924). Born in New York City, Mrs. Gardner collected art from abroad, filling the Venetian palace that she built in Boston's Fenway Court with these great works. The museum still exists and is filled with Renaissance furniture, art, and tapestries. Raphael, Rembrandt, Botticelli, and Monet are just a few of the great painters whose works hang on the walls of Fenway Court.

Literature Connection American author Henry James (1843–1916) was a friend of Isabella Stewart Gardner in the late nineteenth century. James perfected the use of the sentence in literature, molding a single sentence into a work of art. His emphasis on moral themes and the difference between innocence and experience can be identified in all his novels and short stories. *The American, Daisy Miller, The Bostonians*, and the novelette *The Turn of the Screw* are among his best-known works.

Art Connection A friend of Henry James and Isabella Stewart Gardner, the American painter John Singer Sargent (1856–1925) was known for elegant, distinctive portraiture. Born in Florence, Italy, Sargent spent his early years in the major European capitals. In the 1880's, Venice, Italy, was a favorite spot for him, and he painted the city's extraordinary architecture and daily life. Experimenting with the depiction of light, Sargent painted with individual strokes of pure color that made the canvas seem to flicker. His portrait of Isabella Stewart Gardner was done in 1888.

Persuasive Writing Activity: Essay on the Importance of Museums

Write a persuasive essay supporting state and public funding for additional museums in the cities or suburbs in your area. Cite reasons why you think the preservation of art and artifacts is so important. Present your persuasive essay to your class.

Isabella Stewart Gardner (1840–1924), 1888, Isabella Stewart Gardner Museum, Boston, MA, USA

▲ **Critical Viewing**
What do clues in the portrait reveal about Isabella Stewart Gardner, the portrait's subject? **[Interpret]**

Media and Technology Skills

Lesson Objectives

1. To examine the effect of media on constructing one's perception of reality
2. To evaluate and critique the persuasive techniques of media messages
3. To distinguish the purposes of various media forms

Recognizing Persuasion in Media

Activity: Evaluating Internet Advertising

If you have spent much time surfing the Internet, you know that almost every Web site you visit is dotted with eye-catching, sometimes distracting advertisements. However, you might not realize just how many ads you see. Researchers estimate that you will see 360 ads during one hour of using the Internet.

Learn About It Advertisements on Web pages are called banners. Each banner is linked to an advertisement called a "target ad." A target ad can be one Web page or a complete site. For example, a banner ad might take you to an on-line clothing store.

Collect It Conduct an Internet survey to classify the Internet advertising you encounter in a fifteen- or thirty-minute Web session. Complete a chart to describe each advertisement.

Banner Ad	Images	Text	What It Is Advertising

Analyze It After describing each, see how the elements work together to persuade an audience. Look for these examples of persuasive strategies as you analyze the ads you've collected:

- **Animation and Imagery** Many banners use animation and vivid imagery to draw your attention and make you curious about what will happen when you click on the ad.

- **Deceptive or Misleading Layout** Some banner ads try to blend in with the Web page. You may not even be aware that an image is an advertisement until you have already clicked on it.

- **Product Positioning** Even if you never click a banner ad, you can still be affected by Internet advertising. Some Internet advertising is designed to build a product's image or reputation. If you see a name at the top of every Web page in a search engine, you might think that the product being advertised is well known or highly respected.

- **Site Registration** Some Web sites require you to register. The site owners might use your demographic information to target you with specific advertisements.

Watch Where You're Going

Many Internet surfers have experienced this surprise: You click on links without thinking and, before you know it, you're in a Web site that you don't want to be in.

To avoid the problem:
- Pay attention to your cursor, and read before you click.
- Beware of radio buttons that are preset to take you to a site when you hit Back.

To fix the problem:
- Hit GO on the Task Bar, and select from the list of sites already visited the point to which you want to return.

Step-by-Step Teaching Guide

Recognizing Persuasion in Media

Teaching Resources: Writing Support Transparencies, 7-K; Writing Support Activity Book, 7-5

1. Go over the examples of common persuasive strategies listed under Analyze It. If possible, bring students to the computer lab and show them actual examples of banners and other strategies.

2. Display the transparency (7-K) and give students copies of the blank organizer (7-5). Have them work in the computer lab with partners for thirty minutes to fill out the chart. Pairs may choose to start on sites they find interesting, such as sports or movie sites. Have students clear their starting sites with you.

3. Have students compare their charts and discuss the persuasive techniques they encountered. Which technique was used most frequently? Which one was most distracting? Most effective?

Lesson Objectives

1. To write a persuasive letter in response to a prompt
2. To organize ideas in writing to ensure coherence, logical progression, and support for ideas
3. To produce legible work that shows accurate spelling and correct use of the conventions of punctuation, capitalization, and grammar

---

Step-by-Step Teaching Guide

Responding to Persuasive Writing Prompts

Teaching Resources: Standardized Test Preparation Workbook, pp. 13–14

1. Read and discuss the criteria for assessment of a persuasive response.

2. Ask students to read the sample writing situation, and emphasize that the assignment is to compose a letter stating and defending a position.

3. Remind students of the audience (school newspaper) for whom they will be writing. How will this determine their tone?

4. Remind students that they must defend their position with facts. Divide the class into two groups: for the parking lot and against it. Have groups brainstorm for a list of facts that support their position. Students can decide which facts they believe are the strongest and include them in their letters.

5. Assign the writing prompt for completion within a class period.

Standardized Test Preparation Workshop

Responding to Persuasive Writing Prompts

On some standardized tests, you will be evaluated according to your ability to write persuasively. Following are the criteria upon which your persuasive response will be assessed:

- a clearly stated position that directly responds to the essay prompt
- language that appropriately addresses the audience you are targeting
- details that help you achieve your purpose for writing
- a logical and effective organization of ideas
- correct use of grammar, spelling, and punctuation

As you generate standardized test responses, rely on the basic writing process stages—prewriting, drafting, revising, editing, and proofreading—to lead you through the task. Keep an eye on time, however, as you work through each stage.

Below is an example of a standardized test persuasive writing prompt. Before developing your response, read the tips on the next page. Consider them as you write, also noting the time-planning suggestions on the clocks next to each stage.

Sample Writing Situation

> Your school grounds are next to a wooded area inhabited by various forms of wildlife. Recently, the school board decided to expand the school's parking lot into this area in order to solve the congested parking situation. This would have some consequences on the wildlife. What is your position on the situation? Compose a letter to your school newspaper stating your opinion and defending it with compelling reasons.

Test Tips

- Use the opening paragraph of your test prompt response to prepare your audience for your argument, and use your closing paragraph to restate your main points.
- Save your strongest argument for the final body paragraph.

146 • Persuasive Speech

✍ TEST-TAKING TIP

Tell students that after they have made a Pro-and-Con chart as part of prewriting, they should consider numbering their arguments for either side in order of importance. They can then organize their response by saving their strongest argument for last.

Remind students that an argument is more credible when it recognizes the beliefs of the opposition. Encourage students to mention one of the opposition's ideas and clearly explain why it is incorrect.

146

Prewriting

Allow about one quarter of your time for shaping your argument and providing supporting details.

Look at Both Sides To provide you with a fully rounded picture of the topic you are addressing, enter your ideas onto a Pro-and-Con chart. To make a Pro-and-Con chart, write details that support your position in the left column and details that support the opposition's opinion in the right column. Take the opposition's points into account, and address them in your argument, pointing out why your position makes more sense.

Drafting

Allow about half of your time for drafting. Remember to leave space for text you may want to add when revising.

Elaborate State your position clearly at the beginning of the essay, and present your supporting reasons in order of importance. Also, cite specific examples from your personal experience that will help readers visualize the situation as you see it.

Create a Tone The tone of your argument should be persuasive. It should not simply attack any opposing viewpoints. Support your argument with convincing reasons, and present your case in as positive a light as possible. For example, if you are opposed to the expansion of the parking lot onto wildlife-inhabited areas, explain the ways in which the construction would injure the presence of the animals.

Revising

Allow almost one quarter of your time for revising.

Review the Tone Read over your work, and listen to its tone. Replace words with negative, overly critical connotations, which may alienate undecided readers. If possible, recopy your work. Otherwise, insert changes neatly.

Editing and Proofreading

Allow about five minutes to review your work for spelling, punctuation, and grammar errors.

Take Time Work steadily and carefully to review your essay for spelling or punctuation errors. Sometimes reading backward makes these errors easier to spot. Make all changes with proofreader's marks and neatly drawn deletion lines.

Customize for
Less Advanced Students

Remind students that they are not to write about the grounds and parking situation at their own school, but about the school described in the writing prompt.

Customize for
AP Students

Remind students their peers are not the only people who read the school newspaper. Teachers, parents, and school board members read it as well. The tone of their letters should reflect this understanding.

Integrating Speaking and Listening Skills

After they finish, you might organize a class debate about the issue in the writing prompt. Students will be prepared to argue their opinions because they have thought them through while writing their letters. You might quickly review the speaking and listening skills in Chapter 28 before starting the debate.

Chapter 8

Time and Resource Manager

In-Depth Lesson Plan

	LESSON FOCUS	PRINT AND MEDIA RESOURCES
DAY 1	**Introduction to Advertisements** Students learn key elements of an advertisement and analyze the Model From Literature. (pp. 148–150/☐92–94)	*Writers at Work* **DVD**, Persuasion *Writing and Grammar* **Interactive Text**, Ch. 8, Introduction
DAY 2	**Prewriting** Students choose and narrow a topic, consider their audience and purpose, and gather information. (pp. 151–154/☐95–98)	*Writing and Grammar* **Interactive Text**, Section 8.2 **Teaching Resources** *Writing Support Transparencies*, 8-A–C; *Writing Support Activity Book*, 8-1; *Topic Bank for Heterogeneous Classes*, Ch. 8
DAY 3	**Drafting** Students organize their ideas and write their first drafts. (p. 155/☐99)	*Writing and Grammar* **Interactive Text**, Section 8.3
DAY 4	**Revising** Students revise their drafts in terms of overall structure, paragraphs, sentences, and word choice. (pp. 156–158/☐100–102)	*Writing and Grammar* **Interactive Text**, Section 8.4 **Teaching Resources** *Writing Support Transparencies*, 8-D–E; *Writing Support Activity Book*, 8-4
DAY 5	**Editing and Proofreading; Publishing and Presenting** Students check their work for accuracy and present their final drafts. (pp. 159–161/☐103–105)	*Writing and Grammar* **Interactive Text**, Sections 8.5–6 **Teaching Resources** *Scoring Rubrics on Transparency*, Ch. 8; *Writing Assessment and Portfolio Management; Formal Assessment*, Ch. 8

Accelerated Lesson Plan

	LESSON FOCUS	PRINT AND MEDIA RESOURCES
DAY 1	**Introduction Through Drafting** Students review characteristics of an advertisement, select topics, and write drafts. (pp. 148–155/☐92–99)	*Writing and Grammar* **Interactive Text**, Ch. 8, Introduction through Section 8.3 **Teaching Resources** *Writing Support Transparencies*, 8-A–C; *Writing Support Activity Book*, 8-1
DAY 2	**Revising Through Presenting** Students work individually or with peers to revise, edit, and proofread their work for presentation. (pp. 156–161/☐100–105)	*Writing and Grammar* **Interactive Text**, Sections 8.4–6 **Teaching Resources** *Writing Support Transparencies*, 8-D–E; *Writing Support Activity Book*, 8-4; *Scoring Rubrics on Transparency*, Ch. 8; *Writing Assessment and Portfolio Management; Formal Assessment*, Ch. 8

Options for Adapting Lesson Plans

HOMEWORK

Have students complete any stage of the lesson for homework.

FEATURES

Extend coverage with Connected Assignment (p. 162), Spotlight on the Humanities (p. 164), Media and Technology Skills (p. 165), and the Standardized Test Preparation Workshop (p. 166).

TECHNOLOGY

Students can complete any stage of the lesson on the computer, using *Writing and Grammar* Interactive Text or a word-processing program. Have them print out their completed work.

Writing and Grammar Handbook Alignment

Page numbers in Step-by-Step Teaching Guides in this Teacher's Edition refer to pages from the full student text. Handbook page references, indicated with this icon Ⓗ, are provided in Time and Resource Manager boxes and at the bottom of each Teacher's Edition page.

INTEGRATED SKILLS COVERAGE

Integrating Grammar
Abbreviating Dates and Ordinals, SE p. 159/Ⓗ103

Reading/Writing Connection
Evaluate Visuals, SE p. 150/Ⓗ94

Viewing and Representing
Critical Viewing, SE pp. 148, 155, 156, 162, 164/Ⓗ92, 99, 100; ATE p. 164
Identifying Themes in Media, SE p. 164
Using Technology to Extend Meaning, SE p. 165

Speaking and Listening
ATE pp. 153, 161

Vocabulary
ATE p. 158

Technology
SE pp. 158, 160, 163/Ⓗ102, 104

ASSESSMENT SUPPORT

Standardized Test Preparation Workshop, SE p. 166; ATE p. 158
Standardized Test Preparation Workbook, pp. 15–16
Scoring Rubrics on Transparency, Ch. 8
Formal Assessment, Ch. 8
Writing Assessment and Portfolio Management

MEETING INDIVIDUAL NEEDS

Less Advanced Students ATE pp. 154, 163, 167. See also Ongoing Assessments ATE pp. 152, 157.
AP Students ATE p. 167
ESL Students ATE pp. 155, 157, 161, 163
Spatial Learners ATE p. 149
Linguistic Learners ATE p. 154

BLOCK SCHEDULING

Pacing Suggestions
For 90-minute Blocks
• Have students complete the Prewriting and Drafting stages in a single period.
• Focus one class period on Revising and Editing and Publishing and Presenting. Allow at least 30 minutes for peer revision.

Resources for Varying Instruction
• *Writing and Grammar* **Interactive Text** A 90-minute block provides an ideal opportunity for students to work on the computer.
• *Writers at Work* **DVD** Show the Persuasion segment in class.

Professional Development Support
• *How to Manage Instruction in the Block* This teaching resource provides management and activity suggestions.

MEDIA AND TECHNOLOGY

For the Student
• *Writing and Grammar* **Interactive Text**, Ch. 8

For the Teacher
• *Writers at Work* **DVD**, Persuasion
• **Teacher**EXPRESS™ **CD-ROM**

WRITING AND GRAMMAR ON-LINE

Interactive Text (On-line or on CD-ROM)
• Easily navigable instruction with interactive Revision Checkers
• Full use of e-rater™, the essay-scoring system (on-line only)

Companion Web Site PHSchool.com
• Scoring rubrics with models (use Web Code egk-1201)

See the Go On-line! **feature, SE p. iii.**

LITERATURE CONNECTIONS

Related selection from *Prentice Hall Literature, Penguin Edition,* The British Tradition:
Topic Bank Option "Kubla Khan," Samuel Taylor Coleridge, SE p. 151/Ⓗ95

Lesson Objectives

1. To write a persuasive advertisement appropriate to audience and purpose

2. To read to appreciate a writer's craft and to discover models for writing

3. To use prewriting strategies to generate ideas and plan

4. To test and revise a project using questionnaires, group discussions, and feedback forms

5. To organize ideas to ensure coherence, logical progression, and support for ideas

6. To develop and revise drafts in terms of structure, paragraphs, sentences, and word choice

7. To edit and proofread to ensure standard English usage and grammar

8. To refine an advertisement for publication

Critical Viewing

Interpret Possible responses might include comments about the festive, colorful image, or simply the realization that a postcard like this would be sent from a place someone thought was worth visiting.

---

8 Persuasion
Advertisement

Greetings from Route 66, Beth Nobles, Courtesy of the artist

Advertisements in Everyday Life

Take a moment to think about how many advertisements you see or hear every day. What was your guess? Nine? Ninety? Every time you open a newspaper, turn on the television, flip through a magazine, log on the Internet, listen to the radio, check your mail, walk into a store, or drive past a billboard, you are exposed to advertising.

Advertisements (or *ads*, for short) are a form of **persuasion**—writing or speaking that attempts to convince others to accept a position or to take an action. Ads, it seems, are everywhere today.

▲ **Critical Viewing**
In what way does this artwork make Route 66 seem appealing? Explain. **[Interpret]**

148 • Persuasion

⏱ TIME AND RESOURCE MANAGER

Resources
Technology: *Writers at Work* DVD, Persuasion; *Writing and Grammar* Interactive Text, Ch. 8

Using the Full Student Edition	Using the Handbook🖰
• Cover pp. 148–149 in class. • Show the Persuasion section of the *Writers at Work* DVD. • Read the Model From Literature (p. 150) in class, and use it to brainstorm for ideas with students.	• Cover pp. 92–93 in class. • Show the Persuasion section of the *Writers at Work* DVD. • Read the Model From Literature (p. 94) in class, and use it to brainstorm for ideas with students.

What Is an Advertisement?

An **advertisement** tries to persuade an audience to buy a product or service, accept an idea, or support a cause or candidate. Most advertisements have

- an attention-getting opener, such as a startling headline, catchy slogan, or surprising statistic.
- a memorable ending or tag line.
- persuasive and/or informative text.
- striking visual or aural images.

To preview the criteria on which your advertisement may be evaluated, see the Rubric for Self-Assessment on page 160.

Types of Advertisements

Advertisements range from those that sell consumer products to those that educate the public. Whatever the focus, most advertising takes one of the following forms:

- **Print ads** are written advertisements that appear in newspapers and magazines.
- **Posters, flyers, and mailers** are printed on sheets of paper and are either posted or delivered.
- **Television and radio commercials** convey their persuasive messages through dialogue and visual or aural images.
- **On-line ads** contain persuasive messages, some of which employ animation, video, and sound effects.
- **Product packaging,** besides listing a product's contents, may also contain promotional messages and attractively designed labels to entice consumers.

Writers in ACTION

English actor John Cleese is also an expert comedian who was part of the renowned Monty Python troupe. Cleese believes that humor can play an important role in the art of persuasion:

"If I can get you to laugh with me, you like me better, which makes you more open to my ideas. And if I can persuade you to laugh at the particular point I make, by laughing at it you acknowledge its truth."

PREVIEW *Student Work* IN PROGRESS

Matt Bezerman, a student at General Douglas MacArthur High School in Seaford, New York, created an advertisement for a yard sale in his neighborhood. Follow his progress as he gathers details, drafts, and revises his advertisement. Matt's finished advertisement appears at the end of the chapter.

Advertisement • **149**

PREPARE and ENGAGE

Interest GRABBER Ask students to brainstorm for their favorite print, radio, or television advertisements. Have volunteers share their answers and discuss the specific elements that make these ads so successful.

Activate Prior Knowledge

Ask students to recall the last time they had to make a sign or write an advertisement (for example, to sell something they no longer wanted, to promote a car wash or other service, or to support a candidate for a school campaign). What steps and techniques did they use to produce a successful advertisement? After discussing these methods, refer students to the characteristics of an advertisement listed at the top of the page.

More About the Writer

While he is best known for his comedy roles in television shows such as *Monty Python's Flying Circus* and in movies such as *A Fish Called Wanda,* John Cleese has also succeeded in advertising, where he uses humor as a serious tool of persuasion. He is one of the founders of Video Arts, now the world's leading provider of video-based learning programs. Cleese combines humor with scholarship in books such as *Life and How to Survive It,* co-authored with psychiatrist Robin Skynner.

Customize for
Spatial Learners

Have each student bring in an example of product packaging. Examine and discuss the various kinds of advertising on each example.

☑ ONGOING ASSESSMENT: Diagnose

Use one of the following options to diagnose students' current level of proficiency in persuasive writing.

Option 1 Ask students to select their strongest example of persuasive writing (an advertisement, if possible) from last year. Have them read over their work and write a short paragraph on its strong points and its weaknesses. Meet with students and discuss the areas in which they believe they need to improve.

Option 2 Ask students to make a list of three to five important features of an advertisement. Have them share and discuss their answers. Students who have trouble articulating at least three features will need a review of the function and purpose of an advertisement.

Reading\Writing Connection
Evaluate Visuals

Advertisers know that visuals are the first thing to catch a person's eye. If a visual pleases the person, he or she may go on to read or listen to the "sales pitch," the words that describe the product or service and explain why it is, in the advertiser's view, worth having. These visuals may consist simply of large, colorful type, but they often include artwork, from simple starbursts or banners to complex photographic or video images. Visuals can also include more subtle persuasive elements, such as making it appear that your life will improve dramatically (nice cars, more friends) if you use the right shampoo, toothpaste, or soft drink. Be aware of how visuals work on these two levels: selling the product and selling a dream. Determine which technique is being used and whether it is effective and realistic.

Step-by-Step Teaching Guide

Engage Students Through Literature

1. Ask students what they noticed first about this advertisement.

2. Have students discuss how the blend of photographs and names of countries contributes to the impact of the ad.

3. Ask students which elements of the ad they find most appealing: which design elements, which words, which facts.

4. Explain that an ad is successful only if potential consumers remember the product. If an ad is beautiful or amazing, but no one remembers the product, it has not succeeded. Ask students whether they feel that the ad in the text is successful.

8.1 Model From Literature

The following advertisement was placed by a university. The ad promotes the university's Semester at Sea program.

The advertisement features the catchy title of the university's program. The title helps capture readers' interest.

Photographs such as these help convince the audience that the program is interesting and worthwhile.

Words like "voyage" and "discovery" conjure up exciting associations in readers.

Boldfaced text makes exotic country names stand out.

Evaluate Visuals When you look at an advertisement, identify the message that is being conveyed by visual elements such as photographs and art. Then, decide whether or not that message is realistic and truthful.

8.2 *Prewriting*

Choosing Your Topic

Before you can create an advertisement, you need to have a product, a service, or an idea to sell. Use the following strategies to generate a topic:

Strategies for Generating a Topic

1. **Blueprint** Sketch rooms in your home. Then, list the products that you use daily in the various rooms. For example, you might list dish soap and sponges when you consider the kitchen. Then, write an advertisement for the product you like the most.

2. **Listing** Write the heading "Things I Can Do," and list as many items in this category as you can. For example, you might list *play the piano*, *walk the dog*, *cook*, and *baby-sit*, among other things. Then, choose an item from the list, and write an advertisement for that service.

Interactive Textbook

Try it out! List your items using the Essay Builder, accessible from the menu bar, on-line or on CD-ROM.

TOPIC BANK

Following are more topic ideas for advertisements:

1. **Favorite Restaurant** When you get to choose where to eat out, where do you go? Choose to advertise your favorite restaurant.

Responding to Literature

2. Samuel Taylor Coleridge's "Kubla Khan" contains descriptive details that make Xanadu seem magical. Create your own "Xanadu," using your imagination. Then, write an advertisement to encourage tourism to that place. "Kubla Khan" appears in *Prentice Hall Literature, Penguin Edition*, The British Tradition.

Timed Writing Prompt

3. Write a persuasive essay in which you convince a college admissions director to accept you as a student. Mention your academic credentials, such as grades and test scores. You should also discuss your extracurricular activities, such as sports, arts, and student government. Finally, share with the admissions director what you hope to contribute to the college if you are accepted as a student. **(35 minutes)**

Prewriting • 151

Prewriting: Blueprint and Listing

1. Encourage students to share their blueprinting lists and explain why they think their ideas would make good topics for advertisements. This will help them think through and develop their ideas.

2. As students complete the listing activity, encourage them to write freely. They should list not only practical things, but also things they enjoy doing.

3. Have students share and compare their lists in small groups. This might help to spark more ideas for students who are struggling.

⏱ Timed Writing Prompt

• To help students think about their audience, have them reflect on the most recent item/product they have seen advertised.

• Tell them to imagine themselves selling this item to someone who has never used it before. Ask them to consider factors, such as what the product is, who uses it, why they use it over another product of the same type, and how to get more people to purchase the product. Remind students that good spelling and grammar are considered minimum requirements for college.

• Suggest that students allow five minutes for prewriting, twenty-five minutes for writing, and five minutes for reviewing and proofreading.

⏱ TIME AND RESOURCE MANAGER

Resources
Print: *Writing Support Transparencies*, 8-A–C; *Writing Support Activity Book*, 8-1–2
Technology: *Writing and Grammar* Interactive Text, Section 8.2

Using the Full Student Edition	Using the Handbook ⊞
• Work through the Blueprint or the Listing strategy with the class (p. 151).	• Work through the Blueprint or the Listing strategy with the class (p. 95).
• Using the transparencies, do the Audience Profile questionnaire and the Audience Language chart in class.	• Using the transparencies, do the Audience Profile questionnaire and the Audience Language chart in class.

Prewriting: Narrow and Focus Your Topic

1. To help students narrow their topics, you might give examples such as the following:

    Too broad: *clothing*

    Focused: *men's athletic clothing*

    Too broad: *pet watcher*

    Focused: *exotic-bird sitter*

2. Ask volunteers to share topics. If a topic is too broad, list smaller elements of it on the board and invite students to suggest which ideas might make for a more focused topic.

3. Analyze the intended audience to help narrow a topic. Discuss the people who might use the products or services, and narrow topics to include only those elements that would interest the intended audience. For example, the audience for men's athletic clothing might be professional sports teams, school teams, clubs, or individuals.

Prewriting: Identify Your Audience

Teaching Resources: Writing Support Transparencies, 8-A; Writing Support Activity Book, 8-1

1. Display Transparency 8-A and have students answer the questions on the Audience Profile based on the audience they hope to reach with an ad for the topic they have chosen.

2. Ask students to consider which details would be important to the audience they have identified. Give students blank copies of the profile (8-1) for their own use.

3. Encourage students to discuss their ideas and topics with partners or in small groups.

Narrowing Your Topic

Narrow and Focus Your Topic

If you have chosen a particular product or service to advertise, you will not need to narrow your topic further. If your topic is general, however, such as chocolate chip cookies, narrow it by choosing to advertise a specific brand.

It is also helpful to focus your topic. To do this, analyze the product, service, or idea to get a clear sense of what it is you're selling, who might buy it, and why someone might buy it. Keep the answers to those questions in mind as you begin to gather details for your advertisement.

Considering Your Audience and Purpose

Identify Your Audience

Before you begin to gather details to sell your idea, service, or product, think about your audience—the people you are trying to convince. The details you choose to emphasize and the word choices you make will have a great impact on how well your audience responds to your ad.

Fill out an audience profile like the one below to pinpoint the details that will appeal to your audience. Take their responses into consideration as you gather details.

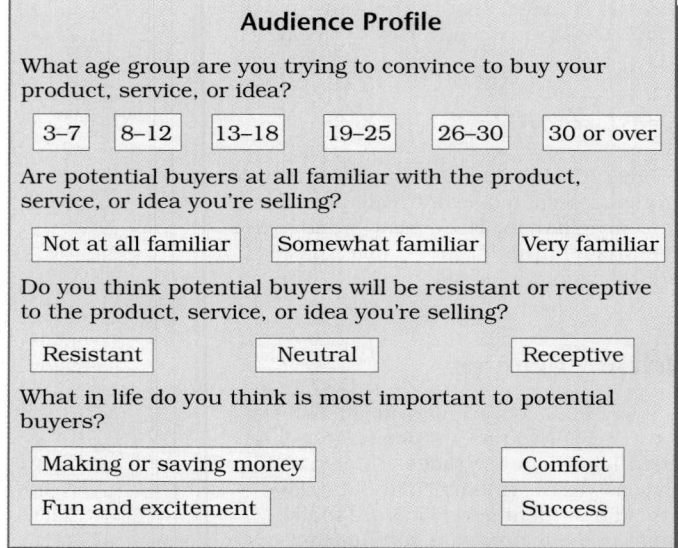

Audience Profile

What age group are you trying to convince to buy your product, service, or idea?

| 3–7 | 8–12 | 13–18 | 19–25 | 26–30 | 30 or over |

Are potential buyers at all familiar with the product, service, or idea you're selling?

| Not at all familiar | Somewhat familiar | Very familiar |

Do you think potential buyers will be resistant or receptive to the product, service, or idea you're selling?

| Resistant | Neutral | Receptive |

What in life do you think is most important to potential buyers?

| Making or saving money | Comfort |
| Fun and excitement | Success |

152 • Advertisement

🗋 Research Tip

Before you write your advertisement, look at ads for products or services similar to the one you plan to advertise. Then, make your advertisement different, so that it stands out from the rest.

☑ **ONGOING ASSESSMENT: Monitor and Reinforce**

If students have trouble identifying their intended audience, try the following strategy.

Most products and services inherently have a clear audience: a pet washing service is aimed at pet owners; a new moisturizing lotion is for people with dry skin. If students are having trouble determining their audience, perhaps their product or service is not clearly defined. Encourage them to work on clarifying their product or service before working on their advertisement.

Consider Your Audience's Taste

Once you have identified your audience, think about what type of word choice or language style will most appeal to the audience you've identified. Then, plan your ad carefully, choosing details, words, and phrases that will help you achieve your purpose: to sell your product, idea, or service.

This chart gives examples of how your language might vary in an advertisement for a restaurant depending on your audience.

	Families With Children	Older, Upscale Crowd	Young Singles
Food	hearty plentiful kids' menus all-you-can-eat salad bar	traditional cuisine	innovative sensational updated nouvelle
Service	fast friendly	attentive exclusive experienced	relaxed knowledge-able
Atmosphere	family fun relaxed	quiet elegant classical luxury reservations required	lively hip new young

Identify Your Audience's Questions

Think about the questions your audience—potential buyers—might have about the product, service, or candidate that you are advertising. Make a list of those questions, and be sure to answer them as you draft and develop your advertisement. Questions that your audience might have may include the following:

- How can I be sure the product, service, or person is reliable?
- Is this product, service, or person recommended by others?
- What do I have to do to learn more about this product, service, or person?

 Timed Writing Hint

Before writing, read the prompt carefully at least twice to make sure you understand the purpose of your writing and its audience.

Step-by-Step Teaching Guide

Prewriting: Considering Your Audience

Teaching Resources: Writing Support Transparencies, 8-B

1. Use the transparency (8-B) to demonstrate how different words and details appeal to different audiences.

2. Have each student make a list of the important details about his or her topic that might interest the intended audience.

3. Ask for volunteers to read their lists. Then, have the class take each detail and shorten it to one representative word. (Example: professional football uniforms that do not rip = durable or long-lasting; league uniforms that do not cost too much = affordable.)

4. If students are having difficulty choosing specific words, try using a well-known product as an example. Write the product and the desired audience on the board. Have the whole class brainstorm for specific words to represent the product in a positive way.

Integrating Vocabulary Skills

Popular Language Advertising frequently affects popular language. Have students bring in examples of print advertisements in which a word or words are being used in a new way. Or, have them share examples of advertising slogans that have found a permanent place in popular language.

Integrating Speaking and Listening Skills

Word Choice It is not only the meanings of words that suggest a specific audience; it can also be the way they sound or the connotations they have acquired. Discuss how the sound of the words in an advertisement for teenagers might be different than the sound of the words in an advertisement for senior citizens. Challenge students to cite specific examples.

Prewriting: Create and Distribute a Questionnaire

Teaching Resources: Writing Support Transparencies, 8-C

1. Draw students' attention to the Student Work in Progress on this page or display Transparency 8-C to review the information Matt's questionnaire generated. Ask students to infer Matt's original questions. (Matt may have asked: *Have you been to a yard sale? If yes, did you buy anything? If no, why not?*)

2. Next, have students consider questions for their own topics. Start this activity by having each student fold a piece of paper in half.

3. On the left, have them list the kinds of details they would like to know about the audience members and their views about the topic.

4. On the right, have them list some questions they could ask in their questionnaires that would generate the information identified in the left-hand column.

Customize for
Linguistic Learners

Some students may find they can more easily talk about a topic than write about it. Have students break into pairs. Suggest that one student ask questions of the other student regarding the proposed topic. Students can use tape recorders to orally "pre-write" their questionnaires.

Customize for
Less Advanced Students

Have the class work together as a whole to create a questionnaire on a sample topic. Small groups can then use this as a model for their own questionnaires.

8.2

Gathering Details

To sell a product or idea successfully, you need to learn everything you can about it and about the people you hope will buy it. Use the following strategy to help you gather detailed information:

Create and Distribute a Questionnaire

One way to find out how people view a product is to create a questionnaire. Distribute the questionnaire to people you think make up the potential market for your product. Use the questionnaire results to help you determine the approach you will take in your ad.

Below, you can see how Matt grouped the responses he received to his questionnaire.

Student Work IN PROGRESS

Name: Matt Bezerman
General Douglas MacArthur High School
Seaford, NY

Creating and Distributing a Questionnaire

Matt Bezerman had been to yard sales before, but he was interested in other people's experiences. He distributed a short questionnaire to several friends and relatives. The results gave him a direction for his advertisement.

6 out of 13 had attended a yard sale in the last two months.

> Matt realized he needed to target the people who don't go to yard sales.

Of those 6:
2 had bought something at the sale they attended.
3 said: "there was nothing good for sale."
1 said: "didn't have any money."

> Matt decided to target this market to those who might not attend based on past experience.

Of the 7 who had not attended a yard sale in the last two months:
5 said: "there's never anything worth buying."
2 said: "too busy."

> This told Matt that he needed to convince the doubters that this was not a typical yard sale. This one would have high-quality merchandise.

154 • Advertisement

8.3 Drafting

Shaping Your Writing

Because advertisements usually have little time or space to make an impression, create a structure that will allow you to capture the audience's attention right away and to underscore your message at the close.

Develop a Main Idea

To shape a written advertisement, develop a main idea to feature. One way to do this is to create a slogan. A good slogan sums up a product or an idea in a few words and is easily recognizable and catchy. Not every product has one, but a good one may make your advertisement more effective. Here are some ways to make a slogan memorable:

- **Word Play** Rhyme, pun, repetition, or other forms of word play can make a slogan memorable. For example, a company that makes baby-food products may use: "Give a Cookie to Your Cookie."

- **Alliteration** Using the same sound for most of the words in a phrase or sentence will grab your readers' attention. For example, "The Cocoa Cookies That Crunch" contains alliteration.

- **Pithiness** *Pith* means "essence" or "gist"; a pithy slogan is one that is short but full of meaning. For example, "Your Favorite Cookie" contains one essential idea about the product.

Providing Elaboration

As your advertisement takes shape, add details to support the claims you make about your product.

Cite Statistics and Experts

Collect and include in your advertisement data about your topic—the percentage of people who use it, the number of doctors who recommend it, awards given to it, and so on. Following is an example:

In a recent poll conducted by Pollard University, 87% of cardiologists recommend swimming to improve health. It strengthens the muscles, especially the back muscles, and it is less damaging than aerobics or jogging.

> This is a statistic.

> Cardiologists are doctors who are experts in the field of heart and health.

Now that you've given your advertisement its rough form, find ways to improve it. Look at it critically, as if you were the audience seeing or hearing the advertisement for the first time.

▲ Critical Viewing What main idea might you convey in a slogan for an ad about this cookie? [Analyze]

Drafting • 155

Revising: Highlighting Key Ideas

1. Explain to students that an advertisement needs to attract attention and maintain the reader's interest. To be successful, the main idea must be obvious to the reader.

2. After students mark their key ideas with highlighters, encourage them to move these ideas to prominent places in the advertisements. They might also consider design elements that would emphasize these ideas.

3. To make sure that main ideas are being communicated as the writers intend, have students trade drafts of their ads with a partner. Then, have each reader identify what he or she believes are the main ideas. Have partners discuss their drafts to determine how successfully their writing communicates the key ideas.

Revising: Cutting Extraneous Information

1. Once students have identified the key words in their advertisements, they can begin to revise and edit.

2. Refer students to the example in the text. Discuss why the information that was removed from the paragraph was deemed to be extraneous.

3. Suggest that students condense a phrase or idea to a single descriptive word. Encourage them to use the dictionary or thesaurus to choose the most precise words they can.

Critical Viewing

Connect Responses will likely focus on music quality or the precision of the marching, because these are the primary reasons one watches a marching band.

8.4 Revising

Revising Your Overall Structure

Your advertisement will not be very persuasive if your main point is hidden where the audience can't find it. Check that your advertisement is structured—both textually and visually—so that the key ideas stand out.

▶ **REVISION STRATEGY**
Highlighting Key Ideas

Using a highlighter, identify the key ideas in your advertisement. Make sure these key points are the most prominent ideas in your advertisement. If they are not, restructure the advertisement to feature your most important points.

Revising Your Paragraphs

Although it is common to see advertisements that are almost completely visual, with just a line or two of text, many advertisers, particularly on the radio, use words skillfully. If your advertisement depends heavily on words, make sure that its message is clear and to the point.

▶ **REVISION STRATEGY**
Cutting Extraneous Information

Read your advertisement, and evaluate each sentence or paragraph carefully. Ask yourself: What is the single most important idea in this paragraph? If it is not obvious, take out unnecessary words and phrases. Cut and rewrite until just the most important ideas are left.

The following paragraph from a radio advertisement contained extraneous information, which was cut to make it more focused and concise.

Galliard High School Marching Band has held an award-winning reputation since it was formed. Over the years, it has won several awards, including ~~Second Prize in the Festival of colors and~~ last year's First Prize at the Boone County Competition of the Bands. Support this band, which has enhanced our local reputation. ~~The students work really hard and deserve the community's support.~~

▲ **Critical Viewing**
If you were to write an ad for a marching band like the one shown, what key idea would you choose to feature? Why? **[Connect]**

156 • Advertisement

⏱ TIME AND RESOURCE MANAGER

Resources
Print: *Writing Support Transparencies,* 8-D–E; *Writing Support Activity Book,* 8-2
Technology: *Writing and Grammar* Interactive Text, Section 8.4

Using the Full Student Edition	Using the Handbook🄷
• Work through the Revision Strategies with students.	• Work through the Revision Strategies with students.
• Demonstrate strategies for correcting run-on sentences by Circling Sentence Subjects (p. 157) and for Revising Weak Words (p. 158).	• Demonstrate strategies for connecting run-on sentences by Circling Sentence Subjects (p. 101) and for Revising Weak Words (p. 102).
• Divide the class into groups for the Peer Review activity (p. 158).	• Divide the class into groups for the Peer Review activity (p. 102).

Revising Your Sentences

Correcting Run-on Sentences

In your advertisement, you may find that you have run two or more main clauses together into a run-on sentence. Run-on sentences are confusing and will detract from the impression you want to make. You can correct this problem by breaking the sentence into two sentences or by revising the sentence so that it becomes a complex or a compound sentence.

Run-on
You must try Horton's Hamburgers they're Hamtastic!

Sentences With End Marks
You must try Horton's hamburgers. They're Hamtastic!

Run-on
We gave the food to the experts they agreed.

Sentences With Commas
We gave the food to the experts, **and** they agreed.

▶ **REVISION STRATEGY**
Circling Sentence Subjects

A run-on sentence is two or more complete sentences that are punctuated as if they were one. One way to spot a run-on sentence is to circle all the sentence subjects you come across in your draft. Then, examine each sentence that contains two or more subjects to be sure that it is not a run-on.

⏱ Timed Writing Hint

When revising your writing under timed conditions, read each sentence slowly but silently to check for run-on sentences.

Student Work
IN PROGRESS

Name: *Matt Bezerman*
General Douglas MacArthur High School
Seaford, NY

Circling to Identify Run-on Sentences

Matt discovered this run-on sentence in the opening of his draft. To fix the problem, he decided to break the run-on sentence into two distinct sentences:

(Everybody) knows yard sales can be a waste of time, however all your preconceived (notions) about yard sales are about to change.

Matt fixed this run-on by making it two sentences.

Revising • 157

Revising: Circling Sentence Subjects

Teaching Resources: Writing Support Transparencies, 8-D

1. Use the transparency to show how circling subjects can help identify run-on sentences.

2. After students have made their corrections, have them exchange papers with a partner to check their work.

3. In addition to checking for run-on sentences, ask peer reviewers to look for sentence fragments. If students need a reminder, explain that a sentence fragment is a group of words punctuated as a sentence that does not contain a subject and a predicate.

4. As students revise their sentences, remind them that sentence length can affect the flow of a written piece. Short sentences can be powerful and to the point. Long sentences can convey complicated ideas. Varying sentence length can help accentuate an important point and maintain reader interest. Encourage students to vary the length of the sentences in their advertisements.

Customize for
ESL Students

Students learning English as a second language may encounter difficulties with sentence structure. Circling nouns, verbs, and clauses in different colors can help these students identify sentence building blocks. Encourage students to use this method to make sure each sentence contains a subject and a verb. Remind them that subordinate clauses cannot stand on their own as sentences.

☑ **ONGOING ASSESSMENT: Monitor and Reinforce**

If students are having difficulty identifying and organizing key ideas, try the following strategy.

Identify a place, product, or service and have the class brainstorm for key ideas that should be highlighted in an advertisement for it. Ask the class which ideas are most important. How would they draw attention to the most important ideas? Suggest that they consider how design elements, such as type size and color, might be used to show the prominence of important points. What one word or phrase would they give special attention?

⏱ **TIME SAVERS!**

🗎 **Writing Support Transparencies**
Use the transparencies for Chapter 8 to facilitate the teaching of strategies.

Revising: Choose Words to Achieve Your Purpose

1. Explain to students that precise adjectives can help create a more distinctive image of a service or product.

2. Point out the difference between "weak" (vague, uninteresting) and "strong" (precise, descriptive, colorful, informative) adjectives. Brainstorm with the class for a list of substitutes for "nice" when describing a car, a movie, or a meal.

3. Ask students to circle all of the adjectives in their advertisements. Have them consider whether any of them could be replaced by a more precise or more vivid adjective.

Integrating Vocabulary Skills

Point out that there is more to vivid language than just finding words that mean the same thing as the weak adjective. However, it is possible that using a thesaurus to find synonyms will help trigger ideas as to which words might work.

Revising: Peer Review

Teaching Resources: Writing Support Transparencies, 8-E; Writing Support Activity Book, 8-2

1. Begin the peer review process by reminding students to identify a draft's strengths before focusing on its drawbacks.

2. Remind students that some errors will be corrected at the proofreading stage, and that the focus here should be on content and ability to persuade.

3. Display the transparency (8-E) and suggest students use a similar survey to gather reactions to their ads.

4. Point out that many comments made during peer review will be helpful to all students. Suggest that students jot down important ideas raised in discussion and share them with the class later.

8.4

Revising Your Word Choice
Choose Words to Achieve Your Purpose

Check the words in your advertisement. Do they achieve the purpose you have set? If not, experiment with other word choices until you are satisfied that you have found just the right ones.

▶ **REVISION STRATEGY**
Revising Weak Words

Your advertisement will have more impact if you avoid using weak or vague adjectives to describe the product or service you are selling.

Peer Review

The goal of advertising is to persuade others to do what you want them to do—whether it is to make a purchase, attend an event, or donate money to a cause. Therefore, the best way to find out whether your advertisement works is to show it to a potential audience. Here's a strategy for getting constructive feedback:

Distribute a Survey and Discuss It

Share your advertisement with a peer group, and distribute a short survey about the effectiveness of the advertisement. Your survey questions might resemble the following:

Survey
1. What do you find appealing about this ad? What do you find unappealing? _____ _____
2. How likely are you to purchase this service after hearing or seeing this advertisement?   **Very Likely   Likely   Not Likely**
3. On a scale of 1 to 5 (with 1 being least likely and 5 being most likely), how likely are you to purchase this service?   **5 4 3 2 1**

💿 Technology Tip

If you have a thesaurus in your word-processing program, use it to investigate possible word choices for your advertisement.

✒ STANDARDIZED TEST PREPARATION WORKSHOP

Synonyms Standardized tests may require students to recognize words with similar meanings. Provide students with opportunities to identify synonyms. Write the following test question on the board.

Match the following word with its synonym.

theory

A reality   **C** science
B hypothesis   **D** truth

Students should recognize that the correct answer is **B** because *hypothesis* is a synonym of *theory*. If they know that *synonym* means "a word with a similar meaning," they will not be misled by the other answer choices.

8.5 Editing and Proofreading

Advertisements are meant to positively impress others. Carefully check spelling, grammar, usage, and mechanics to ensure that your advertisement is error-free.

Focusing on Dates and Times

You do not want to persuade people to attend an event only to have them come on the wrong day! Proofread your advertisement carefully to make sure dates and times are correct.

Grammar in Your Writing
Abbreviating Dates and Ordinals

To save space in your advertisement, abbreviate *dates* and *ordinals* (numbers that rank items in a series, like third and thirtieth). Following is a chart showing correct abbreviations for months and days.

DAYS	Sun.	Mon.	Tues.	Wed.	Thurs.	Fri.	Sat.

MONTHS	Jan.	Feb.	Mar.	Apr.	May	June
	July	Aug.	Sept.	Oct.	Nov.	Dec.

ORDINALS	Add -*st* after 1	*1st* Annual Roadrace
	Add -*nd* after 2	*2nd* Prize
	Add -*rd* after 3	*3rd* Day of the Month
	Add -*th* after all other numbers	*16th* Squadron

Find It in Your Reading Read the advertisement on page 150 to locate an abbreviation of a country name.

Find It in Your Writing As you proofread your advertisement, check to see that all of the dates and ordinals are correctly abbreviated.

For more on abbreviations, see the Abbreviation Guide.

Editing and Proofreading • 159

Step-by-Step Teaching Guide

Editing and Proofreading

1. Remind students that editing and proofreading are essential stages of the writing process.
2. Suggest that students verify correct spelling and grammar. Does the writing use strong and varied adjectives? Does it contain any run-ons or fragments?
3. Have them check the accuracy of any dates, times, costs, or other facts in the advertisement.

Step-by-Step Teaching Guide

Abbreviating Dates and Ordinals

1. Remind students that, although abbreviated dates and ordinals can save space, there are some numbers that should not be abbreviated. For example, the word *First* in *First Lady* should not be abbreviated because *First Lady* is a title. In addition, the impact of a word is sometimes stronger when it is written out rather than abbreviated.
2. Tell students that the abbreviations listed in the chart are not usually acceptable in formal writing.

Find It in Your Reading

The country abbreviation in the advertisement on page 150 is *U.S.* Ask students to think of other ways they have seen *United States* abbreviated (*US, U.S.A.*).

Find It in Your Writing

Have students double-check the accuracy of the abbreviations they used in their advertisements. If some students chose not to use abbreviations, have them explain when they might consider using them.

⏱ TIME AND RESOURCE MANAGER

Resources
Print: *Scoring Rubrics on Transparency,* Ch. 8; *Writing Assessment and Portfolio Management; Formal Assessment,* Ch. 8
Technology: *Writing and Grammar* Interactive Text, Section 8.5

Using the Full Student Edition	Using the Handbook🄷
• Review p. 159 in class, including Grammar in Your Writing.	• Review p. 103 in class, including Grammar in Your Writing.
• Have students complete the Rubric for Self-Assessment (p. 160).	• Have students complete the Rubric for Self-Assessment (p. 104).
• Have them edit and proofread their advertisements in class.	• Have them edit and proofread their advertisements in class.

Publishing and Presenting

1. Remind students that the publishing phase is the true test for advertisements. This is the best way to determine how effective they really are.

2. If the products are fictional, suggest that the class hold a marketing fair. Have other students visit the fair and comment on which ads persuaded them to be interested in the topics being marketed.

ASSESS and CLOSE

Assessment

Teaching Resources: Scoring Rubrics on Transparency, Ch. 8; Writing Assessment and Portfolio Management; Formal Assessment, Ch. 8

1. Display the Scoring Rubric transparency and review the criteria in class.

2. Before students proceed with self-assessment, you may wish to review the Final Draft of the Student Work in Progress on p. 161. Have students score the Final Draft in one or more of the rubric categories. For example, how would students score the advertisement in terms of audience and purpose?

3. In addition to student self-assessment, you may wish to use the following assessment options:

   • score student advertisements yourself, using the rubric and scoring models in *Writing Assessment and Portfolio Management.*

   • review the Standardized Test Preparation Workshop on pp. 166–167 and administer the practice test.

   • administer the Chapter 8 Test from *Formal Assessment* in Teaching Resources to measure students' grasp of concepts presented.

8.6 Publishing and Presenting

Now that your advertisement is finished, share it with the public. Here are some ideas for presenting your ad:

Building Your Portfolio

1. **Post It** If you've created a print advertisement for an actual product or service of your own, get permission to post it in your classroom, school, and around town. You'll soon find out if your ad is effective by the response you get.

2. **Ad Book** Gather together ads your classmates have completed, and bind them together into an ad book. Leave a copy in the classroom for everyone to flip through.

Reflecting on Your Writing

When you've finished your advertisement, think about what it was like to create it. Answer the following questions, and save your responses in your portfolio.

• How did creating your own ad change your view of the advertising you see around you?

• With which aspect of creating an advertisement did you feel more comfortable, the verbal or the visual?

Internet Tip

To see an advertisement scored according to this rubric, go on-line:
PHSchool.com
Enter Web Code:
egk-1201

Rubric for Self-Assessment

Use the following criteria to evaluate your persuasive writing.

	Score 4	Score 3	Score 2	Score 1
Audience and Purpose	Presents effective slogan; clearly addresses persuasive task	Presents good slogan; addresses persuasive task	Presents slogan; minimally addresses persuasive task	Does not present slogan; shows lack of attention to persuasive task
Organization	Uses clear, consistent organizational strategy; clearly presents key ideas	Uses clear organizational strategy with few inconsistencies	Uses inconsistent organizational strategy; creates illogical presentation	Demonstrates lack of organizational strategy; creates confusing presentation
Elaboration	Successfully combines words and images to provide convincing, unified support for a position	Combines words and images to provide unified support for a position	Includes some words or images that detract from a position	Uses words and images that do not support a position
Use of Language	Successfully communicates an idea through clever use of language; includes very few mechanical errors	Conveys an idea through adequate use of language; includes few mechanical errors	Misuses language and lessens impact of ideas; includes many mechanical errors	Demonstrates poor use of language and confuses meaning; includes many mechanical errors

160 • Advertisement

✓ ONGOING ASSESSMENT: Assess Mastery

Use one of the following options to assess the final drafts of students' advertisements.

Self-Assessment	Teacher Assessment
Ask students to score their advertisements using the rubric provided. Then have them write a single paragraph reflecting on the most valuable thing they learned in completing this assignment.	You may wish to use the rubric and the scoring models provided in *Writing Assessment and Portfolio Management* to score the advertisements.

8.7

FINAL DRAFT

Not Your Everyday Yard Sale

Matt Bezerman
General Douglas MacArthur High School
Seaford, New York

NOT YOUR EVERYDAY **YARD SALE**

Everybody knows yard sales can be a waste of time.
However, all your preconceived notions about yard sales are about to change.

THIS WILL BE THE. . .

BIGGEST Four households' worth of goods!

BEST Like-new appliances, never-worn clothes, antiques, collectibles!!!

CHEAPEST Low prices are flexible; make us an offer!

YARD SALE YOU HAVE EVER SEEN!

Saturday, July 20th
10:00 A.M.–5:00 P.M.
Johnson Avenue, Seaford

YOU CAN'T AFFORD TO MISS IT!

The opening line of Matt's ad helps and arouses readers' curiosity.

Matt used an unusual visual element— the yard sign—to make his ad interesting to look at.

These details are persuasive and are centrally placed to catch the readers' eyes.

The ad's ending line is memorable. It also is a pun—the word "afford" makes a connection with the yard sale.

Step-by-Step Teaching Guide

Final Draft

1. Ask students whether the specific language used in the flyer would persuade them to attend the yard sale. Which words did they find most appealing? Explain that a few well-chosen words can provide information, instill curiosity, and persuade readers that a product, event, or service might be of interest to them.

2. Ask students whether they would recommend any other changes to the advertisement. How might they apply these suggestions to their own writing?

Integrating Speaking and Listening Skills

Some students may find art projects difficult. Suggest that two students work together to create a radio advertisement. Have them record their "radio spot" using a tape recorder, so it can be played back to the class. Encourage them to use music, sound effects, or other audio elements to enhance their advertisements.

Customize for
ESL Students

Have English-language learners use tape recorders to create radio commercials in their home languages. Have them translate the "radio spots" into English on paper and then rerecord their commercials.

Lesson Objectives

1. To write an ad campaign appropriate to audience and purpose
2. To use a variety of forms and technologies to communicate specific messages
3. To use a range of techniques to plan and create a media text and reflect critically on the work produced
4. To create media products to engage specific audiences

Step-by-Step Teaching Guide

Ad Campaign

Teaching Resources: Writing Support Transparencies, 8-F; Writing Support Activity Book, 8-4

1. Ask students to think of ad campaigns they have seen. To start the discussion, you may want to suggest they think of soft drinks, sports shoes, or other commonly advertised products, and have students mention the number of places they have seen ads.

2. Display Transparency 8-F to discuss the sample ad campaign for Fizz Cola. Explain that the example is very much like the sort of planning that actually goes into big ad campaigns.

3. Have students brainstorm for ideas about other places ads might possibly appear (television, Internet, shopping bags, in or on buses, train stations, magazines and newspapers, product placement in movies, even signs pulled by airplanes).

continued

Critical Viewing

Connect Students appear to be making print ads. They have already decided on their cause and their slogans.

Connected Assignment
Ad Campaign

Ad campaigns, like other ads, seek to sell you something. Ad campaigns, however, seek to reach potential buyers through various places and forms; for example, through print ads, radio and television ads, T-shirts, bumper stickers, and so on. Usually, an ad campaign focuses on a central idea, slogan, issue, or position, creating a key idea that carries through all the ads.

Create an ad campaign for a real or imaginary product, idea, service, or candidate. Use the writing process tips to guide you as you create your ad campaign.

▲ **Critical Viewing**
What aspect of an ad campaign do these students seem to be working on? **[Connect]**

Ad Campaign for FIZZ COLA

Slogan: Put Some Fizz In Your
(Life, Work, Step, and so on)!

Radio ad:
[sound of Fizz cola being opened followed by the sound of someone drinking and saying "Ah." Lively music in background.]

WOMAN'S VOICE: Put some Fizz in your life. Nothing else can compare.

Billboard:
Picture of a giant bottle of Fizz Cola on a desk. Enthusiastic, determined group—professionally dressed —gathered around in intense discussion. Underneath photo is the slogan: "Put Some Fizz In Your Work."

T-shirt giveaway:
Photo of Fizz Cola bottle centered on the front of the shirt. On the back will read: "Put Some Fizz In Your Step."

162 • Advertisement

☑ ONGOING ASSESSMENT: Prerequisite Skills

Students may find the following resources from Chapter 8 particularly helpful in developing their ad campaigns.

In the Textbook	Print Resources	Technology
Identify Your Audience, Section 8.2 Distribute a Survey, p. 158, Section 8.4	*Writing Support Transparencies,* 8-A, 8–E *Writing Support Activity Book,* 8-4	*Writing and Grammar* Interactive Text, Section 8.2

162

Prewriting To choose a topic, decide on a product, a service, an idea, or a candidate on which to build your ad campaign. To come up with topic ideas, think about the products or services you use often or the people in politics or those who seek public office.

Examples of Products: soap, car, alarm clock, food, towel

Examples of Services: public transportation, gas stations, hair salons

Examples of People: city mayor, school principal, union leader

Focusing Your Ad Campaign Choose an aspect of your product, service, or candidate to build your campaign around. Then, focus on getting that message out. Jot down every advertising outlet you can list in which to sell your product or candidate. Group them into categories, and note the type of details (visual, text, music, sound effect, and so on) that will best work within that medium.

Television	Radio	Magazines	T-shirts
visual aural	aural sound effects	visual text	visual some text

Drafting Experiment with jingles or rhymes to make your slogan memorable. Then, create three ads that are built around this slogan. Use positive and persuasive language to highlight what it is you're selling. Include visuals, if appropriate. Finally, develop and complete a presentation chart to show how the overall campaign will work.

Revising and Editing Post your presentation chart and sample ads on a bulletin board and review them. Enlarge the text for readability, and position the main idea of each ad prominently. Read any text aloud to gauge its aural impact, and punch up language to achieve a friendly but direct tone. Ask a friend or family member to scan your presentation for errors or areas of confusion.

Publishing and Presenting Place your presentation chart and the sample ads in a portfolio. If you have created radio or television ads, consider taping or filming them with the help of your peers. Then, "broadcast" the ads for your class.

⊚ Technology Tip

To make your sample advertisement look professional, work in a page-layout program. Scan in photographs or other visual aids. Then, use interesting fonts and type treatments—such as boldface, italics, and drop shadows—to make your ad's main idea stand out.

Step-by-Step Teaching Guide continued

4. Ask students why they think large campaigns like this are used by advertisers (to make sure their message gets heard in a time when there is so much competition for people's attention).

5. Go over the prewriting steps with students. Explain that a campaign can sell an idea as well as a product. Some students might want to focus on an environmental, safety, or health issue, for example.

6. Using Transparency 8-F, point out how a campaign can be focused and how the message can be tailored to the medium.

7. Hand out copies of the organizer (8-4) or have students create their own charts. Allow time for students to jot down ideas for their campaigns.

8. Tell students to create three treatments of their ad campaign for three different media and then develop a chart or outline to show how the total campaign will work.

9. Have students display or "broadcast" their work for the class.

Customize for
Less Advanced Students

Allow students to work in small groups, brainstorming for ideas and contributing different elements of the ad campaign.

Customize for
ESL Students

Suggest that students create a bilingual ad campaign. They can either create ads with the slogans and text shown in two languages or create two versions of the ad, tailoring each to a different audience.

Step-by-Step Teaching Guide

Identifying Themes in Media

1. Choose one of the Spotlight elements for class discussion, or have students work individually or in groups to research the element of their choice.

2. Students may be interested to know that the Alexandre Dumas who wrote *Camille* (or *La Dame Aux Camelias,* as it was originally titled) was the son of the Alexandre Dumas who wrote *The Three Musketeers* and *The Man in the Iron Mask.*

3. Marguerite, the heroine of *Camille,* is known for the camellias (flowers) she always wears. In the opera, the heroine's name is Violetta.

4. A movie has been made of *La Traviata.* Students may want to compare this film with *Camille.*

5. Students may want to compare and contrast portraying a story on stage as opposed to in a film.

6. Have students note elements of film posters displayed at theatres before they design their own. They may also want to check the library for historic film posters.

Viewing and Representing

Activity Display students' posters in the classroom and ask students to tell why they decided to emphasize certain elements.

Critical Viewing

Connect Students may comment on her beauty or on the fact that she is stylish and elegant.

Spotlight on the Humanities

Identifying Themes in Media

Focus on Film: *Camille*

Today, film producers release aggressive ad campaigns on television, radio, and in newspapers, touting their films as "must sees" and persuading audiences to flock to see them. This was true even in 1936, when *Camille* was released. Starring legendary actress Greta Garbo, it is one of the great romance classics of the twentieth century. Originally a novel written in 1848 by the French novelist Alexandre Dumas, *Camille* is the story of a woman with a questionable past who falls in love with a gentleman, played by Robert Taylor. The heroine, Marguerite (or Camille, as she is known to American audiences) ultimately sacrifices her happiness for his good. George Cukor directed the film, and the New York Film Critics gave Garbo the award for best actress.

Music Connection Italian composer Giuseppe Verdi (1813–1901) immortalized the story of Camille (whom he renamed Violetta) in his opera *La Traviata.* Written in 1853, *La Traviata* is one of Verdi's most popular works and brought him fame on an international scale. Verdi was one of the first operatic composers to combine drama and music into one unified composition.

Theater Connection The actress who made the lead role of Dumas's play famous on the stage was France's Sarah Bernhardt (1844–1923). Educated in a convent and at the Paris Conservatoire, Bernhardt made her acting debut at the Comedie Française. Her first noticeable success came in 1869, in François Coppée's *Le Passant.* Bernhardt went on to become one of the most famous stage actresses of her time. In 1914, she was given membership in the Legion of Honor and continued to act until her death.

Persuasive Writing Activity: Poster for a Film
Create a poster advertising your favorite film. Decide what details from the film to highlight on the advertisement. For example, you may include lines of dialogue, a still photograph from the movie, or feature the names of the starring actors. Also, be sure to include information about where and when the film is playing.

▲ **Critical Viewing** Judging from this photograph, what makes the character of Camille so interesting? **[Connect]**

164 • Advertisement

Media and Technology Skills

Using Technology to Extend Meaning

Activity: Enhance a Video

Even beginning filmmakers can learn to create sophisticated and effective videos. Most video cameras have many built-in special effects; you can create others using sounds, lights, and a little imagination. For your next video project, challenge yourself to use several new techniques that will enhance the overall effect.

Think About It Choose a basic project for a short video. For example, you might create an advertisement for a school event or produce a brief "welcome" video for new students. You might also decide to reshoot a video you previously produced. You can apply several new strategies to create a more effective video.

Plan It Begin by planning the new techniques you will try. Read your camera's manual to find out what effects are built into it. Consider trying the following strategies and tools.

> **Framing Devices:** Your camera might allow you to fade in and out of scenes, as well as to decide on the shape of a frame, such as circular or oval.
>
> **Color Effects:** Shoot a scene in black and white, or choose a sepia tint for an old-fashioned look.
>
> **Titles:** Create titles using an in-camera function, or film hand-drawn or computer-printed titles of your own.
>
> **Lighting Effects:** Use natural lighting effects, such as a sunrise or sunset, to create an intense atmosphere. Artificial lighting, such as a single bare bulb or a desk lamp shining up from the floor, can create unusual or other-worldly effects.

Film It After choosing your techniques, begin filming. Be ready to take advantage of "happy accidents." A sudden storm might produce an effective mood, as might a gust of wind.

Edit It You can create some special effects, like quick cutting between shots, while editing your video. During editing, you can also select the best of several takes, or filmed versions.

Choose an Unusual Point of View

Filming a scene from an unusual point of view can make the difference between a drab video and an exciting one. Suppose you are filming two friends talking in your school parking lot. Any of these angles might make the scene stand out:

- Film from inside a parked car, framing the action with the car window.
- Place the camera on the ground, making the actors loom.
- Use a ladder to view the scene from above.
- Have different students walk past the scene, holding the camera in their hands to create a hand-held, documentary quality.

Step-by-Step Teaching Guide

Using Technology to Extend Meaning

1. Have students jot down a few ideas for a short video project.

2. As students begin to plan their videos, suggest steps for the project: outline, write script, decide on strategies and tools, create titles, film, and edit.

3. Discuss the strategies and tools with students, and direct them to read the sidebar tips. Ask students whether they have seen some of these techniques used in movies. What effect did they have?

4. Set a date by which students should have their short videos completed. Remind students to leave time for editing the film.

5. You may want to schedule class time to show some of the videos.

6. After videos are done, ask students to discuss their experiences: what worked, what did they learn, and so on.

7. It is likely that some students will not have access to a camera. Possible solutions are to have students do this exercise in groups, making certain that at least one person has access to a camera; or to use school equipment during class time.

Media and Technology Skills • 165

Lesson Objectives

1. To evaluate and critique the persuasive techniques of media messages
2. To evaluate the credibility of information sources
3. To recognize logical, deceptive, and/or faulty modes of persuasion in text
4. To describe how a writer's motivation, stance, or position may affect text credibility, structure, and tone

Step-by-Step Teaching Guide

Reading Critically

Teaching Resources: Standardized Test Preparation Workbook, pp. 15–16

1. Go over the three evaluating strategies with students. Students may need to review the following terms:

   • *Overgeneralization* (an inference too broad or sweeping for its limited supporting evidence)

   • *Circular reasoning* (an argument that attempts to prove its point by restating it in other words)

   • *Questionable cause-and-effect reasoning* (statements that mistake a time-order relationship for a cause-and-effect relationship)

   • *Either/or argument* (oversimplified argument that offers a choice of only two extremes)

   • *Bandwagon appeal* (a statement based on the desire of people to conform or be part of a group)

2. Discuss the sample test items and their answers and explanations. Tell students that the key to analyzing persuasive texts effectively is to read carefully and objectively.

3. Assign the practice test. After checking students' answers, discuss any items that gave students trouble.

Standardized Test Preparation Workshop

Reading Critically

Standardized test questions often measure your ability to evaluate an advertisement objectively. All advertisements have the same goal—to get you to believe or do something. As an educated reader, you must discern what information is valid by seeing past the attempts to persuade you. The following strategies will help you evaluate an advertisement:

• See if the argument or claim is supported with facts.

• Check for missing information, vague statements, or partial truths.

• Recognize faulty logic, such as overgeneralizations, circular reasoning, questionable cause-and-effect statements, either/or arguments, or bandwagon appeals.

The following sample test item will give you practice with these types of questions.

Test Tip

Consider what the writer does not say. Omitting details can slant information in a particular direction.

Sample Test Item	Answer and Explanation
Directions: Read the passage, and then choose the letter of the best answer. Buy Brighter toothpaste for a brighter, whiter smile! Three out of five dentists recommend that you use it every day for a healthier, whiter smile.	
1 What important information has been left out of this advertisement? A the name of the toothpaste B the total number of dentists surveyed C how often it should be used D the results of using the toothpaste	The correct answer is *B*. While the advertisement implies that many dentists were asked, it does not tell you how many dentists were asked overall. An advertiser could make this claim even if only five dentists were asked.

166 • Advertisement

⚔ TEST-TAKING TIP

When analyzing a persuasive advertisement, students should be alert to vague statements, partial truths, and missing information. Tax dollars may be going to painting police cars and new trash cans, but no supporting evidence is used to show why this is frivolous. Perhaps these are wise expenditures that the writer simply doesn't like because they deflect dollars from his or her own cause.

Readers are supposed to assume that children will be educationally deprived if the school budget isn't approved, but the writer does not give the amount of next year's school budget or the alternatives to this budget. In addition, the writer could be an employee of the school system whose salary will be increased by the new budget.

▶ **Practice 1**   **Directions:** Read the passage, and then choose the letter of the best answer to each question.

How are your tax dollars best used? Are they best used to paint police cars a new color? Are they best used to replace the functional trash cans on main streets with prettier ones? Either the money goes to these projects or to the schools. Our town's priority should be caring for its children. Town officials have allocated our tax dollars for frivolous expenditures. All of the taxpayers in this town have been given the opportunity to attend school without being deprived of teachers, textbooks, and supplies, yet we would deprive our children of the same. If we don't support education, the children won't have a chance at being successful. Everyone who cares about children will be voting YES for next year's school budget. Vote YES for next year's school budget and give today's children a fair chance at tomorrow.

1 The statement "Either the money goes to these projects or to the schools" is an example of—

A a bandwagon appeal

B circular reasoning

C questionable cause and effect

D either/or argument

2 Which of the following is an example of an overgeneralization—a statement too broad to be backed up by evidence?

F "Vote YES for next year's school budget and give today's children a fair chance at tomorrow."

G "Town officials have allocated our tax dollars for frivolous expenditures."

H Our town's priority should be caring for its children.

J None of the above

3 You can tell from this political advertisement that the writer intends to—

A vote against the school budget

B vote for the school budget

C encourage people to make private donations

D find ways to allocate money to town projects as well as education

4 Which of the following appeals to the emotions and not to logic?

F "All of the taxpayers in this town have been given the opportunity to attend school without being deprived of teachers, textbooks, and supplies, yet we would deprive our children of the same."

G "Either the money goes to these projects or to the schools."

H "Everyone who cares about children will be voting YES . . ."

J None of the above

5 The author implies but does not provide proof that—

A an inadequate amount of money is allocated to education

B the community plans on painting police cars

C the school budget is supported by most town members

D none of the above

6 Which of the following is an example of a bandwagon appeal?

F "Either the money goes to these projects or to the schools."

G "Town officials have allocated our tax dollars for frivolous expenditures."

H "Our town's priority should be caring for its children."

J "Everyone who cares about children will be voting YES for next year's school budget."

Customize for
Less Advanced Students

Students may need more help recognizing types of faulty logic, such as bandwagon appeal or circular reasoning, in order to evaluate a persuasive advertisement. You may want to do the practice test as a group, discussing each of the questions and how students might recognize the best answers. You may also want to discuss how specific items could have been written to make them more precise.

Customize for
AP Students

Ask students to discuss the connotations of the following words: *functional, prettier, frivolous, deprive.* Then, ask students, if the ad writer had included a graphic with the ad, what they think he or she might have chosen.

In-Depth Lesson Plan

FOCUS AND TEKS/TAAS CORRELATIONS	PRINT AND MEDIA RESOURCES
DAY 1 — **Introduction to Comparison-and-Contrast Essays** Students learn key elements of writing comparison-and-contrast essays and analyze the Model from Literature. (pp. 168–173/ⓗ106–107)	*Writers at Work* **DVD**, Exposition *Writing and Grammar* **Interactive Text**, Ch. 9, Introduction
DAY 2 — **Prewriting** Students choose and narrow a topic, consider their audience and purpose, and gather information. (pp. 174–177/ⓗ108–111)	*Writing and Grammar* **Interactive Text**, Section 9.2 **Teaching Resources** *Writing Support Transparencies, 9-A–D; Writing Support Activity Book, 9-1–2; Topic Bank for Heterogeneous Classes,* Ch. 9
DAY 3 — **Drafting** Students organize their ideas and write their first drafts. (pp. 178–179/ⓗ112–113)	*Writing and Grammar* **Interactive Text**, Section 9.3 **Teaching Resources** *Writing Support Transparencies, 9-E–F; Writing Support Activity Book,* 9-3
DAY 4 — **Revising** Students revise their drafts in terms of overall structure, paragraphs, sentences, and word choice. (pp. 180–184/ⓗ114–118)	*Writing and Grammar* **Interactive Text**, Section 9.4 **Teaching Resources** *Writing Support Transparencies,* 9-G–I
DAY 5 — **Editing and Proofreading; Publishing and Presenting** Students check their work for accuracy and correctness and present their final drafts. (pp. 185–188/ⓗ119–120)	*Writing and Grammar* **Interactive Text**, Sections 9.5–6 **Teaching Resources** *Scoring Rubrics on Transparency,* Ch. 9; *Writing Assessment and Portfolio Management; Formal Assessment,* Ch. 9

Accelerated Lesson Plan

FOCUS AND TEKS/TAAS CORRELATIONS	PRINT AND MEDIA RESOURCES
DAY 1 — **Introduction Through Drafting** Students review characteristics of comparison-and-contrast essays, select topics, and write drafts. (pp. 168–179/ⓗ106–113)	*Writing and Grammar* **Interactive Text**, Ch. 9, Introduction through Section 9.3 **Teaching Resources** *Writing Support Transparencies, 9-A–F; Writing Support Activity Book,* 9-1–3
DAY 2 — **Revising Through Presenting** Students work individually or with peers to revise, edit, and proofread their work for presentation. (pp. 180–188/ⓗ114–120)	*Writing and Grammar* **Interactive Text**, Sections 9.4–6 **Teaching Resources** *Writing Support Transparencies, 9-G–I; Scoring Rubrics on Transparency,* Ch. 9; *Writing Assessment and Portfolio Management; Formal Assessment,* Ch. 9

Options for Adapting Lesson Plans

HOMEWORK

Have students complete any stage of the lesson for homework.

FEATURES

Extend coverage with Connected Assignment (p. 189/ⓗ121), Spotlight on the Humanities (p. 190), Media and Technology Skills (p. 191), and the Standardized Test Preparation Workshop (pp. 192–193).

TECHNOLOGY

Students can complete any stage of the lesson on the computer, using *Writing and Grammar* Interactive Text or a word-processing program. Have them print out their completed work.

Writing and Grammar Handbook Alignment

Page numbers in Step-by-Step Teaching Guides in this Teacher's Edition refer to pages from the full student text. Handbook page references, indicated with this icon 🄷, are provided in Time and Resource Manager boxes and at the bottom of each Teacher's Edition page.

INTEGRATED SKILLS COVERAGE

Integrating Grammar
Using Commas, ATE p. 172

Reading/Writing Connection
Identify Author's Tone, SE p. 170
Writing Application, SE p. 173

Viewing and Representing
Critical Viewing, SE pp. 168, 170, 171, 184, 187, 190/🄷106, 118
Connecting Themes in the Arts, SE p. 190
Analyzing Relationships Between Media, SE p. 191

Real-World Connection
ATE p. 172

Technology
SE p. 177/🄷111; ATE p. 188

Workplace Skills
ATE pp. 177, 181

Vocabulary Skills
ATE p. 179

ASSESSMENT SUPPORT

Standardized Test Preparation Workshop SE p. 192; ATE p. 183
Standardized Test Preparation Workbook, pp. 17–18
Scoring Rubrics on Transparency, Ch. 9
Formal Assessment, Ch. 9
Writing Assessment and Portfolio Management

MEETING INDIVIDUAL NEEDS

Less Advanced Students ATE pp. 177, 193. See also Ongoing Assessments ATE pp. 170, 175, 179, 181.
AP Students ATE p. 193
ESL Students ATE pp. 171, 178, 186
Linguistic Learners ATE p. 176
Logical/Mathematical Learners ATE p. 175

BLOCK SCHEDULING

Pacing Suggestions
For 90-minute Blocks
• Have students complete the Prewriting and Drafting stages in a single period.
• Focus one class period on Revising and Editing and Publishing and Presenting. Allow at least 30 minutes for peer revision.

Resources for Varying Instruction
• *Writing and Grammar* Interactive Text A 90-minute block provides an ideal opportunity for students to work on the computer.
• *Writers at Work* DVD Show the Exposition segment in class.

Professional Development Support
• *How to Manage Instruction in the Block* This teaching resource provides management and activity suggestions.

MEDIA AND TECHNOLOGY

For the Student
• *Writing and Grammar* Interactive Text, Ch. 9
• *On-line Exercise Bank,* Sections 19.5, 20.2–3

For the Teacher
• *Writers at Work* DVD, Exposition
• **TeacherEXPRESS** CD-ROM

WRITING AND GRAMMAR ON-LINE

Interactive Text (On-line or on CD-ROM)
• Easily navigable instruction with interactive Revision Checkers
• Full use of e-rater™, the essay-scoring system (on-line only)

Companion Web Site PHSchool.com
• Scoring rubrics with models (use Web Code egk-1201)

See the Go On-line! feature, SE p. iii.

LITERATURE CONNECTIONS

Related selection from *Prentice Hall Literature, Penguin Edition,* The British Tradition:
Professional Model "Birds on the Western Front," Saki, SE p. 171
Topic Bank Options Sonnets 116 and 130, William Shakespeare, SE p. 175/🄷109

Lesson Objectives

1. To write a comparison-and-contrast essay appropriate to audience and purpose
2. To analyze text structures such as compare/contrast for how they influence understanding
3. To read to appreciate a writer's craft and to discover models for writing
4. To use prewriting strategies to generate ideas, develop voice, and plan
5. To use effective sequences and transitions to achieve coherence and meaning
6. To develop and revise drafts in terms of structure, paragraphs, sentences, and word choice
7. To edit and proofread to ensure standard English usage and grammar
8. To evaluate how well writing achieves its purposes
9. To refine a comparison-and-contrast essay for publication

Critical Viewing

Compare and Contrast Students may note that although the dog and cat both have eyes, fur, and tails, the color and size of their eyes, fur, and tails differ.

Chapter
9 Exposition
Comparison-and-Contrast Essay

▲ **Critical Viewing**
What physical similarities do this dog and cat share? What differences do you see? **[Compare and Contrast]**

Comparisons and Contrasts in Everyday Life

Many psychologists say that you can learn about dogs by studying cats. Comparing and contrasting the two animals, rather than studying one in isolation, will give a richer understanding of both animals.

Besides enriching your knowledge, skills in comparing and contrasting also help you make decisions in daily life. You could, for example, compare and contrast sports equipment in order to select the brand that's best for you, or you could choose a college or university to attend by comparing and contrasting several possibilities.

168 • Exposition

⏱ TIME AND RESOURCE MANAGER

Resources
Technology: *Writers at Work* DVD, Exposition; *Writing and Grammar* Interactive Text, Ch. 9

Using the Full Student Edition	Using the Handbook⊞
• Read and discuss pp. 168–171 in class. • Discuss the use of humor, charts, and point-by-point organization in the Model From Literature. • Ask students to discuss comparisons and contrasts they make every day.	• Read and discuss pp. 106–107 in class. • Ask students to discuss comparisons and contrasts they make every day.

What Is a Comparison-and-Contrast Essay?

A **comparison-and-contrast essay** is an expository nonfiction essay that explains how two or more subjects are similar and different. An effective comparison-and-contrast essay

- explores two or more topics that are similar enough to make an effective comparison.
- clearly shows through details and examples how two or more subjects are similar and different.
- is logically and effectively organized.
- clearly indicates the connections among ideas.
- closes with a summary of main points or an evaluation of the subject's overall points of similarity and difference.

To preview the criteria on which your comparison-and-contrast essay may be evaluated, see the Rubric for Self-Assessment on page 186.

Types of Comparison-and-Contrast Essays

Comparison-and-contrast essays exist in a number of specialized forms, including the following:

- **Comparisons of literary works** examine similarities and differences between literary elements, such as characters, setting, or theme, in different works.
- **Consumer reports** may compare and contrast two or more products or services from different companies to evaluate the positive and negative qualities of each.
- **Comparative reviews** evaluate or compare two or more related books, movies, albums, or television programs.

PREVIEW

Student Work
IN PROGRESS

Catherine Bailey and Zach Bucek, students at L. C. Anderson High School in Austin, Texas, used various writing strategies to write a comparison-and-contrast article about shopping for music on-line versus shopping for music in a store. A completed draft appears at the end of this chapter.

Writers in ACTION

An effective comparison-and-contrast essay addresses both similarities and differences. Poet Percy Bysshe Shelley emphasized the importance of addressing both aspects when he said: "Reason respects the differences, and imagination the similitudes of things."

Comparison-and-Contrast Essay • **169**

Interest GRABBER Ask the students to jot down the name of their favorite book or short story. Encourage them to consider such aspects as setting, character, tone, and plot, and list the reasons they enjoy the work. Have volunteers share some of their answers and reasons. Explain that in comparison-and-contrast essays, the writer must address specific qualities of the things he or she is comparing.

Activate Prior Knowledge

Instruct the students to think about an occasion when they had to select a gift for someone they cared about. Discuss the factors they considered. How did they reach their final decision? After discussing these criteria, explain to students that we compare and contrast things for different purposes every day. Can they think of more examples of things they frequently compare and contrast?

More About the Writer

Percy Bysshe Shelley (1792–1822) led a short, troubled life. As a boy, he attended the prestigious Eton School in England and was viewed as something of a loner. He spent much of his time wandering in the countryside, and was nicknamed "Mad Shelley." Later, at Oxford University, he was expelled after six months for his religious views. Shelley went on to find his literary voice through poetry and became a renowned Romantic poet. He drowned in a boating accident at the age of thirty.

✓ ONGOING ASSESSMENT: Diagnose

Use one of the following options to diagnose the students' current level of proficiency in writing comparison-and-contrast essays.

Option 1 Conference with each student to evaluate a sample of comparison-and-contrast writing from his or her portfolio. Using the criteria detailed in the rubric on p. 186, evaluate competence in this genre.

Option 2 Ask students to think about two seasons. Using a Venn diagram, have them show the similarities and differences between these seasons. Next, ask them to choose one point of comparison and develop it in a paragraph. Students who have difficulty with this exercise will need extra support in writing a comparison-and-contrast essay.

Reading: Identify Author's Tone

Ask students to identify the first clue that this essay will have a humorous tone. They should notice that the playful title (the play on the word *bytes* and on the legendary headline "Man Bites Dog") immediately conveys a humorous tone. What can students learn from the title of the Student Final Draft on page 187?

Step-by-Step Teaching Guide

Engage Students Through Literature

1. Ask the students to read "Man, Bytes, Dog" and analyze word choice to identify the author's attitude toward his subject. (Students should note that Gorman uses a humorous approach to express a wary attitude about personal computers. He uses words such as *portability*, *compatibility*, and *software*, which have specific meanings in the context of personal computers, and makes them sound silly by using them in the wrong context.)

2. Have your students discuss the word choice in the title and why it is effective. Point out that the title comes from an old reporter's tale about what's news and what isn't. According to the tale, a story headlined "Dog Bites Man" isn't news, but a story headlined "Man Bites Dog" is.

Critical Viewing

Connect Students may mention the monitor and screen size, keyboard layout, features of the operating systems, and so on.

9.1 Model From Literature

◀ **Critical Viewing**
If you were to compare and contrast this computer with another, what features might you use as points of comparison? **[Connect]**

The following article by James Gorman originally appeared in The New Yorker *magazine.*

Reading Strategy: Identify Author's Tone
Recognizing an author's tone—his or her attitude toward a subject—can help you better understand and appreciate what you read. As you read the following article, look for clues that reveal Gorman's attitude toward the topic of his comparison-and-contrast essay. Clues may include word choice, formality of language, and types of examples given.

Man, Bytes, Dog

James Gorman

Many people have asked me about the Cairn Terrier. How about memory, they want to know. Is it IBM compatible? Why didn't I get the IBM itself, or a Kaypro, Compaq, or Macintosh? I think the best way to answer these questions is to look at the personal computer and the Cairn head on. I almost did buy the personal

Gorman introduces the subjects of his comparison-and-contrast essay: a personal computer and a dog. This essay is humorous because the two subjects are not often thought of as similar enough to compare.

170 • Comparison-and-Contrast Essay

✓ ONGOING ASSESSMENT: Monitor and Reinforce

After previewing the Model From Literature, you may anticipate that some students will have difficulty with some words. If so, use one of the following options.

Option 1 After they read the model independently, have students list any unfamiliar words they encounter. Allow time to look up and discuss pronunciations and definitions in class.	**Option 2** If you or a prepared student read the model aloud in class, take time to define unfamiliar words as you read. Words such as *peripheral, instantaneously, astrophysics, criterion, eponymously,* and *mercifully* might need definition. Work with students to decipher the meanings by using context clues.

computer. It has terrific graphics, good word-processing capabilities, and the mouse. But in the end I decided on the Cairn, and I think I made the right decision.

Let's start out with the basics:

Personal Computer	Cairn Terrier
Weight (without printer): 20 lbs.	Weight (without printer): 14 lbs.
Memory (RAM): 128 K	Memory (RAM): Some
Price (with printer): $3,090	Price (without printer): $250

Just on the basis of price and weight, the choice is obvious. Another plus is that the Cairn Terrier comes in one unit. No printer is necessary, or useful. And—this was a big attraction to me—there is no user's manual.

Here are some of the other qualities I found put the Cairn out ahead of the personal computer.

Portability: To give you a better idea of size, Toto in *The Wizard of Oz* was a Cairn Terrier. So you can see that if the young Judy Garland was able to carry Toto around in that little picnic basket, you will have no trouble at all moving your Cairn from place to place. For short trips it will move under its own power. The personal computer will not. . . .

Compatibility: Cairn Terriers get along with everyone. And for communications with any other dog, of any breed, within a radius of three miles, no additional hardware is necessary. All dogs share a common operating system.

Software: The Cairn will run three standard programs, SIT, COME, and NO, and whatever else you create. It is true that, being microcanine, the Cairn is limited here, but it does load the programs instantaneously. No disk drives. No tapes.

Admittedly, these are peripheral advantages. The real comparison has to be on the basis of capabilities. What can the personal computer and the Cairn do? Let's start on the personal computer's turf—income-tax preparation, recipe storage, graphics, and astrophysics problems:

Charts such as this one allow readers to see supporting details at a glance.

Gorman chose point-by-point organization for his comparison-and-contrast essay.

To read another comparison-and-contrast essay, see "Birds on the Western Front," in which Saki compares and contrasts the reactions of various birds to wartime conditions. The essay appears in *Prentice Hall Literature, Penguin Edition,* The British Tradition.

◀ **Critical Viewing** How does this dog compare and contrast with a dog you know? [**Compare and Contrast**]

Model From Literature • 171

Teaching From the Model

Ask students to determine the purpose of this comparison-and-contrast essay and to support their answers with evidence from the text. (Students should notice that the purpose is to entertain. The humorous tone and the absurdity of comparing a personal computer to a dog make this clear.)

More About the Writer

James Gorman is a contemporary science writer who has written about the phenomena that surround the age of dinosaurs. He has also written extensively about the ecology of Antarctica.

Connections With Literature

If students have read the story, ask them to identify the purpose of "Birds on the Western Front." (Students should note that Saki's cynical, sarcastic tone makes clear his disgust for war. He is trying to inspire similar feelings in his readers.)

Customize for
ESL Students

English-language learners might need help picking up on the homophone in the story title. As a class, create a list of homophones and their definitions. Encourage students to collect other examples of homophones and record them in a reader's journal.

Critical Viewing

Compare and Contrast Answers will vary, but students will probably include information with respect to the dog's size, color, general appearance, and so on.

Real-World Connection

When a consumer magazine evaluates products or services, it decides on the elements to be compared. It then tests these elements and records the data. Finally, this information is evaluated and reported to consumers in a clear manner. Ask students whether they have ever read a comparison of products or services they were thinking about purchasing. What characteristics of each item were compared? How was the information presented? Did the article help them reach a decision?

Integrating Grammar Skills

Using Commas to Separate Items in a Series Have students reread the first paragraph of "Man, Bytes, Dog." Ask them to find a place where Gorman uses commas to separate three items in a series (terrific graphics, good word-processing capabilities, and the mouse). Remind them to use commas to separate three or more words, phrases, or clauses in a series. If the items themselves contain commas, they can prevent confusion by using semicolons to separate the phrases.

9.1

	Taxes	Recipes	Graphics	Astrophysics
Personal Computer	yes	yes	yes	yes
Cairn	no	no	no	no

At first glance it looks bad for the Cairn. But it's important to look beneath the surface with this kind of chart. If you yourself are leaning toward the personal computer, ask yourself these questions: Do you want to do your own income taxes? Do you want to type all your recipes into a computer? In your graph, what would you put on the x-axis? The y-axis? Do you have any astrophysics problems you want solved?

Then consider the Cairn's specialties: playing fetch and tug-of-war, licking your face, and chasing foxes out of rock cairns (eponymously). Note that no software is necessary. All these functions are part of the operating system:

	Fetch	Tug-of-war	Face	Foxes
Cairn	yes	yes	yes	yes
Personal Computer	no	no	no	no

Another point to keep in mind is that computers, even the personal computer, only do what you tell them to do. Cairns perform their functions all on their own. Here are some of the additional capabilities that I discovered once I got the Cairn home and housebroken:

Word Processing: Remarkably, the Cairn seems to understand every word I say. He has a nice way of pricking up his ears at words like "out" or "ball." He also has highly tuned voice recognition.

Education: The Cairn provides children with hands-on experience at an early age, contributing to social interaction, crawling ability, and language skills. At age one, my daughter could say "Sit," "Come," and "No."

Cleaning: This function was a pleasant surprise. But of course cleaning up around the cave is one of the reasons dogs were developed in the first place. Users with young (below age two) children will still find this function useful. The Cairn Terrier cleans the floor, spoons, bib, and baby, and has an unerring ability to distinguish strained peas from ears, nose, and fingers.

Heads like the ones that appear in front of these paragraphs help clarify the point being compared and contrasted.

172 • Comparison-and-Contrast Essay

Psychotherapy: Here the Cairn really shines. And remember, therapy is something that computers have tried.

There is a program that makes the computer ask you questions when you tell it your problems. You say, "I'm afraid of foxes." The computer says, "You're afraid of foxes?"

The Cairn won't give you that kind of echo. Like Freudian analysts, Cairns are mercifully silent; unlike Freudians, they are infinitely sympathetic. I've found that the Cairn will share, in a nonjudgmental fashion, disappointments, joys, and frustrations. And you don't have to know BASIC.

This last capability is related to the Cairn's strongest point, which was the final deciding factor in my decision against the personal computer—user-friendliness. On this criterion, there is simply no comparison. The Cairn Terrier is the essence of user friendliness. It has fur, it doesn't flicker when you look at it, and it wags its tail.

Transitions such as "like" and "unlike" allow readers to clearly connect what's being compared and contrasted.

Reading ▸ Writing Connection

Writing Application: **Identify Author's Tone** Before you begin writing your comparison-and-contrast essay, think for a moment about what subject you might write about and how you would reveal your attitude toward that subject. What words and phrases might you choose to create a tone revealing your attitude?

Reading\Writing Connection

Writing Application: Identify Author's Tone

If students elect a play on words for the title of their essay, suggest that they consult a reference book of homonyms as a starting point. Remind them that in written communication, level of formality and word choice are their primary means of creating tone.

Prewriting: Strategies for Generating Topics

Teaching Resources: Writing Support Transparencies, 9-A; Writing Support Activity Book, 9-1

1. Display Transparency 9-A to model the word association strategy. Give students blank copies of the organizer and have them pair up to do the activity. After they finish, have volunteers write some of their examples on the board. Students might use the words on the board as the basis for more word associations and might possibly come up with more ideas.

2. Students who use the freewriting activity should meet with small groups and share some of what they wrote. Their classmates might help them identify valuable topic ideas within their writing.

3. Students who try the mental shopping strategy should meet in small groups and share their ideas. It is likely that someone in the group will disagree with their evaluation of a certain product. Allow them to discuss their differences of opinion. This discussion might turn into a strong essay topic.

9.2 *Prewriting*

Choosing Your Topic

You need to find two or more related things or ideas to form the topic of your comparison-and-contrast essay. Use these strategies to select a topic you would like to develop:

Strategies for Generating Topics

1. **Word Association** Work with a partner to create a list of pairs. Your pairs might be opposites or closely related subjects. Take turns suggesting a person, character, subject, idea, or product, and allow your partner to respond with the first related idea that comes to mind. After listing ideas and responses, choose as a topic a pair that you could understand better through comparing and contrasting.

Idea	Response
high school	college
Keats	Shelley
Frankenstein	Dracula
sonnet	soliloquy
e-mail	World Wide Web
satire	parody

2. **Writing Marathon** If you have a single subject that interests you but do not know to what you could compare it, perform a "writing marathon." To do this, freewrite about your topic for at least ten minutes. Jot down everything that comes to mind about the subject. When you're finished writing, read what you have written to see if you have generated any possible topics for a comparison. If so, focus your comparison-and-contrast essay on that topic.

3. **Mental Shopping** Imagine yourself shopping in a store. What products might you compare before making a buying decision? You can concentrate on a large purchase, such as a bicycle or jacket, or a small purchase that affects your daily life, such as toothpaste or shampoo. As you visualize the store, jot down notes or sketches to help you focus on two or more products. Choose as a topic the products you find most interesting.

🕐 **Timed Writing Hint**

Most exam prompts provide very specific topics to compare and contrast. Structure your essay so that it addresses the prompt directly.

Get instant help! For assistance in finding a topic, use the Topic Bin, accessible under Topic Generators on the menu bar, on-line or on CD-ROM.

🕐 TIME AND RESOURCE MANAGER

Resources
Print: *Writing Support Transparencies*, 9-A–D; *Writing Support Activity Book*, 9-1–2
Technology: *Writing and Grammar* Interactive Text, Section 9.2

Using the Full Student Edition	Using the Handbook🄷
• Read and discuss pp. 174–177 in class. • Work through the activities on pp. 175–177 so students can choose, evaluate, and narrow their topics and gather details for their essays.	• Read and discuss pp. 108–111 in class. • Work through the activities on pp. 109–111 so students can choose, evaluate, and narrow their topics and gather details for their essays.

TOPIC BANK

Use one of these topics if you are having trouble coming up with your own:

1. **Comparison of Political Leaders** Choose two political leaders who held the same position, and compare their governing style and overall effectiveness. For example, you might choose two U.S. presidents from the same era, such as Abraham Lincoln and Ulysses S. Grant. As an alternative, choose two world leaders who ruled at the same time, such as King George III and George Washington.

2. **Consumer Report** Write a consumer report for a student newspaper. Choose as a topic a specific type of product that many students are interested in buying, such as in-line skates or jeans. Then, compare and contrast two or more brands of that product.

Responding to Fine Art

3. Closely examine *Song of Many Colors* by Michael Woodbury. Then, write a comparison-and-contrast essay in which you discuss the ways in which the artist uses color, shapes, and texture to depict various aspects of nature.

Responding to Literature

4. Read William Shakespeare's Sonnets 116 and 130. Compare the views of love presented in each sonnet. You can find these sonnets in *Prentice Hall Literature, Penguin Edition*, The British Tradition.

Timed Writing Prompt

5. Think about the people you respect the most. Perhaps they are your parents, teachers, politicians, or celebrities. Write an essay in which you compare and contrast two people you admire and respect. First, present the two individuals and explain why you admire and respect them. Then, discuss the ways in which they are similar. Finally, explain the ways in which they are different. Leave your reader with a sense of whether they are more similar or more different from each other. **(40 minutes)**

Song of Many Colors, Michael Woodbury, Courtesy of the artist

Prewriting • 175

Step-by-Step Teaching Guide

Responding to Fine Art
Song of Many Colors by Michael Woodbury

Teaching Resources: Writing Support Transparencies, 9-B

1. Use this artwork as a starting point to help students find an interesting topic for a comparison-and-contrast essay.

2. Display the transparency and engage students in a discussion about it. You may use questions such as these to prompt discussion:

   What kinds of objects can you identify?

   Does the artist repeat a certain color, shape, or pattern? If so, describe it.

   What aspects of nature are suggested in the work?

3. Ask students to brainstorm for subjects suggested by the painting that offer an opportunity to compare and contrast. Some possibilities are: nature, geometric shapes and patterns, and still life.

Timed Writing Prompt

- To help students narrow their focus, have them think about two separate events where another person's work, words, or personal guidance helped them overcome an obstacle, get through a difficult situation, make an important decision, or change their point of view.

- Have students make a list of the characteristics from their own personal experiences for the persons they choose.

- Suggest that students allow five minutes for prewriting, thirty minutes for writing, and five minutes for reviewing and proofreading.

Customize for
Logical/Mathematical Learners

Have students create a consumer report by conducting a survey in your class or school. First, bring in samples from consumer report magazines to show them models of survey questions. Then, have them select a topic, write questions, and conduct the survey. Have them display their results in charts and graphs and share them with the class.

Prewriting: Evaluate Similarities and Differences

Teaching Resources: Writing Support Transparencies, 9-C; Writing Support Activity Book, 9-2

1. If students are having difficulty understanding what makes an effective comparison, choose two familiar movies that have nothing in common and work with them to fill in the chart. Then, choose two familiar movies that have a similar subject or theme and complete the chart again.

2. Tell students that the movies in the second chart would make an effective topic and work with them to explain why (the contrasts between items that are completely different are already apparent; they do not need to be enumerated in an essay).

3. Have students complete a chart with their own topic ideas and evaluate whether they need to make any changes.

Prewriting: Consider Your Purpose

1. Work with students to make a list of various purposes for writing (to inform, to entertain, to warn, to persuade, to motivate).

2. Have students decide on the purpose of their essays, and then meet with other students who chose the same purpose.

3. Have them brainstorm in small groups for a list of words that will help to convey the purpose and tone they are trying to achieve.

Customize for
Linguistic Learners

Talking rather than writing about a subject may be more comfortable for some students. If possible, have students meet with a member of their intended audience (for example, a peer, a parent, a young child) and discuss their topic. It is likely that they will naturally use the appropriate tone and word choice when they talk.

9.2

Evaluating Your Topic

Choose subjects to compare that share enough similarities and have enough differences to make the comparison useful.

Evaluate Similarities and Differences

To evaluate your subjects, use a chart to note similarities and differences. Review your chart to make sure your subjects share enough qualities to make an effective topic for comparison.

Ineffective Comparison
Romeo and Juliet
and
Guys and Dolls

Similarities	Differences
both have been made into movies	one is a tragedy; one is a comedy
both include love stories	written in different eras
	characters have little in common
	plots are different
	themes are different

Effective Comparison
Romeo and Juliet
and
West Side Story

Similarities	Differences
both tell the same story	settings are different
both are plays that have been filmed	time periods are different
related characters	one is a drama; one is a musical
both explore the theme of love overcoming differences	backgrounds of characters are different

Considering Your Audience and Purpose

Select details and choose a style of language that will appeal to your audience and help you achieve your purpose.

Consider Your Purpose

When writing exposition, your general purpose is to inform. However, you must have a more specific purpose to guide your choices as you collect ideas, draft, and revise.

For example, if you are writing a consumer report and your purpose is to educate readers, use words and details that are formal, precise, and factual. If your purpose is to warn readers, include details and language that have strong connotations and a serious impact.

Gathering Details

To create a balanced comparison, make sure you collect details in similar categories about each of your subjects. Remember that your essay will investigate both similarities and differences.

List Your Questions

Write a list of questions to help guide your prewriting investigation. Your questions should focus on specific categories or aspects of your subjects. To achieve a balanced essay, be sure you answer each question relating to both subjects.

For example, suppose you are writing an essay comparing and contrasting two different colleges. You might use some of the following questions to help you gather details:

- Where is each college located?
- How many students attend each school?
- What subject areas are particular strengths for each college?
- How does each school determine financial aid?
- What is the estimated cost of attending each school?

Write each question on note cards or paper, and record answers for each subject. Keep your research plan flexible, because your answers may lead you to additional questions.

 **Technology Tip**

Use the "table" feature in your word-processing program to create a chart in which you list similarities and differences between your subjects.

Student Work IN PROGRESS

Name: *Catherine Bailey and Zach Bucek*
L. C. Anderson High School
Austin, TX

Listing Questions to Gather Details

Catherine and Zach wrote a list of questions before they began researching their article about on-line and traditional music stores

1. What is the procedure for buying CDs?
2. How much does a CD cost?
3. How do you search for a CD?
4. What are the benefits?

Prewriting • 177

Step-by-Step Teaching Guide

Prewriting: List Your Questions

Teaching Resources: Writing Support Transparencies, 9-D

1. Lead a discussion to review the reasons for gathering details in similar categories (example: to develop a balanced comparison between two or more subjects).

2. Ask for volunteers to explain the rationale for listing questions on individual note cards. Point out that questions guide the prewriting investigation and individual note cards offer a place to record the answers.

3. Display Transparency 9-D and discuss the Student Work in Progress. How will the list of questions Catherine and Zach prepared about their topic help them organize their essay?

Customize for
Less Advanced Students

Help students write to a specific audience by creating an audience profile. Have them answer a series of questions about their intended audience, such as level of education, skills, and background knowledge of the topic.

Integrating Workplace Skills

In the workplace, employees often present suggestions in the form of proposals to advocate a particular course of action. For example, a lawyer might try to convince his partners to take on a particularly challenging case. In doing so, they must consider their audience and include details and arguments that the audience will find appealing.

⏱ **TIME SAVERS!**

 Writing Support Transparencies
Use the transparencies for Chapter 9 to facilitate teaching of strategies.

 Writing Support Activity Book
Use the graphic organizers for Chapter 9 to facilitate student planning.

Drafting: Choose an Effective Organization

Teaching Resources: Writing Support Transparencies, 9-E; Writing Support Activity Book, 9-3

1. Display Transparency 9-E and use it to explain the differences between the two organizational techniques. Lead a discussion about the benefits of each method as a way to organize essays. Explain that point-by-point organization focuses attention on specific features of subjects while subject-by-subject organization focuses on the subjects as a whole.

2. Have students think of examples of topics that would be best organized by each of the methods listed. Make sure they explain their choices.

3. Ask students to choose either a point-by-point or subject-by-subject organizational plan for their topics. Once they choose a plan, have them outline their essays and then begin writing.

Customize for
ESL Students

Allow students to draft their essays in their first language. This way, they can concentrate on getting their ideas down. Later, they can focus on organizing the information and translating it into English.

9.3 Drafting

Shaping Your Writing
Choose an Effective Organization

During prewriting, you uncovered various details about the subjects you are comparing and contrasting. Now, decide on a clear organizational strategy to keep those details from becoming jumbled and confusing.

Two common approaches are used to write a comparison-and-contrast essay:

- **Point-by-Point Comparison:** Discuss one feature or aspect of both subjects, and then move on to another feature. Continue until you have covered all of your points.

- **Subject-by-Subject Comparison:** Discuss one subject fully, and then move on to the next subject. Make sure that the sequence of details in the second discussion mirrors that of the first.

Point-by-Point Comparison	Subject-by-Subject Comparison
I. Introduction: Three Portable Stereos	I. Introduction: Three Portable Stereos
II. Sound Quality	II. Product 1
A. Product 1	A. Sound quality
B. Product 2	B. Economy
C. Product 3	C. Additional features
III. Economy	III. Product 2
A. Product 1	A. Sound quality
B. Product 2	B. Economy
C. Product 3	C. Additional features
IV. Additional features	IV. Product 3
A. Product 1	A. Sound quality
B. Product 2	B. Economy
C. Product 3	C. Additional features
V. Recommendation	V. Recommendation

178 • Comparison-and-Contrast Essay

⏱ Timed Writing Hint

Pay close attention to the way a prompt is written. The prompt will often suggest which organizational strategy you should use when drafting your essay.

⏱ TIME AND RESOURCE MANAGER

Resources
Print: *Writing Support Transparencies 9-3–F, Writing Support Activity Book, 9-3*
Technology: *Writing and Grammar* Interactive Text, Section 9.3

Using the Full Student Edition	Using the Handbook⊞
• Read and discuss the forms of organization for a comparison-and-contrast essay.	• Read and discuss the forms of organization for a comparison-and-contrast essay.
• Emphasize the importance of providing details to support statements.	• Emphasize the importance of providing details to support statements.
• Have students draft their comparison-and-contrast essays in class.	• Have students draft their comparison-and-contrast essays in class.

Providing Elaboration

As you draft, create a complete picture of each subject you are comparing and contrasting. Use specific details to show the extent to which or the ways in which your subjects are similar and different.

Support Your Statements

Provide details that emphasize how your subjects are similar and different, and then prove or illustrate those points of similarity or difference. Following are examples of details you could use:

- **Example:** Hugger Jeans faded after just ten washings.
- **Statistic:** Nine out of ten mechanics recommend Ignite Spark Plugs.
- **Quotation:** Skating commentator Dirk Leeland stated, "Romanov is exquisite, but Lewis is perfection."

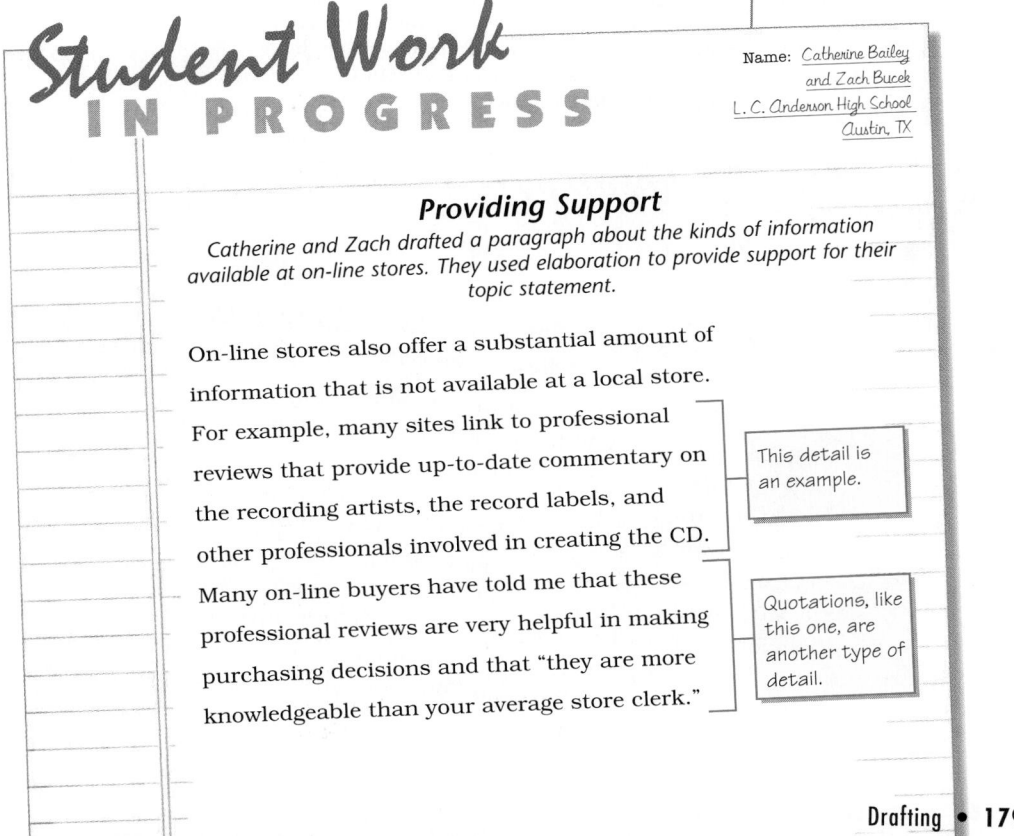

Student Work
IN PROGRESS

Name: *Catherine Bailey and Zach Bucek*
L. C. Anderson High School
Austin, TX

Providing Support

Catherine and Zach drafted a paragraph about the kinds of information available at on-line stores. They used elaboration to provide support for their topic statement.

On-line stores also offer a substantial amount of information that is not available at a local store. For example, many sites link to professional reviews that provide up-to-date commentary on the recording artists, the record labels, and other professionals involved in creating the CD.

> This detail is an example.

Many on-line buyers have told me that these professional reviews are very helpful in making purchasing decisions and that "they are more knowledgeable than your average store clerk."

> Quotations, like this one, are another type of detail.

Drafting • 179

Step-by-Step Teaching Guide

Drafting: Support Your Statements

Teaching Resources: Writing Support Transparencies, 9-F

1. Have the students read the introduction to this section. Discuss with them the different types of details that are used to support statements. If necessary, define the terms *statistics*, *quotations,* and *examples*. Challenge students to think of examples of each.

2. Display Transparency 9-F or direct students to the Student Work in Progress on this page. Point out that this example builds on the questions shown in the Student Work in Progress on page 177.

3. If students cannot think of details to include, have them explain their topic to a partner. Then, have the partner write down five questions he or she has about the topic. The answers to these questions might be useful details to include in their essays.

Integrating Vocabulary Skills

Have students exchange drafts with partners and underline any words they do not recognize. Problems in understanding vocabulary are likely to happen if students choose a topic with a highly specialized vocabulary, such as comparing and contrasting two Web browsers. Have them look up unfamiliar terms and write them in their vocabulary notebooks.

☑ ONGOING ASSESSMENT: Monitor and Reinforce

At times, students have problems recognizing the strengths and weaknesses of their supporting evidence. If students have this difficulty, try the following strategy.

After pairing students, supply them with index cards or self-sticking notes. Have each student write down his or her supporting details. Then, each student should arrange his or her partner's supporting points in order, from strongest to weakest. Encourage them to eliminate any evidence that they both believe is very weak or irrelevant. This will only detract from the overall credibility of their work.

Revising: Circling Topic Sentences

Teaching Resources: Writing Support Transparencies, 9-G

1. Initiate a class discussion of the elements of the revision process. What strategies are students accustomed to using when revising a piece of writing? What parts of their essays do they feel need the most improvement?

2. Point out that the first step in revising is to look at the overall structure of the piece. Every paragraph should work to strengthen the main idea of the essay. If it does not, it should be revised or eliminated.

3. Have a volunteer remind the class of the definition of a topic sentence. Then, have students complete the Circling Topic Sentences strategy. Have them write down every topic sentence on a piece of paper. Do they all relate? Do they connect logically to one another? Should any of them appear in a different order? Should any be eliminated?

9.4 Revising

Improve your first draft by reviewing it from a variety of perspectives. Start by evaluating the big picture, making sure that the overall structure is complete and effective. Once you are sure that the basic structure is solid, evaluate your paragraphs, sentences, and word choices.

Revising Your Overall Structure

Strengthen Unity

A comparison-and-contrast essay needs a strong sense of unity, or singleness of effect, to keep it from seeming like two separate essays. Your overall structure should help make clear how your subjects are related.

▶ **REVISION STRATEGY**
Circling Topic Sentences

With a colored pencil, circle the topic sentence of each paragraph of your essay. Then, review each topic sentence to make sure it directly supports or connects to your essay's topic. If you find a topic sentence that does not belong, delete the sentence and the paragraph in which it appears.

Student Work
IN PROGRESS

Name: Catherine Bailey
and Zach Bucek
L. C. Anderson High School
Austin, TX

Circling Topic Sentences to Strengthen Unity
Catherine and Zach noticed a break in the unity of their first draft.

Another advantage of on-line record stores is their extensive collection of albums. Web sites sell hundreds of thousands of titles. Although it may take some rare selections a few weeks to ship, at least on-line stores can get them for you. No local store can stock such a vast inventory, and many are reluctant to try to locate rare selections for their customers.

MP3s have also contributed to the on-line music boom. MP3 is a format that allows users to download music directly to their hard drives. Songs in MP3 format are available on many Web sites. Because of this innovation, downloading music has become more convenient.

The topic of MP3s is not directly related to the comparison of on-line record stores and retail stores. Catherine and Zach cut the paragraph to create unity.

180 • Comparison-and-Contrast Essay

⏱ TIME AND RESOURCE MANAGER

Resources
Print: *Writing Support Transparencies, 9-G–I*
Technology: *Writing and Grammar* Interactive Text, Section 9.4

Using the Full Student Edition	Using the Handbook Ⓗ
• Read and discuss pp. 180–184 in class. • Give students time in class to complete the revising activities. Answer revising questions as they arise. • Review and discuss sentence types.	• Read and discuss pp.114–118 in class. • Give students time in class to complete the revising activities. Answer revising questions as they arise. • Review and discuss sentence types.

Revising Your Paragraphs

To make your comparison-and-contrast essay effective, make sure you have effectively grouped your thoughts, details, and support into paragraphs.

Identify and Revise Paragraphs

Paragraphs present a unit of thought. Some units are expressed in a single sentence; some are expressed through several. Following are explanations of several types of paragraphs you may use in your comparison-and-contrast essay.

Topical Paragraphs: A topical paragraph revolves around a main idea that is expressed in its topic sentence. All other sentences within this type of paragraph should support or relate to the paragraph's topic sentence.

Functional Paragraphs: A functional paragraph serves a specific purpose. For example, it may emphasize a single point, create a special effect, show a shift from one speaker to another, or provide a transition.

Paragraph Blocks: A paragraph block refers to a topic sentence that is supported by several paragraphs in sequence. Paragraphs blocks are useful when presenting characteristics of a subject, citing causes, distinguishing features, or enumerating components of something.

▶ REVISION STRATEGY
Underlining Main Ideas and Checking Paragraphs

Read through your draft, and underline each main idea.
- If you have more than one main idea within a paragraph, break that paragraph into two paragraphs.
- If a paragraph has no main idea, read it carefully. If it contains support for a main idea presented in another paragraph, combine the two paragraphs. If the paragraph serves a specific function, leave it as is. If the paragraph is part of a paragraph block, leave it as is.

On our road test, we found that the Greystone Lynx X321 is a pleasure to drive. The cab is quiet, even when the engine is pushed to perform. It accelerates swiftly and smoothly and handles curves like a dream. On wet roads, on bumpy roads, on curved roads and straight ones, the Lynx out drives all others in its category.

Now, let's look at the price factors—what you'll get for your money.

> This paragraph is topical. Its sentences support the main idea expressed in its topic sentence.

> This is a functional paragraph. It makes a transition from the previous paragraph to the next.

Learn More

To learn more about effective paragraphs, see Chapter 3.

Identify and Revise Paragraphs

1. Have students carefully read the points making up each of the three kinds of paragraphs. They will probably be most familiar with topical paragraphs, as supporting a paragraph's main idea is the most stressed feature of paragraph development.
2. Point out that writers often make use of paragraphs that are functional rather than topical. Tell students that often a short functional paragraph will help a reader move between the main ideas in two topical paragraphs.
3. For paragraph blocks, point out that sometimes topics are complex and that rather than using one long paragraph, a writer will sometimes use paragraph blocks to break up the idea. Explain, though, that analogous to all the statements within a paragraph, all the information in a paragraph block should support the topical paragraph.

Step-by-Step Teaching Guide

Underlining Main Ideas and Checking Paragraphs

Teaching Resource: Writing Support Transparencies, 9-H

1. Tell students that the underlining they do will let them see at a glance where they might have either too many or not enough main ideas.
2. Display Transparency 9-H. It allows students to see a topical paragraph followed by a functional paragraph and should help reinforce their understanding of how the two kinds of paragraphs work together.

Integrating Workplace Skills

Tell students that many jobs involve research, and the coherent presentation of often complex results will be enhanced by an adept handling of paragraphing. In particular, paragraph blocks used for the presentation of several points to support a point will be frequently used.

✓ ONGOING ASSESSMENT: Monitor and Reinforce

If you observe that students are having difficulty categorizing and varying the supporting details in their paragraphs, use one of the following options.

Option 1 Have students work in pairs. They can exchange papers and color code the supporting details by category. They can then discuss these groupings.

Option 2 Working with their partner's paper, students can suggest other details to enhance the support of the topic. Or, they can simply ask questions about the topic that will help the author think of more details to include. Students can then integrate these suggestions into their essays.

Revising: Coding to Identify Sentence Type

Teaching Resources: Writing Support Transparencies, 9-I

1. Tell students that a good way to determine whether their sentences are too repetitive is to read their essays aloud. This will allow them to hear the rhythm of the essay. If it sounds too choppy, they should consider combining sentences. If it sounds too wordy, have them shorten sentences and vary sentence structures.

2. Have the students code the sentence types in their drafts. They might work in pairs to simplify or add complexity using the suggested techniques. Then, have them read aloud selected paragraphs in their original and revised states to evaluate whether their changes are effective.

9.4

Revising Your Sentences
Vary Your Sentences

During revision, identify sentence patterns that you rely on too heavily and make adjustments. An effective essay uses sentences of various lengths as well as types to create interest and flow.

▶ **REVISION STRATEGY**
Coding to Identify Sentence Type

Read your essay, and bracket each simple sentence you have used. Put a box around compound sentences. Underline the compound-complex sentences. Then, review your draft. If you have relied too heavily on one type of sentence, add complexity to your sentences or simplify them.

To add complexity:
- Combine sentences.
- Add transitions to link ideas.
- Insert clauses into simple sentences.
- Use a question to create variety.

To simplify:
- Separate one sentence into two or more sentences.
- Add a short, emphatic statement between long sentences.
- Delete unnecessary phrases.

Get instant help! Use the Revision Checker for Sentence Length, accessible on the menu bar, on-line or on CD-ROM.

Student Work IN PROGRESS

Name: *Catherine Bailey and Zach Bucek*
L. C. Anderson High School
Austin, TX

Coding to Improve Sentence Variety
Catherine and Zach noticed that every sentence in this paragraph was a simple sentence. They decided to combine some sentences to improve sentence variety and the overall flow of the paragraph.

Although
∧[On-line record stores have created a ∧convenient
more
experience.] However, the atmosphere and feel of ∧tangible record
an ordinary
store is absent.] [For many people, a local record store is like a
favorite coffee shop or bookstore.] [Clerks ∧are familiar with the
who
stock.] [They can offer personal recommendations.]

182 • Comparison-and-Contrast Essay

☑ **ONGOING ASSESSMENT: Prerequisite Skills**

If students have difficulty recognizing sentence types, you may find it helpful to refer them to the following materials to ensure coverage of prerequisite knowledge.

In the Textbook	Print Resources	Technology
Sentences Classified by Structure, Section 19.4 Combining Sentences, Section 20.2 Varying Sentences, Section 20.3	*Grammar Exercise Workbook,* pp. 51–52; 53–60	*On-Line Exercise Bank,* Sections 19.4, 20.2–3

Grammar in Your Writing
Compound and Complex Sentences

Creating sentence variety means using different sentence types. Become familiar with various sentence types so that you know your options as you revise.

A **simple sentence** consists of a single independent clause:

Last night, <u>we</u> <u>watched</u> a movie.

The <u>critic</u> <u>enjoyed</u> the film and <u>recommended</u> it.

Laughing all the way to the bank, the <u>director</u> <u>parodies</u> modern society.

A **compound sentence** consists of two or more independent clauses joined by a comma and a coordinating conjunction or by a semicolon.

<u>Hamlet</u> <u>becomes</u> a tragic hero, but <u>Macbeth</u> <u>becomes</u> a villain.

The two <u>calculators</u> <u>are</u> nearly identical; therefore, <u>I</u> <u>purchased</u> the cheaper model.

A **complex sentence** consists of one independent clause and one or more subordinate clauses.

Independent Clause	Subordinate Clause

<u>She</u> <u>created</u> the Web site <u>that</u> <u>was profiled</u> in *The New York Times.*

Independent Clause

<u>Lady Macbeth</u> <u>encourages</u> her husband to criminal actions, but

Subordinate Clause	Independent Clause

after <u>he</u> <u>kills</u> his enemies, <u>she</u> <u>loses</u> her sanity.

Find It in Your Reading Read through "Man, Bytes, Dog" on pages 170–173 of this chapter. Identify two simple, two compound, and two complex sentences within it. Then, explain how the author's use of sentence variety makes his writing lively.

Find It in Your Writing Classify each sentence in two or three paragraphs of your essay according to its type. If you find too many examples of one type, combine or split several sentences to create greater variety.

For more on sentence variety, see Chapter 20.

Compound and Complex Sentences

1. Review each sentence type with the class. Write a simple sentence on the board as a model for the students.

   We arrived at school on time.

   Then, write a compound sentence.

   She worked hard all summer, but she still needed more money.

   Next, write a compound-complex sentence.

   Ms. Rodriguez, who is a new teacher, has a good grasp of the subject matter.

2. After writing each sentence, discuss its characteristics and ask for volunteers to offer other examples.

3. Have students make sure they've used a variety of sentence types in their own essays.

Find It in Your Reading

There are numerous examples of the three types of sentences in the essay. However, there are also a few sentence fragments ("No disk drives. No tapes."), which will be made especially apparent to students as they comb the essay for simple sentences. You may need to justify their use to students. Explain how this type of light, ironic essay allows for such creative license.

Find It in Your Writing

Remind students to refer to the list on page 182 for methods of making sentences simpler or more complex.

STANDARDIZED TEST PREPARATION WORKSHOP

Standardized tests often require students to recognize sentence types. Give students extra practice in this area.

Read the two sentences below. What type of sentence are they?

Struggling uphill, we carried our equipment to base camp.

I had a great time on the camping trip and would love to go again.

A fragment   **C** compound

B compound-complex   **D** simple

The correct answer is **D.** Both are simple sentences because each consists of a single independent clause.

Step-by-Step Teaching Guide

Revising: Adding Transitions

1. Remind students that transitional phrases in sentences help clarify relationships. For example, in the sentences below, the phrase *in spite of* adds to the meaning because it suggests that the hikers were undaunted in the face of adversity.

2. Write the following sentences on the board.

   The hikers completed their trek up the valley. It rained all day.

   In spite of the all-day rain, the hikers completed their trek up the valley.

3. Ask students to find other examples of effective transitions in novels, biographies, textbooks, or magazines and explain why the transitions help strengthen the writing.

4. Encourage volunteers to give examples of transitional words and phrases *(although, next, then, however, but, despite this, as a result, as time went on)*. Write their suggestions on the board. Students might want to copy this list and keep it in their notebooks for future reference.

5. Have students work in pairs to read each other's essays and identify places where transitional words and phrases can improve the essay. Encourage them to use the list on the board as a resource.

Step-by-Step Teaching Guide

Revising: Peer Review

1. Ask students to read the list of questions to be answered by peer reviewers. Tell them to add some questions that are specific to their essays. For example, they might need help rephrasing a certain sentence or determining whether a paragraph is necessary.

2. Have students read the remarks of their reviewers. Give them time to discuss these remarks if they are unclear.

3. Remind students that they are not required to follow the suggestions of their peer reviewers. If they are unsure whether a suggestion is valuable, they might get another classmate to read their essay and offer a second opinion.

Revising Your Word Choice

Strengthen Connections

It's especially important in a comparison-and-contrast essay to make connections between the similarities and differences you are discussing. Review your draft critically, and strengthen connections between your ideas.

▶ **REVISION STRATEGY**
Adding Transitions

Transitions make the relationships among your ideas clearer to readers. They are words, phrases, and even sentences that help explain the similarities and differences between your subjects or emphasize the relative importance of the details you present. As you review your choice of words, consider adding transitional words, phrases, and sentences to strengthen the connections you are describing.

Transitional Word: The Traveler brand backpack held up under tough conditions, *although* it did get extremely dirty.

Transitional Phrase: The Take-It brand backpack, *on the other hand*, fell apart after getting soaked by rain.

Peer Review

Make a Summary Report

Ask a partner to read your draft and summarize the essay aloud. Listen to your partner's summary to help you evaluate the overall effectiveness of your writing, as well as the points that stand out the most.

After discussing the summary, have your partner respond to specific questions about your essay, like the ones that follow. Then, consider his or her responses as you prepare your final draft.

- Is my topic clear and well supported? Explain.
- Are there enough points of comparison and contrast? If not, explain.
- Which, if any, sections of the essay confused you?
- Was my writing exciting or predictable? Explain.
- If you could make one change to this essay, what would it be?

▼ **Critical Viewing**
Who is the peer reviewer in this photograph? How can you tell? **[Analyze]**

184 • Comparison-and-Contrast Essay

Critical Viewing

Analyze Most students will say that the peer reviewer is the student on the right. She is the one who appears to be speaking.

9.5 Editing and Proofreading

Read your draft carefullly. Make your essay error-free by fixing errors in spelling, punctuation, and grammar.

Focusing on Punctuation

Read your draft carefully, and fix any errors you find in punctuation. Check especially to make sure you have correctly used commas in sentences in which ideas have been combined.

Grammar in Your Writing
Using Commas in Compound and Complex Sentences

A **comma** tells a reader to take a short pause before continuing the sentence. Here are some of the rules you can follow when using commas in compound and complex sentences:

Use a comma before the conjunction that separates two independent clauses in a compound sentence:

I enjoyed the film, but the ending was unbelievable.

Use commas to separate three or more words, phrases, or clauses:

The report stated that security was lax, that lighting was inadequate, and that exits were not clearly marked.

Use commas to set off an introductory adverb clause:

When the bus stopped, the passengers got off.

Do not use a comma to set off adverb clauses in other positions:

The passengers got off when the bus stopped.

Find It in Your Reading Find one example of each of the above usages of the comma in "Man, Bytes, Dog" on pages 170–173. Label each example, and explain why it is punctuated as it is.

Find It in Your Writing Review your draft to find two compound sentences and two complex sentences. Decide whether or not the sentences require commas.

To learn more about using commas, see Chapter 27.

Editing and Proofreading • 185

⏱ **TIME AND RESOURCE MANAGER**

Resources
Technology: *Writing and Grammar* Interactive Text, Section 9.5

Using the Full Student Edition	Using the Handbook🅷
• Read and discuss Grammar in Your Writing. • Have students proofread their own drafts for usage of commas and make necessary revisions. • Give students time in class to edit and proofread their essays.	• Read and discuss Grammar in Your Writing. • Have students proofread their own drafts for usage of commas and make necessary revisions. • Give students time in class to edit and proofread their essays.

Step-by-Step Teaching Guide

Editing and Proofreading

1. Remind students that editing and proofreading are an extension of the writing process. Suggest that they check their punctuation paragraph by paragraph.

2. Students should look carefully at their use of commas and transitions.

Step-by-Step Teaching Guide

Using Commas in Compound and Complex Sentences

1. Write this sentence on the board.

   I walked to the train station to buy a ticket, but the ticket machine was out of order.

   This illustrates the use of a comma before the conjunction to separate independent clauses.

2. Write this sentence on the board.

   She read a book with beautiful illustrations, interesting dialogue, and compelling characters.

   This is an example of using commas to separate three or more phrases in a series.

3. Write this sentence on the board.

   After we played the game, I was exhausted.

   Point out that this shows how commas are used to set off an introductory adverb clause.

4. Have students write and share their own sentences of this type.

Find It in Your Reading

Possible answers:

1. To separate independent clauses: *But in the end, I decided on the Cairn, and I think I made the right decision.*

2. To separate items in a series: *It has terrific graphics, good word-processing capabilities, and the mouse.*

3. To set off an introductory adverb clause: *Just on the basis of height and weight, the choice is obvious.*

Find It in Your Writing

Have students trade papers and evaluate each other's use of commas.

Publishing and Presenting

1. Ask students to think about finding other places where they might publish their essays (magazine essay contests or the school newspaper).

2. Encourage students to create relevant illustrations, charts, and other graphic enhancements to their essays.

ASSESS and CLOSE

Assessment

Teaching Resources: Scoring Rubrics On Transparency, Ch. 9; Writing Assessment and Portfolio Management; Formal Assessment, Ch. 9

1. Display the Scoring Rubric transparency and review the criteria in class.

2. Before students proceed with self-assessment, you may wish to review the Final Draft of the Student Work in Progress on pp. 187–188. Have students score the Final Draft in one or more of the rubric categories.

3. In addition to student self-assessment, you may wish to use the following assessment options:
   - score student essays yourself, using the rubric and scoring models from *Writing Assessment and Portfolio Management.*
   - administer the Chapter 9 assessment from *Formal Assessment* in the Teaching Resources to measure students' grasp of the concepts presented.

Customize for
ESL Students

Students might have trouble understanding some of the criteria in the rubric for self-assessment because they contain a specialized writing vocabulary. Encourage them to identify words they do not recognize and work with a more-fluent English speaker to define them.

9.6 Publishing and Presenting

No matter how you share your comparison-and-contrast essay, you will learn a lot from the reaction of your audience. Use the following ideas for publishing and presenting your essay:

Building Your Portfolio

1. **School Bulletin** Publish your consumer review in a school bulletin to share your findings with an audience. Talk with readers to see whether or not they agree with your conclusions.

2. **Class Essay Contest** Hold a class contest with a panel of student judges to determine the most effective comparison-and-contrast essays. Winning essays can be read aloud, posted, or printed in a pamphlet. Talk as a class about the qualities shared by each of the best entries.

Reflecting on Your Writing

Think about the strategies you used to complete your essay. Then, respond to the following questions, and save your responses in your portfolio.

- What did you learn about your topic as you gathered details?
- What advice would you give to a student who is about to begin a comparison-and-contrast essay?

Internet Tip

To see a comparison-and-contrast essay scored according to this rubric, go on-line: PHSchool.com
Enter Web Code: egk-1201

Rubric for Self-Assessment

Use the following criteria to evaluate your comparison-and-contrast essay.

	Score 4	Score 3	Score 2	Score 1
Audience and Purpose	Clearly provides a reason for a comparison-contrast analysis	Adequately provides a reason for a comparison-contrast analysis	Provides a reason for a comparison-contrast analysis	Does not provide a reason for a comparison-contrast analysis
Organization	Clearly presents information in a consistent organization best suited to the topic	Presents information using an organization suited to the topic	Chooses an organization not suited to comparison and contrast	Shows a lack of organizational strategy
Elaboration	Elaborates several ideas with facts, details, or examples; links all information to comparison and contrast	Elaborates most ideas with facts, details, or examples; links most information to comparison and contrast	Does not elaborate all ideas; does not link some details to comparison and contrast	Does not provide facts or examples to support a comparison and contrast
Use of Language	Demonstrates excellent sentence and vocabulary variety; includes very few mechanical errors	Demonstrates adequate sentence and vocabulary variety; includes few mechanical errors	Demonstrates repetitive use of sentence structure and vocabulary; includes many mechanical errors	Demonstrates poor use of language; generates confusion; includes many mechanical errors

186 • Comparison-and-Contrast Essay

⏱ TIME AND RESOURCE MANAGER

Resources
Print: *Scoring Rubrics on Transparency,* Ch. 9; *Writing Assessment and Portfolio Management; Formal Assessment,* Ch. 9
Technology: *Writing and Grammar* Interactive Text, Section 9.6

Using the Full Student Edition	Using the Handbook🄷
• Discuss the Rubric for Self-Assessment. • Let students practice using the rubric by applying it to "Are Local Music Stores Obsolete?" (pp. 187–188).	• Discuss the Rubric for Self-Assessment.

9.7 Student Work IN PROGRESS

FINAL DRAFT

Are Local Music Stores Obsolete?

Catherine Bailey and Zach Bucek
L. C. Anderson High School
Austin, Texas

In recent years, the fusion of the Internet and the music industry has revolutionized the way many people buy music. Today, Web sites that sell music compete directly with local music stores. But what are the advantages and disadvantages of each shopping experience?

On-line shopping offers unprecedented convenience. Customers can search for and purchase music without leaving their homes. Travel time to these on-line stores is based not on speed limits, location, or traffic, but on the agility of your fingers and the speed of your computer connection. You don't have to check the store hours, either. Web sites operate twenty-four hours a day.

Another advantage of on-line record stores is their extensive collection of albums. Web sites sell hundreds of thousands of titles. Although it may take a few weeks to ship some rare selections, at least on-line stores can get them for you. No local store can stock such a vast inventory, and many are reluctant to try to locate rare selections for their customers.

On-line stores also offer a substantial amount of information that is not available at a local store. For example, many sites link to professional reviews that provide up-to-date commentary on the recording artists, the record labels, and other professionals involved in creating the CD. Many on-line buyers have told me that these professional reviews are very helpful in making purchasing decisions and that "they are more knowledgeable than your average store clerk." There is a lot of information stored in on-line search engines, too. For example, you can search for a specific song title and find out what album it is on. Of course,

▲ **Critical Viewing**
What might you find to compare and contrast within a music store, such as this one? **[Connect]**

The opening paragraph clearly states what Catherine and Zach will compare and contrast: on-line music stores and local music stores.

The sentences of various lengths in the second paragraph help make it lively and interesting.

The essay uses point-by-point organization. Each paragraph discusses one feature or point and how it relates to the two subjects being compared and contrasted.

Final Draft

1. Point out to students that "Are Local Music Stores Obsolete?" incorporates key elements of the comparison-and-contrast essay. A well-written comparison-and-contrast essay offers an original viewpoint on the topic, is written in a logical, organized manner, uses interesting language, and has few errors in spelling, capitalization, and punctuation.

2. Ask the students to apply the rubric from page 186 to "Are Local Music Stores Obsolete?" and write their own assessment.

3. Lead a discussion about the merits and weaknesses of Catherine and Zach's essay. Students may offer suggestions on possible changes to the piece. How might they apply these suggestions to their own writing?

Critical Viewing

Connect Students may mention the actual CDs or cassettes, prices, music categories, artists, and so on.

☑ **ONGOING ASSESSMENT: Assess Mastery**

Use one of the following options to assess final drafts of students' comparison-and-contrast essays.

Self-Assessment Ask students to score their essays using the rubric provided on page 186. Then, have students write a single paragraph reflecting on the most valuable thing they learned in completing this essay.	**Teacher Assessment** You may wish to use the rubric and the scoring models provided in *Writing Assessment and Portfolio Management* to score the comparison-and-contrast essays.

Integrating Technology

On-line Search If possible, have students browse on the Web for examples of some of the features Catherine and Zach mention. For example, can they find an on-line music store that allows the buyer to create a personalized CD? Can they find one that offers professional reviews and personalized recommendations? Can they find other positive and negative features that the authors could have included?

9.4

many record stores have computers that work in the same way, but you might have to wait in line to use it.

Although on-line record stores have created a more convenient experience, the atmosphere and feel of an ordinary record store is absent. For many people, a local record store is like a favorite coffee shop or bookstore. Clerks, who are familiar with the stock, can offer personal recommendations.

Prices are often, but not always, cheaper at on-line stores. You usually have to pay a shipping cost, which decreases the more items you buy. Depending on where the CDs are shipped from, you may not have to pay a sales tax. In our survey, the total cost of a CD was about one dollar less at on-line sites. That's not a huge difference, but it can add up if you are a music collector.

Don't think, however, that on-line stores are impersonal. They, too, can offer personalized services, based on your purchases or album ratings. To shop at most on-line stores, you create an account by giving them information about yourself. You might also provide some album ratings so the database can determine your musical preferences. Once your account is established, the site will keep records of what you buy and provide you with customized recommendations and special offers.

Some on-line stores provide a personalized experience that local stores cannot match: They let you buy single songs to create your own CD. Do you want a CD with your favorite dance music or maybe one with your list of the ten best jazz songs? Some sites allow you to assemble your own CD by choosing songs and selecting the order. Your finished CD will cost much less than it would cost to buy all of the albums that include those songs.

Of course, if you want a CD right away, you'll still have to drive, cycle, or walk to your nearest music store. "People love impulse buying," Bill Jeffrey, the buyer at Waterloo Records, said. "We often hear complaints from our customers concerning the time it takes to receive the product [when ordering on-line]. We have considered starting a Web site because of the competition, but I don't think these on-line music sites are any threat to us or other record stores in general."

For now, however, on-line stores offer an attractive and economical alternative, not a replacement. Even with the convenience and personalization offered by on-line sites, we don't think physical stores are going to disappear any time soon. For many shoppers, the experience of flipping through albums with their glossy packaging is just as vital as convenience.

Results of a statistical survey create support for the main point of this paragraph.

Transitions such as "too," "also," and "once" clarify the connections among ideas.

Catherine and Zach support this topic sentence with a lengthy quotation from a professional in the music industry.

The conclusion presents a recommendation based on Catherine and Zach's findings.

Connected Assignment Consumer Report

Being an informed consumer helps you maximize your spending dollars and avoid costly mistakes. One way to become informed is to read consumer reviews. These articles compare and contrast features of a product or service, drawing on factual information such as testing, experts' opinions, or user surveys. Report writers then reach a conclusion or make a recommendation to readers.

Write your own consumer report, following the writing process steps below to guide you.

Prewriting Make a questionnaire like the one at right, and poll friends or family about their favorite or least favorite services in your community. Ask at local stores about the products people are buying most frequently. Then, choose a product or service to analyze in a consumer report.

Questionnaire

1. Which service do you find more useful?

2. What kind of savings do you get by using that service?

3. How long have you used the service?

Devise a note-taking system, such as index cards or a chart, building your system around such criteria as durability, appearance, and cost. Then, visit stores, conduct surveys, or talk with an expert to gather information about the product or service about which you are reporting.

Drafting In your report's introduction, identify what you are evaluating and introduce the criteria on which it will be judged. Use transitions such as *more, less, equally, identically,* or *differently* to indicate relationships. Also, be sure to include supporting information from your prewriting fact-gathering.

Revising and Editing As you revise, change any language that is unsuitable for your audience, and check to ensure that you've explained technical terms clearly. Delete any details that are unnecessary or misleading, and double-check survey or test results, quotations, and other supporting information.

Publishing and Presenting Share your report with interested friends or peers. To share your report with a wider audience, send it to your school newspaper and ask its editorial board to publish it.

Connected Assignment: Consumer Report • 189

▶ Lesson Objectives

1. To write a consumer report appropriate to audience and purpose

2. To generate relevant, interesting, and researchable questions

3. To produce research projects and reports in varying forms for audiences

4. To compile written ideas and representations into reports, summaries, or other formats and draw conclusions

5. To create, present, test, and revise a project and analyze a response using data-gathering techniques such as questionnaires, group discussions, and feedback forms

Step-by-Step Teaching Guide

Consumer Report

Teaching Resources: Writing Support Transparencies, 9-J; Writing Support Activity Book, 9-4

1. Bring to class and discuss several examples of consumer reports.

2. When each student has chosen a topic, display Transparency 9-J and give students copies of the blank organizer 9-4.

3. Suggest that students review strategies from Chapter 9. See the chart below for resources.

4. Students might benefit by focusing on a particular type of product or service, such as toothpaste, frozen pizza, on-line grocery shopping, or auto repair.

5. Emphasize that after students have surveyed friends or family, they are to analyze one product or service, probably the one most commonly mentioned.

6. Help students focus on the criteria they are using to judge the product or service.

7. Students might compile their consumer reports into a booklet and make a copy for each class member.

☑ ONGOING ASSESSMENT: Prerequisite Skills

Students may find the following resources from Chapter 9 particularly helpful in completing their essays.

In the Textbook	Print Resources	Technology
Evaluating Your Topic, Section 9.2 Drafting, Section 9.3	*Writing Support Transparencies,* 9-E–F *Writing Support Activity Book,* 9-3	*Writing and Grammar* Interactive Text, Sections 9.2–3

Lesson Objectives

1. To recognize and discuss themes and connections that cross cultures

2. To compare and contrast elements of texts such as themes, conflicts, and allusions both within and across texts

3. To use a variety of forms and technologies such as videos, photographs, and web pages to communicate specific messages

Step-by-Step Teaching Guide

Connecting Themes in the Arts

1. Ask students to focus on one of the Spotlight elements and to research further about Shaw, *Pygmalion*, the myth of Pygmalion and Galatea, or *My Fair Lady*.

2. Some students might view the 1938 black-and-white film of *Pygmalion* starring Leslie Howard, Wendy Hiller, and Stanley Holloway.

3. The staging of *My Fair Lady* created stunning effects. Some students may research this aspect.

4. Shaw's play is often produced in regional theaters. Students can research recent productions.

5. Students focusing on historic change for their chart or pictorial might investigate state or national historic preservation information.

Viewing and Representing

Activities Provide ample time for students to present their pictorials, and post them on a bulletin board.

Critical Viewing

Analyze Most students will focus on details of the vehicles (the door Shaw is standing beside; the automobile seen through the window) to set the scene in the early to mid-twentieth century, although they probably can't cite a specific time. The clothing styles may provide a further clue.

Spotlight on the Humanities

Connecting Themes in the Arts
Focus on Theater: *Pygmalion*

Pygmalion Makeovers are great examples of visual comparison and contrast. British playwright George Bernard Shaw (1856–1950) explored such a comparison and contrast in *Pygmalion*, one of his most famous plays. In the play, Shaw tells the story of Professor Henry Higgins and his student, Eliza Doolittle. In the play, Professor Higgins, who teaches phonetics, transforms Eliza from a flower girl with a Cockney accent into a well-spoken, elegant woman.

Literature Connection The myth of Pygmalion and Galatea appears in Ovid's (43 B.C.?–A.D. 17) *Metamorphoses*. Pygmalion was a sculptor who adored his statue of Aphrodite. He appealed to the goddess Venus to give life to the statue— which she did. In 1871, W. S. Gilbert wrote a comedy, *Pygmalion and Galatea*, based upon the myth.

Film Connection In 1964, George Cukor directed a film adaptation of *My Fair Lady*, a Broadway musical that was based on Shaw's *Pygmalion*. Composer Frederick Loewe created the music, and Alan Jay Lerner wrote the book and lyrics. Cukor's film, starring Audrey Hepburn and Rex Harrison, won eight Academy Awards.

Comparison-and-Contrast Writing Application:
Before-and-After Chart or Pictorial

Choose as a topic something that has changed over time. For example, has a playground in your town been refurbished? Perhaps Main Street has undergone a renewal, or a remake of a classic film has just been released. Once you find a topic, visually represent the before-and-after relationship with a chart, illustrations, or photographs. Then, write captions that point out the features that changed for the better or worse over time. When your chart or pictorial is finished, share it with your class.

▲ **Critical Viewing** Based on clues in this photograph, in what time period do you think this photo of George Bernard Shaw was taken? Explain how you arrived at your answer. **[Analyze]**

190 • Comparison-and-Contrast Essay

Media and Technology Skills

Analyzing Relationships Between Media
Activity: Compare Newspapers' Editorial Positions

The people who edit and produce newspapers have opinions that become clear when you read many issues. A newspaper's editorial position might be conservative or liberal, Democratic or Republican, mainstream or progressive. Examining a newspaper's editorial position can help you interpret the articles you read.

Think About It Choose two newspapers to analyze. Then, read several issues of each paper to evaluate each paper's editorial position. Before you begin, write down your first impression of each paper. When you have finished your research, you will be able to decide whether your first impressions were justified.

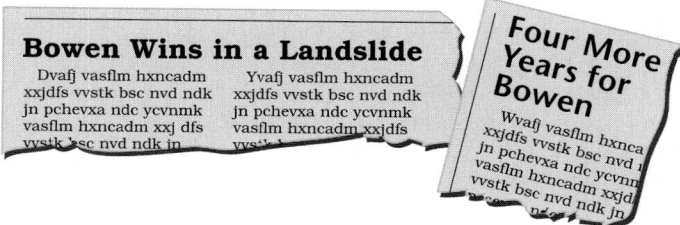

Bowen Wins in a Landslide

Dvafj vasflm hxncadm
xxjdfs vvstk bsc nvd ndk
jn pchevxa ndc ycvnmk
vasflm hxncadm xxj dfs
vvstk bsc nvd ndk jn

Yvafj vasflm hxncadm
xxjdfs vvstk bsc nvd ndk
jn pchevxa ndc ycvnmk
vasflm hxncadm xxjdfs
vvstk b

Four More Years for Bowen

Wvafj vasflm hxnca
xxjdfs vvstk bsc nvd
jn pchevxa ndc ycvnm
vasflm hxncadm xxjd
vvstk bsc nvd ndk jn

Plan It Use several strategies to compare the two newspapers you have selected. Consider these action plans:

- Read issues from the same date. Evaluate the stories that are covered in each paper.
- Keep a list of editorials presented by each paper for one week.
- Research the paper's history of political endorsements.
- Compare published photographs of prominent politicians. Evaluate each photograph to determine whether it presents a positive or negative view of the subject.

Evaluate It After collecting information from several issues of each newspaper, analyze your findings to draw a conclusion about each source's editorial position. For example, a paper might be conservative on financial issues but progressive on conservation.

Create a chart or paragraph to compare your evaluation of the two newspapers. Share your work by displaying the finished project or by holding a presentation for the class.

Media and Technology Skills • 191

191

Lesson Objectives

1. To use prewriting strategies to generate ideas, develop voice, and plan

2. To develop drafts by organizing consent and by refining style to suit occasion, audience, and purpose

3. To produce legible work that shows accurate spelling and correct use of the conventions of punctuation and capitalization such as italics and ellipses

Step-by-Step Teaching Guide

Responding to Comparison-and-Contrast Prompts

Teaching Resource: Standardized Test Preparation Workbook, pp. 17-18

1. Go over the bulleted items with students.

2. Have students point out the most important words in the sample writing prompt *(compare, contrast, two or more philosophies, also point out)*, and emphasize that one key to success on a standardized test is to pay particular attention to what the assignment is.

3. Go over the writing steps on page 193.

4. Your decision to assign this particular sample assignment should depend on your knowledge of students' recent learning or grasp of the topic. However, tell students that this type of writing prompt is fairly typical, although the subject will differ.

Standardized Test Preparation Workshop

Responding to Comparison-and-Contrast Prompts

Standardized writing tests measure your ability to compare-and-contrast two or more subjects. The types of samples you will be prompted to compare and contrast might include two models of literature, two views on a controversial issue, or two reviews of a work of art. Whatever prompt you are offered, your goal is to illuminate both the similarities and differences of the subjects given. You may also be asked to state a position on which of the two you prefer. Within your comparison-and-contrast writing, make sure to address the following:

- similarities and differences among the two or more subjects

- a neat and logical organization of the points of comparison and contrast

- details that successfully support and elaborate upon your comparisons and contrasts

- proper use of spelling and grammar

Use the writing process stages—prewriting, drafting, revising, editing, and proofreading—as you draft your response. Assign a rough amount of time to perform each stage of the writing process.

Following is an example of a comparison-and-contrast writing prompt you may encounter. Use the writing process steps on the next page to guide you as you respond to the prompt. The clocks next to each stage recommend the amount of time you should spend on each suggestion.

Sample Writing Situation

Read the following prompt, and provide an answer in essay form.

In an essay, compare and contrast two or more economic philosophies, ranging from *laissez faire* to total government regulation. Also, point out in your essay which economists supported which philosophies.

192 • Comparison-and-Contrast Essay

✎ TEST-TAKING TIP

Remind students that although they should allow only about a quarter of their test-taking time to prewrite, fifteen minutes or so should be ample time. Depending on the topic, they might want to take ten minutes to decide how to approach the topic and five minutes to jot down and organize details. Emphasize that students should not be afraid to take time to organize their thoughts. When they do so, the writing will be much easier. Difficulties come when the writing has not been well planned.

Stress that if students know they have spelling or punctuation weaknesses, they should allow time to go over their work. In the margin of a paper, they can try out various spellings of a word they are unsure about and decide which spelling looks correct.

Prewriting

Allow about one quarter of your time for developing your position and identifying comparison-and-contrast details.

Identify Details Select two or three criteria against which to evaluate the two opposing views. List details that show the ways in which the subjects are similar and different.

Organize Details Create a two-column chart to help organize the details you have collected in a comparison-and-contrast format. Make sure that you have a balanced number of details that show similarities and differences.

Drafting

Allow about half of your time for drafting. Write neatly, and leave space for any text you may want to insert when revising.

Write an Introduction, Body, and Conclusion As you draft, introduce your thesis, or main idea, and grab the interest of your audience. Also, provide a transition into the first body paragraph of your essay. In the body of your essay, develop your main idea and provide support in the form of details. Conclude memorably by restating your main idea and then posing an interesting question or providing a thought-provoking quotation or observation.

Elaborate As you draft, support your statements by giving specific examples. You should present a variety of support, such as details that show personal observations, statistical data, quotations, and historical facts.

Revising, Editing, and Proofreading

Allow almost one quarter of your time for revising.

Close the Gaps Solidify your argument by adding important details you omitted. Review your prewriting notes to make sure that you have included the details you had planned to include.

Stengthen Unity Read your essay carefully to be sure that each detail relates to your topic. If you find a detail that is beside the point, delete it or add a clarifying sentence to show its connection to your topic.

Clarify Relationships Smooth connections and clarify relationships between your subjects by inserting transitions such as *in addition, as well,* and *unlike.*

Fix Errors Take time to proofread carefully. Look first to catch errors that you make frequently. Then, proofread and correct all errors you find in spelling, punctuation, and grammar.

Customize for
Less Advanced Students

Some students may have difficulty, not with the test directions, but with understanding and thus recalling information with which to formulate an essay for a test of this type. Assure them that tests of this type will not absolutely determine their future in life and that they may be able to retake similar tests.

Customize for
AP Students

If necessary, give students some extra help in writing thesis statements and transitional words or statements.

In-Depth Lesson Plan

	LESSON FOCUS	PRINT AND MEDIA RESOURCES
DAY 1	**Introduction to Cause-and-Effect Essays** Students learn key elements of a cause-and-effect essay and analyze the Model From Literature. (pp. 194–197/H122–123)	*Writers at Work* **DVD**, Exposition *Writing and Grammar* **Interactive Text**, Ch. 10, Introduction
DAY 2	**Prewriting** Students choose and narrow a topic, consider their audience and purpose, and gather information. (pp. 198–201/H124–127)	*Writing and Grammar* **Interactive Text**, Section 10.2 **Teaching Resources** *Writing Support Transparencies*, 10-A–E; *Writing Support Activity Book*, 10-1–2; *Topic Bank for Heterogeneous Classes*, Ch. 10
DAY 3	**Drafting** Students organize their ideas and write their first drafts. (pp. 202–203/H128–129)	*Writing and Grammar* **Interactive Text**, Section 10.3 **Teaching Resources** *Writing Support Transparencies*, 10-F–G
DAY 4	**Revising** Students revise their drafts in terms of overall structure, paragraphs, sentences, and word choice. (pp. 204–207/H130–133)	*Writing and Grammar* **Interactive Text**, Section 10.4 **Teaching Resources** *Writing Support Transparencies*, 10-H
DAY 5	**Editing and Proofreading; Publishing and Presenting** Students check their work for accuracy and correctness and present their final drafts. (pp. 208–211/H134–135)	*Writing and Grammar* **Interactive Text**, Sections 10.5–6 **Teaching Resources** *Scoring Rubrics on Transparency*, Ch. 10; *Writing Assessment and Portfolio Management; Formal Assessment*, Ch. 10

Accelerated Lesson Plan

	LESSON FOCUS	PRINT AND MEDIA RESOURCES
DAY 1	**Introduction Through Drafting** Students review characteristics of a cause-and-effect essay, select topics, and write drafts. (pp. 194–203/H122–129)	*Writing and Grammar* **Interactive Text**, Ch. 10, Introduction through Section 10.3 **Teaching Resources** *Writing Support Transparencies*, 10-A–G; *Writing Support Activity Book*, 10-1–2
DAY 2	**Revising Through Presenting** Students work individually or with peers to revise, edit, and proofread their work for presentation. (pp. 204–211/H130–135)	*Writing and Grammar* **Interactive Text**, Sections 10.4–6 **Teaching Resources** *Writing Support Transparencies*, 10-H; *Scoring Rubrics on Transparency*, Ch. 10; *Writing Assessment and Portfolio Management; Formal Assessment*, Ch. 10

Options for Adapting Lesson Plans

HOMEWORK

Have students complete any stage of the lesson for homework.

FEATURES

Extend coverage with Connected Assignment (p. 212), Spotlight on the Humanities (p. 214), Media and Technology Skills (p. 215), and the Standardized Test Preparation Workshop (pp. 216–217).

TECHNOLOGY

Students can complete any stage of the lesson on the computer, using *Writing and Grammar* Interactive Text or a word-processing program. Have them print out their completed work.

Writing and Grammar Handbook Alignment

Page numbers in Step-by-Step Teaching Guides in this Teacher's Edition refer to pages from the full student text. Handbook page references, indicated with this icon Ⓗ, are provided in Time and Resource Manager boxes and at the bottom of each Teacher's Edition page.

INTEGRATED SKILLS COVERAGE

Integrating Grammar
Independent and Subordinate Clauses, SE p. 206/Ⓗ132
Commas in Essential and Nonessential Expressions, SE p. 208/Ⓗ134

Reading/Writing Connection
Reading: Look for Author's Main Points, SE p. 196
Writing Application, SE p. 197

Viewing and Representing
Critical Viewing, SE pp. 194, 196, 210, 211, 212, 214/Ⓗ122
Appreciating Music, SE p. 214
Examining the Effect of Media on Perceptions of Reality, SE p. 215

Speaking and Listening
ATE p. 201

Real-World Connection
ATE p. 196

Technology Skills SE p. 207/Ⓗ133

ASSESSMENT SUPPORT

Standardized Test Preparation Workshop, SE p. 216; ATE p. 200
Standardized Test Preparation Workbook, pp. 19–20
Scoring Rubrics on Transparency, Ch. 10
Formal Assessment, Ch. 10
Writing Assessment and Portfolio Management

MEETING INDIVIDUAL NEEDS

Less Advanced Students ATE pp. 200, 205, 213, 217. See also Ongoing Assessments ATE pp. 197, 199, 203.
AP Students ATE p. 217
ESL Students ATE pp. 202, 211, 213
Gifted and Talented Students ATE p. 205
Musical Learners ATE p. 210
Interpersonal Learners ATE p. 213

BLOCK SCHEDULING

Pacing Suggestions
For 90-minute Blocks
• Have students complete the Prewriting and Drafting stages in a single period.
• Focus one class period on Revising and Editing and Publishing and Presenting. Allow at least 30 minutes for peer revision.

Resources for Varying Instruction
• *Writing and Grammar* Interactive Text A 90-minute block provides an ideal opportunity for students to work on the computer.
• *Writers at Work* DVD Show the Exposition segment in class.

Professional Development Support
• *How to Manage Instruction in the Block* This teaching resource provides management and activity suggestions.

MEDIA AND TECHNOLOGY

For the Student
• *Writing and Grammar* Interactive Text, Ch. 10
• *On-line Exercise Bank,* Section 19.3

For the Teacher
• *Writers at Work* DVD, Exposition
• TeacherEXPRESS CD-ROM

WRITING AND GRAMMAR ON-LINE

Interactive Text (On-line or on CD-ROM)
• Easily navigable instruction with interactive Revision Checkers
• Full use of e-rater™, the essay-scoring system (on-line only)

Companion Web Site PHSchool.com
• Scoring rubrics with models (use Web Code egk-1201)

See the Go On-line! **feature, SE p. iii.**

LITERATURE CONNECTIONS

Related selections from *Prentice Hall Literature, Penguin Edition,* The British Tradition:
Professional Model *We'll Never Conquer Space,* Arthur C. Clarke, SE p. 197
Topic Bank Option from *The Diary,* Samuel Pepys, SE p. 199/Ⓗ125

Exposition
Cause-and-Effect Essay

Lesson Objectives

1. To write a cause-and-effect essay appropriate to audience and purpose

2. To read to appreciate a writer's craft and to discover models for writing

3. To use prewriting strategies to generate ideas and plan

4. To compile information from primary and secondary sources using available technology

5. To develop and revise drafts in terms of structure, paragraphs, sentences, and word choice

6. To compose increasingly more involved sentences that contain phrases and clauses in their various forms

7. To evaluate how well writing achieves its purpose and to engage in conversations with peers and the teacher about one's writing and the writing of others

8. To edit and proofread to ensure standard English usage and grammar

9. To refine a cause-and-effect essay for publication

Critical Viewing

Analyze Causes and Effects
Students may say that light particles glow in the air, causing the lights to twinkle and glisten.

▲ **Critical Viewing**
Judging from clues in this photograph, what might cause a phenomenon like the Northern Lights? **[Analyze Causes and Effects]**

Cause-and-Effect Relationships in Everyday Life

Have you ever tried to explain to a friend how a series of mishaps caused you to be late? Perhaps you have recounted for your family the game events that led to a basketball victory. In these situations, you explained the cause-and-effect relationships among events. Understanding such relationships helps you to learn about past events as well as to predict future ones.

Cause-and-effect relationships are often explored in various types of writing. For example, a self-help book may explain how certain attitudes produce poor outcomes in life and then tell you why new attitudes might lead to better results. A biography of a rock star might explain what caused each of the ups and downs in her career or tell you what caused her to leave one record label for another.

194 • Exposition

⏱ TIME AND RESOURCE MANAGER

Resources
Technology: *Writers at Work* DVD, Exposition; *Writing and Grammar* Interactive Text, Ch. 10

Using the Full Student Edition	Using the Handbook🄷
• Read and discuss pp. 194–195 in class. • Show the Exposition section of the *Writers at Work* DVD. • Read the Model From Literature (pp. 196–197) in class, and use it to brainstorm for cause-and-effect ideas with students.	• Read and discuss pp. 122–123 in class. • Show the Exposition section of the *Writers at Work* DVD.

What Is a Cause-and-Effect Essay?

Writing that explains or informs is called **expository writing.** One type of expository writing is the **cause-and-effect essay,** which explains the relationship between events or situations that took place in the past and the events or situations that occurred as a result. Sometimes, these essays may look forward, cautioning readers about the likely results of certain current events or situations.

Effective cause-and-effect essays usually contain

- an explanation of how particular causes produced or might produce particular effects.
- examples and other details that support the essay's main ideas.
- transitions that show how various causes and effects are linked.
- a logical organizational strategy.

To preview the criteria on which your cause-and-effect essay may be evaluated, see the Self-Assessment Rubric on page 209.

Types of Cause-and-Effect Essays

Cause-and-effect essays may take the following forms:

- **Historical cause-and-effect essays** may explain causes and effects of major events such as war, drought, and elections.
- **Scientific cause-and-effect essays** often explore the causes of natural phenomena such as hurricanes and volcanoes.
- **General interest cause-and-effect essays** center around the cause-and-effect relationships in the everyday world, such as exercise and fitness or education and success.

PREVIEW

Student Work IN PROGRESS

Follow along as student Carl Byers of Muncie Central High School in Muncie, Indiana, writes an article for his school paper explaining why swing music has risen in popularity. A final draft of Carl's article appears at the end of this chapter.

Writers in ACTION

The Greek philosopher Aristotle was renowned for his wisdom. An astute observer of human nature, Aristotle noted the following: "Every action must be due to one or other of seven causes: chance, nature, compulsion, habit, reasoning, anger, or appetite."

Cause-and-Effect Essay • 195

PREPARE and ENGAGE

Interest GRABBER Show a clip from a television news program that features a cause-and-effect explanation for an event. For example, a reporter might explain the events that caused a plane crash or a rise in the stock market. As they watch, have students take notes on the causes of the event. Have them share their answers.

Activate Prior Knowledge

Remind students of the ending of the last book or story you read in class this year. Have them work backwards to trace the chain of events that led to that ending. Point out that stories are basically a series of causes and effects. How might the story's ending be different if just one of the events in the chain were altered?

More About the Writer

Aristotle (384–322 B.C.) is one of the three most famous philosophers of ancient Greece. (Plato and Socrates are the other two.) His impact on the world during his own lifetime was great, both because of his teaching at Plato's Academy and elsewhere, and because he was the tutor of the young prince who would be known as Alexander the Great. But Aristotle's impact was not limited to his own time. His ideas about science, poetry, literature, politics, education, existence, and cause-and-effect relationships have influenced thought for thousands of years, and are still appreciated today.

☑ ONGOING ASSESSMENT: Diagnose

Use one of the following options to diagnose students' current level of proficiency in cause-and-effect writing.

Option 1 Ask each student to select the best example of their cause-and-effect writing from last year. Hold conferences to review each student's sample and to determine which students will need extra help in developing a cause-and-effect essay.	**Option 2** Tell students to imagine there will be a multiplex cinema opening in their town. Ask them to write down two things that might have caused this event, and two effects it might have. Students who have difficulty with this exercise will need to review the definition of a cause-and-effect essay.

Reading\Writing Connection

Reading: Look for Authors' Main Points

Encourage students to jot down anything that seems like a key idea (either a summarizing phrase of their own or a topic sentence from the model) as they read. Then have them review their notes to see how the main points contribute to building the story.

Step-by-Step Teaching Guide

Engage Students Through Literature

1. Read this essay aloud or have a prepared student read it.
2. Use the following questions to prompt discussion about the essay.

   How did weather conditions contribute to the crash?

   How did pilot error contribute to the crash?

   What were other factors that caused the crash?

3. Then ask students whether any details appear to be missing. Are there any holes in the chain of cause and effect? Remind students that the relationships among the events in their essays must be clearly explained.

Critical Viewing

Analyze Answers will be related to students' familiarity with what a crash site looks like, based on news footage of other crashes they may have seen.

Real-World Connection

After a major catastrophe like the plane crash in "Miracle on 34th Street," an official investigation is conducted to determine its cause. An important step in many investigations involves developing theories about the possible causes of the crash. Investigators then test these theories against the facts they have collected.

Model From Literature

Mario Salvadori is the author of *Why Buildings Stand Up*, as well as *Why Buildings Fall Down*, from which this selection was taken. Matthys Levy, a master of structural design, collaborated with Salvadori on this book.

Reading \ Writing Connection

Reading Strategy: Look for Authors' Main Points As you read, look for the main points the authors are making to help you more thoroughly understand and evaluate their ideas.

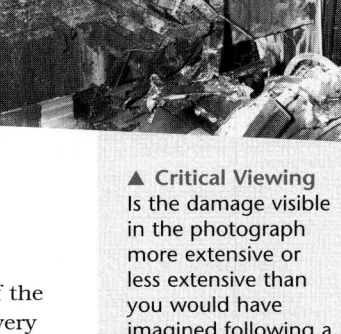

from "Miracle on 34th Street"

Matthys Levy and Mario Salvadori

On July 28, 1945, nearly three months after the defeat of the Nazi government and the end of the war in Europe, on the very day the U.S. Senate ratified the United Nations Charter, Lieutenant Colonel W. F. Smith, Jr., took off at 8:55 A.M. from Bedford, Massachusetts, in a B-25 bomber for a flight to Newark, New Jersey. With two other occupants, the plane flew on the gray morning at an estimated 250 mph, arriving in the New York area less than an hour later. Lieutenant Colonel Smith was advised by the control tower at La Guardia Airport that the ceiling, the distance from the ground to the clouds, was less than 1,000 feet. This implied that clouds and fog would have obscured the tops of New York's skyscrapers, especially the then tallest, the Empire State Building.

The pilot, flying under visual rules, was required to maintain 3 miles forward visibility. If unable to do so between La Guardia and Newark airports, he was required to land at La Guardia. Smith ignored that requirement. Continuing toward Newark, he was seen heading in a southwesterly direction, weaving through the maze of skyscrapers over Manhattan and crossing low-hanging clouds. Heading toward Forty-second Street, the plane

▲ Critical Viewing Is the damage visible in the photograph more extensive or less extensive than you would have imagined following a plane crash? Explain. **[Analyze]**

Here, the first cause-and-effect relationship is revealed: Because of the war, bomber planes were in use by the air force.

Among the details that explain the various causes are those describing the weather conditions.

196 • Cause-and-Effect Essay

flew down out of a cloud at no more than 400 feet above the ground, at which point it started climbing in a right turn. In an effort to slow the plane, the wheels were lowered moments before the plane struck the Empire State Building on the north face of the seventy-ninth floor, 913 feet above the ground, ripping a hole 18 feet wide and 20 feet high in the outer wall of the building. The force of the impact sheared off the wings of the plane and pro-pelled one of the two motors across the width of the building, through the opposite wall, and down through the twelfth-story roof of a building across Thirty-third Street, starting a destructive fire. Two women in an elevator fell seventy-five stories when the cable holding their cab snapped, cut by flying shrapnel. Miraculously they escaped with their lives, although they were seriously injured, when automatic devices sufficiently slowed the free fall of the cab. Flames from the burning gasoline killed most of the thirteen victims, including the crew of the plane.

"I couldn't believe my own eyes," said a witness, looking out from the 103rd-story observatory, "when I saw the plane come out of the overcast. Then it struck the building with a force that sent a tremor through the whole structure." The crash spilled gasoline from the ruptured tanks, which immediately ignited, illuminating the tower of the building for a brief instant before it disappeared again in the mist and the smoke from the burning plane. As the spilled gasoline burned, flaming debris rained down the face of the building. The ebullient mayor of the city, Fiorello La Guardia, arriving, as usual right behind his firefighters, on the scene of the inferno at the seventy-ninth floor, was seen shaking his fist and muttering: "I told them not to fly over the city."

The center of impact aligned almost exactly with a column on the face of the tower. The right motor passed on one side of the column and the left motor on the opposite side. The column itself was barely damaged, although a steel beam supporting the masonry wall struck by the right motor was torn out, and a sec-ond beam supporting the floor slab was bent back 18 inches. The plane apparently struck the seventy-ninth floor dead-on, which explains the lack of damage to the column. Had the plane been just a bit higher or lower, it might have struck and bent the column, and then . . .

Writing Application: State Your Points
When you write your cause-and-effect essay, present your main points clearly and directly.

Supporting details are arranged in chronological order, making it easy to fol-low the cause-and-effect relationships.

"We'll Never Conquer Space," an essay by Arthur C. Clarke, examines cause-and-effect relationships as he predicts space travel possibilities. "We'll Never Conquer Space" appears in *Prentice Hall Literature, Penguin Edition,* The British Tradition.

Elaboration in the form of quotations by eyewitnesses helps bring the event to life for readers.

These details, which help explain the effects of the crash, are factual and statistical.

The final sentence poses an intriguing cause-and-effect "what if" question.

Model From Literature • 197

Teaching From the Model

Use this Model From Literature to show students the importance of including specific details in a cause-and-effect essay. In the model, Levy and Salvadori describe the chain of events that results from an imprudent pilot flying in bad weather. Each detail is significant; a variation in any of them would have affected the outcome. Accurate details in a cause-and-effect essay provide a map that enables the reader to follow the sequence of events and their interconnection. Have each student choose two details from the essay and explain the role of each in causing the disaster.

Connections With Literature

If students read the essay, ask them to think about the effects Clarke predicts (we will reach other planets and maybe other stars; we will not conquer space) and then determine the causes for each effect (humans are curious, determined; space is too vast).

More About the Writers

Italian-born Mario Salvadori (1907–1997) was professor of civil engineering and architecture at Columbia University for fifty years. He wrote several books, including *Why Buildings Stand Up* (1982). Swiss-born Matthys Levy is an architectural engineer. Before Salvadori's death, the two were principals in one of America's leading structural engineering firms. The two men collaborated on three books: *Why Buildings Fall Down* (1992), *Why the Earth Quakes* (1995), and *Earthquake Games* (1997).

Reading\Writing Connection

Writing Application: State Your Points

Suggest that students identify the points they want to make in an outline or on notecards, and make certain that the points not only are included when they write, but that they are also well supported.

Step-by-Step Teaching Guide

Prewriting: Scan a Newspaper or Magazine

1. If you want students to do this activity in class, you might supply newspapers or magazines. Or, tell students ahead of time to bring their own magazines to class. This will make it easier for you to discourage selection of inappropriate topics. Keep in mind, however, that topics of interest to students will yield the best essays. Consider allowing students to use their own news sources, with your approval.

2. Encourage students to discuss with small groups why they think their articles are good topics for cause-and-effect essays. Group members can also help them brainstorm for possible causes and effects of each student's situation.

Step-by-Step Teaching Guide

Prewriting: Freewrite

Teaching Resources: Writing Support Transparencies, 10-A

1. Some students may need a writing prompt to begin the freewriting exercise. Provide an object or photograph and ask them to write whatever comes to mind when they look at it.

2. Display the transparency (10-A) and discuss how Carl Byers used freewriting to develop his topic. Encourage students to consider other topics whose origins they could explain in an essay.

3. Tell students that they can choose a topic they find interesting even if they do not know much about it. If they do this, however, they will have to conduct thorough research.

Choosing Your Topic

Choose a topic for your cause-and-effect essay by selecting a subject or recent event that can be broken down into specific causes and effects.

Following are some strategies that can help you find a topic for a cause-and-effect essay:

Strategies for Generating a Topic

1. **Scan a Newspaper or Magazine** Read quickly through a favorite newspaper or magazine. When you find an interesting topic, ask yourself "What caused this situation?" and "What effects will it have?" Jot down a few notes in answer to those questions. Then, if you find the topic has possibilities, use it for your cause-and-effect essay.

2. **Freewrite** Sometimes, the best way to come up with a topic is to just start writing. Find a quiet place to work, glance at your watch or set a timer, and write without stopping for five minutes. When the time is up, read over what you have written. Choose the idea that interests you most as a topic for your cause-and-effect essay.

interactive Textbook

Try it out! Freewrite using the Essay Builder, accessible from the menu bar, on-line or on CD-ROM.

Student Work
IN PROGRESS

Name: *Carl Byers*
Muncie Central High School
Muncie, IN

Freewriting to Find a Topic

Carl Byers used the freewriting strategy to help him find a topic for his cause-and-effect essay. After he wrote for five minutes, he read though his writing and found a suitable topic. (Because he was freewriting, he jotted down words and phrases. When he drafts, he will use complete sentences.)

Rock music—how it came into being. Elvis Presley, blues bands, Carl Perkins, Cab Calloway, Glenn Miller, and swing music. Jitterbugging, Lindy Hop. Big bands—Harry Connick, Jr. New swing bands. Why swing is popular again today.

198 • Cause-and-Effect Essay

⏱ TIME AND RESOURCE MANAGER

Resources
Print: *Writing Support Transparencies,* 10-A–E; *Writing Support Activity Book,* 10-1–2
Technology: *Writing and Grammar* Interactive Text, Section 10.2

Using the Full Student Edition	Using the Handbook🄷
• Work through pp. 198–201 in class.	• Work through pp. 124–127 in class.
• Use the Responding to Fine Art transparency to generate additional topic ideas.	• Use the Responding to Fine Art transparency to generate additional topic ideas.
• Assign detail gathering as homework.	• Assign detail gathering as homework.

TOPIC BANK

If you are having difficulty coming up with a topic on your own, consider one of the following:

1. **Analysis of a War** Write about the causes that led to a particular war or about the effects that the war had. For example, if you were writing about the Civil War, you might explain how disagreements over slavery, arguments over states' rights, and economic competition all helped cause the war.

2. **Prediction** Advances in technology—television, microwave ovens, the Internet—have had a huge impact on our lives. Think of an invention yet to be created, and explain the effects it will have on the way people live.

Responding to Fine Art

3. *Breakers on the Promontory at Granville* is an artist's depiction of ocean waves. Write an essay explaining the causes and effects of the ocean's tides or the effects that storm tides have on shorelines.

Breakers on the Promontory at Granville,
Paul Huet, Musée du Louvre, Paris

Responding to Literature

4. In Samuel Pepys's *Diary*, he gives an eyewitness account of the Great Fire of London. In a cause-and-effect essay, examine the causes and effects of a notable fire like the one Pepys describes or the ones that devastated Chicago and San Francisco. You can read Pepys's *Diary* in *Prentice Hall Literature, Penguin Edition,* The British Tradition.

🕐 Timed Writing Prompt

5. While the majority of students successfully complete high school, some students drop out before earning a diploma. Write an essay to your state senator explaining the reasons why some students drop out of school. Your essay should also discuss the effects of dropping out of school, both for the student and society. Focus your essay on no more than three causes and three effects. **(40 minutes)**

Prewriting • 199

Prewriting: Create a Web to Narrow Your Topic

Teaching Resources: Writing Support Transparencies, 10-C; Writing Support Activity Book, 10-1

1. Display the transparency. Show students the way a topic is narrowed further with each layer of the web.

2. Point out to students that they may find within the web a topic that is more interesting or manageable than the original idea in the center.

3. If students do find a new topic, encourage them to create another web, using the new topic as the center. This exercise will help them gather details to include in their essays.

Prewriting: Considering Your Audience and Purpose

Teaching Resources: Writing Support Transparencies, 10-D; Writing Support Activity Book, 10-2

1. Give students a blank copy of the organizer, or have students create their own based on the example in the text.

2. Suggest that students consider more than one audience and purpose, both to practice the skill and to clarify the requirements for researching and writing about their topics.

3. Have students look over their completed charts and decide which purpose makes the most sense for the topics they have selected.

Customize for
Less Advanced Students

Help students determine the purpose of their essays by first brainstorming with them for a list of possible purposes. Then, have them choose two or three from the list and fill out the chart to decide which seems the most logical choice.

10.2

Narrowing Your Topic

Once you have a general topic, decide how much of that topic can be covered effectively in a short paper. If you are analyzing a war, for example, you probably can't describe all of its causes fully in a single essay. You could either give a general overview of the most important causes, or you could focus on one type of cause, such as economic conditions.

Create a Web to Narrow Your Topic

Make a web to help you consider ways of narrowing your focus. Start by listing your topic in the center. Surround it by connected subtopics. Then, list details connected to each subtopic. Review your web to see whether any of the subtopics would make a suitable topic for your paper.

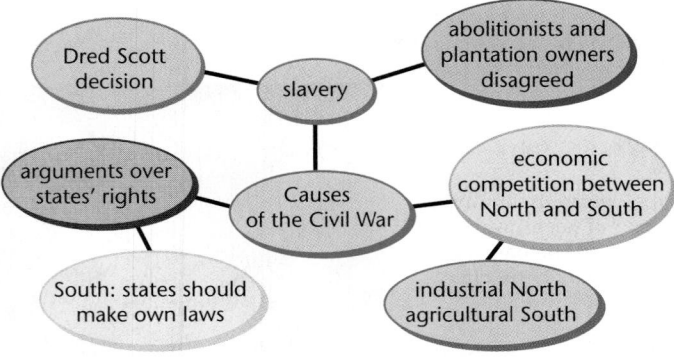

Considering Your Audience and Purpose

Your audience is the people who will read your essay; your purpose is the way you want your writing to affect your audience. As you write, choose details and language that will engage and interest your audience and help you accomplish your purpose.

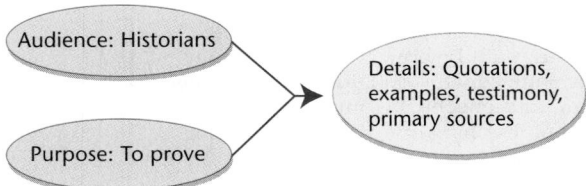

200 • Cause-and-Effect Essay

⏲ **Timed Writing Hint**

When writing with a deadline, use a graphic organizer such as the one on this page. This will help you narrow your focus quickly.

✎ STANDARDIZED TEST PREPARATION WORKSHOP

Organize and Plan Standardized tests may require students to answer questions about how to organize an essay. Help students practice organizing an essay in chronological order.

The Missing Bike

I. The Cyclery Bike Shop sells a record number of the latest model bike in a neon green.

II. Brian is in a hurry when he arrives at school, leaving his bike unlocked. He parks his bike near the school exit near his sixth period classroom, so he will be close to it when he leaves school.

III. School is released early after fourth period.

IV. Melissa forgets to bring her bike lock to school, so she has to leave her bike unlocked and heads to class.

V. Brian finds the green bike outside his classroom and rides home.

VI. Melissa reports her bike missing.

Which item in this outline is out of order?

A I **B** II **C** III **D** IV

Students should recognize that **D** is out of order because Melissa left her bike before school started, not after students were released at the end of fourth period.

Gathering Details

Your general purpose in a cause-and-effect essay is to show how one action or situation led to another. Include concrete, specific details so your readers can see exactly how this process happened.

Research to Gather Details

Of course, you might not know all the details you need in order to write an effective essay. You might need to do research—reading books, magazines, or newspapers; interviewing experts in the field; or looking up a topic on the Internet.

One way to direct your research is to begin with an effect. List all the causes of that effect that you know. Then, use printed materials, interviews, and the Internet to verify those causes and to discover more.

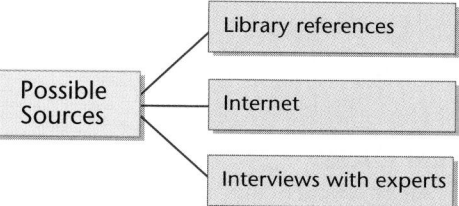

Possible Sources
- Library references
- Internet
- Interviews with experts

Student Work IN PROGRESS

Name: *Carl Byers*
Muncie Central High School
Muncie, IN

Gathering Details Through an Interview

Carl began with an effect that interested him: the rise in popularity of swing music. He made a list of the causes that came to mind. When he reviewed his list, Carl realized he needed to know more. He decided to interview an expert, Ya'kov Eden, a local dance instructor who taught swing classes. Following are a question and a response from the interview.

Interview Questions

Question: Why is swing music becoming popular?

Response: The music is exciting. It has a nice melodic line, and it's very American. I think that some of the music today has lost its edge, but there is something about the energetic beat of swing that's exciting.

Prewriting • 201

Prewriting: Research to Gather Details

1. Point out that access to the Internet makes gathering details easier than ever; however, here as elsewhere, students must make sure they are getting information from credible sources. Encourage them to double-check all information.

2. Have students use a search engine to research their topics. Help students narrow their results by limiting their searches.

3. Have students record useful information from their searches. If possible, give them time to double-check what they learned.

Prewriting: Gathering Details Through an Interview

Teaching Resources: Writing Support Transparencies, 10-E

1. Refer students to the Student Work in Progress or display the transparency. Discuss how Carl's use of listing helped him discover what he needed to know about swing music. How did it help him create interview questions?

2. Ask students to look over their notes and determine the gaps they must fill. Then, have them meet in small groups and brainstorm for ideas about whom to interview.

3. Have students work individually to arrange interviews. Remind them that experts don't always have to be professionals. Sometimes a parent or a good friend will know enough about a topic to answer questions.

4. Have students prepare a list of questions before conducting their interviews.

Integrating Speaking and Listening Skills

Point out to the class the importance of critical listening. When interviewing an expert, effective listening is just as important as speaking clearly and framing specific or targeted questions.

Drafting: Organize Details in Order of Importance

1. Point out to students that ranking details by order of importance is subjective. What one person considers most important may seem irrelevant to someone else.

2. Remind students that the key to successful use of this method is to support one's ranking with details and examples.

3. The use of superlatives can be effective. The claim that the outfield is "the most impressive force in the major leagues," although subjective, demands the reader's attention.

Drafting: Organize Details in Chronological Order

Teaching Resources: Writing Support Transparencies, 10-F

1. Display the transparency and discuss how each event leads to the next in a cause-and-effect relationship.

2. Have students meet in groups to discuss whose topics might best be organized chronologically. Explain that essays, such as "Miracle on 34th Street," which describe a series of events, lend themselves to chronological organization.

3. Ask students to begin drafting their essays using one of the organization techniques above.

Customize for
ESL Students

English language learners may also find it helpful to create a flowchart for their topics. They might make an illustrated chart, writing captions for each illustration in their native language. This way, they can concentrate fully on organizing their thoughts. After that, they can work on translating the captions into English.

10.3 Drafting

Shaping Your Writing

Before you begin writing, decide how you want to organize your details. Consider which of the following organizational strategies will be most effective in enabling readers to follow causes and effects.

Organize Details in Order of Importance

One effective way to organize details is to begin with the least important cause and move up to the most important one. Readers' interest builds as they feel that they are getting closer and closer to the heart of the matter.

If you were writing about the causes of a baseball team winning the World Series, for example, you might choose the following order, from least to most important:

1. Good outfield
2. Outstanding pitcher
3. New coach, who reorganized the team and totally improved morale

Organize Details in Chronological Order

Another logical organization is to give causes or effects in the order in which they occurred. This is especially useful when one cause or effect leads to another. If you were writing about the causes of a rock band's rise to fame, for example, you might want to begin at the beginning of their formation, listing each important milestone to their destination—the top of the charts.

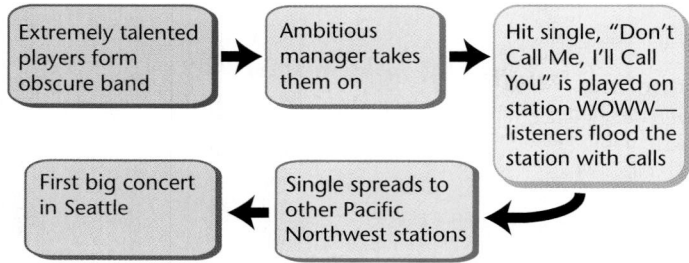

⏱ TIME AND RESOURCE MANAGER

Resources
Print: *Writing Support Transparencies,* 10-F–G
Technology: *Writing and Grammar* Interactive Text, Section 10.3

Using the Full Student Edition	Using the Handbook⊞
• Read and discuss the Shaping Your Writing strategies.	• Read and discuss the Shaping Your Writing strategies.
• Have students organize details in class.	• Have students organize details in class.
• Discuss elaboration strategies.	• Discuss elaboration strategies.
• Have students begin drafting in class.	• Have students begin drafting in class.

Providing Elaboration

As your cause-and-effect essay takes shape, use elaboration—the addition of details—to help your readers understand more clearly the nature of each cause or effect and how they relate to each other.

Provide Data

Specific statistics, dates, names, or places can help your readers fully understand what you are describing. The use of data also adds authority to your writing.

Give Examples

Examples help readers connect information you have given with their own experiences. For example, if you were describing the horrors of a battle, you might compare the battle to one your audience may have seen in a film.

Share Insights

Your own insights and predictions will give your writing a personal touch and help you to convey a tone, or your attitude toward your subject.

Student Work
IN PROGRESS

Name: *Carl Byers*
Muncie Central High School
Muncie, IN

Elaborating by Adding Insights

Carl included hard data on the causes for swing's popularity, but he decided that giving his own insights would help get his main idea across.

type of
"The Swing" is not only a dance step. It's also an attitude, a way of dressing—and a type of very appealing music.

Some of the reasons have to do with the dance itself.

"The Swing" is based on the smooth movement of the ballroom step the foxtrot.

Drafting • 203

Step-by-Step Teaching Guide

Drafting: Providing Elaboration

Teaching Resources: Writing Support Transparencies, 10-G

1. Display Transparency 10-G to show students how Carl used his own insights about swing music to get his point across. Ask students why they think he decided to do this.

2. Explain to students that elaboration must add meaning and substance to the essay, not just make it longer. Help them to distinguish between pertinent and irrelevant details.

3. Have students evaluate their details by using the following criteria:

   How does the detail relate to the main idea?

   Does the detail strengthen the cause-and-effect relationship?

   Does the detail distract from the cause-and-effect relationship?

4. Students are often tempted to include details simply because they are interesting, regardless of their relevance. Remind them that an irrelevant detail, no matter how interesting, distracts the reader from the point of the essay.

☑ ONGOING ASSESSMENT: Monitor and Reinforce

Students sometimes have difficulties recognizing the strengths and weaknesses of their evidence. If this is the case, try the following strategy.

Have students work in pairs. Each student writes down his or her supporting points on note cards or self-sticking notes and asks the other student to place them in order from strongest to weakest. Students can then discuss the priority arrangements before continuing to draft.

⏱ TIME SAVERS!

Writing Support Transparencies
Use the transparencies for Chapter 10 to facilitate teaching of strategies.

Writing Support Activity Book
Use the graphic organizers for Chapter 10 to facilitate student planning.

Revising: Making a New Outline

1. Explain to students that a cause-and-effect essay needs to be logical and interesting. All the details of the essay should support the cause-and-effect relationship. Unnecessary information or details should be eliminated.

2. Refer students to the partial outline in the text, and discuss the elements of the outline. Explain that making a new outline will help them in two ways. First, it will help them identify the main idea of each paragraph. Second, it will help them determine whether the paragraphs are necessary and in the right order.

3. Have students make new outlines of their essays and then determine what changes they will need to make. Give them time to start making these revisions.

Revising: Circling the First and Last Sentences

1. To help students test the logical flow of the sequence of their ideas, have students write the first and last sentences of each paragraph on separate slips of paper. Then have them shuffle the pieces and attempt to place them in order without looking at their essays.

2. Remind students that transition words and phrases help improve the flow from one paragraph to the next.

More About the Writer

Samuel Johnson published his *Dictionary of the English Language* in 1755. He is considered the finest English literary scholar and critic of the eighteenth century.

10.4 Revising

Revising Your Overall Structure

Review Your Essay's Organization

Review the method of organization you chose to be sure it works effectively and that you've used it consistently throughout the essay.

▶ **REVISION STRATEGY**
Making a New Outline

Make a new outline of your work to see whether all the information you have included is in the right place. At the top of the page, write the form of organization you have chosen. Then, make a numbered list, one number for each paragraph in your work. Beside each number, write a few words or a sentence summarizing what's in the paragraph.

Now, look at the list to be sure the ideas are presented in an effective or logical order. If necessary, rearrange paragraphs or sentences within paragraphs.

Revising Your Paragraphs

Improve Paragraph Flow

A coherent essay contains paragraphs that flow together. Review your paragraphs, and revise them so that they work together to develop your main idea.

▶ **REVISION STRATEGY**
Circling the First and Last Sentences

Read through your cause-and-effect essay, using a colored pen to circle the first and last sentences in each paragraph. Then, look at your work, focusing on paragraph flow. Ask yourself whether each sentence that begins a paragraph flows naturally out of the sentence that came before it. If necessary, rewrite one or both sentences in order to show the connection.

Writers in ACTION

Samuel Johnson was known for his brilliant prose style and his keen wit. His famous quotation on the revising process works particularly well for cause-and-effect essays, in which every sentence should contribute to the reader's understanding and nothing should be included simply because it "sounds good":

"Read over your compositions and, when you meet a passage which you think is particularly fine, strike it out."

Order of Importance
1. Poverty
2. Restrictive Laws
3. Revolution in France

⏱ TIME AND RESOURCE MANAGER

Resources
Print: *Writing Support Transparencies*, 10-H
Technology: *Writing and Grammar* Interactive Text, Section 10.4

Using the Full Student Edition	Using the Handbook Ⓗ
• Cover revising strategies in class. • Review Grammar in Your Writing (p. 206). • Divide the class into groups for the peer review activity.	• Cover revising strategies in class. • Review Grammar in Your Writing (p. 132). • Divide the class into groups for the peer review activity.

Revising Your Sentences

Fix Faulty Coordination

Clauses can be connected in various ways. When a writer fails to show the relationship between two clauses in a sentence, it is known as faulty coordination. Changing the connecting words can help make the relationship more clear.

▶ **REVISION STRATEGY**
Changing or Adding a Conjunction

To fix faulty coordination, change an inappropriate conjunction or add a conjunction to better show relationships.

Coordinating conjunctions connect similar kinds of words or groups of words that are grammatically alike. Examples include: *and, but, for, nor or, so,* and *yet.*

Correlative conjunctions are similar to coordinating conjunctions except that they are always used in pairs. Examples include: *but . . . and; either . . . or; neither . . . nor; not only . . . but also.*

Subordinating conjunctions connect two complete ideas by making one of the ideas subordinate to, or less important than, the other. Examples include: *consequently, furthermore, however, indeed, otherwise, therefore, fortunately,* and *moreover.*

🕐 **Timed Writing Hint**

Adapt the Revision Strategy by reading silently to yourself in an exam. "Hear" how your sentences and connecting words sound and improve them when necessary.

Student Work
IN PROGRESS

Name: *Carl Byers*
Muncie Central High School
Muncie, IN

Improving Sentence Coordination

As he reread his work, Carl corrected instances of faulty coordination he found in his writing.

"The Swing" is based on the smooth movement of the ballroom step the foxtrot. ~~And,~~ "the Swing" is not only a ,however, dance ~~step.~~ type of It's also an attitude, a way of dressing—and a a type of very appealing music.

> By deleting And and adding however, Carl highlights the fact that "The Swing" is more than a dance step.

Revising: Changing or Adding a Conjunction

Teaching Resources: Writing Support Transparencies, 10-H

1. Review the three types of conjunctions with the class.

2. Display Transparency 10-H and discuss how Carl fixed faulty coordination in his essay.

3. Give students a copy of an anecdotal magazine article. Have them underline the conjunctions and classify them according to type: coordinating, correlative, or subordinating.

4. Tell students to cross out the conjunctions and reread the passage. Discuss how the omission of conjunctions affects the meaning of the sentences. (The cause-and-effect relationship is no longer clear when a subordinating conjunction is omitted.)

5. Allow students time to check their essays for effective use of conjunctions.

6. After students have reviewed their essays, have them circle all the conjunctions they used. Have them exchange papers so their partners can check their work, making special note of any transitions with inappropriate conjunctions.

Customize for
Less Advanced Students

One way to promote constructive criticism is to have students complete a peer-edit chart. Give them specific points to evaluate, such as clear transitions or varying sentence structure. This will help to eliminate generic comments, such as "It was good" or "It needs a lot of work."

Customize for
Gifted and Talented Students

Some students tend to master assignments quickly and feel satisfied with a first draft. These students may benefit from editing their own work. Have them complete a "peer-edit" review of their own essays. It will make them aware of elements that can be improved.

Independent and Subordinate Clauses

1. Give students copies of a magazine or newspaper article. Have them underline independent clauses and double-underline subordinate clauses. Then, have them circle any conjunctions that begin the subordinate clauses. (Students may want to look back at p. 205 for more examples of subordinating conjunctions.)

2. After students have identified the subordinate clauses in the article, ask them to identify the relationship—time, result, comparison, or condition— each establishes.

3. Remind students that subordinate clauses can be created by combining two sentences that already exist or by adding a clause to a sentence.

4. Encourage students, as they revise their essays, to look for places where they can make relationships clearer by adding or creating subordinate clauses.

Find It in Your Reading

If they have difficulty with this activity, you may want to allow students to work in pairs. There are several subordinating clauses in the excerpt. Possibilities include: ". . . the plane flew . . . above the ground, at which point . . ."; ". . . escaped with their lives, although they were . . ."; ". . . gasoline from ruptured tanks, which immediately ignited."; "The column . . . damaged, although a steel beam . . ."

Find It in Your Writing

Ask students how the relationships shown by subordinate clauses can help establish cause-and-effect relationships. Encourage students to keep these ideas in mind as they review their writing.

10.4

Grammar in Your Writing
Independent and Subordinate Clauses

A **clause** is a group of words with its own subject and verb. An **independent clause** can stand by itself as a complete sentence. An independent clause can be used in several ways:

By Itself

That cat has a striped tail.

With Another Independent Clause

I hope it's true that cats have nine lives; my cat has used up eight.

With a Subordinate Clause

My cat yowled to be helped from the tree because it was scared.

A **subordinate clause,** although it has a complete subject and verb, cannot stand by itself as a complete sentence; it can only be part of a sentence. Subordinate clauses show relationships of time, result, comparison, contrast, or condition; or they simply add information. They begin with conjunctions, such as *while, because, as if,* and *which.*

Relationship of Time

While they were in the store shopping, we were becoming bored.

Relationship of Result

We became bored *because* they spent so much time shopping.

Relationship of Comparison

They shopped *as if* the world were coming to an end tomorrow.

Relationship of Condition

Shopping, *which* is my family's favorite pastime, is not one of my favorite things to do.

Find It in Your Reading Read through "Miracle on 34th Street" on pages 196–197, and locate three sentences containing subordinate clauses. Identify the conjunctions that help indicate the relationship of the subordinate clause to the main clause of the sentence.

Find It in Your Writing Review your draft to find at least two independent and two subordinate clauses. If you can't find them, challenge yourself to add them. Then, make sure that you have used the correct connecting words to show the relationship between clauses.

To learn more about clauses, see Chapter 19.

☑ ONGOING ASSESSMENT: Prerequisite Skills

If students have difficulty identifying independent and subordinate clauses, you might find it helpful to refer them to the following materials to ensure coverage of prerequisite knowledge.

In the Textbook	Print Resources	Technology
Clauses, Section 19.3	*Grammar Exercise Workbook,* pp. 41–46	*On-Line Exercise Bank,* Section 19.3

Revising Your Word Choice
Eliminate Qualifying Words and Phrases

Unnecessary words clutter up writing, making the main points less clear to readers. Qualifying words and phrases are almost always unnecessary. Read your draft, and eliminate all qualifying words and phrases that are not essential to the point you are trying to convey.

UNNECESSARY QUALIFIERS
almost; it seems; kind of; quite; rather; somewhat; sort of; tends

▶ **REVISION STRATEGY**
Underlining Unnecessary Qualifiers

Read through your cause-and-effect essay, looking for the qualifiers listed in the chart above. Underline with red ink those you find. Then, think about whether you simply want to cut them or whether the sentence needs to be rewritten.

Original sentence: The group's rise was somewhat fast, but so was its fall.

Revised sentence: The group's rise was fast, but so was its fall.

Rewritten sentence: The group's rise was fast by today's standards, but so was its fall.

Peer Review
Ask Peers to Summarize

Share your revised work with a group of peers. Once they've read through your essay, ask them to summarize for you the major causes and effects that they understood from reading your work.

If your classmates have not understood the main cause-and-effect relationships, revise your writing to make it more clear.

Technology Tip

Use the Find option in your word-processing program to locate qualifiers. Then, edit on the spot and search for more.

Revising: Underlining Unnecessary Qualifiers

1. Before beginning the activity, ask students to quickly scan their drafts and circle all qualifiers. Do they notice any patterns? (Examples: overuse of the words *very* and *really*)

2. Discuss unnecessary qualifiers. Ask students how they can address this problem. (They can simply delete these qualifiers, or eliminate them and change the word they modify to a stronger word.)

3. Students might be reluctant to eliminate qualifiers from their writing because qualifiers are a comfortable part of most people's daily speech. Encourage them to look for more precise words instead of depending on overused qualifiers. A richer, more diverse vocabulary can intrigue a reader and lend an essay more credibility.

Revising: Peer Review

1. Begin the peer-review process by inviting students to first identify a draft's strengths and then its weaknesses.

2. Remind students to use a separate sheet of paper for peer editing, rather than making corrections on the draft. This way, the writer can read over the suggestions and decide which ones to incorporate.

3. Remind students that minor errors will be corrected at the proofreading stage. The focus of this exercise should be on the logic and effectiveness of the draft's cause-and-effect development.

4. Give students an editing checklist. (Example: spelling, punctuation, good sequencing of details, clear transitions, and use of unnecessary qualifiers.) This will help them make precise, useful suggestions.

Editing and Proofreading

1. Remind students that editing and proofreading are an extension of the writing process. Suggest that students check their punctuation paragraph by paragraph.

2. Be sure students look carefully at conjunctions, qualifiers, and the use of *which* and *that*.

Commas in Essential and Nonessential Expressions

1. Explain that nonessential expressions may convey interesting, even important, information. They are simply not essential to the structure of the sentence.

2. Write on the board "My sister, who is my only sibling, is the youngest member of our family."

3. Ask students what the commas do in this sentence. (They indicate that the phrase between them is not essential. "My sister is the youngest member of our family" still has meaning without the phrase.)

4. Point out that "who is my only sibling" may be vital to a story, but it is not essential to the meaning of the sentence.

5. Suggest that students read sentences without including phrases enclosed in commas, to see whether they still make sense. If they don't, students should determine how to fix the sentences.

Find It in Your Reading

Possible example: "The pilot, flying under visual rules, was required . . ." ("flying . . ." is nonessential). Any expression without commas would be essential.

Find It in Your Writing

Encourage students to use nonessential expressions when they enrich meaning, but to be careful to punctuate them correctly.

10.5 Editing and Proofreading

Edit your work carefully, correcting errors in spelling, punctuation, and grammar before you write your final draft.

Focusing on *Which* and *That*

Which and *that* are frequently misused, even by experienced writers. *That* offers essential information, and *which* indicates nonessential information. As you proofread your work, check your usage to be sure that it is correct.

Grammar in Your Writing
Commas in Essential and Nonessential Expressions

An **essential expression** is a word, phrase, or clause that provides information that cannot be removed without changing the meaning of the sentence. **Nonessential expressions** provide additional, but not essential, information.

1. Essential information does not need to be enclosed in commas. Since the following sentence does not make much sense without the essential expression *Brain*, you don't need commas.

The rock band **Brain** is one of my favorites.

2. Nonessential information must be set off with commas. The following sentence makes sense without the italicized phrase. Therefore, that nonessential expression is set off by commas.

Brain, one of my favorite bands, now rarely plays in concert.

Find It in Your Reading Look for one example each of essential and nonessential expressions in "Miracle on 34th Street" on pages 196–197. Then, explain why each expression is punctuated as it is.

Find It in Your Writing As you proofread your cause-and-effect essay, double-check to be sure your punctuation of essential and nonessential information is correct.

For more on punctuating essential and nonessential information, see Chapter 27.

⏱ TIME AND RESOURCE MANAGER

Resources
Print: *Scoring Rubrics on Transparency,* Ch. 10; *Writing Assessment and Portfolio Management; Formal Assessment,* Ch. 10
Technology: *Writing and Grammar* Interactive Text, Section 10.5

Using the Full Student Edition	Using the Handbook🄷
• Review p. 208 in class, including Grammar in Your Writing. • Read and discuss p. 209. • Analyze the Final Draft on pp. 210–211. • Have students edit and proofread their essays in class.	• Review p. 134 in class, including Grammar in Your Writing. • Read and discuss p. 135. • Have students edit and proofread their essays in class.

10.6 Publishing and Presenting

Building Your Portfolio

Following are some ideas for publishing and presenting your cause-and-effect essay:

1. **Discussion Group** Share your essay with interested peers. Then, lead a discussion about your work. Note which strategies you'll repeat and which you'll change the next time you write a cause-and-effect essay.

2. **Community Publication** If you've written about an event or a situation that affects your community, a community publication might be interested in publishing your work. Find out the guidelines for submitting your writing and prepare your manuscript accordingly.

Reflecting on Your Writing

Think back on your writing experience. Then, respond to the following questions, and save your responses in your portfolio.

- What new information about your topic did you learn as you gathered details for your essay?
- If a friend were writing a cause-and-effect essay, what three pieces of advice would you give to him or her?

 Internet Tip

To see a cause-and-effect essay scored according to this rubric, go on-line:
PHSchool.com
Enter Web Code:
egk-1201

Rubric for Self-Assessment

Use the following criteria to evaluate your cause-and-effect essay.

	Score 4	Score 3	Score 2	Score 1
Audience and Purpose	Consistently targets an audience; clearly identifies purpose in thesis statement	Targets an audience; identifies purpose in thesis statement	Misses a target audience by including a wide range of word choice and details; presents no clear purpose	Addresses no specific audience or purpose
Organization	Presents a clear, consistent organizational strategy to show cause and effect	Presents a clear organizational strategy with occasional inconsistencies; shows cause and effect	Presents an inconsistent organizational strategy; creates illogical presentation of causes and effects	Demonstrates a lack of organizational strategy; creates a confusing presentation
Elaboration	Successfully links causes with effects; fully elaborates connections among ideas	Links causes with effects; elaborates connections among most ideas	Links some causes with some effects; elaborates connections among some ideas	Develops and elaborates no links between causes and effects
Use of Language	Uses words precisely; presents very few mechanical errors	Uses words precisely; presents few mechanical errors	Contains some imprecise words; presents many mechanical errors	Demonstrates poor use of words; presents many mechanical errors

Publishing and Presenting • 209

Publishing and Presenting

1. Explain to students that publishing makes it possible for authors to share their writing with others. Encourage students to find outlets for their work. (Examples: the Internet, magazine writing contests, the school library, or family and friends.)

2. In preparing their essays for publication, students may wish to add illustrations, diagrams, or photos. A flow chart detailing the sequence of events may be effective.

ASSESS and CLOSE

Assessment

Teaching Resources: Scoring Rubrics on Transparency, Ch. 10; Writing Assessment and Portfolio Management; Formal Assessment, Ch. 10

1. Display the Scoring Rubric transparency and review the criteria in class.

2. Before students proceed with self-assessment, you may wish to review the Final Draft of the Student Work in Progress on pages 210–211. Have students score the Final Draft in one or more of the rubric categories. For example, how would students score the essay in terms of audience and purpose?

3. In addition to student self-assessment, you may wish to use the following assessment options:

   - score student essays yourself, using the rubric and scoring models from *Writing Assessment and Portfolio Management*.

   - review the Standardized Test Preparation Workshop on pp. 216–217 and administer a timed writing assignment.

   - administer the Chapter 10 assessment from *Formal Assessment* in Teaching Resources to measure students' grasp of concepts presented.

☑ **ONGOING ASSESSMENT: Assess Mastery**

Use one of the following options to assess final drafts of students' cause-and-effect essays.

Self-Assessment Ask students to score their essays using the rubric provided. Then, have students write a single paragraph reflecting on the most valuable thing they learned in completing this essay.

Teacher Assessment You may wish to use the rubric and the scoring models provided in *Writing Assessment and Portfolio Management* to score the cause-and-effect essays.

Final Draft

1. Help students understand how "Why Swing Is Here to Stay" incorporates key elements of the cause-and-effect essay.

   - The topic is clearly presented and supported by relevant details.
   - Audience and purpose have been carefully considered.
   - The topic appeals to student readers of the school newspaper who are interested in music, fashion, and trends.
   - The details are organized by order of importance, leading to what the author presents as the biggest cause of the rise of swing: the television commercial.
   - The conclusion ties the essay together by clearly stating why the topic is important.

2. Ask students whether they would recommend other changes to make the essay flow better or to improve the language. How might they apply these suggestions to their own writing?

Customize for
Musical Learners

Choose a student with dramatic flair to read the essay to the class, or do the dramatic reading yourself. The animated reading, especially with a swing tune as background music, will convey the excitement and liveliness of swing. Challenge students to add liveliness to their own writing by using varied sentence structures and interesting, precise words.

Critical Viewing

Interpret Responses are likely to include phrases such as "with hands joined overhead" or "circling in opposite directions."

10.7 *Student Work* IN PROGRESS

FINAL DRAFT

▶ **Critical Viewing** If you were describing this dance move to someone, what phrases would you use? **[Interpret]**

Why Swing Is Here to Stay

Carl Byers
Muncie Central High School
Muncie, Indiana

We live in an age in which music is bought and sold by major labels and marketed to the public until nothing is left, after which the majors move on to the next trend and repeat the process. Well, it looks as if the public has done the picking this time. Swing music and its dances have had a renewed interest—and with almost no help from the major labels. I mean, who hasn't heard the latest covers of swing classics by modern rock bands?

You don't see tons of swing bands turning up on the covers of popular music magazines or on music television. Yet swing is everywhere: on TV commercials, in fashion, and in movies. Popular culture is full of swing nowadays.

How did this happen? It was a combination, really: Certain people were in the right place at the right time.

Some of the reasons have to do with the dance itself. "The Swing" is based on the smooth movement of the ballroom step the foxtrot. "The Swing," however, is not only a dance step. It's also

In his introduction, Carl reveals his topic: the causes behind the rise in popularity of swing music.

Carl's essay is organized consistently and logically: He discusses each causative factor, one at a time.

210 • Cause-and-Effect Essay

an attitude, a way of dressing—and a type of very appealing music.

"I think that, when you listen to the music, it's exciting. It has a nice melodic line, and it's very American," said swing instructor Ya'kov Eden. "I think that some of the music today has kind of lost its edge, but there is something about the rock-and-roll beat of swing that's exciting. The nineties swing bands are so exciting in their instrumentation that when you hear them, you can't sit still."

Another factor in the rise of swing was the "Khakis Swing" commercial produced by a popular clothing chain. The popular ad featured "Jump, Jive and Wail," leading to a radio renaissance of singles from various rock bands.

An interest in swing has filtered down to our very own school. Eden offers swing classes to the public at his studio on Monday and Thursday nights, and several Central students have attended.

"I took the class because it sounded like fun," said senior Monica Young.

By offering a fresh, new alternative to the dead-end trends of popular music, swing music is guaranteed to leave a lasting impression.

By mentioning that Central High School students are studying swing, Carl shows his audience—readers of the school newspaper—how they, too, are affected by the rise in swing's popularity.

This conclusion predicts an effect swing music will have in the future.

▼ **Critical Viewing** Why might the dance depicted in the photograph be so popular among young and old? **[Analyze]**

Teaching From the Final Draft

Students should understand that opinions, by definition, are subjective. Even though the essay is largely factual, based on the revival of swing in pop culture, the author adds an energetic flavor by including personal views. (Example: describing swing as "a fresh alternative" and labeling other music trends as "dead-end" are not facts but subjective characterizations.) The essay is an effective blend of factual data and personal taste.

Customize for
ESL Students

Suggest that students translate their essays into their native languages to share them with friends and family who share their native language. If possible, encourage students to read their translated essays to the class.

Critical Viewing

Analyze Responses might include that the dance looks like fun, that it is good exercise, or that it includes elements of both older and newer styles.

Lesson Objectives

1. To write a documentary appropriate to audience and purpose

2. To use a variety of forms and technologies such as videos, photographs, and Web pages, to communicate specific messages

3. To use a range of techniques to plan and create a media text and reflect critically on the work produced

Step-by-Step Teaching Guide

Documentary

Teaching Resources: Writing Support Transparencies, 10-I; Writing Support Activity Book, 10-3

1. Discuss with students any television documentaries that they may have seen recently.

2. Suggest that students review strategies from Chapter 10 as they begin to plan their documentaries. See the chart below for useful resources.

3. Display Transparency 10-I and distribute copies of the blank organizer (10-3) to students for use in their own planning. Explain to students that a major way that documentary writing differs from other types of writing is that elements like camera angles, stage directions, and props need to be included in the script.

4. Set up a schedule for students to screen their documentaries in school, after school, or during a free period.

Critical Viewing

Connect It appears that they are working on a documentary about dinosaurs, perhaps about the cause of their extinction. They are reviewing posters with dinosaurs pictured on them.

Connected Assignment
Documentary

Documentaries are films that examine people's lives, historical events, and scientific phenomena. Today's television schedules are filled with documentaries on every topic from sports to politics to celebrity lifestyles. Many focus on cause-and-effect relationships, such as those that influence a person's career path or lead a country into war.

The writers of documentaries create scripts that help filmmakers shape and mold visual and textual information into the finished film you view. Documentaries can include interviews, historical and current film clips, sound bites and audio excerpts, information footage explained by narration, or primary source documents, such as legal court papers. Stage directions outline the organization of these different elements, while narration is indicated as dialogue.

Imagine that you're a scriptwriter for a popular television newsmagazine. Develop a documentary script using these suggested writing process steps.

▲ **Critical Viewing**
What sort of documentary might the people pictured be working on? How can you tell?
[Connect]

MODEL

Scene 1
Interior. Fade in.

Close-up of female hand writing a letter with a quill pen. A voice-over (Jane Austen character) reads as letter is written:

Dearest Fanny,

I feel quite as doubtful as you could be my dearest Fanny as to *when* my Letter may be finished, for I can command very little quiet time at present, but yet I must begin, for I know you will be glad to hear as soon as possible . . .

Fade out.

NARRATOR: Jane Austen was born in Steventon, Hampshire. Her father was a clergyman . . .

212 • Cause-and-Effect Essay

☑ ONGOING ASSESSMENT: Prerequisite Skills

Students may find the following resources from Chapter 10 particularly helpful in completing their documentaries.

In the Textbook	Print Resources	Technology
Narrowing Your Topic, Section 10.2 Research to Gather Details, Section 10.2	*Writing Support Transparencies,* 10-C–D *Writing Support Activity Book,* 10-1–2	*Writing and Grammar* Interactive Text, Section 10.2

Choosing a Topic Brainstorm for possible documentary topics by scanning the newspaper or talking with neighbors about issues of interest. You might also choose to center your documentary around a person or place within your own community.

Creating a Plan Decide on a plan for your documentary. Make a chart like the one that follows, and show how various elements from your plan will work together as you develop your documentary.

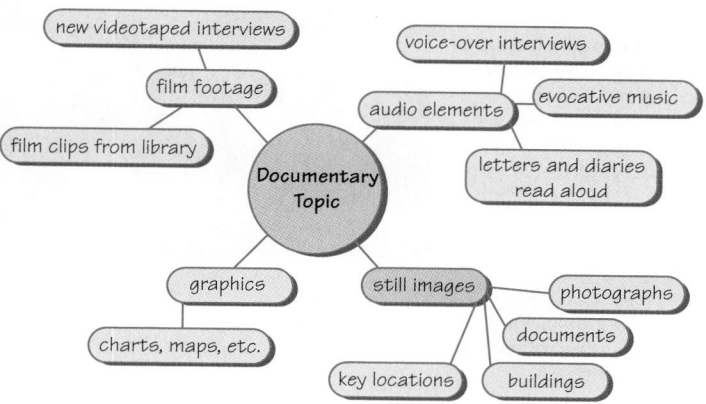

Drafting Follow your plan as you draft, visualizing the images viewers will see as you describe them in words on your script. Orient the filmmaker (and other script readers) to the events by clearly indicating what images are shown when. Add voice-overs to bind the elements into a smooth narrative that emphasizes a cause-and-effect relationship. Keep the narration neutral in tone, even when explaining disturbing or surprising events.

Revising and Editing Have a peer read your script and comment on its coherence and visual impact. Add transitional narration to smoothly move from element to element. Check to be sure that people and places are well explained and that your language suits the audience's knowledge level. Avoid overly emotional appeals; trust viewers to reach reasonable conclusions when presented with compelling evidence.

Publishing and Presenting Film your documentary or a portion of it, and hold a screening for your family and friends.

Customize for
Interpersonal Learners

You will almost certainly want to approach the documentary as a group project. Have students work in teams to select a topic and then plan and produce a documentary segment. If time or equipment is limited, have students videotape selected portions of their planned documentary or produce it on audio tape.

Customize for
Less Advanced Students

Suggest that as students read their scripts they use a watch or timer and note how long each segment will last. This will give them a more precise sense of how much to add or delete from the script to control the pace and duration of their documentary.

Customize for
ESL Students

Suggest that students create a bilingual documentary. They can interview friends and family in their native language and then use a voice over to explain what is being said, as is common in professional documentaries on multinational topics.

1. To analyze relationships, ideas, and cultures as represented in various media

2. To investigate the source of a media presentation, such as who made it and why it was made

3. To demonstrate proficiency in each aspect of the listening process, such as focusing attention, interpreting, and responding

Step-by-Step Teaching Guide

Appreciating Music

1. Choose one of the Spotlight elements for class discussion, or have students work individually or in groups to find the necessary music, poetry, or related information. Ralph Vaughan Williams's most famous work is *Fantasia on "Greensleeves."* Many of his symphonies are programmatic: No. 1, *A Sea Symphony,* is based on Whitman's poetry; No. 2, *A London Symphony,* is a musical picture of the city; No. 3, *A Pastoral Symphony,* describes nature; and No. 7, *Sinfonia Antarctica,* is an adaptation of his music to a film of an exploration of the South Pole. Among other symphonies, his dissonant No. 4 opens with some of the most powerful measures of music ever written, and, in contrast, No. 5 is one of the softest symphonies ever composed.

2. Interested students might research the poets who inspired Vaughan Williams, such as A. E. Housman, George Herbert, William Blake, and Walt Whitman.

Viewing and Representing

Activity Give interested students an opportunity to make class presentations of their descriptions. If possible, have them play a favorite part of the music they chose.

Spotlight on the Humanities

Appreciating Music
Focus on Music: Ralph Vaughan Williams

In a cause-and-effect essay, you consider the reasons something did happen or might happen. According to Ralph Vaughan Williams, one of the reasons he became a composer was that he was profoundly influenced and inspired by English folk songs, as well as the poetry and music of the seventeenth century. British composer Ralph Vaughan Williams (1872–1958) was one of the most important composers of the twentieth century. With a voice all his own and inspired by poetry in much of his work, Vaughan Williams wrote music of almost every type. Some of his major works include *Serenade to Music, Five Mystical Songs,* and *10 Blake Songs.* His nine symphonies include the *London Symphony* and the *Pastoral Symphony.*

Theater Connection Ralph Vaughan Williams's *Serenade to Music,* written in 1938, is based upon a passage in William Shakespeare's *The Merchant of Venice.* Written in 1596–1597, *The Merchant of Venice* is the story of the Venetian merchant Antonio; Portia, a wealthy single woman; and Shylock, the man who has loaned Antonio money. In the drama, the money must be repaid in three months or Shylock may take a pound of flesh from Antonio. However, it is a disguised Portia who brings the plot to an unexpected end.

Literature Connection In 1920, Ralph Vaughan Williams revised a musical piece entitled *The Lark Ascending,* which was based upon the poem of the same name by British author and critic George Meredith (1828–1909). Meredith was a prolific writer who believed that comedy and laughter kept in check the excesses of sentimentality and egotism. Meredith, who began as a newspaper writer and reader for a publisher, became the author of novels and poetry. He was awarded the Order of Merit in 1905.

Cause-and-Effect Writing Activity: Musical Analysis

Listen to a symphony or other work by Ralph Vaughan Williams. Then, describe the effect the music had on you, and analyze how various musical elements—tempo, instruments, volume, or intensity, for example—contributed to that effect.

▲ **Critical Viewing** What type of music might you expect these musicians to play? Why? **[Infer]**

Critical Viewing

Infer Most students would guess classical music for an orchestra, though more knowledgeable students may suggest a broader repertoire.

Media and Technology Skills

Examining the Effect of Media on Perceptions of Reality

Activity: Create a Musical Tour of Current Styles

Popular music is a primary component of our culture. When a song becomes a hit, its musicians become cultural trendsetters through their appearances in videos, television, and magazines. Identify trendsetters of the moment by creating an audio tour of currently popular, "cutting edge" music.

Learn About It Begin by researching which songs are most popular at this time. If you want to analyze how your school's students are affected by their favorite music, conduct a survey to identify the most popular current songs or artists.

Record and Reflect on It Record and listen to three or four popular songs. Use a chart to describe each song. Then, use sources such as television interviews, music and entertainment magazines, and Internet sites to collect information about the performers.

Song Title	Style of Song	Summary of Lyrics	Performers	Performers' Styles (clothing, speech, hair, etc.)

Select and Annotate It Create an anthology tape of influential music to share with classmates. Also, include an annotated track list that contains the information that you gathered in the chart above.

Present It Share your audio tour in a presentation. To create a visual impact, use an overhead projector to show photographs from magazines or other sources. In your presentation, emphasize how the music you are playing has affected current styles and trends.

Materials

Audiocassette Recorder
Overhead Projector

The Future Now
Media analysts use current data to predict future trends. They scramble to identify "the next big thing" before it happens. Discuss current trends with your classmates, and make three predictions about what fashions will be popular next month or next year.

Step-by-Step Teaching Guide

Examining the Effect of Media

Teaching Resources: Writing Support Transparencies, 10-J; Writing Support Activity Book, 10-4

1. Discuss the effect students think their favorite music has on them. Are the performers as influential as the music?

2. Ask students to identify current trends that they recognize. Encourage them to consider the nature of trends, and perhaps why they occur.

3. Ask students to suggest ways they could find out what music is most popular (music stores, radio stations, survey).

4. Display the transparency and point out the categories of information to be included in students' reflections on music.

5. Give students copies of the graphic organizer (10-4) or have them create their own charts.

6. If students are unable to record three or four popular songs, suggest that they listen to the radio and determine which songs are played most often, and research these songs.

7. Allow time in class for students to share the music they have recorded, as well as their comments.

Media and Technology Skills • 215

Lesson Objectives

1. To write in a style appropriate to audience and purpose
2. To organize ideas to ensure coherence, logical progression, and support for ideas
3. To develop and revise drafts in terms of structure, paragraphs, sentences, and word choice
4. To edit and proofread to ensure standard English usage and grammar

Step-by-Step Teaching Guide

Responding to Cause-and-Effect Writing Prompts

Teaching Resources: Standardized Test Preparation Workbook, pp. 19–20

1. Have students read the information on responding to writing prompts and taking tests on pp. 216–217.

2. Emphasize the importance of keeping the main elements of a cause-and-effect essay in mind when responding to this writing prompt.

3. Have students read the writing prompt, and then assign the excerpt from "Miracle on 34th Street."

4. Have students respond to the writing prompt, completing their essays during the class period.

Standardized Test Preparation Workshop

Responding to Cause-and-Effect Writing Prompts

Writing prompts on standardized tests measure your ability to identify and analyze cause-and-effect relationships. For example, you may be asked to analyze the causes of the Great Depression or explain the phenomena that causes a tornado. Your writing will likely be evaluated on the following criteria:

- a clearly stated thesis that answers the prompt
- details that support your thesis
- a logical and effective organizational strategy
- language that is appropriate for your audience and that helps you to achieve your purpose
- appropriate transitions that clearly indicate connections between ideas
- correct grammar, spelling, and punctuation

When writing for a timed test, plan to devote a specified amount of time for prewriting, drafting, revising and proofreading.

Following is an example of a writing prompt that probes your understanding of cause-and-effect relationships. Respond to the prompt, using the writing process steps on the following page as a guide. The clocks next to each stage give a suggestion for how much time you should devote to each step.

Sample Writing Situation

Read the excerpt from "Miracle on 34th Street" on pages 196–197. Then respond to the following prompt in the form of an essay.

In "Miracle on 34th Street," Levy and Salvadori analyze the causes leading up to and the effects following a plane crash. Read the essay, and then comment upon the thoroughness and effectiveness of the authors' work. Use details from the essay to support your evaluation.

216 • Cause-and-Effect Essay

Test Tips

- Organize your thoughts before you begin writing your response.
- Just before you begin drafting, reread the question to be sure that you answer it in your response.

TEST-TAKING TIP

Tell students that, before they begin to write, they should be certain they are responding to what is asked for in the writing prompt. Ask students to pick out the key words in the writing prompt on this page: *causes, effects, thoroughness, and effectiveness of the author's work.*

Emphasize that students should consider using some kind of organizer to jot down their key points before drafting. Outlines, pro and con columns, webs, or listings of chronological events can all be useful, depending on the test prompt. Then, ask students what kind of organizer they might use with this test prompt during the prewriting stage.

Prewriting

Allow about one quarter of your time for prewriting.

Write a Thesis Statement Read the prompt and come up with a thesis statement in response. For example, you might think that the cause-and-effect relationships within "Miracle on 34th Street" could be more clear. If so, your thesis statement might read, "Although Levy and Salvadori provide ample details showing cause and effects, they fail to clearly show the relationships among them." Once you develop your thesis statement, gather details to support it.

Outline Details Take a few moments to outline the details you plan to use in your essay. Rough out the order in which you plan to present your ideas. For example, you may prefer to lead off with your second-most important point, followed by points in descending order of importance, and end with your most important point.

Drafting

Allow about one-half hour to draft your essay.

Create an Introduction, Body, and Conclusion Use a classic essay structure as you draft your response. In your introduction, state your thesis and lead into the body of the essay. In the body of your essay, develop and support your thesis. Then, in the essay's conclusion, restate your main points and conclude with a memorable or intriguing closing statement.

Elaborate As you draft the body of your essay, elaborate on your ideas by providing examples from the text as well as personal observations and examples from real life.

Revising, Editing, and Proofreading

Allow almost one fourth of your time to revise and edit. Use the last few minutes to proofread your work.

Delete Unnecessary Details Read through your draft and delete details that do not support your thesis or that detract from your purpose.

Revise Your Introduction and Conclusion Make sure that your introduction and conclusion match and that they work together to create a unified essay. Be sure that in your introduction that you state your thesis and that in your conclusion you reinforce that statement.

Fix Errors Read carefully through your essay and fix all errors in grammar, spelling, and punctuation that you find. Neatly cross out passages containing errors and write corrections above or in the margins.

In-Depth Lesson Plan

	LESSON FOCUS	PRINT AND MEDIA RESOURCES
DAY 1	**Introduction to Exposition: Problem-and-Solution Essay** Students learn key elements of problem-and-solution essays and analyze the Model From Literature. (pp. 218–223/H136–137)	*Writers at Work* **DVD**, Exposition *Writing and Grammar* **Interactive Text**, Ch. 11, Introduction
DAY 2	**Prewriting** Students choose and narrow a topic, consider their audience and purpose, and gather information. (pp. 224–227/H138–141)	*Writing and Grammar* **Interactive Text**, Section 11.2 **Teaching Resources** *Writing Support Transparencies,* 11-A–D; *Writing Support Activity Book,* 11-1–2; *Topic Bank for Heterogeneous Classes,* Ch. 11
DAY 3	**Drafting** Students organize their ideas and write their first drafts. (pp. 228–229/H142–143)	*Writing and Grammar* **Interactive Text**, Section 11.3 **Teaching Resources** *Writing Support Transparencies,* 11-E–G
DAY 4	**Revising** Students revise their drafts in terms of overall structure, paragraphs, sentences, and word choice. (pp. 230–234/H144–148)	*Writing and Grammar* **Interactive Text**, Section 11.4 **Teaching Resources** *Writing Support Transparencies,* 11-H–K
DAY 5	**Editing and Proofreading; Publishing and Presenting** Students check their work for accuracy and correctness and present their final drafts. (pp. 235–243/H149–153)	*Writing and Grammar* **Interactive Text**, Sections 11.5–6 **Teaching Resources** *Scoring Rubrics on Transparency,* Ch. 11; *Writing Assessment and Portfolio Management; Formal Assessment,* Ch. 11

Accelerated Lesson Plan

	LESSON FOCUS	PRINT AND MEDIA RESOURCES
DAY 1	**Introduction Through Drafting** Students review characteristics of problem-and-solution essays, select topics, and write drafts. (pp. 218–229/H136–143)	*Writers at Work* **DVD**, Exposition *Writing and Grammar* **Interactive Text**, Ch. 11, Introduction through Section 11.3 **Teaching Resources** *Writing Support Transparencies,* 11-A–G; *Writing Support Activity Book,* 11-1–2
DAY 2	**Revising Through Presenting** Students work individually or with peers to revise, edit, and proofread their work for presentation. (pp. 230–243/H144–153)	*Writing and Grammar* **Interactive Text**, Sections 11.4–6 **Teaching Resources** *Writing Support Transparencies,* 11-H–K; *Scoring Rubrics on Transparency,* Ch. 11; *Writing Assessment and Portfolio Management; Formal Assessment,* Ch. 11

Options for Adapting Lesson Plans

HOMEWORK

Have students complete any stage of the lesson for homework.

FEATURES

Extend coverage with the Connected Assignment (p. 240), Spotlight on the Humanities (p. 242), Media and Technology Skills (p. 243), and the Standardized Test Preparation Workshop (pp. 244–245).

TECHNOLOGY

Students can complete any stage of the lesson on the computer, using *Writing and Grammar* Interactive Text or a word-processing program. Have them print out their completed work.

Writing and Grammar Handbook Alignment

Page numbers in Step-by-Step Teaching Guides in this Teacher's Edition refer to pages from the full student text. Handbook page references, indicated with this icon Ⓗ, are provided in Time and Resource Manager boxes and at the bottom of each Teacher's Edition page.

INTEGRATED SKILLS COVERAGE

Integrating Grammar
Using Subject Complements, SE p. 232/Ⓗ146
Using Hyphens and Dashes, SE p. 235/Ⓗ149
Subject-Verb Agreement, ATE p. 231

Reading/Writing Connection
Evaluate the Writer's Statements, SE p. 220
Writing Application, SE p. 223

Vocabulary Skills
ATE p. 238

Viewing and Representing
Critical Viewing, SE pp. 218, 220, 221, 222, 223, 237, 239, 240, 242/Ⓗ136, 151, 153
Recognizing Inspirations for Art, SE p. 242
Using Technology to Find Answers, SE p. 243

Real-World Connection
ATE p. 219

Workplace Skills
ATE p. 226

ASSESSMENT SUPPORT

Standardized Test Preparation Workshop SE p. 244; ATE p. 234
Standardized Test Preparation Workbook, pp. 21–22
Scoring Rubrics on Transparency, Ch. 11
Formal Assessment, Ch. 11
Writing Assessment and Portfolio Management

MEETING INDIVIDUAL NEEDS

Less Advanced Students ATE pp. 222, 241, 245. See also Ongoing Assessments ATE pp. 225, 226.
AP Students ATE pp. 229, 245
ESL Students ATE pp. 221, 227
Gifted and Talented Students, ATE p. 223
Bodily/Kinesthetic Learners ATE p. 238
Logical/Mathematical Learners ATE pp. 222, 233
Spatial Learners ATE p. 228
Linguistic Learners ATE pp. 239, 241

BLOCK SCHEDULING

Pacing Suggestions
For 90-minute Blocks
• Have students complete the Prewriting and Drafting stages in a single period.
• Focus one class period on Revising and Editing and Publishing and Presenting. Allow at least 30 minutes for peer revision.

Resources for Varying Instruction
• *Writing and Grammar* **Interactive Text** A 90-minute block provides an ideal opportunity for students to work on the computer.
• *Writers at Work* **DVD** Show Exposition segment in class.

Professional Development Support
• *How to Manage Instruction in the Block* This teaching resource provides management and activity suggestions.

MEDIA AND TECHNOLOGY

For the Student
• *Writing and Grammar* **Interactive Text**, Ch. 11
• *On-line Exercise Bank,* Section 18.3

For the Teacher
• *Writers at Work* **DVD**, Exposition
• **Teacher**EXPRESS™ **CD-ROM**

WRITING AND GRAMMAR ON-LINE

Interactive Text (On-line or on CD-ROM)
• Easily navigable instruction with interactive Revision Checkers
• Full use of e-rater™, the essay-scoring system (on-line only)

Companion Web Site PHSchool.com
• Scoring rubrics with models (use Web Code egk-1201)

See the Go On-line! **feature, SE p. iii.**

LITERATURE CONNECTIONS

Related selections from *Prentice Hall Literature, Penguin Edition,* The British Tradition:
Professional Model "Wartime Speech," Winston Churchill, SE p. 221
Topic Bank Option "The Train from Rhodesia," Nadine Gordimer, SE p. 225/Ⓗ139

Lesson Objectives

1. To write a problem-and-solution essay appropriate to audience and purpose
2. To read to appreciate a writer's craft and to discover models to use in one's own writing
3. To evaluate the credibility of information sources, including how the writer's motivation may affect that credibility
4. To use prewriting strategies to generate ideas, develop voice, and plan
5. To develop and revise drafts in terms of structure, paragraphs, sentences, and word choice
6. To edit and proofread to ensure standard English usage and grammar
7. To evaluate how well writing achieves its purposes
8. To refine a problem-and-solution essay for publication

Critical Viewing

Analyze Problems include arranging numerous patches in an orderly and visually appealing pattern.

Chapter 11 *Exposition*
Problem-and-Solution Essay

His Grandmother's Quilt, 1998, Phoebe Beasley, Courtesy of the artist

▲ **Critical Viewing**
Quilting is a craft that involves skill as well as creativity. What sort of problems might you encounter while quilting? **[Analyze]**

Problems and Solutions in Everyday Life

Like most people, you probably face major and minor problems every day. You may, for instance, have limited time and too many obligations, or maybe your two closest friends are having a dispute. No matter what the problem is, it won't go away if you ignore it. As commentator Alan Saporta said, "The best way to escape a problem is to solve it."

Writing about problems can help you face difficult challenges and turn them into opportunities. In this chapter, you will learn how to analyze and discuss problem-and-solution topics.

⏱ TIME AND RESOURCE MANAGER

Resources
Technology: *Writers at Work* DVD, Exposition; *Writing and Grammar* Interactive Text, Ch. 11

Using the Full Student Edition	Using the Handbook🅗
• Read and discuss pp. 218–219 in class. • Read the Model From Literature in class, and use it to brainstorm for problem-and-solution ideas with students. • Discuss examples of problem-and-solution issues that affect your class or your school.	• Read and discuss pp. 136–137 in class. • Discuss examples of problem-and-solution issues that affect your class or your school.

What Is a Problem-and-Solution Essay?

Exposition is writing that explains or informs. A **problem-and-solution essay** is a piece of exposition that describes a problem and one or more likely solutions. An effective problem-and-solution essay

- clearly states a specific problem.
- identifies the most important aspects of the problem.
- presents one or more possible solutions.
- supports each solution with specific details and logical reasons.
- is logically and effectively organized.

To preview the criteria on which your problem-and-solution essay may be evaluated, see the Rubric for Self-Assessment on page 236.

Types of Problem-and-Solution Essays

Problem-and-solution essays may address a variety of issues, including the following:

- **Business issues**, which include problems facing a business, such as inventory control and increased competition.
- **Community issues,** which revolve around problems that directly affect the residents of and visitors to your community.
- **Consumer issues,** which address problems related to the operation of products or the quality of services rendered.

PREVIEW
Student Work
IN PROGRESS

Follow along as Gabrielle Frame, a student at Northeast High School in Omaha, Nebraska, writes a problem-and-solution essay about the fear that many students feel when faced with speaking in public. A final draft of her essay appears at the end of this chapter.

Writers in
ACTION

Inventor R. Buckminster Fuller once said: "When I'm working on a problem, I never think about beauty. I think only how to solve the problem. But when I have finished, if the solution is not beautiful, I know it is wrong."

PREPARE and ENGAGE

Interest GRABBER On the board, write a problem that is currently affecting your class or school. (Examples: anxieties about standardized tests, not enough computers, lack of variety in extra-curricular activity choices.) Challenge students to brainstorm for at least three solutions to one of the problems. Have students share and discuss their ideas.

Activate Prior Knowledge

Students have probably heard the proverb "Necessity is the mother of invention." Have students think of some recent inventions, and list them on the board. Then, have them identify the problem or problems that each invention solved. Do students agree with the proverb? Do they think that most useful ideas develop as solutions to some kind of problem or need?

More About the Speaker

R. Buckminster Fuller was an inventor, engineer, author, teacher, and architect who imagined creative solutions to various problems. He used science, technology, and his own imagination to benefit humanity. Some of his most widely-known discoveries include a unique mapping system for showing the earth's surface without size distortion, and the geodesic dome.

Real-World Connection

Almost every profession relies on people who are adept at identifying problems, considering solutions, and explaining ideas in an organized way. For example, an architect might have to determine the best materials and design for creating a sturdy structure in a location with a harsh climate. He then has to communicate these ideas clearly to many people: co-workers, clients, engineers, the construction crew, and more. Can students think of other professions that value problem-solving skills?

Reading\Writing Connection

Reading: Evaluate the Writer's Statements

Explain that readers must determine whether the writer presents statements of fact or statements of opinion. Ask students to check the author's details against other sources. If they can be proven, they are facts. However, a writer might include facts that support his or her point and omit those that do not. Students should be aware of the writer's motivation.

Step-by-Step Teaching Guide

Engage Students Through Literature

1. Invite students to discuss the text. You can use the following questions to prompt discussion.

   What problem affects Swain's garden? (It is being ravaged by birds and animals.)

   What are some of the unsuccessful ways he tries to address this problem? (squashing, drowning, clubbing)

   What is Swain's purpose in mentioning the unsuccessful solutions? (It shows that an easy way out is not possible; the successful solution, although time-consuming, is necessary.)

2. Ask students to brainstorm for problem-and-solution ideas suggested by the essay. Here are some possibilities.

   How to prevent gardening from getting too expensive

   How to fit gardening into a very full schedule

3. Students may add these ideas to their own topic banks. Point out that almost any topic that identifies and offers a solution to a common problem makes for an interesting and useful essay.

Critical Viewing

Draw Conclusions The fence might ward off animals that walk, such as woodchucks, deer, and rabbits, but not birds.

"Warding Off Wildlife" appears in The Practical Gardener *by Roger B. Swain. Swain is the science editor of* Horticulture *magazine, as well as the host of* The Victory Garden, *a popular gardening show on PBS.*

Reading Strategy: Evaluate the Writer's Statements Don't accept as fact everything a writer offers. As you read the following essay, evaluate the details and statements that are given as evidence. Then, decide whether each detail or statement has merit.

▲ **Critical Viewing** What sort of wildlife might the fence shown in this photograph ward off? **[Draw Conclusions]**

Warding Off Wildlife

Roger B. Swain

I am no hunter. It doesn't really matter how many legs are involved—two, four, six, eight. I don't even like to kill slugs, and they have no legs at all. . . . Not that I am unbloodied. I have done my share of squashing, drowning, poisoning, clubbing, and shooting. It was all, however, in self-defense. My garden was being attacked. Even pacifist vegetarians will reach for a rock when their own beans are at stake.

Because I don't have the temperament of a hunter, and because even if I did I doubt whether I could kill all the animals that have a taste for my fruits and vegetables, I put my effort into excluding the larger animals rather than exterminating them. This means finding ways to keep animals at a safe distance from my young lettuce and ripening grapes.

Woodchucks, rabbits, raccoons, porcupines, and assorted birds have all troubled my gardens at one time or another. These can all do a devastating amount of damage in a short time. For completeness I ought to add deer, but, though deer wreak havoc in some people's gardens, so far they haven't in any of mine.

The introduction reveals Swain's problem. Swain uses humor to capture the interest of his audience.

Here, Swain explains a problem—large animals invade his garden.

I have learned as have generations of gardeners before me, that as long as I am actually working in the garden, animals stay away. But if I am gone even a few minutes, let alone a whole night, they move in to feed. Stand-ins for myself, old-fashioned straw men, are notoriously ineffective. Scarcely better are the more modern scarecrows, those vinyl snakes or inflatable owls. All too quickly the enemy becomes habituated to their presence and recognizes these dummies for what they are.

The only practical way to ward off wildlife, I am now convinced, is to erect barriers: fences against the ones that walk, nets against those that fly. These barriers are put up each year before the animals begin to feed in the garden. A naïve woodchuck will be turned back by a wire fence; not so one that has tasted peas.

Over the years I have used different materials for fencing my main vegetable garden, but the one that I have settled on is 48-inch–high chicken wire with a 1-inch mesh. Historically, chicken wire was indestructible stuff. I have been trying to tear up some that has been outdoors for at least half a century, and it is hardly tarnished. But the current lot lasts scarcely five years before it disintegrates into rusty fragments. The falling quality has not, however, prevented a rise in price. Chicken wire now sells for roughly $25 per 50-foot length, or 50¢ a foot. My vegetables are valuable, but my garden is not Fort Knox. To keep the costs of fencing within bounds, I now dismantle the fence every fall, rolling the wire up and storing it under cover until spring. I am hoping that by exposing the wire to weather for only six months of every year it will last at least twice as long.

For fence posts I use 6-foot wooden stakes that are no thicker than a bean pole. Indeed, some of them are ex–bean poles that rotted off at ground level. Instead of trying to drive these slender posts into the ground with a mallet, I ram them into conical holes made by jamming a crowbar 18 inches into the soil and rotating it. I space these posts 8 feet apart, a generous distance that

For a variation of a problem-and-solution essay, see Winston Churchill's "Wartime Speech," in which he addresses the monumental problem of war in Europe. The speech is included in *Prentice Hall Literature, Penguin Edition,* The British Tradition.

These details clearly explain how to make a barrier fence to solve the problem of invading wildlife.

Within this paragraph is another problem-and-solution relationship: Because the posts were so slender, the author found an alternate method of putting them into the ground.

◄ **Critical Viewing**
What sorts of problems might a raccoon like the one pictured cause in a garden? **[Speculate]**

Model From Literature • 221

Teaching From the Model

Use this Model From Literature to introduce the elements of a problem-and-solution essay. The writer identifies a common problem — how to protect his garden from birds and animals who threaten it — and proposes a number of solutions. Have students point out the specific lines in the text that explain problems and suggest solutions.

Customize for
Less Advanced Students

Students might get bogged down in the details and lose track of which solutions were successful and which were not. As they read, have students keep a running list of each solution Swain tried. Next to each one, have them write a one-sentence description of it and tell whether or not it worked.

Customize for
Logical/Mathematical Learners

Swain's solutions are very cost-efficient. Have students research the cost of protecting a similar garden in their area. Have them talk to gardeners and to employees at gardening stores for alternative solutions. Then, have them determine the cost of each solution and compare it with the cost of Swain's plan.

Critical Viewing

Draw Conclusions Students might say the woodchuck looks cute and harmless in the photograph. Others might says he looks eager to cause mischief.

saves on the number of posts needed and guarantees a floppy fence. Animals, I have found, are more reluctant to climb a floppy fence than a taut one.

Once the posts are in, I unroll the fence, leaning it up against the posts. Originally I then bent the bottom foot of the wire at a 90-degree angle because this made a barrier much more difficult for animals to burrow under (because when they began tunneling at the edge of the fence they were stymied by the wire beneath them). This left me with a three-foot-high fence that required no gate, since it was low enough to step over. . . .

My fence does a good job of keeping woodchucks and rabbits and porcupines at bay. It does not, however, keep out raccoons. Raccoons are ordinarily not a problem in the vegetable garden— unless you are growing corn, whereupon they are guaranteed to show up the first night the corn is ripe and begin breaking down even the most robust stalks in pursuit of the sweet kernels.

Innumerable ploys for keeping raccoons away from corn have been tried. The only one that has worked for me is an electric fence, which I use in conjunction with the chicken wire. It need not be up until the corn is nearing maturity, but installing it earlier helps keep out other animals. I purchased a standard electric fence charger intended for livestock, one that runs off a house current, though battery-powered models exist. I then made a large number of 16-inch–long stakes, each topped with a porcelain or plastic insulator. These I drive in a row around the garden about a foot outside the chicken-wire fence. Their height and distance from one another are such that when I string electric-fence wire from insulator to insulator it is always 6 to 8 inches above the ground. The only difficulty with a wire this low is that the grass and weeds grow up and short-circuit the fence. But by using a string trimmer I keep the vegetation down with only a few minutes of attention a week.

The shock that the animal, or for that matter human, gets from an electric fence of this sort is painful but not dangerous. I find it works better to leave mine on all the time, and risk an occasional zap, than to turn it off when I am working in the garden and risk forgetting to turn it on. . . .

My two-ply fence—one woven, the other electrified— stops only those animals that walk. For those that fly, I turn to netting. My introduction to the virtues of netting came when in desperation I covered a bed of strawberries

At this point, the organization of the essay becomes clear: The author is introducing one related problem at a time and then discussing in detail its solution.

▼ **Critical Viewing** Judging from this photograph, would you expect woodchucks to be garden pests? Why or why not? [**Draw Conclusions**]

◄ **Critical Viewing**
What sort of barrier might be effective in keeping crows out of gardens? Explain. **[Speculate]**

with some salvaged fish netting picked up at a nearby seaport. Draped across the bed on low-lying poles, it cut my avian losses enormously. Since then I have purchased netting intended for the purpose, some of which is made of black polypropylene, some from white nylon. I now consider it indispensable in assuring a harvest of grapes, cherries, or blueberries.

Again, netting should be installed before the crop is ripe and birds have acquired a taste for the fruits. And there must be no gaps through which birds can pass. The larger the piece of netting, the less splicing and tying will be needed. Netting that is 14 feet wide is sufficient to drape over a 6-foot-high grape trellis. A medium-size cherry tree can use a piece that is 20 feet or more square. I've found that a long pole with a forked tip serves best to put such a big piece on and take it off a tree.

Netting is even more susceptible to the elements than chicken wire. Plastic, especially polypropylene, breaks down eventually from exposure to sunlight. So I am careful to roll up and store the netting indoors as soon as the crop of fruit has been picked.

All this may sound like a huge endeavor. In season my garden—the fruit trees wrapped in netting, the vegetables encircled by chicken wire and an electric fence—is reminiscent of a Christo project. But now that I know what I am doing the fences and nets go up and down in only a few hours. And the beauty of it is knowing that I am going to be the one who gets to enjoy what I am growing. Some days I can even relax enough to admire a woodchuck eating clover outside the fence.

 **Writing Application: Prepare Your Work for Evaluation** As you prepare to write your problem-and-solution essay, remember to support your statements, so that your readers will give them a positive evaluation.

Swain gives specific details that explain how to install netting, which helps solve the problem of birds invading the garden.

This paragraph introduces another related problem.

The concluding paragraph emphasizes the easiness and successfulness of the solutions.

Model From Literature • 223

Speculate According to Swain, netting is needed to keep winged creatures out of the garden. He purchases fish netting and drapes it over a bed of low-lying poles.

Customize for
Gifted and Talented Students

In the last paragraph, Swain compares his wrapped-up garden to a "Christo project." Challenge students to research Bulgarian artist Christo and bring in some photographs of his projects to share with the class. This will help them better understand Swain's metaphor.

Reading\Writing Connection

Writing Application: Prepare for Evaluation

Explain to students that a strong problem-and-solution essay must be balanced. In other words, it is not enough to identify and clearly explain a problem. The essay must also offer at least one plausible solution. If this proves too difficult, students should consider choosing a new topic.

Step-by-Step Teaching Guide

Prewriting: Scan a Newspaper

1. Have students choose a local or national story and track all of its newspaper coverage for a week. Encourage them to use critical thinking skills to determine whether the solutions posed in any of the articles are adequate.

2. For articles with inadequate solutions, encourage students to devise their own solution and write a problem-and-solution essay about it. They can use the articles they've read as models for various ways of organizing and presenting their material.

3. This assignment can be an opportunity to familiarize students with the elements of newspapers.

Step-by-Step Teaching Guide

Prewriting: Make a List

Teaching Resources: Writing Support Transparencies, 11-A; Writing Support Activity Book, 11-1

1. Display Transparency 11-A and discuss any topic ideas that are unclear. Allow students to add ideas to each category.

2. Students might have trouble working with the broad categories on the chart. If so, give them narrower categories such as these: problems in the education system, problems that affect our health, or problems in transportation. These focused topics will make it easier for students to come up with focused ideas.

3. Remind students that this is a brainstorming activity. In this phase, it is important to be free with ideas.

11.2 *Prewriting*

Choosing Your Topic

Your essay should address an important problem. Challenge yourself to select a topic that has a complex solution. Use the following strategies for help finding a topic:

Strategies for Generating Topics

1. **Scan a Newspaper** Newspapers can provide you with countless examples of issues and problems. For example, you might read about a conflict between a mayor and the school board. After investigating the situation, you might propose a fair compromise. Use a highlighter or self-sticking notes to mark possible articles as you flip through the newspaper. Then, choose the topic you like best for your essay.

2. **Work With a Peer** Work with a partner to find a topic for your problem-and-solution essay. Each of you should create a list of problems. Then, take turns reading each item on your list aloud to your partner. After each item is read, allow time for your partner to write down one or two possible solutions to each problem. Review your responses to find a topic.

3. **Make a List** Make a list to help you find and evaluate a wide variety of possible topics. Once your list is finished, choose the entry you find most promising as the topic for your problem-and-solution essay. Following is an example:

Individual	School	Country	World
• Not enough time to exercise • Too much information about colleges • High levels of stress reduce productivity	• Two student groups want to use the auditorium on the same day • Overenrollment in many school activities	• Crime • Political apathy • Crumbling infrastructure	• Endangered animals • Pollution • Ozone depletion • Oil spills • Unequal distribution of wealth

224 • Problem-and-Solution Essay

Try it out! To list possible topics, use the Essay Builder, accessible from the menu bar, on-line or on CD-ROM.

⏱ TIME AND RESOURCE MANAGER

Resources
Print: *Writing Support Transparencies*, 11-A–D; *Writing Support Activity Book*, 11-1–3
Technology: *Writing and Grammar* Interactive Text, Section 11.2

Using the Full Student Edition	Using the Handbook🄷
• Work through the strategies for generating topics. • Use the Responding to Fine Art transparency to generate additional topics. • Work through the strategies for narrowing topics.	• Work through the strategies for generating topics. • Use the Responding to Fine Art transparency to generate additional topics. • Work through the strategies for narrowing topics.

TOPIC BANK

If you are having difficulty finding a topic, choose one of the topics below:

1. **Essay About Overcoming an Obstacle** Many people face obstacles that restrict and complicate their lives. For example, a person may not have a car, yet need to drive to hold a job. Choose such a situation, and solve it in a problem-and-solution essay.

2. **Letter Resolving a Dispute** Identify a conflict that has occurred within your school or community. Analyze the situation, and determine the best solution to the dispute. Write a letter to both sides explaining why you think your solution is both fair and practical.

Responding to Fine Art

3. Consider how the workers in *Tunnel Workers* by William Low solve problems every day on the job. Write an essay in which you evaluate one problem that workers might face on the job: anything from a dangerous work environment to an unreasonable supervisor.

Tunnel Workers, William Low, Courtesy of the artist

Responding to Literature

4. Read "The Train from Rhodesia" by Nadine Gordimer, and use it as a springboard to consider the problem of conflict between different cultures. Write a problem-and-solution essay based on your reflections. You can find Gordimer's story in *Prentice Hall Literature, Penguin Edition*, The British Tradition.

⏱ Timed Writing Prompt

5. Young adults, aged eighteen to twenty-five, are often passionate about changing the world. Yet as a group, they are underrepresented as voters. In fact, voter turnout is lowest among eighteen-to-twenty-five year-olds. Write an essay on why turnout is so low among young people and propose two strategies that might solve this problem. **(40 minutes)**

Prewriting • 225

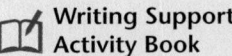

1. Display Transparency 11-C and discuss how the various topics and sub-topics are linked to the main topic. Point out that the topics get narrower as they move away from the web's center. Distribute copies of the blank organizer (11-2).

2. To help students generate their webs, you might invite prepared students to model a game of "free association." Start with a topic of strong interest and encourage the students to take turns listing all the relevant words or phrases that come to mind. Record their responses.

3. Give students an opportunity to pair up and play this game after they have seen it modeled. Have a third student work with each pair to record the responses and help them create their webs.

1. Have students identify their intended audience. Then, have them consider the audience's level of knowledge about the topic.

2. Have them brainstorm for a list of words or concepts the audience might not understand. As they write their essays, they should be sure to explain these ideas.

Integrating Workplace Skills

Point out that an employee can benefit his or her organization by writing a constructive suggestion memo. Many supervisors appreciate short letters that identify a problem and propose a solution. Such letters spur improvements in the workplace and show that a worker is dedicated to improving his or her environment.

Narrowing Your Topic

Many problems are too complex to be described and solved effectively in a single problem-and-solution essay. You may need to narrow your topic to focus on one aspect.

Create a Web

Make a web to help you narrow a topic. Write your broad topic in the center and specific topics in circles branching off from the center. Then, review the specific topics, and choose one as your narrowed topic.

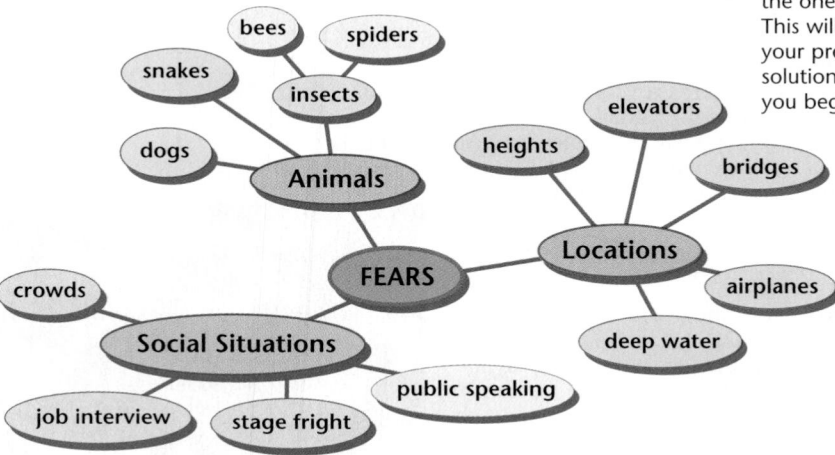

Considering Your Audience and Purpose

Your general purpose for writing a problem-and-solution essay is to share your ideas about how to solve a problem. The way that you share your ideas depends on your specific purpose and on the audience you are addressing.

Suit Details to Your Audience

Always consider your audience's level of familiarity with your topic, and choose details that are appropriate for that audience. For example, if you were writing for an audience of computer experts, you would not need to define computer terminology; but if you were writing for beginning computer students, you would have to explain computer terms in detail.

Timed Writing Hint
When writing under timed conditions, create a web such as the one on this page. This will help narrow your problem-and-solution essay before you begin to write.

226 • Problem-and-Solution Essay

Gathering Evidence

Once you have narrowed your topic, gather details about both the problem and the solution. The deeper you explore your problem, the more likely you are to come up with truly successful solutions. Begin your research and preparation by getting to know each important aspect of your problem.

Complete a T-Chart

Complete a T-chart to collect ideas for your essay. In the left column of the chart, list the problem or problems you will address in your essay. In the right column, list your solution or solutions. Refer to the details that you gather as you draft your problem-and-solution essay.

Writers in ACTION

Edwin Bliss is the author of self-help books. He has the following advice to give when dealing with problems and solutions:

"The precise statement of any problem is the most important step in its solution."

Student Work IN PROGRESS

Name: Gabrielle Frame
Northeast High School
Omaha, NE

Using a T-Chart to Gather Evidence

Gabrielle used a T-chart to gather ideas for her essay on overcoming a fear of public speaking.

Problem	Solution
Fear of public speaking is one of the most common fears	Use note cards (if they're allowed)
Nerves	Practice a lot
Fear of forgetting what you are going to say	Memorize the beginning and end
Classmates become very critical, even if they are your friends	Change your attitude

Prewriting: Complete a T-Chart

Teaching Resources: Writing Support Transparencies, 11-D; Writing Support Activity Book, 11-3

1. Begin this activity by discussing Transparency 11-D. Make sure students see that each of the problems on the left side of the chart has a corresponding solution.

2. Encourage students to identify the various problems presented by their topic. Following the model, have them write each problem on a separate line.

3. Then, have them brainstorm for solutions to each problem and write them down in the appropriate place in the chart. Students who are having trouble can form small groups and work together to discuss solutions.

Customize for
ESL Students

A T-chart provides English language learners with an opportunity to include visual symbols in addition to words. Allow them to sketch their solutions in addition to writing them. This can help them more quickly reference their ideas without having to search for the right words.

More About the Writer

Edwin Bliss is a motivational writer and is the author of *Getting Things Done: The ABCs of Time Management*. Bliss says of achieving success, "Yesterday is a cancelled check; forget it. Tomorrow is a promissory note; don't count on it. Today is ready cash; use it!"

Drafting: Choose an Appropriate Organization

Teaching Resources: Writing Support Transparencies, 11-E

1. Point out that writers may choose from a number of ways to organize the information in their essays. They should choose the method that best suits their topic.

2. Ask students to identify the method of organization used by the author of "Warding Off Wildlife." Students should notice that Swain presents a number of problems and offers a solution for each. Some of the solutions contain many steps, so he uses chronological organization to present each step.

3. Next, have students determine the most appropriate way to organize their own essays. Have them make an outline that follows the method they choose. If the information seems logical in outline form, it will probably be clear and logical in essay form as well.

Customize for
Spatial Learners

Recommend that students choose a problem-and-solution topic that lends itself to logical or spatial organization. Possible topics might include "How to Find Your Way in the Forest Without a Map" or "How to Find a Book Quickly in the Library."

11.3 *Drafting*

Shaping Your Writing

The most common organization for a problem-and-solution essay is suggested by the name itself. Most writers begin by describing the problem and then present one or more solutions. Begin your draft with a clear statement of the problem. Depending on your audience, you might decide to include background information or explanations about how the problem developed, as well as specific descriptions of each important aspect of the problem.

Choose an Appropriate Organization

When describing the solution, choose an organization that will most effectively present to readers the details you have gathered.

- If your solution has several steps, use **chronological order.** Describe all steps completely, in the logical order that they will be carried out, so that your audience will be able to follow your step-by-step description.

- If you are presenting more than one solution, place them in **order of importance.** Begin with the least effective solution, and build to the solution that you believe is most effective. This organization is particularly useful when you are trying to persuade readers that your solution is the best option.

Chronological Organization:

Waterproofing Basement
- A. Strip off old drywall
- B. Apply vapor barrier
- C. Cover with level-10 drywall
- D. Tape joints
- E. Use NoDamp paint

Order of Importance Organization:

Combatting Unemployment
- A. "Stay-in-school" incentives
- B. Adult education scholarships
- C. Tax breaks to businesses that provide training
- D. Create county jobs

⏱ TIME AND RESOURCE MANAGER

Resources
Print: *Writing Support Transparencies*, 11-E–G
Technology: *Writing and Grammar* Interactive Text, Section 11.3

Using the Full Student Edition	Using the Handbook🄷
• Using Transparency 11-E, work through the organization strategies with the class. • Read and discuss the five points of illumination. • Have students draft their essays in class.	• Using Transparency 11-E, work through the organization strategies with the class. • Read and discuss the five points of illumination. • Have students draft their essays in class.

Providing Elaboration
Use Points to Illuminate

As you write your first draft, elaborate on your major points by providing a variety of supporting details. One way to ensure that you use various types of elaboration is to use the Five Points of Illumination strategy as you draft.

Five Points of Illumination When you illuminate something, you reveal its features or qualities. Do the same as you draft your essay. To do so, create the following graphic, and keep it nearby as you draft your essay. As you write each paragraph, try to incorporate at least two different types of details.

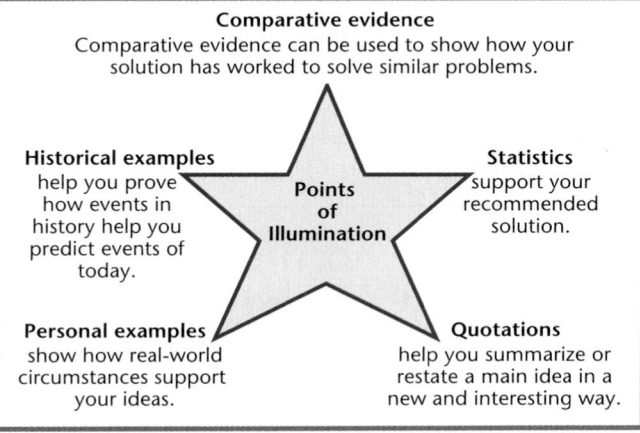

Comparative evidence
Comparative evidence can be used to show how your solution has worked to solve similar problems.

Historical examples help you prove how events in history help you predict events of today.

Points of Illumination

Statistics support your recommended solution.

Personal examples show how real-world circumstances support your ideas.

Quotations help you summarize or restate a main idea in a new and interesting way.

Student Work IN PROGRESS

Name: *Gabrielle Frame*
Northeast High School
Omaha, NE

Using Points to Illuminate
As she drafted her essay, Gabrielle used various kinds of examples to elaborate on her main points.

Class speeches in high school aren't greatly helping students once they reach the business world, either. A recent survey conducted by our local newspaper found that public speaking is the second-most common fear among adults. Only bugs and other creepy-crawly things provoke more anxiety.

> In this paragraph, Gabrielle cited the results of a survey to vary the type of details in her essay.

Drafting • 229

Step-by-Step Teaching Guide

Drafting: Using Points to Illuminate

Teaching Resources: Writing Support Transparencies, 11-F–G

1. Have students share examples of ways they plan to use anecdotes, comparative evidence, statistics, and quotes in their own essays. Help them get started with the following examples.

   Anecdotes: *Tell a brief story about a time someone faced the same kind of dilemma that you are writing about.*

   Comparative evidence: *Ask yourself these questions: Has this problem occurred in another place or time? Was it ever solved successfully? How did those people do it?*

   Statistics: *Use almanacs or census data. You can also find statistical data by looking up a topic on the Internet.*

   Quotations: *Look in your library or on the Internet for a dictionary of quotations such as* Bartlett's Book of Familiar Quotations.

2. Remind students that while these examples can lend authority to your paper, they need to be used thoughtfully and sparingly.

3. Invite students to find examples of problem-and-solution writing that employ these devices. Discuss whether or not each example is effective and why.

Customize for *AP Students*

Have students review a tape or transcript of a political debate between opposing candidates. Have them analyze and evaluate each candidate's use of anecdotes, comparative evidence, statistics, and quotations. What type of elaboration seems to be most persuasive?

Revising: Analyze the Balance of Information

Teaching Resources: Writing Support Transparencies, 11-H

1. Point out that there should be a balance between the detailed exploration of problems and solutions in an essay. Ask students why this is important. What would be ineffective about an essay in which problems received more attention than solutions? What would be wrong with an essay that offered detailed solutions but did not clearly explain the problem?

2. Display the unbalanced essay on Transparency 11-H. Discuss how the essay was revised. Can students think of other ways of adding balance to this essay?

3. You may want to have a supply of colored pencils or highlighters on hand so that students have access to multiple colors for this activity. As an alternative, you can instruct students to circle, underline, or double-underline passages they wish to distinguish from one another.

11.4 Revising

Revising Your Overall Structure
Analyze the Balance of Information

Your essay should present details that explain a problem, as well as details that describe one or more solutions to that problem. If your essay contains lots of details describing a problem and fewer details proposing a solution, fix the balance of details.

▶ **REVISION STRATEGY**
Color-Coding Details to Analyze Balance

Use a highlighter or colored pencil to call out details that relate to the problem you are addressing. If you are discussing more than one problem, use a highlighter or pencil of a different color for each. Use a highlighter or pencil of a different color to call out details that describe your solution or solutions. Then, review your draft. Add details where necessary to improve the balance of information you provide.

Fixing an Unbalanced Essay

The biggest problem related to air travel is getting to the plane. Airport access highways are always crowded, and it's virtually impossible to park in long-term parking, let alone in short-term parking. Once in the terminal, long lines at the baggage check-in torture passengers, as do long lines at the boarding gate.

When rows are called for boarding, everyone rushes to the gate, heedless of whether or not their row has been called. And carry-on bins are always filled with the excess baggage of thoughtless fellow travelers.

~~How do we solve this problem? Make available public transportation to the airport, make curbside check-in mandatory, and enforce one per customer limit on carry-on bags.~~

Make available better public transportation to the airport. Designate area hotels as bus stops, allowing travelers to take public transportation rather than driving rental cars to the airport. Give residents a book of coupons, encouraging them to ride the bus rather than driving to area airports. Make curbside check-in mandatory. When airline tickets are sent to customers, also send along a book of forms for baggage check-in for filling out. That way there will be no delays at curbside. Once at the gate, flight attendants should be made to enforce the one-bag-per-customer limit on carry-on bags. If necessary, security can be increased to deal with belligerent customers. However, once an airline commits to enforcing the rules, fewer and fewer customers will expect the rules to be broken in their favor.

⏱ TIME SAVERS!

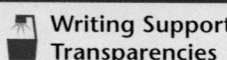 **Writing Support Transparencies**
Use the transparencies for Chapter 11 to facilitate teaching of strategies.

📖 **Writing Support Activity Book**
Use the graphic organizers for Chapter 11 to facilitate student planning.

⏱ TIME AND RESOURCE MANAGER

Resources
Print: *Writing Support Transparencies*, 11-H–K
Technology: *Writing and Grammar* Interactive Text, Section 11.4

Using the Full Student Edition	Using the Handbook Ⓗ
• Use Transparencies 11-H–K to discuss revising strategies. • Have students begin revising their essays in class.	• Use Transparencies 11-H–K to discuss revising strategies. • Have students begin revising their essays in class.

Revising Your Paragraphs

Each topical paragraph in your essay should focus on a single main idea. Functional paragraphs should perform a specific function, such as making a transition or emphasizing a point. In your problem-and-solution essay, many of your paragraphs will be topical. Consider the following strategies as you revise your topical paragraphs:

▶ **REVISION STRATEGY**
Adding, Strengthening, or Moving Topic Sentences

- **Add a topic sentence.** If you find a topical paragraph without a topic sentence, read it carefully. If the point of the paragraph is vague, add a topic sentence to make its meaning clear.

- **Use a subject complement in your topic sentence.** Use a short defining statement as a topic sentence. The following statements, each containing a subject complement, make a strong, clear point: *Teamwork is essential. The only viable solution is recycling.*

- **Change the positions of some topic sentences.** For variety and impact, change the positions of some topic sentences. Although many paragraphs begin with topic sentences, others build to a powerful close by saving the topic sentence for the last statement.

⏱ Timed Writing Hint

When revising a problem-and-solution essay under a deadline, check for vivid topic sentences and topical paragraphs.

Student Work
IN PROGRESS

Name: *Gabrielle Frame*
Northeast High School
Omaha, NE

Adding a Topic Sentence

Gabrielle added a short, emphatic topic sentence to strengthen this paragraph. She also deleted a sentence that was not related to the paragraph's main idea.

Anyone who has ever stood in front of a class and felt numb or panicky has probably had the same thought: "Why didn't I practice more?" The more familiar you are with your material, the more comfortable you'll be when the dreaded hour strikes. ~~Remember to wear something comfortable.~~ Practice in the morning before you go to school. Practice on the bus. Practice in front of the mirror before you go to bed. Keep at it until you feel as if you are speaking in your sleep. Practice is the most effective fear-buster.

Revising: Revising Your Paragraphs

Teaching Resources: Writing Support Transparencies, 11-I

1. Make sure students understand that the purpose of a topic sentence is to state the main idea in a paragraph. While introductory statements are clear places to put topic sentences, they should not lead off every paragraph. Ask students to explain why. (It would make the writing seem stilted and predictable.)

2. Ask students why a subject complement can be effective in a topic sentence. (It is short, clear, and demands attention. It is not wishy-washy or vague.)

3. Point out the Student Work in Progress on page 231 or display Transparency 11-I. Help students see how Gabrielle added a short, emphatic topic sentence to strengthen the end of her paragraph. Discuss why short, emphatic sentences are powerful.

Integrating Grammar Skills

Subject-Verb Agreement Point out that when writing about problems, it is common for the subject of the sentence to be an abstract idea rather than a simple noun. For this reason, it is important for writers to identify the subject and use verbs that match it in number. (Example: "The rising cost of medicines affects senior citizens the most." Note that in this sentence, the subject is *cost*, not *medicines*. The complete subject is *the rising cost of medicines*. It is a singular subject.) Challenge students to review their drafts for subject-verb agreement.

Subject Complements

1. Remind students that linking verbs are useful for connecting subjects with important descriptive information. For example, the linking verbs *is* and *seems* function as equal signs in a sentence.

2. Provide students with examples of newspaper editorials. Have them underline subject complements and draw a line between them and the linking verbs. Challenge students to define each type of subject complement as either predicate nominative or predicate adjective.

3. Point out that this kind of grammatical construction allows writers to identify and expand on the information in their essays.

Find It in Your Reading

Sample answers:
Predicate nominatives: *I am no hunter; chicken wire was indestructible stuff; my garden is not Fort Knox*

Predicate adjectives: *I am unbloodied; I am gone; stand-ins . . . are ineffective*

Find It in Your Writing

Encourage students to use linking verbs such as *appear*, *seem*, and *sound*. Remind them that including predicate nominatives or adjectives helps readers look at things in new ways.

11.4

Grammar in Your Writing
Subject Complements

A **subject complement** is a noun, pronoun, or adjective that appears with a linking verb and tells something about the subject of the sentence. A **linking verb** is a verb that connects a word at or near the beginning of a sentence with a word at or near the end. Common linking verbs are *be, appear, seem, sound, feel, grow,* and *look*.

There are two kinds of subject complements: predicate nominatives and predicate adjectives. A **predicate nominative** is a noun or pronoun that appears with a linking verb and renames, identifies, or explains the subject of the sentence.

The essay in the morning newspaper is an *editorial*.

The best person for the job is *you*.

A **predicate adjective** is an adjective that appears with a linking verb and describes the subject of the sentence.

The problem is *complex*.

The solution to our predicament seems *obvious* to me.

Find It in Your Reading "Warding Off Wildlife" by Roger B. Swain appears on pages 220–223. Read through the essay, and find three predicate nominatives and three predicate adjectives. Explain how they help Swain communicate with the reader.

Find It in Your Writing Look for linking verbs in your draft, and identify whether they connect subjects to predicate nominatives or to predicate adjectives. If your essay is lacking in predicate nouns or predicate adjectives, consider rewriting some sentences to include linking verbs and subject complements.

To learn more about subject complements, see Chapter 18.

☑ ONGOING ASSESSMENT SYSTEM: Prerequisite Skills

If students have difficulty with subject complements, you may find it helpful to review the following materials to ensure coverage of prerequisite knowledge.

In the Textbook	Print Resources	Technology
Subjects and Predicates, Section 18.1	*Grammar Exercise Workbook,* pp. 29–32	*On-Line Exercise Bank,* Section 18.3

Revising Your Sentences

Sentences are an important part of an essay. Review each sentence in your draft to be sure that it contains a subject and verb. If a sentence lacks either a subject or verb, it is a fragment and should be rewritten.

Vary Sentence Lengths

Edit your draft to include sentences of various lengths. A series of short sentences can sound choppy and un-connected. A series of long sentences can be tiring to read. Use the following strategy to help you analyze sentence lengths within your draft.

▶ REVISION STRATEGY
Underlining to Code Sentence Length

Read through your draft, and underline in one color sentences containing fewer than six words. Underline in another color sentences that contain six or more words. Then, review the markings in your draft. If most of your sentences are underlined in the same color, rewrite some of them to add variety to your essay.

For example, to add sophistication, combine some short sentences into longer, complex ones; to add clarity, break some long sentences into shorter, simpler sentences.

Student Work
IN PROGRESS

Name: *Gabrielle Frame*
Northeast High School
Omaha, NE

Underlining to Code Sentence Length

When she used the underlining strategy, Gabrielle discovered that she almost always wrote long sentences. She edited her draft to include a greater variety of sentence lengths.

Of course, once you stand in front of the class, all your preparation can fly right out the window. Utter terror can leave even the best prepared student with a blank mind, a dry mouth, and a roomful of staring eyes. The only way to combat this is to stay calm and concentrate on your breathing. A brain with oxygen is a happy brain, so use calm breathing to make remembering easier and to keep you from passing out, which is not a good thing.

Revising • 233

Revising: Vary Sentence Lengths

Teaching Resources: Writing Support Transparencies, 11-J

1. Read students a brief example of prose with short, choppy sentences and then a second with long, convoluted sentences. Ask them why each piece might be difficult for a reader to follow. (The choppy prose makes it difficult to make connections between ideas. The extended sentences can be tiring to follow.)

2. Display Transparency 11-J. Discuss how Gabrielle underlined long sentences and then edited them to vary their length. Discuss how short sentences improve her writing.

3. Brainstorm for a list of ways to lengthen short sentences and shorten long sentences. Ideas include the following: use commas and conjunctions to combine sentences; insert clauses into simple sentences; add a short and emphatic sentence between two long ones; delete unnecessary phrases.

Customize for
Logical/Mathematical Learners

Encourage students to calculate the average number of words in a sentence in their essays by adding up the total number of words in two paragraphs and then dividing by the number of sentences in those paragraphs. You may also want to have them compare the number of words in each sentence to the length of the "average" sentence they calculated.

Step-by-Step Teaching Guide

Revising: Eliminating Redundancies

Teaching Resources: Writing Support Transparencies, 11-K

1. Explain that editors try to cut unnecessary words from newspaper stories. Discuss with students why this is important in newspapers and in other kinds of writing. Ask students how they feel when they read a book or article with unnecessary words or repetition.

2. Display and discuss Transparency 11-K. Ask students to identify the types of words that were removed during the edit (extra adverbs and prepositional phrases). Make sure students understand why these particular words are redundant. Can they think of other examples of common redundancies?

3. As students look over their drafts, make a list on the board of the redundant phrases they found. Invite volunteers to revise some of these phrases by eliminating words or re-phrasing.

Step-by-Step Teaching Guide

Revising: Peer Review

1. Explain why it is helpful to give each partner a different focus. (It is easier to read closely when there is less to read.)

2. Remind students of the importance of active listening and appropriate feedback.

3. Encourage the writer to jot down notes from the peer review to use during revision. Remind students that writers are not required to use the feedback they receive. Have them weigh it carefully and then decide whether it is valuable.

Revising Your Word Choice

Read your draft, and examine your choice of words. Replace imprecise words with more precise ones, and double-check to be sure you've used unfamiliar words correctly. Be on the lookout for redundancies, and delete them when they occur.

▶ **REVISION STRATEGY**
Eliminating Redundancies

Redundancy is the unnecessary repetition of an idea. To identify a redundancy, look for a passage in your essay that seems wordy or weak. Within that passage, look for repeated words that take away from the impact or meaning of your statement. Eliminate the redundant words and phrases.

Example	Revised Sentence
You can solve the problem *alone by yourself*.	You can solve the problem by yourself.
The flag is a brilliant *red in color*.	The flag is a brilliant red.

Some Common Redundancies

free gift; past history; completely finished; surrounded on all sides; various different; usual custom; first begins; referred back; reflected back; repeated again; advanced forward; speak out loud; unknown stranger

Peer Review

Use "Double Vision"

Ask two partners to read and review your problem-and-solution essay. Give each partner a specific focus. You might try one of these divisions of responsibility:

- **Problem and Solution** One partner evaluates your description of the problem; the other evaluates your presentation of the solution.

- **Clarity and Style** One partner assesses the clarity of what you say; the other considers the effectiveness of the way you say it.

- **Overview and Details** One partner looks at your overall structure; the other inspects the details you present.

234 • Problem-and-Solution Essay

Interactive Textbook

Get instant help! For assistance in identifying repeated words in your essay, use the Revision Checker for Language Variety, accessible from the menu bar, on-line or on CD-ROM.

✎ STANDARDIZED TEST PREPARATION WORKSHOP

Analogies Standardized test questions may require students to answer analogy questions. Provide students with opportunities to practice this skill.

Which response most closely reflects the relationship between the words below?

PAINTER : ARTIST

A fire : firefighter   **C** teacher : student

B poet : writer   **D** athlete : quarterback

Students should recognize that **B** is the right answer. A painter is a type of artist, just as a poet is a type of writer. Answer D is incorrect because the relationship is the same but the words are in reverse order. A and C are incorrect because the relationship is not the same.

11.5 Editing and Proofreading

Carefully read your essay to make sure it is free from errors in grammar, spelling, and punctuation.

Focusing on Punctuation

Proofreading is an important part of the writing process. When you proofread your problem-and-solution essay, check especially to see whether you have used punctuation marks correctly. If you have used hyphens and dashes, check the rules for usage to make sure that you have used them correctly.

Grammar in Your Writing
Using Hyphens and Dashes

Although they look similar, **hyphens** and **dashes** are used for different purposes. Below are some of the most common uses for these punctuation marks:

Use a **dash** to indicate an abrupt change of thought, a dramatic interrupting idea, or a summary statement.

| Examples: | The problem is challenging—no, it's impossible! |
| | The mayor's speech—did you hear it?—was impressive. |

Use a **hyphen** to connect a compound modifier that comes before a noun.

Examples:	well-prepared student
	grayish-blue sky
	all-night diner

Use a **hyphen** in words with the prefixes *all-*, *ex-*, and *self-*.

Examples:	all-powerful
	ex-mayor
	self-addressed

Find It in Your Reading Find two dashes and two hyphens in "Warding Off Wildlife" on pages 220–223. Explain why each punctuation mark is used.

Find It in Your Writing As you proofread, check your usage of dashes and hyphens, and correct any errors.

To learn more about dashes and hyphens, see Chapter 27.

Editing and Proofreading • **235**

⏱ TIME AND RESOURCE MANAGER

Resources
Print: *Scoring Rubrics on Transparency,* Ch. 11; *Writing Assessment and Portfolio Management; Formal Assessment, Ch. 11*
Technology: *Writing and Grammar* Interactive Text, Section 11.5

Using the Full Student Edition	Using the Handbook⊞
• Read and discuss pp. 235–236 in class. Have students edit their essays.	• Read and discuss pp. 149–150 in class. Have students edit their essays.
• Read and analyze the Final Draft.	• Read and analyze the Final Draft.
• Have students analyze their own work using the rubric on p. 236.	• Have students analyze their own work using the rubric on p.150.

Step-by-Step Teaching Guide

Editing and Proofreading

1. Point out that professional proofreaders and editors read a text several times, concentrating on different kinds of errors each time.

2. Challenge students to make a list of possible errors, such as grammatical, spelling, or punctuation. Have them read their work several times, looking for a different kind of error each time.

Step-by-Step Teaching Guide

Using Hyphens and Dashes

1. Make sure students understand the difference between a dash and a hyphen. Also, show them how to make both marks on a computer keyboard.

2. Write the following sentences on the board. Ask students to supply dashes or hyphens as necessary.

   That summer was hot it was the hottest one on record.

   The month long vacation was a blast!

   (Place a dash between *hot* and *it*; place a hyphen between *month* and *long*.)

3. Have students make sure they used dashes and hyphens correctly in their essays. Remind them that one way to combine short, choppy sentences is to use a dash.

Find It in Your Reading

Sample answers:

Hyphens: *1-inch mesh; 50-foot length*

Dashes: *involved—two, four, six, eight; vegetable garden—unless you are growing corn*

Find It in Your Writing

Have students exchange papers with partners and double-check one another's use of hyphens and dashes.

Publishing and Presenting

1. Provide examples of cover letters that students can use as models when they submit their essays.

2. Point out that these letters are important tools in persuading a publication to accept a piece of writing. Discuss the ways that a cover letter can reflect a writer's qualifications and professionalism. Remind students to edit and proofread their cover letters just as they did their essays.

3. Encourage students to work with as many other students as possible. Presenting their ideas to a variety of people will provide writers with a wealth of feedback and opinions.

ASSESS AND CLOSE

Assessment

Teaching Resources: Scoring Rubrics on Transparency, Ch. 11; Writing Assessment and Portfolio Management; Formal Assessment, Ch. 11

1. Display the Scoring Rubric transparency and review the criteria in class.

2. Before students proceed with self-assessment, you may wish to review the Final Draft of the Student Work in Progress on pages 237–239.

3. In addition to student self-assessment, you may wish to use the following options:

   • score student essays yourself, using the rubric and scoring models in *Writing Assessment and Portfolio Management*.

   • review the Standardized Test Preparation Workshop on pages 244–245 and administer a timed writing assignment.

   • administer the Chapter 11 assessment in *Formal Assessment* to measure students' grasp of concepts presented.

11.6 Publishing and Presenting

Share your problem-and-solution essay with an audience to provide a meaningful conclusion to your writing process.

Building Your Portfolio

1. **Local Publication** If your essay addresses a vital contemporary problem, submit it to a local newspaper or student magazine. In your cover letter, you might suggest that the publication could use the essay on an editorial page.

2. **Discussion** Read your essay to students, teachers, and community members who are concerned about your topic. Your essay can be the launching point for an in-depth discussion about the problem and potential solutions.

Reflecting on Your Writing

Pause to reflect on your writing experience. Then, answer the following questions, recording your responses in your portfolio:

• Which strategy did you try for the first time, and how successful was it?

• What discoveries did you make during the revision process that strengthened your writing?

Internet Tip

To see a problem-and-solution essay scored according to this rubric, go on-line: PHSchool.com
Enter Web Code: egk-1201

Rubric for Self-Assessment

Use the following criteria to evaluate your problem-and-solution essay:

	Score 4	Score 3	Score 2	Score 1
Audience and Purpose	Contains language and details to engage audience and accomplish purpose	Contains language and details appropriate for audience and that help contribute to overall effect	Contains some language and details not suited for audience; contains some details that detract from purpose	Contains language and details that are not geared for a particular audience; has an unclear purpose
Organization	Is organized consistently, logically, and effectively	Has consistent organization	Has inconsistent organization	Is disorganized and confusing
Elaboration	Has a solution that is clearly laid out, along with details that support or explain it	Has a solution that is supported with details	Has a stated solution, but it contains few details to support it	Has unclear solution, and no details are given to support it
Use of Language	Contains precise words and no redundancies; contains no errors in grammar, punctuation, or spelling	Contains effective words and few redundancies; contains few errors in grammar, punctuation, and spelling	Contains few precise words and some redundancies; contains some errors in grammar, punctuation, and spelling	Contains imprecise words and many redundancies; contains many errors in grammar, punctuation, and spelling

236 • Problem-and-Solution Essay

☑ ONGOING ASSESSMENT: Assess Mastery

Use one of the following options to assess students' problem-and-solution essays.

Self-Assessment Ask students to score their essays using the rubric provided. Then, have students write a paragraph that discusses the strategy they found most helpful in composing their essays.

Teacher Assessment Use the rubric and the scoring models provided in *Writing Assessment and Portfolio Management* to score students' work.

11.7 Student Work IN PROGRESS

FINAL DRAFT

◀ **Critical Viewing**
How well does the student pictured seem to be handling the pressure of public speaking? Explain. **[Analyze]**

Fear of the Speech

Gabrielle Frame
Northeast High School
Omaha, Nebraska

Gabrielle's introduction humorously reveals the topic of her problem-and-solution essay.

High school can be a scary place. Deadlines loom like stone sentinels in the future. Previous grades and papers haunt the past. Besides academic anxieties, social scares also abound. Above all of these, there is one event that can strike terror into even the most confident student's heart; something that can make the prom queen's knees shake and the valedictorian's hair stand on end. This dreaded occurrence is, yes, a speech in English class.

In theory, classes in public speaking provide an excellent opportunity to become accustomed to speaking in front of people before having to conduct presentations in the business world. After all, one gets to speak in a familiar classroom environment in

Final Draft

1. Help students see that "Fear of the Speech" incorporates key elements of the problem-and-solution essay. It clearly states a specific, real-life problem (anxiety about public speaking); it identifies the most important aspects of the problem; and it presents possible solutions for each.

2. Point out that the essay makes use of varied, emphatic topic sentences throughout. Ask students to discuss why this holds their attention. (Sentence variety keeps the text from becoming monotonous while reading.)

3. Ask students what aspects of the essay were most interesting to them. How did the writer hold their attention? What changes would they suggest? How could they apply these suggestions to their own work?

Critical Viewing

Analyze The student looks comfortable. She makes eye contact with her audience and does not depend on her notes. Her manner seems almost conversational.

Integrating Vocabulary Skills

The word *lectern*, like *lecture*, comes from the Latin word *lectus*, a form of the word *legere*, which means "to read or to gather [information]." A lectern is a reading desk. These desks were used in churches to hold Bibles or prayer books that were read to congregations. Eventually, they were used outside of churches, in schools and public places where speakers needed a place to put their notes or written speeches as they addressed an audience.

Customize for
Bodily/Kinesthetic Learners

Challenge students to identify the main problems and solutions that Gabrielle addresses. Then, have them form small groups and perform a short skit illustrating one of the problem-and-solution relationships in the essay.

Teaching From the Final Draft

The second paragraph on this page introduces Gabrielle's three solutions to the problem of public speaking. She writes that "preparation, a strong will, and some relaxed breathing can help you keep your fear from getting the best of you." Have students stop reading and predict what Gabrielle means by "preparation" and "a strong will." What specific actions will she recommend? How exactly should one prepare for a speech? Encourage students to compare their ideas to Gabrielle's when they continue reading the essay.

front of friends, right? Wrong. First of all, sitting at a desk is completely different from standing in front of the room looking at everyone with everyone looking back. Second, those sweet best friends, no matter how close they are, will enjoy teasing and heckling a poor stuttering classmate all too much. It's all in good fun, but the teasee often doesn't realize the teaser is teasing until his or her feelings are already hurt.

Class speeches in high school aren't greatly helping students once they reach the business world, either. A recent survey conducted by our local newspaper found that public speaking is the second-most common fear among adults. Only bugs and other creepy-crawly things provoke more anxiety.

So, what can be done? Is there anything that can keep a normal, talkative student from becoming absolutely speechless once she steps up to the lectern? You may not be able to completely overcome your fear, but preparation, a strong will, and some relaxed breathing can help you keep your fear from getting the best of you.

Fear of forgetting is a major cause of anxiety for almost all speakers. There are a few things you can do beforehand to make remembering the speech easier. If note cards are allowed, write down key points and statistics, and keep it short. Too much detailed information on the note cards will just get in the way when you are delivering your speech. If the speech must be completely memorized, your best bet is to memorize the opening and closing statements and have a good idea of what you need to say in between. It is almost impossible to try to memorize a speech word for word, and it is better to have a solid, logical outline that can easily be modified on the spot.

Anyone who has ever stood in front of a class and felt numb or panicky has probably had the same thought: "Why didn't I practice more?" The more familiar you are with your material, the more comfortable you'll be when the dreaded hour strikes. Practice in the morning before you go to school. Practice on the bus. Practice in front of the mirror before you go to bed. Keep at it until you feel as if you are speaking in your sleep. Practice is the most effective fear-buster.

Gabrielle provides a description of the various aspects of the problem.

The organization of the essay becomes clear at this point. The essay first discussed aspects of the problem; from this point on, it will address solutions to the problem.

Each aspect of the solution is described in a separate paragraph.

Of course, once you stand in front of the class, all your preparation can fly right out the window. Utter terror can leave even the best-prepared student with a blank mind, a dry mouth, and a roomful of staring eyes. The only way to combat this is to stay calm. Concentrate on your breathing. Calm breathing can make remembering easier and keep you from passing out, which is not a good thing. However, don't overdo it—hyperventilating won't help. Take a few deep breaths before starting the speech, and try to concentrate on speaking slowly and clearly. Do not drink massive doses of soda beforehand. Not only will this energy overload make you nervous and excitable, but the sugar can coat the back of your throat and vocal cords, making it difficult to speak clearly.

Sometimes, a simple psychological placebo can make the difference between a stuttering utterance and a stunning speech. Wearing a "lucky" shirt or necklace or performing a prespeech mental ritual can soothe your nerves. If props or visual aids are allowed, by all means use them. Props give your hands something to do and help shift the audience's gaze away from your face.

There are a few gifted people who have no problems getting up in front of crowds and talking until the cows come home. For the rest of us, learning to speak comfortably in class is an inevitable challenge that we have to face and conquer. Like parachuting out of an airplane, you may not feel truly relieved until it's over, but after one or two jumps, you might even begin to enjoy the journey.

Humor adds to the friendly and supportive tone of the essay.

A brief conclusion summarizes the essay's overall message.

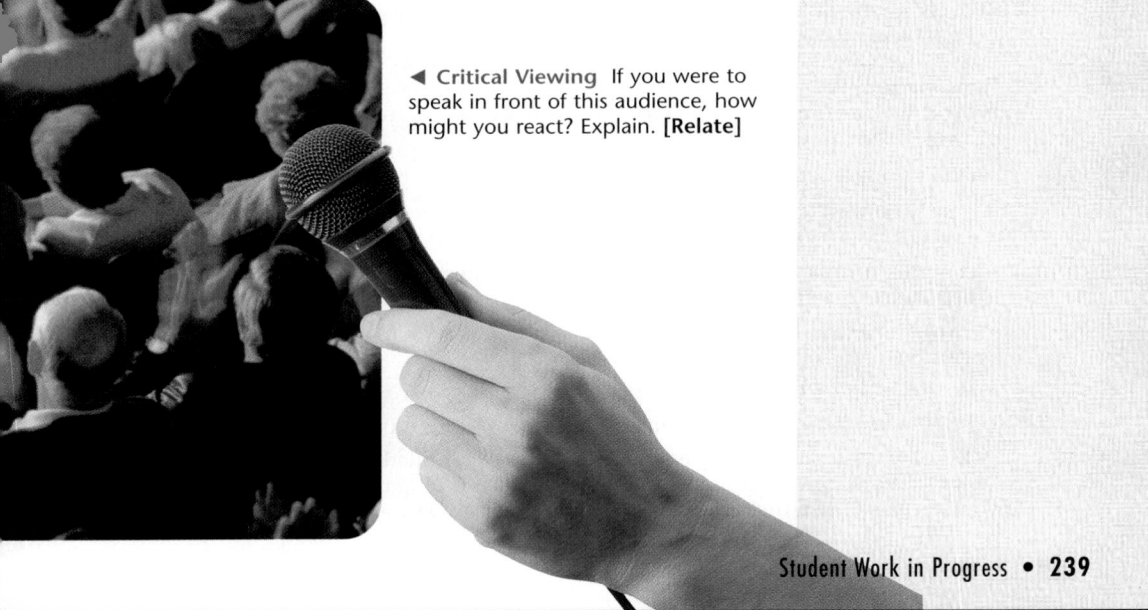

◄ Critical Viewing If you were to speak in front of this audience, how might you react? Explain. **[Relate]**

1. To write a proposal appropriate to audience and purpose
2. To employ precise language to communicate ideas clearly and concisely
3. To organize ideas in writing to ensure coherence, logical progression, and support for ideas

Step-by-Step Teaching Guide

Proposal

1. Ask students why it is important to clearly define the problem. (The audience must be convinced that the problem exists before they will agree to support any type of solution.)

2. Ask students why it is important to correct all mistakes in grammar, spelling, and punctuation. (People often associate careless and sloppy writing with careless and sloppy thinking.)

3. If students have trouble thinking of a problem to write about, have the class brainstorm for a list of problems currently affecting your school or town.

4. Encourage students to present their proposals to the class. Some proposals may be suitable for presenting or mailing to the targeted individual or organization.

Critical Viewing

Relate The speaker is prepared and appears able to answer questions. The group is attentive; it is likely that they will accept the proposal.

Connected Assignment
Proposal

Suppose that you want to suggest some ways to solve a problem shared by yourself and others in a group. A **proposal**—which presents a plan of action for acceptance—is the writing tool you need. In a proposal, you explain the plan in detail and provide specifics on how the plan will solve the problem or meet the identified need. You should also discuss requirements such as human effort, financial contributions, or supplies you'll need to put the plan into action. Proposals sometimes take the form of business letters, memos, or even letters to the editor.

An effective proposal

• clearly defines the problem and the solution or solutions to rectify the problem.

• contains details that appeal to the writer's audience and help achieve a specific purpose.

• provides details that support and explain the writer's main idea.

• is clearly and effectively organized.

• is free from mistakes in grammar, spelling, and punctuation.

Develop a proposal to solve a problem you've identified. Write it in a format that fits your audience. As you prepare your proposal, use the writing process stages to guide you.

▲ **Critical Viewing**
Do you think this group is likely to accept the speaker's proposal? Why do you think as you do? **[Relate]**

240 • Problem-and-Solution Essay

Prewriting

Choosing Your Topic To come up with a topic for a proposal, jot down ideas you have about improving your school, neighborhood, or town. Review what you have written, and choose as a topic the idea that interests you most.

Considering Your Audience and Purpose Defining your audience is critical when writing a proposal. Choose a business-letter format if you are writing to a local business or organization with whom you have had no previous experience. Write a memo to your employer, school, or neighborhood. Then, decide on the details you must emphasize to gain the audience's interest and support.

Gathering Details Once you have a topic for your proposal, gather details that show why your ideas are good ones. For example, gather statistics that prove that there is a problem that needs solving. Then outline, step by step, your proposed solution to the problem—your proposal. You may want to use index cards like the one at right on which to gather and organize details.

> Proposal: Support Volunteerism
>
> 1. Post a sign-up sheet
> 2. Give training
> 3. Prepare a phone list

Drafting As you draft, outline the steps of your proposal in a logical and effective way. For example, if your proposal consists of three stages, present them in the order in which they must occur. Also, make connections as you draft to ensure that your audience will be able to follow your ideas and understand what you are proposing.

Revising and Editing Review your proposal carefully to be sure that it makes sense. Add details where your argument seems thin, and remove details if they are unnecessary. Next, examine your proposal's overall organization. Move chunks of text and details, where necessary, to create a consistent structure. Finally, add transitions to link your ideas and to help the flow of your sentences.

Publishing and Presenting Proofread your proposal carefully, and correct all errors in grammar, spelling, and punctuation. Also, check to be sure that you have consistently and correctly formatted your proposal. Share your completed proposal with interested peers and family members.

Customize for
Less Advanced Students

If possible, bring examples of proposals for students to use as models. Examples of proposals you might find are teachers' proposals for new school policies, students' proposals for funding for a new club, and so on.

Customize for
Linguistic Learners

If their proposals relate to problems in the school, arrange for students to present their proposals orally to the principal, the board of education, a parent group, or another organization that has discretion over the issue.

Lesson Objectives

1. To analyze relationships, ideas, and cultures as represented in various media

2. To investigate the source of a media presentation such as who made it and why it was made

3. To write in a variety of forms

Step-by-Step Teaching Guide

Recognizing Inspirations for Art

1. Choose one of the Spotlight elements for class discussion, or have students work individually or in pairs to research the element of their choice.

2. Interested students might rent the video of *A Room with a View* and discuss their opinions of it.

3. Students researching Forster's works will note that several of his novels, such as *A Passage to India* and *Howard's End*, have been made into films.

4. Students interested in Florence or the Uffizi should limit their research, perhaps to the architecture of one or two famous buildings or to one of the many famous painters whose work is displayed in the Uffizi.

5. Students might work in pairs to complete the problem-and-solution writing activity, with one student writing the questions and the other providing the answers. They can then reverse roles.

Viewing and Representing

Activity Allow class time for volunteers to present their advice columns. Some students may wish to role-play the situations described in their columns.

Critical Viewing

Infer Students might suggest that the clothing and furniture indicate a setting from the past. The character appears pensive.

Recognizing Inspirations for Art

Focus on Film: *A Room With a View*

Just as a problem-and-solution essay focuses on solving a problem, many films are based on a characters' problems and conflicts that require resolution. Released in 1986 and a winner of three Academy Awards, the Merchant-Ivory film *A Room With a View* is a beautifully photographed story of a Victorian girl, Lucy Honeychurch, who must decide whether to follow through with her marriage to her stoic fiancé or follow her heart and her growing attraction to a young man she met on a trip to Florence, Italy. Filmed in England and Florence, the period film is based upon the 1908 novel by British author E. M. Forster (1879–1970).

Literature Connection E. M. Forster's *A Room With a View* was inspired by Forster's first trip to Italy, during the winter of 1901–1902. Over the course of the trip, Forster sketched out ideas for the novel. The novel, however, took several years to finish, and it was finally published in 1908. Although Forster was not entirely satisfied with *A Room With a View*, most critics of the time responded positively to the story.

Art Connection In E. M. Forster's *A Room With a View*, the main character, Lucy Honeychurch, falls under the spell of Florence, Italy, an ancient and beautiful city in Tuscany. One of the main attractions of Florence is the Uffizi, which houses one of the world's largest and most impressive art collections. Masterpieces by Raphael, Botticelli, Caravaggio, and Titian belong to its collection.

Problem-and-Solution Writing Activity: Advice Column
Lucy Honeychurch, the main character in *A Room With a View*, travels with an older companion who does not hesitate to dispense advice. Imagine that you are an advice columnist for your high-school newspaper, and write questions that you have received from students who need advice. Then, provide answers or solutions to them in your column. Share your advice column with your classmates.

▲ **Critical Viewing**
What do the details in this photograph reveal about this character and her circumstances? **[Infer]**

242 • Problem-and-Solution Essay

Media and Technology Skills

Using Technology to Find Answers

Activity: Rate Help Resources

Getting help when you need it is often a matter of knowing where to look. Consulting the wrong source can be a waste of time. Familiarize yourself with the many help resources available. Then, share your knowledge and opinions of those resources in a ratings guide. Make your guide available in your school computer center to help other students get the help they need.

Think About It Choose a common situation in which you might need informational help. Consider these circumstances, or select one that you have experienced:

- A software program is not compatible with your computer.
- You are trying to locate a friend or relative with whom you have lost touch.
- You would like information about how to plan a camping trip.

Research It Consult a variety of sources to get the help you need. You might use any of the following resources:

On-line support: Many companies offer on-line support to their customers. Look for Internet addresses in manuals or advertisements.
Manuals: Many products—from computer hardware and software to audio equipment—come with manuals that provide essential information and list other help resources.
Search engines: These Internet sites can help you locate specific information. Enter a key word or words to search for your topic.
E-mail: Write to a company or expert listed in a manual or on an Internet site. Using a courteous tone, explain your problem completely in your e-mail note.
Telephone hotlines: Many hotlines provide useful information about handling health, safety, or other problems.

Evaluate It After consulting each help source, provide a rating that assesses its ease of use and efficiency. When you have finished researching, write a comparative review that describes your findings. Post your completed ratings guide in your classroom or in your school's computer center.

FAQs
Many Web sites use the abbreviation *FAQ* to stand for Frequently Asked Questions. Take the time to read these entries before you ask a question. You may find the answer is already posted in the FAQs.

Software Help
Remember that most software programs have built-in Help functions that can answer many common questions. Select Help from the software's menu to access this feature.

1. To generate relevant, interesting, and researchable questions
2. To locate appropriate print and non-print information using text and technical resources
3. To evaluate the credibility of information sources and how they fit various needs
4. To produce research projects and reports in varying forms

Step-by-Step Teaching Guide

Using Technology to Find Answers

1. Ask students to suggest some situations in which they might need to find information, and write these on the board. Then, ask for some informational sources that might provide help in each case.
2. Point out the sidebar, and ask students whether they have ever used FAQ entries.
3. Have each student select one of the situations from the board and research possible sources of information. Have them write down the facts they gather.

1. To develop drafts by organizing content and refining style to suit occasion, audience, and purpose

2. To use effective sequences and transitions to achieve coherence and meaning

3. To produce legible work that shows accurate spelling and correct use of the conventions of punctuation and capitalization

4. To demonstrate control over grammatical elements

Step-by-Step Teaching Guide

Teaching Resource: Standardized Test Preparation Workbook, pp. 21–22

1. Read and discuss the criteria on which students' responses will be evaluated. Make sure students can define order-of-importance organization, chronological order, and pro-and-con organization. Have them give an example of a topic that would be suitable for each.

2. Have students read the sample prompt, noting the audience (the student body) and the form in which they are to write (essay). Have them explain how this determines the type of language they will use. How would it differ if the audience were the school principal?

3. Emphasize that preliminary drafting for an essay of this type need not be extensive. Often, jotting down a few key ideas and supporting details will help students remember their main points.

4. Assign the prompt for completion within a class period.

Standardized Test Preparation Workshop

Responding to Expository Writing Prompts

Standardized test prompts often measure your ability to clearly state a problem and offer several solutions. Your response will be evaluated on the following criteria:

- a clearly stated problem, with appropriate language that suits the purpose and audience identified in the response
- a method of organization that allows you to organize your solution in a meaningful and coherent sequence, such as order-of-importance, chronological order, or pro-and-con organization
- appropriate transitions that contribute to your essay's unity and coherence
- clear descriptions, facts, and other details that support your main points
- correct grammar, spelling, and punctuation

When writing for a timed test, plan to devote a specific amount of time to prewriting, drafting, revising, and proofreading.

Following is an example of an expository writing prompt. Use the strategies following to help you respond. The clocks next to each stage show a suggested amount of time to devote to each stage.

Sample Writing Situation

Directions: Read the following prompt, and write an essay in response. Use details to support your response.

Different people have different tastes. This can present a real problem, particularly when it is your job to satisfy many people at once. You are on the organizing committee for a school dance. It is your decision to choose what form the music will take. Write an open essay to the student body, to be published in the school newspaper, in which you clearly state the problem you are facing and possible solutions for selecting the right type of musical format for the dance.

244 • Problem-and-Solution Essay

 TEST-TAKING TIP

Tell students that when writing a problem-and-solution essay, they have two choices: They can present several solutions, support them, and persuade readers that one is the best; or they can present and support several solutions and let readers decide which one is best. Either choice is acceptable on a test of this type.

Encourage students to thoroughly explain each possible solution to a problem. Explanations might include costs; time constraints; people needed; environmental, neighborhood, or ethical concerns; and so on.

Prewriting

Allow close to one quarter of your time for prewriting.

Choose a Topic Sentence Because you are writing an essay for a wide audience, it is important to clearly identify the issue so that everyone who reads it understands it. A topic sentence explains what your essay is about. This is your opportunity to summarize the problem and provide yourself with a foundation for the essay.

Brainstorm There is usually more than one solution to any given problem. Write down every solution you can think of that would solve your problem. Then, decide which solution or solutions are the most practical and why.

Prepare an Outline Once you have arrived at your solution, outline your thought process and how you came to this particular solution. Not only will an outline help you organize your ideas, but it may also serve as a rough sketch for your first draft.

Drafting

Allow half of your time for drafting.

Start Creatively Begin your essay in a creative way. For example, if you begin your essay with a thought-provoking question, you have an immediate attention-grabber.

Present Solutions Let your audience know that you have thought the problem through. Choose several of your choices from your prewriting, and explain each thoroughly. Use examples, details, and anecdotal evidence to support your concern.

Link Your Ideas Coherence makes your essay easier for readers to understand. You can achieve this by using clear transitions between paragraphs. Transitions are words that will help you link ideas from one paragraph or sentence to the next.

Revising, Editing, and Proofreading

Allow almost one quarter of your time to revise and edit.

Revise Where Necessary Delete repetitive or nonvital information. Be honest with yourself about what does and does not belong in your essay. A point may be well written, but it may also be nonessential.

Proofread Your Essay Use the last few minutes to check your writing for errors in spelling, grammar, and punctuation. Add words or phrases neatly in the space above the text, using a caret [^] to indicate the exact placement.

In-Depth Lesson Plan

	LESSON FOCUS	PRINT AND MEDIA RESOURCES
DAY 1	**Introduction to Documented Essays** Students learn key elements of documented essays and analyze the Model From Literature. (pp. 246–251/H154–155)	*Writers at Work* DVD, Research Writing *Writing and Grammar* Interactive Text, Ch. 12, Introduction
DAY 2	**Prewriting** Students choose and narrow a topic, consider their audience and purpose, and gather information. (pp. 252–256/H156–160)	*Writing and Grammar* Interactive Text, Section 12.2 **Teaching Resources** *Writing Support Transparencies*, 12-A–E; *Writing Support Activity Book*, 12-1–2; *Topic Bank for Heterogeneous Classes*
DAY 3	**Drafting** Students organize their ideas and write their first drafts. (pp. 257–258/H161–162)	*Writing and Grammar* Interactive Text, Section 12.3 **Teaching Resources** *Writing Support Transparencies*, 12-F–G
DAY 4	**Revising** Students revise their drafts in terms of overall structure, paragraphs, sentences, and word choice. (pp. 259–264/H163–168)	*Writing and Grammar* Interactive Text, Section 12.4 **Teaching Resources** *Writing Support Transparencies*, 12-H–I
DAY 5	**Editing and Proofreading; Publishing and Presenting** Students check their work for accuracy and correctness and present their final drafts. (pp. 265–268/H169–170)	*Writing and Grammar* Interactive Text, Sections 12.5–6 **Teaching Resources** *Scoring Rubrics on Transparency*, Ch. 12; *Writing Assessment and Portfolio Management; Formal Assessment*, Ch. 12

Accelerated Lesson Plan

	LESSON FOCUS	PRINT AND MEDIA RESOURCES
DAY 1	**Introduction Through Drafting** Students review characteristics of research writing, select topics, and write drafts. (pp. 246–258/H154–162)	*Writing and Grammar* Interactive Text, Ch. 12, Introduction through Section 12.3 **Teaching Resources** *Writing Support Transparencies*, 12-A–G; *Writing Support Activity Book*, 12-1–2
DAY 2	**Revising Through Presenting** Students work individually or with peers to revise, edit, and proofread their work for presentation. (pp. 259–268/H163–170)	*Writing and Grammar* Interactive Text, Sections 12.4–6 **Teaching Resources** *Writing Support Transparencies*, 12-H–I; *Scoring Rubrics on Transparency*, Ch. 12; *Writing Assessment and Portfolio Management; Formal Assessment*, Ch. 12

Options for Adapting Lesson Plans

HOMEWORK

Have students complete any stage of the lesson for homework.

FEATURES

Extend coverage with Connected Assignment (p. 269/H171), Spotlight on the Humanities (p. 270), Media and Technology Skills (p. 271), and the Standardized Test Preparation Workshop (pp. 272–273).

TECHNOLOGY

Students can complete any stage of the lesson on the computer, using *Writing and Grammar* Interactive Text or a word-processing program. Have them print out their completed work.

Writing and Grammar Handbook Alignment

Page numbers in Step-by-Step Teaching Guides in this Teacher's Edition refer to pages from the full student text. Handbook page references, indicated with this icon 🄷, are provided in Time and Resource Manager boxes and at the bottom of each Teacher's Edition page.

INTEGRATED SKILLS COVERAGE

Integrating Grammar
Pronoun-Antecedent Agreement, SE p. 262/🄷166
Direct and Indirect Quotations, SE, p. 265/🄷169; ATE p. 249

Reading/Writing Connection
Read Ahead or Back, SE p. 248
Writing Connection, SE p. 251

Viewing and Representing
Critical Viewing, SE pp. 246, 248, 252, 254, 267, 268, 269, 270/🄷154, 156, 158, 171
Examining Messages in Film, SE p. 270
Using Media to Produce a Documentary, SE p. 271

Technology
SE pp. 256, 265, 266/🄷160, 169, 170; ATE p. 255

Vocabulary ATE pp. 249, 261, 264

Integrating Spelling Skills ATE p. 265

Speaking and Listening ATE p. 260

Real-World Connection ATE p. 256

ASSESSMENT SUPPORT

Standardized Test Preparation Workshop, SE p. 272; ATE p. 264
Standardized Test Preparation Workbook, pp. 23–24
Scoring Rubrics on Transparency, Ch. 12
Formal Assessment, Ch. 12
Writing Assessment and Portfolio Management

MEETING INDIVIDUAL NEEDS

Less Advanced Students ATE pp. 254, 259, 260, 273. See also Ongoing Assessments ATE pp. 248, 253, 258.
AP Students ATE pp. 257, 269, 273
Gifted and Talented Students ATE p. 268
ESL Students ATE pp. 249, 261, 263
Linguistic Learners ATE p. 250
Spatial Learners ATE p. 255

BLOCK SCHEDULING

Pacing Suggestions
For 90-minute Blocks
• Have students complete the Prewriting and Drafting stages in a single period.
• Focus one class period on Revising and Editing and Publishing and Presenting. Allow at least 30 minutes for peer revision.

Resources for Varying Instruction
• *Writing and Grammar* **Interactive Text** A 90-minute block provides an ideal opportunity for students to work on the computer.
• *Writers at Work* **DVD** Show the Research segment in class.

Professional Development Support
• *How to Manage Instruction in the Block* This teaching resource provides management and activity suggestions.

MEDIA AND TECHNOLOGY

For the Student
• *Writing and Grammar* **Interactive Text,** Ch. 12
• *On-line Exercise Bank,* Section 23.2

For the Teacher
• *Writers at Work* **DVD,** Research Writing
• **Teacher**EXPRESS™ **CD-ROM**

WRITING AND GRAMMAR ON-LINE

Interactive Text (On-line or on CD-ROM)
• Easily navigable instruction with interactive Revision Checkers
• Full use of e-rater™, the essay-scoring system (on-line only)

Companion Web Site PHSchool.com
• Scoring rubrics with models (use Web Code egk-1201)

See the Go On-line! **feature, SE p. iii.**

LITERATURE CONNECTIONS

Related selections from *Prentice Hall Literature, Penguin Edition,* The British Tradition:

Professional Model from *A History of the English Church and People,* Bede, SE p. 251
Topic Bank Option "The Chimney Sweeper," William Blake, SE p. 253/🄷157

Lesson Objectives

1. To write a documented essay appropriate to audience and purpose

2. To read to appreciate a writer's craft and to discover models for writing

3. To organize ideas in writing to ensure coherence, logical progression, and support for ideas

4. To use prewriting strategies to generate ideas and plan

5. To use writing to formulate questions, compile information, and support what is known about a topic

6. To develop and revise drafts in terms of structure, paragraphs, sentences, and word choice

7. To edit and proofread to ensure standard English usage and grammar

8. To refine a documented essay for publication

Critical Viewing

Hypothesize Students should mention data and statistics drawn from the scientists' own research and that of others.

Chapter
12 Research
Documented Essay

Documentation in Everyday Life

"Where did you hear that?" "What makes you so sure?" You probably encounter questions like these from time to time in everyday life. In response, you may furnish a name, book, or news article to reveal your source of information.

The same holds true in journalism. When you switch on the radio and hear a news report, chances are you don't question its truthfulness. Perhaps that's because most reporters and journalists, as part of their job, provide documentation to help ensure that what you hear and read in newspapers, news programs, magazines, and journals is accurate.

▲ Critical Viewing
Scientists like those pictured often write reports on their findings. What sort of documentation might they provide in their reports? [Hypothesize]

246 • Research

⏱ TIME AND RESOURCE MANAGER	
Resources	
Technology: *Writers at Work* DVD, Research Writing; *Writing and Grammar* Interactive Text, Ch. 12	
Using the Full Student Edition	**Using the Handbook**🄷
• Read and discuss pp. 246–247 in class.	• Read and discuss pp. 154–155 in class.
• Show the Research Writing section of *Writers at Work* DVD.	• Show the Research Writing section of *Writers at Work* DVD.
• Have students read the Model From Literature, pp. 248–251, and use it to discuss elements of the documented essay.	

What Is a Documented Essay?

A **documented essay** is writing, based on research, about a particular subject. Though it may make use of personal observations and illustrations, the documented essay is a form of research writing and is therefore more formal and authoritative than a personal essay. Most documented essays

- provide detailed information about a specific topic, usually one of current interest.
- are based on research that can be documented, or proved, to be accurate by means of supporting references.
- contain references to source material within the text of the essay.
- have fewer than four sources of information.
- are clearly and effectively organized.

To preview the criteria on which your documented essay may be evaluated, see the Rubric for Self-Assessment on page 266.

Types of Documented Essays

Documented essays may be about a variety of subjects:

- **Biographical profiles** give information about the life, experiences, and career of a notable person.
- **Science articles** explore a wide range of subjects—from weather occurrences to discoveries in outer space to brain research.
- **General information articles** may provide up-to-the-minute information on current fads, fashions, or cultural events.

PREVIEW Student Work IN PROGRESS

Tameeka Mitchem, a student at the Satellite Academy in New York City, wrote a documented essay about volunteerism among teenagers. Her essay was published in a student newspaper called *Spectrum.* Tameeka's completed documented essay appears at the end of this chapter.

Writers in ACTION

Many writers perform research when preparing their manuscripts. Zora Neale Hurston, author and storyteller, showed her understanding of the usefulness of research skills when she said: "Research is formalized curiosity. It is poking and prying with a purpose."

Interest GRABBER Ask students whether they watch news on the television, hear it on the radio, or read it in a newspaper. Have them identify phrases reporters use to let you know where they got their information *(in a release from the office of . . ., in a statement made by . . ., a study released today indicates . . ., AP Wire Service, Reuters).* Ask students why they think reporters identify their sources like this. (It helps people judge whether information is reliable.)

Activate Prior Knowledge

Remind students that when they hear an interesting piece of news about friends or acquaintances, they are likely to ask about the source of the information. Point out that a documented essay is simply a way of formalizing this need to know the source of information, so that the data's reliability can be judged or further research can be conducted.

More About the Writer

Zora Neale Hurston was a respected writer during a period known as the Harlem Renaissance. In the 1930s and 1940s, African American artists gathered in the Harlem section of New York City and rejuvenated interest in the arts. Zora Neale Hurston drew on her childhood, her love of the Caribbean, and the storytelling style of folk tales to write about being a young African American woman in the South. Her best-known novel is *Their Eyes Were Watching God.*

☑ ONGOING ASSESSMENT: Diagnose

Use one of the suggestions below to diagnose the students' level of understanding of how to write a documented essay.

Option 1 Ask each student to select the strongest example of his or her documented research writing. Hold conferences in which you review each student's example. Use the conferences to determine which students may need extra support in writing a documented essay.	**Option 2** Give students a common topic, such as "Soccer in America" or "Women in Rock Music." Have students write one or two paragraphs of a documented essay. If students have difficulty completing this activity, you will need to devote additional time to gathering information, drafting, and providing documentation.

Reading: Read Ahead or Back

Point out that reading ahead or rereading are ways readers can use context clues to determine meaning. Suggest that students keep the general subject of an essay in mind when they encounter an unfamiliar word. Tell them to look at the construction of the sentence. Is the word compared or contrasted to something? (For example, "He used to be strong, but now he is feeble" would indicate that *feeble* means the opposite of *strong*.) Point out that unfamiliar terms and references can also often be ideas for further study—for example, the references to Leif Ericson and the Venerable Bede in the fourth paragraph of the Model.

Engage Students Through Literature

1. Read the Bryson excerpt aloud, or have students read it independently.

2. Ask students to summarize the main idea. (Language achieves its single goal in a myriad of forms.)

3. Ask students to point out the places where the author cites his sources. (The quotations, the citation in brackets, a 1979 poll.)

4. Ask students why the statistics in the last three paragraphs on page 250 do not have documented sources cited. (Aside from his reference to a 1979 poll, the other statistics are familiar enough to be found in many different sources.)

5. Ask students to brainstorm for other topics suggested by this passage. Students may add these topics to their topic banks.

Critical Viewing

Hypothesize Students may guess that the language is Russian or recommend library research to find out.

12.1 Model From Literature

Bill Bryson is the author of several collections of essays, among them A Walk in the Woods *and* The Mother Tongue, *from which the following excerpt comes.*

Reading Strategy: Read Ahead or Back As you read the following essay, you may encounter unfamiliar words or references. To figure out their meaning, read ahead or read back to see whether clues within the text can help you figure out the meaning of troublesome words, phrases, and references.

from
The Mother Tongue

Bill Bryson

All languages have the same purpose—to communicate thoughts—and yet they achieve this single aim in a multiplicity of ways. It appears there is no feature of grammar or syntax that is indispensable or universal. The ways of dealing with matters of number, tense, case, gender, and the like are wondrously various from one tongue to the next. Many languages manage without quite basic grammatical or lexical features, while others burden themselves with remarkable complexities. A Welsh speaker must choose between five ways of saying *than: na, n', nag, mwy,* or *yn fwy.* Finnish has fifteen case forms, so every noun varies depending on whether it is nominative, accusative, allative, inessive, comitative, or one of ten other grammatical conditions. Imagine learning fifteen ways of spelling *cat, dog, house,* and so on. English, by contrast, has abandoned case forms, except for possessives, where we generally add *'s*, and with personal pronouns

▲ **Critical Viewing** What language is printed on the sign in this photograph? How might you find out? **[Hypothesize]**

Bryson presents his thesis in the first sentence of his essay. It is an effective thesis because it is concise and clear.

248 • Documented Essay

☑ **ONGOING ASSESSMENT: Monitor and Reinforce**

Use one of the suggestions below to check students' level of understanding of a documented essay as they read the Model From Literature, pages 248–251.

Option 1 Have students review the basic elements of a documented essay on page 3. Tell them to look for these elements as they read the Model From Literature.	**Option 2** Have students read the Model From Literature. Then have them cite examples of the elements of a documented essay as outlined on page 3.

which can vary by no more than three ways (e.g., *they, their, them*), but often by only two (*you, your*). Similarly, in English *ride* has just five forms (*ride, rides, rode, riding, ridden*); the same verb in German has sixteen. In Russian, nouns can have up to twelve inflections and adjectives as many as sixteen. In English adjectives have just one invariable form with but, I believe, one exception: *blond/blonde*.

Estimates of the number of languages in the world usually fix on a figure of about 2,700, though almost certainly no one has ever made a truly definitive count. In many countries, perhaps the majority, there are at least two native languages, and in some cases—as in Cameroon and Papua New Guinea—there are hundreds. India probably leads the world, with more than 1,600 languages and dialects (it isn't always possible to say which is which). The rarest language as of 1984 was Oubykh, a highly complex Caucasian language with eighty-two consonants but only three vowels, once spoken by 50,000 people in the Crimea. But as of July 1984 there was just one living speaker remaining and he was eighty-two years old.

The number of languages naturally changes as tribes die out or linguistic groups are absorbed. Although new languages, particularly creoles, are born from time to time, the trend is towards absorption and amalgamation. When Columbus arrived in the New World, there were an estimated 1,000 languages. Today there are about 600.

Almost all languages change. A rare exception is written Icelandic, which has changed so little that modern Icelanders can read sagas written a thousand years ago, and if Leif Ericson appeared on the streets of Reykjavik he could find his way around, allowing for certain difficulties over terms like *airport* and *quarter-pound cheeseburger*. In English, by contrast, the change has been much more dramatic. Almost any untrained person looking at a manuscript from the time of, say, the Venerable Bede would be hard pressed to identify it as being in English—and in a sense he or she would be right. Today we have not only a completely different vocabulary and system of spelling, but even a different structure.

Nor are languages any respecters of frontiers. If you drew a map of Europe based on languages it would bear scant resemblance to a conventional map. Switzerland would disappear, becoming part of the surrounding dominions of French, Italian, and German but for a few tiny pockets for Romansh (or Romantsch or Rhaeto-Romanic as it is variously called), which

Bryson's essay is well organized. Each paragraph is devoted to exploring and developing a single aspect of his thesis.

To make his essay interesting and slightly humorous, Bryson cites "rare exceptions"—that the words airport *and* cheeseburger *would be unfamiliar to Leif Erickson.*

The topic sentence of this paragraph is supported by several details.

Model From Literature • 249

Customize for
ESL Students

If students speak one of the languages mentioned in the essay, ask them to volunteer details other thn those Bryson cites. Ask other students to contribute examples from their own first languages of regional differences, dialects, or vocabulary.

Integrating Vocabulary Skills

Word Origins Demonstrate, or have a student demonstrate, how to use the dictionary to find the etymology (history or origin) of words. Have each student take a different letter of the alphabet and scan the page, looking for as many etymologies as he or she can find in a set amount of time. Then have students share which languages they discovered as roots. Do students notice any patterns?

Integrating Grammar Skills

Point out how the author uses italics to highlight focus words and foreign words. Tell students this distinguishes these words from quoted words, which are surrounded by quotation marks. Where else do students notice that Bryson uses italics? (He uses italics to cite the title of one of his sources at the end of this excerpt.)

249

Teaching From the Model

You can use this Model From Literature as one way to find a relevant topic for a documented essay. Bryson discusses the variety of languages and dialects in the world and indicates that language frequently transcends and supercedes national borders. Have students look for obvious references or citations in the essay. How is Bryson's essay organized? What details support his main idea?

Customize for
Linguistic Learners

Ask students to find out some of the other languages spoken in Europe, in addition to the more familiar ones regularly associated with the large countries (for example, Catalan, Basque, Walloon). Encourage them to discover the origins and histories of these languages or the people who speak them.

is spoken as a native language by about half the people in the Graubünden district (or Grisons district—almost everything has two names in Switzerland) at the country's eastern edge. This steep and beautiful area, which takes in the ski resorts of St. Moritz, Davor, and Klosters, was once effectively isolated from the rest of the world by its harsh winters and forbidding geography. Indeed, the isolation was such that even people in neighboring valleys began to speak different versions of the language, so that Romansh is not so much one language as five fragmented and not always mutually intelligible dialects. A person from the valley around Sutselva will say, "Vagned nà qua" for "Come here," while in the next valley he will say, "Vegni neu cheu." [Cited in *The Economist*, February 27, 1988] In other places people will speak the language in the same way but spell it differently depending on whether they are Catholic or Protestant.

German would cover not only its traditional areas of Germany, Austria, and much of Switzerland, but would spill into Belgium, Czechoslovakia, Romania, Hungary, the Soviet Union, and Poland, and it could be further divided into high and low German, which have certain notable differences in terms of vocabulary and syntax. In Bavaria, for instance, *Samstag* is the name for Saturday, but in Berlin it is *Sonnabend*; a plumber in Bavaria is a *spengler*, but a *klempner* in Berlin.

Italy, too, would appear on the map not as one language entity but as a whole variety of broadly related but often mutually incomprehensible dialects. Italian, such as it is, is not a national language, but really only the dialect of Florence and Tuscany, which has slowly been gaining preeminence over other dialects. Not until 1979 did a poll show for the first time that Italian was the dialect spoken at home by more than 50 percent of Italians.

Much the same would be the position in the Soviet Union, which would dissolve into 149 separate languages. Almost half the people in the country speak some language other than Russian as a native tongue, and a full quarter of the people do not speak Russian at all.

Some languages are not so distinct as we are sometimes led to believe. Spanish and Portuguese are closely enough related that the two peoples can read each other's newspapers and books, though they have more difficulty understanding speech. Finns and Estonians can freely understand each other. Danes, Swedes, and Norwegians often insist that their languages are quite distinct and yet, as Mario Pei puts it, there are greater differences between Italian dialects such as Sicilian and Piedmontese than

Since Bryson is a language expert, he needed to cite only two sources in this essay. This internal citation reveals the source of Bryson's information.

The supporting details in this paragraph are statistical and easily proved.

there are between any of the three main Scandinavian languages. Romanian and Moldavian, spoken in the Soviet Union, are essentially the same language with different names. So are Serbian and Croatian, the only real difference being that Serbian uses the Cyrillic alphabet and Croatian uses Western characters.

In many countries people use one language for some activities and a second language for others. In Luxembourg, the inhabitants use French at school, German for reading newspapers, and Luxemburgish, a local Germanic dialect, at home. In Paraguay, people conduct business in Spanish, but tell their jokes in Guarani, the native Indian tongue. In Greece, for a long time children were schooled only in Katharevousa, a formal language so archaic that it was (and indeed still is) no longer spoken anywhere in the country. The language for common discourse was Dhimotiki, yet perversely this everyday language was long held in such low esteem that when the Old Testament was published in Dhimotiki for the first time in 1903, riots broke out all over the country. [Peter Trudgill, *Sociolinguistics*, page 115+] . . .

Reading Writing Connection

Writing Application: Give Clues to Help Readers Understand As you draft your documented essay, include details about your topic to help readers understand it better.

▶ **Critical Viewing** Does any of the information shown on this map surprise you? Explain. **[Relate]**

LITERATURE

To read an essay that contains research, see the excerpt from Bede's *A History of the English Church and People*, which appears in *Prentice Hall Literature, Penguin Edition,* The British Tradition.

INDO-EUROPEAN FAMILY

Balto-Slavic Branch		Romance Branch	Other branches
Bulgarian	Russian	Friulian	Albanian
Croatian	Serbian	Italian	Germanic
Czech	Slovak	Romansh	Greek
Macedonian	Slovene	Romanian	
Polish	Ukrainian		

OTHER FAMILIES

Altaic Turkish   Uralic (Magyar)

Model From Literature • 251

Connections With Literature

If students read the excerpt from *A History of the English Church and People*, ask them to analyze Bede's methods of documentation. What devices does Bede use to present his research and support his facts? Encourage students to review the language and organization of Bede's history.

Critical Viewing

Relate Answers may vary. Some students may be surprised that so many languages are spoken in a relatively small area. Other students may be from or have traveled to the area on the map, and will be aware of the information it contains.

Reading\Writing Connection

Writing Application: Provide Clues to Help Readers

Tell students that they can make it easier for their readers to use context clues to establish the meaning of words. Encourage students to track their use of words that may be unfamiliar to readers and to insert definitions or restatements of these words in their writing.

Prewriting: Write "Invisibly"

1. Explain to students that invisible writing is a strategy that encourages writers to get ideas flowing without getting slowed down by reviewing or judging what has been written.

2. Remind students that, as in freewriting, no one else will see what is written, so they should relax and just get ideas recorded.

3. Encourage students to try invisible writing several times to see if the strategy helps them.

Prewriting: Perform a Flip Test

1. Point out that magazines and newspapers are designed so that the stories they want you to notice will have the biggest or most eye-catching titles. This can be an aid when looking for ideas.

2. Suggest that students use an unfamiliar magazine for a flip test. With an unfamiliar format, topics may be more obvious.

Prewriting: Imagine an Address Book

1. Suggest students run through a typical day in their minds to remind themselves of all the people with whom they come in contact, both in and out of school.

2. Ask students if they know a person to whom something interesting has happened or who is from an interesting place.

3. As they generate ideas for people to interview, tell students they should also think ahead about the kinds of questions they might ask.

Critical Viewing

Infer Students may say that the student is either jotting down ideas from the Flip Test or Imagine an Address Book strategies.

12.2 Prewriting

Choosing Your Topic

To choose a topic for a documented essay, start with subjects that interest you and that you would like to research. Also, think about whether there are likely to be sources of information available about the particular topic you're considering. Use the following strategies for help in choosing a topic:

Strategies for Generating Topics

1. **Write "Invisibly"** When you use the Invisible Writing strategy, you brainstorm for ideas without editing or judging them as you write them down. To perform this activity, turn off your computer monitor or insert carbon paper between two sheets of writing paper and write with an empty pen. When you have finished writing, turn on the monitor or look at the sheet of paper under the carbon paper. Review what you have written, and choose an idea for your documented essay.

2. **Perform a Flip Test** Magazines can be a source of ideas for research. Choose one or more magazines that explore an area of interest to you, such as art or science. Flip through the magazines, and jot down topics that interest you. Consider whether or not you will be able to find information on these topics through library or other sources. Choose to develop the topic that both interests you and for which sources can be found.

3. **Imagine an Address Book** Mentally flip through a book containing the names and addresses of interesting people. Then, write down the names of those you would like to research. Review the list, and base your documented essay on the person about whom information is available or who would be available for an interview.

▶ **Critical Viewing** What strategy for choosing a topic might this student be using? [Infer]

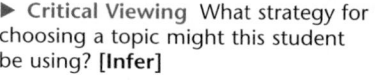

Timed Writing Hint

Most prompts provide very specific topics to write about. Structure your essay so that it addresses the prompt directly.

⏱ TIME AND RESOURCE MANAGER

Resources
Print: *Writing Support Transparencies*, 12-A–E; *Writing Support Activity Book*, 12-1–2; *Topic Bank for Heterogeneous Classes*
Technology: *Writing and Grammar* Interactive Text, Section 12.2

Using the Full Student Edition	Using the Handbook⊞
• Cover pp. 252–256 in class. • Assist students in choosing and narrowing a topic. • Review the sources available for documenting an essay.	• Cover pp. 156–160 in class. • Assist students in choosing and narrowing a topic. • Review the sources available for documenting an essay.

TOPIC BANK

If you are having difficulty coming up with a topic, consider these ideas:

1. **Inspiration From an Inspirational Person** Is there someone you admire for his or her ability to inspire others? Do research, including a personal interview if possible, and write a documented essay about that person.

2. **Essay on a New Trend** Identify a trend that you would like to research. For example, is there a new sports craze, fitness routine, or development in fashion that is significant? Write a documented essay about it based on research and interviews.

Responding to Fine Art

3. The *Chrysler Building Composite at Dusk* depicts a world-famous skyscraper located in New York City. Think about a building you admire, and reveal what makes it special in a documented essay.

Responding to Literature

4. Read "The Chimney Sweeper" by William Blake. This poem deals with a serious problem of Blake's time—child labor. Write a documented essay that centers on one aspect of child labor. Blake's poem appears in *Prentice Hall Literature, Penguin Edition*, The British Tradition.

Chrysler Building Composite at Dusk, Yvonne Jacquette, DC Moore Gallery

Timed Writing Prompt

5. Write an essay in which you describe watching a historic event on television as it unfolds. The event could be the results of a presidential election, a dramatic weather event, or a historic sports game. Discuss what it felt like to witness the event on television. Address whether another medium, such as the radio or a newspaper, could have enabled you to experience the event as fully. Draw a conclusion about the value of television as a communications medium during a crisis or historic event. **(45 minutes)**

Prewriting • 253

Step-by-Step Teaching Guide

Prewriting: Narrow by Looping

Teaching Resources: Writing Support Transparencies, 12-B

1. Point out the free flow of ideas in the sample. Ask students to identify the connection between the people named by the writer. (They are all people who envisioned or enabled space flight.)

2. After displaying and discussing the transparency (12-B), have students try the looping activity on their own and share their results. Ask students the following questions to stimulate discussion.

   Did you eliminate elements that did not relate to the main idea?

   Did this process permit you to effectively narrow the topic for your documented essay?

Customize for
Less Advanced Students

Have students freewrite for a few minutes on a topic they choose or you assign. Ask a volunteer to share his or her freewriting. Then, guide students through a looping process using this sample.

Step-by-Step Teaching Guide

Prewriting: Considering Audience and Purpose

Teaching Resources: Writing Support Transparencies, 12-C; Writing Support Activity Book, 12-1

1. Display Transparency 12-C to remind students how their language and choice of details will be affected by a given audience or purpose.

2. Encourage students to identify their audience and purpose before they begin researching.

Critical Viewing

Assess Students may suggest such topics as the history of space flight or the engineering required to reach space.

Narrowing Your Topic

Think about your topic and whether it is narrow enough to fully develop in the confines of your planned essay. If your topic can be divided into significant subheads, each with its own focus, then it is probably too broad. One way to narrow your topic is by looping.

Narrow by Looping

First, write freely on your topic for two or three minutes, based on what you already know or have learned. Read what you have written, and circle the most important idea. Write for a few minutes on that idea. Again, read what you have written, and circle the most important idea. Continue this process until you arrive at a topic that is narrow enough for your essay.

> Space shuttle missions are interesting. There are many shuttlecraft in the fleet. How dangerous are the missions? How have the shuttle's goals changed since *Challenger?* Who is likely to be the (visionary) behind missions of the twenty-first century?

> Visionaries. Gene Roddenberry. John F. Kennedy. Bill Gates. (George Lucas.) Making special effects realistic. Matching sci-fi with possible reality.

▲ **Critical Viewing** What topic for a documented essay does this photograph inspire? **[Assess]**

Considering Your Audience and Purpose

Before you begin to draft, identify your audience (who will read your essay) and your purpose (what effect you want your writing to have on your audience). Then, begin to gather details that are appropriate for your audience and that will help you to achieve your purpose.

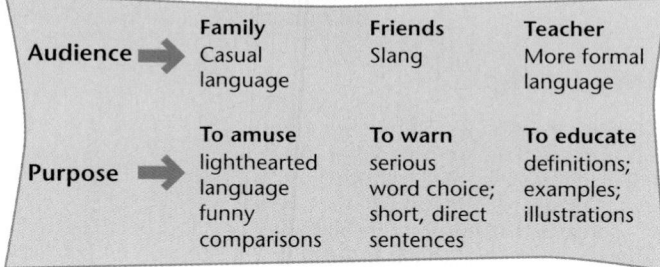

Audience ➡	**Family** Casual language	**Friends** Slang	**Teacher** More formal language
Purpose ➡	**To amuse** lighthearted language funny comparisons	**To warn** serious word choice; short, direct sentences	**To educate** definitions; examples; illustrations

Gathering Details

Make a search plan to direct your search for information from a variety of sources. Use the following tips to help you:

Make a Research Plan

The best way to prepare for research is to list the information you want to find and where you hope to find it. Libraries contain information in both printed and electronic formats.

- To locate **nonfiction books,** use the library's card or computer catalog. In either catalog, you can search for books about your topic by author, title, or subject.
- To locate **current magazine articles,** use the *Readers' Guide to Periodical Literature.* Use a microfiche machine to read the appropriate articles.
- Libraries also have reference sections in which you will find a variety of useful sources, including **indexes, bibliographies, almanacs, atlases,** and **encyclopedias.**
- **CD-ROM encyclopedias** give multimedia presentations on a number of topics.
- The **World Wide Web** contains a wealth of Web pages that give information about a multitude of subjects.

🖥 Research Tip

If you're not sure where to look for what you need, ask a librarian. Librarians are trained to know various places in which to locate information.

Student Work
IN PROGRESS

Name: <u>Tameeka Mitchem</u>
<u>Satellite Academy</u>
<u>New York, NY</u>

Creating a Research Plan
To direct her search for information, Tameeka first made a research plan.

<u>Topic:</u> Volunteerism

<u>Question:</u> How many students volunteer?

<u>Plan:</u> *Readers' Guide:* Search for "volunteering, volunteerism, volunteers, teen volunteering"

<u>Question:</u> What kind of volunteering experiences have local students had?

<u>Plan:</u> Interview two or three local teens who volunteer; contact volunteer groups to get names and numbers of possible interview subjects

Prewriting: Make a Research Plan

Teaching Resources: Writing Support Transparencies, 12-D

1. Display the transparency (12-D) and review with students how Tameeka created her research plan. Point out that she started with basic ideas—to search the Readers' Guide—rather than specific books.

2. Tell students that the first step, after identifying a topic, is to jot down notes on what they want to find out about the topic.

3. If possible, allow for class time in the library. Encourage students to seek help from librarians if they are not certain of all the resources available at the library.

4. Remind students of the importance of keeping detailed notes about their sources. If necessary, provide them with an example of the bibliographic information and page numbers, or Internet reference information appropriate for documenting a source. If students are careful with their documentation, they will not have to go back to a research resource numerous times.

Integrating Technology Skills

An Internet search provides a good method for narrowing a topic. Suggest that students begin their searches by typing in a broad topic in which they are interested. When the search engine returns a list of related pages, they can begin to find out what possible subtopics are related to their original idea. They can then continue to make new searches until they reach their specific topic idea.

Customize for
Spatial Learners

Encourage students to use graphic organizers in their research or in their final documented essays. Remind students that maps, graphs, illustrations, diagrams, charts, and photographs are excellent resources, both for research and for inclusion in the essay. Demonstrate how to cite a graphic organizer printed off the Internet or photocopied from a book or magazine.

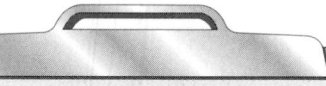

Step-by-Step Teaching Guide

Prewriting: Conduct Interviews

Teaching Resources: Writing Support Transparencies 12-E; Writing Support Activity Book, 12-2

1. Have students think of people who might be resources for their topic. Have them create a list of people they already know and people they might search out to gather information.

2. Display Transparency 12-E or distribute copies of interviewing tips (12-2) to help students plan their interviews.

3. Tell students to prepare a list of questions before they do their interviews. Explain that, during the interview, they can ask any new questions that might arise, but a list will help them remember the key questions, so they leave with the information they need.

Step-by-Step Teaching Guide

Prewriting: Conduct On-line Research

1. Remind students that it is important to make certain that a Web site is posted by a reliable source. Point out that even ".edu" is no guarantee that a site is reliable, since students can post to many .edu sites. They should check to see whether the writer is a professor or researcher.

2. Ask students to share favorite research techniques or search engines with the class.

Real-World Connection

Point out that interviewing is a key element of most jobs. To get a job, an applicant has an interview. As one advances in business, one may interview others. Reporters' jobs consist largely of interviewing. Learning to be comfortable on both sides of the interview is a valuable skill. Pair students up and have each prepare three or four questions to ask their partner, first as a news reporter and then as a job recruiter. Then have them interview each other.

Conduct Interviews

If your documented essay is about a person, interview him or her if you can. If the topic of your essay isn't a person, you still may benefit from interviewing experts, eyewitnesses, or others who have firsthand knowledge about your subject. Follow these tips for interviewing:

Interview Tips

√ Contact each person, and arrange to meet or speak by telephone at his or her convenience.

√ Prepare questions in advance.

√ Design your questions to get as much information as possible.

√ Don't ask "yes or no" questions.

√ Record answers in writing or, with the interviewee's consent, on audiocassette or videotape. Take note of the date, time, and place.

√ Follow up with a thank-you call or note.

Conduct On-line Research

The World Wide Web contains a vast source of information, both reliable and unreliable. To conduct research on-line, keep the following tips in mind:

- Use a search engine to speed and focus your search.

- Always look for the originator of the Web site. Doing so will help you spot biased or one-sided coverage of issues.

- Web addresses with **.gov** are government sponsored; Web addresses with **.edu** stem from educational organizations. They are good places to find information.

- Download and print out pages you plan to use as source material. Double-check facts you plan to use to make sure they are accurate.

256 • Documented Essay

⊛ Technology Tip

If you plan to tape-record an interview, be sure that your tape recorder has fresh batteries. Also, check sound levels prior to the interview to ensure that both you and the interviewee can be clearly heard.

12.3 Drafting

Shaping Your Writing
Write an Introduction, Body, and Conclusion

As you draft, give your writing shape by writing an introduction, a body, and a conclusion.

Introduction Starting to read an essay is like meeting a new person: First impressions count, so plan your introduction carefully. An effective introduction serves two key purposes: It states the essay's main idea, letting readers know what you are planning to discuss, and it captures readers' interest, making them eager to keep reading.

Body The body of an essay is composed of paragraphs that develop and support a main idea. Normally, each body paragraph presents a single main idea that is supported by details. Some paragraphs, however, perform a specific function, such as making a transition or emphasizing an important point. Sometimes, too, when dealing with a long or complicated issue, a single aspect of a topic may be explored over a number of paragraphs known as a paragraph block.

Conclusion Conclusions should leave a lasting, vivid impression on the reader. An effective conclusion sums up or restates an essay's main idea and gives the reader something to think about. Consider ending your essay by offering a recommendation, an intriguing question, or a personal insight.

Student Work
IN PROGRESS

Name: Tameeka Mitchem
Satellite Academy
New York, NY

Writing an Introduction
Tameeka's introduction was designed to capture her audience's interest immediately.

Each day after school, eighteen-year-old Courtney Cauthett of Manhattan spends two hours counseling and tutoring young children at a local community center. Kajal Angras, eighteen, a senior at Curtis High School in Staten Island, volunteers three hours a day, two days a week at Project Hospitality, an organization that helps needy mothers and their kids.

> By giving two examples of local teens who currently volunteer, Tameeka draws the interest of her audience, New York-area teenagers.

Drafting • 257

Step-by-Step Teaching Guide

Drafting: Writing an Introduction
Teaching Resources: Writing Support Transparencies, 12-F

1. Display Transparency 12-F and ask students to evaluate the effectiveness of Tameeka's opening paragraph. Does it grab their attention? Does it give them an idea where the essay might be headed?

2. Point out that Tameeka's opener, aside from catching the reader's interest, also prepares the reader for the body of the essay and the conclusion.

Customize for
AP Students

Share with students that an introduction or opening line can have a tremendous impact on readers. Some, such as the opening line of *Moby-Dick*, "Call me Ishmael," become almost legendary. Have students think of opening lines or paragraphs from favorite stories that really "hooked" them. Ask them to share some of these openers in class.

⏱ TIME AND RESOURCE MANAGER

Resources
Print Resources: Writing Support Transparencies, 12-F–G
Technology: *Writing and Grammar* Interactive Text, Section 12.3

Using the Full Student Edition	Using the Handbook🄷
• Work through the Write an Introduction, Body, and Conclusion and the Providing Elaboration strategies with the class (pp. 257–258). • Have students write their first draft in class.	• Work through the Write an Introduction, Body, and Conclusion and the Providing Elaboration strategies with the class (pp. 161–162). • Have students write their first draft in class.

⏱ TIME SAVERS!

Writing Support Transparencies
Use the transparencies for Chapter 12 to facilitate teaching of strategies.

Writing Support Activity Book
Use the graphic organizers for Chapter 12 to facilitate student planning.

Drafting: Providing Elaboration

Teaching Resources: Writing Support Transparencies, 12-G

1. Display the transparency (12-G) and discuss how Tameeka cited specific details that she found during her research.

2. Help students see that the first sentence in Tameeka's draft is a thesis statement, and that every sentence thereafter cites some evidence that backs up her thesis statement. Discuss how this strengthens the credibility of a writer.

3. Have students review their drafts for suitable places to add elaboration. Ask students to consider whether they could add a sentence or cite a reference to elaborate on a particular idea. Would it make the point clearer, more vivid, or more credible?

12.3

Providing Elaboration

As you draft, elaborate by defining, explaining, or illustrating the points you are making.

Provide Details and Elaborate

In your documented essay, cite facts and statistics and explain how they relate to your main idea. For example, suppose you are writing about the growing popularity of ferrets as house pets. Prove your point by citing a survey (Twenty-five percent of today's teens would like to own a ferret.) or a fact found in your research (Ferrets are banned as house pets in some states). Then, follow up by restating, explaining, defining, or illustrating the fact (Although ferrets can be house pets in one state, in another, they are considered to be wild animals.).

Whenever you cite a fact within your essay, be sure to document it. Immediately following details you got from a source, place in parentheses the title, author, and copyright information of the corresponding source material.

ⓛ Learn More

To learn how to format citations within text, see Citing Sources and Preparing Manuscript on pages 886–892.

Student Work
IN PROGRESS

Name: Tameeka Mitchem
Satellite Academy
New York, NY

Providing Details and Elaboration
As she drafted, Tameeka cited and elaborated on specific details she found while researching her topic.

Many teenagers devote their free hours to volunteering. Last year, for example, nearly 60% of the nation's teens volunteered 2.3 billion hours to a social or political cause. Of those hours, 1.8 billion were given to national organizations while the other 500 million were given to people in their communities. (Philanthropy Journal Online) These statistics are compelling evidence that teenagers care about others.

> Philanthropy Journal Online
> nearly 60% of U.S. teens
> volunteered 2.3 billion hours
> to causes:
> 1.8 billion to national
> organizations / 500 million to
> communities

258 • Documented Essay

☑ ONGOING ASSESSMENT: Monitor and Reinforce

Students may have difficulty recognizing appropriate details for reinforcing points or identifying where sources should be cited. If this is the case, try the following strategy.

Have students work in pairs and write down the points they need to support. Partners can then work together to go through the details each has collected and code them (color coding or number coding) to show which ideas they support. Students can flag with stars or self-sticking notes facts or ideas that require that a source be cited.

12.4 Revising

Now that you have completed your first draft, look at it critically. Then, take steps to improve it.

Revising Your Overall Structure

Improve Unity and Coherence

Effective essays are unified—each paragraph relates to the essay's thesis or main point. Paragraphs should also be coherent—they should link together to build meaning. As you reread your draft, improve your essay's unity and coherence by using the following strategies:

▶ **REVISION STRATEGY**
Eliminating Unnecessary Details to Improve Unity

Read through your draft, and circle your thesis statement or main idea. Then, using another color, circle all details in your draft that support or relate to your main idea. When you are finished, review the details that have not been circled. Either rewrite them to connect with or support your main idea or eliminate those details altogether.

The historic district of Philadelphia has a lot to offer visitors and residents alike. Elfreth's Alley, off 2nd Street, is hailed as being the narrowest street in the United States. ~~Philadelphia is home to some great sports teams, too, like the Phillies and the Eagles.~~ The Liberty Bell can be viewed close up at Independence Park. At the end of the park is Independence Hall, where our nation's founders hammered out the details of the Declaration of Independence. To see some tall ships, stroll over to Penn's Landing, a waterfront park along the Delaware River. . . .

▶ **REVISION STRATEGY**
Linking Paragraphs to Improve External Coherence

External coherence refers to the connections that link paragraphs together. To make your paragraphs coherent:

- Repeat a word or thought from the previous paragraph to emphasize the connection between paragraphs.
- Add sentences or phrases that build bridges, making the connection between paragraphs more clear.

Interactive Textbook

Get instant help! To improve the unity of your essay, use the Revision Checker for Unity and Coherence, accessible from the menu bar, on-line or on CD-ROM.

 Timed Writing Hint

When revising your writing under timed conditions, check that your thesis sentence addresses the essay prompt directly.

Revising • 259

Step-by-Step Teaching Guide

Revising: Improve Unity and Coherence

1. Explain that unity and coherence are what make an essay strong. Everything that is in the essay belongs in the essay and is working to support the thesis.

2. Tell students that, when applying the circling strategy, any sentences that are hard to define may be superfluous and should be considered for deletion.

3. Have students also consider paragraph order as they evaluate the connection between paragraphs. If students find it difficult to create a bridge between paragraphs, suggest that this might indicate that either the order is not ideal or another paragraph should be added. Encourage students to evaluate paragraphs in alternative orders, to find the order that is most effective.

Customize for
Less Advanced Students

Have students write each paragraph on a separate index card, using a pencil to number them according to their current order. Then, ask them to reorder the cards to see whether they make more sense in a different order. Ask students to consider whether each paragraph flows into the next. Once they have determined the most effective paragraph order, ask students to consider how to make a transition from one paragraph to the next. Help them identify their transitions and improve on them where possible.

⏱ TIME AND RESOURCE MANAGER

Resources
Print: *Writing Support Transparencies*, 12-H–I
Technology: *Writing and Grammar* Interactive Text, Section 12.4

Using the Full Student Edition	Using the Handbook🄷
• Cover pp. 259–264 in class, working through each Revision Strategy with students. • Assign Grammar in Your Writing (p. 262). • Allow class time for peer review as students revise their drafts.	• Cover pp. 163–168 in class, working through each Revision Strategy with students. • Assign Grammar in Your Writing (p. 166). • Allow class time for peer review as students revise their drafts.

Revising: Place Topic Sentences Effectively

1. Have students go over their draft and bracket topic sentences.

2. Students may tend to include supporting details as part of the central idea of the topic sentence, thus confusing the central idea. Remind students that a paragraph's central idea is almost always expressed in a single well-focused topic sentence.

3. Suggest that students practice restating central ideas briefly and in their own words, and revising their topic sentences.

4. As an exercise, read supporting details from a paragraph of descriptive writing and invite students to predict what the topic sentence will be. After students do this, invite them to predict where in a paragraph the topic sentence should be placed.

Customize for
Less Advanced Students

Some students may benefit by working with a partner in applying the bracketing strategy. Have students exchange drafts with partners, and ask each partner to bracket topic sentences in the other's draft.

Integrating Speaking and Listening Skills

Encourage students to deliver their documented essays as speeches, putting particular emphasis on quoted sources. Presentations can come to life when the audience gets a sense of the mood of the essay.

12.4

Revising Your Paragraphs
Place Topic Sentences Effectively

Topical paragraphs contain topic sentences. Functional paragraphs perform a specific function, such as making a transition or emphasizing a point. Each topical paragraph of your essay should contain a topic sentence and supporting details, but the placement of these elements is up to you. The topic sentence doesn't necessarily have to come first. You may express your main idea in the first sentence, the last sentence, or the body of the paragraph.

▶ **REVISION STRATEGY**
Bracketing Topic Sentences

Reread each paragraph of your essay carefully. If the paragraph is topical, place a bracket around its topic sentence. Then, review the placement of each topic sentence, considering whether it is positioned effectively. If a paragraph seems dull or unclear, or if a transition between paragraphs can't be made, your topic sentence may need to be moved.

EXAMPLE: Topic Sentence Begins Paragraph

[Prior to the construction of the Newmill Market, there had been several community protests aimed at halting the developer's project.] For example, residents were primarily concerned about increased traffic and the disappearance of wildlife. Built in 2000 on what had been a cow farm, the mall has since been hailed as an example of how the community and developers can work together to erect a well-planned shopping area.

EXAMPLE: Topic Sentence Within Paragraph

The Newmill Market was built in 2000 on the site of what had been a cow farm. [Prior to construction, there had been several community protests aimed at halting the developer's project.] For example, residents were primarily concerned about increased traffic and the disappearance of wildlife. Since its completion, however, the mall has been hailed as an example of how the community and developers can work together to erect a well-planned shopping area.

Learn More

To learn more about writing effective paragraphs, see Chapter 3.

Revising Your Sentences

Improve Sentence Variety

One of the most common problems in writing sentences is the careless repetition of certain words. For example, if you were writing about the United States mail, you might repeat the word *letter* several times. In order to add variety to your sentences, replace some repeated words with synonyms or pronouns to enliven your writing.

DRAFT: The company president receives thousands of *letters* a day. Many *letters* are from companies and corporations, and many *letters* are from private individuals.

REVISION: The company president receives thousands of *letters* a day. Many *of them* are from companies and corporations, and many are from private individuals.

▶ REVISION STRATEGY
Color-Coding to Locate Repeated Words

Read through your draft, and highlight or circle all repeated words you find. Then, replace some of those words with synonyms (words with similar meanings) or with pronouns (words that stand for nouns). When you insert pronouns to take the place of nouns, be sure that you do not introduce errors in pronoun-antecedent agreement.

Student Work
IN PROGRESS

Name: Tameeka Mitchem
Satellite Academy
New York, NY

Color-Coding to Locate Repeated Words
In revising her draft, Tameeka replaced some repeated words with pronouns.

A survey conducted by The Gallup Organization in January said ~~teens~~ are four times more likely to
         they
volunteer when asked than when ~~teens~~ are not asked.
And, according to a recent on-line poll in *Youth Magazine*,
               young people
96 percent of ~~teens~~ feel that they can make a difference
and change the world.

> Tameeka replaced the repeated word *teens* with a pronoun, *they*, and a synonym, *young people*, to add variety to her writing.

Revising: Color-Coding to Locate Repeated Words

Teaching Resources: Writing Support Transparencies, 12-H

1. Display transparency 12-H and discuss how Tameeka located repeated words. Discuss how changing words to eliminate repetition improves and enlivens writing.

2. Explain that, if they are having a difficult time adding variety to their essays, students might want to consult a thesaurus. Warn them, however, that each word should be looked up before being used, because the thesaurus gives words in very broad categories, and it is easy to choose inappropriate words.

3. Remind students that, often, eliminating repeated words requires rewriting a sentence, either to use a different word effectively, or to simply delete the repeated word without changing the sense of the sentence.

Integrating Vocabulary Skills

Ask a student to read a sentence from a previous work. Call on a volunteer to select a word from that sentence and suggest a synonym to replace a word in it. See how many synonyms students can generate for a single word. Try each synonym in turn in the sentence to test which improves the sentence most.

Customize for
ESL Students

This exercise may be difficult for students with limited English vocabularies. Have students work with partners or in small groups to brainstorm for alternatives to repeated words. Make sure students look up proposed alternative words in a dictionary to ensure their precise usage. Encourage them to write the new words in their notebooks.

Step-by-Step Teaching Guide

Pronoun-Antecedent Agreement

1. After reviewing pronouns and antecedents, have students look through their books, especially their textbooks, to find the ways pronouns are handled by the authors.

2. Discuss the problem of using pronouns when the gender of a singular antecedent is not specified. Note the sentence in the fourth paragraph of "The Mother Tongue," in which the writer uses "he or she." Ask students how this sentence could be revised to use plural pronouns. (*Untrained readers looking at manuscripts from the time of . . . and in a sense they would be right.*)

3. Make sure students understand that when the pronoun and antecedents are plural, so are the objects. (Examples: Several guests asked that their rooms be changed. Some decided not to register their complaints after all.)

Find It in Your Reading

Students may cite the following:

First paragraph: *others burden themselves* (plural).

Fourth paragraph: *any untrained person . . . he or she would be right* (singular).

Find It in Your Writing

Have students review their writing either in class or on their own at home. Ask them to show the class some examples of corrections they made during revision.

12.4

Grammar in Your Writing
Pronoun-Antecedent Agreement

Pronouns are an indispensable writing tool. Most pronouns replace words that have already been used and thus help avoid repetition. The word or group of words to which the pronoun refers is called the *antecedent*. **Pronouns and their antecedents must agree in number and gender.**

When the antecedent is an indefinite pronoun, it may be difficult to tell whether the pronoun and antecedent agree. **Indefinite pronouns** refer to nouns or pronouns that are not specifically named. They may be singular or plural or either.

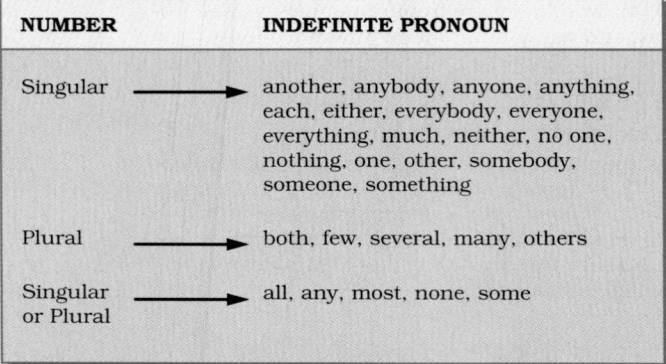

NUMBER	INDEFINITE PRONOUN
Singular	another, anybody, anyone, anything, each, either, everybody, everyone, everything, much, neither, no one, nothing, one, other, somebody, someone, something
Plural	both, few, several, many, others
Singular or Plural	all, any, most, none, some

When an indefinite pronoun is used as an antecedent, make sure the pronoun that refers to it agrees with it in number and gender.

Examples:
Each of the students was given **his or her** own book.
One of the dogs had **its** bowl upside down.
Several guests asked that **their** rooms be changed.
Some of the initial confusion had **its** source in a computer malfunction.
Some decided not to register **their** complaints after all.

Find It in Your Reading Review the excerpt from "Mother Tongue" on pages 248–251. Then, identify two indefinite pronouns used as antecedents and the pronouns that refer to them. Label each *singular* or *plural*.

Find It in Your Writing Review your draft to identify any indefinite pronouns used as antecedents. Be sure that the pronouns that refer to them agree with them in number and gender. Make any necessary corrections.

To learn more about pronoun-antecedent agreement, see Chapter 23.

262 • Documented Essay

☑ ONGOING ASSESSMENT: Prerequisite Skills

If students have difficulty with pronoun-antecedent agreement, you might find it helpful to refer them to the following materials to assure coverage of the subject.

In the Textbook	Print Resources	Technology
Pronoun-Antecedent Agreement, Section 23.2	*Grammar Exercise Workbook,* pp. 99–102	*On-Line Exercise Bank,* Section 23.2

Revising Your Word Choice

Revise to Convey a Tone

Tone is the writer's attitude toward his or her subject. Although most research papers are academic and lack a personal tone, documented essays may be less formal and convey an attitude toward the subject. For example, a writer's tone may be satirical, humorous, or one of warning.

▶**REVISION STRATEGY**

Color-Coding to Check Word Choice

A writer's tone is achieved through his or her word choice. Read through your draft, and circle in color the key words, such as verbs or adjectives and adverbs. Then, review your word choice. Ask yourself the following:

- Do the words work together to create a specific picture?
- Which words, if any, do not fit with the others?
- What other word choice might I make to better convey a single attitude?

Based on the answers to the questions above, revise your draft to create a single, specific tone.

Student Work
IN PROGRESS

Name: Tameeka Mitchem
Satellite Academy
New York, NY

Color-Coding to Identify Word Choice

Tameeka color-coded the words in her essay to get a better idea of her tone. She decided to change her choice of words to better achieve a single tone.

Courtney was told that in order to graduate, she had to do one hundred hours of community service over the summer.

Courtney ~~decided~~ *was determined* to make the most of it. She ~~went~~ *showed up* the first day on time and nervous.

Revising: Color-Coding to Check Word Choice

Teaching Resources: Writing Support Transparencies, 12-I

1. After students read through the textbook material on tone and word choice, ask a volunteer to provide a definition of tone in his or her own words.

2. Challenge students to provide examples of verbs, adjectives, and adverbs that convey the tone in their own drafts. They could also provide examples from previous years.

3. Display Transparency 12-I and point out how Tameeka color-coded her verbs to identify the tone of her essay. How did the revisions improve Tameeka's writing? Does the tone match Tameeka's target audience?

Customize for
ESL Students

Students who are learning English may need extra assistance in determining how word choice affects the tone of writing. Pair students with more fluent speakers of English who can help them with their word choice.

Revising: Check Connotation and Denotation

1. Review the definitions of *connotation* and *denotation*. Ask students to suggest groups of words that have related denotations but different connotations.

2. Have students use the revision strategy to check the words in their drafts. As they look up words, have them share with the class any definitions that were unexpected.

Integrating Vocabulary Skills

Often, words take on a meaning through usage that was not their original definition. For example, the word *personable* once meant "attractive." It has been used to mean "friendly" for so long that now its definition is "having pleasant looks and personality." The word *gregarious* means "living in a herd or flock." It has been used to mean "friendly" so often that now it also means "sociable."

Revision: Peer Review

1. Have students work in class on peer reviews. Students can work in small groups or pairs.

2. Review the two feedback questions, and urge peer reviewers to develop other, more specific questions to ask during group discussion.

3. Encourage students to consider peer suggestions carefully when they revise their work.

12.4

Check Connotation and Denotation

In research writing, accuracy is important. Therefore, you need to be very aware of both the denotation and connotation of the words you choose. A word's *denotation* is its explicit meaning or dictionary definition. A word's *connotation* is its underlying emotional association.

Following are the various denotations and connotations for three similar words:

Word		Connotation
inventor	☞	scientific; neutral
visionary	☞	far-seeing; positive
dreamer	☞	impractical; negative

▶ **REVISION STRATEGY**
Underlining Words and Using a Dictionary and a Thesaurus

Reread your draft, and underline words that have a denotation or connotation of which you are unsure. Then, use a dictionary to check the denotation and a thesaurus to look up alternate word choices and their connotations. Revise your word choices where necessary to make sure you are communicating exactly what you intend.

Peer Review

One of the best ways to find out whether your essay succeeds is to have peers read and respond to it. Your peers may give you a fresh perspective and point out ways to sharpen your ideas and express them more clearly.

Get Group Feedback

Distribute your documented essay to a few of your classmates in advance of meeting as a group. Ask them to read your essay and to jot down their comments about what they have read. Then, when you meet as a group, use these questions to generate discussion:

- How well was the essay's main idea supported?
- How could the essay be made more interesting to a reader?

After you've heard from your classmates, consider using their suggestions to improve your essay.

264 • Documented Essay

⬦ STANDARDIZED TEST PREPARATION WORKSHOP

Standardized tests may require students to identify grammatical errors. Have students read each sentence below and mark the sentence that has a grammatical error.

- **A** The audience applauded the performers' rendition of the play.

- **B** Everyone laughed when the lead player ended her humorous song.

- **C** They all cheered at their great fortune at seeing this performance.

- **D** When the play began, everyone was as quiet as mice.

Students should have selected **D**, where the singular *everyone* does not match the plural *mice*.

12.5 Editing and Proofreading

Before sharing your documented essay with others, proofread it carefully. Correct all errors you find in grammar, spelling, and punctuation.

Focusing on Quotation Marks

Cite sources for all information in your documented essay that does not come directly from you. To avoid plagiarism—using other people's words or ideas without crediting them—be sure you use quotation marks around words, phrases, and sentences that come directly from someone other than yourself. As you proofread, compare each quotation in your essay with the source to make sure that you have recorded exactly what your source said or wrote.

Technology Tip

Use the Find feature in your word-processing program to quickly locate quotation marks within your draft. Then, check each quoted passage against the original to be sure that you have accurately transcribed it.

Grammar in Your Writing
Direct and Indirect Quotations

A **direct quotation** is a word-for-word repetition of what someone said or wrote. Set off direct quotations in one of two ways:

• When a direct quotation is short, enclose it in quotation marks.

Example: Director L. C. Woodgrange remarked, "Shooting a film in an urban location is extremely complicated. That's why we built a set on a soundstage."

• When a direct quotation is four lines or more, precede the quotation with a colon, start the quotation on a new line, and write or type the quoted material to a narrower measure than that used in the rest of the report.

An **indirect quotation** is a restatement, or paraphrase, of someone else's words. It should not be put in quotation marks. However, the source of an indirect quotation must be acknowledged in your essay.

Example: According to director L. C. Woodgrange, he chose to build a set on a soundstage because urban film shoots are complicated.

Find It in Your Writing As you proofread your essay, check that you have set off and correctly punctuated all direct quotations. If you have no direct quotations in your essay, challenge yourself to add a few.

For more on punctuating direct quotations, see Chapter 27.

Editing and Proofreading • 265

Direct and Indirect Quotations

1. After reading the Grammar in Your Writing section, have students look through textbooks to find examples of direct and indirect quotations.

2. Remind students that they may see punctuation outside an ending quotation mark on the Internet or in British works, but the writing style in the United States is to put the comma and period inside a closing quotation mark. The placement of other punctuation, such as a semicolon, question mark, and exclamation point, depends on whether or not they are part of the original quotation.

Find It in Your Writing

Have students use the guidelines to make sure they have correctly cited and punctuated all direct and indirect quotations. Ask them to tell the class whether they have added or deleted quotations from their documented essays.

Integrating Spelling Skills

Remind students that a computer spell checker is useful but cannot replace careful reading when proofing a written work. The spell checker will identify misspelled words, but cannot identify words that are spelled correctly but used incorrectly (examples: *their, there; too, to*).

⏱ TIME AND RESOURCE MANAGER

Resources

Print: *Scoring Rubrics on Transparency*, Ch. 12; *Writing Assessment and Portfolio Management; Formal Assessment*, Ch. 12

Technology: *Writing and Grammar* Interactive Text, Section 12.5

Using the Full Student Edition	Using the Handbook🗎
• Review p. 265 in class, including Grammar in Your Writing. • Give step-by-step coverage to Publishing and Presenting. • Analyze the Final Draft on pp. 267–268.	• Review p. 169 in class, including Grammar in Your Writing. • Give step-by-step coverage to Publishing and Presenting.

1. Discuss presentation options with the group. Ask students to relate ways in which they have published their essays before.

2. Ask students to make a written response to one of the reflecting questions on page 266.

ASSESS and CLOSE

Assessment

Teaching Resources: Scoring Rubrics on Transparency, Ch. 12; Writing Assessment and Portfolio Management; Formal Assessment, Ch. 12

1. Display the Scoring Rubric transparency and review the criteria in class.

2. Before students proceed with self-assessment, you may wish to review the Final Draft of the Student Work in Progress on pages 267–268. Have students score the Final Draft in one or more of the rubric categories.

3. In addition to student self-assessment, you may wish to use the following assessment options.

   • score student essays yourself, using the rubric and scoring models from *Writing Assessment and Portfolio Management*.

   • review the Standardized Test Preparation Workshop on pages 272–273 and administer a timed writing assessment.

   • administer the Chapter 12 assessment from *Formal Assessment* in the Teaching Resources to measure students' grasp of the concepts presented.

12.6 Publishing and Presenting

Building Your Portfolio

Consider these ideas for publishing and presenting your documented essay:

1. **Class Presentation** Contact a teacher who might be interested in having you present your essay to his or her class. Discuss the form of presentation—reading aloud or distributing copies—with the teacher.

2. **Library** If several of your classmates have written profiles of individuals, compile them into an anthology. Protect the essays by putting them in a plastic binder, and put the binder in an accessible place so others can borrow it.

Reflecting on Your Writing

Consider your experience writing a documented essay. Then, respond to the following questions. Record your responses in your portfolio.

• In the process of writing, what did you learn about the topic you chose?

• If you had to research and write a documented essay again, what would you do differently?

Internet Tip

To see a documented essay scored according to this rubric, go on-line:
PHSchool.com
Enter Web Code:
egk-1201

Rubric for Self-Assessment

Use the following criteria to evaluate your documented essay:

	Score 4	Score 3	Score 2	Score 1
Audience and Purpose	Consistently targets a unique audience; clearly identifies purpose in thesis statement	Targets a specific audience; identifies purpose in thesis statement	Misses target audience by including too many details; presents no clear thesis	Addresses no specific audience or purpose
Organization	Presents a clear, consistent organizational strategy	Presents a clear organizational strategy with few inconsistencies	Presents an inconsistent organizational strategy; creates illogical presentation	Demonstrates a lack of organization; creates confusing presentation
Elaboration	Supports thesis statement with several documented sources; elaborates all main points	Supports thesis statement with some documented sources; elaborates most points	Supports the thesis statement with one documented source; elaborates some points	Provides no documented sources; does not provide thesis
Use of Language	Clearly integrates researched information into the writing; presents very few mechanical errors	Integrates most researched information into the writing; presents very few mechanical errors	Does not integrate researched information into the writing; presents many mechanical errors	Demonstrates poor use of language; presents many mechanical errors

266 • Documented Essay

☑ ONGOING ASSESSMENT: Assess Mastery

Use one of the following options to assess drafts of students' essays.

Self-Assessment Ask students to score their stories using the rubric provided. Then, have students write a paragraph that discusses the strategy they found most helpful in composing their documented essays.	**Teacher Assessment** Use the rubric and the scoring models provided in *Writing Assessment and Portfolio Management* to score students' work.

12.7 Student Work IN PROGRESS

FINAL DRAFT

▼ **Critical Viewing**
What benefits does reading to children provide for the children? For the volunteer? [**Generalize**]

Youths Offer a Helping Hand

Tameeka Mitchem
Satellite Academy
New York, New York

Each day after school, eighteen-year-old Courtney Cauthett of Manhattan spends two hours counseling and tutoring young children at a local community center. Kajal Angras, eighteen, a senior at Curtis High School on Staten Island, volunteers three hours a day, two days a week at Project Hospitality, an organization that helps needy mothers and their children.

Courtney and Kajal are among the growing number of teens across the country who are getting up, going out, and getting

Tameeka captures the interest of her audience by giving examples of teenagers who are actively participating in volunteering.

Step-by-Step Teaching Guide

Final Draft

1. Have students read the opening paragraph and paraphrase it. Ask students if this presents the thesis statement. (No, it sets up the thesis with an example.)

2. Have students identify Tameeka's thesis statement. *(Courtney and Kajal are among the growing number of teens across the country who are getting up, going out, and getting involved to help others.)*

3. After reading the essay, have students identify Tameeka's sources. Have them describe how she documents each source.

4. Have students find Tameeka's quotations. Ask them to identify each one as either "direct" or "indirect."

5. Ask students to identify the opening statement, the body, and the conclusion of Tameeka's essay.

6. Have students look for words that have connotations that add to the meaning *(needy, rewarding, tutor,* and *intrigued).*

7. Ask students to describe how Tameeka's closing supports her thesis.

8. Finally, ask students to evaluate Tameeka's essay for its effectiveness. Do they think she did a good job of documenting her thesis? Did they learn something by reading her essay?

9. Ask students to suggest any changes they would make to Tameeka's essay. How might they apply these suggestions to their own writing?

Critical Viewing

Generalize Students may suggest that children will gain a positive experience of reading and the volunteer will gain a sense of accomplishment.

267

Teaching from the Final Draft

Due to space constraints in this textbook, the Final Draft of the documented essay may not be as long as you will require of your students. As you review the Final Draft, be sure to clarify to students your particular requirements regarding length, quantity of quotations and sources, method of citation, and other details.

Customize for
Gifted and Talented Students

Ask students how they would illustrate Tameeka's essay if it were to be published in a general-interest magazine. What photographs and other visual aids might be added? Have students sketch a magazine layout for this essay.

Critical Viewing

Analyze Students may suggest that the volunteer is working in a food pantry of some sort, collecting or distributing food for those in need.

---

involved to help others. Last year, nearly 60 percent of the nation's teens volunteered 2.3 billion hours to a social or political cause. (*Philanthropy Journal Online.* Philanthropy News Network Online. 3 May 20_ **<http://www.pj.org>**) Of those hours, 1.8 billion were given to national organizations, while the other 500 million were given to people in their communities. These statistics present compelling evidence that teenagers care about others.

"The kids make you feel needed," says Courtney McAllister, a senior at The Beacon School, referring to the children she works with in a Police Athletic League program in Harlem. "They really open your eyes to so many things. It feels good when you help them with their homework and they thank you. It is so rewarding." (McAllister, Courtney, Personal interview, 25 March 2000)

Courtney was told that in order to graduate, she had to do 100 hours of community service over the summer. Courtney was determined to make the most of it. She showed up the first day on time and nervous. "I didn't know what to expect from the

kids," she says. But after getting to know them, she became more relaxed and even stayed on after her 100 hours were up.

Kajal says she never expected to be a volunteer. She had been to Project Hospitality once, but only to interview someone for her school paper. After reading about the organization and seeing it in action, she became intrigued and decided to pitch in. Kajal has now been a counselor and tutor there for two years. "I love the kids," said Kajal. "They remind me to be humble and help me to realize what I take for granted."

A survey conducted by The Gallup Organization in January said teens are four times more likely to volunteer when asked than if they are not asked. And, according to a recent poll, 96 percent of teens feel that they can make a difference and change the world.

"Getting out there and helping to contribute something to this planet is what it's all about," says Courtney.

Tameeka follows with her main idea: The number of students volunteering in their communities is increasing.

Source information is provided within parentheses.

The body of Tameeka's essay is clearly organized. Here, she illustrates her thesis with anecdotes and quotations, identifying the source each time.

◀ **Critical Viewing** What sort of volunteer work is this student performing? How can you tell? **[Analyze]**

In conclusion, Tameeka reemphasizes her thesis by citing two surveys that support it.

Ending with this quotation leaves the reader with something to think about.

Connected Assignment *Statistical Report*

A **statistical report** relies on numerical evidence—often presented in tables, charts, or graphs—to make and support its main idea. Sometimes, the main idea may be presented last as a conclusion drawn from the statistical evidence. Other times, writers may state a thesis and use statistical evidence to support it.

Use the writing process skills outlined below to write your own statistical report.

Prewriting

Choosing Your Topic To find a topic for a statistical report, you can either start with the statistics or with a more general topic. To start with statistics, look at a newspaper's business report or flip through an almanac until some numbers catch your eye. To start with a more general topic, think of an event from history or a scientific breakthrough that interests you.

Narrowing Your Topic Once you've chosen a topic, narrow it by asking yourself what you want readers to learn about that topic. Then brainstorm for places to find statistical information. Try subject-linked reference sources, general and specific almanacs, specialty magazines, newspaper articles, and even expert interviews. Respond to the statistics by writing a thesis statement that is supported by the data you have found.

Drafting State your topic and your main idea in the first paragraph. Then, develop your main idea in the body of the report. Support each paragraph's main idea with the evidence you have found. As you draft, connect your statistics to the ideas you've stated. Don't use statistics unless they directly relate to the point you are making.

Revising and Editing Reread your report. If it seems unconvincing, insert more statistical evidence from your sources or from the library if necessary. Replace argumentative language with objective statements that are supported by facts. Review your evidence for accuracy, and check to be sure that charts and graphs are legible and consistently labeled.

Publishing and Presenting Make a neat copy of your report and its accompanying charts, graphs, or other visual evidence. Present your report to a group of interested peers. Keep a copy of your finished report in your portfolio.

▲ **Critical Viewing**
At which stage of the writing process is this student? What makes you think so?
[Speculate]

Connected Assignment: Statistical Report • 269

▶ *Lesson Objectives*

1. To write a statistical report that is appropriate to audience and purpose
2. To use writing to discover, organize, and support what is known and what needs to be learned about a topic
3. To organize and record information in systematic ways, including notes, charts, and graphic organizers

Step-by-Step Teaching Guide

Statistical Report

1. Ask students to brainstorm for statistical report topics or look for possible topics in magazines and newspapers.
2. As students identify topics of interest, list them on the board. Lead students to see connections between the topic areas, student's ideas about possible related statistics that they could look for, and what these may indicate about the subject.
3. Remind students that their writing must still be persuasive or attention-getting. Suggest that students augment their statistics with personal testimony or quotes.

Customize for *AP Students*

Suggest that students develop a topic on the benefits or drawbacks of a school, state, or national policy. Remind students that newspaper articles and editorial pages frequently cite statistical sources that can help students write further on the same issue.

Critical Viewing

Speculate Students may suggest that the student is at the Publishing and Presenting phase, since he appears to be polishing an illustrative graphic.

☑ **ONGOING ASSESSMENT: Prerequisite Skills**

Students may find the following resources from Chapter 12 particularly helpful in completing their assignments.

In the Textbook	Print Resources	Technology
Narrowing a Topic, Section 12.2 Make a Research Plan, Section 12.2	*Writing Support Transparencies,* 12-B–D; Writing Support Activity Book, 12-1–2	*Writing and Grammar* Interactive Text, Section 12.2

Spotlight on the Humanities

Examining Messages in Film

Focus on Film: *Grand Illusion*

Documentary essays tell about real-life people, things, and events. War is a real-life event that is often explored in films and documentaries. French director Jean Renoir (1894–1979), considered to be one of the great filmmakers of all time, directed the masterpiece *Grand Illusion* in 1937. This moving war film defies the characteristics of the genre of war films in that it does not contain a single combat scene. Rather, it focuses on the relations between human beings, both friend and foe. This focus conveys the message that war is an illusion. Renoir's meaningful use of the moving camera, his use of plain yet emphatic music, and his use of middle gray tones to convey meaning make *Grand Illusion* a masterwork in the world of cinema.

Art Connection Jean Renoir's father was French Impressionist painter Pierre-Auguste Renoir (1841–1919). Pierre-Auguste Renoir was famed for his use of brilliant color, his harmony of lines, and his wide range of subjects, to which he brought great intimacy. His early influences were the painters Claude Monet and Eugène Delacroix. Although he was crippled by arthritis for the last years of his life, Renoir continued to paint by strapping a brush to his arm.

Music Connection In 1939, Jean Renoir directed a film version of the classic Italian opera *Tosca* by Giacomo Puccini (1858–1924). *Tosca*, first performed in Rome in 1900, is the operatic tale of a woman whose beloved friend is killed by a heartless sheriff for hiding a fugitive. *Tosca* brought Puccini recognition as the successor to composer Giuseppe Verdi, one of the most important composers of the nineteenth century.

Research Writing Application: Documented Essay on the Renoirs

Imagine that you had been able to interact with and interview Pierre-Auguste and Jean Renoir (instead, you can pull your information from library research). Write a documented essay about their exciting, prolific lives, complete with personal anecdotes about both men.

▲ Critical Viewing Where and when might this scene from *Grand Illusion* have taken place? Explain. **[Analyze]**

Media and Technology Skills

Using Media to Produce a Documentary

Activity: Film a Video Documentary

As you collect information for a documented essay, you may uncover fascinating facts, images, and ideas that are best shared in another medium. Video allows you to combine various types of details to bring a subject to life for your audience.

Think About It Film a 10- to 12-minute documentary based on research into a topic. Choose a topic that will translate well into film. Because interviews are a key element of many documentaries, consider topics for which you know experts to interview.

Research It Collect information about your topic from a number of sources. Take careful notes that identify photographs, artwork, songs, sounds, or other media resources that you intend to include in your documentary.

Storyboard It Make a storyboard like the one shown below to plan and balance the elements you will include in your video.

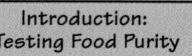

Introduction:
Testing Food Purity

Narrated discussion in the
school cafeteria

Interview with Dr. Alana Klein
in her food-testing lab

Script It Write a script that includes narration, a list of settings, and the images you will include. Write narration that provides essential background information, introduces settings and people, and links scenes. Conduct your video interviews, and select the best sections before finalizing your filming script.

Produce It Shoot the remaining video elements of your documentary. Look for opportunities to incorporate action into your film. Consider conducting an interview while walking, or have the camera pan across a photograph or landscape. Assemble the documentary elements during editing, and script to match your actual footage.

Media and Technology Skills • 271

► *Lesson Objectives*

1. To use a variety of forms and technologies to communicate specific messages
2. To create a ten-to fifteen-minute investigative documentary
3. To present a documentary to an audience and analyze the response

Step-by-Step Teaching Guide

Using Media to Produce a Documentary

Teaching Resources: Writing Support Transparency, 12-J, Writing Support Activity Book, 12-3

1. Students may work more efficiently in small groups to produce a documentary. Give them ample time to settle on a subject and choose a director.
2. Display Transparency 12-J to help them plan their filming. Encourage students to devise their own storyboards by distributing copies of 12-3 from the *Writing Support Activity Book*.
3. If students work in groups, suggest that each person in a group can be responsible for one aspect of the documentary, including the script.
4. Go over the filming tips in the sidebar. If students do not have access to the technologies suggested, encourage them to come up with creative solutions.
5. Give students the opportunity to present their documentaries to the class. Some students may wish to make a presentation for another class as well.

1. To respond to a document-based writing prompt

2. To use prewriting strategies to generate ideas, develop voice, and plan

3. To develop a draft by organizing content such as by paragraphing and outlining and by refining style to suit occasion, audience, and purpose

4. To revise drafts by rethinking content organization and style to better accomplish the task

5. To produce error-free writing in the final draft

Step-by-Step Teaching Guide

Responding to Document-Based Writing Prompts

Teaching Resources: Standardized Test Preparation Workbook, pp. 23–24

1. Go over the first paragraph on this page, clarifying if necessary the terms *analyze, evaluate, draw conclusions,* and *synthesize.*

2. Review the bulleted items with students. These clarify what abilities are measured on the test items they will be practicing.

3. Assign the the writing prompt, and go over the responses with students when they have finished.

4. After students complete their responses to the prompt, ask them which portion of the assignment they had the most difficulty with, and why.

Standardized Test Preparation Workshop

Responding to Document-Based Writing Prompts

Your ability to use evidence from an article to support a response to a writing prompt is often assessed on standardized tests. For example, this type of prompt may require you to analyze an issue, evaluate a writer's position, or draw conclusions. In some cases, you may be required to synthesize information from several documents that are provided. When writing a response, you will be evaluated on your ability to do the following:

- respond directly to the prompt
- show a clear understanding of the included text
- elaborate, using details from the article to support your response
- compare and contrast several documents, where applicable
- organize details logically and effectively
- use correct grammar, spelling, and punctuation

The process of writing for a test, as for any kind of writing, can be divided into stages. Plan to use a specific amount of time for prewriting, drafting, revising, and proofreading.

Following is an example of one type of writing prompt that you might find on a standardized test. Use the suggestions on the following page to help you respond. The clocks next to each stage show a suggested plan for organizing your time.

Reread the excerpt from "Mother Tongue," by Bill Bryson, on pages 248–251. Then, respond to the following test prompt.

Sample Writing Situation

In "Mother Tongue," Bill Bryson discusses how the world would be different if geographic boundaries were based on the languages spoken in different areas. How does language create boundaries between groups of people in the same country? Use details and information from the article in your response.

Test Tip

When analyzing a document provided in a test, don't overuse direct quotations. The basis of the response should be your interpretation of the text.

✐ TEST-TAKING TIP

Ask students to pick out the key phrases in the sample prompt to which they must respond *(how does language create boundaries* and *use details and information from the article in your response).* Encourage students to underline such passages in test prompts and refer to them from time to time during the writing period to ensure that they are answering the question asked.

Then tell students that in a response to a document-based writing prompt, the length of their answers will often depend on how many points they feel they can cite in the time allotted. Assure students they will rarely be asked to invoke every fact in the text. Review with students how they can distinguish which elements are most helpful to their theses.

Prewriting

Allow close to one quarter of your time for prewriting.

Use a T-Chart Before you write, use a T-chart to gather details for your response. On the left side of the chart, list reasons that languages might create boundaries between people. For each reason, list on the right side details from the article that support it.

Make an Outline Review the information on your T-chart, and think about how to best present it. Make an outline that shows the order in which you plan to discuss each detail. Refer to your completed outline as you draft your response.

Drafting

Allow almost half of your time for drafting.

Write a Strong Beginning Begin your response with an effective introduction that lets readers know what you plan to discuss. Include a thesis statement that introduces the main idea of your response. Also, write a sentence that acts as a transition into the body of the response.

Elaborate in the Body In the body of your response, develop and support your thesis statement. In each paragraph, use specific details from the article to support your thesis; then, add your insights to support, explain, or illustrate those details.

Conclude Effectively In your final paragraph, summarize the main points of your essay by restating the thesis. Also, leave a lasting impression on readers by including a recommendation, a provocative question, or a statement of personal insight.

Revising, Editing, and Proofreading

Allow almost one quarter of your time to revise and edit. Use the last few minutes to proofread your work.

Quote Accurately Make sure that all the quotations included in your response are correctly punctuated and enclosed in quotation marks. Also, check to be sure that you have copied each quotation word for word from the article. Finally, make sure that all quotations are incorporated smoothly into the text.

Make Corrections Review your response for errors. Neatly cross out any details that do not support your thesis. Correct all errors you have made in grammar, spelling, and punctuation. When making changes, place one line through text that you want eliminated, and use a caret [^] to indicate where you are adding words.

Chapter 13 Time and Resource Manager

In-Depth Lesson Plan

	LESSON FOCUS	PRINT AND MEDIA RESOURCES
DAY 1	**Introduction to Research Papers** Students learn key elements and types of research papers and analyze the Model From Literature. (pp. 274–279/H172–173)	*Writers at Work* DVD, Research Writing *Writing and Grammar* Interactive Text, Ch. 13, Introduction
DAY 2	**Prewriting** Students choose and narrow a topic, consider their audience and purpose, and gather details. (pp. 280–285/H174–179)	*Writing and Grammar* Interactive Text, Section 13.2 **Teaching Resources** *Writing Support Transparencies, 13-A–E; Writing Support Activity Book, 13-1; Topic Bank for Heterogeneous Classes,* Ch. 13
DAY 3	**Drafting** Students develop a thesis statement, organize to support it, and write their first drafts. (pp. 286–288/H180–182)	*Writing and Grammar* Interactive Text, Section 13.3 **Teaching Resources** *Writing Support Transparencies,* 13-F–H
DAY 4	**Revising** Students revise their drafts in terms of overall structure, paragraphs, sentences, and word choice. (pp. 289–293/H183–187)	*Writing and Grammar* Interactive Text, Section 13.4 **Teaching Resources** *Writing Support Transparencies,* 13-I–J
DAY 5	**Editing and Proofreading; Publishing and Presenting** Students check their work for accuracy and correctness and present their final drafts. (pp. 294–299/H188–193)	*Writing and Grammar* Interactive Text, Sections 13.5–6 **Teaching Resources** *Writing Support Transparencies, 13-K; Scoring Rubrics on Transparency,* Ch. 13; *Writing Assessment and Portfolio Management; Formal Assessment,* Ch. 13

Accelerated Lesson Plan

	LESSON FOCUS	PRINT AND MEDIA RESOURCES
DAY 1	**Introduction Through Drafting** Students review the elements of research writing, select topics, and write drafts. (pp. 274–288/H172–182)	*Writers at Work* DVD, Research Writing *Writing and Grammar* Interactive Text, Ch. 13, Introduction through Section 13.3 **Teaching Resources** *Writing Support Transparencies, 13-A–H; Writing Support Activity Book,* 13-1
DAY 2	**Revising Through Presenting** Students work individually or with peers to revise, edit, and proofread their work for presentation. (pp. 289–296/H183–190)	*Writing and Grammar* Interactive Text, Sections 13.4–6 **Teaching Resources** *Writing Support Transparencies, 13-I–K; Writing Support Activity Book, 13-2; Scoring Rubrics on Transparency,* Ch. 13; *Writing Assessment and Portfolio Management; Formal Assessment,* Ch. 13

Options for Adapting Lesson Plans

HOMEWORK
Have students complete any stage of the lesson for homework.

FEATURES
Extend coverage with Connected Assignment (p. 300), Spotlight on the Humanities (p. 302), Media and Technology Skills (p. 303), and the Standardized Test Preparation Workshop (pp. 304–305).

TECHNOLOGY
Students can complete any stage of the lesson on the computer, using *Writing and Grammar* Interactive Text or a word-processing program. Have them print out their completed work.

Writing and Grammar Handbook Alignment

Page numbers in Step-by-Step Teaching Guides in this Teacher's Edition refer to pages from the full student text. Handbook page references, indicated with this icon 🄷, are provided in Time and Resource Manager boxes and at the bottom of each Teacher's Edition page.

INTEGRATED SKILLS COVERAGE

Integrating Grammar
Dependent and Independent Clauses, SE p. 292/🄷186
Formatting, SE p. 295/🄷189
ATE pp. 285, 298

Reading/Writing Connection
Identify Causes and Effects, SE p. 276
Writing Application, SE p. 279

Viewing and Representing
Critical Viewing, SE pp. 274, 276, 278, 279, 289, 290, 297, 300, 302/🄷172, 183, 184, 191
Recognizing Art Forms, SE p. 302

Technology
Evaluating On-line Resources, SE p. 303
SE pp. 284, 294/🄷178, 188; ATE p. 299

Research SE p. 282/🄷176

Vocabulary ATE pp. 287, 292

Real-World Connection ATE p. 277

Workplace Skills ATE p. 301

ASSESSMENT SUPPORT

Standardized Test Preparation Workshop SE p. 304; ATE p. 290
Standardized Test Preparation Workbook, pp. 25–26
Formal Assessment, Ch. 13
Scoring Rubrics on Transparency, Ch. 13
Writing Assessment and Portfolio Management

MEETING INDIVIDUAL NEEDS

Less Advanced Students ATE pp. 299, 305. See also Ongoing Assessments ATE pp. 281, 285, 287, 291.
AP Students ATE pp. 279, 283, 285, 295, 305
ESL Students ATE pp. 277, 284
Spatial Learners ATE p. 286
Bodily/Kinesthetic Learners ATE pp. 278, 296, 302

BLOCK SCHEDULING

Pacing Suggestions
For 90-minute Blocks
• Have students complete the Prewriting and Drafting stages in a single period.
• Focus one class period on Revising and Editing and Publishing and Presenting. Allow at least 30 minutes for peer revision.

Resources for Varying Instruction
• *Writing and Grammar* **Interactive Text** A 90-minute block provides an ideal opportunity for students to work on the computer.
• *Writers at Work* **DVD** Show the Research Writing segment in class.

Professional Development Support
• *How to Manage Instruction in the Block* This teaching resource provides management and activity suggestions.

MEDIA AND TECHNOLOGY

For the Student
• *Writing and Grammar* **Interactive Text**, Ch. 13
• *On-line Exercise Bank,* Section 19.3

For the Teacher
• *Writers at Work* **DVD**, Research Writing
• **Teacher**EXPRESS™ **CD-ROM**

WRITING AND GRAMMAR ON-LINE

Interactive Text (On-line or on CD-ROM)
• Easily navigable instruction with interactive Revision Checkers
• Full use of e-rater™, the essay-scoring system (on-line only)

Companion Web Site PHSchool.com
• Scoring rubrics with models (use Web Code egk-1201)

See the Go On-line! **feature, SE p. iii.**

LITERATURE CONNECTIONS

Related selection from *Prentice Hall Literature, Penguin Edition,* The British Tradition:

Topic Bank Option from "Defending Nonviolent Resistance," Mohandas K. Gandhi, SE p. 281/🄷175

Lesson Objectives

1. To write a research paper appropriate to audience and purpose
2. To read to appreciate the writer's craft and to discover models for writing
3. To use prewriting strategies to generate ideas and to plan
4. To use writing to formulate questions, refine topics, and clarify ideas
5. To compile and organize information from primary and secondary sources using available technology
6. To develop drafts and revise drafts in terms of structure, paragraphs, sentences, and word choice
7. To edit and proofread to ensure standard English usage and grammar
8. To use a manual of style
9. To refine a research paper for publication

Critical Viewing

Analyze Students may wish to do research on the builder of the castle, on its inhabitants through the centuries, or on its architecture.

Chapter 13 Research
Research Paper

Research in Everyday Life

As a high-school student, you might think it's obvious how research papers fit into your daily life: They are a requirement for many courses. You may even be working on one right now. However, **research writing**—writing based on information gathered from outside sources—also has an important role to play in the world at large. News reports, documentary films, historical fiction, and business reports are an example of the various everyday items that involve some degree of research.

Other activities that involve research are not written at all. For example, checking a map to locate a city, running a web search to learn about a scientific breakthrough, and questioning a grandparent about life in the "olden days" are all forms of research. In the following chapter, you will become more familiar with how to conduct research and write a research-based paper.

▲ **Critical Viewing** Study this photograph of Edinburgh Castle. What three questions come to mind that you would like to research? **[Analyze]**

274 • Research

⏱ TIME AND RESOURCE MANAGER

Resources
Technology: *Writers at Work* DVD, Research Writing; *Writing and Grammar* Interactive Text, Ch. 13

Using the Full Student Edition	Using the Handbook Ⓗ
• Cover pp. 274–275 in class. • Show the Research Writing section of the *Writers at Work* DVD. • Read the Model From Literature (pp. 276–279) in class, and use it to brainstorm for research paper ideas.	• Cover pp. 172–173 in class. • Show the Research Writing section of the *Writers at Work* DVD.

What Is a Research Paper?

A **research paper** is an in-depth, written examination of a topic in which the writer puts forth a thesis, or main point, and supports it with information drawn from several outside sources. A research paper

- brings together factual information from a variety of credible sources.
- develops a thesis, which presents one or more key points or arguments about the topic.
- has a consistent and effective organization.
- uses footnotes, endnotes, or parenthetical notes to credit sources.
- includes a bibliography or "works-cited" page.

To preview the criteria on which your research paper may be evaluated, see the Rubric for Self-Assessment on page 296.

Types of Research Papers

Writing involving research varies in length, formality, and audience and can take many forms:

- **I-Searches** are research papers about a topic of special interest to the writer. An I-Search tells the story of the writer's research path.
- **Academic reports** help educators gauge a student's ability to use research skills as a learning tool.
- **Biographical reports** contain information—such as interview material, quotations, and family history—about a person.
- **Multigenre reports** share insights gained through research. Rather than presenting findings in a traditional report, the writer shares findings through writing spanning several genres, such as poetry, short story, and drama.

PREVIEW
Student Work
IN PROGRESS

Ian Pritchard, a student at Buena High School in Ventura, California, researched and wrote a biographical report on Seamus Heaney, a Pulitzer Prize-winning poet. His completed research paper appears at the end of the chapter.

Writers in ACTION

Sportswriter Peter Ginsburg uses research in his work. He offers the following observations about the types of research that he performs:

"There are a couple of different types of research that I do, and I guess you could call them primary and secondary. Primary research occurs when we talk to the person on whom we want to do the story. . . . The best type of research you can do is going right to the source. Other types of research I do I would consider secondary. It takes place through the newspaper, talking to the sports information director, and then just reading articles and reading books."

Interest GRABBER Write some broad categories on the chalkboard such as Personal Health, All About Cars, Problems Affecting Society, The Arts, Sports, Science, and History. Distribute slips of paper and have students write questions to which they would enjoy finding the answers. Encourage students to share their questions and post them under each category.

Activate Prior Knowledge

Ask students to talk about research papers and projects that they have done in their school careers. What are some of the topics they explored? What difficulties did they encounter in writing their papers? What did they find satisfying or successful in their work? Refer students to the types of research writing on this page.

☑ ONGOING ASSESSMENT: Diagnose

Use the following strategy to diagnose students' current level of proficiency in research paper writing.

Hold a conference with students about their interests and strategies for turning ideas into research projects. Students who are trying to explore questions that are either too broad or too narrow, or those with little idea where to look for supporting factual material may need extra help in completing the assignment.

Identify Causes and Effects

Have students speculate on the reasons that the game of football changed in response to the conditions described in this piece. (Widespread injuries and deaths made it essential that players be protected and rules be changed.)

Step-by-Step Teaching Guide

Engage Students Through Literature

1. Use the following questions to prompt discussion:

   What did Kachur discover about the nature of football at the turn of the century? (Football had become a very brutal sport.)

   How did it differ from the game we know today? (Today's game has rules and regulations to protect players; nineteenth-century football did not.)

   What sources does Kachur cite? (*The New York Times Index, The History of American Football, The Journal of the American Medical Association,* and the *Boston Medical and Surgical Journal*)

2. Ask students to brainstorm for related research paper ideas suggested by the excerpt.

Critical Viewing

Compare and Contrast Student may say the close-fitting jerseys and knee pants are similar, but the absence of heavy protective padding is different.

Model From Literature

13.1

The following research report was written by Matthew Kachur as he pursued his doctorate in American history. Kachur is a writer and editor who works in New York City.

Reading Writing Connection

Reading Strategy: Identify Causes and Effects As you read this paper, deepen your understanding by looking for cause-and-effect relationships.

▲ **Critical Viewing** Examine this photograph taken in the 1890's. In what ways are football uniforms similar to and different from football uniforms today? **[Compare and Contrast]**

Football at the Turn of the Twentieth Century

Matthew Kachur

The indexers for *The New York Times* decided to make a change when compiling the information for the year 1903. Previously, the heading "Football" had been sufficient for coverage of the subject matter. But in 1903, the newspaper had printed a group of related stories with such frequency that the index editors saw the need for a new category under the main head: "Football, Fatal Accidents." Below this subhead runs a list of people who had died while playing football that year (*New York Times Index* 664).

This addition to the index indicates that, by the turn of the twentieth century, football had become a sport of almost unmatched brutality. Fatal injuries, of course, occur in sporting events today. It appears that we as a people are prepared to accept the occasional fatality on the football field or the death of a prizefighter in the ring as long as they are isolated instances. It is difficult to imagine the American public sanctioning a sport in which participants are regularly killed. This last point must be emphasized: In the brand of football played in the 1890's, players

Kachur's introduction grabs the interest of the audience and introduces his topic.

The thesis statement leads off the second paragraph.

regularly sustained fatal injuries. And yet it was a sport that was defended and endorsed by many Americans, some of whom were members of the medical community.

In 1894, an American journal published a French visitor's description of a football game he had witnessed. The account was marked by phrases such as "young bulldogs" and "the demon of conflict." One passage was particularly telling:

> The brutality with which they seize the bearer of the ball is impossible to imagine without having witnessed it. He is seized by the middle of the body, by the head, by the legs, by the feet. He rolls over and his assailants with him, and as they fight for the ball and the two sides come to the rescue, it becomes a whole heap of twenty-two bodies tumbling on top of one another, like a [. . .] heap of serpents with human heads [. . .]. (*Boston Medical and Surgical Journal* 570–571)

American football has its origins in the English games of soccer and rugby. Indeed, the first American match game would seem to a modern observer more like soccer than American football. This game, played in 1869, pitted Rutgers against the College of New Jersey, with 25 players on each side. The ball was moved by kicking or slapping with the hand or head, but could not be carried or passed. By the 1870's, a game more familiar to us had developed, with ball carrying replacing kicking. Still, the game was basically a defensive affair in which serious injuries were common.

In 1882, a reform was instituted that halted play after the ball carrier was knocked down. Before this rule change, his teammates would have dragged him along if he hit the turf.

By the 1890's, football had become well established in the United States, especially at the intercollegiate level. Sixty colleges were playing the game in 1888, a figure that doubled by 1890. Already such institutions as the big Thanksgiving Day game had been established. College alumni supported the teams of their alma maters, and there were widespread rumblings of professionalism in the ranks of college athletes (Danzig; Weyland).

In [an] essay, titled "The American Boy," [vice-president Theodore] Roosevelt addressed the importance of competitive athletics:

> Nowadays, whatever other faults the son of rich parents may tend to develop, he is at least forced [. . .] to bear himself well in many exercises and to develop his body—and therefore, to a certain extent, his character—in the rough sports which call for pluck, endurance, and physical address. (Roosevelt 104)

The [supporters] of the game of football seized on Roosevelt's words, using his rhetoric in their defenses of the sport. Dr. J. William White, writing in *The Outlook*, quoted some remarks Roosevelt made before an audience of Harvard alumni:

Quotation marks around phrases like "young bulldogs" indicate that the words are someone else's.

This quoted passage is correctly set as an excerpt. The internal citation that follows gives the title of the source material because there was no author listed, plus the pages on which the quotation appears.

Historical data such as this help develop Kachur's thesis: that football was a brutal game.

The body of Kachur's report is organized chronologically.

This summary is based on information found in the two works cited.

Model From Literature • 277

Teaching From the Model

Use this Model From Literature as a way of showing the style and format of a research paper. Matthew Kachur explores a historical phenomenon and cites historical developments and contemporary writings on the subject. Have students consider how this formal research paper is different from a newspaper article or a personal essay.

Real-World Connection

Research writing is a standard activity in higher education to assess, test, and make discoveries known. It is also the form that is most commonly used to evaluate whether someone should receive a graduate degree. In the business world, research writing is used to present business proposals and projects. In government, research writing helps officials make public policy decisions.

Customize for
ESL Students

Many students may be unfamiliar with the game known as "American football" and know the game referred to in the U.S. as "soccer." To improve students' comprehension of this selection, provide pictures of contemporary football players and soccer players and discuss the differences between these two games.

Teaching From the Model

Have students note Kachur's frequent use of quotations from nineteenth-century sources. Ask them what purpose these quotes serve in the essay. (They help the reader understand how people in the nineteenth century viewed the game of football.)

Ask students whether they think Kachur chose an interesting topic, and why. Lead them to see that the topic allows interesting comparisons to be made between a cultural phenomenon of the past and of the present.

Customize for
Bodily/Kinesthetic Learners

Encourage students who play in organized sports to discuss the issue of injuries sustained during competition. Do students feel that the risks are worth taking? Why or why not? Do other students agree or disagree?

Critical Viewing

Analyze Students will point out that the absence of heavy padding for chest and shoulders and the lack of a rigid helmet suggests that the uniforms provided little protection for players.

I do not mind in the least that they are rough games, or that those who take part in them are occasionally injured. I have no sympathy whatever with the overwrought sentimentality which would keep a young man in cotton wool, and I have a hearty contempt for him if he counts a broken arm or collarbone as of serious consequence when balanced against the chance of showing that he possesses hardihood, physical address, and courage. (*The Outlook*)

One of the leading critics of football was E. L. Godkin, who as early as 1893 was [protesting] against the sport in the editorials of *The Nation*. Describing a game between Harvard and Yale, it was pointed out that seven out of the twenty-two starting players were injured, a higher casualty rate than at Cold Harbor, Waterloo, or Gravelotte. How, the magazine asked, could the colleges [authorize] a sport in which litters and surgeons were required at every contest (*The Nation*)?

The numerous defenses of football were consistent on a number of points. First, the brutality and violence of football was overstated by its detractors, as were the number of injuries: It just was not as bad as it was said to be. Second, football was good exercise and beneficial to health. But the importance of football to physical health paled in importance to the moral benefits of football. Football built character; it turned boys into men.

William Lee Howard gave a spirited defense of football in "Football and Moral Health," published in 1906. In the article, Howard urged that no barriers beyond the basic minimum necessary to organize the game be placed on football. Indeed, he refers to the many "miserable beings" he has come across in his practice who he feels should have been forced to play football in their younger days (*The Medical Record* 546–547).

There were those doctors who condemned football. It was as an institution, however, that the medical journals expressed dissatisfaction with the sport. *The Medical News*, entitling an 1884 editorial "The Football Disgrace," stated:

> Our postman has brought us from many correspondents and from all over the land an amazing mass of news of deaths, broken bones, wrenches, concussions, dislocations, [and] gambling [. . .] of the victorious; tears and bellowing of the vanquished; and sluggings, sluggings, sluggings—without end. [. . .] Let us hear no more of [. . .] revision and reform. [. . .] there is but one change demanded: abolish them absolutely! (615)

A game between Harvard and Yale prompted *The Boston Medical and Surgical Journal* to write: "That a player may with impunity jump on an antagonist [lying] on the ground with the

When no page number exists in source material, provide the title of the source or author name within parentheses.

Keeping his audience in mind, Kachur gives information about the people who are quoted.

▼ **Critical Viewing**
What sort of protection does this uniform offer the football player? [**Analyze**]

ball, after the whistle has blown, and dislocate his victim's [collar-bone], should be an impossibility." They argued that promises of reform had not been kept and that football would no longer be tolerated if the players were allowed to behave like "brutes" (543).

Finally, *The Journal of the American Medical Association* wondered if football was worth the twelve deaths and over eighty serious injuries, including "torn ears" and "brain injuries resulting in insanity," that occurred in the 1902 season. "To be a cripple or a lunatic for life is paying high for athletic (competition)" (39).

It is interesting to note that some of the strongest defenses of football, such as that of William Lee Howard, occurred after those in control of the sport at the college level were forced to reform the game. According to one source, seven football players died in 1901, fifteen in 1902, fourteen in 1903, fourteen again in 1904, and twenty-four in 1905. Theodore Roosevelt, new President of the United States, was moved by the mounting death toll to pressure those in charge of college football to begin a process of reform. The result was the gradual elimination of football's most vicious characteristics. Although the sport did not change overnight, rule changes that encouraged the pass and discouraged mass play gradually changed the character of the game.

When the source information is mentioned within the text of your paper, provide page number(s) within parentheses.

▲ **Critical Viewing**
Does the violence in this illustration seem excessive to you? Would you rule it legal or illegal in a football rule book? **[Make a Judgment]**

A works-cited listing gives more information about Kachur's source material.

Works Cited

The Boston Medical and Surgical Journal 131 (1894).
Danzig, Allison. *The History of American Football.* Englewood Cliffs, NJ: Prentice Hall, 1956.
The Journal of the American Medical Association 6 Dec. 1902: 39.
The Medical News 1 Dec. 1884: 615.
The Medical Record 7 April 1906: 546–547.
The Nation 29 Nov. 1894.
The New York Times Index for the Published News of 1899–June 1905. New York: (1969).
The Outlook 18 Nov. 1905.
Roosevelt, Theodore. *The Strenuous Life: Essays and Addresses.* New York: The Century Co., 1900.
Weyand, Alexander. *The Saga of American Football.* New York: Macmillan, 1955.

Reading → Writing Connection

Writing Application: Give Causes and Effects As you prepare to write your research paper, consider the cause-and-effect relationships you could explore concerning your topic.

Prewriting: Scan News Headlines

1. Explain to students that each day, newspapers cover a broad range of topics and organize each issue into topic sections such as World and National News, Business, Sports, and Arts and Entertainment.

2. Have students pick a particular section that interests them and note what topics are explored over several issues. Have them jot down the range of subjects they find.

3. Encourage students to focus on a topic that seems most interesting to them from these headlines. Ask them to use that topic as a springboard to ask additional questions or consider related topics that come to mind.

Prewriting: Use Looping

Teaching Resources: Writing Support Transparencies, 13-A

1. Point out that writing is not only a way to share what you know with others; it can also help writers make discoveries for themselves.

2. Provide a timer so that students can begin together and stop after five minutes. By working at the same time, they can receive your guidance and suggestions for how to use this technique, which may be new to them.

3. Display Transparency 13-A and discuss how Ian freewrote, then used looping to narrow his topic. Discuss the relationship between the two looped elements.

4. Encourage students to recognize the discoveries they may make while working on interesting topics or how their topics may be modified to make them more original or more practical to research.

13.2 Prewriting

Choosing Your Topic

Because doing research means immersing yourself in a topic, choose one in which you have a genuine interest. If you are having trouble finding a topic, try one of these strategies:

Strategies for Generating Topics

1. **Scan News Headlines** Sometimes reading about events in the news can trigger a desire to find more in-depth information. Scan news headlines of the previous few days. Read articles of interest, and jot down your questions. Then, choose one of those questions, and base your research around it.

2. **Use Looping** Write freely about a general topic of interest for five minutes. Read what you've written, and circle the most interesting idea. Write for five minutes on that idea. Again, read what you have written, and circle the most important idea. Choose one of the circled items to be the topic for your research paper.

Try it out! Use the interactive Looping to Generate a Topic activity in **Section 13.2**, on-line or on CD-ROM.

Student Work IN PROGRESS

Name: Ian Pritchard
Buena High School
Ventura, CA

Looping to Generate a Topic
By using the looping strategy, Ian was able to find a topic for his research report: a biographical report on poet Seamus Heaney.

I love Britain. Scotland, Ireland, Wales. The Tower, Elizabeth I, and the Armada. Guy Fawkes Day and the Houses of Parliament. Westminster Abbey and Poet's Corner. The Plague.
The Potato Famine. The Industrial Revolution. Poverty. Child Labor and Dickens. Marlowe and Jonson. The Troubles.
Belfast and Dublin. James Joyce. Eavan Boland. Seamus Heaney.
Bombings. U2.

280 • Research Paper

⏱ TIME AND RESOURCE MANAGER

Resources
Print: *Writing Support Transparencies*, 13-A–E
Technology: *Writing and Grammar* Interactive Text, Section 13.2

Using the Full Student Edition	Using the Handbook🄷
• Work through the news headlines or the looping strategy (p. 280) with the class. • Use the Responding to Fine Art (p. 281) transparency to generate additional topics. • Do the Webbing (p. 282) and T-Chart (p. 283) activities in class.	• Work through the news headlines or the looping strategy (p. 174) with the class. • Use the Responding to Fine Art (p. 175) transparency to generate additional topics. • Do the Webbing (p. 176) and T-Chart (p. 177) activities in class.

TOPIC BANK

If you're having trouble coming up with a topic, consider these ideas:

1. **Research Paper on Raising the *Titanic*** Perhaps no disaster in the twentieth century has inspired more interest than the sinking of the *Titanic*. Newly developed technology has kept that interest alive. Develop a thesis, and write a research paper about the raising of the *Titanic*.

2. **Research Paper on Your Town's Origins** Whether you live in New York, Los Angeles, or Anytown, U.S.A., your town has a history. Research and write a paper about your town's beginnings.

Responding to Fine Art

3. Study the people and setting in *Benedict Arnold Escapes on a British Frigate* by Brent Silverman. Then, write a research paper inspired by what you see. For example, you might research the British navy of the 1800's, or you could write a biography of Lord Nelson, a famous British naval hero.

Benedict Arnold Escapes on a British Frigate, Brent Silverman, Courtesy of Silverman Studios, Inc.

Responding to Literature

4. Read "Defending Nonviolent Resistance" by Mohandas K. Gandhi. Then, write a research paper about the influence of Gandhi's nonviolent philosophy on Dr. Martin Luther King, Jr. "Defending Nonviolent Resistance" appears in *Prentice Hall Literature, Penguin Edition*, The British Tradition.

Timed Writing Prompt

5. Write an essay in which you identify a profession that interests you and present a plan for learning more about it. Discuss the questions you have about the profession. Then, explain what research activities you would pursue to answer your questions. Some research activities might include talking to career counselors, reading books and magazines, and talking to professionals in the field you are researching. **(45 minutes)**

Prewriting • 281

Prewriting: Webbing to Narrow a Topic

Teaching Resources: Writing Support Transparencies, 13-C; Writing Support Activity Book, 13-1

1. Encourage students to use print or CD-ROM encyclopedias to find associated topics. Illustrate this process by looking up a particular topic, and then finding the suggested follow-up topics listed at the end of each article.

2. Have students look up some articles of interest and note the related topics listed at the end of those. After two or three rounds of this, you will have enough information to make a web of linked topics. Also refer students to the Research Tip on this page.

3. Display Transparency 13-C and discuss how the subtopics in the web relate to the main topic of World War I.

4. Ask students to apply this strategy and list their main topic and subtopics on their webs. Distribute copies of the graphic organizer (13-1) for this purpose.

Prewriting: Considering Your Audience and Purpose

1. Provide students with some examples of research essays and challenge them to identify the purpose of each of the papers. Remind them that the purpose should be clear from the title, but that this is not always the case.

2. Discuss the fact that the age, education level, and experience of the audience make it necessary to adjust the way writers present information. How might a research paper be different when written for a general audience rather than a college professor? (Writing for a college professor can contain specialized language and references that might be too difficult for a general audience to understand.)

Narrowing Your Topic

Now that you've chosen a topic, consider whether it needs to be narrowed. For example, suppose you have chosen World War I as your topic. A glance at a card or computer catalog on this subject will show you that the research on such a vast topic could take years; the writing could fill volumes. If your own topic can be broken down into several subtopics, each pointing in a different direction for research, then you should narrow it. One technique for narrowing a topic is webbing.

Webbing to Narrow a Topic

Design a web, and write your topic in the center. In the outer circles, write the key aspects of your topic. One of these aspects may become the topic for your paper, or you may need to narrow it further. If so, choose an outer circle topic, and put it in the center of a second web. Repeat the process until you have arrived at a manageable topic for your research paper.

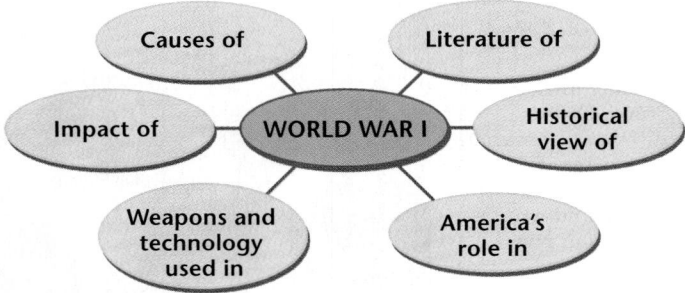

Considering Your Audience and Purpose

Consider your audience to identify the types of details and language they will understand and appreciate. Also, identify your purpose, so that you will be sure to choose details that will have a definite impact on your audience. Ask yourself:

- **For whom am I writing?** Consider the age, education level, and experience of your audience. For example, you would probably take one approach if your paper about pollution in a local lake is to be read by environmental scientists and a very different approach if it is to be read by high-school students.

- **Why am I writing?** Research papers are intended to inform or explain; but if your thesis is a controversial one, you may also have persuasion as a purpose.

282 • Research Paper

Research Tip

Do preliminary research to narrow a topic. Check card and computer catalogs, tables of contents of books, encyclopedia entries, and bibliographies to get a sense of the depth and breadth of a topic and its subtopics.

Gathering Details

Before you start gathering details, make a research plan to guide you. A plan will help you to stay focused and use your time wisely as you make your way through the vast array of information sources available.

Develop a Research Plan

To develop a research plan, make a list of questions about your topic or areas of your topic you want to explore. Identify the types of sources that would be most useful, and find out where they are located. Plan to use a wide variety of sources, such as:

- Library sources
- Internet sites
- Media sources
- Interviews

One way to organize your research is to make a T-chart. Fold a piece of paper in half lengthwise to form two columns. In the left column, write down what you want to know. In the right column, write the possible sources for finding the information.

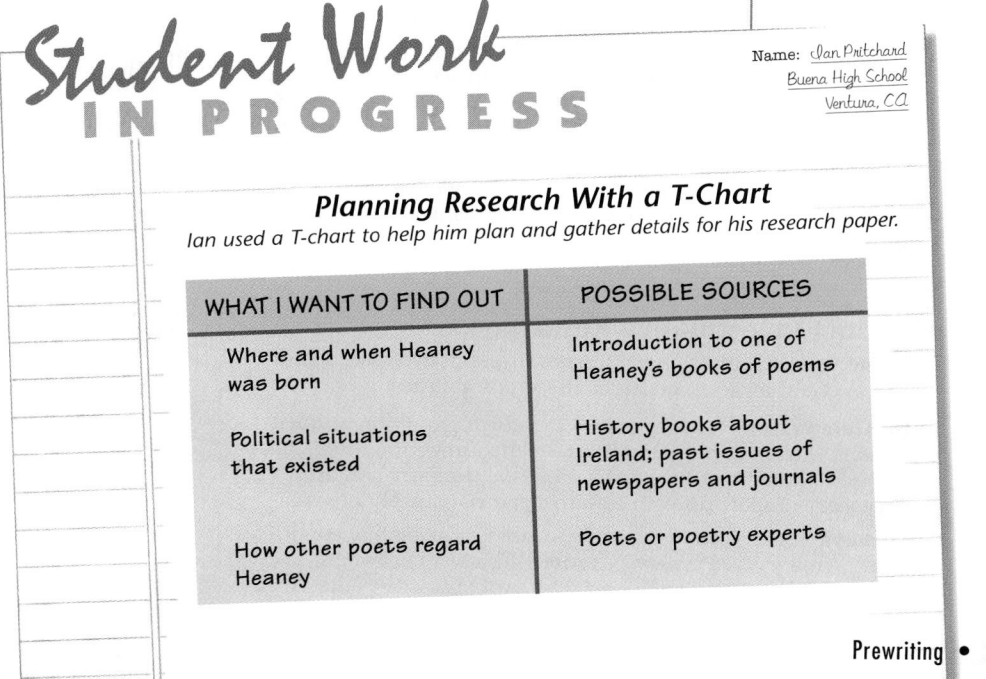

Student Work
IN PROGRESS

Name: *Ian Pritchard*
Buena High School
Ventura, CA

Planning Research With a T-Chart

Ian used a T-chart to help him plan and gather details for his research paper.

WHAT I WANT TO FIND OUT	POSSIBLE SOURCES
Where and when Heaney was born	Introduction to one of Heaney's books of poems
Political situations that existed	History books about Ireland; past issues of newspapers and journals
How other poets regard Heaney	Poets or poetry experts

Prewriting • **283**

Customize for
AP Students

Matthew Kachur's topic used nineteenth- and early twentieth-century sources. Students who are interested in researching similar topics should be warned that finding such sources could be difficult and time-consuming. Nearby college or university libraries may be able to arrange for interlibrary loans of photocopies of relevant sources. Nonetheless, students may wish to focus their research on historical issues in their own communities and use the more easily available archives of local newspapers.

Step-by-Step Teaching Guide

Prewriting: Develop a Research Plan

Teaching Resources: Writing Support Transparencies, 13-D

1. Discuss how making a list of questions related to a research topic helps give the writer an overview of what he or she will need to research and cover in the paper.

2. Discuss Transparency 13-D. Make sure students see that each of Ian's research goals on the left side of the chart has a corresponding information source directly across the line on the right side.

3. As a group, have them chart the relationship between the questions that Matthew Kachur explored in his essay on football and the sources he used to find that information. (Example: What he wanted to find out—How violent was early football? Source he used—*Boston Medical and Surgical Journal.*)

4. Ask students to begin to consider the questions they hope to answer in their research topics and list them on a T-chart. Have students also make preliminary lists of possible sources to find that information.

 TIME SAVERS!

 **Writing Support Transparencies**
Use the transparencies for Chapter 13 to facilitate the teaching of strategies.

Writing Support Activity Book
Use the graphic organizers for Chapter 13 to facilitate student planning.

Prewriting: Use Library and Electronic Resources; Conduct Investigative Research

1. Have students read the material on page 284 in small groups. Define any unknown terminology. Discuss the topics that you could find information about in each of these places.

2. Distribute large sheets of paper and place them around the room. On each, write headings such as Tips for Using Library Resources, Tips for Electronic Research, and Tips for Doing Investigative Research. Then write a different topic on each. Student topics generated during the T-chart exercise could be used here.

3. Station a group at each of the large sheets of paper and give them five minutes to jot down their ideas on the topic labeled on each. Groups should consider the sources they would use to research their topic. Refer students to the Technology Tip on finding source material.

4. Afterwards, have each group present their ideas. Encourage the class to contribute additional ideas their classmates may have missed.

Customize for
ESL Students

Point out to students that they can use the Internet to search for information resources written in their first languages. Encourage them to explore topics related to history, culture, and current events.

More About the Writer

Franklin Pierce Adams was an American journalist and translator whose career spanned nearly the first half of the twentieth century. As a political correspondent, he researched numerous behind-the-scenes activities that led to public policy decisions. He once said, "The trouble with this country is that there are too many politicians who believe, with a conviction based on experience, that you can fool all of the people all of the time."

13.2

Use Library Resources

The library contains extensive information in both print and electronic formats. Before you begin library research, use a T-chart to list the information or sources you want to find and use. Without such a list, you may waste valuable time browsing.

- **Nonfiction Books** Nonfiction books may provide broad overviews of topics, which can be useful when you are beginning your research, or they may explore specialized subjects. Use the library's card or computer catalog to locate nonfiction books. You can search for a topic by author, title, subject, or (in a computer catalog) key word.

- **Periodicals** To locate magazine articles, use the *Readers' Guide to Periodical Literature*.

- **Reference Books** The reference section of a library has a variety of sources that can provide interesting and current information on your topic. Types of reference works include bibliographies, almanacs, atlases, and encyclopedias.

Use Electronic Resources

Computers have become an indispensable research tool. There are two basic ways to use your computer for research:

- **On-line Research** The Internet, which you can access through an on-line service, offers a wealth of sources for information, including museums, news media, colleges and universities, special-interest groups, and government institutions. You can also find links to your topic by using a search engine.

- **CD-ROMs** Many information and reference sources are now available on CD-ROM. Check your library, bookstore, or electronics outlet to see what is available.

Conduct Investigative Research

Some research topics benefit from investigative research. If yours is one that does, consider these possibilities:

- **Interviews** Interview an expert in your topic. Prepare questions in advance, phrasing them to encourage the interviewee to answer at length. Conduct preliminary research if necessary. Follow up with a thank-you note or phone call.

- **Surveys** If the statistics you need are not available, conduct your own survey. Prepare questions in advance, framing questions as neutrally as possible to avoid biased results. Keep track of responses, and tabulate them carefully.

284 • Research Paper

Writers in
ACTION

The noted columnist for the **New York Herald-Tribune** *Franklin P. Adams* said the following about researching:

"I find that a great part of the information I have was acquired by looking up something and finding something else on the way."

Technology Tip

Many articles from past periodicals are stored on microfiche. The *Readers' Guide* will identify the file on which the article you want is located. Request the appropriate file from the librarian, and use a microfiche machine to locate and print out useful articles you find.

Take Notes

As you find information from sources, make note cards and source cards.

Source cards contain publication information of each source you consult in your research. This material will be used in your bibliography. Use one card for each source. Number each source card, and write that number on your note card.

Note cards contain details you might want to use in your report. To make organizing information easier, put only one piece of information on each card. Write the number of the source (written on the source card) on each note card.

Photocopy or Print Source Material

If resources are available, you may prefer to photocopy source material, including the book or journal's title page and copyright information. On the printout, highlight or circle the information you plan to use.

If you get your information from an on-line source or from a CD-ROM, print out the appropriate pages. Then, highlight or circle the information you plan to use.

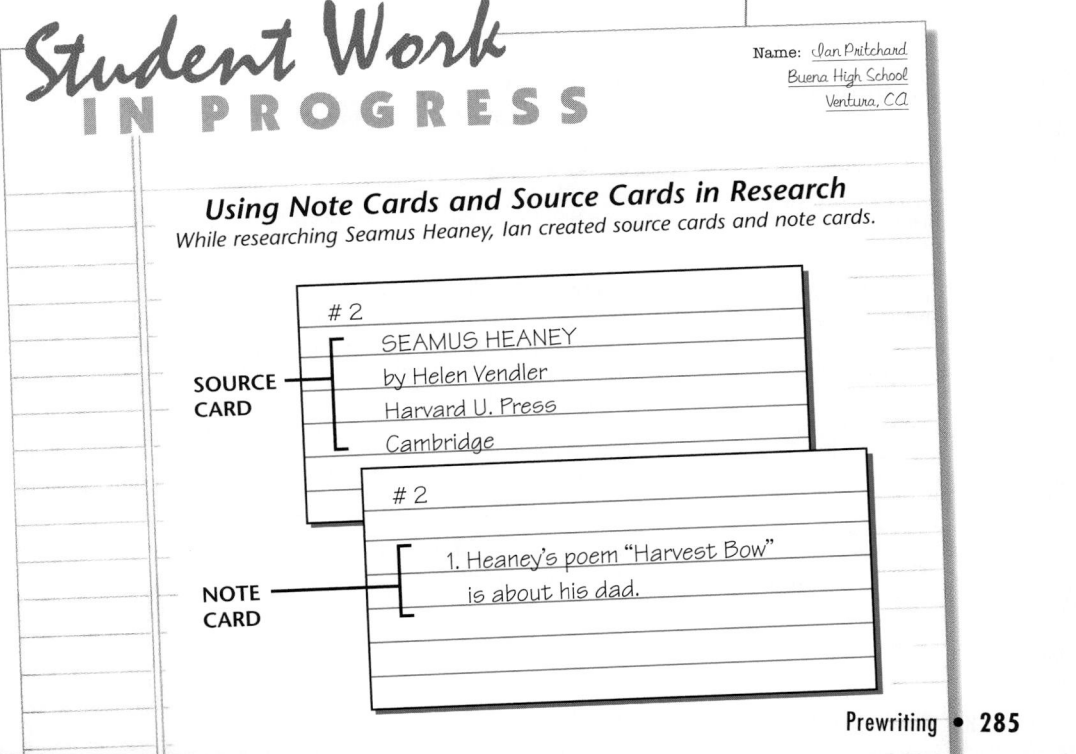

Student Work
IN PROGRESS

Name: Ian Pritchard
Buena High School
Ventura, CA

Using Note Cards and Source Cards in Research
While researching Seamus Heaney, Ian created source cards and note cards.

SOURCE CARD

2

SEAMUS HEANEY
by Helen Vendler
Harvard U. Press
Cambridge

NOTE CARD

2

1. Heaney's poem "Harvest Bow" is about his dad.

Prewriting • 285

Prewriting: Take Notes

Teaching Resources: Writing Support Transparencies, 13-E

1. To help monitor and reinforce comprehension, ask the following questions:

   How might source cards be useful in organizing information used in a research paper? (They remind writers where information originated. They also allow writers to refer to a numbered card rather than a full bibliographic citation when a source is used repeatedly.)

   How are note cards useful? (They organize specific facts and quotations obtained from information sources.)

2. Display Transparency 13-E and discuss the features of source cards and note cards. You may also wish to show students examples of source and note cards that you or students have made.

Customize for
AP Students

Encourage students to familiarize themselves with specialized professional and academic journals in addition to the books and periodicals they are likely to find in your school library. College and university libraries and large public libraries have access to catalogs such as *ERIC* and *Infotrack*, that can lead to specialized and sophisticated information for in-depth scholarship on a topic.

Integrating Grammar

Punctuation Conventions Point out that bibliographic citations have a particular format for punctuating elements. (A comma separates the last and first names of an author; a colon separates the city and the name of the publisher; and a period comes at the end of each individual citation.) These punctuation conventions allow for clarity when searching through a long list of closely arranged pieces of information. Encourage students to review their past work for their use of punctuation conventions.

☑ ONGOING ASSESSMENT: Monitor and Reinforce

If students need help to understand the concept of documentation, use the following option.

Using local magazines or newspapers, refer students to documentation within news articles. Point out, or help students locate, examples of people or places that served as sources of documentation. Make sure students take note of the language used in referring to these examples.

Step-by-Step Teaching Guide

Drafting: Develop a Thesis Statement

1. Tell students that a clear thesis statement will work like a lens, helping them to focus their research and their writing on what is central and relevant.

2. Ask what the possible disadvantages are of attempting research without a clear thesis. (They may gather information that does not help answer important questions or is not organized clearly.)

3. Have students analyze and discuss how thesis statements help writers conduct focused, purposeful research.

Step-by-Step Teaching Guide

Drafting: Organize to Support Your Thesis

Teaching Resources: Writing Support Transparencies, 13-F

1. Display Transparency 13-F and have students define and review the meanings of *chronological, cause-and-effect,* and *order of importance.*

2. Invite students to share their topics. As a class, make suggestions to writers about which organizational forms are best suited to their subjects.

3. Ask individuals to write a brief explanation of which structure they are going to use and to share it with you or a partner before they embark on research.

Customize for
Spatial Learners

As students gather their note cards, encourage them to arrange them on a large surface, such as a table or floor, so they may see them at a glance. Doing this will allow them to more easily consider their information as related groups of ideas rather than as individual facts and quotes.

Shaping Your Writing

With your research finished, you may look at a stack of note cards or photocopied materials and wonder what to do with them. The task now is to organize your information. Start by sorting your notes into various groups. Label the groups, and write subheads, if necessary, beneath the general heads.

Develop a Thesis Statement

As you begin drafting, introduce your topic and state your thesis in the introduction. A *thesis* states the key point or argument you wish to make about your topic. Some writers have a thesis in mind before they even begin to research. Sometimes, the research will point a writer in a new direction.

To create a thesis statement, read your grouped notes carefully. Decide on the most important ideas you have gathered, and summarize them. After deleting unnecessary information, shape your summary into a single, clear statement.

Sample Thesis Statements

The space program of the 1960's helped to unite Americans. The childhood of Queen Elizabeth I of England had a great impact on decisions she made as a ruler.

Organize to Support Your Thesis

Having decided on a thesis, develop an organizational plan that will best support your thesis. There are several methods of organizing a paper, but the "right" plan for you is the one that best matches the content and purpose of your paper. Below are some suggestions for how to organize your research findings:

ORGANIZATIONAL IDEAS	
Use chronological organization if . . .	you are tracing the history of something; you are writing about someone's life.
Use cause-and-effect organization if . . .	you want to emphasize that certain events caused others to happen; you are making a prediction.
Use order-of-importance organization if . . .	you want to build an argument; there are various aspects to your topic.

286 • Research Paper

⏱ TIME AND RESOURCE MANAGER	

Resources
Print: *Writing Support Transparencies,* 13-F–H
Technology: *Writing and Grammar* Interactive Text, Section 13.3

Using the Full Student Edition	Using the Handbook 🄷
• Work through the appropriate organization strategies with the entire class. • Demonstrate the techniques of Giving Details and Citing Sources (p. 288). • Have students begin their research draft in class.	• Work through the appropriate organization strategies with the entire class. • Demonstrate the techniques of Giving Details and Citing Sources (p. 182). • Have students begin their research draft in class.

Make an Outline

Once you've chosen an organizational approach, use an outline or graphic organizer to help you arrange the details to fit your organization. In an outline

- List each main point you will cover next to a Roman numeral.
- Under each main point, enter the topics you'll discuss next to capital letters.
- Under each topic, list details next to Arabic numerals.

Review your outline, and experiment with its organization until you are satisfied with it. Keep your completed outline handy, and refer to it as you draft and revise your research writing.

interactive Textbook

Try it out! Use the interactive Organizing With an Outline activity in **Section 13.3**, on-line or on CD-ROM.

Student Work IN PROGRESS

Name: *Ian Pritchard*
Buena High School
Ventura, CA

Organizing With an Outline

Here is the outline Ian created to support his thesis statement:
"The hard labor that he, his family, and other generations of Irish farmers endured in the cultivation and harvesting of potatoes has had a great influence on Heaney's poetry."

I. Family Background
   A. Ireland
   B. "The Troubles"
   C. Relationship with parents

II. Effect on Poetry
   A. Connection with homeland
   B. Allusion to parents
   C. Haunting imagery

Drafting • **287**

Drafting: Give Details and Cite Sources

Teaching Resources: Writing Support Transparencies, 13-H

1. Have students view Transparency 13-H and discuss with them the various types of details that they may include in a research paper.

2. Discuss the effect of Ian's insertion of direct and indirect quotations on his work. Have students give examples of their use of each of these types of detail. Ask: How did it improve your work? Did your reader feel that you had conducted adequate research?

3. Have students write examples of a fact, a statistic, an example, a quotation, a personal observation, and paraphrased information on blank index cards.

4. Make six columns on the chalkboard titled *Fact, Statistic, Example, Quotation, Paraphrase, Personal Observation*. Invite students to tape their cards under appropriate columns.

5. Ask students to discuss and evaluate whether these cards have been placed in the correct columns.

13.3

Providing Elaboration

As you draft, follow your outline, making sure each body paragraph addresses an aspect of your thesis. Then, develop your ideas by providing supporting details. Insert citations as you draft, revealing the origin of source material.

Give Details and Cite Sources

Support your main points with various types of details:

Facts can be proved. General facts do not need to be cited.

Statistics give information about your topic. Cite the origin of your statistical information.

Examples include situations from life that illustrate the points you are making. Such examples do not need to be cited.

Quotations are word-for-word quotes from someone other than yourself. They must appear in quotation marks and be cited.

Paraphrased information is retelling in your own words information you learned while researching. If paraphrased information is not generally known, you must cite the source material.

Personal observations are your own ideas about what you have learned. Personal observations do not need to be cited.

Student Work IN PROGRESS

Name: Ian Pritchard
Buena High School
Ventura, CA

Giving Details and Citing Sources

Ian incorporated the opinions of several authorities on the works of Heaney, using both direct and indirect quotations. In each case, he cited his sources.

He passed his days either at the local school in Anahorish or next to his father in the fields of Mossbawn, the family farm (Buttel 9). The hard labor that he, his family, and other generations of Irish farmers endured in the cultivation and harvesting of potatoes has had a great influence on Heaney's poetry. The land itself is mirrored in the strength of Heaney's words: As poet and editor Philip Fried has said, "He handles words as if they had the heft of potatoes." (Fried)

13.4 *Revising*

Once you have completed your first draft, start looking for ways to improve it. Take a critical look at each level of writing, from the overall structure to individual word choices. Begin with the big picture.

Revising Your Overall Structure

Evaluate the Variety of Support

One of the hallmarks of an effective research paper is thoroughness. Review your paper to make sure you have completely explored your topic, using a variety of types of support.

▶ **REVISION STRATEGY**
Color-Coding to Identify Supporting Details

Using highlighters, identify the supporting facts and details in your paper. Use a different color of highlighter for each category of detail. Choose categories that suit your topic. You might choose to call out causes and effects in different colors, for example. Another system that works for many research papers is to make details that answer *Who? What? When? Where?* and *Why?* For example:

- **Whos,** or people, might be blue.
- **Whens**—dates, times, and periods in history—might be green.
- **Whats**—or events, developments, effects, things, and objects—might be yellow.
- **Wheres,** or places, might be red.
- **Whys**—or explanations, definitions, or causes—might be purple.

When you are finished, scan your paper. Is it a rainbow of color, or is it predominantly one color or two? If a category is underrepresented, consider why. It may be that your thesis requires you to focus on a particular type of data. On the other hand, it may mean that you've left something out. If that is the case, add details where they are lacking, to elaborate on your points.

▶ Critical Viewing
What are the benefits of revising on a computer? What are the benefits of revising in longhand? [**Generalize**]

Revising • **289**

Step-by-Step Teaching Guide

Revising: Color-Coding to Identify Supporting Details

1. Have a student read this section aloud to the class. Write the words *Who, What, When, Where,* and *Why* on the chalkboard.

2. Provide several sets of colored highlighters or colored pencils for the class. Have students assign each word a separate color, and have them underline, in the appropriate color, sentences or phrases in their drafts that answer the listed questions. If students find that they have not answered all of the questions, they should revise their drafts.

3. Have students discuss how this strategy is useful, and have them share other strategies they might use to evaluate the quality of supporting details in their drafts.

Critical Viewing

Generalize Students may note that revising on computer is fast and convenient but leaves no "paper trail" of original work. While it is slower, revising in longhand leaves a visible record of the revision process.

⏱ TIME AND RESOURCE MANAGER

Resources
Print: *Writing Support Transparencies,* 13-I
Technology: *Writing and Grammar* Interactive Text, Section 13.4

Using the Full Student Edition	Using the Handbook🄷
• Work through revising strategies with the entire class (pp. 289–291). • Assign Grammar in Your Writing (p. 292). • Have students do peer reviews with partners in class (p. 293).	• Work through revising strategies with the entire class (pp. 183–185). • Assign Grammar in Your Writing (p. 186). • Have students do peer reviews with partners in class (p. 187).

Revising: Strengthen Your Paragraph Organization

1. Discuss the TRI/PS/QA paragraph patterns in class. You may wish to show students additional examples of these patterns from published writing or from collected student work. You might also have students review the Model From Literature on pages 276–279 to identify the paragraph patterns Matthew Kachur uses.

2. As students look over their drafts, have them find examples of these paragraph patterns in their own writing. Afterwards, have each write a selected paragraph on a card, and distribute the cards randomly to the class. Have students identify the paragraph pattern on each card.

Critical Viewing

Infer Students may note that the Rockefeller Center is well publicized throughout the country by national media.

13.4

Revising Your Paragraphs
Strengthen Your Paragraph Organization

When you are satisfied with the general structure of your paper, focus on individual paragraphs. In a research paper, body paragraphs are like building blocks: Arranged properly, they will provide solid support for your thesis. If the blocks aren't strong, your paper won't be either.

▶ **REVISION STRATEGY**
Identifying Paragraph Patterns: TRI/PS/QA

Identify the paragraph patterns you have used. Go through your draft, and jot down in the margin the organization pattern of each paragraph. If you cannot identify a specific pattern for a paragraph, reread it closely to make sure it makes sense. If not, revise it. You may want to use an organizational pattern like the ones that follow:

- **TRI: T**opic, **R**estatement, **I**llustration. In this pattern, the topic sentence comes first, followed by a restatement or extension of the main idea, followed by an illustration or an example. This pattern may be altered to TIR, TII, ITR, or TRIT.

- **PS: P**roblem/**S**olution. In this pattern, a problem is posed and one or several solutions follow.

- **QA: Q**uestion/**A**nswer. Paragraphs of this type generally start with a question that is then answered in subsequent sentences.

TRI

Rockefeller Center, an enormous complex of buildings located in midtown Manhattan, is named for its principal financial backers. These were John D. Rockefeller, Jr., and other members of that wealthy family. The Rockefeller family made most of its fortune in the oil industry. . . .

> T
> R
> I

PS

Rockefeller Center is so big, it's hard to know where to begin to take a tour. If you begin, however, on Fifth Avenue between Forty-ninth and Fiftieth streets and follow this path, you will have an enjoyable tour of this fascinating piece of New York City. From Fiftieth Street and Fifth Avenue, walk down the flagstone path into the sunken plaza, which contains an ice rink and a statue of Prometheus.

> P
> S

QA

How did Rockefeller Center get its name? The building complex was named for its principal financial backers—John D. Rockefeller, Jr., and other members of that wealthy family.

> Q
> A

▲ **Critical Viewing** Why do you think Rockefeller Center, pictured here, is such a popular destination for tourists? **[Infer]**

🖋 STANDARDIZED TEST PREPARATION WORKSHOP

Comprehension Questions Standardized test questions may require students to read an informational passage and answer a question to demonstrate their comprehension. Provide students with opportunities to practice this skill by familiarizing them with the format and strategy for making these choices.

Which paragraph pattern does the following paragraph represent?

> *Which paragraph pattern is best for this situation? The answer depends on the nature of your information, the expectations of your readers, and the purpose of your research paper.*

Which paragraph pattern, TRI, PS, or QA, does this paragraph represent?

A TRI paragraph   **C** QA paragraph

B PS paragraph   **D** None of the above.

Students should recognize that **C** is the correct answer. The paragraph starts with a question and goes on to answer it. A is incorrect because it lacks restatement and illustration. B is possible, but not as good as C, which is more precisely a question/answer pattern. D is incorrect because there is a possible answer to the question from among the choices given.

Revising Your Sentences

Create Sentence Variety

When too many sentences in a composition are of the same length, structure, and type, it has a numbing effect on its readers. Examine your draft closely, looking for patterns in your sentences. Provide variety where needed by interrupting patterns with sentences of different lengths or types.

▶ **REVISION STRATEGY**
Color-Coding to Identify Sentence Length

Read through your draft, using a highlighter of one color to mark sentences of fewer than twelve words. Use another highlighter color to mark sentences of twelve or more words.

Review your draft, and locate passages in which you have too many sentences of a particular length. Make those passages more interesting by rewriting or adding sentences to provide variety.

Student Work
IN PROGRESS

Name: *Ian Pritchard*
Buena High School
Ventura, CA

Color-Coding to Identify Sentence Length
Because the highlighting showed that all the sentences in this passage were long, Ian split some of them to add variety to his research paper.

The peat bogs that so fascinated Heaney as a child have come to be a consistent metaphor in his poetry; just as the bogs contain a catalog of objects buried for hundreds of years, Heaney's poems rely heavily on stories and people from the past, which give the reader a sense of modern-day Irish sentiment. *These reflections on the past.* Heaney writes about his country's and his countrymen's violated past in a voice that reflects upon the violence of the present. Persons, animals, and objects resurrected from the brown peat—indeed, the peat itself—have all become the source and subject of Heaney's writings (Tobin 91).

Revising • 291

Dependent and Independent Clauses

1. Have students note that a clause is a group of words with a subject and a verb and that there are a number of variations possible using main clauses, which can stand alone, or combinations of main clauses and subordinate or dependent clauses, which cannot stand alone.

2. Point out that the use of different combinations and types of clauses in sentences allow for more interesting writing and a more sophisticated connecting of ideas.

3. If students have difficulty finding the four kinds of sentence structure, provide them with a range of texts from children's books to scholarly material.

Find It in Your Reading

Answers will vary; samples are given.

Compound:
1. "Football built character; it turned boys into men." (p. 278)

Compound-Complex:
1. "I have no sympathy . . . physical address and courage." (p. 278)

Complex:
1. "Still, the game was . . . serious injuries were common." (p. 277)
2. "In 1882, a reform . . . carrier was knocked down." (p. 277)

Find It in Your Writing

Provide students with phrases that will encourage them to use complex, compound, and compound-complex sentences (*in spite of; on the other hand*). Encourage them to experiment with new sentence structures to see how it changes their prose style.

Integrating Vocabulary Skills

Latin Roots *Subordinate* comes from the Latin *sub*, meaning "under" and *ordinare*, meaning "to order." In other words, a subordinate clause "takes orders," or derives its full meaning, from another (main) clause.

13.4

Grammar in Your Writing
Independent and Subordinate Clauses

When you combine sentences, you form a new sentence structure. The structure of a sentence is determined by the number and kind of clauses it contains. A **clause** is a group of words that contains a subject and a verb. There are two major types of clauses:

Independent Clause: An **independent clause** can stand alone as a sentence: Shakespeare's popularity has never waned.

Subordinate Clause: A **subordinate clause** cannot stand alone because it does not express a complete thought. It must be linked to a main clause: Because Shakespeare is so popular, his plays have been translated into dozens of languages.

Four sentence structures can be formed from these two types of clauses:

1. A **simple sentence** is a independent clause that stands alone:
   Sir Laurence Olivier was a great Shakespearean actor.
2. A **compound sentence** contains two or more independent clauses separated by a semicolon or linked by a comma and a coordinating conjunction such as *and, but, or, for, nor, so,* or *yet*:
   Olivier starred in many stage productions of Shakespeare plays, and he also starred in movies of these plays.
3. A **complex sentence** contains one independent clause and one or more subordinate clauses. The subordinate clauses in the following examples are underlined:
   Because he preferred the stage to film, Olivier made only a handful of films of Shakespeare's plays.
4. A **compound-complex sentence** contains at least one subordinate clause and at least two independent clauses:
   These films, though they were critically acclaimed, did not translate into box office success, so Olivier turned to more commercial films.

Find It in Your Reading Find one compound, one compound-complex, and two complex sentences in "Football at the Turn of the Twentieth Century" on pages 276–279. Identify the clauses in each example.

Find It in Your Writing Find two compound and two complex sentences in your research essay. Identify the clauses in each one. In the complex sentences, be sure the main idea of the sentence is contained in the main clause, not in the subordinate clause.

For more about independent and subordinate clauses, see Chapter 19.

292 • Research Paper

✓ **ONGOING ASSESSMENT: Prerequisite Skills**

If a number of students seem unable to recognize the various kinds of clauses described in the lesson, you might refer them to the following materials to assure coverage of prerequisite knowledge.

In the Textbook	Print Resources	Technology
Dependent and Independent Clauses, Section 19.3	*Grammar Exercise Workbook*, pp. 33–48	*On-Line Exercise Bank*, Section 19.3

Revising Your Word Choice

Review Your Use of *I* and *You*

Formal research papers are almost always written in the third person. Although the use of the first person is sometimes acceptable—in making a personal interpretation, for example—most times, the use of the third person is preferred. A common error, especially when writing about society and social issues, is to unintentionally lapse into the first or second person. For example:

FIRST PERSON: A 1989 study revealed that most of us vote for candidates of our own ethnic group.

THIRD PERSON: A 1989 study revealed that most people vote for candidates of their own ethnic group.

▶ REVISION STRATEGY
Circling Personal Pronouns

Carefully reread your paper. Identify and circle all first- or second-person pronouns: *I, my, we, us, our, you, your, yours.* If switches from third person to first person and second person are unintentional, revise them.

Peer Review

With the process of revision almost completed, step back to get a fresh perspective on your work. A good way to do this is to have a fellow student read your revised draft. At this stage, a peer can be more objective about your work than you can; he or she may help you see things you might have missed.

Work With a Partner

Pair up with another student, and exchange revised drafts. Take turns reviewing each other's work. Read through each other's drafts silently and then aloud before offering suggestions about content and style. You may want to prepare a list of questions such as the following to help your peer respond as he or she reads your report:

- What can make the introduction clearer and more interesting? What is my thesis statement?

- Which passages, if any, in the body could be better organized? Have I included enough facts and details to support the thesis?

- What revisions might make the conclusion stronger and more memorable?

- How can the writing be tightened or trimmed?

- What mistakes, if any, have I made in documenting resources?

⏱ Timed Writing Hint

If you are given forty-five minutes to write an essay, spend ten minutes revising. Check that you have not unintentionally switched pronouns when addressing the prompt.

▶ Speaking and Listening Tip

Slowly read your draft aloud to a partner while your partner jots down comments and suggestions for improvement.

Step-by-Step Teaching Guide

Revising: Circling Personal Pronouns

1. Tell students that writing in the first person or in the second person is considered inappropriate for most academic writing. Point out that when presenting ideas, it is the strength of the information, rather than the personality of the speaker, that conveys authority.

2. Review the examples with students. Talk about how the use of the pronoun *us* changes the tone of the sentence.

3. Ask students to come up with other examples of sentences with *I* or *you* and write them on the chalkboard. Ask students to revise the sentences to give them additional practice in recognizing inappropriate tone and editing it.

4. Have students apply the strategy to their own writing.

Step-by-Step Teaching Guide

Revising: Peer Review

1. Refer students to the Speaking and Listening Tip on this page and encourage students to read their drafts aloud.

2. Encourage all students to take notes during the Peer Review process. These notes can be used to direct their revisions.

Editing and Proofreading

1. Encourage students to see editing and proofreading as a natural and automatic part of the writing process. Suggest that students read through their own, or each other's work, line by line, searching for typographical errors, inconsistencies, misspellings, and usage errors before they submit any work to be read by a teacher or editor.

2. Tell students that in preparing research papers, it is particularly important to proofread quoted material for accuracy of wording and correctness of punctuation.

3. Review the conventions for formatting excerpts. Emphasize the fact that quotations of more than four lines should be double indented and single spaced. Ask students why this format is necessary. (So that the words of sources are more easily distinguished in the text of the paper.)

4. Review the formatting conventions for citations and works cited. The Grammar in Your Writing feature on page 295 will enable you to focus on formatting in greater detail.

13.5 Editing and Proofreading

Errors in spelling, punctuation, grammar, and usage indicate sloppiness and carelessness—qualities you do not want associated with your work. Before creating your final draft, proofread your essay to eliminate such errors.

Focusing on Quotations

Check each quoted line or passage in your research report to ensure that it is transcribed correctly and that it is enclosed in quotation marks or set as an excerpt. Also double-check the names, titles, and other reference information to be sure that each is accurate.

Focusing on Formatting

Research writing contains numerous citations. These may be in parenthetical form, in footnotes, or in endnotes. As you proofread, make sure you have formatted all citations correctly.

Formatting Excerpts Sometimes, the best way to incorporate another person's ideas into your research paper is to quote that person at length. Direct quotations of four lines or more are considered excerpts and must be formatted as such. Proofread your paper to make sure you have formatted excerpts correctly.

Formatting Citations When you credit your sources, it shows that your information is reliable. Use footnotes, endnotes, or parenthetical citations to document your sources whenever you directly or indirectly quote another person, present an idea that is not your own, or report a fact that is available only from one source. You should also prepare a works-cited page, which lists your sources alphabetically by author or, if a work has no credited author, by title.

Formatting a Works-Cited Listing Check your listing of works cited to be sure that it is complete and correctly formatted. Also, double-check the punctuation of entries to ensure that you've consistently and correctly punctuated each one. If in doubt, consult a manual or list of guidelines for preparing a works-cited list.

Technology Tip

Enter author names into the spell-check library of your software program. Then, run the spell-check feature to ensure that you have made no typographical errors in names.

Timed Writing Hint

If you are given forty-five minutes to complete an essay, spend five minutes editing and proofreading carefully.

⏱ TIME AND RESOURCE MANAGER

Resources
Technology: *Writing and Grammar* Interactive Text, Section 13.5

Using the Full Student Edition	Using the Handbook Ⓗ
• Review pp. 294–295 in class, including Grammar in Your Writing.	• Review pp. 188–189 in class, including Grammar in Your Writing.
• Analyze the Final Draft on pp. 297–299.	• Analyze the Final Draft on pp. 191–193.
• Have students edit and proofread their papers in class.	• Have students edit and proofread their papers in class.

Grammar in Your Writing
Formatting

Excerpts: When you have an excerpt of four lines or more, precede the excerpt with a colon; start the excerpt on a new line; write or type the excerpted material to a narrower measure than that used in the rest of the paper; and credit the source of the excerpt using a footnote, endnote, or parenthetical citation.

Parenthetical Citation: This appears in parentheses immediately after the relevant passage in the text of your paper. Include either the author's last name and page number (style of Modern Language Association, the MLA) or give the author's last name, date of publication, and page number (style of American Psychology Association, the APA).

MLA Style   (Coles 306)   **APA Style**   (Coles, 1990, p. 306)

Be sure to include a works-cited listing at the end of your paper.

Footnote: Place a raised number at the end of a cited passage. Place the same raised number at the bottom of the page; next to it, give details about the source of the information. Include the source documentation in full the first time you cite a source and a shortened version for every subsequent citation of that source.

Endnote: Place a raised number at the end of a cited passage. Instead of listing the source information next to a number at the bottom of the page, prepare a separate page for all endnotes.

Works-Cited Listing: This list comes at the end of your paper. It should contain an entry for each work cited in your text. Alphabetize entries by the authors' last names. If the author's name is unknown, alphabetize by the first word in the title of the work. Each entry has three parts: the author, the title, and the publication information. Each part is followed by a period and one space.

Ferrara, Jerry L. "Why Vultures Make Good Neighbors." *National Wildlife*. June–July, 1987: 16–20.

Gerrard, Tabitha. *A Guide to Eastern Seabirds*. Chicago: Agincourt Press, 1999.

Find It in Your Reading Find a passage and its accompanying citation in "Football at the Turn of the Twentieth Century" on pages 276–279. Identify the method of citation. Rewrite the citation using each of the two alternative methods shown above.

Find It in Your Writing Identify all the source citations in your paper. Double-check to make sure that you have included all the pertinent source information in the correct format.

For more about citing sources, see Citing Sources and Preparing Manuscript on pages 918–924.

Formatting

1. Review the conventions for citing sources. If you (or your school) prefers MLA, APA, or some other style, be sure to make that preference clear to students at the outset. If your school has a style manual, refer to it at this point.

2. Discuss the differences among footnotes and endnotes, parenthetical citations, and bibliographic form with students. Model each form on the board and discuss each element within the citations.

3. If you have specific requirements regarding the minimum number of citations or the number and types of sources you expect students to use in their research papers, make those clear to students.

Find It in Your Reading

Students will find many examples of citations in the model. Refer them to the first paragraph on page 276. The sentence beginning "Below this subhead runs a list . . . " contains a parenthetical citation: (*New York Times Index* 664). Challenge students to read textbooks in other subjects and review their citations against these rules.

Find It in Your Writing

You may wish to have students collaborate with partners in checking source citations in their papers.

Customize for
AP Students

Give students excerpts from a research paper on a floppy disk. Save a version of the file that omits punctuation or includes errors. Ask students to revise these pages on the disk and restore it to acceptable form using a stylebook as guide.

Publishing and Presenting

1. Work with the technology consultant in your school or district to provide students with direct help in publishing on the Internet. Your school may have a Web site that would allow students to post their work and receive comments.

2. If students plan to present their research papers in class, set up and post a schedule so that each presenter will know the date and time allotted.

ASSESS and CLOSE

Assessment

Teaching Resources: Scoring Rubrics on Transparency, Ch. 13; Writing Assessment and Portfolio Management; Formal Assessment Ch. 13

1. Display the Scoring Rubric transparency and review the criteria in class.

2. Before students proceed with self-assessment, you may wish to review the Final Draft of the Student Work in Progress on pages 297–299.

3. In addition to student self-assessment, you may wish to use the following options:

   • score student essays yourself, using the rubric and scoring models in *Writing Assessment and Portfolio Management.*

   • administer the Chapter 13 assessment in *Formal Assessment* in the Teaching Resources to evaluate students' grasp of concepts presented.

Customize for
Bodily/Kinesthetic Learners

Encourage students to make their presentations theatrical, using costumes, props, and live action demonstration. This will help deepen the involvement of the audience and will also give students an opportunity to exercise a broader range of skills.

13.6 Publishing and Presenting

Building Your Portfolio

Here are some suggestions for publishing and presenting your work:

1. **Internet** Millions of people around the world are connected electronically through the Internet; no doubt some of them will be interested in reading your paper. Try these ideas for using the Internet: e-mail your paper to a friend; publish it on an electronic bulletin board; submit it to a student publication.

2. **Oral Presentation** Present your research paper orally to your class or to another class that is studying a subject related to your topic. Instead of reading your paper word for word, speak from note cards with key ideas highlighted. Use visual aids to support your presentation.

Reflecting on Your Writing

After you've completed your research paper, spend a few minutes thinking about your writing experience. Then, answer the following questions, and record your answers in your portfolio.

• Did you learn anything about your topic that surprised you?

• If you had to do it over again, what would you do differently?

🖥 Internet Tip

To see a research paper scored according to this rubric, go on-line: PHSchool.com
Enter Web Code: egk-1201

Rubric for Self-Assessment

Use the following criteria to evaluate your research paper.

	Score 4	Score 3	Score 2	Score 1
Audience and Purpose	Focuses on a clearly stated thesis, starting from a well-framed question; gives complete citations	Focuses on a clearly stated thesis; gives citations	Focuses mainly on the chosen topic; gives some citations	Presents information without a clear focus; few or no citations
Organization	Presents information in logical order, emphasizing details of central importance	Presents information in logical order	Presents information logically, but organization is poor in places	Presents information in a scattered, disorganized manner
Elaboration	Draws clear conclusions from information gathered from multiple sources	Draws conclusions from information gathered from multiple sources	Explains and interprets some information	Presents information with little or no interpretation or synthesis
Use of Language	Shows overall clarity and fluency; contains few mechanical errors	Shows good sentence variety; contains some errors in spelling, punctuation, or usage	Uses awkward or overly simple sentences; contains many mechanical errors	Contains incomplete thoughts and many mechanical errors

296 • Research Paper

⏱ TIME AND RESOURCE MANAGER

Resources
Print: *Scoring Rubrics on Transparency,* Ch. 13; *Writing Assessment and Portfolio Management; Formal Assessment,* Ch.13
Technology: *Writing and Grammar* Interactive Text, Section 13.6

Using the Full Student Edition	Using the Handbook Ⓗ
• Discuss presentation options in class. • Read and discuss the Final Draft (pp. 297–299). • Have students apply the Rubric for Self-Assessment to their own research papers.	• Discuss presentation options in class. • Read and discuss the Final Draft (pp. 191–193). • Have students apply the Rubric for Self-Assessment to their own research papers.

13.7 Student Work
IN PROGRESS

FINAL DRAFT

Seamus Heaney: A Literary Biography

Ian Pritchard
Buena High School
Ventura, California

The Irish poet Seamus Heaney spent his youth among fertile farmlands and peat bogs that make up the countryside of County Derry, a small farming community thirty miles northwest of Belfast. Born on April 13, 1939, to Margaret and Patrick Heaney, Seamus was the eldest of nine children. He passed his days either

◄ **Critical Viewing**
Heaney is wearing the medal he received when he was awarded the Nobel Prize. How might you research the symbolism of the medal's design? **[Make a Plan]**

In his report's introduction, Ian introduces the topic of his essay—Seamus Heaney—and his thesis—that Heaney's life has a direct influence on his poetry.

Student Work in Progress • **297**

Teaching From the Final Draft

The author draws a parallel between Heaney "uncovering layers upon layers of peat" and uncovering the layers of his thoughts through poetry. Encourage students to use metaphor in their own writing, as it is a powerful way to make connections between ideas and phenomena.

Integrating Grammar Skills

Punctuation In the citation of some lines of poetry, the author places a forward slash (/) between two words: "Cauldron bog/Our holy ground." Point out to students that the slash is a way of separating words or groups of words that originally appeared on separate lines in a poem. Why is it important to preserve this information? (Poetry is divided into lines for important reasons that affect the meaning, sound, and intent of the words.)

Teaching From the Final Draft

Due to space constraints in this textbook, the Final Draft of this research paper may not be as long and detailed as you will require of your students. As you review the Final Draft, be sure to specify to students your particular requirements regarding length, quantity of quotations and sources, style of citations, and other details.

at the local school in Anahorish or next to his father in the fields of Mossbawn, the family farm (Buttel 9). The hard labor that he, his family, and other generations of Irish farmers endured in the cultivation and harvesting of potatoes has had a great influence on Heaney's poetry. The land itself is mirrored in the strength of Heaney's words. Philip Fried, whose poetry collections include *Mutual Trespasses* and *Quantum Genesis,* has observed the earthiness of Heaney's poetry. In a recent interview, Fried said, "Heaney handles words as if they had the heft of potatoes" (Fried). The tumultuous past and fervent present of Ireland's political situation have also lent substantially to Heaney's work.

The peat bogs that so fascinated Heaney as a child have come to be a consistent metaphor in his poetry: Just as the bogs contain a catalog of objects buried for hundreds of years, Heaney's poems rely heavily on stories and people from the past, which give readers a sense of modern-day Irish sentiment. Heaney writes about his country's and his countrymen's violated past in a voice that reflects upon the violence of the present. Persons, animals, and objects resurrected from the brown peat—indeed, the peat itself— have all become the source and subject of Heaney's writings (Tobin 91). Through his poems, Heaney's strong attachment to the soil is apparent; in "The Tollund Man," Heaney makes reference to "the cauldron bog/Our holy ground," from which the well-preserved body of an old hunter was exhumed. The poet's fascination with things buried and times past parallels his search for answers to not only specifically Irish questions, but to questions that are universal (Vendler 42, 43). The uncovering of layer upon layer of peat is similar to the poet digging down to the depths of his own mind. He seems to discover a truth that comes from both kinds of digging: "The wet centre is bottomless" ("Bogland").

A strong connection with his homeland and his family has given Heaney much material to write upon. His early life was filled with hardships, few of which did not leave an impression on his character, and, thus, on his work. Perhaps it was the joy he found in his life away from Mossbawn with Marie Devlin, whom he married in 1965, and their two children, Michael and Christopher, which made him realize that he had missed the fun of childhood.

Heaney, however, was grateful to his parents and actually in awe of them—his father, in particular. One of his best-known poems, "Harvest Bow," praises his father's creative impulse, glorifies the unspoken joy of shared experiences between father and son, and details the attachment Heaney felt toward his dad (Vendler 74). Among Heaney's more moving poems are those eight

Ian used various types of details to support his thesis. This paragraph contains information from a source, lines of poetry written by the subject, and personal observations.

Ian used MLA style documentation within his report.

Much of the body of Ian's report is organized chronologically, tracing the events of Heaney's life.

sonnets entitled *Clearances,* written shortly after his mother's death.

> When all the others were away at Mass
> I was all hers as we peeled potatoes.
> They broke the silence, let fall one by one
> Like solder weeping off the soldering iron:
> (111, 1–4)

After his parents' deaths, Heaney faced a double challenge. Being thus released from both the weight and the shield of his parents was simultaneously freeing and frightening to Heaney. Heaney's 1991 volume of poetry, *Seeing Things,* is largely a tribute to his father.

Ireland's turbulent past is also a common theme in Heaney's work, and he often draws connections between himself and the past. Heaney relates the killings of those centuries-dead persons to modern-day executions and martyrs, commenting that although the times have changed, very little in public action has. In his poem "Two Lorries," Heaney connects a turbulence in his own life with the violence of Irish history, asking "but which lorry/Was it now? Young Agnew's or that other,/Heavier, deadlier one, set to explode in a time beyond her time in Magherafelt" (31–34).

Seamus Heaney, who, along with William Butler Yeats and Louis MacNeice, is considered among the best of all Irish poets, draws his vital and vivid images from the land he grew up in—Ireland's plagued past and its tormented present. Although Heaney has become successful and famous, it is nonetheless his past and the strong connection he feels with it that will be ever apparent in his poetry. His poem "Tollund Man" reinforces this link.

> Out there in Jutland
> In the old man-killing parishes
> I will feel lost,
> Unhappy and at home. (41–44)

Works Cited

Buttel, Robert. *Seamus Heaney/Irish Writers Series.* Lewisburg: Bucknell University Press, 1975.

Fried, Philip. Personal Interview. 15 Dec. 1999.

Heaney, Seamus. *Opened Ground, Selected Poems,* 1966–1996. New York: Farrar, Straus, and Giroux, 1998.

Tobin, Daniel. *Passage to the Center: Imagination and the Sacred in the Poetry of Seamus Heaney.* Lexington: University Press of Kentucky, 1999.

Vendler, Helen. *Seamus Heaney.* Cambridge: Harvard University Press, 1998.

Because this quotation is four lines long, it is styled as an excerpt.

▲ **Critical Viewing**
What aspects of this Irish landscape might fascinate a poet such as Heaney? **[Connect]**

Ian chose to end his report with some lines of Heaney's poetry. These lines help prove Ian's thesis, and they create a memorable ending for the report.

Ian lists the source information for material that he cited in his report.

Customize for
Less Advanced Students

Point out that reference librarians are skilled and able to help students in all phases of research paper writing. Encourage students to go to them for help in researching, formatting, and finding reference works such as style manuals.

Integrating Technology

Internet Addresses Remind students that when citing an Internet address, it is important to take care to reproduce it exactly. The addition of a space or the omission of a period can make it difficult or impossible for that address to be located.

Critical Viewing

Connect Answers include: The intense greens, the rolling hills, and the lines of trees and hedges marking borders and so recording history might all fascinate a poet.

1. To write a multimedia report in a style appropriate to audience and purpose
2. To use prewriting strategies to generate ideas and plan
3. To use a variety of forms and technologies to communicate specific messages
4. To use a range of techniques to plan and create a media text

Step-by-Step Teaching Guide

Multimedia Report

Teaching Resources: Writing Support Transparency, 13-J; Writing Support Activity Book, 13-2

1. Ask students to read the first three paragraphs on this page and the prewriting directions.
2. Go over the bulleted items, asking students to jot down their own ideas as you discuss the categories.
3. Allow plenty of time for students to decide on a topic and propose a thesis statement.
4. Display Transparency 13-J and distributed copies of the blank organizer 13-2 for students to use in their own planning.
5. Suggest that students review strategies from Chapter 13. See the chart below for resources that may be of particular help.
6. Allow time for students to present their reports in class. Consider videotaping the presentations.

Critical Viewing

Speculate Students may suggest that because the student is pictured using an overhead projector and is apparently writing on a transparency, the material she is presenting is probably suited to being presented in graphic form, such as in an outline or a graphic organizer.

Connected Assignment
Multimedia Report

A **multimedia report** is similar to a research paper in that it states a thesis that is supported with evidence. The difference is in the presentation—a multimedia report conveys its message through visual, auditory, and print media. The preparer of a multimedia report can therefore choose the most suitable medium for the presentation of research findings. For example, you could illustrate a painter's growth by showing slides of paintings completed at different points in the artist's career. If you wanted to make an observation about musical styles popular in the days of King Louis XIV, you could play a recording of such music for the class.

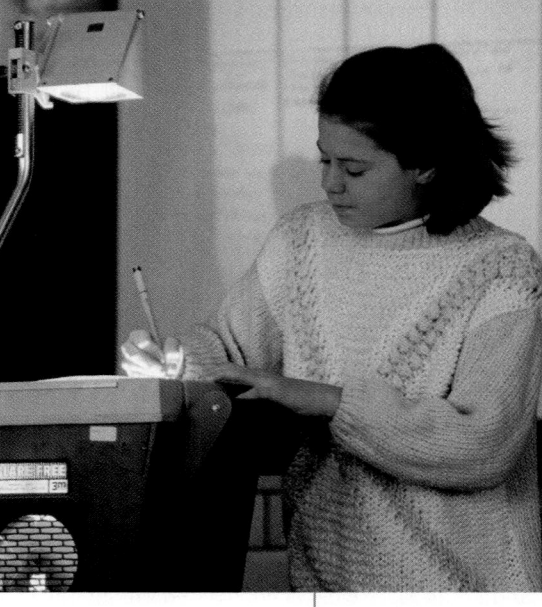

An effective multimedia presentation
• states, develops, and supports a thesis.
• contains a variety of supporting information.
• presents information through a variety of media.
• engages an audience and accomplishes a specific purpose.
• is error free.

Develop your own multimedia report by following the writing process suggestions explained below.

▲ **Critical Viewing** What sort of information might the student pictured be presenting? How can you tell? **[Speculate]**

Prewriting

Choosing Your Topic Make a list of potential topics for your multimedia report. Then, choose two or three entries that interest you most. Copy those entries down on another list. For each, come up with ideas for how you would incorporate multimedia technology in its presentation. Finally, review your list and choose the topic most suited for a multimedia report.

Gathering Details Make a chart like the one on the following page to plan the types of media you will use in your presentation and the types of media you'll have to create and research. As you fill in the chart, strive to use a variety of types of media from a variety of sources.

☑ ONGOING ASSESSMENT: Prerequisite Skills

Students may find the following resources from Chapter 13 particularly helpful in completing their multimedia reports.

In the Textbook	Print Resources	Technology
Webbing to Narrow a Topic, Section 13.2 Planning Research with a T-Chart, Section 13.2	*Writing Support Transparencies,* 13-C–D *Writing Support Activity Book,* 13-1	*Writing and Grammar* Interactive Text, Section 13.2

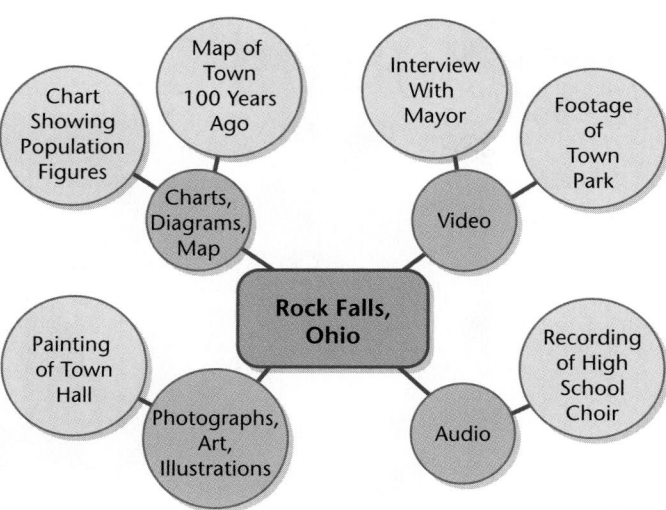

Integrating Workplace Skills

Let students know that multimedia presentation skills are routinely necessary in the workplace. Today's employees must regularly present new material to groups of other employees, and frequently make use of visual and aural aids to do so.

Drafting Because much of the information you find will be presented through visual or auditory media, shape your text in a script format, with your narration shown as dialogue. Within the script, explain the sequence and position of various media in stage direction format. Make sure to indicate what you or other helpers need to do to make alternative media accessible. For example, you may note in your report to point to specific elements or advance the slide projector.

Revising and Editing Critically examine the information you plan to present. Evaluate the information according to the following criteria: Make sure it is accurate; make sure it is interesting; and make sure it relates to your topic. Also, examine your word choice and choice of details to be sure that they are appropriate for your audience and help you to fulfill your purpose.

Publishing and Presenting Rehearse your multimedia presentation beforehand. Ask a family member or friend to watch your rehearsals. Practice using note cards and making eye contact with your audience. Also, make sure that you know how to operate all pieces of equipment you plan to use. Get feedback from your audience, and incorporate their suggestions wherever appropriate. Reduce or expand the time spent on each part of your presentation until it flows smoothly and retains audience interest.

Lesson Objectives

1. To link related information from a variety of sources
2. To analyze relationships and ideas as represented in various media
3. To investigate the source of a media presentation or production

Recognizing Art Forms

1. Show students an excerpt from a video of *Oklahoma!* Discuss with students the qualities of movement in the dance sequences.

2. Encourage students to find and play, or perform, songs from Rogers and Hammerstein musicals such as *Oklahoma!*, *State Fair*, *South Pacific*, *The King and I*, and *Sound of Music* and explore the stories behind these plays.

3. Many books have been written about the behind-the-scenes creation of Cecil B. DeMille's spectacles. Students may wish to write about them, about DeMille's career, or about the relationship between the films and the original sources of his stories.

4. Ask a volunteer to get more information on the DeMille films via Web sites on the history of cinema and share it with the class.

Viewing and Representing

Activity Give interested students an opportunity to make class presentations of their research. Encourage students to use visuals in their presentations.

Customize for
Bodily/Kinesthetic Learners

Have students view a film or video recording of *Oklahoma!* Students may wish to stage a scene or song from this production to perform for classmates.

Spotlight on the Humanities

Recognizing Art Forms

Focus on Dance: Agnes DeMille

If you were to do a research report on a famous family, the DeMille family would be an excellent choice. American choreographer and dancer Agnes DeMille (1905–1993) revolutionized the musical theater in 1943 with the Broadway show *Oklahoma!* by integrating choreography with plot. For the first time, dance numbers furthered the plot of a musical. In 1942, she created a major American ballet in *Rodeo*, which received twenty-two curtain calls at its premiere. The niece of Hollywood film producer Cecil B. DeMille, she danced and continued to tour with her dance company into the 1970's. In 1976, she received the Handel Medallion, which is New York's highest award for achievement in the arts.

Theater Connection Richard Rodgers (composer, 1902–1979) and Oscar Hammerstein (lyricist, 1895–1960) wrote eleven musicals in seventeen years, including the classic *Oklahoma!* with Agnes de Mille as choreographer. Beginning in 1943, Rodgers and Hammerstein created the musicals *Carousel*, *State Fair*, *South Pacific*, *The King and I*, and *Sound of Music*. In their lifetime, they garnered thirty-four Tony Awards, fifteen Academy Awards, two Pulitzer Prizes, and two Grammy Awards.

Film Connection Cecil B. DeMille (1881–1959), uncle of choreographer Agnes DeMille, is renowned for his monumental films, such as *Ten Commandments* (1923, 1956), *King of Kings* (1927), and *Greatest Show on Earth* (1952). Arriving in Hollywood in 1913 with Samuel Goldwyn and Jesse L. Lasky, he directed *The Squaw Man* that same year, which was one of the first full-length movies ever made.

Research Writing Application: Report on a Famous Family
Write a report on a famous family that you find interesting. You might choose to research a family active in politics, like the Roosevelts or the Kennedys, or you may choose to research a show-business family like the Bridgeses or the Baldwins.

▲ **Critical Viewing**
This photograph captures a moment from DeMille's Dream Ballet in *Oklahoma!* Does this scene seem realistic or dreamlike to you? Explain. **[Criticize]**

Critical Viewing

Criticize Students may say the scene seems dreamlike, because of the exaggerated perspective of the backdrop, or that it seems realistic, because of the homely details of the actors' costumes.

Media and Technology Skills

► Lesson Objectives

1. To use writing to formulate questions, refine topics, and clarify ideas

2. To locate appropriate print and non-print information using text and technical resources, including databases and the Internet

3. To compile information from primary and secondary sources using available technology

4. To organize notes from multiple sources in useful and informing ways such as graphics

Evaluating On-line Resources

Activity: Prepare an Annotated Web Index

Using the Internet successfully requires two complementary skills: finding the information you need and assessing the credibility of the information you locate. As you become an experienced Web surfer, you can share your evaluations of search engines and Web sites by building an annotated Web index to share with others.

Think About It Prepare a list of Web sites that you find particularly useful, misleading, poorly organized, or strongly biased. Identify your plan for your index before you sign on. For example, you might decide to review three search engines and six Web sites.

Locate It Search engines allow you to search the World Wide Web for specific information. The engine will search its database and present a list of every Web page that matches your search criteria. The number of matches, or hits, will vary because every engine uses a different search mechanism and has different Web sites in its database. Evaluate different search engines by trying the same search topic in three or four different search engines. Keep a chart like the one below to record the hits.

Search Engine	Search String	Number of Hits	Quality of Hits

Interpret It After evaluating search engines, analyze a set of related Web sites. For example, you might evaluate sites that relate to United States parks. When you enter a site for the first time, find out who has sponsored or produced the site. Evaluating authorship can help you uncover biases.

Many Web pages are written and published quickly. Do not assume that every fact on the Web has been verified. Always try to find at least one additional, reliable source for any fact or statistic you find.

Annotate It Finally, compile your annotated Web index. List the name and URL (address) of each site you visited. Describe the purpose of the content of the site, and explain any biases you uncovered. Finally, provide a rating to help your readers identify particularly helpful Web sites.

Varieties of Search Engines

Not every search engine on the Internet uses the same techniques. Notice the organization of your search results to evaluate a search engine and make use of its strengths.

- **Text searches:** Many search engines search through millions of Web pages to find the search string, or words, you entered. Sites using the string most frequently usually appear first on the list.
- **Category searches:** Some search engines group Web pages into related categories. Results are listed under topic classifications.
- **Group searches:** Some engines combine the results from several different search engines.

Media and Technology Skills • 303

Step-by-Step Teaching Guide

Evaluating On-Line Resources

Teaching Resources: Writing Support Transparencies, 13-K; Writing Support Activity Book, 13-3

1. Review the information on search engines in the sidebar box. Since it is likely that several students in the class will be familiar with search engines, draw on their expertise during discussion.

2. Point out to students that evaluating Internet sites will require the same or similar critical skills called for when they evaluate written texts or television programs.

3. Display Transparency 13-K to demonstrate one system for organizing their evaluations. Distribute copies of the graphic organizer (13-3) for their own use.

4. You might wish to refer students to other annotated texts to give them an understanding of the writers' critical and evaluative style and terminology.

1. To analyze aspects of texts such as patterns of organization and choice of language for their effect on audiences

2. To analyze text structures such as compare/contrast, cause/effect, and chronological order for how they influence understanding

3. To demonstrate a command of accurate spelling and correct use of the conventions of punctuation and capitalization

Step-by-Step Teaching Guide

Revising and Editing

Teaching Resources: Standardized Test Preparation Workbook, pp. 25–26

1. Review the bulleted items with students. These clarify what abilities are measured on the test items they will be practicing.

2. Have students read the sample test item, answer the question, and review the correct answer and explanation.

3. Assign the practice test, and go over the answers with students when they have finished.

4. Ask students to discuss any item or items with which they had difficulty.

Standardized Test Preparation Workshop

Revising and Editing

One of the most important steps in writing a research paper is revising and editing. When taking a standardized test, you may be challenged by questions that test your ability to revise and edit a passage. Following are strategies that can help you address these types of questions:

- Critically evaluate a writer's word choice.
- Decide which information is irrelevant.
- When reading a passage, pay attention to how information could be clarified by adding more information.
- When reading a passage, note information that does not connect to the rest of the information being presented.
- Notice any commas that are placed incorrectly.
- Be sure that the proper tense is being used for verbs in the text.

The following sample test item will give you practice with questions on revising and editing.

Test Tip

Read the passage once and the questions that follow. Then, reread the passage before answering the questions. This will help you identify weaknesses and strengths in the paper.

Sample Test Item	Answer and Explanation
Directions: Read the passage, and then answer the questions that follow. 1Alexander Pope's mock-epic *The Rape of the Lock,* a tale about the theft of a lock of hair, are based on a real incident. 2Two families, the Petres and the Fermors, became involved in a dispute when Robert Petre flirtatiously cut a lock of hair from the head of beautiful Arabella Fermor. 3Pope wrote about this incident, in the hopes that a humorous poem would bring the families together.	
1. Which of the following changes is needed in the above passage? A. Part 1: Change *are based* to *is based*. B. Part 2: Change *became* to *becomes*. C. Part 3: Change *wrote* to *written*. D. Make no changes.	The answer is *A*. Since the subject of the sentence *The Rape of the Lock* refers to a single poem, the verb must also be singular. Therefore, the singular verb phrase *is based* is correct.

304 • Research Writing

✐ TEST-TAKING TIP

Tell students to make a note of any questions they have or any errors they find as they read through a passage. Emphasize that students should look for punctuation errors of all types. Sometimes punctuation will be needed. At other times, a passage may be wrongly punctuated.

Capitalization errors can include words that are capitalized but shouldn't be, as well as words that should be but aren't. Students should also be alert for information that seems extraneous to a passage and sentences that lack parallelism.

> **Practice 1** **Directions:** Read the passage, and then answer the questions that follow. Choose the letter of the best answer.

1The obsession with fashion satirized by Alexander Pope in *The Rape of the Lock* was a genuine phenomenon of the upper classes in the 1700's. 2The world's first fashion magazine dates from 1785, and although it was French, fashion had become an international affair. 3Queen Marie Antoinette's hairdresser, Léonard, had stunned the world. 4He rolled her hair over pads of horse hair, then added accessories such as gauze and feathers to create elegant "hair statues" sometimes as high as four feet. 5His masterpiece, celebrating a French naval victory, transformed, waves of hair into a raging sea battering the sides of a French frigate in full sail. 6It was probably more difficult to do this with knotty hair. 7At war with France in fashion as well as on the battlefield, the English quickly responded to Léonard. 8English hairdressers decorated fashionable heads with horse-drawn carriages, zoos with miniature lions and tigers and, if accounts can be believed, a lit stove complete with pots and pans. 9For the most part, men of the period showed considerably less imagination when it came to hair. 10Among them are the Macaroni Club, a group of young men who wore bizarrely shaped wigs in order to annoy their conservative elders.

1. What is the best change, if any, to make in Part 1?
   A. Change *satirized* to *satirizes*.
   B. Change *lock* to *Lock*.
   C. Change *upper classes* to *upper class*.
   D. Make no change.

2. Which of the following changes, if any, is needed in the passage?
   A. Move Part 10 to the beginning of the passage.
   B. Delete Part 3.
   C. Delete Part 6.
   D. Make no change.

3. Which of the following should have a comma deleted?
   A. Part 2
   B. Part 10
   C. Part 5
   D. Part 8

4. Which of the following is the best way, if any, to combine the sentences in Part 3 and Part 4?
   A. Queen Marie Antoinette's hairdresser, Léonard, had stunned the world when he rolled her hair over pads of horse hair and added accessories such as gauze and feathers to create elegant "hair statues," some as high as four feet.
   B. Queen Marie Antoinette's hairdresser, Léonard, had stunned the world, and he rolled her hair over pads of horse hair, and then added accessories such as gauze and then he added feathers to create elegant "hair statues," sometimes as high as four feet.
   C. Queen Marie Antoinette's hairdresser, Léonard, had stunned the world; he rolled her hair over pads of horse hair and then added accessories such as gauze and feathers to create elegant "hair statues" sometimes as high as four feet.
   D. Make no change.

5. Which of these sentences would best fit after Part 9?
   A. Men weren't as interested in fashion.
   B. There were exceptions, however.
   C. They were very immature.
   D. A line from "Yankee Doodle" refers to these men.

Customize for
Less Advanced Students

Explain that a test that measures revising and editing skills will probably not require that students look for factual details in a passage. For example, this practice test does not ask students to answer a question about the ways Léonard styled Queen Marie Antoinette's hair. Students will, however, be expected to get the main idea of a passage.

Customize for
AP Students

Tell students that carelessness is often a cause of a poor grade on a test. They should always focus on test directions, noting whether they are to choose a letter, underline, write out an answer, circle an item, and so on.

In-Depth Lesson Plan

	LESSON FOCUS	PRINT AND MEDIA RESOURCES
DAY 1	**Introduction to Response to Literature** Students learn key elements of writing responses to literature and analyze the Model From Literature. (pp. 306–309/H194–195)	*Writers at Work* DVD, Response to Literature *Writing and Grammar* Interactive Text, Ch. 14, Introduction
DAY 2	**Prewriting** Students choose and narrow a topic, consider their audience and purpose, and gather information. (pp. 310–314/H196–200)	*Writing and Grammar* Interactive Text, Section 14.2 **Teaching Resources** *Writing Support Transparencies,* 14-A–E; *Writing Support Activity Book,* 14-1–3; *Topic Bank for Heterogeneous Classes,* Ch. 14
DAY 3	**Drafting** Students organize their ideas and write their first drafts. (pp. 315–316/H201–202)	*Writing and Grammar* Interactive Text, Section 14.3 **Teaching Resources** *Writing Support Transparencies,* 14-F–G
DAY 4	**Revising** Students revise their drafts in terms of overall structure, paragraphs, sentences, and word choice. (pp. 317–320/H203–206)	*Writing and Grammar* Interactive Text, Section 14.4 **Teaching Resources** *Writing Support Transparencies,* 14-H; *Writing Support Activity Book,* 14-4
DAY 5	**Editing and Proofreading; Publishing and Presenting** Students check their work for accuracy and correctness and present their final drafts. (pp. 321–322/H207–208)	*Writing and Grammar* Interactive Text, Sections 14.5–6 **Teaching Resources** *Scoring Rubrics on Transparency,* Ch. 14; *Writing Assessment and Portfolio Management; Formal Assessment,* Ch. 14

Accelerated Lesson Plan

	LESSON FOCUS	PRINT AND MEDIA RESOURCES
DAY 1	**Introduction Through Drafting** Students review characteristics of writing a response to literature, select topics, and write drafts. (pp. 306–316/H194–202)	*Writers at Work* DVD, Response to Literature *Writing and Grammar* Interactive Text, Ch. 14, Introduction through Section 14.3 **Teaching Resources** *Writing Support Transparencies,* 14-A–G; *Writing Support Activity Book,* 14-1–3
DAY 2	**Revising Through Presenting** Students work individually or with peers to revise, edit, and proofread their work for presentation. (pp. 317–322/H203–208)	*Writing and Grammar* Interactive Text, Sections 14.4–6 **Teaching Resources** *Writing Support Transparencies,* 14-H; *Scoring Rubrics on Transparency,* Ch. 14; *Writing Assessment and Portfolio Management; Formal Assessment,* Ch. 14

Options for Adapting Lesson Plans

HOMEWORK

Have students complete any stage of the lesson for homework.

FEATURES

Extend coverage with Connected Assignment (p. 325/H209), Spotlight on the Humanities (p. 326), Media and Technology Skills (p. 327), and the Standardized Test Preparation Workshop (pp. 328–329).

TECHNOLOGY

Students can complete any stage of the lesson on the computer, using *Writing and Grammar* Interactive Text or a word-processing program. Have them print out their completed work.

Writing and Grammar Handbook Alignment

Page numbers in Step-by-Step Teaching Guides in this Teacher's Edition refer to pages from the full student text. Handbook page references, indicated with this icon [H], are provided in Time and Resource Manager boxes and at the bottom of each Teacher's Edition page.

INTEGRATED SKILLS COVERAGE

Integrating Grammar
Usage and Mechanics, SE p. 316/[H]202
Comparisons, SE p. 319/[H]205
Quotation Marks, SE p. 321/[H]207

Reading/Writing Connection ATE p. 316
Draw Conclusions, SE p. 308
Writing Application, SE p. 309

Viewing and Representing
Critical Viewing, SE pp. 306, 308, 323, 325, 326, 327/[H]194, 209
Examining Various Media, SE p. 326

Technology Skills
Responding Using Technology, SE p. 327
SE pp. 317, 318, 322/[H]203, 204, 208; ATE p. 317

Workplace Skills ATE p. 315

Real-World Connection ATE p. 313

ASSESSMENT SUPPORT

Standardized Test Preparation Workshop SE p. 328; ATE p. 320
Standardized Test Preparation Workbook, pp. 27–28
Scoring Rubrics on Transparency, Ch. 14
Formal Assessment, Ch. 14
Writing Assessment and Portfolio Management

MEETING INDIVIDUAL NEEDS

Less Advanced Students ATE pp. 325, 329. See also Ongoing Assessments ATE pp. 308, 311, 316, 318.
AP Students ATE p. 329
ESL Students ATE pp. 311, 312
Spatial Learners ATE p. 309
Interpersonal Learners ATE p. 314
Linguistic Learners ATE p. 324

BLOCK SCHEDULING

Pacing Suggestions
For 90-minute Blocks
• Have students complete the Prewriting and Drafting stages in a single period.
• Focus one class period on Revising and Editing and Publishing and Presenting. Allow at least 30 minutes for peer revision.

Resources for Varying Instruction
• *Writing and Grammar* **Interactive Text** A 90-minute block provides an ideal opportunity for students to work on the computer.
• *Writers at Work* **DVD** Show the Response to Literature segment in class.

Professional Development Support
• *How to Manage Instruction in the Block* This teaching resource provides management and activity suggestions.

MEDIA AND TECHNOLOGY

For the Student
• *Writing and Grammar* **Interactive Text,** Ch. 14
• *On-line Exercise Bank,* Sections 24.1–2

For the Teacher
• *Writers at Work* **DVD,** Response to Literature
• **Teacher**EXPRESS™ CD-ROM

WRITING AND GRAMMAR ON-LINE

Interactive Text (On-line or on CD-ROM)
• Easily navigable instruction with interactive Revision Checkers
• Full use of e-rater™, the essay-scoring system (on-line only)

Companion Web Site PHSchool.com
• Scoring rubrics with models (use Web Code egk-1201)

See the Go On-line! **feature, SE p. iii.**

LITERATURE CONNECTIONS

Related selections from *Prentice Hall Literature, Penguin Edition,* The British Tradition:

Professional Model "Outside History," Eavan Boland, SE p. 309
Topic Bank Options Sonnet 116, William Shakespeare, SE p. 311/[H]197
"Love Among the Ruins," Robert Browning, SE p. 311/[H]197
Sonnet 43, Elizabeth Barrett Browning, SE p. 311/[H]197

Lesson Objectives

1. To write a response to literature appropriate to audience and purpose

2. To read to appreciate a writer's craft and to discover models for writing

3. To analyze literary elements for their contributions to meaning

4. To evaluate text through critical analysis

5. To use prewriting strategies to generate ideas, develop voice, and plan

6. To develop drafts independently by organizing content such as by paragraphing and outlining and refining style to suit occasion, audience, and purpose

7. To edit and proofread to ensure standard English usage and grammar

8. To refine selected work for publication

Critical Viewing

Interpret Students may observe that the book seems to prompt a meditative, reflective mood in the woman reading it.

Chapter 14 Response to Literature

Fond Memories, Michael Mortimer Robinson

Responding to Literature in Everyday Life

A talk-show host recommends a book she has been reading, and book sales skyrocket the next day. A rock band records a song based on an old Scottish folk tale. These responses to literature take place in everyday life. When you respond to literature, you might talk with friends about something you read, recommend it in an e-mail note, or write a letter to an author.

306 • Response to Literature

▲ Critical Viewing
Study the woman's expression in this painting. How would you describe her reaction to the book she's reading? [Interpret]

⏱ TIME AND RESOURCE MANAGER

Resources
Technology: *Writers at Work* DVD, Response to Literature; *Writing and Grammar* Interactive Text, Ch. 14

Using the Full Student Edition	Using the Handbook🄷
• Read and discuss pp. 306–307 in class. Discuss how students respond to literature in everyday life. • Read the Model From Literature in class. • Have students work in small groups or pairs to list three literary examples they have read or heard about from others.	• Read and discuss pp. 194–195 in class. Discuss how students respond to literature in everyday life. • Have students work in small groups or pairs to list three literary examples they have read or heard about from others.

What Is a Response to Literature?

A **response to literature** is a nonfiction piece of writing that presents a reaction to or an analysis of one or more literary works. An effective response to literature usually

- identifies the work or works being discussed.
- supports the writer's interpretations with precise examples, citations, or quotations.
- is organized clearly and effectively.
- offers an opinion, a judgment, or an evaluation based on close scrutiny of specific elements.

To preview the criteria on which your response to literature may be evaluated, see the Self-Assessment Rubric on page 322.

Types of Responses to Literature

There are many different types of responses to literature. Your response might fall into one of these specific categories:

- **Reading journals** are notebooks in which to record your reactions and responses to works of literature.
- **Literary analyses** explain the literary elements that appear within a work, such as theme, character, plot, or meter.
- **Comparative analyses** compare two or more literary works, identifying relevant and instructive similarities and differences.
- **Critical reviews** identify a work's strengths and weaknesses and often present the reviewer's overall, supported evaluation.

PREVIEW
Student Work
IN PROGRESS

Samuel Taylor Coleridge's poem "Kubla Khan" has inspired a variety of responses in readers. In this chapter, you will see how Emily Elstad, a student at Tupelo High School in Tupelo, Mississippi, shaped her response to the poem into an effective essay. A completed draft of Emily's response can be found at the end of the chapter.

Writers in ACTION

Poet and critic Eavan Boland emphasizes the strong mutual relationship between literature and readers that keeps texts fresh and vital:

"A poem or other work of literature is a little bit like a field that gets parched....The reader is like the rain, you see, so you want to keep bringing [literature] to the reader's attention and love and interest. This refreshes it. And every new generation brings a new view to it...."

Response to Literature • **307**

PREPARE and ENGAGE

Interest GRABBER Have students name a favorite book, story, or poem. Ask them to tell why they like the piece of literature. Explain that this is an informal response to literature. Ask students to write their thoughts about the favorite piece of writing in a short paragraph, adding a few details to explain their reactions. Explain that their paragraphs are more formal responses to literature.

Activate Prior Knowledge

Ask students whether they have ever seen a movie that was based on a book. If they aren't sure, you might suggest titles of movies that were books first, such as *Tarzan*, *Blade Runner*, or any of the films based on the works of Jane Austen. Explain that adapting a book into a screenplay is a type of literary response that involves sharing one's interpretation of a written work with others.

More About the Writer

Eavan Boland was born in Dublin, Ireland, and was educated in Dublin, London, and New York. An award-winning writer, and one of Ireland's few recognized women poets, she has published twelve books of poetry, as well as other works. Much of her writing addresses Irish national identity and the role of women in Irish culture. She has taught at colleges in the United States and Ireland, and is currently professor of English at Stanford University. Boland's poem "Outside History" can be found in *Prentice Hall Literature, Penguin Edition,* The British Tradition.

☑ ONGOING ASSESSMENT: Diagnose

Use one of the following options to diagnose students' current level of proficiency in responding to literature.

Option 1 Ask students to select their strongest example of literary response writing from last year. Hold conferences in which you review each student's sample. Use the conferences to determine which students will need extra support in writing responses to literature.

Option 2 Ask students to select a familiar literary work and write a short paragraph of literary or character analysis that supports their opinion of or reaction to the work. If students have difficulty completing this exercise, you may need to devote more time to the choosing a topic and elaboration phases of the process.

Reading\Writing Connection

Reading: Draw Conclusions

Point out that drawing conclusions is something most readers do unconsciously—even preferring one character to another is drawing a conclusion. Explain that readers can learn more if they look for clues. Remind students how Sherlock Holmes could look at someone and, based on small clues that others overlooked, tell a great deal about the person. Clues are everywhere in literature, and the more of them a reader can find, the more he or she will know about either the story or the writer.

Step-by-Step Teaching Guide

Engage Students Through Literature

1. After students have read the essay, ask them what clues they discovered about the author and her life or what conclusions they drew. ("Every time I opened the book . . ." is a clue that she enjoyed reading; what she discovered about Dickinson is a clue that she loves learning; the description of the birds in the snow is a clue that she has an eye for detail.)

2. Ask students how Boland constructs an effective response to literature. The following questions might prompt discussion.

   Does Boland support her interpretation of Dickinson's poems with precise examples, citations, or quotations?

   Is the work organized clearly and effectively? Explain.

   Does it offer an opinion, judgment, or evaluation? Explain.

Critical Viewing

Relate Students' responses may focus on the patterns the birds make against the snow.

14.1 Model From Literature

Eavan Boland's love of literature is reflected in her multifaceted writing, from poems to essays and criticism. This essay shares Boland's thoughts and feelings as she puzzled over a poem by Emily Dickinson.

Reading Writing Connection

Reading Strategy: Draw Conclusions As you read, use clues within the text to draw conclusions about the author.

Meanings

Eavan Boland

When I was seventeen my mother gave me a book of Emily Dickinson's poetry. We were standing in a room in a hotel when she handed it to me. It was summer. There was a gray, rainy light outside the window. She was returning to New York where she lived at that time with my father. I was staying in Dublin, getting ready to go back to boarding school for my last year.

She had a reason for giving it. I had gone to school for three years in New York, from age eleven to fourteen. I was beginning to forget the power and noise and drama of New York. I was beginning to forget the little of American poetry I had learned at school there. The whole experience of a different place was beginning to fade. And my mother wanted me to remember.

When she was gone and I was back in school I opened the book and began to read. Immediately I stumbled on one poem. It was so short it almost looked like a riddle:

> *Water is taught by thirst;*
> *Land, by the oceans passed;*
> *Transport by throe;*
> *Peace, by its battles told;*
> *Love by memorial mould;*
> *Birds by the snow.*

308 • Response to Literature

▲ **Critical Viewing** If you were to write a line of poetry inspired by this photograph, how would it go? **[Relate]**

Boland emphasizes the personal perspective of the essay by using the first-person point of view and opening with a description of how she first came to read Dickinson's poem.

Because this poem is short, Boland cites all of it. The citation allows readers to more fully understand Boland's response.

☑ ONGOING ASSESSMENT: Monitor and Reinforce

After reviewing the Model From Literature, you may anticipate that some students will have difficulty following the course of and reasons for Boland's changing responses to Dickinson's poetry. To help them make connections, use the following strategy.

Have students create two columns headed *Where and When* and *Responses*. In the first column students should record words from Boland's account that give the reader clues about her circumstances, such as *staying in Dublin* and *forgetting New York*. In the opposite column, students should record Boland's responses at the time, such as *forgetting American poetry* or *what did the snow tell you about birds?* Encourage students to use the information to construct a chronology for Eavan Boland's literary response.

Now wait a moment, I said to myself—and, of course, by saying that I was already drawn into the poem. I can see perfectly well why you get to know something about water through being thirsty. I can see how you get to know about land by being on the sea. The little traveling I had done made me understand that you appreciated a car more when you had to walk. So that explained *Transport by throe.* And yes, peace became clearer in war. And love in memory. But what did the snow tell you about birds?

I couldn't forget the poem. Every time I opened the book it seemed to open at that page. I was so curious that I began to ask other people—friends, teachers—what they thought the line meant. No matter what they said, I was dissatisfied. I began to read about Emily Dickinson herself: that she lived in Amherst, Massachusetts, in the middle of the nineteenth century. That she was shy and solitary. That when she died her poems were found carefully sorted and tied by ribbon in what were called fascicles and looked like love letters. That out of the 1800 she kept, only ten were published in her lifetime. And that she said, in a letter describing herself, that her eyes were like "the sherry in the glass that the guest leaves."

Soon I knew the poem by heart and I was reading more. I loved the way her lines were short and out-of-breath and yet told so much, like someone who has run all the way to tell important news. And soon enough, the school term was ending. The autumn had become winter. I was excited because I was going back to New York for Christmas, for the first time since I had left. I packed my suitcase, stored her book away carefully.

Two days before I left, it began to snow. For a whole morning a crisp, light snow covered the grass and school buildings and obscured the blue of the Dublin hills. Snow was not an everyday part of an Irish winter. All morning, I kept looking out the window. And then I saw it: All at once I saw the line of poetry as if it had been written in the snow. There were birds outside on the grass. Blackbirds and thrushes, their wings tucked in, their beaks searching for food under the white crust. Suddenly I saw how they were made distinct—were *taught* just as the poem had said— in a way I had never seen before: Their wings. Their movements. Their dark heads. *Birds by the snow.* All at once the poem explained the world. And the world the poem.

Writing Application: As you prepare to write your response to literature, think about the conclusions you would like your readers to draw about you.

Boland presents a line-by-line analysis of the poem, explaining her interpretations.

This essay is organized chronologically, tracing Boland's efforts to assign meaning to the poem's final line.

Personal opinions, like this one, are one type of elaboration.

"Outside History" is a poem by Eavan Boland. You'll find the poem in *Prentice Hall Literature, Penguin Edition,* The British Tradition.

Boland saves her final insight about the poem for the conclusion of her essay.

Teaching From the Model

You can use this Model From Literature as an example of a response to literature. As students read, ask them to jot down things they learn or conclude about Eavan Boland by reading her story. (As a teen she lived apart from her parents; she was from New York City; she went to school in Ireland; she was intellectually curious.)

Customize for
Spatial Learners

You might want to use a map to point out where Dublin, Ireland, and New York are located. You might also want to point out London, England, and Palo Alto, California (where Stanford University is), to show where the author grew up, was educated, and now lives.

Reading\Writing Connection
Writing Application: Draw Conclusions

Ask students to think about how Boland created an awareness of what she was like. Note how she uses details and word choice to create a cheerful mood. Suggest that students jot down a few notes about things that they would like to get across to a reader. Then, have them think of details and words that will provide clues from which readers can draw conclusions.

Prewriting

Prewriting: Review Your Reader's Journal

1. Have students share some of the reactions they've had to literature they've read.

2. Ask students to suggest things that might make them want to write about a work, such as interesting facts or strong emotional appeal.

Prewriting: Compile a List

Teaching Resources: Writing Support Transparencies, 14-A; Writing Support Activity Book, 14-1

1. Display Transparency 14-A and discuss with students factors on which they might base their ratings.

2. Suggest that students develop a strategy for rating listed works.

3. Explain that choosing the work with the highest rating is not necessarily the only way to pick an essay topic. Sometimes it is easier to write a critical essay about something one disliked. Another possibility is an essay that compares a work one enjoys with one he or she dislikes.

Prewriting: Flip Through a Source Book

1. Tell students that, in addition to textbook anthologies, they may bring anthologies from home.

2. Discuss literary works students have enjoyed in order to inspire interest in reading or to help others recall something that they have read.

Integrating Viewing and Representing Skills

Have students name movies they have seen that were adapted from books. Suggest they read the book or story and write a response. Tell them to jot notes as they read about how the movie and book differ.

Choosing Your Topic

A response to literature begins with the literature itself. In some situations, the topic will be assigned. In others, you will choose the literature to which you will respond. Select works about which you feel strongly.

Strategies for Generating Topics

1. **Review Your Reader's Journal** Scan your reading journal to help you recall the works you have read and to revisit your initial reactions. As you browse through your notes, think about whether or not you still agree with everything you wrote. If you have changed your mind about a book or selection, you might write an essay to explain how your response has evolved over time. Choose to develop the topic about which you feel most strongly.

2. **Compile a List** Compile a list of possible works about which to write. When you make your list, add personal comments that record your instinctive reactions. For example, you might give your own ratings on a scale of one to five stars or assign three words that come to mind. When your list is complete, look for entries with high or low ratings or specific and intriguing words. Choose one such entry as a start for your response to literature.

Work	My Rating	Three Words
Frankenstein (Shelley)	★★★★★	fascinating, sad, mankind
The Tyger (Blake)	★★★	symbolic, illustrated, fearful
Infant Sorrow (Blake)	★	pessimistic, dark, depressing
The Rime of the Ancient Mariner (Coleridge)	★★★	rhythmic, long, guilt
Kubla Khan (Coleridge)	★★★★★	hypnotic, compelling, intense

3. **Flip Through a Source Book** You may have a literature anthology that contains works you have read and many that you would like to read. Read the introductory text to help you preview the literature, as well as the response questions to help you review selections you have already read. Use self-sticking notes to mark possible topics for your response. Then, review your notes, and select one topic to develop.

Interactive Textbook

Try it out! Use the interactive Compile a List in **Section 14.2**, on-line or on CD-ROM.

⏱ TIME AND RESOURCE MANAGER

Resources
Print: *Writing Support Transparencies,* 14-A–E; *Writing Support Activity Book,* 14-1–3
Technology: *Writing and Grammar* Interactive Text, Section 14.2

Using the Full Student Edition	Using the Handbook🅗
• Work through the Reader's Journal, Listing, and Source Book strategies with the class.	• Work through the Reader's Journal, Listing, and Source Book strategies with the class.
• Use the Responding to Fine Art transparency to generate additional topics.	• Use the Responding to Fine Art transparency to generate additional topics.
• Complete the Looping and Hexagonal exercises in class.	• Complete the Looping and Hexagonal exercises in class.

TOPIC BANK

For more specific topic suggestions, consider the ones below:

1. **Thematic Comparison** Choose two works that focus on a common theme. Then, describe similarities and differences in each presentation of the theme. You might, for example, consider comparing the theme of greed in Shakespeare's *Macbeth* and Milton's *Paradise Lost.*

2. **Literary Analysis of Character** Choose one literary character that had a strong impact on you, and describe that character's journey from the beginning to the end of the work. Explain how and why the character grew, identifying landmark events and realizations. You might consider title characters, such as Jane Eyre or Oliver Twist.

Responding to Fine Art

3. *Sean, Coco and Rumple*, by March Avery, depicts two interesting characters sharing a book. Study the painting, and then write a response that explores the growth of an interesting character.

Sean, Coco and Rumple, March Avery, Courtesy of the artist

Responding to Literature

4. Read "Sonnet 116," by William Shakespeare; "Love Among the Ruins," by Robert Browning; and "Sonnet 43," by Elizabeth Barrett Browning. Then, write a response in which you examine the speakers' ideas about love.

Timed Writing Prompt

5. Most people, no matter how much they read, have a favorite genre. Perhaps your favorite is science fiction, historical novels, nonfiction, or mystery stories. Write an essay in which you discuss your favorite genre. First, introduce the genre and explain its main characteristics. Then, identify some of your favorite titles and authors. Finally, explain why this genre appeals to you.
(45 minutes)

ONGOING ASSESSMENT: Monitor and Reinforce

If you observe that students are having difficulty choosing a topic, use one of the following options.

Option 1 Suggest that students choose an idea from the Topic Bank, or recommend topics that you have seen students use successfully. You may also wish to offer topics from the *Topic Bank for Heterogeneous Classes* in the Teaching Resources.	**Option 2** Have students work in groups of three or four to discuss possible topics for a response to literature. Encourage students to ask each other questions about the works, such as What is the theme? Who are strong characters? Why do you like or dislike this piece?

Step-by-Step Teaching Guide

Responding to Fine Art

Sean, Coco and Rumple by March Avery

Teaching Resources: Writing Support Transparencies, 14-B

1. Display Transparency 14-B and ask students what thoughts the image triggers.

2. Point out that often two people have different responses to the same information. Suggest that students might consider comparing two works of literature that comment on a similar event, but from different points of view.

Timed Writing Prompt

- To help students choose a favorite genre, ask them to list their three favorite characters from literature, their defining personality traits or personal characteristics, and what makes them memorable.

- Tell students to examine these characters. Do they share any common traits or is each unique from the other? Then, have students examine whether or not these characters come from novels in similar genres.

- Suggest that students allow five minutes for prewriting, thirty-five minutes for writing, and five minutes for reviewing and proofreading.

Customize for
ESL Students

Suggest that students select a book written in their first language and compare it with an English translation of the same book. Their essays should focus on how the work differs in translation.

TIME SAVERS!

Writing Support Transparencies
Use the transparencies for Chapter 14 to facilitate teaching of strategies.

Writing Support Activity Book
Use the graphic organizers for Chapter 14 to facilitate student planning.

Prewriting: Use Looping to Narrow a Topic

Teaching Resources: Writing Support Transparencies, 14-C

1. Display Transparency 14-C. Point out how Emily found her topic by writing down all her ideas first, then selecting the ones that stood out for her, then starting another "loop" by freewriting about the ideas she chose.

2. Remind students that, as with all freewriting activities, they should not stop to judge or edit their work at this point or worry about having complete sentences.

3. Explain that, depending on how broad their initial topic choice is, they may need more "loops" than Emily, or fewer.

4. If students have identified their topics, they can begin this brainstorming process in class. If they have not identified topics, you may want to assign a topic and have them do a practice looping exercise.

Customize for
ESL Students

Students learning English may have a difficult time writing all of their thoughts as they come to them. Allow them to tape-record their initial burst of ideas, then transcribe them on paper. Alternatively, they could do their initial freewriting in their first language, then translate the items that are of greatest interest to them before narrowing the topic further.

14.2

Narrowing Your Topic

Once you have chosen a work of literature to write about, focus your response. You might decide to concentrate on literary elements or on your personal reactions to the work. If you want to discuss literary elements, consider narrowing the scope of your response to a single important element, such as character, theme, setting, or tone. Use the strategy of looping to help you narrow your response to any work of literature.

Use Looping to Narrow a Topic

Looping is a brainstorming technique that helps you identify key ideas. Begin by writing freely on your response-to-literature topic for about five minutes. Read what you have written, and circle the most important or interesting idea. Then, write for five minutes on that idea. Continue this process until you discover a topic that is narrow enough to address fully and effectively in your essay.

Student Work
IN PROGRESS

Name: *Emily Elstad*
Tupelo High School
Tupelo, MS

Using Looping to Focus a Topic

Emily Elstad used looping to find a specific topic for her response to literature.

Broad topic: My response to "Kubla Khan"

Coleridge took medication before writing this poem. Then he fell asleep and when he woke up, wrote the poem. The landscape is very (dreamy.) Lots of detailed descriptions. Some references: Kubla Khan, Greek gods. When I read the poem I feel like I have entered his (dream.)

Dreams: How does Coleridge make me feel like I'm in his dream? He uses fragmented (images) that remind me of dreams. The (sounds) of the poem are hypnotic.

Narrowed topic: How Coleridge uses images and sounds to draw readers into a dream world.

Considering Your Audience and Purpose

Your general purpose in writing your response to literature is to share your reactions with an audience. Choose details and a writing style that will help you accomplish your purpose and appeal to your audience.

Satisfy Audience Expectations

Suppose that you talked about a piece of writing with a teacher, an author, and a friend. Consider how your conversation would change, depending on which person you were speaking to. You should be able to adjust your writing style to reach different audiences, too.

The following chart shows three specific audiences for whom you might write and provides strategies you can use to reach each audience.

Audience	Writing Examples	Audience Expectations	Strategies
Teacher	Class essays	A teacher is familiar with your previous work and will look for signs of growth and new accomplishments.	• Stretch yourself by choosing a more challenging topic. • If you are writing about a work discussed in class, relate additional insights.
Review Panel	Standardized tests College application essays	A review panel does not know your previous work. It is considering the quality of only one piece of your writing.	• Use formal language. • Exercise additional care when reviewing grammar and spelling.
Students	Book review for school newspaper	Students may or may not know you, but they expect that you will share your honest opinions.	• Use direct language that will appeal to student readers. • State your opinion clearly, and explain why you feel this way.

 **Timed Writing Hint**

When writing under a deadline, use a diagram like the one on this page to shape your audience expectations and strategies quickly.

Prewriting: Satisfy Audience Expectations

Teaching Resources: Writing Support Transparencies, 14-D; Writing Support Activity Book, 14-2

1. Ask students to talk about how their language varies when talking to teachers, family members, and friends. Why does it vary?

2. Explain to students that, while it is easier to identify one's audience when speaking (there is usually a specific person in front of you or on the other end of the phone), it may involve more thought to determine the audience when writing.

3. Display Transparency 14-D. Let students know that these are not the only audiences they might ever write for—there are general audiences, organizations and clubs, employers, and others.

4. Distribute copies of the audience chart (14-2) to students. Encourage students to keep the information on audience expectations in mind when writing.

5. You have the option of identifying the audience for whom you wish students to write, if you would like to see them vary their approach. You will then need to assess the writing based on the expectations identified in the chart.

Real-World Connection

Ask students whether they have ever read an instruction manual (perhaps for a computer or for assembling a piece of equipment) that did not seem to have been written with non-technical readers in mind. Why do they think this happened? How could such writing be remedied? Point out that there has been a recent explosion of books that explain technical things in simpler terms or with a level of detail that makes the technology more accessible.

Prewriting: Use the Hexagonal Writing Strategy

Teaching Resources: Writing Support Transparencies, 14-E; Writing Support Activity Book, 14-3

1. Explain to students that the hexagonal figure is designed to remind them that there are six levels to consider when collecting details. Give students copies of the hexagonal graphic (14-3) to help them plan.

2. Display Transparency 14-E and point out how Emily used hexagonal writing to gather details about her topic.

3. Point out that not all levels will apply to all topics.

4. List the six levels on the board and ask students to think of good examples (from any story) that might be used to illustrate each level. Suggestions may be related to the topic students have selected or to any other literature that offers good illustrations of levels.

Customize for
Interpersonal Learners

Have students demonstrate by writing on the board how they have used (or would use) the hexagonal writing strategy to gather details for this or another writing project. If there are several students, each could take a different level to describe, and then show how they applied the strategy to their own topics.

Gathering Details

Once you have decided on a narrow topic and considered your audience, gather details that will support your response.

Use the Hexagonal Writing Strategy

Use hexagonal writing to explore various aspects of your response to literature. Doing so will help you fully understand your response and will give maturity and depth to your writing. Following are the six levels of hexagonal writing:

Literal Level: Plot, Character, and Setting Give a concise retelling of plot events. Describe the characters and settings.

Personal Allusions Reveal the associations or memories this piece of literature brings to mind.

Themes Explore the theme or themes revealed in the literature.

Analysis of Literary Devices Explain the ways in which plot, setting, character, and theme work as separate elements, as well as how they work together.

Literary Allusions Describe other works that have similar elements or that come to mind when you read this work.

Evaluation Judge the work based on how well its literary elements combine to create an effective, fresh piece of literature.

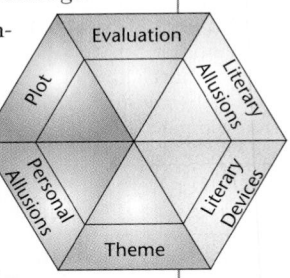

Student Work
IN PROGRESS

Name: Emily Elstad
Tupelo High School
Tupelo, MS

Using Hexagonal Writing to Gather Details
Emily began gathering details for her response through hexagonal writing.

Literal level: Kubla Khan decreed that a pleasure dome be built. The place it was built was "savage," "holy," "enchanted." A girl playing a dulcimer was singing.

Personal allusions: The Wizard of Oz; Pickeral Forest

Theme: Beware of excess; nature is savage

Analyze: Plot unfinished, seems rambling; speaker uses lush, magical language, is omniscient; the language and theme work well together; imagery is appealing yet frightening.

14.3 Drafting

Shaping Your Writing
Use Nestorian Organization

"Saving the best for last" can be an effective organizational strategy for your response to literature. For example, in Nestorian organization, a proposition is presented in the introduction. Then, the second-best example or idea is developed, followed by reasons that decrease in impact or importance. The best example, the one that makes the strongest case, is saved for the conclusion.

SAMPLE OUTLINE SHOWING NESTORIAN ORGANIZATION

I. Introduction: Some readers believe that *Macbeth* shows the title character slowly losing his mind.

    A. "Some say he's mad," says one character.

    B. I disagree. I believe that Macbeth is weak, but not insane. — Proposition

II. Lady Macbeth is mad.

    A. Lady Macbeth definitely goes mad, driven insane by her guilt.

    B. Shakespeare wants us to compare and contrast Macbeth and his wife. The contrast shows that Macbeth is not mad. — 2nd most important point

III. Everything Macbeth does has a clear motivation.

    A. He kills the king to become king.

    B. He believes the witches because they tell him what he wants to hear. — 3rd most important point

IV. Madness would weaken the point.

    A. The point of the play is that Macbeth was once noble, but is corrupted by ambition.

    B. That idea would be severely weakened if Macbeth is not accountable for his actions. Shakespeare clearly intends for us to hold Macbeth accountable. — Most important point

Step-by-Step Teaching Guide

Drafting: Shaping Your Writing

Teaching Resources: Writing Support Transparencies, 14-F

1. Display Transparency 14-F. Review the example, pointing out how each step in the outline relates to the definition of Nestorian order.

2. Ask students to discuss the types of arguments for which they feel Nestorian organization might work best. (Possible answers: situations where there is a particularly strong argument and other, interesting points would appear weak if they followed it; situations where the writer wants to surprise the audience; or situations where the writer wants the last thing readers hear—and therefore the thing most likely to be remembered—to be the strongest point.)

Integrating Workplace Skills

Nestorian organization is often used by speakers, since people who are listening, rather than reading, are most likely to remember the last thing they hear.

⏱ TIME AND RESOURCE MANAGER

Resources
Print: *Writing Support Transparencies,* 14-F–G
Technology: *Writing and Grammar* Interactive Text, Section 14.3

Using the Full Student Edition	Using the Handbook 🄷
• Read and discuss the Nestorian Organization and Citing Passages strategies in class. • Have students work in small groups or pairs to practice the strategies and discuss the findings as they work.	• Read and discuss the Nestorian Organization and Citing Passages strategies in class. • Have students work in small groups or pairs to practice the strategies and discuss the findings as they work.

⏱ TIME SAVERS!

 Writing Support Transparencies
Use the transparencies for Chapter 14 to facilitate teaching of strategies.

 Writing Support Activity Book
Use the graphic organizers for Chapter 14 to facilitate student planning.

Step-by-Step Teaching Guide

Drafting: Cite Passages

Teaching Resources: Writing Support Transparencies, 14-G

1. Display Transparency 14-G. Read the quotation and have students discuss how Emily introduced or explained the quote.

2. Explain that examples from the writing help support the viewpoint of the person writing about the literature, just as lawyers and scientists use evidence and data to prove a thesis.

3. Extend the ideas on the page by asking students to suggest other sources that might be quoted when writing about a piece of literature. (Example: The writer might quote comments by a critic, historian, or fellow reader.)

4. Encourage students to use the strategies in the text both to choose their quotes and to use them to good advantage in their essays.

Integrating Grammar Skills

Usage and Mechanics Remind students that when they use a quote of four lines or more and set it in narrower margins, they need not begin and end the passage with quotation marks. As an example, point out the poem quoted by Eavan Boland in the Model From Literature.

Providing Elaboration

Elaborate on key ideas or statements by giving examples, referencing personal and literary allusions, and citing relevant passages from the text.

Cite Passages

You can use passages from the original text to provide an example of an author's style or tone, to highlight a specific literary device, or to support an interpretation. Consider these strategies when choosing passages to illustrate your ideas:

- Look for passages that are typical of the writer or work.
- Make sure the passages clearly show the characteristics you plan to discuss.
- Provide an introduction or context if your quotation needs it.
- Set off short passages with quotation marks. If you plan to use a quotation that is four lines or longer, set the passage off by using a narrower margin than you do for the rest of your response.

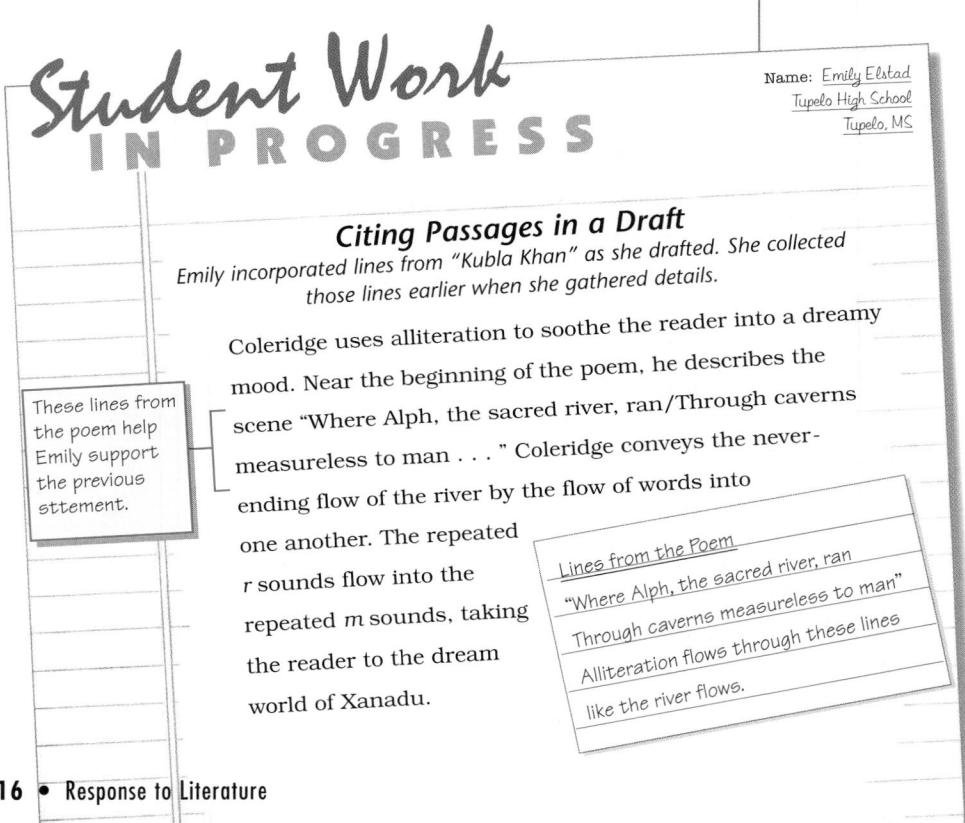

Student Work IN PROGRESS

Name: Emily Elstad
Tupelo High School
Tupelo, MS

Citing Passages in a Draft

Emily incorporated lines from "Kubla Khan" as she drafted. She collected those lines earlier when she gathered details.

Coleridge uses alliteration to soothe the reader into a dreamy mood. Near the beginning of the poem, he describes the scene "Where Alph, the sacred river, ran/Through caverns measureless to man . . . " Coleridge conveys the never-ending flow of the river by the flow of words into one another. The repeated *r* sounds flow into the repeated *m* sounds, taking the reader to the dream world of Xanadu.

> These lines from the poem help Emily support the previous sttement.

> Lines from the Poem
> "Where Alph, the sacred river, ran
> Through caverns measureless to man"
> Alliteration flows through these lines like the river flows.

316 • Response to Literature

☑ ONGOING ASSESSMENT: Monitor and Reinforce

If students appear to be having difficulty with writing their drafts or elaborating on their topics, use one of the following options.

Option 1 Have students recall and discuss previous drafting strategies they have learned and used successfully. Reinforce the concept of using effective strategies to gather and organize information in a way that has the best results for the topic and purpose.	**Option 2** Let students work independently to make an organizational plan of the materials they expect to use in their response to literature. Give them the opportunity to discuss ideas with you or their peers as they determine how they will organize content.

14.4 Revising

During revision, find ways to strengthen your writing so that it communicates directly and effectively with your audience.

Revising Your Overall Structure

Consider Paragraph Order

As you review your draft, think about each paragraph as a unit, or chunk, of information. Ask yourself whether a different organization would strengthen the flow of ideas.

▶ **REVISION STRATEGY**
Rereading and Rearranging

If your response is organized in Nestorian order, evaluate the importance and effectiveness of each idea you present. You may find that what you thought would be your strongest argument or point is weaker than you had planned. If an earlier argument is more effective, move it to the end of the essay, to build to a powerful conclusion.

Revising Your Paragraphs

Eliminate Digressions

Each paragraph in your response should develop one central idea or perform a specific function, such as provide a transition. Identify the topic sentence or the function of each paragraph.

- If the paragraph has a topic sentence, make sure that all of the sentences and details relate directly to that topic. If not, eliminate or move unnecessary details.

- If the paragraph is functional, make sure that the details within it help it to perform that function. Eliminate any ideas that stray from the main purpose of the paragraph.

▶ **REVISION STRATEGY**
Coding Supporting Material in Topical Paragraphs

As you review topical paragraphs, use two different-colored pencils or use circling and underlining. Circle the topic sentence in each paragraph. Circle in another color or underline all the details within that paragraph that support the topic sentence.

When you have finished, examine your markings. Look closely at material that has not been circled or underlined. Consider eliminating that material, or revise it so that it has a purpose for being there.

🖭 Technology Tip

If you are using a word processor, rearrange paragraphs using cut-and-paste tools. Try several different ways to present your paragraphs. Then, choose the organization you find most effective.

Revising • 317

Step-by-Step Teaching Guide

Revising: Rereading and Rearranging

1. Explain to students that rereading and rearranging are good strategies even if they have not used Nestorian order. All types of organization benefit from a review of how, and in what order, the points are presented.

2. If applicable, work with students to evaluate their use of Nestorian order.

3. Suggest that, if a computer is not available, students list their paragraphs on note cards and reorder them until they achieve an organization that appears effective.

Step-by-Step Teaching Guide

Revising: Coding Supporting Material in Topical Paragraphs

1. Suggest that students watch for content that does not code easily; if they can't determine the connection, the reader probably won't be able to either.

2. Tell students that if a point does not fit into a paragraph but is something they feel is important to the essay, they should consider moving it elsewhere, possibly using it to construct another paragraph.

Integrating Technology Skills

Students who are using a word processor to cut and paste their paragraphs can benefit from using the numbers and bullets feature to review their organization. Explain that students can block text and set the program to number each point in an outline fashion or to bullet each new concept. After they have used this strategy for visual organization and their paragraphs are in the order they select, they can block the text again and remove the numbers or bullets.

⏱ TIME AND RESOURCE MANAGER

Resources
Print: *Writing Support Transparencies, 14-H*
Technology: *Writing and Grammar* Interactive Text, Section 14.4

Using the Full Student Edition	Using the Handbook 🄷
• Work through the revising strategies of Rearranging, Coding, and Circling and Boxing with the class (pp. 317–320). • Divide the class into small groups for the Peer Review activity (p. 320).	• Work through the revising strategies of Rearranging, Coding, and Circling and Boxing with the class (pp. 203–206). • Divide the class into small groups for the Peer Review activity (p. 206).

Revising: Circling and Boxing Comparisons

Teaching Resources: Writing Support Transparencies, 14-H

1. After they read the page, have students discuss the example in the Student Work in Progress. Display Transparency 14-H during discussion. How did Emily define the elements she decided to compare? How did she then strengthen her essay?

2. Select a topic that is familiar to students, and do a practice activity comparing it with another familiar topic. Remind students that making comparisons requires students to show how the two things are similar and how they are different.

14.4

Revising Your Sentences
Clarify Your Comparisons

You will make many different kinds of comparisons when you write a response to literature. You might compare two works by the same author, two lines from the same poem, or two different techniques used in the same work. Regardless of what you are comparing, you need to make sure that your audience can easily understand your comparison.

▶ **REVISION STRATEGY**
Circling and Boxing Comparisons

Use this strategy to check that your comparisons are clear and logical:

1. Circle any comparisons you make in your draft. Look for adjectives or adverbs in the comparative or superlative (scan for *more, most, -er, -est,* and common irregulars).
2. When you find a comparison, draw a box around the names of the things being compared.
3. Make sure that if you have boxed two items, you use the comparative degree. If you have boxed three or more items, use the superlative degree.

Technology Tip

Use the Find feature in your word-processing program to locate words with *-er* and *-est* endings. Then, if the word found is a comparison, check to be sure you have used the correct comparative form.

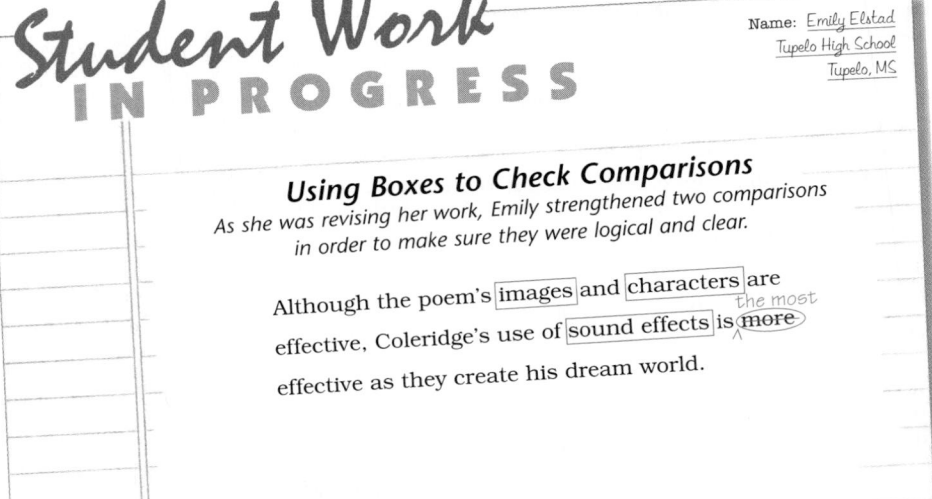

Student Work
IN PROGRESS

Name: *Emily Elstad*
Tupelo High School
Tupelo, MS

Using Boxes to Check Comparisons
As she was revising her work, Emily strengthened two comparisons in order to make sure they were logical and clear.

Although the poem's images and characters are
effective, Coleridge's use of sound effects is more *the most*
effective as they create his dream world.

318 • Response to Literature

☑ ONGOING ASSESSMENT: Monitor and Reinforce

If you observe that students are having difficulty revising their drafts, use the following strategy.

Ask students to trade their drafts with partners. Have each student read his or her partner's paper and make notes about things he or she discovers, such as reordering ideas, deleting material that does not fit in a paragraph, or finding comparisons that the writer overlooked during the circling exercise. Partners can then discuss the discoveries they've made about each other's papers and use the information gained to further refine their own drafts.

Grammar in Your Writing
Comparisons

You will use adjectives and adverbs to make **comparisons.** Most adjectives and adverbs have different forms to show degrees of comparison. The three degrees of comparison are the *positive,* the *comparative,* and the *superlative.*

	Positive	Comparative	Superlative
Regular			
Adjectives	fast	faster	fastest
	beautiful	more beautiful	most beautiful
Adverbs	quickly	more quickly	most quickly
Irregular			
Adjectives	bad	worse	worst
	good	better	best
Adverbs	much	more	most
	well	better	best

- Use the **comparative degree** to compare two people, places, or things:

  Lady Macbeth becomes corrupt more quickly than Macbeth.

- Use the **superlative degree** to compare three or more people, places, or things:

  Macbeth is the most fascinating character in the play. (The superlative degree is used to compare Macbeth with all the other characters in the play.)

- When comparing one of a group with the rest of the group, make sure that your sentence contains the word *other* or the word *else.* In the example below, you need to add the word *other* because the poem is one of the poems *she wrote:*

Illogical: The poem is more romantic than any poem she wrote.

Logical: The poem is more romantic than any other poem she wrote.

Find It in Your Reading Read through "Meanings" on pages 308–309 to find a comparison in the comparative degree. Explain why Boland chose the comparative rather than the superlative degree.

Find It in Your Writing Review your draft to identify any comparisons you make. Make sure that your comparisons are correct and logical.

For more on comparisons, see Chapter 24.

Comparisons

1. Review making comparisons with students. Point out that the guidelines given here do not simply apply to the irregular comparative words in the chart, but also include adjectives or adverbs that are made comparative by the adding *-er* or *-est*.

2. For each bulleted point, ask volunteers to cite examples. Write the examples on the board to reinforce correct usage. (If an incorrect example is offered, guide the student to correct usage by asking him or her to determine the number of things being compared.)

Find It in Your Reading

In her initial description of the poem, Boland reflects that "you appreciated a car more when you had to walk" and "peace became clearer in war." The comparative degree was used because there were only two things being compared.

Find It in Your Writing

Have students review their drafts once again to evaluate any comparisons they have made. If there are no comparisons, encourage them to consider whether they might be able to strengthen an analysis or argument by including a comparison.

☑ ONGOING ASSESSMENT: Prerequisite Skills

If students have difficulty with comparisons, you might find it helpful to refer them to the following materials to assure coverage of prerequisite knowledge.

In the Textbook	Print Resources	Technology
Using Modifiers, Section 24.1–2	*Grammar Exercise Workbook,* pp. 107-116	*On-Line Exercise Bank,* Section 24.1–2

Step-by-Step Teaching Guide

Revising: Circling and Replacing Dull Words

1. Give students some examples of words that are more powerful or descriptive. For example: "he went fast" is not as strong as "he raced" or "he rocketed toward"; "it rained really hard" is not as strong as "the rain was torrential," and so on. Encourage students to contribute examples as well.

2. Give students time in class to use the revision strategy to replace dull words with more powerful or meaningful words.

Step-by-Step Teaching Guide

Revising: Peer Review

Teaching Resources: Writing Support Transparencies 14-I; Writing Support Activity Book, 14-4

1. Have students work in pairs on the peer review.

2. Display the transparency (14-I) and review the questions. Ask students to use the response chart to evaluate each other's written works.

3. Remind each writer to consider peer suggestions objectively before making changes. Sometimes a suggestion is a step toward finding a solution, but is not the best fix. Remind students that the writer is responsible for making final choices and decisions about his or her written work.

Revising Your Word Choice

Revise Words to Achieve Your Purpose

Review the word choices you have made in your response. Replace any words that are inaccurate, dull, or vague with better choices.

▶ **REVISION STRATEGY**
Circling and Replacing Dull Words

Reread your draft, focusing on your choice of words. When you come to a word that seems dull, obvious, or predictable, circle it. When you have read through your entire draft, replace circled words with more effective alternatives. Be careful, however, not to select alternate words simply because they are interesting. Make sure that your vivid word choices really say what you mean to say.

Peer Review

A peer reviewer can make suggestions for improving your writing. Share your response to literature with a peer before you share it with the world.

Prepare a Response Sheet

Give a copy of your revised draft to a partner. When your partner has read your response, ask him or her to fill in a response sheet like the following to identify strong elements in your writing, as well as those that could use improvement.

> **Response Sheet**
>
> 1. What is the main idea of my essay?
>
> 2. Are any passages confusing? Explain.
>
> 3. Is my word choice interesting and appropriate? Explain.

Timed Writing Hint

When revising your work, include at least one vivid detail per paragraph.

⏱ TIME SAVERS!

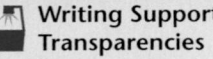
Writing Support Transparencies
Use the transparencies for Chapter 14 to facilitate teaching of strategies.

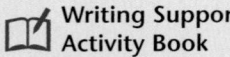
Writing Support Activity Book
Use the graphic organizers for Chapter 14 to facilitate student planning.

◇ STANDARDIZED TEST PREPARATION WORKSHOP

Adjectives Standardized test questions may require students to distinguish which words in a sentence are adjectives. Use the following question to give students practice finding adjectives in descriptive writing.

1. Which word is an adjective in the sentence?

   The chipped paint on the house peeled slowly.

A paint

B chipped

C slowly

D peeled

Students should recognize that **B** is the correct answer because it modifies the noun "paint." Students should also recognize that A is a noun, C is an adverb, and D is a verb.

14.5 Editing and Proofreading

Make sure that your writing is error-free by fixing errors in spelling, punctuation, and grammar.

Focusing on Proofreading

Double-check every text citation and quotation you have included. Make sure that you copied passages and quotations accurately from the original source. Also, check to be sure you have placed quotation marks around the author's exact words.

Grammar in Your Writing
Quotation Marks

Quotation marks are used frequently in responses to literature. Following are some guidelines for using quotation marks:

Titles of Short Works: Use quotation marks around the titles of short poems, stories, or essays.

> "Kubla Khan"   "The Rocking-Horse Winner"

Titles of Long Works—such as novels, plays, nonfiction books, or long poems. Underline or use italics to indicate these titles.

> Oliver Twist   Macbeth   Walden   Paradise Lost

Cited Passages: Use quotation marks around any words, lines, or passages you quote directly from another source.

> Coleridge refers to a "woman wailing."
>
> How did you feel when you first read "In Xanadu did Kubla Khan/A stately pleasure dome decree"?

Find It in Your Reading In "Meanings" by Eavan Boland, on pages 308–309, one passage is enclosed in quotation marks. Locate the passage, and explain why quotation marks are necessary.

Find It in Your Writing As you proofread your response to literature, review your usage of quotation marks to be sure they are correct.

To learn more about using quotation marks, see Chapter 27.

Editing and Proofreading • 321

⏱ TIME AND RESOURCE MANAGER

Resources
Print: *Scoring Rubrics on Transparency,* Ch. 14; *Writing Assessment and Portfolio Management; Formal Assessment,* Ch. 14

Using the Full Student Edition	Using the Handbook Ⓗ
• Review p. 321 in class, including Grammar in Your Writing. • Give step-by-step coverage to Publishing and Presenting (p. 322). • Analyze the Final Draft (pp. 323–324). • Have students edit and proofread their responses in class.	• Review p. 207 in class, including Grammar in Your Writing. • Give step-by-step coverage to Publishing and Presenting (p. 208). • Have students edit and proofread their responses in class.

Publishing and Presenting

1. If possible, allow students to choose how they wish to present their written works.

2. Encourage students to develop illustrative material such as drawings or photos to elaborate on their essays.

3. Give students time to discuss how their audience(s) responded to their essays. Did the audience appear to share or understand the opinions or viewpoints expressed?

ASSESS and CLOSE

Assessment

Teaching Resources: Scoring Rubrics on Transparency, Ch. 14; Writing Assessment and Portfolio Management; Formal Assessment, Ch. 14

1. Display the Scoring Rubric transparency and review the criteria in class.

2. Before students proceed with self-assessment, you may wish to use the rubric to evaluate the Final Draft of the Student Work in Progress on pages 323–324. Have students score the Final Draft in one or more of the rubric categories.

3. In addition to student self-assessment, you may wish to use the following assessment options:

   • score student essays yourself, using the rubric and scoring models from *Writing Assessment and Portfolio Management*.

   • review the Standardized Test Preparation Workshop on pages 328–329 and administer a timed writing assessment.

   • administer the Chapter 14 assessment from *Formal Assessment* in the Teaching Resources to measure students' grasp of the concepts presented.

14.6 Publishing and Presenting

Consider these ideas for publishing and presenting your writing:

Building Your Portfolio

1. **Discussion Group** Share your responses with a group of readers. Allow all group members to read from their responses or to summarize their most important ideas. Then, take turns asking questions to compare and contrast opinions within the group.

2. **Critical Anthology** Compile responses in a classroom anthology. Decide on the order in which to present the responses, and compile a table of contents. Design a cover for the anthology, and put a copy in the school library.

Reflecting on Your Writing

Reflect on the experience of writing a response to literature. Use these questions to spark your reflection:

• How did your response to the work change or develop from the time you finished reading to the time you finished writing?

• What aspects of the work became clearer to you through writing about them?

Internet Tip

To see a response to literature scored according to this rubric, go on-line: PHSchool.com Enter Web Code: egk-1201

Rubric for Self-Assessment

Use the following criteria to evaluate your response to literature.

	Score 4	Score 3	Score 2	Score 1
Audience and Purpose	Presents sufficient background on the work(s); presents the writer's reactions forcefully	Presents background on the work(s); presents the writer's reactions clearly	Presents some background on the work(s); presents the writer's reactions at points	Presents little or no background on the work(s); presents few of the writer's reactions
Organization	Presents points in logical order, smoothly connecting them to the overall focus	Presents points in logical order and connects them to the overall focus	Organizes points poorly in places; connects some points to an overall focus	Presents information in a scattered, disorganized manner
Elaboration	Supports reactions and evaluations with elaborated reasons and well-chosen examples	Supports reactions and evaluations with specific reasons and examples	Supports some reactions and evaluations with reasons and examples	Offers little support for reactions and evaluations
Use of Language	Shows overall clarity and fluency; uses precise, evaluative words; makes few mechanical errors	Shows good sentence variety; uses some precise evaluative terms; makes some mechanical errors	Uses awkward or overly simple sentence structures and vague evaluative terms; makes many mechanical errors	Presents incomplete thoughts; makes mechanical errors that cause confusion

322 • Response to Literature

14.7 Student Work IN PROGRESS

FINAL DRAFT

Paisaje, (Cinco Pagodas), Alejandro Solar

"Kubla Khan": A Response

Emily Elstad
Tupelo High School
Tupelo, Mississippi

In his short but intense poem "Kubla Khan," Samuel Taylor Coleridge envisions a dream world filled with exotic landscapes and creatures. The cumulative effect of the poet's rich use of language and imagery is hypnotizing and nearly overwhelming. It is a re-creation of a dark dream—a product of Coleridge's unique imagination.

The origin of the poem explains the source of the dreamy quality. Coleridge apparently wrote this poem while in a medicat-

◄ **Critical Viewing**
What sort of poem might this landscape inspire? Explain.
[Analyze]

Emily identifies the poem, author, and her thesis in the opening paragraph.

Student Work in Progress • 323

Step-by-Step Teaching Guide

Final Draft

1. As you discuss Emily's Final Draft, point out that she
   • identifies the poem and its author in the opening paragraph;
   • makes a statement of her thesis followed by a statement that vividly expresses her feelings and the poem's impact;
   • makes good use of quotes from the poem to illustrate and support her main thesis;
   • continues to back up her thesis with powerful proof and citations.

2. Make sure students understand that the use of the ellipses in a quote means that the sentence goes on, but the quoted part ends here.

3. Help students recognize that Emily uses the Nestorian style. Point out how the less important points set the essay up for greater impact when the strongest point is reached.

4. Ask students to evaluate their response to the final draft. Does the writer present a strong thesis and then back it up sufficiently to convince the audience? Are Emily's feelings conveyed well? What words does she use to reveal feelings? *(intense poem, overwhelming, hypnotizing)*

5. Encourage students to use these points, as well as their own observations, when revising their own essays or when doing peer reviews.

Critical Viewing

Analyze Students may suggest that the landscape might inspire a poem about quest or adventure in an exotic location.

323

ed daze. Falling asleep while reading about Kubla Khan, he awoke with his head filled with richly poetic lines. This background is sufficient explanation for the lack of narrative in the poem. The poet simply paints the picture of his dream.

These details came from researching the life of Coleridge.

The description of the landscape reminds me of the deep but fading details of a remembered dream. Coleridge describes a garden surrounded by a wall that encloses caves of ice. He envisions fountains, flowers, forests, and crevices. In addition to this lush and exotic scenery, Coleridge includes fragmented characters. He describes a "damsel with a dulcimer" playing "symphony and song." Coleridge (or the speaker) suggests that he could turn her song into the pleasure dome in the air. These odd and specific details contribute to the overall imagery of a dream.

In the final image, the dream turns into a nightmare. Coleridge gives a picture of Kubla Khan as a man with "flashing eyes" and "floating hair." He is diabolical; he has drunken the "milk of Paradise" and, one assumes, has gained some sort of magical or unworldly power—possibly immortality. He seems to have an inexorable power, one that casts a trance over the women in the poem.

Passages from the poem are cited to illustrate and support Emily's statements.

Although the poem's visuals are effective, Coleridge's use of sound effects is even more effective as they help create his dream world. The sounds and rhythms of the poem work together to hypnotize the reader. Repetition is one of the key devices Coleridge uses to create this effect. The phrase "the sacred river, ran through caverns measureless to man" is repeated twice, changed only slightly. This emphasizes the fact that the cavern, as well as the whole fantastical world, is incomprehensible to humans; it is a world for immortals only.

This paragraph opens with a statement of opinion, which Emily supports in the rest of the paragraph.

Alliteration, too, is a key device that transports the reader into Coleridge's dream world. Take, for example, the lines near the beginning of the poem, "Where Alph, the sacred river, ran/ Through caverns measureless to man . . ." The lines help convey the never-ending flow of the river because the words themselves flow into each other. The repeated *r* sounds flow into the repeated *m* sounds, lulling the reader into a dreamlike state. "Kubla Khan" contains many such examples of alliteration, such as "sunny spots," "woman wailing," and "meandering with a mazy motion."

Emily has chosen Nestorian organization for her response to literature. She began with her second-most important point, following with points in descending order of importance. She saved her strongest point for last.

Although "Kubla Khan" is said to have been written in one draft as a transcription of a dream of Coleridge, it is a short masterpiece, in which the poet's use of imagery and sound effects draws the reader into the realm of the fantastic. The kingdom of Xanadu is vivid and unforgettable—as, perhaps, was Coleridge's fateful dream.

Emily concludes with a restatement of her insights.

324 • Response to Literature

Connected Assignment *Music Review*

Before buying the latest CD by your favorite band, do you read the critic's reviews? Like other responses to literature, **music reviews** analyze the features of a work and put forth an opinion about that work. Rather than merely summarizing the work, music reviews analyze the music, the lyrics, the originality and effectiveness. Reviews also give credit to the album's key creative forces and recommend it (or not) to readers.

Write a music review about a song, concert, or CD you've heard. Use the writing process skills outlined below as a guide.

Prewriting Choose a song or CD about which to write a review. Then, begin gathering details about the work. As you gather details, organize them into "pro" and "con" categories, listing them, if you wish, on a two-column chart. For each entry, provide one or more specific details from the music that exemplify your reaction. Review your chart or list to decide whether it supports a positive or a negative recommendation to your readers.

Drafting Start by identifying the work's title and artist. Establish your opinion or recommendation to readers directly by stating it in the first paragraph. Then, describe the music, using descriptive nouns, verbs, and modifiers to help readers "hear" the music and understand its structure and message. Elaborate on your initially stated opinion by analyzing specific features such as lyrics, pacing, or arrangement.

Revising and Editing Ask a peer to read your review for clarity and impact. If necessary, reword your opinion statement, insert more precise evaluative modifiers, or add examples to support your views. Check your title punctuation, using quotation marks for specific song titles but underlining or italics for CD or album titles.

Publishing and Presenting Hold a music discussion group with classmates. Take turns playing selections of music that you are reviewing and reading your review aloud to peers. After each presentation, briefly discuss the opinions of group members.

▲ **Critical Viewing** What unique aspects of this performance would you address in a music review? **[Analyze]**

Connected Assignment: Music Review • **325**

► *Lesson Objectives*

1. To write a music review appropriate to audience and purpose
2. To organize ideas in writing to ensure coherence, logical progression, and purpose, and support for ideas
3. To develop drafts by organizing content such as paragraphing and outlining and by refining style to suit occasion, audience, and purpose

---

Step-by-Step Teaching Guide

Music Review

1. Bring sample music reviews to class or have students do so. Review several examples with students.
2. Suggest that students briefly review the writing strategies from this chapter. See the chart below for useful resources.
3. Remind students that a music review may have a less formal tone and language than an essay about literature.
4. Compile all reviews into a class newsletter, or encourage students to submit their reviews to the school newspaper.

Customize for
Less Advanced Students

You may wish to have students who have listened to the same music to work in pairs or small groups to discuss the impact of the music on the listener before they draft individual reviews.

Critical Viewing

Analyze Answers will vary. Students may mention the attire of the musicians and the casual setting in which they are performing.

☑ **ONGOING ASSESSMENT: Prerequisite Skills**

Students may find the following resources from Chapter 14 particularly helpful in completing their music reviews.

In the Textbook	Print Resources	Technology
Narrowing Your Topic, Section 14.2 Gathering Details, Section 14.2	*Writing Support Transparencies,* 14-C, 14-E *Writing Support Activity Book,* 14-3	*Writing and Grammar* Interactive Text, Section 14.2

Lesson Objectives

1. To analyze strategies that writers in different fields use to compose

2. To recognize how writers represent and reveal their cultures and traditions in texts

3. To analyze the melodies of literary language, including its use of evocative words and rhythms

4. To analyze relationships and ideas as represented in various media

Examining Various Media

1. Choose one of the Spotlight elements for class discussion, or have students work individually or in groups on the elements of their choice.

2. Some students might research additional information about Stéphane Mallarmé. Mallarmé's ideas about poetry gave rise to the Symbolist movement. Suggest that students research Symbolism and present their discoveries to the class.

3. Students who are interested in learning more about Franz Liszt might obtain recordings of his symphonic poems such as *Orpheus, Tasso,* or *Faust,* and play selected portions for the class.

Viewing and Representing

Activity Encourage students to present their responses to the class. They might play portions of the tone poems as part of their presentations.

Critical Viewing

Examine Causes and Effects
Answers will vary. Students may note that the colors seem appropriate to the apparent somberness of the subject.

Spotlight on the Humanities

Examining Various Media
Focus on Music: Tone Poems

Just as a good book or powerful painting may stir a response from the reader or viewer, artists often respond to other art forms by creating another work of art inspired by the original piece. Written from ideas that came from poems, paintings, dramas, natural landscapes, or sources other than music, the **tone poem** is a nineteenth- and twentieth-century musical phenomenon that consists of one movement, or section. Its early composers were the Hungarian piano virtuoso and composer Franz Liszt (1811–1886) and the French composer Hector Berlioz (1803–1869). Claude Debussy's tone poem *Prelude to the Afternoon of a Faun* (1894) was inspired by the French poet Stéphane Mallarmé.

Literature Connection French poet Stéphane Mallarmé (1842–1898) was a teacher most of his life who supplemented his income as a poet. His work explored the differences between an ideal world and the natural world. Rather than having a sunlit day in reality, Mallarmé believed that the poet could create the "notion" of a sunlit day. In 1876, he completed his dramatic poem "Afternoon of a Faun," which inspired Claude Debussy's tone poem years later.

Art Connection German painter and illustrator Wilhelm von Kaulbach (1805–1874) was a prolific artist who was part of the German Romantic movement in the nineteenth century. He illustrated the poetry of such great writers as William Shakespeare and Johann Goethe. On walls in Berlin and Munich, he created huge murals that resembled the work of the Renaissance artist Raphael. Composer Franz Liszt's tone poem *Hunnenschlacht* (1857) was inspired by Kaulbach's historical painting *The Battle of the Huns.*

Response Writing Activity: Response to a Tone Poem

Listen to one of the tone poems mentioned above or another tone poem that a music teacher recommends. Then, write a response to the piece. Discuss what you liked about it and how it differed from the music you usually listen to. Did the piece capture the feel of the art that influenced it? Why or why not?

Claude Debussy, Marcel Baschet

▲ Critical Viewing
What effect does this painting's colors have on its overall mood? Explain.
[Examine Causes and Effects]

Media and Technology Skills

Responding Using Technology

Activity: Video Adaptation of a Story

A memorable story, character, or theme can often be transplanted from a historical setting to a contemporary one in order to emphasize common threads between eras. Use your response to a short story or novel as a jumping off point to create a video adaptation set today.

Think About It Choose a work that you believe has a strong relevance for today's viewers, regardless of its original setting. Choose a short story or a section of a longer novel or play. For example, rather than update all of *Frankenstein*, you might produce an updated version of the scene in which the scientist confronts his creation.

Update It Begin by choosing an overall setting for your updated retelling. In addition to changing the setting, you might also alter the ages of the central characters to reflect your peer group. For example, you might update *The Tragedy of Macbeth* by writing a drama about the drastic steps a high-school student takes to achieve political power at school.

Next, brainstorm ideas for your modernization by listing the key elements of your source material. Think of how you can maintain the essential qualities of a character or background in your chosen environment.

Script It You might improvise with other students to help you write dialogue for your script. Use the original story as a launching point for key plot events, but try to generate dialogue that clearly reflects your new setting. Record your improvisations with audio- or video-cassettes, and then transcribe the best lines for use in your shooting script.

Film It Rehearse your script, and then film it in appropriate locations. Shoot several versions of each scene, selecting the best takes during editing. Share the finished film with an audience without identifying the original source. After the screening, discuss the project and see whether viewers recognized the inspiration for your film.

Materials
- video camera
- single-deck or double-deck video-cassette recorder
- audio recorder

Updating Tips
Try these strategies to remove any "old" feeling from the source you are modernizing.
- Use contemporary music in the soundtrack.
- Rename characters with historical or literary names. For example, you might change Hamlet to Henry or Hannah.
- Choose settings that feel modern, such as a computer lab, airport, or electronics store.

◀ **Critical Viewing** This still is from a film adaptation of Jane Austen's *Emma*. What details in this still reveal that it takes place in the past? **[Analyze]**

▶ *Lesson Objectives*

1. To use a variety of forms and technologies such as videos to communicate messages
2. To recognize how visual and sound techniques or design convey messages in media
3. To use elements of text to defend, clarify, and negotiate responses and interpretations

Step-by-Step Teaching Guide

Responding Using Technology

1. Review the steps to the video response activity with students, and help them generate a realistic shooting schedule.
2. Encourage students to work in teams to produce their videos. Students might decide to complete a class video about a work of literature that was assigned in class.
3. After students have finished their video responses, ask them to tell what they learned from the experience. Has their understanding of the work changed or deepened as a result of their adaptation?

Critical Viewing

Analyze Students may mention clothing and hairstyle as details that establish a setting in the past.

Lesson Objectives

1. To use prewriting strategies to generate ideas, develop voice, and plan
2. To develop drafts by organizing content with paragraphing and outlining and by refining style to suit occasion, audience, and purpose
3. To produce legible work that shows accurate spelling and correct use of the conventions of punctuation and capitalization, and to demonstrate control over grammatical elements

Step-by-Step Teaching Guide

Responding to Prompts About Literature

Teaching Resources: Standardized Test Preparation Workbook, pp. 27–28

1. Go over the bulleted criteria with students.
2. Have students read the sample writing situation. Define and clarify terms such as *damasked, reeks,* and *false compare.* To make sure students understand the assignment, have them rephrase it in their own words.
3. Assign the sample writing situation for completion within a set time period.

Standardized Test Preparation Workshop

Responding to Prompts About Literature

You will frequently be asked on standardized tests to write in response to a literary prompt—to comment on a provided piece of literature and support your analysis with examples. You will be evaluated on your ability to do the following:

- develop a clearly stated responsive position
- present effective supporting examples and details
- organize ideas in a logical manner
- apply proper grammar, usage, and mechanics

When you write for a test, use the same writing stages as you would for any writing assignment, but be aware of how much time you devote to each. Below is a poem followed by a standardized test writing prompt. Use the suggestions on the next page to help you formulate your response.

Sample Writing Situation

Read the following sonnet by William Shakespeare:

Sonnet 130

My mistress' eyes are nothing like the sun,
Coral is far more red than her lips' red;
If snow be white, why then her breasts are dun;
If hairs be wires, black wires grow on her head.
5 I have seen roses damasked, red and white,
But no such roses see I in her cheeks;
And in some perfumes is there more delight
Than in the breath that from my mistress reeks.
I love to hear her speak. Yet well I know
10 That music hath a far more pleasing sound.
I grant I never saw a goddess go;
My mistress, when she walks, treads on the ground.
And yet, by heaven, I think my love as rare
As any she belied with false compare.

Many traditional love sonnets place the object of their devotion upon a pedestal. "Sonnet 130" describes a different attitude toward love. Write a literary analysis of the poem in which you examine its structure, sentiment, and effectiveness. Use specific examples from the sonnet as support.

⚓ TEST-TAKING TIP

Explain that a good essay begins with a clear and strong thesis statement. Students should express their opinion about the sonnet's structure, sentiment, and effectiveness in their first paragraphs, and give some indication of their reasons for their point of view.

Students should then continue by providing specific details and quotes supporting their thesis statements. Remind them that when they use quotes, they must explain how the quotes back up their arguments, rather than simply citing them.

Prewriting

Allow about one quarter of your time for developing your response and identifying supporting details.

Write a Thesis Statement Your thesis statement lets your readers know the main idea of your response. Write a statement that clearly states your main idea about the sonnet.

List Details After writing your thesis statement, generate a list of details from the poem that directly support your main idea. Also, list your own opinions as well as personal and literary allusions and suitable examples and quotations.

Drafting

Allow about half of your time for drafting. Write neatly, and allow space for revision changes.

Organize Ideas Introduce your main idea or thesis statement in your introduction. Using the ideas in your list, organize them into groups. Discuss each of these groups in one of the body paragraphs. Finally, summarize your main points in your conclusion.

Elaborate As you draft, weave together details that reveal and support your ideas. Give examples, both from the sonnet as well as from your own experience and prior knowledge.

Revising

Allow about one quarter of your time for revising.

Check for Clarity As you review your work, make sure your references to the poem are clear. If a reference to the poem is not clearly explained, either omit it or neatly add necessary information.

Check Support Reread your response, and carefully discriminate between details that directly relate to the prompt and those that do not. Although some details may provide interesting insights, they may be distracting because they do not relate directly to the prompt. Eliminate these details by neatly drawing a line through them.

Editing and Proofreading

Allow about five minutes to review your essay for spelling, punctuation, and grammar errors.

Make Final Changes Read your response a final time, checking for errors in spelling or punctuation. Make changes by neatly placing a line through text to be omitted and using a caret [^] to show where new text should be inserted.

Customize for
AP Students

After students have completed the assignments within the allotted time, have them exchange papers with a partner. They can then use the scoring rubric on page 322 to evaluate the essays.

Customize for
Less Advanced Students

Help students budget their time as they respond to the prompt by announcing elapsed time at ten-minute intervals and suggesting at what stage of the process they should be at each interval. As students gain more practice in responding to timed assessments, this help will become unnecessary.

In-Depth Lesson Plan

	LESSON FOCUS	PRINT AND MEDIA RESOURCES
DAY 1	**Introduction to Writing for Assessment** Students learn key elements of writing for assessment. (pp. 330–331/H210–211)	*Writers at Work* DVD, Practical and Technical Writing *Writing and Grammar* Interactive Text, Ch. 15, Introduction
DAY 2	**Prewriting** Students choose and narrow a topic, consider their audience and purpose, and gather information. (pp. 332–333/H212–213)	*Writing and Grammar* Interactive Text, Section 15.1 **Teaching Resources** *Writing Support Transparencies*, 15-A; *Topic Bank for Heterogeneous Classes*, Ch. 15
DAY 3	**Drafting** Students organize their ideas and write their first drafts. (pp. 334–335/H214–215)	*Writing and Grammar* Interactive Text, Section 15.2 **Teaching Resources** *Writing Support Transparencies*, 15-B–C; *Writing Support Activity Book*, 15-1
DAY 4	**Revising** Students revise their drafts in terms of overall structure, paragraphs, sentences, and word choice. (pp. 336–337/H216–217)	*Writing and Grammar* Interactive Text, Section 15.3 **Teaching Resources** *Writing Support Transparencies*, 15-D
DAY 5	**Editing and Proofreading; Publishing and Presenting** Students check their work for accuracy and correctness and present their final drafts. (pp. 338–341/H218–219)	*Writing and Grammar* Interactive Text, Sections 15.4–5 **Teaching Resources** *Scoring Rubrics on Transparency*, Ch. 15; *Writing Assessment and Portfolio Management; Formal Assessment*, Ch. 15

Accelerated Lesson Plan

	LESSON FOCUS	PRINT AND MEDIA RESOURCES
DAY 1	**Introduction Through Drafting** Students review characteristics of writing for assessment, select topics, and write drafts. (pp. 330–335/H210–215)	*Writing and Grammar* Interactive Text, Ch. 15, Introduction through Section 15.2 **Teaching Resources** *Writing Support Transparencies*, 15-A–C; *Writing Support Activity Book*, 15-1
DAY 2	**Revising Through Presenting** Students revise, edit, and proofread their work for presentation. (pp. 336–341/H216–219)	*Writing and Grammar* Interactive Text, Sections 15.3–4 **Teaching Resources** *Writing Support Transparencies*, 15-D; *Scoring Rubrics on Transparency*, Ch. 15; *Writing Assessment and Portfolio Management; Formal Assessment*, Ch. 15

Options for Adapting Lesson Plans

HOMEWORK

Have students complete any stage of the lesson for homework.

FEATURES

Extend coverage with Connected Assignment (p. 342), Spotlight on the Humanities (p. 344), Media and Technology Skills (p. 345), and the Standardized Test Preparation Workshop (pp. 346–347).

TECHNOLOGY

Students can complete any stage of the lesson on the computer, using *Writing and Grammar* Interactive Text or a word-processing program. Have them print out their completed work.

Writing and Grammar Handbook Alignment

Page numbers in Step-by-Step Teaching Guides in this Teacher's Edition refer to pages from the full student text. Handbook page references, indicated with this icon 🄷, are provided in Time and Resource Manager boxes and at the bottom of each Teacher's Edition page.

INTEGRATED SKILLS COVERAGE

Integrating Grammar
Homophones, SE p. 338/🄷218
SE p. 343; ATE pp. 333, 336, 341

Viewing and Representing
Critical Viewing, SE pp. 330, 340, 341, 342, 344/🄷210
Understanding History Through Media, SE p. 344

Speaking and Listening
ATE p. 339

Spelling
ATE p. 335

Technology
SE p. 334/🄷214; ATE p. 345

Real-World Connection
ATE p. 332

ASSESSMENT SUPPORT

Standardized Test Preparation Workshop, SE p. 346; ATE p. 337

Standardized Test Preparation Workbook, pp. 29–30

Scoring Rubrics on Transparency, Ch. 15

Formal Assessment, Ch. 15

Writing Assessment and Portfolio Management

MEETING INDIVIDUAL NEEDS

Less Advanced Students ATE pp. 337, 341, 343, 347. See also Ongoing Assessments ATE pp. 333, 335.

AP Students ATE pp. 343, 347

ESL Students ATE pp. 332, 338, 340

Spatial Learners ATE p. 334

Logical/Mathematical Learners ATE p. 341

BLOCK SCHEDULING

Pacing Suggestions
For 90-minute Blocks
• Have students complete the Prewriting and Drafting stages in a single period.
• Focus one class period on Revising and Editing and Publishing and Presenting. Allow at least 30 minutes for peer revision.

Resources for Varying Instruction
• *Writing and Grammar* Interactive Text A 90-minute block provides an ideal opportunity for students to work on the computer.
• *Writers at Work* DVD Show the Practical and Technical Writing segment in class.

Professional Development Support
• *How to Manage Instruction in the Block* This teaching resource provides management and activity suggestions.

MEDIA AND TECHNOLOGY

For the Student
• *Writing and Grammar* Interactive Text, Ch. 15

For the Teacher
• *Writers at Work* DVD, Practical and Technical Writing
• Teacher EXPRESS CD-ROM

WRITING AND GRAMMAR ON-LINE

Interactive Text (On-line or on CD-ROM)
• Easily navigable instruction with interactive Revision Checkers
• Full use of e-rater™, the essay-scoring system (on-line only)

Companion Web Site PHSchool.com
• Scoring rubrics with models (use Web Code egk-1201)

See the Go On-line! **feature, SE p. iii.**

▶ **Lesson Objectives**

1. To write for assessment, organizing ideas in writing to ensure coherence, logical progression, and support for ideas
2. To use prewriting strategies to generate ideas and plan
3. To write in a voice and style appropriate to the audience
4. To develop and revise drafts in terms of structure, paragraphs, sentences, and word choice
5. To edit and proofread to ensure standard English usage and grammar

Critical Viewing

Criticize Most students will probably say that this is an idealized portrayal of a classroom. Students may mention the classroom size, arrangement and size of the desks, and wall decorations.

Chapter 15 Writing for Assessment

Before the Nine O'Clock Bell, Jane Wooster Scott, Buckley School Collection

Assessment in School

How often have you heard or uttered these sentences: "Did you study for the science exam?" "Did you finish your history essay?" "I hope the test is multiple choice."

You have probably become used to being tested frequently. Tests may take many forms—from essays to short-answer quizzes to standardized timed tests. With some preparation and some basic test-taking skills, most students can perform well on tests—both timed and nontimed—enabling their teachers to evaluate accurately how much students have learned.

▲ **Critical Viewing** Would you say this is a realistic portrayal of a classroom or an idealized one? Explain. **[Criticize]**

🕐 TIME AND RESOURCE MANAGER

Resources
Technology: *Writers at Work* DVD, Practical and Technical Writing; *Writing and Grammar* Interactive Text, Ch. 15

Using the Full Student Edition	Using the Handbook🄷
• Cover pp. 330–331 in class.	• Cover pp. 210–211 in class.
• Show the Practical and Technical Writing section of the *Writers at Work* DVD.	• Show the Practical and Technical Writing section of the *Writers at Work* DVD.
• Discuss what assessment is and what it seeks to accomplish.	• Discuss what assessment is and what it seeks to accomplish.
• Discuss ways in which work is assessed in school and on the job.	• Discuss ways in which work is assessed in school and on the job.

What Is Assessment?

An **assessment** is an evaluation. You might be assessed on the amount of information you have acquired, how well you can solve problems, or where you stand academically compared with other students in your class.

Most people who make assessments look for

- correct answers or responses that match the question asked.
- clearly stated main points that are supported with details.
- writing that is organized logically.
- correct grammar, spelling, and punctuation.

To preview the criteria on which your writing may be evaluated, see the Rubric for Self-Assessment on page 339.

Types of Assessment

Many types of tests and essays help educators assess your ability to write. Among the tests you may be asked to take are the following:

- **Timed tests** may take many forms. They access a student's familiarity with the tested topics.
- **Short-answer tests** require brief answers, ranging from a word or phrase to a few sentences for each question.
- **Analyses** are critical papers in which the structural components of a work are examined and evaluated or compared and contrasted.
- **Personal essays** reveal the unique experiences and insights of the writer.

Writers in ACTION

No matter what type of writing you do, if it is read by someone, it will be assessed or evaluated. Writer Bill Wheeler has the following to say about what makes writing effective:

"Good writing is clear thinking made visible."

PREVIEW Student Work IN PROGRESS

Scott Sang-Hyun Lee, a student at Duncanville High School in Duncanville, Texas, wrote a personal essay for a college application. Follow along as he drafts and revises his essay. Scott's completed essay appears at the end of the chapter.

Writing for Assessment • 331

Interest GRABBER Ask students what they do to prepare for a test (go over notes, work with a partner, reread the material). Make a list of techniques on the chalkboard. Have students refer to the types of assessment on page 331 and discuss whether they use different techniques for different types of tests. Group the study techniques with the type of test. Focus the discussion on the essay as an assessment tool.

Activate Prior Knowledge

Ask students to recall the types of tests that they have had over the years (multiple choice, true/false, fill in the blank, essay). Ask them to tell which tests required the most preparation. Request explanations for their responses. Discuss how essay responses frequently require the most preparation and are the most difficult for students. Explain that this chapter is designed to help students prepare to answer essay questions well.

TEACH

Step-by-Step Teaching Guide

What Is Assessment?

1. Ask students the following questions to promote discussion:

   Which, if any, of the bulleted elements surprised you?

   Which of the elements do you feel most directly corresponds to the idea behind Bill Wheeler's quotation? Why? (Most students should feel that the idea behind either bullet two or three is what Wheeler is addressing.)

2. Have students review the Rubric for Self-Assessment, page 339.

3. Discuss with students the purposes or uses of assessment at school, in the workplace, in military service, and in other places they mention.

✓ ONGOING ASSESSMENT: Diagnose

Use one of the following options to diagnose students' current level of proficiency in writing for assessment.

Option 1 Ask each student to select the strongest example of his or her writing for assessment from the previous year. Hold conferences to review each student's sample. Use the conferences to determine which students will need extra support during this chapter.	**Option 2** Ask students to write a thesis statement and three topic sentences for paragraphs of support for the following topic: "The Impact of the Computer on the Present." If students have difficulty completing this exercise, you will need to devote more time to organization and elaboration.

Prewriting: Choosing Your Topic

1. Discuss the four strategies for choosing a topic. Which strategies have students used before? Which strategy has helped them the most?

2. Encourage students to jot down ideas as they read an essay question.

3. Read each question from the Topic Bank. Have students make notes about their ideas.

4. Use questions provided by teachers in other disciplines to expand this activity.

5. Discuss the observations that students made when reading and writing notes for the questions.

Real-World Connection

In expectation of having students prepare essays to include with college applications or to apply for scholarships, invite a guidance counselor to present his or her perspective on effective application essays.

Customize for
ESL Students

Being able to answer essay questions depends on knowledge of the vocabulary in the questions. Provide students with a list of words that frequently appear in essay questions and their definitions (Examples: *define, compare, explain*). Encourage students to study these words and allow them to use the list when analyzing essay questions. Provide students with a list of sample essay questions that teachers from all disciplines have submitted and ask students to explain those questions.

15.1 Prewriting

Choosing Your Topic

On some tests, you will be given one or more essay prompts to which you have to respond. In other instances, you will be given a choice of topics. Following are strategies to help you make this decision:

Strategies for Choosing an Essay Prompt

- **Read all of the prompts and then decide:** Don't simply read the first prompt and decide to answer it. Take the time to read all of the prompts. Then, choose to answer the prompt to which you can best respond.

- **Eliminate first:** Read the prompts and decide which questions baffle you or about which you're unsure, and avoid them.

- **Choose the question for which you have the most answers:** As you read the list of questions, rapidly think of evidence or details you could use to make your point. Choose to answer the question for which you have the most support.

- **Pay attention to what the question is asking:** If one question requires you to compare and contrast two or more topics and another asks you to trace the causes of an event, choose to answer the one you can organize more clearly in your mind.

TOPIC BANK

Following are some essay-test questions. If you plan to practice writing for assessment, choose one of these or ask your teacher to provide you with one.

1. In an essay, examine the impact that the Great Depression had on American politics in the decades that followed.
2. In a letter to the school board, argue for or against school newspapers being given absolute free speech, with no censorship from faculty advisors.
3. Explain "magical realism," and identify and examine a literary work that falls within that category.
4. Compare and contrast the literary contributions of the Romantic poets William Wordsworth and Samuel Taylor Coleridge.

⏱ TIME AND RESOURCE MANAGER

Resources
Print: *Writing Support Transparencies,* 15-A; *Topic Bank for Heterogeneous Classes*
Technology: *Writing and Grammar* Interactive Text, Section 15.1

Using the Full Student Edition	Using the Handbook🄷
• Discuss the four factors to keep in mind when choosing a topic. • Collect sample essay questions from teachers in other disciplines and provide copies for students. • Practice thesis writing with the Topic Bank suggestions or those from other teachers.	• Discuss the four factors to keep in mind when choosing a topic. • Collect sample essay questions from teachers in other disciplines and provide copies for students. • Practice thesis writing with the Topic Bank suggestions or those from other teachers.

Narrowing Your Response

Before you start writing your response, take a few moments to identify what the focus of your response will be.

Locate Key Words

Reread the question you're answering, and locate what you're being asked to do. For example, are you being asked to compare and contrast, analyze, reflect, trace the history of something, support an idea, or argue against an idea?

Form a Main Idea

Once you locate the key word, write down the main idea, or thesis, you will present in your response. Keep this idea in mind as you quickly gather details and plan an organization for your response.

Identify Your Audience and Purpose

Reread the prompt to see whether an audience or purpose has been specified. If so, keep them in mind as you gather details for your essay. If an audience and purpose have not been specified, identify them for yourself and gather details accordingly.

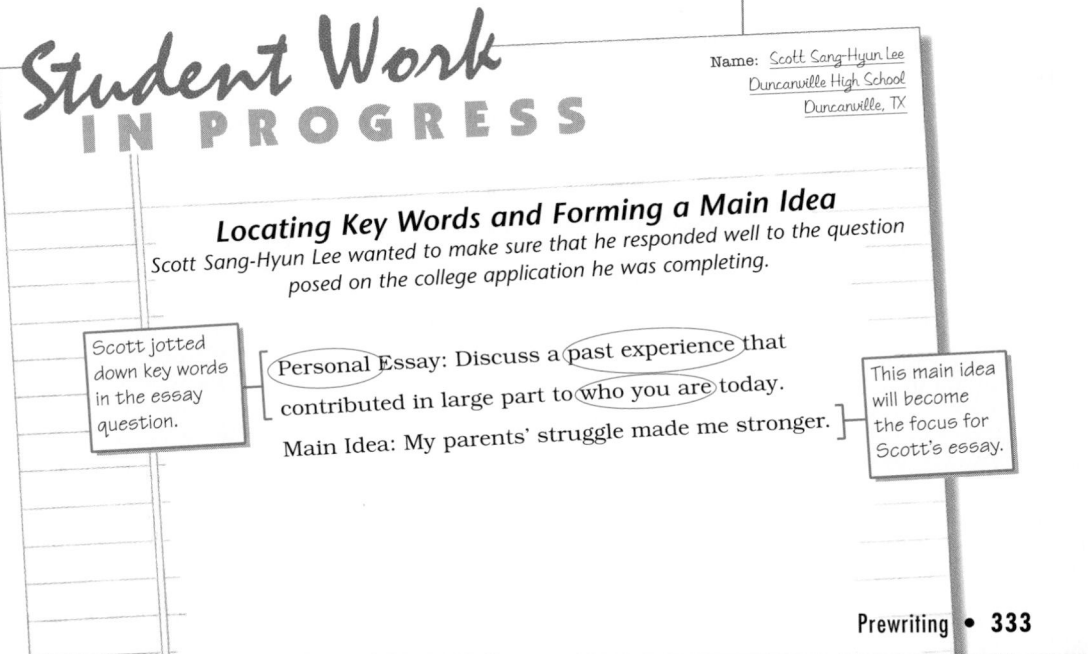

Student Work
IN PROGRESS

Name: Scott Sang-Hyun Lee
Duncanville High School
Duncanville, TX

Locating Key Words and Forming a Main Idea

Scott Sang-Hyun Lee wanted to make sure that he responded well to the question posed on the college application he was completing.

Scott jotted down key words in the essay question.

Personal Essay: Discuss a past experience that contributed in large part to who you are today.

Main Idea: My parents' struggle made me stronger.

This main idea will become the focus for Scott's essay.

Prewriting • 333

If you observe that some students are having difficulty choosing a topic, use one of the following options.

Option 1 Suggest that students choose an idea from the Topic Bank. If many students are having trouble, work with the whole class on one idea selected from the Topic Bank or from ideas suggested by students or by other teachers.	**Option 2** If the Topic Bank ideas seem too difficult, suggest that students try one of the assignments from the *Topic Bank for Heterogeneous Classes* in the Teaching Resources.

Prewriting: Narrowing Your Response

Teaching Resources: Writing Support Transparencies, 15-A

1. Ask students why it is important to identify the key words (so they know what is expected).

2. Display the transparency and discuss the key words that Scott identified. Using this information, have students identify what it is that they are actually looking for (words of direction, such as *compare* or *analyze*, plus any other clues to what is expected, such as *opinion, fact, personal experience, response to literature,* and so on).

3. Discuss how identifying these key words and ideas helped Scott form a main idea for the sample essay. How do students think they could apply this strategy?

4. Tell students that if no audience or purpose is identified, either in the question or by the situation (such as a college application), they should imagine an audience and purpose that is important to them. They should also use formal English.

5. Ask students to identify the key words for the four topics listed on page 332, and select one for which they can create a main idea.

Integrating Grammar Skills

Pronouns In formal writing, students should be encouraged to avoid the use of the personal pronouns *you, it,* and *they.* Using *you* should be discouraged in all cases because the second person is inappropriate in formal writing. *It* and *they* should be used only if they have a definite antecedent. If possible, have students review their portfolios to locate the inappropriate use of these pronouns. For additional practice, have students revise sentences that you compile.

Drafting: Plan a Structure

Teaching Resources: Writing Support Transparencies, 15-B; Writing Support Activity Book, 15-1

1. Discuss *comparison* and *contrast*. Define the terms to be certain everyone in class understands the difference. Ask students to comment on how a point-by-point approach differs from subject by subject. Do they think one approach is better, or does it depend on the topic? (Opinions will vary, but students should be able to comment on the purpose of each.) Have students suggest topics that lend themselves to comparison-and-contrast development.

2. Discuss chronological organization. Have students suggest topics that lend themselves to chronological development (autobiographies, histories).

3. Display Transparency 15-B as you discuss Nestorian organization. Point out that the strongest argument comes at the end. Ask students why someone might use this organizational form (to place the best point last, so the reader remembers it; to build to a strong conclusion).

4. Place students in groups with a list of possible topics. Have students determine the best method of organization and present it to the class. As a class, discuss the students' conclusions.

5. Have students select a topic, determine the type of structure to be used in the essay, and develop a thesis statement.

Customize for
Spatial Learners

When students have a time limit, they need to get the ideas flowing and on paper. Rather than have these students try to organize an outline, recommend that they use a graphic organizer. Suggest that students make a map, drawing connecting lines to join ideas.

15.2 Drafting

Shaping Your Writing
Plan a Structure

Before you draft, quickly sketch an organizational plan. You may want to make an outline or some other type of graphic organizer to be sure that your points are clearly and logically organized. Following are some organizations you might consider:

Comparison and Contrast Use this method of organization if you are asked to examine similarities and differences, choose one option from among several, compare an author's works, or argue for one thing over another.

Point by Point: Within each paragraph, examine one point of similarity or difference.

Subject by Subject: First examine all the features of one topic. Then, examine all the features of the second.

Chronological Organization This method of organization is effective when you're asked to trace causes and effects, examine the history of something, or tell a personal story.

Nestorian Organization When you are writing persuasively, this type of organization can be very effective.

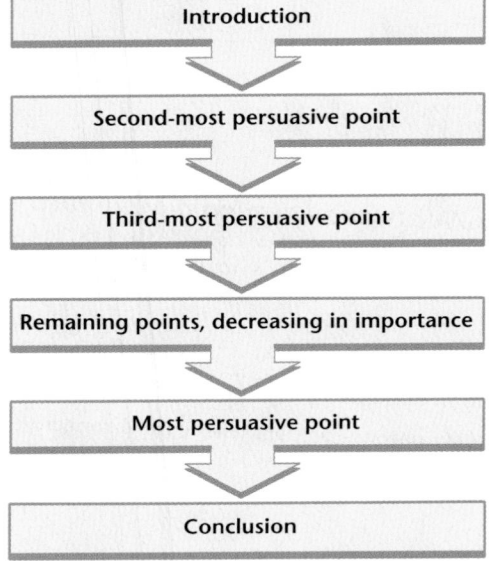

Technology Tip

If you are taking your test on-line, use the cut-and-paste feature to help you move around material to fit your organization.

⏱ TIME AND RESOURCE MANAGER

Resources
Print: *Writing Support Transparencies,* 15-B–C; *Writing Support Activity Book,* 15-1
Technology: *Writing and Grammar* Interactive Text, Section 15.2

Using the Full Student Edition	Using the Handbook 🄷
• Cover pp. 334–335 by discussing the methods of organization and practicing categorizing topics. • Require students to select a topic and develop a thesis statement. • As students prepare details, have them categorize the types of support that best apply to their essays.	• Cover pp. 214–215 by discussing the methods of organization and practicing categorizing topics. • Require students to select a topic and develop a thesis statement. • As students prepare details, have them categorize the types of support that best apply to their essays.

Providing Elaboration

As you draft, make your writing convincing and give it depth by providing elaboration—details that define, explain, support, or illustrate your points.

Include Various Details

- **Details That Define** Be specific in your writing. Provide definitions to show that you fully understand the subject matter about which you're writing.
- **Details That Explain** Give reasons for your statements.
- **Details That Support** Cite statistics, expert testimony, and examples from life to make your arguments strong and convincing.
- **Details That Illustrate** Create graphs, sketches, or charts that present your points clearly and effectively.

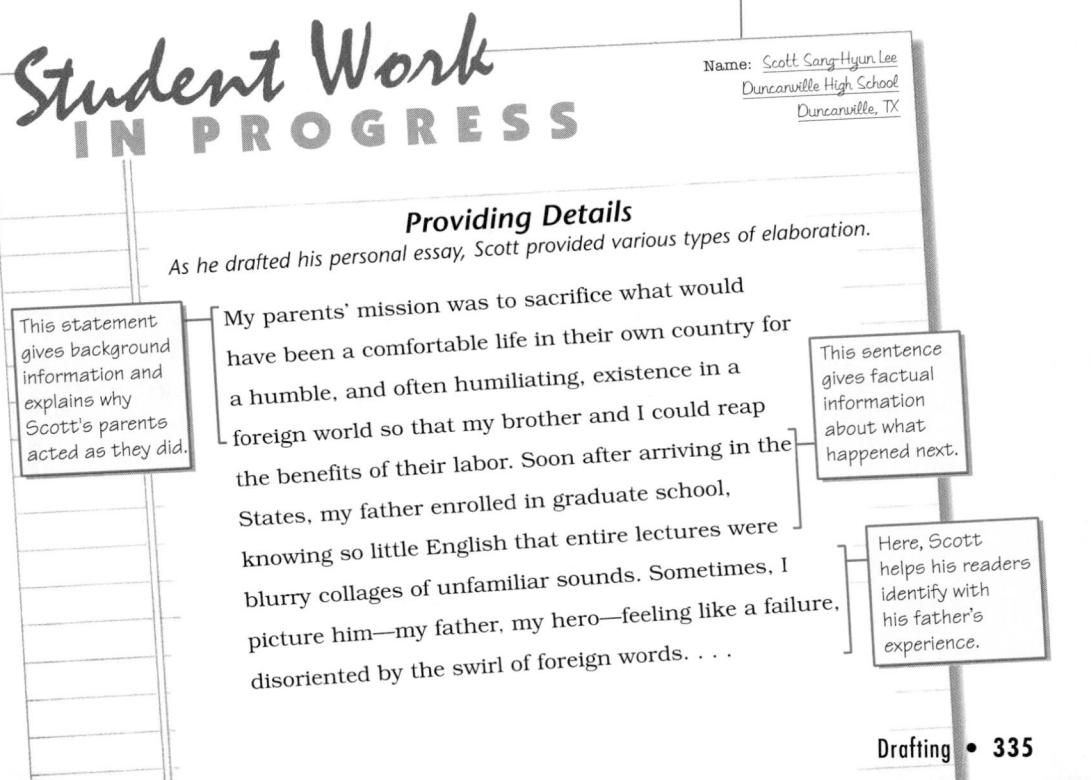

Student Work
IN PROGRESS

Name: Scott Sang-Hyun Lee
Duncanville High School
Duncanville, TX

Providing Details

As he drafted his personal essay, Scott provided various types of elaboration.

This statement gives background information and explains why Scott's parents acted as they did.

My parents' mission was to sacrifice what would have been a comfortable life in their own country for a humble, and often humiliating, existence in a foreign world so that my brother and I could reap the benefits of their labor. Soon after arriving in the States, my father enrolled in graduate school, knowing so little English that entire lectures were blurry collages of unfamiliar sounds. Sometimes, I picture him—my father, my hero—feeling like a failure, disoriented by the swirl of foreign words. . . .

This sentence gives factual information about what happened next.

Here, Scott helps his readers identify with his father's experience.

Drafting • 335

Drafting: Include Various Details

Teaching Resources: Writing Support Transparencies, 15-C

1. Display Transparency 15-C and discuss types of support. Discuss how Scott elaborated on various points and, therefore, strengthened his essay.
2. Provide students with newspaper or magazine article excerpts and have students identify the types of details.
3. Have students discuss the effectiveness of the support for each main point.
4. Have students include and identify at least one of each type of support as they write their first drafts.

Integrating Spelling Skills

In English there are several words that are spelled the same but are pronounced differently depending on the part of speech (examples: *address, affix, conflict, desert, elaborate, peaked, permit, present,* and *project*). Ask students to identify other words that change pronunciation but not spelling when they change part of speech. Most dictionaries indicate the different entries with an exponential number. Ask students to locate examples of these words in a dictionary. Have students work in pairs to create sentences that include both pronunciations and to identify the part of speech of each pronunciation. (Example: The *produce* farm will *produce* a surplus of lettuce this year. [adjective/verb])

☑ **ONGOING ASSESSMENT: Monitor and Reinforce**

Students sometimes have problems recognizing the strengths and weaknesses of their supporting evidence. If this is the case with your students, try the following strategy.

Provide pairs of students with a thesis statement that you have prepared. Have students write five supporting points on note cards. Then, have the students exchange cards and ask the partners to order the cards from strongest to weakest. Students can then discuss the effectiveness of their organization before continuing to draft.

⏱ **TIME SAVERS!**

 **Writing Support Transparencies**
Use the transparencies for Chapter 15 to facilitate teaching of strategies.

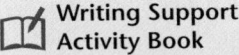 **Writing Support Activity Book**
Use the organizers for Chapter 15 to facilitate student planning.

Revising: Revisiting Your Introduction and Conclusion

1. Discuss the importance of introductions and conclusions.

2. Provide students with examples of introductions that grab interest and provide a transition into the first body paragraph.

3. Put students in pairs. Have them read and critique each other's introductions and conclusions.

4. Have students revise their drafts.

Revising: Deleting Unnecessary Details to Create Unity

Teaching Resources: Writing Support Transparencies, 15-D

1. Read and discuss Transparency 15-D. Have students examine how Scott created unity by deleting unnecessary details.

2. Give students highlighters and have them read their drafts for unity. Instruct them to highlight statements that do not seem to fit.

3. Encourage students to be aware of other improvements they could make at this time to improve organization and flow.

Integrating Grammar Skills

Alert students to conjunctive adverbs: connective, transitional words that establish a more formal, sophisticated tone. Remind students that connective words that join two independent clauses require a semicolon before the connector and a comma after it (examples: *however*, *furthermore*, *consequently*, and *therefore*). Help students develop a comparison list of coordinating conjunctions and conjunctive adverbs (examples: *therefore, so, furthermore, and*). Provide students with pairs of sentences and have them combine them with conjunctive adverbs. Have students return to their essays and find at least one coordinating conjunction they can replace with a conjunctive adverb.

15.3 Revising

Revising Your Overall Structure

If you are writing under a time restriction, you may not be able to spend much time revising. Use your own knowledge of your writing habits to decide on the areas of your essay most likely to require revision.

▶ **REVISION STRATEGY**
Revisiting Your Introduction and Conclusion

Introductions and conclusions can have a great impact on how well your writing is judged. The following ideas can help you to strengthen your introduction and conclusion: (1) Add an interest-grabbing sentence to the introduction. (2) Write a transitional sentence to lead from the introduction to the body of your writing. (3) Reword the final sentence in the conclusion to give it more impact.

Revising Your Paragraphs

▶ **REVISION STRATEGY**
Deleting Unnecessary Details to Create Unity

Check to be sure that each paragraph helps develop or explain the main point of your essay. If not, delete or rewrite the paragraph. Then, read each paragraph carefully. If any sentences within the paragraph do not support the topic, move or delete them.

Student Work
IN PROGRESS

Name: Scott Sang-Hyun Lee
Duncanville High School
Duncanville, TX

Deleting Unnecessary Details to Create Unity
After reviewing his paragraphs, Scott made the following changes to create unity.

It is a challenge I accept because they first accepted it. ~~Their selfless love affects me in broader ways.~~ My fulfillment of their dream is not an idyllic state that I will reach only in adulthood; instead, it is something I achieve every day in who I am and what I do. ~~My happiness now comes in living humbly.~~

⏱ TIME AND RESOURCE MANAGER

Resources
Print: *Writing Support Transparencies*, 15-D
Technology: *Writing and Grammar* Interactive Text, Section 15.3

Using the Full Student Edition	Using the Handbook🅗
• Discuss the Revision Strategies with the class.	• Discuss the Revision Strategies with the class.
• Demonstrate each of the strategies and have students employ them in their drafts.	• Demonstrate each of the strategies and have students employ them in their drafts.

Revising Your Sentences

When writing quickly, it is easy to make mistakes. One common mistake is the unintentional switch of verb tenses. When you revise, be sure that you correct such mistakes.

▶ **REVISION STRATEGY**
Scanning Verbs to Check for Unintentional Switches

One way to tell whether you've switched verb tenses is to scan your writing, looking for verbs. Identify the tense of each verb as you read. If, for instance, within one paragraph you find three past tense verbs and one present tense verb, you may have made an unintentional tense change.

> **EXAMPLE:**
>
> Participation in sports promotes teamwork, helps build leadership, and teaches players to strive for victory yet accept defeat gracefully. When you join a team, you learn life lessons. You~~will have built~~ build self-confidence, too.

Revising Your Word Choice

Each word counts when you write for assessment. Critically examine the word choices you have made, and make sure that you have used transitions to connect your ideas.

▶ **REVISION STRATEGY**
Adding Transitions to Make Connections Clear

Transitional words and phrases indicate relationships between ideas, enabling readers to follow your thoughts.

- If you have used comparison-and-contrast organization, you may want to add transitions such as *on the other hand*, *similarly*, *likewise*, or *contrary to*.
- If you have used chronological organization, you may want to add transitions such as *first*, *next*, *last*, *finally*, and *after that*.
- If you have used cause-and-effect organization, you may want to add transitions such as *consequently*, *because*, *after that*, and *due to*.

Revising • **337**

Revising: Scanning Verbs to Check for Unintentional Switches

1. Discuss the example. Ask students why the change is an improvement (the tense of the verb now matches that of the other verbs in the passage).

2. Remind students that tenses don't have to be identical, but they should be logical and appropriate. Use the following examples to illustrate:

   I went to the store and bought tomatoes. (parallel)

   I had been shopping for an hour when I found them. (logical progression)

Revising: Adding Transitions to Make Connections Clear

1. To illustrate and provide practice, suggest sentences and organizational options, and then have students suggest a sentence that could follow, using an appropriate transition. For example:

   Going to a movie was tempting. (comparison and contrast)

   Sample response: *Going to a movie was tempting. On the other hand, renting a video was cheaper.*

2. Have students review their drafts to make certain transitions are clear.

Customize for
Less Advanced Students

Provide students with a simple reading passage that is missing transitions. Ask them to read the passage aloud to help them hear how disjointed the writing sounds. Have them determine what transitions to use and where to use them. After revising, solicit volunteers to read the passage aloud again to hear the improvement.

✎ STANDARDIZED TEST PREPARATION WORKSHOP

Transitions Standardized tests may require students to recognize which transitions make meaning clear. Provide students with practice in using transitions.

Select the transition that most effectively communicates the relationship between the two sentences.

We had to take Juan to the emergency room. He had a broken arm.

A although   **C** until

B because   **D** before

Students should recognize that the best response is **B**, as it establishes a logical cause-and-effect relationship. Responses A, C, and D would produce illogical relationships.

338 • 218Ⓗ

Editing and Proofreading

1. Discuss the importance of correct spelling. Provide examples of how easily typographical errors can be made on a computer keyboard. Such errors can often bring nonsense to a sentence.

2. Have students exchange papers and read them word for word, looking for spelling errors and typographical errors.

Grammar in Your Writing: Homophones

1. Remind students that homophone errors must be identified by careful proofreading. They will not be picked up by a computer spell-checking function since the words are used incorrectly but not spelled incorrectly.

2. Have students pay particular attention to the examples on page 338. Ask students to suggest other homophone errors.

3. Assign students to review their essays for homophone errors.

Find It in Your Writing

Challenge students to develop lists of commonly misspelled homophones for reference during proofreading.

Customize for
ESL Students

Distinguishing between homophones can be a challenge to some students. Help them create homophone lists, with homophones listed together and defined. Encourage students to add to the list as they discover new homophones.

15.4 # Editing and Proofreading

Focusing on Spelling

Misspellings and typographical errors convey to readers that your work is sloppy and carelessly written. Be sure to proofread carefully to catch such mistakes. Use the following strategies, depending on your assignment:

Open-Book and Nontimed Essays Use the spell-check tool if you are working electronically. Use a dictionary if you are writing in longhand.

Timed-Test Essays If you are aware of the mistakes you most often make in spelling, peruse your writing for such mistakes now. Otherwise, check for common errors, such as misspellings in "*i* before *e* words" and homophones.

Grammar in Your Writing
Homophones

Homophones are words that sound alike but have different spellings and meanings. When you write quickly, as in test-taking situations, you might mistakenly write the wrong homophone. Proofread your essay, and pay special attention to homophones such as *it's* and *its; there, their,* and *they're; to, too,* and *two;* and *your* and *you're.* Be sure that you've correctly spelled the homophone you intend.

its/it's	To give the organization **its** due, they employ many young students. **It's** a good idea to pack lightly.
your/you're	It is **your** responsibility. **You're** the only one who can make a difference.
hear/here	Can you **hear** the music? Put the empty boxes over **here**.
sight/cite	The tourist went to see the **sights**. Don't forget to **cite** your sources.

Find It in Your Writing As you proofread your essay, check that you have written all homophones correctly.

For more on spelling homophones, see Chapter 29.

⏱ TIME AND RESOURCE MANAGER

Resources
Print: *Scoring Rubrics on Transparency,* Ch. 15; *Writing Assessment and Portfolio Management; Formal Assessment,* Ch. 15
Technology: *Writing and Grammar* Interactive Text, Section 15.4

Using the Full Student Edition	Using the HandbookⒽ
• Cover pp. 338–341 in class. • Have students complete the Rubric for Self-Assessment. • Have students edit and proofread their essays in class.	• Cover pp. 218–219 in class. • Have students complete the Rubric for Self-Assessment. • Have students edit and proofread their essays in class.

15.5 Publishing and Presenting

Building Your Portfolio

1. **Portfolio** Save your completed essay in your portfolio. Attach a small note on which you describe when and where you took this test.
2. **Guidance Counselor** Give a copy of your writing to your guidance counselor for his or her review. Then, make an appointment with the counselor to discuss how best to take advantage of your writing skills.

Reflecting on Your Writing

Take a few moments to think about writing for assessment. Then, answer the following questions, and save your responses in your portfolio.

- Were you satisfied with the question you chose to answer? Why or why not?
- Which stage of the writing process did you find most useful as you wrote for assessment? Why?

 Internet Tip

To see an essay scored according to this rubric, go on-line:
PHSchool.com
Enter Web Code:
egk-1201

Rubric for Self-Assessment

Use the following criteria to evaluate your writing:

	Score 4	Score 3	Score 2	Score 1
Audience and Purpose	Uses appropriately formal diction; clearly addresses writing prompt	Uses mostly formal diction; adequately addresses writing prompt	Uses some informal diction; addresses writing prompt	Uses inappropriately informal diction; does not address writing prompt
Organization	Presents a clear, consistent organizational strategy	Presents a clear organizational strategy with few inconsistencies	Presents an inconsistent organizational strategy	Shows a lack of organizational strategy
Elaboration	Provides several ideas to support the thesis; elaborates each idea; links all information to thesis	Provides several ideas to support the thesis; elaborates most ideas with facts, details, or examples; links most information to thesis	Provides some ideas to support the thesis; does not elaborate some ideas; does not link some details to thesis	Provides no thesis; does not elaborate ideas
Use of Language	Uses excellent sentence and vocabulary variety; includes very few mechanical errors	Uses adequate sentence and vocabulary variety; includes few mechanical errors	Uses repetitive use of sentence structure and vocabulary; includes many mechanical errors	Demonstrates poor use of language; generates confusion; includes many mechanical errors

Publishing and Presenting • 339

Publishing and Presenting

1. Have students add their completed assessment essays to their portfolios. Encourage them to consider illustrative material such as photos, illustrations, and graphic organizers that could illuminate their main topics.
2. Encourage students to schedule a meeting with a guidance counselor. Consider inviting the counselors to come to class to listen to students read finished products.

ASSESS and CLOSE

Assessment

Teaching Resources: Scoring Rubrics on Transparency, Ch. 15; Writing Assessment and Portfolio Management; Formal Assessment, Ch. 15

1. Display the Scoring Rubric transparency and review the criteria.
2. Before students proceed with self-assessment, you may wish to review the Final Draft of the Student Work in Progress, pages 340-341, and have students score it in one or more of the rubric categories.
3. In addition to student self-assessment, you may wish to use the following assessment options:
   - score student essays yourself, using the rubric and scoring models from *Writing Assessment and Portfolio Management*.
   - administer the Chapter 15 assessment from *Formal Assessment* in the Teaching Resources to measure students' grasp of the concepts presented.

Integrating Speaking and Listening Skills

Before students read their finished essays aloud, suggest that they practice the presentation. Encourage them to be aware of intonation, eye contact, and delivery speed as they present. Have the listening students jot down and report at least one thing that they learn from each presentation.

Final Draft

1. Read the essay aloud or have a prepared student read it to the class.

2. Begin helping students see how this model exemplifies the characteristics of a well-written essay response by pointing out how Scott's introduction grabs the reader's attention and clearly states the thesis.

3. Have students name some of the transitional devices (conjunctive adverbs, repetition of key phrases).

4. Together, evaluate the sentence structure. Is there adequate variety? Does Scott use a mix of simple, compound, and complex sentences?

5. Have students find examples of effective word choice.

6. Ask students to analyze the supporting evidence in each paragraph of the student model. Which paragraph is the strongest? Why?

7. Based on what they have read, how might students improve their own writing?

Critical Viewing

Relate Students may mention such associations as graduation, ceremonies, photographs, celebrations, and good-byes.

Customize for
ESL Students

Provide an opportunity for students to discuss their experiences of coming to the United States. Encourage these students to answer questions from their peers. To prevent anxiety, prepare questions as a class that students would like to have answered. Provide students an opportunity to prepare answers for the questions. Then, allow the students to practice their oral presentation skills.

15.6 *Student Work*
IN PROGRESS

FINAL DRAFT

Dream and Dreamer

**Scott Sang-Hyun Lee
Duncanville High School
Duncanville, Texas**

My parents, hoping to establish richer lives for my brother and me, moved the family to the United States when I was ten months old. We were the classic American immigrant family— poor and sustained only by the bread of hopes and dreams. My parents' mission was to sacrifice what would have been a comfortable life in their own country for a humble, and often humiliating, existence in a foreign world so that my brother and I could reap the benefits of their labor.

Soon after arriving in the United States, my father enrolled in graduate school, knowing so little English that entire lectures were blurry collages of unfamiliar sounds. Sometimes I picture him—my father, my hero—feeling like a failure, disoriented by the swirl of foreign words and unable to voice his confusion. My mother, needing to earn money as my father was studying, worked as a custodian at the local mall. Sometimes I picture her—my mother, my hero—cleaning up public restrooms. Thinking of her backbreaking task fills me with tears.

340 • Writing for Assessment

◄ **Critical Viewing**
What associations do the cap and diploma shown on this page call to mind? **[Relate]**

In the opening paragraph, Scott reveals the main point of his essay.

Scott's essay is logically and effectively organized. Each paragraph deals with a single main idea that he supports with examples and details.

My mother and father no longer have to work at jobs for which they are overqualified. Nevertheless, it is the memory of their past that pushes me forward. Every day, I strive to reward their sacrifice. Though it is not my only goal, nor my only motivation, I now consider it a duty to serve them as they have served me. I now willingly live with the weight of their dream upon my shoulders.

It is a challenge I accept because they first accepted it. My fulfillment of their dream is not an idyllic state that I will reach only in adulthood; instead, it is something I achieve every day in who I am and what I do. In one sense, I have already justified my parents' toils in committing myself to serving others. Yet commitment without deeds is meaningless; I still must equip myself in preparation for a life of service.

The memory of my past will serve as my vision for the future. I will always hold dearly my parents' dream and live to attain it—not only in submission to it, but also in ownership of it. The sacrifice of many years of their lives for my own is something I can never fully comprehend. However, I at least know that their lives have been planted in my heart, and that I have been entrusted as the deliverer of their defined hope. I am what they have sown, but I am also what I sow. I am both seed and reaper; I am both dream and dreamer.

Strong word choices, like "committing," "justified," and "serving" help Scott achieve his purpose.

The final sentences of Scott's conclusion are powerful and memorable.

▶ **Critical Viewing** How would you describe this student's mood upon graduation? Explain. **[Interpret]**

Integrating Grammar Skills

Parallel Structure Remind students that *parallel structure* means using equivalent structures of words, phrases, and clauses to emphasize the similarities or differences among items. In his paper, Scott uses numerous instances of parallel structure. (For example: *The memory of my past* will serve as *my vision for the future.*) Ask students to point out those examples in each paragraph and discuss the effectiveness of each structure. Examine the last sentence of the essay. What does the parallel structure do for the conclusion?

Customize for
Less Advanced Students

A full discussion of parallelism, and how to correct faulty parallelism, can be found on pages 505–508. You may want to review and discuss in class how parallel structure is created. Then, have students write (in class or for homework) two or more sentences to illustrate parallel structure.

Customize for
Logical/Mathematical Learners

Point out that parallelism in sentence structure is similar to parallelism in mathematics. Making words, phrases, or clauses parallel is similar to having both sides of an equation equal.

Critical Viewing

Interpret Students may suggest the mood is one of joy, pride, and anticipation of the future.

Lesson Objectives

1. To write an essay for an open-book test
2. To use prewriting strategies to generate ideas and plan
3. To develop drafts by organizing and reorganizing content and by refining style to suit purpose
4. To produce legible work that shows accurate spelling and correct use of the conventions of punctuation and capitalization
5. To demonstrate control over grammatical elements

Step-by-Step Teaching Guide

Open-Book Test

1. Tell students that, in a test situation, they should decide quickly on their general response to the test question. It will help to write one or two sentences that describe their general response. This will become their main idea.

2. Encourage students to bring self-sticking notes to the testing room and to use them in marking passages to which they will refer as they gather details for writing.

3. When students have compiled a list of supporting details and have begun writing paragraphs, remind them to explain how the details support their main idea.

4. Tell students to use clear transitions to link one idea to the next. You may wish to review transitional words and phrases with students.

5. Walk students through a response to a sample test question. Brainstorm for supporting details and organize them into logical groups on the board.

Critical Viewing

Connect Students might say that an open-book test allows them to spend time organizing their ideas rather than memorizing information.

Connected Assignment
Open-Book Test

Do you feel anxious when taking a test? If you do, an open-book test may be a welcome change. In these tests, you're allowed to refer to specific materials such as textbooks and study notes. As a result, the process of developing supporting details rests more on scanning than on memory, but expectations for factual support may be higher. In most other ways, open-book tests require the same skills as traditional tests. You must plan your time, write efficiently, and express meaningful ideas and accurate information.

Practice writing an essay for an open-book test by following the writing process steps identified below.

▲ **Critical Viewing** How does the chance to refer to textbooks change the way you approach an exam? Explain. [Connect]

Prewriting

Gather Materials Before test time, verify the ground rules and then locate the books or materials that you are allowed to use during the test. If you know the test topics, think about these in advance and highlight relevant sections of your study materials. If topics are presented only at test time, choose to develop the topic about which you know the most.

Write Your Thesis Be sure that you write a thesis statement that matches the question being asked. Below is an example of an essay question for an open-book test followed by a thesis statement that addresses the question.

Sample Question:	Was King Richard III of England indeed a murderous villain, as portrayed by Sir Thomas More and William Shakespeare, or was he falsely maligned, as many modern historians claim? Support your views using at least four reliable sources.
Sample Thesis:	King Richard III of England was unfairly depicted as a murderer and villain. Indeed, he was a great counselor, battlefield commander, and trusted friend to many of his contemporaries.

Find Support Once you've written your thesis statement, make a plan for finding information that will support it. Use self-sticking tags to mark materials from books or in your notes that you plan to use in your essay.

342 • Writing for Assessment

☑ **ONGOING ASSESSMENT: Prerequisite Skills**

Students may find the following resources from Chapter 15 particularly helpful in completing their open-book tests.

In the Textbook	Print Resources	Technology
Locate Key Words, Section 15.1 Plan a Structure, Section 15.2	*Writing Support Transparencies,* 15-A–B *Writing Support Activity Book,* 15-1	*Writing and Grammar* Interactive Text, Sections 15.1–2

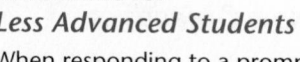

Make an Outline Finally, prepare an outline to help you organize and present your ideas in an clear and effective way. When you are finished with your outline, use it as a guide as you gather supporting details.

SAMPLE OUTLINE

I. Introduction

    A. Quotation from Plato

    B. Thesis Statement: Jeremy Bentham's philosophies are ridiculed by Dickens in *Hard Times*

II. Utilitarianism

    A. Utilitarianism defined

    B. Utilitarianism—followers

III. Dickens

    A. Dickens's childhood

    B. Dickens's philosophies

Drafting Refer often to your outline and the earmarked reference materials as you draft. As with any essay, start by stating your thesis. Take full advantage of the open-book format to support your main idea with vivid, specific, and accurate details. If you cannot locate a particular fact or detail when you need it, leave yourself a reminder and continue drafting. As you write, look out for additional details or appropriate substitutes as you check notes and texts for information.

Revising and Editing Reread your essay, and adjust its organization, if necessary, to emphasize and develop your thesis. Use text resources to verify the accuracy of your supporting details. Add details where necessary to help support or explain your ideas. Delete details that stray from your purpose or the point you are making. Be sure to proofread your essay to locate and fix all errors you have made in grammar, spelling, and punctuation.

Publishing and Presenting Neatly write or print out a copy of your essay and hand it in when test time is over. To give your essay a professional look, enclose it in a folder or put a cover on it.

Grammar and Style Tip

Reread the test question and decide on an appropriate tone—a writer's attitude toward a topic—for your response. Then, choose words and phrases that will help create that tone.

Customize for
Less Advanced Students

When responding to a prompt, students should be sure they understand each part of what they are being asked to do. Tell students that, often, they will find writing prompts that contain more than one question or topic to be addressed. For example, students may be asked to discuss both their own opinions about a topic and a writer's opinion about the same topic, and then to compare and contrast them. In other prompts, students may need to explain a theme before moving on to explain how the writing supports it.

Customize for
AP Students

Students may want to revise their topic sentence as they work. They should be careful, however, to stay with their original main idea.

1. To recognize distinctive and shared characteristics of cultures through reading
2. To recognize and discuss themes and connections that cross cultures
3. To analyze ideas and cultures as represented in various media
4. To compile written ideas and representations into reports and draw conclusions

Step-by-Step Teaching Guide

Understanding History Through Media

1. Have students find examples of Curtis's photographs in the library or on the Internet. Have them examine the photos and then explain what Theodore Roosevelt meant when he said that Curtis " . . . has been able to do what no man has ever done."

2. If possible, show students clips from *The Squaw Man* and other films about Native American cultures, such as *Return of a Man Called Horse* or *Smoke Signals*. Encourage students to compare and contrast the depiction of Native Americans in these films.

3. Give students copies of excerpts from N. Scott Momaday's work, such as *The Way to Rainy Mountain*, *House Made of Dawn* or *The Ancient Child*. What can students learn about Kiowa culture from reading these selections?

Viewing and Representing

Activity Encourage students to learn about the art made by the tribe they are studying. What are some of the common images and what do they represent? What materials did the artists use? Students may want to illustrate their essays with photographs.

Spotlight on the Humanities

Understanding History Through Media

Focus on Photography: Edward S. Curtis

While the history of Native Americans may form the subject for an essay-test question, artists, photographers, and playwrights have used our nation's history as a springboard for their creative work. American photographer Edward S. Curtis (1868–1952) took about 40,000 pictures of Native Americans over the span of thirty years. Theodore Roosevelt said that Curtis ". . . has been able to do what no other man has ever done; what, as far as we can see, no other man could do." Curtis spent more than thirty years in remote areas of the United States and Canada photographing Native Americans.

Film Connection In 1920, Edward S. Curtis moved to Los Angeles and assisted noted film director Cecil B. DeMille, whose first silent film in 1914 was called *The Squaw Man.* In 1976, film director Robert Altman brought Arthur Kopit's play *Indians* to the screen. The film, starring Paul Newman, was called *Buffalo Bill and the Indians.*

Literature Connection Author N. Scott Momaday has devoted himself to preserving Kiowa culture. Through essays, poetry, and retellings of Kiowa legends, Momaday provides his audience with a deeper understanding of Native American culture, both past and present.

Writing for Assessment Writing Activity: Essay on Native American History

Using several resources, research the history of a Native American group, perhaps one that originated in your home state. Then, write an essay—giving yourself a time limit as if you were being tested—discussing the history and tradition of the group.

▲ **Critical Viewing** What aspects of this photograph increase your understanding of Native American life? [**Distinguish**]

344 • Writing for Assessment

Critical Viewing

Distinguish The photograph offers information about the clothing, housing, and method of transportation of one Native American culture.

Media and Technology Skills

Taking Computerized Tests

Activity: Share Test-Taking Strategies

Many tests—from aptitude tests to driving exams—are computerized. Some test-taking skills can be easily applied to computerized situations, but some are specific to computerized testing. Talking about test-taking strategies can help you focus on the distinctions between computerized and traditional testing.

Think About It Review your own experiences with computerized tests. Think about what features helped ensure your success. List three points you would like to share during a team discussion.

Discuss It Share your ideas about computerized tests. In addition to talking about your team's ideas, discuss these strategies:

- **Read instructions:** Take time to read the test rules carefully. For example, find out what happens if you skip a question. How can you change an answer?

- **Read automatic feedback:** Some tests provide feedback while the test is in progress. Be sure to read feedback carefully, and apply any hints or suggestions provided.

- **Print out results:** After taking a test, print out the results. You might use the results to help you prepare for a final.

List It Compile a list of test-taking strategies. Use a chart like this one to organize strategies according to the type of test.

Computerized Tests Only	All Tests	Print Tests Only
• Print out your results to review later.	• Preview the test before you start answering. • Reserve some time to review your test.	• Underline key words in multiple-choice questions.

Share It Prepare a short presentation in which to share your test-taking strategies with your class. Identify the similarities and differences between forms of tests, and provide a list of the strategies you believe are most effective.

▶ *Lesson Objectives*

1. To use technology for writing essays and answering test questions

2. To establish and adjust purpose for reading such as to understand and to solve problems

3. To make relevant contributions in conversations and discussions

---

Step-by-Step Teaching Guide

Taking Computerized Tests

Teaching Resources: Writing Support Transparencies, 15-E; Writing Support Activity Book, 15-2

1. Ask students to make a list of the tests they expect to have to take in the next few years. Which of these tests will be computerized?

2. Have each student generate three tips for taking computerized tests and share his or her tips with the class. Students can record these tips in the blank organizer (15-2).

3. If possible, show students an example of a standardized test on CD-ROM or the Internet. You might obtain this material from test-preparation booklets that contain CD-ROMs. Allow students time to practice taking these tests.

Integrating Technology Skills

If possible, administer a test on computer. For essay tests, have students compose their essays in the computer lab during class. For objective tests, have them fill in their answers on an electronic file rather than on a hard copy. This will help students feel familiar with the use of a computer in testing situations.

Lesson Objectives

1. To use prewriting strategies to generate ideas and plan

2. To develop drafts by organizing and reorganizing content and by refining style to suit purpose

3. To produce legible work that shows accurate spelling and correct use of the conventions of punctuation and capitalization

4. To demonstrate control over grammatical elements

Step-by-Step Teaching Guide

Responding to Writing Prompts for Assessment

Teaching Resources: Standardized Test Preparation Workbook, pp. 29–30

1. Go over the bulleted criteria with students.

2. Point out that the keys to success are simply steps students have already covered in learning to write essays, and they are all things that can be improved upon with practice.

3. Remind students to pace themselves, budgeting their time over the various steps of the writing activity.

4. Depending on students' familiarity with the space program, you may want to list some of the benefits (commercial products, many medical techniques, such as MRIs, greater knowledge of the solar system) and costs (in the billions) on the board, so that students have details to use in their essays.

5. Assign the sample writing situation for completion within a class period.

Standardized Test Preparation Workshop

Responding to Writing Prompts for Assessment

Test Tip

Before you begin to write, reread the prompt to ensure that you answer it fully.

The writing prompts on standardized tests often measure your ability to write effectively. Some tests measure your ability to respond to literature; some measure your ability to write persuasively. The following are the criteria upon which your writing will be evaluated:

• varied word and sentence choice for the purpose and audience named in the response
• a method of organization that allows you to organize details in a meaningful and coherent sequence, such as pro-and-con organization or cause-and-effect organization
• appropriate transitions so ideas will flow and your persuasive writing will be unified and coherent
• elaboration through effective use of description, facts, and other details
• correct grammar, spelling, and punctuation

When writing for a timed test, plan to devote a specified amount of time to prewriting, drafting, revising, and proofreading.

Following is an example of a persuasive writing prompt. Use the suggestions on the following page to help you respond. The clocks next to each stage show a suggested percentage of time to devote to each stage.

Sample Writing Situation

Space exploration has always been a hot topic for debate. Some people believe that government funding for space missions is a waste of money because there are so many domestic issues that need to be addressed. Yet some of our most innovative technology and advanced scientific understanding have evolved from the exploration of space.

Write a detailed letter to your state senator presenting your side of the argument for or against the federal funding of space exploration. Be sure to clearly state your position and to support it with reasons and facts.

346 • Writing for Assessment

✎ TEST-TAKING TIP

You may want to model a strong thesis statement for a test of this kind. For example, *I feel strongly that this nation should/should not fund further missions in space because* (students insert their main idea or chief supporting detail). Students should then continue with more details that support the thesis, first addressing the main advantage or disadvantage of funding for such missions, then discussing reasons for the success or failure of them. Encourage students to avoid general summaries until their conclusions.

Prewriting

Allow close to one quarter of your time for prewriting.

Identify Your Thesis A thesis reveals your main idea about the topic. Your thesis will help you summarize the issue and provide you with a foundation for the letter.

Gather Details Debatable statements are not factual statements but statements of opinion. When you are writing a persuasive letter, it is your job to convince your reader to agree with your thesis. You can do this by gathering details that support your position.

Drafting

Allow almost half of your time for drafting.

Write for Your Reader Since you are writing a letter to a senator, keep your language formal and your ideas concise. The choice and presentation of your words are important.

Introduce Your Topic Start your letter with a strong introduction. Although your premise does not have to be the first sentence, make sure it is included in the first paragraph. Then, give a brief description of the points you intend to make in the following paragraphs.

Present Your Argument In the letter's body paragraphs, present supporting arguments for your main premise. You may also address opposing arguments and illustrate why your argument is better. In your concluding paragraph, restate your topic sentence in a different way. Then, briefly summarize each of the points you've made, making sure that your last sentence will grab the reader's attention.

Revising, Editing, and Proofreading

Allow almost one quarter of your time to revise and edit. Use the last few minutes to check your work.

Review Your Writing Does what you've written make sense? If not, how can you reword it to sound more convincing? Delete any extra words, ideas, or sentences that repeat points already made or that don't belong.

Do a Final Check Use the last few minutes to check your letter for errors in spelling, grammar, and punctuation. Draw a line through the text you want to delete, and add the new choices neatly in the space above the text, using a caret [^] to indicate the exact placement.

Customize for
Less Advanced Students

If you did not list details of the space program's costs and benefits for the class as a whole, supply this information to students who would be unable to do the exercise at all without the information. Alternatively, you could assign a writing prompt for a topic with which less advanced students might be more familiar.

Customize for
AP Students

After students have completed the assignment within the allotted time, ask them to go back and review their thesis statements and conclusions. How could they be improved? What other parts of the essay could be strengthened?

Time and Resource Manager

In-Depth Lesson Plan

	LESSON FOCUS	PRINT AND MEDIA RESOURCES
DAY 1	**Introduction; Business Letter** Students are introduced to workplace writing. They analyze and then write a business letter. (pp. 348–351/H220–223)	*Writers at Work* DVD, Practical and Technical Writing *Writing and Grammar* Interactive Text, Ch. 16, Introduction through Section 16.1 **Teaching Resources** *Writing Support Transparencies,* 16-A
DAY 2	**Memo** Students analyze a model and write a business memo. (pp. 352–353/H224–225)	*Writing and Grammar* Interactive Text, Section 16.2 **Teaching Resources** *Writing Support Transparencies,* 16-B
DAY 3	**Résumé** Students analyze a model and write a résumé. (pp. 354–355/H226–227)	*Writing and Grammar* Interactive Text, Section 16.3 **Teaching Resources** *Writing Support Transparencies,* 16-C
DAY 4	**Forms and Applications** Students review and complete forms and applications. (pp. 356–357/H228–229)	*Writing and Grammar* Interactive Text, Section 16.4 **Teaching Resources** *Writing Support Transparencies,* 16-D–E; *Writing Support Activity Book,* 16-1–2; *Writing Assessment and Portfolio Management; Formal Assessment,* Ch. 16

Accelerated Lesson Plan

	LESSON FOCUS	PRINT AND MEDIA RESOURCES
DAY 1	**Business Letter; Memo** Students review models in class and then draft a business letter and a memo as homework. (pp. 348–353/H220–225)	*Writers at Work* DVD, Practical and Technical Writing *Writing and Grammar* Interactive Text, Ch. 16, Introduction through Section 16.2 **Teaching Resources** *Writing Support Transparencies,* 16-A–B
DAY 2	**Résumé; Forms and Applications** Students review models in class and then draft a résumé and complete an application as homework. (pp. 354–357/H226–229)	*Writing and Grammar* Interactive Text, Sections 16.3–4 **Teaching Resources** *Writing Support Transparencies,* 16-C–E; *Writing Support Activity Book,* 16-1–2; *Writing Assessment and Portfolio Management; Formal Assessment,* Ch. 16

Options for Adapting Lesson Plans

HOMEWORK

Have students complete any stage of the lesson for homework.

FEATURES

Extend coverage with Connected Assignment (p. 358), Spotlight on the Humanities (p. 360), Media and Technology Skills (p. 361), and the Standardized Test Preparation Workshop (pp. 362–363).

TECHNOLOGY

Students can complete any stage of the lesson on the computer, using *Writing and Grammar* Interactive Text or a word-processing program. Have them print out their completed work.

Writing and Grammar Handbook Alignment

Page numbers in Step-by-Step Teaching Guides in this Teacher's Edition refer to pages from the full student text. Handbook page references, indicated with this icon 🅷, are provided in Time and Resource Manager boxes and at the bottom of each Teacher's Edition page.

INTEGRATED SKILLS COVERAGE

Integrating Grammar Skills
Grammar and Style, SE p. 359
Abbreviations, ATE p. 357

Viewing and Representing
Critical Viewing, SE pp. 348, 358, 360/🅷220
Comparing Art Forms, SE p. 360
ATE pp. 354, 360

Vocabulary
ATE p. 350

Technology
ATE p. 354

Real-World Connection
ATE pp. 352, 357

Workplace Skills
ATE p. 357

ASSESSMENT SUPPORT

Standardized Test Preparation Workshop SE p. 362; ATE p. 353
Standardized Test Preparation Workbook, pp. 31–32
Scoring Rubrics on Transparency, Ch. 16
Formal Assessment, Ch. 16
Writing Assessment and Portfolio Management

MEETING INDIVIDUAL NEEDS

Less Advanced Students ATE pp. 355, 363. See also Ongoing Assessments ATE pp. 351, 355.
ESL Students ATE pp. 351, 353, 359
AP Students ATE p. 363
Spatial Learners ATE p. 357

BLOCK SCHEDULING

Pacing Suggestions
For 90-minute Blocks
• Follow the Accelerated Lesson Plan, and cover the business letter and memo in one class period and the résumé and forms and applications in a second class period.
• Allow class time for students to refine one form of workplace writing for inclusion in their portfolios.

Resources for Varying Instruction
• *Writing and Grammar* **Interactive Text** A 90-minute block provides an ideal opportunity for students to work on the computer.
• *Writers at Work* **DVD** Show the Practical and Technical Writing segment in class.

Professional Development Support
• *How to Manage Instruction in the Block* This teaching resource provides management and activity suggestions.

MEDIA AND TECHNOLOGY

For the Student
• *Writing and Grammar* **Interactive Text**, Ch. 16

For the Teacher
• *Writers at Work* **DVD**, Practical and Technical Writing
• **Teacher**EXPRESS™ **CD-ROM**

WRITING AND GRAMMAR ON-LINE

Interactive Text (On-line or on CD-ROM)
• Easily navigable instruction with interactive Revision Checkers
• Full use of e-rater™, the essay-scoring system (on-line only)

Companion Web Site PHSchool.com
• Scoring rubrics with models (use Web Code egk-1201)

See the Go On-line! **feature, SE p. iii.**

▶ *Lesson Objectives*

1. To write in various forms with particular emphasis on workplace writing such as a report, a memo, and a résumé

2. To use prewriting strategies to generate ideas, develop voice, and plan

3. To write in a voice and style appropriate to audience and purpose

4. To organize ideas in writing to ensure coherence, logical progression, and support for ideas

5. To develop and revise drafts in terms of structure, paragraphs, sentences, and word choice

6. To edit and proofread to ensure standard English usage and grammar

7. To produce legible work that shows accurate spelling and correct use of the conventions of punctuation and capitalization

8. To refine work-related writing to publish for general and specific audiences

Critical Viewing

Analyze Students may note that people in the photograph seem to be demonstrating communication skills, computer skills, and research skills.

Chapter 16 *Workplace Writing*

Workplace Writing in Everyday Life

When you send a letter to the editor of the local newspaper or complete an application for financial aid for a summer-school program, you are using workplace writing skills. Workplace writing links the exits and entrances on today's information highway, and it keeps the lines of communication open between co-workers, classmates, businesses, and even governments. Effective workplace writing can lead to job advancement, ensure accurate and speedy financial transactions, persuade potential customers of a product's merit, or warn readers about an urgent problem.

In this chapter, you will examine various types of workplace writing and learn about the features that help make each successful.

▲ **Critical Viewing** What sort of workplace skills do the people working in this office demonstrate? **[Analyze]**

348 • Workplace Writing

⏱ TIME AND RESOURCE MANAGER

Resources
Print: *Writing Support Transparencies,* 16-A
Technology: *Writers at Work* DVD, Practical and Technical Writing; *Writing and Grammar* Interactive Text, Ch. 16

Using the Full Student Edition	Using the Handbook Ⓗ
• Discuss the types of workplace writing on pp. 348–349. • Read and identify elements of the business letter on p. 350. • Review the Topic Bank on p. 351 and make sure each student has a topic.	• Discuss the types of workplace writing on pp. 220–221. • Read and identify elements of the business letter on p. 222. • Review the Topic Bank on p. 223 and make sure each student has a topic.

What Is Workplace Writing?

The term **workplace writing** refers to fact-based written products that communicate specific information in a structured format. Effective workplace writing

- presents a core message and anticipates the readers' questions.
- communicates essential details in a concise way.
- is neatly and effectively organized.
- is free from errors in grammar, spelling, and punctuation.

Types of Workplace Writing

From the accident report a police officer generates at the scene of an accident to the memo a teacher submits requesting science lab supplies, workplace writing is an important part of life. Several types of workplace writing are listed below. Each reflects its own particular audience and purpose:

- **Business letters** introduce documents, communicate specific information, or discuss particular issues of concern to the writer.
- **Memorandums (memos)** are used to circulate information within a business.
- **Résumés** list a job applicant's skills, qualifications, and educational background.
- **Forms and applications** provide specific factual information requested by the issuing company or employer.

PREVIEW
Chapter Contents

In this chapter, you will review and analyze several examples of workplace writing. These examples include real-life situations, such as a letter of recommendation for a school program, an office memo about appropriate dress, the résumé of a college student seeking employment after graduation, an application for college admission, and the forms typically used to accompany facsimiles (faxes) and record phone messages.

Writers in ACTION

In 1978, writer Isaac Bashevis Singer was awarded the Nobel Prize for Literature. He had the following advice for aspiring writers:

"The wastebasket is a writer's best friend."

This may be especially true in workplace writing, where mistakes can cost more than merely injured pride. Revising and editing, and even starting over, are well worth the time they take.

PREPARE and ENGAGE

Interest GRABBER Ask students to suggest four or five very different occupations. Write these on the board. Brainstorm for the different kinds of workplace writing applicable to each occupation. (Examples: *Lawyer:* legal briefs, memos, business letters, legal forms, client records, e-mail, law journal articles; *Sports Newscaster:* score sheets, interview questions, memos, e-mail.)

Activate Prior Knowledge

Encourage students to recall the last item they wrote outside of school. Remind them that notes, letters, directions, and e-mails are all writing. How could their examples be transferred to a business environment or occupation? (A college entrance form is like an employment application. Club or school government meeting minutes are similar to business meeting minutes.)

More About the Writer

Polish-born Isaac Bashevis Singer immigrated to America in 1935 at the age of thirty-one. Though he lived the remainder of his life in the United States, Singer continued to write novels and short stories in his native Yiddish language. Despite his many awards, Singer said, "I keep on struggling today as I did fifty years ago, because there is no guarantee, even if you have written ten good books, that the eleventh is going to be good. You have to work on it, rewrite, and improve, and ponder about it, until it comes out right."

Business Letter

Teaching Resources: Writing Support Transparencies, 16-A

1. Tell students that workplace writing has a specific audience and purpose, and that these must be kept in mind.

2. Explain that it is wise to always use a formal writing style.

3. If possible, bring in examples of business letters, so that students can see that the format is basically the same in all formal letters. (Even offers for credit cards or magazine subscriptions follow this format.)

4. Have students identify each part of the letter. Which elements are similar to other types of writing they've done and which are different?

5. Point out that, in the salutation, the colon is used in a formal letter. In a letter to a friend, a comma is appropriate.

6. Ask students to describe the language used by Kim in this letter (enthusiastic but formal and business-like, clear, well-chosen for the intended audience).

Integrating Vocabulary Skills

"Sincerely" is probably the most common closing for business letters. It means "genuinely, honestly, free from pretense or deceit." Closings such as "Warmest regards" are saved for friends and close acquaintances.

🕐 TIME SAVERS!

📋 **Writing Support Transparencies**
Use the transparencies for Chapter 16 to facilitate teaching of business letters and other forms of workplace writing.

16.1 *Business Letter*

What Is a Business Letter?

Business letters are formally written letters in which the content is other than personal. Business letters can address any topic, in any industry, in any language. An effective business letter

- has six parts: the heading, the inside address, the salutation, the body, the closing, and the signature.
- follows one of several acceptable formats. In block format, each section of the letter begins at the left margin. In modified block format, the heading, the closing, and the signature are indented to the center of the page.
- contains formal and courteous language.

Model Business Letter

This letter was written from one librarian to another, recommending a job applicant for a position.

> The header should include the recipient's company name and address as well as the date.

Covington Consolidated Libraries
900 Baker Street
Covington, KY 41010

July 31, 20_ _

Derek Henderson
Crowell Public Library
1400 Locke Lane
Charleston, SC 29407

> A colon follows the name of the recipient. Address the recipients by title, if known.

Dear Mr. Henderson:

I would like to recommend Ericka Alonso for a position at your library. I am the children's librarian for the several branches of the Covington Library System. As the supervisor of her work in our libraries, I have seen Ericka's sense of responsibility, initiative, and humor in action.

> In the body, briefly communicate your purpose for writing as well as other important details.

Ericka began as an assistant in the story-hour program, helping children with projects. She quickly captivated her audiences with creative ideas and contagious enthusiasm. In addition, Ericka has mastered the complicated workings of our interlibrary loan, computer cataloging, and shelving systems and has acquired transferable skills in the process.

> Formal language is appropriate for business communications.

The independence Ericka has shown, paired with her strong intellectual curiosity, should serve her well in her library career. I am pleased to recommend Ericka to you, and I look forward to hearing about her successes.

> A polite closing should be followed by a signature as well as your typed name and title, if applicable.

Sincerely,

Kim Adams

Kim Adams
Head Children's Librarian

350 • Workplace Writing

TOPIC BANK

To write a business letter that accomplishes your goals, choose a manageable and appropriate issue. If you're having trouble deciding on your own topic, consider these possibilities:

1. **Letter to an Author** Write a letter to an author in response to something he or she has written. In the letter, you may comment on the quality of the author's writing or the development of the book's main character or the work's theme.

2. **Community Service Letter** Many young people today have become involved in improving their communities and solving local problems. Think of a way you could help in your community. Then, write a business letter to residents or community officials introducing your idea and inviting their support.

Prewriting Jot down notes about your purpose for writing—what you want to accomplish. Then, gather the facts or statistics to ensure that your audience has the necessary information to respond to your letter. Also, take note of the recipient's name, title, and business address.

Drafting Decide on a format—block or modified block—and begin drafting. Refer to your prewriting notes to be sure you include necessary information.

Revising Review your letter critically. Be sure that you have clearly and briefly introduced yourself and stated your purpose for writing. Also, confirm that the details you've included support your main point and purpose. If not, delete them. Check your use of language, and change any words or phrases that are too informal.

Editing and Proofreading Use the model on the opposite page to check your letter's format. Verify the accuracy and correct spelling of names and addresses. Proofread to correct errors in spelling, grammar, and punctuation.

Publishing If you wrote your letter by hand, type or word-process it before mailing. Use 8 1/2 x 11 inch paper in a neutral color. Make sure to sign your finished letter. Then, fold it neatly and enclose it in an envelope that matches the paper. Apply correct postage, and mail it.

Business Letter • **351**

Choosing a Topic

1. Have students brainstorm for ideas about the sort of people to whom they might write business letters. Suggest that they think about local service providers, magazines, stores, or other businesses with which they interact.

2. Discuss the reasons people write business letters (to complain, to ask questions, to get information, to express opinions, and, within the corporate world, to deliver information or tell others what needs to be done).

3. Have students pick one business from the brainstorming (audience) and combine it with one reason for writing from the discussion (purpose) for their business letter.

Customize for
ESL Students

Suggest that students choose a topic with which they are very familiar, so that their focus is on language, not on worrying about details. They might consider a letter to the maker of a daily-use item or a food product, a company for which a friend or parent works, or an employer for whom they would like to work.

The Writing Process

1. Remind students to apply each writing process step when writing their business letters.

2. Discuss how to find the appropriate person to address by using the library, Internet, or customer service departments.

3. Encourage students to notice how the model letter's purpose is stated in the first sentence. Each paragraph focuses on a specific point that helps support the main purpose. As they revise, encourage students to do the same thing in their own letters.

4. Remind students to be aware of language, style, grammar, and punctuation in their letters.

☑ **ONGOING ASSESSMENT: Monitor and Reinforce**

If you observe that some students are having difficulty completing any of the writing assignments in this chapter, try one of the following options.

Option 1 Suggest that students imitate the models fairly closely, changing only the name of the recipient, name of the company or organization, and perhaps one other item in the piece.	**Option 2** Suggest that students think of any subject or cause that is important to them and freewrite about it. Then have them use the freewriting to help them create a letter to an editor.

Memo

Teaching Resources: Writing Support Transparencies, 16-B

1. Ask students to tell about any memos they may have received or written. If you have any in-school memos, share those in class.

2. Tell students that one difference between a business letter and a memo is that the memo writer usually knows or has something in common with the audience.

3. Point out that, though the structure of a memo is informal (there is no formal address, salutation, or close), the language is still generally formal.

4. Have students examine the sample memo and identify parallels to the business letter. For example, the "TO:" line parallels the addressee.

5. Explain that memos can cover a wide range of business topics, from new employees to rule changes to general information to good news. Audiences will vary, too, from one individual who needs instruction to a general announcement to the whole company.

6. Remind students that a memo is not private. While the writer might have a specific audience in mind, many other readers may see the memo as well. Tell students to keep this in mind as they choose the language and content covered in their memos.

Real-World Connection

Many large companies circulate memos via e-mail. Ask students how the memo's format might be different if it were an e-mail. (E-mail messages appear in a mailbox with a short subject line.) Which line from the model memo would most likely go in the e-mail subject line? (the "RE:" line)

16.2 Memo

What Is a Memorandum?

Accurate communication of information among team members or co-workers is necessary for the successful completion of a task or a project. Memos (memorandums) are one tool colleagues can use to achieve that communication. Memorandums are usually brief letters or messages that offer information or communicate company policy. An effective memo

- communicates pertinent information.
- follows standard memo format to clearly present the topic and date along with names of sender(s) and addressee(s).
- quickly elaborates on the topic line and specifically directs any requested responses.

Model Memo

Angela Schwers heads the Human Resources department for a large bank. In this memo, she clarifies the company's dress code.

> Most memos follow this format: To, From, Date, and Re (Regarding). The memo's topic appears in the " Re:" line.

> Angela uses the company letterhead for a professional appearance and to command respect.

Memo

Global Bank

TO: Global Bank Employees
FROM: Angela Schwers
              Vice President/Director
DATE: April 28, 1999
RE: Casual Business Dress

It has been several years now since we introduced the policy of "casual business attire" on Fridays. Most employees are pleased with this policy, and similar practices appear to be growing within our industry.

The objective of casual dress days is to be comfortable, while still maintaining a professional business environment. Casual businesswear encompasses many looks, but it really means casual clothing that is appropriate for an office environment. It is clothing that allows you to feel comfortable at work, yet always looks neat and professional. Clothing such as casual slacks, polo shirts, sweaters, and casual shoes would be appropriate. To maintain our professional image, we ask that you use discretion when determining what to wear. If you are expected to interact with customers, vendors, authors, or other business guests, you should dress in a manner that is professional and appropriate.

Please use good, professional judgment in selecting your casual business attire. Casual business dress is not an exemption from the Company's neat and appropriate standards of dress. If you have any questions regarding appropriate business attire, please direct them to your manager or your Human Resources representative.

Angela Schwers

> The body of a memo should be brief and informative.

> Most memos are signed to indicate that the contents have been approved by the sender.

352 • Workplace Writing

⏱ TIME AND RESOURCE MANAGER

Resources:
Print: *Writing Support Transparencies,* 16-B
Technology: *Writing and Grammar* Interactive Text, Section 16.2

Using the Full Student Edition	Using the Handbook 🄷
• Read and discuss the memo on p. 352 in class. • Ask students to compare and contrast a memo with a business letter. • Assist students in selecting topics for a memo. • Review the steps in the writing process, and have students apply each step while writing their memos.	• Read and discuss the memo on p. 224 in class. • Ask students to compare and contrast a memo with a business letter. • Assist students in selecting topics for a memo. • Review the steps in the writing process, and have students apply each step while writing their memos.

TOPIC BANK

Choose a topic about which to write a memo. If you're having trouble finding a topic, consider these possibilities:

1. **Memo to Sports Director** In many communities, high-school students play important staff roles in intramural sports programs for children. As a staffer in such a program, write a memo to the regional sports director asking for clarification of program rules.

2. **Memo to Events Committee** Community organizations frequently raise funds through events such as auctions, fairs, and sponsored sporting events. Choose an organization or issue that interests you, and write a memo concerning plans for an upcoming fund-raiser.

Prewriting What would the title line for your memo's topic be? If you cannot easily summarize the topic this way, it's probably too broad for a memo. Think also about your audience's interest and knowledge level. How much do they know? How much do they need to know? Use questions such as *Who? What? When? Where?* and *Why?* to gather necessary details.

Drafting Present your main point as concisely and clearly as possible. Depending on the kind of information you need to communicate, charts or bulleted lists can convey a lot of information in a highly accessible format.

Revising Look to be sure that you have filled in the *TO:, FROM:, DATE:,* and *RE:* lines completely and accurately. Then, review the body of your memo to be sure that you have stated your main idea briefly and clearly. If your memo is long, delete unnecessary information. You might also reformat the information in a numbered or bulleted list for clarity.

Editing and Proofreading Revise inconsistent or confusing formatting. Also, proofread to correct errors in spelling, grammar, and punctuation.

Publishing Memos are useless unless they are shared with others. Print out and distribute your memo to interested peers. As an alternative, publish your memo via e-mail.

Memo • 353

STANDARDIZED TEST PREPARATION WORKSHOP

Vocabulary Standardized test questions may require students to identify words that have more than one meaning. Use the following sample test item to give students practice in this skill.

Which of the words below makes sense in both sentences?

The girls paid the entrance fee and were granted ___ to the movie.

The mayor's ___ of guilt caused him to resign.

A confession

B access

C revelation

D admission

Students should recognize that **D**, *admission,* is the only word that fits both sentences. The other words fit one sentence, but not both.

Résumé

Teaching Resources: Writing Support Transparencies, 16-C

1. Ask students whether they have ever read or written a résumé or shared in someone's experience of writing one.

2. Review the elements of the model résumé. Encourage students to think about the types of things, other than work experience, that might tell an employer what kind of employee they would be (grade point average, scholastic honors, science fairs, outside activities, charity work, tutoring, establishing or running clubs or programs, organizing events).

3. Explain that, while this organization is ideal for someone just getting out of school, organization will change as time goes by. For instance, education will follow work experience once a student has a considerable amount of work experience to show.

4. Point out that the writer doesn't write "I handled" but rather "handled." This phrasing is standard for résumé writing.

5. Emphasize that it is vital to be honest on a résumé. If an employer finds out that someone lied on a résumé, they will not trust them with anything. Also, it often constitutes grounds for dismissal.

Integrating Viewing and Representing Skills

Visual Focus In the résumé model, the name is visually identified as being key information by the use of bold type and a centered position. Point out how capitalization, bold type, and white space are used to highlight important information. The appearance of a résumé affects the impression the reader has of the writer.

Integrating Technology Skills

Point out that this résumé looks clean. Today, employers often use scanners to load résumés into computers for sorting, so having a clean, "scannable" résumé—with no fancy type, italics, or underlining—is vital.

16.3 Résumé

What Is a Résumé?

If you haven't compiled a résumé yet, you will probably need to do so soon. A *résumé* summarizes your educational background, work experiences, pertinent skills, and other employment qualifications. It also tells potential employers how to contact you. An effective résumé

- presents the applicant's name, address, and phone number.
- follows an accepted résumé organization, using labels and headings to guide readers.
- outlines the applicant's educational background, life experiences, and related qualifications using precise and active language.

> Put contact information such as name, address, telephone number, and e-mail address at the top of the résumé.

Model Résumé

With this résumé, college student Jon-Paul hoped to find a full-time job.

> Jon-Paul used heads with capital letters to identify each section of his résumé.

> Entries on a résumé should be brief and to the point, like those on Jon-Paul's.

JON-PAUL CIAMBRA
1234 Greene Street, Apt #3
Columbia, SC 29201

EDUCATION
University of South Carolina, Columbia, SC
Bachelor of Science in Administrative Information Management
Expected: December, 20_ _

SKILLS
Computer Languages: Cobol, HTML
Internet: Dial-Up Networking and most e-mail or WWWeb applications

WORK EXPERIENCE
Fall 1997 — Computer Services Department
University of South Carolina, Columbia, SC
Computer Lab Technician: Assisted students in the use of software and hardware; responded to user questions and problems
1995 – 1998 (summers and breaks) — Gen X Wireless Services
Paramus, NJ
Receivables Management Representative: Handled incoming accounts-receivable calls for cellular phone accounts in the New York, New Jersey, and Connecticut markets; trained and facilitated other representatives

Summer 1999 — P.E.S. Engineering
Charleston, SC
Intern: Designed a customized record management system for the engineers; trained in the data entry department

REFERENCES
Furnished on request

354 • Workplace Writing

⏱ TIME AND RESOURCE MANAGER

Resources:
Print: *Writing Support Transparencies,* 16-C
Technology: *Writing and Grammar* Interactive Text, Section 16.3

Using the Full Student Edition	Using the Handbook Ⓗ
• Read through the résumé on pp. 354–355 in class. • Point out the elements of a résumé. • Read the Topic Bank and have students list suggestions for writing a sample résumé.	• Read through the résumé on pp. 226–227 in class. • Point out the elements of a résumé. • Read the Topic Bank and have students list suggestions for writing a sample résumé.

TOPIC BANK

Create a résumé that emphasizes the ways in which you are unique and special. If you're not sure how to write a résumé, practice with the following assignments:

1. **Résumé for a Job** Is there a job that needs to be done in your family, school, community, or part-time workplace? Define that job, and then write a résumé for the ideal candidate.

2. **Résumé for a Fictional or Historical Job** Find a job from your reading or from historical research that you would like to have. Write your own résumé for that job, using real and imaginary qualifications.

Prewriting Gather information with self-questioning. What skills do I have? Where and when did I use them? You might talk with a family member or friend to jog your memory about informal job experiences, such as tutoring a younger sibling with homework or driving in a carpool.

Drafting Experiment with the organization and design, but once you choose a format, stick with it consistently. Consider opening each job description with a vivid, active verb that describes your efforts. Consult a thesaurus to add variety and precision to these verbs.

Revising Review your organizing priorities, and make sure that your design supports your goals. For example, make sure that your most significant achievements are readily visible. Then, review the information you've provided. Cut out extraneous wording and add important details, if they're lacking.

Editing and Proofreading Verify names and addresses of former employers or educational institutions. If you are working on a computer, print out a copy of your résumé to check for centering, line spacing, and general readability.

Publishing Find out to whom the résumé should be sent. Print out a clean copy on good quality paper. Then, create a cover letter (see the Business Letter on page 350). Use a paper clip to attach the cover letter to your résumé. Mail both in a properly addressed and stamped matching business envelope.

Résumé • 355

Step-by-Step Teaching Guide

Topic Bank

1. After reading the Topic Bank, discuss other possible résumé topics. Students might want to try creating actual résumés based on their own experiences and skills.

2. Elicit discussion about shaping résumé content to suit the job. (For example, if Jon Paul had been more interested in a people-oriented job, like sales, he could have highlighted the relational skills learned in his training positions under the "Skills" heading, rather than just noting technical skills.)

3. Bring in want ads from local papers and have students read them to learn the language of job searching.

Step-by-Step Teaching Guide

The Writing Process

1. Encourage students to use prewriting to organize information. Suggest that they use note cards with different headings: education, work experience, skills, goals, awards, and so on.

2. To begin drafting, students can try different arrangements of the information cards. Remind them to think about their audience. What information is most important to the potential employer?

3. Focus during revision on what should be highlighted, boldfaced, centered, or set in larger print. Urge students to delete anything unrelated to the audience and the purpose.

4. Remind students to be aware of language, style, grammar, and punctuation.

Customize for
Less Advanced Students

Have students suggest three or four jobs that could be filled by most high school students. Write these on the board, and have each student pick one. Form groups by job choice. Ask students in each group to work together to create a general résumé, and then have individuals personalize it for themselves.

☑ **ONGOING ASSESSMENT: Monitor and Reinforce**

If you find that students are having difficulty with ideas for completing a résumé, use one of the following options.

Option 1 Have students work in pairs, asking each other questions about what they've done and what type of work would interest them. Have each student jot down résumé items for their partner. Then, have partners show each other the things that might be included in a résumé.	**Option 2** Direct students to one of the many books that cover the topic of résumé writing in detail, and suggest that they use the "skills" worksheets to uncover skills they might not realize are valuable. (Alternatively, you could supply copies of one of these worksheets.)

Forms and Applications

Teaching Resources: Writing Support Transparencies, 16-D–E; Writing Support Activity Book, 16-1–2

1. Some students may have filled out applications for driver's licenses, jobs, college admission, or scholarships. Encourage them to share their experiences.

2. As students review the bulleted points, ask them to explain further why each point is important. (Examples: A person looking at a job application might get discouraged if the handwriting is illegible. Missing information delays any process and makes a bad impression.)

3. Explain that a fax needs a cover sheet because, unlike e-mail, most faxes do not identify the sender, and there is no "reply" button. If someone doesn't know who sent a fax, or doesn't know the fax number of the sender, it may be impossible for him or her to respond.

4. Point out that, for applications, it is vital that students read directions and determine not only what information is needed, but also what format it should be in (block letters, month or day first for dates, last name first). Also, tell students to be aware of where the information goes—it is not always immediately obvious whether entries should go above or below the direction line, so scan the form for clues.

5. Explain that forms that require signatures are legal contracts. The signer is legally liable to abide by the rules stated or to supply accurate information. There can be serious consequences if one signs such a form without being honest.

16.4 Forms and Applications

What Are Business Forms?

Forms are preprinted documents that contain spaces in which the user enters specific information. Sometimes, forms contain directions or explanations to help users respond accurately. Two common forms in the workplace are **fax cover sheets** and **applications**. An effectively completed form

- is legible and neat so that reviewers can easily read information.
- responds specifically to the information requested by each instruction or heading.
- provides only the requested information.

Model Fax Cover Sheet

A fax (short for facsimile) is an electronically transmitted document. Most faxes are two part: They contain a cover sheet and an accompanying document. Below is an example of a fax cover sheet:

PITTSBURGH SASH & DOOR
2 Kate Street • Pittsburgh, PA 15235
phone 151.773.8600 • fax 151.773.2104
e-mail: PSD@panct.com

PS&D

Fax

FACSIMILE COVER SHEET

DATE: *4/5/20--*

TO: *Marshall Burnett, Clinton Glass*

FAX NUMBER: *860-669-1230*

FAX SOURCE TRANSMISSION NUMBER: *151-773-2104*

FROM: *Rhonda Henebry*

TOTAL NUMBER OF PAGES (including this cover sheet): *3*

REMARKS:

Marshall—We need prices for the window glass in order to submit an important fee proposal. I've attached all the info and specifications you need. Can you get prices to me later today? Please call with questions. Thanks! Rhonda

Fill in fax cover sheets completely, neatly, and accurately. This will ensure that the addressee actually receives the fax transmission.

A brief message tells the recipient what the fax is about and gives other important information.

356 • Workplace Writing

⏱ TIME AND RESOURCE MANAGER

Resources
Print: *Writing Support Transparencies*, 16-D–E; *Writing Support Activity Book*, 16-1–2
Technology: *Writing and Grammar* Interactive Text, Section 16.4

Using the Full Student Edition	Using the Handbook 🄷
• Read Forms and Applications, pp. 356–357, with the entire class.	• Read Forms and Applications, pp. 228–229, with the entire class.
• Using the models, point out the elements of a fax form and an application.	• Using the models, point out the elements of a fax form and an application.
• Review the writing process and ways to apply each step to forms and applications.	• Review the writing process and ways to apply each step to forms and applications.

Model Application

In recent years, colleges and universities around the country have accepted the Common Application. This straightforward form allows high-school students to complete one basic college application form and use it for several institutions. Below is an example:

1999-2000 Common Application

Application for Undergraduate Admission

Member colleges and universities encourage the use of this application. No distinction will be made between it and the college's own form. The accompanying instructions tell you how to complete, copy, and file your application with any one or several of the colleges.

Personal Data
Legal Name: _____Stelk_____ _____Samuel_____ _____Jacob_____ _____ ☐
              Last/Family   First   Middle (complete)   Jr, etc.

Prefer to be called: _Sam_ (nickname) Former Last name(s) if any: _N/A_
                                        For the term beginning: _____
Applying as a ☒ Freshman ☐ Transfer

Permanent home address: _45 Vincent Street_

Eugene   _OR_   _USA_   _97401_
City or Town   State   Country   Zip Code + 4 or Postal Code

E-mail address: _SamJS@gene.com_

Birth date (mm/dd/yy): _1/25/83_ ☒ Citizenship: U.S./dual U.S. citizen
                        If dual, specify other citizenship: _____

☐ U.S. Permanent resident visa. Citizen of: _____ ☐ Other citizenship.

Please specify country: _____

If you are not a U.S. citizen and live in the United States, how long have you been in the country? _____ Visa Type: _____

Possible area(s)of academic concentration/major: _physics_ ☐ Or undecided

Special college or division if applicable: _____

Possible career or professional plans: _teaching_ ☐ Or undecided
Will you be a candidate for financial aid? ☒ Yes ☐ No If yes, the appropriate form(s) was/will be filed on (mm/dd/yy): _10/15/20--_

Callout notes:

Because space is limited, print clearly and neatly in small letters.

If any items do not pertain to your situation, write N/A for "not applicable" in the space provided.

Use a check mark or an X to signal a choice.

To avoid errors, double-check labels before filling in spaces.

Customize for *Spatial Learners*

Have the students examine the visual layout of the fax model. Point out that the fax's important elements should be obvious at a glance. Challenge students to alter the model's visual layout and design their own personal fax cover sheet. Remind them that they must integrate all of the necessary information.

Real-World Connection

College applications are important forms. Encourage students to represent themselves as positively as possible by taking extra care when filling out these and other important applications. Suggest that students make a photocopy of the blank form and write out their answers first on the copy. Urge students to have someone else proofread their drafts. After revising, they can transfer the information to the application. Encourage them to proofread it one last time, to make certain that errors didn't occur during copying.

Integrating Grammar Skills

Abbreviations Point out places in the application where words are abbreviated to save space. Remind students to abbreviate properly. If necessary, review some words that are commonly abbreviated, such as Street (St.), Boulevard (Blvd.), Avenue (Ave.), Post Office Box (P.O.), Rural Route (RR.). For state names, students need to know the correct two-letter abbreviation.

Integrating Workplace Skills

Just like the other forms of workplace writing, prewriting applies when filling out an application. Suggest that students always look over the entire document before they begin. As they read, they should ask these questions: *Will information be written above or below the line? Are check-off boxes located to the left or right of the answer? Is information required that I will have to supply from another source?*

Lesson Objectives

1. To write an e-mail appropriate to audience and purpose.
2. To use technology for aspects of creating, revising, and editing texts
3. To produce legible work that shows accurate spelling and correct use of the conventions of punctuation and capitalization

Step-by-Step Teaching Guide

E-Mail

Teaching Resources: Writing Support Transparencies, 16-F; Writing Support Activity Book, 16-3

1. Ask students whether they have ever sent e-mail. For what reasons do they generally use e-mail?

2. Use Transparency 16-F or direct students' attention to the text and have them read the model e-mail. Ask students how it is similar to and different from other business communication they have studied (formatted like a memo, organized and to the point, relatively short, somewhat less formal).

3. Explain that a common problem with e-mail is that, because people work quickly and casually, there are often several misspelled words and typos. This can interfere with communication. For example, a common typo is to type *not* instead of *now,* and this can make a big difference if the writer wants the reader to take action of some sort.

continued

Critical Viewing

Generalize Students may mention that many people now compose and send messages on a computer instead of sitting down with pen, paper, envelopes, and stamps. The difference in speed and convenience is enormous.

Connected Assignment
E-mail

The pace of communication in today's workplace has gotten faster and faster due to technological innovations. E-mail, short for electronic mail, is an extremely effective workplace writing tool that enables messages and documents to be sent around the world to multiple recipients simultaneously and almost instantaneously. E-mail is composed in a software program and transmitted through a modem over the Internet.

Effective e-mails

• are brief and to the point.

• are simply formatted.

• contain a description of the contents in the Subject line.

Practice composing and sending effective e-mail messages with the help of the suggestions below.

▲ **Critical Viewing** In what ways have computers changed people's lifestyles? **[Generalize]**

MODEL

From:	Leland, Rebecca
Sent:	Friday, March 11, 20_ _
To:	Gandry, Evan; Jackson, Nicola; Parker, Theresa
Subject:	Tuesday's Fund-raiser

Hello!

Only four days left until the "big night," so I'm checking with you to make sure that the arrangements are proceeding according to schedule. In particular, I want to confirm the following:

• Flowers have been ordered.
• The podium and microphone have been requisitioned from facilities.
• Programs have been printed and delivered.

Let me know immediately if you foresee any difficulties ahead.

Thanks.

Rebecca

Prewriting Identify a topic or main message you want to convey in your e-mail. Possible topics include conveying interest in a summer job or asking a research librarian for guidance. Then, think carefully about your audience before writing. How well do you know the recipient? What supporting information, such as your order number, might he or she need in order to respond effectively? Finally, review your e-mail program's format, consulting electronic or printed directions if necessary. Gather necessary information such as e-mail addresses to complete the memo-style address section.

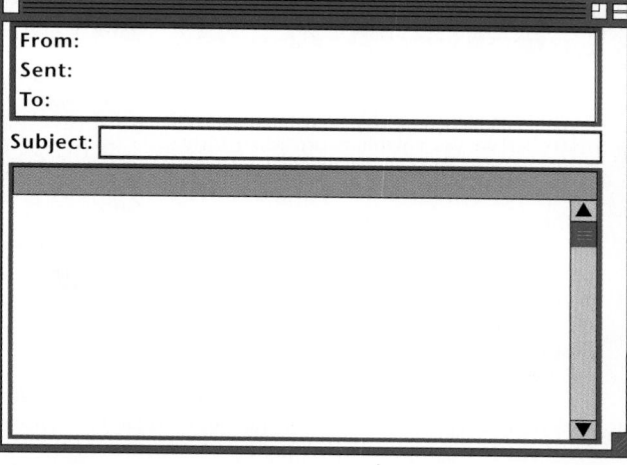

From:
Sent:
To:

Subject:

Drafting Although you'll need to be on-line to send your e-mail, consider drafting off-line to free up your phone line and limit on-line time. After completing the address section, open your letter much as you would a memo or personal note. For example, while you should address business recipients by their full name, you need not insert street addresses. Set a formality level appropriate to the recipient as you develop the letter's message. Keep the formatting simple to avoid translation problems at the receiving computer.

Revising and Editing Reread your letter carefully to be sure that its message is clearly stated. Change inappropriate language to better suit its recipients. Add details where it is lacking, and delete unnecessary information.

Also, check your e-mail for spelling and typographical errors. Use a pencil or your finger on the screen to verify e-mail addresses character by character. One mistake and your communication may come back undelivered.

Publishing and Presenting When you're satisfied with your e-mail message, find and attach any necessary documents. For important correspondence, print out or copy your letter into a desktop folder before sending it. To ensure that your e-mail gets delivered, you may want to click the optional Get Receipt feature from the software program you are using.

4. Point out that reading text onscreen is difficult. As noted in the "Grammar and Style Tip," brevity is helpful. This advice does not simply apply to sentences. In e-mail, paragraphs should be kept fairly short, too, and bulleted points (as in the example) can help, as well.

5. Students may use the form in the activity book or draft their e-mails before entering them on the computer. Alternatively, they may want to draft the body of the e-mail in a word-processing program, and then copy and paste the spell-checked, edited text into the e-mail form.

Customize for
ESL Students

Since the spell checkers on most computers will be set up for American English spelling, some students will not be able to check work if they write in their first language. Hence, they will need to check carefully if they are not writing in English. Encourage students to work with a dictionary near at hand, so that they can check for correctness when the spell-checking program challenges a word they have used.

🌸 Grammar
🌸 and Style Tip

When reading text on screen, shorter and simpler is better. Review the length and complexity of your sentences, and consider shortening and simplifying them to ensure that your message gets across to your readers.

Comparing Art Forms

1. If you are aware of any students being particularly sensitive, you may want to steer them toward the Dali, rather than the Buñuel, whose images can be unsettling, or Lorca, whose plays are generally grim.

2. Have students find a definition of *surrealism* and discuss it in class. Then, have students work individually or in groups to research the Spotlight element of their choice.

3. Encourage interested students to find other artists or writers who represent surrealism. What does their work have in common? What is their message?

4. Reassure students that their ideas for films need not be surrealist. However, encourage them to at least consider how a favorite image, such as a painting or photograph, or favorite piece of writing, perhaps a poem, play, or short story, might inspire ideas for a film writer.

5. Students may wish to work with partners or in small groups to discuss a possible film project and to compose an e-mail describing it.

Viewing and Representing

Activity Have students print out their e-mail movie descriptions, read them aloud, and post them on the classroom bulletin board.

Spotlight on the Humanities

Comparing Art Forms

Focus on Film: Luis Buñuel

Workplace writing skills can be useful no matter what your profession. Most film directors, for example, write memos, scenarios, and directions for setup shots in the course of producing a film. One of the greatest filmmakers of the twentieth century, Spanish film director Luis Buñuel (1900–1983), produced films with a simple narrative behind which he placed powerful on-screen imagery. In the 1960's and 1970's, Buñuel created some of his finest work, including *The Exterminating Angel* (1962), *The Discreet Charm of the Bourgeoisie* (1972), and *The Phantom of Liberty* (1974). *The Discreet Charm of the Bourgeoisie* won the Academy Award for Best Foreign Language Film of 1972.

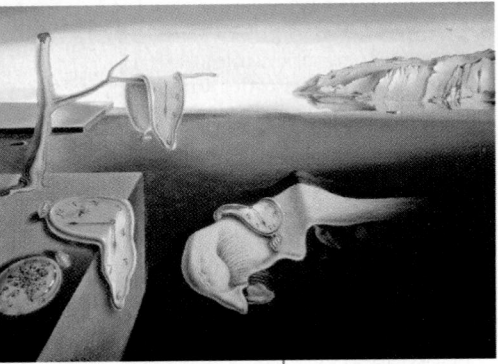

The Persistence of Memory, Salvador Dali

▲ **Critical Viewing** What sort of film might this painting inspire? Why? **[Analyze]**

Art Connection Luis Buñuel collaborated with the Spanish artist Salvador Dali (1904–1989) on the 1928 film *Un Chien Andalou*. Dali's paintings are known for their strong depiction of dream imagery in which daily objects appear in unexpected forms. One of his most famous paintings, *The Persistence of Memory* (1931), shows limp, melting watches falling across the canvas. His later paintings reflect a more classical style. Using bright colors covered with transparent glazes, he is remembered as a master of the Surrealist art movement.

Literature Connection While at the University of Madrid, Luis Buñuel met the most popular poet of the Spanish-speaking world, Federico García Lorca (1898–1936). Lorca lived in Madrid from 1919 to 1934, where he often gave readings of his poems. In 1922, he organized the festival of the "deep song," or *cante jondo*, which was based upon an ancient Gypsy song, and this form heavily influenced his own poetry. Like Buñuel, Lorca's work is filled with startling images.

Workplace Writing Activity: E-mail That "Pitches" a Film

Even artists like filmmakers find workplace writing skills useful as they plan and produce their films. Think of an interesting idea you would like to make into a movie. Then, in an e-mail to a film production company, write a description of the movie, explaining why it would be a success and requesting financial backing.

Critical Viewing

Analyze Answers will vary. Students should note the blend of realistic and surrealistic images in the painting.

Media and Technology Skills

Utilizing Business Technology

Activity: Compile a Technology Glossary

Understanding terminology is crucial when using technology. Whether you are learning to log onto a new computer system, operate a word processor, or search the Internet, you need to be familiar with specialized vocabulary. Creating a technology glossary can help you remember new words and phrases and share your knowledge with others.

Think About It Brainstorm for a list of technology terms. Include both terms you understand and those that confuse you. Keep in mind that your glossary may be used by people with little or no technology experience.

Expand It The best way to expand your list of terms is to work with several different technologies. As you work, add unfamiliar or specialized terms to your list. Find words from at least three of the following technologies:

- **Server:** If your school has access to a server, use this system to store material you have written.
- **Database:** Find information in a database, or prepare a database using your own information.
- **Page Layout Software:** Use the program to design a simple poster, greeting card, or flyer.
- **Graphics Software:** Create an original digital artwork or modify a scanned photograph.

Define It After exploring several technologies, review your list of terms. Write definitions for those you already understand. Use reference sources—such as instruction manuals, books, and the Internet—to find definitions for the other terms. Make sure that your definitions will be understood by someone who has not used the technology.

Organize It Finally, organize your glossary so that it will be easy to use. You might choose alphabetical order or a modified organization in which terms are grouped by category, such as the Internet or graphics, and then alphabetized. Make your final version available to students in your school's computer center.

Some Terms to Consider

Consider adding these terms to your technology glossary:

- bitmap
- cache
- central processing unit (CPU)
- daemon
- desktop
- domain
- e-mail attachment
- firewall
- footer
- footprint
- hardware
- header
- host
- HTML
- hypertext
- ISP
- memory
- menu
- MIME
- monitor
- network
- operating system
- peripheral
- RAM
- shareware
- software
- URL
- utility
- wallpaper

Lesson Objectives

1. To link related information and ideas from a variety of sources
2. To compile information into reports, summaries, and other formats using available technology
3. To use reference material to determine precise meanings and usage

---

Step-by-Step Teaching Guide

Utilizing Business Technology

1. Have students review the suggested terms in the sidebar. Ask students how many of the terms they have seen before.
2. Define and discuss terms that students do not understand.
3. Suggest that, to find additional terms, students check the menus associated with various software or talk to people they know who are computer experts.
4. Divide students into small groups to work on the glossary. Each group might work on terms related to a specific technology. Encourage them to check even terms they think they know, in case there are multiple or newer meanings.
5. Suggest that students check training manuals, "help" functions on computers, or scan the Internet to find definitions, and possibly more terms.
6. Give students ample time to compile their lists and definitions, ask for suggestions about organization of the glossary, and then ask for volunteers to put the list in final form.

Lesson Objectives

1. To produce legible work that shows accurate spelling and correct use of the conventions of punctuation and capitalization

2. To demonstrate control over grammatical elements such as subject-verb agreement and pronoun-antecedent agreement

Step-by-Step Teaching Guide

Applying Usage Rules to Writing

Teaching Resources: Standardized Test Preparation Workbook, pp. 31–32

1. Go over the two sample test items with students, and discuss the explanations for the correct answers. If necessary, review the concepts of subject-verb agreement and the definitions of common and proper nouns.

2. Tell students that the practice tests will measure their ability to use proper verb tenses and subject-verb agreement, as well as their ability to locate spelling, capitalization, and punctuation errors.

3. Assign the two practice items, and go over the answers with students.

Standardized Test Preparation Workshop

Applying Usage Rules to Writing

Writing in the workplace should be error-free and follow the rules of grammar, usage, and mechanics. Standardized tests often measure your ability to recognize errors in grammar, spelling, or punctuation. The following strategies will help you address commonly tested usage problems:

- Check verbs to make sure they agree with their subjects.
- Make sure that verb tense is consistent.
- Look for homophones.
- Check pronoun-antecedent agreement.

Use the following sample test items to practice identifying usage problems.

Test Tip

Read each sentence to yourself several times. Each time, substitute one of the answer choices for the blank. Then, choose the word or group of words that best completes the sentence.

Sample Test Items	Answers and Explanations

Directions: Read the passage, and choose the word or words that belong in each space. Choose the appropriate letter for your answer.
 	
On Friday, Haley and I ___(1)___ to the meeting for the senior banquet.
 	
1 A is going
   B were going
   C was going
   D are going
	The correct answer is *D, are going.* This verb phrase is correct in both tense—present progressive—and number—plural.

Directions: Read each passage, and decide which type of error, if any, appears in each underlined section. Choose the letter for your answer.
 	
Both Haley and Caroline will <u>lead the Work</u>
                           (1)
<u>Group for the banquet.</u>
 	
1 A Spelling error
   B Capitalization error
   C Punctuation error
   D No error
	The correct answer is *B.* The words *work group* are not proper nouns and should not be capitalized.

TEST-TAKING TIP

Emphasize that students need to read test items like these carefully. One way to be sure of a correct answer on a test that measures the ability to use verb tenses correctly is to try out each choice to see whether it makes sense in the sentence. Clues to verb tenses are dates and words that refer to times, such as *when, then,* and *finally.*

When analyzing a passage for punctuation errors, it's important to look for missing punctuation as well as for punctuation that shouldn't appear. Also, remind students that they should look for missing capitalization as well as for words that shouldn't be capitalized but are.

▶ **Practice 1** **Directions:** Read the passage, and choose the word or group of words that belongs in each space. Choose the appropriate letter for your answer.

My first college interview ___(1)___ place last Friday afternoon at Grove University. I ___(2)___ nervous, but my mood ___(3)___ as soon as I entered the room. When I saw the posters for the school hockey team, I ___(4)___ I was in the right place. I then told the interviewer that I loved hockey and ___(5)___ out for the team if accepted to the school.

1 A take
   B have taken
   C took
   D will take

2 F were
   G is
   H was
   J are

3 A change
   B changes
   C changed
   D will change

4 F knew
   G know
   H will know
   J knowing

5 A tried
   B have been trying
   C would be trying
   D try

▶ **Practice 2** **Directions:** Read each passage, and decide which type of error, if any, appears in each underlined section. Choose the letter for your answer.

Our committee must create a Proposal for
                                (1)
the March dance. The first section will

describe the theme of the dance and Marys
                          (2)
plan for decorations. Next, each member

should write a description of his or her role
         (3)
on the comittee. Finally, let's include a
 (4)
description of our overall plan for the
                    (5)
evening.

1 A Spelling error
   B Capitalization error
   C Punctuation error
   D No error

2 F Spelling error
   G Capitalization error
   H Punctuation error
   J No error

3 A Spelling error
   B Capitalization error
   C Punctuation error
   D No error

4 F Spelling error
   G Capitalization error
   H Punctuation error
   J No error

5 A Spelling error
   B Capitalization error
   C Punctuation error
   D No error

Answer Key

▶ **Practice 1**
1. C
2. H
3. C
4. F
5. C

▶ **Practice 2**
1. B (*Proposal* should not be capitalized)
2. H (*Mary's* needs an apostrophe)
3. D
4. F (*committee* is misspelled)
5. D

Customize for
Less Advanced Students

Some students may have difficulty with the format of tests of this type. Be sure they understand that the numbers within the test correspond to the numbers below the test.

Customize for
AP Students

To prepare for a test of this type, students might review past errors on graded papers to see where their weaknesses in grammar, usage, and mechanics lie. They can then brush up on the applicable rules.

▶ *Lesson Objectives*

1. To understand parts of speech and basic sentence patterns and to apply relevant concepts to one's own writing

2. To learn and apply key concepts governing usage of verbs

3. To understand concepts of agreement relating to subjects and verbs and pronouns and antecedents, and to apply this understanding to one's own writing

4. To compose sentences of increasing sophistication and appropriateness

5. To analyze works of literature as models of appropriate and effective English usage

6. To recognize appropriate English usage in one's own reading and writing

7. To use "hands-on" strategies to reinforce understanding of grammar and usage concepts

8. To master the conventions of capitalization, punctuation, and spelling, and to apply them accurately to one's own writing

Waterfront Landscape, 1936, Stuart Davis, National Museum of American Art, Washington, D.C.

PART

2

Grammar, Usage, and Mechanics

Grammar, Usage, and Mechanics • 365

Responding to Fine Art

Waterfront Landscape (1936)
by **Stuart Davis**

Use this artwork to start a discussion about the functions of grammar, usage, and mechanics.

1. You might use the following questions to prompt discussion about the painting:

   How many different items can you see in this basically abstract painting? (Students may cite lamps, tarps, cables, ropes, tethers, rope ladders, tongs, a scale.)

   The title indicates a "waterfront." What parts of a waterfront are suggested? (Students may note a pier or waterfront loading dock; the color blue suggests water.)

   How does the interplay of bright colors and shapes affect you?

2. As dashes, exclamation points, question marks, parentheses, commas, and other elements of punctuation are the "shapes" of grammar, so curves, circles, triangles, and rectangles are the elements of Davis's artistic "grammar." Carrying this analogy forward, students should express how punctuation shows connections and separations among thoughts the way that geometric shapes connect and separate the images in Davis's canvas.

About the Artist

Philadelphia-born Stuart Davis (1894–1964) was among the first American abstract painters. The "hardware" of urbanized 1930's America—billboards, neon lights, boxed office buildings—was the major influence on Davis's style. His paintings seem created from interlocking "cut-outs" of bright colors that feature symbols, straight lines, and sharp points. There is an undeniable influence of the nervous energy of jazz in his work, which some claim was the precursor for the Pop-Art movement of the 1960's.

Time and Resource Manager

In-Depth Lesson Plan

	LESSON FOCUS	PRINT AND MEDIA RESOURCES
DAY 1	**Parts of Speech; Nouns and Pronouns** Students review the eight parts of speech and learn and apply concepts relating to nouns and pronouns. (pp. 368–378/ Ⓗ234–244)	***Writing and Grammar** Interactive Text,* Section 17.1; *On-line Exercise Bank,* Section 17.1 **Teaching Resources** *Grammar Exercise Workbook,* pp. 1–4; *Grammar Exercises Answers on Transparencies,* Ch. 17
DAY 2	**Verbs** Students learn and apply concepts relating to verbs and verb phrases. (pp. 379–385/Ⓗ245–251)	***Writing and Grammar** Interactive Text,* Section 17.2; *On-line Exercise Bank,* Section 17.2 **Teaching Resources** *Grammar Exercise Workbook,* pp. 5–10
DAY 3	**Adjectives and Adverbs** Students learn and apply concepts relating to adjectives and adverbs. (pp. 386–393/Ⓗ252–259)	***Writing and Grammar** Interactive Text,* Section 17.3; *On-line Exercise Bank,* Section 17.3 **Teaching Resources** *Grammar Exercise Workbook,* pp. 11–14
DAY 4	**Prepositions, Conjunctions, and Interjections** Students learn and apply concepts relating to the function of prepositions, conjunctions, and interjections. (pp. 394–405/ Ⓗ260–271)	***Writing and Grammar** Interactive Text,* Sections 17.4–5; *On-line Exercise Bank,* Sections 17.4–5 **Teaching Resources** *Grammar Exercise Workbook,* pp. 15–22; *Hands-on Grammar Activity Book,* Ch. 17
DAY 5	**Review and Assess** Students review the chapter and demonstrate mastery of parts of speech. (pp. 406–407)	**Teaching Resources** *Formal Assessment,* Ch. 17

Accelerated Lesson Plan

	LESSON FOCUS	PRINT AND MEDIA RESOURCES
DAY 1	**Nouns, Pronouns, and Verbs** Students review the eight parts of speech and focus on nouns, pronouns, and verbs, as determined by their performance on the Diagnostic Test. (pp. 368–385/Ⓗ234–251)	***Writing and Grammar** Interactive Text,* Sections 17.1–2; *On-line Exercise Bank,* Sections 17.1–2 **Teaching Resources** *Grammar Exercise Workbook,* pp. 1–10; *Grammar Exercises Answers on Transparencies,* Ch. 17
DAY 2	**Adjectives to Interjections** Students cover adjectives, adverbs, prepositions, conjunctions, and interjections. (pp. 386–405/Ⓗ252–271)	***Writing and Grammar** Interactive Text,* Sections 17.3–5; *On-line Exercise Bank,* Sections 17.3–5 **Teaching Resources** *Grammar Exercise Workbook,* pp. 11–22
DAY 3	**Review and Assess** Students review the chapter and demonstrate mastery of concepts. (pp. 406–407)	**Teaching Resources** *Formal Assessment,* Ch. 17

Options for Adapting Lesson Plans

HOMEWORK

Have students complete any section of the chapter for homework.

FEATURES

Extend coverage with the Grammar in Literature features (pp. 368, 381, 398/Ⓗ234, 247, 264) and the Standardized Test Preparation Workshop (p. 408).

TECHNOLOGY

Students can use *Writing and Grammar* Interactive Text to complete the exercises interactively on computer. They can complete additional exercises in the *On-line Exercise Bank:* The Auto Check feature will grade their work. Go on-line: PHSchool.com Use Web Code: egk-1202

Writing and Grammar Handbook Alignment

Page numbers in Step-by-Step Teaching Guides in this Teacher's Edition refer to pages from the full student text. Handbook page references, indicated with this icon 🄷, are provided in Time and Resource Manager boxes and at the bottom of each Teacher's Edition page.

INTEGRATED SKILLS COVERAGE

Grammar in Literature
SE pp. 368, 381, 398/🄷234, 247, 264

Writing
Integrating Writing, ATE p. 375
Find It in Your Writing, SE pp. 378, 385, 393, 401, 404, 405/
🄷244, 251, 259, 267, 270, 271
Writing Application, SE pp. 378, 385, 393, 401, 405, 407/
🄷244, 251, 259, 267, 271; ATE p. 375

Research
SE p. 380/🄷246

Vocabulary
ATE pp. 370, 371, 376, 382

Spelling
SE p. 397/🄷263; ATE p. 387

Viewing and Representing
Critical Viewing, SE pp. 366, 368, 371, 377, 379, 381, 382, 386, 389, 392, 395, 399, 400, 403/🄷232, 234, 237, 243, 245, 247, 248, 252, 255, 258, 261, 265, 266, 269

Technology
SE pp. 390, 396/🄷256, 262

Real-World Connection
ATE p. 396

ASSESSMENT SUPPORT

Standardized Test Preparation Workshop SE p. 408; ATE p. 372
Standardized Test Preparation Workbook, pp. 33–34
Formal Assessment, Ch. 17

MEETING INDIVIDUAL NEEDS

Less Advanced Students ATE pp. 382, 390, 409. See also Ongoing Assessments ATE pp. 370, 377, 381, 383, 389, 392, 395, 396, 399, 403.
AP Students ATE pp. 369, 390, 409
ESL Students ATE pp. 383, 395
Gifted and Talented Students ATE p. 380
Linguistic Learners ATE pp. 369, 372

BLOCK SCHEDULING

Pacing Suggestions
For 90-minute Blocks
• Administer the Diagnostic Test to students to determine instructional coverage.
• Have students complete necessary exercises in class. Use the Hands-on Grammar activity to provide a change of pace.

Resources for Varying Instruction
• *Writing and Grammar* Interactive Text; *On-line Exercise Bank* A 90-minute block provides an ideal opportunity for students to work on the computer.

Professional Development Support
• *How to Manage Instruction in the Block* This teaching resource provides management and activity suggestions.

MEDIA AND TECHNOLOGY

For the Student
• *Writing and Grammar* Interactive Text, Ch. 17
• *On-line Exercise Bank,* Sections 17.1–5

For the Teacher
• Teacher**EXPRESS** CD-ROM

WRITING AND GRAMMAR ON-LINE

Interactive Text (On-line or on CD-ROM)
• Easily navigable instruction with on-line supporting resources
• Self-scoring exercises and diagnostic tests

Companion Web Site PHSchool.com
• On-line Exercise Bank (use Web Code egk-1202)

See the Go On-line! feature, SE p. iii.

LITERATURE CONNECTIONS

Grammar in Literature selections from *Prentice Hall Literature, Penguin Edition,* The British Tradition:
from "Outside History," Eavan Boland, SE p. 368/🄷234
from *The Tragedy of Macbeth,* William Shakespeare, SE p. 381/🄷247
from "Progress in Personal Comfort," Sydney Smith, SE p. 398/🄷264

▶ **Lesson Objectives**

1. To identify and distinguish among the various types of nouns and pronouns

2. To distinguish among the various types of verbs and to use helping verbs to create verb phrases

3. To identify and use all types of adjectives and adverbs

4. To identify and use prepositions, conjunctions, and interjections

5. To understand that words act as different parts of speech depending on how they are used in a sentence

6. To demonstrate control over grammatical elements

7. To evaluate how well writing achieves its purposes

Critical Viewing

Deduce Student estimates of the number of words in English will vary. The language includes more than 600,000 words. Students are likely to think correctly that the number of words is increasing because new words are constantly being coined to describe new technologies, but remind them to consider the number of words that have fallen out of use.

Chapter 17 The Parts of Speech

There are thousands of words in the English language. Different combinations of these words in sentences can produce almost as many different meanings as there are stars in the sky.

On the other hand, every word in the English language can be assigned to at least one of only eight categories called the *parts of speech*, which are shown in the following chart.

THE EIGHT PARTS OF SPEECH		
nouns	adjectives	prepositions
pronouns	adverbs	conjunctions
verbs		interjections

The meaning of a word and the way it is used in a sentence determines its part of speech. This chapter discusses each of the eight parts of speech.

▲ Critical Viewing The Andromeda Galaxy contains as many as 200 billion stars. How many words do you think there are in the English language? Do you think the number is increasing or decreasing? Why? [Deduce]

366 • The Parts of Speech

✓ ONGOING ASSESSMENT: Diagnose

If students miss more than one item in any category, direct them to the relevant pages of the textbook and assign exercises for practice and review.

Skill Check A	Diagnostic Test Items	Teach	Practice	Section Review	Chapter Review
Nouns		pp. 368–370/ 🄷 234–236	Ex. 1–2	Ex. 6	Ex. 52
Pronouns	A 1–5	pp. 372–375/ 🄷 238–241	Ex. 4–5	Ex. 7–8	Ex. 53
Antecedents	A 1–5	pp. 372–375/ 🄷 238–241	Ex. 3	Ex. 7	Ex. 53
Skill Check B					
Action and Linking Verbs	B 6–10	pp. 379–380/ 🄷 245–246	Ex. 12	Ex. 16	Ex. 54
Transitive and Intransitive Verbs	B 6–10	p. 382/ 🄷 248	Ex. 13–14	Ex. 17	

Diagnostic Test

Directions: Write all answers on a separate sheet of paper.

Skill Check A. Write the pronouns and their antecedents (if any). Then, identify each pronoun as *personal, reflexive, intensive, demonstrative, relative, interrogative,* or *indefinite.*

(1) Which civilizations made the first discoveries about the stars? (2) It is the ancient Egyptians, Babylonians, and Greeks who made contributions to our knowledge of the stars. (3) The Greek astronomer Aristarchus of Samos found himself alone in the belief that the planets revolved around the sun. (4) According to Copernicus, the Earth revolved around the sun and the sun itself was the center of the universe. (5) However, in the eighteenth and nineteenth centuries, others would discover thousands of galaxies beyond this.

Skill Check B. Write the complete verb or verb phrase. Then, write *AV* or *LV* to indicate whether the word is an *action verb* or *linking verb* and *T* or *I* to indicate whether it is *transitive* or *intransitive.*

(6) Scientists classify galaxies by appearance. (7) Elliptical galaxies appear globular and have a bright center. (8) Spiral galaxies look flat. (9) Gravitational pull affects the appearance of irregular galaxies. (10) Large amounts of gas and dust exist in an irregular galaxy, but there are no spiral forms.

Skill Check C. Write the adjectives and adverbs in the following sentences. Beside each, write the word or words it modifies.

(11) Improved telescopes have greatly increased our knowledge. (12) In the 1960's, two British astronomers discovered pulsars. (13) Pulsars are widely believed to be the last stage in a star's life before eventual extinction as a black hole. (14) The Hubble Space Telescope provided very convincing evidence of a black hole's existence. (15) This Earth-orbiting telescope can peer through the deep recesses of space.

Skill Check D. Identify the conjunctions, prepositions, and interjections in the following sentences. Write whether the conjunctions are *coordinating, correlative,* or *subordinating.*

(16) The first images transmitted from the X-ray telescopes of the Chandra X-ray Observatory were of an exploding star. (17) Say, did you know that this star, Cassiopeia A, actually exploded around 300 years ago, but its light is only now reaching the Earth? (18) Not only did they capture a clear, detailed image of a supernova, they also found strong evidence of a black hole near its center. (19) In addition to this, a second image shows a long stream of X-rays jetting from a quasar about 6 billion light-years from Earth. (20) Wow! After I saw those pictures, I certainly felt small and insignificant in regard to my place in the universe.

The Parts of Speech • **367**

Diagnostic Test

Each item in the Diagnostic Test corresponds to a specific section in this chapter. This will enable you to tailor instruction to the particular needs of your students. See "Ongoing Assessment: Diagnose" below for further details. Answers for the Diagnostic Test and all chapter exercises are available in *Grammar Exercises Answers on Transparencies* in your Teaching Resources.

Skill Check A

1. Which–none, interrogative
2. It–none, personal; who–Egyptians, Babylonians, Greeks, relative; our–none, personal
3. himself–Aristarchus, reflexive; that–belief, relative
4. itself–sun, intensive
5. others–none, indefinite; this–none, demonstrative

Skill Check B

6. classify–AV, T
7. appear–LV, I; have–AV, T
8. look–LV, I
9. affects–AV, T
10. exist–AV, I; are–LV, I

Skill Check C

11. ADJS: Improved–telescopes; our–knowledge; ADVS: greatly–have increased
12. ADJS: the–1960s; two, British–astronomers; ADVS: none
13. ADJS: the, last–stage, a, star's–life, eventual–extinction, a, black–hole ADVS: widely–believed
14. ADJS: The–Hubble Space Telescope; convincing–evidence; a–black hole; black hole's existence; ADVS: very–convincing
15. ADJS: This, Earth-orbiting–telescope; the, deep–recesses; ADVS: none

Skill Check D

16. from, of, of–PREP
17. Say–INTJ; that–CONJ, subordinating; but–CONJ, coordinating
18. Not only . . . also–CONJ, correlative; of–PREP; of–PREP, near–PREP
19. In addition to, of, from, about, from–PREP
20. Wow–INTJ; After–CONJ, subordinating; in, to, in–PREP

✓ ONGOING ASSESSMENT: Diagnose *continued*					
Skill Check C	**Diagnostic Test Items**	**Teach**	**Practice**	**Section Review**	**Chapter Review**
Adjectives	C 11–15	pp. 386–389/ ⊞252–255	Ex. 22	Ex.26, 28	Ex. 55
Adverbs	C 11–15	pp. 390–391/ ⊞256–257	Ex. 23–25	Ex. 27–28	
Skill Check D					
Prepositions	D 16–20	pp. 394–396/ ⊞260–262	Ex. 32–33	Ex. 37–38	Ex. 56
Conjunctions	D 16–20	pp. 397–398/ ⊞263–264	Ex. 34–35	Ex. 38	Ex. 57
Interjections	D 16–20	p. 400/ ⊞266	Ex. 36	Ex. 39	
Cumulative Review and Application				Ex. 9–11, 19–21, 29–31, 40–51	Ex. 58–60

Give students one minute to list as many objects and people in the classroom as they can. Then have student volunteers share their answers and place several on the board. Ask students to help you label each noun *concrete* or *abstract*, *singular* or *plural*, *common* or *proper*, *compound*, or *collective*.

Activate Prior Knowledge

Using either the list of nouns generated in the Interest Grabber or one that you provide, have students offer at least one pronoun that could take the place of each noun. Tell them that they will be learning how to differentiate among many types of pronouns. Ask what they remember about the various types of pronouns.

TEACH

Step-by-Step Teaching Guide

Nouns

1. Have a student read aloud the definition of *noun* and ask for examples of nouns that name people, places, and things.

2. As you hear examples of nouns that name people, point out that some are general names such as *girl*, *policeman*, *astronaut*, and some are specific names, or proper nouns, such as *Juanita*, *Mrs. Fine*, *John Glenn*.

3. Ask students to offer examples of common nouns that name places or things (*river, country, school, team*). Then have them name five specific examples of each (*Mississippi River, China, George Washington Middle School, New York Jets*).

Step-by-Step Teaching Guide

Grammar in Literature

1. Have a student read the excerpt from "Outside History" aloud.

2. Draw two columns on the board headed "Concrete Nouns" and "Abstract Nouns." Ask students to place each of the concrete and abstract nouns in the passage into the appropriate column.

Section 17.1 — *Nouns and Pronouns*

Nouns

Nouns constitute the largest category of the parts of speech.

▶ **KEY CONCEPT** A **noun** is the name of a person, place, or thing. ■

The classification of things encompasses visible things, ideas, actions, conditions, and qualities.

VISIBLE THINGS:	crater, rocket, camera
IDEAS:	scholasticism, militarism, evolution
ACTIONS:	exploration, research, ignition
CONDITIONS:	excitement, command, anticipation
QUALITIES:	courage, integrity, ability

Knowing the endings often attached to nouns can help you identify them. Some of the most common noun suffixes are *-dom, -ics, -ion, -ism, -ment, -ness,* and *-ship.*

EXAMPLES:	aeronau*tics*	free*dom*
	cyni*cism*	fu*sion*
	fit*ness*	commit*ment*
	fellow*ship*	

GRAMMAR IN LITERATURE

from Outside History
Eavan Boland

Read the following lines from Eavan Boland's poem. She uses concrete nouns such as light, stars, *and* inklings. These things can be perceived with the sense of sight. She also uses an abstract noun, history.

There are outsiders, always. These stars—
these iron inklings of an Irish January,
whose light happened

thousands of years before
our pain did: they are, they have always been
outside history.

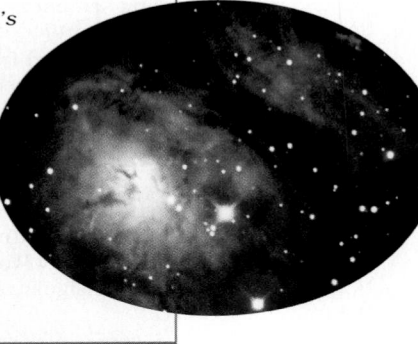

Theme: Stars

In this section, you will learn how to classify nouns and pronouns. You will learn how to identify the antecedents of pronouns. The examples and exercises in this section are about stars and space.

Cross-Curricular Connection: Science

▼ **Critical Viewing**
The Lagoon Nebula is an interstellar cloud in the region of the constellation Sagittarius. What kind of a noun is *nebula?* Think of an adjective that is related. **[Classify]**

More About the Writer

Eavan Boland is a contemporary Irish poet. In her poetry, Boland considers the role of women in the context of Irish history. In an essay, she writes that the literary heritage of a nation is formed from its visible elements and that women are not particularly visible in Ireland. One of her goals is to help change this. The complete text of "Outside History" may be found in *Prentice Hall Literature: Penguin Edition*, The British Tradition.

Critical Viewing

Classify Possible answers: A nebula is a visible thing; *nebula* is a singular concrete noun. Related adjective: *nebulous*.

Concrete and Abstract Nouns

Nouns are sometimes grouped according to the characteristics of the things they name. A *concrete* noun names something that you can physically see, touch, taste, hear, or smell. An *abstract* noun names something that is nonphysical, or that you cannot readily perceive through any of your five senses.

Concrete Nouns	Abstract Nouns
nebula	distance
gas	light-year
scientist	discovery
telescope	infinity

Singular and Plural Nouns

Nouns can indicate number. *Singular* nouns name one person, place, or thing. *Plural* nouns name more than one. Most plural nouns are formed by the addition of *-s* or *-es* to the singular form. Some plural nouns, however, are formed irregularly and must be memorized.

SINGULAR: valley, sky, mouse
PLURAL: valleys, skies, mice

SINGULAR NOUNS	
Regular	Irregular
valley	mouse
lash	ox
sky	nucleus
PLURAL NOUNS	
valleys	mice
lashes	oxen
skies	nuclei

Collective Nouns

Nouns that name *groups* of people or things are called *collective nouns*. Although a collective noun looks singular, its meaning may be either singular or plural depending on how it is used in a sentence.

COLLECTIVE NOUNS	
council	orchestra
delegation	team
entourage	troop

Nouns and Pronouns • **369**

Step-by-Step Teaching Guide

Concrete and Abstract Nouns

1. Point out the difference between a concrete and abstract noun: A concrete noun names something that can be perceived using the five senses. An abstract noun names something that cannot.

2. Use this example:

   You can see a scientist, but you cannot see science.

   Point out that *scientist* is concrete, but *science* is abstract. Ask a student to explain why.

Step-by-Step Teaching Guide

Singular, Plural, and Collective Nouns

1. Point out that most plural nouns are formed by adding *-s* or *-es,* but that some plurals are formed in irregular ways. These need to be memorized.

2. Explain that *jury* is singular if the members of the jury are acting in concert. For example: The *jury has reached* a decision (singular). However, if the members act as individuals, the noun is plural. For example: The *jury have been arguing* among themselves (plural).

Customize for
AP Students

Ask students to classify each underlined word as a concrete or abstract noun and to explain their choices.

Consider a star in space, the gases that make it up, and the distance from it to Earth in light-years.

(*star, Earth,* and *gases* are concrete; *space* and *distance* are abstract)

Customize for
Linguistic Learners

Give students the following terms and ask them to locate and learn the collective noun for each.

ants (colony)	geese (gaggle)
bees (swarm)	monkeys (troop)
lions (pride)	sheep (flock)

⏱ TIME AND RESOURCE MANAGER

Resources
Print: *Grammar Exercise Workbook,* pp. 1–4; *Grammar Exercises Answers on Transparencies,* Ch. 17
Technology: *Writing and Grammar* Interactive Text, Section 17.1; *On-Line Exercise Bank,* Section 17.1

Using the Full Student Edition	Using the Handbook 🖽
• Work through all key concepts, pp. 368–375.	• Work through all key concepts, pp. 234–241.
• Assign and review Exercises 1–5.	• Assign and review Exercises 1–5.
• Read and discuss Grammar in Literature, p. 368.	• Read and discuss Grammar in Literature, p. 234.

Compound Nouns

1. Remind students that compound nouns may appear in three forms: as separate words, as hyphenated words, or as combined words (*space shuttle, space-time, spaceship*).

2. Have students brainstorm for other compound nouns and look in the dictionary to determine the correct spelling of each.

3. Next, have them read the definition of each compound noun and explain how it differs from the meaning of the individual nouns that make it up. For example, an *earmark* is a mark, often placed on the ear of an animal, that shows ownership. This definition is different from the definitions for *ear* and *mark*.

Common and Proper Nouns

1. Explain the difference between *mom* and *Mom*. (Example: "*Mom*, have you talked to Sue's *mom* yet?")

2. Have students offer more examples of nouns used in direct address and as family titles, as shown on the bottom of the student page. If students need a reminder of the capitalization rules for family members and titles, refer them to Chapter 26.

Integrating Vocabulary Skills

Offer a full definition of a noun of direct address: *a noun that names a person being spoken to but that is not part of the basic structure of the sentence.* Give students this example:

Please rake the lawn, George, after you mow the grass.

Point out that *George* is not the subject of either clause: *You* is the understood subject of the first clause; its verb is *rake*. In the dependent clause, *you* is the subject and *mow* is the verb. The words *lawn* and *grass* are direct objects. The proper noun *George* is not a basic sentence part.

17.1

Compound Nouns

A noun that is composed of two or more words acting as a single unit is called a *compound noun*. For example, the noun *space* and the noun *ship* can act together to name a particular object—a *spaceship*.

Compound nouns are usually entered in dictionaries because they name something other than what the individual words suggest. An expression such as *space movie*, on the other hand, is not generally considered a compound noun because it means nothing more than what the two words suggest: "a movie about space."

Compound nouns may appear in three forms: as separate words, as hyphenated words, or as combined words.

COMPOUND NOUNS	
Separated	crab grass, player piano, space shuttle
Hyphenated	jack-in-the-box, light-year, sister-in-law
Combined	dragonfly, eardrum, earthquake

If you are in doubt about the spelling of a compound noun, check a dictionary.

Common and Proper Nouns

All nouns can be categorized as either common or proper. A *common noun* names any one of a class of people, places, or things. A *proper noun* names a specific person, place, or thing.

Common Nouns	Proper Nouns
astronomer	William Herschel, Charles Messier
nation	India, France
building	National Observatory, Taj Mahal

As you can see from these examples, proper nouns are always capitalized, whereas common nouns are not. (See Chapter 26 for rules on capitalization.)

A noun of direct address—the name of a person to whom you are directly speaking—is always a proper noun, as is a family title before a name.

COMMON NOUN: My aunt is a pilot.
DIRECT ADDRESS: Please, Dad, tell us about your spacewalk.
FAMILY TITLE: For years, Aunt Sarah has worked for NASA.

● Grammar ● and Style Tip

Specific dates (*e.g.*, 1994) are also considered nouns.

☑ ONGOING ASSESSMENT: Monitor and Reinforce

If students miss more than two items in Exercise 1 or 2, refer them to the following for additional practice.

In the Textbook	Print Resources	Technology
Section Review Ex. 6, Section 17.1	*Grammar Exercise Workbook*, pp. 1–2	*On-Line Exercise Bank*, Section 17.1

Exercise 1 Identifying the Types of Nouns Copy the following list of nouns. Then, identify each according to whether it (1) names a person, place, or thing, (2) is concrete or abstract, (3) is singular or plural, (4) is collective, (5) is compound, and (6) is common or proper.

EXAMPLE: light
ANSWER: (1) thing, (2) concrete, (3) singular, (4) not collective, (5) not compound, (6) common

1. spacesuit
2. star
3. telescope
4. Alpha Centauri
5. astronomer
6. theory
7. light-year
8. Andromeda
9. universe
10. brown dwarf
11. cluster
12. Dr. Carl Sagan
13. cosmos
14. Milky Way
15. stargazer
16. astronomy
17. supernova
18. Pleiades
19. moonscape
20. system

▼ **Critical Viewing**
The Hubble Space Telescope is seen suspended in space above Earth. What nouns name images the telescope might transmit? [**Speculate**]

Exercise 2 Recognizing Compound Nouns Look up the following expressions. If an expression is in your dictionary, write *compound* and give a brief definition. If an expression is not in your dictionary, simply define the expression from common knowledge.

EXAMPLE: word of honor   solemn promise
ANSWER: compound   oath

1. star tracker
2. star system
3. stellar voyage
4. stellar wind
5. white light
6. white dwarf
7. black light
8. black hole
9. cosmic dimensions
10. cosmic dust

More Practice
Grammar Exercise Workbook
• pp. 1–2
On-line Exercise Bank
• Section 17.1
Go on-line:
PHSchool.com
Enter Web Code:
egk-1202

Textbook

Complete the exercises on-line! Exercises 1 and 2 are available on-line or on CD-ROM.

Integrating Vocabulary Skills

Some nouns, such as the names of certain animals (*bison, deer, sheep, moose*), have the same form in the singular and the plural. Ask students to locate more nouns that do not change form from singular to plural.

Critical Viewing

Speculate Students might list such nouns as *planets, moons, stars, white dwarfs, sunspots, asteroids,* and other extraterrestrial objects.

Answer Key

> **Exercise 1**

1. thing, concrete, singular, compound, common
2. thing, concrete, singular, common
3. thing, concrete, singular, common
4. place or thing, concrete, singular, compound, proper
5. person, concrete, singular, common
6. thing, abstract, singular, common
7. thing, abstract, singular, compound, common
8. place, concrete, singular, proper
9. place, concrete, singular, common
10. thing, concrete, singular, compound, common
11. thing, abstract, singular, common
12. person, concrete, singular, compound, proper
13. thing, concrete, singular or plural, common
14. place or thing, concrete, compound, singular, proper
15. person, concrete, singular, compound, common
16. thing, abstract, singular, common
17. thing, concrete, singular, common
18. place or thing, concrete, plural, collective, proper
19. thing, concrete, singular, compound, common
20. thing, abstract, singular, common

> **Exercise 2**

Answers may vary; samples are given.

1. a telescopic instrument
2. compound, a group of stars
3. a journey through space
4. compound, the flow of plasma ejected from a star's surface into space
5. a spectrum of light
6. compound, a faint, dense star
7. compound, invisible ultraviolet or infrared radiation
8. compound, a theoretical collapsed star with an intense gravitational field
9. vastness
10. compound, fine, solid-matter particles in outer space

⏱ **TIME SAVERS!**

📋 **Answers on Transparencies** Use the *Grammar Exercises Answers on Transparencies* for Chapter 17 to facilitate correction by students.

🖥 **On-Line Exercise Bank** Have students complete the exercises on computer. The Auto Check feature will grade their work for you!

Pronouns

1. Write the following sentences on the board and ask students to revise them.

   Joan's favorite movie was playing near Joan's house. Joan asked Joe if Joe wanted to see it with Joan, and Joe said that Joe would.

2. Have students rewrite the sentences, making any revisions they deem necessary. (They will likely suggest using pronouns such as *she*, *her*, and *he*.) Point out that these words, which take the place of nouns, are called pronouns. If necessary, form equations to demonstrate, such as *Joan's = her, Joan = she, Joe = he.*

3. Remind students that the term *antecedent* refers to the noun that has been replaced by the pronoun.

Customize for
Linguistic Learners

Ask students to describe a scene from a book or movie they recently enjoyed. Have a student offer his or her description orally, and then have him or her do it again, without using any pronouns. Other students can raise their hands if they hear the speaker use a pronoun. This exercise will demonstrate the usefulness of pronouns in everyday conversation.

Personal Pronouns

1. Using the chart on page 373, show students that first- and third-person pronouns change form to show singular and plural.

2. Point out also that some third-person pronouns change form to show gender.

3. Have students write five sentences using personal pronouns. Then have them exchange papers with a partner and label each pronoun first, second, or third person and singular or plural.

17.1

Pronouns

Pronouns help people avoid awkward repetition of nouns.

> **KEY CONCEPT** **Pronouns** are words that stand for nouns or for words that take the place of nouns. ■

In the examples below, the italicized words are pronouns. The arrows point to the words that the pronouns stand for.

EXAMPLES: Michelle and Ken went to the observatory. *They*

thought *it* was the clearest night so far this year.

The words that the arrows point to in the examples are called *antecedents*.

> **KEY CONCEPT** **Antecedents** are nouns (or words that take the place of nouns) for which pronouns stand. ■

Although an antecedent usually precedes its pronoun, it can also follow the pronoun.

EXAMPLE: After their conference, the astronomers went to a party.

There are several kinds of pronouns in English. Most have antecedents; a few do not.

Personal Pronouns

> **KEY CONCEPT** **Personal pronouns** are used to refer to (1) the person speaking, (2) the person spoken to, or (3) the person, place, or thing spoken about. ■

All of the personal pronouns are listed in the chart on the next page. *First-person pronouns* refer to the person speaking; *second-person pronouns* refer to the person spoken to; and *third-person pronouns* refer to the person, place, or thing spoken about. The personal pronouns in the chart that are italicized are sometimes called *possessive pronouns*.

372 • The Parts of Speech

✎ STANDARDIZED TEST PREPARATION WORKSHOP

Grammar and Usage Many standardized tests require students to recognize and correct errors in sentences. Use the following example to demonstrate:

Read the sentence below and choose the answer that shows which revision, if any, is needed.

Have you thought Susan about the consequences of your actions?

A Place a comma after *Susan.*

B Place a comma after *thought.*

C Place commas after *thought* and *Susan.*

D No correction is needed.

The answer is **C** because *Susan* is a noun used in direct address. Because the noun is not part of the structure of the sentence, it should be set off on both sides by commas.

PERSONAL PRONOUNS		
	Singular	Plural
First Person	I, me *my, mine*	we, us *our, ours*
Second Person	you *your, yours*	you *your, yours*
Third Person	he, she, it him, her *his, her, hers, its*	they, them *their, theirs*

The antecedent of a personal pronoun may or may not be directly stated. In the following examples, only the last one has a stated antecedent. In the first two, the antecedents are implied.

FIRST PERSON: *We* read about the origin of the universe.

SECOND PERSON: *You* must submit *your* paper soon.

THIRD PERSON: The technicians ate *their* lunch at noon.

Reflexive and Intensive Pronouns

KEY CONCEPTS **Reflexive pronouns** are used to add information to a sentence by pointing back to a noun or pronoun near the beginning of the sentence. **Intensive pronouns** are used simply to add emphasis to a noun or pronoun. ■

REFLEXIVE: Cosmologists ready themselves for discovery.

INTENSIVE: You yourself agreed with the theory.

REFLEXIVE AND INTENSIVE PRONOUNS		
	Singular	Plural
First Person	myself	ourselves
Second Person	yourself	yourselves
Third Person	himself, herself, itself	themselves

Reflexive and Intensive Pronouns

1. Use the word *intensify* to help students remember the function of intensive pronouns; the pronoun *intensifies*, or stresses, the word it renames.

2. Have students choose two pronouns from the chart and write two sentences for each: one that uses the word as an intensive pronoun and one that uses it as a reflexive pronoun. Have them label each pronoun they use.

Demonstrative Pronouns

1. Tell students to use the word *demonstrate* to remember the function of a demonstrative pronoun: It *demonstrates*, or points out, a particular person, place, or thing.

   You may want to point out to students that demonstrative pronouns become adjectives when they directly precede nouns (*that* book, *this* chair).

2. Have students write a sentence using each of the four demonstrative pronouns in the chart. Caution them that the word *that* may be used as either a relative or a demonstrative pronoun. Use these sentences to demonstrate:

   Here is the book that you gave me. (relative)

   That is the worst book I've ever read! (demonstrative)

   In the first sentence, *that* links, or relates, the information in the subordinate clause (*that you gave me*) to the information in the main clause (*Here is the book*). In the second sentence, *that* points out, or demonstrates, a specific thing.

Relative Pronouns

1. Use the word *relate* to help students understand the function of relative pronouns: They *relate*, or link, one group of words to another within a sentence.

2. Remind students of the definitions of independent and subordinate clauses. An independent clause is a group of words with a subject and a verb that can stand on its own as a complete sentence; a subordinate clause cannot. Subordinate clauses must be linked to independent clauses in order to make sense, and relative pronouns can provide that link.

3. Have students write a sentence using each of the five relative pronouns on this page. Then have them exchange papers with a partner and circle the relative pronouns, underline the independent clauses, and double-underline the subordinate clauses.

17.1

Demonstrative Pronouns

▶ **KEY CONCEPT** A **demonstrative pronoun** is used to point out a specific person, place, or thing. ∎

DEMONSTRATIVE PRONOUNS	
Singular	Plural
this, that	these, those

Demonstrative pronouns may be located before or after their antecedents.

BEFORE: *That* is a newly discovered galaxy.

AFTER: A star to steer by—*this* was all I had.

Relative Pronouns

▶ **KEY CONCEPT** A **relative pronoun** is used to begin a subordinate clause and relate it to another idea in the sentence. ∎

RELATIVE PRONOUNS				
that	which	who	whom	whose

As the following sentences show, the antecedent for a relative pronoun is located in another clause of the sentence. Each relative pronoun links the information in a subordinate clause to a word in an independent clause.

Independent Clause	Subordinate Clause
We began reading *The Cyclops*,	*which* is a play by Euripides.
I wish to thank Sir John Herschel,	to *whom* we are grateful.
The show focused on scientists	*whose* discoveries changed our view of the universe.

374 • The Parts of Speech

Interrogative Pronouns

▶ **KEY CONCEPT** An **interrogative pronoun** is used to begin a direct or indirect question. ■

The five interrogative pronouns are listed in the following chart.

INTERROGATIVE PRONOUNS				
what	which	who	whom	whose

The antecedent for an interrogative pronoun may not always be known, as the first of the following examples illustrates.

DIRECT QUESTION: *What* fell from the sky?

INDIRECT QUESTION: He had two problems. I asked *which* needed to be solved first.

Indefinite Pronouns

▶ **KEY CONCEPT** **Indefinite pronouns** are used to refer to persons, places, or things, often without specifying which ones. ■

NO SPECIFIC ANTECEDENT: *Nobody* was required to clean up, but *many* offered to assist.

SPECIFIC ANTECEDENT: I bought new book covers, but *none* was the right size.

The chart below lists the most commonly used indefinite pronouns.

INDEFINITE PRONOUNS				
Singular			**Plural**	**Singular or Plural**
another	everyone	nothing	both	all
anybody	everything	one	few	any
anyone	little	other	many	more
anything	much	somebody	others	most
each	neither	someone	several	none
either	nobody	something		some
everybody	no one			such

⚙ Grammar and Style Tip

For more on pronouns, see Chapter 22, "Pronoun Usage."

Interrogative Pronouns

1. Ask students whether they know the verb *interrogate* (to question formally), and suggest that they use this definition to help them remember that interrogative pronouns begin questions.

2. Point out that the questions begun by interrogative pronouns may be direct or indirect. Use the following sentences to clarify the difference between direct and indirect questions. (An indirect question is a statement that shows that someone has asked a question. A direct question states the speaker's exact words.)

   Who spoke to you? (direct)

   I asked whom he spoke to. (indirect)

3. Have students study the examples on this page and write two sentences for each interrogative pronoun—one used in a direct question and one in an indirect.

Indefinite Pronouns

1. Point out the difference between an indefinite pronoun and an indefinite adjective. Write this sentence on the board: *Our math teacher gave us another assignment, but he told us we could use either book.* Show students that in *another assignment* and *either book*, *another* and *either* are adjectives modifying nouns; they are not indefinite pronouns. Then demonstrate the same words used as indefinite pronouns: *He assigned us another. I will read either.*

2. Have students choose two of the indefinite pronouns in the chart on page 375 and write two sentences for each: one as an indefinite pronoun and one as an indefinite adjective.

Integrating Writing Skills

Explain the difference between *who* and *whom*: *Who* is nominative and is used as a subject; *whom* is objective and is used as a direct or indirect object or the object of a preposition. Examples:

Who won the game? (nominative, subject)

The game was won by whom? (objective, object of a preposition)

Remind students to be aware of this distinction as they write.

Integrating Vocabulary Skills

Review the definitions of prefixes, suffixes, and word roots. Then have students look up the Latin derivations of the following words:

antecedent	demonstrative
interrogatory	relative
reflexive	intensive

Have them explain how either the derivations or modern meanings help clarify the concepts presented in this section. Based on their answers, point out that the functions of pronouns can be learned from their names. For instance, the Latin *reflectere* (from which the word *reflexive* comes) means "to bend (back)."

Answer Key

Exercise 3

1. one–none
2. them–stars
3. itself–Milky Way
4. which–gases
5. its–a star's surface; these–reactions
6. anybody–none; which–star
7. That–star; which–sun
8. Many–none
9. that–stars; each other–stars; that, their–stars
10. some–binary systems

Exercise 4

Answers will vary. Sample responses:

1. Many
2. I, you
3. us
4. He
5. Which, those

17.1

▶ **Exercise 3** **Identifying Antecedents of Pronouns** Write each underlined pronoun and its antecedent. If a pronoun does not have an antecedent, write *none* after the pronoun. If the pronoun refers to the speaker, write *speaker*. Note that an antecedent may appear in a preceding sentence.

EXAMPLE: I know that a star gets hotter and denser near its core.

ANSWER: I (speaker)   its (star)

1. From the Earth, one can see about 3,000 stars without the assistance of a telescope.
2. However, there are actually hundreds of billions of them within the Milky Way alone.
3. The Milky Way itself is actually only one of hundreds of millions of galaxies in the universe.
4. A star is composed of extremely hot gases such as hydrogen and helium, which are held together by gravity.
5. Beneath its surface, nuclear reactions rumble, and these cause the gases to emit electromagnetic radiation, especially light.
6. Does anybody know which star is nearest?
7. That would be the sun, which is considered a typical star.
8. Many of the stars are actually multiple or binary systems.
9. A binary system comprises two stars that are in close proximity to each other and that orbit around their common center of mass.
10. These usually look like single stars when viewed from Earth, although some can be seen as doubles through a telescope.

▶ **Exercise 4** **Supplying Pronouns** Fill in each blank below with an appropriate pronoun.

1. ___?___ of the stars have been in existence for millions—and, in some cases, billions—of years.
2. ___?___ suspect that it is difficult for ___?___ to imagine that new stars are still forming all across the galaxy.
3. An astronomer told ___?___ that meteors, called "falling stars," are actually burning lumps of metal and rock.
4. ___?___ should write an essay on the formation of meteors.
5. ___?___ of ___?___ stars can be called a supergiant?

▶ **More Practice**

Grammar Exercise Workbook
• pp. 3–4
On-line Exercise Bank
• Section 17.1
  Go on-line:
  PHSchool.com
  Enter Web Code:
  egk-1202

Get instant feedback! Exercises 3, 4, and 5 are available on-line or on CD-ROM.

☑ ONGOING ASSESSMENT: Monitor and Reinforce

If students have difficulty with Exercise 3, 4, or 5, refer them to the following for additional practice.

In the Textbook	Print Resources	Technology
Section Review, Ex. 7–8, Section 17.1	*Grammar Exercise Workbook,* pp. 3–4	*On-Line Exercise Bank,* Section 17.1

Exercise 5 Identifying the Different Types of Pronouns
Identify each underlined pronoun as *personal, reflexive, intensive, demonstrative, relative, interrogative,* or *indefinite.*

EXAMPLE: We sat on the grass and gazed at the stars.
ANSWER: personal

When (1) you walk outside and look up at the stars, do you notice (2) that (3) their brightness often appears to fluctuate? Some of these variable stars change greatly, while (4) others vary only slightly. It can take hours, days, or even years for (5) them to return to their original brightness. All stars, even the sun (6) itself, are variable stars.

The nova, however, varies the most violently and fantastically of (7) all. (8) It may become thousands of times brighter than (9) our sun. The supernova, on the other hand, is an explosion (10) that, for all intents and purposes, marks the end of a star's life. (11) It may be billions of times brighter than the sun but burns out over time. In (12) its wake are left glowing gaseous clouds called nebulae or small stars known as pulsars.

A pulsar emits radio pulses that are so steady, (13) one could set a clock by them. Exactly (14) what are pulsars? Scientists think that (15) they are rotating neutron stars that are up to 10 miles in diameter. (16) This belies the fact, however, that they are among the densest objects known to (17) us.

A star's life generally ends when (18) nothing remains of it to produce energy. When all of their hydrogen is consumed, stars swell up to become red giants, but (19) those, too, do not last. As the high temperature causes fusion of its helium nucleus, a star contracts and becomes denser, and (20) many may ultimately become white dwarfs.

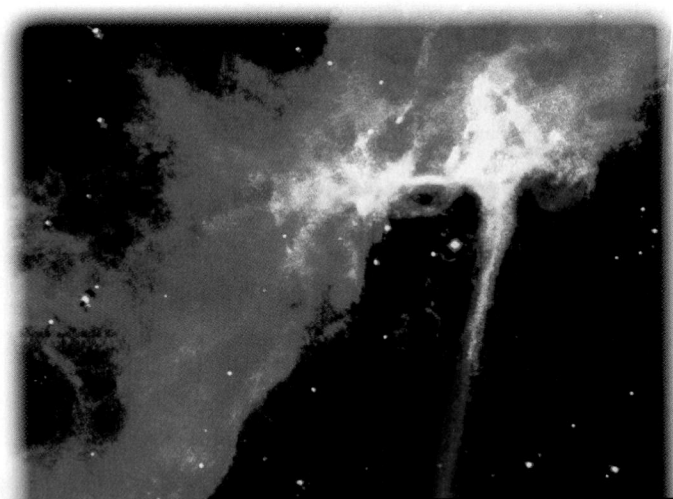

◄ **Critical Viewing**
This supernova, in a picture taken by the Hubble Space Telescope, is part of the Cygnus Loop. Ask three questions about the picture. Begin each question with an interrogative pronoun. **[Connect]**

Nouns and Pronouns • 377

Answer Key

▶ **Exercise 5**

1. personal
2. relative
3. personal
4. indefinite
5. personal
6. intensive
7. indefinite
8. personal
9. personal
10. relative
11. personal
12. personal
13. indefinite
14. interrogative
15. personal
16. demonstrative
17. personal
18. indefinite
19. demonstrative
20. indefinite

Critical Viewing

Connect Possible answers: What is a supernova? Who discovered this one? Which part of the sky holds the constellation Cygnus?

☑ **ONGOING ASSESSMENT: Assess Mastery**

Use the following resources to assess student mastery of nouns and pronouns.

In the Textbook	Technology
Chapter Review, Ex. 52–53	*Writing and Grammar* Interactive Text, Section 17.1, Section Review; *On-Line Exercise Bank,* Section 17.1

⏱ **TIME SAVERS!**

🔳 **Answers on Transparencies**
Use the *Grammar Exercises Answers on Transparencies* for Chapter 17 to facilitate correction by students.

🖥 **On-Line Exercise Bank**
Have students complete the exercises on computer. The Auto Check feature will grade their work for you!

Section Review

Each of these exercises correlates to the instruction on nouns and pronouns, pages 368–375. These exercises may be used for more practice, for reteaching, or for review of the key concepts presented.

Answer Key

Exercise 6

1. abstract, singular, common
2. concrete, singular, compound, proper
3. concrete, singular, compound, common
4. concrete, singular, compound, proper
5. concrete, singular, common
6. concrete, singular, compound, proper
7. concrete, singular, common
8. abstract, plural, compound, common
9. abstract, singular, common
10. concrete, plural, compound, common

Exercise 7

1. What–star
2. That–star or sun; which–sun
3. Its–sun
4. Many–none; it–Alpha Centauri
5. Which–none; these–stars; our–none *or* the speaker

Exercise 8

1. relative
2. personal
3. personal
4. indefinite, personal
5. personal, personal, relative, personal, personal
6. interrogative
7. demonstrative
8. personal
9. relative
10. intensive

Exercise 9

Find It in Your Reading
These = (acts as an adjective)
these = (acts as an adjective)
whose = stars
our = none
they = stars
they = stars

Section 17.1 Section Review

GRAMMAR EXERCISES 6–11

Exercise 6 Identifying the Types of Nouns Identify each noun according to whether it (1) is *concrete* or *abstract*, (2) is *singular* or *plural*, (3) is *collective*, (4) is *compound*, and (5) is *common* or *proper*.

1. magnitude
2. Stephen Hawking
3. cosmic ray
4. Proxima Centauri
5. neighbor
6. Barnard's Star
7. observatory
8. dog days
9. matter
10. sunspots

Exercise 7 Recognizing Antecedents Write each underlined pronoun and its antecedent. If a pronoun does not have an antecedent, write *none* after the pronoun.

1. <u>What</u> is the closest star to the Earth?
2. <u>That</u> is the sun, <u>which</u> helps sustain life on Earth.
3. <u>Its</u> nearest neighboring star system is the Alpha Centauri system.
4. <u>Many</u> say <u>it</u> looks like a single star when viewed with the unaided eye, but Alpha Centauri is really a triple star system.
5. <u>Which</u> of <u>these</u> is <u>our</u> sun's nearest neighbor?

Exercise 8 Identifying Different Types of Pronouns Identify each underlined pronoun in the paragraphs that follow as *personal*, *intensive*, *demonstrative*, *relative*, *interrogative*, or *indefinite*.

The sun is the star (1) <u>that</u> is at the center of (2) <u>our</u> solar system. Because (3) <u>it</u> is so near and is a typical star, (4) <u>many</u> consider <u>it</u> the greatest resource for cosmological study. Over the centuries, (5) <u>we</u> have studied and even worshiped the sun, but <u>it</u> is only relatively recently <u>that we</u> have gained in-depth knowledge about <u>it</u>.

(6) <u>Who</u> were the first people to gain quantitative knowledge about the sun? (7) <u>That</u> would have been Chinese astronomers more than 2,000 years ago. (8) <u>They</u> first reported the discovery of sunspots, (9) <u>which</u> are dark spots on the sun's surface. About 1,900 years later, German physicist Gustav Kirchhoff showed that the sun (10) <u>itself</u> was composed of ordinary matter by studying the light it emitted.

Exercise 9 Find It in Your Reading
Reread the poem in the Grammar in Literature box on page 368. On your paper, write each pronoun and its antecedent. If a pronoun has no antecedent, write *none*.

Exercise 10 Find It in Your Writing Review a short story from your writing portfolio. Check to see that you have used pronouns correctly, and rewrite to clarify antecedents.

Exercise 11 Writing Application Write a description of a typical school week. Use pronouns to avoid repeating the same nouns over and over. Challenge yourself to use each category of pronouns discussed in this section.

Exercise 10

Find It in Your Writing
After students finish, have them circle each pronoun and label it either *personal, reflexive, intensive, demonstrative, relative, interrogative,* or *indefinite*.

Exercise 11

Writing Application
If students need a reminder about the function or purpose of a certain type of pronoun, suggest that they consult their textbooks.

Section 17.2 *Verbs*

Every complete sentence contains at least one verb, which may consist of as many as four words.

▶ **KEY CONCEPT** A **verb** is a word or group of words that expresses time while showing an action, a condition, or the fact that something exists. ■

Action Verbs and Linking Verbs

Action verbs, as their name suggests, express either physical or mental action—that is, what someone or something does, did, or will do. *Linking verbs* serve a more passive function, expressing a condition. Verbs used as linking verbs may also be used simply to show that something does exist.

▶ **KEY CONCEPT** An **action verb** tells what action someone or something is performing. ■

ACTION VERBS: The enemy *attacked.*
                 The soldiers *considered* their position.

In the first example, the verb tells what the enemy did; in the second example, the verb describes a mental action of the soldiers. The person or thing that performs the action is called the *subject* of the verb. *Enemy* is the subject of *attacked. Soldiers* is the subject of *considered.*

▶ **KEY CONCEPT** A **linking verb** connects its subject with a word generally found near the end of the sentence and identifies, renames, or describes the subject. ■

LINKING VERBS: Augustus *was* emperor.

                  Augustus *was* powerful.

In the first example, *emperor* identifies or renames *Augustus.* In the second example, *powerful* describes *Augustus.*

The verb *be* is the most common linking verb. Study the many forms of this verb in the chart at the top of the next page.

Theme: Historic Leaders

In this section, you will learn how to classify verbs. You will learn about linking and action verbs and transitive and intransitive verbs. The examples and exercises in this section are about historic leaders.

Cross-Curricular Connection: Social Studies

▼ **Critical Viewing** Use linking verbs in sentences describing Caesar Augustus as rendered by the sculptor. **[Analyze]**

Verbs • **379**

⏲ **TIME AND RESOURCE MANAGER**

Resources
Print: *Grammar Exercise Workbook,* pp. 5–10; *Grammar Exercises Answers on Transparencies,* Ch. 17
Technology: *Writing and Grammar* Interactive Text, Section 17.2; *On-Line Exercise Bank,* Section 17.2

Using the Full Student Edition	Using the Handbook
• Work through all key concepts, pp. 379–384.	• Work through all key concepts, pp. 245–250.
• Assign and review Exercises 12–15.	• Assign and review Exercises 12–15.
• Read and discuss Grammar in Literature, p. 381.	• Read and discuss Grammar in Literature, p. 247.

PREPARE and ENGAGE

☀ Interest GRABBER Write the following groups of words on the board:

1. *The large house with three chimneys*
2. *The man going into the house*
3. *Go*

Ask students which group of words states a complete idea. Elicit that only number three, which contains the verb *Go* and the understood subject *you,* states a complete idea.

Activate Prior Knowledge

Ask students to recall exciting things they have seen. As students offer examples, place some clauses you hear onto the board, such as "she rode a horse bareback" or "he skied on one ski." When you have written several, ask which word in each best communicates the action. Point out that these action words are verbs.

TEACH

Step-by-Step Teaching Guide

Action and Linking Verbs

1. Ask students to write three sentences that can be used as examples of how verbs change form to show time. Sample sentences:

   He runs home. (present)

   He ran home. (past)

   He will run home. (future)

2. Give examples of verbs showing action, condition, and the existence of something:

   He ran into the street. (*Ran* expresses action.)

   The soup tasted salty. (*Tasted* shows a condition.)

   The desk is in the corner. (*Is* shows that something exists.)

   Ask students for additional examples.

Critical Viewing

Analyze Possible answers: Caesar Augustus looks imposing. His armor is highly decorated. Is the statue bronze?

The Forms of *Be*

1. Explain to students that certain verbs can be either action verbs or linking verbs, depending on how they are used in a sentence. An action verb expresses or describes an action; a linking verb connects the subject with a word in the predicate.

2. Have students decide whether the verbs in the following sentences are action verbs or linking verbs. Remind them that they can replace the verb with *am, are,* or *is,* as explained on page 380, or they can consider the function of the verb in the sentence.

   The air smelled fresh and clean. (linking)

   She smelled the scent of apple pie in the air. (action)

   The students stayed alert throughout the lecture. (linking)

   She stayed on the same topic for two hours! (action)

Customize for
Gifted and Talented Students

Have students rewrite the passage from *Macbeth* on the next page in modern English. Tell them to exchange their passages with a partner, underline all of the verbs, and label them either *action* or *linking*. Students can then compare their passages. Did they use any of the same verbs?

17.2

THE FORMS OF *BE*			
am	am being	can be	have been
are	are being	could be	has been
is	is being	may be	had been
was	was being	might be	could have been
were	were being	must be	may have been
		shall be	might have been
		should be	shall have been
		will be	should have been
		would be	will have been
			would have been

When the forms of *be* act as linking verbs, they express the condition of the subject. Sometimes, however, they may merely express existence, usually by working with other words to show where the subject is located.

EXAMPLES: The queen *is* in the castle.
Alexander's armies *will be* here soon.

Other verbs can also function as linking verbs. The following list shows some of these verbs.

OTHER LINKING VERBS

appear	come	feel	grow	look	remain
seem	smell	sound	stay	taste	turn

EXAMPLES: Before the battle, the soldiers *grew* anxious.

The leader *looked* determined.

Most of these verbs can also serve as action verbs. To determine the function of such a verb, insert *am, are,* or *is* in its place. If the resulting sentence makes sense while linking two words, then the verb is serving as a linking verb.

LINKING VERB: Caesar *looks* busy. (Caesar *is* busy.)
ACTION VERB: The conspirators *looked* for an opportunity.

Research Tip

You can find lists of current and former world leaders in almanacs, which typically are published yearly.

GRAMMAR IN LITERATURE

from **The Tragedy of Macbeth**
William Shakespeare

In the following passage from Macbeth, *the linking verbs are highlighted in blue.*

Good sir, why do you start, and *seem* to fear
Things that *do sound* so fair? I' th' name of truth,
Are you fantastical, or that indeed
Which outwardly ye show? My noble partner
You greet with present grace . . .

◀ **Critical Viewing**
Use three forms of *be* in three sentences about this statue of William Shakespeare. **[Compare]**

> **Exercise 12** Identifying Action and Linking Verbs Identify each underlined verb as an action verb or a linking verb.

EXAMPLE: Conspirators in the Roman senate <u>plotted</u> the assassination of Julius Caesar.

ANSWER: action verb

1. Born into a powerful family, Julius Caesar <u>seemed</u> destined for glory after an early career in public office.
2. His power <u>grew</u> when he formed an alliance with Pompey the Great and Marcus Licinius Crassus in 60 B.C.
3. After several successful foreign campaigns and the death of Crassus, Caesar and Pompey <u>turned</u> against each other in a quest for the ultimate power in Rome.
4. In 48 B.C., Caesar <u>crushed</u> Pompey's armies at Pharsalus, and Pompey himself was later assassinated.
5. It <u>appeared</u> that Caesar was set to assume power, but wary senators assassinated him on the Ides of March in 44 B.C.
6. Rome <u>was</u> filled with turmoil and unrest after his death.
7. The following year, Caesar's grandnephew Octavian, Mark Antony, and Marcus Aemilius Lepidus <u>banded</u> together to defeat the armies of the assassins.
8. Soon, however, Octavian <u>became</u> the first Roman emperor, after successively defeating Antony and then Lepidus.
9. Under Octavian, Rome <u>enjoyed</u> peace and prosperity.
10. Octavian <u>remained</u> emperor for the rest of his days, and in 27 B.C., the Roman senate gave him the name Augustus.

> **More Practice**

Grammar Exercise Workbook
• pp. 5–6
On-line Exercise Bank
• Section 17.2
Go on-line:
PHSchool.com
Enter Web Code:
egk-1202

Get instant feedback!
Exercise 12 is available on-line or on CD-ROM.

Verbs • 381

Step-by-Step Teaching Guide

Grammar in Literature
1. Have one student read the passage aloud.
2. Ask students to identify the action verbs in the selection (*start, show, greet*).
3. Ask students to identify the linking verbs and to indicate the words that they connect.
   seem—links *you* and *to fear*
   do sound—links *things* and *fair*
   are—links *you* and *fantastical*

More About the Writer
Shakespeare's influence on the English language is incalculable. Words such as *accommodation, indistinguishable,* and *premeditated* are only a few of the words that first appeared in his plays. Some of our everyday expressions are Shakespeare's inventions, including *refuse to budge an inch, green-eyed jealousy, tongue-tied, tower of strength,* and *laugh yourself into stitches.*

Critical Viewing
Compare Possible answers: This statue is very old. It might have been an early statue of Shakespeare. Is it being left outside in the weather?

Connections With Literature
Students will find the complete *Macbeth* in *Prentice Hall Literature, Penguin Edition,* The British Tradition.

Answer Key
> **Exercise 12**
1. linking verb   6. linking verb
2. action verb   7. action verb
3. action verb   8. linking verb
4. action verb   9. action verb
5. action verb   10. linking verb

⏱ **TIME SAVERS!**

Answers on Transparencies Use the *Grammar Exercises Answers on Transparencies* for Chapter 17 to facilitate correction by students.

On-Line Exercise Bank Have students complete the exercises on computer. The Auto Check feature will grade their work for you!

☑ **ONGOING ASSESSMENT: Monitor and Reinforce**

If students miss more than two items in Exercise 12, refer them to the following for additional practice.

In the Textbook	Print Resources	Technology
Section Review, Ex. 16, Section 17.2	*Grammar Exercise Workbook,* pp. 5–6	*On-Line Exercise Bank,* Section 17.2

Transitive and Intransitive Verbs

1. Explain to students that the object of the preposition *to* is not the object of a transitive verb. Use this sentence as an example: She wrote *to* the manager.

2. Since a transitive verb is defined as a verb that transfers action to something else, students might think *wrote* transfers action to the manager. However, *manager* is the object of a preposition, so *wrote* is an intransitive verb.

3. Ask students to rewrite the sentence so that *wrote* is a transitive verb. Sample answer: She wrote a letter to the manager. (The action of *wrote* is transferred to *letter*.)

Integrating Vocabulary Skills

Roots Use the word *intransitive* to suggest new words, such as *transit*, *transition*, and *transportation*. Ask students what root these words have in common (*-trans-*, to move across), what each word means, and how the meaning of *-trans-* helps them understand the concept of transitive and intransitive verbs. (The action "moves across" the verb to an object.)

Customize for
Less Advanced Students

Give students more practice in identifying transitive and intransitive verbs. Have each student cut out a magazine article of personal interest. Then have them underline all linking and action verbs and circle each word that receives the action of a verb.

Critical Viewing

Infer Possible answer: *Wears* is a transitive verb because it conveys the action of the subject, *Alexander*, to the direct object, *crown*.

17.2

Transitive and Intransitive Verbs

All verbs can be described as either *transitive* or *intransitive*, depending on whether they transfer action to another word in a sentence.

▶ **KEY CONCEPTS** A verb is transitive if it directs action toward someone or something named in the same sentence. ■

A verb is intransitive if it does not direct action toward someone or something named in the same sentence. ■

The word toward which a transitive verb directs its action is called the *object* of the verb. Intransitive verbs never have objects. You can determine whether a verb has an object and is thus transitive by asking *Whom?* or *What?* after the verb. (See Section 18.3 for more about objects of verbs.)

TRANSITIVE:	OBJ He *wrote* a proclamation. Wrote *what?* Answer: proclamation
	OBJ The general *questioned* the soldier. Questioned *whom?* Answer: soldier
INTRANSITIVE:	The army *marched* south. Marched *what?* Answer: none
	He *fights* for his king. Fights *what?* Answer: none

Notice in the examples that the action of the transitive verbs is done *to* something. The writing is done to the proclamation; the questioning is done to the soldier. The action of the intransitive verbs, however, is just done. Nothing receives it.

Linking verbs, which do not express action, are always intransitive. Most action verbs, however, can be either transitive or intransitive, depending on their use in a sentence. Some are either always transitive or always intransitive.

TRANSITIVE OR INTRANSITIVE:	OBJ The commander *exercised* his authority. He *exercises* before battle.
ALWAYS TRANSITIVE:	OBJ A stone wall *encloses* the village.
ALWAYS INTRANSITIVE:	They *cringed* in fear.

Grammar and Style Tip

Remember: Verbs functioning as linking verbs are always intransitive.

▼ **Critical Viewing** Alexander the Great possessed one of the greatest military minds. In this picture, he wears a crown of laurels. Explain why *wears* is a transitive verb in this sentence. **[Infer]**

☑ **ONGOING ASSESSMENT: Monitor and Reinforce**

If students miss more than two items in Exercise 13 or 14, refer them to the following for additional practice.

In the Textbook	Print Resources	Technology

Section Review, Ex. 17,
   Section 17.2
	Grammar Exercise Workbook,
	   pp. 7–8
		On-Line Exercise Bank,
		   Section 17.2

Exercise 13 Identifying Transitive and Intransitive Verbs

Write the verb or verbs in the following sentences, and label each *transitive* or *intransitive*.

EXAMPLE: Alexander the Great conquered much of the Mediterranean world.

ANSWER: conquered (transitive)

1. Alexander the Great was the son of Philip II, king of Macedonia.
2. The great Greek philosopher Aristotle taught him rhetoric, literature, science, and philosophy.
3. Conspirators assassinated King Philip in 336 B.C.
4. At the young age of twenty, Alexander became the new king.
5. He quickly strengthened his position by quelling revolts at home and in Thessaly and Thebes.
6. His armies marched into Persia in 334 B.C. and defeated the main Persian army at Issus in northeastern Syria.
7. Alexander then traveled south, and by 332 B.C., he controlled much of the Middle East.
8. He next took Egypt and established the city of Alexandria at the mouth of the Nile River.
9. Alexandria quickly grew into the commercial and cultural center of the Greek world, and its culture and language spread throughout the lands.
10. After his armies waged war upon India, Alexander traveled to Babylon, where he contracted a fever and died.

Exercise 14 Using Verbs as Transitive or Intransitive

Write sentences using each of the following verbs. Use the verb as a transitive verb and as an intransitive verb. If the verb can be used only one way, identify that one way.

1. taste
2. fight
3. exist
4. leave
5. include
6. gather
7. encourage
8. march
9. pass
10. diminish
11. remember
12. travel
13. take
14. rise
15. name

▶ **More Practice**

Grammar Exercise Workbook
• pp. 7–8
On-line Exercise Bank
• Section 17.2
Go on-line:
PHSchool.com
Enter Web Code:
egk-1202

Get instant feedback! Exercises 13 and 14 are available on-line or on CD-ROM.

Verbs • **383**

Answer Key

▶ **Exercise 13**

1. was (intransitive)
2. taught (transitive)
3. assassinated (transitive)
4. became (intransitive)
5. strengthened (transitive)
6. marched (intransitive); defeated (transitive)
7. traveled (intransitive); controlled (transitive)
8. took (transitive); established (transitive)
9. grew (intransitive); spread (intransitive)
10. waged (transitive); traveled (intransitive); contracted (transitive); died (intransitive)

▶ **Exercise 14**

Answers will vary. Sample answers:

1a. He tasted the soup.
1b. The soup tastes salty.
2a. The Romans fought the Carthaginians.
2b. She will fight for her rights.
3. Did dodo birds exist in 1800? (Can only be intransitive.)
4a. Where did he leave my books?
4b. Did he leave on the bus?
5. That price includes a keyboard, a monitor, and a modem. (Can only be transitive.)
6a. We will gather flowers.
6b. We will gather at 6:00.
7. My piano teacher encourages me to practice daily. (Can only be transitive.)
8a. He marched his regiment toward the enemy lines.
8b. We marched through the rain.
9a. Please pass the potatoes.
9b. Let's pass through the tunnel.
10a. Well-rooted grass can diminish soil erosion.
10b. The rain will diminish soon.
11a. Do you remember last summer?
11b. I don't remember.
12a. We traveled the roads of Europe.
12b. Did you travel to Scotland?
13a. Can we take a break?
13b. I will take to the road next year.
14. The river is rising toward flood stage. (Can only be intransitive.)
15. Can you name all of the presidents of the United States? (Can only be transitive.)

Customize for
ESL Students

Have students use English dictionaries to help them decide whether the verbs in these exercises are transitive or intransitive. Show them that dictionaries distinguish between transitive and intransitive verbs with the abbreviations *vt* and *vi*. Remind them, though, that many action verbs can be either intransitive or transitive depending on how they are used in a sentence.

Verb Phrases

1. Ask students to explain the difference between a main verb and a helping verb. (Main verbs indicate action or condition, while helpers clarify such things as time and number.)

   Use the example sentences on this page to contrast a single, or main, verb with a verb phrase.

2. Ask students to substitute another verb for *instituted* (*passed*, *implemented*) and to form three verb phrases similar to the model on this page.

3. Point out that verb phrases are sometimes interrupted by other words, usually adverbs. Direct students' attention to the example of interrupted verb phrases on this page. Ask whether they can explain why *probably* and *not* are adverbs. (They are adverbs because they answer the question *To what extent?* about the verb *will institute*.)

Answer Key

▶ **Exercise 15**

Answers may vary; samples are given.

1. was . . . born
2. would have shared
3. Did . . . rule
4. would conquer
5. would have done

17.2

Verb Phrases

When a verb consists of more than one word, it is called a *verb phrase.*

▶ **KEY CONCEPT** A **verb phrase** is a verb with one, two, or three helping verbs before it. ■

Helping verbs, also known as *auxiliary verbs* or *auxiliaries*, add meaning to other verbs.

SINGLE VERB: The nation *instituted* a new law.
VERB PHRASES: The nation *will institute* a new law.
The nation *should have instituted* a new law.
A new law *might have been instituted* by the nation.

Any of the forms of the verb *be* that are listed on page 380 can be used as helping verbs, as can these words listed below.

HELPING VERBS OTHER THAN *BE*

do	have	shall	will	can	may
does	has	should	would	could	might
did	had				must

Verb phrases are often interrupted by other words. To find the complete verb in a sentence, locate the main verb first; then, check for helping verbs that may precede it.

INTERRUPTED
VERB PHRASES: They *will* probably not *institute* a new law.

▶ **Exercise 15** Using Verb Phrases Complete each of the following sentences with an appropriate verb phrase using a form of the verb in parentheses.

EXAMPLE: ___?___ you ___?___ the knight's tales? (hear)
ANSWER: Have you heard the knight's tales?

1. The son of a Frankish king, Charlemagne ___?___ probably ___?___ in Aachen about A.D. 742. (born)
2. King Charlemagne and his brother Carloman ___?___ ___?___ ___?___ power had not Carloman died in A.D. 771. (share)
3. ___?___ Charlemagne ___?___ without his brother? (rule)
4. Over the next 30 years, he ___?___ ___?___ most of Europe. (conquer)
5. His knights were extremely loyal and ___?___ ___?___ ___?___ anything for the glory of their king. (do)

384 • The Parts of Speech

⚲ **Learn More**

For more on verbs, see Chapter 21, "Verb Usage."

▶ **More Practice**

Grammar Exercise Workbook
• pp. 9–10
On-line Exercise Bank
• Section 17.2
  Go on-line:
  PHSchool.com
  Enter Web Code:
  egk-1202

Complete the exercise on-line! Exercise 15 is available on-line or on CD-ROM.

☑ **ONGOING ASSESSMENT: Assess Mastery**

Use the following resources to assess student mastery of verbs.

In the Textbook	Technology
Chapter Review, Ex. 54	*Writing and Grammar* Interactive Text, Section 17.2, Section Review; *On-Line Exercise Bank,* Section 17.2

Section 17.2 Section Review

GRAMMAR EXERCISES 16–21

Exercise 16 Identifying Action and Linking Verbs Identify each of the underlined verbs or verb phrases in the following sentences as either an *action* or a *linking* verb.

1. Born in 1533, Elizabeth I <u>was</u> the daughter of King Henry VIII.
2. After Henry's death, her brother, Edward VI, <u>became</u> king.
3. Edward <u>ruled</u> briefly, and after his death, Mary I <u>ascended</u> to the throne.
4. Elizabeth <u>would have become</u> queen immediately, but Mary was older.
5. Queen Mary I <u>professed</u> Catholicism and had her Protestant sister jailed.

Exercise 17 Identifying Transitive and Intransitive Verbs Write the verbs or verb phrases in the following sentences, and label each *transitive* or *intransitive*.

1. During the French Revolution, Napoleon commanded the French forces.
2. A brilliant general, Napoleon defeated the Austrians in Italy.
3. He returned to France in 1798 and later led a successful coup d'état.
4. After years of successful warfare against the Austrians, peace was declared in 1801.
5. For two years, tranquillity reigned as Napoleon reorganized and simplified the government, courts, and schools.

Exercise 18 Using Verbs in Sentences Write sentences using the verb given as instructed in parentheses.

1. seem (linking verb phrase)
2. smell (action verb)
3. smell (linking verb phrase)
4. write (transitive verb)

5. write (intransitive verb phrase)
6. drive (intransitive verb)
7. drive (transitive verb phrase)
8. grow (linking and action verb phrases)
9. sound (intransitive, linking verb)
10. sound (action, transitive verb phrase)

Exercise 19 Find It in Your Reading Reread the excerpt from "Outside History" by Eavan Boland on page 368. Has Boland used transitive or intransitive verbs? Judging from this example, what differences might you expect to find between poetry that uses primarily transitive verbs and poetry that uses primarily intransitive verbs?

Exercise 20 Find It in Your Writing Review an autobiographical essay from your writing portfolio. In recounting events in your life, have you tended to use more action verbs or linking verbs? How do you think the verbs you use affect your reader? Consider revising your work to include more action verbs.

Exercise 21 Writing Application Draft a college application essay. As you write, monitor the balance of action and linking verbs and transitive and intransitive verbs. Why do you think successful applications tend to be those that make extensive use of action verbs and transitive verbs?

Section Review • 385

Interest GRABBER Write a common noun such as *flower* on the board and ask students to make this word more specific or interesting. Write their better suggestions in a web around *flower* until you have seven or eight (*yellow, very bright, wilted, robust*). Remind students that these words, which modify or slightly change the meaning of other words, are called adjectives and adverbs.

Activate Prior Knowledge

Ask students whether they remember the difference between adjectives and adverbs. Then, using the modifiers from the Interest Grabber or a list that you provide, have them circle each adjective and underline each adverb. Ask them to defend their choices.

TEACH

Step-by-Step Teaching Guide

Adjectives

1. Explain to students that adjectives often appear before the nouns they modify. However, some writers vary the placement of adjectives in order to create different rhythms in their writing. Show students these examples:

   The nervous and excited woman took her baby home from the hospital.

   Nervous and excited, the woman took her baby home from the hospital.

   The woman, nervous and excited, took her baby home from the hospital.

2. Have students choose a paragraph from their portfolios and rewrite it so that some adjectives follow the nouns they modify.

Critical Viewing

Describe Possible answers: *colorful* garden, *carved* basin, *showy* tulips, *dense* foliage, *lovely* sight.

Section 17.3 Adjectives and Adverbs

Adjectives and adverbs are the two parts of speech known as *modifiers*—that is, they slightly change the meaning of other words by adding description or by making them more precise.

Adjectives

An adjective qualifies the meaning of a noun or pronoun by providing information about its appearance, location, and so on.

▶ **KEY CONCEPT** An **adjective** is a word used to describe a noun or pronoun or to give it a more specific meaning. ■

An adjective answers one of four questions about a noun or pronoun: *What kind? Which one? How many?* and *How much?*

EXAMPLES: *green* fields (*What kind* of fields?)
             the *flower* garden (*Which* garden?)
             six roses (*How many* roses?)
             extensive rainfall (*How much* rainfall?)

When an adjective modifies a noun, it usually precedes the noun. Occasionally, though, the adjective may follow the noun.

EXAMPLES: The naturalist was *tactful* about my knowledge.

             I considered the naturalist *tactful*.

An adjective that modifies a pronoun usually follows it. Sometimes, however, the adjective may precede the pronoun.

AFTER: They were *brokenhearted* by the early frost.

BEFORE: *Brokenhearted* by the early frost, they left for Florida.

More than one adjective may modify a single noun or pronoun.

EXAMPLE: We hired a *competent, enthusiastic* gardener.

386 • The Parts of Speech

Theme: Gardens

In this section, you will learn about adjectives and adverbs. The examples and exercises in this section are about gardens.

Cross-Curricular Connection: Science

▲ **Critical Viewing** List five adjectives you would use in a description of this picture. **[Describe]**

⏱ TIME AND RESOURCE MANAGER

Resources
Print: *Grammar Exercise Workbook*, pp. 11–14; *Grammar Exercises Answers on Transparencies*, Ch. 17
Technology: *Writing and Grammar* Interactive Text, Section 17.3; *On-Line Exercise Bank*, Section 17.3

Using the Full Student Edition	Using the Handbook🕮
• Work through all key concepts, pp. 386–391.	• Work through all key concepts, pp. 252–257.
• Assign and review Exercises 22–25.	• Assign and review Exercises 22–25.

Articles

Three common *adjectives*—*a*, *an*, and *the*—are known as *articles*. *A* and *an* are called *indefinite articles* because they refer to any one of a class of nouns. *The* refers to a specific noun and, therefore, is called the *definite article*.

INDEFINITE: *a* daisy
                   an orchid

DEFINITE: *the* stem

Nouns Used as Adjectives

Words that are usually nouns sometimes act as adjectives. In this case, the noun answers the questions *What kind?* or *Which one?* about another noun.

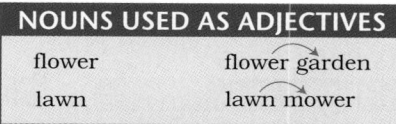

NOUNS USED AS ADJECTIVES	
flower	flower garden
lawn	lawn mower

Proper Adjectives

Adjectives can also be proper. Proper adjectives are proper nouns used as adjectives or adjectives formed from proper nouns. They usually begin with capital letters.

Proper Nouns	Proper Adjectives
Monday	Monday morning
San Francisco	San Francisco streets
Europe	European roses
Rome	Roman hyacinth

Compound Adjectives

Adjectives can be compound. Most are hyphenated; others are combined or are separate words.

HYPHENATED: *rain-forest* plants; *water-soluble* pigments
COMBINED: *airborne* pollen; *evergreen* shrubs
SEPARATED: *North American* rhododendrons

⚙ Grammar and Style Tip

While some adjectives and nouns many seem interchangeable, that is not always the case. For example, *flower* can be both a noun and an adjective, but *flowery* is only an adjective.

Adjectives and Adverbs • **387**

Integrating Spelling Skills

Explain to students that a compound adjective generally does not need to be hyphenated when it follows a noun (*the woman is strong willed*). If the dictionary spells the word with a hyphen, however, it should always be hyphenated (*that hat is up-to-date*).

Pronouns Used as Adjectives

1. Give students practice determining the difference between pronouns used as pronouns and those used as adjectives. Use this example:

   This is the game I bought. (*This* is a pronoun; it is the subject.)

   This game is the one I bought. (*This* is an adjective; it answers the question *Which one?* about the noun *game*.)

2. Tell students that looking at the word after the pronoun provides a clue as to whether the word is used as a pronoun or as an adjective. When pronouns act as adjectives, they always stand directly before the nouns they modify. In the first example, *This* is next to the verb, so it is not an adjective. In the second, *This* is next to *game*, the word it modifies, so it is an adjective.

3. Have students choose three of the pronouns in the chart and write two sentences for each: one with the pronoun used as a pronoun and one with it used as an adjective.

17.3

Pronouns Used as Adjectives

Certain pronouns can also function as adjectives. The seven personal pronouns, known as either *possessive adjectives* or *possessive pronouns*, fill two capacities in a sentence. They act as pronouns because they have antecedents. They also act as adjectives because they modify nouns by answering *Which one?* The other pronouns become adjectives instead of pronouns when they stand before nouns and answer the question *Which one?*

▶ **KEY CONCEPT** A pronoun is used as an adjective if it modifies a noun.■

Possessive pronouns, demonstrative pronouns, interrogative pronouns, and indefinite pronouns can all function as adjectives when they modify nouns. The chart below shows examples of each type.

PRONOUNS USED AS ADJECTIVES

Possessive Pronouns or Adjectives	
my, your, his, her, its, our, their	The bride threw *her* bouquet.
Demonstrative Adjectives	
this, that, these, those	*This* lettuce and *these* dandelions are composite flowers.
Interrogative Adjectives	
which, what, whose	*Which* orchard do you own?
Indefinite Adjectives	
Used with singular nouns: another, each, either, little, much, neither, one	*Each* rose had thorns.
Used with plural nouns: both, few, many, several	*Several* plants bloomed this spring.
Used with singular or plural nouns: all, any, more, most, other, some	Buy *any* fertilizer that you want.
	We appreciate *any* donations.

▶ **More Practice**

Grammar Exercise Workbook
• pp. 11–12
On-line Exercise Bank
• Section 17.3
Go on-line:
PHSchool.com
Enter Web Code:
egk-1202

Verb Forms Used as Adjectives

Verb forms used as adjectives usually end in *-ing* or *-ed* and are called *participles*.

EXAMPLE: I pruned the *wilting* flowers.

Nouns, pronouns, and verb forms function as adjectives only when they modify other nouns or pronouns. The following examples show how their function in a sentence can shift.

	Regular Function	As an Adjective
Noun	The *deck* of the boat tilted.	I sat in the *deck* chair.
Pronoun	*This* was an idyllic life.	*This* life was idyllic.
Verb	I *arranged* the flowers.	The *arranged* flowers were admired.

▶ **Exercise 22** **Identifying Adjectives** Copy each underlined noun or pronoun in the following paragraph, and write all the adjectives, if any, that modify it. Write *none* if the noun or pronoun has no modifiers.

EXAMPLE: Collections of great art treasures have been preserved in many <u>places</u> around the world.

ANSWER: places (many)

(1) <u>Plants</u> are grown for scientific and educational (2) <u>purposes</u> in botanical (3) <u>gardens</u>. Living (4) <u>plants</u> are grown outdoors or in temperature-controlled (5) <u>greenhouses</u> and indoor (6) <u>conservatories</u>. The (7) <u>plants</u> are displayed in systematic, ecological, and geographic (8) <u>arrangements</u>. Rock, water, and wildflower (9) <u>gardens</u> are included at the larger botanical (10) <u>gardens</u>. In ancient (11) <u>Athens</u>, Aristotle founded one of the earliest botanical (12) <u>gardens</u>. Pisa, an Italian (13) <u>city</u>, houses the oldest public botanical (14) <u>gardens</u>. In the sixteenth and seventeenth (15) <u>centuries</u>, curious (16) <u>herbalists</u> cultivated medicinal (17) <u>herbs</u> in private (18) <u>gardens</u> for scientific (19) <u>research</u>. The (20) <u>Chelsea Physic Garden</u> provided research (21) <u>materials</u>. In the (22) <u>United States</u>, an American (23) <u>botanist</u> founded an experimental (24) <u>garden</u> near (25) <u>Philadelphia</u>.

Adjectives and Adverbs • **389**

✿ Grammar and Style Tip

Numbers can also be used as adjectives. In formal writing, numbers are usually written out: *forty* acres or a *dozen* roses.

▼ **Critical Viewing**
Compare this garden with the one pictured on page 386. Which adjectives could be used to describe both? Which adjectives would describe only one? **[Compare and Contrast]**

Step-by-Step Teaching Guide

Adverbs

1. Review the questions that adverbs answer: *Where? When? In what manner? To what extent?* Have students write five examples of adverbs and the words they modify for each category (Where? = sat *down*, ran *around*, went *home*, slept *there*, traveled *everywhere*).

2. Students might have been taught that adverbs end in *-ly*. Point out that while many adverbs do end in *-ly* (*softly, quietly, nearly*), this is not true of all adverbs. Refer them to their answers in step 1 to illustrate this point.

Customize for
Less Advanced Students

Students may have trouble recognizing adverbs that do not end in *-ly.* Remind them that the best way to determine whether a word is an adverb is to ask whether it answers one of the four questions answered by adverbs.

Customize for
AP Students

Have students explore words that are often misused as adjectives and adverbs. Have them use dictionaries to define which word in each pair is an adjective and which is an adverb: *good/well, real/really, clear/clearly, bad/badly,* and *true/truly.* Then, have them write sentences that demonstrate the words' correct uses.

Step-by-Step Teaching Guide

Adverbs as Parts of Verbs

1. Tell students that they can recognize verbs that require an adverb, such as *point out,* because the word has a different meaning without the adverb. *Point out* and *point* are very different actions.

2. Have students think of more examples of adverbs used as parts of verbs. (*take up, run out*)

3. Remind students that in other situations, the adverb remains an adverb:

   She pointed out the right answer. (part of verb)

   She left at noon to take her dog out. (adverb)

Adverbs

Adverbs, like adjectives, describe other words or make other words more specific.

▶ **KEY CONCEPT** An **adverb** is a word that modifies a verb, an adjective, or another adverb. ■

When an adverb modifies a verb, it will answer any one of the following questions: *Where? When? In what way?* or *To what extent?* An adverb answers only one question, however, when modifying an adjective or another adverb: *To what extent?* Because it specifies the degree or intensity of the modified adjective or adverb, such an adverb is often called an *intensifier.*

As the following charts show, the position of an adverb in relation to the word it modifies can vary in a sentence. If the adverb modifies a verb, it may precede or follow it or even interrupt a verb phrase. Normally, adverbs modifying adjectives and adverbs will immediately precede the words they modify.

Adverbs Modifying Verbs	
Where?	**When?**
The plant grew *upward.*	She *never* raked the leaves.
The bushes were planted *there.*	*Later,* we toured the greenhouses.
In what way?	**To what extent?**
He *officially* announced it.	The bees were *still* buzzing.
She was *graciously* helping.	He *always* did it right.
Adverbs Modifying Adjectives	**Adverbs Modifying Adverbs**
To what extent?	**To what extent?**
The solution was *quite* logical.	He worked *very* competently.
It was an *extremely* overgrown garden.	I am *not* completely finished.

Adverbs as Parts of Verbs Some verbs require an adverb to complete their meaning. Adverbs used this way are considered part of the verb. An adverb functioning as part of a verb does not answer the usual questions for adverbs.

EXAMPLE: The tractor *backed up* alongside the field.

Learn More

For more about correctly placing your modifiers within a sentence, see Chapter 24.

Technology Tip

To keep your writing fresh, use your word processor's thesaurus to find new and exciting modifiers.

Exercise 23 Identifying Adverbs Identify the adverb or adverbs in each sentence, and write whether each modifies a verb, another adverb, or an adjective, or whether it is itself part of a verb.

1. Japanese flower arranging is a very ancient art form.
2. Lately, westerners have taken up the practice.
3. It requires an exquisitely balanced sense of form.
4. When I tried it, I ran out of roses.
5. Nonetheless, I was so thrilled with the results.

Nouns Functioning as Adverbs

Several nouns can function as adverbs that answer the questions *Where?* or *When?* Some of these words are *home, yesterday, today, tomorrow, mornings, afternoons, evenings, nights, week, month,* and *year.*

NOUNS USED AS ADVERBS	
Nouns	**As Adverbs**
Evenings are restful times.	I work *evenings.*
My *home* is miles from here.	Let's head *home.*

Adverb or Adjective?

Adverbs usually have different forms from adjectives and thus are easily identified. Many adverbs are formed by the addition of *-ly* to an adjective.

ADJECTIVE: Our professor looked *pensive.*

ADVERB: The professor looked at her notes *pensively.*

Some adjectives, however, also end in *-ly.* Therefore, you cannot assume that every word ending in *-ly* is an adverb.

ADJECTIVES: an *ugly* scene
                     a *nightly* bloom

Some adjectives and adverbs share the same form. You can determine the part of speech of such words by checking their function in the sentence. An adverb will modify a verb, adjective, or adverb; an adjective will modify a noun or pronoun.

ADVERB: The concert ran late.

ADJECTIVE: We enjoyed the late dinners in Spain.

More Practice

Grammar Exercise Workbook
• pp. 13–14
On-line Exercise Bank
• Section 17.3
Go on-line:
PHSchool.com
Enter Web Code:
egk-1202

Get instant feedback! Exercise 23 is available on-line or on CD-ROM.

Adjectives and Adverbs • 391

Answer Key

Exercise 23

1. very–adjective
2. Lately–verb; up–part of verb
3. exquisitely–adjective
4. When–verb; out–part of verb
5. Nonetheless–verb; so–adjective

Step-by-Step Teaching Guide

Nouns Functioning as Adverbs

1. Ask students to explain why *home,* which names a place, can act as an adverb, but other nouns that name places, such as *store* or *park,* cannot.

2. Students should say that *home* does not require a preposition, while the other nouns do. *Let's go home* makes sense but *Let's go store* does not. A preposition such as *to, inside,* or *around* is necessary for this sentence to make sense: *Let's go to the store.* Remind students that the object of a preposition is always a noun or a pronoun; it cannot be an adverb.

Step-by-Step Teaching Guide

Adverb or Adjective?

1. Remind students that the best way to decide whether a word is an adverb or an adjective is not to examine its form, but to determine its function in a sentence.

2. List the following words on the board and ask students to write two sentences for each, one that uses them as adjectives and the other as adverbs. They may change the form of the word, if necessary.

    Example: *open*

    Matt walked through the open door. (adjective)

    The committee discussed the matter openly. (adverb)

    Words: *inside, correct, cool, far, thoughtful*

Answer Key

ASSESS

Section Review

Each of the exercises on page 393 correlates to the instruction on adjectives and adverbs (pages 386–392). These exercises may be used for more practice, for reteaching, or for review of the key concepts presented.

17.3

▶ Exercise 24 Identifying Adverbs Each of the following sentences contains one or more adverbs. Write each adverb, and then write the word or words that it modifies.

EXAMPLE: We sailed the boat all afternoon.
ANSWER: all (afternoon)   afternoon (sailed)

1. Composite flowers are particularly well adapted to semi-arid regions.
2. Their name refers directly to the clusters of small flowers in their compact heads.
3. The flowers are always grouped into an "inflorescence," called the head, that resembles a single flower.
4. The numerous petals effectively make the flower more conspicuous to insects and other pollinators.
5. They are poorly represented in the tropical rain forests.
6. Also, composite flowers are not found on Antarctica, where only two species of grass grow.
7. The composite family contains nearly 10 percent of all flowering plants.
8. Economically, the importance of these plants is quite small.
9. Lettuce is certainly the most important crop, but the family also contains artichokes, endives, and tarragon.
10. Horticulturally important composite flowers include marigolds, daisies, dahlias, and zinnias.

▶ Exercise 25 Revising Sentences by Adding Adverbs Add one adverb from the line below the example to each of the sentences below. Do not use an adverb more than once.

EXAMPLE: People visit botanical gardens.
ANSWER: People *often* visit botanical gardens.

then—later—also—actually—originally

(1) The Royal Botanical Gardens, known as Kew Gardens, are situated on the banks of the River Thames. (2) They consist of two estates, the Richmond Estate and Kew Estate. (3) Augusta, Dowager Princess of Wales, laid out a section of her estate as a botanical garden. (4) The architect Sir William Chambers designed several buildings for the gardens and grounds. (5) When King George III inherited the gardens, Sir Joseph Banks became the unofficial director.

392 • The Parts of Speech

▲ **Critical Viewing**
What adverb would you use to describe how this plant has been cared for? **[Infer]**

Get instant feedback! Exercises 24 and 25 are available on-line or on CD-ROM.

☑ ONGOING ASSESSMENT: Monitor and Reinforce

If students have difficulty with Exercise 24 or 25, refer them to the following for additional practice.

In the Textbook	Print Resources	Technology
Section Review, Ex. 27–28, Section 17.3	*Grammar Exercise Workbook,* pp. 13–14	*On-Line Exercise Bank,* Section 17.3

Section 17.3 Section Review

GRAMMAR EXERCISES 26–31

Exercise 26 Identifying **Adjectives** Write each noun, and list all the adjectives, if any, that modify it. Write *none* if the noun has no adjectives.

1. After visiting the Royal Botanical Gardens in London, a Columbia University botanist decided that New York should possess a similar garden.
2. A site was selected in the northern section of the Bronx.
3. The State Legislature set aside this land for the creation of "a public botanic garden of the highest class."
4. Many prominent civic leaders agreed to contribute funds.
5. At the New York Botanical Gardens, there are 250 acres of floral beauty and hands-on fun.

Exercise 27 Identifying Adverbs Write each adverb, and then write the word or words that it modifies.

1. The New York Botanical Garden has always had a commitment to public education.
2. Today, the garden effectively combines modern technology with traditional scientific research.
3. Its scientists travel extensively around the plant world.
4. They collect data to identify and save already endangered plant species.
5. Almost daily, schoolchildren visit and tour the garden.

Exercise 28 Identifying **Adjectives and Adverbs** Write and label each adjective (except articles) and adverbs in the following paragraph. Then, write the word each modifies.

(1) Gardens in medieval Europe were generally small and enclosed within fortified walls. (2) Castles had a kitchen garden, a private ornamental garden, and a large grassy area for entertaining the entire court. (3) Without the constant threat of war and upheaval, gardens in Renaissance Italy were extensively landscaped areas. (4) The architect designed both the garden and the house, for a harmonious relationship between the inside and outside.

Exercise 29 Find It in Your **Reading** Reread the passage from *Macbeth* in the Grammar in Literature on page 381, and identify the adjectives and adverbs in it. Tell which word is modified by each adjective and adverb you find.

Exercise 30 Find It in Your **Writing** Look through a personal-response piece from your writing portfolio, and find examples of adjective and adverb usage. Challenge yourself to revise at least two sentences to contain a verb form used as an adjective and a noun that functions as an adverb.

Exercise 31 Writing Application Briefly describe a private or public garden in your community. Make sure your descriptions contain examples of nouns, pronouns, and verb forms as adjectives; of nouns used as adverbs; and adverbs functioning as parts of verbs.

Section Review • 393

Answer Key

Exercise 26

1. Royal Botanical Gardens–the; London–none; botanist–a, Columbia University; New York–none; garden–a, similar
2. site–a; section–the, northern; Bronx–the
3. State Legislature–the; land–this; creation–the; garden–a, public, botanic; class–the, highest
4. leaders–many, prominent, civic; funds–none
5. New York Botanical Gardens–the; acres–250; beauty–floral; fun–hands-on

Exercise 27

1. always–has had
2. Today–combines; effectively–combines
3. extensively–travel
4. already–endangered
5. almost–daily; daily–visit, tour

Exercise 28

1. medieval (adj)–Europe; generally (adv)–small, enclosed; small, enclosed (adj)–gardens; fortified (adj)–walls
2. kitchen (adj)–garden; private (adj)–garden; ornamental (adj)–garden; large (adj)–area; grassy (adj)–area; entire (adj)-court
3. constant (adj)–threat; Renaissance (adj)–Italy; extensively (adv)–landscaped; landscaped (adj)–areas
4. harmonious (adj)–relationship

Exercise 29

Find It in Your Reading
Good (adj)–sir; so (adv)–fair; fair (adj)–that; fantastical (adj)–you; indeed (adv)–are; outwardly (adv)–show; noble (adj)–partner; present (adj)–grace

Exercise 30

Find It in Your Writing
If students need to review verbs used as adjectives and nouns used as adverbs, refer them to the relevant pages in this section.

Exercise 31

Writing Application
Encourage students to use only as many modifiers as are needed to clearly convey their ideas.

☑ **ONGOING ASSESSMENT: Assess Mastery**

Use the following resources to assess student mastery of adjectives and adverbs.

In the Textbook	Technology
Chapter Review, Ex. 55	*On-Line Exercise Bank,* Section 17.3

The lioness waited in the tall grass.

The lioness peered through the trees.

Ask students for their answers and write some of them on the board, circling all conjunctions. Remind students that conjunctions are used to connect words or groups of words.

Activate Prior Knowledge

Write the following questions on the board and ask students to answer each with a phrase that indicates location:

Where do you keep your shoes at home?

Where do you do your homework?

Where is your best friend's house?

As students offer their answers, write the phrases on the board and underline the prepositions. (<u>under</u> the bed, <u>in</u> my room, <u>around</u> the corner) Point out that these words are prepositions and prepositional phrases. Ask students whether they remember the definition of a preposition.

TEACH

Step-by-Step Teaching Guide

Prepositions

1. Use the following examples to show students the various types of relationships that prepositions can show. Have them add at least one example to each category.

   Location *(underneath, beside)*

   Direction *(toward, away from)*

   Time *(during, after)*

   Cause *(instead of, because of)*

   Possession *(with, together with)*

2. Point out that some prepositions are made up of more than one word. Have students locate the examples in the chart on page 395. Explain that those prepositions function exactly as single-word prepositions do.

Section 17.4

Prepositions, Conjunctions, and Interjections

Two of the final three parts of speech—prepositions and conjunctions—function in sentences as connectors. *Prepositions* express relationships between words or ideas, whereas *conjunctions* join words, groups of words, or even entire sentences. The last part of speech, *interjections*, functions by itself, independent of other words in a sentence.

Prepositions and Prepositional Phrases

Prepositions make it possible to show relationships between words. The relationships shown may involve, for example, location, direction, time, cause, or possession.

▶ **KEY CONCEPT** A **preposition** relates the noun or pronoun that appears with it to another word in the sentence. ■ See how the prepositions below relate to the italicized words.

LOCATION: Inventions *are made* around the *world*.

DIRECTION: Small discoveries *lead* toward new *inventions*.

TIME: Some inventions *last* for *centuries*.

CAUSE: People *invent* because of their *curiosity*.

POSSESSION: *Changes* from new *inventions* help many people.

▶ **KEY CONCEPT** A **prepositional phrase** is a group of words that includes a preposition and a noun or pronoun. ■

The noun or pronoun with a preposition is called the *object of the preposition*. Objects may have one or more modifiers. A prepositional phrase may also have more than one object.

EXAMPLES: Alexander Graham Bell and Elisha Gray applied
for telephone patents *on* the same day.

During his lifetime, Bell resided *in* Scotland and Canada.

Theme: Inventions

In this section, you will learn about prepositions, conjunctions, and interjections. The examples and exercises in this section are about inventors and inventions.

Cross-Curricular Connection: Science

⏱ TIME AND RESOURCE MANAGER

Resources
Print: *Grammar Exercise Workbook,* pp. 15–20; *Grammar Exercises Answers on Transparencies,* Ch. 17
Technology: *Writing and Grammar* Interactive Text, Section 17.4; *On-Line Exercise Bank,* Section 17.4

Using the Full Student Edition	Using the Handbook Ⓗ
• Work through all key concepts, pp. 394–400.	• Work through all key concepts, pp. 260–266.
• Assign and review Exercises 32–36.	• Assign and review Exercises 32–36.
• Read and discuss Grammar in Literature, p. 398.	• Read and discuss Grammar in Literature, p. 264.

PREPOSITIONS

aboard	before	in front of	over
about	behind	in place of	owing to
above	below	in regard to	past
according to	beneath	inside	prior to
across from	beside	in spite of	regarding
across	besides	instead of	round
after	between	into	since
against	beyond	in view of	through
ahead of	but	like	throughout
along	by	near	till
alongside	by means of	nearby	to
along with	concerning	next to	together with
amid	considering	of	toward
among	despite	off	under
apart from	down	on	underneath
around	during	on account of	until
aside from	except	onto	unto
as of	for	on top of	up
at	from	opposite	upon
atop	in	out	with
barring	in addition to	out of	within
because of	in back of	outside	without

▶ **Exercise 32** Identifying Prepositional Phrases Write the prepositional phrases in the following paragraph, and circle each preposition. If there are no prepositional phrases, write *none*.

EXAMPLE: The Machine Age began with the Industrial Revolution and continues to this day.

ANSWER: (with) the Industrial Revolution; (to) this day

(1) At the time, Thomas Edison was selling newspapers on the Grand Trunk Railway. (2) From a freight car, he started publishing a weekly newspaper called the *Grand Trunk Herald*. (3) After he saved the life of a child, Edison was taught telegraphy by the child's father. (4) Then, Edison made his first important invention, a telegraphic repeating instrument. (5) It could transmit messages over a second line without an operator.

More Practice

Grammar Exercise
Workbook
• pp. 15–16
On-line Exercise Bank
• Section 17.4
Go on-line:
PHSchool.com
Enter Web Code:
egk-1202

interactive Textbook

Get instant feedback! Exercise 32 is available on-line or on CD-ROM.

▼ Critical Viewing
Describe the clutter in Thomas Edison's office. What prepositions would you use? [Analyze]

Prepositions, Conjunctions, and Interjections • 395

Prepositional Phrases

1. Tell students that although a prepositional phrase can consist of as few as two words, it is often longer because of the addition of words to modify the object of the preposition. Use this example to illustrate this idea:

   above ground

   above the ground

   above the frozen, dangerous ground

2. Remind students that the object of a preposition must be a noun or pronoun. In all three examples above, the object of *above* is *ground*. *The*, *frozen*, and *dangerous* are words that modify the object; however, they are not considered part of the object.

Customize for
ESL Students

Have students draw simple diagrams that illustrate prepositions that show location. Alongside each drawing, have students write the prepositional phrase it illustrates.

The book is (1) on the table

(2) under the table

(3) alongside the table

Answer Key

▶ Exercise 32

Prepositions are underlined.

1. At the time; on the Grand Trunk Railway
2. From a freight car
3. of a child
4. none
5. over a second line; without an operator

Critical Viewing

Analyze Possible answers: behind Edison, on the desk, on top of the roll-top desk, in the pigeonholes of the desk

---

If students miss more than one item in Exercise 32, refer them to the following for additional practice.

In the Textbook	Print Resources	Technology
Section Review, Ex. 37, Section 17.4	*Grammar Exercise Workbook*, pp. 15–16	*On-Line Exercise Bank*, Section 17.4

Preposition or Adverb?

1. Remind students that prepositions are never used alone; they are always followed by a noun or pronoun that acts as the object of the preposition. If a word that seems to be a preposition does not have an object, it is probably acting as an adverb.

2. Give students the following prepositions and have them write a sentence with each one. Then have them exchange papers with a partner, circle each preposition, and label it *P* if it acts as a preposition or *A* if it acts as an adverb.

   Prepositions: *around, down, in, off, on, out, over, up*

Real-World Connection

In many social and work situations, people need to direct others—to give directions, clarify locations, or express conditions. Perhaps more than any other part of speech, the preposition helps direct the traffic of ideas. Present this concept to students and ask them to suggest situations in which the right prepositions are needed for precision in directing others. Examples: providing directions for lost tourists, directing furniture movers, peer-editing writing for classmates.

Answer Key

> **Exercise 33**

1. adverb
2. preposition–public
3. preposition–cylinder
4. preposition–exhibition
5. preposition–perfection
6. preposition–improvement
7. adverb
8. adverb
9. adverb
10. preposition–succession

17.4

Preposition or Adverb?

Because prepositions and adverbs occasionally take the same form, they may be difficult to tell apart. Words that can function in either role include *around, before, behind, down, in, off, on, out, over,* and *up.* To determine the part of speech of these words, see whether an object accompanies the word. If so, the word is used as a preposition.

PREPOSITION: The Machine Age developed *around a*
                                                    OBJ
                       group of inventions.

ADVERB: My thoughts went *around* and *around.*

▶ **Exercise 33** Distinguishing Between Prepositions and Adverbs Identify the underlined word in each sentence as either a *preposition* or an *adverb.* If the word is a preposition, write its object on your paper as well.

EXAMPLE: They are waiting <u>near</u> the door.
ANSWER: preposition (door)

1. After Edison set up his own laboratory, his successful inventions took <u>off</u>.
2. In 1877, Edison announced <u>to</u> the public his invention of a phonograph.
3. Sound could be recorded <u>on</u> a tinfoil cylinder.
4. The incandescent electric light was ready <u>for</u> exhibition two years later.
5. <u>Before</u> its perfection, it required careful research and extensive experimentation.
6. He occupied himself <u>with</u> the improvement of the bulbs.
7. Edison <u>next</u> developed the first central electric-power station.
8. He experimented early with direct current, which was left <u>behind</u> when other inventors developed the alternating current system.
9. Later, he moved away <u>from</u> Menlo Park to West Orange, New Jersey.
10. In 1888, he invented the kinetoscope, which produced motion pictures <u>by</u> a succession of individual views.

396 • The Parts of Speech

🖥 Internet Tip

To find information about other inventions, use Internet search words like *inventions, patents,* and *Industrial Age.*

▶ **More Practice**

Grammar Exercise Workbook
• pp. 15–16
On-line Exercise Bank
• Section 17.4
  Go on-line:
  PHSchool.com
  Enter Web Code:
  egk-1202

Get instant feedback! Exercise 33 is available on-line or on CD-ROM.

☑ **ONGOING ASSESSMENT: Monitor and Reinforce**

If students miss more than two items in Exercise 33, refer them to the following for additional practice.

In the Textbook	Print Resources	Technology
Section Review, Ex. 38, Section 17.4	*Grammar Exercise Workbook,* pp. 15–16	*On-Line Exercise Bank,* Section 17.4

Conjunctions

There are three main kinds of conjunctions: *coordinating, correlative,* and *subordinating.* Sometimes a kind of adverb, the conjunctive adverb, is also considered a conjunction.

▶ **KEY CONCEPT** A **conjunction** is a word used to connect other words or groups of words. ■

Coordinating Conjunctions The seven coordinating conjunctions are used to connect similar parts of speech or groups of words of equal grammatical weight.

COORDINATING CONJUNCTIONS						
and	but	for	nor	or	so	yet

Correlative Conjunctions The five paired correlative conjunctions join elements of equal grammatical weight.

CORRELATIVE CONJUNCTIONS		
both . . . and	either . . . or	neither . . . nor
not only . . . but also	whether . . . or	

Subordinating Conjunctions Subordinating conjunctions join two complete ideas by making one of the ideas subordinate to or dependent upon the other.

SUBORDINATING CONJUNCTIONS			
after	because	lest	till
although	before	now that	unless
as	even if	provided	until
as if	even though	since	when
as long as	how	so that	whenever
as much as	if	than	where
as soon as	inasmuch as	that	wherever
as though	in order that	though	while

The subordinate idea in a sentence always begins with a subordinating conjunction and makes up what is known as a subordinate clause. A subordinate clause may either follow or precede the main idea in a sentence.

🖋 Spelling Tip

Be careful when writing some subordinating conjunctions. Words like *inasmuch* are written without spaces, but other words, like *as much as,* do have spaces.

Step-by-Step Teaching Guide

Coordinating Conjunctions

1. Remind students that conjunctions can join many types of words or groups of words:

   Nouns and Pronouns: *She and her friends attended the lecture.*

   Verbs: *Our dog whined and scratched at the door.*

   Adjectives: *The steak was tender, large, and tasteless.*

   Adverbs: *The man responded quickly and truthfully.*

   Prepositional Phrases: *I will go to Greece or to Spain.*

   Complete Ideas: *He seemed distressed, so we discussed his problem.*

2. Review the examples above and have students offer one more example for each. Point out that when a coordinating conjunction connects two complete ideas, it must be preceded by a comma.

Step-by-Step Teaching Guide

Correlative and Subordinating Conjunctions

1. Show students that, even though they are made up of more than one word, correlative conjunctions act like coordinating conjunctions in that they connect words of equal grammatical weight.

2. Review the definition of a subordinate clause. It is a group of words with a subject and verb that cannot stand on its own.

3. Ask students to write sentences of their own using some of the subordinating conjunctions in the chart.

Language Highlight

The word *conjunction* comes from the Latin words *con-* (with) and *jugare* (to join or marry). This combination helps create the modern meaning: "a joining together." Ask students to think of other words with one or both of these roots.

Conjunctive Adverbs

1. Ask students to define some of the words in the chart on this page. Examples: *consequently* means "as a result," *however* means "on the other hand," *therefore* means "in summary" or "as a result."

2. Have students write sentences using some of the conjunctive adverbs in the chart. When they finish, have students trade papers with a partner and make sure that all conjunctive adverbs are punctuated correctly.

Grammar in Literature

1. Have a volunteer read aloud the excerpt from "Progress in Personal Comfort."

2. Ask students to eliminate all the coordinating conjunctions from the passage. Then, have them express the same ideas in other ways. They might replace the coordinating conjunctions with commas, or they might separate longer sentences into a series of shorter ones.

3. Have students read this new version aloud to a partner. Ask them to discuss how the writing changes when the conjunctions are omitted. (Students might say that the writing becomes more choppy and that related ideas are not linked very clearly.)

More About the Writer

Born in 1771, Sydney Smith was a clergyman and writer who helped found the *Edinburgh Review*, a literary magazine. He later gained fame as a preacher, a lecturer, and an admired wit. His writings include a series of articles printed in the *Edinburgh Review* and later republished for English audiences. Smith was known for his belief in religious tolerance and for championing the rights of the oppressed.

Connections With Literature

Students can find Sydney Smith's article in *Prentice Hall Literature, Penguin Edition,* The British Tradition.

Conjunctive Adverbs Conjunctive adverbs act as transitions between complete ideas by indicating comparisons, contrasts, results, and other relationships. The chart below lists the most common conjunctive adverbs.

CONJUNCTIVE ADVERBS		
accordingly	finally	nevertheless
again	furthermore	otherwise
also	however	then
besides	indeed	therefore
consequently	moreover	thus

As shown in the following examples, punctuation is usually required both before and after conjunctive adverbs.

EXAMPLES: The Marconi Wireless Telegraph Co., Inc., was very successful. *Nevertheless*, Marconi continued to pursue other inventions.
He also invented several types of aerials; *however*, he will be remembered for the wireless telegraph.

GRAMMAR IN LITERATURE

from **Progress in Personal Comfort**
Sydney Smith

In the passage below, note how, by using coordinating conjunctions (highlighted in blue italics), the author presents a rapid series of images depicting a vanished way of life.

I can walk, by the assistance of the police, from one end of London to the other, without molestation; *or,* if tired, get into a cheap *and* active cab, instead of those cottages on wheels, which the hackney coaches were at the beginning of my life.

I had no umbrella! They were little used, *and* very dear. There were no waterproof hats, *and* my hat has often been reduced by rains into its primitive pulp.

Exercise 34 Identifying Conjunctions in Sentences Write the conjunctions in each sentence and label each *coordinating*, *correlative*, or *subordinating*.

EXAMPLE: They could not decide whether their films of everyday life would bore people or would interest people.

ANSWER: whether or (correlative)

1. Louis and Auguste Lumière contributed to the birth of film.
2. Their camera was a machine for both film projection and development.
3. Not only could the camera perform two tasks, but the box was much lighter than its rival, the Kinematoscope.
4. Because it was portable, the camera was suitable for outdoor use.
5. The camera was notable because it ran quietly and smoothly.

Exercise 35 Revising Sentences by Adding Conjunctive Adverbs Write the following pairs of sentences, adding appropriate conjunctive adverbs.

EXAMPLE: Many scholars believe that Homer wrote the *Iliad* and the *Odyssey*. Some scholars claim that he never existed.

ANSWER: Many scholars believe that Homer wrote the *Iliad* and the *Odyssey*. Some scholars, however, claim that he never existed.

1. A device called the Praxinoscope consisted of a revolving drum with mirrors at the center. When it revolved, the images appeared to be living.
2. People across Europe were working on similar theories at that time. In 1839, the photographic process was perfected.
3. Photographs replaced drawings in viewing machines. Coleman Sellers patented the Kinematoscope for this viewing.
4. The Kinematoscope made it possible to photograph movement instead of poses. In 1877, Eadweard Muybridge used multiple cameras to record the image of a running horse.
5. The chronophotographe moved a band of images past an opening at a steady speed. This invention was a major step toward the motion-picture camera.

More Practice

Grammar Exercise Workbook
• pp. 17–18
On-line Exercise Bank
• Section 17.4
  Go on-line:
  PHSchool.com
  Enter Web Code:
  egk-1202

interactive Textbook

Get instant feedback! Exercises 34 and 35 are available on-line or on CD-ROM.

▼ Critical Viewing Use a conjunctive adverb in a sentence that contrasts the way this Kinematoscope technology would have been considered in the 1800's with the way we consider it today. **[Contrast]**

Prepositions, Conjunctions, and Interjections • 399

Answer Key

▶ **Exercise 34**

1. and–coordinating
2. both . . . and–correlative
3. Not only . . . but–correlative
4. Because–subordinating
5. because–subordinating; and–coordinating

▶ **Exercise 35**

Answers will vary. Samples are given.

1. A device called the Praxinoscope consisted of a revolving drum with mirrors at the center. *Thus*, when it revolved, the images appeared to be living.
2. People across Europe were working on similar theories at that time. *Consequently*, in 1839 the photographic process was perfected.
3. Photographs replaced drawings in viewing machines. *Accordingly*, Coleman Sellers patented the Kinematoscope for this viewing.
4. The Kinematoscope made it possible to photograph movement instead of poses. *Then*, in 1877, Eadweard Muybridge used multiple cameras to record the image of a running horse.
5. The chronophotographe moved a band of images past an opening at a steady speed. *Consequently*, this invention was a major step toward the motion-picture camera.

Critical Viewing

Contrast Possible answer: People in the 1800's might have considered the Kinematoscope a technological marvel; however, many modern viewers consider it an amusing antique.

☑ **ONGOING ASSESSMENT: Monitor and Reinforce**

If students miss more than one item in Exercise 34 or 35, refer them to the following for additional practice.

In the Textbook	Print Resources	Technology
Section Review, Ex. 38, 40, Section 17.4	*Grammar Exercise Workbook*, pp. 17–18	*On-Line Exercise Bank*, Section 17.4

⏰ **TIME SAVERS!**

Answers on Transparencies Use the *Grammar Exercises Answers on Transparencies* for Chapter 17 to facilitate correction by students.

On-Line Exercise Bank Have students complete the exercises on computer. The Auto Check feature will grade their work for you!

Interjections

1. Point out that the word interjection comes from the Latin words *inter-* (between) and *jacere* (to throw). An interjection, therefore, is a word that is inserted, or thrown into, a sentence. Its purpose is to express emotion.

2. Because they are thrown into sentences, interjections have no grammatical connection to other words in a sentence and can be punctuated as though they are complete thoughts.

3. Refer students to the chart on this page and ask them to write original sentences that appropriately reflect the meaning of three of the interjections.

    Example: Hey! Don't touch that dial.

Critical Viewing

Speculate Possible answers: Aha! Hurray! Whew!

Answer Key

> **Exercise 36**

Answers will vary. Samples are given.

1. *Well*, I guess Porter could be the father of the story film.
2. *Alas*, I wasn't able to see his films in a theater.
3. *Hey*, if we hurry we can visit the old nickelodeon.
4. *Whew*, I can't believe we watched all those one-reel movies.
5. *Ah!* I thought the train was going to jump out of the screen!

17.4

Interjections

Interjections express emotion. Unlike most words, they have no grammatical connection to other words in a sentence.

▶ **KEY CONCEPT** An **interjection** is a word that expresses feeling or emotion and functions independently of a sentence. ■

Interjections can express a variety of sentiments, such as happiness, fear, anger, pain, surprise, sorrow, exhaustion, or hesitation.

SOME COMMON INTERJECTIONS				
ah	dear	hey	ouch	well
aha	goodness	hurray	psst	whew
alas	gracious	oh	tsk	wow

Exclamation marks or commas usually set off an interjection from the rest of the sentence, as the following examples show.

EXAMPLES: *Ouch!* That machine is very hot.
Goodness, if you didn't see *The Great Train Robbery,* you haven't seen the first major American movie!

▶ **Exercise 36** Using Interjections Write five sentences containing interjections that express the following general emotions. Underline the interjections in your sentences.

EXAMPLE: surprise
ANSWER: <u>Oh</u>, was that by Edwin Porter?

1. indecision
2. sorrow
3. urgency
4. exhaustion
5. fear

▶ Critical Viewing
Thomas Edison inspects film as he sits next to an early projector. How do you think it would feel to discover that one of your inventions actually worked? What interjections might you use to express your feelings? **[Speculate]**

400 • The Parts of Speech

Grammar and Style Tip

When choosing the method of punctuating your interjections, be sure that your period, comma, question mark, or exclamation mark matches the content of your sentence.

▶ **More Practice**

Grammar Exercise Workbook
• pp. 19–20
On-line Exercise Bank
• Section 17.4
Go on-line:
PHSchool.com
Enter Web Code:
egk-1202

✓ ONGOING ASSESSMENT: Assess Mastery	
Use the following resources to assess student mastery of prepositions, conjunctions, and interjections.	
In the Textbook	**Technology**
Chapter Review, Ex. 56–57	*On-Line Exercise Bank,* Section 17.4

Section 17.4 *Section Review*

GRAMMAR EXERCISES 37–42

Exercise 37 Identifying Prepositional Phrases Write the prepositional phrases from the following paragraph, and circle each preposition.

(1) A glider stays afloat by means of the aerodynamic forces acting upon it. (2) Glider wings, when compared to airplane wings, are longer and narrower. (3) Early experiments with gliders influenced the design of the first aircraft. (4) Starting in the 1870's, successful gliders provided information about wings and controls for flying. (5) Otto Lilienthal discovered the advantages of curved surfaces on wings.

Exercise 38 Distinguishing Among Subordinating Conjunctions, Prepositions, and Adverbs Identify each underlined word as a *subordinating conjunction, preposition, adverb,* or *conjunctive adverb.*

1. France and Germany focused <u>on</u> the internal-combustion engine.
2. Nikolaus Otto, who had already developed an efficient gas engine <u>before</u>, built a four-cycle engine in 1876.
3. <u>However</u>, it was Daimler's high-speed motor that aided development.
4. In 1891, Emile Levassor produced an automobile with parts arranged <u>in</u> the same order still used today.
5. Henry Ford brought <u>out</u> his first experimental car in 1896.

Exercise 39 Revising Sentences by Adding Interjections Insert an appropriate interjection into each sentence.

1. X-rays were discovered accidentally!
2. Wasn't Wilhelm Roentgen studying cathode rays?

3. The fluorescent light was quite a surprise!
4. He named the radiation "X ray" because it was so unknown.
5. I hope it didn't hurt him.

Exercise 40 Find It in Your Reading Identify the prepositions and conjunctions in the following excerpt from "Progress in Personal Comfort."

It is of some importance at what period a man is born. A young man, alive at this period, hardly knows to what improvements of human life he has been introduced; and I would bring before his notice the following eighteen changes which have taken place in England since I first began to breathe in it the breath of life—a period amounting now to nearly seventy-three years.

Exercise 41 Find It in Your Writing Review a comparison-and-contrast essay from your writing portfolio. How many correlative conjunctions did you use? Challenge yourself to revise at least five sentences to include correlative conjunctions.

Exercise 42 Writing Application Write a brief dialogue among three or more characters. Use at least three different interjections, four prepositions, and two conjunctions. Underline each of these words and identify the part of speech. For each conjunction, tell what kind it is.

Section Review • 401

Answer Key continued

Exercise 41

Find It in Your Writing
Ask students why a compare-and-contrast essay is an ideal place to use correlative conjunctions. (Students should note that this kind of essay shows the specific ways in which two or more things relate, and correlative conjunctions show the same thing.)

Exercise 42

Writing Application
Remind students to use interjections judiciously in their writing. If too many interjections are used, they will stand out less and therefore have less of an impact. Use interjections only to express strong emotion.

ASSESS

Section Review
Each of these exercises correlates to the instruction on prepositions, conjunctions, and interjections, pages 394–400. These exercises may be used for more practice, for reteaching, or for review of the key concepts presented.

Answer Key

Exercise 37

Prepositions are underlined.
1. <u>by</u> means; <u>of</u> the aerodynamic forces; <u>upon</u> it
2. <u>to</u> airplane wings
3. <u>with</u> gliders; <u>of</u> the first aircraft
4. <u>in</u> the 1870's; <u>about</u> wings and controls; <u>for</u> flying
5. <u>of</u> curved surfaces; <u>on</u> wings

Exercise 38

1. preposition
2. adverb
3. conjunctive adverb
4. preposition
5. adverb

Exercise 39

Answers will vary. Samples are given.
1. *Wow!* X-rays were discovered accidentally!
2. *Well*, wasn't Wilhelm Roentgen studying cathode rays?
3. *Oh!* The fluorescent light was quite a surprise!
4. *Aha!* He named the radiation "X ray" because it was so unknown.
5. *Ouch!* I hope it didn't hurt him.

Exercise 40

Find It in Your Reading
Prepositions are underlined.
Conjunctions are double underlined.

It is <u>of</u> some importance <u>at</u> what period a man is born. A young man, alive <u>at</u> this period, hardly knows <u>to</u> what improvements <u>of</u> human life <u>he</u> has been introduced; <u><u>and</u></u> I would bring <u>before</u> his notice the following eighteen changes which have taken place <u>in</u> England <u><u>since</u></u> I first began to breathe <u>in</u> it the <u>breath</u> <u>of</u> life—a period amounting now <u>to</u> nearly seventy-three years.

continued

Interest GRABBER Ask students for the part of speech of *green*. (Most will say adjective.) Then ask what other part of speech it might be. (Possibilities: verb and noun.) Challenge students to use it as a noun. (*The golf ball lay on the green.*) Then challenge students to use the word as a verb. Suggest that they can change its tense. (*The desert greened after years of irrigation.*)

Activate Prior Knowledge

Ask students to think of as many different uses as they can for the word *bat*. As students offer examples, place enough on the board so that the word acts as two or three parts of speech. Examples:

The bats were lined up in the dugout. (noun)

Larry bats fourth in the lineup. (verb)

Have you ever seen a bat cave? (adjective)

Ask students to brainstorm for more words that they have used in different ways.

TEACH

Step-by-Step Teaching Guide

Words as Different Parts of Speech

1. Explain that some words can operate as different parts of speech because they have alternate meanings that can be put to use differently depending on the sentence.

2. Have students use the chart on this page to review the questions they must ask themselves when determining the use of a word and therefore its part of speech.

3. Give students some additional words that can be used as different parts of speech and ask them to use each at least two ways:

play	game	bowling
goodness	either	trade
by	lost	opening

Section 17.5 Reviewing Parts of Speech

Words are flexible, often serving as one part of speech in one sentence and as another part of speech in another.

Words as Different Parts of Speech

A word's part of speech should be determined only by the way it is used in a sentence.

▶ **KEY CONCEPT** How a word is used in a sentence determines its part of speech. ■

Notice, for example, the many functions of the word *outside*.

AS A NOUN: The *outside* of the house is brick.
AS AN ADJECTIVE: It was an *outside* chance, but I took it.
AS AN ADVERB: The children played *outside*.
AS A PREPOSITION: We went sightseeing *outside* the city limits.

The following chart suggests questions to ask yourself when you are trying to identify a word's part of speech.

Parts of Speech	Questions to Ask Yourself
Noun	Does the word name a person, place, or thing?
Pronoun	Does the word stand for a noun?
Verb	Does the word tell what someone or something did? Does the word link one word with another word that identifies or describes it? Does the word merely show that something exists?
Adjective	Does the word tell *what kind, which one, how many,* or *how much*?
Adverb	Does the word tell *where, when, in what way,* or *to what extent*?
Preposition	Is the word part of a phrase that includes a noun or pronoun?
Conjunction	Does the word connect other words in the sentence?
Interjection	Does the word express emotion and function independently of the sentence?

402 • The Parts of Speech

Theme: Volcanoes

In this section, you will practice using words as different parts of speech. The examples and exercises in this section are about volcanoes.

Cross-Curricular Connection: Science

Grammar and Style Tip

In formal writing, try to vary your word choice rather than repeating the same words as different parts of speech.

⏱ TIME AND RESOURCE MANAGER

Resources
Print: *Grammar Exercise Workbook*, pp. 21–22; *Grammar Exercises Answers on Transparencies*, Ch. 17; *Hands-on Grammar Activity Book*, Ch. 17
Technology: *Writing and Grammar* Interactive Text, Section 17.5; *On-Line Exercise Bank*, Section 17.5

Using the Full Student Edition	Using the Handbook🄷
• Work through all key concepts, p. 402.	• Work through all key concepts, p. 268.
• Assign and review Exercises 43–44.	• Assign and review Exercises 43–44.
• Do the Hands-on Grammar activity, p. 404.	• Do the Hands-on Grammar activity, p. 270.

Exercise 43 Identifying Parts of Speech Identify the part of speech of each underlined word.

EXAMPLE: Take <u>care</u> where you walk if you <u>care</u> about your safety

ANSWER: noun   verb

1. <u>Many</u> of us felt the <u>many</u> dangers brewing in the volcano.
2. <u>Well</u>, I think it would <u>serve</u> us <u>well</u> to evacuate.
3. If the Earth's <u>rock</u> layer is disrupted, the island <u>rocks</u>.
4. We tried to take everything <u>but</u> the furniture, <u>but</u> there was not enough time.
5. The volcano let out a mighty <u>groan</u> while the departing boat <u>groaned</u> under the weight of the fleeing residents.

Exercise 44 More Work With Parts of Speech Identify the part of speech of each underlined word.

EXAMPLE: In the distance, we saw the <u>smoking</u> volcano.
ANSWER: adjective

  Volcanoes can erupt in (1) <u>different</u> ways at different times. (2) <u>Some</u> are more violent than (3) <u>others</u>. They blast ash, rock, and lava (4) <u>into</u> the atmosphere. Puffs of ash and gases (5) <u>are</u> released from the more gentle eruptions without causing much damage to the (6) <u>surrounding</u> landscape. The materials in the volcano's magma (7) <u>chamber</u> will determine the type of eruption. (8) <u>When</u> lava flows (9) <u>out of</u> a volcano, (10) <u>that</u> is called an effusive eruption. A (11) <u>steam</u> eruption, the more violent type, (12) <u>occurs</u> when water mixes with the molten rock. Some pieces of rock spin (13) <u>around</u> and (14) <u>become</u> more streamlined. These are called (15) <u>volcanic</u> bombs. Giant clouds of dust (16) <u>and</u> ash are produced in a (17) <u>Plinian</u> explosion. Pumice is a rock with holes (18) <u>where</u> there used to be gas bubbles. It is so (19) <u>light</u> that it can (20) <u>even</u> float on water.

More Practice

Grammar Exercise Workbook
• pp. 21–22
On-line Exercise Bank
• Section 17.5
  Go on-line:
  PHSchool.com
  Enter Web Code:
  egk-1202

*i*nteractive Textbook

Get instant feedback! Exercises 43 and 44 are available on-line or on CD-ROM.

◄ Critical Viewing Compare this volcanic explosion with the explosion of the supernova on page 377. Which verbs apply to both events? [Compare]

Answer Key

► **Exercise 43**

1. pronoun, adjective
2. interjection, adverb
3. adjective, verb
4. preposition, conjunction
5. noun, verb

► **Exercise 44**

1. adjective
2. pronoun
3. pronoun
4. preposition
5. verb
6. adjective
7. noun
8. (subordinating) conjunction
9. preposition
10. pronoun
11. adjective
12. verb
13. adverb
14. verb
15. adjective
16. conjunction
17. adjective
18. (subordinating) conjunction
19. adjective
20. adverb

Critical Viewing

Compare Possible answers: explode, burn, spread, glow, expand, burst, destroy

---

☑ **ONGOING ASSESSMENT: Monitor and Reinforce**

If students have difficulty with Exercise 43 or 44, refer them to the following for additional practice.

In the Textbook	Print Resources	Technology
Section Review, Ex. 45–48, Section 17.5	*Grammar Exercise Workbook,* pp. 21–22	*On-Line Exercise Bank,* Section 17.5

⏱ **TIME SAVERS!**

🗔 **Answers on Transparencies** Use the *Grammar Exercises Answers on Transparencies* for Chapter 17 to facilitate correction by students.

🖥 **On-Line Exercise Bank** Have students complete the exercises on computer. The Auto Check feature will grade their work for you!

Hands-on Grammar

Teaching Resources: Hands-on Grammar Activity Book, Ch. 17

1. Be prepared with index cards for the students. Give each student a copy of the Hands-on Grammar activity sheet.

2. Have students follow the directions to prepare the index cards and to play the game.

3. Possible answers:

   past: adjective, noun, preposition, adverb

   present: adjective, noun, verb

   last: adjective, adverb, noun, verb

   stop: adjective, verb, noun

   opposite: adjective, noun, adverb, preposition

   after: adverb, preposition, conjunction, adjective

   dry: adjective, noun, verb

   left: adjective, noun, adverb, verb

   fast: adjective, adverb, noun, verb

   beyond: preposition, adverb, noun

   outside: noun, adjective, adverb, preposition

   down: adverb, adjective, preposition, verb, noun

   before: adverb, preposition, conjunction

   look: verb, noun, interjection

   which: pronoun, adjective

Find It in Your Writing

If students have difficulty recognizing words that could be used as other parts of speech, encourage them to work in pairs and suggest other uses of words they find.

Find It in Your Reading

Students might compose a grid with words down the side, the seven parts of speech across the top, and illustrations of the word used as a particular part of speech in the box where the row and column intersect.

17.5

Hands-on Grammar

Parts-of-Speech Points

Write each of the following words on an index card: *past, present, last, stop, opposite, after, dry, left, fast, beyond, outside, down, before, look, which.* Put the cards in a box, and shake them all around.

Divide your class into groups of three or four students so that there are an even number of groups. One group of students plays against another group. The object of the game is to use each word in as many ways as possible.

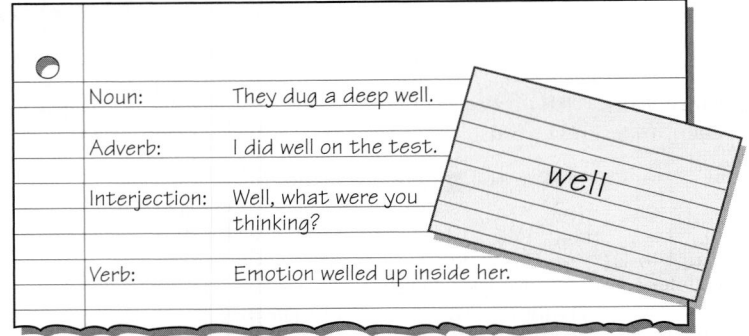

Pick a card. Set your timer for five minutes. See how many different ways the word can function. Students may brainstorm within their group for possible parts of speech the word may be used as. Each group is to write a sentence illustrating the use of the word as that part of speech.

The group that comes up with the most correct uses of the word within a sentence in five minutes gets a point. The team with the most points wins.

Find It in Your Writing Look through your portfolio to find examples of words used as more than one part of speech. Write the words on index cards, and add them to your collection for another round of the game.

Find It in Your Reading Record examples of words used as more than one part of speech as you discover them in your reading. Write them down, identify the parts of speech they are used as, and challenge yourself to think of other ways they could be used.

☑ ONGOING ASSESSMENT: Assess Mastery

Use the following resources to assess student mastery of the parts of speech.

In the Textbook	Print Resources	Technology
Chapter Review, Ex. 58–59	*Formal Assessment*, Ch. 17	*On-Line Exercise Bank,* Chapter 17

⏱ TIME SAVERS!

✋ **Hands-on Grammar**
Use the Hands-on Grammar activity sheet for Chapter 17 to facilitate this activity.

Section 17.5 Section Review

GRAMMAR EXERCISES 45–51

Exercise 45 Identifying Parts of Speech Identify the part of speech of each underlined word.

1. Volcanic explosions rock the area around <u>them</u>.
2. Lava <u>escapes</u> from cracks called fissures.
3. The lava floods <u>from</u> the fissures, which may be miles long.
4. It pours <u>down</u> the mountain.
5. As the lava continues to move <u>down</u>, it begins to cool.
6. <u>Cooling</u> lava cracks into columns with four, five, or six sides.
7. Basalt <u>is</u> a type of rock that forms when lava hardens.
8. <u>Flood</u> basalts may be hundreds of feet thick.
9. They will cover the <u>landscape</u>.
10. Much <u>basalt</u> cover was formed millions of years ago.

Exercise 46 Supplying Parts of Speech Supply the part of speech indicated in parentheses to complete each sentence.

1. Flowing (adv.), fluid lava races down a mountain at 660 feet per second.
2. Some lava resembles piles and coils (prep.) rope when it cools.
3. The speed of a lava flow (verb) upon its composition.
4. (Adj.) minerals and gases make up lava.
5. Silica, the most common mineral in the Earth's crust, is found more often in slowly flowing (noun).

Exercise 47 Using Parts of Speech Write sentences using each of the words that follow as the part of speech indicated.

1. like (verb)
2. like (preposition)
3. today (noun)
4. today (adverb)
5. after (preposition)
6. after (adverb)
7. train (verb)
8. train (noun)
9. early (adjective)
10. early (adverb)

Exercise 48 Revising Sentences Revise each sentence by adding adjectives, adverbs, and prepositional phrases.

1. The volcano exploded.
2. Lava is hot.
3. Lava is running.
4. The mountain is tall.
5. Eruptions are dangerous.

Exercise 49 Find It in Your Reading Identify the nouns, adjectives, adverbs, and prepositions in the excerpt from "Progress in Personal Comfort" on page 398.

Exercise 50 Find It in Your Writing Review a single paragraph from a finished piece of work in your writing portfolio. Determine the part of speech each word fills. Do you tend to use the same parts of speech over and over?

Exercise 51 Writing Application Revise the paragraph you reviewed for the preceding exercise to vary the parts of speech. Make a point of revising to include parts of speech that were missing or little used in the original.

Section Review • 405

Section Review

Each of these exercises correlates to the instruction on words as different parts of speech, pages 402–404.

Answer Key

Exercise 45

1. pronoun	6. adjective
2. verb	7. verb
3. preposition	8. adjective
4. preposition	9. noun
5. adverb	10. adjective

Exercise 46

Answers will vary. Sample answers:

1. quickly	4. Many
2. of	5. lava
3. depends	

Exercise 47

Answers may vary. Sample answers:

1. I like reading about volcanoes.
2. He floats like a butterfly.
3. Today is colder than usual.
4. Let's go to the mall today.
5. What shall we do after lunch?
6. He ate dinner and left shortly after.
7. He is training for the marathon.
8. That train just left the station.
9. I often weed the garden in the early morning.
10. We will arrive early for the meeting.

Exercise 48

Answers may vary. Sample answers:

1. The smoking volcano exploded suddenly in the middle of the night.
2. The glowing lava on the east slope is extremely hot.
3. The hot lava is running rapidly toward the ocean.
4. The beautiful, snow-capped mountain on the horizon is extremely tall.
5. Steam eruptions of volcanoes are the most dangerous of all.

Exercise 49

Find It in Your Reading
I can walk, by (Prep) the (Adj) assistance (N) of (Prep) the (Adj) police (N), from (Prep) one (Adj) end of (Prep) London (N) to (Prep) the (Adj) other, without (Prep) molestation (N); or, if tired (Adj), get into (Prep) a (Adj) cheap (Adj) and active (Adj) cab (N), instead of (Prep)

continued

Answer Key continued

Exercise 49

those (Adj) cottages (N) on (Prep) wheels (N), which the (Adj) hackney (Adj) coaches (N) were at (Prep) the (Adj) beginning (N) of (Prep) my (Adj) life (N).

I had no (Adj) umbrella (N)! They were little (Adv) used, and very (Adv) dear (Adj). There were no (Adj) waterproof (Adj) hats (N), and my (Adj) hat (N) has often (Adv) been reduced by (Prep) rains (N) into (Prep) its (Adj) primitive (Adj) pulp (N).

Exercise 50

Find It in Your Writing
Have students exchange papers with a partner and check that all words have been correctly identified. Challenge them to add one adjective, one adverb, and one interjection to appropriate places in their writing.

Exercise 51

Writing Application
Have students closely examine each modifier they used to determine whether it is necessary and precise. If it is not, have them replace it with a more precise modifier or omit it altogether.

Each of these exercises correlates to a section of the chapter on the parts of speech, pages 368–407. The exercises may be used for more practice, for reteaching, or for review of the key concepts presented. Answers for all chapter exercises are available in *Grammar Exercises Answers on Transparencies* in your Teaching Resources.

Answer Key

▶ Exercise 52

1. thing, concrete, singular, common
2. place, concrete, singular, compound, proper
3. thing, concrete, singular, compound, common
4. thing, concrete, singular, common
5. thing, concrete, plural, compound, common
6. thing, concrete, singular, common
7. thing, abstract, singular, collective, common
8. thing, concrete, plural, common
9. thing, concrete, singular, common
10. thing, concrete, singular, compound, proper

▶ Exercise 53

1. their–personal; volcanoes
2. they–personal; lines
3. it–personal; volcano
4. these–demonstrative; island arches
5. That–demonstrative; ridge
6. they–personal; plates
7. their–personal; plates
8. What–interrogative; none
9. that–relative; shapes
10. Which–interrogative; none

▶ Exercise 54

1. was considered–linking; intransitive
2. had remained–linking; intransitive
   exploded–action; intransitive
3. wrecked–action; transitive
   poured–action; intransitive
4. forced–action; transitive
5. opened–action; intransitive
   feared–action; transitive

▶ Exercise 55

1. one (adj)–eruption; giant (adj)–eruption; completely (adv)–can change
2. 1980 (adj)–eruption; perfect (adj)–cone
3. violent (adj)–eruption; out (adv)–blew; one (adj)–side

GRAMMAR EXERCISES 52–60

▶ Exercise 52 Classifying Nouns

For each noun in the following list, identify it according to whether it (1) names a person, place, or thing; (2) is concrete or abstract; (3) is singular or plural; (4) is collective; (5) is compound; and (6) is common or proper.

1. crater
2. Mount Vesuvius
3. carbon monoxide
4. volcano
5. hot spots
6. basalt
7. organization
8. gases
9. magma
10. Mount Etna

▶ Exercise 53 Identifying Pronouns and Their Antecedents Write each pronoun and identify it as *personal*, *reflexive*, *intensive*, *demonstrative*, *relative*, *interrogative*, or *indefinite*. Then, write its antecedent. If the pronoun does not have an antecedent, write *none*.

1. Volcanoes are not found everywhere. Their locations follow patterns.
2. Lines of volcanoes spread for miles. Sometimes, they are where a continent meets an ocean.
3. When a volcano is seen alone, it doesn't seem to belong to a chain.
4. Island arches are groups of volcanoes. Japan is one example of these.
5. There is a ridge in the middle of the Atlantic Ocean. That is where two of the Earth's plates meet.
6. As the plates move apart, they cause another line of volcanoes.
7. Their actions continue to move Europe and North American farther apart.
8. What produces the volcanic cones?
9. The magma cools into shapes that are called pillow lava.
10. Which volcanoes are still active?

▶ Exercise 54 Identifying Verbs

Identify the verbs or verb phrases in the following sentences, and label them *action* or *linking*, *transitive* or *intransitive*.

1. Mount Pinatubo, a Philippine volcano, was not considered dangerous.
2. It had remained dormant for 600 years before it exploded in 1991.
3. The lava wrecked homes as it poured down the slopes.
4. The 30-mile-long stream forced 75,000 people to flee.
5. When a fissure opened on the side of the volcano, people in the 25-mile danger zone feared the worst.

▶ Exercise 55 Identifying Adjectives and Adverbs Write each adverb and adjective, not including articles, in the following sentences. Write the word that each adverb or adjective modifies.

1. One giant eruption can completely change the shape of a volcano.
2. Mount St. Helens, before the 1980 eruption, was a perfect cone.
3. The violent eruption blew out one side.
4. The snowy mountain quickly lost 1,300 feet off the top.
5. The north side fell swiftly as an avalanche while ash clouds blasted out.
6. Mudflows and other debris filled in surrounding river valleys and lakes.
7. Entire forests of trees were blown flat.
8. Today, the shape continues to change.
9. Inside, there is now a new vent, and lava is building a new cone.
10. Rain and ice wear away the slopes to carve new valleys into the landscape.

4. snowy (adj)–mountain; quickly (adv)–lost; 1,300 (adj)–feet
5. north (adj)–side; swiftly (adv)–fell; ash (adj)–clouds; out (adv)–blasted
6. other (adj)–debris; in (adv)–filled; surrounding (adj)–valleys and lakes; river (adj)–valleys and lakes
7. Entire (adj)–forests; flat (adv)–were blown
8. Today (adv)–continues
9. Inside (adv)–is; now (adv)–is; new (adj)–vent; new (adj)–cone
10. away (adv)–wear; new (adj)–valleys

Exercise 56 Using Prepositions

Complete each prepositional phrase with an appropriate preposition.

1. Earth is not the only planet ___?___ volcanoes.
2. The highest and largest volcano, called Olympus Mons, is found ___?___ Mars.
3. It is more than 16 miles high and 370 miles ___?___ the base.
4. It may have been very active ___?___ a very long period of time, longer than any volcanoes on Earth.
5. The entire area looks like it may have been formed ___?___ lava flows.

Exercise 57 Writing Sentences With Conjunctions

Write five sentences about volcanoes, earthquakes, or other natural phenomena, using at least eight of the conjunctions listed below. Make sure that each one functions correctly as a coordinating, correlative, or subordinating conjunction or as a conjunctive adverb.

and	but
or	yet
neither . . . nor	either . . . or
not only . . . but also	because
provided that	while
when	until
since	even though
therefore	consequently
moreover	finally
nevertheless	otherwise

Exercise 58 Supplying All Parts of Speech

Fill in the blanks in the following paragraph with the appropriate parts of speech.

Flying into the ___?___ of Managua, ___?___ is the capital of Nicaragua, I ___?___ see the volcanoes. There ___?___ the middle of Lake Nicaragua was a volcano! Later, we ___?___ a bus trip to the volcano. ___?___ below, ___?___ looked like a smoking cone. ___?___ hiked to the top. Looking ___?___ from the rim, ___?___ view was obscured by the smoke. I just ___?___ imagine living next to ___?___ active volcano!

Exercise 59 Recognizing All Parts of Speech

Identify the part of speech of the underlined word.

Pompeii, in ancient Italy, (1) was located a few miles south of Mount Vesuvius. Vesuvius is the only (2) currently active volcano on the (3) European mainland. Other (4) nearby cities included Herculaneum and Stabiae. Pliny the Younger, from his (5) vantage point across the bay in Naples, observed the (6) A.D. 79 eruption of Mount Vesuvius. Winds (7) carried a tall (8) column of ash and dust (9) directly over Pompeii. Pumice, ash, and dust caused (10) complete darkness. The next stage of the eruption (11) brought hot, rocky avalanches and (12) then mudflows. The (13) glowing avalanches advanced (14) slowly, (15) until they surged toward Herculaneum and then (16) again toward Pompeii. The dark cloud covered the entire area and dropped (17) ash on the surrounding landscape. (18) Hot ashes and cinders showered (19) down for days. (20) Furthermore, the deep coverings preserved (21) these towns (22) for modern archaeologists. Digs and excavations (23) have unearthed historical information about first-century (24) Italian life and (25) about the volcanic eruption.

Exercise 60 Writing Application

Write a paragraph about the Earth, using at least three prepositional phrases, three conjunctions, two interjections, three adverbs, and three adjectives. Underline all nouns once, underline all verbs twice, and circle all prepositions.

Chapter Review • 407

Answer Key

Exercise 56

Answers may vary; samples are given.
1. with   4. for
2. on   5. by
3. around

Exercise 57

Answers will vary. Have students research volcanoes in the school library or on the Internet if they need information to include in their sentences.

Exercise 58

Answers may vary. Sample answers:
1. city   7. it
2. which   8. We
3. could   9. down
4. in   10. our
5. took   11. can't
6. From   12. an

Exercise 59

1. verb
2. adverb
3. adjective
4. adjective
5. noun
6. adjective
7. verb
8. noun
9. adverb
10. adjective
11. verb
12. adverb
13. adjective
14. adverb
15. (subordinating) conjunction
16. adverb
17. noun
18. adjective
19. adverb
20. conjunctive adverb
21. adjective
22. preposition
23. verb
24. adjective
25. preposition

Exercise 60

Writing Application
When students finish, have them identify the following words in their paragraphs:
1. objects of prepositions
2. words or groups of words linked by conjunctions
3. all words modified by adjectives
4. all words modified by adverbs

Step-by-Step Teaching Guide

Analogies

Teaching Resources: Standardized Test Preparation Workbook, pp. 33–34

1. Discuss with students the definition of an analogy as the relationships between pairs of words. Review each type of relationship described in the student textbook. Have students come up with additional examples for each type of relationship.

2. Tell students to identify the type of relationship in the first word pair given in a test item. Then, they can consider and eliminate any word pair that describes a different type of relationship.

3. Point out that parts of speech in the first word pair usually match the parts of speech of the pair in the correct response.

Standardized Test Preparation Workshop

Analogies

Analogy questions test your ability to determine a relationship between a given pair of words and to identify a similar relationship between the words in the second pair.

The words in the correct answer choice will usually, but not always, be the same parts of speech combination (nouns, pronouns, verbs, adjectives, or adverbs) as the original pair. To answer correctly, find the more specific relationship between the words.

Types of word relationships include:

- *Antonyms*, such as *infuriate : please*
- *Part-Whole* or *Whole-Part*, such as *vest : buttons*
- *Definitional/ Synonyms*, such as *tacit : unspoken*
- *Cause-Effect or Effect-Cause*, such as *deceit : mistrust*
- *Functional Relationship*, such as *needle : knitting*
- *Relationship of Degrees*, such as *rivulet : torrent*

Sample Test Item	**Answer and Explanation**
Directions: The question below consists of a related pair of words, followed by five pairs of words labeled *A* through *E*. Select the pair that *best* expresses a relationship similar to that expressed in the original pair. CRUMB : BREAD :: (A) ounce : unit (B) splinter : wood (C) water : bucket (D) twine : rope (E) cream : butter	The correct answer is *B*. A crumb is a tiny, broken off bit of a piece of bread. In the same way, a splinter is a tiny, broken off bit of a piece of wood.

408 • The Parts of Speech

408

Practice 1 **Directions:** Each question below consists of a related pair of words or phrases, followed by five pairs of word or phrases labeled *A* through *E*. Select the pair that best expresses a relationship similar to that expressed in the original pair.

1. SUBMERGE : WATER ::
   (A) parch : soil
   (B) bury : earth
   (C) suffocate : air
   (D) disperse : gas
   (E) extinguish : fire

2. TACIT : WORDS ::
   (A) visible : scenes
   (B) inevitable : facts
   (C) colorful : hues
   (D) suspicious : clues
   (E) unanimous : disagreements

3. DEFECTOR : CAUSE ::
   (A) counterfeit : money
   (B) deserter : army
   (C) critic : book
   (D) advertiser : sale
   (E) intruder : meeting

4. COMPATRIOTS : COUNTRY ::
   (A) transients : home
   (B) kinsfolk : family
   (C) competitors : team
   (D) performers : audience
   (E) figureheads : government

Practice 2 **Directions:** Each question below consists of a related pair of words or phrases, followed by five pairs of words or phrases labeled *A* through *E*. Select the pair that best expresses a relationship similar to that expressed in the original pair.

1. UNFETTER : PINIONED ::
   (A) recite : practiced
   (B) sully : impure
   (C) enlighten : ignorant
   (D) revere : unrecognized
   (E) adore : cordial

2. CHIEF : HIERARCHY ::
   (A) office : rank
   (B) platoon : army
   (C) president : term
   (D) lawyer : court
   (E) summit : mountain

3. SHOVE : NUDGE ::
   (A) vex : mutter
   (B) calm : quell
   (C) teach : lecture
   (D) push : fight
   (E) stare : glance

4. BARLEY : GRAIN ::
   (A) yeast : bread
   (B) pine : tree
   (C) vine : fruit
   (D) knot : rope
   (E) twig : nest

Answer Key

Practice 1
1. B
2. E
3. B
4. B

Practice 2
1. C
2. E
3. E
4. B

Customize for
Less Advanced Students

Give students sample analogies with which to practice identifying types of relationships. Tell them to begin by identifying each word's part of speech and its function.

Customize for
AP Students

Have students make up practice analogies and identify their types of relationships. They might exchange their analogies with a partner and discuss their conclusions.

In-Depth Lesson Plan

LESSON FOCUS	PRINT AND MEDIA RESOURCES
DAY 1 **Subjects and Predicates** Students learn and apply concepts relating to simple and compound subjects and predicates. (pp. 412–419/Ⓗ274–281)	*Writing and Grammar* Interactive Text, Section 18.1; *On-line Exercise Bank*, Section 18.1 **Teaching Resources** *Grammar Exercise Workbook*, pp. 23–26; *Grammar Exercises Answers on Transparencies*, Ch. 18
DAY 2 **Hard-to-Find Subjects** Students learn and apply concepts relating to hard-to-find subjects and do the Hands-on Grammar activity. (pp. 420–425/Ⓗ282–287)	*Writing and Grammar* Interactive Text, Section 18.2; *On-line Exercise Bank*, Section 18.2 **Teaching Resources** *Grammar Exercise Workbook*, pp. 27–28; *Hands-on Grammar Activity Book*, Ch. 18
DAY 3 **Complements** Students learn and apply concepts relating to direct and indirect objects and objective and subject complements. (pp. 426–433/Ⓗ288–295)	*Writing and Grammar* Interactive Text, Section 18.3; *On-line Exercise Bank*, Section 18.3 **Teaching Resources** *Grammar Exercise Workbook*, pp. 29–32
DAY 4 **Review and Assess** Students review the chapter and demonstrate mastery of basic sentence parts. (pp. 434–435)	**Teaching Resources** *Formal Assessment*, Ch. 18

Accelerated Lesson Plan

LESSON FOCUS	PRINT AND MEDIA RESOURCES
DAY 1 **Subjects and Predicates; Hard-to-Find Subjects** Students cover subjects, predicates, and hard-to-find subjects as determined by the Diagnostic Test. (pp. 412–425/Ⓗ274–287)	*Writing and Grammar* Interactive Text, Sections 18.1–2; *On-line Exercise Bank*, Sections 18.1–2 **Teaching Resources** *Grammar Exercise Workbook*, pp. 23–28; *Grammar Exercises Answers on Transparencies*, Ch. 18
DAY 2 **Complements** Students cover complements as determined by the Diagnostic Test. (pp. 426–433/Ⓗ288–295)	*Writing and Grammar* Interactive Text, Section 18.3; *On-line Exercise Bank*, Section 18.3 **Teaching Resources** *Grammar Exercise Workbook*, pp. 29–32
DAY 3 **Review and Assess** Students review the chapter and demonstrate mastery of concepts. (pp. 434–435)	**Teaching Resources** *Formal Assessment*, Ch. 18

Options for Adapting Lesson Plans

HOMEWORK

Have students complete any section of the chapter for homework.

FEATURES

Extend coverage with the Grammar in Literature features (pp. 418, 423, 431/Ⓗ280, 285, 293) and the Standardized Test Preparation Workshop (p. 436).

TECHNOLOGY

Students can use *Writing and Grammar* Interactive Text to complete the exercises interactively on computer. They can complete additional exercises in the *On-line Exercise Bank:* The Auto Check feature will grade their work. Go on-line: PHSchool.com Use Web Code: egk-1202

Writing and Grammar Handbook Alignment

Page numbers in Step-by-Step Teaching Guides in this Teacher's Edition refer to pages from the full student text. Handbook page references, indicated with this icon **H**, are provided in Time and Resource Manager boxes and at the bottom of each Teacher's Edition page.

INTEGRATED SKILLS COVERAGE

Grammar in Literature
SE pp. 418, 423, 431/**H**280, 285, 293

Writing
Find It in Your Writing, SE pp. 419, 424, 425, 433/**H**281, 286, 287, 295
Writing Application, SE pp. 419, 425, 433, 435/**H**281, 287, 295
Grammar and Style, SE p. 417/**H**279
Integrating Writing Skills, ATE p. 424

Spelling
SE p. 427/**H**289

Viewing and Representing
Critical Viewing, SE pp. 410, 413, 415, 416, 418, 421, 423, 426, 429, 431/**H**272, 275, 277, 278, 280, 283, 285, 288, 291, 293

Real-World Connection
ATE p. 417

Technology
SE p. 428/**H**290

Workplace Skills
ATE p. 432

Speaking, Listening, and Viewing Skills
ATE p. 413

Vocabulary
ATE p. 416

ASSESSMENT SUPPORT

Standardized Test Preparation Workshop SE p. 436; ATE p. 428
Standardized Test Preparation Workbook, pp. 35–36
Formal Assessment, Ch. 18

MEETING INDIVIDUAL NEEDS

Less Advanced Students ATE p. 437. See also Ongoing Assessments ATE pp. 413, 415, 417, 418, 423, 427, 429, 432.
AP Students ATE pp. 430, 437
ESL Students ATE pp. 416, 432
Linguistic Learners ATE p. 427
Spatial Learners ATE p. 429

BLOCK SCHEDULING

Pacing Suggestions
For 90-minute Blocks
• Administer the Diagnostic Test to students to determine instructional coverage.
• Have students complete the necessary exercises in class. Use the Hands-on Grammar activity to provide a change of pace.

Resources for Varying Instruction
• *Writing and Grammar* Interactive Text; *On-Line Exercise Bank*
A 90-minute block provides an ideal opportunity for students to work on the computer.

Professional Development Support
• *How to Manage Instruction in the Block* This teaching resource provides management and activity suggestions.

MEDIA AND TECHNOLOGY

For the Student
• *Writing and Grammar* Interactive Text, Ch. 18
• *On-line Exercise Bank,* Sections 18.1–3

For the Teacher
• Teacher**EXPRESS** CD-ROM

WRITING AND GRAMMAR ON-LINE

Interactive Text (On-line or on CD-ROM)
• Easily navigable instruction with on-line supporting resources
• Self-scoring exercises and diagnostic tests

Companion Web Site PHSchool.com
• On-line Exercise Bank (use Web Code egk-1202)

See the Go On-line! **feature, SE p. iii.**

LITERATURE CONNECTIONS

Grammar in Literature selections from *Prentice Hall Literature, Penguin Edition,* The British Tradition:
from *Macbeth,* Act III, William Shakespeare, SE p. 423/**H**285
from "We'll Never Conquer Space," Arthur C. Clarke, SE p. 431/**H**293

▶ **Lesson Objectives**

1. To locate and identify complete and simple subjects and predicates
2. To recognize and correct sentence fragments
3. To recognize compound subjects and verbs
4. To locate and identify hard-to-find subjects
5. To understand the function of complements in sentences
6. To use varied sentence structure to express meanings and achieve desired effect
7. To analyze the characteristics of clear texts such as conciseness, correctness, and completeness

Critical Viewing

Speculate Sample response: These ants want to use the leaf for food. They are trying to figure out a way to transport it.

Chapter 18 Basic Sentence Parts

When words combine to form a sentence, they can convey great meaning. As sentences increase in complexity and sophistication, they take on even greater meaning.

In many ways, words are like ants. An ant, though an extraordinary creature in itself, is still limited in size and strength. However, ants are social creatures. They live in colonies inhabited by thousands of other ants and share the workload of the entire colony. They combine their efforts, each ant carrying out a specific task, to produce more work as a whole than any individual ant could accomplish alone in a lifetime. Like ants, words work together to form limitless possibilities.

This chapter will focus on how words are combined to form sentences and to convey meaning.

▲ **Critical Viewing** In two complete sentences, explain what these ants could be doing. **[Speculate]**

410 • Basic Sentence Parts

☑ **ONGOING ASSESSMENT: Diagnose**

If students miss more than one item in any category, direct them to the relevant pages of the textbook and assign exercises for practice and review.

Basic Sentence Parts	Diagnostic Test Items	Teach	Practice	Section Review	Chapter Review
Skill Check A					
Subjects and Predicates	A 1–5	pp. 412–417/Ⓗ274–279	Ex. 1–4	Ex. 5–7	Ex. 30, 32, 34
Skill Check B					
Hard-to-Find Subjects	B 6–10	pp. 420–422/Ⓗ282–284	Ex. 11	Ex. 11–14	Ex. 31
Skill Check C					
Direct and Indirect Objects	C 11–13	pp. 426–428/Ⓗ288–290	Ex. 18–20	Ex. 24	Ex. 32–33

Diagnostic Test

Directions: Write all answers on a separate sheet of paper.

Skill Check A. Copy the following sentences, drawing a vertical line between the subject and the complete predicate.

1. Ants are very closely related to wasps.
2. They have similar body structures.
3. Their antennae are jointed in the middle.
4. Like wasps, some ant species have a functional sting for the defense of their colony.
5. Because of their physical similarities, both wasps and ants belong to the Hymenoptera order of insect classification.

Skill Check B. Write each sentence, underlining the subject once and the verb twice. Include in parentheses any word that is understood.

6. There is a nest of fire ants in our basement.
7. In every corner of the basement crawled the busy ants.
8. Have you ever been bitten by a fire ant?
9. In case of a bite, apply alcohol.
10. Please, get me my antihistamine.

Skill Check C. Identify the complement(s) in each sentence as *direct object, indirect object, objective complement, predicate nominative,* or *predicate adjective.*

11. Ants improve the environment.
12. Some ants give their prey vicious bites.
13. Scientists call ants social creatures.
14. Ants are foragers and builders.
15. Ants appear ugly, but most are harmless.

Skill Check D. Write each sentence, underlining the subject once, underlining the verb twice, and circling each complement.

16. I gave my brother an ant farm for his birthday.
17. Ants are members of the Formicidae family.
18. Some ants construct nests in mounds of soil.
19. One often sees the mounds in sidewalk cracks.
20. Ant colonies include workers, males, and a queen.
21. Small, younger workers are nurse ants.
22. Some workers feed other ants honeydew, a substance secreted by other insects.
23. Farmers find some ants useful.
24. In a house, however, ants are a nuisance.
25. Ants are highly intelligent.

Basic Sentence Parts • **411**

ONGOING ASSESSMENT: Diagnose *continued*

Basic Sentence Parts	Diagnostic Test Items	Teach	Practice	Section Review	Chapter Review
Objective Complements and Subject Complements	C 13–15	pp. 430–432/ Ⓗ292–294	Ex. 21–23	Ex. 25–26	Ex. 32–33
Skill Check D					
Direct and Indirect Objects	D 16, 18–20, 22	pp. 426–428/ Ⓗ288–290	Ex. 18–20	Ex. 24	Ex. 32–33
Objective Complements and Subject Complements	D 17, 21, 23–25	pp. 430–432/ Ⓗ292–294	Ex. 21–23	Ex. 25–26	Ex. 32–33
Cumulative Reviews and Applications				Ex. 8–10, 15–17, 27–29	Ex. 35–36

Interest GRABBER Have students build original sentences about insects. Ask for volunteers to provide words to complete these patterns:

article/adjective/adjective/noun/verb
article/adjective/noun

pronoun/linking verb/adverb/ adjective

(Sample responses: *The small black ants attacked an invading beetle. They were absolutely voracious.*) Have students make up similar sentence patterns for other students to complete, using no prepositions.

Activate Prior Knowledge

Ask each student to write two original sentences. One should have a subject of five or more words and a one-word predicate. The other should have a one-word subject and a predicate of five or more words. Have students read their sentences aloud.

TEACH

Step-by-Step Teaching Guide

Subjects and Predicates

1. Reiterate that the complete subject and the complete predicate may consist of one word or many words.

2. Advise students not to let introductory prepositional phrases confuse them; the subject is the word that tells what the sentence is about. Mention that a noun following a preposition cannot be the subject of a sentence.

continued

Answer Key

▶ Exercise 1

1. Cicadas I adapt well to their surroundings.
2. From tropical to temperate regions, I they I survive in a wide range of climates.
3. In the United States, I cicadas I are most abundant in the East and Midwest.
4. Some cicada species I are known as locusts or harvest flies.
5. These species I are neither true locusts nor flies.

Section 18.1 *Subjects and Predicates*

A sentence is a group of words that expresses meaning. In English, every sentence has two essential parts, a *complete subject* and a *complete predicate*. Being aware of these parts can help you avoid letting the order of your words get in the way of your ideas.

▶ **KEY CONCEPT** A **sentence** is a group of words with two main parts: a complete subject and a complete predicate. Together, these parts express a complete thought. ■

The complete subject contains the noun, pronoun, or group of words acting as a noun, plus their modifiers, that tells *who* or *what* the sentence is about. The complete predicate consists of the verb or verb phrase, plus any modifiers and complements, that tells what the complete subject *does* or *is*.

Complete Subjects	Complete Predicates
Critters	creep.
A bell-clanging streetcar	moved through the intersection.
Wood or cellulose	is a delicious meal for a termite.
The candidate's pragmatic approach to fiscal problems	impressed the voters attending the rally last Thursday.

In some sentences, a portion of the predicate may precede the complete subject.

COMPLETE   COMPLETE SUBJ   PREDICATE

EXAMPLE: At midnight, | the multitude of spiders | spun webs.

▶ **Exercise 1** Recognizing Complete Subjects and Complete Predicates Copy the following paragraph, drawing a vertical line between each complete subject and each complete predicate. Some sentences may require more than one line.

EXAMPLE: Suddenly, | the trilling of the cicadas | filled the room.

(1) Cicadas adapt well to their surroundings. (2) From tropical to temperate regions, they survive in a wide range of climates. (3) In the United States, cicadas are most abundant in the East and Midwest. (4) Some cicada species are known as locusts or harvest flies. (5) These species are neither true locusts nor flies.

Theme: Insects

In this section, you will learn about simple and complete subjects and predicates. The examples and exercises in this section are about insects.

Cross-Curricular Connection: Science

Interactive Textbook

Get instant feedback! Exercise 1 is available on-line or on CD-ROM.

▶ **More Practice**

Grammar Exercise Workbook
• pp. 23–24
On-line Exercise Bank
• Section 18.1
Go on-line:
PHSchool.com
Enter Web Code:
egk-1202

🕐 **TIME AND RESOURCE MANAGER**

Resources
Print: *Grammar Exercise Workbook,* pp. 23–26; *Grammar Exercises Answers on Transparencies,* Ch. 18
Technology: *Writing and Grammar* Interactive Text, Section 18.1; *On-Line Exercise Bank,* Section 18.1

Using the Full Student Edition	Using the HandbookⒽ
• Work through all key concepts, pp. 412–417. • Assign and review Exercises 1–4. • Read and discuss Grammar in Literature, p. 418.	• Work through all key concepts, pp. 274–279. • Assign and review Exercises 1–4. • Read and discuss Grammar in Literature, p. 280.

Simple Subjects and Predicates

When all modifiers and complements are removed from a complete subject and complete predicate, an essential word or group of words remains in each. These essential elements, called the *simple subject* and *simple predicate*, are the core around which sentences are developed.

▶ **KEY CONCEPTS** The **simple subject** is the essential noun, pronoun, or group of words acting as a noun that cannot be left out of the complete subject. The **simple predicate** is the essential verb or verb phrase that cannot be left out of the complete predicate. ■

The following chart shows simple subjects underlined once and simple predicates underlined twice. Notice how any remaining words either modify the simple subject and simple predicate or help to complete the meaning of the sentence.

SIMPLE SUBJECTS AND SIMPLE PREDICATES	
Complete Subjects	**Complete Predicates**
Small <u>mice</u>	<u>fit</u> nicely into coat pockets.
Many horror <u>films</u>	<u>have used</u> bugs to terrifying effect.
<u>Studies</u> of insects	<u>have</u> certainly <u>revealed</u> much about their behavior.

Notice in the last example that the simple subject is *studies*, not *insects*, which is the object of the preposition *of*. Objects of prepositions never function as simple subjects. In this same example, notice also that the simple predicate is a verb phrase.

NOTE: In this textbook, the term *subject* will be used to refer to a simple subject and the term *verb* will be used to refer to a simple predicate.

(Learn More)

Learn More

For a review of nouns, pronouns, and verbs, see Chapter 17.

▼ **Critical Viewing**
How is a bee's diet different from an ant's? Respond in one or more complete sentences. **[Contrast]**

---

3. Prepositional phrases following the simple subject can be confusing. Provide these sentences for extra practice:

   A swarm of insects moved toward the spilled cereal.

   A small puddle of milk also attracted their attention.

   Though *insects* and *milk* may seem to be what the sentences are about, reiterate yet again that the object of a preposition cannot be the simple subject.

4. If students need further practice in identifying simple subjects and predicates, have them analyze the sentences in the chart on the preceding page.

Critical Viewing

Contrast Sample response: An ant may eat items like crumbs. A bee eats the nectar from flowers.

Integrating Speaking, Listening, and Viewing Skills

Have volunteers look for photos of unusual animals or insects. Students should work in pairs to write two or three simple sentences about each photo. Student A reads a sentence, and Student B listens and repeats the simple subject and verb. Then Student B reads and Student A answers. Have students keep track of how many they get correct and incorrect. Put some of the ones missed on the board, and ask students to decide on the correct answers.

☑ ONGOING ASSESSMENT: Monitor and Reinforce		
If students miss more than one item in Exercise 1, refer them to the following for additional practice.		
In the Textbook	**Print Resources**	**Technology**
Section Review, Ex. 5, Section 18.1	*Grammar Exercise Workbook*, pp. 23–24	*On-Line Exercise Bank*, Section 18.1

Fragments

1. Have students review the chart to see the ways sentence fragments can be corrected.

2. For practice, ask students to provide different subjects and predicates to complete the missing fragments in the chart.

3. Mention that sometimes sentence fragments can also be corrected by connecting them to nearby sentences. Have students apply this technique to the following example:

    I spent the evening with my little brother. Who needed help with his report on insects.

18.1

Fragments

When either the complete subject or complete predicate is missing, the resulting group of words does not constitute a sentence. Instead, it is called a fragment, which is usually considered an error in writing.

▶ **KEY CONCEPT** A fragment is a group of words that does not express a complete thought. ■

You can correct a fragment by adding the missing parts, as in the following chart.

FRAGMENTS	COMPLETE SENTENCES
People allergic to bug bites. (complete predicate missing)	People allergic to bug bites *should avoid the outdoors.* (complete predicate added)
Thrive in the rain forests. (complete subject missing)	*Tarantulas* thrive in the rain forests. (complete subject added)
From the barn. (complete subject and complete predicate missing)	*Flies* from the barn *made their way into the house.* (complete predicate and rest of complete subject added)

In conversations, fragments usually do not present a problem because repetition, tone of voice, gestures, and facial expressions help to communicate meaning. In writing, however, fragments should be avoided because the reader is alone with the words on the page and cannot go to the writer for clarification. An exception, of course, is writing that represents speech, such as the dialogue in a play or short story. Even then, fragments must be used carefully so that the reader can follow the flow of ideas.

Another exception to the rule of avoiding fragments is the occasional use of elliptical sentences.

▶ **KEY CONCEPT** An elliptical sentence is one in which the missing word or words can be easily understood. ■

ELLIPTICAL   Until later.
SENTENCES: Why such a sad face?

📖 Journal Tip

This section contains a variety of information about insects. In your journal, note some of the facts that interest you; review them later to find a topic for an essay or a report.

Exercise 2 Revising to Correct Sentence Fragments

Decide whether each item is a sentence or a fragment. If it is a sentence, write *sentence*. If it is a fragment, revise it to make it a sentence. Label the elliptical sentence.

EXAMPLE: Because of the noise from the cicadas.
ANSWER: Because of the noise from the cicadas, we could hardly have a conversation.

1. The loudest of all insects.
2. Some heard a quarter of a mile away.
3. Males produce a whirring sound.
4. Longest cycle of development of any known insect.
5. Females lay up to 600 eggs high up in trees.
6. The eggs usually hatch within six weeks.
7. Then drop to the ground.
8. The wingless young are called nymphs.
9. Work their way a few centimeters into the soil and feed on the sap of tree roots.
10. Emerge from the ground after thirteen to seventeen years, big enough to climb up the tree trunk.
11. By fastening themselves securely to tree trunks to molt their outer cases.
12. Easy to hear but hard to find.
13. Trying to stay out of sight, move around a branch, hiding from view.
14. They live only one month.
15. Long development cycle but short life.

More Practice

Grammar Exercise Workbook
• pp. 23–24
On-line Exercise Bank
• Section 18.1
  Go on-line:
  PHSchool.com
  Enter Web Code:
  egk-1202

▼ Critical Viewing
Add a predicate to complete a sentence about the picture: The cicada, emerging slowly **[Relate]**

Subjects and Predicates • **415**

Answer Key

▶ **Exercise 2**

Revisions of fragments will vary. Samples are given.

1. The cicada is the loudest of all insects.
2. Some can be heard a quarter of a mile away.
3. sentence
4. Cicadas have the longest cycle of development of any known insect.
5. sentence
6. sentence
7. Then, the newly hatched insects drop to the ground.
8. sentence
9. The young work their way a few centimeters into the soil and feed on the sap of tree roots.
10. Cicadas emerge from the ground after thirteen to seventeen years. They are now big enough to climb up the tree trunk.
11. The cicadas take the next step in their development by fastening themselves securely to tree trunks to molt their outer cases.
12. elliptical sentence *or* They are easy to hear but hard to find.
13. Trying to stay out of sight, they move around a branch, hiding from view.
14. sentence
15. They have a long development cycle but a short life.

Critical Viewing

Relate Sample response: The cicada, emerging slowly, leaves its outer shell behind and spreads its wings to dry.

☑ **ONGOING ASSESSMENT: Monitor and Reinforce**

If students miss more than two items in Exercise 2, refer them to the following for additional practice.

In the Textbook	Print Resources	Technology
Section Review, Ex. 6, Section 18.1	*Grammar Exercise Workbook,* pp. 23–24	*On-Line Exercise Bank,* Section 18.1

⏱ **TIME SAVERS!**

📠 **Answers on Transparencies**
Use the *Grammar Exercises Answers on Transparencies* for Chapter 18 to facilitate correction by students.

🖥 **On-Line Exercise Bank**
Have students complete the exercises on computer. The Auto Check feature will grade their work for you!

Step-by-Step Teaching Guide

Locating Subjects and Verbs

1. One tip for students having difficulty locating subjects and verbs is to revamp the sentence so no parts of the predicate precede the subject. Have students reorder this example:

   Because of their short lives, insects seem inconsequential to some people. (Insects seem . . . people because of their . . .)

2. Give students more practice with locating subjects and verbs in lengthy sentences. Use the following (subjects are underlined; verbs are in boldface):

   A thorough knowledge of the life cycles of insects **can** *easily* **involve** *years of study.*

   Without a great deal of dedication, the student **may lose** *interest in this field of study.*

Customize for
ESL Students

Students will recognize verbs more easily if they are reminded of words and endings that may be verb markers. Discuss how the *-ed* ending is often the sign of a past tense verb and ask students to give examples. Then refer students to page 384 to review the list of auxiliary, or helping, verbs. With students' help, compile a list of verbs using auxiliaries. Remind them that several may be used together, and give examples like *should have asked* and *will be going.*

Critical Viewing

Draw Conclusions Sample response: A large swarm of desperately hungry grasshoppers can virtually destroy a crop of ripe, harvest-ready wheat.

18.1

Locating Subjects and Verbs To help you check your own writing to avoid fragments, employ either of two methods for locating subjects and verbs in sentences. The first method involves locating the subject. Ask, "Which word tells what this sentence is about?" Once you have the answer—in other words, the subject—then ask, "What does the subject do?" This gives you the verb.

Some people, however, prefer to find the verb first. In this case, ask, "Which word states the action or condition in this sentence?" This question should give you the verb. Then ask, "Who or what?" before it. The resulting word or words will be the subject.

Notice how these methods are applied to the example:

EXAMPLE: Grasshoppers often feed on corn, cotton, clover, and grasses.

To find the subject first, ask, "Which word tells what this sentence is about?"

ANSWER: Grasshoppers (*Grasshoppers* is the subject.)

Then ask, "What do the grasshoppers do?"

ANSWER: feed (*Feed* is the verb.)

To find the verb first, ask, "Which word states the action or condition in the sentence?"

ANSWER: feed (*Feed* states the action and is therefore the action verb.)

Then ask, "Who or what feed?"

ANSWER: Grasshoppers (*Grasshoppers* is the subject.)

Sometimes, a sentence contains numerous modifiers, making isolation of the subject and verb difficult. Simplify these sentences by mentally crossing out adjectives, adverbs, and prepositional phrases.

EXAMPLE: The science of entomology should grow extensively in the next ten years.

The science of entomology should grow extensively in the next ten years.

With the skeletal sentence that remains, you can easily use one of the two methods just introduced to determine the subject and verb.

▲ **Critical Viewing** What happens if large numbers of grasshoppers attack a crop? Respond in a complete sentence with several modifiers. **[Draw Conclusions]**

416 • Basic Sentence Parts

Integrating Vocabulary Skills

Have students use a dictionary to determine the Greek root words for the scientific names of each class of insect listed below. Ask them to write out the etymologies of the root words. (Example: Orthoptera: crickets; *ortho*, meaning "straight" and *pteron*, meaning "wing")

Lepidoptera: butterflies and moths (*lepidos*, meaning "scale," and *pteron*, meaning "wing")

Siphonaptera: fleas (*siphon*, meaning "tube," and *pteron*, meaning "wing")

Diptera: flies (*di*, meaning "two," and *pteron*, meaning "wing")

Coleoptera: beetles (*koleos*, meaning "sheath," and *pteron*, meaning "wing")

More Than One Subject or Verb So far, the examples in this section have contained only one subject and one verb. Sometimes, however, a sentence may contain a *compound subject* or *compound verb*.

▶ **KEY CONCEPT** A **compound subject** is two or more subjects that have the same verb and are joined by a conjunction such as *and* or *or*. ■

EXAMPLE: The <u>campers</u> and <u>hikers</u> <u>repelled</u> the mosquitoes with insect spray.
<u>Flies</u>, <u>gnats</u>, or <u>bees</u> <u>are</u> always <u>buzzing</u> around the garbage can.

▶ **KEY CONCEPT** A **compound verb** is two or more verbs that have the same subject and are joined by a conjunction such as *and* or *or*. ■

EXAMPLE: <u>I</u> neither <u>saw</u> them nor <u>heard</u> them.
<u>Most</u> of the bees <u>left</u> their hive and <u>flew</u> to the nearest flower patch.

Some sentences may contain both a compound subject and a compound verb.

EXAMPLE: Both my <u>father</u> and <u>brother</u> <u>swatted</u> at the fly, <u>missed</u> it, and <u>smacked</u> each other in the head.

▶ **Exercise 3** Identifying Subjects and Verbs Copy each of the following sentences, drawing a vertical line between the complete subject and complete predicate. Then, underline each subject once and each verb twice.

EXAMPLE: The <u>state</u> with the most people | <u>is</u> California.

1. Mosquitoes inhabit most areas of the world.
2. Their nasty bites cause swelling and itching.
3. Their bites also cause many deaths each year.
4. Mosquitoes transmit a number of diseases.
5. Many viral and bacterial infections can result from mosquito bites.
6. Mosquitoes must bite and feed on blood to live.
7. The females need protein for the production of eggs.
8. Unfed females weigh only one ten-thousandth of an ounce.
9. A single bite can cause them to triple in weight.
10. Only one bite is needed for the production of seventy-five eggs.

🔧 **Grammar and Style Tip**

Compound subjects joined with *and* take the plural form of a verb. Compound subjects joined with *or* take the form of the verb that agrees with the subject closest to the verb.

▶ **More Practice**

Grammar Exercise Workbook
• pp. 25–26
On-line Exercise Bank
• Section 18.1
Go on-line:
PHSchool.com
Enter Web Code:
egk-1202

Interactive Textbook

Get instant feedback! Exercise 3 is available on-line or on CD-ROM.

Subjects and Predicates • **417**

Step-by-Step Teaching Guide

More Than One Subject or Verb

1. If necessary, review coordinating conjunctions before examining the examples on this page.
2. Write the following predicate on the board: . . . *ravage a farmer's tomatoes*. Have students suggest several compound subjects consisting of two or three nouns to complete the sentence. (Example: *Worms, caterpillars, or slugs ravage a farmer's tomatoes.*)
3. Perform the same procedure with this subject: *The angry hornets . . .* Have students suggest a variety of compound verbs. (Example: *The angry hornets emerged from the nest and swarmed down.*)
4. You may need to help students see that the simple subject or predicate of a sentence may still be compound. Remind them that the simple subject or predicate is simply the main word without modifiers. In a compound subject or predicate, there are two or more main words.

Real-World Connection

Have students compile a list of people who have been famous in pairs or groups. Examples might include married couples, actors, musicians, politicians, world leaders, and so on. Then, ask students to create sentences with compound subjects about these people. (Example: *Jerry Lewis and Dean Martin were a popular comedy team during the 1960's.*)

Answer Key

▶ **Exercise 3**

1. <u>Mosquitoes</u> | <u>inhabit</u> most areas of the world.
2. Their nasty <u>bites</u> | <u>cause</u> swelling and itching.
3. Their <u>bites</u> | also <u>cause</u> many deaths each year.
4. <u>Mosquitoes</u> | <u>transmit</u> a number of diseases.
5. Many viral and bacterial <u>infections</u> | <u>can result</u> from mosquito bites.
6. <u>Mosquitoes</u> | <u>must bite</u> and <u>feed</u> on blood to live.
7. The <u>females</u> | <u>need</u> protein . . .
8. Unfed <u>females</u> | <u>weigh</u> . . .
9. A single <u>bite</u> | <u>can cause</u> . . .
10. Only one <u>bite</u> | <u>is needed</u> . . .

▶ **Exercise 4**

1. Beetles, insects
2. examine, study
3. was practiced, did develop
4. research, planning; have driven, made
5. Rain forests, swamps, ecosystems

Step-by-Step Teaching Guide

Grammar in Literature

1. Have one student read the excerpt aloud. Then have another reread it one sentence at a time, emphasizing the compound verbs.

2. Ask students for the subject of each compound verb (*soul, brother*).

3. Ask students to suggest reasons why the author might have chosen to use compound verbs (for example, to convey a sense of urgency).

More About the Translator

The translations of Burton Raffel are noted for their rare combination of linguistic accuracy and fresh, readable style. In his 1988 book *The Art of Translating Poetry*, Raffel attributes his success at capturing a poem's original flavor to his painstaking re-creation of each poet's characteristic syntax. Raffel has also practiced law on Wall Street; taught in the United States, Canada, and Indonesia; and published a volume of his own poems. In addition to *The Seafarer*, he has translated *Beowulf* and works by such literary giants as Horace, Rabelais, Cervantes, and Balzac. He currently holds an endowed chair in the University of Louisiana English Department.

Connections With Literature

To read more of *The Seafarer*, see *Prentice Hall Literature, Penguin Edition*, The British Tradition.

Critical Viewing

Relate Sample response: I would throw myself on the ground and cover my head.

18.1

▶ **Exercise 4** Locating Compound Subjects and Compound Verbs Write the parts of each compound subject and compound verb. Notice that some sentences may have both.

EXAMPLE: The babies kicked their feet and gurgled.
ANSWER: kicked gurgled

1. Beetles and other insects are studied by entomologists.
2. Entomologists examine insect anatomy and study insect behavior.
3. The study of insects was practiced as early as the fourth century B.C. but did not develop into an organized science until the seventeenth century A.D.
4. In recent years, medical research and agricultural planning have driven entomology further into the scientific mainstream and made it the largest branch of zoology.
5. Rain forests, swamps, and other delicate ecosystems are being explored for their exotic insect species.

GRAMMAR IN LITERATURE

from The Seafarer
Translated by Burton Raffel

In the following passage, the compound verbs are italicized and highlighted in blue.

The soul stripped of its flesh *knows* nothing
Of sweetness or sour, *feels* no pain,
Bends neither its hand nor its brain.
A brother
Opens his palms and *pours* down gold
On his kinsman's grave, strewing his coffin
With treasures intended for Heaven, but nothing
Golden shakes the wrath of God
For a soul overflowing with sin, and nothing
Hidden on earth rises to Heaven.

418 • Basic Sentence Parts

▶ **More Practice**

Grammar Exercise Workbook
• pp. 23–24
On-line Exercise Bank
• Section 18.1
Go on-line:
PHSchool.com
Enter Web Code:
egk-1202

▼ **Critical Viewing**
Using a compound verb, describe your likely reaction to encountering a swarm of locusts, such as the one in this photograph. **[Relate]**

☑ **ONGOING ASSESSMENT: Monitor and Reinforce**

If students miss more than one item in Exercise 4, refer them to the following for additional practice.

In the Textbook	Print Resources	Technology
Section Review, Ex. 7, Section 18.1	*Grammar Exercise Workbook,* pp. 25–26	*On-Line Exercise Bank,* Section 18.1

Section Review

GRAMMAR EXERCISES 5–10

Exercise 5 Recognizing Complete Subjects and Predicates Copy the following paragraph, drawing a vertical line between each complete subject and complete predicate. Then, underline each subject once and each verb twice.

(1) *Locust* is the common name of a number of jumping insects. (2) However, true locusts are migratory grasshoppers. (3) Farmers revile them. (4) True locusts swarm in great numbers. (5) In a brief span of time, they can destroy vast expanses of crops.

Exercise 6 Revising to Eliminate Fragments Revise this paragraph, eliminating the fragments. Then, underline each subject once and each verb twice.

Mosquitoes in most areas of the world. Their nasty bites! Cause swelling and itching. The buzzing of mosquitoes in a darkened room annoying. More than mere irritants, also cause many deaths each year. In people with allergies or because of disease. Some viral and bacterial infections from mosquito bites. Including malaria.

Exercise 7 Locating Compound Subjects and Compound Verbs Write the parts of each compound subject and compound verb.

1. Termites live in tropical countries but also inhabit temperate regions of the Americas and Europe.
2. A colony has anywhere from one hundred to one million termites and possesses a rigid caste structure.

3. The king and queen, the soldiers, and the workers perform specialized roles for the good of the colony.
4. The workers provide for the nest, tend to the queen's eggs, and feed the other members of the colony.
5. The soldiers grow huge heads and are equipped for the protection and defense of the colony.

Exercise 8 Find It in Your Reading Reread the excerpt from "The Seafarer," translated by Burton Raffel, on the preceding page. Then, on your paper, list the simple subjects that you find in the excerpt.

Exercise 9 Find It in Your Writing Review a piece of work from your writing portfolio. Revise at least four sentences by adding either compound subjects, compound verbs, or both. Notice the effect the revision has on your writing.

Exercise 10 Writing Application In Czech author Franz Kafka's story *The Metamorphosis*, the protagonist awakens one morning to find that he has been transformed into a giant cockroach. Imagine that you awake one morning to find that you are transformed into a giant insect. Write a brief description of the experience from the moment of your discovery. Use complete sentences to convey the experience clearly and meaningfully.

Section Review • **419**

✓ ONGOING ASSESSMENT: Assess Mastery

Use the following resources to assess student mastery of subjects and predicates.

In the Textbook	Technology
Chapter Review, Ex. 30	*On-Line Exercise Bank,* Section 18.1

ASSESS

Section Review

Each of these exercises correlates to the instruction on subjects and predicates, pages 412–418. These exercises may be used for more practice, for reteaching, or for review of the key concepts presented.

Answer Key

Exercise 5

(1) *Locust* / is the common name of a number of jumping insects. (2) However, / true locusts / are migratory grasshoppers. (3) Farmers / revile them. (4) True locusts / swarm in great numbers. (5) In a brief span of time, / they / can destroy vast expanses of crops.

Exercise 6

Answers may vary; samples are given.

Mosquitoes inhabit most areas of the world. Their nasty bites cause swelling and itching. The buzzing of mosquitoes in a darkened room can be annoying. More than mere irritants, their bites also cause many deaths each year in people with allergies or because of disease. Some viral and bacterial infections, including malaria, can result from mosquito bites.

Exercise 7

1. live, inhabit
2. has, possesses
3. king, queen, soldiers, workers
4. provide, tend, feed
5. grow, are equipped

Exercise 8

Find It in Your Reading
Simple subjects include *soul, brother,* and *nothing.*

Exercise 9

Find It in Your Writing
When students have finished, have them discuss what kinds of sentences worked best with compounds.

Exercise 10

Writing Application
Before students begin writing, discuss the point of view this assignment requires (first person). Suggest that students use compound verbs wherever they can.

Ask students to suggest statements related to trains that illustrate the four kinds of sentences. Here are some examples.

Declarative: *The train is long.*

Imperative: *Give me your ticket.*

Exclamatory: *Get off the tracks!*

Interrogative: *Is that an electric train?*

Once you have all four types on the board, ask students how each differs from the others (possible answers: different functions, different subject-verb order, different construction).

Activating Prior Knowledge

Have students work in pairs. One student should choose one kind of sentence (declarative, imperative, exclamatory, interrogative) and write a statement about transportation. The student's partner should then write a reply or reaction using another kind of sentence and hand it back to the first student. Passing the paper back and forth, students should create a dialogue on paper that eventually uses all four kinds of sentences.

TEACH

Step-by-Step Teaching Guide

Subjects in Declarative Sentences

1. Ask students to explain why *here* and *there* are never subjects (a subject is a noun or pronoun, and these words are neither).

2. Direct students' attention to the chart on this page for examples of declarative sentences beginning with *here* or *there* written in inverted word order.

3. Point out that in either order, the subject and the verb of each sentence remain the same.

continued

Section 18.2 *Hard-to-Find Subjects*

The position of a subject in relation to its verb may vary according to the function of the sentence. Some subjects, therefore, are more difficult to find than others.

Subjects in Declarative Sentences In most declarative sentences, the subject precedes the verb. This subject-verb order is the normal pattern for declarative sentences. There are, however, two exceptions: sentences beginning with *there* or *here* and sentences that are inverted for emphasis.

When *there* or *here* begins a declarative sentence, it is often erroneously identified as the subject.

▶ **KEY CONCEPT** The subject of a sentence is never *there* or *here*. ■

There and *here* usually serve as adverbs that modify the verb by explaining *where*. The most effective technique for making the subjects visible in these kinds of sentences is to rearrange the sentence in your mind so that *there* or *here* comes after the verb. If *there* sounds awkward after the verb, it is an *expletive*, a device used merely to get the sentence started. In this case, simply drop *there* from the sentence when you rearrange it.

Sentences Beginning With *There* or *Here*	Sentences Rearranged With Subject Before Verb
There <u>are</u> my subway <u>tokens</u>.	My subway <u>tokens</u> <u>are</u> there.
Here <u>is</u> your <u>ticket</u> to the Bedford Falls station.	Your <u>ticket</u> to the Bedford Falls station <u>is</u> here.
There <u>was</u> <u>room</u> to sit down.	<u>Room</u> to sit down <u>was</u> there.

Occasionally, a sentence beginning with *there* or *here* may be in normal word order, with the subject coming before the verb.

EXAMPLES: Here <u>you</u> <u>are</u> at last!
There <u>it</u> <u>goes</u>, out of the station.

Theme: Train Travel
In this section, you will learn to locate hard-to-find subjects. The examples and exercises are about train travel.

Cross-Curricular Connection: Social Studies

⏱ TIME AND RESOURCE MANAGER

Resources
Print: *Grammar Exercise Workbook*, pp. 27–28; *Grammar Exercises Answers on Transparencies*, Ch. 18; *Hands-on Grammar Activity Book*, Ch. 18
Technology: *Writing and Grammar* Interactive Text, Section 18.2; *On-Line Exercise Bank*, Section 18.2

Using the Full Student Edition	Using the Handbook🄷
• Work through all key concepts, pp. 420–422.	• Work through all key concepts, pp. 282–284.
• Assign and review Exercise 11.	• Assign and review Exercise 11.
• Read and discuss Grammar in Literature, p. 423.	• Read and discuss Grammar in Literature, p. 285.
• Do the Hands-on Grammar activity, p. 424.	• Do the Hands-on Grammar activity, p. 286.

KEY CONCEPT In some declarative sentences, the subject follows the verb. ■

Often, prepositional phrases begin such inverted sentences. Mentally shifting the words at the beginning of the sentence to the middle or to the end makes the subject easier to detect.

Sentences Inverted for Emphasis	Sentences Rephrased With Subject Before Verb
Deep into the cavernous tunnel <u>went</u> the <u>subway crew</u>.	The subway <u>crew</u> <u>went</u> deep into the cavernous tunnel.
Around my head <u>buzzed</u> the most persistent <u>fly</u>.	The most persistent <u>fly</u> <u>buzzed</u> around my head.

Subjects in Interrogative Sentences Many interrogative sentences follow the usual subject-verb order, making the subject easy to identify.

EXAMPLE: Which train <u>lines</u> <u>are traveled</u> the most?

Almost as often, however, an inversion occurs, changing the subject's location within the sentence.

KEY CONCEPT In interrogative sentences, the subject often follows the verb. ■

Inverted interrogative sentences will commonly begin with a verb, a helping verb, or one of the following words: *how, what, when, where, which, who, whose,* or *why*. When looking for the subject in these sentences, mentally change the interrogative sentence into a declarative sentence, as in the following examples.

Questions	Rephrased as Statements
<u>Is</u> the <u>coffee</u> ready?	The <u>coffee</u> <u>is</u> ready.
<u>Will</u> <u>you</u> <u>prepare</u> the monthly train schedule?	<u>You</u> <u>will prepare</u> the monthly train schedule.
<u>Should</u> this <u>line</u> <u>be read</u> now?	This <u>line</u> <u>should be read</u> now.

▼ **Critical Viewing**
The gloved hand on the right belongs to a person hired to help Tokyo commuters squeeze into the subway car. Will this "shover" succeed? Use *there is* or *there are* in your response. [Judge]

Hard-to-Find Subjects • 421

Step-by-Step Teaching Guide continued

4. Explain that some sentences beginning with *here* or *there* may be written with normal subject-verb order. (Example: *Here the colonists <u>fought</u> a brave battle.*) This construction may be used to heighten the drama of a sentence.

5. Using the next chart for examples of inverted order, ask students why or when they think this construction would be used (dramatic effect, changed emphasis).

Step-by-Step Teaching Guide

Subjects in Interrogative Sentences

1. Explain that in interrogative sentences the inversion is, in many cases, precisely what makes the sentence a question. The difference between *It is time* and *Is it time* is the inversion, but we recognize the second as a question.

2. Write the following on the board and have students identify the subject and verb *(train/is)*.

   The last train to New York is on track number nine.

3. Then write:

   <u>Is</u> the last <u>train</u> to New York on track number nine?

   Point out that the subject and verb remain the same but have changed positions.

4. Remind students that some pronouns are interrogative. Words like *who, what,* and *whose* can make finding the subject trickier, because they might modify the subject *(What train lines provided service to Des Moines?)* but could also be the subject *(What fell from that tree?)*.

Critical Viewing

Judge Sample response: There is a good likelihood this "shover" will succeed, because shoving is the person's job.

Step-by-Step Teaching Guide

Subjects in Imperative Sentences

1. Ask students if they have ever heard *imperative* used somewhere other than a grammar lesson — perhaps in a movie (*It is imperative that we take out that bridge*). Explain that the word indicates that something must be done, is necessary, or even urgent.

2. Explain that in grammar, *imperative* relates to requests or commands. So, though less urgent than the first definition, the word still indicates that something needs to happen.

3. Have students suggest imperative sentences where the subject is not "understood" (*You get out of here; You two men have to leave*). Point out that a command is given to a person that the speaker is addressing directly — hence, *you*, whether singular or plural, is the subject.

Language Highlight

The common imperative statement *Sleep tight*, which means "sleep well," most likely originated in the 1700's. At that time, bed mattresses rested upon a series of taut ropes. Over time, the ropes would become loose and cause the mattress to sag. Adjusting the ropes to keep them tight would ensure a more comfortable night.

Step-by-Step Teaching Guide

Subjects in Exclamatory Sentences

1. Ask students to define *exclaim*, "speak suddenly in surprise or strong feeling," or define it for them. Ask how this definition helps explain exclamatory sentences.

2. Ask students to define *elliptical*, "omitting words." Explain that an elliptical sentence is not the same as a sentence fragment.

3. Point out that in some exclamatory sentences both subject and verb are understood. After students read the examples in the chart (*Quickly!* and *Air!*), have them suggest more (*Fire! Now!*). Point out that context often helps in identifying understood sentence parts.

Subjects in Imperative Sentences Subjects in imperative sentences are usually implied, not specifically stated.

▶ **KEY CONCEPT** In imperative sentences, the subject is understood to be *you*. ■

In the following chart, the left side shows imperative sentences in which the subjects are implied. The right side shows the positions where the understood subjects logically occur.

Imperative Sentences	With Understood *You* Added
<u>Wait</u> for the conductor, please.	[You] <u>wait</u> for the conductor, please.
In an earthquake, <u>crawl</u> under a sturdy table.	In an earthquake, [you] <u>crawl</u> under a sturdy table.
Carolyn, <u>take</u> the A-train to Park Slope.	Carolyn, [you] <u>take</u> the A-train to Park Slope.

In the last example, the person addressed is named. However, *Carolyn*, a noun of direct address, is not the subject of the sentence. The subject is still understood to be *you*.

Subjects in Exclamatory Sentences In exclamatory sentences, subjects may come after verbs or be missing entirely.

▶ **KEY CONCEPT** In an exclamatory sentence, the subject may come after the verb or may be understood. ■

The same technique employed to find subjects in interrogative sentences can be used to find the subject in many exclamatory sentences.

EXAMPLES: What could <u>I</u> <u>have done</u>! (I <u>could have done</u> what.)
<u>Can</u> <u>this</u> <u>be</u> real! (This <u>can be</u> real.)

Some exclamatory sentences may be so elliptical that both the subject *and* the verb are implied. For such sentences as these, common sense and context serve as your best guides for determining the unstated subject and verb.

Exclamatory Sentences	With Understood Parts Added
Quickly!	[You <u>come</u> here] quickly!
Air!	[I] <u>need</u>] air!

422 • Basic Sentence Parts

✎ STANDARDIZED TEST PREPARATION WORKSHOP

Grammar and Usage Many standardized tests require students to use their knowledge of subjects and verbs to respond correctly. Use the following example to demonstrate:

(1) The opium poppy has been called both a blessing and a curse. (2) From this plant comes codeine and morphine, which doctors prescribe for pain. (3) However, the drug heroin, which also comes from the poppy, has been seriously abused.

Which sentence in the above passage contains an error in usage?

A 1   **C** 3

B 2   **D** None

The correct answer is **B**. In this inverted order sentence, the subject *codeine and morphine* is compound and plural. Because the verb must also be plural, the correct verb form should be *come*.

GRAMMAR IN LITERATURE

from **The Tragedy of Macbeth**
William Shakespeare

In the following passage, imperative sentences are italicized in blue. What is the understood subject of each?

Prithee, see there!
Behold! Look! Lo! How say you?
Why, what care I? *If thou canst nod, speak too.*

▲ **Critical Viewing**
Describe the state of these train passengers. Answer using an inverted sentence beginning with a prepositional phrase, such as "In repose . . . " [Relate]

▶ **Exercise 11** Locating Hard-to-Find Subjects Write the subject and verb in each sentence. Include in parentheses any words that are understood or implied. Underline each subject once and each verb twice.

EXAMPLE: Here is my report.
ANSWER: <u>report</u> is

1. Where is the train schedule?
2. On the counter lay the schedule.
3. There beside the schedule is your train pass.
4. To the station walked the sleepy commuters.
5. There are thousands of them taking the train to the city every day.
6. Does your father commute to work by train?
7. No!
8. Where does he work?
9. Are the conductors adequately prepared in case of an emergency?
10. After work, take the train home.

▶ **More Practice**

Grammar Exercise Workbook
• pp. 27–28
On-line Exercise Bank
• Section 18.2
Go on-line:
PHSchool.com
Enter Web Code:
egk-1202

Hard-to-Find Subjects • **423**

✓ **ONGOING ASSESSMENT: Monitor and Reinforce**

If students miss more than two items in Exercise 11, refer them to the following for additional practice.

In the Textbook	Print Resources	Technology
Section Review, Ex. 12, Section 18.2	*Grammar Exercise Workbook,* pp. 27–28	*On-Line Exercise Bank,* Section 18.2

Hands-on Grammar

Teaching Resources: Hands-on Grammar Activity Book, Ch. 18

1. If you wish to do this activity in class, be prepared with scissors, a ruler, and construction paper.

2. Working in pairs, students should follow the directions to prepare and label a Subject Locator.

3. After students have inserted the verbs, work with the class to come up with prepositional phrases or introductory words, as well as subjects, for the first two or three verbs.

4. Have students continue the activity with their partners until they have filled in the Subject Locator.

5. Ask for volunteers from various pairs to read their completed sentences aloud.

Find It in Your Reading

Use your current literature textbook and have students work in pairs or groups. Mention that it may be easier to find inverted-order sentences in older, rather than modern, poetry.

Find It in Your Writing

Before students perform this activity, remind them that good inverted-order sentences do not sound awkward or forced. Have volunteers read their new sentences aloud, and ask other students to comment on how effective the new sentences are.

Integrating Writing Skills

Explain to students that becoming comfortable with the different types of sentences has important applications in writing. First, it is important to know how to express both the ideas and the tone one wishes to convey. Second, a variety of sentences is needed not only for meaning but for interest. In addition, if the writer doesn't keep track of the subject well enough and remain consistent, he or she may create confusion that will lose the reader.

⏱ TIME SAVERS!

Hands-on Grammar
Use the Hands-on Grammar activity sheet for Chapter 18 to facilitate this activity.

18.2

Hands-on Grammar

Dual-Direction Subject Locator

Make and use a Dual-Direction Subject Locater to reinforce your ability to locate subjects in sentences where the subject and verb are inverted. Use a sheet of 6 1/2" x 8 1/2" paper and fold in each side edge 1 3/4", leaving a space of 1 1/2" in the middle. Next, draw 11 lines across the folds at 1/2" intervals. Then, open the folds and finish drawing the lines on the inside from crease to crease. Now, print 8 of the following verbs down the middle section:

SITS	RUN	ARE	PLAYED	FLIES	DROVE
CAME	GOES	DANCED	SLEEPS	SHOUTED	FELL

Next, on each line on the outside of the left fold, write a prepositional phrase, a question word (*who, what, where,* etc.), the word *there,* or the word *here.* On the right fold, write a subject that makes sense with the words on the left and the verb. Examples: **Here SITS my loyal dog. Finally, at night CAME the storm.** Cut on the lines as far as the fold on each side, creating a double "fringe." Under each piece of fringe on the left, write the subject from the outside right piece of fringe. Under each piece of fringe on the right, write the words from the outside left piece of fringe. (See illustration.)

Finally, with a partner or alone, practice reading your inverted sentences and the same sentences in normal word order underneath. Notice what happens to the subjects.

Find It in Your Reading Poets often use inverted word order to maintain rhythm or rhyme in their poems. Find examples of inverted word order in a poem; then, restate the sentence in subject-verb order.

Find It in Your Writing Add interest to a piece of your own writing by revising some sentences to invert the word order.

424 • Basic Sentence Parts

☑ ONGOING ASSESSMENT: Assess Mastery

Use the following resources to assess student mastery of subjects and predicates.

In the Textbook	Technology
Chapter Review, Ex. 31	*On-Line Exercise Bank,* Section 18.2

Section Review

GRAMMAR EXERCISES 12–17

Exercise 12 Identifying Subjects and Verbs in Interrogative Sentences
Write the subject and verb in each sentence. Include in parentheses any words that are understood or implied. Underline each subject once and each verb twice.

1. Will we take a train across the country?
2. Where are we going?
3. Have you packed your bags?
4. Did you remember to take your toothbrush?
5. How much will the train cost?
6. Where are some maps of the route?
7. Will we have a sleeping car?
8. How will we eat?
9. Will we see the majestic scenery of the American countryside?
10. Having fun?

Exercise 13 Revising to Invert Subjects and Verbs Revise each sentence, inverting the word order according to the instructions given in parentheses.

1. A family of four was in line for tickets. (Begin with a prepositional phrase.)
2. They will have to buy tickets for the children. (Ask a question.)
3. Will you please pay quickly? (Turn into an imperative.)
4. Ten more people are in line. (Begin with *There.*)
5. We must wait for the train [for what length of time]. (Ask a question.)
6. The express train is pulling into the station now. (Begin with *There.*)
7. The porter is helping them with their luggage. (Ask a question.)
8. The children jump into the train first. (Begin with a prepositional phrase.)
9. This is the right car. (Ask a question.)
10. Our seats are here. (Begin with *Here.*)

Exercise 14 Revising to Form Imperative Sentences Revise these sentences, turning each one into an imperative.

1. Hey, can we go now?
2. I wish you wouldn't walk quite so fast.
3. I want you to put that down now.
4. You turn left here to reach the station.
5. Would you please pick me up at noon?
6. If you leave early, you'll arrive before the crowds.
7. You shouldn't wait to buy your ticket.
8. I ask that you write to me soon.
9. You need to get the form signed if you want to attend.
10. We can all go together and have fun!

Exercise 15 Find It in Your Reading Reread the excerpt from William Shakespeare's *Macbeth* on page 423. Identify the interrogative sentences and their subjects.

Exercise 16 Find It in Your Writing Revise a piece of written dialogue to include at least one interrogative, one exclamatory, and one imperative sentence. Notice how changing the sentences affects the presentation of your characters and the tone of the dialogue.

Exercise 17 Writing Application Consider the different types of jobs associated with trains, such as conductor, engineer, stationmaster, and track maintenance crew. Write a brief essay detailing which job you think would be the best and why. Use each of the four sentence functions in your essay.

Section Review • 425

ASSESS

Section Review

Each of these exercises correlates to the instruction on hard-to-find subjects, pages 420–424. These exercises may be used for more practice, for reteaching, or for review of the key concepts presented.

Answer Key

Exercise 12

1. we <u>Will take</u>
2. we <u>are going</u>
3. you <u>Have packed</u>
4. you <u>Did remember</u>
5. train <u>will cost</u>
6. maps <u>are</u>
7. we <u>Will have</u>
8. we <u>will eat</u>
9. we <u>Will see</u>
10. (you <u>are</u>) <u>Having</u>

Exercise 13

Answers may vary. Sample answers:

1. In line for tickets was a family of four.
2. Will they have to buy tickets for the children?
3. (you) Please pay quickly.
4. There are ten more people in line.
5. How long must we wait for the train?
6. There is the express train pulling into the station now.
7. Is the porter helping them with their luggage?
8. Into the train jump the children first.
9. Is this the right car?
10. Here are our seats.

Exercise 14

Answers may vary. Sample answers:

1. Hey, let's go now!
2. Do not walk quite so fast, please.
3. Put that down now.
4. Turn left here to reach the station.
5. Please pick me up at noon.
6. Leave early so you can arrive before the crowds.
7. Don't wait to buy your ticket.
8. Do write to me soon.
9. Get the form signed if you want to attend.
10. Let's all go together and have fun!

Answer Key continued

Exercise 15

Find It in Your Reading
"How say you?" The subject is *you*.
"Why, what care I?" The subject is *I*.

Exercise 16

Find It in Your Writing
If students have written dialogues that contain a variety of these sentence types, ask them to comment on why each type was appropriate for the character and/or the situation. Or, suggest that students write a short dialogue.

Exercise 17

Writing Application
Ask students to identify the sentence functions that were easiest and most difficult to work into essay writing. (Exclamations may be the most difficult to work into an essay, while declarative sentences are probably the easiest.) Discuss the types of writing that lend themselves most readily to the use of the different functions (dialogue, persuasive writing, etc.).

Interest GRABBER Write the following on the board:

The satellite circled the (noun).

The scientists showed the (noun) their new invention.

The moon was (adjective).

Ask students to complete each sentence by supplying words that logically fill each blank. Circle each word they supply and explain that these are called complements. Identify the type of complement that completes each sentence. (DO, IO, Predicate Adj.)

Activate Prior Knowledge

Write on the board:

compliment/complement

Ask students to define these frequently confused words. (*Compliment* has to do with praise or politeness; *complement* means that something completes or makes something perfect or is required to create a whole.) You may wish to point out that *complement*, like *complete*, has two *e*'s. Then discuss why a sentence might need words other than subjects and verbs to be complete.

Critical Viewing

Draw Conclusions Sample response: The astronaut might be seeing the clouds below him. Through the clouds, he might also get a glimpse of Earth.

TEACH

Step-by-Step Teaching Guide

Complements

1. Write on the board:

   He is . . .

   I swung . . .

   She handed . . .

2. Point out that, even though each of these phrases has a subject and a verb, we recognize that the thoughts are incomplete.

3. Explain that, because a sentence is "a group of words that expresses a complete thought," these phrases need something to make them complete—they need complements.

Section 18.3

Complements

Some sentences are complete with just a subject and a verb or with a subject, verb, and modifiers, as in *The crowd cheered.*

The meaning of many sentences, however, depends on additional words to finish the idea begun by the subject and verb. For example, *The satellite continually sends . . .* is confusing and incomplete, even though it has a subject and verb. To complete the meaning of the predicate parts of those sentences, a writer must add *complements*.

▶ **KEY CONCEPT** A **complement** is a word or group of words that completes the meaning of the predicate of a sentence. ■

There are five different kinds of complements in English: *direct objects, indirect objects, objective complements, predicate nominatives,* and *predicate adjectives.* The first three occur in sentences with transitive action verbs, whereas the last two, often grouped together as *subject complements,* are found only with linking verbs. (See Chapter 17 for more information about action and linking verbs.)

Direct Objects

Direct objects, the most common of the five types of complements, complete the meaning of action verbs by telling *who* or *what* receives the action.

▶ **KEY CONCEPT** A **direct object** is a noun, pronoun, or group of words acting as a noun that receives the action of a transitive verb. ■

EXAMPLES:
                    DO
      I <u>visited</u> the Air and Space Museum.

                      DO
      <u>Mud</u> and <u>leaves</u> <u>clogged</u> the gutters.

To determine the direct object of a sentence, ask *Whom?* or *What?* after an action verb. If the sentence offers no answer, the action verb is intransitive and there is no direct object in the sentence.

EXAMPLES:
      The <u>curator</u> of the museum <u>led</u> the tour. (Led *what? Answer:* tour)
      The <u>satellite</u> <u>spun</u> beyond the atmosphere. (Spun *what? Answer:* none; the verb is intransitive)

426 • Basic Sentence Parts

Theme: NASA

In this section, you will learn about direct and indirect objects and objective and subject complements. The examples and exercises are about NASA.

Cross-Curricular Connection: Science

▲ **Critical Viewing** What are some of the things this astronaut might be seeing as he maneuvers this massive satellite? Use direct objects in your answer. **[Draw Conclusions]**

⏱ TIME AND RESOURCE MANAGER

Resources
Print: *Grammar Exercise Workbook,* pp. 29–32; *Grammar Exercises Answers on Transparencies,* Ch. 18
Technology: *Writing and Grammar* Interactive Text, Section 18.3; *On-Line Exercise Bank,* Section 18.3

Using the Full Student Edition	Using the Handbook🄷
• Work through all key concepts, pp. 426–432. • Assign and review Exercises 18–23. • Read and discuss Grammar in Literature, p. 431.	• Work through all key concepts, pp. 288–294. • Assign and review Exercises 18–23. • Read and discuss Grammar in Literature, p. 293.

KEY CONCEPT In some inverted questions, the direct object may appear before the verb. Rephrase such questions as statements in normal word order to locate the direct objects. ∎

INVERTED QUESTION:

DO
Which rocket <u>did</u> <u>they</u> <u>launch</u>?

REWORDED AS A STATEMENT:

DO
<u>They</u> <u>did launch</u> which rocket?

Keep alert for sentences with more than one direct object, known as a *compound direct object.* If a sentence contains a compound direct object, asking *Whom?* or *What?* after the action verb will yield two or more answers.

EXAMPLES:

DO   DO
The <u>astronaut</u> <u>wore</u> a helmet and a spacesuit.

DO
NASA's <u>programs</u> <u>have included</u> the Mercury, the

DO   DO
Gemini, and the Apollo during the last forty years.

In the last example, *years* is the object of the preposition *during.* The object of a preposition is never a direct object.

Exercise 18 **Recognizing Direct Objects** Read the paragraph below, and then write the direct objects in each sentence, including all parts of any compound direct objects.

EXAMPLE: Often, space shuttle astronauts conduct scientific experiments.

ANSWER   experiments

(1) In 1958, the United States Congress created the National Aeronautics and Space Administration (NASA). (2) The National Aeronautics and Space Act established the organization. (3) NASA plans, directs, and conducts all non-military U.S. space activity. (4) The President appoints a civilian administrator to the organization. (5) The U.S. Senate, however, must approve the President's selection. (6) NASA coordinates all research and study of the cosmos. (7) Then, it disseminates the results of the research. (8) Under the President's guidance, NASA also develops cooperative space programs with other countries. (9) With the advent of the space shuttle program, NASA increasingly began work on military projects, despite its original mandate as a civilian agency. (10) Because of the 1986 *Challenger* shuttle disaster, however, the military expanded its own separate fleet of rockets.

💡 **Spelling Tip**

NASA is an acronym that stands for the **N**ational **A**eronautics and **S**pace **A**dministration. When an acronym is three or more letters, it is usually written without periods after each letter.

More Practice

Grammar Exercise Workbook
• pp. 29–30
On-line Exercise Bank
• Section 18.3
Go on-line:
PHSchool.com
Enter Web Code:
egk-1202

ⓘnteractive
Textbook

Get instant feedback!
Exercise 18 is available on-line or on CD-ROM.

Complements • 427

☑ **ONGOING ASSESSMENT: Monitor and Reinforce**

If students miss more than two items in Exercise 18, refer them to the following for additional practice.

In the Textbook	Print Resources	Technology
Section Review, Ex. 24, Section 18.3	*Grammar Exercise Workbook,* pp. 29–30	*On-Line Exercise Bank,* Section 18.3

Indirect Objects

1. Point out that an indirect object almost always precedes a direct object. In the literal context of the sentence, it receives the direct object.

2. Write the following sentences on the board:

   The astronauts brought the equipment.

   The astronauts brought me the equipment.

   Have students identify the subject, verb, and direct object in each sentence. Show them that, by asking the question *To whom was the equipment brought?*, they can determine what the indirect object is. Point out that the indirect object of the second sentence, *me*, precedes the direct object, *equipment*.

3. Explain that, because the indirect object generally precedes the direct object, students should be aware that an object that follows the direct object may not be an indirect object. Use the examples at the bottom of the page to demonstrate the difference between indirect objects and objects of prepositions.

4. Remind students that indirect objects may have their own modifiers, such as prepositional phrases and adjectives. Give this example: *I promised my brother Ian a ride in my car.* The indirect object, (*my brother*), has an appositive, (*Ian*).

5. Review the verbs commonly associated with indirect objects (located beneath the key concept). Ask students if they can think of others (*take, offer, sell, send*). Have students suggest sentences that contain both indirect objects and objects of prepositions, with and without modifiers.

18.3

Indirect Objects

Indirect objects are found in sentences with direct objects.

▶ **KEY CONCEPT** An **indirect object** is a noun or pronoun that appears with a direct object and names the person or thing that something is given to or done for. ■

Indirect objects are common with such verbs as *ask, bring, buy, give, lend, make, promise, show, teach, tell,* and *write.*

EXAMPLES:
IO   DO
NASA gave the astronauts a course correction.

                    IO   DO
The satellite sent the television stations its signal.

Like direct objects, indirect objects can be compound.

EXAMPLE:
           IO   IO   DO
I showed my mom and dad the NASA poster.

To locate an indirect object, first be sure the sentence contains a direct object. Then, ask one of these questions after the verb and direct object: *To or for whom?* or *To or for what?*

EXAMPLES:
           IO   DO
The teacher taught our class astrophysics.
(Taught astrophysics *to whom? Answer:* class)

           IO   DO
We made the couch a slipcover.
(Made slipcover *for what? Answer:* couch)

To avoid confusing an indirect object with a direct object, always remember to ask the right questions in the correct order. First, ask *Whom?* or *What?* after the verb to find the direct object. If the sentence contains a direct object, then ask *To or for whom?* or *To or for what?* after the verb and direct object to find the indirect object.

EXAMPLE:
           IO   DO
Pat gave Doug a model space shuttle. (Gave *what? Answer:* shuttle) (Gave shuttle *to whom? Answer:* Doug)

Remember also that an indirect object almost always sits squarely between the verb and direct object. In a sentence in normal word order, it will never follow the direct object nor will it ever be the object of the preposition *to* or *for.*

EXAMPLES:
               DO   OBJ OF PREP
NASA sent the poster to me.

               IO   DO
NASA sent me the poster.

428 • Basic Sentence Parts

Internet Tip

Most search engines on the Internet recognize common acronyms such as NASA and NATO. However, initiating a second search using the spelled-out version of an organization's abbreviated name sometimes generates more or different results.

✒ STANDARDIZED TEST PREPARATION WORKSHOP

Grammar and Usage Many standardized tests require students to use their knowledge of basic sentence parts to respond correctly. Use the following example to demonstrate:

A good mystery author develops an intricate story line, and a cast of unusual characters for us to follow and analyze.

How is the underlined portion correctly written?

A story line and a cast of unusual characters

B story line; and a cast of unusual characters

C story line — a cast of unusual characters

D Correct as is

The correct answer is **A**. The comma must be removed because it interrupts the compound direct object of this sentence (*story line* and *cast*). B and C are wrong because they create an even greater separation between the two parts of the compound direct object.

Exercise 19 Recognizing Indirect Objects Write the underlined words in each sentence, and identify each as a *direct object*, *indirect object*, or *object of a preposition*.

EXAMPLE: Frank gave his <u>friends</u> rock <u>samples</u> from the moon.

ANSWER: friends (indirect object) samples (direct object)

1. NASA designed the <u>space shuttle</u> for human and cargo <u>transport</u>.
2. Congress granted <u>NASA</u> <u>funds</u> for the spacecraft in the 1970's.
3. A reusable spacecraft, the space shuttle gave <u>scientists</u> a <u>way</u> to study the effects of repeated space exposure.
4. Because of the shuttle's reusability, the program marked a major <u>departure</u> from previous space <u>programs</u>.
5. After ten years of preparation, NASA presented the <u>country</u> its first <u>shuttle</u> in 1981.
6. NASA now keeps four <u>shuttles</u> in <u>operation</u>.
7. In response to NASA's <u>shuttles</u>, the Soviet Union started a shuttle <u>program</u> themselves.
8. However, a scarcity of funds halted the <u>program</u> in 1993.
9. At first, NASA's space shuttle deployed <u>satellites</u> into <u>orbit</u>.
10. As the program matured, the space shuttle retrieved ailing <u>satellites</u> for <u>repair</u>.

Exercise 20 Writing Sentences With Indirect Objects Write sentences with indirect objects using the verbs given below. Then, underline each indirect object, and draw a circle around the direct object.

EXAMPLE: wrote

ANSWER: I wrote <u>NASA</u> a (letter.)

1. promise
2. gave
3. told
4. lend
5. will show

▶ Critical Viewing
What role does the rocket play in the shuttle launch? Use an indirect object in your response. [Interpret]

More Practice

Grammar Exercise Workbook
• pp. 29–30
On-line Exercise Bank
• Section 18.3
Go on-line:
PHSchool.com
Enter Web Code:
egk-1202

Complements • 429

Answer Key

▶ **Exercise 19**

1. space shuttle (direct object), transport (object of preposition)
2. NASA (indirect object), funds (direct object)
3. scientists (indirect object), way (direct object)
4. departure (direct object), programs (object of preposition)
5. country (indirect object), shuttle (direct object)
6. shuttles (direct object), operation (object of preposition)
7. shuttles (object of preposition), program (direct object)
8. program (direct object)
9. satellites (direct object), orbit (object of preposition)
10. satellites (direct object), repair (object of preposition)

▶ **Exercise 20**

Answers will vary; samples are given. Indirect objects are underlined; direct objects are double underlined.

1. I promise <u>you</u> a quick <u>answer</u> to your inquiry.
2. She gave <u>him</u> her <u>word</u> of honor.
3. Who told <u>Laura</u> the <u>truth</u> about the telegram?
4. Please lend <u>Peter</u> some <u>money</u>.
5. They will show <u>us</u> the <u>results</u> of the survey.

Critical Viewing

Interpret Sample response: The rocket gives the shuttle a boost.

Customize for
Spatial Learners
On the board, create a series of four boxes. In order, label the boxes *subject*, *verb*, *indirect object*, and *direct object*. Call on students to suggest nouns, pronouns, and verbs for each box. Once you have created a sentence (Example: *Bill showed me the telescope.*), pick a box and ask students to suggest another appropriate word (Example: *Bill showed Albert the telescope.*). After you have worked through several variations, expand the sentences by adding adjective and adverb boxes and prepositional phrase boxes. Use a second color of chalk when you make these additions. This activity will help students see that the basic grammatical pattern remains the same.

☑ **ONGOING ASSESSMENT: Monitor and Reinforce**

If students have difficulty with Exercise 19 or 20, refer them to the following for additional practice.

In the Textbook	Print Resources	Technology
Section Review, Ex. 24, Section 18.3	*Grammar Exercise Workbook,* pp. 29–30	*On-Line Exercise Bank,* Section 18.3

Objective Complements

1. Explain to students that the first step in identifying an objective complement is finding the direct object. If there is no direct object, there can be no objective complement.

2. Write on the board: *I consider her a great scientist.* Ask students to identify the direct object (*her*), and then ask how the words that follow relate to the direct object (they tell us what they speaker thinks of "her"). Point out that the objective complement here, *scientist*, has modifiers.

3. Write the following on the board:

    The pilot called him a hero.

    Commander Pepper considered the mission difficult and dangerous.

    Have students identify the direct object and objective complement(s) in each. (DO = him, OC = hero; DO = mission, OC = difficult/dangerous)

Customize for
AP Students

Ask students to write sentences that use more complicated structures for complements (gerunds and infinitives). Begin with these models:

*Scientists declared the lunar **landing** a great **success**. (DO = landing (gerund); OC = success)*

*The magician tried **to make the rabbit disappear**. (DO = to make the rabbit disappear (infinitive); **rabbit** is the object of the infinitive)*

Answer Key

Exercise 21

Answers will vary; samples are given.

1. . . . one space shuttle *Enterprise*.
2. . . . early missions promising.
3. . . . a scientist administrator of NASA.
4. . . . Cape Kennedy a treasure.
5. . . . spacecraft exciting.
6. . . . has made space less unknown and incomprehensible.
7. Scientists consider one another brilliant and lucky.
8. . . . U.S. space program a success.
9. . . . NASA's research excellent.
10. . . . have made life on Earth better.

18.3

Objective Complements

Whereas an indirect object almost always comes before a direct object, an *objective complement* almost always follows a direct object. As its name implies, the objective complement "complements," or adds to the meaning of, the direct object.

> **KEY CONCEPT** An objective complement is an adjective or noun that appears with a direct object and describes or renames it. ■

A sentence containing an objective complement may at first glance seem to have two direct objects. Identifying objective complements is simplified when you know they occur only with such verbs as *appoint, call, consider, declare, elect, judge, label, make, name, select,* or *think.*

EXAMPLES:
The <u>directors</u> of the launch <u>declared</u> it successful. (DO = it, OC = successful)

The <u>President</u> <u>appointed</u> him NASA administrator. (DO = him, OC = administrator)

Like other sentence parts, objective complements can be compound.

EXAMPLE:
I <u>called</u> Dave a very talented swimmer and a brilliant astronaut. (DO = Dave, OC = swimmer / astronaut)

> **Exercise 21** Revising to Add Objective Complements
Revise each sentence, adding an objective complement of the type indicated.

EXAMPLE:
The committee judged that entry (<u>noun</u>).
The committee judged that entry the winner.

1. NASA named one space shuttle (noun).
2. It considered the early missions (adjective).
3. The President appoints a scientist (noun) of NASA.
4. Florida considers Cape Kennedy (noun).
5. Many children find spacecraft (adjective).
6. NASA's research has made space less (adjective) and (adjective).
7. Scientists consider one another (adjective) and (adjective).
8. NASA's work has made the U.S. space program (noun).
9. In fact, scientists generally consider NASA's research (adjective).
10. New advancements from NASA's research have made life on Earth (adjective).

> **More Practice**

Grammar Exercise Workbook
• pp. 31–32
On-line Exercise Bank
• Section 18.3
 Go on-line:
 PHSchool.com
 Enter Web Code:
 egk-1202

Interactive Textbook

Complete the exercise on-line! Exercise 21 is available on-line or on CD-ROM.

☑ ONGOING ASSESSMENT: Monitor and Reinforce

If students miss more than two items in Exercise 21, refer them to the following for additional practice.

In the Textbook	Print Resources	Technology
Section Review, Ex. 25, Section 18.3	*Grammar Exercise Workbook,* pp. 31–32	*On-Line Exercise Bank,* Section 18.3

GRAMMAR IN LITERATURE

from **We'll Never Conquer Space**

Arthur C. Clarke

Notice how the author has used several subject complements (predicate nominatives and predicate adjectives) in the passage.

To our ancestors, the vastness of the earth was a dominant *fact* controlling their thoughts and lives. In all earlier ages than ours, the world was *wide* indeed, and no man could ever see more than a tiny fraction of its immensity. A few hundred miles—a thousand, at the most—was *infinity*. Only a lifetime ago, parents waved farewell to their emigrating children in the virtual certainty that they would never meet again.

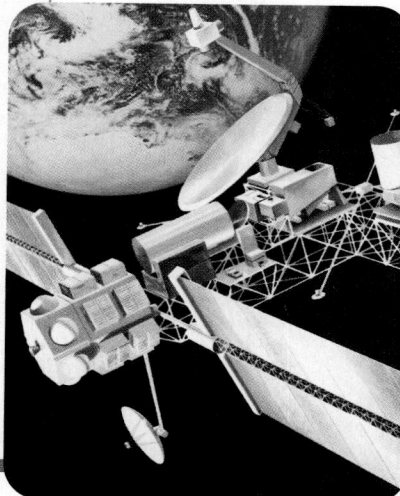

▲ **Critical Viewing**
Using subject complements, describe some of the features of this satellite. **[Analyze]**

Subject Complements

Linking verbs require *subject complements* to complete their meaning.

▶ **KEY CONCEPT** A **subject complement** is a noun, pronoun, or adjective that appears with a linking verb and tells something about the subject. ■

Predicate Nominatives The subject and the predicate nominative refer to the same person, place, or thing.

▶ **KEY CONCEPT** A **predicate nominative** is a noun or pronoun that appears with a linking verb and renames, identifies, or explains the subject. ■

The last example has a compound predicate nominative.

EXAMPLES:

                PN
Ann Pace <u>became</u> a scientist for NASA.

        PN
The <u>winner</u> <u>is</u> you.

              PN   PN
<u>John Glenn</u> <u>is</u> a politician and former astronaut.

Complements • 431

Predicate Adjectives

1. Explain that, if the word following the linking verb is an adjective instead of a noun, the complement is a predicate adjective.

2. Write on the board

    The scientist became an astronaut. (PN)

    The scientist was brilliant. (PA)

    Have students identify the type of subject complement in each.

Customize for
ESL Students

Explain to students that predicate nominatives are a little like translations. For example, in the sentence "*Rojo* is "red" in Spanish," *rojo* is the subject, which is connected by the linking verb *is* to the predicate nominative, "red." In the case of predicate nominatives, the renaming stays in the same language (any language), but fulfills the same function.

Integrating Workplace Skills

Have students look for books that describe applying for jobs or creating résumés. Have them scan examples in the books to find complements. (For example: *I am a good student.* [PN]; *I am eager to learn.* [PA])

Answer Key

Exercise 22

1. stargazer (PN)
2. distant, inviting (PA)
3. intense (PA)
4. fervent (PA)
5. major (PN)
6. good (PA)
7. candidate (PN)
8. strict, demanding (PA)
9. challenging, exciting (PA)
10. dream (PN)

Exercise 23

Answers will vary; samples are given.

1. I will become a <u>nurse</u> in two years.
2. I grow <u>excited</u> at the thought of it.
3. I felt <u>nervous</u> at first.
4. I will be an <u>expert</u> like my sister.
5. A wonderful <u>nurse</u> is <u>she</u>.

18.3

Predicate Adjectives As the name indicates, a predicate adjective is not a noun or a pronoun but an adjective.

> **KEY CONCEPT** A **predicate adjective** is an adjective that appears with a linking verb and describes the subject of the sentence. ∎

A predicate adjective refers to the subject by describing it in much the same way any adjective modifies a noun or pronoun.

EXAMPLES: Your <u>reasoning</u> <u>seems</u> logical.
                                          PA

                                  PA   PA
The <u>launch</u> <u>sounded</u> loud and thunderous.

> **Exercise 22** Identifying Subject Complements Write the subject complement or complements in each sentence. Then, identify each as a *predicate nominative* or *predicate adjective*.

EXAMPLE: Jean should become a successful college student.
ANSWER: student (predicate nominative)

1. After a high-school course in astronomy, I became an avid stargazer.
2. The heavens appeared distant yet inviting.
3. My interest grew more intense in college.
4. Following a series of difficult advanced astronomy courses, I remained fervent in my passion for the heavens.
5. With enough credits, I had become an astronomy major.
6. Graduate school looked good to me after graduation.
7. With my degree, I will be a candidate for a post at NASA.
8. NASA's requirements are strict and demanding.
9. A future with NASA appears challenging but exciting.
10. Working with NASA is a dream of mine.

> **Exercise 23** Writing Sentences With Subject Complement Write sentences with the verbs and types of subject complements indicated. Then, underline each subject complement.

EXAMPLE: was (predicate pronoun)
ANSWER: The first shuttle captain was <u>he</u>.

1. become (predicate noun)
2. grow (predicate adjective)
3. felt (predicate adjective)
4. will be (predicate noun)
5. is (predicate pronoun)

432 • Basic Sentence Parts

> **More Practice**

Grammar Exercise Workbook
• pp. 31–32
On-line Exercise Bank
• Section 18.3
Go on-line:
PHSchool.com
Enter Web Code:
egk-1202

Get instant feedback! Exercises 22 and 23 are available on-line or on CD-ROM.

☑ **ONGOING ASSESSMENT: Monitor and Reinforce**

If students have difficulty with Exercise 22 or 23, refer them to the following for additional practice.

In the Textbook	Print Resources	Technology
Section Review, Ex. 26, Section 18.3	*Grammar Exercise Workbook,* pp. 31–32	*On-Line Exercise Bank,* Section 18.3

Section 18.3 Section Review

GRAMMAR EXERCISES 24–29

Exercise 24 Recognizing Direct Objects and Indirect Objects Write the underlined words in each sentence, and identify each as a *direct object*, *indirect object*, or *object of a preposition*.

1. The Russians designed their space station <u>Mir</u> for long-term space <u>habitation</u>.
2. They launched the <u>station</u> into <u>orbit</u> on February 20, 1986.
3. Russian spacecraft and American space shuttles bring crew <u>members</u> instant <u>fame</u>.
4. Through the *Salyut* series, the Russians developed the <u>technology</u> for <u>Mir</u>.
5. The series gave the <u>Russians</u> valuable <u>information</u> about living in space.

Exercise 25 Identifying Objective Complements Write the objective complement(s) in each of the following sentences. Then, identify them as *nouns* or *adjectives*.

1. NASA named the first American space station Skylab.
2. NASA considers its astronauts hard-working.
3. For each mission, the administration appoints astronauts crew members.
4. Most people think an astronaut's training impossible.
5. The difficult training makes astronauts tough and alert.
6. The astronaut must consider the hardships of the job necessary.
7. Astronauts consider space an adventure.
8. NASA has made astronauts heroes.
9. NASA has declared satellites a priority.
10. Communications and industry have made the continual development of satellites vital.

Exercise 26 Supplying Subject Complements Complete each sentence with an appropriate subject complement. Then, identify each as a *predicate nominative* or *predicate adjective*.

1. Satellites have become ___?___ of modern life.
2. Circling beyond the atmosphere, satellites seem ___?___ than they are.
3. They are ___?___ for virtually all communication.
4. Since 1962, satellites have become ___?___ in the telephone and television industries.
5. Satellites appear ___?___ for voice, data, and image transfer.

Exercise 27 Find It in Your Reading Identify the subject complements in the following passage from Arthur C. Clarke's "We'll Never Conquer Space."

. . .For it seems as certain as anything can be that no signal—still less any material object—can ever travel faster than light. The velocity of light is the ultimate speed limit, being part of the very structure of space and time.

Exercise 28 Find It in Your Writing Review one of your lab reports for a science class, and underline each direct object.

Exercise 29 Writing Application Write a brief story about space travel. Underline any complements you use.

Section Review • 433

ONGOING ASSESSMENT: Assess Mastery

Use the following resources to assess student mastery of basic sentence parts.

In the Textbook	Print Resources	Technology
Chapter Review, Ex. 32–33 Standardized Test Preparation Workshop	*Formal Assessment*, Chapter 18	*On-Line Exercise Bank*, Chapter 18

ASSESS and CLOSE

Section Review

Each of these exercises correlates to the instruction on complements, pages 426–432. These exercises may be used for more practice, for reteaching, or for review of the key concepts presented.

Answer Key

Exercise 24

1. space station (direct object), habitation (object of preposition)
2. station (direct object), orbit (object of preposition)
3. members (indirect object), fame (direct object)
4. technology (direct object), *Mir* (object of preposition)
5. Russians (indirect object), information (direct object)

Exercise 25

1. Skylab (noun)
2. hard-working (adjective)
3. astronauts (noun)
4. impossible (adjective)
5. tough, alert (adjectives)
6. necessary (adjective)
7. adventure (noun)
8. heroes (noun)
9. priority (noun)
10. vital (adjective)

Exercise 26

Answers will vary; samples are given.

1. part (PN)
2. smaller (PA)
3. links (PN)
4. significant (PA)
5. useful (PA)

Exercise 27

Find It in Your Reading
certain (predicate adjective)
limit (predicate nominative)

Exercise 28

Find It in Your Writing
Ask students why they think a lab report is a good place to look for direct objects (much lab work involves actions directed toward something). Have students share some of the direct objects they found.

Exercise 29

Writing Application
Have students trade stories with partners, and have each identify the types of complements underlined in the other's work.

CHAPTER REVIEW

Each of these exercises correlates to a section of the chapter on basic sentence parts, pages 410–433. The exercises may be used for more practice, for reteaching, or for review of the key concepts presented in the chapter. Answers for all chapter exercises are available in *Grammar Exercises Answers on Transparencies* in your Teaching Resources.

Answer Key

▶ Exercise 30

1. The Canadian <u>province</u> of Alberta I <u>is</u> rich in natural beauty.
2. <u>Nothing</u> I <u>proves</u> this more than Banff National Park.
3. <u>Banff</u> I <u>is located</u> in the southwestern part of the province.
4. Canada's oldest national park, <u>it</u> I <u>was</u> formally <u>established</u> in 1885.
5. Famous for its spectacular scenery, glaciers, hot springs, and lakes, <u>Banff</u> I <u>is nestled</u> in the Rocky Mountains.
6. Perfect for exploration, the <u>mountains</u> I <u>provide</u> a spectacular environment for outdoor recreation.
7. Its pristine <u>lakes</u>, mountainous <u>terrain</u>, and intricate <u>network</u> of <u>trails</u> I <u>make</u> it suitable as both a summer and winter resort.
8. <u>Wildlife</u>, such as elk, cougar, and bighorn sheep I <u>populate</u> Banff.
9. With an area of more than 2,500 square miles, I <u>Banff</u> I <u>is</u> Canada's eleventh largest <u>nature</u> preserve.
10. Nature <u>lovers</u> of all kinds I <u>should find</u> Banff a fulfilling destination.

▶ Exercise 31

1. There <u>are</u> <u>dozens</u> of national parks in the United States.
2. Deep into the cavern <u>trekked</u> the brave <u>spelunkers</u>.
3. <u>Are</u> <u>you</u> <u>planning</u> to visit Howe Caverns this summer?
4. (You) <u>Wait</u> for your guide, please.
5. (You) <u>Help</u>!
6. Here <u>are</u> our <u>backpacks</u>.
7. In the event of a storm, (<u>you</u>) <u>find</u> shelter immediately.
8. Over the rapids <u>surged</u> a <u>group</u> of white-water rafters.
9. <u>Was</u> <u>Yellowstone</u> worth the trip?
10. (You) <u>Hammer</u> the tent stakes securely into the ground.

Chapter 18 Chapter Review

GRAMMAR EXERCISES 30–36

▶ **Exercise 30** Identifying Complete Subjects and Predicates Copy each of the following sentences, drawing a vertical line between the complete subject and complete predicate. Then, underline each subject once and each verb twice.

1. The Canadian province of Alberta is rich in natural beauty.
2. Nothing proves this more than Banff National Park.
3. Banff is located in the southwestern part of the province.
4. Canada's oldest national park, it was formally established in 1885.
5. Famous for its spectacular scenery, glaciers, hot springs, and lakes, Banff is nestled in the Rocky Mountains.
6. Perfect for exploration, the mountains provide a spectacular environment for outdoor recreation.
7. Its pristine lakes, mountainous terrain, and intricate network of trails make it suitable as both a summer and winter resort.
8. Wildlife such as elk, cougar, and bighorn sheep populate Banff.
9. With an area of more than 2,500 square miles, Banff is Canada's eleventh largest nature preserve.
10. Nature lovers of all kinds should find Banff a fulfilling destination.

▶ **Exercise 31** Identifying Hard-to-Find Subjects Copy the following sentences, underlining each subject once and each verb twice. Include in parentheses any words that are understood or implied.

1. There are dozens of national parks in the United States.
2. Deep into the cavern trekked the brave spelunkers.

434 • Basic Sentence Parts

3. Are you planning to visit Howe Caverns this summer?
4. Wait for your guide, please.
5. Help!
6. Here are our backpacks.
7. In the event of a storm, find shelter immediately.
8. Over the rapids surged a group of white-water rafters.
9. Was Yellowstone worth the trip?
10. Hammer the tent stakes securely into the ground.

▶ **Exercise 32** Recognizing Sentence Parts Label each of the underlined sentence parts *subject, verb, direct object, indirect object, objective complement, predicate nominative,* or *predicate adjective.*

1. The Gir National Park and Lion Sanctuary <u>is</u> in western India.
2. It was declared a forest <u>reserve</u> in 1913, a wildlife <u>sanctuary</u> in 1965, and a national <u>park</u> in 1975.
3. The lion <u>sanctuary</u> occupies 445 square <u>miles</u> in the Kathiawar Peninsula.
4. Within that area, the national park <u>comprises</u> 100 square miles.
5. This conservation area is <u>one</u> of the largest in India.
6. The region's climate is <u>hot</u> and <u>arid</u>.
7. The area's scrublike vegetation includes teak <u>trees</u> and thorn <u>forests</u>.
8. In 1948, the local ruler, the nawab of Junagadh, gave the endangered Asiatic <u>lions</u> a larger <u>area</u> in which to roam.
9. Later agricultural considerations made the <u>area</u> <u>smaller</u>.
10. Despite the shrinking preserve lands, conservation <u>efforts</u> took effect about fifty years later.

▶ Exercise 32

1. verb
2. PN, PN, PN
3. subject, DO
4. verb
5. PN
6. PA, PA
7. DO, DO
8. IO, DO
9. DO, OC
10. subject

continued

434

11. From a low of about 20 Asiatic lions in the area, 300 lions now <u>roam</u> the sanctuary.
12. Unfortunately, the growing numbers of lions <u>present</u> difficulties for the park authorities.
13. The sanctuary is not <u>large</u> enough to accommodate them, and some <u>have moved</u> beyond the park.
14. The park and sanctuary are also <u>home</u> to many other animals.
15. These include <u>antelope</u> and several <u>species</u> of reptiles.

Exercise 33 Writing Sentences

With Complements On your paper, write sentences following the instructions given below.

1. Use *mountain* as a direct object.
2. Use *campers* as an indirect object.
3. Use *brisk* as a predicate adjective.
4. Use *campsite* as a predicate noun.
5. Use *adventure* as an objective complement.

Exercise 34 Revision Practice On

a separate sheet of paper, revise the following paragraph. Where appropriate, combine sentences, using compound subjects and predicates. Eliminate fragments.

Many African countries are working to protect elephants. Many preservation groups are also trying to protect elephants. Although elephants can sometimes be dangerous to people. People have turned out to be much more dangerous to elephants. Loggers have eliminated elephant habitats. Farmers have done the same. Hunters have killed elephants for their valuable ivory tusks. Elephants now in danger of extinction. Some nations have banned any trade in ivory. In addition, they have discouraged poaching by helping communities to profit from tourism. Many countries have set aside parklands and preserves to protect elephants. They also protect other endangered species. Hoping for success.

Exercise 35 Writing Application

Imagine that you are a reporter writing about the activities of an environmental conservation club in your community. Craft a feature-length story (about 200 words) describing the club's projects and their overall effect. Edit and proofread your work, and as you revise, make sure you have used a variety of sentence patterns.

Exercise 36 CUMULATIVE REVIEW

Parts of Speech and Basic Sentence Parts On your paper, write the part of speech of each underlined word, including those that are boldfaced. Then, revise the passage, changing each underlined word to a more precise word in the same part of speech. Finally, underline the subject once and the verb twice in each sentence, and circle elliptical sentences.

Every <u>February</u>, the Mahoney family gathers at Lake Tahoe to ski. <u>Among</u> the family <u>members</u>, some are <u>great</u> skiers, <u>some</u> are <u>good</u>, and two <u>are forever</u> on the beginners' slope. No matter. The object of the <u>trip</u> is to have fun, and, *boy*, what fun they have!

Renting cabins <u>near</u> the <u>pretty</u> lake, the family rises <u>every</u> clear, <u>nice</u> morning to a view of <u>rich</u> blue water, forests of <u>tall</u> pines and cedars, and the <u>great</u> <u>Sierra Nevada</u> <u>and</u> Carson range of <u>granite</u> mountains covered with <u>bright</u> snow. After a <u>big</u> breakfast, <u>everyone</u> <u>goes</u> to the <u>slopes</u>. <u>Some</u> days, the sun <u>is</u> <u>so</u> warm <u>that</u> the skiers wear <u>only</u> sweaters.

In the afternoon, the <u>tired</u> <u>adults</u> and <u>children</u> <u>go</u> to the lodge to <u>have</u> <u>hot</u> chocolate and warm <u>themselves</u> <u>by</u> the fire. Often, the teenagers <u>go</u> to Emerald Bay, where some take photographs of this <u>very</u> <u>lovely</u> natural <u>place</u>. Well-read cousin Daniel Mahoney <u>admires</u> the view and <u>quotes</u> <u>Mark Twain</u>, <u>who</u> described Lake Tahoe as "a noble <u>sheet</u> of blue water . . . it must <u>surely</u> be the <u>fairest</u> picture the <u>whole</u> earth affords." What a life!

Chapter Review • 435

Exercise 32

11. verb
12. verb
13. PA, verb
14. PN
15. DO, DO

Exercise 33

Answers will vary; samples are given.

1. We climbed the highest mountain in the park.
2. A ranger gave the campers water.
3. The wind felt brisk on our faces.
4. This ridge will be a good campsite.
5. We called our trip a great adventure.

Exercise 34

Answers will vary; a sample is given.

Many African countries, as well as preservation groups, are working to protect elephants. Although elephants can sometimes be dangerous to people, people have turned out to be much more dangerous to elephants. Loggers and farmers have eliminated elephant habitats, and hunters have killed elephants for their valuable ivory tusks. Because elephants are now in danger of extinction, some nations have banned any trade in ivory. They have also discouraged poaching by helping communities to profit from tourism. Many countries have set aside parklands and preserves to protect elephants and other endangered species. These countries are hoping for success.

Exercise 35

Writing Application
When students have finished, have volunteers read their compositions aloud. The class should listen for use of different sentence patterns.

Exercise 36

Cumulative Review
Parts of speech: February – noun; Among – preposition; members – noun; great – adjective; some – pronoun; good – adjective; are – verb; forever – adverb; trip – noun; boy – interjection;

near – preposition; pretty – adjective; every – adjective; nice – adjective; rich – adjective; tall – adjective; great – adjective;

continued

Exercise 36

Sierra Nevada – noun; and – conjunction; granite – adjective; bright – adjective; big – adjective; everyone – pronoun; goes – verb; slopes – noun; Some – adjective; is – verb; so – adverb; that – pronoun; only – adverb;

tired – adjective; adults – noun; children – noun; go – verb; have – verb; hot – adjective; themselves – pronoun; by – preposition; go – verb; very – adverb; lovely – adjective; place – noun; admires – verb; quotes – verb; Mark Twain – noun; who – pronoun; sheet – noun; surely – adverb; fairest – adjective; whole – adjective

Students' replacements for underlined words will vary.

Subjects and verbs: family gathers; some are; some are; two are; object is; they have; family rises; everyone goes; sun is; adults [and] children go; teenagers go; cousin admires, quotes

Elliptical sentences: No matter. What a life!

Recognizing Appropriate Sentence Construction

Teaching Resources: Standardized Test Preparation Workbook, pp. 35–36

1. Practice with students locating the subject and verb in simple sentences. Point out that verbs can be mental actions (such as *believe, know, imagine*) as well as physical actions.

2. Using some dependent clauses as examples, remind students that some sentence fragments do contain a subject and verb. Practice adding to dependent clauses in order to form a complete thought. For example, *After the boys ran home, they had a snack.*

3. In going over the Sample Test Item, discuss with students some ways a sentence or group of sentences can be awkward. For example, it may be choppy, as in answer A. Answer C contains a misplaced modifier which makes the sentence awkward and confusing.

4. Point out that sometimes, in trying to combine sentence fragments, writers create run-on sentences. Review run-on sentences with students. There is an example of a run-on in Practice 1, Answer 3C.

Standardized Test Preparation Workshop

Recognizing Appropriate Sentence Construction

Knowing how to use the basic parts of a sentence correctly is the foundation of good writing. Standardized tests measure your ability to identify a complete sentence. Every sentence must contain a subject—the *who* or *what* that performs the action—and a verb—the action the subject is performing—to express a complete thought. If one of these parts is missing, you have an incomplete sentence, or a fragment.

When answering these test questions, check each group of words for a subject and verb. Then, determine whether the group of words expresses a complete thought. Finally, choose the group of words that contains all of the elements of a complete sentence to replace any sentence fragments.

The following questions will give you practice with the format used for testing your knowledge of basic sentence parts.

Test Tip

Remember that a verb can either follow or come before its subject. Also, a form of *be* can be the main verb of a sentence, but it does not express action; instead, it links words together.

Sample Test Item	Answer and Explanation
Directions: Choose the letter of the best way to write each underlined section. If the underlined section needs no change, choose "Correct as is." The guests were given birdseed. To throw at (1) the bride and groom. Instead of rice. **1 A** The guests were given birdseed. They were supposed to throw it at the bride and groom. It was instead of rice. **B** The guests were given birdseed to throw at the bride and groom instead of rice. **C** To throw at the bride and groom, the guests were given birdseed and not rice. **D** Correct as is	The correct answer is *B.* This answer choice smoothly combines the two fragments with the sentence that precedes them and successfully integrates all the information into a complete thought. Choice *A,* on the other hand, eliminates the fragments but makes three choppy sentences. Choice C contains a misplaced modifier that changes the meaning of the sentence.

436 • Basic Sentence Parts

TEST-TAKING TIP

Review with students the form of the verb *be* and its use as a linking verb. You might compare simple sentences. (Sandy is a good athlete. Sandy runs very fast.) Point out how the verb *is* links the subject and its complement, whereas *runs* is an action of the subject. Review some additional linking verbs, such as *feel, seem, look, appear,* and *sound.*

Practice 1 **Directions:** Choose the letter of the best way to write each underlined section. If the underlined section needs no change, choose "Correct as is."

A century ago. A family boarded an emi-
(1)
grant ship. Sailed from Ireland. The ship
                                    (2)
was bound for America. And was

rickety. The O'Connells were a strong
       (3)
bunch, Eight in all, the youngest named

Connor.

1 A A century ago, a family boarded an emigrant ship. It sailed from Ireland.

B A century ago. A family boarded an emigrant ship that sailed from Ireland.

C A century ago. when a family boarded an emigrant ship, it sailed from Ireland.

D Correct as is

2 F The ship was bound for America, and the ship was rickety.

G The ship, bound for America, was a rickety ship.

H The rickety ship was bound for America.

J Correct as is

3 A The O'Connells were a strong, bunch. There were eight in all. The youngest was named Connor.

B The O'Connells were a strong bunch, eight in all. The youngest was named Connor.

C There were eight strong O'Connells in all, the youngest was named Connor.

D Correct as is

Practice 2 **Directions:** Choose the letter of the best way to write each underlined section. If the underlined section needs no change, choose "Correct as is."

The sound system. It was all set up. It
(1)
was ready to go. Rafik tested the bass levels
                    (2)
one more time. Nothing like a lot of bass.

Gets people dancing. He closed his eyes
                       (3)
and saw the dance floor. Packed with people.

1 A The sound system was all set up. And ready to go.

B The sound system was all set up and ready to go.

C The sound system, was all set up, and it was ready to go.

D Correct as is

2 F Rafik tested the bass levels one more time. There is nothing like a lot of bass to get people dancing.

G Rafik tested the bass levels one more time. Nothing like a lot of bass to get people dancing.

H Rafik tested the bass levels one more time, and nothing like a lot of bass got people dancing.

J Correct as is

3 A He closed his eyes, and there he saw the dance floor packed with people.

B He closed his eyes and saw the dance floor. It was packed with people.

C He closed his eyes and saw the dance floor packed with people.

D Correct as is

Answer Key

Practice 1

1. A
2. C
3. B

Practice 2

1. B
2. A
3. C

Customize for
Less Advanced Students

The possible answers in sentence construction tests are often lengthy. When students read through answer choices, they should learn to move quickly to the next choice as soon as they spot a certain error.

Customize for
AP Students

Tell students to note sentence fragments and run-ons as they read the test passages. Doing so will enable them to evaluate the answer possibilities more quickly and accurately, without spending a lot of time rereading.

Chapter 19 Time and Resource Manager

In-Depth Lesson Plan

	LESSON FOCUS	PRINT AND MEDIA RESOURCES
DAY 1	**Prepositional Phrases and Appositive Phrases** Students learn and apply concepts relating to prepositional phrases, appositives, and appositive phrases. (pp. 440–445/H298–303)	*Writing and Grammar* Interactive Text, Section 19.1; *On-line Exercise Bank,* Section 19.1 Teaching Resources *Grammar Exercise Workbook,* pp. 33–36; *Grammar Exercises Answers on Transparencies,* Ch. 19
DAY 2	**Verbals and Verbal Phrases** Students learn and apply concepts relating to participles, gerunds, infinitives, and their respective phrases. (pp. 446–457/ H304–315)	*Writing and Grammar* Interactive Text, Section 19.2; *On-line Exercise Bank,* Section 19.2 Teaching Resources *Grammar Exercise Workbook,* pp. 37–40; *Hands-on Grammar Activity Book,* Ch. 19
DAY 3	**Clauses** Students learn and apply concepts relating to independent and subordinate clauses. (pp. 458–467/H316–325)	*Writing and Grammar* Interactive Text, Section 19.3; *On-line Exercise Bank,* Section 19.3 Teaching Resources *Grammar Exercise Workbook,* pp. 41–46
DAY 4	**Sentences Classified by Structure** Students identify simple, compound, complex, and compound-complex sentences. (pp. 468–471/H326–329)	*Writing and Grammar* Interactive Text, Section 19.4; *On-line Exercise Bank,* Section 19.4 Teaching Resources *Grammar Exercise Workbook,* pp. 47–48
DAY 5	**Review and Assess** Students review the chapter and demonstrate mastery of phrases, clauses, and sentence structures. (pp. 472–473)	Teaching Resources *Formal Assessment,* Ch. 19

Accelerated Lesson Plan

	LESSON FOCUS	PRINT AND MEDIA RESOURCES
DAY 1	**Prepositional and Appositive Phrases; Verbals and Verbal Phrases** Students cover concepts relating to phrases as determined by the Diagnostic Test. (pp. 440–457/H298–315)	*Writing and Grammar* Interactive Text, Sections 19.1–2; *On-line Exercise Bank,* Sections 19.1–2 Teaching Resources *Grammar Exercise Workbook,* pp. 33–40; *Grammar Exercises Answers on Transparencies,* Ch. 19
DAY 2	**Clauses** Students cover concepts relating to clauses. (pp. 458–467/ H316–325)	*Writing and Grammar* Interactive Text, Section 19.3; *On-line Exercise Bank,* Section 19.3 Teaching Resources *Grammar Exercise Workbook,* pp. 41–46
DAY 3	**Sentence Structure; Review and Assess** Students identify the four sentence structures and demonstrate mastery of concepts. (pp. 468–473/H326–329)	*Writing and Grammar* Interactive Text, Section 19.4; *On-line Exercise Bank,* Section 19.4 Teaching Resources *Grammar Exercise Workbook,* pp. 47–48; *Formal Assessment,* Ch.19

Options for Adapting Lesson Plans

HOMEWORK

Have students complete any section of the chapter for homework.

FEATURES

Extend coverage with the Grammar in Literature features (pp. 455, 466/H313, 324) and the Standardized Test Preparation Workshop (p. 474).

TECHNOLOGY

Students can use *Writing and Grammar* Interactive Text to complete the exercises interactively on computer. They can complete additional exercises in the *On-line Exercise Bank:* The Auto Check feature will grade their work. Go on-line: PHSchool.com Use Web Code: egk-1202

Writing and Grammar Handbook Alignment

Page numbers in Step-by-Step Teaching Guides in this Teacher's Edition refer to pages from the full student text. Handbook page references, indicated with this icon **H**, are provided in Time and Resource Manager boxes and at the bottom of each Teacher's Edition page.

INTEGRATED SKILLS COVERAGE

Grammar in Literature
SE pp. 455, 466/**H**313, 324

Writing
Find It in Your Writing, SE pp. 445, 457, 467, 471/**H**303, 315, 325, 329
Writing Application, SE pp. 445, 457, 467, 471, 473/**H**303, 315, 325, 329
Grammar and Style, SE pp. 465, 469/**H**323, 327

Vocabulary Skills
ATE p. 444

Viewing and Representing
Critical Viewing, SE pp. 438, 440, 443, 448, 450, 453, 458, 464, 468, 470/**H**296, 298, 301, 306, 308, 311, 316, 322, 326, 328

Technology Skills
SE p. 442/**H**300

Speaking and Listening
ATE pp. 443, 448

Real-World Connection
ATE p. 469

ASSESSMENT SUPPORT

Standardized Test Preparation Workshop SE p. 474; ATE pp. 443, 469

Standardized Test Preparation Workbook, pp. 37–38

Formal Assessment, Ch. 19

MEETING INDIVIDUAL NEEDS

Less Advanced Students ATE pp. 447, 475. See also Ongoing Assessments ATE pp. 441, 444, 447, 449, 450, 452, 455, 459, 461, 463, 465.

AP Students ATE pp. 454, 475

ESL Students ATE pp. 441, 459

Linguistic Learners ATE p. 451

BLOCK SCHEDULING

Pacing Suggestions
For 90-minute Blocks
- Administer the Diagnostic Test to students to determine instructional coverage.
- Have students complete the necessary exercises in class. Use the Hands-on Grammar activity to provide a change of pace.

Resources for Varying Instruction
- *Writing and Grammar* **Interactive Text** A 90-minute block provides an ideal opportunity for students to work on the computer.

Professional Development Support
- *How to Manage Instruction in the Block* This teaching resource provides management and activity suggestions.

MEDIA AND TECHNOLOGY

For the Teacher
- *Writing and Grammar* **Interactive Text**, Ch. 19
- *On-line Exercise Bank,* Sections 19.1–4

For the Teacher
- **Teacher**EXPRESS™ CD-ROM

WRITING AND GRAMMAR ON-LINE

Interactive Text (On-line or on CD-ROM)
- Easily navigable instruction with on-line supporting resources
- Self-scoring exercises and diagnostic tests

Companion Web Site PHSchool.com
- On-line Exercise Bank (use Web Code egk-1202)

See the Go On-line! **feature, SE p. iii.**

LITERATURE CONNECTIONS

Grammar in Literature selections from *Prentice Hall Literature, Penguin Edition,* The British Tradition:
from "The Parable of the Prodigal Son," The King James Bible, SE p. 455/**H**313
from "The Second Coming," William Butler Yeats, SE p. 466/**H**324

Objectives

1. To identify prepositional phrases and to recognize whether they are used as adjectives or adverbs
2. To identify appositives and appositive phrases and use them to combine sentences
3. To identify and use verbals and verbal phrases
4. To identify independent and subordinate clauses and to recognize adjective clauses, adverb clauses, and noun clauses
5. To recognize and identify the four structures of sentences
6. To analyze the characteristics of clear texts such as conciseness, correctness, and completeness
7. To recognize appropriate English usage within the context of a written passage

Critical Viewing

Describe Sample response: How many people would be willing to pass through the archway? Other possible descriptive phrases: *with little light, through fantastic formations.*

Chapter 19 Phrases and Clauses

Previous chapters have discussed the essential materials at a writer's command: the parts of speech and the basic English sentence patterns. This chapter will describe additional elements—phrases and clauses—that writers can use to expand these basic patterns and to achieve richer communication.

Phrases and clauses function in sentences in much the same way as passageways in a cave. The various chambers are connected by passageways, which expand the overall size and scope of the cave. At the same time, they also add to the detail and beauty of the cave.

In this chapter, you will learn how phrases and clauses add meaning to sentences and make a writer's work more interesting and informative.

438 • Phrases and Clauses

▲ Critical Viewing Use the phrase "through the archway" in a sentence about this picture. What other phrases could you use to describe the features of the cave? [Describe]

☑ **ONGOING ASSESSMENT: Diagnose**

If students miss more than one item in any category, direct them to the relevant pages of the textbook and assign exercises for practice and review.

	Diagnostic Test Items	Teach	Practice	Section Reviews	Chapter Review
Skill Check A					
Prepositional Phrases	A 1–5	pp. 440–441/Ⓗ298–299	Ex. 1	Ex. 4, 6	Ex. 39
Appositives	A 2, 4, 5	pp. 442–443/Ⓗ300–301	Ex. 2–3	Ex. 5, 6	Ex. 40
Skill Check B					
Verbals and Verbal Phrases	B 6–10	pp. 446–454/Ⓗ304–312	Ex. 10–14	Ex. 15–16	Ex. 41, 44–45

Each item in the Diagnostic Test corresponds to a specific section in the phrases and clauses chapter, enabling you to tailor instruction as needed. See "Ongoing Assessment: Diagnose" below for further details.

Diagnostic Test

Directions: Write all answers on a separate sheet of paper.

Skill Check A. List prepositional phrases or appositives in each of the following sentences. Label each prepositional phrase *adjective* or *adverb*, and identify the word each appositive modifies.

1. Many of the world's caves have been discovered by accident.
2. Carlsbad Caverns, a series of caves in the American Southwest, was discovered by a cowboy who noticed a large swarm of bats.
3. While looking for a stray goat, two men in Jordan stumbled upon a very important cave near the Dead Sea.
4. Another famous cave, Lascaux, was discovered by four French teenagers who were looking for an underground passage.
5. Altamira, a town in Spain, was made famous by a five-year-old girl's discovery of prehistoric paintings on a cave's ceiling.

Skill Check B. Identify the verbal or verbal phrase in each of the following sentences. Tell whether each one is an *infinitive*, a *gerund*, a *participle*, or a *nominative absolute*.

6. The fascinating story of the cave paintings at Altamira, Spain, begins in 1879.
7. The cave having been discovered years earlier, Don Marcelino DeSautuola was searching for artifacts on the cave floor.
8. DeSautuola brought his young daughter along to help him.
9. Digging in the dirt tired her, so she lay down on the ground.
10. She looked up and saw the ancient paintings staring back at her.

Skill Check C. In each of the following sentences, identify the subordinate clause, and then tell whether it is an *adjective*, an *adverb*, a *noun*, or an *elliptical clause*.

11. In 1901, a cowboy named Jim White, who worked on a ranch in New Mexico, stumbled upon Carlsbad Caverns.
12. On a warm summer day, White was riding across the desert when he noticed an enormous dark cloud billowing out of the ground.
13. Whatever was causing the cloud puzzled the young cowboy.
14. In fact, the "cloud" that White saw was actually an enormous swarm of bats, and they were coming from a large cave.
15. This cave proved to be one of the largest in the country.

Skill Check D. Identify each of the following sentences as *simple*, *compound*, *complex*, or *compound-complex*.

16. In 1940, four French teenaged boys made a startling discovery.
17. The boys, who were from the small town of Montignac, were exploring a dark, deep hole near a dead tree.
18. The boys were looking for an underground passage.
19. They cleared the ground around the opening and then ventured into the hole.
20. The boys, who had an oil lamp with them, squeezed into the tight opening, and they soon discovered the prehistoric paintings that have made the cave famous.

Phrases and Clauses • 439

Skill Check A

1. of the world's caves: adj.; by accident: adv.
2. a series of caves . . . Southwest: modifies *Carlsbad Caverns*; in the American Southwest: adj.; by a cowboy: adv.; of bats: adj.
3. for a stray goat: adv.; in Jordan: adj.; upon . . . cave: adv.; near the Dead Sea: adj.
4. Lascaux: modifies *cave*; by . . . teenagers: adv.; for . . . passage: adv.
5. a town in Spain: modifies *Altamira*; in Spain: adj.; by . . . discovery: adv.; of prehistoric paintings: adj.; on a cave's ceiling: adj.

Skill Check B

6. fascinating: participle
7. The cave . . . earlier: nom. abs.
8. to help him: infinitive
9. Digging . . . dirt: gerund
10. staring . . . her: participle

Skill Check C

11. who worked . . . New Mexico: adj.
12. when he . . . ground: adv.
13. Whatever . . . cloud: noun
14. that White saw: adj.
15. one of . . . country: ellipt, adj.

Skill Check D

16. simple
17. complex
18. simple
19. complex
20. compound-complex

✓ ONGOING ASSESSMENT: Diagnose *continued*

	Diagnostic Test Items	Teach	Practice	Section Reviews	Chapter Review
Skill Check C					
Clauses	C 11–15	pp. 458–465/ H316–323	Ex. 20–25	Ex. 26–28	Ex. 42, 44–45
Skill Check D					
Sentences Classified by Structure	D 16–20	pp. 468–469/ H326–327	Ex. 32	Ex. 33–35	Ex. 43
Cumulative Review and Application				Ex. 7–9, Ex. 17–19 Ex. 29–31 Ex. 36–38	Ex. 46

⏱ TIME SAVERS!

Answers on Transparencies Use the *Grammar Exercises Answers on Transparencies* for Chapter 19 to facilitate correction by students.

On-Line Exercise Bank Have students complete the Diagnostic Test on computer. The Auto Check feature will grade their work for you!

Demonstrate uses of prepositional phrases by giving one student a prop such as a set of car keys to place in various locations. Ask students to identify these locations using only prepositional phrases. Give another student a round object to roll in various directions. Have students use prepositional phrases such as *to the corner* to tell the object's direction.

Activate Prior Knowledge

Remind students that prepositional phrases and appositives can add more information to a sentence. Write this sentence on the board: *The explorers discovered a cave.* Have students suggests two or more prepositional phrases and at least one appositive phrase to expand the sentence.

TEACH

Step-by-Step Teaching Guide

Prepositional Phrases

1. Explain that the easiest way to recognize a prepositional phrase is to look for the preposition that begins it. List common prepositions such as *in*, *on*, *for*, *about*, and *under* on the board and ask students to add more.

2. Explain that prepositional phrases can be lengthy or as short as two words (*for me*). Prepositions themselves may contain several words (*on top of*).

3. Tell students that adjective phrases usually come just after the nouns or pronouns they modify. Present this sentence:

   We noticed a rock with strange carvings in bright red.

   Explain that *with strange carvings* modifies *rock* and *in bright red* modifies *carvings*.

continued

Critical Viewing

Connect Sample response: Stalactites hang down *from the ceiling*, and stalagmites point up *from the ground*.

Prepositional Phrases and Appositives

When one-word adjectives and adverbs cannot convey all of the details and relationships that a writer needs to express, the writer can use a *phrase* to express the precise idea.

▶ **KEY CONCEPT** A **phrase** is a group of words that functions in a sentence as a part of speech. ∎

Two common types of phrases that add to the meaning of sentences are *prepositional phrases* and *appositive phrases.*

Prepositional Phrases

As shown in Section 17.4, prepositional phrases contain a preposition and a noun or pronoun called the object of the preposition. The object may have modifiers and be compound.

	PREP	OBJ OF PREP
EXAMPLES:	on the ancient limestone floor	

	PREP	OBJ OF PREP	OBJ OF PREP
	beside the underground stream and rocks		

Prepositional phrases function as either adjectives or adverbs.

Adjective Phrases Like adjectives, adjective phrases modify nouns and pronouns.

▶ **KEY CONCEPT** An **adjective phrase** is a prepositional phrase that modifies a noun or pronoun by stating *what kind* or *which one.* ∎

Adjective phrases can modify any sentence part that is acting as a noun.

EXAMPLES:

S
An etching *of a cave bear* was found. *(What kind* of etching?)

DO
I have a fear *of the dark.* *(What kind* of fear?)

IO
I sent my friend *in Iowa* a picture. *(Which* friend?)

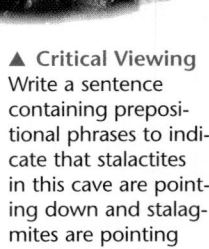

Theme: Caves and Caverns

In this section, you will learn to recognize prepositional phrases and appositive phrases. The examples and exercises are about caves and caverns.

Cross-Curricular Connection: Science

▲ **Critical Viewing** Write a sentence containing prepositional phrases to indicate that stalactites in this cave are pointing down and stalagmites are pointing up. **[Connect]**

⏱ **TIME AND RESOURCE MANAGER**

Resources
Print: *Grammar Exercise Workbook,* pp. 33–36; *Grammar Exercises Answers on Transparencies,* Ch. 19
Technology: *Writing and Grammar* Interactive Text, Section 19.1; *On-Line Exercise Bank,* Section 19.1

Using the Full Student Edition	Using the Handbook 🖽
• Work through all key concepts, pp. 440–443.	• Work through all key concepts, pp. 298–301.
• Assign and review Exercises 1–3.	• Assign and review Exercises 1–3.

Adverb Phrases Like adverbs, adverb phrases modify verbs, adjectives, and other adverbs.

▶ **KEY CONCEPT** An **adverb phrase** is a prepositional phrase that modifies a verb, an adjective, or an adverb by pointing out *where, when, in what way,* or *to what extent.* ■

When modifying a verb, an adverb phrase may come before or after the modified word.

MODIFYING A VERB:	*In Mammoth Cave National Park*, you can tour the caves. (Can tour *where?*)
	Except for one section, the cave had been mapped. (Was mapped *to what extent?*)
MODIFYING AN ADJECTIVE:	I am angry *beyond belief.* (Angry *to what extent?*)
MODIFYING AN ADVERB:	The shovel bit well *into the earth.* (Well *where?*)

As with adjective phrases, more than one adverb phrase can modify the same word.

EXAMPLE:	*Before breakfast*, the smell of bacon drifted *into our campsite.* (Drifted *when?* Drifted *where?*)

▶ **Exercise 1** Identifying Adjective and Adverb Phrases Write the prepositional phrases in the following sentences. Then, identify each prepositional phrase as *adjective* or *adverb.*

EXAMPLE:	Have you ever been to the cave?
	to the cave (adverb)

1. Caves occurring in nature can be formed in different ways.
2. Caves formed by the long-term effect of acidic water are called solution caves.
3. Most of these caves are formed from limestone, which dissolves easily in slightly acidic water.
4. In certain geographic areas, water tends to absorb large amounts of carbon dioxide and other acidic compounds.
5. Over time, this acidic ground water eventually eats away at the rock, leaving an underground chamber, or cave.

Interactive Textbook

Get instant feedback! Exercise 1 is available on-line or on CD-ROM.

▶ **More Practice**

Grammar Exercise Workbook
• pp. 33–34
On-line Exercise Bank
• Section 19.1
Go on-line:
PHSchool.com
Enter Web Code:
egk-1202

Prepositional Phrases and Appositives • 441

Step-by-Step Teaching Guide continued

4. Explain to students that many of the words that introduce adverb phrases, such as *near*, *below*, *down*, and *across*, may also be used as adverbs. The way to distinguish them is to look for an object. Have students tell how *down* is used in these sentences.

   We set the map down. (adv.)

   Rainwater ran down the path. (preposition)

Customize for
ESL Students

Ask students to make flashcards from index cards. On one side of each card, have students create a simple drawing that depicts the location, direction, or condition of something, such as a man leaping over a puddle or a boat sailing under a bridge. On the other side, have students write prepositional phrases to describe what is going on: *over a puddle*, *under a bridge*. Students can quiz each other on prepositions and prepositional phrases with the cards.

Language Highlight

Before A.D. 750, Old English, the language spoken by Anglo-Saxons, featured word endings that changed to show differences in meanings. For example, the Old English words *se cyning* meant "the king," and the phrase *thaem cyninge* was the equivalent of today's prepositional phrase "to the king." We now use only prepositions such as *to*, *with*, and *from*—not changes in word endings—to indicate direction or location.

Answer Key

▶ **Exercise 1**

1. in nature: adv.; in . . . ways: adv.
2. by . . . effect: adv.; of . . . water: adj.
3. of these caves: adj.; from limestone: adv.; in . . . water: adv.
4. In . . . areas: adv.; of carbon . . . compounds: adj.
5. Over time: adv.; at the rock: adv.

✔ **ONGOING ASSESSMENT: Monitor and Reinforce**

If students miss more than one item in Exercise 1, refer them to the following for additional practice.

In the Textbook	Print Resources	Technology
Section Review, Ex. 4, Section 19.1	*Grammar Exercise Workbook,* pp. 33–34	*On-Line Exercise Bank,* Section 19.1

Appositives and Appositive Phrases

1. Mention to students that one-word appositives, as in the sentence *My brother Bob visited his first cave at age ten*, can sometimes be difficult to identify. The key is to look for two nouns in a row where one renames the other.

2. Explain that to decide whether an appositive is nonessential and thus should be set off with commas, it can be helpful to read the sentence aloud. If you pause before the appositive, you probably need commas.

3. Explain that the most likely sentence pairs to be combined with an appositive are those in which one sentence has a form of *be* as its verb. Have students decide which of these pairs is easier to combine:

   Ted is an experienced explorer. He was lost in the cave for three days.

   Ted loves exploring caves. He visits local ones whenever he can.

Customize for
Gifted and Talented Students

Students might enjoy writing short, amusing monologues or dialogues in which most or all of the sentences use negative appositives. These examples could get them started:

"I decided to buy the blue shirt, not the red one."

"But it was the red one, not the blue one, that didn't look two sizes too big for you."

19.1

Appositives and Appositive Phrases

To *appose* means "to place near or next to." Appositives and appositive phrases are words placed next to nouns and pronouns to provide additional information.

Appositives When you name something and then immediately rename it to give further information, you are using an appositive.

> **KEY CONCEPT** An **appositive** is a noun or pronoun placed next to another noun or pronoun in order to identify, rename, or explain it. ■

EXAMPLES: My dog, *a pointer*, stood silently outside the cave.

She did not care for his hobby, *spelunking*.

These examples show appositives set off by commas. Dashes and colons can also be used to set off appositives. Punctuation is used to set off an appositive only when the appositive contains *nonessential* (or *nonrestrictive*) material—that is, material that can be removed from the sentence without altering its meaning. If the material is *essential* (or *restrictive*), no commas are used.

EXAMPLE: My friend *Marilyn* enjoyed the tour of the cavern.

Appositive Phrases When an appositive is accompanied by one or more modifiers, it becomes a phrase.

> **KEY CONCEPT** An **appositive phrase** is a noun or pronoun with modifiers placed next to a noun or pronoun in order to add information and details. ■

One-word adjectives, adjective phrases, or other groups of words acting as adjectives can modify an appositive.

EXAMPLE: The explorer, *a daring scientist*, braved the dark recesses of the cave.

442 • Phrases and Clauses

🖥 Internet Tip

Specific information about most large caves, such as Mammoth Cave National Park or Luray Caverns, can be found on numerous Web sites.

KEY CONCEPT Appositives and appositive phrases can modify or rename any sentence part that is acting as a noun. ∎

WITH A SUBJECT: My jacket, *a windbreaker*, keeps me perfectly warm in the cool, damp cave.

WITH A DIRECT OBJECT: I bought a book, *an atlas of famous caves.*

WITH AN INDIRECT OBJECT: The man gave his fellow caving enthusiast, *his friend for ten years*, a brand-new flashlight.

WITH AN OBJECTIVE COMPLEMENT: I called my friend Caruso, *the name of a famous operatic tenor*, because he likes to sing in the caves.

WITH A PREDICATE NOMINATIVE: She is an archaeologist, *a historic explorer.*

WITH THE OBJECT OF A PREPOSITION: In a shady area, *a small cave in the side of the hill*, I ate my lunch.

Appositives and appositive phrases can be compound.

EXAMPLE: The family—*Mr. Trapp, his wife, and his children*—spent their vacation at Mammoth Cave in Kentucky.

Use appositives and appositive phrases to tighten your writing. Often, two sentences can be combined by turning the information in one sentence into an appositive.

TWO SENTENCES: Tarantulas were hiding in the cave. Tarantulas are large, hairy spiders.

SENTENCE WITH APPOSITIVE PHRASE: Tarantulas—*large, hairy spiders*—were hiding in the cave.

▼ Critical Viewing How can appositives and appositive phrases help a writer describe a single element in a larger scene, such as this cave entrance set in the mountainside? [Connect]

Integrating Speaking and Listening Skills

Point out to students that appositive phrases are nearly always nonessential sentence elements. When we read sentences with appositive phrases aloud, we usually incorporate a brief pause before the appositive and a slight change in tone to indicate its presence. Have students read aloud the example sentences on this page in a way that does not cue the listener to the presence of an appositive phrase. Then, have them discuss what clarity of meaning is lost without the pauses.

Critical Viewing

Connect Appositives and appositive phrases allow writers to be more descriptive in their writing. Sample sentence with appositive: The cave entrance, a huge opening in the mountainside, allows spelunkers to explore a majestic site.

STANDARDIZED TEST PREPARATION WORKSHOP

Grammar and Usage Many standardized tests require students to punctuate appositives and appositive phrases properly within the context of a passage. Use the following example to demonstrate.

Decide which type of error, if any, appears in the underlined section:

My friend Carolyn has been exploring caves for two years. Her <u>brother an expert spelunker,</u> *first introduced her to the sport.*

A Spelling error   B Punctuation error

C Capitalization error   D No error

The correct answer is **B**. The group of words *an expert spelunker* is an appositive phrase. Because it is not needed to identify *brother*, it is nonessential and should be set off on both sides by commas.

Integrating Vocabulary Skills

Apposite and Appositive Have students find the Latin word from which *appositive* is derived, and ask them to identify other words that share this origin. (The Latin word *apponere* means "to place near to." Related words include *apposite*, meaning "suitable," and *apposition*, meaning "placement alongside.")

Answer Key

> **Exercise 2** Identifying Appositives and Appositive Phrases
Write each appositive or appositive phrase.

EXAMPLE: The tour guide, a very knowledgeable fellow, explained the history of the cave.

a very knowledgeable fellow

1. Caves, natural subterranean cavities, have many unique characteristics.
2. Calcium carbonate, a chemical compound, leaches from rock to form structures found only in caves.
3. Speleothems, the scientific name for these structures, form after the cave itself has developed.
4. Stalactites, hanging formations on the roof of a cave, are formed when water rich in calcium carbonate drips through cracks in the rock above.
5. Stalagmites, formations on the ground, are formed when this mineral-rich water drips to the floor of the cave.

> **Exercise 3** Combining Sentences With Appositives and Appositive Phrases Combine each pair of sentences by turning one into an appositive or appositive phrase.

EXAMPLE: Washington, D.C., is fascinating. It is our capital.
Washington, D.C., our capital, is fascinating.

1. Carlsbad Caverns is located in southeast New Mexico. It is a national park.
2. Carlsbad Caverns is very interesting. It contains one of the largest caves in the world.
3. Jim White explored the caves in the 1890's. He was a cowboy.
4. A group of scientists first explored the caves in 1924. They were members of the National Geographic Society.
5. Today, tourists flock to Carlsbad Caverns. It is a beautiful vacation spot with much to see.
6. The Big Room is the largest chamber in the cave. It is 1,800 feet long and 1,100 feet wide.
7. It is home to the Giant Dome. The Giant Dome is a massive column of rock 16 feet thick and 62 feet high.
8. The temperature in the cave rarely varies. It is a constant 56°F.
9. The fee to enter the cave is relatively inexpensive. It is only six dollars.
10. Call the park's phone number to make reservations for a special tour. The park has a toll-free number.

> **More Practice**

Grammar Exercise Workbook
• pp. 35–36
On-line Exercise Bank
• Section 19.1
Go on-line:
PHSchool.com
Enter Web Code:
egk-1202

Get instant feedback! Exercises 2 and 3 are available on-line or on CD-ROM.

 **Learn More**

To learn more about properly punctuating appositives and appositive phrases, refer to Sections 27.2 and 27.5.

☑ ONGOING ASSESSMENT: Monitor and Reinforce

If students have difficulty with Exercise 2 or 3, refer them to the following for additional practice.

In the Textbook	Print Resources	Technology
Section Review, Ex. 5–6, Section 19.1	*Grammar Exercise Workbook,* pp. 35–36	*On-Line Exercise Bank,* Section 19.1

Section 19.1 Section Review

GRAMMAR EXERCISES 4–9

Exercise 4 Identifying Adjective and Adverb Phrases Write the prepositional phrases in the following sentences. Then, identify each prepositional phrase as *adjective* or *adverb*.

1. For some 32,000 years, people have been drawing on cave walls.
2. The first example of cave art was discovered in a Spanish cave in 1879.
3. At first, people did not believe that the realistic pictures of animals could have been drawn by prehistoric peoples.
4. It was only after the discovery of art in caves that had been sealed off for thousands of years that skeptics were disproved.
5. Today, more than 230 caves are known to contain examples of cave art.

Exercise 5 Identifying Appositive Phrases On your paper, write each appositive phrase you find in the following sentences and the word it identifies.

1. The Ice Cave near Grants, a small town in western New Mexico, attracts thousands of tourists each year.
2. The temperature in the cave never gets above 32° F, the freezing point of water.
3. As rainwater and snow melt seep into the cave, its floor—a solid block of ice 20 feet deep—continues to thicken.
4. The unique green tint of the ice, the result of Arctic algae trapped within, often fascinates tourists.
5. Pueblo Indians, who explored the cave hundreds of years ago, gave it a special name—"Winter Lake."

Exercise 6 Combining Sentences by Using Prepositional Phrases and Appositive Phrases Combine each group of sentences by turning one or more into a prepositional phrase or an appositive phrase.

1. Bats live throughout the United States. Caves are home to many of them.
2. Their seclusion makes them seem more mysterious. Caves are where they are secluded. People wonder about them.
3. Two main groups of bats exist in the world. The two main groups are Megachiroptera and Microchiroptera.
4. While most "megabats" have excellent eyesight, "microbats" rely on echolocation to find their way. Echolocation is a form of natural sonar.
5. The smallest bat weighs about two grams. Its size resembles a bumblebee's. Its weight is less than a dime's.

Exercise 7 Find It in Your Reading Reread the first paragraph on page 438. Locate and identify the two appositives in the paragraph. Hint: Neither is punctuated with commas.

Exercise 8 Find It in Your Writing Revise sentences in one of your social studies essays by using appositives and appositive phrases to combine sentences.

Exercise 9 Writing Application Compose a descriptive passage of an outdoor scene. Use adjective and adverb phrases to characterize and locate the scene you have chosen.

Section Review • 445

Section Review

Each of these exercises correlates to the instruction on prepositional phrases and appositives, pages 440–443. The exercises may be used for more practice, for reteaching, or for review of the key concepts presented.

Answer Key

Exercise 4

1. For some . . . years: adv.; on cave walls: adv.
2. of cave art: adj.; in a Spanish cave: adv.; in 1879: adv.
3. At first: adv.; of animals: adj.; by . . . peoples: adv.
4. after the discovery: adv.; of art: adj.; in caves: adj.; for thousands: adv.; of years: adj.
5. of cave art: adj.

Exercise 5

1. a small . . . Mexico: Grants
2. the freezing . . . water: 32°F
3. a solid . . . deep: floor
4. the result . . . within: tint
5. "Winter Lake": name

Exercise 6

Answers will vary; samples are given.

1. Many bats live in caves throughout the United States.
2. Their seclusion in caves makes them seem more mysterious to people.
3. Two main groups . . . world, Megachiroptera and . . .
4. . . . rely on echolocation, a form of natural sonar, to find their way.
5. The smallest bat—the size of a bumblebee—weighs . . .

Exercise 7

Find It in Your Reading
1. the parts of speech and the basic English sentence patterns
2. phrases and clauses

Exercise 8

Find It in Your Writing
Have students review their revisions to see how often they used appositives rather than appositive phrases.

Exercise 9

Writing Application
Students should exchange papers with a writing partner and comment on each other's use of prepositional phrases.

☑ **ONGOING ASSESSMENT: Assess Mastery**

Use the following resources to assess student mastery of prepositional phrases and appositives.

In the Textbook	Technology
Chapter Review, Ex. 39–40	*Writing and Grammar* Interactive Text, Section 19.1, Section Review; *On-Line Exercise Bank,* Section 19.1

Verbals and Verbal Phrases

Interest GRABBER On the board, write the film titles *Driving Miss Daisy* and *Saving Private Ryan* and have students notice the *-ing* word in each. Then ask them to volunteer other similar titles of movies, books, or television shows. Explain that the *-ing* word in each title resembles a verb but does not function as one because it does not have an auxiliary verb such as *is* or *was*.

Activate Prior Knowledge

Mention that stand-alone verb forms such as *driving* and *saving*, as well as forms like *to drive* and *to save*, are called *verbals*. Write these sentences on the board and see if students can tell whether the underlined verbal in each is a participle, a gerund, or an infinitive.

<u>Driving Miss Daisy</u> *was an enjoyable movie.* (gerund)

A man was hired <u>to drive Miss Daisy</u>. (infinitive)

The man <u>driving Miss Daisy</u> became her friend. (participle)

TEACH

Participles and Participial Phrases

1. Have students notice in the chart that only present participle forms end in *-ing*. Many past participles end in *-ed*, but make sure students understand that quite a few commonly used ones (*broken*, *stolen*) do not.

2. Explain that almost any present participle may be used as a modifier but not that many past participles are commonly used in this way. Ask students to give examples of some that are.

continued

> **KEY CONCEPT** A **verbal** is a word derived from a verb but used as a noun, an adjective, or an adverb. ∎

Like verbs, verbals may be modified by adverbs and adverb phrases or have complements. A verbal with modifiers or a complement is called a *verbal phrase*.

Participles and Participial Phrases

Many adjectives are actually verbals known as *participles*.

> **KEY CONCEPT** A **participle** is a form of a verb that can act as an adjective. ∎

EXAMPLES: A *devastating* fire swept through the valley.
A *frightened* doe bounded into the woods.

Forms of Participles Participles come in three forms: *present participles*, *past participles*, and *perfect participles*.

Kinds of Participles	Forms	Examples
Present Participle	Ends in *-ing*	The *burning* embers fell to the ground. The water shone with *glimmering* phosphorescence.
Past Participle	Usually ends in *-ed*; sometimes *-t*, *-en*, or another irregular ending	The *scorched* forest eventually regenerated itself. The *exhausted* firefighter didn't hear the alarm.
Perfect Participle	Includes *having* or *having been* before a past participle	*Having tested the smoke detector*, I replaced its cover. *Having been asked*, he gave his opinion.

Participles precede or follow the words they modify, answering *Which one?* or *What kind?* as do one-word adjectives.
A verb has a subject and expresses the main action; a participle acting as an adjective describes a noun or pronoun.

Theme: Fires and Firefighters

In this section, you will learn to recognize participals, gerunds, infinitives, and various verbal phrases. The examples and exercises are about fires and firefighters.

Cross-Curricular Connection: Social Studies

Functioning as a Verb	Functioning as a Participle
The firefighter's muscles are *aching*.	The firefighter rubbed her *aching* muscles.
The firefighters *respected* their chief.	The *respected chief* had the firefighters' support.

Participial Phrases The addition of modifiers and complements to a participle produces a *participial phrase*.

▶ **KEY CONCEPT** A **participial phrase** is a participle modified by an adverb or adverb phrase or accompanied by a complement. The entire phrase acts as an adjective. ∎

The following examples show different modifiers and complements that a participial phrase can have.

WITH AN ADVERB: *Burning brightly*, the fire lit up the room.

WITH AN ADVERB PHRASE: The bone, *broken in two places*, healed slowly.

WITH A DIRECT OBJECT: *Holding the high-pressure hose*, I struggled to stand still.

A comma usually sets off a participial phrase at the beginning of a sentence. Within the sentence, however, a participial phrase is set off by commas only if it is *nonessential* to the sentence.

The sentence on the left side of the chart below would still make sense even if the participial phrase were removed. The phrase in the sentence on the right is necessary to identify the specific man being discussed.

Nonessential Participial Phrase	Essential Participial Phrase
Mr. Sharp, *driving that fire engine*, is well trained.	The man *driving that fire engine* is well trained.

🔍 Learn More

Refer to Section 27.2 for more information about punctuating participial phrases.

Step-by-Step Teaching Guide continued

3. Remind students that because a participle is a verb form, it can take modifiers or complements just as a verb can. To reinforce the concept, have students identify the elements in the participial phrases in these sentences:

   Smothering the fire with a pan lid, the woman avoided a disaster. (direct object and adverb phrase)

   We noticed the firefighter talking quietly with our neighbors. (adverb and adverb phrase)

4. Explain to students that when combining two sentences with a participial phrase (as on page 448), they should determine what their main point is. That point should go in the main part of the sentence, while the less important point should go in the participial phrase.

Customize for
Less Advanced Students

Combining a few simple sentences into sentences with participles may help students recognize participles on their own. Present the following pairs and have students reformat the second sentence in each into a participle. Have students experiment with placing the phrases both before and after the words they modify.

The student volunteers put out the fire. They were led by Jason Smith.

One old man almost wasn't rescued. He was sleeping near a noisy heater.

☑ ONGOING ASSESSMENT: Prerequisite Skills

If students have difficulty with verbals, you may find it necessary to review the following to ensure coverage of prerequisite knowledge.

In the Textbook	Print Resources	Technology
Verbs, Section 17.2 Complements, Section 18.3	*Grammar Exercise Workbook* pp. 5–6, 29–32, 37–40	*On-Line Exercise Bank,* Sections 17.2, 18.3

Nominative Absolutes

1. Reiterate these basic distinctions between nominative absolutes and participial phrases:
   - the first word (plus modifiers) in a nominative absolute is always a noun or pronoun;
   - a participial phrase must always modify a word in the sentence, but a nominative absolute never does.

2. Explain that nominative absolutes function independently from the rest of the sentence only in terms of their grammatical construction. They must still have some relation to the meaning of the sentence.

Critical Viewing

Analyze Sample response: A match having been dropped on the ground, the gasoline quickly caught fire.

Integrating Speaking and Listening Skills

Have students work in pairs to continue a brief script of a conversation between a character (boy or girl) named Nomy Solute, who speaks only in nominative absolutes, and his or her parents. Offer students this opener:

Parent: *Why were you late?*

Nomy: *My car being unreliable, I decided to walk back from the mall.*

Parent: *Why didn't you call me?*

Nomy: *The phones were broken, someone having cut the phone cords.*

Have students continue, adding at least three more lines with nominative absolutes.

KEY CONCEPT Participial phrases can be used to combine the information in two sentences into one sentence. ■

TWO SENTENCES:	The fire marshal's speech expressed her opinion about several important issues. It convinced many people to vote for her.
COMBINED SENTENCE:	The fire marshal's speech, convincing many people to vote for her, expressed her opinions about several important issues.
	The fire marshal's speech, expressing her opinions about several important issues, convinced many people to vote for her.

Nominative Absolutes Sometimes, participles occur in phrases that are grammatically separate from the rest of the sentence. These phrases, called *nominative absolutes*, can show time, reason, or circumstance.

KEY CONCEPT A **nominative absolute** is a noun or pronoun followed by a participle or participial phrase that functions independently of the rest of the sentence. ■

The following examples show nominative absolutes.

TIME:	*Precious minutes having been lost,* I decided to call the fire department.
REASON:	*My stomach growling with hunger,* I made a sandwich.
CIRCUMSTANCE:	Many cadets missed final exams, *the flu epidemic having struck at the end of the semester.*

The participle *being* is sometimes understood rather than expressed in some nominative absolutes.

EXAMPLE:	*The camera [being] out of film,* we stopped taking pictures of the forest fire.

Do not mistake a nominative absolute for the main subject and verb in a sentence. As a phrase, a nominative absolute cannot stand independently as a complete sentence.

▲ **Critical Viewing** Write a sentence introduced by a nominative absolute to explain how this fire may have started. **[Analyze]**

448 • Phrases and Clauses

▶ **Exercise 10** Recognizing Participles and Participial Phrases Write the participle or participial phrase in each sentence. Then, label it *present, past,* or *perfect.*

EXAMPLE: Led by the captain, the firefighters ran to the building.
Led by the captain (past)

1. Besieged by drought for several months, the city of Chicago was ripe for a major fire in the fall of 1871.
2. On September 30, 1871, the Burlington Warehouse burned down, causing $600,000 damage.
3. A few days later, a devastating fire destroyed four city blocks.
4. Having battled both of these blazes, the firefighters were exhausted.
5. The exhausted firefighters were unprepared for another fire.
6. Additionally, the beleaguered fire department had lost several pieces of badly needed equipment.
7. Mrs. O'Leary's cow was once blamed for accidentally starting the Great Chicago Fire on October 8, having knocked over a lantern in the barn at 8:30 P.M.
8. Once started, the fire was carried by high winds throughout the city.
9. Spreading quickly, the fire soon ravaged the west side of Chicago.
10. After three days, the raging fire eventually burned itself out.

▶ **Exercise 11** Revising Sentences by Using Participial Phrases Revise the following sentences by changing the underlined verb into a participial phrase.

EXAMPLE: The town elected a fire chief, and he is a fearless leader.
The fire chief elected by the town is a fearless leader.

1. On the morning of April 18, 1906, a massive earthquake rocked San Francisco and destroyed much of the city.
2. The earthquake lasted approximately one minute but caused extensive damage.
3. Gas mains, stoves, and fireplaces were soon initiating fires all across the city, and these fires contributed to a larger blaze.
4. More than fifty small fires contributed to the larger blaze and resulted in the Great San Francisco Fire.
5. The firemen responded to the numerous fires, but they were hampered by broken water mains and high winds.

▶ **More Practice**

Grammar Exercise Workbook
• pp. 37–38
On-line Exercise Bank
• Section 19.2
Go on-line:
PHSchool.com
Enter Web Code:
egk-1202

Interactive Textbook

Get instant feedback! Exercises 10 and 11 are available on-line or on CD-ROM.

Verbals and Verbal Phrases • **449**

Answer Key

▶ **Exercise 10**

1. Besieged by drought for several months: past
2. causing $600,000 damage: present
3. devastating: present
4. Having battled both of these blazes: perfect
5. exhausted: past
6. beleaguered: past; needed: past
7. having knocked over a lantern in the barn at 8:30 P.M.: perfect
8. Once started: past
9. Spreading quickly: present
10. raging: present

▶ **Exercise 11**

Responses will vary. Emphasize to students that their participles must modify words in the sentence and must be close to those words. The following are possible responses.

1. Rocking San Francisco on the morning of April 18, 1906, a massive earthquake destroyed much of the city.
2. Lasting approximately one minute, the earthquake caused extensive damage.
3. Gas mains, stoves, and fireplaces, initiating fires all across the city, contributed to a larger blaze.
4. Contributing to the larger blaze, more than fifty small fires resulted in the Great San Francisco fire.
5. Responding to the numerous fires, the firemen were hampered by broken water mains and high winds.

☑ **ONGOING ASSESSMENT: Monitor and Reinforce**

If students have difficulty with Exercise 10 or 11, refer them to the following for additional practice.

In the Textbook	Print Resources	Technology
Section Review, Ex. 15–16, Section 19.2	*Grammar Exercise Workbook*, pp. 37–38	*On-Line Exercise Bank*, Section 19.2

⏱ **TIME SAVERS!**

🖼 **Answers on Transparencies** Use the *Grammar Exercises Answers on Transparencies* for Chapter 19 to facilitate correction by students.

🖥 **On-Line Exercise Bank** Have students complete the exercises on computer. The Auto Check feature will grade their work for you!

Answer Key

▶ **Exercise 12**

1. (The freighter *Grandcamp* having docked at Texas City, Texas,) <u>workers</u> <u><u>were</u></u> loading its cargo on April 16, 1947.
2. (The ship having transported a cargo of ammonium nitrate,) an onboard <u>fire</u> <u><u>caused</u></u> a tremendous explosion.
3. (Most <u>townspeople having been</u> far enough away,) <u>casualties</u> in the town <u><u>were kept</u></u> to a minimum.
4. (The blast having damaged much of the town,) <u>people</u> <u><u>were evacuated</u></u> because of the prospect of a second explosion.
5. (Most people having left,) a second <u>explosion</u> <u><u>did</u></u> not <u><u>cause</u></u> many casualties.
6. (The dock engulfed in flames,) the <u>ship</u> *High Flyer* eventually <u><u>exploded</u></u> early the next morning.
7. (The city's fire department having been destroyed in the first explosion,) many <u>buildings</u> <u><u>could</u></u> not <u><u>be saved</u></u>.
8. (The blast having originated on the outskirts of the town,) the <u>fires</u> <u><u>were</u></u> not as destructive as those in Chicago or San Francisco.
9. (Nearly six hundred people having died,) the <u>town</u> <u><u>was</u></u> in a state of shock.
10. (The fire on the *Grandcamp* having been caused by careless actions,) the <u>event</u> <u><u>could</u></u> easily <u><u>have been prevented</u></u>.

Critical Viewing

Connect Sample response: *Watching the city burn,* the firefighter, *exhausted* from hours of work, watched the buildings *burning* in the distance.

19.2

▶ **Exercise 12** **Recognizing Nominative Absolutes** Write each sentence, underlining the subject once, underlining the verb twice, and circling the nominative absolute.

EXAMPLE: (<u>Lightning having struck the dry forest,</u>) a <u>fire</u> <u><u>swept</u></u> through twenty acres.

1. The freighter *Grandcamp* having docked at Texas City, Texas, workers were loading its cargo on April 16, 1947.
2. The ship having transported a cargo of ammonium nitrate, an onboard fire caused a tremendous explosion.
3. Most townspeople having been far enough away, casualties in the town were kept to a minimum.
4. The blast having damaged much of the town, people were evacuated because of the prospect of a second explosion.
5. Most people having left, a second explosion did not cause many casualties.
6. The dock engulfed in flames, the ship *High Flyer* eventually exploded early the next morning.
7. The city's fire department having been destroyed in the first explosion, many buildings could not be saved.
8. The blast having originated on the outskirts of the town, the fires were not as destructive as those in Chicago or San Francisco.
9. Nearly six hundred people having died, the town was in a state of shock.
10. The fire on the *Grandcamp* having been caused by careless actions, the event could easily have been prevented.

▶ **Critical Viewing** Create participial phrases from the verbs *burn, watch,* and *exhaust* in sentences to describe this picture. **[Connect]**

☑ **ONGOING ASSESSMENT: Monitor and Reinforce**

If students miss more than two items in Exercise 12, refer them to the following for additional practice.

In the Textbook	Print Resources	Technology
Section Review, Ex. 15–16, Section 19.2	*Grammar Exercise Workbook,* pp. 37–38	*On-Line Exercise Bank,* Section 19.2

Gerunds and Gerund Phrases

Verbs ending in *-ing* can be used as nouns called *gerunds*.

▶ **KEY CONCEPT** A **gerund** is a form of a verb that acts as a noun. ■

EXAMPLES: *Training* is the fire department's favorite activity.
Climbing is an important part of the job.

The Function of Gerunds in Sentences By themselves, gerunds function in sentences like any other nouns.

SOME USES OF GERUNDS IN SENTENCES	
As a Subject	*Firefighting* is often dangerous.
As a Direct Object	A successful firefighter must enjoy *firefighting*.
As an Indirect Object	He gives *studying* all of his attention.
As a Predicate Nominative	Her favorite pastime is *reading*.
As an Object of a Preposition	Check the smoke detector before *leaving*.
As an Appositive	One field, *engineering*, has made great advances in fire safety.

To avoid confusing verbs, participles, and gerunds—which all can end in *-ing*—check the word's use in the sentence.

VERB PHRASE: My friends *are fighting* the fire.
PARTICIPLE: A *fighting* spirit permeated the fire station.
GERUND: *Firefighting* tires me out.

Note About *Gerunds and Possessive Pronouns:* Only the possessive form of a personal pronoun is appropriate before a gerund.

INCORRECT: *Them* risking their lives is heroic.
CORRECT: *Their* risking their lives is heroic.

Gerunds

1. Students often have trouble differentiating gerunds from present participles and actual verbs with *-ing* endings. To further reinforce the concept, present these sentences. Have students identify how the *-ing* form in each is used.

   No one was working at the fire station. (verb; part of verb phrase *was working*)

   One rookie had a working knowledge of procedures. (participle; modifies *knowledge*)

   Working had tired everyone out. (gerund; used as subject)

2. Ask students to write their own groups of sentences like those above. Suggest verbs that carry their own meaning, such as *shoveling, swimming, cooking,* and *snoring*.

Customize for
Linguistic Learners

Have students take turns reading aloud to a partner the three sentences they wrote in step 2 above. The partner should identify how the *-ing* form in each sentence was used.

Gerund Phrases

1. Direct students' attention to the chart on the page. Have them identify the gerund in each gerund phrase. Remind them that a gerund phrase can fill the same noun functions in sentences as a single-word gerund can.

2. Have students tell the function of each gerund phrase in the chart.

3. For additional practice, write this on the board:

   My favorite chores do not include washing dishes.

   Have students identify the gerund (*washing*), the complete phrase (*washing dishes*), components of the phrase (*dishes*, direct object), and the function of the phrase in the sentence (direct object).

Integrating Workplace Skills

Explain to students that verbals may come in handy when applying and interviewing for jobs. Ask for examples of gerunds and gerund phrases that applicants might write to express their goals and abilities. (Examples: *working for a large corporation, developing my interpersonal skills, meeting new challenges*.) Once students generate a list of phrases, have them use them in sentences that might appear on résumés or letters of application.

Answer Key

Exercise 13

1. Fighting fires: subject
2. protecting buildings . . . fire: predicate nominative
3. Arriving at . . . minutes: subject
4. Risking . . . lives: subject
5. leaving: object of preposition
6. Handling a fire hose: subject
7. rescuing people: predicate nominative
8. ascending ladders: direct object
9. The showering . . . hoses: subject
10. salvaging property: subject

19.2

Gerund Phrases A gerund with modifiers or a complement is called a *gerund phrase*.

▶ **KEY CONCEPT** A **gerund phrase** is a gerund with modifiers or a complement, all acting together as a noun. ■

In the following chart, notice the variety of different kinds of modifiers and complements that a gerund phrase can contain.

GERUND PHRASES	
With Adjectives	*His loud, persistent snoring* disrupted the entire fire station.
With an Adjective Phrase	*Worrying about the next fire* prevented the captain from sleeping.
With an Adverb	I contacted the fire department by *dialing quickly.*
With an Adverb Phrase	*Fishing from the pier* is permitted.
With a Direct Object	*Battling arson* grows more expensive each year.
With Indirect and Direct Objects	The teacher suggested *writing the firemen a letter.*

▶ **Exercise 13** Identifying Gerunds and Gerund Phrases
Write the gerund or gerund phrase in each sentence. Then, identify its function in the sentence.

EXAMPLE: Taking this shortcut will save firefighters time.
Taking this shortcut (subject)

1. Fighting fires is a dangerous profession that requires courage and dedication.
2. The job of the fire department is protecting buildings and people from the ravages of a fire.
3. Arriving at a fire within a few minutes is the goal of the fire department.
4. Risking their lives is a regular part of firefighters' jobs.
5. They completely extinguish the flames before leaving.
6. Handling a fire hose is difficult because the water is under such high pressure.
7. An important part of a firefighter's job is rescuing people.
8. Firefighters are often seen ascending ladders.
9. The showering of water from the high-pressure hoses is impressive to see.
10. After the fire is extinguished, salvaging property becomes the main focus of the firefighters.

452 • Phrases and Clauses

▶ **More Practice**

Grammar Exercise Workbook
• pp. 39–40
On-line Exercise Bank
• Section 19.2
  Go on-line:
  PHSchool.com
  Enter Web Code:
  egk-1202

Get instant feedback! Exercise 13 is available on-line or on CD-ROM.

☑ **ONGOING ASSESSMENT: Monitor and Reinforce**

If students miss more than two items in Exercise 13, refer them to the following for additional practice.

In the Textbook	Print Resources	Technology
Section Review, Ex. 15–16, Section 19.2	*Grammar Exercise Workbook,* pp. 39–40	*On-Line Exercise Bank,* Section 19.2

Infinitives and Infinitive Phrases

Infinitives, the third type of verbal, can function as three parts of speech.

KEY CONCEPT An *infinitive* is a form of a verb that generally appears with the word *to* and acts as a noun, an adjective, or an adverb. ∎

EXAMPLES: The firefighter would like *to sleep*.
The instructor gave them an assignment *to do*.

Forms of Infinitives There are two kinds of infinitives—*present infinitives* and *perfect infinitives*.

Kinds of Infinitives	Forms	Examples
Present Infinitive	*To* plus the base form of a verb	I like *to debate. To concede* is *to lose.*
Perfect Infinitive	*To have* or *to have been* plus a past participle	I would have liked *to have gone. To have been mentioned* would have sufficed.

Do not mistake prepositional phrases for infinitives. In an infinitive, a verb follows the word *to*. In a prepositional phrase beginning with the word *to*, a noun or pronoun follows the word *to*.

INFINITIVES: to fight, to have excelled
PREPOSITIONAL PHRASES: to them, to a friend

Sometimes infinitives do not include the word *to*. After the verbs *dare, hear, help, let, make, please, see,* and *watch*, the *to* will usually be understood rather than stated.

EXAMPLES: The student helped *extinguish* the fire.
No one dared *rush* into the blazing building.

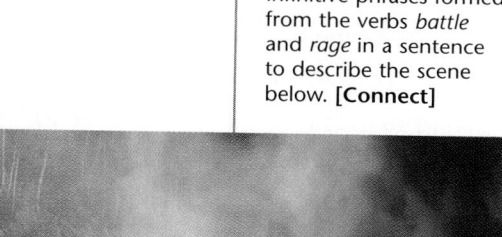

▼ **Critical Viewing**
Use infinitives and infinitive phrases formed from the verbs *battle* and *rage* in a sentence to describe the scene below. **[Connect]**

Verbals and Verbal Phrases • **453**

Forms of Infinitives

1. Students may be more familiar with present than with perfect infinitives. Use the chart to review the two kinds of infinitives and how they are formed.

2. Ask students to write the perfect infinitive forms of several verbs. You might use *notice, drive, write,* or other verbs of your choice. (Perfect infinitive forms of these verbs: *to have noticed, to have been noticed; to have driven, to have been driven; to have written, to have been written*)

3. Ask for volunteers to create sentences using infinitives without *to* after the verbs *hear, help, let,* and *see.*

Critical Viewing

Connect Sample response: As the fire continued *to rage out of control,* the fire fighters had no choice but to continue *to battle it.*

Infinitive Phrases

1. Explain that infinitive phrases are like other verbal phrases in that they take modifiers and objects.

2. Remind students that infinitive phrases can function as nouns, adjectives, or adverbs in sentences. Have them review the use of the phrases in the chart.

3. The concept of infinitives used as nouns should not seem unusual to students. Remind them that they have seen the same sort of usage with gerunds.

4. Infinitives used as modifiers may be more difficult for students to recognize. Unless they introduce a sentence, in which case they probably modify the verb, such forms nearly always come just after the words they modify. It is common for adverb infinitives to modify adjectives.

5. Offer additional practice using infinitives and infinitive phrases by asking students to write three infinitive phrases for each of the following: *to see, to practice, to understand.* (Examples: *to see well, to practice on Saturday mornings, to understand math*)

Customizing for
AP Students

Introduce the concept of infinitive clause, in which the infinitive has its own subject. Use this example:

The girl asked the firefighter to rescue her cat.

Ask students to identify the direct object of the sentence (*the firefighter to rescue her cat*), and point out that this is an infinitive clause because it has a subject (*firefighter*) and a verb (*to rescue*) even though the entire clause operates as a noun. Then ask students to construct five sentences of their own with infinitive clauses.

19.2

Infinitive Phrases When you add modifiers, complements, or subjects to an infinitive, an infinitive becomes an *infinitive phrase.*

▶ **KEY CONCEPT** An **infinitive phrase** is an infinitive with modifiers, a complement, or a subject, all acting together as a single part of speech. ■

WITH AN ADVERB:	The firefighters at the scene needed *to act quickly.*
WITH AN ADVERB PHRASE:	They hoped *to finish within a few minutes.*
WITH A COMPLEMENT:	They tried *to confine the blaze.*
WITH A SUBJECT AND COMPLEMENT:	The firefighters asked *the crowd to leave the area.*

The Function of Infinitives in Sentences The flexibility of infinitives enables them to be used in almost any capacity. Note in the chart below that infinitives, like gerunds, often function as nouns. Unlike gerunds, however, infinitives can also act as adjectives or adverbs in sentences.

INFINITIVES AND INFINITIVE PHRASES USED AS NOUNS AND MODIFIERS	
As a Subject	*To play with matches* is wrong.
As a Direct Object	The fire inspector decided *to leave the scene.*
As a Predicate Nominative	Our best protection against a fire was *to have been prepared.*
As an Object of a Preposition	I was about *to speak.*
As an Appositive	The fire department's intention, *to save the house,* intensified quickly.
As an Adjective	The fireman gave us some safety advice *to follow.*
As an Adverb	Fires are hard *to contain.*

▦ **Internet Tip**

Most city and county fire departments have their own Web sites. To learn more about firefighting, search for the site of a fire department in your city or in a city near your home.

GRAMMAR IN LITERATURE

from **The Parable of the Prodigal Son**
The King James Bible

In the following passage, two infinitive phrases and an infinitive are highlighted in blue italics. What part of speech is each used as?

14 And when he had spent all, there arose a mighty famine in that land; and he began *to be in want.*

15 And he went and joined himself to a citizen of that country; and he sent him into his fields *to feed swine.* . . .

17 And when he came to himself, he said, How many hired servants of my father's have bread enough and *to spare,* and I perish with hunger!

> **Exercise 14** Identifying Infinitives and Infinitive Phrases

Write each infinitive or infinitive phrase. Then, label its part of speech *noun, adjective,* or *adverb.* If the infinitive or infinitive phrase is used as a noun, further identify its function as a *subject, direct object, predicate nominative, object of a preposition,* or *appositive.*

EXAMPLE: We tried for two hours to start the campfire.
              to start the campfire (noun, direct object)

1. Here are the facts to understand about the tragic fire at Peshtigo, Wisconsin, in 1871.
2. The hot, arid summer had managed to drain the surrounding forest of any moisture.
3. Just one day before the fire, the local newspaper chose to declare, "Without rain, a conflagration may ensue."
4. Initially, it was difficult to perceive the fire as a threat, but it soon developed into an all-consuming blaze.
5. To make matters worse, a strong wind propelled the fire through the forest with great speed.
6. The town's only fire engine was called to stop the flames.
7. The firemen were quick to realize that they could not save the town.
8. To save their own lives, the firemen fled to the river.
9. To return to the ashes of the town was difficult for the citizens of Peshtigo.
10. A memorial was built to honor the men and women who perished.

> **More Practice**

Grammar Exercise Workbook
• pp. 39–40
On-line Exercise Bank
• Section 19.2
  Go on-line:
  PHSchool.com
  Enter Web Code:
  egk-1202

interactive Textbook

Get instant feedback! Exercise 14 is available on-line or on CD-ROM.

Verbals and Verbal Phrases • **455**

Step-by-Step Teaching Guide

Grammar in Literature

1. Have a volunteer read the passage aloud. Then ask students if these are complete sentences. (No.)

2. Have students discuss the effect created by these infinitive phrases. (There is a repetitious, almost singsong quality.)

Connections With Literature

Students will find a complete "The Parable of the Prodigal Son" in *Prentice Hall Literature, Penguin Edition,* The British Tradition.

Answer Key

> **Exercise 14**

1. to understand . . . 1871: adj.
2. to drain . . . moisture: noun, direct object
3. to declare . . . ensue": noun, direct object
4. to perceive . . . threat: adv.
5. To make matters worse: adv.
6. to stop the flames: adv.
7. to realize . . . town: adv.
8. To save . . . lives: adv.
9. To return . . . town: noun, subject
10. to honor . . . perished: adv.

☑ ONGOING ASSESSMENT: Monitor and Reinforce

If students miss more than two items in Exercise 14, refer them to the following for additional practice.

In the Textbook	Print Resources	Technology
Section Review, Ex. 15–16, Section 19.2	*Grammar Exercise Workbook,* pp. 39–40	*On-Line Exercise Bank,* Section 19.2

Step-by-Step Teaching Guide

Hands-on Grammar

Teaching Resources: Hands-on Grammar Activity Book, Ch. 19

1. If you wish to do this activity in class, be prepared with scissors and construction paper. Assign students to work in pairs.

2. Go through the directions and the samples with the whole class. Then have students work with their partners to combine the remaining sentences on the page.

3. When students have finished, see if they came up with these combinations:

   To reach the top of the rock wall was his goal.

   Frightened of heights, Alice wouldn't attempt the climb.

   Cheryl had her own secret method: keeping her eyes shut.

   Exhausted by the effort, Sal almost gave up.

   Sal was determined to reach the top of the rock face.

4. Ask student pairs to write several of their own sentences for combining and present them to other pairs to work with.

Find It in Your Reading

After all students have found their examples of verbals, have them discuss which type—participle, gerund, or infinitive—seems to be used most commonly.

Find It in Your Writing

Have students work individually with sentences from their own writing. They can then share the results with their partners.

Hands-on Grammar

Verbal-Phrase Folds

One way to write sentences that are longer and more varied is to use verbal phrases in your writing. Often, you can change part of the predicate of one sentence into a participial, gerund, or infinitive phrase that you can incorporate into a second sentence. To practice this sentence-combining technique, try the following activity.

Cut out a series of long, thin strips of paper. On one strip, write the following pair of sentences: *He was climbing the rock face. He fell and broke his leg.* Bend under the first two words of the first sentence to form a combined sentence that starts with a participle: *Climbing the steep rock face, he fell and broke his leg.* On the strip, correct the capitalization and punctuation as needed.

> He was climbing the rock face. He fell and broke his leg.

> climbing the rock face, He fell and broke his leg.

Complete a second strip with the following pair of sentences: *He was losing his grip on the rocks. That led to his accident.* Bend under the first two words of the first sentence and fold the paper over to cover the word *That* at the beginning of the second sentence. The result is a combined sentence that starts with a gerund phrase: *Losing his grip on the rocks led to his accident.*

> He was losing his grip on the rocks. That led to his accident.

> losing his grip on the rocks, led to his accident.

Use the following sentences to create more verbal phrase folds. Some sentences can be folded in more than one way. For each folded strip, identify the type of verbal phrase you have formed and its function in the new sentence.

> *He hoped to reach the top of the rock wall. That was his goal.*
> *Alice was frightened of heights. Alice wouldn't attempt the climb.*
> *Cheryl had her own secret method. She was keeping her eyes shut.*
> *Sal was exhausted by the effort. Sal almost gave up.*
> *Sal was determined. Sal wanted to reach the top of the rock face.*

Find It in Your Reading Find examples of sentences in a short story or novel that contain verbal phrases. For each one you find, identify the type of phrase and its function in the sentence.

Find It in Your Writing Review a piece of writing from your portfolio. Combine at least two pairs of sentences using phrases.

456 • Phrases and Clauses

☑ ONGOING ASSESSMENT: Assess Mastery

Use the following resources to assess student mastery of verbals and verbal phrases.

In the Textbook	Technology
Chapter Review, Ex. 41	*Writing and Grammar* Interactive Text, Section 19.2, Section Review; *On-Line Exercise Bank*, Section 19.2

⏱ TIME SAVERS!

✋ **Hands-on Grammar**
Use the Hands-on Grammar activity sheet for Chapter 19 to facilitate this activity.

Section 19.2 Section Review

GRAMMAR EXERCISES 15–19

Exercise 15 Identifying Verbals and Verbal Phrases Identify the underlined verbals in the following sentences as either a *gerund phrase*, an *infinitive phrase*, a *participle*, a *participial phrase*, or a *nominative absolute*. Identify the way each gerund or infinitive functions in the sentence.

1. The movie <u>having ended</u>, my friend and I walked to our homes.
2. On the way, I noticed a <u>burning</u> smell.
3. <u>Originating above an old, empty warehouse</u> was a cloud of smoke.
4. As we got closer to the building, I could see smoke <u>billowing from the top floor</u>.
5. My friend ran to the nearest pay phone <u>to call the fire department</u>.
6. Soon after he returned, we could hear the <u>blaring</u> sirens of the fire engines.
7. By now, sparks could be seen <u>falling to the ground</u>.
8. Two brightly <u>painted</u> fire engines came to a stop in front of the building.
9. The firefighters knew exactly how <u>to handle the situation</u>.
10. Several immediately began <u>unraveling the long hoses</u>.
11. Another one ran <u>to open the nearby fire hydrant</u>.
12. <u>Dousing the fire with water</u> immediately reduced the level of the blaze.
13. The ladder truck <u>having been moved into position</u>, one person climbed up to the top floor of the building.
14. <u>Wielding an axe</u>, she shattered the windows so the others could douse the flames with water from the hoses.
15. <u>Witnessing the firefighters' skills</u> made us feel more secure.

Exercise 16 Revising Sentences by Using Verbal Phrases On your paper, rewrite each sentence that follows using the directions in parentheses.

1. A fire damaged and destroyed much of London in 1666. (Change *damaged* to a present participle.)
2. The fire started in a bakery, and the smell of burnt bread soon filled the air. (Change the first clause into a nominative absolute.)
3. Londoners who lived nearby saw the blaze. The sight frightened them. (Change *frightened* into a participle.)
4. London's citizens were unprepared to battle the fire. They stood by helplessly. (Combine by using a participial phrase.)
5. We discovered that very few people died in the fire. That was amazing. (Combine with an infinitive subject.)

Exercise 17 Find It in Your Reading Identify the verbals and verbal phrases in this passage from Samuel Pepys's diary.

. . . [T]o see how the streets and the highways are crowded with people running and riding, and the getting of carts at any rate to fetch away things.

Exercise 18 Find It in Your Writing Review a piece of writing from your portfolio. Identify at least two gerunds or gerund phrases. If you have not used any gerunds, challenge yourself to include at least two.

Exercise 19 Writing Application Write a newspaper article describing a fire or other tragedy. Use several types of verbal phrases to make your writing more interesting and descriptive.

Section Review • 457

Answer Key continued

Exercise 19

Writing Application
When students analyze their completed writing, tell them to be especially careful that all participial phrases modify some noun in a sentence and that each phrase is placed close to the word it modifies.

ASSESS

Section Review

Each of these exercises correlates to the instruction on verbals and verbal phrases, pages 446–454. The exercises may be used for more practice, for reteaching, or for review of the key concepts presented. Answers for all chapter exercises are available in *Grammar Exercises Answers on Transparencies* in your Teaching Resources.

Answer Key

Exercise 15

1. nominative absolute
2. participle
3. gerund, subject
4. participial phrase
5. infinitive, adverb
6. participle
7. participial phrase
8. participle
9. infinitive, direct object
10. gerund, direct object
11. infinitive, adverb
12. gerund, subject
13. nominative absolute
14. participial phrase
15. gerund, subject

Exercise 16

Expect some variation in response.

1. A damaging fire destroyed . . .
2. The fire having started in a bakery, the smell of . . .
3. Frightened Londoners who lived nearby watched the blaze.
4. London's citizens, standing by helplessly, were unprepared . . .
5. To discover that very few people died in the fire was amazing.

Exercise 17

Find It in Your Reading
[T]o see how the streets and the highways are crowded—inf.; running—part.; riding—part.; the getting of carts at any—gerund; to fetch away things—inf.

Exercise 18

Find It in Your Writing
After students have added gerunds to their piece of writing, have them analyze how they used the gerunds—as subjects, direct objects, and so on.

continued

PREPARE and ENGAGE

Interest GRABBER Ask students to recall song lyrics, titles of works, or jingles that are incomplete ideas but contain subjects and verbs (Examples: "When you wish upon a star," "If I were a rich man.") Write the examples on the board. Point out that these lyrics are subordinate clauses; they cannot stand alone. Then have students offer an original clause to add to each in order to form a complete sentence.

Activate Prior Knowledge

Present this sentence and ask students to find three subordinate clauses in it: *Though it astonishes some students, that I love grammar is well known by everyone that I've taught.* Have students identify each subordinate clause and tell the type it is. (*Though it astonishes some students:* adverb; *that I love grammar:* noun; *that I've taught:* adjective.)

TEACH

Step-by-Step Teaching Guide

Clauses

1. If students need practice distinguishing independent from subordinate clauses, ask them to identify each of the following

   The dog and cat fought. (independent)

   Everybody heard them. (independent)

   As soon as they saw each other. (subordinate)

   Which attracted everybody's attention. (subordinate)

2. Have students combine these clauses into new sentences.

Critical Viewing

Analyze Sample response: This flag, *which represents the United States,* inspires awe in many people.

Section 19.3

Clauses

Clauses, like phrases, are groups of related words, but unlike phrases, they have a subject and a verb.

> **KEY CONCEPT** A **clause** is a group of words with its own subject and verb. ■

There are two basic kinds of clauses: *independent* and *subordinate* clauses.

> **KEY CONCEPT** An **independent clause** has a subject and a verb and can stand by itself as a complete sentence. ■

All complete sentences must contain at least one independent clause; additional independent or subordinate clauses may be added. *The flag will be lowered at sundown* is an independent clause. *I bought a flag, but I didn't have a flag pole* is one independent clause added to another. *The flagpole was barren after the banner was removed* is an example of an independent clause followed by a subordinate clause. Though *after the banner was removed* contains a subject *(banner)* and a verb *(was removed)*, the clause cannot stand alone.

> **KEY CONCEPT** A **subordinate clause** cannot stand by itself as a complete sentence; it is only part of a sentence. ■

Subordinate clauses can add important details to sentences and show relationships between ideas. Within sentences, subordinate clauses act as either adjectives, adverbs, or nouns.

458 • Phrases and Clauses

Theme: Flags

In this section, you will learn to recognize adjective, adverb, and noun clauses. The examples and exercises are about flags.

Cross-Curricular Connection: Social Studies

▼ **Critical Viewing** What fact about this flag could be set off in a nonessential adjective clause? Write a sentence that includes that clause. **[Analyze]**

⏱ TIME AND RESOURCE MANAGER

Resources
Print: *Grammar Exercise Workbook*, pp. 41–46; *Grammar Exercises Answers on Transparencies*, Ch. 19
Technology: *Writing and Grammar* Interactive Text, Section 19.3; *On-Line Exercise Bank*, Section 19.3

Using the Full Student Edition	Using the Handbook⊞
• Work through all key concepts, pp. 458–465.	• Work through all key concepts, pp. 316–323.
• Assign and review Exercises 20–25.	• Assign and review Exercises 20–25.
• Read and discuss Grammar in Literature, p. 466.	• Read and discuss Grammar in Literature, p. 324.

Adjective Clauses

Adjective clauses modify nouns or pronouns in ways often not possible with one-word adjectives or adjective phrases.

KEY CONCEPT An **adjective clause** is a subordinate clause that modifies a noun or pronoun. ■

An adjective clause appears after the noun or pronoun it modifies. It usually begins with a relative pronoun *(that, which, who, whom, or whose)* or with a relative adverb (such as *before, since, when, where,* or *why).*

EXAMPLES: The flag, *which was created in 1847,* is striped.

There was a time *when the flag had only thirteen stars.*

Essential and Nonessential Adjective Clauses

Adjectives clauses are punctuated according to whether they add *essential* or *nonessential* information to a sentence.

KEY CONCEPTS An adjective clause that is not essential to the basic meaning of a sentence is set off by commas. An essential clause is not set off. ■

The following chart demonstrates the difference between nonessential and essential clauses.

Nonessential Adjective Clauses	Essential Adjective Clauses
The tattered flag, which inspired Francis Scott Key, was on display at the museum.	The tattered flag that inspired Francis Scott Key was on display at the museum.

You can often combine two sentences into one by using either a nonessential or an essential adjective clause.

TWO SENTENCES: "The Star-Spangled Banner" is a patriotic song about the American flag. It became the national anthem in 1931.

ADJECTIVE CLAUSE: "The Star-Spangled Banner," which became the national anthem in 1931, is a patriotic song about the American flag.

Learn More

For more information about punctuating adjective clauses, see Chapter 27.

Clauses • 459

Adjective Clauses

1. Remind students that adjective clauses function similarly to single-word adjectives: They tell which one, what kind, how much, or how many. Use the example in the text to demonstrate that this is true even when the clause begins with a relative adverb.

2. Explain to students that the more specific the word being modified, the less likely the adjective clause will be essential to meaning. For example, clauses following proper nouns are virtually always nonessential.

3. Tell students that when combining two sentences with an adjective clause, they should decide which idea is more important. That idea should go in the independent clause, while the less important point should go in the adjective clause.

Customize for
ESL Students

To emphasize the distinction between independent and subordinate clauses, have students list everyday greetings and common expressions like *Good morning, Excuse me, Whatever you say,* and *When I'm ready.* Then ask which sayings are independent clauses, which are subordinate clauses, and which are simply phrases without subjects or verbs. For each clause, have students underline the subject and double-underline the verb. (For expressions like *Excuse me,* point out that the subject is understood.) For the subordinate clauses, ask students to add independent clauses to them to form complete sentences.

✓ **ONGOING ASSESSMENT: Prerequisite Skills**

If students have difficulty with clauses, you may find it necessary to review the following to ensure coverage of prerequisite knowledge.

In the Textbook	Print Resources	Technology
Subordinating Conjunctions, Section 17.4	*Grammar Exercise Workbook,* pp. 17–18	*On-Line Exercise Bank,* Section 17.4

Introductory Words in Adjective Clauses

1. In identifying parts of clauses, students often have difficulty with relative pronouns used as objects. For reinforcement, present these portions of sentences (clauses are underlined for your reference):

   the flag that she hung in the window (*that* is direct object)

   the worker to whom we spoke (*whom* is object of the preposition *to*)

   the flag book I bought in the museum store (understood *that* is direct object)

   Have students identify the clauses and rearrange them in order to determine the objects. (For the third sentence, students may need to be told that the relative pronoun, *that*, is understood.)

2. Following the patterns in step 1, have students write three original sentences of their own.

19.3

Introductory Words in Adjective Clauses *Relative pronouns* and *relative adverbs* not only begin adjective clauses but also function within the subordinate clause.

▶ **KEY CONCEPT** **Relative pronouns** connect adjective clauses to the words they modify and act as subjects, direct objects, objects of prepositions, or adjectives in the clauses. ■

Relative pronouns act as an introduction to the clause and as a subject, direct object, object of a preposition, or adjective *within* the clause. The role of the relative pronoun can be determined by isolating the adjective clause from the rest of the sentence and then by identifying its subject and verb. Because adjective clauses are sometimes in inverted order, you may need to rearrange the words mentally.

THE USES OF RELATIVE PRONOUNS WITHIN ADJECTIVE CLAUSES	
As a Subject	*Sentence:* The flag *that was just lowered* is the Italian flag. *Clause:* <u>that</u> <u>was</u> just <u>lowered</u>
As a Direct Object	*Sentence:* Someone scratched the flagpole *that I recently painted.* *Reworded clause:* <u>I</u> recently <u>painted</u> that (DO)
As the Object of a Preposition	*Sentence:* This is the flag designer *of whom I have spoken.* *Reworded clause:* <u>I</u> <u>have spoken</u> of whom (OBJ OF PREP)
As an Adjective	*Sentence:* I have a friend *whose grandfather raised the flag at San Juan Hill.* *Clause:* whose <u>grandfather</u> <u>raised</u> the flag at San Juan Hill

Note About *Understood Relative Pronouns:* In some adjective clauses, the relative pronoun may be understood.

EXAMPLE: The flag *[that] I own* is from the War of 1812.

▶ **KEY CONCEPT** **Relative adverbs** function only as adverbs within clauses. ■

THE USE OF RELATIVE ADVERBS WITHIN ADJECTIVE CLAUSES

As an Adverb	*Sentence:* The spot *where we stood* afforded us an excellent view of the flag. *Reworded clause:* <u>we</u> <u>stood</u> where

▶ **Exercise 20** **Identifying Adjective Clauses** Write each adjective clause, underlining its subject once and its verb twice. Then, circle the relative pronoun or relative adverb and identify its function in the clause.

EXAMPLE: I salute the same flag that my forefathers saluted.
            (that) my <u>forefathers</u> <u>saluted</u> (direct object)

1. A flag is a piece of fabric that functions as a symbol.
2. Historians know surprisingly little about the first flags that ancient peoples used.
3. The first place where flags are known to have been used was China.
4. The Chinese, who made flags from silk, began using them more than 3,000 years ago.
5. Roman flags, which developed at a later date, were called *vexilla*.

▶ **Exercise 21** **Punctuating Adjective Clauses** On your paper, underline each adjective clause and add commas if necessary.

EXAMPLE: We wrote to Ms. Gomez who was our instructor.
            We wrote to Ms. Gomez, <u>who was our instructor</u>.

1. The flag of the United States which is often called the Stars and Stripes originated during the Revolutionary War.
2. Congress passed a resolution on June 14, 1777, that prescribed the official design of the new flag.
3. The flag's design consisted of thirteen stars and stripes which represented the thirteen colonies.
4. Historians who study flags are unable to determine the first flag's creator.
5. According to popular legend, Betsy Ross who was a seamstress made the first American flag.

More Practice

Grammar Exercise Workbook
• pp. 41–42
On-line Exercise Bank
• Section 19.3
 Go on-line:
 PHSchool.com
 Enter Web Code:
 egk-1202

interactive
Textbook

Get instant feedback! Exercises 20 and 21 are available on-line or on CD-ROM.

Clauses • 461

☑ **ONGOING ASSESSMENT: Monitor and Reinforce**

If students miss more than one item in Exercise 20 or 21, refer them to the following for additional practice.

In the Textbook	Print Resources	Technology
Section Review, Ex. 26, 29, Section 19.3	*Grammar Exercise Workbook,* pp. 41–42	*On-Line Exercise Bank,* Section 19.3

Adverb Clauses

1. Students will find it easier to recognize adverb clauses once they have reviewed subordinating conjunctions. Begin a list on the board (*before, if, unless*) and have volunteers add to it, or refer students to the list on page 397 of their textbooks.

2. Tell students that the subordinating conjunction is important because it tells the relationship between the ideas in the independent and subordinate clauses. Have students give at least one subordinating conjunction that shows each of these relationships: why (*because*), under what condition (*although, unless*), and when (*before, after, since*).

3. To give students extra practice, have them use some of the subordinating conjunctions you have identified or listed in new sentences.

continued

19.3

Adverb Clauses

An *adverb clause* functions in a sentence in much the same way one-word adverbs and adverb phrases do.

> **KEY CONCEPT** An **adverb clause** is a subordinate clause that modifies a verb, an adjective, an adverb, or a verbal. It does this by pointing out *where, when, in what way, to what extent, under what condition,* or *why.* ■

An adverb clause begins with a subordinating conjunction and contains a subject and a verb, although they are not the main subject and verb in the sentence. This kind of subordinate clause may modify any word that an adverb can.

ADVERB CLAUSES

Modified Words	Examples
Verb	We saluted *because the flag had been raised.*
Adjective	The veteran appeared proud *as he saluted the flag.*
Adverb	The flag ceremony ended sooner *than we expected.*
Participle	The flag, flapping in the wind *as I attempted to do my studies,* made concentration impossible.
Gerund	I relax by sitting under the flagpole *after I study.*
Infinitive	I wanted to visit the museum *while "The Star-Spangled Banner" was still being displayed.*

⊘ Learn More

Refer to Section 17.4 for a list of subordinating conjunctions.

Adverb clauses can be used to combine two sentences into one and to show relationships between ideas.

TWO SENTENCES: The design was used by the king. It was added to the flag in 1924.

COMBINED: The design was used by the king before it was added to the flag in 1924.

▶ **KEY CONCEPT** Some adverb clauses beginning with *as* or *than* are **elliptical**. The verb or both the subject and the verb in the clause are understood but not stated. ■

VERB UNDERSTOOD:	I recognized as many flags *as he* [did].
SUBJECT AND VERB UNDERSTOOD:	The UN building has more flags *than* [it has] *rooms*.

▶ **Exercise 22** Identifying Adverb Clauses Write the adverb clause in each sentence. Then, indicate whether it modifies a *verb*, an *adjective*, an *adverb*, or a *verbal*.

EXAMPLE: Although rain had been predicted, the flag was still raised.
            Although rain had been predicted (verb)

1. There are specific rules to know before you display the American flag.
2. Although the flag should always be raised quickly, it should be lowered slowly.
3. The flag is generally raised after the sun has risen.
4. It should be lowered when the sun sets.
5. The flag should be flown every day unless it is raining.
6. The American flag should be displayed on the right-hand side of any other flags if it is carried in a procession.
7. Marchers, parading while they hold the American flag, may also carry it in front of the procession.
8. A public building, such as a courthouse, should display the flag once the building has been occupied.
9. The flag is often flown prominently wherever U.S. troops are stationed.
10. Folding the flag into a small triangular-shaped bundle is appropriate unless it is being displayed.

▶ **Exercise 23** Recognizing Elliptical Clauses Write each elliptical adverb clause, showing understood words in parentheses.

EXAMPLE: I enjoyed making this banner more than that one.
            than (I did) that one

1. Not all flags are the same shape as the American flag.
2. However, there are more rectangular national flags than square national flags.
3. The width of most of these flags is usually longer than the height.
4. Horizontal stripes are as common to national flags as vertical stripes.
5. Some national flags contain more colors than others.

▶ **More Practice**

Grammar Exercise Workbook
• pp. 43–44
On-line Exercise Bank
• Section 19.3
 Go on-line:
 PHSchool.com
 Enter Web Code:
 egk-1202

Get instant feedback! Exercises 22 and 23 are available on-line or on CD-ROM.

 **Learn More**

Refer to Section 22.2 for rules about the correct use of pronouns in elliptical clauses.

Clauses • **463**

4. To recognize elliptical clauses, have students look for word groups beginning with *as* or *than* in which a complete idea is not stated. They can mentally supply the understood words.

Answer Key

▶ **Exercise 22**
1. before you display the American flag: verbal
2. Although the flag should always be raised quickly: verb
3. after the sun has risen: verb
4. when the sun sets: verb
5. unless it is raining: verb
6. if it is carried in a procession: verb
7. while they hold the American flag: verbal
8. once the building has been occupied: verb
9. wherever U.S. troops are stationed: verb
10. unless it is being displayed: adjective

▶ **Exercise 23**
1. as the American flag (is)
2. than (there are) square national flags
3. than the height (is)
4. as vertical stripes (are)
5. than others (do)

✓ **ONGOING ASSESSMENT: Monitor and Reinforce**

If students have difficulty with Exercise 22 or 23, refer them to the following for additional practice.

In the Textbook	Print Resources	Technology
Section Review, Ex. 26, 29, Section 19.3	*Grammar Exercise Workbook,* pp. 43–44	*On-Line Exercise Bank,* Section 19.3

⏱ **TIME SAVERS!**

Answers on Transparencies Use the *Grammar Exercises Answers on Transparencies* for Chapter 19 to facilitate correction by students.

On-Line Exercise Bank Have students complete the exercises on computer. The Auto Check feature will grade their work for you!

Noun Clauses

1. To reinforce the concept of clauses functioning as nouns, have students replace the noun clauses in the chart with single nouns and pronouns. (Example: *Information* can be found in this book.)

2. Since noun clauses may begin with words that also introduce adjective or adverb clauses (*that, which, who, whom, whose, how, if, when, where, whether*), students may have trouble identifying noun clauses. Point out that if the clause can be replaced by a single noun, it probably is a noun clause.

3. To understand the function of words within a noun clause, recommend that students isolate the clause and, if necessary, put the words in it into natural order. Follow this procedure to have students identify the subject, verb, and direct object (if there is one) of each noun clause in the charts on pages 464 and 465.

Critical Viewing

Apply Sample response: The flag of Wales clearly shows *what a red dragon looks like.*

Noun Clauses

The *noun clause* is the third kind of subordinate clause.

▶ **KEY CONCEPT** A **noun clause** is a subordinate clause that acts as a noun in a sentence. ■

As the following chart shows, a noun clause can perform any function in a sentence that any other kind of noun can.

USES OF NOUN CLAUSES IN SENTENCES

Functions in Sentences	Examples
Subject	*Whatever information you need* can be found in this book.
Direct Object	The soldiers carried *whichever flag belonged to their country.*
Indirect Object	The group sent *whoever requested information* a brochure about the history of flags.
Predicate Nominative	To change the design of the ensign is *what I would like.*
Object of a Preposition	I will cut the banner to *whatever length you desire.*

Noun clauses frequently begin with *that, which, who, whom,* or *whose,* the same words that can begin adjective clauses. Other words that can begin noun clauses are *how, if, what, whatever, when, where, whether, whichever, whoever,* or *whomever.* Besides serving to introduce a noun clause, these words sometimes serve a function within the clause as well.

▼ Critical Viewing Use the noun clause "what a red dragon looks like" in a sentence about the flag of Wales. **[Apply]**

464 • Phrases and Clauses

SOME USES OF INTRODUCTORY WORDS IN NOUN CLAUSES

Functions in Clauses	Examples
Adjective	She could not decide *which Scandinavian flag was her favorite.*
Adverb	I do not know *when the flag pole was painted.*
Subject	*Whoever recognizes the American flag* should treat it with respect.
Direct Object	*Whatever my supervisor advised,* I did.
No Function	The historian said *that the flag was two hundred years old.*

When the word *that* has no function within the clause except to introduce it, it is often omitted.

EXAMPLE: We remembered [*that*] *you wanted to raise the flag in the morning.*

Because some of the words that introduce noun clauses also introduce adjective and adverb clauses, do not let the introductory word be your only guide in determining the type of clause. Always check the function of the clause in the sentence.

> **Exercise 24** Identifying Noun Clauses Write each noun clause. Then, identify the function of each noun clause as *subject, direct object, indirect object, predicate nominative, object of a preposition,* or *appositive.*

EXAMPLE: A symbolic flag is what everyone wants.
           what everyone wants (predicate nominative)

1. A ship at sea traditionally flies whichever flag represents its country of origin.
2. Specific guidelines often govern how flags should be displayed on ships.
3. Whichever national flag is flown at the front of a ship is called the jack.
4. An ensign is what the national flag is called on the rear of a ship.
5. As a courtesy, most ships usually fly the national flag of whichever country they are visiting.

Grammar and Style Tip

With noun clauses, you can also try substituting the words *fact, it, thing,* or *you* for the clause. If the sentence retains its smoothness, the clause is probably a noun clause. I knew *the flag was waving.* I knew *it.*

> **More Practice**

Grammar Exercise Workbook
• pp. 45–46
On-line Exercise Bank
• Section 19.3
  Go on-line:
  PHSchool.com
  Enter Web Code:
  egk-1202

Complete the exercise on-line! Exercise 24 is available on-line or on CD-ROM.

Clauses • 465

☑ ONGOING ASSESSMENT: Monitor and Reinforce

If students have difficulty with Exercise 24 or 25, refer them to the following for additional practice.

In the Textbook	Print Resources	Technology
Section Review, Ex. 27–28, Section 19.3	*Grammar Exercise Workbook,* pp. 45–46	*On-Line Exercise Bank,* Section 19.3

⏱ TIME SAVERS!

Answers on Transparencies Use the *Grammar Exercises Answers on Transparencies* for Chapter 19 to facilitate correction by students.

On-Line Exercise Bank Have students complete the exercises on computer. The Auto Check feature will grade their work for you!

Each of these exercises correlates to a section of the chapter on phrases and clauses, pages 438–470. These exercises may be used for more practice, for reteaching, or for review of the key concepts presented. Answers for all exercises are available in the *Grammar Exercises Answers on Transparencies* in your Teaching Resources.

Answer Key

> **Exercise 39**

1. in the isolated area: adv.; in the mountains: adv.; of northern India: adj. 2. on the north side: adv.; of the Himalayan mountain range: adj. 3. of high mountains, vast snowfields, glaciers, and cliffs: adj. 4. in the wild: adv. 5. During the summer: adv.; in the mountains: adv.; above the timberline: adv.

> **Exercise 40**

1. another name for the snow leopard: identifies *ounce*
2. a protection against the bitter environment: identifies *Hair cushions*
3. a device used by the snow leopard to keep its balance on rocky terrain: identifies *tail*
4. bitter cold in winter and scorching heat in summer: identifies [*weather*] *conditions*
5. black rosettes and small spots: identifies *marks*

> **Exercise 41**

1. infinitive phrase
2. participial phrase
3. infinitive phrase
4. gerund phrase
5. nominative absolute
6. gerund phrase
7. participial phrase
8. gerund phrase
9. participial phrase
10. nominative absolute

> **Exercise 42**

1. than most species of wildcats (are): adverb
2. In the Sahara and other African deserts where they live: adverb

continued

Chapter **19** *Chapter Review*

GRAMMAR EXERCISES 39–46

> **Exercise 39** Identifying Adjective and Adverb Phrases Write the prepositional phrases in the following sentences. Then, identify each prepositional phrase as *adjective* or *adverb*.

(1) Snow leopards live in the isolated area high in the mountains of northern India. (2) They are most common on the north side of the Himalayan mountain range. (3) This habitat contains numbers of high mountains, vast snowfields, glaciers, and cliffs. (4) This territory is so vast and wide that humans rarely will glimpse a snow leopard in the wild. (5) During the summer, they have been spotted in the mountains when they run above the timberline.

> **Exercise 40** Identifying Appositives and Appositive Phrases Write each sentence, underlining the appositive or appositive phrase. Then, draw an arrow to the noun for which it provides extra information.

1. The ounce, another name for the snow leopard, is a member of the cat family.
2. Hair cushions, a protection against the bitter environment, are located on its paws.
3. The furry tail, a device used by the snow leopard to keep its balance on rocky terrain, is about three feet long.
4. The thick, furry coat protects the snow leopard from extreme weather conditions—bitter cold in winter and scorching heat in summer.
5. It has camouflaging marks: black rosettes and small spots.

> **Exercise 41** Recognizing Verbal Phrases On your paper, identify the underlined phrase in each sentence below as a *participial phrase*, a *nominative absolute*, a *gerund phrase*, or an *infinitive phrase*.

1. To find information about cougars, you can also look up *puma*, *catamount*, or *mountain lion*.
2. Outweighing the lynx and the bobcat, jaguars are the biggest wildcats in North America.
3. They can grow to weigh up to 250 pounds.
4. Running long distances after prey can tire out a cougar.
5. It being easier to hide and hunt deer, cougars roam in hills and forests.
6. Cougars can swim but prefer jumping across water to avoid getting wet.
7. Once thriving throughout the United States, cougars now live mainly in the West.
8. Hunting cougars became very popular in the 1800's.
9. By 1900, most cougars formerly living in the East and Midwest had been killed.
10. The existence of the cougar being threatened, several organizations have created Internet alerts.

> **Exercise 42** Identifying Subordinate Clauses On your paper, write the subordinate clause in each sentence and identify it as *adjective*, *adverb*, or *noun*. If it is an *elliptical clause*, place parentheses around the understood words.

1. Sand cats are smaller than most species of wildcats.
2. In the Sahara and other African deserts where they live, there are sand dunes.

SOME USES OF INTRODUCTORY WORDS IN NOUN CLAUSES

Functions in Clauses	Examples
Adjective	She could not decide *which Scandinavian flag* was her favorite.
Adverb	I do not know *when the flag pole was painted.*
Subject	*Whoever recognizes the American flag* should treat it with respect.
Direct Object	*Whatever my supervisor advised,* I did.
No Function	The historian said *that the flag was two hundred years old.*

When the word *that* has no function within the clause except to introduce it, it is often omitted.

EXAMPLE: We remembered [*that*] *you wanted to raise the flag in the morning.*

Because some of the words that introduce noun clauses also introduce adjective and adverb clauses, do not let the introductory word be your only guide in determining the type of clause. Always check the function of the clause in the sentence.

▶ **Exercise 24** Identifying Noun Clauses Write each noun clause. Then, identify the function of each noun clause as *subject, direct object, indirect object, predicate nominative, object of a preposition,* or *appositive.*

EXAMPLE: A symbolic flag is what everyone wants.
            what everyone wants (predicate nominative)

1. A ship at sea traditionally flies whichever flag represents its country of origin.
2. Specific guidelines often govern how flags should be displayed on ships.
3. Whichever national flag is flown at the front of a ship is called the jack.
4. An ensign is what the national flag is called on the rear of a ship.
5. As a courtesy, most ships usually fly the national flag of whichever country they are visiting.

Grammar and Style Tip

With noun clauses, you can also try substituting the words *fact, it, thing,* or *you* for the clause. If the sentence retains its smoothness, the clause is probably a noun clause. I knew *the flag was waving.* I knew *it.*

▶ **More Practice**

Grammar Exercise Workbook
• pp. 45–46
On-line Exercise Bank
• Section 19.3
Go on-line:
PHSchool.com
Enter Web Code:
egk-1202

Interactive Textbook

Complete the exercise on-line! Exercise 24 is available on-line or on CD-ROM.

Clauses • **465**

☑ **ONGOING ASSESSMENT: Monitor and Reinforce**

If students have difficulty with Exercise 24 or 25, refer them to the following for additional practice.

In the Textbook	Print Resources	Technology
Section Review, Ex. 27–28, Section 19.3	*Grammar Exercise Workbook,* pp. 45–46	*On-Line Exercise Bank,* Section 19.3

⏱ **TIME SAVERS!**

 **Answers on Transparencies** Use the *Grammar Exercises Answers on Transparencies* for Chapter 19 to facilitate correction by students.

💻 **On-Line Exercise Bank** Have students complete the exercises on computer. The Auto Check feature will grade their work for you!

Grammar in Literature

1. Have a volunteer read the passage aloud.

2. Have students identify the word that begins the noun clause (That) and explain this word's function in the clause.

More About the Writer

Irish-born poet William Butler Yeats wrote "The Second Coming" in the aftermath of World War I. The hauntingly ominous poem reflects his devotion to politics and history, and his fascination with mythology and mysticism. These influences produced bold, multilayered symbolism that is as mysterious today as it was when Yeats wrote the poem.

Connections With Literature

The full text of "The Second Coming" is in *Prentice Hall Literature, Penguin Edition,* The British Tradition.

Answer Key

> **Exercise 25**

Answers will vary; samples are given.

1. That flags have been used since ancient times to signal messages at sea may surprise you: noun

2. Before radio was invented, signal flags were one . . . : adv.

3. In the fifth century B.C., Greeks were using signal flags that communicated attack plans: adj.

4. One thing that researchers don't completely understand is the way these flags were used: adj.

5. Because the Italian . . . Mediterranean Sea, by the Middle Ages they had . . . : adv.

6. In 1369, the British created a new flag that was used . . . : adj.

7. The admiral used the flag when he summoned his officers . . . : adv.

8. That the British . . . signals is widely held . . . : noun

9. In 1812, Sir Home . . . flags that represented . . . : adj.

10. After the twentieth century had begun, the first . . . : adv.

19.3

GRAMMAR IN LITERATURE

from **The Second Coming**
William Butler Yeats

In the following passage from Yeats's poem, a noun clause that serves as a direct object is highlighted in blue italics.

> The darkness drops again; but now I know
> *That twenty centuries of stony sleep*
> *Were vexed to nightmare by a rocking cradle, . . .*

▶ **Exercise 25** **Combining Sentences With Subordinate Clauses** Combine each pair of sentences by using a subordinate clause. You may need to change or rearrange words or make other minor changes. Underline the subordinate clause and label it *adjective, adverb,* or *noun.*

1. Flags have been used to signal messages at sea. They have been used since ancient times.
2. Signal flags were used before radio was invented. It was one way for ships to communicate.
3. In the fifth century B.C., Greeks were using signal flags. These flags communicated attack plans.
4. There is one thing researchers don't completely understand. They don't understand the way these flags were used.
5. The Italian city-states had ships roaming the Mediterranean Sea. By the Middle Ages, they had developed a more sophisticated system of signaling.
6. In 1369, the British created a new flag. The flag was used only as a signal flag.
7. The admiral used the flag. With this flag, he summoned his officers to his ship.
8. The British created the first true code of flag signals. This fact is widely held to be an accurate statement.
9. In 1812, Sir Home Popham created a system of flags. The system represented all twenty-six letters and each numeral.
10. The first international signal flag code was recognized by most nations. It was introduced after the twentieth century had begun.

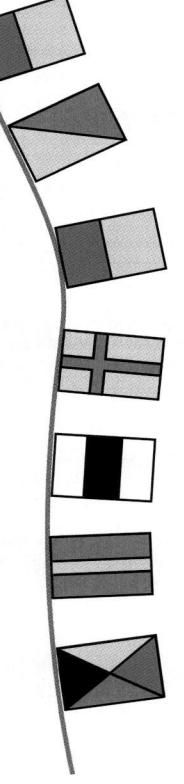

466 • Phrases and Clauses

☑ **ONGOING ASSESSMENT: Assess Mastery**

Use the following resources to assess student mastery of clauses.

In the Textbook	Technology
Chapter Review, Ex. 42	*Writing and Grammar* Interactive Text, Section 19.3, Section Review; *On-Line Exercise Bank,* Section 19.3

Section 19.3 Section Review

GRAMMAR EXERCISES 26–31

Exercise 26 **Identifying Adjective and Adverb Clauses** Write each adjective or adverb clause, underlining its subject once and its verb twice. If a clause is elliptical, add the understood words in parentheses.

1. The flag that the British fly today is called the Union Jack.
2. This flag, which incorporates the flags of England, Scotland, and Ireland, has been in use since 1801.
3. Ireland's tricolor flag has been flown almost fifty years less than the Union Jack.
4. When the Irish rose against England, the tricolor became a symbol of unity and national pride in Ireland.
5. Wales is the only U.K. member that is not represented on the Union Jack.

Exercise 27 **Identifying Noun Clauses** Write each noun clause. Then, identify the function of each noun clause as *subject, direct object, indirect object, predicate nominative,* or *object of a preposition.*

1. That the Dutch flag is the first modern national flag is an accepted fact.
2. The flag commemorates when the Dutch rebelled against the Spanish in 1568.
3. Who created the flag is not known.
4. The flag of red, white, and blue stripes is what vexillologists call a tricolor flag.
5. For nearly 500 years, the tricolor flag has functioned as the national flag for whoever lives in the Netherlands.

Exercise 28 **Revising Sentences by Using Subordinate Clauses** Rewrite the following pairs of sentences by converting one sentence into the type of clause indicated in parentheses.

1. An army indicates its intention to surrender. It waves a white flag. (adverb)
2. A flag is flown upside down. It is a signal of distress. (noun)
3. Some groups fly flags upside down. They want to indicate a political protest. (adverb)
4. The Mexican flag is a tricolor flag. It has a strip of white between green and red bands. (adjective)
5. The person salutes the flag. The person should stand at attention. (noun)

Exercise 29 **Find It in Your Reading** Identify an adjective clause and an adverb clause in this passage from "The Distant Past" by William Trevor. What word does each clause modify?

But as the town increased its prosperity, Carraveagh continued its decline. The Middletons were in their middle sixties now and were reconciled to a life that became more uncomfortable with every passing year.

Exercise 30 **Find It in Your Writing** Look through your portfolio for a paragraph that consists mostly of short sentences. Challenge yourself to combine some sentences by using subordinate clauses.

Exercise 31 **Writing Application** Write a short biography of a friend or family member. Add details and provide characterization by making use of each type of phrase and clause discussed in this chapter. Check your work carefully to ensure that you have used phrases and clauses correctly.

Section Review • 467

Interest GRABBER Write this sentence on the board:

Last summer during the worst heat wave on record in this state, I went to the mall every day and spent hour after hour walking in and out of the air-conditioned stores in search of a little relief from the absolutely stifling temperatures.

Tell students that even though this sentence has forty-four words, it is only a simple sentence. Challenge students to analyze it to see why. (It has only one subject and a compound verb.) Then have students write their own similar sentences.

Activate Prior Knowledge

Using their sentences from the preceding activity or new ones, ask students to write four-sentence paragraphs, using each of the four kinds of sentences once. When they finish, have volunteers read their paragraphs aloud and identify the kinds of sentences.

TEACH

Step-by-Step Teaching Guide

The Four Structures of Sentences

1. Review the characteristics of independent and subordinate clauses. Remind students that independent clauses can stand alone as complete sentences while subordinate clauses cannot.

2. Explain to students that in addition to compound elements such as subjects and predicates, simple sentences may also contain gerunds, participles, and infinitives.

continued

Critical Viewing

Analyze Sample response: The king's crown is a simple symbol of royalty. It communicates complex ideas of authority and lineage.

Section 19.4

Sentences Classified by Structure

Sentences may be classified according to the kind and number of clauses they contain.

The Four Structures of Sentences

Different combinations of independent and subordinate clauses form four basic sentence structures. You should try to use all four types of sentences in your writing.

▶ **KEY CONCEPTS** A **simple sentence** consists of a single independent clause. A simple sentence can still have a compound subject or compound verb. ■

A **compound sentence** consists of two or more independent clauses joined by a comma and a coordinating conjunction or by a semicolon. ■

A **complex sentence** consists of one independent clause and one or more subordinate clauses. ■

A **compound-complex sentence** consists of two or more independent clauses and one or more subordinate clauses. ■

Study the examples of each type of sentence structure in the chart on page 469. Notice that simple sentences can contain compound subjects, compound verbs, or both. Notice also that a subordinate clause may fall between the parts of an independent clause or even within an independent clause.

As you can see in the examples of complex sentences, independent clauses in complex sentences are often called *main clauses* to distinguish them from subordinate clauses. The subject and verb of a main clause are often respectively called the *subject of the sentence* and the *main verb* to distinguish them from the other subjects and verbs that appear in the sentence.

Henry III

▶ **Critical Viewing** What simple symbol of royalty does this king display? What complex ideas does that royal symbol convey? **[Analyze]**

Theme: Royal Symbols

In this section, you will learn to classify sentences according to their structure. The examples and exercises are about royal symbols, such as crowns, sceptres, and thrones.

Cross-Curricular Connection: Social Studies

⏱ **TIME AND RESOURCE MANAGER**

Resources
Print: *Grammar Exercise Workbook*, pp. 47–48; *Grammar Exercises Answers on Transparencies*, Ch. 19
Technology: *Writing and Grammar* Interactive Text, Section 19.4; *On-Line Exercise Bank*, Section 19.4

Using the Full Student Edition	Using the Handbook🄷
• Work through all key concepts, pp. 468–469. • Assign and review Exercise 32.	• Work through all key concepts, pp. 326–327. • Assign and review Exercise 32.

FOUR STRUCTURES OF SENTENCES

Simple Sentences	The <u>king</u> <u>ruled</u> for forty years. Either the firstborn <u>son</u> or the firstborn <u>daughter</u> <u>will become</u> the new ruler.
Compound Sentences	The <u>duke</u> <u>was</u> courageous on the battlefield, so the <u>king</u> <u>rewarded</u> him. The <u>prince</u> <u>was</u> unfit to rule; nevertheless, <u>he</u> <u>became</u> king upon his father's death.
Complex Sentences	SUBORDINATE CLAUSE Although the <u>king</u> <u>had ruled</u> MAIN CLAUSE compassionately, the <u>people</u> still <u>wanted</u> to abolish the monarchy. MAIN SUBORDINATE CLAUSE The <u>queen</u>, who <u>raised</u> taxes to new MAIN CLAUSE levels, <u>was</u> no longer popular with the SUBORDINATE CLAUSE people whom <u>she</u> <u>ruled</u>. MAIN CLAUSE SUBORDINATE CLAUSE The <u>people</u> <u>will do</u> whatever the <u>king</u> <u>says</u>.
Compound-Complex Sentences	INDEPENDENT CLAUSE The <u>prince</u> <u>dismissed</u> all of his advisors SUBORDINATE CLAUSE as soon as <u>he</u> <u>became</u> king, and INDEPENDENT CLAUSE <u>he</u> <u>began making</u> his own decisions. SUBORDINATE CLAUSE When the <u>queen</u> <u>entered</u> the room, INDEPENDENT CLAUSE everyone <u>bowed</u> according to custom, INDEPENDENT CLAUSE but <u>many</u> <u>were resentful</u> of her power.

Grammar and Style Tip

Using a variety of sentence structures demonstrates a mature writing style. Varied sentence patterns make your writing richer and, therefore, more interesting to read.

Step-by-Step Teaching Guide continued

3. Referring to the chart, have students notice that each independent clause in a compound sentence is complete in itself and could stand alone.

4. To help students distinguish between compound sentences and simple sentences with compound elements, present these sentences:

   The ruler of England in A.D. 1000 is called Ethelred the Unready, but he does not deserve his nickname.

   Ethelred ruled effectively for many years but had trouble subduing the Vikings.

   Point out that the first sentence is compound because it has two subjects and two predicates. The second sentence has two predicates but only one subject.

5. Students may need to be told that even though the noun clause in a sentence like *We learned that Ethelred ruled for almost forty years* plays an integral part in conveying meaning, such a sentence is still considered complex.

Real-World Connection

Public speakers know the power of certain kinds of sentence structures. They frequently use compound sentences with repeated elements to hammer home their points. Students probably know John F. Kennedy's "Ask not what your country can do for you; ask what you can do for your country." You might also give them this example from Winston Churchill:

"We shall fight on the beaches; we shall fight on the landing grounds, we shall fight in the fields and in the streets, we shall fight in the hills; we shall never surrender."

Have students listen for similar uses of repetitive compounds in formal, prepared speeches.

STANDARDIZED TEST PREPARATION WORKSHOP

Grammar and Usage Many standardized tests require students to be familiar with the structures of sentences. Use the following example to demonstrate.

Some people think baby raccoons make good pets, usually, they don't. Indeed, raccoons are sometimes pests to farmers because they raid poultry houses.

What revision, if any, is needed in this passage?

A Place a semicolon after *pets*.
B Place a comma after *farmers*.
C Capitalize *Raccoons*.
D No correction is needed.

The correct answer is **A**. The first sentence in the passage is a run-on. The two independent clauses need to be separated by a semicolon or else by a comma and a coordinating conjunction.

Answer Key

Exercise 32

1. complex
2. simple
3. compound
4. simple
5. simple
6. complex
7. complex
8. compound
9. compound-complex
10. compound

Critical Viewing

Analyze Sample response: This picture shows a ruler holding a scepter and a castle. The scepter often represents authority, and the castle might be seen to represent lineage.

19.4

Exercise 32 Identifying the Four Structures of Sentences

Identify each sentence as *simple, compound, complex,* or *compound-complex.*

EXAMPLE: Whenever the king makes a decision, there is no changing his mind.
complex

1. Monarchy is a form of government that is based upon the idea of a person's hereditary right to rule.
2. There are many different types of monarchical governments.
3. Some monarchs have complete control of their government, but other monarchs have very limited power.
4. Throughout the course of history, most monarchs have exercised absolute power over their subjects.
5. During the Middle Ages, this system of government spread across Europe.
6. Most of these European monarchies were ruled by one family who passed control of the country down from one generation to the next.
7. Initially, most of these governments were supported by the middle class, who prospered from the stability that a strong central government brought to the country.
8. By the end of the eighteenth century, many absolute rulers, such as Louis XVI, had become too abusive and self-centered, and several of them were overthrown by republican revolutionaries.
9. As World War I drew to a close, many European monarchies were eliminated altogether, and they were replaced by constitutional governments.
10. Today, a few countries maintain monarchs as symbols of national unity, but most have little, if any, real power.

▶ **Critical Viewing** Write a simple sentence describing this piece of art. Write a compound or complex sentence about the symbols of royalty shown in the painting. **[Analyze]**

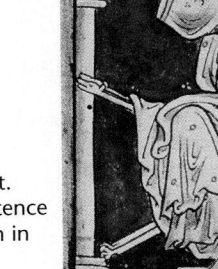

More Practice

Grammar Exercise Workbook
• pp. 47–48
On-line Exercise Bank
• Section 19.4
Go on-line:
PHSchool.com
Enter Web Code:
egk-1202

🌐 **Learn More**

To learn more about properly punctuating the various types of sentence structures, refer to Chapter 27.

☑ ONGOING ASSESSMENT: Assess Mastery

Use the following resources to assess student mastery of phrases and clauses.

In the Textbook	Print Resources	Technology
Chapter Review, Ex. 43–45 Standardized Test Preparation Workshop	*Formal Assessment,* Chapter 19	*On-Line Exercise Bank,* Chapter 19

Section 19.4 Section Review

GRAMMAR EXERCISES 33–38

Exercise 33 Identifying the Four Structures of Sentences Identify each of the following sentences as *simple, compound, complex,* or *compound-complex.*

1. Elizabeth I was the daughter of Henry VIII, the king of England, and his second wife, Anne Boleyn.
2. Elizabeth was born in 1533, and she spent the better part of her childhood away from London.
3. Shortly before the death of her father in 1547, Elizabeth returned to the court in London, where Henry's sixth wife, Katherine Parr, took care of her.
4. Elizabeth's two siblings, Edward VI and Mary I, ruled England for the next eleven years.
5. During her short reign, Mary suspected that Elizabeth, who was her half sister, had supported a revolt against the throne; consequently, Mary had Elizabeth imprisoned.

Exercise 34 Forming Complex Sentences Add a subordinate clause to each of the following sentences to form a complex sentence.

1. The country is ruled by a queen.
2. The queen is respected by her subjects.
3. She has ruled the country for ten years.
4. The monarch has initiated many excellent policies.
5. She is a generous and thoughtful ruler.

Exercise 35 Forming Compound-Complex Sentences Add a subordinate clause to each of the following sentences to form a compound-complex sentence.

1. The king of England ruled over a large empire in the 1700's, and America was a part of that empire.

2. The American colonies wanted to form an independent nation, but the king wanted them to remain a part of his empire.
3. The king would not change his position, nor would the colonies alter theirs.
4. In 1776, the colonies revolted against the king's authority, so he sent soldiers to stop their independence movement.
5. Ultimately, the colonies were victorious over the king, and he was forced to admit defeat.

Exercise 36 Find It in Your Reading Read the following advice to a monarch from Sir Thomas More's *Utopia.* Identify whether the sentence is *compound, complex,* or *compound-complex.*

He ought to shake off either his sloth or his pride, for the people's hatred and scorn arise from these faults in him.

Exercise 37 Find It in Your Writing Review a social studies essay from your writing portfolio. Evaluate the ratio of simple sentences to compound, complex, and compound-complex sentences. If you have mostly simple sentences, decide which sentences could be combined or expanded into other types.

Exercise 38 Writing Application Rewrite some or all of the social studies essay you reviewed in Find It in Your Writing. Revise and combine sentences to form compound, complex, and compound-complex sentences.

Section Review • 471

ASSESS and CLOSE

Section Review

Each of these exercises correlates to the instruction on sentences classified by structure, pages 468–469. The exercises may be used for more practice, for reteaching, or for review of the key concepts presented.

Answer Key

Exercise 33
1. simple
2. compound
3. complex
4. simple
5. compound-complex

Exercise 34
The following are possible responses.
1. The country is ruled by a queen who ascended to the throne at the age of nineteen.
2. Though she is still rather young, the queen is respected by her subjects.
3. She has ruled the country, which is located in Asia, for ten years.
4. During the time she has reigned, the monarch has initiated many excellent policies.
5. According to all who know her, she is a generous and thoughtful ruler.

Exercise 35
The following are possible responses.
1. The king of England ruled over a large empire in the 1700's, and America, though it was thousands of miles away, was part of that empire.
2. The American colonies wanted to form an independent nation in which the people would govern themselves, but the king wanted them to remain part of his empire.
3. The king, who was a stubborn man, would not change his position, nor would the colonies alter theirs.
4. In 1776, the colonies, which were fed up with foreign dominance, revolted against the king's authority, so he sent soldiers to stop their independence movement.
5. Ultimately, the colonies were victorious over the king, and though it was a bitter pill to swallow, he was forced to admit defeat.

continued

Answer Key continued

Exercise 36

Find It in Your Reading
The sentence is compound.

Exercise 37

Find It in Your Writing
When students have finished their review, have them write a brief analysis of what it tells them about their style. Is there anything about it they would like to change or improve?

Exercise 38

Writing Application
After completing their revisions, students could exchange their work with partners. How much did the revision actually improve the paper? Were the new sentences varied or all essentially of the same type?

Each of these exercises correlates to a section of the chapter on phrases and clauses, pages 438–470. These exercises may be used for more practice, for reteaching, or for review of the key concepts presented. Answers for all exercises are available in the *Grammar Exercises Answers on Transparencies* in your Teaching Resources.

Answer Key

> **Exercise 39**

1. in the isolated area: adv.; in the mountains: adv.; of northern India: adj. 2. on the north side: adv.; of the Himalayan mountain range: adj. 3. of high mountains, vast snowfields, glaciers, and cliffs: adj. 4. in the wild: adv. 5. During the summer: adv.; in the mountains: adv.; above the timberline: adv.

> **Exercise 40**

1. another name for the snow leopard: identifies *ounce*
2. a protection against the bitter environment: identifies *Hair cushions*
3. a device used by the snow leopard to keep its balance on rocky terrain: identifies *tail*
4. bitter cold in winter and scorching heat in summer: identifies [*weather*] *conditions*
5. black rosettes and small spots: identifies *marks*

> **Exercise 41**

1. infinitive phrase
2. participial phrase
3. infinitive phrase
4. gerund phrase
5. nominative absolute
6. gerund phrase
7. participial phrase
8. gerund phrase
9. participial phrase
10. nominative absolute

> **Exercise 42**

1. than most species of wildcats (are): adverb
2. In the Sahara and other African deserts where they live: adverb

continued

Chapter

19 *Chapter Review*

GRAMMAR EXERCISES 39–46

> **Exercise 39** Identifying Adjective and Adverb Phrases Write the prepositional phrases in the following sentences. Then, identify each prepositional phrase as *adjective* or *adverb*.

(1) Snow leopards live in the isolated area high in the mountains of northern India. (2) They are most common on the north side of the Himalayan mountain range. (3) This habitat contains numbers of high mountains, vast snowfields, glaciers, and cliffs. (4) This territory is so vast and wide that humans rarely will glimpse a snow leopard in the wild. (5) During the summer, they have been spotted in the mountains when they run above the timberline.

> **Exercise 40** Identifying Appositives and Appositive Phrases Write each sentence, underlining the appositive or appositive phrase. Then, draw an arrow to the noun for which it provides extra information.

1. The ounce, another name for the snow leopard, is a member of the cat family.
2. Hair cushions, a protection against the bitter environment, are located on its paws.
3. The furry tail, a device used by the snow leopard to keep its balance on rocky terrain, is about three feet long.
4. The thick, furry coat protects the snow leopard from extreme weather conditions—bitter cold in winter and scorching heat in summer.
5. It has camouflaging marks: black rosettes and small spots.

> **Exercise 41** Recognizing Verbal Phrases On your paper, identify the underlined phrase in each sentence below as a *participial phrase*, a *nominative absolute*, a *gerund phrase*, or an *infinitive phrase*.

1. To find information about cougars, you can also look up *puma*, *catamount*, or *mountain lion*.
2. Outweighing the lynx and the bobcat, jaguars are the biggest wildcats in North America.
3. They can grow to weigh up to 250 pounds.
4. Running long distances after prey can tire out a cougar.
5. It being easier to hide and hunt deer, cougars roam in hills and forests.
6. Cougars can swim but prefer jumping across water to avoid getting wet.
7. Once thriving throughout the United States, cougars now live mainly in the West.
8. Hunting cougars became very popular in the 1800's.
9. By 1900, most cougars formerly living in the East and Midwest had been killed.
10. The existence of the cougar being threatened, several organizations have created Internet alerts.

> **Exercise 42** Identifying Subordinate Clauses On your paper, write the subordinate clause in each sentence and identify it as *adjective*, *adverb*, or *noun*. If it is an *elliptical clause*, place parentheses around the understood words.

1. Sand cats are smaller than most species of wildcats.
2. In the Sahara and other African deserts where they live, there are sand dunes.

3. Their coloring, which is sandy-yellow or yellowish-gray, blends in well with their surroundings.
4. They hunt for whatever prey is available, including small rodents, lizards, small snakes, and insects.
5. Occasionally, they supplement their diet when they catch hares and birds.

> **Exercise 43** **Combining Simple Sentences to Form the Four Structures of Sentences** Combine the simple sentences in each item to form the type of sentence indicated in parentheses.

1. The caracal is also known as the Persian lynx. It is native to Africa and Asia. (complex)
2. Caracals prey on rodents, birds, and small antelope. In India and Iran, they are sometimes trained to keep areas pest-free. (complex).
3. They have speed and agility. They are accomplished hunters. (simple)
4. Caracals have been known to chase birds. The birds flocked together on the ground. They have even been known to attack eagles. (compound-complex)
5. A caracal's coat is reddish-brown with a white belly. There are tufts of black hair on the tips of its ears. (compound)

> **Exercise 44** **Revising Sentences by Using Phrases and Clauses** Rewrite the following sentences so that they include the types of phrases or clauses indicated in parentheses.

1. Several private and governmental efforts have been enacted. Their aim is saving species that are threatened. (infinitive phrase)
2. The Endangered Species Act was passed in 1973. It provided steps for the conservation of ecosystems containing endangered species. (adjective clause, gerund phrase)

3. The Endangered Species Act also banned the importation and trade of any product made from an endangered animal. (compound infinitive phrase)
4. Two other nations have joined with the United States in agreements that protect migratory birds. These nations are Canada and Mexico. (appositive phrase)
5. The Convention on International Trade in Endangered Species of Wild Flora and Fauna (CITES) has become the center of international conservation efforts. It was ratified by the United States and fifty-one other nations in 1973. (participial phrase)

> **Exercise 45** **Revision Practice: Using Phrases and Clauses** On a separate sheet of paper, revise the following paragraph, combining sentences as appropriate. You may need to change or rearrange words and make other minor changes. Identify the structure of each sentence in your final revision.

A park ranger has many duties. He or she patrols the park, maintains park grounds, and enforces park rules. A park ranger often lives in the park. The park is the place the park ranger works. Rangers face some dangers. This is the reason some people don't want the job. Rangers are often alone. They live in the wilderness. Sometimes they need supplies or help. They use the radio to call for supplies or help.

> **Exercise 46** **Writing Application** Write a short description of a park or natural area near your home. Include two simple sentences, one complex sentence, one compound sentence, and one compound-complex sentence in your description.

> **Exercise 42**

3. which is sandy-yellow or yellowish-gray: adjective
4. whatever prey is available, including small rodents, lizards, small snakes, and insects: noun
5. when they catch hares and birds: adverb

> **Exercise 43**

Answers will vary; samples are given.

1. The caracal, which is also known . . . lynx, is native to Africa . . .
2. Because caracals prey on . . . , in India and Iran they are . . .
3. They have speed and agility and are accomplished hunters.
4. Caracals have been known to chase birds when the birds are flocked together on the ground and they have even been . . .
5. A caracal's coat is reddish-brown with a white belly, and there are . . .

> **Exercise 44**

Answers will vary; samples are given.

1. Several private and governmental efforts have been enacted to save species threatened.
2. The Endangered Species Act, which was passed in 1973, provided steps for conserving ecosystems . . .
3. The Endangered Species Act also forbade merchants to import or trade any product . . .
4. Two other nations, Mexico and Canada, have joined with . . .
5. Ratified by the United States . . . 1973, the Convention . . .

> **Exercise 45**

Answers will vary; samples are given.

A park ranger has many duties, including patrolling the park, maintaining park grounds, and enforcing park rules. *[simple]* A park ranger often lives and works in the park. *[simple]* Because rangers face some dangers, some people don't want the job. *[complex]* Because they live in the wilderness, rangers are often alone. *[complex]* When rangers need supplies or help, they use their radios to call for them. *[complex]*
continued

> **Exercise 46**

Writing Application
When students have finished, have them exchange compositions with partners. Partners should check to see that all sentence types have been covered appropriately.

1. Review with students some types of phrases and clauses. You might go over prepositional phrases, adjective and adverb phrases, and verbal phrases, giving examples of each.

2. Review the differences between a subordinate clause and an independent clause. Remind students that although all clauses contain subjects and verbs, subordinate clauses cannot stand alone.

3. Help students learn to recognize awkwardly written sentences by reading aloud the Sample Test Item and the Practice items. Ask them to listen carefully in order to identify the main ideas and to describe ways in which the passage sounds awkward. Students should notice that many of the sentences are short and choppy and that ideas do not always follow each other logically.

4. Discuss the response choices in the Practice items in terms of the areas students identified as needing improvement. Ask students to read the main idea and explain how it has been recast. Have them point out phrases and clauses in the responses.

Standardized Test Preparation Workshop

Recognizing Appropriate Sentence Construction

Knowledge of grammar is tested on standardized tests. Questions that measure your ability to use phrases and clauses show your understanding of basic sentence construction and style. When faced with these types of questions, first read the entire passage to get an idea of the author's purpose. Focus on the underlined group of words, and note any ways they can be combined without changing the meaning. Then, choose a rewrite that uses a phrase or clause to combine similar ideas without changing the meaning of the author's message.

The following will give you practice with the format of questions that test rules of standard grammar.

Test Tip

Although an answer choice may make sense, it may not be the best way to rewrite the original. Read each choice carefully before deciding on your answer.

Sample Test Item	Answer and Explanation
Directions: Read the passage, and choose the letter of the best way to write the underlined sentences. New England is known for its beautiful (1) foliage. There is no sight more breathtaking than New England in the autumn.	
A There is no sight more breathtaking than the foliage for which New England is known. **B** New England is known for breathtaking foliage, and there nothing is more beautiful than New England in the autumn. **C** There is no sight more breathtaking than New England's beautiful autumn foliage. **D** New England is known for its beautiful foliage, and it's breathtaking.	The correct answer is *C*. This is the best rewrite of the two sentences because it combines related ideas in a direct way without changing the meaning of the original sentence or changing the author's intent.

474 • Phrases and Clauses

⬥ TEST-TAKING TIP

Tell students that as they read through response choices, they should make sure each idea in the designated section of the original is represented.

They should look also for combinations of sentences that present ideas in a logical order and that flow smoothly from one idea to the next.

▶ **Practice 1** **Directions:** Read the passage, and choose the letter of the best way to write the underlined sentences.

Reggie's father taught him to box. He was
(1)
a former pro boxer. Reggie was only six

years old. Reggie had great speed and
(2)
agility. He was so young. He caught on to

the sport quickly.

1 A Reggie's father was a pro boxer, and he taught Reggie to box, and Reggie was only six years old.

B Reggie's father, a former pro boxer, taught Reggie to box at the age of six.

C When Reggie was only six years old, his father taught him how to box, and he was a former pro boxer.

D Being a former pro boxer, Reggie learned how to box from his father when he was only six.

2 F Reggie caught on to the sport quickly because he was so young and his speed and agility were so great.

G Reggie had great speed and agility because he was so young; therefore, he caught on to the sport quickly.

H Reggie had great speed and agility for someone who was so young, and he caught on to the sport quickly.

J Being young, Reggie caught onto the sport quickly because of his great speed and agility.

▶ **Practice 2** **Directions:** Read the passage, and choose the letter of the best way to rewrite the underlined sentences.

It was morning. It was the day after the
(1)
school dance. Marianne had danced for
(2)
hours. She had danced the jitterbug. Her

feet felt as if they would fall off. She woke
(3)
up. She was exhausted. She was happy.

1 A It was in the morning, and it was the day after the school dance.

B It was after the school dance.

C The next morning, it was the day after the school dance.

D It was the morning after the school dance.

2 F Marianne had danced for hours, doing the jitterbug until her feet felt as if they would fall off.

G Marianne had danced for hours, and she did the jitterbug until her feet felt as if they would fall off.

H Dancing the jitterbug, Marianne had danced for hours when her feet felt as if they would fall off.

J Marianne danced the jitterbug until her feet felt as if they would fall off for hours.

3 A She woke up and she was exhausted and she was happy.

B She woke up when she was exhausted she was happy.

C She woke up exhausted but happy.

D She, exhausted, woke up happy.

▶ **Practice 1**
1. B
2. F

▶ **Practice 2**
1. D
2. F
3. C

Customize for
Less Advanced Students

Tell students to pick out the most important point being made in the designated test sentences. This idea most often will be stated first in a rewrite.

Customize for
AP Students

Remind students that one effective way to combine sentences is to use a subordinate clause. You might show them some examples of these.

CUMULATIVE REVIEW

Each of these exercises reviews concepts taught in the chapters on the parts of speech, basic sentence parts, and phrases and clauses. The exercises may be used for more practice, for review of the key concepts presented, or for assessment of student mastery of the major concepts.

Answer Key

▶ **Exercise A**

1. history, N, Subj.; periods, N, Obj. of Prep.; Middle, Adj., modifies kingdoms
2. Ptolemaic, Adj., priest; which, Conj., Subord.; roughly, Adv., modifies corresponded
3. spanned, V, action; centuries, N, D. Obj.; and, Conj., Coord.
4. this, Adj., modifies capital; exercised, V, action; over, Prep.
5. Step Pyramid, N, Subj.; Egyptians, N, D. Obj.; today, Adv., modifies gives
6. early, Adj., modifies king; king, N, Pred. Nom.; prosperity, N, D. Obj.
7. It, Pron., Subj.; his, Adj., modifies son; who, Pron., Subj.
8. Yes, Interj.; reportedly, Adj., modifies introduced
9. These, Pron., Subj.; are, V, linking; when, Conj., Subord.; not only . . . but also, Conj., Correl.; astronomy, N, Obj. of Prep.
10. solar, Adj., modifies calendar; furthermore, Conj., Conj. Adv.; demonstrated, V, action

▶ **Exercise B**

1. Mentuhotep, Subj.; unified and ruled, V; kingdoms, D Obj.
2. Amenemhet I, Subj.; established and favored, V; Memphis, Obj. of Prep.
3. He, Subj.; considered, V; deity, Objtv. Comp.
4. literature, Subj.; was, V; that, Subj.; was, V; propaganda, Pred. Nom.
5. Amenemhet, Subj.; named, V; co-regent, Objtv. Comp.
6. He, Subj.; built and established, V; people, Ind. Obj.
7. Architecture, art, and designs, Subj.; were, V; graceful and delicate, Pred. Adj.
8. rulers, Subj.; were, V; ineffective, Pred. Adj.
9. people, Subj., challenged and took, V; portions, Obj. of Prep.
10. Hyksos, Subj.; were conquered, V; who, Subj.; reunited, V; Egypt, D Obj.

Cumulative Review

GRAMMAR

▶ **Exercise A** Recognizing the Part of Speech and Function of Words in Sentences Identify the part of speech of each underlined word in the following sentences. Indicate the function in the sentence or clause of any underlined noun or pronoun, whether an underlined verb is action or linking, what word any adjective or adverb modifies, and whether any conjunction is coordinating, subordinate, correlative, or a conjunctive adverb.

1. Egyptian history has been divided into three periods, the Old, Middle, and New kingdoms.
2. Manetho, a Ptolemaic priest, organized the country's rulers into 30 dynasties, which roughly corresponded to different ruling families.
3. The Old Kingdom spanned five centuries, from 2755–2255 B.C., and was centered at the city of Memphis.
4. From this capital, monarchs exercised absolute power over the people.
5. The Step Pyramid, built by the ruler Zoser, still gives Egyptians pride today.
6. King Snefru was an early warrior king; through his military campaigns, he brought prosperity to the kingdom.
7. It was his son, Khufu, also known as Cheops, who built the Great Pyramid at Giza.
8. Yes, one of Khufu's sons, Redjedef, reportedly introduced a religion centered around the sun god Ra.
9. These are men who ruled during the 4th Dynasty, when Egypt reached a cultural zenith not only in architecture and engineering, but also in sculpture, painting, astronomy, and surgery.
10. Astronomers created a solar calendar based on a year with 365 days; furthermore, physicians demonstrated broad knowledge of the body's circulatory system.

▶ **Exercise B** Recognizing Basic Sentence Parts Identify the simple subject and simple predicate in each sentence. Then, identify the word underlined in the sentence as *direct object*, *indirect object*, *objective complement*, *object of a preposition*, *predicate nominative*, or *predicate adjective*.

1. Starting the Middle Kingdom, Mentuhotep unified the kingdoms and ruled for more than fifty years.
2. Amenemhet I established a capital near Memphis and favored national unity.
3. He considered Amon, a Theban god, the principal deity for the people.
4. There was literature at the time that was propaganda in support of the king.
5. Amenemhet named his son, Sesostris I, co-regent in the twentieth year of his reign.
6. He then built his people fortresses and established trade with foreign lands.
7. Architecture, art, and jewelry designs of the period were graceful and delicate.
8. However, succeeding rulers were weak and ineffective.
9. The Hyksos people challenged and eventually took control of the middle and northern portions of the country.
10. The Hyksos were later conquered by forces of Ahmose I, who reunited Egypt.

▶ **Exercise C** Identifying Phrases and Clauses Identify the underlined group of words in each of the following sentences as a phrase or a clause. Tell whether each phrase is a *gerund phrase*, *prepositional phrase*, *appositive phrase*, *infinitive phrase*, or *participial phrase*. Tell whether each clause is an *independent clause, adjective clause, adverb clause,* or *noun clause.*

1. Unifying Egypt was the first step Ahmose I took to begin the New Kingdom.
2. His rule featured a revived balance of power; in addition, it saw an increasingly important role for women.
3. Hatshepsut, a royal princess and the wife of Thutmose II, governed as regent, and she then crowned herself king.
4. Although he had ruled with his mother, Thutmose III attempted to remove her image and name from Egyptian records and monuments.
5. Growing in strength, forces of the Hittite states later threatened the kingdom of Thutmose IV.
6. The 19th Dynasty began with Ramses I, who had earlier commanded the army.
7. When Ramses died after only two years on the throne, his son, Seti I, replaced him.
8. As the next several centuries went by, power usually passed to whoever was the eldest son of the royal family.
9. Ramses II was more interested in establishing peace with the Hittites than his predecessors were.
10. His son, Merneptah, fought whoever invaded the area, and in the thirteenth century B.C., he worked on extending the empire he had inherited.

▶ Exercise D   Revision Practice: Combining Sentences to Vary Structure
Combine the sentences in each item to form the type of sentence indicated in parentheses.

1. Merneptah ruled a large empire. His successors were unable to preserve it. (complex)
2. Ramses III won several key victories. Royal power was beginning to decline. (compound)

3. Priests and nobles began dividing the country into sections. Royal power weakened. Egypt soon became the target of numerous invasions. (compound-complex)
4. A series of rulers controlled Egypt for the next 700 years. Many of these rulers were from outside nations. (simple)
5. In 332 B.C., Alexander the Great conquered Egypt. He was from Macedonia. (complex)

▶ Exercise E   Revising a Paragraph
Write the paragraph below on a separate sheet of paper. Revise by using phrases and clauses to vary sentence length and structure. You may need to change or rearrange some words and make other minor changes.

Alexander died in 323 B.C. His generals divided up his empire. Ptolemy was one of the generals. He gained power over Egypt. He soon took the title of king. He founded a new dynasty. Alexandria became Egypt's capital. This happened under Ptolemy. He built a magnificent library and museum in Alexandria. This was done to spread Greek knowledge and culture. Soon, Alexandria became the cultural center. It was the center of not only Egypt. It was the center of the rest of the ancient world. Scholars from many countries came to Egypt. They were hoping to study in the library. Whoever studied in Alexandria had a responsibility. Their responsibility was to add new volumes to the library.

▶ Exercise F   Writing Application
Write a description of an imaginary trip to see the Great Pyramids in Egypt or some other unusual sight. Include all four structures of sentences. Underline each simple subject once and each simple predicate twice. Circle at least three phrases and three subordinate clauses.

Answer Key

▶ Exercise C
1. gerund phrase
2. prepositional phrase
3. appositive phrase
4. infinitive phrase
5. participial phrase
6. adjective clause
7. adverb clause
8. adverb clause
9. adverb clause
10. noun clause

▶ Exercise D
1. Merneptah ruled a large empire that his successors were unable to preserve.
2. Rameses III won several key victories, but royal power was beginning to decline.
3. When priests and nobles began dividing the country into sections, royal power weakened, and Egypt soon became the target of numerous invasions.
4. A series of rulers, many from outside nations, controlled Egypt for the next 700 years.
5. In 332 B.C., Alexander the Great, who was from Macedonia, conquered Egypt.

▶ Exercise E
Revisions will vary. Possible revision:

When Alexander died in 323 B.C., his generals divided up his empire. Ptolemy, one of the generals, gained power over Egypt and soon took the title of king, founding a new dynasty. He made Alexandria Egypt's capital and built a magnificent library and museum there to spread Greek knowledge and culture. Soon Alexandria became the cultural center not only of Egypt but also of the rest of the ancient world. Scholars from many countries came to Egypt hoping to study in the library. Whoever studied in Alexandria had a responsibility to add new volumes to the library.

▶ Exercise F
When students finish, have them exchange papers and identify the sentence structures, phrases, and subordinate clauses that their partners have used.

Time and Resource Manager

In-Depth Lesson Plan

	LESSON FOCUS	PRINT AND MEDIA RESOURCES
DAY 1	**Effective Sentences; Sentence Combining** Students learn and classify the four functions of a sentence and then combine sentences for sentence variety. (pp. 480–487/⊞ 332–339)	*Writing and Grammar* **Interactive Text,** Sections 20.1–2; *On-line Exercise Bank,* Sections 20.1–2 **Teaching Resources** *Grammar Exercise Workbook,* pp. 49–52; *Grammar Exercises Answers on Transparencies,* Ch. 20
DAY 2	**Varying Sentences** Students learn to vary sentences by adjusting lengths and beginnings. (pp. 488–491/⊞340–343)	*Writing and Grammar* **Interactive Text,** Section 20.3; *On-line Exercise Bank,* Section 20.3 **Teaching Resources** *Grammar Exercise Workbook,* pp. 53–60
DAY 3	**Avoiding Fragments and Run-ons** Students learn to recognize and correct sentence fragments and run-ons. (pp. 492–500/⊞344–352)	*Writing and Grammar* **Interactive Text,** Section 20.4; *On-line Exercise Bank,* Section 20.4 **Teaching Resources** *Grammar Exercise Workbook,* pp. 61–64; *Hands-on Grammar Activity Book,* Ch. 20
DAY 4	**Misplaced and Dangling Modifiers; Faulty Parallelism** Students learn to recognize and correct modifier errors and faulty parallelism. (pp. 501–509/⊞353–361)	*Writing and Grammar* **Interactive Text,** Sections 20.5–6; *On-line Exercise Bank,* Sections 20.5–6 **Teaching Resources** *Grammar Exercise Workbook,* pp. 65–68
DAY 5	**Faulty Coordination; Review and Assess** Students learn to recognize and correct faulty coordination in sentences, review the chapter, and demonstrate mastery of concepts. (pp. 510–515/⊞362–365)	*Writing and Grammar* **Interactive Text,** Section 20.7; *On-line Exercise Bank,* Section 20.7 **Teaching Resources** *Grammar Exercise Workbook,* pp. 69–70; *Formal Assessment,* Ch. 20

Accelerated Lesson Plan

	LESSON FOCUS	PRINT AND MEDIA RESOURCES
DAY 1	**Combining and Varying Sentences; Avoiding Fragments and Run-ons** Students learn the functions of a sentence, sentence combining, varying sentence beginnings and length, and correcting sentence fragments and run-ons. (pp. 480–500/⊞332–352)	*Writing and Grammar* **Interactive Text,** Sections 20.1–4; *On-line Exercise Bank,* Sections 20.1–4 **Teaching Resources** *Grammar Exercise Workbook,* pp. 49–64; *Grammar Exercises Answers on Transparencies,* Ch. 20
DAY 2	**Modifiers, Parallelism, and Coordination** Students cover modifier errors and faulty parallelism and coordination. (pp. 501–513/⊞353–365)	*Writing and Grammar* **Interactive Text,** Sections 20.5–7; *On-line Exercise Bank,* Sections 20.5–7 **Teaching Resources** *Grammar Exercise Workbook,* pp. 65–70
DAY 3	**Review and Assess** Students review the chapter and demonstrate mastery of concepts. (pp. 514–515)	**Teaching Resources** *Formal Assessment,* Ch. 20

Options for Adapting Lesson Plans

FEATURES

Extend coverage with the Grammar in Literature features (pp. 489, 508/⊞341, 360) and the Standardized Test Preparation Workshop (p. 516).

TECHNOLOGY

Students can use *Writing and Grammar* Interactive Text to complete the exercises interactively on computer. They can complete additional exercises in the *On-line Exercise Bank:* The Auto Check feature will grade their work. Go on-line: PHSchool.com Use Web Code: egk-1202

Writing and Grammar Handbook Alignment

Page numbers in Step-by-Step Teaching Guides in this Teacher's Edition refer to pages from the full student text. Handbook page references, indicated with this icon **H**, are provided in Time and Resource Manager boxes and at the bottom of each Teacher's Edition page.

INTEGRATED SKILLS COVERAGE

Grammar in Literature
SE pp. 489, 508/**H**341, 360

Writing
Find It in Your Writing SE pp. 482, 487, 491, 499, 500, 504, 509, 513/**H**334, 339, 343, 351, 352, 356, 361, 365
Writing Application SE pp. 482, 487, 491, 500, 504, 509, 513, 515/**H**334, 339, 343, 352, 356, 361, 365
Grammar and Style SE pp. 488, 493, 494, 501, 502, 507, 512/**H**340, 345, 346, 353, 354, 359, 364

Viewing and Representing
Critical Viewing, SE pp. 478, 480, 483, 486, 490, 495, 497, 498, 501, 502, 505, 508, 510, 511/**H**330, 332, 335, 338, 342, 347, 349, 350, 353, 354, 357, 360, 362, 363; ATE p. 501

Real-World Connection ATE p. 488

Vocabulary Skills
ATE p. 510

Speaking and Listening ATE p. 492

Spelling SE pp. 484, 492/**H**336, 344

Workplace Skills ATE pp. 502, 511

ASSESSMENT SUPPORT

Standardized Test Preparation Workshop SE p. 516; ATE pp. 484, 507, 516

Standardized Test Preparation Workbook, pp. 39–40

Formal Assessment, Ch. 20

MEETING INDIVIDUAL NEEDS

Less Advanced Students ATE pp. 493, 506, 517. See also Ongoing Assessments, ATE pp. 481, 485, 489, 490, 495, 497, 498, 502, 506, 511.

Gifted and Talented Students ATE p. 489

AP Students ATE p. 517

ESL Students ATE p. 481

Spatial Learners ATE p. 494

Linguistic Learners ATE p. 496

BLOCK SCHEDULING

Pacing Suggestions
For 90-minute Blocks
• Administer the Diagnostic Test to students to determine instructional coverage needed.
• Have students complete necessary exercises in class. Use the Hands-on Grammar activity for a change of pace.

Resources for Varying Instruction
• *Writing and Grammar* **Interactive Text** A 90-minute block provides an ideal opportunity for students to work on the computer.

Professional Development Support
• *How to Manage Instruction in the Block* This teaching resource provides management and activity suggestions.

MEDIA AND TECHNOLOGY

For the Student
• *Writing and Grammar* **Interactive Text**, Ch. 20
• *On-line Exercise Bank,* Sections 20.1–7

For the Teacher
• **Teacher**EXPRESS™ CD-ROM

WRITING AND GRAMMAR ON-LINE

Interactive Text (On-line or on CD-ROM)
• Easily navigable instruction with on-line supporting resources
• Self-scoring exercises and diagnostic tests

Companion Web Site PHSchool.com
• On-line Exercise Bank (use Web Code egk-1202)

See the Go On-line! **feature, SE p. iii.**

LITERATURE CONNECTIONS

Grammar in Literature selections from *Prentice Hall Literature, Penguin Edition,* The British Tradition:

from "Mary Chestnut's Civil War," Mary Chestnut, SE p. 489/**H**341

from "Defending Nonviolent Resistance," Mohandas K. Gandhi, SE p. 508/**H**360

▶ Lesson Objectives

1. To understand the four functions of sentences

2. To use varied sentence structure to express meanings and achieve a desired effect

3. To demonstrate control over grammatical elements such as parallelism

4. To combine sentences using basic sentence parts, phrases, and clauses

5. To compose increasingly more involved sentences that contain gerunds, participles, and infinitives in their various functions

6. To revise sentences to eliminate misplaced or dangling modifiers, faulty parallelism, and faulty coordination

7. To analyze the characteristics of clear text such as conciseness, correctness, and completeness

Critical Viewing

Analyze Possible answer: The crown and the scepter are both symbols of royal power.

Chapter 20 Effective Sentences

JOHANNES REX :

◀ **Critical Viewing**
What details indicate that this is a portrait of a powerful man?
[Analyze]

Sentences are a basic unit of communication. You use sentences every day—to make statements, ask questions, express emotions, give directions, or share information. Using different types of sentences, varying the length of your sentences, and varying their structure can give your writing style more sophistication and help you hold a reader's attention. These techniques for writing effective sentences can help you communicate in a clear and interesting way.

Effective sentences are the key to written communication, just as England's monarchs were the key individuals throughout much of that nation's history.

Like a strong monarchy, whose clear decisions and swift action helped to maintain an efficient government in England, effective sentences are the surest, strongest means to ensure that your ideas are understood clearly.

478 • Effective Sentences

✓ ONGOING ASSESSMENT: Diagnose

If students miss more than one item in any category, direct them to the relevant pages of the textbook and assign exercises for practice and review.

Effective Sentences	Diagnostic Test Items	Teach	Practice	Section Review	Chapter Review
Skill Check A					
Identifying the Four Functions of a Sentence	A 1–5	p. 480/Ⓗ332	Ex. 1–2	Ex. 3–5	Ex. 57
Skill Check B					
Combining Sentences	B 6–10	pp. 483–486/Ⓗ335–338	Ex. 8–12	Ex. 13–15	Ex. 58
Skill Check C					
Varying Sentences	C 11–15	pp. 488–490/Ⓗ340–342	Ex. 19–21	Ex. 22–24	Ex. 58

Diagnostic Test

Directions: Write all answers on a separate sheet of paper.

Skill Check A. Rewrite each sentence using the proper end mark. Then, identify the sentence as *declarative, interrogative, exclamatory,* or *imperative.*

1. Elizabeth II was crowned as Queen of Great Britain in 1953
2. What an amazing coronation ceremony that was
3. Look at the photographs of the wedding in this book
4. Why are so many people fascinated by the British monarchy
5. Give me your answer immediately

Skill Check B. Combine each pair of sentences to form one sentence. Try to use several different combining methods.

6. Prince Charles has the official title of Prince of Wales. He is the heir apparent to the English throne.
7. Charles graduated from Cambridge University. He is the first heir to the British crown to earn a university degree.
8. Charles served in the Royal Air Force and the Royal Navy from 1971 to 1976. He is often photographed in military uniform.
9. Charles will assume the throne after his mother dies. She may also decide to resign and turn over the crown to him.
10. Will a huge coronation ceremony be held for Charles? I wonder.

Skill Check C. Rewrite each sentence to begin with the part of speech indicated in parentheses.

11. The British Empire has undergone many changes during the reign of Elizabeth II. (preposition)
12. There has been constant turmoil in Northern Ireland, beginning in the 1950's. (participle)
13. More than forty former colonies and territories are newly independent. (adverb)
14. Britain joined the European Economic Community in 1973 as a way to improve its economic status. (infinitive)
15. Elizabeth II has overseen these changes as queen. (preposition)

Skill Check D. Identify the sentence errors below. Write *F* for fragment, *RO* for run-on, *MM* for misplaced modifier, *FP* for faulty parallelism, and *FC* for faulty coordination.

16. Windsor Castle is situated west of London, and the area became popular.
17. Windsor Castle is steeped in tradition and history, King Arthur gathered his Knights of the Round Table in the general vicinity.
18. Soon after arriving from France, a stockade was built on the site in 1070 by William the Conqueror.
19. The Round Tower, or Keep, was used as a prison in the seventeenth century, is still surrounded by a moat, and the tower is the dominant structure of Windsor Castle.
20. In 1992, Windsor Castle seriously damaged by fire and not yet restored to its former glory.

Effective Sentences • 479

Diagnostic Test

Each item in the Diagnostic Test correlates to a specific section in the effective sentences chapter, enabling you to tailor instruction to the particular needs of your students. See "Ongoing Assessment: Diagnose" below.

Skill Check A

1. . . . in 1953. *declarative*
2. . . . that was! e*xclamatory*
3. . . . in this book. *imperative*
4. . . . the British monarchy? *interrogative*
5. . . . answer immediately. *or* ! *imperative* or *exclamatory*

Skill Check B

Answers will vary; samples are given.

6. Prince Charles, heir apparent to the English throne, has the official title of Prince of Wales.
7. Charles, who graduated from Cambridge University, is the first heir to the British crown to earn a university degree.
8. Charles served in the Royal Air Force and the Royal Navy from 1971 to 1976 and is often photographed in military uniform.
9. Charles will assume the throne after his mother dies, or she may decide to resign and turn over the crown to him.
10. I wonder whether a huge coronation ceremony will be held for Charles.

Skill Check C

Answers may vary slightly.

11. During the reign of Elizabeth II, the British Empire has undergone many changes.
12. Beginning in the 1950's, there has been constant turmoil in Northern Ireland.
13. Currently, more than forty former colonies and territories are newly independent.
14. To improve its economic status, Britain joined the European Economic Community in 1973.
15. As queen, Elizabeth II has overseen these changes.

Skill Check D

16. FC
17. RO
18. MM
19. FP
20. F

ONGOING ASSESSMENT: Diagnose *continued*

Agreement	Diagnostic Test Items	Teach	Practice	Section Review	Chapter Review
Skill Check D					
Identifying Fragments	D 20	pp. 492–494/⊞344–346	Ex. 28	Ex. 31, 33	Ex. 59
Identifying Run-ons	D 17	p. 496/⊞348	Ex. 29–30	Ex. 32–33	Ex. 59
Id. Misplaced Modifiers	D 18	pp. 501–502/⊞353–354	Ex. 36–37	Ex. 38–39	Ex. 60
Id. Faulty Parallelism	D 19	pp. 505–507/⊞357–359	Ex. 43–44	Ex. 45–46	Ex. 61–62
Id. Faulty Coordination	D 16	pp. 510–512/⊞362–364	Ex. 50–51	Ex. 52–54	Ex. 61–62
Cumulative Reviews and Applications				Ex. 5–7, 16–18, 25–27 34–35, 41–42, 55–56	Ex. 63

Read aloud or write on the chalkboard the following dialogue:

How much does this cost?

It costs forty-nine dollars.

What a bargain!

Wrap it carefully.

Remind students that sentences are classified according to their function, and ask students to name the function of each sentence.

Activate Prior Knowledge

Have students draft a list of interview questions and answers. To get them started, provide some examples and label them.

Tell me how long you've been playing the violin. (imperative)

I've played since I was three. (declarative)

How much do you practice? (interrogative)

That's amazing! (exclamatory)

TEACH

Step-by-Step Teaching Guide

The Four Functions of a Sentence

1. Write on the chalkboard:

   Who is the queen

   I know who is queen

   Find out who is queen

   She will be queen

2. Have students use the words *declarative, interrogative, imperative,* and *exclamatory* to label the sentences and choose the appropriate end marks.

Critical Viewing

Interpret Sample responses: Show me a king more honest and brave than he! The king appears ready for war because he is carrying a sword. Was he a war leader? He was so brave in battle!

The Four Functions of a Sentence

Sentences can be classified according to what they do. The four types of sentences in English are *declarative, interrogative, imperative,* and *exclamatory.* Each type of sentence has a different purpose and is constructed in a different way. You can indicate what type of sentence you are writing by the punctuation mark you use to end the sentence.

▶ **KEY CONCEPT** A **declarative sentence** states an idea and ends with a period. ■

Declarative sentences are the most common type. They are used to "declare," or state facts.

DECLARATIVE: Windsor has been the surname of the British royal family since 1917.

▶ **KEY CONCEPT** An **interrogative sentence** asks a question and ends with a question mark. ■

Interrogative means "asking." An interrogative sentence is a question.

INTERROGATIVE: In which direction is Windsor Castle?

▶ **KEY CONCEPT** An **imperative sentence** gives an order or a direction and ends with either a period or an exclamation mark. ■

The word *imperative* is related to the word *emperor,* a person who gives commands. *Imperative* sentences are like emperors: They give commands. Most imperative sentences start with a verb. In this type of imperative sentence, the subject is understood to be *you.*

IMPERATIVE: Wait for me!
Turn left at the corner, and walk three blocks east.

▶ **KEY CONCEPT** An **exclamatory sentence** conveys strong emotion and ends with an exclamation mark. ■

To *exclaim* means to "shout out." *Exclamatory sentences* are used to "shout out" emotions, such as happiness, fear, delight, and anger.

EXCLAMATORY: The palace is on fire!
What a tiring night that was!

480 • Effective Sentences

Theme: Rulers of England

In this section, you will learn about the four functions sentences can perform. The examples and exercises are about rulers of England.

Cross-Curricular Connection: Social Studies

▼ **Critical Viewing** King Richard I of England was known as Richard the Lion-Hearted. Write one of each type of sentence about him, based on the picture. **[Interpret]**

▶ **Exercise 1** Supplying the Appropriate End Marks Rewrite the following paragraphs, putting in the appropriate end marks. Then, identify each sentence as *declarative, interrogative, imperative,* or *exclamatory.*

Since the 1720's, England has had six kings named George What was George I's greatest drawback as British monarch He did not speak English That's unbelievable Actually, George's mother was from the German state of Hanover, and German was his most comfortable language You should look at a map of eighteenth-century Europe if you want to find where Hanover is located

What were the most significant events during the reign of his son, George II The Industrial Revolution changed manufacturing and transportation in Europe, and England extended its rule over India What an amazing time that was Have you ever heard about George III's weaknesses He had a gigantic ego and suffered from mental illness during parts of his life He dissolved the Irish Parliament in 1801 and established stronger British rule over Ireland

Is it true that George IV's extravagant spending and loose lifestyle weakened the British monarchy in the 1820's He became a very unpopular ruler who seldom left his palace Nearly eighty years passed before another George held the British throne George V's reign lasted from before World War I until just before World War II Did he do more or less than other European monarchs to help avoid war His son George VI was the father of England's current monarch, Elizabeth II

▶ **Exercise 2** Writing Sentences With Different Functions Write the type of sentence indicated about the topic that is given.
1. television (declarative)
2. television (interrogative)
3. politics (imperative)
4. politics (exclamatory)
5. trains (declarative)
6. trains (exclamatory)
7. baseball (interrogative)
8. baseball (imperative)
9. subways (declarative)
10. subways (exclamatory)

▶ **More Practice**

Grammar Exercise Workbook
• pp. 49–50
On-line Exercise Bank
• Section 20.1
Go on-line:
PHSchool.com
Enter Web Code:
egk-1202

interactive Textbook

Get instant feedback! Exercises 1 and 2 are available on-line or on CD-ROM.

The Four Functions of a Sentence • 481

Customize for
ESL Students

When identifying the functions of unpunctuated sentences, students may quickly recognize statements but need help recognizing questions. Have students look at the beginnings of sentences for helping verbs or interrogative words, such as *where, when, why, how,* or *what.* Give students practice rewording declarative sentences into interrogatives, and vice versa.

Answer Key

▶ **Exercise 1**
1. named George. [Declarative]
2. British monarch? [Interrogative]
3. speak English. [Declarative]
4. unbelievable! [Exclamatory]
5. language. [Declarative]
6. is located. [Declarative]
7. George II? [Interrogative]
8. over India. [Declarative]
9. that was! [Exclamatory]
10. weaknesses? [Interrogative]
11. of his life. [Declarative]
12. over Ireland. [Declarative]
13. in the 1820's? [Interrogative]
14. his palace. [Declarative]
15. British throne. [Declarative]
16. World War II. [Declarative]
17. avoid war? [Interrogative]
18. Elizabeth II. [Declarative]

▶ **Exercise 2**
Answers will vary; samples are given.
1. I watch too much television.
2. What is your favorite show?
3. Vote in the election this year.
4. What a close race for governor that was!
5. I caught the train to Montreal in White River Junction, Vermont.
6. How the scenery did zoom past our windows!
7. Did you watch the World Series in October?
8. Pay attention to the pitching changes next time.
9. The number 4 subway stops right at the stadium.
10. We missed our subway stop!

☑ **ONGOING ASSESSMENT: Monitor and Reinforce**

If students miss more than two items in Exercise 1 or 2, refer them to the following for additional practice.

In the Textbook	Print Resources	Technology
Section Review, Ex. 3–4, Section 20.1	*Grammar Exercise Workbook,* pp. 49–50	*On-Line Exercise Bank,* Section 20.1

Section Review

Each of these exercises correlates with the instruction on the four functions of a sentence, page 480. The exercises may be used for more practice, for reteaching, or for review of the key concepts presented.

Answer Key

> **Exercise 3**

1. interrogative;?
2. declarative;.
3. imperative;. *or* exclamatory;!
4. declarative;.
5. imperative;.
6. declarative;.
7. interrogative;?
8. declarative;.
9. declarative;.
10. exclamatory;!

> **Exercise 4**

Answers will vary; samples are given.

1. Visit Buckingham Palace when you go to England.
2. George III originally bought it in 1761 as a home for his family.
3. Was George IV the one who paid a fortune to transform the house into a palace?
4. The renovation cost nearly half a million pounds!
5. Is it true that George IV never got to live in the palace?
6. His niece Victoria was the first royal occupant of the palace.
7. Did Victoria make certain changes to the palace?
8. She added bedrooms for visitors and a nursery for her children.
9. It was amazing that Victoria made sure the renovation came in 50,000 pounds under budget!
10. Read more about the palace by clicking on this Web site.

> **Exercise 5**

Find It in Your Reading
The passage contains all four types of sentences.

> **Exercise 6**

Find It in Your Writing
Encourage students to write a short assessment of their work.

> **Exercise 7**

Writing Application
Students might research travel writing to prepare for the assignment.

GRAMMAR EXERCISES 3–7

> **Exercise 3** Identifying the Four Functions of Sentences Label each sentence *declarative, interrogative, imperative,* or *exclamatory.* Then, write the end mark.

1. Have you ever attended the changing of the guard at Buckingham Palace
2. We thought it was fantastic
3. Imagine watching two groups of soldiers in bright red tunics and bearskin hats marching smartly together
4. The whole process takes about 45 minutes to complete
5. Make sure you bring your camera and have fast film
6. Unbelievably, the same ceremony has been followed for nearly 700 years
7. Was the ceremony of the keys at the Tower of London as interesting to watch
8. After locking the tower gates at night, the chief yeoman warder must pass by an armed guard and be recognized
9. The guard says, "Pass Queen Elizabeth's keys, and all's well"
10. What an interesting tradition that is

> **Exercise 4** Revising Sentences to Fit a Different Function Rewrite each sentence to fit the function indicated in parentheses. Add the appropriate end mark.

1. You might visit Buckingham Palace when you go to England. (imperative)
2. Did George III originally buy it in 1761 as a home for his family? (declarative)
3. George IV was the one who paid a fortune to transform the house into a palace. (interrogative).
4. Did the renovation really cost nearly half a million pounds? (exclamatory)
5. It is true that George IV never got to live in the palace. (interrogative)
6. Was his niece Victoria the first royal occupant of the palace? (declarative)

482 • Effective Sentences

7. Victoria made certain changes to the palace. (interrogative)
8. Did she add bedrooms for visitors and a nursery for her children? (declarative)
9. Was it amazing that Victoria made sure the renovation came in 50,000 pounds under budget? (exclamatory)
10. You can read more about the palace by clicking on this Web site. (imperative)

> **Exercise 5** Find It in Your Reading
Read this short speech from *Macbeth* by William Shakespeare. Which of the four types of sentences does it contain?

MACBETH. Bring me no more reports; let them fly all!
Till Birnam Wood remove to Dunsinane
I cannot taint with fear. What's the boy Malcolm?
Was he not born of woman? The spirits that know
All mortal consequences have pronounced me thus:
"Fear not, Macbeth; no man that's born of woman
Shall e'er have power upon thee." Then fly, false thanes,
And mingle with the English epicures.

> **Exercise 6** Find It in Your Writing
Look through your portfolio for examples of all four types of sentences. How does varying the types of sentences make your writing more interesting to read?

> **Exercise 7** Writing Application
Think of a tourist attraction you have visited. Write a paragraph for a guidebook to the attraction. Include all four types of sentences in your comments, and be sure to use appropriate end marks.

✓ ONGOING ASSESSMENT: Assess Mastery

Use the following resources to assess student mastery of the four functions of a sentence.

In the Textbook	Technology
Chapter Review, p. 514	*On-Line Exercise Bank*, Section 20.1

Section 20.2 Combining Sentences

Books written for very young readers present information in short, direct sentences. While this style makes the book easy to read, it doesn't make it enjoyable or interesting to mature readers. Writing intended for mature readers should include sentences of varying lengths and complexity to produce a flow of ideas. One way to achieve sentence variety is to combine sentences—to express two or more related ideas or pieces of information in a single sentence.

EXAMPLE:	We went to Scotland. We saw castles.
COMBINED:	We went to Scotland and saw castles. We saw castles in Scotland. We saw castles when we went to Scotland.

Combining Sentence Parts

Sometimes, the best way to combine ideas from several sentences into one is to join parts of the two sentences to form compound subjects, verbs, or objects.

▶ **KEY CONCEPT** Sentences can be combined by using a compound subject, a compound verb, or a compound object. ■

EXAMPLE:	Maura enjoyed seeing the castles. Tony enjoyed seeing the castles.
COMPOUND SUBJECT:	Maura and Tony enjoyed seeing the castles.
EXAMPLE:	Latrell climbed the turret stairs. Latrell saw the countryside.
COMPOUND VERB:	Latrell climbed the turret stairs and saw the countryside.
EXAMPLE:	Scott visited Jolly Old England. Scott visited Wales.
COMPOUND OBJECT:	Scott visited Jolly Old England and Wales.

Theme: England's History

In this section, you will learn different ways to combine sentences to make your writing more interesting. The examples and exercises are about events in the history of England.

Cross-Curricular Connection: Social Studies

▶ Critical Viewing How many different shapes and forms are combined in the design of this castle in Scotland? [Analyze]

Combining Sentences • 483

TIME AND RESOURCE MANAGER

Resources
Print: *Grammar Exercise Workbook*, pp. 51–52; *Grammar Exercises Answers on Transparencies,* Ch. 20
Technology: *Writing and Grammar* Interactive Text, Section 20.2; *On-Line Exercise Bank,* Section 20.2

Using the Full Student Edition	Using the Handbook⊞
• Work through key concepts, pp. 483–486. • Assign and review Exercises 8–12.	• Work through key concepts, pp. 335–338. • Assign and review Exercises 8–12.

PREPARE and ENGAGE

Interest GRABBER Challenge students to make this information more succinct, readable, or interesting:

One of Dickens's best-known characters is Charles Darnay.

Charles Darnay is a character in Dickens's A Tale of Two Cities.

Write a combination on the chalkboard *(One of Dickens's best-known characters is Charles Darnay from A Tale of Two Cities)*. Point out that combining the two sentences eliminates repetitions of some words.

Activate Prior Knowledge

In order to combine sentences, a review of types of sentence structure will be helpful. To reinforce the idea of classifying sentences by structure, write the following patterns on the chalkboard:

S V

S V, but S V

S V because S V

S V because S V, but S V

Ask students to suggest subjects and verbs and any other words needed to complete the patterns. Then, review the four terms (*simple, compound, complex,* and *compound-complex*) and ask students to classify the patterns and examples accordingly.

TEACH

Step-by-Step Teaching Guide

Combine Sentence Parts

1. Ask students to identify the compound elements in each of these sentences. *I read an article and a biography.* (object) *Mary and Elizabeth ruled their countries during the 1560's.* (subject) *Mary Queen of Scots enjoyed music and read widely.* (verb)

2. Remind students that any of the coordinating conjunctions they have studied (*and, but, or, nor, so, for, yet*) can be used to join elements in sentences.

Critical Viewing

Analyze Possible answer: The castle includes rectangles, squares, circles, and cylinders.

Answer Key

▶ Exercise 8

Answers may vary slightly.

1. <u>My brother and I</u> traveled to England. (subjects)
2. We went <u>to relax and to see the sights</u>. (infinitives)
3. In a guidebook, we learned about <u>the island's early occupants and its naming</u>. (objects of a preposition)
4. In A.D. 449, Anglo-Saxons <u>invaded the island and occupied its southeastern part</u>. (predicates)
5. The island <u>was originally called "Angle-land" and later became known as "England."</u> (predicates)

Step-by-Step Teaching Guide

Combining Clauses

1. Have a student define a *compound sentence* (two or more independent clauses joined by a comma and a coordinating conjunction or by a semicolon). Be sure students remember both methods of forming compound sentences: semicolon and comma plus conjunction.

2. Write on the chalkboard: *I walk to school in the mornings. In the afternoon, I take the bus home.* Have students use both methods to form compound sentences.

3. Remind students that a comma rarely precedes a coordinating conjunction when combining two subjects, verbs, objects, or other lesser constructions.

continued

Answer Key

▶ Exercise 9

Answers may vary slightly.

1. Britain had long been known to the Romans as a source of tin, but the island . . .
2. That year, Julius Caesar invaded the island; it was a fitting . . .
3. Emperor Claudius invaded Britain in A.D. 43, and his . . .
4. In 122, the Romans wanted a way to defend their settlements from northern attacks, so they . . .
5. Under Roman rule, many new towns sprang up near Roman army camps, and London . . .

▶ **Exercise 8** Combining Sentence Parts Combine each pair of sentences in a logical way. Identify the parts of the two sentences you have made compound as you combined them.

EXAMPLE: Frank met the queen. Freida met the queen.
ANSWER: Frank and Freida met the queen. (subject)

1. I traveled to England. My brother traveled with me.
2. We went to relax. We went to see the sights.
3. In a guidebook, we learned about the island's early occupants. We also learned how it was named.
4. In A.D. 449, Anglo-Saxons invaded the island. The Anglo-Saxons occupied its southeastern part.
5. The island was originally called "Angle-land." The island later became known as "England."

Combining Clauses

▶ **KEY CONCEPT** Sentences can be combined by joining two independent clauses to form a compound sentence. ■

Use a compound sentence to combine ideas that are related but independent. Join two independent clauses with a comma and a coordinating conjunction or with a semicolon. Coordinating conjunctions include *and, but, or, for, nor, yet,* and *so.*

EXAMPLE: The clouds crossed the English Channel. The rain beat down on England.

COMPOUND   The clouds crossed the English Channel, and the
SENTENCE: rain beat down on England.

▶ **Exercise 9** Combining Ideas of Equal Weight Combine the following sentences, following the directions in parentheses.
1. Britain had long been known to the Romans as a source of tin. The island did not come under Roman rule until 55 B.C. (comma and conjunction)
2. That year, Julius Caesar invaded the island. It was a fitting follow-up to his conquest of Gaul. (semicolon)
3. Emperor Claudius had invaded Britain in A.D. 43. His army easily conquered Celtic tribes there. (comma and conjunction)
4. In 122, the Romans wanted a way to defend their settlements from northern attacks. They built Hadrian's Wall near the border of Scotland. (comma and conjunction)
5. Under Roman rule, many new towns sprang up near Roman army camps. London developed into a prosperous port city. (comma and conjunction)

484 • Effective Sentences

💡 Spelling Tip

Some words are spelled differently in England than they are in America. For instance, the American word "color" is spelled "colour" in the UK. If you are not sure whether you are using the proper American spelling, check your dictionary. Most dictionaries list the British spelling.

✎ STANDARDIZED TEST PREPARATION WORKSHOP

Grammar and Usage Many standardized tests require students to revise errors in compositions. Write the following on the chalkboard.

Only one package arrived in the mail. The other items never came.

What is the best way to combine these two sentences?

A Only one package arrived in the mail, the other items never came.

B The other items never came because only one package arrived in the mail.

C Arriving in the mail, the other items never came.

D Only one package arrived in the mail; the other items never came.

The correct answer is **D**. Two complete sentences are joined correctly by a semicolon.

KEY CONCEPT Sentences can be combined by changing one of them into a subordinate clause. ■

You can combine sentences to form one complex sentence that shows the relationship between ideas. The subordinating conjunction will help readers understand the relationship. Subordinating conjunctions include *after, although, because, before, even though, if, since, until, when,* and *while.*

EXAMPLE: We were frightened. We thought the castle was haunted.

COMBINED WITH   We were frightened because we
A SUBORDINATE CLAUSE: thought the castle was haunted.

Exercise 10 Combining Sentences Using Subordinate Clauses Combine the following sentences using the subordinating conjunction indicated in parentheses.

EXAMPLE: Julius Caesar invaded Britain. He had conquered Gaul. (after)

ANSWER: Julius Caesar invaded Britain after he had conquered Gaul.

1. The Roman Empire began to decline in the third and fourth centuries. It was overextended. (because)
2. The Romans abandoned Britain in 410. They left behind a superb network of roads and many growing towns. (when)
3. Roman engineering was advanced for its time. Britain was able to use Roman roads for hundreds of years. (because)
4. Warriors from Ireland, Scotland, and Germany invaded Britain. The Romans left the island. (after)
5. Tribes of Britons fought hard to protect their lands. Most of the island was conquered by the invaders. (although)

Exercise 11 Combining Using Subordinate Clauses Combine the following sentences using a logical subordinating conjunction.
1. The Angles and Saxons were the most powerful of the invaders. They soon took over most of the territory.
2. The Angles and Saxons were not a united group. They divided the land into seven separate kingdoms.
3. The seven kingdoms were not Greek. Historians have given them a Greek name, the Heptarchy.
4. The Heptarchy lasted for 300 years. Raiders from Denmark invaded and conquered six of the kingdoms.
5. The Danes tried to conquer Wessex. Its king, Alfred the Great, defeated the Danes and forced them to retreat.

▶ **More Practice**

Grammar Exercise Workbook
• pp. 51–52
On-line Exercise Bank
• Section 20.2
Go on-line:
PHSchool.com
Enter Web Code:
egk-1202

interactive Textbook

Complete the exercises on-line! Exercises 8, 9, 10, and 11 are available on-line or on CD-ROM.

Step-by-Step Teaching Guide continued

4. Write on the chalkboard: *We opened the front door. We mounted the stairs.* Have students suggest subordinating conjunctions that express the relationship between the two clauses (*before, then, after*). Point out the different meanings that different conjunctions will establish in the sentence.

Answer Key

▶ **Exercise 10**

Answers may vary slightly.

1. The Roman Empire began to decline in the third and fourth centuries because it was . . .
2. When the Romans abandoned Britain in 410, they left . . .
3. Because Roman engineering was advanced for its time, Britain was . . .
4. Warriors from Ireland, Scotland, and Germany invaded Britain after the Romans . . .
5. Although tribes of Britons fought hard to protect their lands, most of the island . . .

▶ **Exercise 11**

Answers will vary; samples are given.

1. Because the Angles and Saxons were the most powerful of the invaders, they soon . . .
2. Because the Angles and Saxons were not a united group, they divided . . .
3. Although the seven kingdoms were not Greek, historians have . . .
4. The Heptarchy lasted for 300 years, until raiders . . .
5. As soon as the Danes tried to conquer Wessex, its king, Alfred the Great, defeated them . . .

☑ **ONGOING ASSESSMENT: Monitor and Reinforce**

If students miss more than one item in Exercise 8, 9, 10, 11, or 12, refer them to the following for additional practice.

In the Textbook	Print Resources	Technology
Section Review, Ex. 13–14, Section 20.2	*Grammar Exercise Workbook,* pp. 51–52	*On-Line Exercise Bank,* Section 20.2

⏱ **TIME SAVERS!**

Answers on Transparencies
Use the *Grammar Exercises Answers on Transparencies* for Chapter 20 to facilitate correction by students.

On-Line Exercise Bank
Have students complete the exercises on computer. The Auto Check feature will grade their work for you!

Combining Using Phrases

1. Have students list the various types of phrases (prepositional, appositive, gerund, infinitive, participial) and identify the types used in the examples (appositive and prepositional).

2. Point out that phrases add detail to the main sentence and that sometimes they can be removed from the new sentence without changing meaning.

Answer Key

▶ Exercise 12

Answers will vary; samples are given.

1. Alfred I ruled for nearly twenty years, from A.D. 871 to 899.
2. He justly deserves the title of Alfred the Great.
3. Many English political and educational reforms began under Alfred, the most powerful Anglo-Saxon king.
4. Showing his interest in education, Alfred built many schools.
5. He also brought in scholars to translate Latin books into Anglo-Saxon, the common language of his subjects.
6. Historians give Alfred credit for establishing the first English naval fleet.
7. Alfred also commissioned the *Anglo-Saxon Chronicles*, an extensive written history of England.
8. Scholars continued to add to the *Chronicles* for more than 250 years after Alfred's death.
9. Alfred organized his kingdom into local divisions, which were known as shires.
10. Under Alfred, English common law, the basis of the legal system in England and the United States, developed.

Critical Viewing

Connect Sample responses: Britain, an island nation, offered many landing sites to invaders. Britain's nearness to the European continent invited attack.

20.2

Combining Using Phrases

▶ **KEY CONCEPT** Sentences can be combined by changing one of them into a phrase. ■

Change one of the sentences into a phrase when you are combining sentences in which one of the sentences just adds detail.

EXAMPLES: The Anglo-Saxon kings feared the Jutes. The Jutes were a tribe of seafaring raiders.
The Jutes' homeland was in Denmark. Denmark was to the east.

CORRECTED SENTENCES: The Anglo-Saxon kings feared the Jutes, a tribe of seafaring raiders. The Jutes' homeland was in Denmark, to the east.

The Anglo-Saxon Kingdoms

▶ **Exercise 12** Combining Using Phrases Combine the following sentences by changing one into a phrase.

EXAMPLE: Alfred was the king of Wessex. Wessex was a region in the southwestern part of England.

ANSWER: Alfred was the king of Wessex, a region in the southwestern part of England.

1. Alfred I ruled for nearly twenty years. He ruled from A.D. 871 to 899.
2. He is known as Alfred the Great. He justly deserves that title.
3. Many English political and educational reforms began under Alfred. Alfred was the most powerful Anglo-Saxon king.
4. Alfred showed his interest in education. He built many schools.
5. He also brought in scholars to translate Latin books into Anglo-Saxon. Anglo-Saxon was the common language of his subjects.
6. Historians give credit to Alfred. Alfred established the first English naval fleet.
7. Alfred also commissioned the *Anglo-Saxon Chronicles*. This book was an extensive written history of England.
8. Scholars continued to add to the *Chronicles*. They added to the *Chronicles* for more than 250 years after Alfred's death.
9. Alfred organized his kingdom into local divisions. These divisions were known as "shires."
10. Under Alfred, English common law developed. English common law is the basis of the legal system in England and the United States.

486 • Effective Sentences

▲ **Critical Viewing** Write two sentences containing phrases that describe why the British Isles could easily be invaded. **[Connect]**

▶ **More Practice**

Grammar Exercise Workbook
• pp. 51–52
On-line Exercise Bank
• Section 20.2
Go on-line:
PHSchool.com
Enter Web Code:
egk-1202

☑ **ONGOING ASSESSMENT: Assess Mastery**

Use the following resources to assess student mastery of combining sentences.

In the Textbook	Technology
Chapter Review, Ex. 57	*On-Line Exercise Bank*, Section 20.2

Section 20.2 Section Review

GRAMMAR EXERCISES 13–18

▶ **Exercise 13** Combining Sentences Using Compound Subjects, Verbs, and Objects Combine each of the pairs of sentences. Revise as necessary for clarity.

1. In the mid-1200's, Edward I restored royal control. He made many reforms.
2. He limited special rights of the powerful. He limited privileges of the wealthy.
3. Edward I established English control over Wales. His son, Edward II, helped establish English control over Wales.
4. Edward II tried to conquer Scotland. He tried to make the Scots pay taxes.
5. The Scots were conquered. The Scots continued to rebel against his rule.

▶ **Exercise 14** Combining Sentences Using Clauses Combine each pair of sentences with a comma and coordinating conjunction, a semicolon, or a subordinating conjunction.

1. Edward II was a poor ruler. He was forced to give up the throne.
2. Edward III took over after his father. He proved to be more effective.
3. Edward III hoped to rule France. He sent an army across the English Channel.
4. The English developed a new weapon. They fought with the longbow.
5. The war continued for one hundred years. Its expense nearly broke England.
6. Henry VII became king in 1485. He was the first of the Tudor line.
7. He married Elizabeth of York. He wanted the support of her powerful family.
8. Henry promoted foreign trade. He hoped to increase England's wealth.
9. Henry avoided foreign wars. England enjoyed a strong government and a stable economy during his rule.
10. Henry was respected by his people. He was never really loved.

▶ **Exercise 15** Combining Sentences Using Phrases Combine the following sentences by changing one of each pair into a phrase.

1. Henry VIII was born in 1491. He was the second son of Henry VII and Elizabeth of York.
2. He became heir to the throne in 1502. This followed his brother's death.
3. Henry is known for his great appetites. The appetites were for food, hunting, and music.
4. Henry dramatically increased the size of the Royal Navy. It was increased from five to fifty-three ships.
5. He strengthened England. He made separate alliances with France and Spain.

▶ **Exercise 16** Find It in Your Reading Find three or more ideas combined in this sentence from a *London Times* article "Elizabeth II: A New Queen."

. . . She did not go to school but was taught, under the close personal direction of the Queen, by a governess, Miss Marion Crawford, who joined the household in 1933.

▶ **Exercise 17** Find It in Your Writing Look through your portfolio for a paragraph that contains several short sentences. Combine two of the short sentences to form one longer sentence.

▶ **Exercise 18** Writing Application Write a brief description of a famous world ruler. First, use only short sentences in your description. Then, rewrite it, combining some of the short sentences into longer, more interesting ones.

Section Review • 487

ASSESS

Section Review

Each of these exercises correlates with the instruction on sentence combining, pages 483–486. The exercises may be used for more practice, for reteaching, or for review of the key concepts presented.

Answer Key

▶ **Exercise 13**

Answers will vary; samples are given.

1. In the mid-1200's, Edward I restored royal control and made . . .
2. He limited special rights of the powerful and privileges of . . .
3. Edward I and Edward II established English control over Wales.
4. Edward tried to conquer Scotland and to make the Scots pay taxes.
5. The Scots were conquered but continued to rebel against his rule.

▶ **Exercise 14**

Answers will vary; samples are given.

1. Because Edward II was a poor ruler, he . . .
2. Edward III took over after his father; he proved . . .
3. Edward III hoped to rule France, so he sent an army . . .
4. After the English developed the longbow, they fought with this new weapon.
5. The war continued for one hundred years, and its expense . . .
6. Henry VII, who became king in 1485, was the first of . . .
7. He married Elizabeth of York because he wanted the support . . .
8. Henry promoted foreign trade because he hoped to . . .
9. Because Henry avoided foreign wars, England enjoyed . . .
10. Although Henry was respected by his people, he was never . . .

▶ **Exercise 15**

Answers will vary; samples are given.

1. Henry VIII, the second son of Henry VII and Elizabeth of York, was born in 1491.
2. He became heir to the throne in 1502 following his . . .
3. Henry is known for his great appetites for food, . . .
4. Henry dramatically increased the size of the Royal Navy from five to fifty-three ships.
5. Making separate alliances with France and Spain, he . . .

continued

Answer Key continued

▶ **Exercise 16**

Find It in Your Reading
Students should identify the following ideas:

She did not go to school.

She was taught under the close personal direction of the Queen.

She was taught by Miss Marion Crawford, a governess.

Miss Crawford joined the household in 1933.

▶ **Exercise 17**

Find It in Your Writing
Challenge students to construct at least three combined sentences.

▶ **Exercise 18**

Writing Application
Encourage students to add their descriptions to their writing portfolios.

Interest GRABBER Challenge students to vary this sentence in at least two ways: *The hikers returned exhausted from their journey.* (Possible variations: *Exhausted, the hikers returned from their journey. The hikers returned from their journey exhausted.*)

Activate Prior Knowledge

Write the phrase *the man in the dark overcoat* on the chalkboard. Challenge students to complete the sentence and to vary it in at least two ways by using different sentence openers. (Examples: *Under a dimly lit street lamp stood the man in the dark overcoat. Looking uneasy, the man in the dark overcoat stood alone.*) Tell students that varying sentence beginnings is but one way to add interest to written work.

TEACH

Step-by-Step Teaching Guide

Vary Sentence Length

1. Draw students' attention to the number of clauses and phrases in each sentence in the example cluster (8 phrases and 2 clauses; 6 phrases and 1 clause; 6 phrases and 1 clause; 2 phrases and 1 clause).

2. Ask students to read the two long sentences and their corrections. Have them describe the changes that were made (changing a wordy compound sentence into a simple sentence; breaking a long compound-complex sentence into two sentences—one simple, one compound).

Real-World Connection

Explain that speakers include sentences of varying lengths and structures to make their presentations interesting and enjoyable. Demonstrate by taping several stories from a newscast. Ask students to classify each sentence by structure and then discuss how each sentence begins. Discuss how coherence has been achieved by varying sentence lengths, structures, and openers.

Section 20.3

Varying Sentences

Vary your sentences to develop a rhythm, to achieve an effect, or to emphasize the connections between ideas.
There are several ways you can vary your sentences.

Varying Sentence Length

You have already learned that you can combine several short, choppy sentences to form a longer, more interesting, and more mature sentence. However, too many long sentences in a row can be as uninteresting to read as too many short sentences. When you want to emphasize a point or surprise a reader, insert a short, direct sentence to interrupt the flow of long sentences. Take note of the following writing sample:

EXAMPLE: The Jacobites derived their name from *Jacobus,* the Latin name for King James II of England, who was dethroned in 1688 by William of Orange during the Glorious Revolution. An unpopular king in England because of his Catholicism and autocratic ruling style, James fled to France to seek the aid of King Louis XIV. In 1690, James, along with a small body of French troops, landed in Ireland in an attempt to regain his throne. His hopes ended at the Battle of the Boyne.

Some sentences contain only one idea and can't be broken. It may be possible, however, to state the idea in a shorter sentence. Other sentences contain two or more ideas and might be shortened by breaking up the ideas.

LONGER SENTENCE: Many of James I's predecessors were able to avoid major economic problems, but James had serious economic problems.

MORE DIRECT: Unlike many of his predecessors, James I was unable to avoid major economic problems.

LONGER SENTENCE: James tried to work with Parliament to develop a plan for taxation that would be fair and reasonable, but members of Parliament rejected his efforts, and James dissolved the Parliament.

SHORTER SENTENCES: James tried to work with Parliament to develop a fair and reasonable taxation plan. Members of Parliament rejected his efforts, and James dissolved the Parliament.

488 • **Effective Sentences**

Theme: England's History

In this section, you will learn how to make your writing more interesting by varying the length and beginnings of the sentences you write. The examples and exercises are about more events in the history of England.

Cross-Curricular Connection: Social Studies

⚙ Grammar and Style Tip

When revising your work to include a variety of sentence lengths and structures, make sure you do not introduce an error. Long sentences can turn into run-on sentences; inverted sentences can inadvertently contain misplaced or dangling modifiers. Proofread carefully.

⏱ TIME AND RESOURCE MANAGER

Resources
Print: *Grammar Exercise Workbook,* pp. 53–60; *Grammar Exercises Answers on Transparencies,* Ch. 20
Technology: *Writing and Grammar* Interactive Text, Section 20.3; *On-Line Exercise Bank,* Section 20.3

Using the Full Student Edition	Using the Handbook Ⓗ
• Work through key concepts, pp. 488–490. • Assign and review Exercises 19–21. • Read and discuss Grammar in Literature, p. 489.	• Work through key concepts, pp. 340–342. • Assign and review Exercises 19–21. • Read and discuss Grammar in Literature, p. 341.

Exercise 19 Revising to Vary Sentence Length In the following items, break up long sentences into two or more shorter sentences or restate long sentences more simply.

EXAMPLE: Oliver Cromwell was a man who did not have any military training, yet he was able to direct the army that had a loyalty to Parliament in many stunning victories during the English Civil War.

ANSWER: Though he had no military training, Oliver Cromwell led the army loyal to Parliament in many stunning victories during the English Civil War.

1. Oliver Cromwell came from a wealthy background and, following attendance at Cambridge University, he served his country in two ways, both as a member of Parliament and as a spokesperson for religious freedom.
2. Cromwell was a member of Parliament in 1640, and as a member of Parliament, he spoke out against King Charles and voiced disagreements with the king's policies.
3. Cromwell was a decisive leader, and he was very successful in military circles and in political circles.
4. Cromwell directed the army in the military campaigns that led to the final defeat of Charles I, and he afterward served as the chief advocate at the king's trial and execution.
5. For the next ten years, Cromwell served as chief executive, and he was a ruthless and effective leader.

GRAMMAR IN LITERATURE

from **Mary Chesnut's Civil War**
Mary Chesnut

Notice how the addition of a long sentence (in blue italics) between several short ones not only creates a more varied and fluid rhythm in this passage, but also intensifies the dramatic impact of the final statement.

These men all talked so delightfully. For once in my life I listened.

That over, business began. *In earnest, Governor Means rummaged a sword and red sash from somewhere and brought it for Colonel Chesnut, who has gone to demand the surrender of Fort Sumter.*

And now, patience—we must wait.

More Practice

Grammar Exercise Workbook
• pp. 53–54
On-line Exercise Bank
• Section 20.3
  Go on-line:
  PHSchool.com
  Enter Web Code:
  egk-1202

interactive Textbook

Complete the exercise on-line! Exercise 19 is available on-line or on CD-ROM.

Answer Key

▶ **Exercise 19**

Answers will vary; samples are given.

1. Oliver Cromwell, who came from a wealthy background, attended Cambridge University. Afterwards, he served his country as a member of Parliament and as a spokesperson for religious freedom.
2. In 1640, as a member of Parliament, Cromwell spoke out against King Charles, voicing disagreements with the king's policies.
3. A decisive leader, Cromwell was very successful in both military and political circles.
4. After directing the army in the military campaigns that led to the final defeat of Charles I, Cromwell served as the chief advocate at the king's trial and execution.
5. As chief executive for the next ten years, Cromwell was a ruthless and effective leader.

Step-by-Step Teaching Guide

Grammar in Literature

1. Ask students to analyze each sentence's structure (simple, compound, and so forth).
2. Help students list the types of sentences, including the number of clauses and phrases in each (simple: 1 clause, 1 phrase; simple: 1 clause, 1 phrase; simple: 1 clause; 1 phrase; compound-complex: 3 clauses, 3 phrases; compound: two clauses [note that the verb *have* is understood in the first clause], 1 phrase).

Connections With Literature

Students can read more of "Mary Chesnut's Civil War" in *Prentice Hall Literature, Penguin Edition,* The British Tradition.

Customize for
Gifted and Talented Students

Have students find a paragraph in a history textbook that contains many long sentences. Ask them to rewrite the paragraph, varying the lengths of sentences to make the paragraph more interesting.

☑ **ONGOING ASSESSMENT: Monitor and Reinforce**

If students miss more than one item in Exercise 19, refer them to the following for additional practice.

In the Textbook	Print Resources	Technology
Section Review, Ex. 22, Section 20.3	*Grammar Exercise Workbook,* pp. 53–54	*On-Line Exercise Bank,* Section 20.3

Vary Sentence Beginnings; Use Inverted Word Order

1. Write on the chalkboard: *The sun set slowly in the west and signaled that the day was over.* Have students rewrite this sentence beginning with an adverb, a participle, and a prepositional phrase (*Slowly . . . ; Setting . . .* or *Signaling …; In the west . . .*). Have them read aloud some examples and help the class decide which changes flow effectively and preserve meaning.

2. Ask students where they have seen inverted subject-verb order (interrogative sentences). Write on the chalkboard: *Crystal ran after the bus.* Ask students to rewrite it as an interrogative (*Did Crystal run . . .*) and as a declarative with inverted subject-verb order (*After the bus ran Crystal*).

Critical Viewing

Describe Possible answer: The guard marches stiffly. Rewritings: Stiffly, the guard marches in front of the palace. Swinging one straight arm, the guard marches to his post.

Answer Key

Answers may vary; samples are given.

1. In 1558, Queen Elizabeth I came to power.
2. Challenged by her cousin Mary, Queen of Scots, was Elizabeth's right to the throne.
3. An attack by a fleet of Spanish ships added to her problems.
4. Rapidly, the English fleet put down the attack.
5. To the problems she faced, Elizabeth brought intelligence and keen diplomatic instincts.

Answers may vary; samples are given.

1. Filled with fascinating stories is the history of British royal families.
2. Particularly interesting are the lives . . .
3. Through the Tower of London walks a class . . .
4. Among themselves talk the students animatedly.
5. Next on their agenda is a tour . . .

20.3

Varying Sentence Beginnings

Another way to create sentence variety is to avoid starting each sentence in the same way. You can start sentences with different parts of speech.

START WITH A NOUN:	Parliament's authority grew and eventually exceeded royal power.
START WITH AN ADVERB:	Eventually, Parliament's authority grew to exceed royal power.
START WITH A PARTICIPLE:	Growing over time, Parliament's authority finally exceeded royal power.
START WITH A PREPOSITIONAL PHRASE:	In time, Parliament's authority grew to exceed royal power.

▶ **Exercise 20** Revising to Vary Sentence Beginnings
Rewrite each sentence to begin with the part of speech indicated in parentheses.
1. Queen Elizabeth I came to power in 1558. (preposition)
2. Her right to the throne was challenged by her cousin Mary, Queen of Scots. (participle)
3. Adding to her problems was an attack by a fleet of Spanish ships. (article and noun)
4. The English fleet put down the attack rapidly. (adverb)
5. Elizabeth brought intelligence and keen diplomatic instincts to the problems she faced. (preposition)

Using Inverted Word Order

You can also vary sentence beginnings by reversing the traditional subject-verb order.

SUBJECT-VERB ORDER:	The queen was waiting for the attack. The royal armada sailed into the bay.
INVERTED ORDER:	Waiting for the attack was the queen. Into the bay sailed the royal armada.

▶ **Exercise 21** Revising Using Inverted Word Order Rewrite the following sentences by inverting the subject-verb order. Rearrange the rest of the words of the sentence as needed.
1. The history of British royal families is filled with fascinating stories.
2. The lives of Queens Elizabeth I, Anne, and Victoria are particularly interesting.
3. A class of students walks through the Tower of London.
4. The students talk animatedly among themselves.
5. A tour of Buckingham Palace is next on their agenda.

490 • Effective Sentences

▲ **Critical Viewing**
Write a sentence describing how this guard marches. Then, rewrite the sentence twice. First, begin with an adverb; next, with a participle. **[Describe]**

▶ **More Practice**

Grammar Exercise Workbook
• pp. 55–60
On-line Exercise Bank
• Section 20.3
Go on-line:
PHSchool.com
Enter Web Code:
egk-1202

✓ **ONGOING ASSESSMENT: Monitor and Reinforce**

If students miss more than one item in Exercise 20 or 21, refer them to the following for additional practice.

In the Textbook	Print Resources	Technology
Section Review, Ex. 23–24, Section 20.3	*Grammar Exercise Workbook*, pp. 55–60	*On-Line Exercise Bank*, Section 20.3

Section 20.3 Section Review

GRAMMAR EXERCISES 22–27

▶ **Exercise 22** Revising Sentence Length Rewrite the following sentences by breaking each into two sentences or writing a simpler, more direct sentence.

1. Born Alexandrina Victoria on May 24, 1819, Queen Victoria was the only daughter of Edward, Duke of Kent, fourth son of George III.
2. She became queen at the age of 18, and she succeeded her uncle, William IV.
3. She had two main advisors early in her reign, and they were her husband, Prince Albert, and the Prime Minister, Lord Melbourne.
4. Melbourne was the leader of the branch of the Whig party that later became known as the Liberal party, and he exercised a strong influence on the political thinking of the queen.
5. Victoria's marriage to Albert was an arranged marriage, but the couple loved each other very much, and she became very depressed when he died in 1861.

▶ **Exercise 23** Revising Sentence Beginnings Rewrite each sentence below to begin with the part of speech indicated in parentheses.

1. Victoria remained in mourning for several years following Albert's death. (participle)
2. It disturbed her to be seen in public. (infinitive)
3. Victoria remained in seclusion in the palace and allowed her son, the Prince of Wales, to represent her at most ceremonial functions. (participle)
4. She was eventually convinced to return to public life by Prime Minister Benjamin Disraeli. (adverb)
5. Victoria's popularity grew as a result of her concern for the welfare of the poor and needy. (preposition)

▶ **Exercise 24** Inverting Sentences to Vary Beginnings Rewrite each of the following sentences by inverting subject-verb order to be verb-subject order.

1. The Round Tower at Windsor Castle is old.
2. The Royal Family strolled through Windsor Great Park.
3. A magnificent tree-lined avenue leads to the castle grounds.
4. The Round Tower has a fascinating history.
5. The Throne Room was magnificent.

▶ **Exercise 25** Find It in Your Reading Notice the use of long and short sentences in this passage from "Elizabeth II: A New Queen":

Early in the New Year they set out on their public life together, and in May paid an official visit to Paris, where they were greeted with a welcome of great warmth and spontaneity. Then early in June it was announced that the Princess would soon cancel all her engagements. On November 14 her son, Prince Charles, was born.

▶ **Exercise 26** Find It in Your Writing Look in your portfolio for examples of long sentences. Rewrite some of the sentences to form shorter, more direct ones.

▶ **Exercise 27** Writing Application Write a short essay about a powerful political leader. Use both long and short sentences in your essay.

Section Review • 491

ASSESS

Section Review

Each of these exercises correlates with the instruction on varying sentences, pages 488–490. The exercises may be used for more practice, for reteaching, or for review of the key concepts presented.

Answer Key

▶ **Exercise 22**

Answers will vary; samples are given.

1. Queen Victoria was born Alexandrina Victoria on May 24, 1819. She was the only daughter of Edward, Duke of Kent, fourth son of George III.
2. At the age of 18, she became queen, succeeding her uncle, William IV.
3. Prince Albert, her husband, and the Prime Minister, Lord Melbourne, were her two main advisors early in her reign.
4. Melbourne was the leader of the branch of the Whig Party that became known as the Liberal Party. He exercised a strong influence on the political thinking of the queen.
5. Though their marriage was arranged, Victoria and Albert loved each other very much. She became very depressed when he died in 1861.

▶ **Exercise 23**

Answers may vary; samples are given.

1. Following Albert's death, Victoria remained . . .
2. To be seen in public disturbed her.
3. Remaining in seclusion in the palace, Victoria allowed her son, the Prince of Wales, to . . .
4. Eventually, she was convinced . . .
5. As a result of her concern for the welfare of the poor and needy, Victoria's popularity grew.

▶ **Exercise 24**

Answers may very; samples are given.

1. Old is the Round Tower at Windsor Castle.
2. Through Windsor Great Park strolled the Royal Family.
3. To the castle grounds leads a magnificent tree-lined avenue.
4. A fascinating history has the Round Tower.
5. Magnificent was the Throne Room.

continued

Answer Key continued

▶ **Exercise 25**

Find It in Your Reading
Have students also note the author's use of inference.

▶ **Exercise 26**

Find It in Your Writing
Encourage students to develop an eye for a judicious mix of long and short sentences in their writing.

▶ **Exercise 27**

Writing Application
You may wish to allow students to use class time to use the library.

Write the clause *When Aunt Dolly stepped from the train* on the chalkboard. Ask students to identify the verb (*stepped*), identify the subject (*Aunt Dolly*), and tell what punctuation mark belongs at the end (none, because this is not a complete sentence). Discuss the fact that even though this clause contains a subject and a verb, it is not a sentence because it does not express a complete thought.

Activate Prior Knowledge

Point out that because they contain subjects and verbs, subordinate clauses are sometimes mistaken for complete sentences. Write the following clauses on the chalkboard, and ask students for a way to change each into a sentence:

that he wanted to use (Add an independent clause.)

since you are going to London (Drop the subordinating conjunction or add an independent clause.)

who won the prize last year (Add a question mark or add an independent clause.)

TEACH

Step-by-Step Teaching Guide

Recognizing Fragments

1. Point out that there are several options for fixing a fragment depending on the context of the surrounding sentences.

continued

Integrating Speaking and Listening Skills

Sentence Fragments Read these items to students. For each, have a volunteer identify it as a sentence or a fragment:

The person waiting for us at the bus stop (F)

A beautiful baby smiling at us (F)

Are you going to the play? (S)

Have students write complete sentences out of the fragments.

Section 20.4

Avoiding Fragments and Run-ons

Hasty writers sometimes omit crucial words, punctuate awkwardly, or leave their thoughts unfinished, causing two common sentence errors: fragments and run-ons.

Recognizing Fragments

Although some writers use fragments purposefully for a stylistic effect, fragments are generally considered writing errors.

▶ **KEY CONCEPT** Do not capitalize and punctuate phrases, subordinate clauses, or words in a series as if they were complete sentences. ■

Reading your work aloud and listening to the natural pauses and stops should help you avoid fragments. Sometimes, you can repair a fragment by connecting it to words that come before or after it.

▶ **KEY CONCEPT** One way to correct a fragment is to connect it to the words in a nearby sentence. ■

PARTICIPIAL FRAGMENT:	Inspired by the grace of the dancer.
ADDED TO A NEARBY SENTENCE:	*Inspired by the grace of the dancer,* Linda saw the performance again.
PREPOSITIONAL FRAGMENT:	Before her partner.
ADDED TO A NEARBY SENTENCE:	The *ballerina* came on stage *before her partner.*

A fragment containing a pronoun and a participial phrase can often be repaired by dropping the pronoun and adding the participial phrase to a nearby sentence.

PRONOUN AND PARTICIPIAL FRAGMENT:	The one hanging in the closet.
ADDED TO NEARBY SENTENCE:	I wore the leotard *hanging in the closet.*

Sometimes, you may need to add missing sentence parts. Remember that every complete sentence must have both a subject and a verb and express a complete thought. Check to see that each of your sentences contains all of the parts necessary to be complete.

492 • Effective Sentences

Theme: Ballet

In this section, you will learn how to avoid two problems that can make your sentences incorrect or hard to understand. The examples and exercises are about ballet and ballet dancers.

Cross-Curricular Connection: Performing Arts

💡 Spelling Tip

Two essential steps in improving your spelling are proofreading carefully and using a dictionary. To catch misspelled words, try proofreading your draft backward, word by word. Use a dictionary to confirm the spelling of unfamiliar words.

⏱ TIME AND RESOURCE MANAGER	
Resources	
Print: *Grammar Exercise Workbook*, pp. 61–64; *Grammar Exercises Answers on Transparencies*, Ch. 20	
Technology: *Writing and Grammar* Interactive Text, Section 20.4; *On-Line Exercise Bank*, Section 20.4	

Using the Full Student Edition	Using the Handbook 🄷
• Work through all key concepts, pp. 492–496. • Assign and review Exercises 28–30. • Do the Hands-on Grammar activity, p. 499.	• Work through all key concepts, pp. 344–348. • Assign and review Exercises 28–30. • Do the Hands-on Grammar activity, p. 351.

KEY CONCEPT Another way to correct a fragment is to add any missing sentence part that is needed to make the fragment a complete sentence. ∎

One typical fragment error involves writing a noun phrase (a noun with its modifiers) as if it were a sentence. However, a noun phrase will need a verb if it is to be used as a subject. If the noun phrase is to be used as a complement, an object of a preposition, or an appositive, it will need both a subject and a verb.

NOUN FRAGMENT: The troupe of lively young dancers.

COMPLETED SENTENCES: The troupe of lively young dancers moved across the stage.
We excitedly watched the troupe of lively young dancers.

Notice what missing sentence parts must be added to the following types of phrase fragments to make them complete.

NOUN FRAGMENT WITH PARTICIPIAL PHRASE: The food eaten by us.
COMPLETED SENTENCE: The food was eaten by us.

VERB FRAGMENT: Will be at the rehearsal today.
COMPLETED SENTENCE: I will be at the rehearsal today.

PREPOSITIONAL FRAGMENT: In the hall closet.
COMPLETED SENTENCE: I put the toe shoes in the hall closet.

PARTICIPIAL FRAGMENT: Found under the desk.
COMPLETED SENTENCES: The dance books found under the desk were mine.
The dance books were found under the desk.

GERUND FRAGMENT: Teaching children to dance.
COMPLETED SENTENCES: Teaching children to dance can be rewarding.
She enjoys teaching children to dance.

INFINITIVE FRAGMENT: To see the new ballet.
COMPLETED SENTENCES: To see the new ballet is my goal.
I expect to see the new ballet.

Grammar and Style Tip

Sentence fragments are easier to identify when they appear out of context than when they appear with related sentences. Read each of your sentences individually, aloud if necessary, to isolate fragments.

2. Write on the chalkboard: *Dropped into the well; Into the well he dropped the stone; The stone dropped into the well; Into the well the stone.* Ask students to identify these as complete sentences or fragments and to defend their answers (F, Sent, Sent, F).

3. Remind students that participles, gerunds, and infinitives are verb forms used as other parts of speech. Be sure they understand that, if used as verbals, participial, gerund, and infinitive fragments still require a verb elsewhere in the sentence.

4. Write on the chalkboard: *learning to speak Spanish; to learn Spanish; fluency in Spanish.* Have students complete these fragments and then identify how they use each in their sentences. Point out that the same verb (e.g., *is a goal of mine*) could complete all three phrase fragments. Additionally, the first two fragments can be corrected by combining them with verbs (*I am learning . . . , I wanted to learn . . .*).

Customize for
Less Advanced Students

To identify and correct fragments and run-ons, students must be able to recognize prepositions, participles, gerunds, and infinitives and their phrases. Point out that *-ing* forms are not verbs unless they are used with helping verbs; alone, they perform other functions in sentences. Then, give students a series of examples and have them use each in original sentences:

eating chocolate

on the front page

to sing professionally

looking straight at me

Correcting Clause and Series Fragments

1. Caution students against writing a subordinate clause to answer a question; students should not begin an answer with "Because . . ." and fail to add an independent clause. Give students practice answering questions with complete sentences, such as this:

   Why did colonists throw tea into Boston harbor? (Because they were angry at the tax imposed by the King, colonists protested by throwing the tea overboard.)

2. Have volunteers suggest lists of related prepositional phrases and demonstrate how these may become series fragments. Then, have the class use the fragments in complete sentences.

3. Caution students against writing series fragments in answer to questions on exams. Point out that test examiners will expect complete sentences, not fragments.

Customize for
Spatial Learners

Have students design and draw charts that demonstrate each type of phrase fragment (prepositional, participial, gerund, infinitive) and another chart for each type of clause fragment (adjective, adverb, noun). Have students include an example of each kind of fragment, and tell them to leave space in their charts to add still more examples. Here are examples:

Phrase fragments

Prepositional: *on a fast train*

Participial: *bought for a few dollars*

Gerund: *growing flowers*

Infinitive: *to sing well*

Clause Fragments

Adjective: *that you gave me*

Adverb: *if they decide to leave soon*

Noun: *whoever is first*

When each student has completed a chart with one example for each type of fragment, have students exchange charts and add examples to each other's.

20.4

> **KEY CONCEPT** You may need to attach a subordinate clause to an independent clause to correct a fragment. ■

A subordinate clause contains a subject and a verb but does not express a complete thought. Therefore, it cannot stand alone as a sentence. Link the subordinate clause to an independent clause to make the sentence complete.

ADJECTIVE CLAUSE FRAGMENT:	Which was being performed outdoors.
COMPLETED SENTENCE:	I enjoyed watching the dance rehearsal, *which was being performed outdoors.*
ADVERB CLAUSE FRAGMENT:	After she practiced the new dance routine.
COMPLETED SENTENCE:	*After she practiced the new dance routine,* she was ready for the show.
NOUN CLAUSE FRAGMENT:	Whatever ballet we see in this theater.
COMPLETED SENTENCE:	We always enjoy *whatever ballet we see in this theater.*

A fragment does not always contain a small number of words. If a series of words seems long enough to be a sentence, you still need to make sure that it contains a subject and a verb and expresses a complete thought. It may be a long fragment masquerading as a sentence.

> **KEY CONCEPT** Some series fragments may look long enough to be sentences, but they may still not express a complete thought. ■

SERIES FRAGMENT:	After reading Steinbeck's novel, with its probing look at poverty and greed, in the style so typical of this master storyteller.
COMPLETED SENTENCE:	After reading Steinbeck's novel, with its probing look at poverty and greed, in the style so typical of this master storyteller, I was able to prepare an interesting oral presentation.

494 • Effective Sentences

Grammar and Style Tip

Do not confuse verbals and verbs! Fragments are often verbal phrases; make sure that you can differentiate between verbal phrases and verbs. Review Chapter 17 if you need extra help.

Exercise 28 Identifying and Correcting Fragments If an item contains only complete sentences, write *correct*. If the item contains a fragment, rewrite it to make a complete sentence.

EXAMPLE: Pleased by the applause of the audience. The ballerina danced an encore.

ANSWER: Pleased by the applause of the audience, the ballerina danced an encore.

1. An ice-skating champion at the age of ten. Nina Ananiashvili was encouraged to study in Moscow.
2. She studied dance at the Moscow Ballet School. From which she graduated in 1981.
3. To win a Gold Medal at the age of seventeen in an international competition, she had to work very hard.
4. After she graduated from the Moscow Ballet School, Nina fulfilled her dream of joining the Bolshoi Ballet.
5. Miss Ananiashvili has danced in the United States. With the New York City Ballet.
6. She made her debut with the Boston Ballet. In a performance of *Swan Lake*.
7. She has danced with troupes all over the world. Making the audience gasp in Finland, awing her peers in Portugal, and earning great respect in England.
8. Her debut with the Royal Ballet in *The Nutcracker*.
9. Such a great honor to be named a People's Artist of the Georgia Republic.
10. The first Russian ballerina to appear in a United States production of George Balanchine's *Apollo*.

▶ **More Practice**

Grammar Exercise Workbook
• pp. 61–62
On-line Exercise Bank
• Section 20.4
Go on-line:
PHSchool.com
Enter Web Code:
egk-1202

Interactive Textbook

Complete the exercise on-line! Exercise 28 is available on-line or on CD-ROM.

◀ **Critical Viewing**
Write a fragment describing these dancers. Then, correct your fragment by making it into a complete sentence. **[Describe]**

Avoiding Fragments and Run-ons • **495**

✓ ONGOING ASSESSMENT: Monitor and Reinforce

If students miss more than two items in Exercise 28, refer them to the following for additional practice.

In the Textbook	Print Resources	Technology
Section Review, Ex. 31, Section 20.4	*Grammar Exercise Workbook*, pp. 61–62	*On-Line Exercise Bank*, Section 20.4

Avoiding Run-on Sentences

1. As you use the chart to help students recognize methods of correcting run-ons, have them identify the grammatical structures involved. For instance, they should recognize that the phrase *in the gym* in the chart's first example could be included in either the first or second revised sentence.

2. Explain to students that correcting run-ons sometimes will involve adding words, such as conjunctions, and eliminating unnecessary or repetitious words.

Customize for
Linguistic Learners

Prepare for this activity by choosing an excerpt from a short story or nonfiction selection that students have recently read. Duplicate the excerpt and rewrite it by eliminating all punctuation marks. In class, distribute copies to students and have them reread the passage carefully, inserting punctuation where they believe it belongs. Have volunteers read their punctuated excerpts to the class (or place them on overheads). With the class, check these passages for fragments and run-on sentences. Students may find that the passage may be punctuated correctly in different ways. Discuss how different punctuation of the same passage can not only change the flow of ideas but its meaning as well. Finally, display the original passage (on handouts or on the overhead) with its punctuation in place.

20.4

Avoiding Run-on Sentences

A run-on sentence is two or more sentences capitalized and punctuated as if they were one.

▶ **KEY CONCEPT** Use punctuation and conjunctions to join or separate parts of a run-on sentence correctly. ■

There are two kinds of run-ons: *fused sentences*, which are two or more sentences joined with no punctuation, and *comma splices*, which have two or more sentences separated only by commas rather than by commas and conjunctions.

FUSED SENTENCE: The dancers practiced every day they were soon the best in the state.

COMMA SPLICE: Only one package arrived in the mail, the other items never came.

As with fragments, proofreading or reading your work aloud will usually help you spot run-ons. Once found, they can be corrected by adding punctuation and conjunctions or by rewording the sentences. Four ways to correct run-ons are described below.

FOUR WAYS TO CORRECT RUN-ONS	
With End Marks and Capitals	
Run-on: The dance was in full swing in the gym people crowded together.	*Sentence:* The dance was in full swing. In the gym, people crowded together.
With Commas and Conjunctions	
Run-on: The wrapping paper needed cutting we could not locate the scissors.	*Sentence:* The wrapping paper needed cutting, but we could not locate the scissors.
With Semicolons	
Run-on: Our city has many cultural activities, for example it hosts the National Ballet.	*Sentence:* Our city has many cultural activities; for example, it hosts the National Ballet.
By Rewriting	
Run-on: The horse show began late, someone had misplaced the registration forms.	*Sentence:* The horse show began late because someone had misplaced the registration forms. (Changed to complex sentence)
Run-on: We replaced the sparkplugs, the filter was also bad.	*Sentence:* We replaced the sparkplugs and the filter. (Changed to simple sentence with compound direct object)

496 • Effective Sentences

▶ **Exercise 29** Revising to Eliminate Run-on Sentences Correct each run-on. Use each of the four methods for correcting run-ons at least once. If an item is correct as written, write *correct*.

EXAMPLE: I want to study dance it is a beautiful art form.

ANSWER: I want to study dance, a beautiful art form.

1. Ballet as an art form began in Italy in the 1400's, this was during the Renaissance.
2. Many Italian dukes were successful businessmen they were willing to spend some of the money they earned to support the arts.
3. Each duke wanted to outdo the others, they sponsored elaborate song-and-dance performances.
4. Ballet moved from Italy to France Catherine de Medici, a Florence noblewoman, brought ballet with her when she became Queen of France in 1547.
5. Some people consider French King Louis XIV to be the father of modern ballet, he ruled in the seventeenth century.
6. Louis founded the *Academie Royale de Musique et de Danse* in 1661 it trained musicians and dancers to perform for the royal court.
7. In the mid-nineteenth century, the ballet centers of the world shifted from Paris and Milan, they moved to St. Petersburg and Moscow in Russia.
8. Marius Petipa, a Frenchman, Christian Johansson, a Swede, and Enrico Cecchetti, an Italian, developed a new style of ballet in Russia.
9. These three men worked with generations of Russian dancers the dancers developed the most precise techniques in the world.
10. Two of the world's most famous dancers began their careers in St. Petersburg, they were Anna Pavlova and Vaslav Nijinsky.

▲ **Critical Viewing**
In what ways does writing correct sentences relate to dancing ballet routines correctly?
[Compare]

▶ **More Practice**

Grammar Exercise Workbook
• pp. 63–64
On-line Exercise Bank
• Section 20.4
  Go on-line:
  PHSchool.com
  Enter Web Code:
  egk-1202

interactive **Textbook**

Complete the exercise on-line! Exercise 29 is available on-line or on CD-ROM.

Avoiding Fragments and Run-ons • **497**

Answer Key

▶ **Exercise 29**

Answers may vary; samples are given.

1. Ballet as an art form began in Renaissance Italy in the 1400's.
2. Many Italian dukes were successful businessmen. They were willing to spend some of the money they earned to support the arts.
3. Each duke wanted to outdo the others by sponsoring elaborate song-and-dance performances.
4. Ballet moved from Italy to France. Catherine de Medici, a Florence noblewoman, brought ballet with her when she became Queen of France in 1547.
5. Some people consider French King Louis XIV, who ruled in the seventeenth century, to be the father of modern ballet.
6. Louis founded the *Academie Royale de Musique et de Danse* in 1661; it trained musicians and dancers to perform for the royal court.
7. In the mid-nineteenth century, the ballet centers of the world shifted from Paris and Milan to St. Petersburg and Moscow in Russia.
8. correct
9. These three men worked with generations of Russian dancers, who developed the most precise techniques in the world.
10. Two of the world's most famous dancers, Anna Pavlova and Vaslav Nijinsky, began their careers in St. Petersburg.

Critical Viewing

Compare Possible answer: Errors in grammar and in dance can be both easy to miss by the performer and glaringly obvious to the audience; therefore, the rules must be learned and followed precisely.

☑ **ONGOING ASSESSMENT: Monitor and Reinforce**

If students miss more than two items in Exercise 29, refer them to the following for additional practice.

In the Textbook	Print Resources	Technology
Section Review, Ex. 32, Section 20.4	*Grammar Exercise Workbook*, pp. 63–64	*On-Line Exercise Bank*, Section 20.4

⏱ **TIME SAVERS!**

Answers on Transparencies Use the *Grammar Exercises Answers on Transparencies* for Chapter 20 to facilitate correction by students.

On-Line Exercise Bank Have students complete the exercises on computer. The Auto Check feature will grade their work for you!

Exercise 30

Sample answers are given.

Toe dancing was developed in the early nineteenth century, but it did not become widely used until the 1830's. Swedish-Italian ballerina Marie Taglioni demonstrated its potential for poetic effect. Toe dancing, also known as *pointe* work, is almost exclusively used by women, although male dancers may use it as well.

The term *line* in ballet refers to the configuration of the dancer's body, whether it is in motion or at rest. Good line is partly a matter of physique—a dancer is born with a certain physical stature—but it can also be developed and enhanced by training. In ballet, the arms, legs, head, and torso are expected to work together in harmony. Large movements of a whole limb are preferred over small isolated movements of individual body parts. Ballet is often described in terms of moving upward and outward; ideally, the dancer's limbs should appear to extend into infinity. Ballet dancers will carry out many movements and poses during a performance. Jumps and turns are important parts of a ballet as well and add to its excitement. All of these movements take years to learn, and they require extensive practice. With all of its intricate moves and romantic expressions, ballet is a beautiful art form.

Critical Viewing

Apply Possible answer: The ballerinas move gracefully as they extend their arms.

20.4

Exercise 30 Revising to Eliminate Fragments and Run-ons

Rewrite the two paragraphs below, correcting all fragments and run-ons. You may combine items and add or delete words to revise the paragraphs.

Toe dancing was developed in the early nineteenth century it did not become widely used until the 1830's. When Swedish-Italian ballerina Marie Taglioni demonstrated its potential for poetic effect. Also known as *pointe* work, Almost exclusively used by women, although male dancers may use it as well.

The term *line* in ballet refers to the configuration of the dancer's body. Whether it is in motion or at rest. Good line is partly a matter of physique a dancer is born with a certain physical stature, Can also be developed and enhanced by training. In ballet, the arms, legs, head, and torso expected to work together in harmony. Large movements of a whole limb are preferred. Over small isolated movements of individual body parts. Ballet is often described in terms of moving upward and outward, ideally, the dancer's limbs should appear to extend into infinity. Ballet dancers will carry out many movements and poses. During a performance. Jumps and turns an important part of a ballet as well and add to its excitement. All of these movements take years to learn, they require extensive practice. With all of its intricate moves and romantic expressions, a beautiful art form.

More Practice

Grammar Exercise Workbook
• pp. 61–64
On-line Exercise Bank
• Section 20.4
Go on-line:
PHSchool.com
Enter Web Code:
egk-1202

▼ **Critical Viewing** Correct the following fragment by adding an independent clause: *as they extend their arms.* **[Apply]**

498 • Effective Sentences

☑ **ONGOING ASSESSMENT: Monitor and Reinforce**

If students have difficulty with Exercise 30, refer them to the following for additional practice.

In the Textbook	Print Resources	Technology
Section Review, Ex. 33, Section 20.4	*Grammar Exercise Workbook,* pp. 61–64	*On-Line Exercise Bank,* Section 20.4

Hands-on Grammar

Fragment Completion

Practice correcting sentence fragments by doing this activity.

First, cut twelve pieces of paper approximately 3" x 2 1/2" each.
On six of the pieces, write the following fragments:

with his hand in the cookie jar
the one waiting nearby
the food eaten by us
on the kitchen table
a hurricane with fierce winds and rain
angered by the injustice of the remark

On the other six pieces of paper, write the following:

she argued with her friend
the forecaster predicted
I put the groceries
was prepared by my aunt
the child was caught
was the bus downtown

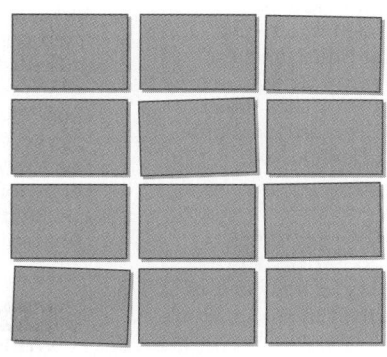

Then, shuffle the pieces of
paper around and arrange them
face down, as shown in the drawing. Take turns with a classmate
trying to match a fragment from
the first group with something
from the second group that will
complete it and make sense. The
first person turns over two pieces of paper. If they work together,
the person removes them and tries two more. If they do not work
together, it is the next person's turn. Continue like this until all
fragments have been completed.

Find It in Your Reading Fragments do not normally occur in
formal writing. However, they often do appear in the dialogue of a
story. Look through a story you have read, and identify six fragments. Write completions for the fragments.

Find It in Your Writing Review some writing from your portfolio
to see if you have used sentence fragments. If you find any, correct
them by making them complete sentences.

Hands-on Grammar

*Teaching Resources: Hands-on
Grammar Activity Book, Ch. 20*

1. If you wish to do this activity in
   class, bring in scissors and
   construction paper for students to
   use.

2. Have students work with a partner
   to combine the pieces into
   sentences. The following are likely
   responses:

   *The child was caught with his
   hand in the cookie jar.*

   *The one waiting nearby was the
   bus downtown.*

   *The food eaten by us was
   prepared by my aunt.*

   *I put the groceries on the kitchen
   table.*

   *The forecaster predicted a
   hurricane with fierce winds and
   rain.*

   *Angered by the injustice of the
   remark, she argued with her
   friend.*

3. When students have finished,
   have them compare their results
   with those of other students.

Find It in Your Reading

Students might do this activity alone
or with a partner.

Find It in Your Writing

Students might analyze their writing
to note the kinds of fragments they
most often write. They should then
work out strategies to avoid these
errors.

☑ ONGOING ASSESSMENT: Assess Mastery

Use the following resources to assess student mastery of avoiding fragments and run-ons.

In the Textbook	Technology
Chapter Review, Ex. 59	*Writing and Grammar* Interactive Text, Section 20.4, Section Review; *On-Line Exercise Bank,* Section 20.4

⏱ TIME SAVERS!

✋ **Hands-on Grammar**
Use the Hands-on Grammar
activity sheet for Chapter 20 to
facilitate this activity.

Section Review

Each of these exercises correlates to the instruction on avoiding fragments and run-ons, pages 492–496. The exercises may be used for more practice, for reteaching, or for review of the key concepts presented.

Answer Key

> **Exercise 31**

Answers may vary; samples are given.

George Balanchine, a Russian-born American choreographer, is one of the foremost choreographers in the history of ballet. The son of a composer, Balanchine was born in Saint Petersburg, Russia. . . . In 1933, Balanchine moved to New York City, where he co-founded the School of American Ballet and the American Ballet Company. . . .

> **Exercise 32**

Answers will vary; samples are given.

1. The Bolshoi Ballet is one of the oldest Russian ballet companies. It is famous . . .
2. In the 1770's, the Bolshoi Ballet began with classes given at a Moscow orphanage.
3. The company gave its first performance in 1776, and it . . .
4. In the 1950's, the company began to tour the world, entertaining and impressing . . .
5. The two dancers Rudolph Nureyev and Margot Fonteyn became celebrities; they were . . .

> **Exercise 33**

Answers will vary; samples are given.

Ballet consists . . . of the feet, which form . . . ballet steps. Corresponding . . . the arms, which should . . . elbows. All of the movements . . . vertical axis, and all . . . aligned. Ballet dancers . . . gravity; they jump . . . positions. Ballet possesses . . . steps, including . . . leg position. Although steps . . . are different, neither is easier . . . other. All require . . .

> **Exercise 34**

Find It in Your Writing
Suggest that explanations be entered in the left margins of students' compositions for future reference.

GRAMMAR EXERCISES 31–35

> **Exercise 31** Proofreading to Eliminate Fragments Read the following paragraph. Rewrite any sentences that are fragments.

George Balanchine, a Russian-born American choreographer, one of the foremost choreographers in the history of ballet. The son of a composer, Balanchine, born in Saint Petersburg, Russia. In 1925, while touring Europe with his small ballet company, he joined the Diaghilev Company as a choreographer. In 1933, Balanchine moved to New York City. Where he co-founded the School of American Ballet and the American Ballet Company. He also helped create the New York City Ballet, which performed new, exciting versions of *The Nutcracker* and *Don Quixote.*

> **Exercise 32** Identifying and Correcting Run-on Sentences Correct the following run-ons. Try to use each of the four methods described in the chart on page 496.

1. The Bolshoi Ballet is one of the oldest Russian ballet companies, it is famous for its dramatic performances of classic ballets.
2. The Bolshoi Ballet began with classes given at a Moscow orphanage, the classes were held in the 1770's.
3. The Petrovsky Theatre Ballet gave its first performance in 1776 it became the Bolshoi Ballet in 1825.
4. In the 1950's, the company began to tour the world, it entertained and impressed audiences around the globe.
5. The two dancers Rudolf Nureyev and Margot Fonteyn became celebrities, they were featured on magazine covers worldwide.

> **Exercise 33** Revising to Eliminate Sentence Errors Rewrite the paragraph below, correcting all fragments and run-ons as needed.

Ballet consists of five numbered positions of the feet. Which form the basis of almost all ballet steps. Corresponding positions exist for the arms. Which should generally be held with gently curved elbows. All of the movements of the dancer's limbs flow from the body's vertical axis, all of the dancer's body parts must be correctly aligned. Ballet dancers must often resist gravity, they jump and twist in difficult but graceful positions. Ballet possesses many such steps it even includes those that require the dancers, while in midair, to turn, beat their legs or feet together, or change their leg position. Steps for male and female dancers different. Neither easier than the other. Require constant practice and repetition.

> **Exercise 34** Find It in Your Writing Look through your portfolio to see if you have used fragments or run-ons in any compositions. Rewrite the incorrect sentences, and explain how you corrected your errors.

> **Exercise 35** Writing Application Write a brief narrative about a live performance you once saw. Write complete sentences that use varied structures to relate information about the performance. Be sure to include details about the performance, the performer(s), and perhaps even the audience.

> **Exercise 35**

Writing Application
Encourage students to add their narratives to their portfolios.

Section 20.6 Faulty Parallelism

Good writers try to present a series of ideas in similar grammatical structures so that they will read smoothly. If one element in a series is not parallel with the others, the result may be jarring and its meaning may be unclear.

Recognizing the Correct Use of Parallelism

To present a series of ideas of equal importance, you should use parallel grammatical structures.

▶ **KEY CONCEPT** *Parallelism* involves presenting equal ideas in words, phrases, or clauses of similar types. ■

Parallel grammatical structures may be two or more words of the same part of speech, two or more phrases of the same type, two or more clauses of the same type, or even two or more sentences of the same type.

PARALLEL WORDS:	The surfer looked *strong, fit,* and *agile.*
PARALLEL PHRASES:	The greatest feeling I know is *to ride a giant wave flawlessly* and *to have all my friends watch me enviously.*
PARALLEL CLAUSES:	The surfboard *that you recommended* and *that my brother wants* is on sale.
PARALLEL SENTENCES:	*It couldn't be, of course. It could never, never be.* —Dorothy Parker

Examine the following paragraph, which begins *A Tale of Two Cities* by Charles Dickens, a novel about the French Revolution. Notice how the parallel structures set up vivid contrasts.

EXAMPLE: It was the best of times, it was the worst of times, it was the age of wisdom, it was the age of foolishness, it was the epoch of belief, it was the epoch of incredulity, it was the season of Light, it was the season of Darkness, it was the spring of hope, it was the winter of despair, we had everything before us, we had nothing before us, we were all going direct to Heaven, we were all going direct the other way—in short, the period was so far like the present period, that some of its noisiest authorities insisted on its being received, for good or for evil, in the superlative degree of comparison only.

Theme: Surfing

In this section, you will learn how to place equal ideas in sentences so that they are balanced correctly. The examples and exercises are about surfing and surfboards.

**Cross-Curricular Connection:
Physical Education**

▼ Critical Viewing
Think of three equal adjectives or phrases that you might use in a sentence describing this surfer or his actions. **[Analyze]**

Faulty Parallelism • **505**

PREPARE and ENGAGE

Interest GRABBER Challenge students to find the error in this sentence:

Steve likes hiking for long distances and to climb mountains.

To help students recognize the structures that need to be parallel, ask them what two things Steve likes. Point out that the first (*hiking for long distances*) is a gerund phrase but that the second is not. Ask a volunteer to change *to climb* into a gerund (*climbing*) and then to complete the gerund phrase (*climbing mountains*).

Activate Prior Knowledge

Write on the chalkboard the following constructions with underlines for missing structures:

Good speech must be audible, logical, and ___.

To try hard is more important than ___.

Remind students that correct parallelism relies on equal structures, and ask them for suggestions on how to complete the sentences.

TEACH

Step-by-Step Teaching Guide

Recognizing the Correct Use of Parallelism

1. Tell students that they should take special care to maintain correct parallelism in compound sentences and sentences with lists (structures with two or more words, phrases, or clauses) because these are structures that can easily go awry.

2. Write on the chalkboard: *I packed my bags, grabbed my ticket, and run for a taxi.* Have students identify the error (faulty phrase parallelism) and offer suggestions for correcting it.

Critical Viewing

Analyze Possible answer: He is standing on the board, balancing carefully, and riding the wave.

⏱ TIME AND RESOURCE MANAGER

Resources
Print: *Grammar Exercise Workbook,* pp. 67–68; *Grammar Exercises Answers on Transparencies,* Ch. 20
Technology: *Writing and Grammar* Interactive Text, Section 20.6; *On-Line Exercise Bank,* Section 20.6

Using the Full Student Edition	Using the Handbook 🄷
• Work through key concepts, pp. 505–507. • Assign Exercises 43–44 and review in class. • Read and discuss Grammar in Literature, p. 508.	• Work through key concepts, pp. 357–359. • Assign Exercises 43–44 and review in class. • Read and discuss Grammar in Literature, p. 360.

Answer Key

Step-by-Step Teaching Guide

Correcting Faulty Parallelism in Series

1. Remind students that coordinating and correlative conjunctions are frequently used to form a series. Use the example on the bottom of this page to demonstrate how word placement is very important when connecting two ideas with a correlative conjunction.

2. Write on the chalkboard: *I discovered that we had missed two answers, but it didn't affect the results.* Have students identify the missing word (*that*) and explain the error (*noun clause + independent clause* rather than *noun clause + noun clause*).

3. Use the chart on the following student page for examples of correcting faulty parallelism.

Customize for
Less Advanced Students

Distribute a worksheet of two groups of sentences, the first group containing parallel structures and the second nonparallel. Have students underline the parallel structures in the first group before assigning the second. As you review their answers, ask students to identify the kinds of parallel structures in each (prepositional phrases, infinitive phrases, adverb clauses). Then assign the second group of sentences. Again have students underline and identify the structures that should be parallel before rewriting each.

20.6

Exercise 43 Recognizing Parallel Structures Write the parallel structures in the following sentences. Then, identify each as *words*, *phrases*, *clauses*, or *sentences*.

EXAMPLE: They leaped to their feet, sprinted toward the water, and jumped onto their boards.

ANSWER: leaped to their feet, sprinted toward the water, jumped onto their boards (phrases)

1. People can surf with their bodies or on their surfboards.
2. Lying, kneeling, or standing on a surfboard requires practice.
3. Because it can be enjoyed in many areas and because it is inexpensive, surfing is a very popular sport.
4. Surfing requires no formal training, but it requires practice.
5. Riding waves takes skill, stamina, and agility.

Correcting Faulty Parallelism

Faulty parallelism occurs when a writer uses unequal grammatical structures to express related ideas.

KEY CONCEPT Correct a sentence containing faulty parallelism by rewriting it so that each parallel idea is expressed in the same grammatical structure. ■

Faulty parallelism can involve words, phrases, and clauses in a series or in comparisons.

Nonparallel Words, Phrases, and Clauses in a Series

Always check a series of ideas in your writing for parallelism. If, for example, you begin a series with a prepositional phrase, make all the items in the series prepositional phrases.

The chart at the top of the next page presents some nonparallel structures and shows how they can be rephrased to restore smoothness and clarity to the sentence. Notice how coordinating conjunctions (such as *and*, *but*, *or*) often connect the items in a series and can signal you to check the connected items for parallelism.

Another potential problem to note involves correlative conjunctions, such as *both . . . and* or *not only . . . but also*. Though these conjunctions connect two related items, writers sometimes misplace or split the first part of the conjunction. The result is faulty parallelism.

NONPARALLEL: Our lifeguard not only won the local surfing championship but also the state title.

PARALLEL: Our lifeguard won not only the local surfing championship but also the state title.

506 • Effective Sentences

More Practice

Grammar Exercise Workbook
• pp. 67–68
On-line Exercise Bank
• Section 20.6
Go on-line:
PHSchool.com
Enter Web Code:
egk-1202

Get instant feedback! Exercise 43 is available on-line or on CD-ROM.

✓ **ONGOING ASSESSMENT: Monitor and Reinforce**

If students have difficulty with Exercise 43 or 44, refer them to the following for additional practice.

In the Textbook	Print Resources	Technology
Section Review, Ex. 45–46, Section 20.6	*Grammar Exercise Workbook*, pp. 67–68	*On-Line Exercise Bank*, Section 20.6

CORRECTING FAULTY PARALLELISM IN A SERIES

Nonparallel Structures	Corrected Sentences
GERUND GERUND *Planning, drafting,* and NOUN *revision* are three steps in the writing process.	GERUND GERUND *Planning, drafting,* and GERUND *revising* are three steps in the writing process.
INFIN I could not wait *to try my* PHRASE INFIN *new surfboard, to catch* PHRASE PART PHRASE *some waves,* and *visiting the* beach.	INFIN I could not wait *to try my* PHRASE INFIN *new surfboard, to catch* PHRASE INFIN *some waves,* and *to visit the* PHRASE beach.
NOUN Some people feel *that surfing* CLAUSE *is not a sport,* but *it* INDEP CLAUSE *requires athleticism.*	NOUN Some experts feel *that surfing* CLAUSE *is not a sport* but NOUN CLAUSE *that it requires athleticism.*

Nonparallel Words, Phrases, and Clauses in Comparisons

As the old saying goes, you cannot compare apples with oranges. In writing comparisons, you generally should compare a phrase with the same type of phrase and a clause with the same type of clause. Furthermore, you should make sure your ideas themselves, as well as the structures you use to express them, are logically parallel.

CORRECTING FAULTY PARALLELISM IN COMPARISONS

Nonparallel Structures	Correlated Sentences
NOUN Most people prefer *corn* to GERUND PHRASE *eating Brussels sprouts.*	NOUN Most people prefer *corn* to NOUN *Brussels sprouts.*
PREP PHRASE I left my job *at 7:00 P.M.* PART rather than *stopping work* PHRASE *at 5:00 P.M.*	PREP PHRASE I left my job *at 7:00 P.M.* PREP rather than *at the usual* PHRASE *5:00 P.M.*
S PREP PHRASE *I* delight *in foggy days* as S much as sunny *days* delight DO other *people.*	S PREP PHRASE *I* delight *in foggy days* as S much as other *people* delight PREP PHRASE *in sunny days.*

⚙ Grammar and Style Tip

You may want to use parallel structure for emphasis, for emotional effect, or for humor. An unexpected item at the end of a series can have a significant impact. Consider James Thurber's take on a familiar proverb: "Early to bed and early to rise makes a man healthy, wealthy, and dead."

Correcting Faulty Parallelism in Comparisons

1. Explain to students that the word *comparison* is derived from the Latin verb *comparare,* which means "to match." Then remind them that the elements being compared must match or be parallel. This rule applies to ideas as well as to grammatical structures: clauses, phrases, and words.

2. As you work with the examples in the chart, point out that correcting nonparallel comparisons often involves omitting unnecessary words or adding words to make the parallel structures match.

3. Write on the chalkboard: *I prefer studying faulty parallelism to the lesson on faulty coordination.* Have students identify the error and create at least two examples of correctly correlated sentences.

🖉 STANDARDIZED TEST PREPARATION WORKSHOP

Grammar and Usage Many standardized tests require students to revise errors in composition. Write the following on the chalkboard, and ask students to identify the correct answer.

Dear Mr. Smithers:

[A] *We have received your letter and request for information about our college.* [B] *Having expressed an interest in Thompson College, we have enclosed the requested materials along with an application form.* [C] *Our first open house will be held on May 5th, and we are looking forward to meeting you.*

Which sentence, if any, in the above passage contains a common usage error?

A	B
C	D No error

The correct answer is **B**. The participial phrase *Having expressed an interest in Thompson College,* is a dangling modifier; a word it would logically modify does not appear in the sentence. The sentence should begin: *Because you have expressed an interest in . . .*

Exercise 44

Answers may vary; samples are given.

1. . . . shaped by hand and covered by a shell . . .
2. Individual surfboards vary in length, width, and weight.
3. Top professional surfers use shortboards. Amateur surfers usually use longboards.
4. . . . three feet longer, three inches wider, and twice as heavy.
5. . . . to provide stability and to enhance performance.
6. . . . for recreation rather than for competition.
7. . . . the size of the wave, the distance of the ride, and the difficulty of their maneuvers.
8. . . . can take place not only at the shore but also in . . .
9. Paddling out to waves and catching waves, a surfer . . .
10. Turning sharply, gaining momentum, and riding gently are . . .

Step-by-Step Teaching Guide

Grammar in Literature

1. Read the passage aloud, emphasizing the fluid rhythm created by the parallel elements.
2. Have students identify the parallel elements in each sentence (parallel adjectives and participial phrases; parallel predicates).

More About the Author

India's Mohandas K. Gandhi began to work for social and political justice in the early 1900's in South Africa. He later led his country's fight for independence from British rule. His pacifist philosophy and methods influenced future activists, including Martin Luther King, Jr.

Critical Viewing

Connect Possible answer:
This tale is of wave and rock. It tells
How waves pound rocks, sweep over them,
Punish them, wear them away.
Incessant pounding through centuries
Turns rock to boulder, to stone, to pebble, to sand.

20.6

Exercise 44 Correcting Faulty Parallelism Rewrite each sentence to correct the faulty parallelism.

EXAMPLE: On the beach, they not only play volleyball but also soccer.

ANSWER: On the beach, they play not only soccer but also volleyball.

1. Surfboards are made of a plastic foam core that is shaped by hand and then a shell of fiberglass and resin covers it.
2. Individual surfboards vary in length, width, and how much they weigh.
3. Top professional surfers use shortboards; longboards are usually used by amateur surfers.
4. Compared to shortboards, longboards are three feet longer, three inches wider, and they weigh twice as much.
5. The bottom of a surfboard has fins to provide stability and for enhancing performance.
6. Most surfers use longboards for recreation rather than competing with them.
7. In competition, surfers are judged on the size of the wave, the distance of the ride, and how difficult their maneuvers are.
8. Surfing competitions not only can take place at the shore but also in artificial indoor wavepools.
9. Paddling out to waves and to catch a wave, a surfer prepares for competition.
10. Turning sharply, gaining momentum, and to gently ride are a few surfing maneuvers.

GRAMMAR IN LITERATURE

from **Defending Nonviolent Resistance**
Mohandas K. Gandhi

Notice how the parallel elements (in blue italics) in these lines from a speech by Mohandas K. Gandhi help put forth his argument in a clear, balanced, and eloquent style.

I gave the government my *voluntary* and *hearty* cooperation, ...

Consequently, when the existence of the empire was threatened in 1899 by the Boer challenge, I *offered my services* to it, *raised a volunteer ambulance corps*, and *served at several actions* that took place for the relief of Ladysmith.

508 • Effective Sentences

More Practice

Grammar Exercise Workbook
• pp. 67–68
On-line Exercise Bank
• Section 20.6
Go on-line:
PHSchool.com
Enter Web Code:
egk-1202

▼ Critical Viewing Write a short poem describing in parallel structure the ocean waves in this photograph. [Connect]

☑ **ONGOING ASSESSMENT: Assess Mastery**

Use the following resources to assess student mastery of faulty parallelism.

In the Textbook	Technology
Chapter Review, Ex. 61	*On-Line Exercise Bank*, Section 20.6

Section Review

GRAMMAR EXERCISES 45–49

> **Exercise 45** Recognizing Parallel Structures Write the parallel structures in the following sentences. Then, identify each as *words*, *phrases*, *clauses*, or *sentences*.

1. Duke Kahanamoku surfed fast. He swam fast. He sailed fast.
2. Duke Kahanamoku, who broke a world record in freestyle swimming in 1912 and who was a talented surfer, popularized surfing in Hawaii.
3. Kahanamoku promoted, popularized, and expanded the sport of surfing.
4. Kahanamoku is credited with inventing windsurfing and perfecting wakesurfing.
5. Teaching water safety, swimming to break records, and acting in movies, Kahanamoku traveled all over the world.

> **Exercise 46** Revising to Eliminate Faulty Parallelism Rewrite each sentence to correct any nonparallel structures.

1. In the 1950's, some people said surfers were illiterate, lazy, and they were not responsible.
2. Surfing in the California sun had a bad image. A better image was working in an office.
3. By the 1960's, however, surfing became more popular, and more respect was given to surfers.
4. A counterculture emerged that admired, emulated, and was promoting the surfing lifestyle.
5. This lifestyle was easygoing, youth centered, and loved to have fun.
6. Popular music in the 1960's was about cars, love, and they sang about surfing.
7. Watching surfing movies, singing surfing songs, and to have a tan were very popular.

8. Bands that sang surfing songs and they looked like surfers grew famous.
9. Young people on the West Coast, in the Midwest, and who lived in the East all listened to surfing songs on the radio.
10. The surfing look was featured in television ads. To have a lifestyle of a surfer was considered admirable.

> **Exercise 47** Find It in Your Reading Notice parallel structures in these lines from the poem "The Seafarer":

But there isn't a man on earth so proud, / So born to greatness, so bold with his youth, / Grown so brave, or so graced by God, / That he feels no fear as the sails unfurl, / Wondering what Fate has willed and will do.

> **Exercise 48** Find It in Your Writing Look through your portfolio for sentences in which you have presented a series of two or more related ideas. Correct any sentences with faulty parallelism.

> **Exercise 49** Writing Application Follow the instructions in parentheses to expand each sentence, making sure the new sentences contain parallel structures.

1. Riding the wave, Mandy was thrilled. (Add another participial phrase.)
2. I surfed in Hawaii last spring. (Add another independent clause.)
3. The surfer caught a wave. (Add three adjectives.)
4. I love surfing. (Compare surfing to something else.)
5. Before wiping out, Ted rode on top of the wave. (Add two more verbs with prepositional phrases.)

Section Review

Each of these exercises correlates to the instruction on faulty parallelism, pages 505–507. The exercises may be used for more practice, for reteaching, or for review of the key concepts presented. Answers for all chapter exercises are available in *Grammar Exercises Answers on Transparencies* in your Teaching Resources.

Answer Key

> **Exercise 45**

1. Duke Kahanamoku surfed fast. He swam fast. He sailed fast.—sentences
2. who broke a world record in freestyle swimming in 1912, who was a talented surfer—clauses
3. promoted, popularized, expanded—words
4. inventing windsurfing, perfecting wakesurfing—phrases
5. Teaching water safety, swimming to break records, acting in movies—phrases

> **Exercise 46**

Answers may vary; samples are given.

1. In the 1950's, some people said surfers were illiterate, lazy, and irresponsible.
2. Surfing in the California sun had a bad image; working in an office had a better image.
3. By the 1960's, however, surfing became more popular and surfers became more respectable.
4. A counterculture emerged that admired, emulated, and promoted the surfing lifestyle.
5. This lifestyle was easygoing, youth centered, and fun loving.
6. Popular music in the 1960's was about cars, love, and surfing.
7. Watching surfing movies, singing surfing songs, and having a tan were very popular.
8. Bands that sang surfing songs and looked like surfers grew famous.
9. Young people on the West Coast, in the Midwest, and in the East all listened to surfing songs on the radio.
10. The surfing look was featured in television ads. The surfing lifestyle was considered admirable.

continued

Answer Key continued

> **Exercise 47**

Find It in Your Reading
Parallel structures include (1) *so proud/ so born/ so bold,* perhaps including *grown so brave/ so graced by God;* (2) *has willed/ will do.*

> **Exercise 48**

Find It in Your Writing
Challenge students to add parallel structures to their writing.

> **Exercise 49**

Writing Application
Answers will vary. Sample answers:

1. Riding the wave and feeling the surge of the ocean, Mandy was thrilled.
2. I surfed in Hawaii last spring, and the waves were the biggest I have ever seen.
3. The fit, tan, muscular surfer caught a wave.
4. I love surfing more than skiing.
5. Before wiping out, Ted rode on top of the wave, swooped down its face, and shot through the tube.

Interest GRABBER Write the following sentence on the chalkboard:

I felt comfortable lying in the sun, and the ocean was too cold for swimming.

Let students know the clauses are joined incorrectly because the two ideas do not follow logically. Ask how these two independent clauses can be joined more logically (change *and* to *but*).

Activate Prior Knowledge

Write the headings *Coordinating Conjunction* and *Subordinating Conjunction* on the chalkboard and ask students to recall examples. Practice correct coordination by having students join structures two ways. Example:

Coordinated: Beagles and collies make good pets.

Subordinated: Beagles are smaller than collies are.

TEACH

Step-by-Step Teaching Guide

Recognizing Faulty Coordination

1. Remind students that they use coordination when they join independent clauses with a coordinating conjunction. (Discuss other options for combining sentences.)

2. Explain that the principle of coordination is similar to that of parallelism.

Critical Viewing

Describe Possible answer: The planes have teeth painted on their noses, and they have sunbursts painted on their wings.

Integrating Vocabulary

Latin Roots The prefix *co-* is a Latin prefix derived from the Latin *cum*, meaning "with." It generally signifies "together, in conjunction, or jointly." Ask students to think of words that begin with the prefix *co-* that represent various parts of speech: verb (*cooperate*), adjective (*cooperative*), adverb (*cogently*), noun (*co-worker*).

510 • 362⊞

Section 20.7 # Faulty Coordination

When two or more independent clauses of unequal importance are joined by *and*, the result is *faulty coordination*.

Recognizing Faulty Coordination

To *coordinate* means to "place side by side in equal rank." Two independent clauses that are joined by the coordinating conjunction *and*, therefore, should have equal rank.

▶ **KEY CONCEPT** Use *and* or other coordinating conjunctions only to connect ideas of equal importance. ■

The following example shows ideas of equal importance joined by the conjunction *and*.

CORRECT COORDINATION: Otis designed an airplane, and Oliver built it.

Sometimes, however, writers carelessly use *and* to join independent clauses that either should not be joined or should be joined in another way so that the real relationship between the clauses will be clear. The faulty coordination puts all the ideas on the same level of importance, even though logically they should not be.

FAULTY COORDINATION: Production of aircraft accelerated in World War II, *and* aircraft became a decisive factor in the war.
I didn't do well, *and* the race was very easy.
The dog looked ferocious, *and* it was snarling and snapping at me.

Occasionally, writers will also string together so many ideas with *and*'s that the reader is left breathless.

STRINGY SENTENCE: The plane that flew over the field did a few dips and turns, *and* the people on the ground craned their necks to watch, *and* everyone laughed and cheered, *and* then the pilot made one more circle of the field and landed, *and* he walked toward us, *and* everyone cheered even louder.

510 • Effective Sentences

▲ **Critical Viewing** In a sentence that describes these planes, use a coordinating conjunction to connect ideas of equal importance. **[Describe]**

Theme: World War II Planes

In this section, you will learn how to place unrelated ideas properly in sentences. The examples and exercises are about World War II fighter planes.

Cross-Curricular Connection: Social Studies

⏱ TIME AND RESOURCE MANAGER

Resources
Print: *Grammar Exercise Workbook*, pp. 69–70; *Grammar Exercises Answers on Transparencies*, Ch. 20
Technology: *Writing and Grammar* Interactive Text, Section 20.7; *On-Line Exercise Bank*, Section 20.7

Using the Full Student Edition	Using the Handbook⊞
• Work through key concepts, pp. 510–512. • Assign Exercises 50–51 and review in class.	• Work through key concepts, pp. 362–364. • Assign Exercises 50–51 and review in class.

▶ **Exercise 50** Identifying Faulty Coordination For the sentences in which *and* is used improperly, write *faulty*. For the sentences in which *and* is used properly, write correct.

EXAMPLE: He builds model airplanes, and he displays them in shows.

ANSWER: correct

1. When World War II began, private airlines expanded their facilities and trained thousands of students, and these new pilots became the backbone of the army, navy, and marine air operation.
2. Aircraft designed for personal use were refitted for military use, and civilian pilots were trained for military duty.
3. Important advances were made in the development of planes for bombing and combat, and small aircraft were produced rapidly.
4. American military aircraft were in action on all fronts, and the number of people employed in the American aviation industry totaled 450,000.
5. At the end of the war, airplane production reached an all-time high, and air warfare increased in intensity.

Correcting Faulty Coordination

Faulty coordination can be corrected in the following ways:

▶ **KEY CONCEPT** One way to correct faulty coordination is to put unrelated ideas into separate sentences. ■

When faulty coordination occurs in a sentence in which the independent clauses are not closely related, separate the clauses and omit the coordinating conjunction.

| FAULTY COORDINATION: | Production of aircraft accelerated in World War II, *and* aircraft became a decisive factor in the war. |
| CORRECTED SENTENCES: | Production of aircraft accelerated in World War II. Aircraft became a decisive factor in the war. |

▶ **More Practice**

Grammar Exercise Workbook
• pp. 69–70
On-line Exercise Bank
• Section 20.7
   Go on-line:
   PHSchool.com
   Enter Web Code:
   egk-1202

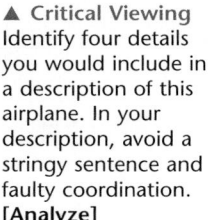

▲ **Critical Viewing** Identify four details you would include in a description of this airplane. In your description, avoid a stringy sentence and faulty coordination. **[Analyze]**

Faulty Coordination • 511

Answer Key

▶ **Exercise 50**

1. correct
2. correct
3. faulty
4. faulty
5. correct

Critical Viewing

Analyze The plane has a propeller, a streamlined body, slightly angled wings, and fixed wheels.

Step-by-Step Teaching Guide

Correcting Faulty Coordination

1. Direct students' attention to the example of faulty coordination. Be sure they understand that the ideas in the sentence are not closely related. Explain that the example of faulty coordination is grammatically correct, in a technical sense, but that the two ideas are sufficiently apart in meaning that creating two independent sentences keeps the reader from making more of a logical connection than is intended.

2. Have students explain why it would not be appropriate to correct the faulty coordination by replacing the comma and coordinating conjunction with a semicolon (the ideas aren't closely related).

Integrating Workplace Skills

Sequence Good sentence coordination requires students to understand the sequence of ideas of greater and lesser importance. Recipes and instructions are often written in numbered steps, which is a form of coordination. Ask students to bring a recipe or a paragraph of instructions to class. Have them rewrite the recipe or instructions, eliminating the numbers and scrambling the sentences. Then ask them to exchange papers and reorder the sentences logically. Have them use transitions that show time sequence. Write these transitions on the chalkboard for reference: *after, at the same time, before, during, earlier, finally, first, second, third, in a few minutes, later, meanwhile, next, then.*

☑ **ONGOING ASSESSMENT: Monitor and Reinforce**

If students miss more than one item in Exercise 50 or 51, refer them to the following for additional practice.

In the Textbook	Print Resources	Technology
Section Review, Ex. 52–54, Section 20.7	*Grammar Exercise Workbook,* pp. 69–70	*On-Line Exercise Bank,* Section 20.7

Using Clauses and Phrases to Correct Faulty Coordination

1. Give students the example from the previous page: *Production of aircraft accelerated in World War II, and aircraft became a decisive factor in the war.* Ask them to try to fix the faulty coordination using a clause or phrase. (*Production of aircraft accelerated as aircraft became a decisive factor in the war.*) Point out that they have converted a compound sentence into a complex sentence and that the revision shows a more meaningful (subordinate) relationship between the ideas.

2. Remind students that stringy sentences are not necessarily examples of faulty coordination, nor are they always run-on sentences. Discuss how the corrected examples on this page have become clearer.

Answer Key

> **Exercise 51**

Answers may vary; samples are given.

1. High-speed offense bombers were developed during the 1930's, including America's long-range Boeing B-17 Flying Fortress.
2. Between 1935 and 1936, Great Britain and Germany developed prototypes of more advanced fighters, including the Hawker Hurricane, the Supermarine Spitfire, and the Messerschmitt Bf 109.
3. In 1939, the German *Luftwaffe* (air force) defeated the Polish air force and bombed major Polish cities, beginning World War II.
4. In 1940, Denmark, Norway, Holland, Belgium, and France were defeated by Germany's troops, who were helped largely through air support.
5. The Battle of Britain, when Britain's Royal Air Force defeated Germany's *Luftwaffe,* was a turning point in World War II.

20.7

> **KEY CONCEPT** You can correct faulty coordination by putting less important ideas into subordinate clauses or phrases. ■

If one independent clause is less important or subordinate to the other, turn it into a subordinate clause.

| FAULTY COORDINATION: | I didn't do well, *and* the race was very easy. |
| CORRECTED SENTENCE: | I didn't do well, even though the race was very easy. |

You can also reduce a less important idea to a phrase—that is, change the compound sentence into a simple sentence.

| FAULTY COORDINATION: | The dog looked ferocious, *and* it was snarling and snapping at me. |
| CORRECTED SENTENCE: | Snarling and snapping at me, the dog looked ferocious. |

Stringy sentences should be broken up and revised using any of the three methods just described. Experiment with a few possibilities before making a choice. Following is one way that the stringy sentence presented earlier can be revised.

| REVISION OF A STRINGY SENTENCE: | The plane that flew over the field did a few dips and turns. Craning their necks to watch, the people on the ground laughed and cheered. The pilot made one more circle of the field and landed. Everyone cheered even louder when he walked toward us. |

> **Exercise 51** Correcting Faulty Coordination Rewrite each sentence, correcting the faulty coordination.
> 1. High-speed offense bombers were developed during the 1930's, and America's long-range Boeing B-17 Flying Fortress was also developed.
> 2. Between 1935 and 1936, Great Britain and Germany developed prototypes of more advanced fighters, and these fighters included the Hawker Hurricane, Supermarine Spitfire, and the Messerschmitt Bf 109.
> 3. The German Luftwaffe (air force) defeated the Polish Air Force and bombed major Polish cities, and World War II began in 1939.
> 4. Denmark, Norway, Holland, Belgium, and France were defeated by Germany's troops in 1940, and the troops were helped largely through air support.
> 5. The Battle of Britain was a turning point in World War II, and Britain's Royal Air Force defeated Germany's Luftwaffe.

512 • Effective Sentences

✿ Grammar and Style Tip

Stringy sentences are connected not only by *and; so* is also often overused as a connector. Be careful not to turn a series of sentences that are causally related into a stringy sentence with too many *so's.*

> **More Practice**

Grammar Exercise Workbook
• pp. 69–70
On-line Exercise Bank
• Section 20.7
Go on-line:
PHSchool.com
Enter Web Code:
egk-1202

Complete the exercise on-line! Exercise 51 is available on-line or on CD-ROM.

☑ ONGOING ASSESSMENT: Assess Mastery		
Use the following resources to assess student mastery of effective sentences.		
In the Textbook	**Print Resources**	**Technology**
Chapter Review, Ex. 61–62 Standardized Test Preparation Workshop	*Formal Assessment,* Chapter 20	*On-Line Exercise Bank,* Chapter 20

Section 20.7 *Section Review*

GRAMMAR EXERCISES 52–56

Exercise 52 Recognizing Faulty Coordination For the sentences in which *and* is used improperly, write *faulty*. For the sentences in which *and* is used properly, write *correct*.

1. The *Spirit of St. Louis* was the plane that Charles Lindbergh used to fly nonstop from New York to Paris, and it is on display at the Smithsonian Institution in Washington, D.C.
2. The plane was built by the Ryan Aeronautical Company of San Diego, and it was specially built for the transatlantic flight.
3. Lindbergh had been an airmail pilot for a corporation, and he was born in Detroit.
4. After his historic nonstop flight, Lindbergh flew the *Spirit of St. Louis* on "goodwill" tours, and he flew 22,000 miles.
5. In 1927, Lindbergh published a book entitled *We*, and it was about his transatlantic flight.

Exercise 53 Revising to Eliminate Faulty Coordination Rewrite each sentence, correcting the faulty coordination.

1. The Boeing B-17 Flying Fortress is one of the most famous airplanes ever built, and the prototype first flew on July 28, 1935.
2. Few B-17's were in service when the U.S. entered World War II, and production quickly accelerated.
3. The Flying Fortress served in every World War II combat zone, and bombing German industrial targets in daylight was its claim to fame.
4. Germany's main air weapon early in the war was the Messerschmitt Bf 109, and that plane was used to bomb London during the Battle of Britain.

5. The British Spitfire prevailed over the Bf 109 at the Battle of Britain, and it was faster and lighter.

Exercise 54 Combining Sentences Effectively Combine each pair of sentences, avoiding faulty coordination.

1. The Me 262 was the world's first operational turbojet aircraft. It was much faster than conventional aircraft.
2. There were delays in production of the Me 262. Development problems, Allied bombings, and cautious Luftwaffe leadership contributed.
3. In July 1944, an Me 262 became the first fighter jet used in combat. It attacked a British reconnaissance plane flying over Munich.
4. More than 1,400 Me 262's were produced. Fewer than 300 saw combat.
5. Many of the German jets were destroyed by Allied bombing raids. The jets were still on the ground.

Exercise 55 Find It in Your Writing Look through your portfolio to see if you have written any "stringy" sentences that contain too many *and*'s or *so*'s. Rewrite the sentences using some of the techniques described in this section.

Exercise 56 Writing Application Imagine that you are a newspaper reporter who has been assigned to cover a local air show. Describe the planes that are on display, the stunts that the pilots perform, and the general atmosphere of the show. Remember to vary your sentence structure, and be sure to use proper coordination.

Section Review • 513

ASSESS and CLOSE

Section Review

Each of these exercises correlates to the instruction on faulty coordination, pages 510–512. The exercises may be used for more practice, for reteaching, or for review of the key concepts presented. Answers for all chapter exercises are available in *Grammar Exercises Answers on Transparencies* in your Teaching Resources.

Answer Key

Exercise 52

1. faulty
2. faulty
3. faulty
4. faulty
5. faulty

Exercise 53

Answers may vary; samples are given.

1. The Boeing B-17 Flying Fortress is one of the most famous airplanes ever built. The prototype first flew on July 28, 1935.
2. Few B-17's were in service when the U.S. entered World War II, but production quickly accelerated.
3. While the Flying Fortress served in every World War II combat zone, bombing German industrial targets in daylight was its claim to fame.
4. Germany's main air weapon early in the war was the Messerschmitt Bf 109, which was used to bomb London during the Battle of Britain.
5. The British Spitfire prevailed over the Bf 109 at the Battle of Britain because it was lighter and faster.

Exercise 54

Answers will vary; samples are given.

1. The Me 262, the world's first operational turbojet, was much faster than conventional aircraft.
2. Contributing to delays in production of the Me 262 were development problems, Allied bombings, and cautious Luftwaffe leadership.
3. In July 1944, an Me 262 became the first fighter jet used in combat when it attacked a British reconnaissance plane flying over Munich.

continued

Answer Key continued

Exercise 54

4. Although more that 1,400 Me 262's were produced, fewer than 300 saw combat.
5. Allied bombing raids destroyed many of the German jets while the jets were still on the ground.

Exercise 55

Find It in Your Writing
Have students form pairs to check each other's revisions.

Exercise 56

Writing Application
You may wish to allow students library time for research.

CHAPTER REVIEW

Each of these exercises correlates to a section of the chapter on effective sentences. The exercises may be used for more practice, for reteaching, or for review of the key concepts presented. Answers for all chapter exercises are available in *Grammar Exercises Answers on Transparencies* in your Teaching Resources.

Answer Key

Exercise 57

Answers will vary; samples are given.

1. Were the ancient Greeks the first civilization to experiment with flying machines?
2. They conducted their first experiments around 400 B.C.
3. Did the Chinese invent kites at around the same time?
4. Imagine how it felt to be the first kite flyer.
5. How exciting it must have been to make a machine fly!

Exercise 58

Answers will vary; samples are given.

Try this experiment. Insert about two inches of a long, thin strip of paper between the pages of a book. Hold the book right up in front of your mouth so the paper hangs over the side of the book farthest from you. See what happens when you blow gently over the top of the paper. If you do this experiment correctly, the paper will be pushed upward, or lifted. You have demonstrated a principle formulated by Daniel Bernouli, an eighteenth-century Swiss scholar, that explains why flight is possible. The pressure in a moving stream of air is less than the pressure in the surrounding air; therefore, the air pressure under the paper was greater than the pressure above it, which pushed the paper upward into the moving air.

Exercise 59

Answers will vary; samples are given.

If the Wright Brothers were the fathers of the airplane, Sir George Cayley was its grandfather. Living and working during the beginning of the nineteenth century, Cayley studied many different theories of flight. He carefully examined Leonardo da Vinci's wing-flapping ornithopter. He measured birds' muscles and wing patterns, studied human muscle activity, and determined that people

514

Chapter 20 Chapter Review

GRAMMAR EXERCISES 57–63

Exercise 57 Writing the Four Types of Sentences Rewrite each sentence to fit the function indicated in parentheses. Add the appropriate end marks to the rewritten sentences.

1. The ancient Greeks were the first civilization to experiment with flying machines (interrogative)
2. Did they conduct their first experiments around 400 B.C. (declarative)
3. The Chinese invented kites at around the same time (interrogative)
4. Can you imagine how it felt to be the first kite flyer (imperative)
5. Making a machine fly must have been so exciting (exclamatory)

Exercise 58 Revising to Combine and Vary Sentence Length Rewrite this paragraph, combining some short sentences and leaving others short for emphasis.

Try this experiment. Get a long, thin strip of paper, and put the paper in a book. Insert about two inches of the paper between the pages of the book. Hold the book right up in front of your mouth. The paper should hang over the side of the book farthest from you. Blow gently over the top of the paper, and see what happens. You do this experiment correctly. The paper will be pushed upward, or lifted. You have demonstrated a principle. The principle was formulated by an eighteenth-century Swiss scholar. The scholar was named Daniel Bernoulli. Bernoulli's principle explains why flight is possible. The pressure in a moving stream of air is less than the pressure in the surrounding air. The air pressure under the paper was greater than the pressure above it. The paper was pushed upward into the moving air.

514 • Effective Sentences

Exercise 59 Revising to Eliminate Fragments and Run-ons Rewrite this paragraph, correcting any fragments or run-ons.

If the Wright brothers were the fathers of the airplane. Sir George Cayley was its grandfather. Lived and worked during the beginning of the nineteenth century. Cayley studied many different theories of flight, he carefully examined Leonardo da Vinci's wing-flapping ornithopter. He measured birds' muscles and wing patterns he also studied human muscle activity and he determined that people could not strap on wings and be able to fly as birds did. Cayley suggested that airplanes needed a fixed-wing design, they also should have a self-contained system for propelling the craft, and a tail to help control it. The only engines available in Cayley's time were steam engines these were too heavy to permit the plane to get off the ground. Using Cayley's theories and the new technological developments. The Wright brothers were able to build a self-propelled plane that could carry a man into the air. And bring him back down safely.

Exercise 60 Revising to Correct Modifiers Rewrite the following sentences, correcting any misplaced or dangling modifiers.

1. Sailing gracefully, the first manned balloon flight took place with two aviators in Paris in November 1783.
2. Invented by the Montgolfier brothers, two French adventurers sailed a hot-air balloon for twenty-two minutes.
3. Inspired by watching wood chips float over a fire, the idea of a hot-air balloon was first conceived.
4. The Montgolfiers believed that forcing

---

could not strap on wings and fly as birds did. Cayley suggested that airplanes needed a fixed wing design, a self-contained system of propelling the craft, and a tail to help control it. The only engines available in Cayley's time were steam engines, which were too heavy to permit the plane to get off the ground. Using Cayley's theories and new technological developments, the Wright Brothers were able to build a self-propelled plane that could carry a man into the air and bring him back down safely.

Exercise 60

Answers will vary; samples are given.

1. The first manned balloon flight took place as two aviators sailed gracefully in Paris in November 1783.
2. The Montgolfier brothers, two French adventurers, invented the hot-air balloon and sailed it for twenty-two minutes.
3. The idea of a hot-air balloon was inspired by watching wood chips float over a fire.
4. The Montgolfiers believed that forcing air heated by a coal stove into a lightweight bag would cause the bag to rise.

continued

air into a lightweight bag heated by a coal stove would cause the bag to rise.

5. Testing materials, many experiments were conducted by the Montgolfiers.
6. Showing off their invention in Paris in 1783, King Louis XVI was impressed.
7. The two pilots reached an altitude over the rooftops of Paris of 500 feet.
8. Watching the men sail over their fields, fear was felt by many French farmers.
9. A Frenchman and an American teamed up over the English Channel in 1785 to make the first international flight.
10. The first hot-air-balloon flight took place in North America in 1793.

> **Exercise 61** Proofreading to Correct Errors in Sentence Structure

Correct any errors in parallelism or coordination in the following sentences.

1. At first, people who believed humans could fly were considered fools, madmen, or those who dreamed.
2. Otto Lilienthal brought respectability to flight invention, and he was a well-respected engineer.
3. Lilienthal once said: "To invent an airplane is nothing, to build one is something, but flying is everything."
4. Lilienthal's flying machines were hanggliders, and you can see similar craft in use today.
5. Lilienthal built 18 gliders, flew 2,500 successful glider flights, and he wrote a book about his experiments.
6. Some of Lilienthal's gliders had one level of wings, and two levels of wings were on some of the others.
7. The Wright brothers read Lilienthal's book, and they made the first successful airplane flight in 1903.
8. Lilienthal inspired the Wrights, and he was courageous and thoughtful.
9. Lilienthal died in a glider accident, and his work was carried on by the Wrights.
10. Today, Lilienthal is honored as a technician, for being a scientist, and a pioneer.

> **Exercise 62** Revising Sentences

Rewrite the following paragraph, combining or revising sentences and correcting any errors in sentence structure.

Amelia Earhart saw her first airplane at the Iowa State Fair, and it was in 1909, and she was twelve years old, and she was not impressed. It was not until eleven years later. That she took her first plane ride. She was up in the air only for a few minutes, and she knew she wanted to become a pilot. Adventurous and headstrong, a plane was purchased by her a few weeks later. Earhart had several accidents, her instructor doubted her talents as a pilot. She kept practicing soon she was breaking altitude records for women fliers. In 1928, Earhart part of a three-person crew that flew across the Atlantic. As the first woman to make a transatlantic flight. She became a celebrity. She was asked to give lectures, written up in newspapers, and people cheered for her everywhere she went. After flying solo from Hawaii to California in 1935, President Roosevelt honored her. He praised her for proving that to men aviation is not limited. Earhart began making plans for a round-the-world flight, she undertook the flight in 1937, and there was a disappearance over the Pacific. Neither body nor plane ever found.

> **Exercise 63** Writing Application

Imagine that you are one of the first people to fly a balloon, a glider, or an airplane. Write a narrative of your first flight. Try to vary the length of your sentences, and include at least two examples of parallel structure. Proofread your narration carefully to make sure that you have no fragments, run-ons, or misplaced modifiers.

Chapter Review • 515

> **Exercise 60**

5. Testing materials, the Montgolfiers conducted many experiments.
6. King Louis XVI was impressed when they showed off their invention in Paris in 1783.
7. The two pilots reached an altitude of 500 feet over the rooftops of Paris.
8. Watching the men sail over their fields, many French farmers were afraid.
9. A Frenchman and an American teamed up in 1785 to make the first international flight over the English Channel.
10. The first hot-air-balloon flight in North America took place in 1793.

> **Exercise 61**

Answers will vary; samples are given.

1. At first, people who believed humans could fly were considered fools, madmen, or dreamers.
2. Otto Lilienthal, a well-respected engineer, brought respectability to flight invention.
3. Lilienthal once said: "To invent an airplane is nothing, to build one is something, but to fly one is everything."
4. Lilienthal's flying machines were hang gliders. You can see similar craft in use today.
5. Lilienthal built 18 gliders, flew 2,500 successful glider flights, and wrote a book about his experiments.
6. Some of Lilienthal's gliders had one level of wings, while others had two levels of wings.
7. The Wright Brothers read Lilienthal's book before they made the first successful airplane flight in 1903.
8. Courageous and thoughtful, Lilienthal inspired the Wrights.
9. After Lilienthal died in a glider accident, his work was carried on by the Wrights.
10. Today, Lilienthal is honored as a technician, a scientist, and a pioneer.

> **Exercise 62**

Answers will vary; samples are given.

In 1909, when Amelia Earhart was twelve years old, she saw her first airplane at the Iowa State Fair but was not impressed. It was not until
continued

> **Exercise 62**

eleven years later that she took her first plane ride. Although she was up in the air for only a few minutes, she knew she wanted to become a pilot. Adventurous and headstrong, Amelia purchased a plane a few weeks later. Because Amelia had several accidents, her instructor doubted her talents as a pilot. She kept practicing, and soon she was breaking altitude records for women flyers. In 1928, Amelia was part of a three-person crew that flew across the Atlantic. As the first woman to make a transatlantic flight, she became a celebrity. She was asked to give lectures, was written up in newspapers, and was cheered for everywhere she went. After flying solo from Hawaii to California in 1935, she was honored by President Roosevelt, who praised her for proving that aviation is not limited to men. Amelia began making plans for a round-the-world flight that she undertook in 1937. She disappeared over the Pacific, and neither her body nor her plane was ever found.

> **Exercise 63**

Writing Application
Encourage students to add their narratives to their writing portfolios.

515

1. To produce work that shows accurate spelling and correct use of the conventions of punctuation and capitalization

2. To use varied sentence structure to express meanings and achieve desired effect

3. To compose increasingly more involved sentences that contain gerunds, participles, and infinitives in their various functions

Step-by-Step Teaching Guide

Recognizing Appropriate Sentence Construction

Teaching Resources: Standardized Test Preparation Workbook, pp. 39–40

1. Make sure students can define the four types of sentences. Ask why it is helpful to know these definitions. (Students are reminded that there are many possible ways to construct sentences.)

2. Ask students why it is important to correct run-on sentences. (Run-on sentences tend to blur ideas. Revising them makes a passage easier for a reader to understand.)

3. Have students read the sample test item and the corresponding explanation. Make sure they can explain why choice **D** is incorrect. (As it is, the sentence is a run-on.)

Standardized Test Preparation Workshop

Recognizing Appropriate Sentence Construction

Standardized tests will measure your ability to write by providing a written passage with numbered sentences. You will be asked to read the passage and to choose from several possible revisions of each sentence. The following tips for writing effective sentences should help you.

- **Avoid choppy sentences** by using a variety of simple, compound, complex, and compound-complex sentences.

- **Correct run-on sentences** by inserting a comma and coordinating conjunction, by inserting a semicolon, or by making one or two distinct, properly punctuated sentences.

- **Correct misplaced modifiers** by placing adverbs and adjectives as close as possible to the words they modify.

- **Varying the beginnings** of your sentences by starting some sentences with adverbs, some with prepositional phrases, some with verbs or verbal phrases, and some with subordinate clauses.

Test Tip

Be sure that the rewrite you have chosen does not change the meaning of the passage.

Sample Test Item	Answer and Explanation
Directions: Read the passage, and choose the best rewrite of each numbered sentence. (1) Susan Williams-Ellis founded Portmeirion Pottery in 1960 since then she and her family have designed many different patterns.	
1 A Susan Williams-Ellis founded Portmeirion Pottery. In 1960, since then she and her family have designed many different patterns. **B** Susan Williams-Ellis was the founder of Portmeirion Pottery in 1960. She designed many different patterns. **C** Since founding Portmeirion Pottery in 1960, Susan Williams-Ellis and her family have designed many different patterns. **D** Correct as is	Choice *A* breaks the passage at an illogical point, and choice *B* slightly changes the meaning of the passage. In the correct choice, *C,* the run-on passage is rewritten as a grammatically correct sentence.

516 • Effective Sentences

⬛ TEST-TAKING TIP

Tell students to read all of the answer choices even if they think the passage is correct as is. Sometimes, when we read a poorly written sentence, our minds will make the necessary corrections for us without our noticing.

Remind students that the key to answering these questions is to choose the best answer, not just any answer that is grammatically correct. Students should choose the revision that is the most clear and concise version of the original sentence.

▶ **Practice 1** **Directions:** Read the following passage. Choose the best rewrite in the questions that follow.

(1) Resistant strains of bacteria develop. (2) If a prescribed antibiotic fails to kill all the bacteria in an infection. (3) Experts fear that these resistant strains are becoming stronger and stronger the overuse of antibiotics can be blamed for this serious danger. (4) Bacterial infections are being seen by doctors that do not respond to traditional antibiotics. (5) Although much research is being done to formulate stronger antibiotics, experts fear that future strains of bacteria will continue to develop. (6) Future bacteria may be deadly. (7) Future bacteria will almost surely develop faster. (8) Than the antibiotics needed to combat them.

1 Which of the following is the best rewrite of passages 1 and 2?

  A Resistant strains of bacteria develop; if a prescribed antibiotic fails to kill all the bacteria in an infection.

  B Resistant strains of bacteria develop if a prescribed antibiotic fails to kill all the bacteria in an infection.

  C Strains of bacteria develop if an antibiotic fails to kill all an infection.

  D Correct as is

2 Which of the following is the best rewrite of passage 3?

  F Experts fear these stronger resistant strains can be blamed for this serious danger.

  G The strong overuse of antibiotics can be blamed for the fear of experts.

  H Experts fear that these resistant strains are becoming stronger and stronger. The overuse of antibiotics can be blamed for this serious danger.

  J Correct as is

3 Which of the following is the best rewrite of passage 4?

  A Doctors are seeing bacterial infections that do not respond to traditional antibiotics.

  B Bacterial infections are being seen by doctors. Bacterial infections that do not respond to traditional antibiotics.

  C Bacterial infections are being seen that do not respond to traditional antibiotics by doctors.

  D Correct as is

4 Which of the following is the best rewrite of passage 5?

  F Although much research is being done to create stronger antibiotics, experts fear the developing future strains of bacteria.

  G Experts who are doing much research fear developing future bacteria.

  H Experts fear that future strains of bacteria; although much research is being done to create stronger antibiotics, will continue to develop.

  J Correct as is

5 Which of the following is the best rewrite of passages 6, 7, and 8?

  A Future bacteria may be deadly; future bacteria will almost surely develop faster than the antibiotics needed to combat them.

  B Future bacteria will almost surely develop faster than the antibiotics needed to combat them.

  C Future bacteria may be deadly, because they will almost surely develop faster than the antibiotics needed to combat them.

  D Correct as is

Customize for
Less Advanced Students

Make sure students understand that Sentences 1 and 2 show a cause-and-effect relationship. If the antibiotic fails to kill all the bacteria in an infection (cause), resistant strains of bacteria develop (effect). Ask students to find another example of a cause-and-effect relationship in the passage. (Sentences 6–8: *Future bacteria may be deadly* [effect] *because they will almost surely develop faster than the antibiotics needed to combat them* [cause].)

Customize for
AP Students

Ask students to identify the tone of the passage and to give at least two examples from the text to support their answer. (Students should note that the passage has a formal, serious tone. The specialized language and the sense of urgency help to convey this tone.) Whom do they think is the writer's intended audience? Why? (Because these terms are used but not explained, the intended audience probably consists of medical professionals.)

Chapter 21 · Time and Resource Manager

In-Depth Lesson Plan

LESSON FOCUS	PRINT AND MEDIA RESOURCES
DAY 1 — **Introduction; Verb Tenses** Students learn and apply concepts relating to the six tenses and four principal parts of verbs. (pp. 518–522/H366–370)	*Writing and Grammar* **Interactive Text**, Section 21.1; *On-line Exercise Bank*, Section 21.1 **Teaching Resources** *Grammar Exercise Workbook*, pp. 71–72; *Grammar Exercises Answers on Transparencies*, Ch. 21
DAY 2 — **Verb Tenses** *continued* Students learn and apply concepts relating to regular and irregular verbs and verb conjugation. (pp. 523–531/H371–379)	**Teaching Resources** *Grammar Exercise Workbook*, pp. 73–76
DAY 3 — **The Correct Use of Tenses** Students learn to use tenses to express time in the basic, progressive, and emphatic forms. (pp. 532–538/H380–386)	*Writing and Grammar* **Interactive Text**, Section 21.2; *On-line Exercise Bank*, Section 21.2 **Teaching Resources** *Grammar Exercise Workbook*, pp. 77–78
DAY 4 — **The Correct Use of Tenses** *continued* Students learn sequence of tenses, time sequence with participles and infinitives, and the use of modifiers to clarify tense, and do the Hands-on Grammar activity. (pp. 539–547/H387–395)	**Teaching Resources** *Grammar Exercise Workbook*, pp. 79–80; *Hands-on Grammar Activity Book*, Ch. 21
DAY 5 — **Subjunctive Mood and Voice; Review and Assess** Students learn the use of the subjunctive mood and of active and passive voice; students review the chapter and demonstrate mastery of concepts. (pp. 548–556; 557–559/H396–405)	*Writing and Grammar* **Interactive Text**, Sections 21.3–4; *On-line Exercise Bank*, Sections 21.3–4 **Teaching Resources** *Grammar Exercise Workbook*, pp. 81–84; *Formal Assessment*, Ch. 21

Accelerated Lesson Plan

LESSON FOCUS	PRINT AND MEDIA RESOURCES
DAY 1 — **Verb Tenses** Students review verb tenses, with coverage determined by their performance on the Diagnostic Test. (pp. 518–531/H366–379)	*Writing and Grammar* **Interactive Text**, Sections 21.1–2; *On-line Exercise Bank*, Sections 21.1–2 **Teaching Resources** *Grammar Exercise Workbook*, pp. 71–78; *Grammar Exercises Answers on Transparencies*, Ch. 21
DAY 2 — **The Correct Use of Tenses; Subjunctive Mood** Students cover sequence of tenses, modifiers that clarify tense, and uses of the subjunctive mood. (pp. 532–551/H380–399)	*Writing and Grammar* **Interactive Text**, Sections 21.2–3; *On-line Exercise Bank*, Sections 21.2–3 **Teaching Resources** *Grammar Exercise Workbook*, pp. 79–82
DAY 3 — **Voice; Review and Assess** Students cover active and passive voice and then review the chapter and demonstrate mastery of concepts. (pp. 552–559/ H400–405)	*Writing and Grammar* **Interactive Text**, Section 21.4; *On-line Exercise Bank*, Section 21.4 **Teaching Resources** *Grammar Exercise Workbook*, pp. 83–84; *Formal Assessment*, Ch. 21

Options for Adapting Lesson Plans

FEATURES

Extend coverage with Grammar in Literature features (pp. 530, 538, 555/H378, 386, 403) and the Standardized Test Preparation Workshop (p. 560).

TECHNOLOGY

Students can use *Writing and Grammar* Interactive Text to complete the exercises interactively on computer. They can complete additional exercises in the *On-line Exercise Bank:* The Auto Check feature will grade their work. Go on-line: PHSchool.com Use Web Code: egk-1202

Writing and Grammar Handbook Alignment

Page numbers in Step-by-Step Teaching Guides in this Teacher's Edition refer to pages from the full student text. Handbook page references, indicated with this icon ⒣, are provided in Time and Resource Manager boxes and at the bottom of each Teacher's Edition page.

INTEGRATED SKILLS COVERAGE

Grammar in Literature
SE pp. 530, 538, 555/⒣378, 386, 403

Writing
Find It in Your Writing SE pp. 531, 545, 547, 551, 556/⒣379, 393, 395, 399, 404
Writing Application SE pp. 531, 547, 551, 556, 559/⒣379, 395, 399, 404
Grammar and Style SE p. 540/⒣388

Vocabulary ATE p. 526

Spelling ATE p. 526

Viewing and Representing
Critical Viewing, SE pp. 518, 522, 525, 527, 528, 537, 539, 542, 544, 549, 550, 552, 555/⒣366, 370, 373, 375, 376, 385, 390, 392, 397, 398, 400, 403

Speaking and Listening SE p. 529/⒣377; ATE p. 523

Technology SE pp. 526, 548/⒣374, 396

Real-World Connection ATE p. 553

Workplace Skills ATE p. 533

ASSESSMENT SUPPORT

Standardized Test Preparation Workshop, SE p. 560; ATE pp. 526, 546, 551

Standardized Test Preparation Workbook, pp. 41–42

Formal Assessment, Ch. 21

MEETING INDIVIDUAL NEEDS

Less Advanced Students ATE pp. 549, 561. See also Ongoing Assessments, ATE pp. 521, 522, 527, 528, 529, 537, 538, 542, 543, 544, 549, 550, 554.

ESL Students ATE pp. 521, 537, 561

Logical/Mathematical Learners ATE p. 542

Gifted and Talented Students ATE p. 525

Linguistic Learners ATE p. 550

BLOCK SCHEDULING

Pacing Suggestions
For 90-minute Blocks
- Administer the Diagnostic Test to students to determine instructional coverage needed.
- Have students complete necessary exercises in class. Use the Hands-on Grammar activity to provide a change of pace.

Resources for Varying Instruction
- *Writing and Grammar* **Interactive Text** A 90-minute block provides an ideal opportunity for students to work on the computer.

Professional Development Support
- *How to Manage Instruction in the Block* This teaching resource provides management and activity suggestions.

MEDIA AND TECHNOLOGY

For the Student
- *Writing and Grammar* **Interactive Text,** Ch. 21
- *On-Line Exercise Bank,* Sections 21.1–4

For the Teacher
- **Teacher**EXPRESS™ CD-ROM

WRITING AND GRAMMAR ON-LINE

Interactive Text (On-line or on CD-ROM)
- Easily navigable instruction with on-line supporting resources
- Self-scoring exercises and diagnostic tests

Companion Web Site PHSchool.com
- On-line Exercise Bank (use Web Code egk-1202)

See the Go On-line! feature, SE p. iii.

LITERATURE CONNECTIONS

Grammar in Literature selections from *Prentice Hall Literature, Penguin Edition,* The British Tradition:

from "An Arundel Tomb," Philip Larkin, SE p. 530/⒣378

from *The Canterbury Tales:* "The Prologue," Geoffrey Chaucer, SE p. 538/⒣386

from "Meditation 17," John Donne, SE p. 555/⒣403

Chapter
21 Verb Usage

▶ Lesson Objectives

1. To recognize the basic and progressive forms of the six verb tenses and to identify the emphatic forms of the present and past tenses

2. To recognize and use tenses and modifiers correctly to show present, past, and future time

3. To recognize and write the correct sequence of tenses when writing sentences with more than one verb

4. To identify and use the subjunctive mood

5. To recognize and use the active voice and the passive voice

6. To demonstrate control over grammatical elements such as verb forms

7. To use varied sentence structure to express meanings and achieve desired effect

8. To use effective sequences and transitions to achieve coherence and meaning

9. To compose increasingly more involved sentences that contain gerunds, participles, and infinitives

Critical Viewing

Relate Possible answer: A verb is the principal, or guiding, element of a sentence's architecture. Without verbs, the direction, purpose, and beauty of a sentence are compromised or structurally unsound.

▲ **Critical Viewing**
A solid understanding of architectural principles was necessary to build the Taj Mahal. In what way is a solid understanding of verbs necessary for clear communication? **[Relate]**

Monuments have long served to remind us of people and events of importance. Throughout history, monuments have been erected to commemorate great battles, to celebrate various religions, and to honor myriad heroes. Although various cultures have built many different types of monuments—pyramids, statues, museums, and churches—the rules regarding construction methods have developed in a remarkably similar way by every civilization.

In the same way, the rules concerning the use of verbs and verb tenses have been developed to allow for more effective communication. Like the individual building blocks that form the foundation of even the largest monument, the rules concerning verb usage form a basic support structure that enables you to communicate effectively.

A solid understanding of verbs and their uses is necessary in order to speak and write well. Generally, native speakers of English tend to use correct verb forms automatically when they speak, but many grammatical situations are tricky.

In this chapter, you will study how verbs are formed and how they show time. You will also learn how verbs express facts, commands, and wishes or possibilities, as well as how verbs indicate whether subjects perform or receive actions.

518 • Verb Usage

☑ ONGOING ASSESSMENT: Diagnose					
If students miss more than one item in any category, direct them to the relevant pages of the textbook and assign exercises for practice and review.					
Verb Usage	**Diagnostic Test Items**	**Teach**	**Practice**	**Section Review**	**Chapter Review**
Skill Check A					
Six Verb Tenses and the Basic, Progressive, and Emphatic Forms	A 1–5	pp. 520–521/ 🖽368–369	Ex. 1–2	Ex. 10, 13	Ex. 53
Skill Check B					
Uses of Tense in Past, Present, and Future Time	B 6–10	pp. 532–538/ 🖽380–386	Ex. 18–20	Ex. 25–27	Ex. 56

Diagnostic Test

Directions: Write all answers on a separate sheet of paper.

Skill Check A. Identify the tense of the italicized verbs, and tell whether the form is *basic*, *progressive*, or *emphatic*.

1. Gary *did travel* to many sports arenas during his vacation.
2. Some arenas *have been* tourist attractions for many decades.
3. At this very moment, people *are visiting* famous sports arenas.
4. Many communities *have been trying* to build new arenas.
5. Someday, these arenas *will serve* as monuments to our society's fascination with sports.

Skill Check B. On your paper, form the tenses listed using the pronouns in parentheses as their subjects.

6. past progressive of *borrow* (*we*)
7. past perfect of *sing* (*they*)
8. present progressive of *acknowledge* (*it*)
9. future perfect of *investigate* (*you*)
10. future perfect progressive of *hope* (*I*)

Skill Check C. For each sentence, write the verbs and their tenses, and tell whether the sentence describes simultaneous or sequential events.

11. We know that people have always enjoyed seeing monuments.
12. We learned that the White House was completed in 1800.
13. It has been called the President's House.
14. Now that I have learned about this famous building, I will add the information to my knowledge of our nation's history.
15. By the time this class ends, we will have learned a lot about famous buildings in the nation's capital.

Skill Check D. Rewrite the following sentences, changing the verbs to the subjunctive mood as necessary.

16. If I was to travel back in time, I would go to the early 1930's.
17. Then, as if I was a citizen of the period, I could witness the construction of the National Archives Building in Washington, D.C.
18. If the National Archives Building was damaged by a fire, many of the nation's most famous documents might be destroyed.
19. I would prefer that these famous documents are protected from all possible damage.
20. It is crucial that the heritage of our nation is preserved for the sake of posterity.

Skill Check E. On your paper, identify whether the verbs in the following sentences are in the active or passive voice.

21. Many people have visited the Library of Congress.
22. The Library of Congress was founded by Thomas Jefferson.
23. Numerous books are held in storage by the Library of Congress.
24. Over the years, much information has been provided by the Library of Congress to scholars.
25. In 2000, the Library of Congress celebrated its bicentennial.

Verb Usage • 519

Diagnostic Test

Each item in the Diagnostic Test corresponds with a specific section in the verb usage chapter, enabling you to tailor instruction to the particular needs of your students. See "Ongoing Assessment: Diagnose" below for further details. Answers for the Diagnostic Test and all chapter exercises are available in *Grammar Exercises Answers on Transparencies* in your Teaching Resources.

Skill Check A

1. past emphatic
2. present perfect (basic)
3. present progressive
4. present perfect progressive
5. future (basic)

Skill Check B

6. were borrowing
7. had sung
8. is acknowledging
9. will have investigated
10. will have been hoping

Skill Check C

11. know (present), have enjoyed (present perfect)—sequential
12. learned (past), was built (past)—sequential
13. has been called (present perfect)
14. have learned (present perfect), will add (future)—sequential
15. ends (present), will have learned (future perfect)—sequential

Skill Check D

16. If I *were* to travel back in time . . .
17. Then, as if I *were* a citizen . . .
18. If the National Archives Building *were* damaged by a fire . . .
19. I would prefer that these famous documents *be* protected . . .
20. It is crucial that the heritage of our nation *be* preserved . . .

Skill Check E

21. active
22. passive
23. passive
24. passive
25. active

☑ ONGOING ASSESSMENT: Diagnose *continued*					
Verb Usage	Diagnostic Test Items	Teach	Practice	Section Review	Chapter Review
Skill Check C					
Sequences of Tenses	C 11–15	pp. 539–542/⊞387–390	Ex. 21–23	Ex. 28	Ex. 57–58
Skill Check D					
Subjunctive Mood	D 16–20	pp. 548–550/⊞396–398	Ex. 36–37	Ex. 38–39	Ex. 59–60
Skill Check E					
Active and Passive Voices	E 21–25	pp. 552–554/⊞400–402	Ex. 43–46	Ex. 47–49	Ex. 61
Cumulative Reviews and Applications				Ex. 15–17, 33–35, 40–42, 50–52	Ex. 63–64

Interest GRABBER Place these examples on the board and ask for the adverb in each that indicates time:

We played rugby yesterday. (yesterday)

We play rugby today. (today)

We will play rugby tomorrow. (tomorrow)

Eliminate the adverbs, and ask whether students can still determine time and what clues or words they use to do so. Point out that verbs change their forms specifically to show time and to clarify time relationships between events.

Activate Prior Knowledge

Have students recall famous phrases originally derived from the popular media. ("Don't touch that dial. We'll be right back.") First, have students determine the time (past, present, future) of each statement. Then, have students rewrite each sentence two ways: one for each of the remaining tenses. (Example: *You did not touch that dial. You will not touch that dial.*) Explain that verbs employ certain helping verbs to make them time specific.

TEACH

Step-by-Step Teaching Guide

The Six Verb Tenses

1. When students have identified the six basic verb tenses, point out the helping verbs that form the future and the perfect tenses.

2. Have students try forming each progressive form by using another verb, such as *talking*, and by saying each form aloud: *I am talking, I was talking,* and so on.

Answer Key

Exercise 1

Student sentences will vary. If students have trouble getting started, brainstorm to choose a monument or building and to name words (*visit, build*) that would be appropriate.

Section 21.1 Verb Tenses

Besides expressing actions or conditions, verbs have different *tenses* to indicate when the action or condition occurred.

▶ **KEY CONCEPT** A **tense** is the form of a verb that shows the time of an action or a condition. ■

The Six Verb Tenses

There are six tenses that indicate when an action or a condition of a verb is, was, or will be in effect. Each of these six tenses has at least two forms:

▶ **KEY CONCEPT** Each tense has a basic and a progressive form. ■

The chart that follows shows the *basic* forms of the six tenses:

THE BASIC FORMS OF THE SIX TENSES	
Present	I visit the Statue of Liberty.
Past	I visited Ellis Island last Sunday.
Future	I will visit the Washington Monument next week.
Present Perfect	I have visited the children at the hospital for almost a year now.
Past Perfect	I had visited my grandmother on weekends until this past month.
Future Perfect	I will have visited my aunt once a week for a year by the end of May.

▶ **Exercise 1** Writing Sentences in All Six Tenses Write six sentences on the subject of a monument or an important building in your town. Use a different verb tense in each sentence, and indicate the tense.

EXAMPLE: The Veterans' Memorial *has stood* in the middle of town for more than fifty years. (present perfect)

Notice in the next chart that all of the progressive forms end in *-ing*.

520 • Verb Usage

Theme: World Monuments

In this section, you will learn about the six verb tenses and the progressive and emphatic forms. The examples and exercises in this section are about great monuments around the world.

Cross-Curricular Connection: Social Studies

⏱ TIME AND RESOURCE MANAGER

Resources
Print: *Grammar Exercise Workbook,* pp. 71–78; *Grammar Exercises Answers on Transparencies,* Ch. 21
Technology: *Writing and Grammar* Interactive Text, Section 21.1; *On-Line Exercise Bank,* Section 21.1

Using the Full Student Edition	Using the Handbook🄷
• Work through all key concepts, pp. 520–530.	• Work through all key concepts, pp. 368–378.
• Assign and review Exercises 1–9.	• Assign and review Exercises 1–9.
• Read and discuss Grammar in Literature, p. 530.	• Read and discuss Grammar in Literature, p. 378.

THE PROGRESSIVE FORMS OF THE SIX TENSES	
Present Progressive	I *am drawing* right now.
Past Progressive	I *was drawing* when you called.
Future Progressive	I *will be drawing* all weekend.
Present Perfect Progressive	I *have been drawing* more than usual lately.
Past Perfect Progressive	I *had been drawing* apples until the art teacher suggested that I draw boats.
Future Perfect Progressive	I *will have been drawing* in my spare time for two years by the end of this month.

There is also a third form, the *emphatic*, which exists only for the present and past tenses. The present emphatic is formed with the helping verbs *do* or *does*, depending on the subject. The past emphatic is formed with *did*.

THE EMPHATIC FORMS OF THE PRESENT AND THE PAST	
Present Emphatic	I *do exercise* more frequently than you.
Past Emphatic	I *did exercise* last night to burn more calories.

▶ **Exercise 2** Recognizing Verb Tenses and Their Forms
Identify the tense of each verb. Identify its form as well, if the form is not basic.

EXAMPLE: We *have been learning* about monuments.
ANSWER: present perfect progressive

1. We traveled for nearly two days.
2. Jerry has viewed the pyramids at Giza.
3. In fact, my mother did visit the Valley of the Kings.
4. The Egyptians had been building tombs and temples along the Nile River thousands of years ago.
5. The obelisk will have been standing for 4,000 years by the early part of this century.

Interactive Textbook

Get instant feedback! Exercises 1 and 2 are available on-line or on CD-ROM.

▶ **More Practice**

Grammar Exercise Workbook
• pp. 71–72
On-line Exercise Bank
• Section 21.1
  Go on-line:
  PHSchool.com
  Enter Web Code:
  egk-1202

Verb Tenses • **521**

☑ **ONGOING ASSESSMENT: Monitor and Reinforce**		
If students miss more than one item in Exercise 2, refer them to the following for additional practice.		
In the Textbook	**Print Resources**	**Technology**
Section Review, Ex. 10, Section 21.1	*Grammar Exercise Workbook,* pp. 71–72	*On-Line Exercise Bank,* Section 21.1

The Four Principal Parts

1. Read aloud the chart on this page so that students can hear the differences among the four principal parts. Then, use additional examples. Give students the present tense form of a verb and have them supply the remaining principal parts. (Example: *do–doing, did, done*.)

2. This can be an ongoing oral drill throughout the school year. The more students respond to such prompts, the more quickly they will develop an ear for the correct use of verb tenses.

Critical Viewing

Connect Students may note that biographies, obituaries, and newspaper and magazine articles can all serve to honor someone or something from the past. Point out that these works will necessarily depend heavily on the use of past tense verbs.

Answer Key

Exercise 3

1. <u>traveled</u>, past
2. <u>viewed</u>, past participle
3. <u>visit</u>, present
4. <u>building</u>, present participle
5. <u>standing</u>, present participle

21.1

The Four Principal Parts of Verbs

Every verb in the English language has four *principal parts* from which all of the tenses are formed.

▶ **KEY CONCEPT** A verb has four principal parts: the *present*, the *present participle*, the *past*, and the *past participle*. ■

The chart below shows the principal parts of two verbs:

THE FOUR PRINCIPAL PARTS			
Present	Present Participle	Past	Past Participle
talk	talking	talked	talked
draw	drawing	drew	drawn

The first principal part is used for the basic forms of the present and future tenses, as well as for the emphatic forms. The present tense is formed by adding an -s or -es when the subject is *he, she, it,* or a singular noun. The future tense is formed with the helping verb *will* (*I will talk, Mary will draw*). The present emphatic is formed with the helping verbs *do* or *does* (*I do talk, Mary does draw*). The past emphatic is formed with the helping verb *did* (*I did talk, Mary did draw*).

The second principal part is used with various helping verbs for all six of the progressive forms (*I am talking, Mary was drawing,* and so on).

The third principal part is used to form the past tense (*I talked, Mary drew*).

The fourth principal part, with helping verbs, is used for the basic forms of the perfect tenses (*I have talked, Mary had drawn,* and so on).

▶ **Exercise 3** Recognizing
Principal Parts Underline and identify the principal part used to form each verb in Exercise 2.

EXAMPLE: We have been <u>learning</u> about movements.

ANSWER: present participle

Jefferson Memorial, Washington, D.C.

522 • Verb Usage

▼ Critical Viewing
A memorial such as this one is built to honor something or someone from the past. What types of written works serve the same purpose? What tense or tenses would predominate in such works? **[Connect]**

☑ **ONGOING ASSESSMENT: Monitor and Reinforce**

If students miss more than one item in Exercise 3, refer them to the following for additional practice.

In the Textbook	Print Resources	Technology
Section Review, Ex. 11, Section 21.1	*Grammar Exercise Workbook,* pp. 71–72	*On-Line Exercise Bank,* Section 21.1

Regular and Irregular Verbs

The way the past and past participle of a verb are formed determines whether the verb is classified as *regular* or *irregular*.

Regular Verbs The majority of verbs are regular; their past and past participles are formed according to a predictable pattern.

KEY CONCEPT A **regular verb** is one for which the past and past participle are formed by adding *-ed* or *-d* to the present form. ■

The chart that follows shows the principal parts of three regular verbs. Pay particular attention to the spelling. Notice that a final consonant is sometimes doubled to form the present participle (*stopping*), as well as the past and past participle (*stopped*). A final *e* may also be dropped to form the present participle (*managing*).

PRINCIPAL PARTS OF REGULAR VERBS

Present	Present Participle	Past	Past Participle
contend	contending	contended	(have) contended
manage	managing	managed	(have) managed
stop	stopping	stopped	(have) stopped

Irregular Verbs Although most verbs are regular, many of the most common verbs are irregular.

KEY CONCEPT An **irregular verb** is one whose past and past participle are not formed by adding *-ed* or *-d* to the present form. ■

The charts that follow group a number of irregular verbs according to common characteristics. It is important to master the principal parts of irregular verbs to avoid usage problems. One common problem is using a principal part that is non-standard.

INCORRECT: They *knowed* about the Jefferson Memorial.
CORRECT: They *knew* about the Jefferson Memorial.

A second problem is confusing the past and past participle when they are different.

INCORRECT: She *done* the right thing.
CORRECT: She *did* the right thing.

⟳ Learn More

To review basic information about verbs and verb phrases, turn to Chapter 17.

Verb Tenses • **523**

Step-by-Step Teaching Guide

Regular Verbs

1. Model for students the fact that the past tense and past participle of regular verbs are formed by adding *-ed* or *-d* to the end of the present form.

2. Stress the idea that, although the past and past participle of regular verbs are the same, the past participle is used with a form of the verb *to have.*

Integrating Speaking and Listening Skills

Have students practice the past and past participle of five regular verbs other than those on the chart by saying the past and past participle of each verb aloud. Make sure they include the helping verb with the past participle. (Examples: *iron–ironed, (have) ironed; push–pushed, (have) pushed; experience–experienced, (have) experienced; sail–sailed, (have) sailed; touch–touched, (have) touched*)

Step-by-Step Teaching Guide

Irregular Verbs

1. Explain to students that *irregular verbs* form the past and past participle with irregular spellings, not by adding *-ed* or *-d* to the present form.

2. Encourage students to consult the chart frequently to ensure the correct use and spelling of irregular verb forms.

☑ ONGOING ASSESSMENT: Prerequisite Skills

If students have difficulty with principal parts of verbs, you may find it necessary to review the following to ensure coverage of prerequisite knowledge.

In the Textbook	Print Resources	Technology
Verbs, Section 17.2	*Grammar Exercise Workbook,* pp. 73–74	*On-Line Exercise Bank,* Section 17.2

⏱ TIME SAVERS!

Answers on Transparencies Use the *Grammar Exercises Answers on Transparencies* for Chapter 21 to facilitate correction by students.

On-Line Exercise Bank Have students complete the exercises on computer. The Auto Check feature will grade their work for you!

Irregular Verbs

1. Have students find partners and test one another's knowledge of irregular verbs. Have one student say the present form of a verb out loud. Then, have the other student respond with the remaining three parts, making sure to say *have* as they form the past participle.

2. Point out that the correct usage of principal parts is essential to written and oral communication. Say, "I have teached for many years." Then, ask a student to point out the error in your sentence. Observe that the incorrect use of principal parts signals an inferior grasp of English.

3. Encourage students to use the dictionary to check the correct forms of the principal parts of verbs. For example: *burst, let, be, dive, forbid, get, hide, spread, think, tell,* or *wake.*

Section
21.1

IRREGULAR VERBS WITH THE SAME PAST AND PAST PARTICIPLE			
Present	**Present Participle**	**Past**	**Past Participle**
bind	binding	bound	(have) bound
bring	bringing	brought	(have) brought
build	building	built	(have) built
buy	buying	bought	(have) bought
catch	catching	caught	(have) caught
cling	clinging	clung	(have) clung
creep	creeping	crept	(have) crept
fight	fighting	fought	(have) fought
find	finding	found	(have) found
fling	flinging	flung	(have) flung
get	getting	got	(have) got or (have) gotten
grind	grinding	ground	(have) ground
hang	hanging	hung	(have) hung
hold	holding	held	(have) held
keep	keeping	kept	(have) kept
lay	laying	laid	(have) laid
lead	leading	led	(have) led
leave	leaving	left	(have) left
lend	lending	lent	(have) lent
lose	losing	lost	(have) lost
pay	paying	paid	(have) paid
say	saying	said	(have) said
seek	seeking	sought	(have) sought
sell	selling	sold	(have) sold
send	sending	sent	(have) sent
shine	shining	shone or shined	(have) shone or (have) shined
sit	sitting	sat	(have) sat
sleep	sleeping	slept	(have) slept
spend	spending	spent	(have) spent
spin	spinning	spun	(have) spun
stand	standing	stood	(have) stood
stick	sticking	stuck	(have) stuck
sting	stinging	stung	(have) stung
strike	striking	struck	(have) struck
swing	swinging	swung	(have) swung
teach	teaching	taught	(have) taught
win	winning	won	(have) won
wind	winding	wound	(have) wound
wring	wringing	wrung	(have) wrung

524 • Verb Usage

Language Highlight

The first English dictionary was published in 1604 with the title *A Table Alphabeticall*, a 120-page book compiled by Robert Cawdray of England. The book included mostly scholarly words and was intended to help users to seem and to become well educated. Dictionaries continue to aid people who wish to use words correctly. Ask students if they know the name for a writer of dictionaries (lexicographer).

Customize for
Gifted and Talented Students

Point out that many past and present participles rhyme with each other. Have students write short poems or rap songs that utilize participle forms to produce rhyming effects. (Example: *Wintertime's when snow starts falling / That's when old north wind comes calling.*) Have students share or perform their rhymes with the class individually or in groups.

Answer Key

▶ **Exercise 4**

1. has stood
2. have sought
3. built
4. have found
5. had held
6. have said
7. caught
8. had spent
9. left
10. will have taught

Critical Viewing

Draw Conclusions Possible answer: It is remarkable to see what people long ago have built without using our modern technology.

▶ **Exercise 4** **Supplying Past Tenses of Irregular Verbs With the Same Past and Past Participles** Supply the verb and tense indicated to complete each sentence.

EXAMPLE: We (get—past) our map and headed for Stonehenge.
ANSWER: We got our map and headed for Stonehenge.

1. This ancient monument of huge stones (stand—present perfect) on Salisbury Plain in Wiltshire, England, for 4,000 years.
2. Over hundreds of years, investigators (seek—present perfect) to learn the origins of Stonehenge.
3. Theories about who (build—past) it have included the Druids, Greeks, Phoenicians, and Atlantians.
4. Investigators (find—present perfect) that it was constructed in stages from 2000 to 1500 B.C.
5. Some believe that the ancient population (hold—past perfect) ceremonies of worship at Stonehenge.
6. Others (say—present perfect) that it was used to observe astronomical phenomena.
7. Stonehenge certainly (catch—past) our imagination.
8. We (spend—past perfect) only three days in England before we went to visit it.
9. We (leave—past) with a feeling that we had had a close encounter with ancient history.
10. As time goes on, we wonder what people from the past (teach—future perfect) us.

▲ **Critical Viewing** Stonehenge is a great tourist attraction. What makes this and other remnants of the past so intriguing? In your response, use the perfect tense of at least one irregular verb from the chart on page 524. **[Draw Conclusions]**

▶ **More Practice**

Grammar Exercise Workbook
• pp. 73–74
On-line Exercise Bank
• Section 21.1
Go on-line:
PHSchool.com
Enter Web Code:
egk-1202

Integrating Vocabulary Skills

Verbs as Other Parts of Speech
Explain to students that many present participle and past participle forms of verbs can also be used as adjectives and nouns. Point out that *winning*, for instance, can be used as an adjective (The *winning* team celebrated joyously) or as a noun (*Winning* isn't everything). Have students use lists of irregular verbs to choose participles that they can use as adjectives and nouns.

Integrating Spelling Skills

Verb Forms Point out that, when forming the present participle of verbs that end in -*e* (*shake, ride, strive*), delete the -*e* before adding the -*ing* (*shaking, riding, striving*). Add that the final consonant of the present forms of some short verbs ending in -*t* or -*d* is doubled, especially when it has a short vowel sound (*cut, cutting; bid, bidding*). Finally, dictate the present form of regular and irregular verbs and have students practice writing the present participle of those words, using the correct spelling.

21.1 IRREGULAR VERBS THAT CHANGE IN OTHER WAYS

Present	Present Participle	Past	Past Participle
arise	arising	arose	(have) arisen
bear	bearing	bore	(have) borne
beat	beating	beat	(have) beaten or (have) beat
become	becoming	became	(have) become
begin	beginning	began	(have) begun
bite	biting	bit	(have) bitten
blow	blowing	blew	(have) blown
break	breaking	broke	(have) broken
choose	choosing	chose	(have) chosen
come	coming	came	(have) come
do	doing	did	(have) done
draw	drawing	drew	(have) drawn
drink	drinking	drank	(have) drunk
drive	driving	drove	(have) driven
eat	eating	ate	(have) eaten
fall	falling	fell	(have) fallen
fly	flying	flew	(have) flown
forget	forgetting	forgot	(have) forgotten or forgot
freeze	freezing	froze	(have) frozen
give	giving	gave	(have) given
go	going	went	(have) gone
grow	growing	grew	(have) grown
know	knowing	knew	(have) known
lie	lying	lay	(have) lain
ride	riding	rode	(have) ridden
ring	ringing	rang	(have) rung
rise	rising	rose	(have) risen
run	running	ran	(have) run
see	seeing	saw	(have) seen
shake	shaking	shook	(have) shaken
shrink	shrinking	shrank	(have) shrunk
sing	singing	sang	(have) sung
sink	sinking	sank	(have) sunk
slay	slaying	slew	(have) slain
speak	speaking	spoke	(have) spoken
spring	springing	sprang	(have) sprung
steal	stealing	stole	(have) stolen
stride	striding	strode	(have) stridden
strive	striving	strove	(have) striven
swear	swearing	swore	(have) sworn
swim	swimming	swam	(have) swum
take	taking	took	(have) taken
tear	tearing	tore	(have) torn
throw	throwing	threw	(have) thrown
wear	wearing	wore	(have) worn
weave	weaving	wove	(have) woven or (have) wove
write	writing	wrote	(have) written

526 • Verb Usage

 **Internet Tip**

You can use the present participle of verbs to find information about activities that may interest you. For instance, to find information about Ellis Island, you can type "visiting Ellis Island" in the query field of your search engine.

✎ STANDARDIZED TEST PREPARATION WORKSHOP

Grammar and Usage Many standardized tests require students to draw upon their knowledge of verb forms and tenses to respond correctly. Use the following to demonstrate:

Choose the word or group of words that belongs in each space in the following passage.

Augusto and his sister had (1) to the lake to fish through the ice. They (2) enough food for lunch and planned to stay until dinnertime.

1. **A** went
   B gone
   C been gone
   D to be going

2. **A** brung
   B had been bringing
   C were bringing
   D brought

1. The correct answer is **B**. The writer needs to use the past participle (gone) with the helping verb *had* to place this action in the past.

2. The correct answer is **D**. The other past tenses (B and C) use present participles to suggest continuing actions. The use of *brung* is an incorrect spelling.

Exercise 5 Learning the Principal Parts of Irregular Verbs

Write the present participle, the past, and the past participle of each verb.

EXAMPLE: become

ANSWER: becoming became become

1. feel
2. teach
3. lead
4. bring
5. win
6. pay
7. hold
8. strike
9. choose
10. bear

Exercise 6 Using the Correct Forms of Irregular Verbs

On your paper, write the form of the verb indicated in parentheses.

1. People throughout the world (build—present perfect progressive) monuments for thousands of years.
2. Remarkably, people of ancient civilizations (build—past) some of the world's most impressive monuments before the advent of industrial machinery.
3. From around 221 B.C. to 214 B.C., the Chinese emperor Shih Huang-ti (oversee—past) the construction of walls to connect a single wall about 1,650 miles long.
4. Since its construction, the Great Wall of China (be—present perfect) one of the world's largest constructions.
5. By the year 2800, people (stand—future perfect) upon the Great Wall of China for about 3,000 years.
6. Stonehenge is another famous monument that (leave—present perfect) visitors with a strong impression for many years.
7. No one who has visited the monument (forget—future progressive) its mysterious beauty.
8. Scholars (set—present perfect progressive) forth theories about Stonehenge's original function for decades.
9. By the time we arrived in Athens, our friends already (spend—past perfect) many hours viewing the Parthenon.
10. This majestic monument (stand—present perfect progressive) atop the Acropolis for nearly 2,500 years.

More Practice

Grammar Exercise Workbook
• pp. 73–74
On-line Exercise Bank
• Section 21.1
Go on-line:
PHSchool.com
Enter Web Code:
egk-1202

▼ Critical Viewing
Although millions of people visit the Great Wall of China every year, this photograph shows a solitary person on the wall. What effect might the photographer have hoped to achieve by doing so? Use at least one irregular verb in your response. [Analyze]

Verb Tenses • 527

Answer Key

Exercise 5
1. feeling, felt, (have) felt
2. teaching, taught, (have) taught
3. leading, led, (have) led
4. bringing, brought, (have) brought
5. winning, won, (have) won
6. paying, paid, (have) paid
7. holding, held, (have) held
8. striking, struck, (have) struck
9. choosing, chose, (have) chosen
10. bearing, bore, (have) borne

Exercise 6
1. have been building
2. built
3. oversaw
4. has been
5. will have stood
6. has left
7. will be forgetting
8. have been setting
9. had spent
10. has been standing

Critical Viewing

Analyze Possible answer: The photographer chose a solitary figure to create an atmosphere of a forbidding loneliness.

☑ ONGOING ASSESSMENT: Monitor and Reinforce

If students miss more than two items in Exercise 5 or 6, refer them to the following for additional practice.

In the Textbook	Print Resources	Technology
Section Review, Ex. 12–13, Section 21.1	*Grammar Exercise Workbook,* pp. 73–74	*On-Line Exercise Bank,* Section 21.1

⏱ TIME SAVERS!

Answers on Transparencies
Use the *Grammar Exercises Answers on Transparencies* for Chapter 21 to facilitate correction by students.

On-Line Exercise Bank
Have students complete the exercises on computer. The Auto Check feature will grade their work for you!

21.1

▶ **Exercise 7** Supplying the Correct Forms of Regular and Irregular Verbs Write the appropriate past or past participle for each verb in parentheses.

EXAMPLE: The development of new and stronger materials (bring) about vast improvements in building construction.

ANSWER: brought

1. Monuments have often (function) as reminders of an important cause or a famous historical figure.
2. The efforts of a group of ordinary people (be) instrumental in the building of a famous American monument.
3. In 1833, concerned citizens (form) the Washington National Monument Society to raise funds for a memorial to George Washington.
4. These people (want) to be sure that future generations would remember the "father" of their country.
5. In 1848, the United States Congress (authorize) the building of the Washington Monument in Washington, D.C.
6. The American architect Robert Mills had initially (design) the monument, but other architects reconceived it.
7. The Civil War (delay) the completion of the monument until 1884.
8. Since its completion, it has (stand) out as a distinct landmark in Washington, D.C.
9. The monument, which is covered on the outside by marble, has also (become) an irreplaceable part of Washington, D.C.'s, skyline.
10. Not surprisingly, thousands of visitors have (pay) the monument a visit since it was opened to the public in 1888.

▶ **Critical Viewing** The Washington Monument evokes images of an American leader. Similarly, how can the tense of a verb evoke a certain time period in the mind of a reader? [**Relate**]

More Practice

Grammar Exercise Workbook
• pp. 73–74
On-line Exercise Bank
• Section 21.1
Go on-line:
PHSchool.com
Enter Web Code:
egk-1202

528 • Verb Usage

☑ **ONGOING ASSESSMENT: Monitor and Reinforce**

If students have difficulty with Exercise 7, refer them to the following for additional practice.

In the Textbook	Print Resources	Technology
Section Review, Ex. 12–13, Section 21.1	*Grammar Exercise Workbook,* pp. 73–74	*On-Line Exercise Bank,* Section 21.1

Verb Conjugation

The *conjugation* of a verb presents all its different forms.

▶ KEY CONCEPT A **conjugation** is a complete list of the singular and plural forms of a verb in a particular tense. ■

The singular forms of a verb correspond to the singular personal pronouns (*I, you, he, she, it*), and the plural forms correspond to the plural personal pronouns (*we, you, they*).

The chart that follows conjugates the irregular verb *to go*. To conjugate a verb, you need the principal parts: the present (*go*), the past participle (*going*), the past (*went*), and the past participle (*gone*). You also need various helping verbs, such as *has, have, or will*.

The chart below conjugates the verb *to go* in its basic forms. Notice that only three principal parts—the present, the past, and the past participle—are used to conjugate all six of the basic forms.

CONJUGATION OF THE BASIC FORMS OF *GO*		
Present	**Singular**	**Plural**
First Person	I go	we go
Second Person	you go	you go
Third Person	he, she, it goes	they go
Past		
First Person	I went	we went
Second Person	you went	you went
Third Person	he, she, it went	they went
Future		
First Person	I will go	we will go
Second Person	you will go	you will go
Third Person	he, she, it will go	they will go
Present Perfect		
First Person	I have gone	we have gone
Second Person	you have gone	you have gone
Third Person	he, she, it has gone	they have gone
Past Perfect		
First Person	I had gone	we had gone
Second Person	you had gone	you had gone
Third Person	he, she, it had gone	they had gone
Future Perfect		
First Person	I will have gone	we will have gone
Second Person	you will have gone	you will have gone
Third Person	he, she, it will have gone	they will have gone

▶ Speaking and Listening Tip

People often misuse the past participle of *go*. For example, instead of saying, "I should've gone," they say, "I should've went." To accustom yourself to hearing and using the correct past participle of *go*, team up with a classmate and take turns making up sentences using the perfect tenses in the third column of this chart.

Verb Tenses • **529**

Step-by-Step Teaching Guide

Verb Conjugation

1. Have students read the key concept on this page. Explain to students that conjugating a verb can help them form and write tenses correctly.

2. Have student volunteers read aloud from the chart. Review the terms *first person, second person,* and *third person,* and point out that each "person" can be singular or plural.

3. Have students conjugate the verbs *sing* and *build* using the chart on the page as a model.

☑ **ONGOING ASSESSMENT: Monitor and Reinforce**		
If students have difficulty with Exercise 8 or 9, refer them to the following for additional practice.		
In the Textbook	**Print Resources**	**Technology**
Section Review, Ex. 14, Section 21.1	*Grammar Exercise Workbook,* pp. 75–76	*On-Line Exercise Bank,* Section 21.1

Grammar in Literature

1. Have a student read this passage and ask for the tense of each verb. (*has transfigured*–present perfect; *meant*–past; *has come*–present perfect; *will survive*–future, *is*–present. Students might note that there are two infinitives: *to be, to prove*)

2. Discuss with students how time changes in the poem. What action carries forward to the present? (*fidelity has come to be*) What occurs in the future? (*love will survive*)

Connections With Literature

"An Arundel Tomb" can be found in *Prentice Hall Literature: Timeless Voices, Timeless Themes,* The British Tradition.

Conjugating the Verb *Be*

1. Emphasize to students that *be* is an irregular verb that has many forms.

2. Explain that the present participle (*being*) and past participle (*been*) are used the same way that these parts are used for all other verbs. For example, *he was being; they are being; it has been; we have been.*

Answer Key

Exercise 8

1. swims, swim
2. swam, swam
3. will swim, will swim
4. have swum, swim
5. had swum

GRAMMAR IN LITERATURE

from **An Arundel Tomb**
Philip Larkin

Notice how the poet has used verbs in different tenses to show events in present, past, and future time.

Time *has transfigured* them into
Untruth. The stone fidelity
They hardly *meant has come* to be
Their final blazon, and to prove
Our almost-instinct almost true:
What *will survive* of us *is* love.

Note About *Be*: The present participle of *be* is *being*. The past participle is *been*. The present and the past depend on the subject and tense of the verb.

PRESENT:	I *am*	we *are*
	you *are*	you *are*
	he, she, it *is*	they *are*
PAST:	I *was*	we *were*
	you *were*	you *were*
	he, she, it *was*	they *were*
FUTURE:	I *will be*	we *will be*
	you *will be*	you *will be*
	he, she, it *will be*	they *will be*

> **Exercise 8** Supplying Conjugated Forms Complete these sentences with forms of the conjugation of the verb *swim*.
> 1. Who __?__? We __?__. (present tense)
> 2. You __?__ yesterday, right? No, they __?__ yesterday. (past tense)
> 3. They __?__ again tomorrow, too, and you __?__ with them, right? (future tense)
> 4. You __?__ with the team on Fridays. (present perfect tense)
> 5. I __?__ __?__ in several meets before the new coach arrived. (past perfect tense)

> **Exercise 9** Conjugating Verbs Conjugate the verbs below in their basic, progressive, and emphatic forms.
> 1. bring   3. leave   5. stay
> 2. believe   4. stride

530 • Verb Usage

Exercise 9

Responses should include all three persons, singular and plural, in the three forms. Correct parts for these verbs, from which conjugations should be formed, are shown.

1. bring, bringing, brought, (have) brought
2. believe, believing, believed, (have) believed
3. leave, leaving, left, (have) left
4. stride, striding, strode, (have) stridden
5. stay, staying, stayed, (have) stayed

Section 21.1 *Section Review*

GRAMMAR EXERCISES 10–17

▶ **Exercise 10** Identifying Verb Tenses and Their Forms Identify the tense of each verb. Identify its form as well if the form is not basic.

1. Angkor Wat has been one of the most famous Hindu temples in Southeast Asia for more than 800 years.
2. The temple stands sixty meters tall.
3. The people of central Cambodia built Angkor Wat in the twelfth century.
4. Earlier, Cambodians had practiced their religion in smaller temples.
5. People in Southeast Asia have been practicing Buddhism for centuries.

▶ **Exercise 11** Identifying Principal Parts and Tenses Identify the principal part used to form each verb; then identify the tense.

1. One of England's most famous attractions is the Tower of London.
2. The Tower of London was *built* over many years.
3. After its construction, royal families did *use* the tower as a royal residence.
4. Today, the tower has been *converted* into a museum.
5. Architecture experts will be *restoring* parts of the tower in the future.

▶ **Exercise 12** Writing Sentences With Irregular Verbs Write sentences using the verbs in the tenses and forms indicated.

1. read (past perfect)
2. take (future perfect)
3. catch (past emphatic)
4. sit (present perfect)
5. do (future perfect progressive)

▶ **Exercise 13** Supplying the Correct Forms of Verbs Write the form of the italicized verb indicated in parentheses.

1. Arlington National Cemetery *be* (present perfect) one of northern Virginia's most popular attractions for decades.
2. Next year, around four million people *visit* (future) Arlington.
3. The cemetery *occupy* (present emphatic) more than 600 acres.
4. Until recently, most of the cemetery *be* (past perfect) devoted to the graves of soldiers who died in combat.
5. In 1932, the government *dedicate* (past) the Tomb of the Unknown Soldier, now the Tomb of the Unknowns.

▶ **Exercise 14** Conjugating Verbs On your paper, conjugate these verbs:

1. sing   2. forget

▶ **Exercise 15** Find It in Your Reading Reread the excerpt from "An Arundel Tomb" on page 530. Write down the tense of at least three of the verbs.

▶ **Exercise 16** Find It in Your Writing Look through your portfolio for a paragraph written in the present tense. Rewrite it first in the past tense and then in the future tense.

▶ **Exercise 17** Writing Application Imagine that you are a sportswriter. Write a prediction of how the local team will fare this season. Use at least three of the following verb forms: *past emphatic, present emphatic, present progressive, future progressive, future perfect progressive.*

ASSESS

Section Review

Each of these exercises correlates to the instruction on verb tenses, pages 520–530. The exercises may be used for more practice, for reteaching, or for review of the key concepts presented. Answers for all chapter exercises are available in *Grammar Exercises Answers on Transparencies* in your Teaching Resources.

Answer Key

▶ **Exercise 10**

1. present perfect
2. present
3. past
4. past perfect
5. present perfect progressive

▶ **Exercise 11**

1. present (present tense)
2. past (past)
3. present (past emphatic)
4. past participle (present perfect)
5. present participle (future progressive)

▶ **Exercise 12**

Sentences will vary. Sample sentences:

1. I had read the assignment before Tim even started it.
2. By the end of this year I will have taken all the required courses.
3. The receiver insisted that he did catch the ball before it touched the ground.
4. Dave has sat at the end of the bench all season.
5. At the end of this month, I will have been doing the crossword puzzle daily for a year.

▶ **Exercise 13**

1. has been
2. will visit
3. does occupy
4. had been
5. dedicated

▶ **Exercise 14**

Sing and *forget* follow the same pattern as *go* on page 529, using *sing, sings, sang, sung,* and *singing* and *forget, forgets, forgot, forgotten,* and *forgetting,* respectively.

continued

Answer Key continued

▶ **Exercise 15**

Find It In Your Reading
has transfigured—present perfect
meant—past
has come—present perfect
will survive—future
is—present

▶ **Exercise 16**

Find It In Your Writing
More advanced students might experiment with rewriting their paragraphs using the subjunctive mood or progressive tense.

▶ **Exercise 17**

Writing Application
Have volunteers share their predictions. Discuss how changing verb tense affected the narration.

Interest GRABBER Ask students to identify the errors in the following sentence:

When I will wake up yesterday, I am feeling very tired.

(The verbs do not express a logical sequence of time.) Ask students to identify the tense of the first verb (*will wake:* future) and to locate other words that are not consistent with it (*yesterday; am feeling*). Have students write the verbs in a different tense so that the sentence makes sense. Ask students to identify the tenses (*woke, was feeling*—past, past progressive).

Activate Prior Knowledge

Have students recall a sentence or phrase from a children's song that describes an action or condition that is taking place in the present. (Example: "London Bridge *is falling* down.") In this example, observe that *is falling* expresses a present action that is continuing (present progressive tense).

TEACH

Step-by-Step Teaching Guide

Uses of Tense in Present Time

1. As students read the key concept, emphasize that present events and conditions can be expressed in the basic, progressive, and emphatic forms.

2. Have students read aloud from the first chart and point out that the progressive form ends in *-ing* and takes a present form of the helping verb *be* and the emphatic form takes the base verb and requires a present form of the helping verb *do.*

3. Ask students questions that they must answer using the three forms. (Examples: *What do you do before speaking?* I listen. *What are you doing now?* I am listening. *Do you really listen?* I do listen.)

4. Have student volunteers read aloud from the second chart. For each example, have students supply an original sentence to reflect that use of the present.

Section 21.2 The Correct Use of Tenses

The basic, progressive, and emphatic forms of the six tenses show time within one of three general categories: present, past, and future. This section will explain how each verb form has a specific use that distinguishes it from the other forms.

Present, Past, and Future Time

Good usage depends on an understanding of how each form works within its general category of time to express meaning.

Uses of Tense in Present Time Three different forms can be used to express present time.

▶ **KEY CONCEPT** The three forms of the present tense show present actions or conditions as well as various continuing actions or conditions. ∎

The chart below gives an example of each of these forms:

FORMS EXPRESSING PRESENT TIME	
Present:	I weld.
Present Progressive:	I am welding.
Present Emphatic:	I do weld.

The main uses of the basic form of the present tense are shown in the chart below:

FORMS EXPRESSING PRESENT TIME	
Present action:	The shopper *strolls* down the aisle.
Present condition:	My head *is* aching.
Regularly occurring action:	They frequently *drive* to Maine.
Regularly occurring condition:	This road *is* slippery in winter.
Constant action:	Fish *breathe* through gills.
Constant condition:	Human beings *are* primates.

The present may also be used to express historical events. This use of the present, called the *historical present*, is occasionally used in narration to make past actions or conditions come to life.

532 • Verb Usage

Theme: World Monuments

In this section, you will learn the many uses of verb tenses and forms. The examples and exercises in this section tell more about great monuments around the world.

••••••••••••••••••••

Cross-Curricular Connection: Social Studies

⏱ TIME AND RESOURCE MANAGER

Resources
Print: *Grammar Exercise Workbook,* pp. 77–80; *Grammar Exercises Answers on Transparencies,* Ch. 21
Technology: *Writing and Grammar* Interactive Text, Section 21.2; *On-Line Exercise Bank,* Section 21.2

Using the Full Student Edition	Using the Handbook⊞
• Work through all key concepts, pp. 532–544.	• Work through all key concepts, pp. 380–392.
• Assign and review Ex. 18–24.	• Assign and review Exercises 18–24.
• Read and discuss Grammar in Literature, p. 538.	• Read and discuss Grammar in Literature, p. 386.
• Do the Hands-on Grammar activity, p. 545.	• Do the Hands-on Grammar activity, p. 393.

THE HISTORICAL PRESENT

Past action expressed in historical present:
In the late 1800's, thousands of immigrants pass through Ellis Island before starting their lives anew in the U.S.

Past condition expressed in historical present:
The exodus of middle-class people from the cities in the 1960's is one of the factors in the decline of urban areas.

The *critical present* is most often used to discuss deceased authors and their literary achievements.

THE CRITICAL PRESENT

Action expressed in critical present:
Dame Agatha Christie writes with a skill that makes her stories classics.

Condition expressed in critical present:
In addition to his novels, Thomas Hardy is the author of several volumes of poetry.

The *present progressive* is used to show a continuing action or condition of a long or short duration.

USES OF THE PRESENT PROGRESSIVE

Long continuing action:	I *am working* at the visitors' center this summer.
Short continuing action:	I *am watering* the plants.
Continuing condition:	Julio *is being* very helpful.

USES OF THE PRESENT EMPHATIC

Emphasizing a statement:	I *do intend* to meet her at the airport.
Denying a contrary assertion:	No, he *does* not *have* the answer.
Asking a question:	*Do* you *guide* people to the pyramids?
Making a sentence negative:	She *does* not *have* our blessing.

The Correct Use of Tenses • 533

☑ **ONGOING ASSESSMENT: Prerequisite Skills**

If students have difficulty with the correct use of tenses, you may find it necessary to review the following to ensure coverage of prerequisite knowledge.

In the Textbook	Print Resources	Technology
Action Verbs, Section 17.2	*Grammar Exercise Workbook,* pp. 77–78	*On-Line Exercise Bank,* Section 17.2

Historical Present and Critical Present

1. Ask students why writers might use the historical or critical present tenses (to make historical events seem relevant or more compelling).

2. As students read about the critical present, explain that this form is used to discuss deceased writers and their works. Ask students why they might write in this form. (Possible answer: Writers may be gone, but their works live on.)

3. Have students practice using this form in sentences about writers they know. (Example: *William Shakespeare uses free verse.*)

Present Progressive and Present Emphatic

1. Have students supply additional examples of the present progressive and present emphatic tenses. Examples: *The bear is hibernating.* (long duration); *I am yawning.* (short duration)

2. Provide additional examples, as needed:

   I am working on my uncle's farm all summer. (long continuing action)

   I am washing the dishes. (short continuing action)

3. Finally, have students read the four examples of present emphatic and ask them to supply original sentences for each.

Integrating Workplace Skills

The Progressive Form Point out that media announcers often use the progressive form of the present tense to tell about live events. Have students imagine that they are television journalists covering a live event and write paragraphs using the present progressive and present emphatic forms to relay information.

Uses of the Past

1. Use the first chart to show students how each form is assembled. Point out that the past and perfect use the past participle, and that the progressives use the present participle.

2. Have students practice these six forms by substituting different verbs: *choose, begin, believe.*

3. As you read the second chart aloud, remind students that *action* and *condition* are different. Add that conditions are often expressed by a form of the verb *be.*

4. Point out that these verbs are not specific about time, but that they can be made more exact with adverbs such as *last month* or *two days ago.*

5. Have students add a modifier like *last month* or *two days ago* to each sentence in the chart to make the time of the action or condition definite. (Example: *They halted work on the new bridge* last year.)

Uses of the Present Perfect and Past Perfect

1. Use the chart on this page (Present Perfect) and the next (Past Perfect) to demonstrate how each tense is formed. Pay special attention to the helping verbs.

2. Then, focus on present perfect. Ask students why this tense is considered a form of the present. (As with the emphatic, the tense is established by the helping verbs, the present tense *has* and *have*.)

3. Next, have student volunteers read aloud the Past Perfect chart on the next page and point out that each sentence contains two actions, both in the past. Ask what the two tenses are (past and past perfect). Then, ask students to explain the function of the past perfect. (It places its action before the other in time.)

21.2

Uses of Tense in Past Time There are seven verb forms that express past actions or conditions.

▶ **KEY CONCEPT** The seven forms that express past time show actions and conditions beginning in the past. ∎

FORMS EXPRESSING PAST TIME	
Past	I drew.
Present Perfect	I have drawn.
Past Perfect	I had drawn.
Past Progressive	I was drawing.
Present Perfect Progressive	I have been drawing.
Past Perfect Progressive	I had been drawing.
Past Emphatic	I did draw.

The uses of the most common form, the past, are shown in the next chart:

USES OF THE PAST	
Completed action:	They halted work on the new bridge.
Completed condition:	Several apartments were empty.

Notice in the chart above that the time of the action or the condition could be changed from indefinite to definite if such words as *last week* or *yesterday* were added to the sentences.

The *present perfect* always expresses indefinite time. Use it to show action or conditions continuing from the past to the present.

USES OF THE PRESENT PERFECT	
Completed action: (indefinite time)	They have befriended us.
Completed condition: (indefinite time)	I have been here before.
Action continuing to present:	It has rained intermittently for two days now.
Condition continuing to present:	I have felt sluggish all day.

The *past perfect* expresses a past action that took place before another.

USES OF THE PAST PERFECT

Action completed before another past action:
Perhaps the nomadic hunters had drawn on the ground before they drew on the cave walls.

Condition completed before another past condition:
Rhoda had been a photographer until she became ill.

These charts show the past progressive and emphatic forms.

USES OF THE PROGRESSIVE FORMS THAT EXPRESS PAST TIME	
Past Progressive	**Long continuing action in the past:** She *was going* to China that year. **Short continuing action in the past:** I *was talking* to Mary when you tried to call. **Continuous condition in the past:** I *was being* honest when I said I was sorry about the incident.
Present Perfect Progressive	**Action continuing to the present:** Edith *has been visiting* more monuments this summer.
Past Perfect Progressive	**Continuing action interrupted by another:** He *had been dreaming* of victory until reality interrupted his dreams.

USES OF THE PAST EMPHATIC

Emphasizing a statement:
The cactus *did grow* without any water.

Denying a contrary assertion:
But I *did hike* to the ancient ruins!

Asking a question:
When *did* the United States *recognize* Vietnam?

Making a sentence negative:
He *did* not *appreciate* her hard work.

Journal Tip

The past perfect and past progressive forms often serve as intriguing beginnings to a story. For example, "It had been raining all morning when Jillian first noticed the stranger. . . . " In your journal, jot down several similar sentences. Perhaps one of them will inspire an idea for a short story.

Uses of the Progressive Forms That Express Past Time

1. Focus on the three examples of the past progressive tense. Observe that continuous actions in the past may be of long or short duration.

2. Discuss the similarities and differences of the three progressive forms. (*Similarities:* all three show continuing action; past progressive and past perfect progressive are both completed before the present. *Differences:* past progressive was finished before now, present perfect progressive continues until now, and past perfect progressive finished before something else in the past occurred.)

3. Finally, have students write original sentences for each of the three forms.

Uses of the Past Emphatic

1. Point out that the past emphatic behaves in many ways like the present emphatic, but with past actions and with a past tense helping verb, *did*.

2. Have students suggest questions that may have prompted each sentence in the chart as a response. (Example: *Did the cactus grow without any water?*) Remind students that the question itself is in the past emphatic form because it has all the elements of the sentence, *The cactus* did *grow without any water.*

Uses of Tense in Future Time

1. Remind students that the perfect tense uses the past participle and that the progressive tenses use the present participle. Then, point out the helping verbs.

2. Give students practice forming these four future forms using the following verbs: *vote, eat, rise.* (Example: *will vote, will have voted, will be voting, will have been voting*)

3. Next, have student volunteers read aloud from the chart that distinguishes *future* from *future perfect.*

4. Ask students to describe the difference between the future and future perfect tenses. (The *future tense* describes an action that will occur in the future. The *future perfect* describes a future action completed before another future action.)

5. Have students identify the words and phrases that help identify sequence of events. (Examples: by the time you arrive, for a month, season begins)

6. Read the chart on *future progressive* and *future perfect progressive*. Ask students how these compare and contrast with the future and future perfect. (*Similarities:* all four are taking place in the future, both perfect forms are completed before something else happens. *Differences:* the progressive form expresses continuing action, the others do not.)

7. Discuss the expression of future time using the present tense. Ask what words show the future in the examples (*next weekend, next month*). Point out that the example for future perfect progressive contains a present tense verb that expresses future time. In this case, it is the future perfect progressive that points to the fact that *embarks* must be in the future.

21.2

▶ **KEY CONCEPT** The four forms that express future time show future actions or conditions. ■

FORMS EXPRESSING FUTURE TIME

Future	I will walk.
Future Perfect	I will have walked.
Future Progressive	I will be walking.
Future Perfect Progressive	I will have been walking.

USES OF THE FUTURE AND THE FUTURE PERFECT

Future	**Future action:** I *will jog* in the morning. **Future condition:** I *will be* late for the meeting.
Future Perfect	**Future action completed before another:** I *will have run* a mile by the time you arrive. **Future condition completed before another:** The orchestra *will have been* on tour for a month before the new concert season begins.

Notice in the next chart that the *future progressive* and the *future perfect progressive* express only future actions.

USES OF THE PROGRESSIVE FORMS THAT EXPRESS FUTURE TIME

Future Progressive	**Continuing future action:** Rita *will be studying* all weekend.
Future Perfect Progressive	**Continuing future action completed before another:** Sharon *will have been preparing* for ten years before she embarks on her trip around the world.

Note About *Expressing Future Time With the Present Tense:* The basic form of the *present* and the *present progressive* are often used with other words to express future time.

EXAMPLES: The new store *opens* next weekend.
              That family *is leaving* next month for Hawaii.

536 • Verb Usage

▶ **Exercise 18** Identifying the Uses of Tense in Present and
Past Time Identify the use of the verb in each
sentence, using the labels in the charts on pages
532–535.

1. The sphinx is a creature found in Greek and
   Egyptian mythology.
2. Greeks envision the sphinx as a monster
   with the head of a woman, the body of a lion,
   and the wings of a bird.
3. For Egyptians, sphinxes are statues that represent rulers.
4. Egypt is a country in northeast Africa.
5. People from around the world often visit
   Egypt's many sphinxes.
6. Around 2500 B.C., the ancient Egyptians
   built the Great Sphinx of Giza.
7. That sphinx stands more than 60 feet high.
8. At this very moment, many people may be
   visiting sphinxes.
9. The ancient Greek historian Herodotus writes
   eloquently about Egypt.
10. Do you like the sphinxes of Egypt?

▶ **Exercise 19** Using Tense in Past Time Write the indicated
form of each verb in parentheses.

1. Many people (believe—present perfect) that pyramids are
   found only in Egypt.
2. In fact, ancient peoples (erect—past) their own pyramids
   throughout Central America thousands of years ago.
3. The Mayas (build—past) their earliest pyramid in Central
   America between 600 and 400 B.C.
4. The Mayas (construct—past progressive) four-sided pyramids
   with flat platforms on the top while ancient Egyptians
   were building pyramids with four sides that met at a point
   on the top.
5. Unlike the ancient Egyptians, the Mayas (use—past
   emphatic) their pyramids as ceremonial platforms.
6. The Mayas (perform—past progressive) elaborate ceremonies
   on their pyramids when ancient Egyptians were using
   their pyramids as burial tombs.
7. The Mayas (thrive—past perfect progressive) for many
   centuries before the arrival of Europeans.
8. People (travel—present perfect) to Mexico to visit these
   sites for many years.
9. Archaeologists (wonder—present perfect progressive) for
   a long time just how the Mayas were able to build such
   formidable structures.
10. (see—past emphatic asking a question) you a Mayan pyra-
    mid during your trip to Mexico last year?

▲ Critical Viewing
How does this sphinx
compare to present-day
monuments? Use a
different form of a
present-tense verb in
each sentence.
**[Compare and
Contrast]**

▶ **More Practice**

**Grammar Exercise
Workbook**
• pp. 77–78
On-line Exercise Bank
• Section 21.2
  Go on-line:
  PHSchool.com
  Enter Web Code:
  egk-1202

The Correct Use of Tenses • 537

☑ **ONGOING ASSESSMENT: Monitor and Reinforce**

If students have difficulty with Exercise 18 or 19, refer them to the following for additional practice.

In the Textbook	Print Resources	Technology
Section Review, Ex. 25–26, Section 21.1	*Grammar Exercise Workbook,* pp. 77–78	*On-Line Exercise Bank,* Section 21.2

Grammar in Literature

1. Have a different student read each line and (1) identify the verb, if any, (2) identify its tense, and (3) distinguish verb forms not used as verbs.

2. Ask why some of the present and past participles are not used as verbs. (They are used as adjectives and nouns.)

3. Have student volunteers change some verbs to the past perfect tense. (Example: No one *had talked* as well as he did.)

More About the Writer

Geoffrey Chaucer was born in 1340 to a family that worked in the wine trade. After a long service to the king of England as a translator and record keeper, he wrote *The Canterbury Tales,* a collection of poems that tell the story of a group of travelers who amuse themselves by telling stories to one another while on pilgrimage. He wrote in English at a time when many others wrote in French, and most official documents were still written in French. Chaucer is regarded by many as the first great writer and poet in English. He died on October 25, 1400, and was buried in Westminster Abbey.

Connections With Literature

The Canterbury Tales: The Prologue can be found in *Prentice Hall Literature, Penguin Edition,* The British Tradition.

Answer Key

Exercise 20

1. takes
2. is increasing
3. will continue
4. will be planning
5. will serve

21.2

GRAMMAR IN LITERATURE

from The Canterbury Tales: The Prologue
Geoffrey Chaucer

The verbs highlighted in blue type show the translator's use of the past tense.

A *Doctor* too *emerged* as we *proceeded*;
No one alive could talk as well as he *did*
On points of medicine and of surgery,
For, being grounded in astronomy,
He *watched* his patient's favorable star
And, by his Natural Magic, *knew* what are
The lucky hours and planetary degrees
For making charms and magic effigies.
The cause of every malady you'd got
He *knew*, and whether dry, cold, moist or hot;
He *knew* their seat, their humor and condition.
He *was* a perfect practicing physician.
These causes being known for what they *were*,
He *gave* the man his medicine then and there.

▶ **Exercise 20** Using Tense in Future Time Write the verb in parentheses in the tense indicated.

1. Downtown, a sign indicates the dedication of the new skyscraper that (take—express future time with present tense) place next year.

2. Everywhere one goes these days, the rate of new construction (increase—express future time with present progressive) rapidly.

3. Improvements in construction materials and methods (continue—future) to change the landscape of modern cities for many years.

4. Architects and city planners (plan—future progressive) great changes for cities like Tokyo, New York, and Chicago in the near future.

5. Towering skyscrapers (serve—future) as monuments to the immense impact of both technology and increased urbanization on the lives of ordinary people worldwide.

▶ **More Practice**

Grammar Exercise Workbook
• pp. 77–78

On-line Exercise Bank
• Section 21.2
  Go on-line:
  PHSchool.com
  Enter Web Code:
  egk-1202

Interactive Textbook

Get instant feedback! Exercise 20 is available on-line or on CD-ROM.

☑ **ONGOING ASSESSMENT: Monitor and Reinforce**

If students miss more than one item in Exercise 20, refer them to the following for additional practice.

In the Textbook	Print Resources	Technology
Section Review, Ex. 27, Section 21.2	*Grammar Exercise Workbook,* pp. 77–78	*On-Line Exercise Bank,* Section 21.2

Sequence of Tenses

A sentence with more than one verb must be consistent in its time sequence.

▶ **KEY CONCEPT** When showing a sequence of events, do not shift tenses unnecessarily. ■

It is, however, sometimes necessary to shift tenses, especially when a sentence is complex or compound-complex. The tense of the main verb often determines the tense of the subordinate verb. Moreover, the form of a participle or infinitive often depends on the tense of the main verb in the sentence.

Verbs in Subordinate Clauses It is frequently necessary to look at the tense of the main verb in a sentence before deciding the tense of the verb in the subordinate clause.

▶ **KEY CONCEPT** The tense of a verb in a subordinate clause should follow logically from the tense of the main verb. ■

As you study the combinations of tenses in the charts that follow, notice that the choice of tenses affects the logical relationship between the events being expressed. Some combinations indicate that the events are *simultaneous*—meaning that they occur at the same time. Other combinations indicate that the events are *sequential*—meaning that one event occurs before or after the other.

▼ Critical Viewing
Mt. Rushmore honors presidents from different time periods. How can you use verbs to show different time periods within a single sentence? **[Analyze]**

The Correct Use of Tenses • **539**

Sequence of Tenses

1. Ask students from what noun the adjective *sequential* derives (sequence).

2. Emphasize for students that verbs in complex or compound-complex sentences often establish a sequence of events and that the wrong tense progression can confuse a reader.

3. You may wish to review complex and compound-complex sentences with the class.

Critical Viewing

Analyze Possible answer: Since verbs can show continuing action (progressive) or action that was completed before another action took place (perfect), it is possible to establish a logical flow of time within a sentence. For example: *George Washington had been dead for nearly sixty years when Theodore Roosevelt was born.*

☑ ONGOING ASSESSMENT: Prerequisite Skills

If students have difficulty with subordinate clauses, you may find it necessary to review the following to ensure coverage of prerequisite knowledge.

In the Textbook	Print Resources	Technology
Clauses, Section 19.3 Sentence Structure, Section 19.4	*Grammar Exercise Workbook,* pp. 79–80	*On-Line Exercise Bank,* Sections 19.3–4

Subordinate Clauses With Main Verb in Present Tense

1. If necessary, briefly review complex and compound-complex sentences.

2. Use the models in the chart on page 540 to illustrate how the tense of the verb in the main clause establishes the time sequence of the sentence. Point out that the verb in the subordinate clause must be fitted to the verb in the main clause, not the other way around.

3. Have students suggest modifiers to add to the clauses. (Example: I understand _now_ that you are writing a novel _today_.)

4. Remind students to analyze the actions and conditions presented in the sentences to determine correct verb choices.

Subordinate Clauses With Main Verb in Past Tense

1. For the first example, point out that the actions described by the two verbs are simultaneous because one action did not occur before the other.

2. For the second example, have students add modifiers that clarify the sense of time in both clauses. (Example: I understood _last week_ that you had written a novel _many years ago_.) Point out that the tense of the verb in the subordinate clause (_had written_) tells us that the writing took place further in the past than the speaker's understanding, which happened in the more recent past.

3. Suggest to students that they can insert modifiers into their writing, or mentally insert them into other people's sentences, to determine correct time sequence.

21.2

SEQUENCE OF TENSES

Main Verb in Present		
Main Verb	Subordinate Verb	Meaning
I understand. . .	PRESENT that he _writes_ novels. PRESENT PROG that he _is writing_ a novel. PRESENT EMPH that he _does write_ novels.	Simultaneous events: All events occur in present time.
I understand. . .	PAST that he _wrote_ a novel. PRESENT PERF that he _has written_ a novel. PAST PERF that he _had written_ a novel. PAST PROG that he _was writing_ a novel. PRESENT PERF PROG that he _has been writing_ a novel. PAST PERF PROG that he _had been writing_ a novel. PAST EMP that he _did write_ a novel.	Sequential events: The writing comes before the understanding.
I understand . . .	FUTURE that he _will write_ a novel. FUTURE PERF that he _will have written_ a novel. FUTURE PROG that he _will be writing_ a novel. FUTURE PERF PROG that he _will have been writing_ a novel.	Sequential events: The understanding comes before the writing.
Main Verb in Past		
I understood. . .	PAST that he _wrote_ a novel. PAST PROG that he _was writing_ a novel. PAST EMP that he _did write_ a novel.	Simultaneous events: All events take place in past time.
I understood. . .	PAST PERF that he _had written_ a novel. PAST PERF PROG that he _had been writing_ a novel.	Sequential events: The writing came before the understanding.

Grammar and Style Tip

When relating the events of a story, generally try to keep your verbs consistently in either past or present tenses to avoid confusing your reader.

540 • Verb Usage

Main Verb in Future		
I will understand. . .	PRESENT if he *writes* a novel. PRESENT PROG if he *is writing* a novel. PRESENT EMPH if he *does write* a novel.	Simultaneous events: All events take place in future time.
I will understand. . .	PAST if he *wrote* a novel. PRESENT PERF if he *has written* a novel. PRESENT PERF PROG if he *has been writing* a novel. PAST EMP if he *did write* a novel.	Sequential events: The writing comes before the understanding.

Time Sequence With Participles and Infinitives

Frequently, the form of a participle or infinitive determines whether the events are simultaneous or sequential. Participles can be present *(seeing)*, past *(seen)*, or perfect *(having seen)*. Infinitives can be present *(to see)* or perfect *(to have seen)*.

KEY CONCEPTS The form of a participle or an infinitive should set up a logical time sequence in relation to a verb in the same clause or sentence. ■

To show simultaneous events, you will generally need to use the present participle or the present infinitive, whether the main verb is present, past, or future.

SIMULTANEOUS EVENTS	
In Present Time	PRESENT PRESENT *Seeing* the results, she *laughs.* PRESENT PRESENT He *needs to confirm* the results.
In Past Time	PRESENT PAST *Seeing* the results, she *laughed.* PAST PRESENT He *needed to confirm* the results.
In Future Time	PRESENT FUTURE *Seeing* the results, she *will laugh.* FUTURE PRESENT He *will need to confirm* the results.

Step-by-Step Teaching Guide

Subordinate Clauses With Main Verb in Future Tense

1. As students read the examples aloud, have them explain how some sentences express simultaneous events while others express sequential ones. (For simultaneous events, verbs and modifiers reflect the same time—events in each clause overlap. For sequential events, verbs and modifiers in each clause reflect a different time, though the two times must be logically related.)

2. Have students analyze time sequence with additional examples:

   I will drive if you pay the tolls. (simultaneous)

   I will drive once you have buckled your seat belts. (sequential)

Step-by-Step Teaching Guide

Simultaneous and Sequential Events

1. Have students read aloud the examples in the chart. Remind them to think logically about the time expressed in each.

2. As students read sentences on p. 542 that describe sequential events, have them reread only the words in each clause that help identify time (for example, *having seen, is laughing*) and ask them to describe the sequence in their own words.

Time Sequence With Participles and Infinitives

1. Remind students that the infinitive of a verb is a basic form with "to" in front. For example, the infinitive of the verb *be* is *to be*.

2. Point out that, as with all other instances of time, relation between clauses must remain logical.

3. As students review the charts on this and the previous page, ask them to suggest other examples of both simultaneous and sequential events that can be described using participles and infinitives.

Customize for
Logical/Mathematical Learners

Let students practice determining time sequence between ideas in sentences by using Exercise 19 on p. 537. For each sentence, have students write the verb, then the other verb or other words that indicate time, then an equal sign (=), and finally, the word *sequential* or *simultaneous*. The first answer would look like this:

have believed / are found = simultaneous

Critical Viewing

Connect Students may cite adjectives, adverbs, adverb phrases, and other modifiers that express time, as well as specific details, such as dates.

Answer Key

Exercise 21

1. to decipher
2. Seeing
3. to have seen
4. to find
5. to have been

21.2

SEQUENTIAL EVENTS	
In Present Time	PERFECT PRESENT PROG *Having seen* the results, she *is laughing.* (The seeing comes before the laughing.) PRESENT PERFECT He *is* fortunate *to have worked* with you. (The working comes before the being fortunate.)
In Past Time	PERFECT PAST *Having seen* the results, *she laughed.* (The seeing came before the laughing.) PAST PERFECT He *was* fortunate *to have worked* with you. (The working came before the being fortunate.)
Spanning Past and Future Time	PERFECT FUTURE *Having seen* her work, I *will recommend* her. (The seeing comes before the recommending.) FUTURE PERFECT He *will be* fortunate *to have worked* with you. (The working comes before the being fortunate.)

To show sequential events, you will generally need to use the perfect form of the participle and infinitive, regardless of the tense of the main verb.

Exercise 21 Using the Correct Forms of Subordinate Verbs, Participles, and Infinitives Rewrite each sentence, following the instructions in parentheses.

EXAMPLE: The architect was sad he had planned so poorly. (Change *had planned* to a perfect infinitive.)

ANSWER: The architect was sad to have planned so poorly.

1. Many scholars have attempted deciphering the mystery of the large stone monuments on Easter Island. (Change *deciphering* to a present infinitive.)
2. Having seen the stone statues, many visitors are overcome by awe. (Change *having seen* to a present participle).
3. Many visitors feel fortunate to see these stone monuments. (Change *to see* to a perfect infinitive.)
4. Archaeologists have tried finding out just who made these magnificent statues. (Change *finding* to present infinitive.)
5. The statues seem to be carved between A.D. 1000 and 1600. (Change *to be* to a perfect infinitive.)

542 • Verb Usage

▼ Critical Viewing Scientists used clues to determine that these Easter Island statues were carved between A.D. 1000 and 1600. In addition to verbs, what clues can you look for in a sentence to determine the time period to which it refers? **[Connect]**

✓ ONGOING ASSESSMENT: Monitor and Reinforce		
If students have difficulty with Exercise 21, refer them to the following for additional practice.		
In the Textbook	**Print Resources**	**Technology**
Section Review, Ex. 29, Section 21.2	*Grammar Exercise Workbook,* pp. 79–80	*On-Line Exercise Bank,* Section 21.2

Exercise 22 Supplying Correct Verb Tenses Supply the correct form of the verb indicated to complete each sentence.

1. Joan of Arc is a patron saint of France who (lead) the resistance to the English invasion of France in the Hundred Years War.
2. Joan was born around 1412 and (grow) up on her father's tenant farm.
3. By the time she was thirteen, she already (begin) to believe that her mission was to save France from the English.
4. She (be) still remembered today for her success at the 1429 battle of Orleans, where she led French troops in a miraculous defeat of the English.
5. There is little doubt that French people always (consider) Joan of Arc a great heroine of France.

Exercise 23 Revising to Correct Errors in Tense Revise the following sentences, correcting unnecessary shifts in tense. If the tense does not shift, write *correct*.

1. Mount Saint Helens is an active volcano, which *will have been lying* in southwest Washington.
2. Before erupting in 1857, the volcano *have* not *been erupting* for more than 100 years.
3. Not surprisingly, most people *have* not *expected* it to erupt ever again.
4. To the people who used Mount Saint Helens for recreation, it *will have been* simply a pristine mountain.
5. However, on May 18, 1980, the volcano *has erupted* with extreme force, surprising nearby residents.
6. A cloud of ash and gases *had shot up* around 12 miles into the sky.
7. The eruption *comes* as a surprise and *resulted* in great destruction.
8. The eruption *was destroying* much animal and plant life in an area of some 230 square miles.
9. In 1982, the U.S. government *established* the National Volcanic Monument there.
10. Today, the volcano *will be continuing* to have small eruptions.

More Practice

Grammar Exercise Workbook
• pp. 79–80
On-line Exercise Bank
• Section 21.2
  Go on-line:
  PHSchool.com
  Enter Web Code:
  egk-1202

Interactive Textbook

Get instant feedback! Exercises 21, 22, and 23 are available on-line or on CD-ROM.

Answer Key

Exercise 22
1. led
2. grew
3. had begun
4. is
5. have considered *or* will consider

Exercise 23
1. lies
2. had not erupted
3. had not expected
4. was
5. erupted *or* did erupt
6. shot up
7. came
8. destroyed
9. correct
10. continues

The Correct Use of Tenses • 543

✓ **ONGOING ASSESSMENT: Monitor and Reinforce**

If students have difficulty with Exercise 22 or 23, refer them to the following for additional practice.

In the Textbook	Print Resources	Technology
Section Review, Ex. 30, Section 21.2	*Grammar Exercise Workbook,* pp. 79–80	*On-Line Exercise Bank,* Section 21.2

⏱ **TIME SAVERS!**

📄 **Answers on Transparencies** Use the *Grammar Exercises Answers on Transparencies* for Chapter 21 to facilitate correction by students.

🖥 **On-Line Exercise Bank** Have students complete the exercises on computer. The Auto Check feature will grade their work for you!

Modifiers That Help Clarify Tense

1. Explain to students that verbs are not the only words that can provide information about the sense of time in sentences.

2. Ask students to suggest additional modifiers. Examples: *today, tomorrow, recently, next year, sometimes, many years ago*.

3. Have students rewrite the examples in the book, replacing the modifiers with modifiers of their own.

Answer Key

▶ **Exercise 24**

Answers will vary. Samples are given.

1. Every year, thousands of people travel to Washington, D.C., to visit the city's many famous monuments.
2. Hundreds of tourists each day visit the Washington Monument, the Lincoln Memorial, the Jefferson Memorial, and the Franklin D. Roosevelt Memorial.
3. People often take photographs at these and other famous sites in our nation's capital.
4. There are always long lines for the tour of the White House.
5. The United States flag is raised each morning outside all the memorials and government office buildings.
6. Because we're studying United States history this year, our class is visiting Washington, D.C.
7. Many of the monuments frequently remind us of the contributions of men who served as president.
8. Other monuments commemorate the daily sacrifices of men and women who have served during wars.
9. In addition to the monuments and memorials, there are frequent special celebrations.
10. Recently, there was an important celebration to honor foreign dignitaries who had come to see the monuments.

Critical Viewing

Speculate Possible answer: Every year, thousands of people visit the Lincoln Memorial.

21.2

Modifiers That Help Clarify Tense

The time expressed by a verb can often be clarified by adverbs such as *always* or *frequently* and phrases such as *last week* or *now and then*.

▶ **KEY CONCEPTS** Use modifiers when they can help clarify tense. ■

EXAMPLES: We read about great monuments *every weekend*.
My brother practices singing *once a week*.

▶ **Exercise 24** Using Modifiers to Improve Meaning

Rewrite each sentence by adding a modifier that indicates time. (*Note:* There are no right or wrong modifiers, but all sentences must make sense once rewritten.)

1. Millions of people travel to Washington, D.C., to visit the city's many famous monuments.
2. Thousands of tourists visit the Washington Monument, the Lincoln Memorial, the Jefferson Memorial, and the Franklin D. Roosevelt Memorial.
3. People take photographs at these and other famous sites in our nation's capital.
4. There are often long lines for tickets to tour the White House.
5. The United States flag is raised outside all memorials and government office buildings.
6. Because we're studying United States history, our class is visiting Washington, D.C.
7. Many of the monuments remind us of the contributions of men who served as president.
8. Other monuments commemorate the sacrifices of men and women who have served during wars.
9. In addition to the monuments and memorials, there are special celebrations.
10. There was an important celebration to honor foreign dignitaries who had come to see the monuments.

▶ **Critical Viewing** Using a modifier to clarify tense, speculate on the number of visitors to the Lincoln Memorial. **[Speculate]**

544 • Verb Usage

More Practice

Grammar Exercise Workbook
• pp. 79–80
On-line Exercise Bank
• Section 21.2
  Go on-line:
  PHSchool.com
  Enter Web Code:
  egk-1202

Interactive Textbook

Complete the exercise on-line! Exercise 24 is available on-line or on CD-ROM.

☑ **ONGOING ASSESSMENT: Monitor and Reinforce**

If students have difficulty with Exercise 24, refer them to the following for additional practice.

In the Textbook	Print Resources	Technology
Section Review, Ex. 31, Section 21.2	*Grammar Exercise Workbook,* pp. 79–80	*On-Line Exercise Bank,* Section 21.2

Hands-on Grammar

Two-Way Modifier Slide

Make and use a Two-Way Modifier Slide to see how modifiers clarify the time expressed by a verb. To begin, fold a piece of lined notebook paper in half the long way, and then unfold it. Next, fold the right side of the paper in half to the crease, cut in 1 1/4" on every third line, and unfold. You should have 12 2 1/2" slits. At the top of the left side of the paper, print the title "Present and Past Tenses." Turn the paper over, and print "Future Tenses" at the top of the right side. Then, cut a 2 1/4" x 8 1/2" strip of colored paper, and draw 16 lines across it at 1/2" intervals on both sides. Now, on one side of the strip, write modifiers that would clarify present or past tense verbs: *today, every day, this year, on Monday, last week, yesterday, before dinner,* and so on.

On the other side, write modifiers that would clarify future tense verbs: *tomorrow, next week, in an hour, in 2030, after lunch,* and so on. (Some modifiers will serve all purposes.) Then, weave the strip through the slits, making sure that the "present and past" modifiers face the appropriate head to the left. Finally, on the notebook paper lines parallel to the modifiers, write short sentences using present and past tense verbs on one side and future

tense verbs on the other. Now, slide the strip of paper through the slits, seeing how many ways the meaning of a sentence can change by adding a modifier. On the "future" side, the modifiers will begin the sentences. Note that not every modifier will work with every sentence.

Find It in Your Reading Look through a recent news article, and note how modifiers are used to clarify the time of the events.

Find It in Your Writing See if you can use modifiers to clarify the times of events in an essay or story in your portfolio.

Hands-on Grammar

Teaching Resources: Hands-on Grammar Activity Book, Ch. 21

1. If you wish to do this activity in class, be prepared with scissors, lined notebook paper, and colored paper for students. Give each student a copy of the Hands-on Grammar activity sheet.
2. Have students follow the directions to prepare the modifier slides.
3. Encourage students to choose a variety of modifiers for the verb tenses.

Find It in Your Reading

You may wish to photocopy an article for each student to work on as a class activity.

Find It in Your Writing

Have students work in pairs or small groups for this activity.

✓ ONGOING ASSESSMENT: Prerequisite Skills

If students have difficulty with modifiers, you may find it necessary to review the following to ensure coverage of prerequisite knowledge.

In the Textbook	Print Resources	Technology
Adjectives, Section 17.3 Adverbs, Section 17.3	*Grammar Exercise Workbook,* pp. 11–14	*On-Line Exercise Bank,* Section 17.3

⏱ TIME SAVERS!

✋ **Hands-on Grammar** Use the Hands-on Grammar activity sheet for Chapter 21 to facilitate this activity.

Section Review

Each of these exercises correlates to the instruction on correct use of tenses, pages 532–545. The exercises may be used for more practice, for reteaching, or for review of the key concepts presented. Answers for all chapter exercises are available in *Grammar Exercises Answers on Transparencies* in your Teaching Resources.

Answer Key

> **Exercise 25**

1. present condition
2. constant condition
3. short continuing action
4. constant condition
5. critical present

> **Exercise 26**

1. labored
2. were completing
3. has been
4. had been worshipping
5. have established

> **Exercise 27**

1. will change
2. will have established
3. will be using
4. will choose
5. will have been admiring

> **Exercise 28**

1. sequential, island was a military prison before it was a federal prison
2. sequential, prison closing occurred before tourists visit
3. simultaneous
4. sequential, prison closing occurred forty years before the anticipated anniversary
5. sequential, its becoming part of the parks system occurred after the island was empty for many years

---

Section **21.2** *Section Review*

GRAMMAR EXERCISES 25–35

> **Exercise 25** **Identifying the Uses of Tense in Present Time** Referring to the charts on pages 532–533, identify the use of the verb in each sentence.

1. Pyramids are among the most impressive monuments in the world.
2. Some pyramids in Egypt stand more than 400 feet tall.
3. People are visiting Egyptian pyramids at this very moment.
4. There is a famous group of pyramids near Cairo, Egypt.
5. The Egyptologist Samuel Mercer writes in great detail about the artifacts found in these pyramids.

> **Exercise 26** **Supplying Verbs in Past Time** On your paper, write the indicated form of each verb in parentheses.

1. From A.D. 532 to 537, during the reign of Emperor Justinian I, thousands of workers (labor—past) to build Hagia Sophia.
2. These workers (complete—past progressive) Hagia Sophia in the Turkish city of Istanbul, which was once known as Constantinople.
3. Hagia Sophia, also known as the Church of Holy Wisdom, (is—present perfect) one of the most famous structures of the Byzantine Empire for nearly 1,500 years.
4. Prior to the completion of the majestic church, worshippers of the Orthodox Christian faith in Constantinople (worship—past perfect progressive) in smaller churches.
5. Hagia Sophia's large size and rich history (establish—present perfect) it as one of the world's most impressive monuments.

> **Exercise 27** **Supplying Verbs in Future Time** Rewrite each sentence, changing each underlined verb as indicated in parentheses.

1. It is inevitable that the landscape of cities and entire nations changes (future) with the passage of time.
2. By the next century, people establish (future perfect) dozens of monuments.
3. It is likely that people of the future use (future progressive) different materials to create monuments.
4. It is possible that they choose (future) different types of events and people to honor.
5. By the time the next generation is grown, they admire (future perfect progressive) for years the monuments that don't even exist now.

> **Exercise 28** **Identifying the Time Sequence in Sentences With More Than One Verb** Identify whether the time sequence of events described by the two verbs in each sentence is sequential or simultaneous. If it is sequential, identify which event occurs before the other.

1. Before it became a federal prison, Alcatraz Island served as the site of a military prison from 1868 to 1933.
2. The prison finally closed in 1963, and the island now lures thousands of tourists to its grounds each year.
3. At the time it was a prison, reformers demanded that government officials improve conditions.
4. Soon it will have been forty years since the prison closed.
5. Although it was left empty for many years, the island became a part of the Golden Gate National Recreation Area in 1972.

✎ STANDARDIZED TEST PREPARATION WORKSHOP

Grammar and Usage Many standardized tests require students to recognize forms, tenses, and sequences of verbs in sentences. Write the following on the board and ask students to identify the correct answer.

By the end of the second semester, underline{students will read} William Thackeray's novel Vanity Fair *and Dickens's* Bleak House.

How should the underlined portion be written?

A Correct as is

B students are reading

C students will have read

D students would have been reading

The correct answer is **C**. The future perfect *will have read* clarifies the sequence of two actions: the reading of the novel happens before the end of the semester.

▶ **Exercise 29** Using the Correct Forms of Subordinate Verbs, Participles, and Infinitives On your paper, rewrite the sentences, following the instructions in parentheses.

1. People have long needed reminding themselves of their place in history. (Replace *reminding* with a present infinitive.)
2. Ancient people are known for building structures commemorating important events. (Change *for building* to a perfect infinitive.)
3. Having wanted to show their power, rulers built monuments for themselves. (Change *having wanted* to a present participle.)
4. Creating these monuments often involved the mobilization of thousands of workers. (Change *the mobilization of* to a present participle.)
5. These people worked hard creating astonishingly huge structures. (Change *creating* to a present infinitive.)

▶ **Exercise 30** Revising to Correct Errors in Tense Revise these sentences, correcting unnecessary shifts in tense.

1. Monuments provide information and are serving as guideposts in research.
2. Monuments often had been commemorating heroic deeds and people.
3. In ancient times, people built structures that were reminding them of their stories.
4. Monuments had been serving a similar function today.
5. Early this century, entire historic battlefields are being designated as monuments in the United States.

▶ **Exercise 31** Revising to Add Modifiers to Enhance Meaning Revise each sentence, adding a modifier to indicate time.

1. Ellis Island was the headquarters of the immigrant processing center.
2. Around twelve million immigrants passed through Ellis Island.
3. Back then, thousands of people from all over the world came to New York.
4. Due to increased use of U.S. Consulates abroad, the United States Immigration Service closed the center.
5. The immigration station on the island was turned into a museum.

▶ **Exercise 32** Writing Sentences With Correct Verb Tenses In the tenses given, write sentences on the topic of monuments or tourist attractions.

1. past and past perfect
2. present perfect and past
3. present and future progressive
4. past progressive and past
5. present and future perfect progressive

▶ **Exercise 33** Find It in Your Reading Reread the excerpt from "The Canterbury Tales" on page 538. List the verbs that would change if the speaker and doctor were with you now relating the story.

▶ **Exercise 34** Find It in Your Writing Looking through your portfolio, find any sentences with more than one verb and check to see that the verbs are correctly sequenced. Rewrite any sentences not consistent in their time sequence.

▶ **Exercise 35** Writing Application Write a paragraph about something interesting a friend of yours did. Use at least five verbs in the past tense, and use verbs to show sequential events at least once.

Section Review • 547

Answer Key

▶ **Exercise 29**

1. to remind
2. to have built
3. Wanting
4. mobilizing
5. to create

▶ **Exercise 30**

1. serve
2. commemorate
3. reminded
4. serve
5. were designated

▶ **Exercise 31**

Answers will vary. Samples are given.

1. Years ago, Ellis Island was the headquarters of the immigrant processing center.
2. Over the years, around twenty million immigrants passed through Ellis Island.
3. Back then, thousands of people from all over the world came to New York every year.
4. Due to declining immigration, the U.S. Immigration Service eventually closed the center.
5. The immigration station on the island was finally turned into a museum.

▶ **Exercise 32**

Sentences will vary. Check for correct use of verb tenses. Encourage students who have difficulty to refer to the charts in the textbook.

▶ **Exercise 33**

Find It In Your Reading

emerges, proceed, can talk, does, watches, knows, knows, knows, is, are, gives

▶ **Exercise 34**

Find It In Your Writing
You may wish to encourage students to review sentence combining (Chapter 20) in order to help them add sentences with more than one verb.

▶ **Exercise 35**

Writing Application
To help students complete the assignment, suggest that they write from their own present point of view about their friends' experiences.

☑ **ONGOING ASSESSMENT: Assess Mastery**

Use the following resources to assess student mastery of tenses.

In the Textbook	Technology
Chapter Review, Ex. 56–58	*Writing and Grammar* Interactive Text, Section 21.2, Section Review; *On-Line Exercise Bank,* Section 21.2

Interest GRABBER On the board, write:

There is only one house on the island.

Her children are all very similar.

If I were at home, I would be asleep.

Ask students what these three sentences have in common. (They all use forms of the verb *be*.) Then, ask whether they notice an unusual use of the verb *to be*. (Sentence 3 is in the subjunctive mood.) Have students explain why *were* in sentence 3 is not *was*, when normally we would say or write *I was*. (The subjunctive mood often uses *were* to express a condition or something contrary to fact.)

Activate Prior Knowledge

Ask students to volunteer statements expressing wishes or conditions. As you hear a subjunctive verb used correctly (or incorrectly), place some of these statements on the board. For instance, if you hear "If I was rich, I'd travel," write this on the board, and then ask how the verb could be changed to help show that this statement is not now true: "If I *were* rich, I'd travel."

TEACH

Step-by-Step Teaching Guide

The Correct Use of the Subjunctive Mood

1. Point out that the subjunctive mood expresses either ideas contrary to fact or requests, demands, and proposals.

2. Have students identify into which category the sentences in the chart fall (*I suggest* and *He insists* are requests/demands; *If she were* expresses an idea contrary to fact).

3. Explain that a statement that is untrue at the moment it is made is subjunctive. For example: *I wish I were home.*

4. Remind students that not every clause with "if" signals the subjunctive. For example: *If you want to come, get your coat.*

The Subjunctive Mood

There are three *moods*, or ways in which a verb can express an action or condition: indicative, imperative, and subjunctive. The *indicative* mood, the most common, is used to make factual statements ("Karl *is* helpful.") and to ask questions ("*Is* Karl helpful?"). The *imperative* mood is limited to sentences that give orders or directions ("*Be* helpful."). This section will focus on the correct uses of the subjunctive mood.

The Correct Use of the Subjunctive Mood

There are two important differences between verbs in the subjunctive mood and those in the indicative mood. First, in the present tense, third-person singular verbs in the subjunctive mood do not have the usual *-s* or *-es* ending. Second, the subjunctive mood of *be* in the present tense is *be* and in the past tense it is *were*, regardless of the subject.

Indicative Mood	Subjunctive Mood
He *listens* to me.	I suggest that he *listen* to me.
They *are* ready.	He insists that they *be* ready.
She *was* impatient.	If she *were* impatient, she would not be suited for this work.

There are two general uses of the subjunctive mood:

> **KEY CONCEPT** Use the subjunctive mood (1) in clauses beginning with *if* or *that* to express an idea contrary to fact or (2) in clauses beginning with *that* to express a request, a demand, or a proposal. ■

To use the subjunctive mood correctly, you must remember to check the *if* and *that* clauses in your sentences.

Expressing Ideas Contrary to Fact Ideas contrary to fact are commonly expressed as wishes or conditions. Using the subjunctive mood in these situations helps to show that the idea expressed is not now true and may never be true.

EXAMPLES: He wishes that the climate *were* more mild.
He talks about meteorology as if he *were* an expert.

Theme: Weather

In this section, you will learn the forms and uses of the subjunctive mood. The examples and exercises in this section are about weather.

Cross-Curricular Connection: Science

Internet Tip

You can use the Internet to look up weather forecasts. Use key words like *weather report* and *regional weather* in the query field of your search engine.

⏱ TIME AND RESOURCE MANAGER

Resources
Print: *Grammar Exercise Workbook*, pp. 81–82; *Grammar Exercises Answers on Transparencies*, Ch. 21
Technology: *Writing and Grammar* Interactive Text, Section 21.3; *On-Line Exercise Bank*, Section 21.3

Using the Full Student Edition	Using the Handbook🄗
• Work through all key concepts, pp. 548–550. • Assign and review Exercises 36–37.	• Work through all key concepts, pp. 396–398. • Assign and review Exercises 36–37.

KEY CONCEPT Not all *if* clauses take a subjunctive verb. If the idea expressed may be true, an indicative form is used.

EXAMPLES: I said that *if* the weather was bad, we'd leave early, so let's go.
You'd know *if* a storm was coming *if* you looked up and saw black clouds.

This use of the indicative in *if* clauses suggests that the ideas expressed could or should be.

Expressing Requests, Demands, and Proposals
Most verbs that request, demand, or propose are often followed by a noun clause beginning with *that*, containing a verb in the subjunctive mood.

REQUEST: She requests that we *be* on time for the trip.
DEMAND: It is required that each student *wear* a uniform.
PROPOSAL: He proposed that a motion *be* made to adjourn.

▶ **Exercise 36** Using the Subjunctive Mood Rewrite each sentence, changing the verb to the subjunctive mood as necessary. Write *correct* if no change is needed.

EXAMPLE: She wished that she *was* famous.
ANSWER: She wished that she *were* famous.

1. Most people hope that the weather stays pleasant, particularly while they are on vacation.
2. It is proposed that one consults weather forecasts to learn what the weather will be before planning outdoor activities.
3. We suggest that a person heeds the advice of a capable meteorologist.
4. If the future was evident to all, people would have no need for weather forecasts.
5. On the other hand, if it was easier to predict the weather, people would be able to prepare better for extreme weather events like hurricanes, blizzards, and hailstorms.

▼ Critical Viewing
If you could have a career in weather, what type of "weather person" would you be? Respond using the subjunctive mood. [Connect]

▶ **More Practice**
Grammar Exercise Workbook
• pp. 81–82
On-line Exercise Bank
• Section 21.3
Go on-line:
PHSchool.com
Enter Web Code:
egk-1202

The Subjunctive Mood • **549**

Expressing Requests, Demands, and Proposals

1. Point out that requests, demands, and proposals are expressed using the present tense subjunctive forms: this is where *be* and third person forms without –*s* or –*es* come into play.

2. Ask students how requests, demands, and proposals are similar to ideas that are contrary to fact. (Requests express things that the speaker would like to see happen, but that are not true at the moment.)

3. Explain that not all sentences with *that* are subjunctive. For example, *I noticed that he eats pizza* is indicative; *I asked that he eat with a fork* expresses a request.

Customize for
Less Advanced Students
Ask students to practice making requests using the subjunctive mood. Start by having students think of people of whom they might make requests, demands, or proposals (a teacher, parent, a friend, a younger sibling). Then discuss how requests could be phrased for each of these people (p. 550).

Answer Key

▶ **Exercise 36**

1. correct
2. It is proposed that one consult weather forecasts before planning outdoor activities . . .
3. We suggest that a person heed the advice . . .
4. If the future were evident . . .
5. On the other hand, if it were easier to predict . . .

Critical Viewing

Connect Sample answer: If I were to have a career in weather, I would be a . . .

☑ ONGOING ASSESSMENT: Monitor and Reinforce

If students miss more than one item in Exercise 36, refer them to the following for additional practice.

In the Textbook	Print Resources	Technology
Section Review, Ex. 38, Section 21.3	*Grammar Exercise Workbook,* pp. 81–82	*On-Line Exercise Bank,* Section 21.3

Auxiliary Verbs That Help Express the Subjunctive Mood

1. As students read each example in the chart, ask how the subjunctive verbs and helping verbs affect the meanings. (They express ideas that are contrary to fact.)

2. Then, have students rewrite the sentences in the chart, replacing the subordinate clause with the main clause and vice versa. (Example: *If we'd act decisively, the future would be clear.*)

Customize for
Linguistic Learners

On the board write three versions of a subjunctive:

I could visit my grandmother.

I would visit my grandmother.

I should visit my grandmother.

Ask students to explain the differences in meaning among the three. (*Could* refers to capability. *Would* refers to desire. *Should* suggests an ethical or moral imperative.) Finally, have students create three versions of their own statements using *could, would,* and *should.*

Answer Key

> **Exercise 37**

1. If I could get the car out of the snowbank, we wouldn't be in this predicament.
2. Last winter, John said that he would come and help any time if I would call him.
3. You know, if this weather would warm up a bit, some of this snow might melt.
4. However, if you would pick up that shovel over there, maybe together we could clear the car.
5. I see that you would be happier if I could lend a hand.

Critical Viewing

Relate Sample sentences: "It is suggested that you stay indoors." "We propose that bottled water be available." "It is proposed that, in the event of an emergency, the National Guard be available to assist."

21.3

Auxiliary Verbs That Help Express the Subjunctive Mood

Because certain helping verbs suggest conditions contrary to fact, they can often be used in place of the subjunctive mood.

> **KEY CONCEPT** *Could, would,* or *should* can be used to help a verb express the subjunctive mood. ∎

The sentences on the left in the chart below have the usual subjunctive form of the verb *be: were.* The sentences on the right have been reworded with *could, would,* and *should.*

THE SUBJUNCTIVE MOOD EXPRESSED THROUGH AUXILIARY VERBS	
If the future were clear, we'd act decisively.	If the future <u>could</u> be clear, we'd act decisively.
If someone were to escort her, she would go.	If someone <u>would</u> escort her, she would go.
If you were to move, would you write to me?	If you <u>should</u> move, would you write to me?

> **Exercise 37** Using Auxiliary Verbs to Express the Subjunctive Mood On your paper, rewrite these sentences, replacing the subjunctive verb form with one using an auxiliary.

1. If I were able to get the car out of the snowbank, we wouldn't be in this predicament.
2. Last winter, John said that he would come and help any time if I were to call him.
3. You know, if this weather were to warm up a bit, some of this snow might melt.
4. However, if you were to pick up that shovel over there, maybe together we could clear the car.
5. I see that you would be happier if I were able to lend a hand.

▶ Critical Viewing Using verbs such as *suggest, require, request, propose,* write three sentences that explain how people can protect themselves from a dangerous weather event such as a hurricane. For example: "It is required that people evacuate coastal areas." **[Relate]**

☑ ONGOING ASSESSMENT: Monitor and Reinforce

If students miss more than one item in Exercise 37, refer them to the following for additional practice.

In the Textbook	Print Resources	Technology
Section Review, Ex. 39, Section 21.3	*Grammar Exercise Workbook,* pp. 81–82	*On-Line Exercise Bank,* Section 21.3

Section 21.3 *Section Review*

GRAMMAR EXERCISES 38–42

> **Exercise 38** Revising to Correct the Mood of Verbs Rewrite the following sentences, changing verbs to the subjunctive mood as necessary.

1. Even with the emergence of meteorology as a rigorous science, many people still view weather forecasting as if it was a matter of luck or chance.
2. Prior to modern weather forecasting methods, people often recommended that folk methods are used to predict the weather.
3. Predicting weather was an important activity for sailors, since a sea voyage could be disastrous if there was a typhoon.
4. If bad weather was coming, my uncle would know it by the aches in his bones.
5. Actually, today there is a new science called biometeorology, and some scientists now propose that these aches and pains are acknowledged as weather predictors.

> **Exercise 39** Using Auxiliary Verbs to Express the Subjunctive Mood On your paper, rewrite each of the following sentences using an auxiliary verb to express the subjunctive mood.

1. It is hoped that information about weather and climate be utilized to prepare for trips overseas.
2. For example, a trip to the South Pacific would be less pleasant if a traveler were there during the typhoon season.
3. Most people wish they were able to be spared from disastrous weather calamities like tornadoes and droughts.

4. If you were aware of the weather at your destination, you would have an easier time deciding what to pack.
5. Of course, if you were to study meteorology, you might want to pick a destination with extreme weather.

> **Exercise 40** Find It in Your Reading Scan a few newspaper or magazine articles, looking for uses (or abuses) of the subjunctive mood. The subjunctive mood is sometimes misused or forgotten when writers are in a hurry. Try to find at least one instance where this mood was used correctly and another where it should have been used but wasn't.

> **Exercise 41** Find It in Your Writing Look through your writing portfolio to find places where you used the subjunctive mood. If you find any instances where you should have used it but didn't, correct the sentence. If you can find no example, rewrite a paragraph (or create a new one) using at least one instance of the subjunctive mood.

> **Exercise 42** Writing Application Imagine that you are a meteorologist reporting for your local newspaper. Write a weather forecast for the next five days. Make sure to use the following phrases with a corresponding verb in the subjunctive mood.

1. suggests that
2. seems as if
3. that people be
4. It is recommended that

Section Review • 551

ASSESS

Section Review

Each of these exercises correlates to the instruction on the subjunctive mood, pages 548–550. The exercises may be used for more practice, for reteaching, or for review of the key concepts presented.

Answer Key

> **Exercise 38**

1. . . . as if it were a matter . . .
2. . . . that folk methods be used . . .
3. . . . if there were a typhoon.
4. If bad weather were coming . . .
5. . . . that these aches and pains be acknowledged . . .

> **Exercise 39**

1. . . . would be utilized . . .
2. . . . a traveler should be there . . .
3. . . . wish they could be spared . . .
4. . . . could be aware . . .
5. . . . if you would study . . .

> **Exercise 40**

Find It In Your Reading
Encourage students to examine publications targeted to teenagers and children.

> **Exercise 41**

Find It In Your Writing
In order to increase opportunities for the use of the subjunctive mood, you might suggest that students write their new paragraphs as science fiction.

> **Exercise 42**

Writing Application
Encourage students to read the weather pages from their local newspapers for examples.

✏️ STANDARDIZED TEST PREPARATION WORKSHOP

Grammar and Usage Many standardized tests require students to draw upon their knowledge and understanding of the subjunctive mood to write sentences correctly. Write the following on the board and ask students to identify the correct answer.

If the house was less expensive, we would be able to purchase it today.

What is the best change, if any, to make in this sentence?

A Correct as is
B Change *was* to *wasn't*.
C Change *was* to *was not*.
D Change *was* to *were*.

The correct answer is **D**. The phrase "If the house was less expensive" should be written in the subjunctive mood because it describes a condition that is contrary to fact.

⏱ TIME SAVERS!

📖 **Answers on Transparencies** Use the *Grammar Exercises Answers on Transparencies* for Chapter 21 to facilitate correction by students.

💻 **On-Line Exercise Bank** Have students complete the exercises on computer. The Auto Check feature will grade their work for you!

Interest GRABBER Write these two sentences on the board and ask students to discuss the differences between them:

The grand prize was won by me.

I won the grand prize.

Make sure they answer these questions: Is the information the same in both? (yes) What is the first sentence about primarily? (the prize) And the second sentence? (the speaker) Point out that *passive voice* (the first sentence) emphasizes the recipient of an action.

Activate Prior Knowledge

Model examples of the use of the passive voice. (Examples: Are you being helped?; I was driven to school today; We have been invited to Aunt Mary's house.) Have each student write at least three passive voice sentences and identify the recipient and the initiator of each action.

Critical Viewing

Analyze, Cause and Effect Students may note that people now carry their own telephones and can place and receive calls no matter where they are.

TEACH

Step-by-Step Teaching Guide

Active and Passive Voice

1. Have students read the definitions of active and passive voice, then have them state the difference. (In active voice, the subject acts; in passive, the subject is acted upon.)

2. Have students compare the examples of the same situations for both voices. What happens with the change? (The emphasis changes.)

3. Point out that, though there are many situations in which only the passive voice works (*The car was abandoned*), the active voice is generally preferred in writing, because it is stronger and more interesting, and is better at showing action.

continued

Section 21.4 *Voice*

This section discusses a characteristic of verbs called *voice.*

▶ **KEY CONCEPT** **Voice** is the form of a verb that shows whether the subject is performing the action. ■

In English, there are two voices: *active* and *passive.* Only action verbs can indicate the active voice; linking verbs cannot.

Active and Passive Voice

If the subject of a verb performs the action, the verb is *active*; if the subject receives the action, the verb is *passive.*

Active Voice Any action verb can be in the active voice. The action verb may be transitive (that is, it may have a direct object) or intransitive (without a direct object).

▶ **KEY CONCEPT** A verb is active if its subject performs the action. ■

In both examples below, the subject performs the action. In the first example, the verb *telephoned* is transitive; *team* is the direct object, which receives the action. In the second example, the verb *gathered* is intransitive; it has no direct object.

ACTIVE VOICE: The captain *telephoned* the team.
Telegraph messages *gathered* on the desk.

Passive Voice Most action verbs can also be passive.

▶ **KEY CONCEPT** A verb is passive if its action is performed upon the subject. ■

In the following examples, the subjects are the receivers of the action. The first example names the performer, the captain, as the object of the preposition *by* instead of the subject. In the second example, no performer of the action is mentioned.

PASSIVE VOICE: The team *was telephoned* by the captain.
The telegraph messages *were gathered* into neat piles.

Theme: The Telephone

In this section, you will learn the forms and uses of the active and passive voices. The examples and exercises in this section are about the telephone.

······························

Cross-Curricular Connection: Social Studies

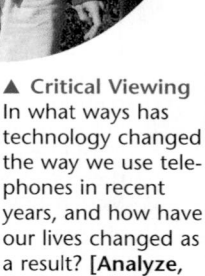

▲ **Critical Viewing** In what ways has technology changed the way we use telephones in recent years, and how have our lives changed as a result? **[Analyze, Cause and Effect]**

⏱ TIME AND RESOURCE MANAGER

Resources
Print: *Grammar Exercise Workbook*, pp. 83–84; *Grammar Exercises Answers on Transparencies*, Ch. 21
Technology: *Writing and Grammar* Interactive Text, Section 21.4; *On-Line Exercise Bank*, Section 21.4

Using the Full Student Edition	Using the Handbook🄷
• Work through all key concepts, pp. 552–555.	• Work through all key concepts, pp. 400–403.
• Assign and review Exercises 43–46.	• Assign and review Exercises 43–46.
• Read and discuss Grammar In Literature, p. 555.	• Read and discuss Grammar in Literature, p. 403.

Step-by-Step Teaching Guide
continued

4. Review the chart that shows *believe* in the passive voice. Point out that the past participle of the verb remains the same in all tenses, while the helping verb *be* undergoes changes depending on tense.

5. Have students write two original sentences in the active voice, one with and one without a direct object, and two in the passive, one with and one without a performer of the action.

KEY CONCEPT A passive verb is always a verb phrase made from a form of *be* plus the past participle of a verb. The tense of the helping verb *be* determines the tense of a passive verb. ■

The chart below provides a short conjugation in the passive voice of the verb *believe* in the three moods. Notice in the chart that there are only two progressive forms and no emphatic form.

THE VERB *BELIEVE* IN THE PASSIVE VOICE	
Present Indicative	he is believed
Past Indicative	he was believed
Future Indicative	he will be believed
Present Perfect Indicative	he has been believed
Past Perfect Indicative	he had been believed
Future Perfect Indicative	he will have been believed
Present Progressive Indicative	he is being believed
Past Progressive Indicative	he was being believed
Present Imperative	(you) be believed
Present Subjunctive	(if) he be believed
Past Subjunctive	(if) he were believed

Exercise 43 Distinguishing Between the Active and Passive Voice Identify each verb as *active* or *passive*.
1. The telephone makes communication easier.
2. Convenience and efficiency have been delivered by the telephone.
3. The telephone affects life today in many ways.
4. This great device was invented by Alexander Graham Bell more than 100 years ago.
5. In 1876, Bell patented his invention with the United States government.
6. In 1854, the principles behind the transmission of human speech by electronic means had been developed by Charles Bourseul of France.
7. In 1878, the world's first commercial telephone company was opened by entrepreneurs in New Haven, Connecticut.
8. In 1915, a telephone link between New York City and San Francisco was established by engineers.
9. In 1955, engineers placed the first transatlantic telephone cable between Newfoundland, Canada, and Scotland.
10. In the near future, more advances in telephone technology will be made by scientists.

More Practice
Grammar Exercise Workbook
• pp. 83–84
On-line Exercise Bank
• Section 21.4
Go on-line:
PHSchool.com
Enter Web Code:
egk-1202

Get instant feedback! Exercise 43 is available on-line or on CD-ROM.

Real-World Connection

Point out that advertisements and other sales pitches frequently use the passive voice, often in questions. Examples: "Have you been given a mess to clean up?" "Were you ever injured through no fault of your own?" Ask students to suggest a sales pitch for an imaginary product that includes statements using passive voice. Discuss why the passive voice may be more effective than the active voice in this instance.

Answer Key

Exercise 43
1. active
2. passive
3. active
4. passive
5. active
6. passive
7. passive
8. passive
9. active
10. passive

Voice • 553

☑ **ONGOING ASSESSMENT: Prerequisite Skills**

If students have difficulty with active and passive voice, you may find it necessary to review the following to ensure coverage of prerequisite knowledge.

In the Textbook	Print Resources	Technology
Action Verbs and Linking Verbs, Section 17.2	*Grammar Exercise Workbook*, pp. 83–84	*On-Line Exercise Bank*, Section 17.2

Answer Key

Students' answers should follow the models on page 553, using the past participle of each verb: *confirmed, praised, proved* or *proven,* and *selected.*

Step-by-Step Teaching Guide

Using Active and Passive Voice

1. Ask students why they think most good writers prefer to use the active voice as much as possible. (Possible answers: it is more dynamic; it is more concise; generally, a writer would want to emphasize the person or thing that was acting, rather than the thing acted upon.)

2. Have students explain why the passive voice is the best choice in the three examples given. What would happen if they tried to make them active? (When the performer is unknown, the sentence can't be made active; for the other two examples, the emphasis would be on the wrong things.)

Answer Key

▶ **Exercise 45**

Answers may vary. Possible answers:

2. The telephone has delivered convenience and efficiency.
4. Alexander Graham Bell invented this great device more than one hundred years ago.
6. In 1854, Charles Bourseul of France developed the principles behind the transmission of human speech by electronic means.
7. Entrepreneurs in New Haven, Connecticut, opened the world's first telephone company in 1878.
8. Engineers established a telephone link between New York City and San Francisco in 1915.
10. Scientists will make more advances in telephone technology in the near future.

▶ **Exercise 44** Forming the Tenses of Passive Verbs On your paper, conjugate each verb in the passive voice, using the first eight entries in the chart on page 553 as your model.
1. confirm (with *it*)
2. praise (with *you*)
3. prove (with *they*)
4. select (with *I*)

Using Active and Passive Voice

As soon as you can distinguish between the active and passive voice, you can use this knowledge to improve your own writing. Most good writers prefer the active voice to the passive voice.

▶ **KEY CONCEPT** Use the active voice whenever possible. ■

The active voice is usually more direct and economical. The first sentence below is shorter and more direct than the second.

ACTIVE VOICE: Finally, Debbie *repaired* the telephone.
PASSIVE VOICE: Finally, the telephone *was repaired* by Debbie.

The passive voice has two important uses in English:

▶ **KEY CONCEPTS** Use the passive voice to emphasize the *receiver* of an action rather than the *performer* of an action. Use the passive voice to point out the receiver of an action whenever the performer is not important or not easily identified. ■

RECEIVER EMPHASIZED: Lori *was mystified* by the new computer program.
PERFORMER UNKNOWN: A telegram *was tacked* to the front door.
PERFORMER UNIMPORTANT: The potholes on our street *will be repaired* soon.

▶ **Exercise 45** Using the Active Voice On your paper, rewrite each of the six sentences in Exercise 43 that have verbs in the passive voice. Change or add words as necessary in order to put each verb in the active voice.

More Practice
Grammar Exercise Workbook
• pp. 83–84
On-line Exercise Bank
• Section 21.4
  Go on-line:
  PHSchool.com
  Enter Web Code:
  egk-1202

interactive Textbook

Get instant feedback! Exercises 44, 45, and 46 are available on-line or on CD-ROM.

✓ ONGOING ASSESSMENT: Monitor and Reinforce

If students have difficulty with Exercise 43, 44, 45, or 46, refer them to the following for additional practice.

In the Textbook	Print Resources	Technology
Section Review, Ex. 47–49, Section 21.4	*Grammar Exercise Workbook,* pp. 83–84	*On-Line Exercise Bank,* Section 21.4

GRAMMAR IN LITERATURE

from **Meditation 17**
John Donne

Notice the use of active voice verbs (in blue) and passive voice verbs (in red) in the passage.

. . . when one man *dies*, one chapter *is* not *torn* out of the book, but *translated* into a better language; and every chapter must be so translated; God *employs* several translators; some pieces *are translated* by age, some by sickness, some by war, some by justice; but God's hand is in every translation, and his hand *shall bind* up all our scattered leaves again for that library where every book *shall lie* open to one another.

▶ **Exercise 46** Revising to Correct Unnecessary Use of the Passive Voice Rewrite the following sentences, changing the passive voice to active when passive is used. If active voice is used, write *active*.

1. Before the inventions of the telephone and the telegraph, people communicated primarily by mail.
2. In the mid-1800's, a daring attempt to improve mail delivery in the western part of the United States was made by a group of brave people.
3. From April 1860 to October 1861, mail was delivered from Missouri to California by the pony express.
4. Mail sent from Missouri was delivered to Sacramento, California, by the pony express in ten days.
5. Boats ferried mail from Sacramento to San Francisco.

▼ **Critical Viewing**
The pony express made improvements to communications in the West, but it also presented dangers and inconveniences. Explain instances of both, using the active voice and then the passive voice. **[Evaluate]**

The Coming and Going of the Pony Express, Frederic Remington

Voice • 555

Step-by-Step Teaching Guide

Grammar in Literature

1. Have a student read the passage one clause at a time, stopping after each to tell whether the verb construction is active or passive.

2. For each passive voice construction, ask students to identify both the recipient and initiator of the action. Point out that some initiators will be unknown.

More About the Writer

John Donne entered the University of Oxford in 1583 when he was eleven years old and later studied at Cambridge University. During his life, Donne was both a poet and a preacher. "Meditation 17" was written when he was dean of St. Paul's Cathedral.

Connections With Literature

"Meditation 17" can be found in *Prentice Hall Literature, Penguin Edition,* The British Tradition.

Answer Key

▶ **Exercise 46**

1. active
2. In the mid-1800's, a group of brave people made a daring attempt to improve mail delivery in the western part of the United States.
3. From April 1860 to October 1861, the pony express delivered mail from Missouri to California.
4. The pony express delivered mail sent from Missouri to Sacramento, California, in ten days.
5. active

Critical Viewing

Evaluate Sample sentences: The pony express brought mail to remote places at improved speeds. However, riders were confronted by dangers such as extreme weather, fatigue, and bandits.

Section Review

Each of these exercises correlates to the instruction on voice, pages 552–555. The exercises may be used for more practice, for reteaching, or for review of the key concepts presented. Answers for all chapter exercises are available in *Grammar Exercises Answers on Transparencies* in your Teaching Resources.

Answer Key

Exercise 47

1. passive
2. passive
3. passive
4. passive
5. active

Exercise 48

Students' answers should follow the models in the chart on p. 553.

Exercise 49

1. Long ago, messages were written on clay tablets or animal hide.
2. The Chinese developed papermaking around A.D. 105.
3. Merchants and travelers introduced paper to Europe more than 1,000 years later.
4. Then, in the fifteenth century, Johannes Gutenberg, a German printer, made a great breakthrough in printing.
5. Movable type was utilized by Gutenberg to print books.

Exercise 50

Find It in Your Reading
Students should note that Donne's use of the active voice is largely restricted to describing the role of God.

Exercise 51

Find It in Your Writing
Ask students to describe the changes they notice in their writing when they rewrite in the active voice.

Exercise 52

Writing Application
Have students read their speeches aloud to the class. What changes do other students suggest?

Section 21.4 Section Review

GRAMMAR EXERCISES 47–52

Exercise 47 Distinguishing Between the Active and Passive Voice
On your paper, identify each verb in the following sentences as *active* or *passive*.

1. In 1837, the electric telegraph was invented by the American inventor Samuel F.B. Morse.
2. In 1844, Morse's telegraph was used to send the world's first telegram.
3. The electric telegraph was eventually supplanted by wireless radio-wave transmission and the telephone.
4. In wireless transmission, electromagnetic waves are sent over the airwaves by a system of transmitters.
5. Guglielmo Marconi, an Italian engineer, perfected this radio technology.

Exercise 48 Conjugating Verbs in the Passive Voice
On your paper, conjugate each of the following verbs in the passive voice, using the tenses and pronouns given.

1. analyze (present; it, me)
2. spare (past; he, you)
3. show (future; it, them)
4. promote (past perfect; we, him)
5. applaud (future progressive; they, us)

Exercise 49 Using the Active and Passive Voice
On your paper, change each sentence in active voice to passive voice and change each sentence in passive voice to active voice.

1. Long ago, people wrote messages on clay tablets or animal hides.
2. Around A.D. 105, papermaking was developed by the Chinese.

3. Paper was introduced to Europe by Moors more than 1,000 years later.
4. Then, in the fifteenth century, a great breakthrough was made in printing by Johannes Gutenberg, a German printer.
5. Gutenberg utilized movable type to print books.

Exercise 50 Find It in Your Reading
Reread the excerpt from John Donne's "Meditation 17" on page 555. In small groups, discuss the use of active and passive voice. Why is the use of the passive voice effective in a work like this? How does it add to the meaning? In what types of writing would it be less effective?

Exercise 51 Find It in Your Writing
Looking through your portfolio, examine your use of passive and active voice. Are there sentences that could be made stronger by switching them to the active voice? Try to find at least one example of each voice, and either explain why the voice used is appropriate or rewrite the sentence to change the voice.

Exercise 52 Writing Application
Imagine that you are on your way to an awards show to accept an award for something you have invented. Write an acceptance speech, thanking the people who have supported you over the years. Be sure to use verbs effectively in both the passive voice and the active voice in your speech.

☑ ONGOING ASSESSMENT: Assess Mastery

Use the following resources to assess student mastery of voice.

In the Textbook	Print Resources	Technology
Chapter Review, Ex. 61–62	*Formal Assessment,* Ch. 21	*On-Line Exercise Bank,* Section 21.4

Chapter 21 Chapter Review

GRAMMAR EXERCISES 53–64

▶ **Exercise 53** Recognizing Verb Tenses and Their Forms On your paper, identify the tense of each italicized verb, and tell whether the form is *basic, progressive,* or *emphatic.*

1. Television *has played* a significant role in the lives of Americans for more than fifty years.
2. In 1927, Philo T. Farnsworth, an American engineer, *developed* the basic elements of an all-electronic television system.
3. It's true that Farnsworth *did invent* the dissector tube, which makes television transmission and reception possible.
4. Farnsworth *had been working* for many years to perfect his invention.
5. By the postwar years, television *was supplanting* radio as the primary source of entertainment in most homes.
6. Just as people *had gathered* around the radio, people began to gather around the television set.
7. In 1955, around 63 percent of American households *owned* a television set.
8. By 1960, that figure *had increased* to around 85 percent.
9. It is likely that future inventors *will be looking* to Farnsworth for inspiration.
10. By the year 2027, people *will have been using* Farnsworth's invention for 100 years.

▶ **Exercise 54** Supplying the Correct Forms of Irregular Verbs On your paper, write the appropriate past or past participle for each verb in parentheses.

1. Around 1500, a German locksmith's invention of the mainspring (bring) about a new timepiece—the watch.
2. The first watches, about 5 inches across and 3 inches deep, were not (wear)—they were carried in the hand.
3. Like clocks of the period, these watches (strike) the hour.
4. However, the owner never (know) the exact time because early watches had only an hour hand.
5. By 1675, the English had (begin) the custom of having a special vest pocket made for their watches.

▶ **Exercise 55** Conjugating Verbs Conjugate the verbs below in their basic, progressive, and emphatic forms in the tenses indicated.

1. plan (present)   2. go (past)

▶ **Exercise 56** Using Tense in Past, Present, and Future Time Write the tense indicated for each verb in parentheses.

1. Before the invention of the hearing aid, people who could not hear well (have—past) few options for improving their hearing.
2. Those who (seek—past perfect) a way to help those with hearing loss were delighted when the hearing aid was invented.
3. Indeed, the hearing aid (change—past emphatic) the way many people deal with hearing loss.
4. For many decades, the simple device (amplify—present perfect progressive) sounds for people who cannot hear well.

CHAPTER REVIEW

Each of these exercises correlates to a section of the chapter on using verbs, pages 518–556. The exercises may be used for more practice, for reteaching, or for review of the key concepts presented.

▶ **Exercise 53**

1. past perfect, basic
2. past, basic
3. past, emphatic
4. past perfect, progressive
5. past, progressive
6. past perfect, basic
7. past, basic
8. past perfect, basic
9. future, progressive
10. future perfect, progressive

▶ **Exercise 54**

1. brought
2. worn
3. struck
4. knew
5. begun

▶ **Exercise 55**

If a verb takes the same form with all pronouns, only the verb form is given.

1. I, you, we, they plan
   he, she, it plans
   I, you, we, they have planned
   he, she, it has planned
   I am planning
   we, you, they are planning
   he, she, it is planning
   I, you, we, they have been planning
   he, she, it has been planning
   I, you, we, they do plan
   he, she, it, does plan
2. went
   had gone
   I, he, she, it was going
   we, you, they were going
   had been going
   did go

continued

Answer Key continued

▶ **Exercise 56**

1. had
2. had sought
3. did change
4. has been amplifying
5. has made
6. does do
7. have managed
8. are hearing
9. will be making
10. will have helped

Answer Key

Exercise 57

1. simultaneous
2. simultaneous
3. sequential; expectation occurs before building
4. sequential; experimentation took place before the network was built
5. sequential; diligent work occurs before the development of the Internet

Exercise 58

Answers will vary. Samples are given.

1. The U.S. Postal Service (USPS) now handles millions of pieces of mail every day.
2. The federal postal system, which was created in 1789 by the U.S. Congress, has undergone numerous changes lately.
3. Long ago, mail was carried by stagecoach.
4. Today, to connect people worldwide, the USPS uses airmail.
5. The USPS will soon make more changes to improve efficiency and service.

Exercise 59

1. . . . as if it were only . . .
2. . . . that the Internet meet . . .
3. . . . wished she were . . .
4. . . . if she were to teach . . .
5. If someone were . . . he or she would be . . .

Chapter Review Exercises cont'd.

5. The hearing aid (make—present perfect) it possible for people with partial to nearly full hearing loss to experience sounds again.
6. Moreover, it (do—present emphatic) so in an unobtrusive way.
7. With incredible ingenuity, engineers (manage—present perfect) to squeeze together the components of a public-address system into a device that fits neatly in or around a person's ear.
8. Thousands of people (hear—present progressive) better because of this wonderful device.
9. Scientists (make—future progressive) additional improvements in aiding those with hearing loss in the future.
10. By the next century, the hearing aid (help—future perfect) millions of people around the world.

Exercise 57 Recognizing and Correcting a Sequence of Events On your paper, identify whether the events described by the verbs in the following sentences describe simultaneous or sequential events. If the events are sequential, identify which action occurred first and which event occurred second.

1. In the 1960's, the U.S. Department of Defense began to search for ways to connect computers to a single network.
2. Recognizing the impressive progress of university research, the U.S. Department of Defense funded research at many university computer science departments.
3. Many of these researchers expected to build a functioning computer network before the 1970's.
4. By the late 1960's, a functioning computer network was built after researchers had experimented greatly.
5. If these researchers had worked less diligently, the Internet would have been developed at a later time.

Exercise 58 Using Modifiers to Improve Meaning On your paper, rewrite the following sentences by adding adverbs or adverb phrases that indicate time.

1. The U.S. Postal Service (USPS) handles millions of pieces of mail every day.
2. The federal postal system, which was created in 1789 by the U.S. Congress, has undergone numerous changes.
3. Mail was carried by stagecoach.
4. To connect people worldwide, the USPS uses airmail.
5. The USPS will make more changes to improve efficiency and service.

Exercise 59 Revising to Correct the Mood of Verbs On your paper, rewrite the following sentences by changing verbs to the subjunctive mood as necessary.

1. Some people talk as if it was only young people using the Internet, but the fastest growing segment of users is people over fifty.
2. This growing segment demands that the Internet meets the needs and interests of an older population.
3. One woman who is sixty said she wished she was a Web site developer.
4. Today, if she was to teach a class, many would be interested in learning what she knows.
5. If someone was developing Web sites, you could be sure that he or she was familiar with the Internet.

Exercise 60 Subjunctive and Auxiliary Verbs Rewrite these sentences using auxiliary verbs to express the subjunctive mood.

1. Many people wish it were easier to learn a foreign language.

558 • Verb Usage

2. If such study were encouraged more, perhaps more people would try.
3. If you were to study another language, which would you choose?
4. It might be easier if you were to have a friend learn with you.
5. Imagine what fun you could have if you were able to speak another language fluently!

Exercise 61 Using the Active and Passive Voice
Identify the voice of these sentences. Then, rewrite each, changing the active voice to the passive and changing the passive voice to the active.

1. A blind French teenager, Louis Braille, invented an ingenious writing and printing system for the blind.
2. At a school in Paris, Braille was taught by nuns to read by touching raised letters on a page.
3. However, Braille could not distinguish between letters like *O* and *Q*.
4. A better method was developed by Braille to allow blind people to read more easily.
5. In the Braille system, clusters of raised dots are utilized to represent letters, numerals, and punctuation marks.

Exercise 62 Revising to Correct Verb Usage
Rewrite the following sentences to correct all improper verb usage.

1. The facsimile transmission process, commonly known as the fax, is transmitting printed material through telephone cables.
2. Prior to the 1980's, people will use facsimile machines primarily for the transmission of news photographs.
3. Everyone said, "If it was faster, more people would use it."

4. With improvements in transmission speed and a decline in cost, the fax machine becomes a staple of businesses in the 1980's.
5. By the 1980's, large businesses routinely have send and receive hundreds of faxes in a typical day.

Exercise 63 Writing Application
Imagine that you are an advice columnist for a newspaper. Write a response to a person who has requested your advice about studying for exams. Be sure to use the active voice and the passive voice, as well as the subjunctive mood.

Exercise 64 CUMULATIVE REVIEW
Verb Usage and Writing Effective Sentences Revise the following paragraph, correcting errors in verb usage and in sentence structure. Make changes as needed to improve the flow of the sentences.

Computers increasingly part of the communication equation. E-mail and the Internet are important communication tools, but the use of computers is going in so many new directions, that sometimes it's hard to keep up with the latest developments, which have occurred continually. Computers are reading printed matter out loud for those who cannot see using a scanner. Spoken words are being translated by them into characters on a screen for those who cannot hear. Even now, computers can be used like televisions, they can also transmit live video. Some people propose that a computer handles even more complex communication tasks.

Answer Key continued

Exercise 64
5. Even now, computers can be used like televisions to transmit live video.
6. It is proposed that computers handle even more complex communication tasks.

Answer Key

Exercise 60
1. . . . wish it could be . . .
2. If such study would be . . .
3. If you could study . . .
4. . . . if you could have . . .
5. . . . if you could speak . . .

Exercise 61
1. Active. An ingenious writing and printing system for the blind was invented by Louis Braille, a blind French teenager.
2. Passive. Nuns at a school in Paris taught Braille to read by touching raised letters on a page.
3. Active. However, letters like Q and O could not be distinguished by Braille.
4. Passive. Braille developed a better method to allow blind people to read more easily.
5. Passive. The Braille system utilizes clusters of raised dots to represent letters, numerals, and punctuation marks.

Exercise 62
1. . . . transmits printed material . . .
2. . . . people used facsimile machines . . .
3. "If it were faster, more people . . .
4. . . . the fax machine became . . .
5. . . . routinely sent and received . . .

Exercise 63
Writing Application
Suggest to students that they use hypothetical examples of study skills in their replies to the imaginary letter writer. This will enable them to more naturally use the subjunctive mood.

Exercise 64
Cumulative Review
Answers will vary. Samples are given.

1. Computers have increasingly become a part of the communication equation.
2. E-mail and the Internet are important communication tools. The use of computers, however, is going in so many new directions, that sometimes it's hard to keep up with the latest developments, which have occurred continually.
3. Computers, using a scanner, are reading printed matter out loud for those who cannot see.
4. Computers are translating spoken words into characters on a screen for those who cannot hear.

continued

Lesson Objectives

1. To demonstrate control over grammatical elements such as verb forms
2. To recognize appropriate English usage within the context of a written passage

Step-by-Step Teaching Guide

Standard English Usage: Using Verbs

Teaching Resources: Standardized Test Preparation Workbook, pp. 41–42

1. Briefly review the verb tenses and the times they convey. Remind students of the rule to avoid unnecessary shifts of tense.
2. Have students read the sample test items, and review the correct answers and explanations.
3. Assign Practices 1 and 2. Check students' answers and go over any incorrect answers with the class. You may wish to provide students with standardized test answer sheets so that they can practice the mechanics of marking in answers.

Standardized Test Preparation Workshop

Standard English Usage: Using Verbs

Your knowledge of verb usage is often measured on standardized tests. Your ability to determine the correct tense of a verb (present, present perfect, past, past perfect, future, or future perfect or their progressive forms) or the correct mood (indicative or subjunctive) is tested when you must choose a verb or verb phrase to complete a sentence. When choosing a verb, first read the sentence silently to yourself and determine when it is taking place. Then, choose a verb that indicates the same time or tense of the sentence.

The following test items will give you practice with the format of questions that test verb usage.

Sample Test Items	Answers and Explanations

Directions: Read the passage, and choose the letter of the word or group of words that belongs in each space.
 	
My brother Mark ___(1)___ the baseball team since he ___(2)___ high school four years ago.
 	
1   A   dominates
     B   will dominate
     C   had dominated
     D   has dominated
	The correct answer is *D*. The word *since* at the beginning of the second clause gives a clue that the action is one that began in the past and is continuing in the present; therefore, the present perfect tense is needed.

2   F   started
     G   had started
     H   will have started
     J   was starting
	The correct answer is *F, started.* Because the event began and ended in the past, the past tense is used. Answer *G* and *J* are also past tense forms; however, *G* (the past perfect) would be used to indicate an action that preceded another past action, and *J* (past progressive) indicates a continuing action in the past.

560 • Verb Usage

TEST-TAKING TIP

Tell students to look for transitional words and phrases in a test that measures knowledge of verb tenses. These will help them know which tenses to use. Ask students to reread the paragraph in Practice 1 and note how many clues there are to time: the transitional words *yesterday* and *however,* as well as the three actual times cited. In Practice 2, the words and phrases *tomorrow, as a result,* and *tonight* are transitional words indicating time.

Students who missed item 4 in the second practice may have to be reminded about the subjunctive mood.

Practice 1 **Directions:** Read the following passage. Choose the letter of the verb or verb phrase that belongs in each space.

Yesterday, the baseball game almost ___(1)___ place on time. The league ___(2)___ it to start at 3:00 P.M. However, it ___(3)___ raining at 11:00, and at 1:00 it ___(4)___ down. We ___(5)___ to ourselves, "We ___(6)___ to play this game."

1 A doesn't take
   B hasn't taken
   C wasn't taking
   D didn't take

2 F had scheduled
   G was scheduling
   H has scheduled
   J had been scheduling

3 A begins
   B began
   C has begun
   D is beginning

4 F will still have been coming
   G still came
   H has still come
   J was still coming

5 A were thinking
   B had been thinking
   C will think
   D will have been thinking

6 F will never have gotten
   G have never gotten
   H will never get
   J were never getting

Practice 2 **Directions:** Read the following passage. Choose the letter of the verb or verb phrase that belongs in each space.

Tomorrow afternoon, we ___(1)___ the second-round tournament game. I ___(2)___ for it all week. As a result, I ___(3)___ in top condition. The coach said that if I ___(4)___ smart, I ___(5)___ to bed early tonight. I certainly ___(6)___ his advice.

1 A play
   B would play
   C were to play
   D will have been playing

2 F had practiced
   G have been practicing
   H will practice
   J was practicing

3 A will have been
   B had been
   C have been
   D am

4 F was
   G were
   H had been
   J will be

5 A would go
   B will go
   C may go
   D am going

6 F took
   G take
   H have taken
   J will take

Answer Key

Practice 1

1. D
2. F
3. B
4. J
5. A
6. H

Practice 2

1. A
2. G
3. D
4. G
5. A
6. J

Customize for
ESL Students

Many of these students will need practice with verb tenses, especially those of irregular verbs, before taking a test on verb usage. For example, give students the following sentences to practice saying aloud:

I am here now.

I was here yesterday.

I will be here tomorrow.

I have been here for twenty minutes.

I will have been here for thirty minutes when the clock strikes three.

I would have been here, but I missed my ride.

Customize for
Less Advanced Students

Ask students to read the two practice paragraphs to themselves, inserting the correct answers as they read. They might also rewrite the first practice paragraph, inserting the correct phrases.

Time and Resource Manager

In-Depth Lesson Plan

	LESSON FOCUS	PRINT AND MEDIA RESOURCES
DAY 1	**Pronoun Case: Nominative and Objective** Students learn and apply concepts relating to the nominative and objective cases of pronouns. (pp. 564–569/⊞408–413)	*Writing and Grammar* Interactive Text, Section 22.1; *On-line Exercise Bank,* Section 22.1 **Teaching Resources** *Grammar Exercise Workbook,* pp. 85–88; *Grammar Exercises Answers on Transparencies,* Ch. 22
DAY 2	**Pronoun Case: Possessive** Students learn and apply concepts relating to the possessive case of pronouns and do the Hands-on Grammar activity. (pp. 570–573/⊞414–417)	**Teaching Resources** *Grammar Exercise Workbook,* pp. 89–90; *Hands-on Grammar Activity Workbook,* Ch. 22
DAY 3	**Special Problems With Pronouns** Students learn and apply concepts relating to the use of *who* and *whom* and pronouns in elliptical clauses. (pp. 574–579/⊞418–423)	*Writing and Grammar* Interactive Text, Section 22.2; *On-line Exercise Bank,* Section 22.2 **Teaching Resources** *Grammar Exercise Workbook,* pp. 91–92
DAY 4	**Review and Assess** Students review the chapter and demonstrate mastery of pronoun usage. (pp. 580–581)	**Teaching Resources** *Formal Assessment,* Ch. 22; *Texas Test Preparation Workbook,* pp. 43–44

Accelerated Lesson Plan

	LESSON FOCUS	PRINT AND MEDIA RESOURCES
DAY 1	**Pronoun Case: Nominative, Objective, and Possessive** Students cover concepts of pronoun case as determined by the Diagnostic Test. (pp. 562–573/⊞406–417)	*Writing and Grammar* Interactive Text, Section 22.1; *On-line Exercise Bank,* Section 22.1 **Teaching Resources** *Grammar Exercise Workbook,* pp. 85–90; *Grammar Exercises Answers on Transparencies,* Ch. 22
DAY 2	**Special Problems With Pronouns; Review and Assess** Students cover special problems with pronouns and then review the chapter and demonstrate mastery of concepts. (pp. 574–581/⊞418–423)	*Writing and Grammar* Interactive Text, Section 22.2; *On-line Exercise Bank,* Section 22.2 **Teaching Resources** *Grammar Exercise Workbook,* pp. 91–92; *Formal Assessment,* Ch. 22

Options for Adapting Lesson Plans

HOMEWORK
Have students complete any section of the chapter for homework.

FEATURES
Extend coverage with the Grammar in Literature features (pp. 571, 577/⊞415, 421) and the Standardized Test Preparation Workshop (p. 582).

TECHNOLOGY
Students can use *Writing and Grammar* Interactive Text to complete the exercises interactively on computer. They can complete additional exercises in the *On-line Exercise Bank:* The Auto Check feature will grade their work. Go on-line: PHSchool.com Use Web Code: egk-1202

Writing and Grammar Handbook Alignment

Page numbers in Step-by-Step Teaching Guides in this Teacher's Edition refer to pages from the full student text. Handbook page references, indicated with this icon ⬚, are provided in Time and Resource Manager boxes and at the bottom of each Teacher's Edition page.

INTEGRATED SKILLS COVERAGE

Grammar in Literature
SE pp. 571, 577/⬚415, 421

Writing
Find It in Your Writing, SE pp. 573, 579/⬚417, 423
Writing Application, SE pp. 573, 579/⬚417, 423

Viewing and Representing
Critical Viewing, SE pp. 562, 565, 567, 569, 570, 575, 576/⬚406, 409, 411, 413, 414, 419, 420

Speaking and Listening
ATE p. 578

Vocabulary
ATE p. 568

Real-World Connection
ATE p. 566

Technology
SE pp. 566, 574/⬚410, 418

Workplace Skills
ATE pp. 567, 575

ASSESSMENT SUPPORT

Standardized Test Preparation Workshop SE p. 582; ATE pp. 570, 577

Standardized Test Preparation Workbook, pp. 43–44

Formal Assessment, Ch. 22

MEETING INDIVIDUAL NEEDS

Less Advanced Students ATE pp. 570, 583. See also Ongoing Assessments ATE pp. 565, 567, 569, 571, 576, 578.

AP Students ATE pp. 569, 583

ESL Students ATE p. 576

Gifted and Talented Students ATE p. 575

Linguistic Learners ATE p. 569

BLOCK SCHEDULING

Pacing Suggestions
For 90-minute Blocks
• Administer the Diagnostic Test to students to determine instructional coverage.
• Have students complete the necessary exercises in class. Use the Hands-on Grammar activity to provide a change of pace.

Resources for Varying Instruction
• *Writing and Grammar* Interactive Text A 90-minute block provides an ideal opportunity for students to work on the computer.

Professional Development Support
• *How to Manage Instruction in the Block* This teaching resource provides management and activity suggestions.

MEDIA AND TECHNOLOGY

For the Student
• *Writing and Grammar* Interactive Text, Ch. 22
• *On-line Exercise Bank,* Sections 22.1–2

For the Teacher
• TeacherEXPRESS™ CD-ROM

WRITING AND GRAMMAR ON-LINE

Interactive Text (On-line or on CD-ROM)
• Easily navigable instruction with on-line supporting resources
• Self-scoring exercises and diagnostic tests

Companion Web Site PHSchool.com
• On-line Exercise Bank (use Web Code egk-1202)

See the Go On-line! **feature, SE p. iii.**

LITERATURE CONNECTIONS

Grammar in Literature selections from *Prentice Hall Literature, Penguin Edition,* The British Tradition:
from "B. Wordsworth," V. S. Naipaul, SE p. 571/⬚415
from *Paradise Lost,* John Milton, SE p. 577/⬚421

Lesson Objectives

1. To recognize and use pronouns in the nominative, objective, and possessive cases

2. To use *who* and *whom* correctly in sentences

3. To determine case in subordinate clauses with parenthetical expressions

4. To identify and use pronouns correctly in elliptical clauses

5. To recognize appropriate English usage within the context of a written passage

Critical Viewing

Analyze Possible answer: Traveling through Nova Scotia was a thrill for the cyclists. They loved the views of its rocky shores, and people in seaside towns welcomed them.

Chapter 22 Pronoun Usage

At one time in the English language, the form of both nouns and pronouns was changed according to their use in a sentence. For example, the form that a noun would have as a subject was different from the form it would have as a direct object. Today, the form of a noun is changed only to show possession. There are a variety of forms that indicate how pronouns are used, however.

In this chapter, you will study the various forms of pronouns and the rules that govern their use.

▲ **Critical Viewing** Imagine that you are one of the travelers in the picture. Write a caption for the photo that includes at least three pronouns. **[Analyze]**

✓ **ONGOING ASSESSMENT: Diagnose**					
If students miss more than one item in any category, direct them to the relevant pages of the textbook and assign exercises for practice and review.					

Pronoun Usage	Diagnostic Test Items	Teach	Practice Review	Section Review	Chapter
Skill Check A					
The Three Cases	A 1–5	pp. 564–565/Ⓗ408–409	Ex. 1	Ex. 10	Ex. 28
Skill Check B					
Nominative Pronouns	B 7, 10–11, 13	p. 566/Ⓗ410	Ex. 2–4	Ex. 11–12	Ex. 29–30
Objective Pronouns	B 9, 13–14	pp. 568–569/Ⓗ412–413	Ex. 5–7	Ex. 11–12	Ex. 29–30
Possessive Pronouns	B 6, 8, 12, 15	pp. 570–571/Ⓗ414–415	Ex. 8–9	Ex. 12	Ex. 31

Diagnostic Test

Directions: Write all answers on a separate sheet of paper.

Skill Check A. Write the pronoun, and tell whether its case is *nominative*, *objective*, or *possessive*.

1. our atlas
2. sent the map to him
3. dedicated it to the benefactor
4. We consulted the map.
5. your best student

Skill Check B. Identify the case of each underlined pronoun in the following sentences, and tell how it is used in the sentence.

6. <u>My</u> aunt is studying to be a cartographer.
7. <u>She</u> is very interested in maps.
8. The professors at <u>her</u> school have been teaching cartography for several decades.
9. Drawing maps gives <u>her</u> pleasure.
10. The two most diligent students in the class are <u>she</u> and her best friend.
11. They hope that <u>they</u> will earn scholarships.
12. They can use <u>their</u> knowledge to make interesting new maps.
13. <u>They</u> gave <u>me</u> maps to study, too.
14. My aunt bought an atlas for <u>me</u> as a birthday present.
15. Studying the atlas has helped <u>me</u> to get *A's* on geography tests.

Skill Check C. Write the correct pronoun in parentheses, and identify its function in the sentence or clause.

16. (Who, Whom) gave you the directions to the cartography school?
17. (Who, Whom) are we expecting?
18. Do you know (who, whom) made the first map of your town?
19. From (who, whom) have you received the correct directions?
20. (Who, Whom) will they hire at their school?

Skill Check D. Choose the correct pronoun in parentheses. Then, write any words or phrases that are understood to be included in the sentences.

21. I was less skilled in reading maps than (she, her).
22. The cartography student was as dedicated to making maps as (we, us).
23. The physical features of the Great Lakes were as familiar to the mapmaker as to (I, me).
24. No living cartographer is as famous as (she, her).
25. This collection of maps from ancient Egypt is more important to the students from Cairo than to (we, us).

Diagnostic Test

Each item in the Diagnostic Test corresponds to a specific section in the pronoun usage chapter, enabling you to tailor instruction as needed. See "Ongoing Assessment: Diagnose" below for further details.

Skill Check A

1. our: possessive
2. him: objective
3. it: objective
4. we: nominative
5. your: possessive

Skill Check B

6. My: possessive, shows ownership
7. She: nominative, subject
8. her: possessive, shows ownership
9. her: objective, indirect object
10. she: nominative, predicate nominative
11. they: nominative, subject (of subordinate clause)
12. their: possessive, shows ownership
13. They: nominative, subject; me: objective, indirect object
14. me: objective, object of preposition
15. me: objective, subject of infinitive

Skill Check C

16. Who: subject
17. Whom: direct object
18. who: subject (of subordinate clause)
19. whom: object of preposition
20. Whom: direct object

Skill Check D

21. she (was)
22. we (were)
23. (they were) to me
24. she (is)
25. (it is) to us

✓ ONGOING ASSESSMENT: Diagnose *continued*

Pronoun Usage	Diagnostic Test Items	Teach	Practice	Section Review	Chapter Review
Skill Check C					
Pronouns *Who* and *Whom*	C 16–20	pp. 574–575/ H418–419	Ex. 16–18	Ex. 21–22, 24	Ex. 32–33, 35
Skill Check D					
Pronouns in Elliptical Clauses	D 21–25	pp. 577–578/ H421–422	Ex. 19–20	Ex. 23–24	Ex. 34–35
Cumulative Reviews and Applications				Ex. 13–15, 25–27	Ex. 35–37

⏱ **TIME SAVERS!**

🖼 **Answers on Transparencies**
Use the *Grammar Exercises Answers on Transparencies* for Chapter 22 to facilitate correction by students.

💻 **On-Line Exercise Bank**
Have students complete the Diagnostic Test on computer. The Auto Check feature will grade their work for you!

Ask students to write a paragraph about a boy and girl and a disagreement they had about a movie or book. After identifying the book or movie (and possibly the individuals) by name, challenge students to use pronouns rather than nouns, in as many different forms as they can, to tell about the conversation. When they finish, have them list all the pronouns they used.

Activate Prior Knowledge

Copy these sentences and have students replace the underlined nouns with pronouns. Then have students identify the case of each pronoun they use. (Answers are provided in parentheses.)

Darnell and Evan like to study maps. (he: nominative)

María told Darnell and Evan about a new atlas. (him: objective)

Evan's mother may buy the book as a birthday gift. (His: possessive)

TEACH

Step-by-Step Teaching Guide

The Three Cases

1. Make the point that pronouns are different from nouns in that their form changes according to how they are used in a sentence.

2. After students have reviewed the two charts, ask for examples of some of the more common case uses, such as pronouns used as subjects, direct objects, and objects of prepositions. Put their examples on the board and have them tell how pronouns are used.

3. Point out the two possessive forms shown for each pronoun in the second chart. Review that *my, your, her, our,* and *their* precede nouns (*my* coat); *mine, yours, hers, ours,* and *theirs* are used alone (the coat is *mine*). Explain that *his* is used both ways.

4. Have students identify in the chart on page 565 the two pronouns with the same nominative and objective form (*you, it*).

Section 22.1 Case

The only parts of speech that have *case* are nouns and pronouns.

▶ **KEY CONCEPT** Case is the form of a noun or a pronoun that indicates its use in a sentence. ■

The Three Cases

Both nouns and pronouns have three cases, each of which has its own distinctive uses.

▶ **KEY CONCEPT** The three cases of a noun or pronoun are the *nominative*, the *objective*, and the *possessive*. ■

The uses of the three cases are explained in the following chart.

Case	Use in Sentence
Nominative	Subject of a Verb, Predicate Nominative, or Nominative Absolute
Objective	Direct Object, Indirect Object, Object of a Preposition, Object of a Verbal, or Subject of an Infinitive
Possessive	To Show Ownership

Nouns generally pose no difficulty because their form is changed only to show possession.

NOMINATIVE: The *map* had been hidden for years.
OBJECTIVE: We tried to find the *map*.
POSSESSIVE: The *map's* location could not be determined.

In the first sentence, *map* is nominative because it is the subject of the verb. In the second sentence, *map* is objective because it is the object of the infinitive *to find.* The form changes only in the possessive case when an *'s* is added.

Notice in the chart on the next page that personal pronouns often have different forms for all three cases. The pronoun that you use depends upon its function in a sentence.

Theme: Maps

In this section, you will learn about the three cases of pronouns and their uses. The examples and exercises in this section are about ancient and modern maps.

Cross-Curricular Connection: Social Studies

⏱ TIME AND RESOURCE MANAGER

Resources
Print: *Grammar Exercise Workbook*, pp. 85–90
Technology: *Writing and Grammar* Interactive Text, Section 22.1; *On-Line Exercise Bank*, Section 22.1

Using the Full Student Edition	Using the Handbook Ⓗ
• Work through all key concepts, pp. 564–571. • Assign and review Exercises 1–9. • Read and discuss Grammar in Literature, p. 571. • Do the Hands-on Grammar activity, p. 572.	• Work through all key concepts, pp. 408–415. • Assign and review Exercises 1–9. • Read and discuss Grammar in Literature, p. 415 • Do the Hands-on Grammar activity, p. 416.

Nominative	Objective	Possessive
I	me	my, mine
you	you	your, yours
he, she, it	him, her, it	his, her, hers, its
we	us	our, ours
they	them	their, theirs

Exercise 1 **Identifying Case** Write the case of each under-lined pronoun. Then, indicate its use in the sentence.

EXAMPLE: The letter was addressed to <u>me</u>.
                    objective (object of a preposition)

1. Travelers often carry maps and study <u>them</u>.
2. <u>We</u> have been making maps to represent the physical world for thousands of years.
3. Around 1000 B.C., the ancient Babylonians drew circular disks on clay tablets to represent <u>their</u> world.
4. <u>They</u> were among the first mapmakers in history.
5. Around A.D.150, the Greek scientist Ptolemy helped to make advances in mapmaking for <u>his</u> contemporaries.
6. They came to <u>him</u> for information about the natural world.
7. Another important mapmaker of the past was the Muslim scholar Al-Idrisi, who advanced the work of <u>his</u> predecessors.
8. It was <u>he</u> who made one of the first maps of the world.
9. He made many advances in cartography, and later mapmakers admired <u>him</u>.
10. Despite developments in mapmaking, <u>it</u> did not become an exact science until several centuries later.

▶ **Critical Viewing** What do the different symbols on the map represent? How is the purpose that the symbols serve similar to that served by pronouns? **[Connect]**

More Practice

Grammar Exercise Workbook
• pp. 85–86
On-line Exercise Bank
• Section 22.1
Go on-line:
PHSchool.com
Enter Web Code:
egk-1202

Case • 565

Answer Key

▶ **Exercise 1**

1. objective (direct object)
2. nominative (subject)
3. possessive (shows ownership)
4. nominative (subject)
5. possessive (shows ownership)
6. objective (object of preposition)
7. possessive (shows ownership)
8. nominative (predicate nominative)
9. objective (direct object)
10. nominative (subject)

Critical Viewing

Connect Possible answer: The symbols on the map are difficult to decipher; some seem to represent mountains, roads, and people. As map symbols stand for physical features, so pronouns stand in the place of nouns.

Language Highlight

The English spoken in the United States has been influenced by many waves of immigration. One influential immigrant group was the Scotch-Irish, who flocked to the United States in the eighteenth century. Their legacy may be found in an expression such as *you-all (y'all)*, which derives from a translation of the Scotch-Irish plural *yous*. Have students identify the plural form of *you (you)*; then explain that although *you-all* may be heard in less formal speech in many parts of the United States, it should not be used in formal speech or writing.

☑ ONGOING ASSESSMENT: Monitor and Reinforce

If students miss more than two items in Exercise 1, refer them to the following for additional practice.

In the Textbook	Print Resources	Technology
Section Review, Ex. 10, Section 22.1	*Grammar Exercise Workbook*, pp. 85–86	*On-Line Exercise Bank*, Section 22.1

⏱ TIME SAVERS!

Answers on Transparencies Use the *Grammar Exercises Answers on Transparencies* for Chapter 22 to facilitate correction by students.

On-Line Exercise Bank Have students complete the exercises on computer. The Auto Check feature will grade their work for you!

The Nominative Case

1. If students need more review of nominative absolutes, provide these examples:

   The mapmaker being busy, we decided not to interrupt his work. A co-worker having stopped with a question, the mapmaker politely gave her an answer.

   Have students identify the noun in the nominative absolute in each sentence *(mapmaker, co-worker)* and then replace each one with an appropriate pronoun *(he, she)*.

2. Tell students that in informal English, especially informal speech, an objective pronoun is often used after a noun *(It's me; That was him)*. Advise students to avoid this use in writing and in any speaking situations where they are not certain of their audience. Constructions like "It was ___ who ..." call for the nominative case; so does identifying oneself on the phone *("This is she")*.

Real-World Connection

Explain to students that organizations such as environmental groups often write petitions and letters about their causes on behalf of numerous members. Consequently, such letters and petitions often begin with *We* followed by an appositive *("We concerned citizens wish to...")* Have students give other examples and tell when they might be used.

22.1

The Nominative Case

The nominative case is used when a personal pronoun acts in one of three ways:

> **KEY CONCEPT** Use the **nominative case** for the subject of a verb, for a predicate nominative, and for the pronoun in a nominative absolute. ■

These uses are illustrated in the chart below.

NOMINATIVE PRONOUNS	
As the Subject of a Verb	*I* will consult the map while *she* asks for directions.
As a Predicate Nominative	The finalists were *he* and *she*.
In a Nominative Absolute	*She* having finished the meal, the waiter cleared her table.

You have learned a lot about subjects and predicate nominatives. The third use of nominative case pronouns is a little more unusual. A *nominative absolute* consists of a noun or nominative pronoun followed by a participial phrase. It functions independently from the rest of the sentence.

EXAMPLE: We having opened our textbooks, the geography teacher pointed out the map on page 435.

Nominative Pronouns in Compounds When you use a pronoun in a compound subject or predicate nominative, check the case by mentally removing the other part of the compound or by mentally inverting the sentence.

COMPOUND SUBJECT: The teacher and *I* inspected the map.
(*I* inspected the map.)
His father and *he* sailed the boat.
(*He* sailed the boat.)

COMPOUND PREDICATE NOMINATIVE: The fastest sailors were Jody and *he*.
(Jody and *he* were the fastest sailors.)
The surveyors were Lin and *I*.
(Lin and *I* were the surveyors.)

Nominative Pronouns With Appositives When an appositive follows a pronoun used as a subject or predicate nominative, the pronoun should stay in the nominative case.

SUBJECT: *We* mapmakers are using more technology.

PREDICATE NOMINATIVE: The programmers were *we* seniors.

Internet Tip

The designation ".gov" as part of a Web address lets you know that the Web site is a part of a government organization. Official Web sites of local, state, and federal governments all have the ".gov" designation as part of their addresses.

> **Exercise 2** Choosing Pronouns in the Nominative Case
Choose the pronoun in the nominative case to complete each sentence. Then, write the use of the pronoun.
1. (We, Us) cartographers have been traveling to remote regions for many years.
2. Two veteran explorers and (I, me) traveled to a remote region of the Amazon River to map it.
3. The participants on that trip were they and (I, me).
4. (They, Them) having traveled throughout the world, their understanding of the world was greater than mine.
5. The most inexperienced traveler was (I, me).

> **Exercise 3** Using Pronouns in the Nominative Case Write a nominative pronoun to complete each sentence. Then, write the use of the pronoun.
1. ___?___ students have been admiring the contributions of cartographers since the beginning of civilization.
2. My classmates and ___?___ learned that prehistoric maps may date to around 6200 B.C.
3. ___?___ were amazed to learn that numerous advances in mapmaking have been made.
4. ___?___ having made many advances in mapmaking, people celebrated their achievements.
5. It was ___?___ who developed latitude and longitude grids to indicate exact locations on the surface of Earth.

> **Exercise 4** Revising Sentences With Pronouns in the Nominative Case Revise these sentences where necessary, correcting errors in pronoun usage. Write *correct* if no revision is needed.
1. Latitude is a system of imaginary lines placed east to west around Earth; it allows you to measure how far a particular location is from the equator.
2. Longitude lines are placed north to south from the North Pole to the South Pole; them help you measure distances east to west or west to east.
3. After several attempts, Joanne and me determined the exact location of the source of the Amazon River.
4. Early cartographers made improvements that were passed on by they to later generations.
5. The Egyptians developed useful mapmaking techniques; some of the best early cartographers were they.

More Practice

Grammar Exercise Workbook
• pp. 87–88
On-line Exercise Bank
• Section 22.1
  Go on-line:
  PHSchool.com
  Enter Web Code:
  egk-1202

Interactive Textbook

Get instant feedback! Exercises 2, 3, and 4 are available on-line or on CD-ROM.

▼ **Critical Viewing**
Use several pronouns to answer the question: What do the lines that cross this map indicate?
[Identify]

Case • 567

> **Exercise 2**
1. We (subject)
2. I (subject)
3. I (predicate nominative)
4. They (nominative absolute)
5. I (predicate nominative)

> **Exercise 3**
Allow some variation in response. The following are likely answers.
1. We (subject)
2. I (subject)
3. We (subject)
4. They (nominative absolute)
5. they (predicate nominative)

> **Exercise 4**
1. correct
2. Replace *them* with *they*
3. Replace *me* with *I*
4. Replace *they* with *them*
5. correct

Integrating Workplace Skills

Explain to students that employers often try to foster a sense of teamwork among employees. Consequently, managers frequently use the nominative plural pronoun *we* when talking to individuals about team projects. (Example: *We're not working hard enough, Bill. We need to put more effort into this project.*) Have students discuss the effectiveness of such a method of communication. Then, have them recall other instances where they have heard pronouns used in this way.

Critical Viewing

Identify Possible answer: They indicate latitude (it is the angular distance north or south of the equator), longitude (it is the angular distance east or west of the prime meridian), and the equator (it is the line around the Earth that is always the same distance from both poles).

⏱ TIME SAVERS!

Answers on Transparencies Use the *Grammar Exercises Answers on Transparencies* for Chapter 22 to facilitate correction by students.

On-Line Exercise Bank Have students complete the exercises on computer. The Auto Check feature will grade their work for you!

☑ ONGOING ASSESSMENT: Monitor and Reinforce

If students miss more than one item in Exercise 2, 3, or 4, refer them to the following for additional practice.

In the Textbook	Print Resources	Technology
Section Review, Ex. 11–12, Section 22.1	*Grammar Exercise Workbook,* pp. 87–88	*On-Line Exercise Bank,* Section 22.1

The Objective Case

1. If students need more review of verbals with direct objects, provide these examples:

   Having bought the old map at a junk store, we weren't sure of its value.

   Someone suggested contacting the store owner for information.

   My friend wanted to contact a professional appraiser.

   Have students identify the direct object noun in each sentence (*map, owner, appraiser*) and then replace each one with an appropriate pronoun (*it, him* or *her, him* or *her*).

2. To further emphasize that the objective case follows the preposition *between*, have students reread the correct sentence at the bottom of this page, replacing *me* with other objective pronouns (*her, him, us, them*).

3. Tell students that in the same way as with compounds, the correct pronoun form for appositives can be determined by dropping the appositive. To demonstrate, have volunteers read aloud the example sentences on page 569, dropping *students, amazed nieces,* and *stragglers.*

4. Direct students' attention to the final appositive example. Point out that here *us* is the subject of the infinitive (*us stragglers to hurry*). Explain that this is an exception: An objective case pronoun may be used as a subject only of an infinitive.

Integrating Vocabulary Skills

Latin Roots As they study pronouns in compounds, have students consult a dictionary for the derivation of the word *compound*. (It comes from the Latin word *componere*, "to put together.") Have students explain how the definition of *componere* relates to compound subjects and objects. (Two or more words are put together to form multiple subjects and objects.)

22.1

The Objective Case

Objective pronouns are used for any kind of object in a sentence as well as for the subject of an infinitive.

▶ **KEY CONCEPT** Use the **objective case** for the object of any verb, preposition, or verbal or for the subject of an infinitive. ■

The chart below illustrates the uses of objective pronouns.

OBJECTIVE PRONOUNS	
Direct Object	A piece of plaster hit *him* on the head.
Indirect Object	My uncle sent *me* a lace fan from Hong Kong.
Object of Preposition	Three very tall men sat in front of *us* in the movie theater.
Object of Participle	The sharks following *them* were very hungry.
Object of Gerund	Meeting *you* will be a great pleasure.
Object of Infinitive	I am obligated to help *her* move this Saturday.
Subject of Infinitive	The firm wanted *her* to work the graveyard shift.

Objective Pronouns in Compounds As with the nominative case, errors with objective pronouns most often occur in compounds. To check yourself, mentally remove the other part of the compound.

EXAMPLES: Cracking ice floes alarmed Burt and *him.*
(Cracking ice floes alarmed *him.*)
Sally drew Laurie and me a map to her house.
(Sally drew *me* a map.)

Take special care to use the objective case after the preposition *between.*

INCORRECT: This argument is just between you and *I.*

CORRECT: This argument is just between you and *me.*

✓ ONGOING ASSESSMENT: Prerequisite Skills

If students have difficulty with some of the constructions requiring the objective case, you may need to review the following to ensure coverage of prerequisite knowledge.

In the Textbook	Print Resources	Technology
Verbals and Verbal Phrases, Section 19.2	*Grammar Exercise Workbook,* pp. 37–40	*On-Line Exercise Bank,* Section 19.2

Objective Pronouns With Appositives When a pronoun used as an object or as the subject of an infinitive is followed by an appositive, remember to use the objective case.

EXAMPLES: The mapmaking quiz intimidated *us* students.
She brought *us* amazed nieces a pet iguana
from her trip to Central America.
The guide asked *us* stragglers to hurry.

▶ **Exercise 5** Choosing Pronouns in the Objective Case
Choose the pronoun in the objective case to complete each
sentence. Then, write the use of the pronoun.
1. Aerial photographs have aided (we, us)
   cartographers.
2. Taking (I, me) up in the bad weather
   worried the pilot.
3. We asked (he, him) to fly over the
   uncharted area.
4. The dangers hovering over (we, us)
   travelers were great.
5. I informed (he, him) that I needed to
   take aerial photographs for my sister.

▶ **Exercise 6** Using Pronouns in the
Objective Case Complete these sentences
by adding objective pronouns.
1. I was determined to take ___?___ on
   the next flight.
2. Asking ___?___ to fly with me on a mapping expedition
   would not be easy.
3. The problem stopping ___?___ was a fear of crashing.
4. She remembered that during our last trip, an unexpected
   air pocket had given ___?___ and ___?___ a scare.
5. Still, I think that she secretly wanted ___?___ to invite her
   to join the flight

▶ **Exercise 7** Revising a Paragraph With Pronouns in the
Objective Case Correct the errors in pronoun usage. Write
correct if no change is needed.
(1) In school today, my geography teacher showed we several topographical maps. (2) She asked Charlayne and me to point out some of the features on the maps. (3) Examining they carefully, we were able to point out such features as hills, valleys, lakes, and streams. (4) Helping us was a key located at the bottom of each map. (5) We students in the geography class will be expected to create a topographical map of our county.

▼ **Critical Viewing**
If you were in a plane looking down on this landscape, how would you describe the experience? What pronouns would you use? [Describe]

▶ **More Practice**

Grammar Exercise Workbook
• pp. 87–88
On-line Exercise Bank
• Section 22.1
   Go on-line:
   PHSchool.com
   Enter Web Code:
   egk-1202

Case • 569

Critical Viewing

Describe Possible description of the landscape: It is a patchwork of farm fields. They stretch away to the horizon. What do farmers grow in them?

Answer Key

▶ **Exercise 5**

1. us (direct object)
2. me (object of gerund)
3. him (subject of infinitive)
4. us (object of preposition)
5. him (direct object)

▶ **Exercise 6**

1. her
2. her
3. her, me
4. her, me
5. me *or* us

▶ **Exercise 7**

Allow some variation in response. The following are likely answers.

1. Replace *we* with *us*
2. correct
3. Replace *they* with *them*
4. correct
5. correct

☑ **ONGOING ASSESSMENT: Monitor and Reinforce**

If students miss more than one item in Exercise 5, 6, or 7, refer them to the following for additional practice.

In the Textbook	Print Resources	Technology
Section Review, Ex. 11–12, Section 22.1	*Grammar Exercise Workbook*, pp. 87–88	*On-Line Exercise Bank*, Section 22.1

The Possessive Case

1. Have students identify the functions of the gerunds in the example sentences (subject, OP, OP). Remind them that not all words that end in *-ing* are gerunds.

2. Reemphasize that possessive pronouns do not use apostrophes to indicate possession. Suggest that when they have a choice between *it's* and *its* and *your* and *you're*, they mentally substitute the uncontracted form (*it is, you are*). If this form does not make sense in the sentence, then they should use the spelling without the apostrophe.

3. Have the class come up with sample sentences to differentiate *their*, *they're*, and *there*. Mention that these words are the source of the most common spelling errors in English.

Customize for
Less Advanced Students

Some students may not be aware how possessive pronouns combine with *-self* or *-selves*. Provide practice by having students correct the errors in these sentences:

He bought hisself a map.(himself)

We promised ourself a vacation.
(ourselves)

They will go by theirselves.
(themselves)

Critical Viewing

Describe Possible description of the map: It shows parts of Spain and North Africa. Its coastlines seem accurate. Why are there straight lines from some points on it?

22.1

The Possessive Case

Although errors are less common in the possessive case than they are in the other two cases, you should take care to use the possessive case before gerunds. A *gerund* is a verbal form ending in *-ing* that is used as a noun.

▶ **KEY CONCEPT** Use the possessive case before gerunds. ■

EXAMPLES: *Your* tracing of the map was sloppy.
We objected to *his* insinuating that we were lazy.
Ms. Malin insists on *our* attending her slide presentation.

Another mistake to avoid is using an apostrophe with possessive pronouns, which already show ownership. Spellings such as *her's*, *our's*, *their's*, and *your's* are incorrect. In addition, do not confuse a possessive pronoun with a contraction that sounds almost the same. *It's* (with an apostrophe) is the contraction for *it is* or *it has*. *Its* (without the apostrophe) is a possessive pronoun that means "belonging to it." *You're* is a contraction of *you are*; the possessive form of *you* is *your*.

POSSESSIVE PRONOUNS: The map had served *its* purpose.
The students displayed *their* maps.

CONTRACTIONS: *It's* not likely that we will become lost.
You're the only ones who refused to consult the map.

▼ **Critical Viewing** Describe this map using pronouns in at least two different cases. **[Describe]**

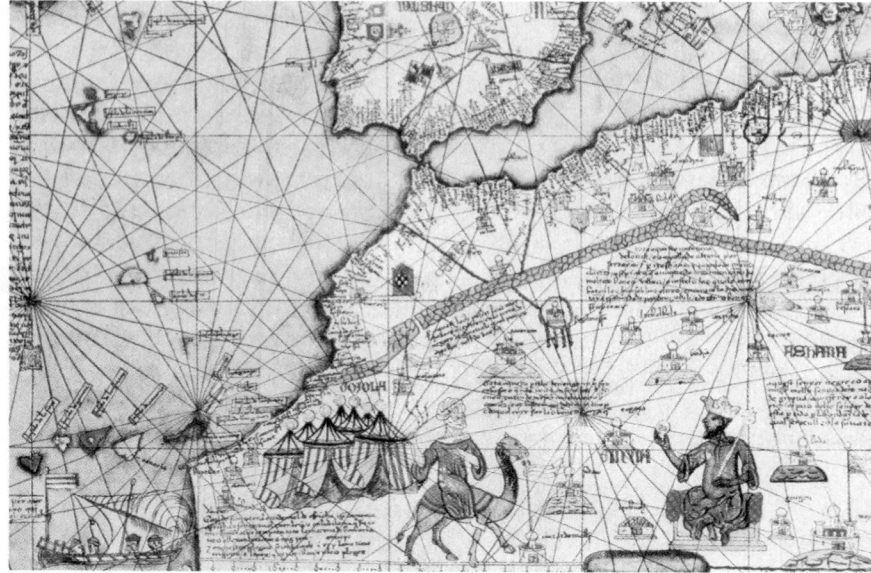

570 • Pronoun Usage

♦ STANDARDIZED TEST PREPARATION WORKSHOP

Grammar and Usage Many standardized tests require students to draw upon their knowledge of pronoun case. Use the following example to demonstrate.

The sisters shared everything. They played together. They ate together. They're closeness was remarkable to us observers.

How would you correct the underlined sentence in the above passage?

A Correct as is.

B Change *us* to *we*.

C Take out the apostrophe in *They're*.

D Replace *They're* with *Their*.

The correct answer is **D**. The word *they're* is a contraction of *they are* and does not show possession; the pronoun form, *their*, does. *Us* is used correctly as an object of a preposition in the objective case.

GRAMMAR IN LITERATURE

from **B. Wordsworth**

V. S. Naipaul

V. S. Naipaul has used pronouns in all three cases in this passage. What is the case of each of the pronouns in blue italics?

I gave *him my* word and I kept *it*.
I liked *his* little room. *It* had no more furniture than George's front room, but *it* looked cleaner and healthier. But *it* also looked lonely.
One day I asked *him*, "Mister Wordsworth, why *you* does keep all this bush in *your* yard? . . ."

Exercise 8 Using Pronouns in the Possessive Case Choose the correct word in each set of parentheses.
1. If (your, you're) looking for an interesting world map, you should consult this book.
2. The history of mapmaking is filled with (it's, its) share of innovators.
3. These innovators used (they're, their) talents to improve existing maps and to create new maps.
4. (Their, Them) experimenting with new mapmaking techniques helped to change the way people viewed the world.
5. Gerardus Mercator was profiled in (your, you're) geography book.

Exercise 9 Revising Sentences With Pronouns in the Possessive Case Revise these sentences where necessary to correct errors in pronoun usage. Write *correct* if no revision is needed.
1. Mercator, who lived in the 1500's, sought to improve the maps of he's era.
2. He is known for his' unique system of drawing maps over grids of lines.
3. This type of map became popular because its easy to use.
4. Ms. Lassiter supervised us posting of the class maps on the school Web site.
5. Her specifying dates for completing each part of the assignment forced us to stay on schedule.

> **More Practice**
>
> **Grammar Exercise Workbook**
> • pp. 89–90
> **On-line Exercise Bank**
> • Section 22.1
> *Go on-line:*
> PHSchool.com
> *Enter Web Code:*
> egk-1202

Case • 571

✅ **ONGOING ASSESSMENT: Monitor and Reinforce**

If students miss more than one item in Exercise 8 or 9, refer them to the following for additional practice.

In the Textbook	Print Resources	Technology
Section Review, Ex. 12, Section 22.1	*Grammar Exercise Workbook,* pp. 89–90	*On-Line Exercise Bank,* Section 22.1

Hands-on Grammar

Teaching Resources: Hands-on Grammar Activity Book, Ch. 22

1. If you wish to do this activity in class, be prepared with scissors and index cards for the students. Give each student a copy of the Hands-on Grammar activity sheet for Chapter 22.

2. Have students follow the directions to prepare the sentence slides.

3. Possible additional sentences:

   Christopher Columbus reached America before Amerigo Vespucci.

   Columbus was sponsored by King Ferdinand.

   Martina Navratilova often played tennis against Chris Evert.

4. You may wish to expand this activity by using sentences with common nouns that are located in positions other than the beginnings and ends of sentences.

Find It in Your Reading

Encourage students to look for sentences that use nouns in a variety of functions, including indirect objects and subjects and objects of verbals.

Find It in Your Writing

As students review their portfolios, suggest that they test for correct pronoun usage with a mental version of the pronoun sentence slide.

22.1

Hands-on Grammar

Pronoun Sentence Slide

To help you see how the use of a pronoun in a sentence determines its case, complete the following activity. Fold a sheet of paper in half lengthwise. Make several cuts, approximately 2 inches apart, from the fold to the open edge. Do not cut all the way to the open edge.

Next, cut from index cards or construction paper pronoun slides. For each pronoun, cut one card as shown. On one side of the card, write the nominative case. On the other side, write the objective case.

Unfold the paper, and write a sentence along each cut. Use a proper noun at each end of the sentence—in some sentences, have the second proper noun be the subject of a clause; in others, the object. Both nouns should be the same number and gender. Use the pronoun slide to cover and replace the noun acting as the subject. Then, slide the pronoun to the other end of the sentence to replace the object. Flip the card to show the objective case.

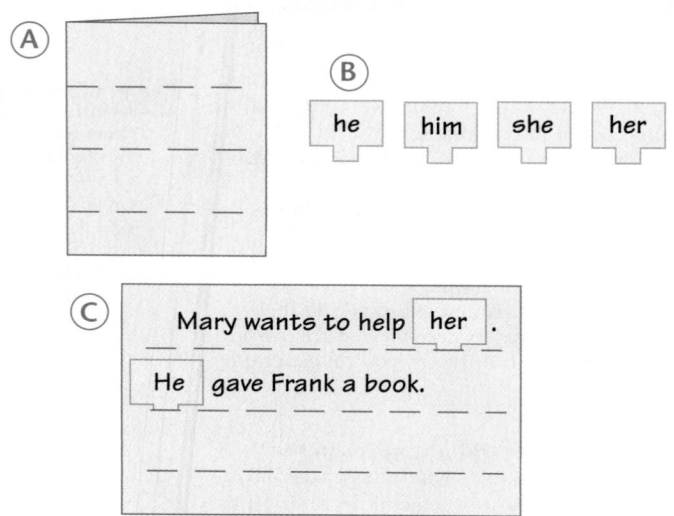

Find It in Your Reading Prepare additional slide sheets to do this activity with sentences from a short story or novel you are currently reading.

Find It in Your Writing Choose from your portfolio a piece of writing in which you use many pronouns. Revise sentences to eliminate any errors in pronoun usage.

572 • Pronoun Usage

☑ ONGOING ASSESSMENT: Assess Mastery

Use the following resources to assess student mastery of pronoun case.

In the Textbook	Technology
Chapter Review, Ex. 28–31	*Writing and Grammar* Interactive Text, Section 22.1, Section Review; *On-Line Exercise Bank*, Section 22.1

⏱ TIME SAVERS!

✋ **Hands-on Grammar**
Use the Hands-on Grammar activity sheet for Chapter 22 to facilitate this activity.

Section 22.1 Section Review

GRAMMAR EXERCISES 10–15

> **Exercise 10** Identifying Case

Write the case of each underlined pronoun. Then, write its use.

1. I saw a time-zone map in <u>my</u> planner.
2. This map shows <u>me</u> what time it is in different parts of the world.
3. <u>We</u> having brought up the subject, our teacher discussed time zones.
4. <u>Our</u> asking her prompted an interesting discussion.
5. She started by providing some background information for <u>us</u> students.
6. In 1884, an international conference proposed <u>its</u> system for twenty-four time zones.
7. Look in the mid-Pacific Ocean, and <u>you</u> can locate the International Date Line.
8. This line was <u>their</u> marker for where each day began.
9. As travelers go eastward, the system requires <u>them</u> to adjust their watches forward.
10. The first people on our plane to adjust their watches were Helene and <u>she</u>.

> **Exercise 11** Using Pronouns

Choose the correct pronoun to complete each sentence. Then, identify its use.

1. Most cities with public transit systems provide maps for (we, us) riders.
2. Bus and subway maps help (we, us) to plan the easiest and fastest routes.
3. To assist riders, maps also show (they, them) where to make bus transfers.
4. Mapmakers hope (we, us) will consult their maps more frequently.
5. However, reading (they, them) is often difficult and confusing.

> **Exercise 12** Correcting Errors in Pronoun Usage Revise the following sentences as necessary to correct errors in pronoun usage. Write *correct* if no revision is needed.

1. Us requesting better maps may lead to improvements.
2. The Transit Authority asked Jill and me to serve on a riders' council.
3. Between her and I, we came up with twelve suggestions.
4. The only people to challenge our suggestions were them.
5. In the end, the Transit Authority was grateful for we help.

> **Exercise 13** Find It in Your Reading In these lines from *The Canterbury Tales*, label at least two pronouns in each case and tell how each is used. Then, rewrite the lines, changing the male pronouns to female pronouns.

"He woke and told his friend what had occurred
And begged him that the journey be deferred
At least a day, implored him not to start.
But his companion, lying there apart,
Began to laugh and treat him to derision.
'I'm not afraid,' he said, 'of any vision, . . .'"

> **Exercise 14** Find It in Your Writing In your portfolio, find two examples of pronouns in each of the three cases. Check to make sure each is used correctly. Then, write down each pronoun, its case, and its use in the sentence.

> **Exercise 15** Writing Application Write a short letter describing a real or imaginary adventure you had that involved following a map. Be sure to describe the adventure using pronouns in all three cases. Circle each pronoun in your letter.

Section Review • 573

ASSESS and CLOSE

Section Review

Each of these exercises correlates to the instruction on case, pages 564–572. The exercises may be used for more practice, for reteaching, or for review of the key concepts presented.

Answer Key

> **Exercise 10**

1. possessive (shows ownership)
2. objective (indirect object)
3. nominative (nominative absolute)
4. possessive (precedes gerund)
5. objective (object of preposition)
6. possessive (shows ownership)
7. nominative (subject)
8. possessive (shows ownership)
9. objective (subject of infinitive)
10. nominative (predicate nominative)

> **Exercise 11**

1. us (object of preposition)
2. us (subject of infinitive)
3. them (indirect object)
4. we (subject)
5. them (direct object of gerund)

> **Exercise 12**

1. Replace *Us* with *Our*.
2. correct
3. Replace *I* with *me*.
4. Replace *them* with *they*.
5. Replace *we* with *our*.

> **Exercise 13**

Find It in Your Reading
The nominatives *He, I,* and *he* are used as subjects; the possessive *his* is used to show ownership (twice); the objective *him* is used as an indirect object, as a direct object, and as a subject of infinitive.

continued

Answer Key continued

> **Exercise 13**

*She woke and told <u>her</u> friend what had occurred
And begged <u>her</u> that the journey be deferred
At least a day, implored <u>her</u> not to start.
But <u>her</u> companion, lying there apart,
Began to laugh and treat <u>her</u> to derision.
"I'm not afraid," <u>she</u> said, "of any vision, . . ."*

> **Exercise 14**

Find It in Your Writing
When students list the pronouns in their work, have them underline them as well. Then ask them to trade their compositions and lists with a partner to see if the partner agrees with how the pronouns are used.

> **Exercise 15**

Writing Application
Have volunteers read their letters aloud, and ask other students to keep tallies of how many pronouns were used.

⏱ TIME SAVERS!

🖨 **Answers on Transparencies** Use the *Grammar Exercises Answers on Transparencies* for Chapter 22 to facilitate correction by students.

💻 **On-Line Exercise Bank** Have students complete the exercises on computer. The Auto Check feature will grade their work for you!

Who Do You Trust?

Tell students that *Who Do You Trust?* was the name of a 1950's television quiz show hosted by Johnny Carson. Ask them to identify the blooper in the title (*Who* should be *Whom*) and tell them that the title was eventually corrected. Students may volunteer other television or movie titles using *who* or *whom*, such as *Who Wants to Be a Millionaire?*

Activate Prior Knowledge

Have students assume the role of the host on any television quiz show and write at least three questions to ask a new contestant. One question should use *who*; the other two should use *whom*. Have volunteers read sentences aloud.

TEACH

Step-by-Step Teaching Guide

Using *Who* and *Whom* Correctly

1. Tell students that they will not confuse *who's* and *whose* if they remember that personal pronouns do not use apostrophes to show possession. Suggest that when they have a choice between *whose* and *who's*, they mentally substitute the uncontracted form (*who is* or *has*). If *who is* or *has* does not make sense in the sentence, then they should use *whose*.

continued

Integrating Vocabulary Skills

Whoever Explain to students that in addition to the forms of *whoever* (*whoever, whomever*), they may also encounter the words *whoso*, *whosoever*, and *whomsoever*. Explain that although these words are not commonly used, they may be found in formal writing. Have students consult the dictionary for their definitions. (*Whoso* and *whosoever* both mean *whoever*; *whomsoever* means *whomever*.)

Special Problems With Pronouns

Choosing the correct form of a pronoun is not always a matter of choosing the form that sounds correct. For example, would it be correct to say, "John is smarter than *me*"? Though the sentence may sound right to you, it is incorrect because an objective pronoun has been used when a nominative one is needed. Several words are understood in the sentence, which reads, in full, "John is smarter than I (am)."

This section will discuss two special pronoun problems: the proper uses of *who* and *whom* and the use of pronouns in clauses where some words are omitted but understood.

Using *Who* and *Whom* Correctly

In order to decide when to use *who* or *whom* and the related forms *whoever* and *whomever*, you need to know how the pronoun is used in a sentence and what case is appropriate.

▶ **KEY CONCEPT** *Who* is used for the subjective case. *Whom* is used for the objective case. ■

The chart below shows the forms and uses of these pronouns.

CASE	PRONOUNS	USE IN SENTENCES
Nominative	who, whoever	Subject of a Verb Predicate Nominative
Objective	whom, whomever	Direct Object Object of a Verbal Object of a Preposition Subject of an Infinitive
Possessive	whose, whosever	To Show Ownership

Note About *Whose*: Do not confuse the possessive pronoun *whose* with the contraction *who's*, which means "who is" or "who has."

POSSESSIVE PRONOUN: *Whose* umbrella is this?
CONTRACTION: *Who's* taken my umbrella?

The nominative and objective cases are the real source of problems. Get into the habit of analyzing the structure of your sentences when you use these pronouns. There are two kinds of sentences in which these pronouns can appear: direct questions and complex sentences.

In this section, you will learn how to determine which pronouns to use in certain problem situations. The examples and exercises are about types of whales.

Cross-Curricular Connection: Science

💿 Technology Tip

Because a computer spell-check feature may not discern between *whose* and *who's*, remember that *whose* is possessive and *who's* means "who is."

⏱ TIME AND RESOURCE MANAGER

Resources
Print: *Grammar Exercise Workbook*, pp. 91–92; *Grammar Exercises Answers on Transparencies*, Ch. 22
Technology: *Writing and Grammar* Interactive Text, Section 22.2; *On-Line Exercise Bank*, Section 22.2

Using the Full Student Edition	Using the Handbook 🕨
• Work through all key concepts, pp. 574–578. • Assign and review Exercises 16–20. • Do the Grammar in Literature activity, p. 577.	• Work through all key concepts, pp. 418–422. • Assign and review Exercises 16–20. • Do the Grammar in Literature activity, p. 421.

In Direct Questions *Who* is the correct form when the pronoun is the subject of a simple question. *Whom* is the correct form when the pronoun is the direct object, object of a verbal, or object of a preposition. A question in the normal subject-verb order will always correctly begin with *who*.

EXAMPLE: *Who* wants a free ticket to the whaling museum?

A question in inverted order will never correctly begin with *who*. To see if you should use *whom* instead of *who*, reword the question as a statement. If you change the order of the words, you often find that you need to use *whom*.

EXAMPLES: *Whom* were you discussing?
             (You were discussing *whom*.)
             Whom did you take with you?
             (You did take *whom* with you.)

In Complex Sentences Choosing the correct case of *who* and *whom* is easier if you remember that the pronoun's use within the subordinate clause determines its case.

EXAMPLE: They screened *whoever* applied for the scholarship.

In the example above, the pronoun appears to be the direct object of *screened*. A closer look at the pronoun's position, however, reveals that it is the subject of the subordinate clause *whoever applied for the scholarship*. Thus, the nominative form *whoever* is correct. The entire subordinate clause is the direct object of the sentence.

Follow these steps to see if the case of a pronoun in a subordinate clause is correct. First, isolate the subordinate clause. (If the complex sentence is a question, rearrange it in normal subject-verb order.) Second, if the subordinate clause itself is inverted, rearrange the words in their usual order. Finally, determine the pronoun's use within the subordinate clause.

EXAMPLE: *Who*, may I ask, has seen a whale?
             Reworded sentence: I may ask *who* has seen a whale.
             Use of pronoun: subject of the verb *has seen*

EXAMPLE: Is the tall man the one *whom* they selected to captain the ship?
             Reworded clause: They selected *whom* to captain the ship.
             Use of pronoun: object of *selected*

▼ **Critical Viewing**
Pose several questions about this whale show, using either *who* or *whom* in each question. **[Analyze]**

Special Problems With Pronouns • 575

Step-by-Step Teaching Guide continued

2. Students often have trouble deciding when to use *whom* because it is rarely used in informal speech. If changing a question into a statement is not enough help, suggest that they substitute another pronoun in the statement. Demonstrate with the sentence (*Who/Whom*) *will you be contacting?* Have students
   • invert the statement: *You will be contacting (who/whom).*
   • substitute another pronoun: *You will be contacting them.*

   Because *them* is in the objective case, the objective form *whom* is correct.

3. Students may be confused when parenthetical expressions like *I think* or *they say* interrupt clauses. Use the example near the bottom of the page to explain that such expressions do not affect pronoun case. Students should mentally omit the parenthetical expression.

Integrating Workplace Skills

Telephone Communication Explain that working in an office may require frequent communication on the phone. In such an auditory medium, errors in pronoun usage can cast a bad light on the speaker. Have students list three different ways to ask someone to identify the person to whom they wish to speak, using the objective pronoun *whom*. (Examples: To *whom* do you wish to speak? *Whom* would you like to speak to?)

Customize for
Gifted and Talented Students

Students with a dramatic flair might enjoy finding a copy of the famous Abbott and Costello routine "Who's on First?" and performing it for the class.

Critical Viewing

Analyze Possible answers: <u>Who</u> trained this whale? For <u>whom</u> does he perform? From <u>whom</u> does the whale get food?

Customize for
ESL Students

Have students practice using *who* and *whom* by memorizing some common expressions such as *With whom will you be coming?*, *Who's calling, please?*, and *To whom am I speaking?* Then have students write a brief skit using these expressions, simulating a telephone call to make an appointment. Have students act out the skit, taking turns playing different parts. Repeated practice with these expressions will help students become accustomed to the patterns followed by *who* and *whom*.

Answer Key

Exercise 16
1. Who
2. Who
3. whom
4. Whom
5. Who

Exercise 17
1. who wrote the book *Moby-Dick* (subject)
2. who is obsessed with killing a giant sperm whale (subject)
3. for whom killing whales is a goal (object of preposition)
4. whom we have met (direct object)
5. whoever offers them a good price (subject)

Exercise 18
1. With whom . . .
2. Who has been . . .
3. Correct
4. By whom . . .
5. . . . expert on whales is who?
6. . . . by those who . . .
7. Whomever I ask . . .
8. Correct
9. Correct
10. Correct

Critical Viewing

Analyze Possible answers: I can't imagine who approves of whale hunting. There may be isolated groups for whom whale hunting is still necessary.

22.2

> **Exercise 16** Using *Who* and *Whom* Correctly in Questions

On your paper, write the correct pronoun in each sentence.
1. (Who, Whom) would like to learn about whales?
2. (Who, Whom) is hoping to go on the whaling expedition?
3. From (who, whom) did you borrow the book about whales?
4. (Who, Whom) did you contact for information?
5. (Who, Whom) told you that a whale's heart rate slows when it dives to the depths of the ocean?

> **Exercise 17** Using *Who* and *Whom* Correctly in Clauses

On your paper, write the subordinate clause in each sentence. Then, indicate how the form of *who* or *whom* is used.
1. Do you know who wrote the book *Moby-Dick*?
2. It is about a sea captain who is obsessed with killing a giant sperm whale.
3. That sea captain is not the only person for whom killing whales is a goal.
4. Many whalers whom we have met hunt whales for money.
5. They sell parts of the whales they catch to whoever offers them a good price.

> **Exercise 18** Revising to Correct Errors in the Use of *Who* and *Whom* Revise the following sentences as necessary to correct errors in pronoun usage. Write *correct* if no revision is needed.
1. With who are you doing the assignment?
2. Whom has been the whale's most threatening predator?
3. Whom should we ask about efforts to save whales?
4. By who were the pictures of whales taken?
5. The world's leading expert on whales is whom?
6. Whalers are opposed by those whom want to help preserve whales and conserve the environment.
7. Whoever I ask insists that whales are highly intelligent and communicative.
8. An oceanographer whom I interviewed described the song of the humpback whale.
9. The scientist is working with a navy team who are studying whale communication.
10. Team members, who are based in Hawaii, made recordings of whale songs.

576 • Pronoun Usage

> **More Practice**

Grammar Exercise Workbook
• pp. 91-92
On-line Exercise Bank
• Section 22.2
  Go on-line:
  PHSchool.com
  Enter Web Code:
  egk-1202

Interactive Textbook

Get instant feedback! Exercises 16, 17, and 18 are available on-line or on CD-ROM.

▼ **Critical Viewing** Describe your feelings about whale hunters and those opposed to them. Use *who* in one sentence and *whom* in another. **[Analyze]**

☑ **ONGOING ASSESSMENT: Monitor and Reinforce**

If students have difficulty with Exercise 16, 17, or 18, refer them to the following for additional practice.

In the Textbook	Print Resources	Technology
Section Review, Ex. 21–22, Section 22.2	*Grammar Exercise Workbook,* pp. 91–92	*On-Line Exercise Bank,* Section 22.2

GRAMMAR IN LITERATURE

from **Paradise Lost**

John Milton

John Milton published the first edition of Paradise Lost *in
1667, not long after England had endured eighteen years of
war and several changes of government. In his epic, Milton
seems to have his nation's strife in mind as he offers a
poetic explanation for the suffering and unhappiness in the
world. Notice in this excerpt how Milton has used* whom
rather than who *in the passage. How is* whom *used?*

Titanian, or Earthborn, that warred on Jove,
Briareos or Typhon, *whom* the den
By ancient Tarsus held, or that sea beast
Leviathan, which God of all his works
Created hugest that swim the ocean stream: . . .

Pronouns in Elliptical Clauses

An *elliptical clause* is one in which some words are omitted
but still understood. Errors in pronoun usage can easily be
made when an elliptical clause that begins with *than* or *as* is
used in making a comparison.

▶ **KEY CONCEPT** In elliptical clauses beginning with *than*
or *as*, use the form of the pronoun that you would use if the
clause were fully stated. ∎

The case of the pronoun depends on whether the omitted
words belong after or before the pronoun. The omitted words
in the examples below are supplied in brackets.

WORDS LEFT OUT AFTER PRONOUN:	Ray is as dedicated as *he*. Ray is as dedicated as he [is].
WORDS LEFT OUT BEFORE PRONOUN:	You gave Lewis more than *me*. You gave Lewis more than [you gave] me.

Mentally add the missing words. If they come after the
pronoun, choose a nominative pronoun. If they come before
the pronoun, choose an objective pronoun.

Special Problems With Pronouns • 577

Grammar in Literature

1. After reading the excerpt, ask
students to whom the pronoun
whom in line 2 refers. (Typhon)

2. Ask a student volunteer to explain
why an objective pronoun is
necessary (*whom* is the direct
object of the verb *held*).

More About the Writer

John Milton, one of English literature's
greatest visionaries and poets, was
born in 1608 to a wealthy family in
London. He excelled in his studies at
the University of Cambridge and
earned an M.A. degree with honors in
1632. Milton wrote both prose treatises
on political questions and haunting
poems that addressed questions
about religion and human nature,
even after he lost his sight in 1652.
Paradise Lost is generally considered
to be his most powerful work.

Connections With Literature

A longer excerpt from *Paradise Lost*
can be found in *Prentice Hall
Literature, Penguin Edition,* The British
Tradition.

Pronouns in Elliptical Clauses

1. Students may think that statements
like *I am as smart as him* or *He was
more angry than me* are correct
because they think *as* and *than*
are prepositions. Point out that *as*
and *than* are subordinating
conjunctions introducing new
clauses.

2. As another example of how
pronoun case can change
sentence meaning, have students
change the case of the pronoun in
the last example on this page
from objective (*me*) to nominative
(*I*). Have them state the complete
clause to determine how the
meaning of the sentence has
changed. (*You gave Lewis more
than [I gave Lewis.]*)

✎ STANDARDIZED TEST PREPARATION WORKSHOP

Grammar and Usage Many standardized tests
require students to draw upon their knowledge
and understanding of pronoun usage to
recognize errors in sentences. Use the following
example to demonstrate.

Jane picked up the phone on the third ring.

*The voice on the other end said, "Who am I
speaking to?"*

Which of the following is the BEST way to revise
the underlined sentence?

A Change *"Who am I speaking to?"* to
"To whom am I speaking?"

B Change *Who* to *Whom*.

C Change *said* to *asked*.

D Correct as is

The correct answer is **A**. While B is also correct,
A is better. *Whom* is the correct pronoun form
because it is the object of a preposition. A is
preferable because it keeps the prepositional
phrase intact.

Integrating Speaking and Listening Skills

Elliptical Clauses Have students use the models on these pages to help them write five original sentences containing pronouns in elliptical clauses. Then have them work in pairs and read their sentences to one another. The partner should state the complete sentence, supplying the omitted words. Have students repeat this oral activity to become comfortable with pronouns in elliptical clauses.

Answer Key

▶ **Exercise 19**

1. . . . than I can.
2. . . . than it is to her.
3. . . . than it can about them.
4. . . . as we human beings behave.
5. . . . as we can be.

▶ **Exercise 20**

Expect some variation in response. The following are likely answers.

1. we
2. we
3. I
4. we
5. him

CHOOSING A PRONOUN IN ELLIPTICAL CLAUSES

1. Consider the choices of pronouns: nominative or objective.
2. Mentally complete the elliptical clause.
3. Base your choice on what you find.

As you can see in the examples below, the case of the pronoun can sometimes change the entire meaning of the sentence.

NOMINATIVE PRONOUN: He liked whales more than *I.*
                                        He liked whales more than I [did].

OBJECTIVE PRONOUN: He liked whales more than *me.*
                                     He liked whales more than
                                     [he liked] me.

▶ **Exercise 19** Identifying the Correct Pronoun in Elliptical Clauses Rewrite each sentence, choosing one of the pronouns in parentheses and completing the elliptical clause.

EXAMPLE: She wrote a better report on whales than (I, me)
ANSWER: She wrote a better report on whales than I did.

1. Your science teacher can help you learn more about whales than (I, me).
2. The need to preserve whales is more pressing to them than (she, her).
3. Studying whales can actually help us learn more about us than (they, them).
4. In many ways, whales behave as (we, us) human beings.
5. Whales can be as nurturing as (we, us).

▶ **Exercise 20** Supplying Correct Pronouns in Elliptical Clauses Complete each sentence by supplying the appropriate nominative or objective pronoun.

1. Whales are as well suited to their surroundings as ___?___ to ours.
2. Because they rely more on their hearing than ___?___ humans, whales can navigate through dark waters.
3. Whales can move in the dark better than you or ___?___ because they use sound to navigate.
4. The biologist cares more about whales than ___?___.
5. Whales are less interesting to me than ___?___.

▶ **More Practice**

Grammar Exercise Workbook
• pp. 91–92
On-line Exercise Bank
• Section 22.2
  Go on-line:
  PHSchool.com
  Enter Web Code:
  egk-1202

Get instant feedback! Exercises 19 and 20 are available on-line or on CD-ROM.

⏱ TIME SAVERS!

📠 **Answers on Transparencies**
Use the *Grammar Exercises Answers on Transparencies* for Chapter 22 to facilitate correction by students.

💻 **On-Line Exercise Bank**
Have students complete the exercises on computer. The Auto Check feature will grade their work for you!

☑ ONGOING ASSESSMENT: Monitor and Reinforce

If students miss more than one item in Exercise 19 or 20, refer them to the following for additional practice.

In the Textbook	Print Resources	Technology
Section Review, Ex. 23–24, Section 22.2	*Grammar Exercise Workbook,* pp. 91–92	*On-Line Exercise Bank,* Section 22.2

Section 22.2 Section Review

GRAMMAR EXERCISES 21–27

Exercise 21 Using *Who* and *Whom* in Questions Write the pronoun that completes each question.

1. To (who, whom) did you send the article about the history of whaling?
2. (Who, Whom) told you about the whaling museum in Massachusetts?
3. With (who, whom) are you sitting on the class trip to the museum?
4. The most interested visitors to the museum were (who, whom)?
5. (Who, Whom) did the teacher ask to narrate our slides of the trip?

Exercise 22 Using *Who* and *Whom* in Clauses Complete each sentence by choosing the correct pronoun.

1. We aren't sure (who, whom) first wrote about whales and their social habits.
2. Anyone (who, whom) likes science will enjoy learning about whales.
3. That's the oceanographer (who, whom) they visited in the Arctic.
4. He is the one (who, whom), I heard, had been studying beluga whales.
5. Those are the scientists (who, whom) have been studying white whales.

Exercise 23 Using Pronouns in Elliptical Clauses Complete each sentence by choosing the correct pronoun.

1. Whalers of the 1800's were more skilled with boats than (we, us).
2. The average whaler was a better sailor than you and (I, me).
3. Sailing was a more vital skill to them than to (we, us).
4. Most people today know far less about whales than (they, them).
5. No one enjoyed *Moby-Dick* more than (I, me).

Exercise 24 Revising to Correct Special Problems With Pronouns Revise this passage, correcting errors in pronoun usage.

Whom would be interested in going on a whale-watching trip? I know that no one is more interested in the trip than me. The people who went on an earlier trip had a great time. Based on what they told me, I think that whomever isn't going is crazy.

Exercise 25 Find It in Your Reading How are *who* and *whom* used in this passage from *Paradise Lost?*

. . . Be it so, since he
Who now is sovereign can dispose and bid
What shall be right: farthest from him is best,
Whom reason hath equaled, force hath made supreme
Above his equals.

Exercise 26 Find It in Your Writing Look through your portfolio, and identify five sentences or questions in which you have used *who* or *whom*. Make sure you used the pronouns correctly.

Exercise 27 Writing Application Imagine that you are interviewing a nineteenth-century whaling captain. Write five to ten questions and answers from your interview. Use *who, whom, whoever,* and *whomever* at least once. Include at least one elliptical clause.

☑ ONGOING ASSESSMENT: Assess Mastery

Use the following resources to assess student mastery of pronoun usage.

In the Textbook	Print Resources	Technology
Chapter Review, Ex. 32–35 Standardized Test Preparation Workshop	*Formal Assessment*, Ch. 22	*Writing and Grammar* Interactive Text, Section 22.2, Section Review; *On-Line Exercise Bank*, Section 22.2

ASSESS and CLOSE

Section Review

Each of these exercises correlates to the instruction on special problems with pronouns, pages 574–578. The exercises may be used for more practice, for reteaching, or for review of the key concepts presented. Answers for all chapter exercises are available in *Grammar Exercises Answers on Transparencies* in your Teaching Resources.

Answer Key

Exercise 21

1. whom   4. who
2. Who   5. Whom
3. whom

Exercise 22

1. who
2. who
3. whom
4. who
5. who

Exercise 23

1. we
2. I
3. us
4. they
5. I

Exercise 24

1. Who would be . . .
2. . . . interested in the trip than I.
3. Correct
4. . . . I think that whoever isn't going . . .

Exercise 25

Find It in Your Reading
Who is used as a subject. *Whom* is the direct object of *hath equaled.*

Exercise 26

Find It in Your Writing
Have students bring to class *who/whom* sentences, correct or not, that they have found in their writing. Have them present samples to the class, and have the class decide whether the usage is correct.

Exercise 27

Writing Application
When students have finished, have them exchange papers and comment on each other's work. Have them look for any incorrect uses of *who* and *whom.*

Each of these exercises correlates to a section of the chapter on pronoun usage, pages 562–579. The exercises may be used for more practice, for reteaching, or for review of the key concepts presented. Answers for all chapter exercises are available in *Grammar Exercises Answers on Transparencies* in your Teaching Resources.

Answer Key

Exercise 28

1. possessive (shows ownership)
2. objective (object of infinitive)
3. nominative (subject)
4. nominative (subject)
5. nominative (nominative absolute)
6. objective (direct object)
7. objective (indirect object)
8. objective (object of preposition)
9. possessive (shows ownership)
10. nominative (predicate nominative)

Exercise 29

1. We (subject)
2. them (direct object)
3. they (subject)
4. us (direct object)
5. They (nominative absolute)

Exercise 30

1. we
2. correct
3. Your
4. correct
5. us

Exercise 31

1. its
2. they're
3. their
4. You're
5. your

Chapter 22 *Chapter Review*

GRAMMAR EXERCISES 28–37

Exercise 28 Identifying Cases of Pronouns On your paper, write the case of each underlined pronoun. Then, write its use.

1. My brother bought <u>his</u> friend expensive perfume made with ambergris.
2. He thought she would be thrilled to receive <u>it</u>.
3. Instead, <u>she</u> became extremely upset.
4. She could not believe that <u>he</u> would purchase something made from a whale.
5. My brother should have realized that he had insulted his friend, <u>she</u> having worked for years to protect whales.
6. The impact of his blunder hit <u>him</u> two days later.
7. She sent <u>him</u> a brochure from a conservation organization.
8. Attached was a letter from <u>her</u> that explained her concerns about animals.
9. The brochure writers noted <u>their</u> worries about the future of some whales.
10. It is <u>they</u>, the brochure warns, that may become extinct someday.

Exercise 29 Using Pronouns Correctly On your paper, write the appropriate pronoun in the following sentences. Then, write its use.

1. (We, Us) humans have been hunting whales for hundreds of years.
2. In the nineteenth century, whalers hunted (them, they) for oil and whalebone.
3. Because the whales were heavily hunted, (they, them) soon disappeared from many ocean areas.
4. Their diminishing numbers alarmed (we, us) environmentalists.
5. (They, Them) having noticed the problem, other people decided to help.

Exercise 30 Revising to Correct Errors in Pronoun Usage Revise these sentences as necessary to correct errors in pronoun usage. Write *correct* if no revision is needed.

1. The people most concerned with improving conditions are us.
2. Have we spoken with you and her about the Endangered Species Act?
3. You being interested is certain to enhance our work.
4. The beneficiaries of today's conservation efforts will be you and me.
5. What would the impact of a world without these magnificent creatures be on we human beings?

Exercise 31 Adding Possessive Pronouns or Contractions to Sentences On your paper, rewrite each sentence, supplying a possessive pronoun or a contraction to fill the blank.

1. The whale's large size makes ___?___ movements relatively easy to follow in captivity.
2. However, their size helps scientists only slightly when ___?___ studying whales in the vast oceans of the world.
3. Whales are fascinating to study because of ___?___ large brains.
4. ___?___ probably wondering just how large a whale's brain is.
5. The brain of an average adult blue whale weighs up to twenty pounds, or more than six times the weight of ___?___ brain.

Exercise 32 Using *Who* and *Whom* Correctly Write the correct pronoun from each set of parentheses in the following sentences.

1. (Who, Whom) is reading the book on beluga whales?
2. (Who, whom) did you ask?
3. With (who, whom) are you working on the whale project?
4. To (who, whom) should we direct our questions about the life span of the beluga whale?
5. The best person to letter the posters is (who, whom)?

Exercise 33 Identifying Subordinate Clauses in Sentences On your paper, write the subordinate clause in each sentence. Then, write how the form of *who* is used in the clause.

1. We are not sure who will be coming to the marine biology exhibit.
2. We have invited only people whom we greatly admire.
3. Most of the guests are oceanographers who have accomplished great things in their field.
4. They are certain to impress whomever they meet.
5. After the exhibit, we will interview whoever has time to answer questions.

Exercise 34 Using Pronouns in Elliptical Clauses On your paper, write two versions of each elliptical sentence—one for each pronoun in parentheses. Include the words that are understood in each version.

1. My brother Rodrigo likes whales more than (I, me).
2. Sometimes, I suspect that he would enjoy living with whales more than (we, us).
3. He does spend more time with books about whales than (we, us).
4. He told me that whales can communicate more clearly with each other than (we, us).
5. My annoying sister says Rodrigo looks more similar to a whale than (we, us).

Exercise 35 Revising to Correct All Types of Errors in Pronoun Usage Copy the paragraph below on a separate sheet of paper. Revise by correcting errors in pronoun usage.

The ocean has long captured the imagination of we writers. Two prominent novelists for who the sea was important were Herman Melville and Ernest Hemingway. Hemingway's fisherman in *The Old Man and the Sea* is memorable; no character is more touching than him. Hemingway was familiar with whoever he was writing about, him having lived and fished in Cuba for many years. In *Moby-Dick*, Melville's sea captain's struggle is both with himself and with a giant whale who is called Moby-Dick.

Exercise 36 Writing Application Write a paragraph about an animal that interests you. Use pronouns in all three cases in your paragraph, and include either *who* or *whom* in at least one sentence. Underline the pronouns you use.

Exercise 37 CUMULATIVE REVIEW Effective Sentence, Verb, and Pronoun Usage Rewrite the following paragraph, correcting any errors in verb and pronoun usage.

(1) My aunt and uncle took they're last vacation on a freighter. (2) They boarded the boat in San Diego, sailed to Hawaii, and then continue on to Japan. (3) Over three months. (4) The trip was exciting it was also hard work. (5) The captain expected they to help the crew load and unload cargo. (6) My uncle even assist with the cooking. (7) My aunt wanted to learn how to tie knots she did. (8) She has teached me how to tie knots, too. (9) Brought me many gifts. (10) If I was older, I'd be able to go on a trip like there's.

Chapter Review • 581

Lesson Objectives

1. To demonstrate control over grammatical elements such as pronoun usage

2. To recognize appropriate English usage within the context of a written passage

Step-by-Step Teaching Guide

Pronoun Usage

Teaching Resources: Standardized Test Preparation Workbook, pp. 43–44

1. Review the three kinds of pronouns described in the student text: nominative, objective, and possessive. Give several examples of each and ask students to compose sentences using them correctly.

2. You may wish to highlight some common situations in which pronoun errors occur. One situation might be using the correct pronoun as the object of a preposition. (Example: *Sally gave the letter to Mary and me.*) Another situation might be the use of *who* and *whom*. (Examples: *Who left the door open? Whom did the boy call for help?*)

3. Review the rules that apply to showing possession. Remind students that possessive personal pronouns do not contain apostrophes.

Standardized Test Preparation Workshop

Pronoun Usage

Standardized tests measure your knowledge of the rules of standard grammar, such as correct pronoun usage. Questions test your ability to use the three cases of personal pronouns correctly. When answering these questions, determine what type of pronoun is needed in the sentence—nominative case pronouns are used as subjects or predicate pronouns; objective case pronouns are used as direct objects, indirect objects, or objects of prepositions; and possessive case pronouns are used to show ownership.

The following test item will give you practice with the format of questions that test your knowledge of pronoun usage.

Test Tip

A possessive pronoun will never have an apostrophe or change form. The possessor in the sentence always determines possessive case pronouns.

Sample Test Items	Answers and Explanations
Directions: Read the passage, and choose the letter of the word or group of words that belongs in each space. Lou and ___(1)___ tried out for the lead role in our school play. I automatically assumed the role would be ___(2)___.	

1 A I
   B me
   C her
   D us
	The correct answer is *A*. Because the pronoun is part of a compound subject, a nominative case pronoun is the correct choice. Therefore, the pronoun *I* best completes the compound subject.

2 F my
   G mine
   H ours
   J him
	The correct answer is *G*. Because the sentence shows ownership, a possessive case pronoun is the correct choice. Therefore, the pronoun *mine* best completes the sentence.

TEST-TAKING TIP

Tell students to read silently the entire passage in a test item before choosing a response for each question. As they read, they should try to fill in the blanks with pronouns that seem to fit. This process will give students a sense of the topic so that the appropriate pronouns can be more easily identified.

> **Practice 1** **Directions:** Read the passage, and choose the letter of the word or group of words that belongs in each space.

The director, Mr. King, said it wasn't an easy decision for ___(1)___ to make. I thought I'd get it, but he chose Lou, ___(2)___ also deserved it. ___(3)___ had more acting experience than I did. I got the role of understudy, and as the rehearsals progressed, ___(4)___ director was pleased. He said he felt confident that either of ___(5)___ could play the lead well.

1 **A** us
   B he
   C me
   D him

2 **F** whom
   G who
   H they
   J we

3 **A** They
   B Him
   C He
   D I

4 **F** its
   G her
   H their
   J our

5 **A** us
   B whom
   C our
   D they

> **Practice 2** **Directions:** Read the passage, and choose the letter of the word or group of words that belongs in each space.

On opening night, Mr. King gave a gift to both Lou and ___(1)___. Lou said it was one of the nicest things anyone had ever done for ___(2)___. One night, Lou was out with the flu, so ___(3)___ had to replace him. I've never been so nervous in all ___(4)___ life. But the audience loved it. ___(5)___ applause lasted through two curtain calls!

1 **A** me
   B she
   C I
   D her

2 **F** them
   G him
   H us
   J he

3 **A** they
   B I
   C we
   D me

4 **F** our
   G their
   H his
   J my

5 **A** Her
   B Its
   C Their
   D Our

Answer Key

> **Practice 1**

1. D
2. G
3. C
4. J
5. A

> **Practice 2**

1. A
2. G
3. B
4. J
5. C

Customize for
Less Advanced Students

Give students a chart of the singular and plural forms of nominative, objective, and possessive pronouns. This visual representation can serve to help some students organize information in order to improve memory.

Customize for
AP Students

Have students practice possessive pronoun usage by making up sentences in which they use the various forms. You might use their sentences as review samples for the class.

In-Depth Lesson Plan

	LESSON FOCUS	PRINT AND MEDIA RESOURCES
DAY 1	**Subject and Verb Agreement** Students learn and apply agreement concepts covering singular and plural subjects and compound subjects. (pp. 586–593/H426–433)	*Writing and Grammar* Interactive Text, Section 23.1; *On-line Exercise Bank,* Section 23.1 **Teaching Resources** *Grammar Exercise Workbook,* pp. 93–98; *Grammar Exercises Answers on Transparencies,* Ch. 23
DAY 2	**Subject and Verb Agreement (continued)** Students learn and apply concepts covering confusing subjects, subjects of linking verbs, collective nouns, indefinite pronouns, and amounts and measurements. (pp. 594–599/H434–439)	**Teaching Resources** *Grammar Exercise Workbook,* pp. 93–98
DAY 3	**Pronoun and Antecedent Agreement** Students learn and apply agreement concepts covering personal pronouns and antecedents, agreement in number, indefinite pronouns, and reflexive pronouns. (pp. 600–607/H440–447)	*Writing and Grammar* Interactive Text, Section 23.2; *On-line Exercise Bank,* Section 23.2 **Teaching Resources** *Grammar Exercise Workbook,* pp. 99–102
DAY 4	**Special Problems With Pronoun Agreement** Students learn and apply agreement concepts covering vague and ambiguous pronoun references, avoiding distant pronoun references, and do the Hands-on Grammar activity. (pp. 608–615/H448–455)	*Writing and Grammar* Interactive Text, Section 23.3; *On-line Exercise Bank,* Section 23.3 **Teaching Resources** *Grammar Exercise Workbook,* pp. 103–106; *Hands-on Grammar Activity Book,* Ch. 23
DAY 5	**Review and Assess** Students review the chapter and demonstrate mastery of agreement concepts. (pp. 616–617)	**Teaching Resources** *Formal Assessment,* Ch. 23

Accelerated Lesson Plan

	LESSON FOCUS	PRINT AND MEDIA RESOURCES
DAY 1	**Subject and Verb Agreement** Students cover subject and verb agreement concepts as determined by the Diagnostic Test. (pp. 586–599/H426–439)	*Writing and Grammar* Interactive Text, Section 23.1; *On-line Exercise Bank,* Section 23.1 **Teaching Resources** *Grammar Exercise Workbook,* pp. 93–98; *Grammar Exercises Answers on Transparencies,* Ch. 23
DAY 2	**Pronoun and Antecedent Agreement; Special Problems With Pronoun Agreement** Students cover pronoun and antecedent agreement and special problems with pronoun agreement concepts. (pp. 600–615/H440–455)	*Writing and Grammar* Interactive Text, Sections 23.2–3; *On-line Exercise Bank,* Sections 23.2–3 **Teaching Resources** *Grammar Exercise Workbook,* pp. 99–106
DAY 3	**Review and Assess** Students review the chapter and demonstrate mastery of concepts. (pp. 616–617)	**Teaching Resources** *Formal Assessment,* Ch. 23

Options for Adapting Lesson Plans

HOMEWORK
Have students complete any section of the chapter for homework.

FEATURES
Extend coverage with the Grammar in Literature feature (p. 590/H430) and the Standardized Test Preparation Workshop (p. 618).

TECHNOLOGY
Students can use *Writing and Grammar* Interactive Text to complete the exercises interactively on computer. They can complete additional exercises in the *On-line Exercise Bank:* The Auto Check feature will grade their work. Go on-line: PHSchool.com Use Web Code: egk-1202

Writing and Grammar Handbook Alignment

Page numbers in Step-by-Step Teaching Guides in this Teacher's Edition refer to pages from the full student text. Handbook page references, indicated with this icon **H**, are provided in Time and Resource Manager boxes and at the bottom of each Teacher's Edition page.

INTEGRATED SKILLS COVERAGE

Grammar in Literature SE p. 590/**H**430

Writing
Find It in Your Writing, SE pp. 599, 607, 614, 615/**H**439, 447, 454, 455
Writing Application, SE pp. 599, 607, 615, 617/**H**439, 447, 455

Viewing and Representing
Critical Viewing, SE pp. 584, 587, 588, 591, 597, 600, 603, 605, 610, 613/**H**424, 427, 428, 431, 437, 440, 443, 445, 450, 453

Speaking and Listening SE p. 594/**H**434

Technology SE p. 595/**H**435

Workplace Skills ATE p. 611

Real-World Connection ATE p. 612

Spelling
SE p. 589/**H**429; ATE pp. 592, 595

Vocabulary
ATE p. 602

ASSESSMENT SUPPORT

Standardized Test Preparation Workshop, SE p. 618; ATE pp. 594, 618

Standardized Test Preparation Workbook, pp. 45–46

Formal Assessment, Ch. 23

MEETING INDIVIDUAL NEEDS

Less Advanced Students ATE p. 619. See also Ongoing Assessments ATE pp. 587, 589, 591, 593, 597, 603, 605, 606, 611, 613.

AP Students ATE p. 601

ESL Students ATE pp. 587, 601, 619

Logical/Mathematical Learners ATE p. 588

Linguistic Learners ATE p. 589

BLOCK SCHEDULING

Pacing Suggestions
For 90-minute Blocks
• Administer the Diagnostic Test to students to determine instructional coverage.
• Have students complete the necessary exercises in class. Use the Hands-on Grammar activity to provide a change of pace.

Resources for Varying Instruction
• *Writing and Grammar* Interactive Text A 90-minute block provides an ideal opportunity for students to work on the computer.

Professional Development Support
• *How to Manage Instruction in the Block* This teaching resource provides management and activity suggestions.

MEDIA AND TECHNOLOGY

For the Student
• *Writing and Grammar* Interactive Text, Ch. 23
• *On-line Exercise Bank,* Sections 23.1–3

For the Teacher
• **Teacher**EXPRESS™ CD-ROM

WRITING AND GRAMMAR ON-LINE

Interactive Text (On-line or on CD-ROM)
• Easily navigable instruction with on-line supporting resources
• Self-scoring exercises and diagnostic tests

Companion Web Site PHSchool.com
• On-line Exercise Bank (use Web Code egk-1202)

See the Go On-line! **feature, SE p. iii.**

LITERATURE CONNECTIONS

Grammar in Literature selection from *Prentice Hall Literature, Penguin Edition,* The British Tradition: from *Don Juan,* George Gordon, Lord Byron, SE p. 590/**H**430

Lesson Objectives

1. To recognize singular and plural nouns, pronouns, and verbs

2. To make verbs agree with their subjects, including singular and plural subjects, compound subjects, confusing subjects, collective nouns, and indefinite pronouns

3. To make pronouns agree with their antecedents in number, person, and gender

4. To make personal, relative, indefinite, and reflexive pronouns agree with their antecedents

5. To recognize and correct vague, ambiguous, and distant pronoun references

6. To demonstrate control over grammatical elements such as subject-verb agreement and pronoun-antecedent agreement

7. To analyze the characteristics of clear texts such as conciseness, correctness, and completeness

Critical Viewing

Classify, Distinguish Possible answer: The pyramid was built by ancient Egyptians. The subject, *pyramid*, and the verb, *was built*, are both singular; therefore, they agree in number.

Chapter
23 Agreement

When the ancient Egyptian pyramids were constructed, each stone had to fit perfectly into the next. Similarly, when you write a sentence, you need to make sure that all of the words fit together just right. For the words in a sentence to fit together properly, the subject and verb must agree, and any pronouns and antecedents must also agree. In this chapter, you will review the rules of agreement and see how to apply these rules to your writing.

▲ **Critical Viewing**
Think of a sentence that gives historical information about this pyramid. What are the subject and verb of your sentence? How do they agree in number?
[Classify, Distinguish]

584 • Agreement

☑ ONGOING ASSESSMENT: Diagnose

If students miss more than one item in any category, direct them to the relevant pages of the textbook and assign exercises for practice and review.

Agreement	Diagnostic Test Items	Teach	Practice	Section Review	Chapter Review
Skill Check A					
Making Subjects and Verbs Agree	A 1–15	pp. 586–597/ ⊞426–437	Ex. 1–10	Ex. 11–17	Ex. 43–45
Skill Check B					
Correcting Pronoun-Antecedent Agreement	B 16–20	pp. 600–606/ ⊞440–446	Ex. 21–26	Ex. 27–30	Ex. 46–47

Diagnostic Test

Directions: Write all answers on a separate sheet of paper.

Skill Check A. Choose the verb in parentheses that agrees with the subject in each sentence.

1. The pyramids at Giza (is, are) among the most famous attractions in the world.
2. The Sphinx and the Great Pyramid (is, are) located at Giza.
3. Over the centuries, the pyramids (has, have) experienced decay and abuse.
4. The forces of nature (has, have) been difficult to control.
5. Desert winds and the hot sun (erodes, erode) the pyramids.
6. While nature is one enemy, another (is, are) people.
7. For centuries, grave robbers (has, have) stolen treasures from the pyramids.
8. The Turks, who invaded Egypt in the early 1500's, (was, were) responsible for using the Sphinx for target practice.
9. Tourists to Egypt, who (arrives, arrive) by the thousands, are also responsible for causing damage.
10. Neither signs nor a guard (deters, deter) tourists from climbing the pyramids.
11. Not all tourists who (enters, enter) a pyramid show respect for the site.
12. (There's, There are) other issues affecting the preservation of the pyramids.
13. What (has, have) been the impact of air and noise pollution?
14. Experts on the environment (agrees, agree) that pollution from vehicles and vibrations from traffic are eroding the pyramids.
15. A joint committee of Egyptian government leaders, scientists, and archaeologists (is, are) trying to remedy the problems.

Skill Check B. Choose the correct pronoun in each sentence.

16. The government has (its, their) problem of reducing pollution.
17. The joint committee offered (its, their) own suggestions, too.
18. According to the new plan, most people must make (its, their) trips to the pyramids in electric buses.
19. The tourist who tries to take (his or her, their) car to a pyramid site will be turned back.
20. This plan met with the approval of my father and (me, myself).

Skill Check C. Rewrite the following sentences, correcting the vague, ambiguous, or distant pronoun references.

21. If tourists visit Egypt, you should certainly tour the pyramids.
22. The Sphinx stands near the Great Pyramid, and it is impressive.
23. Our tour guide told us about the ancient pharaohs and about the building of the pyramids, which impressed me.
24. On the news, it talked about the flooding of the Nile.
25. Dams have been built on the river, and they hope they will ease the flooding problem.

Answer Key

Diagnostic Test

Each item in the Diagnostic Test corresponds to a specific section in the agreement chapter, enabling you to tailor instruction to the particular needs of your students. See "Ongoing Assessment: Diagnose" below for further details.

Skill Check A

1. are	9. arrive
2. are	10. deters
3. have	11. enter
4. have	12. There are
5. erode	13. has
6. is	14. agree
7. have	15. is
8. were	

Skill Check B

16. its	19. his or her
17. its	20. me
18. their	

Skill Check C

Answers will vary; samples are given.

21. If tourists visit Egypt, they should certainly tour the pyramids.
22. The Sphinx, which stands near the Great Pyramid, is impressive.
23. Our tour guide's talk about the ancient pharaohs and the building of the pyramids impressed me.
24. On the news, announcers talked about the flooding of the Nile.
25. Dams have been built on the river, and Egyptians hope those dams will ease the flooding problem.

✓ ONGOING ASSESSMENT: Diagnose *continued*

Agreement	Diagnostic Test Items	Teach	Practice	Section Review	Chapter Review
Skill Check C					
Avoiding Special Problems with Agreement	C 21–25	pp. 608–612/ Ⓗ448–452	Ex. 34–36	Ex. 37–39	Ex. 48
Cumulative Reviews and Applications				Ex. 18–20, 31–33, 40–42	Ex. 49–51

⏱ TIME SAVERS!

Answers on Transparencies Use the *Grammar Exercises Answers on Transparencies* for Chapter 23 to facilitate correction by students.

On-Line Exercise Bank Have students complete the Diagnostic Test on computer. The Auto Check feature will grade their work for you!

*Each little flower, candle, and ribbon (*was* or were) in place.*

*Mathematics (*is* or are) easy for me, and English is hard.*

Have students explain the contextual clues that led to their answers. Help them identify the subject of each sentence, if necessary.

Activate Prior Knowledge

Ask students to identify parts of sentences that should be balanced grammatically (for example, items in a series, independent clauses in a compound sentence). Then draw a simple pan scale or balance on the board. Write the word *subject* over the left pan and *verb* over the right pan. Ask students to explain the significance of your drawing (for balance, the weights on both pans must be equal). Then explain that singular subjects balance singular verbs and plural subjects balance plural verbs.

TEACH

Step-by-Step Teaching Guide

Recognizing the Number of Nouns, Pronouns, and Verbs

1. Ask students to recall the methods for making a noun plural (adding -s or -es) and have them think of irregular nouns that use a different method (*geese, children*).

2. Explain that personal pronouns have different forms to indicate their number. These words function like nouns.

3. Remind students that verb number can be difficult. Many singular verbs already end in -s, so students must not assume that a final -s indicates a plural verb.

Section 23.1

Subject and Verb Agreement

Recognizing the Number of Nouns, Pronouns, and Verbs

In grammar, *number* indicates whether a word is singular or plural. Only three parts of speech have different forms to indicate number: nouns, pronouns, and verbs.

Recognizing the number of most nouns is seldom a problem. The plural of most nouns is formed by adding -s or -es. Some, such as *mouse* or *ox*, form their plurals irregularly: *mice, oxen.*

Many pronouns have different forms to indicate their number. The chart below shows the different forms of personal pronouns in the case used for subjects.

PERSONAL PRONOUNS		
Singular	Plural	Singular or Plural
I he, she, it	we they	you

The grammatical number of verbs is sometimes more difficult to determine. The form of many verbs can be either singular or plural, depending on the number of the subject.

SINGULAR: She *sees.*   She has *seen.*
PLURAL: We *see.*   We *have seen.*

The verb *be* in the present tense has special forms to agree with singular subjects. The pronoun *I* has its own singular form of *be.* So do *he, she, it,* and singular nouns.

ALWAYS SINGULAR: I *am.*   He *is.*

All singular subjects except *you* share the same past tense verb form of *be.*

ALWAYS SINGULAR: I *was.*   He *was.*

The chart on the next page shows those verb forms that are always singular and those that can be singular or plural, depending on the subject.

Theme: Pyramids of Egypt

In this section, you will learn how to recognize and correct errors in subject-verb agreement. The examples and exercises are about the pyramids of ancient Egypt.

Cross-Curricular Connection: Social Studies

⏱ TIME AND RESOURCE MANAGER

Resources
Print: *Grammar Exercise Workbook*, pp. 93–98; *Grammar Exercises Answers on Transparencies*, Ch. 23
Technology: *Writing and Grammar* Interactive Text, Section 23.1; *On-Line Exercise Bank*, Section 23.1

Using the Full Student Edition	Using the Handbook🄷
• Work through all key concepts, pp. 586–597.	• Work through all key concepts, pp. 426–437.
• Assign and review Exercises 1–10.	• Assign and review Exercises 1–10.
• Read and discuss Grammar in Literature, p. 590.	• Read and discuss Grammar in Literature, p. 430.

VERBS	
Always Singular	**Singular or Plural**
(he, Jane) sees	(I, you, we, they) see
(he, Jane) has seen	(I, you, we, they) have seen
(I) am (he, Jane) is	(you, we, they) are
(I, he, Jane) was	(you, we, they) were

A verb form will always be singular if it has had an *-s* or *-es* added to it or if it includes the words *has*, *am*, *is*, or *was*. The number of any other verb depends on its subject.

▶ **Exercise 1** Determining the Number of Nouns, Pronouns, and Verbs Identify each item as *singular, plural,* or *both.*

EXAMPLE: explodes
ANSWER: singular

1. pyramid
2. digs (verb)
3. am
4. pharaohs
5. you
6. builds
7. is
8. they
9. construct (verb)
10. mummies
11. tomb
12. are
13. bricks
14. will be
15. purifies
16. capstone
17. has fallen
18. was carving
19. have
20. measured

▶ **Critical Viewing** Use the words *rocks* and *statue* in a sentence about this photograph. What verbs did you use? **[Connect]**

▷ **More Practice**

Grammar Exercise Workbook
• pp. 93–94
On-line Exercise Bank
• Section 23.1
Go on-line:
PHSchool.com
Enter Web Code:
egk-1202

Subject and Verb Agreement • 587

Customize for
ESL Students

Students may have difficulty distinguishing the singular and plural forms of present-tense verbs. Begin by having them practice third-person singular and plural forms. Use these words: *play, plays, sing, sings, write, writes* with *he, they,* and *Ann, both girls.* Then substitute nouns and include compounds. For example:

My aunt plays *the piano.*

My uncle also plays *the piano.*

My aunt and uncle play *the piano.*

Have students mentally substitute a pronoun for the simple or compound subject and vice versa. For example:

My aunt (she) plays *the piano.*

My aunt and uncle (they) play *the piano.*

Answer Key

▷ **Exercise 1**

1. singular	11. singular
2. singular	12. both
3. singular	13. plural
4. plural	14. both
5. both	15. singular
6. singular	16. singular
7. singular	17. singular
8. plural	18. singular
9. both	19. both
10. plural	20. both

Critical Viewing

Connect, Draw Conclusions Sample answer: This statue stands amid many rocks. The verb, *stands,* is singular.

☑ **ONGOING ASSESSMENT: Monitor and Reinforce**

If students miss more than two items in Exercise 1, refer them to the following for additional practice.

In the Textbook	Print Resources	Technology
Section Review, Ex. 11, Section 23.1	*Grammar Exercise Workbook,* pp. 93–94	*On-Line Exercise Bank,* Section 23.1

🕐 **TIME SAVERS!**

📄 **Answers on Transparencies** Use the *Grammar Exercises Answers on Transparencies* for Chapter 23 to facilitate correction by students.

🖥 **On-Line Exercise Bank** Have students complete the exercises on computer. The Auto Check feature will grade their work for you!

Singular and Plural Subjects

1. Emphasize the two logical rules of subject and verb agreement: a singular subject takes a verb in singular form; a plural subject takes a verb in plural form.

2. Write on the board: *Paula runs every morning. They practice each afternoon.* Have students identify the subjects and verbs and the number of each.

3. Give students additional examples of singular subjects (e.g., *teenager, coach, Mr. Chavez*) and have them make these agree with the verbs *want, work, begin, organize.*

Customize for
Logical/Mathematical Learners

Explain that the rules of agreement can be expressed by simple formulas. When two singular subjects are connected by *and*, the resulting verb must be plural (1+1=2). However, when two singular subjects are connected by *or*, the resulting verb must be singular (1 *or* 1=1). Ask students to create formula expressions for many varieties of compound subjects (with any number higher than 1 following the equal sign meaning that a plural verb is needed). For example, a plural noun connected to a singular noun by *and* results in a plural verb (2+1=3). Have students share some of these formulations with the class and ask for other methods of representing the rules of agreement.

Answer Key

> **Exercise 2**

1. is   4. come
2. meet   5. demonstrate
3. is

> **Exercise 3**

1. Laborers <u>were</u> employed to build the pyramids more than four thousand years ago.
2. The three largest of the Giza Plateau pyramids <u>rise</u> hundreds of feet above the plain.
3. The pharaohs Khufu, his son Khafre, and his grandson Menkaure <u>are</u> buried in these pyramids.
4. Correct
5. He chose the site at Giza because it <u>was</u> close to the royal city of Memphis.

23.1

Singular and Plural Subjects

Two general rules of subject and verb agreement cover all of the more specific rules:

> **KEY CONCEPTS** (1) A singular subject must have a singular verb. (2) A plural subject must have a plural verb. ∎

In the following examples, subjects are underlined once; verbs, twice.

SINGULAR SUBJECT
AND VERB:
The <u>archaeologist</u> <u>works</u> in Egypt.
<u>She</u> <u>was being</u> mysterious about the dig's location.

PLURAL SUBJECT
AND VERB:
These <u>archaeologists</u> <u>work</u> in Egypt.
<u>They</u> <u>were being</u> mysterious about the dig's location.

> **Exercise 2** Making Subjects Agree With Their Verbs
Choose the verb in parentheses that agrees with the subject of each sentence.
1. A pyramid (is, are) a four-sided structure.
2. Its triangular walls (meets, meet) in a point at the top.
3. Egypt's Giza Plateau (is, are) the site of the best-known pyramids.
4. Nearly two million tourists (comes, come) to see the pyramids at Giza each year.
5. The Giza pyramids (demonstrates, demonstrate) the best examples of ancient Egyptian pyramid building.

> **Exercise 3** Proofreading for
Agreement Errors Revise this passage, correcting errors in subject-verb agreement. If there are no errors, write *correct*.

(1) Laborers was employed to build the Giza pyramids more than four thousand years ago. (2) The three largest of the Giza Plateau pyramids rises hundreds of feet above the plain. (3) The pharaohs Khufu, his son Khafre, and his grandson Menkaure is buried in these pyramids. (4) Khufu was Egypt's ruler from approximately 2550 B.C. to 2525 B.C. (5) He chose the site at Giza because it were close to the royal city of Memphis.

▼ Critical Viewing
Write two sentences about this photograph: one that includes a singular subject and verb and one with a plural subject and verb. **[Connect, Identify]**

Critical Viewing

Connect, Identify Sample answers: The <u>man</u> working near the pyramid <u>takes</u> detailed notes. Those <u>stones</u> <u>have been standing</u> in place for centuries.

Intervening Phrases and Clauses

When a sentence contains a phrase or clause that separates the subject from its verb, simply ignore the intervening group of words when you check for agreement.

▶ **KEY CONCEPT** A phrase or clause that interrupts a subject and its verb does not affect subject-verb agreement. ■

In the first example below, the singular subject *discovery* agrees with the singular verb *interests* despite the intervening prepositional phrase that contains a plural noun. In the second example, the plural subject *archaeologists* agrees with the plural verb *require* despite the intervening clause.

EXAMPLES: The <u>discovery</u> of mummies <u>interests</u> many people.
The <u>archaeologists</u>, whose work is nearly complete, <u>require</u> a bit more funding.

Intervening parenthetical expressions—such as those beginning with *as well as, in addition to, in spite of,* or *including*—also have no effect on the agreement of the subject and its verb.

EXAMPLE: Your <u>information</u>, in addition to the data gathered by those working at the site, <u>is helping</u> to solve the mystery surrounding the pyramid.

▶ **Exercise 4** Making Separated Subjects and Verbs Agree
Choose the verb that agrees with the subject of each sentence.
1. The Egyptian pyramids, many of which are found at the Giza Plateau, (are, is) an example of precise planning.
2. A chief architect, along with many assistants, (was, were) usually in charge of planning and design.
3. Imhotep, one of ancient Egypt's greatest architects, (was, were) responsible for pioneering the pyramid form.
4. Remarkably, the sides of an Egyptian pyramid, no matter where it is located, (is, are) almost perfectly equal.
5. Today's engineers, accustomed to modern technology, (considers, consider) Egyptian tools to be somewhat crude.

▶ **Exercise 5** Proofreading for Errors in Agreement Revise this passage, correcting errors in subject and verb agreement. If there are no errors, write *correct*.
(1) An ancient Egyptian stonecutter, working with copper and dolerite tools, were especially skillful. (2) Dolerite, as well as other hard stones, was used by workers to chip away at limestone and granite. (3) One of the most difficult tasks facing pyramid builders were moving stones. (4) A fact that people have a hard time believing is that the ancient Egyptians did not use the wheel. (5) Instead, workers, laboring under the hot Egyptian sun, was pulling cut stones on giant sleds.

✏ Spelling Tip

Remember not to confuse *were* and *we're*. *Were* is the past principal form of *to be*. *We're* is a contraction meaning "we are."

▶ **More Practice**

Grammar Exercise Workbook
• pp. 93–94
On-line Exercise Bank
• Section 23.1
Go on-line:
PHSchool.com
Enter Web Code:
egk-1202

interactive
Textbook

Get instant feedback!
Exercises 2, 3, 4, and 5 are available on-line or on CD-ROM.

Subject and Verb Agreement • **589**

Intervening Phrases and Clauses

1. Write on the board: *That essay, which had several spelling errors, (was, were) not my best work.* Have students identify the subject (*essay*) and the correct verb (*was*).

2. Ask them to identify the grammatical structure of the underlined words (subordinate clause) and explain why neither *which* nor *errors* is the subject of the sentence (the former is the subject of the subordinate clause; the latter is its direct object).

3. Remind students that any interrupting phrases or clauses that can be removed without changing the meaning do not affect subject-verb agreement.

4. Point out that the examples on this page show intervening prepositional phrases and an intervening adjective clause.

Customize for
Linguistic Learners

Point out that a phrase or clause interrupting a subject and verb does not affect subject-verb agreement. Have students write five sentences using intervening phrases, clauses, and parenthetical expressions to separate subject from verb. Challenge them to make their phrases as complex as possible. Have volunteers read aloud some of their sentences.

Answer Key

▶ **Exercise 4**

1. are	4. are
2. was	5. consider
3. was	

▶ **Exercise 5**

1. An ancient Egyptian stonecutter, working with copper and dolerite tools, <u>was</u> especially skillful.
2. Correct
3. One of the most difficult tasks facing pyramid builders <u>was</u> moving stones.
4. Correct
5. Instead, workers, laboring under the hot Egyptian sun, <u>were</u> pulling cut stones on giant sleds.

✓ ONGOING ASSESSMENT: Monitor and Reinforce

If students miss more than one item in Exercise 2, 3, 4, or 5, refer them to the following for additional practice.

In the Textbook	Print Resources	Technology
Section Review, Ex. 12–13, Section 23.1	*Grammar Exercise Workbook,* pp. 93–94	*On-Line Exercise Bank,* Section 23.1

Relative Pronouns as Subjects

1. Have students list as many relative pronouns as they can remember *(that, which, who, whom, whose)* and define their use (to relate a subordinate clause to an idea in the independent clause).

2. Remind students that these pronouns rely on antecedents to give them meaning. Write on the board: *The cashier, who was new, did not know how to work the cash register.* Have students identify the relative pronoun *(who)*, the antecedent *(cashier)*, and the subject of the independent clause *(cashier)*.

3. Use the example on this page to help students reason why *Chuck* is not the antecedent in either sentence.

Grammar in Literature

1. Have students read the excerpt and examine what is underlined. In the first line, have students rearrange the inverted word order if they are having difficulty. *(The hopes of man are what?)*

2. Be sure they understand that in the last line "of dust" is an intervening phrase that doesn't affect subject-verb agreement.

More About the Writer

Lord Byron was born George Gordon in England in 1788. The publication of sections of his long poem *Childe Harold's Pilgrimage* brought him fame. Byron left England in 1816 and settled in Italy. In 1823 he joined the Greek revolt for independence from Turkey. He became a leader of Greek forces just before his death in 1824 and is today a Greek national hero.

Connections With Literature

A longer passage from *Don Juan* can be found in *Prentice Hall Literature, Penguin Edition,* The British Tradition.

Relative Pronouns as Subjects

When *who, which,* or *that* acts as a subject of a subordinate clause, its verb will be singular or plural depending on the number of the antecedent.

▶ **KEY CONCEPT** The antecedent of a relative pronoun determines its agreement with a verb. ■

In the first example below, the antecedent of *who* is *one;* therefore, the singular verb *has* is used. In the second example, the antecedent of *who* is *archaeologists;* therefore, the plural verb *have* is used

EXAMPLES: Chuck is *the only one* of those archaeologists <u>who</u> <u>has</u> prior experience working in Egypt.

Chuck is only *one of several archaeologists* <u>who</u> <u>have</u> prior experience working in Egypt.

GRAMMAR IN
LITERATURE

from Don Juan
George Gordon, Lord Byron

Notice that the plural subject hopes *agrees with the plural verb* are *in the first line, and the singular noun* pinch *agrees with the singular verb* remains *in the last line.*

What <u>are</u> the <u>hopes</u> of man? Old Egypt's King
   Cheops erected the first pyramid
And largest, thinking it was just the thing
   To keep his memory whole, and mummy hid:
But somebody or other rummaging
   Burglariously broke his coffin's lid:
Let not a monument give you or me hopes,
   Since not a <u>pinch</u> of dust <u>remains</u> of Cheops.

Exercise 6 Making Relative Pronouns Agree With Their Verbs Choose the verb in parentheses that agrees with the subject of each subordinate clause.

1. The Great Sphinx of Giza, which (is, are) located near the Great Pyramid, seems to stand on guard.
2. Those who (has, have) studied the Sphinx estimate that it was built about the same time as the pyramids of Giza.
3. How the Sphinx was carved from a single giant block of limestone is a mystery that (continues, continue) to puzzle archaeologists.
4. The name *Sphinx* was given to the statue by the Greeks, who (was, were) associating it with a monster from an ancient Greek myth.
5. The Sphinx was also the subject of attacks by invading soldiers of Turkey and France, who (was, were) trying out their weapons on the sculpture.

Exercise 7 Proofreading for Agreement Errors Revise this passage, correcting errors in subject-verb agreement. If there are no errors, write *correct.*

(1) Long exposure to sand and wind has worn down the face that adorns the Great Sphinx. (2) In addition, the shifting desert sands, which has covered the Sphinx nearly to its neck, need to be cleared from the Sphinx from time to time.

(3) The Great Sphinx is not the only statue of its kind that exist in Egypt. (4) There are other statues similar to the Great Sphinx that has rams' heads or hawks' heads set on animallike bodies. (5) Ram-headed sphinxes line the main avenue near the Great Temple of Amon-Re, which are located in southern Egypt.

More Practice

Grammar Exercise Workbook
• pp. 93–94
On-line Exercise Bank
• Section 23.1

Go on-line:
PHSchool.com
Enter Web Code:
egk-1202

Get instant feedback! Exercises 6 and 7 are available on-line or on CD-ROM.

◀ Critical Viewing How does seeing this photograph of the Great Sphinx add to what you learned in Exercises 6 and 7? [Analyze]

Answer Key

▶ **Exercise 6**

1. is
2. have
3. continues
4. were
5. were

▶ **Exercise 7**

1. Correct
2. In addition, the shifting desert sands, which <u>have</u> covered the Sphinx nearly to its neck, need to be cleared from the Sphinx from time to time.
3. The Great Sphinx is not the only statue of its kind that <u>exists</u> in Egypt.
4. There are other statues similar to the Great Sphinx that <u>have</u> rams' heads or hawks' heads set on animallike bodies.
5. Ram-headed sphinxes line the main avenue near the Great Temple of Amon-Re, which is located in southern Egypt.

Critical Viewing

Analyze Sample answer: The photograph gives me a better sense of what the Sphinx looks like today.

☑ **ONGOING ASSESSMENT: Monitor and Reinforce**

If students miss more than one item in Exercise 6 or 7, refer them to the following for additional practice.

In the Textbook	Print Resources	Technology
Section Review, Ex. 12–13, Section 23.1	*Grammar Exercise Workbook,* pp. 93–94, 97–98	*On-Line Exercise Bank,* Section 23.1

⏱ **TIME SAVERS!**

Answers on Transparencies Use the *Grammar Exercises Answers on Transparencies* for Chapter 23 to facilitate correction by students.

🖥 **On-Line Exercise Bank** Have students complete the exercises on computer. The Auto Check feature will grade their work for you!

Compound Subjects

1. Remind students of the coordinating conjunctions that are most frequently used to join subjects: *or, nor, and.* Explain that there are several rules that apply when using these words with compound subjects. For instance, when *or* or *nor* is used to create compound subjects, the subject closer to the verb determines the number of the verb. This rule applies to two singular subjects (singular verb), two plural subjects (plural verb), and mixed number subjects (singular or plural verb depending on which subject is closer to the verb).

2. Write on the board: *Neither the mother nor her children (was, were) ready to go.* Ask students to choose the correct verb and explain their choice (*were,* because *children* is plural). Now change *children* to *son* (*was* should be used because *son* is singular); now change *mother* to *parents* and *her* to *their* (*were,* because *children* is plural).

Integrating Spelling Skills

Compound Words Subject and verb agreement depends upon recognizing nouns and verbs as singular or plural. Point out that compound words written as single words follow the rule for spelling regular plurals (*baseballs*) unless one part of the compound is irregular (*Welshmen*). These rules are important for correct agreement. To form the plurals of compound words written with hyphens or written as separate words, make the modified word in the compound plural (*passersby, field mice*). Have students make a list of compound words and show how each word forms its plural. Tell students to check a dictionary if they are unsure of any plural forms.

23.1

Compound Subjects

Different rules of agreement apply when the words *or, nor,* or *and* are used to join two or more subjects:

Singular Subjects Joined by *or* or *nor*

When two singular subjects are joined by *or* or *nor,* use a singular verb.

▶ **KEY CONCEPT** Two or more singular subjects joined by *or* or *nor* must have a singular verb. ∎

EXAMPLE: Either the <u>Step Pyramid</u> or the <u>Bent Pyramid</u> <u>is</u> open to tourists.

Plural Subjects Joined by *or* or *nor*

A compound consisting of two plural subjects requires a plural verb.

▶ **KEY CONCEPT** Two or more plural subjects joined by *or* or *nor* must have a plural verb. ∎

EXAMPLE: Neither the <u>pyramids</u> at Giza *nor* the <u>pyramids</u> at Dahshur <u>have escaped</u> the ravages of weather.

Subjects of Mixed Number Joined by *or* or *nor*

If a compound subject consists of a singular subject and a plural subject, determining the number of the verb is more difficult.

▶ **KEY CONCEPT** If one or more singular subjects are joined to one or more plural subjects by *or* or *nor,* the subject closest to the verb determines agreement. ∎

EXAMPLES: Either a <u>lantern</u> or <u>candles</u> <u>are used</u> to see into the pyramid's burial chamber.
Either <u>candles</u> or a <u>lantern</u> <u>is used</u> to see into the pyramid's burial chamber.
Neither the <u>candles</u> *nor* the <u>lantern</u> <u>was</u> very helpful.

Subjects Joined by *and*

A single rule applies to most situations in which *and* joins two or more subjects.

KEY CONCEPTS A compound subject joined by *and* is generally plural and must have a plural verb. ■

Whether the parts of the compound subject are all singular, all plural, or mixed in number, the conjunction *and* usually acts as a plus sign and indicates the need for a plural verb.

EXAMPLES: A <u>lantern</u> *and* a <u>candle</u> <u>are used</u> to see into the pyramid's burial chamber.

<u>Candles</u> *and* <u>lanterns</u> <u>are used</u> to see into the pyramid's burial chamber.

<u>Candles</u> *and* a <u>lantern</u> <u>are used</u> to see into the pyramid's burial chamber.

Exceptions occur when the parts of the compound subject equal one thing or when the word *each* or *every* is used before a compound subject. Each of these situations requires a singular verb.

EXAMPLES: <u>Bread and butter</u> <u>was</u> all the workers were fed.
Every <u>chart and diagram</u> <u>was</u> precise.

Exercise 8 Making Compound Subjects Agree With Their Verbs Choose the verb in parentheses that agrees with the subject in each sentence.

1. Either Saqquarah or Giza (is, are) a good place to study pyramid-building techniques.
2. The burial grounds and the step pyramid at Saqquarah (fascinates, fascinate) me.
3. Archaeologists and historians (has, have) found *mastabas*, or royal tombs, at Saqquarah 's burial grounds.
4. Mud or stones (is, are) used to build a mastaba.
5. The mastaba and the pyramids (protects, protect) bodies buried below ground.
6. In a mastaba, weapons or food (was, were) stored in the above-ground chambers.
7. I doubt that macaroni and cheese (was, were) among the dishes stored for a pharaoh.
8. Either the pharaoh or other members of the royal family (lies, lie) in the mastaba's underground chambers.
9. The size and complexity of the mastaba (varies, vary) depending on the importance of the pharaoh buried inside.
10. Grave robbers or dishonest guards (was, were) responsible for stealing treasures from many mastabas.

More Practice

Grammar Exercise Workbook
• pp. 95–96
On-line Exercise Bank
• Section 23.1
Go on-line:
PHSchool.com
Enter Web Code:
egk-1202

Interactive Textbook

Get instant feedback! Exercise 8 is available on-line or on CD-ROM.

☑ **ONGOING ASSESSMENT: Monitor and Reinforce**

If students miss more than two items in Exercise 8, refer them to the following for additional practice.

In the Textbook	Print Resources	Technology
Section Review, Ex. 14–15, Section 23.1	*Grammar Exercise Workbook,* pp. 95–96	*On-Line Exercise Bank,* Section 23.1

Hard-to-Find Subjects

1. Have students recall the kinds of structures having hard-to-find subjects (questions, imperatives, inverted sentences, sentences beginning with *there* and *here*). Point out that these kinds of sentences present special challenges in making subjects and verbs agree in number.

2. Remind students that rearranging the word order will help them locate the subject and determine the number of the verb for agreement.

3. Write on the board: *There are the teachers and the students from Asia.* Have students rearrange the word order to locate the subject and to determine the proper agreement (*the teachers and the students from Asia are there*).

4. Have students read the note about *there's* and *here's*. Be sure they remember not to confuse *there* with *their* or *they're*.

Subjects of Linking Verbs

1. Write on the board: *Aggressive drivers were the cause of the accident.* Remind students that the verb *to be* is a linking verb. Have them locate the subject (*drivers*) and the predicate nominative (*cause*). Point out that the subject is plural and so the verb (*were*) must be plural even though the predicate nominative is singular.

2. Explain that if the sentence were rearranged (*The cause of the accident was aggressive drivers*), the number of the verb would be changed because the subject (*cause*) is now singular.

23.1

Using Confusing Subjects

Certain confusing subjects require special attention.

Hard-to-Find Subjects

If a subject comes after its verb, you must still make sure they agree in number.

▶ **KEY CONCEPT** A subject that comes after its verb must still agree with it in number. ■

If a subject comes after its verb, the sentence is said to be inverted. Check the agreement of the subject and verb by mentally putting the sentence in the usual subject-verb order.

EXAMPLES: Under the mummy's bandages <u>was</u> a <u>pendant</u>.
(A pendant was under the mummy's bandages.)

Which pyramid <u>is</u> <u>he</u> visiting?
(He does visit which pyramid.)

There <u>are</u> no more <u>pharaohs</u> in Egypt.
(No more pharaohs are in Egypt.)

Note About *There's* and *Here's*: A common mistake is the misuse of *there's* and *here's*, contractions for *there is* and *here is*. They cannot be used with plural subjects.

INCORRECT: Here'<u>s</u> <u>Ann</u> and <u>Tanya</u> now, both ready to leave for Egypt as soon as possible.

CORRECT: Here <u>are</u> <u>Ann</u> and <u>Tanya</u> now, both ready to leave for Egypt as soon as possible.

Subjects of Linking Verbs

Another agreement problem involves linking verbs and predicate nominatives—words that rename the subject. Do not be confused by the number of the predicate nominative. Make sure the verb agrees in number with the subject.

▶ **KEY CONCEPT** A linking verb must agree with its subject, regardless of the number of its predicate nominative. ■

EXAMPLES: Religious <u>beliefs</u> <u>were</u> the motivation for the ancient Egyptians to build pyramids.

(The <u>motivation</u> for the ancient Egyptians to build pyramids <u>was</u> religious beliefs.)

594 • Agreement

Speaking and Listening Tip

Avoid using *there's* and *here's* for plural subjects in your speaking as well as in your writing.

STANDARDIZED TEST PREPARATION WORKSHOP

Grammar and Usage Many standardized tests require students to recognize and solve common usage problems. Use the following example to demonstrate.

Which sentence in the following passage contains a common usage error?

A In the northern regions lies an area called the taiga.

B Throughout the taiga, there is large forests of evergreen trees.

C The evergreen trees never lose all their leaves at one time.

D They remain green throughout the year.

The answer is **B**. The subject of the inverted sentence, *forests*, is plural and takes a plural verb. The sentence should be written "Throughout the taiga, there *are* large forests of evergreen trees."

Collective Nouns

Collective nouns—words such as *jury, family,* or *committee*—name groups of persons or things. They may be either singular or plural, depending on their use in the sentence.

▶ **KEY CONCEPTS** A collective noun takes a singular verb when the group it names acts as a single unit. A collective noun takes a plural verb when the group it names act as individuals with different points of view. ■

SINGULAR: The <u>team</u> of archaeologists <u>has made</u> a discovery.
            The royal <u>family is buried</u> under the pyramid.
PLURAL: The <u>team</u> of archaeologists <u>are quarreling</u>.
            The royal <u>family are debating</u> the tomb's location.

One collective noun, *number,* deserves special attention. When used with *the, number* is always singular; when used with *a, number* is always plural.

SINGULAR: *The* <u>number</u> of digs in Egypt <u>has been increasing</u>.
PLURAL: *A* <u>number</u> of digs <u>have unearthed</u> ancient artifacts.

Nouns That Look Like Plurals

Nouns that look plural but are actually singular can also cause agreement problems.

▶ **KEY CONCEPT** Nouns that are plural in form but singular in meaning agree with singular verbs. ■

Some of these nouns name branches of knowledge: *acoustics, aesthetics, civics, economics, gymnastics, mathematics, physics, politics,* and *social studies.* Others are singular in meaning because, like collective nouns, they name singular units: *confetti, macaroni, measles, molasses, news, rickets,* and so on.

SINGULAR: <u>Mathematics is</u> my most difficult subject.
            <u>Measles threatens</u> unborn babies.

Some of these words are especially tricky. When *ethics* and *politics,* for example, name characteristics or qualities rather than branches of knowledge, their meanings are plural. Also, such words as *eyeglasses, pliers, scissors,* and *trousers* generally take plural verbs although they name single items.

PLURAL: Nina's <u>ethics change</u> to fit any occasion.
            Jack's <u>politics were</u> not our concern.
            The <u>scissors are</u> in the sewing box.

⊙ Technology Tip

A grammar check feature in a word-processing program can help you find errors in subject-verb agreement. However, using a grammar checker is not a substitute for proofreading your work carefully.

Collective Nouns

1. Remind students that *collective nouns* name groups of people or things and can be treated as either singular or plural subjects.

2. Explain the two situations: The collective noun can refer to a group acting as a single unit or to a group acting as individuals.

3. Point out that if the phrase *with the archaeologists* were added to the end of the example *The royal family are debating . . .,* the subject *family* would again be singular. This is because it would then be known that the family was not debating among its own individual members.

Nouns That Look Like Plurals

1. Have students think of other examples of nouns that look like plurals (*aeronautics, spaghetti*).

2. Have students think of other examples of exceptions (*pants, tweezers*).

3. This explanation may help students think of the exceptions as plurals: *Eyeglasses* have two lenses; *pliers* and *scissors* have two halves; and *trousers* have two legs.

Integrating Spelling Skills

Irregular Plural Forms To write using correct agreement, it is important to be able to identify plural nouns; however, inconsistent rules of English can make this difficult. Ask students to practice forming plurals of words ending in *-f* or *-fe* by using words like *scarf* and *life.* Give examples of irregularities: *leaf* becomes *leaves.* Have students make a list of words ending in *-f* and *-fe* and show how each forms its plural. Ask students to think of other nouns that have irregular plural forms that may be difficult to identify (*mice, geese*). Discuss words that do not change their spellings in their plural form (*fish, deer*).

Indefinite Pronouns

1. Ask students to recall some of the *indefinite pronouns* they have learned (*some, little, much, none*). Remind them that indefinite pronouns are used to refer to persons, places, or things, often without specifying which ones. Distinguish these from indefinite adjectives, which are the same words used not as pronouns but as adjectives.

2. Point out that some indefinite pronouns are always plural, some are always singular, and those that can be either will depend upon their antecedents for their number.

3. Write on the board: *Danny baked four desserts, and most (were, was) eaten.* Have students identify the indefinite pronoun (*most*) and the antecedent (*desserts*) and choose the correct verb (*were*). Point out that the plural antecedent makes this indefinite pronoun plural.

Titles

1. Explain that titles of works can sound plural but that they are always singular, requiring singular verbs.

2. Have students read the examples and provide other examples of titles that sound plural. Explain that the rule applies also to such things as paintings, CDs, and movie and television shows — anything with an official title (The X-Files *is the scariest television show ever made*).

Indefinite Pronouns

Some indefinite pronouns are always singular, including those that end in -*one* (*anyone, everyone, someone*), those that end in -*body* (*anybody, everybody, somebody*), and those that imply one (*each, either*). Others are always plural: *both, few, many, others,* and *several.*

▶ **KEY CONCEPTS** Singular indefinite pronouns take singular verbs. Plural indefinite pronouns take plural verbs. ■

ALWAYS SINGULAR: Almost <u>everyone</u> <u>is</u> interested in his report on Egyptian pyramids.
<u>Everybody</u> <u>is</u> expected to hear him speak.
<u>Neither</u> of the pyramids <u>has been</u> pillaged by thieves.

ALWAYS PLURAL: <u>Both</u> of these tombs <u>are</u> thousands of years old.
<u>Many</u> in the class <u>excel</u> in Egyptian history.
<u>Others</u> <u>overlook</u> the difficulties of studying ancient history.

Some indefinite pronouns can be either singular or plural, depending on the antecedent.

▶ **KEY CONCEPT** The pronouns *all, any, more, most, none,* and *some* usually take a singular verb if the antecedent is singular and a plural verb if the antecedent is plural. ■

In the first example below, the antecedent of *most* is *pyramid,* a singular noun, so *most* is singular. In the second, the antecedent of *most* is *chambers,* a plural noun, so *most* is plural.

SINGULAR: <u>Most</u> of the pyramid <u>was explored.</u>
PLURAL: <u>Most</u> of the inner chambers <u>have been examined.</u>

Titles

The titles of books and other works of art can be misleading if they sound plural or consist of many words.

▶ **KEY CONCEPT** A title is singular and must have a singular verb. ■

EXAMPLES: *Dr. Jekyll and Mr. Hyde* <u>is</u> a psychological thriller.
The Bunner Sisters <u>is</u> a novel by Edith Wharton.

Amounts and Measurements

▶ **KEY CONCEPT** A noun expressing an amount or measurement is usually singular and requires a singular verb. ∎

In the first two examples below—a single sum and a part of a whole—the subjects agree with singular verbs. In the third example, *half* refers to many individual items, so it is plural.

EXAMPLES: Twenty-five cents <u>buys</u> an Egyptian postcard.
<u>Three fourths</u> of that nation <u>is impoverished</u>.
<u>Half</u> of the brochures <u>were mailed</u> yesterday.

▶ **Exercise 9** Making Confusing Subjects Agree With Their Verbs Choose the correct verb to complete each sentence.

1. On which side of the Nile (does, do) the pyramids lie?
2. Just beyond the Nile's west bank (is, are) the pyramids.
3. (There's, There are) reasons the pyramids were built on the west side of the Nile.
4. Everybody (knows, know) that the sun sets in the west.
5. All of the ancient Egyptians (was, were) convinced that the West was the Realm of the Dead.

▶ **Exercise 10** Proofreading for Agreement With Confusing Subjects Revise this passage, correcting errors in agreement. If there are no errors, write *correct*.

(1) Most archaeologists knows about Egyptian methods of mummification, (2) yet no original accounts of the process of mummification exists today. (3) Each of the steps have been determined by examining physical evidence. (4) A deceased member of a royal family were sure to be mummified. (5) A team of priests was assigned to mummify a dead pharaoh. (6) Placed inside the wrappings of a mummy were charms and jewels. (7) Here is some facts about the pyramids. (8) The *Arabian Nights* mention the Great Pyramid of Khufu. (9) About 480 feet are the height of the Great Pyramid. (10) None of the tours of the pyramids leave after 8:30.

▶ **More Practice**

Grammar Exercise Workbook
• pp. 97–98
On-line Exercise Bank
• Section 23.1

Go on-line:
PHSchool.com
Enter Web Code:
egk-1202

▼ **Critical Viewing**
Write two sentences about this photograph. Begin one with *both* and the other with *each*. What is the number of the verb in each sentence? **[Connect, Identify]**

Subject and Verb Agreement • **597**

Step-by-Step Teaching Guide

Amounts and Measurements

1. Explain that most amounts and measurements consist of plural nouns that form one single unit. Looking at the first example, the subject *twenty-five cents* denotes one single amount that is required to buy a postcard.

2. Write on the board: *Half of the apple is rotten.* Explain that here the *half* refers to part of a whole (*apple*), which makes it a singular subject. Compare this to the final example on the page where *half* is plural.

Answer Key

▶ **Exercise 9**

1. do
2. are
3. There are
4. knows
5. were

▶ **Exercise 10**

1. Most archaeologists know
2. yet no original accounts . . . exist
3. Each of the steps has
4. royal family was
5. correct
6. correct
7. Here are some facts
8. The *Arabian Nights* mentions
9. About 480 feet is the height
10. correct

Critical Viewing

Connect, Identify Sample answer: *Both* are famous. (Plural verb *are*.) *Each* has its own story. (Singular verb *has*.)

☑ **ONGOING ASSESSMENT: Monitor and Reinforce**

If students have difficulty with Exercise 9 or 10, refer them to the following for additional practice.

In the Textbook	Print Resources	Technology
Section Review, Ex. 16–17, Section 23.1	*Grammar Exercise Workbook*, pp. 97–98	*On-Line Exercise Bank*, Section 23.1

⏱ **TIME SAVERS!**

Answers on Transparencies Use the *Grammar Exercises Answers on Transparencies* for Chapter 23 to facilitate correction by students.

On-Line Exercise Bank Have students complete the exercises on computer. The Auto Check feature will grade their work for you!

Section Review

Each of these exercises correlates to the instruction on subject-verb agreement, pages 586–597. These exercises may be used for more practice, for reteaching, or for review of the key concepts presented.

Answer Key

Exercise 11

1. plural subject and verb
2. plural subject and verb
3. singular subject and verb
4. plural subject and verb
5. singular subject and verb

Exercise 12

1. were
2. writes
3. were
4. was
5. were
6. was
7. was
8. were
9. cut
10. was

Exercise 13

1. were used
2. was unloaded
3. correct
4. were
5. were
6. have studied
7. believe
8. correct
9. was
10. was

Exercise 14

1. were
2. was
3. were
4. were
5. was

continued

Section 23.1 Section Review

GRAMMAR EXERCISES 11–20

Exercise 11 Determining Number of Nouns, Pronouns, and Verbs Identify the subject and verb in each sentence as singular or plural.

1. The pyramids were built as monuments to house the pharaohs' tombs.
2. Pictures on the wall of a tomb describe events in the lives of the pharaohs.
3. According to some archaeologists, the Great Pyramid was built in 23 years.
4. Peasant farmers were the majority of unskilled laborers building a pyramid.
5. Each was usually paid in cloth and food.

Exercise 12 Making Subjects and Verbs Agree Choose the verb that agrees with the subject of each sentence.

1. Scribes, or people who knew how to read and write, (was, were) very important to pyramid builders.
2. A scribe (writes, write) a list that includes the amount and sizes of stones needed to build the pyramid.
3. Jobs as scribe (was, were) in demand.
4. Every worker, both skilled and unskilled, (was, were) valued.
5. The quarrymen (was, were) among the strongest workers who labored to build the pyramids.
6. Limestone (was, were) quarried for many pyramids built in the Nile valley.
7. The best quality stone (was, were) available on the east bank of the Nile.
8. To quarry the best stone, tunnels (was, were) dug into the face of cliffs.
9. Workers, who labored deep in the quarry, (cuts, cut) the blocks that would be used for the pyramid.
10. Each worker who labored in the quarry (was, were) an important part of the team.

598 • Agreement

Exercise 13 Proofreading for Agreement Errors Revise these paragraphs, correcting errors in agreement. If there are no errors, write *correct.*

(1) Boats, which crossed the Nile regularly, was used to transport the stones from the quarry to the pyramid site. (2) After reaching one of the pyramid sites, each boat were unloaded. (3) The blocks of limestone were chiseled smooth. (4) The paving stones was the first group to be laid. (5) The casing stones, which was to form the outer walls, had to be cut perfectly.

(6) Historians who has studied the pyramids are not exactly sure how the Egyptians built the structures. (7) Most believes that the Egyptians built ramps to haul the stones up to each level. (8) One historian performed an experiment that was quite clever. (9) He were able to re-create the ramps thought to be used by pyramid makers and asked his staff to haul stones up the ramps. (10) The staff concluded that the best way to haul stones up a ramp were to lubricate the ramp with liquid.

Exercise 14 Making Compound Subjects Agree With Their Verbs Choose the verb in parentheses that agrees with the subject of the sentence.

1. The architect and his surveyors (was, were) expected to carefully examine the location of the pyramid.
2. Next, the pharaoh or his chief advisor (was, were) called to approve the site.
3. After their approval, prayers and animal sacrifices (was, were) offered by priests to the gods.
4. Leveling the site and laying the foundations (was, were) the next major tasks.

ONGOING ASSESSMENT: Assess Mastery

Use the following resources to assess mastery of subject-verb agreement.

In the Textbook	Technology
Chapter Review, Ex. 43–45	*Writing and Grammar* Interactive Text, Section 23.1, Section Review; *On-Line Exercise Bank,* Section 23.1

5. A channel or trench system (was, were) dug to help level the site.
6. A mortuary temple and a causeway (was, were) also constructed.
7. Neither the skilled nor unskilled workers (was, were) usually slaves.
8. Instead, either an unemployed laborer or a farmer (was, were) usually added to a construction gang.
9. Accidents and injury (was, were) common during the construction process.
10. Both my sister and my brother (enjoys, enjoy) learning about the pyramids.

Exercise 15 **Proofreading for Agreement Errors With Compound Subjects** Revise this paragraph, correcting errors in agreement.

Limestone or granite were the typical stone used to build pyramids. Prayers and incense was presented by priests when the capstone was placed atop the pyramid. After the capstone was positioned, grinding and polishing the surface was the next steps. Tunneling and creating burial chambers was done while the pyramid was being built.

Exercise 16 **Making Confusing Subjects Agree With Their Verbs** Choose the verb in parentheses that agrees with the subject of the sentence.

1. This gang of workers (is, are) responsible for maintaining the supply ramps that surround the pyramid.
2. The gang (is, are) unable to agree on how to complete the work.
3. (There's, There are) several ways to proceed.
4. At least half of the pyramid's stones (was, were) from the mines at Tura.
5. Everyone (agrees, agree) that thousands of laborers were needed to build a pyramid.

Exercise 17 **Proofreading for Agreement Errors With Confusing Subjects** Revise this paragraph, correcting errors in agreement.

The exact number of workers who constructed a pyramid are unknown. No matter how many workers it took, all of the experts concludes that it was a monumental task. Only after years of planning and construction were a pyramid completed. *The Pyramids of Giza* by Tim McNeese explain many of these details.

Exercise 18 **Find It in Your Reading** Identify the subjects and verbs in these lines from Byron's "Don Juan." Identify each as singular or plural.

What is the end of fame? 'tis but to fill
  A certain portion of uncertain paper:
Some liken it to climbing up a hill,
  Whose summit, like all hills, is lost in vapor;
For this men write, speak, preach, and heroes kill,
  And bards burn what they call their "midnight taper," . . .

Exercise 19 **Find It in Your Writing** Review a piece of writing from your portfolio to find examples of at least four of the agreement rules in this chapter. Check to see that you have applied the rules correctly.

Exercise 20 **Writing Application** Write a summary of what you know about the pyramids of Egypt. After you have completed the paragraph, underline the subject of each sentence once and the verb twice. Tell whether each subject and verb is singular or plural, and make sure that they agree in number.

Answer Key continued

Exercise 14

6. were
7. were
8. was
9. were
10. enjoy

Exercise 15

Limestone or granite was . . . Prayers and incense were presented . . . grinding and polishing the surface were . . . Tunneling and creating burial chambers were done . . .

Exercise 16

1. is
2. are
3. There are
4. were
5. agrees

Exercise 17

The exact number . . . is unknown. . . . all of the experts conclude . . . planning and construction was . . . by Tim McNeese explains . . .

Exercise 18

Find It in Your Reading
Subjects are underlined once. Verbs are underlined twice.

What is the end of fame? It is but to fill (singular, singular)

A certain portion of uncertain paper: Some liken it to climbing up a hill, (plural)

Whose summit, like all hills, is lost in vapor; (singular)

For this men write, steal, preach, and heroes kill, (plural; plural)

And bards burn what they call their "midnight taper . . ." (plural; plural)

continued

Answer Key continued

Exercise 19

Find It in Your Writing
Have students underline their examples. When they have finished, have them exchange papers with a writing partner for a review of subject and verb agreement.

Exercise 20

Writing Application
Ask volunteers to share their summaries. Instruct students to listen carefully for correct subject-verb agreement. Have students share any strategies they used for determining agreement in more complex sentences.

TIME SAVERS!

Answers on Transparencies Use the *Grammar Exercises Answers on Transparencies* for Chapter 23 to facilitate correction by students.

On-Line Exercise Bank Have students complete the exercises on computer. The Auto Check feature will grade their work for you!

Write the sentence *The eagles flapped their wings as they left their nest* on the board and ask students to change it to refer to only one eagle. (*The eagle flapped its wings . . .*) Have students point out the words they have changed. Tell them that the pronouns needed to be changed to make them agree with their antecedent in number.

Activate Prior Knowledge

Remind students that they already know what pronouns are. Explain that without pronouns, sentences would sound extremely awkward. Have them attempt to say this sentence spoken by someone named Sarah without using any pronouns: *My father gave me the car keys.* (Possible response: *The father of Sarah, the person saying this sentence, gave Sarah the car keys.*)

TEACH

Step-by-Step Teaching Guide

Agreement Between Personal Pronouns and Antecedents

1. Explain to students that personal pronouns have three qualities: *number* (singular or plural), *person* (first, second, or third), and *gender* (masculine, feminine, or neuter).

2. Remind students that in the English language, gender of personal pronouns varies only in the third-person singular.

Language Highlight

Explain to students that *antecedent,* meaning "that which comes before," is derived from the Latin words *ante,* which means "before," and *cedere,* which means "to go." *Pronoun* is derived from the Latin and Greek word *pro,* meaning "before," and the Latin word *nomen,* "name."

Critical Viewing

Connect Sample answer: *she, her, their, them.*

Section 23.2 — Pronoun and Antecedent Agreement

Like a subject and its verb, a pronoun and its antecedent must agree. An antecedent is the word or group of words for which the pronoun stands.

Agreement Between Personal Pronouns and Antecedents

While a subject and verb must agree only in number, a personal pronoun and its antecedent must agree in three ways:

▶ **KEY CONCEPT** A personal pronoun must agree with its antecedent in number, person, and gender. ∎

The *number* of a pronoun indicates whether it is singular or plural. *Person* refers to a pronoun's ability to indicate either the person speaking (first person); the person spoken to (second person); or the person, place, or thing spoken about (third person). *Gender* is the characteristic of nouns and pronouns that indicates whether the word is *masculine* (referring to males); *feminine* (referring to females); or *neuter* (referring to neither males nor females).

The only pronouns that indicate gender are third-person singular personal pronouns.

GENDER OF THIRD-PERSON SINGULAR PRONOUNS		
Masculine	Feminine	Neuter
he, him, his	she, her, hers	it, its

In the example below, the pronoun *her* agrees with the antecedent *Queen* in number (both are singular), in person (both are third person), and in gender (both are feminine).

EXAMPLE: The *Queen* of England has opened some of *her* castles to the public.

600 • Agreement

Theme: Medieval Times

In this section, you will learn how to make sure that pronouns agree in number, case, and gender with their antecedents. The examples and exercises are about castles in medieval times.

Cross-Curricular Connection: Social Studies

▼ **Critical Viewing** What personal pronouns might you use in writing about this British castle? [**Connect**]

⏱ **TIME AND RESOURCE MANAGER**

Resources
Print: *Grammar Exercise Workbook,* pp. 99–102; *Grammar Exercises Answers on Transparencies,* Ch. 23
Technology: *Writing and Grammar* Interactive Text, Section 23.2; *On-Line Exercise Bank,* Section 23.2

Using the Full Student Edition	Using the Handbook Ⓗ
• Work through all key concepts, pp. 600–606.	• Work through all key concepts, pp. 440–446.
• Assign and review Exercises 21–26.	• Assign and review Exercises 21–26.

Agreement in Number

When an antecedent is compound, making the pronoun agree can be a problem. There are three rules to keep in mind to determine the number of compound antecedents.

KEY CONCEPT Use a singular personal pronoun with two or more singular antecedents joined by *or* or *nor*. ■

EXAMPLE: Either Craig *or* Todd will bring *his* model of a castle to class.

KEY CONCEPT Use a plural personal pronoun with two or more antecedents joined by *and*. ■

EXAMPLE: Melissa *and* I are studying for *our* examinations in medieval history.

An exception occurs when a distinction must be made between individual and joint ownership. If individual ownership is intended, use a singular pronoun to refer to a compound antecedent. If joint ownership is intended, use a plural pronoun.

SINGULAR: *Sir Thomas* and *Lady Cecily* practiced playing *her* lyre.
(Lady Cecily owns the lyre.)

PLURAL: *Sir Thomas* and *Lady Cecily* practiced playing *their* lyre.
(Both Thomas and Cecily own the lyre.)

SINGULAR: Neither my *brother* nor my *father* let me ride *his* horse in the jousting tournament.
(The brother and father each own a horse.)

PLURAL: Neither my *brother* nor my *father* let me ride *their* horse in the jousting tournament.
(The brother and father own the same horse.)

The third rule applies to compound antecedents whose parts are mixed in number.

KEY CONCEPT Use a plural personal pronoun if any part of a compound antecedent joined by *or* or *nor* is plural. ■

PLURAL: When the *princesses* or the *queen* comes home, offer *them* refreshments.

Agreement in Number

1. Have students read the first two key concepts. Explain that these rules are similar to the ones for compound subjects.

2. Be sure students understand the exception about individual and joint ownership. Use the examples to demonstrate proper use of the singular and plural possessive pronouns.

3. Read the third key concept aloud. Point out that this rule refers only to *or* and *nor*. Explain that when mixed antecedents are joined by *or* or *nor*, the agreeing pronoun is always plural. It does not matter which antecedent is closer to the pronoun.

Customize for
AP Students

To practice pronoun and antecedent agreement, have students imagine that they have been transported in time from one hundred years ago and have just arrived in a modern kitchen. Ask them to choose one modern appliance that they find particularly interesting and write about it for their friends back in their original time. Be sure they describe the appliance's appearance and its uses clearly, while using pronouns and antecedents correctly.

Real-World Connection

Explain to students that proper agreement is a key to good speech and writing. Discuss with students the effects of errors in agreement (altering and confusing meaning) that they might hear in the media.

Pronoun and Antecedent Agreement • 601

Step-by-Step Teaching Guide

Agreement in Person and Gender

1. Direct students' attention to the first example sentence. Explain that the error has nothing to do with gender: *You* can be either male or female. The error was in shifting from third person to second person.

2. Have students notice in the second pair of sentences that *its* is considered correct. Many people make masculine or feminine pronoun references when speaking of animals when the sex is known, but the neuter *it* is preferred.

Step-by-Step Teaching Guide

Generic Masculine Pronouns

1. Explain to students that there are two pronoun choices when an antecedent's gender is not specified. Traditionally the masculine pronouns are used, but the phrase *his or her* is also an acceptable choice. Suggest that, when possible, students rewrite a sentence making both pronoun and antecedent plural to avoid having to choose between *his* or the phrase *his or her*.

2. Remind students that when the gender is unknown for a third-person plural antecedent, there is no confusion since there is only one option: *they* and *them*.

Integrating Vocabulary Skills

Latin Roots *Person* is derived from the Latin word *persona*, which originally referred only to the characters in a drama or play. *Gender* is from the Latin word *genus*, meaning "kind."

Answer Key

Exercise 21

1. his
2. it
3. they
4. her
5. their

Agreement in Person and Gender

Try to avoid shifts in person or gender of pronouns.

KEY CONCEPT As part of pronoun-antecedent agreement, take care not to shift either person or gender. ■

SHIFT IN PERSON:	*Mike* is planning to visit Windsor Castle so *you* can see how royalty lives.
CORRECT:	*Mike* is planning to visit Windsor Castle so *he* can see how royalty lives.
SHIFT IN GENDER:	The *horse* threw *its* head back and stood on *his* hind legs.
CORRECT:	The *horse* threw *its* head back and stood on *its* hind legs.

Generic Masculine Pronouns

Traditionally, a masculine pronoun has been used to refer to a singular antecedent whose gender is unknown. Such use is called *generic* because it applies to both masculine and feminine genders. Although using the generic masculine pronoun is still acceptable, many writers prefer to use *his or her* or to rephrase the sentence.

KEY CONCEPT When gender is not specified, use *his or her* or rewrite the sentence. ■

EXAMPLES: Each *student* found a useful Web site on which to research *his or her* report on castles.
Each *student* found a useful Web site on which to research the report on castles.
Students found useful Web sites on which to research *their* reports on castles.

Exercise 21 Making Personal Pronouns Agree With Their Antecedents Write an appropriate personal pronoun to complete each sentence.

1. A castle was both fortress and home to a lord and ___?___ family.
2. A huge wall and a moat surrounded the castle to protect ___?___ from invaders.
3. A lord and lady usually had a huge great room in which ___?___ entertained hundreds of guests.
4. Neither a woman nor a young girl living in the castle was permitted to spend ___?___ days in a frivolous manner.
5. Either a queen or noblewomen were accustomed to servants attending to most of ___?___ needs.

602 • Agreement

Get instant feedback! Exercises 21 and 22 are available on-line or on CD-ROM.

More Practice

Grammar Exercise Workbook
• pp. 99–100
On-line Exercise Bank
• Section 23.2
Go on-line:
PHSchool.com
Enter Web Code:
egk-1202

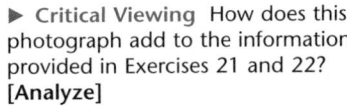 **Exercise 22** Revising to Eliminate Shifts in Person and Gender Rewrite each sentence, correcting the unnecessary shift in person or gender. In some instances, you may need to change only a pronoun, while in others you may want to rephrase the sentence.

EXAMPLE: The ideal castle was a self-sufficient village that met all of their residents' needs.

ANSWER: The ideal castle was a self-sufficient village that met all of its residents' needs.

1. Each lord had to provide their king or queen with soldiers, called knights.
2. In exchange, the ruler gave their loyal nobles an estate.
3. The nobles built his castles on these grants of land.
4. Nobles would usually encourage their followers to develop villages on his land.
5. A lord had the right to demand that peasants living on an estate pay them in work, rents, and taxes.
6. Peasants farmed plots of land around the castle, paying the lord with a portion of the produce he grew.
7. Some peasants, called serfs, were agricultural workers who were tied to a lord's land and bound to serve it for life.
8. A village resident would often use their special skills to serve as a blacksmith, herbalist, cook, seamstress, or musician.
9. Inside the walls of a great castle, a lord or lady could find everything you wanted.
10. Villagers' sons might hope to use his intelligence to become a page and then a knight.

▶ Critical Viewing How does this photograph add to the information provided in Exercises 21 and 22? [Analyze]

Pronoun and Antecedent Agreement • 603

☑ **ONGOING ASSESSMENT: Monitor and Reinforce**

If students have difficulty with Exercise 21 or 22, refer them to the following for additional practice.

In the Textbook	Print Resources	Technology
Section Review, Ex. 27–28, Section 23.2	*Grammar Exercise Workbook,* pp. 99–100	*On-Line Exercise Bank,* Section 23.2

Agreement With Indefinite Pronouns

1. Explain to students that indefinite pronouns can serve as antecedents for personal pronouns.

2. Point out that they must follow the rules of agreement: A singular indefinite pronoun takes a singular personal pronoun; a plural indefinite pronoun takes a plural personal pronoun. Point out also that intervening material does not affect agreement.

3. Write on the board: *Most of the castles were robbed of their decorations.* Ask students if the rules of pronoun-antecedent agreement have been followed correctly (yes). Remind students that some indefinite pronouns can be either singular or plural; their number depends upon their antecedent. Then, change the indefinite pronoun *Most* to *One* and ask students to restate the sentence correctly *(One of the castles was robbed of its decorations).*

4. Looking at the final example on this page, explain that the pronoun *neither* might suggest a singular pronoun *(neither one . . . it)*, but the meaning of the sentence indicates that they left two *windows* (plural) open.

Customize for
ESL Students

To help students recognize the number of indefinite pronouns, ask them to recall or locate examples of indefinite pronouns from their study of parts of speech. Write these words on the board until you have a sizable list. Ask students to speculate on the number of each (singular or plural), and then pick five of the indefinite pronouns to use in sentences about people and things they encountered last weekend. Have students exchange papers and check the agreement of their indefinite pronouns with antecedents in their sentences.

23.2

Agreement With Indefinite Pronouns

When an indefinite pronoun—such as *each, one,* or *several* — is the antecedent of a personal pronoun, both pronouns must agree. Errors are rare when both pronouns are plural.

> **KEY CONCEPT** Use a plural personal pronoun when the antecedent is a plural indefinite pronoun. ■

EXAMPLE: *All* of the knights left *their* weapons outside.

A similar rule applies when both pronouns are singular.

> **KEY CONCEPT** Use a singular personal pronoun when the antecedent is a singular indefinite pronoun. ■

As in subject-verb agreement, an intervening phrase or clause does not affect agreement in number between a personal pronoun and its antecedent.

EXAMPLES: *Either* of the horses will perform in battle for *its* knight. (*Either* is a singular antecedent.)
One of the noblewomen volunteered *her* time to nurse the sick. (*One* is a singular antecedent.)

If other words in the sentence do not indicate gender, use *he or she, him or her, his or her,* or rephrase the sentence.

EXAMPLES: *Each* of the villagers gave *his or her* opinion to the lord of the estate.
All of the villagers gave *their* opinions to the lord of the estate.

For indefinite pronouns that can be either singular or plural (*all, any, more, most, none,* and *some*), agreement depends on the number of the antecedent. In the first example below, the antecedent of *some* is *estate,* a singular noun. In the second example, the antecedent of *some* is *pages,* a plural noun.

EXAMPLES: *Some* of the estate had lost *its* value.
Some of the pages disliked *their* jobs.

Sometimes, strict grammatical agreement may be illogical. In these situations, you should let the meaning of the sentence determine the number of the personal pronoun.

ILLOGICAL: Because *neither* of the windows would budge, we had to leave *it* open.
CORRECT: Because *neither* of the windows would budge, we had to leave *them* open.

604 • Agreement

Exercise 23 Making Personal Pronouns Agree With Indefinite Pronouns Choose the correct pronoun in parentheses for each sentence.

1. Each of the castles had (its, their) own army of knights.
2. Many of the knights were vassals who received (its, their) plots of land by pledging loyalty and service to the lord.
3. All of the dukes selected the best knights to join (his, their) armies.
4. Most of the knights began (his, their) careers as pages.
5. Some of the pages started (his, their) service at eight years of age.
6. Most learned to read while (he, they) lived in the castle.
7. All of the pages served (his, their) knights with dignity.
8. Not one of the boys took (his, their) duties lightly.
9. Most of the knights had to become accustomed to wearing (his, their) heavy suits of armor.
10. All of the horses were carefully trained by the knights who owned (it, them).

Exercise 24 Proofreading for Errors in Agreement With Indefinite Pronouns Revise the two paragraphs, correcting agreement errors.

(1) Before knights engaged in battle, each raised their weapon in unison with the others. (2) In a battle, when every one of the knights charges at once, he has a better chance of defeating the enemy. (3) In addition to knights, each of the lords used foot-soldiers in their army. (4) None of the knights or the foot-soldiers could win battles on his own. (5) Only the best of the foot-soldiers could use his cross-bows effectively. (6) Each of the knights looked out for their fellow soldiers.

(7) Each of a knight's family members often visited the castle of their lord. (8) Each of a knight's daughters hoped they would be wed to a wealthy and sophisticated husband. (9) Every one of the children was expected to abide by their parents' wishes. (10) Only a few of the children ever traveled far from her village.

▶ Critical Viewing What indefinite pronouns and personal pronouns might you use in two sentences describing this knight? [**Analyze, Identify**]

More Practice

Grammar Exercise Workbook
• pp. 101–102
On-line Exercise Bank
• Section 23.2
  Go on-line:
  PHSchool.com
  Enter Web Code:
  egk-1202

Interactive Textbook

Get instant feedback! Exercises 23 and 24 are available on-line or on CD-ROM.

Pronoun and Antecedent Agreement • 605

Answer Key

▶ **Exercise 23**

1. its
2. their
3. their
4. their
5. their
6. they
7. their
8. his
9. their
10. them

▶ **Exercise 24**

Allow some variation in response.

1. his
2. they have
3. his
4. their
5. their
6. his
7. his or her
8. she
9. his or her
10. their

Critical Viewing

Analyze, Identify Sample answer: *Most* of the knights rode *their* own horses into battle. *Each* of the knights wore armor made to fit *his* own body.

☑ **ONGOING ASSESSMENT: Monitor and Reinforce**

If students miss more than two items in Exercise 23 or 24, refer them to the following for additional practice.

In the Textbook	Print Resources	Technology
Section Review, Ex. 29, Section 23.2	*Grammar Exercise Workbook,* pp. 101–102	*On-Line Exercise Bank,* Section 23.2

⏱ **TIME SAVERS!**

🖨 **Answers on Transparencies** Use the *Grammar Exercises Answers on Transparencies* for Chapter 23 to facilitate correction by students.

🖥 **On-Line Exercise Bank** Have students complete the exercises on computer. The Auto Check feature will grade their work for you!

Agreement With Reflexive Pronouns

1. Remind students that reflexive pronouns add information to a sentence by referring to a noun or pronoun near the beginning of the sentence.

2. Explain that reflexive pronouns must agree with their antecedents in gender, number, and person.

3. Caution students to avoid using a reflexive pronoun if they cannot find its antecedent.

4. Give students practice forming the plurals of reflexive pronouns: *ourselves, themselves, yourselves.* Challenge students to use these in original sentences and to identify their antecedents. Ask if *theirselves* is a plural reflexive pronoun (it is an incorrect form and should not be used).

Answer Key

▶ **Exercise 25**

Answers may vary; samples are given.

1. I
2. ourselves
3. myself
4. I
5. herself

▶ **Exercise 26**

1. Ann and I learned that castle building in Europe began in earnest after William the Conqueror invaded England in 1066.
2. correct
3. The only person who could have conquered and unified England was he.
4. May Sarah and I study for the history test with you?
5. Who besides her has ever visited a castle?

23.2

Agreement With Reflexive Pronouns

Reflexive pronouns end in *-self* or *-selves* and are used correctly only when they refer to a word appearing earlier in the same sentence.

EXAMPLE: A *knight* who wins every battle should refrain from congratulating *himself*.

▶ **KEY CONCEPT** A reflexive pronoun must agree with an antecedent that is clearly stated. ■

Do not use a reflexive pronoun if a personal pronoun can logically be used instead. In the example below, *myself* has no antecedent. The personal pronoun *me* should be used instead.

INCORRECT: The hard work was done by Leslie and *myself*.
CORRECT: The hard work was done by Leslie and *me*.

▶ **Exercise 25** Supplying Correct Pronouns On your paper, write a reflexive or personal pronoun to fill each blank.
1. My family and ___?___ decided to tour an English castle this summer.
2. My parents said we had to agree among ___?___ which castle we wanted to visit.
3. At first, I wasn't sure which castle I would prefer ___?___.
4. However, after ___?___ saw pictures of Rochester Castle near London, I knew that would be my choice.
5. My sister arrived at the same choice ___?___.

▶ **Exercise 26** Proofreading to Correct Errors in the Use of Reflexive Pronouns Rewrite each sentence, correcting the misused reflexive pronoun. If a sentence is correct, write *correct*.
1. Ann and myself learned that castle building in Europe began in earnest after William the Conqueror invaded England in 1066.
2. William built castles to defend the territory recently conquered by his armies and himself.
3. The only person who could have conquered and unified England was himself.
4. May Sarah and I study for the history test with yourself?
5. Who besides herself has ever visited a castle?

▶ **More Practice**

Grammar Exercise Workbook
• pp. 101–102
On-line Exercise Bank
• Section 23.2
  Go on-line:
  PHSchool.com
  Enter Web Code:
  egk-1202

Get instant feedback! Exercises 25 and 26 are available on-line or on CD-ROM.

☑ ONGOING ASSESSMENT: Monitor and Reinforce

If students miss more than one item in either Exercise 25 or 26, refer them to the following for additional practice.

In the Textbook	Print Resources	Technology
Section Review, Ex. 30, Section 23.2	*Grammar Exercise Workbook,* pp. 101–102	*On-Line Exercise Bank,* Section 23.2

Section 23.2 Section Review

GRAMMAR EXERCISES 27–33

Exercise 27 Supplying Personal Pronouns That Agree With Their Antecedents Write an appropriate personal pronoun to complete each sentence.

1. Nobles built castles to protect ___?___ lives and property from enemies.
2. A castle's moat also served to protect ___?___ from attack.
3. Attackers staged sieges against ___?___ enemies.
4. A knight fought bravely to defend ___?___ lord's castle.
5. A noblewoman might assist ___?___ husband in defending the castle.

Exercise 28 Avoiding Shifts in Person and Gender Choose the correct pronoun in parentheses for each sentence.

1. Each of the estates had (its, their) own routine.
2. A peasant's wife or daughter might plant (her, their) garden in early spring.
3. In August, everyone joined the harvest so that (he or she, they) would not go hungry.
4. During September, peasants picked grapes near (its, their) lord's castle.
5. Each of the animals relied on (its, their) owners to cut hay in September.

Exercise 29 Making Personal Pronouns Agree With Indefinite Pronouns Choose the correct pronoun in parentheses to complete each sentence.

1. Some of the nobles had several castles under (his, their) control.
2. Each of the castles had a large staff to see to (its, their) upkeep.
3. Every one of the lords served (his, their) peasants by acting as judges of disputes.
4. Each of the noblewomen learned to run a household from (her, their) mother.
5. Neither of the sexes had much choice in (his or her, their) future spouses.

Exercise 30 Using Reflexive Pronouns Correctly Rewrite any sentence that contains an incorrectly used reflexive pronoun. Write *correct* if a sentence is correct.

1. A noble relied on his wife, his clerks, and himself to run the castle.
2. The lord's wife looked after matters that were important to herself.
3. The lord and herself would make plans.
4. Clerks and himself handled accounts.
5. Together, themselves managed the estate efficiently.

Exercise 31 Find It in Your Reading Identify the pronouns and antecedents in these lines from Thomas Gray's "Elegy Written in a Country Churchyard," and explain why they agree.

No children run to lisp their sire's return, Or climb his knees the envied kiss to share.

Exercise 32 Find It in Your Writing Go through your portfolio to find examples of personal and indefinite pronouns. Draw an arrow from each pronoun to its antecedent, and check that they agree in number, gender, and case.

Exercise 33 Writing Application Write a paragraph about people who live in an unusual place. Describe their daily routine. Use several personal and indefinite pronouns, and check for agreement.

Section Review • 607

ONGOING ASSESSMENT: Assess Mastery

Use the following resources to assess student mastery of pronoun and antecedent agreement.

In the Textbook	Technology
Chapter Review, Ex. 46–47	*Writing and Grammar* Interactive Text, Section 23.2, Section Review; *On-Line Exercise Bank,* Section 23.2

ASSESS

Section Review

Each of these exercises correlates to the instruction on pronoun and antecedent agreement, pages 600–606. These exercises may be used for more practice, for reteaching, or for review of the key concepts presented.

Answer Key

Exercise 27
1. their
2. it
3. their
4. his
5. her

Exercise 28
1. its
2. her
3. they
4. their
5. its

Exercise 29
1. their
2. its
3. their
4. her
5. their

Exercise 30
1. correct
2. The lord's wife looked after matters that were important to her.
3. The lord and she would make plans.
4. Clerks and he handled accounts.
5. Together, they managed the estate efficiently.

Exercise 31

Find It in Your Reading
Their agrees with *children; his* agrees with *sire's.*

Exercise 32

Find It in Your Writing
Ask students which personal and indefinite pronouns they found most often. Have them imagine that someone else is reading their writing. Is their use of personal and indefinite pronouns clear to another person?

Exercise 33

Writing Application
Have students trade paragraphs with a partner. Ask the partner to check the paragraph for pronoun agreement. If agreement is not found, have partners discuss needed changes.

Special Problems With Pronoun Agreement

PREPARE and ENGAGE

Interest GRABBER Tell students to imagine that they were reading an article about exploring a cave when they came across this sentence: *This was something we had never expected.* Explain that the sentence illustrates an ineffective use of a pronoun because the pronoun has no clear reference and raises the question of what the sentence is referring to. Have students suggest words that might replace the indefinite pronoun *This* to make the sentence meaningful. (*A locked and rusting old trunk was something we had never expected.*)

Activate Prior Knowledge

Have students recall facts about relative and demonstrative pronouns. Point out that the meanings of these pronouns are formed by their antecedents but that their antecedents cannot always be placed alongside them. Ask students what can happen to the meaning of a pronoun if its antecedent is several words away — or missing entirely (meanings can be confused). Then write this on the board: *The hike was long, the view was breathtaking, and this was tiring* and ask students what the demonstrative pronoun *this* appears to refer to (*view*). Explain that the confusion is caused by a vague and distant pronoun reference. *This* appears to refer to *the view* because it is closer, but logic dictates that a view cannot be *tiring*.

TEACH

Step-by-Step Teaching Guide

Antecedents for *Which, This, That,* and *These*

1. Remind students that the listed pronouns must refer to definite antecedents. Use the example to point out that a vague pronoun reference raises questions.

2. Explain that demonstrative pronouns can be converted into demonstrative adjectives, which can clarify their meaning, as in the first correct example.

Pronouns whose antecedents are vague, ambiguous, or too distant can cloud the meaning of a sentence. This section will show you how to avoid these special problems or how to correct them in your writing.

Vague Pronoun References

For the meaning of a sentence to be clear, the antecedent of any pronoun needs to be clearly stated or understood.

▶ **KEY CONCEPT** A pronoun requires an antecedent that is either stated or clearly understood. ■

Antecedents for *Which, This, That,* and *These*

The pronouns *which, this, that,* and *these* can cause confusion if their antecedents are unclear or too general.

▶ **KEY CONCEPT** The pronouns *which, this, that,* and *these* should not be used to refer to a vague or overly general idea. ■

In the following sentence, it is impossible to point to exactly what the pronoun *this* stands for.

VAGUE REFERENCE: During his trip to Kenya, Mr. Winter climbed Mount Kenya, toured Nairobi, and visited a coffee plantation. *This* made his trip exciting.

"*This* what?" a reader might ask. The answer is not stated nor is it clearly understood. You can correct such vague, overly general references by turning the pronoun into an adjective that modifies a specific noun or by revising the sentence to eliminate the vague pronoun.

CORRECT: During his trip to Kenya, Mr. Winter climbed Mount Kenya, toured Nairobi, and visited a coffee plantation. This variety of activities made his trip exciting.

Climbing Mount Kenya, touring Nairobi, and visiting a coffee plantation all made Mr. Winter's trip to Kenya exciting.

Theme: Kenya

In this section, you will learn how to recognize and correct problems involving vague or ambiguous pronoun meaning. The examples and exercises are about the African nation of Kenya.

Cross-Curricular Connection: Social Studies

⏱ TIME AND RESOURCE MANAGER

Resources
Print: *Grammar Exercise Workbook,* pp. 103–106; *Grammar Exercises Answers on Transparencies,* Ch. 23
Technology: *Writing and Grammar* Interactive Text, Section 23.3; *On-Line Exercise Bank,* Section 23.3

Using the Full Student Edition	Using the Handbook🄷
• Work through all key concepts, pp. 608–612. • Assign and review Exercises 34–36. • Do the Hands-on Grammar activity, p. 614.	• Work through all key concepts, pp. 448–452. • Assign and review Exercises 34–36. • Do the Hands-On Grammar activity, p. 454.

Antecedents for *It, They,* and *You*

The personal pronouns *it, they,* and *you* can also confuse readers if the antecedents are not stated clearly.

> **KEY CONCEPT** The personal pronouns *it, they,* and *you* should not be used with vague antecedents. ■

Errors with these pronouns can be corrected either by replacing the pronoun with a specific noun or rewriting the sentence to eliminate the imprecise pronoun.

In the example below, the pronoun *it* has no clearly stated antecedent. The pronoun should be replaced with a precise noun or the sentence should be rephrased in order to eliminate the pronoun altogether.

VAGUE REFERENCE: When I rode on a *matatu* in Nairobi, *it* traveled on the left side of the road.

CORRECT: When I rode on a *matatu* in Nairobi, the minibus traveled on the left side of the road.
The *matatu* I rode on in Nairobi traveled on the left side of the road.

In the next example, the pronoun *they* is used without an accurate antecedent.

VAGUE REFERENCE: When we arrived in Mombasa, they described the port city's long history.

CORRECT: When we arrived in Mombasa, the tour guide described the port city's long history.

A somewhat different problem occurs when the personal pronoun *you* is misused. The use of *you* is valid only when it refers directly to the reader or listener.

VAGUE REFERENCE: The gathering was so somber *you* dared not speak.

CORRECT: The gathering was so somber *one* dared not speak.

VAGUE REFERENCE: Before homes had modern plumbing, *you* had to pump water from a well.

CORRECT: Before homes had modern plumbing, *people* had to pump water from a well.

Note About *It:* In a number of idiomatic expressions, *it* is used correctly without an antecedent. In phrases such as "*It* is dark," "*It* is time," and "*It* is raining," the idiomatic use of *it* is accepted as standard English.

1. Remind students that the meaning of personal pronouns like *it, they,* and *you* depends on the accuracy of their antecedents. Point out the two methods for correcting these pronoun-antecedent errors.

2. Explain that the pronouns *it, they,* and *you* can be replaced with a specific noun or the sentence can be rewritten to avoid an agreement error. Direct students' attention to the corrected examples to demonstrate these two methods.

3. Emphasize that the second-person plural or singular pronoun *you* refers to the person being spoken to and is incorrectly used in reference to a general body of people. Explain that the word *one* can replace a singular *you* in many situations. Encourage students to look for more precise nouns whenever possible.

4. Have students offer a definition of the word *idiom* (a mode of expression peculiar to a language and not logically or grammatically explicable). Direct students' attention to the note about *it* to remind them that *it* can be used vaguely and yet correctly in several idiomatic expressions.

Answer Key

Answers may vary; samples are given.

1. Swahili, which I cannot speak, and English are familiar languages in Kenya.
2. The British, who granted Kenya independence in 1963, and the Portuguese both controlled Kenya at different times.
3. To appreciate the beauty of Kenya, one has to go there.
4. Kenya contains valuable reserves of gold, silver, and gemstones.
5. Kenya, which has fourteen vast national parks, has much open land.
6. The equator divides Kenya into almost equal parts that have different climates.
7. Roughly eleven percent of Kenya's land is suitable for agriculture. Kenyan farmers grow crops on one third of that territory.
8. The hot and dry northern region has several deserts.
9. In recent years, many rural Kenyans have moved to Nairobi and Mombasa. This migration has led to overcrowding.
10. Though only about 4 percent of Kenya's land is arable, one can grow almost every basic foodstuff there.
11. Kenya has lowland forests containing teak and baobab trees.
12. Kenya has two main rivers, the Tana and the Galana, and also contains a small portion of Lake Victoria.
13. Kenya is famous for wildlife such as giraffes and lions.
14. Kenya also has elephants and rhinoceroses, both of which have been threatened by hunters.
15. Kenya abounds in birds and reptiles, a situation that attracts many zoologists to the country.

23.3

► **Exercise 34** **Revising Vague Pronoun References** Rewrite the sentences below, correcting the vague pronouns.

EXAMPLE: I visited areas where they live in *shambas*.
ANSWER: I visited areas where the people live in *shambas*.

1. English and Swahili, which I cannot speak, are familiar languages in Kenya.
2. The Portuguese and, later, the British controlled Kenya at different times. They granted Kenya independence in 1963.
3. To appreciate the beauty of Kenya, you have to go there.
4. Kenya contains reserves of gold, silver, and gemstones. This is very valuable.
5. In Kenya, there is much open land. It has fourteen vast national parks.
6. Kenya is divided into almost equal parts by the equator. They have different climates.
7. Roughly 11 percent of Kenya's land is suitable for agriculture. They grow crops on one third of that territory.
8. The northern region has several deserts. This is hot and dry.
9. In recent years, many rural Kenyans have moved to Nairobi and Mombasa. This has led to overcrowding.
10. Though only about 4 percent of Kenya's land is arable, you can grow almost every basic foodstuff there.
11. Kenya has forests containing teak and forests containing baobab trees. These are found in the lowlands.
12. Kenya has two main rivers, the Tana and the Galana. It also contains a small portion of Lake Victoria.
13. Kenya is famous for wildlife. They have giraffes and lions.
14. Kenya also has elephants and rhinoceroses that have been threatened by hunters.
15. Kenya abounds in birds and reptiles. This attracts many zoologists to the country.
16. The southern part of Kenya has three distinct climactic regions: humid, tropical, and temperate. This leads to a wide variety of plant and animal life.
17. Native Kenyans belong to more than thirty different ethnic groups. They almost all have a different language.
18. Many tourists visit Kenya's parks that want to see wildlife.
19. Kenya is a member of the Commonwealth of Nations, which has a modified parliamentary form of government.
20. The giraffe has a long neck and is a herbivore. That means it eats plants.

▲ **Critical Viewing**
Write two sentences describing these elephants. Use a pronoun in the second sentence. **[Describe]**

---

16. The southern part of Kenya has three distinct climatic regions: humid, tropical, and temperate. These climates lead to a wide variety of plant and animal life.
17. Native Kenyans belong to more than thirty different ethnic groups, nearly all of which have different languages.
18. Many tourists who want to see wildlife visit Kenya's parks.
19. Kenya, which has a modified parliamentary form of government, is a member of the Commonwealth of Nations.
20. The giraffe has a long neck and is a herbivore — a plant eater.

Critical Viewing

Describe Sample answer: The elephants are huge and impressive. In this photograph they appear to be standing still.

Ambiguous Pronoun References

A pronoun is *ambiguous* if it can refer to more than one possible antecedent.

Personal Pronouns With Two or More Antecedents

A personal pronoun's antecedent should be unmistakable.

> **KEY CONCEPT** A personal pronoun should always be tied to a single, obvious antecedent. ∎

In the example below, the pronoun *he* is confusing because it can refer to either *Sam* or *Steve*.

AMBIGUOUS REFERENCE:	Sam reminded Steve that *he* had some remarkable photos of Kenya.
CORRECT:	Sam reminded Steve that Steve had some remarkable photos of Kenya. In talking with Steve, Sam said that he himself had some remarkable photos of Kenya.

Ambiguous Repetition of Personal Pronouns

Sometimes, repetition of the same pronoun within a sentence can create confusion.

> **KEY CONCEPT** Do not repeat a personal pronoun in a sentence if it can refer each time to a different antecedent. ∎

In the example below, the second use of *she* is unclear. The sentence needs to be rephrased to clarify the meaning.

AMBIGUOUS REPETITION:	Janet shouted to Kelly when *she* saw that *she* was about to be splashed by a bus.
CORRECT:	Janet shouted to Kelly when *she* saw that *Kelly* was about to be splashed by a bus. Janet shouted to Kelly when *Janet* saw that *she herself* was about to be splashed by a bus.

> **More Practice**
>
> **Grammar Exercise Workbook**
> • pp. 105–106
> **On-line Exercise Bank**
> • Section 23.3
>   *Go on-line:*
>   PHSchool.com
>   *Enter Web Code:*
>   egk-1202

Interactive Textbook

Complete the exercise on-line! Exercise 34 is available on-line or on CD-ROM.

Ambiguous Pronoun References

1. Offer students a definition of the word *ambiguous* (doubtful; undetermined; indistinct). Then have them compare this to the meaning of the word *vague* (lacking precision or sharpness of definition).

2. Have students read the first example of an ambiguous reference. Be sure they understand that *he* could refer to either *Sam* or *Steve* and that the best revision is to replace the pronoun with a noun. If you feel that students would be comfortable using an appositive, suggest that the *he* of the first sentence could also be clarified with an appositive reference to either Sam or Steve after the word *he* (*that he, Sam, had* or *that he, Steve, had*).

3. Explain to students that the repetition of pronouns within a sentence is not only poor writing, but also can cause confusion. Direct students to the example of ambiguous repetition and ask them to explain the differences in meanings created by substitutions of more precise words.

4. For the final example on the page, ask students for the antecedent of *herself* (Janet).

Integrating Workplace Skills

Instruction Manuals Tell students that correct agreement between subject-verb and pronoun-antecedent is especially important in a manual that explains how to operate or care for an appliance or machine. Divide the class into groups of three or four students. Have each group find a manual for an appliance, a car, or some other piece of equipment. Ask each group member to evaluate several paragraphs in the manual, looking for examples of singular and plural agreement and noting any errors in agreement. Then have each group report its findings to the class.

☑ **ONGOING ASSESSMENT: Monitor and Reinforce**

If students miss more than two items in Exercise 34, refer them to the following for additional practice.

In the Textbook	Print Resources	Technology
Section Review, Ex. 37, Section 23.3	*Grammar Exercise Workbook*, pp. 103–104	*On-Line Exercise Bank*, Section 23.3

Answer Key

Exercise 35

Answers may vary; samples are given.

1. Sarita told Denise that Denise had gotten an A on her geography project on Kenya.
2. When Denise read her report to Anna, Anna seemed very interested.
3. The report mentioned key facts about Kenya's climate, landforms, and population. All these topics were well covered.
4. Denise noted that Lake Victoria and Lake Turkana are both in Kenya, but it doesn't contain all of either lake.
5. The temperature in Nairobi is quite warm, even though this temperature is different from that on the coast.
6. The coastal region, which is much smaller than the plains area, is more densely populated.
7. There are both Christians, many of whom are Roman Catholics, and Muslims in Kenya.
8. Only Mount Kilimanjaro (in Tanzania), whose peak is over 17,000 feet above sea level, is higher than Mount Kenya.
9. Coffee as well as tea grows abundantly in the highland region. Coffee is one of Kenya's chief exports.
10. Sarita and Denise promised to help Cathy and Liz with their project, but Cathy and Liz never got started.

Step-by-Step Teaching Guide

Avoiding Distant Pronoun References

1. Explain that distant pronoun references refer to pronouns that are so far from their antecedents that confusion results.

2. Be sure students understand that a distant pronoun reference is similar to a misplaced modifier.

Exercise 35 Revising Sentences With Ambiguous Pronoun References Rewrite the following sentences, correcting the ambiguous pronoun references.

1. Sarita told Denise that she had gotten an *A* on her geography project on Kenya.
2. When Denise read her report to Anna, she seemed very interested.
3. The report mentioned key facts about Kenya's climate, landforms, and population, and they were well covered.
4. Denise noted that Lake Victoria and Lake Turkana are both in Kenya, but it doesn't contain all of them.
5. The temperature in Nairobi is different from the temperature on the coast, but it is still quite warm.
6. The coastal region is much smaller than the plains area. It is more densely populated.
7. There are both Christians and Muslims in Kenya. Many of them are Roman Catholics.
8. Only Mount Kilimanjaro in Tanzania is higher than Mount Kenya. Its peak is more than 17,000 feet above sea level.
9. Coffee as well as tea grows abundantly in the highland region. It is one of Kenya's chief exports.
10. Sarita and Denise promised to help Cathy and Liz with their project, but they never got started.

Avoid Distant Pronoun References

A pronoun that is too far away from its antecedent can also confuse a reader.

KEY CONCEPT A personal pronoun should always be close enough to its antecedent to prevent confusion. ∎

A distant pronoun reference can be corrected by moving the pronoun closer to its antecedent or by changing the pronoun to a noun.

DISTANT REFERENCE:	Two chickens moved about in the doorway. On the porch, an old rocker creaked slightly back and forth. *They* pecked aimlessly at the floor.
CORRECT:	As the two chickens moved about in the doorway, *they* pecked aimlessly at the floor. On the porch, an old rocker creaked slightly back and forth.
	Two chickens moved about in the doorway. On the porch, an old rocker creaked slightly back and forth. The *chickens* pecked aimlessly at the floor.

More Practice

Grammar Exercise Workbook
• pp. 105–106
On-line Exercise Bank
• Section 23.3
Go on-line:
PHSchool.com
Enter Web Code:
egk-1202

Complete the exercises on-line! Exercises 35 and 36 are available on-line or on CD-ROM.

▶ **Exercise 36** Correcting Distant Pronoun References
Rewrite the following sentences, correcting the distant
pronoun references.

1. The Great Rift Valley is found in the west of Kenya, while
   the south of the country is heavily forested. It is defined by
   steep cliffs.
2. Volcanic mountain chains are formed to the west of the
   plateau that rises gradually from the coast and covers
   most of the country. Their principal peak is Mount Kenya.
3. The population of Kenya has a majority of Africans of different ethnic groups. There are also Europeans, Asians,
   and Arabs. Some of its largest ethnic groups are the
   Kikuyu, Luhya, and Kamba.
4. Nairobi is home to the National Museums of Kenya, the
   Kenya National Archives, and the McMillan Memorial
   Library, which houses a large collection of Africana. It is
   the capital of Kenya.
5. Kenya's exports total around $1 billion per year. The
   exports go principally to Uganda, England, Germany,
   Rwanda, and Pakistan. Its largest cash crop is tea.
6. Mombasa is the chief port of Kenya, a country that has little river transportation. It serves Uganda and Ethiopia as
   well as Kenya.
7. Kenya has four universities, as well as an extensive system of grade schools for younger children. Close to 40,000
   students were enrolled in them in the early 1990's.
8. Bantu- and Arabic-speaking peoples lived together for
   centuries on the Kenyan coast. Many of the Arabs were
   traders who came originally from northern Africa.
   Eventually, they formed a
   hybrid language,
   Swahili.
9. A region of plains covers
   about three fourths of
   Kenya. The northern
   part of this region is hot
   and dry. It is the country's largest and least-
   populated area.
10. There are vast tracts of
    savanna, or grasslands,
    in Kenya. The country
    has a wide variety of
    wildlife. It supports ele-
    phants, rhinoceroses,
    giraffes, lions, and other
    big cats.

▼ **Critical Viewing**
Describe this scene in
downtown Nairobi
with a pair of sen-
tences that contain the
pronoun *they* and a
clear antecedent.
[Connect]

Special Problems With Pronoun Agreement • **613**

✓ **ONGOING ASSESSMENT: Monitor and Reinforce**

If students miss more than two items in Exercise 35 or 36, refer them to the following for additional
practice.

In the Textbook	Print Resources	Technology
Section Review, Ex. 38–39, Section 23.3	*Grammar Exercise Workbook*, pp. 105-106	*On-Line Exercise Bank*, Section 23.3

Answer Key

▶ **Exercise 36**

Answers may vary; samples are given.

1. The Great Rift Valley, defined by
   steep cliffs, is found in the west
   of Kenya. The south of the
   country is heavily forested.
2. Volcanic mountain chains, with
   the principal peak of Mount
   Kenya, are formed to the west of
   the plateau that rises gradually
   from the coast and covers most
   of the country.
3. The population of Kenya has a
   majority of Africans of different
   ethnic groups, including the
   Kikuyu, Luhya, and Kamba.
   Kenya also has Europeans,
   Asians, and Arabs.
4. Nairobi, the capital of Kenya, is
   home to the National Museums
   of Kenya, the Kenya National
   Archives, and the McMillan
   Memorial Library, which houses
   a large collection of Africana.
5. Kenya's exports total around
   $1 billion per year, the largest
   cash crop being tea. The exports
   go principally to Uganda, England,
   Germany, Rwanda, and Pakistan.
6. Mombasa is the chief port of
   Kenya, a country that has little
   river transportation. Mombasa
   serves Uganda and Ethiopia
   as well.
7. Close to forty thousand students
   were enrolled in Kenya's four
   universities in the early 1990s.
   Kenya also has an extensive
   system of grade schools for
   younger children.
8. Bantu- and Arabic-speaking
   peoples lived together for
   centuries on the Kenyan coast
   and eventually formed a hybrid
   language, Swahili. Many of the
   Arabs were traders who came
   originally from northern Africa.
9. A region of plains, the country's
   largest and least-populated area,
   covers about three fourths of
   Kenya. The northern part of this
   region is hot and dry.
10. Kenya, with vast tracts of savanna,
    or grasslands, supports a wide
    variety of wildlife including
    elephants, rhinoceroses, giraffes,
    lions, and other big cats.

Critical Viewing

Connect Sample answer. Buses are
sitting in the street. They are waiting
for passengers.

Hands-on Grammar

Teaching Resources: Hands-on Grammar Activity Book, Ch. 23

1. If you wish to do this activity in class, be prepared with construction paper and scissors. Put students into groups of four or five students.

2. Go through the sample with the whole class so that they know how to prepare their sentences.

3. When students have finished the activity, have volunteers read some of their sentences aloud so that the whole class can comment on and correct them.

Find It in Your Reading

You might wish to have magazines and newspapers available for student reference.

Find It in Your Writing

Students could check the samples they found in their writing to see if there is a consistent error they make in pronoun reference. They could then try to find ways to avoid this error.

23.3

Hands-on Grammar

Vague-Pronoun Cutouts

Complete the following activity to practice eliminating vague pronoun references. Work with a group of classmates to come up with a series of sentences that contain vague pronoun references. Write each sentence on a separate strip of paper. Place the vague pronoun in the lower left corner, as shown in the example.

Exchange your sentences with those of another group. Then, work with your group to correct the vague pronoun references by replacing each pronoun with an appropriate noun. Cut out the vague pronoun, and tape on a piece of paper containing the noun that is replacing the pronoun. Share your answers with the group that originated the sentences.

> When the team arrived at the competition, they told them that their game would be the next day.

> When the team arrived at the competition, officials told them that their game would the next day.

To get started, use the following sentences:
When we arrived at the zoo, they told us it was closed.
This book is so interesting you can't put it down.
The book is in my bag; it is very heavy.

Find It in Your Reading Sometimes, articles appearing in publications contain vague pronoun references. Look through a newspaper, and find any examples you can. Use these examples as part of your activity.

Find It in Your Writing Go through your portfolio in search of vague pronoun references. Use any you find as sample sentences for this activity. Revise your writing to eliminate the vague pronoun references.

614 • Agreement

☑ ONGOING ASSESSMENT: Assess Mastery		
Use the following resources to assess student mastery of agreement.		
In the Textbook	**Print Resources**	**Technology**
Chapter Review, Ex. 48–49 Standardized Test Preparation Workshop	*Formal Assessment,* Chapter 23	*Writing and Grammar* Interactive Text, Section 23.3, Section Review; *On-Line Exercise Bank,* Section 23.3

⏱ TIME SAVERS!

✋ **Hands-on Grammar**
Use the Hands-on Grammar activity sheet for Chapter 23 to facilitate this activity.

Section 23.3 Section Review

GRAMMAR EXERCISES 37–42

Exercise 37 Revising to Eliminate Vague Pronoun References Rewrite the following sentences, correcting vague pronoun references.

1. I heard they have elephants in Kenya.
2. In the savanna, you have to be careful of wild animals.
3. The tour guide told us that the Great Rift Valley is more than 2,000 miles long and more than 400 miles wide. That impressed us.
4. Kenya attracts more than one-half million tourists annually, mostly to its national parks. They may also visit its Indian Ocean beaches.
5. Kenyan radio and television stations broadcast programs in English and show African- and Asian-language programs. This is because of the many languages spoken in the country.

Exercise 38 Revising to Correct Ambiguous and Vague Pronouns Rewrite the following paragraph, rephrasing and combining sentences to eliminate ambiguous and vague pronouns.

(1) Nairobi is Kenya's capital, and it is also its largest city. (2) Nairobi is now more populous than the city of Chicago. (3) It has grown very rapidly in recent years. (4) Many of Nairobi's residents used to live in rural villages. (5) They were very poor. (6) Life in Nairobi is much more hectic than in the rural villages. (7) This has had an impact on many of the new residents. (8) They spend weekdays working in Nairobi, and then they often return to their villages on the weekend to see friends and family. (9) They are happy to see them again. (10) It can be a difficult and confusing lifestyle.

Exercise 39 Revising Distant Pronoun References Rewrite each sentence, correcting the distant pronouns.

1. Kenya has more than 30 million people, and its rate of growth is very fast. Most of them live in rural areas.
2. Kenya's tourist industry centers around popular beaches and national parks. It has been growing steadily.
3. Agricultural products are also an important part of the economy, which include coffee, tea, and pineapples.
4. Most roads in Kenya are unpaved. Because very few people drive cars, they have not caused much inconvenience.
5. Kenya has two major cities. The rest of the country is primarily rural. They are Nairobi and Mombasa.

Exercise 40 Find It in Your Reading Identify the pronouns and their antecedents in this excerpt from "No Witchcraft for Sale" by Doris Lessing.

. . . Teddy had been on his scooter, and had come to a rest with his foot on the side of a big tub of plants. A tree-snake, hanging by its tail from the roof, had spat full into his eyes.

Exercise 41 Find It in Your Writing Review a piece of narrative writing from your portfolio. Find all of the pronouns you've used, and identify their antecedents. Revise any pronouns that don't have clear antecedents.

Exercise 42 Writing Application Write a description of an interesting place you have visited. Check that all of your pronouns have clear antecedents.

Section Review • 615

ASSESS and CLOSE

Section Review

Answer Key

Exercise 37

Answers may vary; samples are given.

1. I heard there are elephants in Kenya.
2. In the savanna, one has to be careful of wild animals.
3. We were impressed when the tour guide told us that the Great Rift Valley is more than 2,000 miles long and more than 400 miles wide.
4. Kenya attracts more than one-half million tourists annually, mostly to its national parks, but tourists may also visit its Indian Ocean beaches.
5. Because of the many languages spoken in Kenya, its radio and television stations broadcast programs in English and show African- and Asian-language programs.

Exercise 38

Answers may vary; samples are given.

(1) Nairobi is Kenya's capital and largest city. (2–3) Having grown very rapidly in recent years, Nairobi is now more populous than the city of Chicago. (4–5) Many of Nairobi's residents used to live in poor rural villages. (6) Life in Nairobi is much more hectic than in the rural villages. (7) This fast pace has had an impact on many of the new residents. (8) New residents often spend weekdays working in Nairobi and then return to their villages on the weekend to see friends and family. (9–10) The Nairobi workers are happy to see their friends and family again, but splitting time between city and village can be a difficult and confusing lifestyle.

Exercise 39

Answers may vary; samples are given.

1. Kenya has more than 30 million people, most of whom live in rural areas. Kenya's rate of growth is very fast.
2. Kenya's tourist industry, which has been growing steadily, centers around popular beaches and national parks.
3. Agricultural products, including coffee, tea, and pineapples, are also an important part of the economy.

continued

Answer Key continued

Exercise 39

4. Most roads in Kenya are unpaved. Because very few people drive cars, unpaved roads have not caused much inconvenience.
5. Kenya has two major cities, Nairobi and Mombasa. The rest of the country is primarily rural.

Exercise 40

Find It in Your Reading
his refers to *Teddy*; *his* refers to *Teddy*; *its* refers to the *tree-snake*; *his* refers to *Teddy*.

Exercise 41

Find It in Your Writing
Suggest that students look through pieces they wrote before studying this chapter. Suggest that a constant review of pronouns in their own writing will help them catch vague and misleading pronoun references.

Exercise 42

Writing Application
Ask one or two volunteers to read their descriptions out loud.

CHAPTER REVIEW

Each of these exercises correlates to a section of the chapter on agreement, pages 584–615. The exercises may be used for more practice, for reteaching, or for review of the key concepts presented. Answers for all chapter exercises are available in *Grammar Exercises Answers on Transparencies* in your Teaching Resources.

Answer Key

> **Exercise 43**

1. comprises
2. are
3. undergoes
4. are
5. faces

> **Exercise 44**

Answers may vary; samples are given.

1. Either Kenya or Tanzania provides excellent opportunities to view animals living naturally on the savanna.
2. Both the flora and the fauna of Kenya seem to flourish in its national park reserves.
3. Neither a tourist nor a Kenyan citizen is permitted to hunt within a reserve.
4. Park rangers and officials of the government attempt to regulate poaching, the illegal killing of protected animals.
5. correct

> **Exercise 45**

1. is
2. are
3. balance
4. is
5. keeps

> **Exercise 46**

Answers may vary; samples are given.

1. they
2. his or her
3. their
4. I; our
5. its

> **Exercise 47**

Answers may vary; samples are given.

1. My brother and I are planning a trip to Kenya.
2. correct
3. Who besides you can join our trip?
4. Sara and they may join us.
5. The person who has the best itinerary for Kenya is she.

616

Chapter **23** *Chapter Review*

GRAMMAR EXERCISES 43–51

> **Exercise 43** Making Subjects Agree With Their Verbs Choose the verb in parentheses that agrees with the subject of each sentence.

1. Kenya's largest ethnic group, the Kikuyu, (comprises, comprise) about 16 percent of the country's population.
2. Family and tradition (is, are) very important to Kikuyu culture.
3. Traditionally, a young man of one of the Kikuyu tribes (undergoes, undergo) an adulthood ceremony at age eighteen.
4. There (is, are) three things the young man must do: have his ears pierced, his head shaved, and his face marked with white earth.
5. A young woman, who does not undergo the same ceremonies as a man, (faces, face) several challenging tests of endurance.

> **Exercise 44** Revising Sentences to Make Compound Subjects Agree With Their Verbs Rewrite any sentence that contains a subject-verb agreement error. Write *correct* if a sentence is correct.

1. Either Kenya or Tanzania provide excellent opportunities to view animals living naturally on the savanna.
2. Both the flora and fauna of Kenya seems to flourish in its national park reserves.
3. Neither a tourist nor a Kenyan citizen are permitted to hunt within a reserve.
4. Park rangers and officials of the government attempts to regulate poaching, the illegal killing of protected animals.
5. The high value of both tusks and skins tempts poachers to act against the law.

616 • Agreement

> **Exercise 45** Making Confusing Subjects Agree With Their Verbs Chose the verb in parentheses that agrees with the subject of each sentence.

1. One of Kenya's top priorities (is, are) to educate its people.
2. Which of the government's tasks (is, are) more important than this one?
3. Many in a village (balances, balance) schoolwork with their farming chores.
4. Swahili and English are both spoken throughout Kenya. Each (is, are) taught to Kenyan students.
5. Experts have noted at least eighty different languages spoken in Kenya, and the number (keeps, keep) going up.

> **Exercise 46** Supplying Personal Pronouns That Agree With Their Antecedents Write an appropriate personal pronoun to complete each sentence.

1. The people of Kenya enjoy traditional dancing, singing, and storytelling when __?__ have free time.
2. A Kenyan dancer or singer might perform __?__ act for tourists at a hotel.
3. Good storytellers not only entertained, but also educated with __?__ stories.
4. When my family and __?__ visited Kenya, we agreed that __?__ favorite entertainment was Kenyan music.
5. Neither Kenyan music nor Tanzanian music has found __?__ niche in the United States.

> **Exercise 47** Revising to Use Reflexive Pronouns Correctly Rewrite any of the following sentences that contain a misused reflexive pronoun. Write *correct* if a sentence is correct.

1. My brother and myself are planning a trip to Kenya.
2. My brother planned our visit to the Meru Game Reserve himself.
3. Who besides yourself can join our trip?
4. Sara and themselves may join ourselves.
5. The person who has the best itinerary for Kenya is herself.

▶ **Exercise 48** Correcting Pronoun References Rewrite the sentences below correcting the vague, ambiguous, or distant pronoun references.

1. Soccer in Kenya is a very popular sport that you play as a child or an adult.
2. Schools, towns, and companies sponsor soccer teams in Kenya much as they do in the United States.
3. Kenya's national soccer team competes in the Pan-African Games and in World Cup matches. However, these seem to be dominated by teams from west and central Africa.
4. It is difficult for young Kenyans to receive good athletic instruction and coaching, for few schools have athletic programs to train them.
5. Many of Kenya's athletes have received coaching and education at American universities. This has helped them succeed.

▶ **Exercise 49** Using All the Rules of Agreement Revise the following passage, correcting all errors in agreement. Underline each correction.

(1) Between A.D. 700 and 900, the coast between Kenya and Tanzania were settled by Arab traders. (2) Wars in their homelands prompted them to move to east Africa. (3) For several centuries, the Arabs faced no competition for trade with tribes in the interior of the country, and this helped them prosper. (4) During the fifteenth century, however, ships from Portugal were finding their way to east Africa. (5) It meant

that things were bound to change. (6) The Portuguese established trading centers and built forts, several of which you can still see today. (7) They were intent on controlling the east African coast. (8) Each of the groups were trying to monopolize trade in the area. (9) The Arabs finally succeeded in overthrowing the Portuguese during the early 1700's. (10) Soon, however, they were joined by groups from England, France, and Germany, who was interested in expanding its trade and colonization.

▶ **Exercise 50** Writing Application Write a brief essay comparing people or places in another country with what you know about Kenya. Proofread your essay carefully for errors in subject-verb or pronoun agreement.

▶ **Exercise 51** CUMULATIVE REVIEW Verb and Pronoun Usage and Agreement Revise the following sentences, correcting all errors in verb usage, pronoun usage, and agreement. If a sentence has no errors, write *correct*.

1. In 1963, Jomo Kenyatta become the first president of independent Kenya.
2. It's no coincidence that his last name contain "Kenya."
3. He changed its name after he begin to participate in national politics.
4. Early on, Kenyatta seen the need for his country to be independent.
5. A book about Kenyan tribal life was written by him in the 1930's.
6. He described how life would be if Kenya was independent.
7. Kenyatta represented his country at political meetings in England.
8. He spoke eloquently and explains their people's point of view well.
9. At one time, the British accuse Kenyatta of inciting riots and throwed them in jail.
10. He was released in 1961 and lead his party to victory in Kenya's first election.

▶ **Exercise 51**

Answers may vary; samples are given.

1. In 1963, Jomo Kenyatta <u>became</u> the first president of independent Kenya.
2. It's no coincidence that his last name <u>contains</u> "Kenya."
3. He changed <u>his</u> name after he <u>began</u> to participate in national politics.
4. Early on, Kenyatta <u>saw</u> the need for his country to be independent.

5. correct
6. He described how life would be if Kenya <u>were</u> independent.
7. correct
8. He spoke eloquently and <u>explained</u> <u>his</u> people's point of view well.
9. At one time, the British <u>accused</u> Kenyatta of inciting riots and <u>threw</u> <u>him</u> in jail.
10. He was released in 1961 and <u>led</u> his party to victory in Kenya's first election.

Answer Key

▶ **Exercise 48**

Answers may vary; samples are given.

1. Soccer in Kenya is a very popular sport that one plays as a child or an adult.
2. Schools, towns, and companies sponsor soccer teams in Kenya, much as similar organizations do in the United States.
3. Kenya's national soccer team competes in the Pan-African Games and in World Cup matches. However, these competitions seem to be dominated by teams from west and central Africa.
4. Because few schools in Kenya have athletic training programs, young Kenyans find it difficult to receive good athletic instruction and coaching.
5. Many of Kenya's athletes have received coaching and education at U.S. universities. This training has helped them succeed.

▶ **Exercise 49**

Answers may vary; samples are given.

(1) Between A.D. 700 and 900, the coast between Kenya and Tanzania <u>was</u> settled by Arab traders. (2) Wars in their homelands prompted <u>these traders</u> to move to East Africa. (3) For several centuries, the Arabs faced no competition for trade with tribes in the interior of the country, and this <u>lack of competition</u> helped <u>the Arabs</u> prosper. (4) During the fifteenth century, however, ships from Portugal were finding their way to east Africa. (correct) (5) <u>This development</u> meant that things were bound to change. (6) The Portuguese established trading centers and built forts, <u>the latter</u> of which one can still see today. (7) The <u>Portuguese</u> were intent on controlling the east African coast. (8) Each of the groups <u>was</u> trying to monopolize trade in the area. (9) The Arabs finally succeeded in overthrowing the Portuguese during the early 1700's. (correct) (10) Soon, however, the <u>Portuguese</u> were joined by groups from England, France, and Germany, who <u>were</u> interested in expanding <u>their</u> trade and colonization.

▶ **Exercise 50**

Writing Application Consider having students work in pairs and read each other's essays to check for errors in subject-verb and pronoun-antecedent agreement.

continued

Standardized Test Preparation Workshop

Standard English Usage: Agreement

Many standardized tests call on you to demonstrate your knowledge of the rules of agreement. For example, some tests contain sections in which you are asked to identify the part of a sentence that contains an error. Often, the errors are problems with agreement. In other tests, you will be called on to identify the best way to rewrite a sentence or a passage. In some cases, the revision will involve correcting agreement errors. Below are samples of these two formats, along with the answers and an explanation of the answers.

Sample Test Items	Answers and Explanations
Directions: Identify which of the underlined words and phrases in the following sentence contains an error. Neither Brendan nor Claudia are interested in (A) (B) (C) traveling to Boston for the reunion. (D) No error (E)	The correct answer is *C—are interested.* The subject, *Brendan nor Claudia,* is a compound subject made up of two singular subjects joined by *or* or *nor.* Such a subject takes a singular verb; in this case, *is.*
Directions: Choose the revised version of the following sentence that eliminates all errors in grammar, usage, and mechanics. Neither Brendan nor Claudia are interested in traveling to Boston for the reunion. **A** Neither Brendan nor Claudia is interested in traveling to Boston for the reunion. **B** Both Brendan and Claudia is interested in traveling to Boston for the reunion. **C** Neither Brendan and Claudia are interested in traveling to Boston for the reunion. **D** Brendan or Claudia are not interested in traveling to Boston for the reunion.	The correct answer is *A.* The subject, *Brendan nor Claudia,* is a compound subject made up of two singular subjects joined by *or* or *nor.* Such a subject takes a singular verb; in this case, *is.*

618 • Agreement

 TEST-TAKING TIP

Answer Key

> **Practice 1**

1. B
2. B
3. E
4. B
5. C

> **Practice 2**

1. A
2. F

Customize for
Less Advanced Students

In addition to choosing the correct answers in Practice 1, have students write a one-sentence explanation of each answer. Doing so will help them develop a thorough understanding of the rules of agreement.

Customize for
ESL Students

For Practice 2, encourage students to revise the sentences on their own before perusing the answer choices. Then, they can see whether one of the answer choices matches their revision. This will prevent them from having to read and reread the answer choices.

> **Practice 1** **Directions:** Identify which of the underlined words and phrases in each of the following sentences contains an error.

1. Our environment are full of natural
   (A)   (B)   (C)(D)
   resources. No error.
              (E)

2. Because water evaporate into the air
   (A)   (B)
   and falls as rain, snow, hail, and
   (C)
   sleet, it is considered a recyclable
   (D)
   resource. No error.
              (E)

3. Plants and animals are considered
   (A)   (B)
   renewable resources because they
   (C)
   can be used up if they are not
   (D)
   replaced. No error.
             (E)

4. Some timber companies has helped
   (A)   (B)
   keep up a steady supply of renewable
   (C)
   resources by planting new trees to
   (D)
   replace the ones they cut. No error.
                            (E)

5. When nonrenewable resources like
   (A)   (B)
   minerals, natural gas, and oil

   is used up, they cannot be replaced.
   (C)   (D)
   No error.
   (E)

> **Practice 2** **Directions:** Choose the revised version of each numbered sentence that eliminates all errors in grammar, usage, and mechanics.

1. Because aluminum cans and plastic bottles are made of nonrenewable resources, city recycling programs is often eager to recycle them.

   A Because aluminum cans and plastic bottles are made of nonrenewable resources, city recycling programs are often eager to recycle them.

   B Because aluminum cans and plastic bottles is made of nonrenewable resources, city recycling programs is often eager to recycle them.

   C Because aluminum cans and plastic bottles was made of nonrenewable resources, city recycling programs is often eager to recycle them.

   D Because aluminum cans and plastic bottles are made of nonrenewable resources, city recycling programs was often eager to recycle them.

2. People has always been dependent on water. Although it is a recyclable resource, we need to conserve it as much as possible.

   E People have always been dependent on water. Although it are a recyclable resource, we need to conserve it as much as possible.

   F People have always been dependent on water. Although it is a recyclable resource, we need to conserve it as much as possible.

   G People have always been dependent on water. Although it is a recyclable resource, we needs to conserve it as much as possible.

   H People has always been dependent on water. Although it are a recyclable resource, we need to conserve it as much as possible.

In-Depth Lesson Plan

	LESSON FOCUS	PRINT AND MEDIA RESOURCES
DAY 1	**Degrees of Comparison** Students learn and apply the three degrees of comparison using both regular and irregular forms. (pp. 622–627/H458–463)	*Writing and Grammar* Interactive Text, Section 24.1; *On-line Exercise Bank*, Section 24.1 **Teaching Resources** *Grammar Exercise Workbook*, pp. 107–110; *Grammar Exercises Answers on Transparencies*, Ch. 24
DAY 2	**Making Clear Comparisons** Students learn and make logical comparisons, understand absolute modifiers, and do the Hands-on Grammar activity. (pp. 628–633/H464–469)	*Writing and Grammar* Interactive Text, Section 24.2; *On-line Exercise Bank*, Section 24.2 **Teaching Resources** *Grammar Exercise Workbook*, pp. 111–116; *Hands-on Grammar Activity Book*, Ch. 24
DAY 3	**Review and Assess** Students review the chapter and demonstrate mastery of modifiers indicating comparisons. (pp. 634–635)	**Teaching Resources** *Formal Assessment*, Ch. 24

Accelerated Lesson Plan

	LESSON FOCUS	PRINT AND MEDIA RESOURCES
DAY 1	**Degrees of Comparison** Students learn and apply the three degrees of comparison using both regular and irregular forms. (pp. 622–627/H458–463)	*Writing and Grammar* Interactive Text, Section 24.1; *On-line Exercise Bank*, Section 24.1 **Teaching Resources** *Grammar Exercise Workbook*, pp. 107–110; *Grammar Exercises Answers on Transparencies*, Ch. 24
DAY 2	**Making Clear Comparisons; Review and Assess** Students cover logical comparisons and absolute modifiers; they review the chapter and demonstrate mastery of concepts. (pp. 628–635/H464–469)	*Writing and Grammar* Interactive Text, Section 24.2; *On-line Exercise Bank*, Section 24.2 **Teaching Resources** *Grammar Exercise Workbook*, pp. 111–116; *Formal Assessment*, Ch. 24

Options for Adapting Lesson Plans

HOMEWORK

Have students complete any section of the chapter for homework.

FEATURES

Extend coverage with the Grammar in Literature feature (p. 628/H464) and the Standardized Test Preparation Workshop (p. 636).

TECHNOLOGY

Students can use *Writing and Grammar* Interactive Text to complete the exercises interactively on computer. They can complete additional exercises in the *On-line Exercise Bank:* The Auto Check feature will grade their work. Go on-line: PHSchool.com Use Web Code: egk-1202

Writing and Grammar Handbook Alignment

Page numbers in Step-by-Step Teaching Guides in this Teacher's Edition refer to pages from the full student text. Handbook page references, indicated with this icon Ⓗ, are provided in Time and Resource Manager boxes and at the bottom of each Teacher's Edition page.

INTEGRATED SKILLS COVERAGE

Grammar in Literature
SE p. 628/Ⓗ464

Writing
Find It in Your Writing, SE pp. 627, 633/Ⓗ463, 469
Writing Application, SE pp. 627, 633, 635/Ⓗ463, 469
Grammar and Style, SE pp. 623, 632/Ⓗ459, 468

Spelling
SE pp. 623, 624/Ⓗ459, 460
ATE p. 624

Viewing and Representing
Critical Viewing, SE pp. 620, 625, 629/Ⓗ456, 461, 465
ATE p. 630

Vocabulary
ATE p. 632

Writing
ATE p. 629

Real-World Connection
ATE p. 625

ASSESSMENT SUPPORT

Standardized Test Preparation Workshop SE p. 636; ATE pp. 624, 630

Standardized Test Preparation Workbook, pp. 47–48

Formal Assessment, Ch. 24

MEETING INDIVIDUAL NEEDS

Less Advanced Students ATE p. 637. See also Ongoing Assessments ATE pp. 623, 625, 629, 631, 632.

ESL Students ATE p. 629

AP Students ATE pp. 624, 637

Bodily/Kinesthetic Learners ATE p. 623

Gifted and Talented Students ATE p. 629

BLOCK SCHEDULING

Pacing Suggestions
For 90-minute Blocks
• Administer the Diagnostic Test to students to determine instructional coverage.
• Have students complete the necessary exercises in class. Use the Hands-on Grammar activity to provide a change of pace.

Resources for Varying Instruction
• *Writing and Grammar* Interactive Text A 90-minute block provides an ideal opportunity for students to work on the computer.

Professional Development Support
• *How to Manage Instruction in the Block* This teaching resource provides management and activity suggestions.

MEDIA AND TECHNOLOGY

For the Student
• *Writing and Grammar* Interactive Text, Ch. 24
• *On-line Exercise Bank,* Sections 24.1–2

For the Teacher
• TeacherEXPRESS™ CD-ROM

WRITING AND GRAMMAR ON-LINE

Interactive Text (On-line or on CD-ROM)
• Easily navigable instruction with on-line supporting resources
• Self-scoring exercises and diagnostic tests

Companion Web Site PHSchool.com
• On-line Exercise Bank (use Web Code egk-1202)

See the Go On-line! feature, SE p. iii.

LITERATURE CONNECTIONS

Grammar in Literature selection from *Prentice Hall Literature, Penguin Edition,* The British Tradition: from "To the Virgins, to Make Much of Time," Robert Herrick, SE p. 628/Ⓗ464

Lesson Objectives

1. To recognize and use the three degrees of comparison: positive, comparative, and superlative

2. To recognize and use comparative and superlative forms of regular and irregular adjectives and adverbs

3. To make logical, balanced comparisons and to use absolute modifiers correctly

4. To analyze the characteristics of clear texts such as conciseness, correctness, and completeness

5. To recognize appropriate English usage within the context of a written passage

Critical Viewing

Describe Sample responses: One woman's dress is darker and plainer than the other dresses. One dress is fuller at the bottom than the others.

Chapter 24 Using Modifiers

You have probably noticed that you must sometimes change the form of adjectives and adverbs, especially in comparisons. You might say, for example, "Sir Percival traveled *farther* than Sir Gawain, but Sir Hector traveled the *farthest* of them all." The form of the adjective depends on whether two things or more than two things are being compared.

This chapter will show you how to form various adjectives and adverbs and how to avoid some specific errors that often occur in comparisons.

▲ Critical Viewing
"Who is the fairest of them all?" Compare the gowns of the ladies in this photograph. **[Describe]**

☑ ONGOING ASSESSMENT: Diagnose

If students miss more than one item in any category, direct them to the relevant pages of the textbook and assign exercises for practice and review.

Using Modifiers	Diagnostic Test Items	Teach	Practice	Section Review	Chapter Review
Skill Check A					
Forming Regular Comparatives and Superlatives	A 1–5	p. 623/Ⓗ459	Ex. 2	Ex. 6–7	Ex. 24
Skill Check B					
Recognizing Degrees of Comparison	B 6–10	p. 622/Ⓗ458	Ex. 1	Ex. 5	Ex. 23
Skill Check C					

Diagnostic Test

Directions: Write all answers on a separate sheet of paper.

Skill Check A. Write the comparative and superlative degrees of the following modifiers.

1. strong
2. valiantly
3. enduring
4. generous
5. safe

Skill Check B. Identify the degree of each underlined modifier as *positive*, *comparative*, or *superlative*.

6. The earliest knights were usually of <u>noble</u> birth.
7. As armor grew <u>more sophisticated</u>, it also became <u>more expensive</u>.
8. Because of the expense involved, <u>fewer</u> noblemen wanted to become knights.
9. A knight's battle armor was usually <u>less shiny</u> than is popularly imagined.
10. After armor became expensive, nobles <u>most commonly</u> relied on hired men-at-arms for defense purposes.

Skill Check C. Choose the correct comparative or superlative modifier in each sentence.

11. Tournaments were (more/most) popular in the twelfth century than they were in the thirteenth.
12. Because of the expense involved, knighthood became restricted to only the (wealthier/wealthiest) noblemen.
13. Decorative armor was (heavier/heaviest) than battle armor.
14. Today's armor weighs (less/least) than medieval armor.
15. Mobility was the (better/best) attribute a suit of armor could have.

Skill Check D. Write the correct form of the modifier in parentheses to complete each sentence.

16. In England, the coronation of a king or queen is (ceremonious) than the dubbing of a knight.
17. Today, a person of (little) noble birth than royalty can be dubbed a knight in recognition of personal merit or service to society.
18. The (good) recent examples of such pageantry are the British royal weddings.
19. The (bad) aspect of such ceremonies is the expense involved.
20. You would travel a long distance to go to England to witness such pageantry, but the ceremony takes you even (far) back in history.

Skill Check E. Rewrite the following sentences to make the comparisons logical.

21. The shield is older than any protective device.
22. Bad weather could be fatal to a tournament.
23. Medieval armor was much heavier than today.
24. The helmet is a more enduring piece of armor than any.
25. Kings were of nobler birth than anyone.

Using Modifiers • 621

Diagnostic Test

Each item in the Diagnostic Test corresponds with a specific section in the using modifiers chapter. This will enable you to tailor instruction to the particular needs of your students. See "Ongoing Assessment: Diagnose" below for further details.

Skill Check A

1. stronger, strongest
2. more valiantly, most valiantly
3. more enduring, most enduring
4. more generous, most generous
5. safer, safest

Skill Check B

6. positive
7. comparative, comparative
8. comparative
9. comparative
10. superlative

Skill Check C

11. more	14. less
12. wealthiest	15. best
13. heavier	

Skill Check D

16. more ceremonious	19. worst
17. less noble	20. further
18. best	

Skill Check E

Allow some variation in wording.

21. The shield is older than any other protective device.
22. Bad weather could be detrimental to a tournament.
23. Medieval armor was much heavier than armor is today.
24. The helmet is a more enduring piece of armor than any other.
25. Kings were of nobler birth than anyone else was.

☑ ONGOING ASSESSMENT: Diagnose *continued*

Using Modifiers	Diagnostic Test Items	Teach	Practice	Section Review	Chapter Review
Choosing Regular and Irregular Forms	C 11–15	pp. 623–624/Ⓗ459–460	Ex. 2–4	Ex. 6–7	Ex. 25
Skill Check D					
Using Correct Forms of Modifiers	D 16–20	p. 628/Ⓗ464	Ex. 11–12	Ex. 17	Ex. 26–27, 29
Skill Check E					
Forming Logical Comparisons	E 21–25	pp. 630–632/Ⓗ466–468	Ex. 13–16	Ex. 18–19	Ex. 28
Cumulative Reviews and Applications				Ex. 8–10, 20–22	Ex. 30

🕐 **TIME SAVERS!**

📄 **Answers on Transparencies** Use the *Grammar Exercises Answers on Transparencies* for Chapter 24 to facilitate correction by students.

💻 **On-Line Exercise Bank** Have students complete the Diagnostic Test on computer. The Auto Check feature will grade their work for you!

Activate Prior Knowledge

Ask students to form groups of two or three according to their similar interests—for instance, sports enthusiasts, readers, film critics. Groups should work together to write at least three sentences comparing the likes and dislikes among the members of their group. Volunteers might place their best two sentences on the board as a basis for discussion of comparative and superlative degrees.

TEACH

Step-by-Step Teaching Guide

Recognizing Degrees of Comparison

1. Explain that adjectives and adverbs change form when they are used to indicate the three degrees of comparison and that these forms may be regular or irregular.

2. Demonstrate how a modifier may change form. Read aloud from the examples in the chart, and give students additional modifiers in the positive degree (*happy, careless, easily, fast*) for practice in using the comparative and superlative degrees.

3. As students read the forms of each modifier, point out that *-er* or *more* is added to compare two items, but *-est* or *most* is added to compare three or more.

Answer Key

Exercise 1

1. positive
2. superlative
3. superlative
4. comparative
5. comparative

Section 24.1 Degrees of Comparison

In the English language, there are three *degrees*, or forms, of most adjectives and adverbs that are used in comparisons.

Recognizing Degrees of Comparison

In order to write effective comparisons, you first need to know the three degrees.

KEY CONCEPT The three degrees of comparison are the *positive*, the *comparative*, and the *superlative*. ∎

In the following chart, both adjectives and adverbs are shown in each of the three degrees. Notice the three different ways that the words change form: (1) with *-er* and *-est*, (2) with *more* and *most*, and (3) with entirely different words.

DEGREES OF ADJECTIVES		
Positive	**Comparative**	**Superlative**
slow	slower	slowest
disagreeable	more disagreeable	most disagreeable
good	better	best
DEGREES OF ADVERBS		
slowly	more slowly	most slowly
disagreeably	more disagreeably	most disagreeably
well	better	best

Exercise 1 Recognizing Positive, Comparative, and Superlative Degrees Identify the degree of each underlined modifier.

EXAMPLE: Armor was <u>most commonly</u> made of metal.
ANSWER: superlative

1. *Armor* is the name given to any <u>protective</u> body equipment.
2. The <u>oldest</u> protective device is the shield.
3. Medieval knights are <u>most frequently</u> shown wearing armor.
4. Tournament armor was <u>heavier</u> than battle armor.
5. It was also <u>more highly</u> decorated.

Theme: Knights

In this section, you will learn how to form the comparative and superlative degrees of adjectives and adverbs. The examples and exercises in this section are about knights and armor.

Cross-Curricular Connection: Social Studies

Get instant feedback! Exercises 1 and 2 are available on-line or on CD-ROM.

More Practice

Grammar Exercise Workbook
• pp. 107–108
On-line Exercise Bank
• Section 24.1
Go on-line:
PHSchool.com
Enter Web Code:
egk-1202

⏱ TIME AND RESOURCE MANAGER

Resources
Print: *Grammar Exercise Workbook*, pp. 107–110; *Grammar Exercises Answers on Transparencies*, Ch. 24
Technology: *Writing and Grammar* Interactive Text, Section 24.1; *On-Line Exercise Bank*, Section 24.1

Using the Full Student Edition	Using the Handbook H
• Work through all key concepts, pp. 622–624. • Assign and review Exercises 1–4. • Do the Hands-on Grammar activity in class, p. 626.	• Work through all key concepts, pp. 458–460. • Assign and review Exercises 1–4. • Do the Hands-on Grammar activity in class, p. 462.

Regular Forms

Like verbs, adjectives and adverbs can be either regular or irregular. The number of syllables in regular modifiers determines how their degrees form.

KEY CONCEPT Use *-er* or *more* to form the comparative degree and *-est* or *most* to form the superlative degree of most one- and two-syllable modifiers. ■

EXAMPLES:	smart	smarter	smartest
	funny	funnier	funniest
	brisk	more brisk	most brisk
	spiteful	more spiteful	most spiteful

KEY CONCEPT All adverbs that end in *-ly* form their comparative and superlative degrees with *more* and *most* regardless of the number of syllables. ■

EXAMPLES:	curtly	more curtly	most curtly
	shrewdly	more shrewdly	most shrewdly

KEY CONCEPT Use *more* and *most* to form the comparative and superlative degrees of all modifiers with three or more syllables. ■

EXAMPLES:	beautiful	more beautiful	most beautiful
	generous	more generous	most generous

Note About *Comparisons With* Less *and* Least: *Less* and *least* can be used to form another version of the comparative and superlative degrees of most modifiers.

EXAMPLES:	soft	less soft	least soft
	appetizing	less appetizing	least appetizing

Exercise 2 Forming Regular Comparative and Superlative Degrees Write the comparative and the superlative forms of each modifier.

EXAMPLE: wise
ANSWER: wiser, wisest

1. strong	6. classical
2. protective	7. modified
3. durable	8. resistant
4. acceptable	9. convenient
5. heavy	10. festive

Grammar and Style Tip

Choosing vivid, descriptive modifiers to compare people, places, things, and ideas can enhance your writing and make it more interesting.

Spelling Tip

When comparing two things, add the suffix *-er* or the word *more,* but never add both together.

Degrees of Comparison • 623

ONGOING ASSESSMENT: Monitor and Reinforce

If students have difficulty with Exercise 1 or 2, refer them to the following for additional practice.

In the Textbook	Print Resources	Technology
Section Review, Ex. 5, Section 24.1	*Grammar Exercise Workbook,* pp. 107–108	*On-Line Exercise Bank,* Section 24.1

Irregular Forms

1. Give students practice with the modifiers in the chart. Have one volunteer at a time say the three forms of a modifier and then use these forms in three simple sentences. Continue until you have used all the examples.

2. Next, encourage students to form these modifiers without consulting their textbooks. For instance, read one form of a modifier and have students supply the other two.

3. Remind students that they can consult the chart on this page whenever they are in doubt about forming irregular modifiers.

Customize for
AP Students

Ask students to identify two or three related things they have studied or observed—such as various members of a system of organisms, or various world leaders during a historical crisis—and then to write a paragraph or two comparing and contrasting them. When students finish, have volunteers read their paragraphs for the class, and together determine the degrees of modifiers and their use in constructing a compare-and-contrast essay.

Integrating Spelling

To form regular and irregular forms of modifiers that end in *-y*, have students practice adding *-er*, *-ier*, and *more* correctly. Give examples to illustrate the range of irregularities: *gray* becomes *grayer*, *lonely* may become both *lonelier* and *more lonely*, but *loudly* becomes *more loudly* and cannot be *loudlier*. Have students generate a list of modifiers ending in *-y*, and then demonstrate how each forms its comparative and superlative forms.

24.1

Irregular Forms

Because several adjectives and adverbs form their comparative and superlative degrees in unpredictable ways, it is necessary to memorize them.

> **KEY CONCEPT** The irregular comparative and superlative forms of certain adjectives and adverbs must be memorized. ■

As you read the following chart, separate the irregular modifiers that cause problems for you from the ones you already use correctly. Then, study and memorize those that cause problems for you. Notice that some modifiers differ only in the positive degree. *Bad*, *badly*, and *ill*, for example, all have the same comparative and superlative forms (*worse*, *worst*).

IRREGULAR MODIFIERS		
Positive	**Comparative**	**Superlative**
bad	worse	worst
badly	worse	worst
far (distance)	farther	farthest
far (extent)	further	furthest
good	better	best
ill	worse	worst
late	later	last *or* latest
little (amount)	less	least
many	more	most
much	more	most
well	better	best

Note About *Bad* and *Badly*: *Bad* is an adjective; *badly* is an adverb. *Bad* cannot be used as an adverb after an action verb.

EXAMPLES:
ADVERB
The children behaved *badly*.

ADJECTIVE
The children felt *bad* about it.

Note About *Good* and *Well*: *Good* is an adjective; *well* can be used as an adjective or an adverb. *Good* cannot be used as an adverb after an action verb.

EXAMPLES:
ADJECTIVE
The children felt *good* about it.

ADVERB
The children behaved *well*.

ADJECTIVE
The children did not feel *well* after eating candy.

624 • Using Modifiers

💡 Spelling Tip

When comparing three or more things, add the suffix *-est* or the word *most*, but never add both together.

> **More Practice**
>
> Grammar Exercise Workbook
> • pp. 109–110
> On-line Exercise Bank
> • Section 24.1
> *Go on-line:*
> PHSchool.com
> *Enter Web Code:*
> egk-1202

 STANDARDIZED TEST PREPARATION WORKSHOP

Grammar and Usage Many standardized tests require students to recognize correct usage of modifiers within the context of a passage. Use the following example to demonstrate.

Once she was named vice president, Joan Donnelly moved to a highest floor but still hungered for the presidency.

What revision, if any, is required in this sentence?

A Place a comma after *Donnelly*
B Change *highest* to *higher*
C Capitalize *Presidency*
D No revision is required

The correct answer is **B**. Because the statement refers to a new floor compared to the one where she was previously, the comparison is between two things. Accordingly, the comparative form *higher* is correct.

▶ **Exercise 3** Forming Irregular Comparative and Superlative Degrees Write the appropriate form of the underlined modifier to complete each sentence.

EXAMPLE: Battle armor did not cost too <u>much</u> money, but tournament armor cost ___?___ .

ANSWER: more

1. <u>Some</u> knights fought without armor, but many ___?___ knights wore armor.
2. When a knight was in full armor, <u>little</u> of his body and even ___?___ of his face showed.
3. Wealthy knights wore <u>good</u> suits of armor, but they wore their ___?___ armor to a tournament.
4. Knights traveled <u>far</u> in their homeland, but those who went to the Crusades traveled ___?___ .
5. When a boy became a page, he had <u>far</u> to go to become a squire but even ___?___ to become a knight.
6. A wound from a sword was <u>bad</u>, but a wound from a bullet was ___?___ .
7. A battle had <u>some</u> ceremony, but a tournament had much ___?___ ceremony.
8. Medieval armor was a <u>good</u> protective device, but today's armor is ___?___ and lighter.
9. Tournament armor was designed to allow <u>some</u> mobility, but safety was the ___?___ important concern.
10 Tournament armor was a <u>little</u> cumbersome, but battle armor had to be ___?___ so.

▶ **Exercise 4** Writing Sentences With Comparative and Superlative Degrees Write a sentence for each of the following.
1. secretive (comparative)
2. good (superlative)
3. well (comparative)
4. jocular (comparative)
5. malicious (superlative)
6. likely (comparative)
7. funny (superlative)
8. badly (superlative)
9. calmly (comparative)
10. heroic (superlative)

▼ Critical Viewing
Compare the armor worn by this knight with the safety gear worn by people on skateboards or rollerblades. Use the comparative and superlative degrees in your sentences. [**Compare and Contrast**]

Degrees of Comparison • 625

Answer Key

▶ **Exercise 3**

1. more   6. worse
2. less   7. more
3. best   8. better
4. farther   9. most
5. further   10. less

▶ **Exercise 4**

Answers will vary; samples are given.

1. A cat is more secretive than a dog.
2. This is the best pie I've ever had.
3. The lamp will work better if you plug it in.
4. Ed is more jocular than Amy.
5. He was the most malicious prisoner in the jail.
6. He is more likely to fail than she.
7. Of all the jokes, his is the funniest.
8. He played worst of all the cellists.
9. The wind is blowing more calmly now than it was earlier.
10. That was the most heroic rescue I've ever seen.

Real-World Connection

Many job applications—as well as many jobs—require making oral and written comparisons. Ask students to generate a list of comparisons they may be required to make when applying for or performing certain tasks such as interviewing, giving presentations, writing reports, and creating charts and graphs.

Language Highlight

Similes and Metaphors In addition to using appropriate forms of modifiers, writers often use similes (comparisons using *like* or *as*) and metaphors (statements that equate two things to connote their similarity) to make comparisons. Ask students to search through *Prentice Hall Literature, Penguin Edtion,* The British Tradition to find one statement that uses each of these devices to make comparisons: a simile, a metaphor, a comparative modifier, and a superlative modifier.

Critical Viewing

Compare and Contrast Sample responses: The knight would be safer from harm with this equipment than a skateboarder would be with modern protection. The knight's gear, however, is surely the heaviest protective gear.

ONGOING ASSESSMENT: Monitor and Reinforce

If students miss more than two items in Exercise 3 or 4, refer them to the following for additional practice.

In the Textbook	Print Resources	Technology
Section Review, Ex. 6–7, Section 24.1	*Grammar Exercise Workbook,* pp. 109–110	*On-Line Exercise Bank,* Section 24.1

Hands-on Grammar

Teaching Resources: Hands-on Grammar Activity Book, Ch. 24

1. If you wish to do this activity in class, be prepared with construction paper. Have students work in pairs, and give each pair a sheet of paper.

2. Go through the directions and diagrams with students so that they understand how to make the pocket fold.

3. When students have finished working with the irregular modifiers they have written into their pocket folds, you might have them work with regular modifiers requiring spelling changes, such as *dry, nasty, red,* or *flat.*

Find It in Your Reading

You might wish to have students find comparatives and superlatives in selections from a literature unit they have recently studied.

Find It in Your Writing

Students could work with their partners to read each other's writing and evaluate the use of modifiers.

24.1

Hands-on Grammar

Irregular-Modifier Pocket Fold

Practice using irregular comparative and superlative forms of modifiers with a pocket fold. Take a $6\frac{1}{2}$"-inch-square sheet of paper, and fold in the corners so that they meet in the middle. Turn the paper over, and again fold in the corners. Then, crease the paper by folding it in half and in half again. You will have a small square. Unfold only the small square, and lay the paper flat so that four square sections are facing upward. Write the positive degree of a different irregular modifier on each of the four squares. (See example A.)

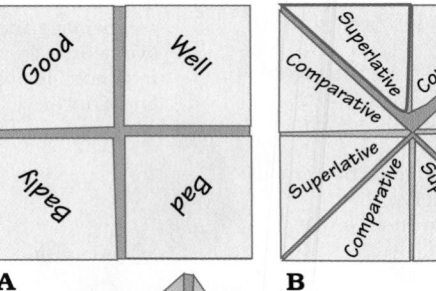

Next, turn the paper over, and on each of the eight triangular sections, write *comparative* or *superlative.* (See example B.) Then, lift up each triangle, and write underneath it the corresponding forms of the comparative or superlative on the back of the square. Each modifier will have two forms.

Finally, refold the square so that the positives are on the outside. Place your thumbs and index fingers in each of the four slots formed by the small squares, and pinch them together. You should be able to open and close the square in two directions, exposing either the comparative or the superlative form each time. (See example C.)

With a partner, take turns choosing a modifier from the other's pocket fold. After opening and closing the square in different directions four or five times, each person must give the form of the modifier indicated on the triangle. Check your answers by lifting up the triangle.

Find It in Your Reading Read two or three paragraphs of a story or article, and see how many comparative and superlative forms you recognize.

Find It in Your Writing Review the use of modifiers in a piece of your writing, and make sure that you used and formed the modifiers

---

Section 24.1 Section Review

GRAMMAR EXERCISES 5–10

▶ **Exercise 5** Recognizing Positive, Comparative, and Superlative Degrees Identify the degree of each underlined modifier.

1. <u>Knightly</u> behavior was regulated by a code of conduct known as chivalry.
2. Tournaments involved <u>much</u> pageantry.
3. Pageantry is <u>difficult</u> to define.
4. It is one of the <u>most ritualistic</u> features of any society.
5. Early pageants were religious in origin, but that aspect is <u>less emphasized</u> now.

▶ **Exercise 6** Supplying the Comparative and Superlative Degrees Write the appropriate comparative or superlative degree of the modifier in parentheses.

1. Becoming a knight involved (much) ceremony in the thirteenth century than it did in the twelfth.
2. In the twelfth century, a squire became a knight when his abilities were recognized by another knight, but in the thirteenth century, he was dubbed by someone of (noble) birth.
3. A good suit of armor weighed around 65 pounds, but carrying a lance, sword, and shield made the load (heavy).
4. Interlinked iron rings known as mail was the (common) armor.
5. It was useful against a sword blow, but (little) so against the point of a lance or an arrow.

▶ **Exercise 7** Revising to Eliminate Errors in Comparisons Revise the following paragraph, correcting any errors in comparison you find.

In his own lifetime, Geoffrey Chaucer was considered one of the most greatest English poets. His more wider read work, *The Canterbury Tales*, is a story told by pilgrims on the way to the cathedral of Canterbury. In medieval Christianity, pilgrimages were considered well things to do. Some pilgrims would travel as far as Rome, and some would travel even further. *The Canterbury Tales* is written in Middle English, which is more easier to read than Old English but not as easy as modern English.

▶ **Exercise 8** Find It in Your Reading Identify the comparatives and superlatives in this passage from *Sir Gawain and the Green Knight*, which was translated by Marie Borroff.

That no host under heaven is hardier of will, / Nor better brothers-in-arms where battle is joined; / I am the weakest, well I know, and of wit feeblest; / And the loss of my life would be least of any; . . .

▶ **Exercise 9** Find It in Your Writing Review a poem from your writing portfolio, and locate the positive, comparative, and superlative modifiers. Check for correct usage. Could adding or intensifying modifiers improve your work?

▶ **Exercise 10** Writing Application Write a comparison-and-contrast essay using positive, comparative, and superlative forms of appropriate modifiers. Check your work for correct usage.

Section Review • 627

✓ ONGOING ASSESSMENT: Assess Mastery

Use the following resources to assess student mastery of degrees of comparison.

In the Textbook	Technology
Chapter Review, Ex. 23–26	*On-Line Exercise Bank,* Section 24.1

ASSESS and CLOSE

Section Review

Each of these exercises correlates to the instruction on regular and irregular comparative forms, pages 622–624. The exercises may be used for more practice, for reteaching, or for review of the key concepts presented.

Answer Key

▶ **Exercise 5**

1. positive   4. superlative
2. positive   5. comparative
3. positive

▶ **Exercise 6**

1. more   4. most common
2. nobler   5. less
3. heavier

▶ **Exercise 7**

one of the greatest
most widely read
good things to do
travel even farther
easier to read

▶ **Exercise 8**

Find It in Your Reading
hardier—comparative
better—comparative
weakest—superlative
feeblest—superlative
least—superlative

▶ **Exercise 9**

Find It in Your Writing
Encourage students to reread their writing and revise their poems to include more modifiers.

▶ **Exercise 10**

Writing Application
Give students the option of posting their essays in the classroom or on a Web site for review by the rest of the class.

⏱ TIME SAVERS!

Answers on Transparencies Use the *Grammar Exercises Answers on Transparencies* for Chapter 24 to facilitate correction by students.

On-Line Exercise Bank Have students complete the exercises on computer. The Auto Check feature will grade their work for you!

Ask students to explain the meaning of the expression "comparing apples and oranges." (You can't compare unlike things.) Then offer this comparison:

I hate oatmeal more than my brother.

Ask students to identify the literal meaning. (My brother is compared to oatmeal.) Ask for solutions.

Activate Prior Knowledge

Ask each student to make a brief list of characteristics—word- or phrase-modifiers—to compare family members. Have students use these modifiers to write statements of comparison using the word *than*. (Example: *My brother is taller than my mother is.*)

TEACH

Step-by-Step Teaching Guide

Using Comparative and Superlative Degrees

1. Quickly review the examples on this page, having students read them aloud.
2. Caution students to avoid using *-er* with *more* or *-est* with *most* to form comparisons.

Step-by-Step Teaching Guide

Grammar in Literature

1. Read the lines aloud to the class.
2. Discuss how the use of comparative and superlative forms heightens meaning.

More About the Writer

The poet who advised, "Gather ye rosebuds while ye may," was a seventeenth-century Anglican priest. His exquisitely crafted love poems failed to impress his contemporaries but are much admired today.

Connections With Literature

The complete "To the Virgins, to Make Much of Time" can be found in *Prentice Hall Literature, Penguin Edition,* The British Tradition.

Section 24.2

Making Clear Comparisons

In this section, you will learn the proper uses of the comparative and superlative degrees and how to avoid making illogical comparisons.

Using Comparative and Superlative Degrees

One basic rule that has two parts covers the correct use of comparative and superlative forms:

▶ **KEY CONCEPT** Use the comparative degree to compare two persons, places, or things. Use the superlative degree to compare three or more persons, places, or things. ■

As the following examples illustrate, the number of items being compared is often indicated in the context of the sentence.

COMPARATIVE: Orange will be *more conspicuous* than blue.
I am *less talented* than Sheila.

SUPERLATIVE: Orange is the *most conspicuous* color of all.
I am the *least talented* person for this work.

Note About *Double Comparisons*: A *double comparison* is a usage error caused by using both *-er* and *more* or both *-est* and *most* to form a regular modifier. A double comparison can also be created by adding any of these endings to an irregular modifier.

INCORRECT: This is the *most happiest* day of my life.
My cold is *worser* today than it was yesterday.

CORRECT: This is the *happiest* day of my life.
My cold is *worse* today than it was yesterday.

GRAMMAR IN LITERATURE

from To the Virgins, to Make Much of Time
Robert Herrick

This verse from Herrick's poem contains comparative and superlative adjectives (in blue italics). Identify which of these adjectives is regular and which is irregular.

That age is *best* which is the first,
    When youth and blood are *warmer*;
But being spent, the *worse*, and *worst*
    Times still succeed the former.

628 • Using Modifiers

Theme: Skyscrapers

In this section, you will learn how to use comparatives and superlatives of adjectives and adverbs correctly. The examples and exercises in this section are about skyscrapers around the world.

Cross-Curricular Connection: Social Studies

 **Internet Tip**

To find out more about skyscrapers, use search words like *skyscraper, construction,* and *architecture.* You can even learn what massive buildings are planned for the future!

⏱ TIME AND RESOURCE MANAGER

Resources
Print: *Grammar Exercise Workbook,* pp. 111–116; *Grammar Exercises Answers on Transparencies,* Ch. 24
Technology: *Writing and Grammar* Interactive Text, Section 24.2; *On-Line Exercise Bank,* Section 24.2

Using the Full Student Edition	Using the Handbook🄷
• Work through all key concepts, pp. 628–632. • Assign and review Exercises 11–16. • Read and discuss Grammar in Literature, p. 628.	• Work through all key concepts, pp. 464–468. • Assign and review Exercises 11–16. • Read and discuss Grammar in Literature, p. 464.

► **Exercise 11** Supplying the Comparative and Superlative Degrees Write the appropriate comparative or superlative degree of the modifier in parentheses.

EXAMPLE: Winston is the (funny) student in our class.
ANSWER: funniest

1. The world's (old) skyscrapers were built in Chicago.
2. They were much (small) than modern buildings.
3. Many were demolished to make room for (new) structures.
4. Unlike today's skyscrapers, the (early) structures were built of solid masonry construction.
5. It was discovered that using a steel skeleton would make possible the construction of (high) buildings.
6. A steel skeleton is (well) able to bear the load of the walls and floors than masonry alone.
7. The antennae added to the Empire State Building make it (tall) now than when it was first built.
8. Is the (tall) building in the United States still the Sears Tower in Chicago?
9. Which is the (high) building in the world?
10. One of the (important) design concerns is the type of air currents that will be hitting the top of the building.

► **Exercise 12** Using the Comparative and Superlative Degrees Correctly Choose the correct comparative or superlative form in each sentence.
1. The (taller/tallest) buildings in the world are skyscrapers.
2. They can be found in (more/most) big cities.
3. The (earlier/earliest) skyscrapers were built in the United States.
4. Today's skyscrapers are much (higher/highest) than those early versions.
5. The invention of the electric elevator made it (more feasible/most feasible) to design taller buildings.

► Critical Viewing The Sears Tower in Chicago is the tallest building in the United States. Compare the Sears Tower with a tall building in a city near you. Use comparatives and superlatives in your sentences. [Compare and Contrast]

► **More Practice**

Grammar Exercise Workbook
• pp. 111–112
On-line Exercise Bank
• Section 24.2
Go on-line:
PHSchool.com
Enter Web Code:
egk-1202

Clear Comparisons • 629

Answer Key

► **Exercise 11**
1. oldest   6. better
2. smaller   7. taller
3. newer   8. tallest
4. earlier   9. highest
5. higher   10. most important

► **Exercise 12**
1. tallest   4. higher
2. most   5. more feasible
3. earliest

Customize for
Gifted and Talented Students

Students can search newspapers and magazines for examples of advertisements that use comparative and superlative degrees of modifiers. Students should present their examples and identify the kinds of comparisons being made. Then have students create advertisements of their own for imaginary new products. Tell them to use every degree of comparative modifiers to extol their products' attributes.

Customize for
ESL Students

Have students use their notebooks or a log to record spoken comparisons they hear around them. Have them record these in two columns: one for correctly formed comparisons and one for comparisons they think are incorrect. Then, as a class or in small groups have students present their lists to decide which comparisons are correct and which should be corrected. Ask students to look specifically for unbalanced comparisons.

Integrating Writing Skills

Ask students to think of items that they can compare in twos and then in threes or more (for example, several buildings, cars, or films). Have them write an essay in which they compare two of the items and then compare one with all the rest. Encourage them to use comparative and superlative modifiers appropriately.

Critical Viewing

Compare and Contrast Sample response: Though the Sears Tower is the <u>tallest</u> building in the United States, we have a <u>shorter</u> building with a <u>more unusual</u> shape.

☑ **ONGOING ASSESSMENT: Monitor and Reinforce**

If students have difficulty with Exercise 11 or 12, refer them to the following for additional practice.

In the Textbook	Print Resources	Technology
Section Review, Ex. 17, Section 24.2	*Grammar Exercise Workbook,* pp. 111–112	*On-Line Exercise Bank,* Section 24.2

Logical Comparisons

1. Explain to students that a faulty comparison—that is, unbalanced or otherwise illogical—is often the result of incomplete or omitted ideas. Something must be added.

2. Have students read the example sentences aloud. For each, have students tell why the comparison is unbalanced. Ask students to identify what element or part of speech has been added to the correct examples.

3. For additional practice with unbalanced comparisons, have students reword the following:

   Feeding the monkeys is more fun than the alligators. (than feeding the alligators is)

   I like the television shows on Monday better than Tuesday. (better than I like those on Tuesday)

4. Have students explain the problem with each illogical comparison example. (The Grand Canyon is one of the parks visited, so it can't be compared to itself. If Corey is on the team, he can't run faster than himself.)

Integrating Viewing and Representing Skills

Ask students to keep a log with them as they watch television commercials for the next two or three days. Have them listen for comparisons—one product compared to another, for example. Students should note the comparisons they hear, and answer these questions: What things are being compared? What is the message, or point, of the comparison? Is the comparison fair or accurate? Why? How would you rewrite this comparison?

Have students present the comparisons to the class as well as their answers to the questions.

24.2

Logical Comparisons

In order to write logical comparisons, you must make sure that you do not unintentionally compare unrelated items or compare something with itself.

KEY CONCEPT Make sure that your sentences compare only items of a similar kind. ■

In the following unbalanced examples, the sentences illogically compare dissimilar things: *Message* cannot be compared with *postcard*, and *plants* in a greenhouse cannot be compared with an entire *greenhouse*.

UNBALANCED:	A *message* conveyed by telephone is more private than a *postcard*.
CORRECT:	A *message* conveyed by telephone is more private than *one* written on a postcard.
UNBALANCED:	The *plants* in this greenhouse are fresher than the *greenhouse* down the road.
BALANCED:	The *plants* in this greenhouse are fresher than *those* in the greenhouse down the road.

***Other* and *Else* in Comparisons** Another kind of illogical comparison results when something is unintentionally compared with itself.

KEY CONCEPT When comparing one of a group with the rest of the group, make sure that your sentence contains the word *other* or the word *else*. ■

In the first example below, the *Grand Canyon*, which is one of the national parks, cannot be compared with all national parks. Adding *other* excludes the Grand Canyon from the rest of the national parks. In the second example, *Corey* cannot be compared to all the members on the team because *Corey* is one of those people. Adding *else* separates *Corey* from the rest of the group.

ILLOGICAL:	We thought the Grand Canyon was *more beautiful than any* national park we visited.
LOGICAL:	We thought the Grand Canyon was *more beautiful than any other* national park we visited.
ILLOGICAL:	Corey runs *faster than anyone* on the team.
LOGICAL:	Corey runs *faster than anyone else* on the team.

630 • Using Modifiers

STANDARDIZED TEST PREPARATION WORKSHOP

Grammar and Usage Many standardized tests require students to recognize correct formations of comparisons within the context of a passage. Use the following example to demonstrate.

(1) Thursday evening's art exhibition drew record crowds. (2) On hand were dignitaries from at least five foreign countries. (3) More than anyone, the artist found herself astonished by the enthusiasm for her work.

How would you correct the underlined portion of sentence 3?

A More than anyone, the artist found him or herself

B More than anyone else, the artist found herself

C More than anyone the artist found herself

D Correct as is.

The correct answer is **B**. Sentence 3 creates an unbalanced comparison because the artist cannot be compared to anyone because she is part of that group. The word *else* clarifies the distinction between the artist and everyone else: She was *more* astonished.

> **Exercise 13** Making Balanced Comparisons Rewrite each sentence, correcting the unbalanced comparison.

EXAMPLE: Shelly's voice is better than Ted.
ANSWER: Shelly's voice is better than Ted's.

1. There are more floors in the Empire State Building than the Flatiron Building.
2. The shape of the Petronas Towers in Malaysia is different from the Empire State Building.
3. Skyscrapers are taller now than the beginning of the last century.
4. The tallest building in Paris is smaller than New York.
5. Building a skyscraper is harder than a house.

> **Exercise 14** Revising Sentences Using *Other* and *Else* in Comparisons Rewrite each sentence, correcting the illogical comparison.

1. The Petronas Towers in Kuala Lumpur are taller than almost any building.
2. Builders in California are more concerned about earth-quakes than builders anywhere in the United States.
3. The United States has more skyscrapers than any country.
4. Tall buildings were being built in the United States earlier than they were anywhere.
5. The Paris skyline is more beautiful than that of any city.
6. By the turn of the century, steel was more abundant than at any time.
7. Tokyo may have more plans for extremely high buildings than any city.
8. In 1990, Chicago had the tallest building of any city.
9. In 1913, the Woolworth Building was taller than any building.
10. Because of the large numbers of people living and working in skyscrapers, safety is more important than almost anything.

> **Exercise 15** Writing Sentences With Logical Comparisons
Write a sentence comparing the given items in a logical way.
1. skyscrapers of New York and Chicago
2. dogs and cats
3. inches and centimeters
4. your town with all others
5. chocolate with all other candy

> **More Practice**

Grammar Exercise Workbook
• pp. 113–114
On-line Exercise Bank
• Section 24.2
Go on-line:
PHSchool.com
Enter Web Code:
egk-1202

interactive Textbook

Complete the exercises on-line! Exercises 13, 14, and 15 are available on-line or on CD-ROM.

Clear Comparisons • 631

Answer Key

> **Exercise 13**
Allow some variation in wording.
1. There are more floors in the Empire State Building than there are in the Flatiron Building.
2. The shape of the Petronas Towers in Malaysia is different from that of the Empire State Building.
3. Skyscrapers are taller now than they were at the beginning of the last century.
4. The tallest building in Paris is smaller than the tallest building in New York.
5. Building a skyscraper is harder than building a house.

> **Exercise 14**
Allow some variation in wording.
1. The Petronas Towers in Kuala Lampur are taller than almost any other building.
2. Builders in California are more concerned about earthquakes than builders anywhere else in the United States.
3. The United States has more skyscrapers than any other country.
4. Tall buildings were being built in the United States sooner than they were anywhere else.
5. The Paris skyline is more beautiful than that of any other city.
6. By the turn of the century, steel was more abundant than at any other time.
7. Tokyo may have more plans for extremely high buildings than any other city.
8. In 1990, Chicago had the tallest building of any other city.
9. In 1913, the Woolworth Building was taller than any other building.
10. Because of the large numbers of people living and working in skyscrapers, safety is more important than almost anything else.

> **Exercise 15**
Answers will vary; samples are given.
1. The two highest skyscrapers in Chicago are higher than any in New York.
2. Dogs are more outgoing than cats.
3. Inches are longer than centimeters.
4. Our town has more public gardens than all other towns in the area.
5. I think chocolate is better tasting than all other candy.

☑ **ONGOING ASSESSMENT: Monitor and Reinforce**

If students have difficulty with Exercise 13, 14, or 15, refer them to the following for additional practice.

In the Textbook	Print Resources	Technology
Section Review, Ex. 18, Section 24.2	*Grammar Exercise Workbook,* pp. 113–114	*On-Line Exercise Bank,* Section 24.2

Absolute Modifiers

1. Absolute modifiers have only one form: positive. They should never be written as comparatives or superlatives.

2. Point out that an absolute describes something that cannot be more or less than it already is. It is for this reason that words like *more, most, less* and *least* cannot be added to them.

3. Clarify for students that absolute modifiers need not describe extreme conditions such as death or eternity. Modifiers such as *vertical* and *opposite* are also absolute, because they describe unchanging conditions.

4. Give students additional examples of absolutes such as *complete, correct, immortal,* and *pointless.* Have students form sentences using these.

Integrating Vocabulary Skills

Ask students to define *absolute* ("perfect, pure, or complete in quality or nature") and to look up the origin of the word (Latin: *absolvere*). Then, have students locate additional uses of the word (Example: absolute zero). Have students use the words and ideas associated with *absolute* to explain why this kind of modifier, paradoxically, should not be modified.

Answer Key

> **Exercise 16**

Allow some variation in response.

1. The top of the Sears Tower is better designed . . .
2. The Empire State Building was unusual when first built.
3. Its design is closer to the Chrysler Building's than to any other building's.
4. He was more affected by the view from the Eiffel Tower than . . .
5. For the greatest safety, tall . . .
6. The design of the Hancock Building in Boston is said by some to be more traditional . . .
7. The architectural plans for the new music center are further along than they were last month.
8. He is closer to finishing . . .
9. The view from the observation deck is the most expansive.
10. The houses of Frank Lloyd Wright are more elegant . . .

24.2

Absolute Modifiers

A few modifiers cannot be used in comparisons because they are *absolute* in meaning; that is, their meanings are entirely contained in the positive degree. If, for example, one vase is *priceless,* another vase cannot be *more priceless.*

▶ **KEY CONCEPT** Avoid using absolute modifiers illogically in comparisons. ■

Among the most common absolute modifiers are the words *dead, entirely, eternal, fatal, final, identical, infinite, mortal, opposite, perfect,* and *unique.* Rather than use words such as these in comparisons, try to find similar words whose meanings are not absolute.

ILLOGICAL:	This truth is *more eternal* than any other.
LOGICAL :	This truth is *more enduring* than any other.
ILLOGICAL:	Your thesis is *more unique* than anyone else's.
LOGICAL:	Your thesis is *more original* than anyone else's.

▶ **Exercise 16** Avoiding Absolute Modifiers in Comparisons

Rewrite each sentence, correcting the illogical comparison.

1. The top of the Sears Tower is more perfect than the top of the Empire State Building.
2. The Empire State Building was most unique when first built.
3. It is more identical to the Chrysler Building than to any other building.
4. He was more overwhelmed by the view from the Eiffel Tower than he was by the view from the Sears Tower.
5. For the most utmost in safety, tall buildings are required to have protected stairways as a means of escape.
6. The design of the Hancock Building in Boston is said by some to be more eternal than that of the Art Institute.
7. The architectural plans for the new music center are more final than they were last month.
8. He is more finished with the drawings of the building's facade than he was last week.
9. The view from the observation deck is the most infinite.
10. The houses of Frank Lloyd Wright are more immortal than any others.

632 • Using Modifiers

🔧 Grammar and Style Tip

An absolute modifier can never be more or less absolute than it is already. Never add the suffix *-er* or *-est* or the words *more* and *most* to words like *unique* or *impossible.*

▶ **More Practice**

Grammar Exercise Workbook
• pp. 115–116
On-line Exercise Bank
• Section 24.2
   Go on-line:
   PHSchool.com
   Enter Web Code:
   egk-1202

ⓘnteractive Textbook

Complete the exercise on-line! Exercise 16 is available on-line or on CD-ROM.

☑ **ONGOING ASSESSMENT: Monitor and Reinforce**

If students miss more than two items in Exercise 16, refer them to the following for additional practice.

In the Textbook	Print Resources	Technology
Section Review, Ex. 19, Section 24.2	*Grammar Exercise Workbook,* pp. 115–116	*On-Line Exercise Bank,* Section 24.2

Section 24.2 Section Review

GRAMMAR EXERCISES 17–22

Exercise 17 Supplying the Comparative and Superlative Degrees
Write the appropriate comparative or superlative degree of the modifier in parentheses.

1. Skyscrapers are subject to (some) rigorous building standards than smaller structures are.
2. Before the use of steel frames, buildings were (small) than they are now.
3. It seems as though there is a competition to see who can build the (high) building.
4. Is Hong Kong's Central Plaza (far) away than the Eiffel Tower?
5. I wonder which building receives the (some) visitors each year?

Exercise 18 Revising Sentences to Make Logical Comparisons Revise each sentence, correcting the illogical comparison.

1. Singapore's new bank building was completed sooner than Toronto.
2. It is harder to climb stairs than an escalator.
3. Do more people work at the Sears Tower than your office?
4. Are there more skyscrapers in New York than Paris?
5. The skyscrapers in New York are nearer than Tokyo.
6. Which building is taller than any?
7. Do more people go to the Sears Tower than anywhere in Chicago?
8. In 1930, the Empire State Building was taller than any building.
9. Is the Eiffel Tower taller than any Parisian structure?
10. He will design a larger building than anyone.

Exercise 19 Revising to Avoid Absolute Modifiers in Comparisons
Rewrite each sentence, correcting the illogical comparison.

1. Skyscrapers are the most eternal feature of a city's skyline.
2. Buildings are more infinitely higher today than they were in the 1930's.
3. Skyscrapers are given the most complete inspection before they open.
4. The skyscraper is the most unique form of architecture.
5. Use of substandard materials could be more fatal to a building's occupants.

Exercise 20 Find It in Your Reading Reread the passage from Robert Herrick's poem "To the Virgins, to Make Much of Time" on page 628. Identify the noun that each adjective modifies. Then, if the adjective is comparative, give its superlative form; if it is superlative, give its comparative form.

Exercise 21 Find It in Your Writing Review a story that you have written. Are comparative modifiers used correctly? Revise your work to add comparative modifiers.

Exercise 22 Writing Application Write a description of a fictional character from one of your reading assignments. Challenge yourself to use adjectives and adverbs logically and in every degree of comparison.

Section Review • 633

ASSESS and CLOSE

Section Review

Each of these exercises correlates to the instruction on clear comparisons, pages 628–632. The exercises may be used for more practice, for reteaching, or for review of the key concepts presented. Answers are available in *Grammar Exercises Answers on Transparencies* in your Teaching Resources.

Answer Key

Exercise 17

1. more
2. smaller
3. highest
4. farther
5. most

Exercise 18

Allow some variation in wording.

1. Singapore's new bank building was completed sooner than Toronto's.
2. It is harder to climb stairs than it is to use an escalator.
3. Do more people work at the Sears Tower than work in your office?
4. Are there more skyscrapers in New York than there are in Paris?
5. The skyscrapers in New York are nearer than those of Tokyo.
6. Which building is taller than any other?
7. Do more people go to the Sears Tower than to anywhere else in Chicago?
8. In 1930, the Empire State Building was taller than any other building.
9. Is the Eiffel Tower taller than any other Parisian structure?
10. He will design a larger building than anyone else.

Exercise 19

Allow some variation in wording.

1. Skyscrapers are the most enduring feature of a city's skyline.
2. Buildings are considerably higher today than they were in the 1930's.
3. Skyscrapers are given a complete inspection before they open.
4. The skyscraper is a very unusual form of architecture.
5. Use of substandard materials could be fatal to a building's occupants.
continued

Answer Key continued

Exercise 20

Find It in Your Reading

Noun: *age*, best (better); noun: *youth* and *blood*, warmer (warmest); noun: *times*, worse (worst) and worst (worse).

Exercise 21

Find It in Your Writing

Challenge students to check their use of comparative and absolute modifiers and add more examples of them.

Exercise 22

Writing Application

You might suggest that students compile a list of unlikely or comic modifiers (*wasp-waisted, sidewalk-oriented, less irascible, steel-belted*) and challenge a partner to use them in revising a character study or in composing a short story.

CHAPTER REVIEW

Each of these exercises correlates to a section of the chapter on using modifiers, pages 620–632. The exercises may be used for more practice, for reteaching, or for review of the key concepts presented. Answers for all chapter exercises are available in *Grammar Exercises Answers on Transparencies* in your Teaching Resources.

Answer Key

Exercise 23

1. comparative
2. positive
3. comparative
4. superlative
5. superlative

Exercise 24

1. more fearfully, most fearfully
2. more regular, most regular
3. more expensive, most expensive
4. more durable, most durable
5. more decisive, most decisive
6. uneasier, uneasiest
7. more dangerous, most dangerous
8. windier, windiest
9. more slyly, most slyly
10. more innovative, most innovative

Exercise 25

1. best
2. farther
3. further
4. worse
5. more
6. worse
7. worst
8. better
9. most
10. farther

Exercise 26

1. most
2. better
3. prettiest
4. cleaner
5. least
6. prouder
7. most
8. finest
9. later
10. older

Chapter
24 Chapter Review

GRAMMAR EXERCISES 23–30

Exercise 23 Recognizing Positive, Comparative, and Superlative Degrees
Identify the degree of each underlined modifier.

1. Elevators travel <u>faster</u> now than ever before.
2. They travel so fast it makes some people feel <u>ill</u>.
3. Other people are <u>more afraid</u> of the confined space.
4. This fear is <u>most commonly</u> known as claustrophobia.
5. There are people whose <u>greatest</u> fear is of heights.

Exercise 24 Forming Regular Comparative and Superlative Degrees
Write the comparative and superlative forms of each modifier.

1. fearfully
2. regular
3. expensive
4. durable
5. decisive
6. uneasy
7. dangerous
8. windy
9. slyly
10. innovative

Exercise 25 Forming Irregular Comparative and Superlative Degrees
Write the correct form of the underlined modifier to complete each sentence.

1. Masonry construction gives <u>good</u> support, but in comparison, a steel frame gives the ___?___ .
2. The Eiffel Tower is <u>far</u> away, but the Petronas Towers are even ___?___ .
3. High-rise building technology has advanced very <u>far</u>, and it appears it will go even ___?___ .
4. He felt <u>ill</u> in the elevator but ___?___ when he reached the top.

634 • Using Modifiers

5. There are <u>some</u> skyscrapers in Paris but ___?___ in New York.
6. Many Parisians feel <u>bad</u> about demolishing old buildings but even ___?___ about building skyscrapers.
7. Some say the tall buildings of Montparnasse are <u>bad</u>-looking, but others believe the Pompidou Center is the ___?___ -looking building in Paris.
8. Not all Parisians think <u>well</u> of the new tall buildings; they believe the city was ___?___ as it was.
9. The Sacre Coeur cathedral has <u>some</u> renown, but the ___?___ famous Paris landmark of all is the Eiffel Tower.
10. London is <u>far</u> away; is Paris even ___?___ ?

Exercise 26 Using the Comparative and Superlative Degrees Correctly Choose the correct comparative or superlative form in each sentence.

1. Which city has the (more/most) skyscrapers?
2. There are (better/best) construction methods today than there were in 1920.
3. Is Paris the (prettier/prettiest) city you have ever seen?
4. The buildings seem (cleaner/cleanest) there than anywhere else.
5. One of the city's (less/least) familiar ordinances requires regular cleaning of buildings.
6. Parisians are (prouder/proudest) of their city than inhabitants of almost any other city.
7. It has some of the (more/most) beautiful buildings in the world.
8. The Notre Dame cathedral is one of the (finer/finest) examples of French Gothic architecture.

☑ ONGOING ASSESSMENT SYSTEM: Assess Mastery

Use the following resources to assess student mastery of modifier usage.

In the Textbook	Print Resources	Technology
Chapter Review, Ex. 27–29 Standardized Test Preparation Workshop	*Formal Assessment*, Ch. 24	*On-Line Exercise Bank*, Chapter 24

9. The cornerstone was laid in 1163, and the building was finally completed more than 30 years (later/latest).

10. Notre Dame is (older/oldest) than another famous Parisian church: Sacre Coeur.

Exercise 27 Supplying the Comparative and Superlative Degrees Write the appropriate degree of the modifier in parentheses.

1. Skyscrapers rise to (great) heights now than ever before.
2. Some people think being on top of a skyscraper is the (scary) thing that could happen to them.
3. Phobias are usually (irrational) than other fears.
4. He is (afraid) of heights than of anything else.
5. Which do you think is (bad)—claustrophobia or acrophobia?
6. Doctors sometimes can help people handle their fears (well) than people can handle them by themselves.
7. What was the (bad) fright you have ever had?
8. Arachnophobia is my (big) fear.
9. There are probably (few) spiders on top of a skyscraper than there are on the ground.
10. She is (little) afraid of heights than he is.

Exercise 28 Revising Sentences to Make Comparisons Clear Revise each sentence, making sure that the comparisons are clear.

1. There are more tall buildings in London than Dublin.
2. London's skyscrapers are smaller than New York.
3. Do you like London better than anywhere?
4. Westminster Abbey is one of England's most perfect examples of Gothic architecture.
5. Is London larger than any city?

6. Its history is older than New York.
7. After World War II, the alteration of the London skyline was most permanent.
8. London lost more buildings to wartime damage than Paris.
9. It suffered more wartime damage than any English city.
10. There have been more monarchs crowned at Westminster Abbey than buried.

Exercise 29 Writing Sentences With Comparatives Write at least two comparative sentences for each set of facts.

1. Largest States:
   Texas, 261,914 square miles
   Alaska, 570,374 square miles
   California, 155,973 square miles
2. Smallest States:
   Rhode Island, 1,045 square miles
   Delaware, 1,982 square miles
   Connecticut, 4,845 square miles
3. Largest Cities:
   Los Angeles, CA, population: 3,485,398
   New York, NY, population: 7,322,564
   Chicago, IL, population: 2,783,726
4. Highest Recorded Temperatures:
   California, 134 degrees Fahrenheit
   Arizona, 128 degrees Fahrenheit
   Nevada, 125 degrees Fahrenheit
   New Mexico, 122 degrees Fahrenheit
5. Lowest Recorded Temperatures:
   Alaska, -80 degrees Fahrenheit
   Montana, -70 degrees Fahrenheit
   Utah, -69 degrees Fahrenheit

Exercise 30 Writing Application Write a brief comparison in which you compare an actor or actress with several others. Make sure that you use modifiers correctly.

Answer Key

Exercise 27

1. greater
2. scariest
3. more irrational
4. more afraid
5. worse
6. better
7. worst
8. biggest
9. fewer
10. less

Exercise 28

Answers will vary; samples are given.

1. There are more tall buildings in London than there are in Dublin.
2. London's skyscrapers are smaller than those in New York are.
3. Do you like London better than anywhere else?
4. Westminster Abbey is one of England's most inspiring examples of Gothic architecture.
5. Is London larger than any other city?
6. Its history is older than that of New York.
7. After World War II, the alteration of the London skyline was permanent.
8. London lost more buildings to wartime damage than Paris did.
9. It suffered more wartime damage than any other English city.
10. There have been more monarchs crowned at Westminster Abbey than have been buried there.

Exercise 29

Answers will vary; samples are given.

1. Texas is larger in area than California. Of the three states, Alaska has the largest area.
2. Connecticut has more square miles than Delaware or Rhode Island. Of the three states, Rhode Island has the fewest square miles.
3. Chicago has a smaller population than Los Angeles or New York. New York has the largest population of the three.
4. The highest temperature ever recorded in the United States was in California. This temperature was higher than the highest recorded temperatures in Nevada and Arizona.
5. The lowest temperature ever recorded in the United States was in Alaska. It was lower than the lowest temperatures recorded in Montana and Utah.

Exercise 30

Writing Application

Ask students to exchange papers with a partner, check for correct usage, and suggest additional comparisons.

1. To employ precise language to communicate ideas clearly and concisely
2. To demonstrate control over grammatical elements
3. To recognize appropriate English usage within the context of a written passage

Step-by-Step Teaching Guide

Standard English Usage: Modifiers

Teaching Resources: Standardized Test Preparation Workbook, pp. 47–48

1. Review with students that a modifier is an adjective or adverb, a word that makes another word's meaning more definite or clear. This lesson focuses on forms of modifiers that are used to compare two or more things or actions.

2. Go over the explanation of the use of the suffixes *-er* and *-est*. Remind students that when something is merely being described, not compared to anything else, neither suffix is necessary.

3. Review some irregular adjectives and adverbs (*bad-worse-worst; good-better-best*) and have students come up with sentences in which they are used correctly.

Standardized Test Preparation Workshop

Standard English Usage: Modifiers

Standardized test questions often measure your ability to use modifiers correctly. Use the following strategies to help you determine which form to use in a sentence:

- If no comparison is being made, use the positive form of the modifier.
- If one thing or action is compared to another thing or action, use the comparative form of the modifier—ending in *-er* or preceded by *more*.
- If one thing or action is being compared to more than one other thing or action, use the superlative form of the modifier—ending in *-est* or preceded by *most*.
- Be aware that some modifiers, such as *good, bad, much,* and *many*, have irregular forms.

Test Tip

Be careful not to choose a double comparison, such as *more easier*, to complete a sentence. The correct forms are *more easy* or *easier*.

Sample Test Items	Answers and Explanations

Directions: Read the passage, and choose the word or group of words that belongs in each space.
 	
Jamaica has always been one of the ___(1)___ tourist destinations in the Caribbean. True, the beaches are beautiful, but the ___(2)___ culture is also a main attraction.
 	
1 A popularest
   B popular
   C mostest popular
   D most popular
	The correct answer for item 1 is *D, most popular*. Because Jamaica is being compared to multiple tourist destinations, the superlative form should be used.

2 F diverser
   G most diverse
   H more diverse
   J diverse
	The correct answer for item 2 is *J, diverse*. Because no comparison is being made, the positive form of the modifier is used.

636 • Using Modifiers

🖊 TEST-TAKING TIP

Tell students that when they take a standardized test, they should eliminate immediately answers that are clearly wrong, such as double comparisons or inaccurate words. Point out some examples of these in Practices 1 and 2. A double comparison is *more better*; inaccurate words include *importantest* and *furthier*.

▶ **Practice 1** **Directions:** Read the passage, and choose the word or group of words that belongs in each space.

Jamaica has an abundant musical history, even compared to __(1)__ countries. Although some forms of music from the island are known __(2)__ than others, the __(3)__ known music is called reggae. Even people with the __(4)__ bit of knowledge about Jamaican music have heard of Bob Marley. Marley is considered one of the __(5)__ Jamaican musicians in the history of the island.

1 A many large
  B many larger
  C more large
  D largest

2 F good
  G better
  H best
  J more better

3 A good
  B better
  C best
  D more better

4 F less
  G little
  H least
  J littler

5 A most important
  B importantest
  C importanter
  D important

▶ **Practice 2** **Directions:** Read the passage, and choose the word or group of words that belongs in each space.

Jamaican music didn't begin with reggae. Nothing could be __(1)__ from the truth. There were __(2)__ forms of Jamaican music that influenced reggae. Mento, one of the first recorded Jamaican sounds, may be the __(3)__ of all of them. To an untrained ear, it resembles music from Trinidad called calypso. But mento was __(4)__ by Jamaican folk music than by calypso. Today, the popularity of Jamaican music is growing __(5)__ than ever.

1 A more far
  B furthest
  C further
  D furthier

2 F old
  G more old
  H older
  J more older

3 A least known
  B lesser known
  C lesser
  D least

4 F influenced
  G mostly influenced
  H most influenced
  J more influenced

5 A most fast
  B faster
  C fastest
  D more fast

Answer Key

▶ **Practice 1**
  1. B
  2. G
  3. C
  4. H
  5. A

▶ **Practice 2**
  1. C
  2. H
  3. A
  4. J
  5. B

Customize for
Less Advanced Students

Tell students to read the entire test passage before going back to complete the first sentence. If they have a clear idea of the main idea of the passage, the correct response also will be clearer. Be sure to test possible choices by reading the completed sentence silently once more.

Customize for
AP Students

Point out some words and phrases that signal comparisons, such as *than*, *one of the*, *compared to*, and *even*. Tell students to be aware of these words as they read in order to alert themselves to modifiers.

In-Depth Lesson Plan

	LESSON FOCUS	PRINT AND MEDIA RESOURCES
DAY 1	**Negative Sentences** Students learn to recognize double negatives, to properly form negatives, to use understatement, and do a Hands-on Grammar activity. (pp. 640–645/H472–477)	*Writing and Grammar* **Interactive Text,** Section 25.1; *On-line Exercise Bank,* Section 25.1 **Teaching Resources** *Grammar Exercise Workbook,* pp. 117–120; *Grammar Exercises Answers on Transparencies,* Ch. 25; *Hands-on Grammar Activity Book,* Ch. 25
DAY 2	**Common Usage Problems** Students learn to avoid common mistakes, such as nonstandard usage (e.g., *alright*) and easily confused words (e.g., *all together/ altogether*) and practice correct usage. (pp. 646–651/H478–483)	*Writing and Grammar* **Interactive Text,** Section 25.2; *On-line Exercise Bank,* Section 25.2 **Teaching Resources** *Grammar Exercise Workbook,* p. 121
DAY 3	**Common Usage Problems (continued)** Students learn to avoid common mistakes, such as nonstandard usage (e.g., *irregardless*) and easily confused words (e.g., *lie/lay*), and practice correct usage. (pp. 652–659/H484–491)	**Teaching Resources** *Grammar Exercise Workbook,* p. 122
DAY 4	**Review and Assess** Students review the chapter and demonstrate mastery of common usage problems. (pp. 660–661)	**Teaching Resources** *Formal Assessment,* Ch. 25

Accelerated Lesson Plan

	LESSON FOCUS	PRINT AND MEDIA RESOURCES
DAY 1	**Negative Sentences; Common Usage Problems** Students cover double negatives, properly formed negative sentences, understatement, and common usage problems. (pp. 638–651/H470–483)	*Writing and Grammar* **Interactive Text,** Sections 25.1–2; *On-line Exercise Bank,* Sections 25.1–2 **Teaching Resources** *Grammar Exercise Workbook,* pp. 117–122; *Grammar Exercises Answers on Transparencies,* Ch. 25
DAY 2	**Common Usage Problems (continued); Review and Assess** Students complete a study of common usage problems and then review the entire chapter and demonstrate mastery of concepts. (pp. 652–661/H484–491)	*Writing and Grammar* **Interactive Text,** Section 25.2; *On-line Exercise Bank,* Section 25.2 **Teaching Resources** *Grammar Exercise Workbook,* pp. 121–122; *Formal Assessment,* Ch. 25

Options for Adapting Lesson Plans

HOMEWORK

Have students complete any section of the chapter for homework.

FEATURES

Extend coverage with the Standardized Test Preparation Workshop (p. 662).

TECHNOLOGY

Students can use *Writing and Grammar* Interactive Text to complete the exercises interactively on computer. They can complete additional exercises in the *On-line Exercise Bank:* The Auto Check feature will grade their work. Go on-line: PHSchool.com Use Web Code: egk-1202

Writing and Grammar Handbook Alignment

Page numbers in Step-by-Step Teaching Guides in this Teacher's Edition refer to pages from the full student text. Handbook page references, indicated with this icon 🄷, are provided in Time and Resource Manager boxes and at the bottom of each Teacher's Edition page.

INTEGRATED SKILLS COVERAGE

Writing
Find It in Your Writing, SE pp. 644, 645, 659/🄷476, 477, 491
Writing Application, SE pp. 645, 659, 661/🄷477, 491
Grammar and Style, SE p. 643/🄷475
Integrating Writing Skills, ATE p. 657

Vocabulary
ATE p. 648

Spelling
SE pp. 640, 656/🄷472, 488; ATE p. 643

Viewing and Representing
Critical Viewing, SE pp. 638, 641, 642, 647, 649, 650, 652, 655, 658/🄷470, 473, 474, 479, 481, 482, 484, 487, 490; ATE p. 652

Technology
SE pp. 641, 648, 652/🄷473, 480, 484

Real-World Connection
ATE p. 652

ASSESSMENT SUPPORT

Standardized Test Preparation Workshop, SE p. 662; ATE pp. 644, 650

Standardized Test Preparation Workbook, pp. 49–50

Formal Assessment, Ch. 25

MEETING INDIVIDUAL NEEDS

Less Advanced Students ATE pp. 641, 647, 651, 663. See also Ongoing Assessments ATE pp. 641, 642, 643, 647, 649, 651, 653, 655, 658

AP Students ATE pp. 646, 663

ESL Students ATE pp. 641, 647

Logical/Mathematical Learners ATE p. 648

BLOCK SCHEDULING

Pacing Suggestions
For 90-minute Blocks
• Administer the Diagnostic Test to students to determine instructional coverage.
• Have students complete the necessary exercises in class. Use the Hands-on Grammar activity to provide a change of pace.

Resources for Varying Instruction
• *Writing and Grammar* Interactive Text A 90-minute block provides an ideal opportunity for students to work on the computer.

Professional Development Support
• *How to Manage Instruction in the Block* This teaching resource provides management and activity suggestions.

MEDIA AND TECHNOLOGY

For the Student
• *Writing and Grammar* Interactive Text, Ch. 25
• *On-line Exercise Bank,* Sections 25.1–2

For the Teacher
• Teacher EXPRESS™ CD-ROM

WRITING AND GRAMMAR ON-LINE

Interactive Text (On-line or on CD-ROM)
• Easily navigable instruction with on-line supporting resources
• Self-scoring exercises and diagnostic tests

Companion Web Site PHSchool.com
• On-line Exercise Bank (use Web Code egk-1202)

See the Go On-line! feature, SE p. iii.

▶ **Lesson Objectives**

1. To recognize double negatives and to form negative sentences correctly

2. To identify and use negatives for expressing understatement

3. To recognize and avoid common usage problems with troublesome words and expressions

4. To demonstate control over grammatical elements

5. To evaluate how well writing achieves its purposes

6. To analyze the characteristics of clear texts such as conciseness, correctness, and completeness

Critical Viewing

Analyze Sample response: One *effect* the moon has on some people is to make them feel romantic.

Chapter 25 Miscellaneous Problems in Usage

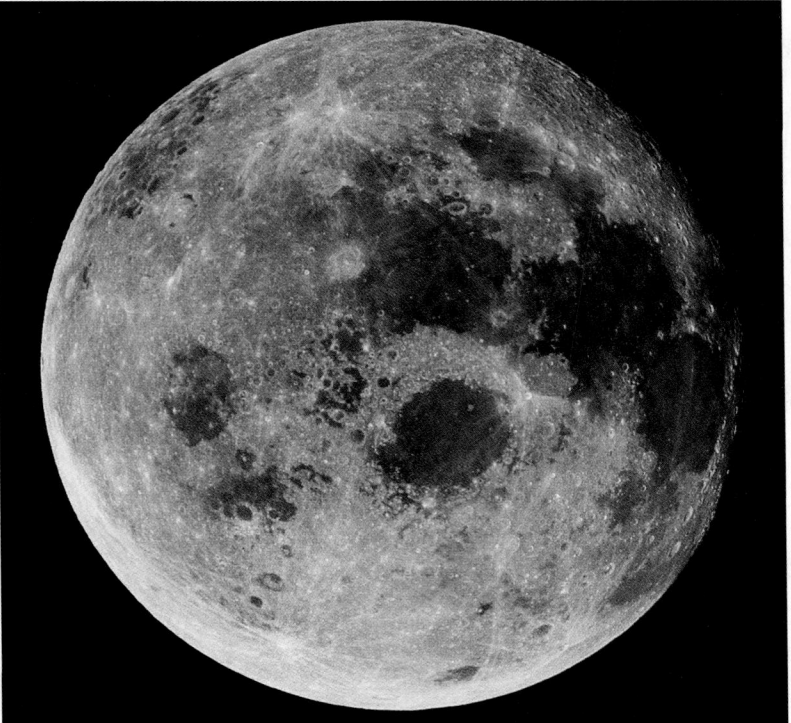

For centuries, the moon's luminous presence in the night sky has fascinated Earth's inhabitants and encouraged the study of our nearest neighbor. Today, we have developed technology that has allowed us to learn much about the moon. Just as we have striven to bring the moon into focus, we must strive to bring clarity and precision to our writing.

Many small problems that can spoil the clarity of speaking or writing do not fall into any of the broad categories of usage that were covered in preceding chapters. Some of these problems involve distinctions between standard and nonstandard usage. Others involve similar spellings or meanings. The next two sections will help you improve your mastery of certain details that contribute to effective speaking and writing.

▲ **Critical Viewing** Write a sentence explaining how the moon influences some people's behavior. Use either *affect* or *effect* correctly in your sentence. **[Analyze]**

638 • Miscellaneous Problems in Usage

☑ ONGOING ASSESSMENT: Diagnose

If students miss more than one item in any category, direct them to the relevant pages of the textbook and assign exercises for practice and review.

Miscellaneous Problems in Usage	Diagnostic Test Items	Teach	Practice	Section Review	Chapter Review
Skill Check A					
Avoiding Double Negatives	A 1–5	pp. 640–641 ⊞472–473	Ex. 1–3	Ex. 6–7	Ex. 24–26
Skill Check B					
Recognizing Understatement	B 6–10	p. 643/⊞475	Ex. 4–5		Ex. 27

Diagnostic Test

Directions: Write all answers on a separate sheet of paper.

Skill Check A. Choose the word in parentheses that best completes each sentence.

1. Because early civilizations didn't know (nothing, anything) about the moon, they devised their own theories.
2. Without a single visit to the moon, they hadn't (no, any) facts.
3. The absence of facts, however, (won't, will) hardly stop people from devising explanations for the unknown.
4. There (is, isn't) no end to people's fascination with the moon.
5. These days, astronauts can visit the moon, but they can't stay for (any, no) length of time.

Skill Check B. Indicate whether or not each of these sentences uses understatement.

6. Once, people thought the shapes on the surface of the moon looked like cheese.
7. That's not to say that there weren't other explanations for the shapes.
8. Some people thought creatures lived on the moon.
9. They didn't believe there wasn't anybody else in the universe.
10. It seems there wasn't anyone who didn't have some theory.

Skill Check C. Choose the word in parentheses that correctly completes each sentence.

11. Sometimes, people's beliefs about the moon (affected, effected) the way they lived their lives.
12. Myths about the moon are (a, an) universal tie among cultures.
13. Some people tried to (adapt, adopt) their theories to fit the scientific facts they learned.
14. Philosophers and kings also stated (they're, their) theories.
15. Musicians have been fascinated with the moon, (too, to).
16. There is agreement (among, between) music lovers that "Blue Moon" is one of the best songs written about the moon.
17. (Beside, Besides) inspiring songs, the moon has also motivated writers to compose stories and poems.
18. Since the first person landed on the moon in 1969, scientists have made (further, farther) discoveries.
19. Scientists in many nations often share information with (each other, one another).
20. With today's technology, scientists (may, can) communicate more easily than ever before.
21. Someday, space travel may (bring, take) tourists to the moon.
22. Plans for lunar vacations will most likely take (awhile, a while).
23. After all, the moon is much (farther, further) than any earthly holiday spot.
24. New studies about the moon (proceed, precede) at a steady rate.
25. Many of us are (all ready, already) for a trip to the moon!

Diagnostic Test

Each item in the Diagnostic Test corresponds to a section in the miscellaneous problems in usage chapter. This will enable you to tailor instruction to the particular needs of your students. See "Ongoing Assessment: Diagnose" below for further details.

Skill Check A

1. anything	4. is
2. any	5. any
3. will	

Skill Check B

6. does not use understatement
7. does use understatement
8. does not
9. does
10. does

Skill Check C

11. affected	19. one another
12. a	20. can
13. adapt	21. take
14. their	22. awhile
15. too	23. farther
16. among	24. proceed
17. Besides	25. all ready
18. further	

✓ ONGOING ASSESSMENT: Diagnose *continued*

Miscellaneous Problems in Usage	Diagnostic Test Items	Teach	Practice	Section Review	Chapter Review
Skill Check C					
Avoiding Common Usage Problems 1–20	C 11–13, 16, 22, 25	pp. 646–649/ Ⓗ478–481	Ex. 11–12	Ex. 18–20	
Avoiding Common Usage Problems 21–40	C 17–21, 23	pp. 650–653/ Ⓗ482–485	Ex. 13–14	Ex. 19–20	Ex. 28–30
Avoiding Common Usage Problems 41–60	C 14–15, 24	pp. 654–657/ Ⓗ486–489	Ex. 15–17	Ex. 19–20	
Cumulative Reviews and Applications				Ex. 8–10, 21–23	Ex. 31

⏱ TIME SAVERS!

📄 **Answers on Transparencies** Use the *Grammar Exercises Answers on Transparencies* for Chapter 25 to facilitate correction by students.

🖥 **On-Line Exercise Bank** Have students complete the Diagnostic Test on computer. The Auto Check feature will grade their work for you!

PREPARE and ENGAGE

 Interest GRABBER Write on the board:

We don't need no education.

Ask if anyone is familiar with this line from an old rock song. Explain that this song became almost an anthem for young people in the 1980's, and ask what is ironic about it (if you use double negatives, you probably do need an education). Ask students for other nonstandard rock lyrics.

Activate Prior Knowledge

Have students mention words and phrases they use to indicate that an idea is not true. List some of the negative words you hear (*no, not, don't, isn't*) and then ask students to use them in making the following sentences into truthful statements.

We visited Mars last week.

All our classrooms are on the moon.

I have been to Saturn.

TEACH

Step-by-Step Teaching Guide

Negative Sentences

1. Remind students that there are other words besides *not* and *never* that are negative. Have them list negative forms of *everybody* (nobody), *anything* (nothing), *any* (no), and *either* (neither). Point out the similarities that these negatives share (the *n*).

2. Write the following on the board: *The sun, which hasn't been seen in days, didn't shine this morning either.* Have students point out the negative words *(hadn't, didn't)* and ask them to explain why this sentence is correct (there are two clauses; each is negative in itself).

continued

Answer Key

> **Exercise 1**

1. any   4. is
2. is   5. can
3. can

Negative Sentences

In today's English, a clause usually needs just one negative word to convey a negative idea. More than one negative word can be redundant and confusing.

Recognizing Double Negatives

A clause containing two negative words when only one is needed is said to contain a *double negative.*

▶ **KEY CONCEPT** Do not write sentences with double negatives. ■

The following chart provides examples of double negatives and the two ways of correcting each double negative.

CORRECTING DOUBLE NEGATIVES	
Double Negatives	**Corrections**
The moon *doesn't never* produce its own light.	The moon *never* produces its own light. The moon *doesn't ever* produce its own light.
You *can't* grow *nothing* on the moon.	You *can't* grow *anything* on the moon. You can grow *nothing* on the moon.
I *didn't* know *nothing* about the moon.	I knew *nothing* about the moon. I *didn't* know *anything* about the moon.

Sentences containing more than one clause can correctly contain more than one negative word. Each clause, however, should contain no more than one negative word.

EXAMPLE: Because the moon *doesn't* revolve around the sun, it *isn't* considered a planet.

▶ **Exercise 1** Avoiding Double Negatives Choose the word in parentheses that makes each sentence negative without forming a double negative.
1. There aren't (no, any) life forms on the moon.
2. The atmosphere (isn't, is) no good for Earth organisms.
3. Nobody (can't, can) breathe on the moon.
4. There (is, isn't) no free-moving water there.
5. Nothing (can, can't) live on the moon.

Theme: The Moon

In this section, you will learn the proper way to write sentences that express negatives. The examples and exercises are about the moon.

Cross-Curricular Connection: Science

🖋 Spelling Tip

Most helping verbs can be made negative by adding *n't*, but watch out for some exceptions, such as *am, may, might, shall,* and *will.*

▶ **More Practice**

Grammar Exercise Workbook
• pp. 117–118
On-line Exercise Bank
• Section 25.1
Go on-line:
PHSchool.com
Enter Web Code:
egk-1202

⏱ TIME AND RESOURCE MANAGER

Resources
Print: *Grammar Exercise Workbook,* pp. 117–120; *Grammar Exercises Answers on Transparencies,* Ch. 25
Technology: *Writing and Grammar* Interactive Text, Section 25.1; *On-Line Exercise Bank,* Section 25.1

Using the Full Student Edition	Using the HandbookⒽ
• Work through all key concepts, pp. 640–643.	• Work through all key concepts, pp. 472–475.
• Assign and review Exercises 1–5.	• Assign and review Exercises 1–5.
• Assign the Hands-on Grammar activity, p. 644.	• Assign the Hands-on Grammar activity, p. 476.

Forming Negative Sentences Correctly

A negative sentence can be formed correctly in one of three ways:

Using One Negative Word The most common way to form a negative sentence is to use a single negative word, such as *never, no, nobody, nothing, nowhere, not,* or the contraction *n't* added to a helping verb.

▶ **KEY CONCEPT** Do not use two negative words in the same clause. ■

DOUBLE NEGATIVE:	The moon *doesn't* have *no* satellites of its own.
CORRECT:	The moon has *no* satellites of its own. The moon *doesn't* have any satellites of its own.

Using *But* in a Negative Sense *But* used negatively means *only* and should not be used with another negative word.

▶ **KEY CONCEPT** Do not use *but* in its negative sense with another negative. ■

DOUBLE NEGATIVE:	Earth hasn't but one moon.
CORRECT:	The Earth has *but* one moon. The Earth has *only* one moon.

Using *Barely, Hardly,* and *Scarcely* Each of these words also makes a sentence negative.

▶ **KEY CONCEPT** Do not use *barely, hardly,* or *scarcely* with another negative. ■

DOUBLE NEGATIVE:	We *haven't barely* begun our hands-on study of the moon.
CORRECT:	We have *barely* begun our hands-on study of the moon.
DOUBLE NEGATIVE:	The moon *isn't hardly* as big as the sun.
CORRECT:	The moon is *hardly* as big as the sun.
DOUBLE NEGATIVE:	Earth *hasn't scarcely* as many moons as Jupiter.
CORRECT:	Earth has *scarcely* as many moons as Jupiter.

💿 Technology Tip

In formal writing, it is better to write out the negative than to use a contraction. On your computer, use the search feature to find *n't* and change it to *not.* Be careful with the words *can't* and *won't.*

▼ **Critical Viewing**
Write two sentences about the moon in this picture, using *isn't* in one sentence and *doesn't* in the other. Watch out for double negatives. **[Analyze]**

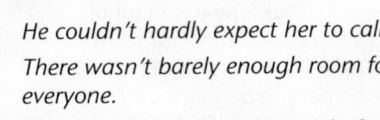
Negative Sentences • 641

Customize for *ESL Students*

Some students may need practice recognizing that certain contractions contain negative words. Give them a list of very brief sentences such as the following.

She will not sing.

They were not happy.

Did you not hear me?

First have students circle the negative word in each sentence, and then ask them to form a contraction for each sentence. Write the contraction alongside the sentence, and then have students rewrite the sentence using the contraction. Point out that each sentence remains negative, but the negative word now is part of a contraction.

Customize for *Less Advanced Students*

Because *hardly* and *barely* look different from other negative words, students may need special drill with them. The use of expressions like *can't hardly wait* or *isn't barely enough* are common errors. Give students sentences like the following to correct:

He couldn't hardly expect her to call.

There wasn't barely enough room for everyone.

Ask students to make up several of their own sentences using *hardly* and *barely* correctly.

Critical Viewing

Analyze Sample response: The moon *doesn't* usually seem as big as it is in this picture. It *isn't* quite so noticeable from Earth.

☑ **ONGOING ASSESSMENT SYSTEM: Monitor and Reinforce**

If students miss more than one item in Exercise 1, refer them to the following for additional practice.

In the Textbook	Print Resources	Technology
Section Review, Ex. 6, Section 25.1	*Grammar Exercise Workbook,* pp. 117–118	*On-Line Exercise Bank,* Section 25.1

Answer Key

> **Exercise 2**

Answers will vary; samples are given.

1. I can see but half of the moon.
2. Nobody can see well in this fog.
3. It doesn't look anything like my drawings.
4. I can barely make out the craters.
5. It isn't devoid of land forms.
6. Some don't appear anywhere but in space.
7. Craters are but the most numerous features.
8. They don't appear to the unaided eye.
9. Such craters are scarcely found on Earth.
10. There aren't any seas on the moon.

> **Exercise 3**

Answers may vary slightly.

1. There is no celestial body
2. nobody knew anything concrete
3. People didn't have any idea
4. early humans couldn't get anywhere
5. couldn't see anything except
6. observers had but a telescope
7. No one had any idea
8. photographs hardly stopped
9. could scarcely stop for directions
10. was but the first extraterrestrial body

Language Highlight

The restriction against double negatives is one more example of a grammatical rule that has changed during the history of the English language. Double negatives were quite acceptable during the period of the English Renaissance; you can find them in Shakespeare. Double negatives were thought to make the negative more emphatic. It was only when people began to follow the mathematical dictum that two negatives make a positive that correct usage began to change.

Critical Viewing

Connect Sample response: The Earth has barely risen above the horizon.

25.1

> **Exercise 2** Correcting Double Negatives Eliminate the error in each of the following phrases, and expand the corrected phrase into a sentence of your own.
>   1. can't see but half
>   2. nobody can't see
>   3. doesn't look nothing like
>   4. can't barely make out
>   5. isn't hardly devoid
>   6. don't appear nowhere
>   7. aren't but the most numerous
>   8. don't hardly appear
>   9. aren't scarcely found
>   10. aren't no seas

> **Exercise 3** Revising Sentences to Avoid Double Negatives Revise each of the sentences, eliminating any problems with negatives.
>   1. There isn't no celestial body closer to Earth than the moon.
>   2. At first, nobody knew nothing concrete about the moon.
>   3. People didn't have no idea how to get there.
>   4. With only primitive technology, early humans couldn't get nowhere close to it.
>   5. Ancient admirers of the moon couldn't see nothing except what they could see with their eyes.
>   6. Renaissance observers hadn't but a telescope to aid them.
>   7. No one had no idea what to expect when the manned spacecraft went to the moon.
>   8. The first close-range photographs didn't hardly stop further lunar exploration.
>   9. Once airborne, the first astronauts to land on the moon couldn't scarcely stop for directions.
>   10. The moon wasn't but the first extraterrestrial body visited by humans.

▼ **Critical Viewing** Write a sentence describing how the Earth seems from the moon. Use the word *hardly* or *barely* in your sentence without creating a double negative. **[Connect]**

☑ ONGOING ASSESSMENT SYSTEM: Monitor and Reinforce

If students miss more than two items in Exercise 2 or 3, refer them to the following for additional practice.

In the Textbook	Print Resources	Technology
Section Review, Ex. 6–7, Section 25.1	*Grammar Exercise Workbook*, pp. 117–118	*On-Line Exercise Bank*, Section 25.1

Using Understatement

Occasionally, a speaker or writer may want to imply a positive idea without actually stating it. This indirect method is called *understatement*. Understatement may be used to minimize the importance of an idea or, conversely, to emphasize its importance.

▶ **KEY CONCEPT** Understatement can be achieved by using a negative word and a word with a negative prefix. ■

EXAMPLES: The study of the moon is *hardly* an *uninteresting* subject.
The moon's light *isn't* completely *unromantic*.

▶ **Exercise 4** Revising Sentences to Create Understatement
Rewrite each sentence so that it achieves understatement.
1. The phases of the moon are interesting.
2. The sliver after a new moon is recognizable.
3. The waxing of the moon from new to full is graceful.
4. The light of the full moon is inviting.
5. Many people who are intelligent have lost their hearts in the light of the full moon.
6. They find their love is requited.
7. A blue moon, the second full moon in one calendar month, seldom occurs.
8. A harvest moon rises soon after sunset and is appreciated by farmers.
9. They are pleased with the extra hours of light.
10. The waning of the moon can be a sad occasion.

▶ **Exercise 5** Writing Negative Sentences Use each item in a negative sentence of your own. Proofread carefully to make sure you have not created a double negative.
1. hardly deserved
2. no one had walked
3. wasn't upsetting
4. never wore
5. can't carry
6. barely finished
7. but one choice
8. scarcely upset
9. nobody can imagine
10. never cared

⚙ Grammar and Style Tip

You can use negatives to add emphasis to an idea by accomplishing the opposite of understatement. For example, "She is definitely *not* a friend of mine."

▶ **More Practice**

Grammar Exercise Workbook
• pp. 119–120
On-line Exercise Bank
• Section 25.1
 Go on-line:
 PHSchool.com
 Enter Web Code:
 egk-1202

Interactive Textbook

Complete the exercises on-line! Exercises 2, 3, 4, and 5 are available on-line or on CD-ROM.

✓ ONGOING ASSESSMENT SYSTEM: Monitor and Reinforce

If students miss more than two items in Exercise 4 or 5, refer them to the following for additional practice.

In the Textbook	Print Resources	Technology
Chapter Review, Ex. 27	*Grammar Exercise Workbook,* pp. 119–120	*On-Line Exercise Bank,* Section 25.1

Understatement

1. Tell students that they will most often encounter understatement in formal speech and writing. It is an interesting device but may lose its effectiveness if overused.
2. Point out that understatement works best in clauses or sentences containing a linking verb. Present these examples:

   Diving is exciting.

   Diving is hardly unexciting.

   The food seemed tasty.

   The food seemed not untasty.

3. Ask students to suggest three or four positive sentences. Write them on the board and, as a class, recast them with understatement.

Integrating Spelling Skills

Prefixes Prefixes like *dis-, in-, un-,* and *ir-* may be added to words to mean "not." Point out that the spelling of the word root does not change when these prefixes are added. Have students correctly spell *dissimilar, unnecessary,* and *irresponsible.*

Answer Key

▶ **Exercise 4**

Wording may vary slightly.
1. are never uninteresting
2. isn't unrecognizable
3. is hardly ungraceful
4. is never uninviting
5. who are not unintelligent
6. is hardly unrequited
7. comes not frequently
8. is not unappreciated by farmers
9. They are hardly displeased
10. can hardly be a happy

▶ **Exercise 5**

Answers will vary; samples are given.
1. My reward was hardly deserved.
2. No one had walked on the path.
3. The news wasn't upsetting.
4. I never wore outfits like that.
5. I can't carry such a big box.
6. I am barely finished with the job.
7. He had but one choice to make.
8. I was scarcely upset by my loss.
9. Nobody can imagine my sorrow.
10. I never cared about the results.

Hands-on Grammar

Teaching Resources: Hands-on Grammar Activity Book, Ch. 25

1. If you wish to do this activity in class, be prepared with scissors and index cards. Each student can create his or her own puzzle.

2. Go through the directions and the samples with the whole class. Then have students cut up and label their own cards.

3. If students need more work with negative sentences, present several examples, some containing double negatives. Have students use their puzzle pieces to decide which sentences need correction.

Find It in Your Reading

For this activity, have students work with their partners to go through the stories or articles, or ask each student to find the negative words independently and then discuss them with a partner.

Find It in Your Writing

Have students work individually with sentences from their own writing. They can then share the results with their partners.

25.1

Hands-on Grammar

Unpuzzling Double Negatives

When you want to convey a negative idea, you should use only one negative adverb in a clause. Putting two negative words together leads to a confusing error called a *double negative*. To help you remember which words you can and cannot put together in a clause, try the following activity:

Make several squares out of paper or index cards. Cut each square into two interlocking L shapes (see diagram).

On the left *L*, write a negative word or a verb connected to a negative word (*hardly, doesn't, wasn't*). On the right (upside down) *L*, write a positive word that creates a phrase with the negative word (*any, anybody, ever*). Flip each square over. This time, write a positive word or verb on the left (*has, almost, was*) and a negative word on the right to create a phrase (*no, nobody, never*).

Mix and match the negative and positive L's. If you try to put two negatives together, you will not be able to complete the puzzle and form a square.

Put your puzzles into an envelope, and store them in your notebook. You can refer to the puzzles to help you avoid forming double negatives in your writing.

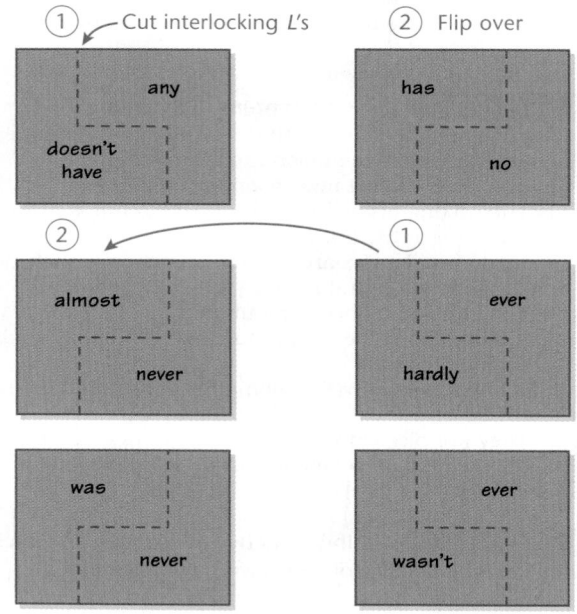

Find It in Your Reading Search a short story, newspaper article, or textbook chapter for negative words. Use your puzzle pieces to explore which words can and can't be used with the negative word. Discuss with a partner how each of the words you can use might affect the meaning of the sentence in which the negative word was originally used.

Find It in Your Writing Choose a piece of writing from your portfolio. Proofread it for double negatives. Identify any negative words you have used correctly.

644 • Miscellaneous Problems in Usage

⟨✎⟩ STANDARDIZED TEST PREPARATION WORKSHOP

Grammar and Usage Many standardized tests require students to correct double negatives in a passage. Use the following to demonstrate.

Because Mars has an atmosphere incapable of supporting human life, <u>humans can't never expect to live there</u> without bringing oxygen with them.

How would you correct the underlined portion of this sentence?

A humans couldn't never expect to live there

B humans can't ever expect to live there

C no humans can never expect to live there

D Correct as is

The correct answer is **B** because it contains only one negative word. The underlined portion and options A and C contain double negatives.

✋ **Hands-on Grammar**
Use the Hands-on Grammar activity sheet for Chapter 25 to facilitate this activity.

Section 25.1 Section Review

GRAMMAR EXERCISES 6–10

> **Exercise 6** Proofreading to Avoid Double Negatives Rewrite any sentence that contains a double negative. If a sentence is correct, write *correct*.

1. A complete eclipse isn't hardly a common experience.
2. There aren't but two kinds of eclipses involving Earth and the moon.
3. A lunar eclipse can't occur if the moon isn't completely in Earth's shadow.
4. If the moon is nowhere near Earth's shadow, it won't be obscured.
5. Lunar eclipses don't never occur when the moon isn't anywhere near the umbra.
6. Yes, a complete lunar eclipse doesn't last but two hours.
7. The sun is so bright it seems as if nothing couldn't block out its light.
8. The moon doesn't scarcely seem big enough for the job.
9. You shouldn't watch any solar eclipses without protective eyewear.
10. Eclipses aren't hardly random occurrences.

> **Exercise 7** Revising to Eliminate Double Negatives Revise each sentence to eliminate the double negatives.

1. There aren't but two types of tide that occur daily: high tide and low tide.
2. The flow of Earth's tides isn't never left to its own devices.
3. They don't never occur without a little help from the moon and the sun.
4. The sun isn't nowhere near as close to Earth as the moon is.
5. Therefore, the sun's gravitational pull isn't scarcely as strong as the moon's.
6. Ordinarily, high tide isn't never as high as at spring tide, when the moon, sun, and Earth form a straight line and the moon and sun work together on the tides.

7. When the moon and sun form right angles with Earth, there aren't no spring tides.
8. During those neap tides, high tide isn't hardly considered all that high.
9. There aren't but two high tides and two low tides a day.
10. Nothing else doesn't consistently exert such powers on Earth's tides.

> **Exercise 8** Find It in Your Reading Read the following excerpt from "We'll Never Conquer Space" by Arthur C. Clarke. Identify the negative word in the sentence. Then, identify the word that should be changed to a negative word if the original negative word were replaced with *a*.

> . . . For it seems as certain as anything can be that no signal—still less any material object—can ever travel faster than light.

> **Exercise 9** Find It in Your Writing Choose a piece of persuasive writing from your portfolio. Identify the negative sentences you have used. If you cannot find examples, add a sentence to elaborate on your position or show your opposition.

> **Exercise 10** Writing Application Use each item in a correctly worded negative sentence of your own.

1. couldn't ask
2. was hardly ready
3. had but one reason
4. could never go
5. hadn't any

Section Review • 645

✓ ONGOING ASSESSMENT: Assess Mastery

Use the following resources to assess student mastery of negative sentences.

In the Textbook	Technology
Chapter Review, Ex. 24–27	*Writing and Grammar* Interactive Text, Section 25.1, Section Review; *On-Line Exercise Bank*, Section 25.1

Common Usage Problems

Interest GRABBER Write this sentence on the board, and challenge students to find the errors in it. Tell them that there are six.

After awhile, we three decided between ourselves that we were already to except the full affects of they're harsh criticism.

(Answer: *After <u>a while</u>, we three decided <u>among</u> ourselves that we were <u>all ready</u> to <u>accept</u> the full <u>effects</u> of <u>their</u> harsh criticism.*)

Activate Prior Knowledge

Ask students to think of as many word pairs as they can that cause confusion in meaning (*accept/except, all ready/already, precede/proceed, principal/principle,* and *than/then* are possibilities). Then have volunteers use all words correctly in sentences.

TEACH

Step-by-Step Teaching Guide

Common Usage Problems 1–10

1. Ask students to note the parts of speech of *accept* (verb) and *except* (preposition). Ask them to use both words correctly in one sentence. *(He accepted all the requests except the last one.)*

2. To simplify usage of *affect* and *effect*, tell students not to be concerned with *effect* as a verb, as they will rarely use it this way. For all practical purposes, they can simply remember that *effect* is a noun and *affect* is a verb.

continued

Customize for
AP Students

Many forms in this section, such as *ain't*, are unacceptable today but were not always so. Have students search for other forms that have fallen out of grammatical favor or popular use. (Examples: *whence, thee, thou, amongst, betwixt*) Have students find why this change has happened or suggest their own reasons. Based on their research, ask them to predict what forms in use today may not survive one hundred years from now.

---

(1) a, an The article *a* is used before consonant sounds; *an,* before vowel sounds. Words beginning with *h, o,* or *u* may have either a consonant sound or a vowel sound.

EXAMPLES: a *h*ighwayman (*h* sound)
                a *o*ne-day excursion (*w* sound)
                a *u*tensil (*y* sound)
                an *h*onest peddler (no *h* sound)
                an *o*men (*o* sound)
                an *u*rchin (*u* sound)

(2) accept, except *Accept,* a verb, means "to receive." *Except,* a preposition, means "leaving out" or "other than."

VERB: I *accept* your offer to teach me about archaic careers.

PREPOSITION: All the apprentices, *except* the youngest, learned the new techniques.

(3) adapt, adopt *Adapt,* a verb, means "to change." *Adopt,* also a verb, means "to take as one's own."

EXAMPLES: Some craftsmen *adapt* new technologies to produce old-looking items.
                Purists prefer to *adopt* the old methods instead.

(4) affect, effect *Affect* is almost always a verb meaning "to influence." *Effect,* usually a noun, means "result." Occasionally, *effect* is a verb meaning "to bring about" or "to cause."

EXAMPLES: The success of a country's privateers could *affect* the outcome of a war.
                He suffered no ill *effects* from traveling.
                The Declaration of Paris *effected* a change in the status of privateers.

(5) aggravate *Aggravate* means "to make worse." Avoid using this word to mean "to annoy."

LESS ACCEPTABLE: The success of the privateers *aggravated* their enemies.

PREFERRED: Their successes *aggravated* the strained relationship.

(6) ain't *Ain't,* originally a contraction of *am not,* is no longer considered acceptable standard English.

NONSTANDARD: Privateers who work for the government *ain't* pirates.

CORRECT: Privateers who work for the government *aren't* pirates.

⏱ TIME AND RESOURCE MANAGER

Resources
Print: *Grammar Exercise Workbook,* pp. 121–122; *Grammar Exercises Answers on Transparencies,* Ch. 25
Technology: *Writing and Grammar* Interactive Text, Section 25.2; *On-Line Exercise Bank,* Section 25.2

Using the Full Student Edition	Using the Handbook Ⓗ
• Work through all key concepts, pp. 646–657. • Assign and review Exercises 11–17.	• Work through all key concepts, pp. 478–489. • Assign and review Exercises 11–17.

(7) all ready, already *All ready* is an expression that functions as an adjective and means "ready." *Already* is an adverb meaning "by or before this time" or "even now."

ADJECTIVE: Many sea captains were *all ready* to try their fortunes as pirates.

ADVERB: Many privateers were *already* pirates when their sovereigns granted them legitimacy.

(8) all right, alright *Alright* is a nonstandard spelling.

NONSTANDARD: The escapades of Sir Francis Drake were *alright* with his sovereign, Queen Elizabeth I.

CORRECT: The escapades of Sir Francis Drake were *all right* with his sovereign, Queen Elizabeth I.

(9) all together, altogether *All together* means "all at once." *Altogether* means "completely" or "in all."

EXAMPLES: The crew decided to mutiny *all together*.
The captain was *altogether* mistaken.

(10) among, between *Among* and *between* are both prepositions. *Among* always implies three or more. *Between* is generally used with just two items.

EXAMPLES: There is a code *among* pirates and privateers.
The pay rate for each voyage was determined *between* the crew's leader and the captain.

▼ **Critical Viewing**
If you were writing about preparing to board this ship, would you use *all ready* or *already* in your sentence? **[Distinguish]**

▶ **Exercise 11** Avoiding Usage Problems Choose the word or expression that most correctly completes each sentence.
1. The sailor (ain't, hasn't) come home since last winter.
2. He knew what (effect, affect) his absence would have.
3. His wife has (all ready, already) prepared for a reunion.
4. Howard considered himself (an, a) honorable peddler.
5. Sometimes, his customers would not (accept, except) his prices.
6. It (aggravated, annoyed) him to lose money.
7. He was good at (adapting, adopting) to the moods around him.
8. Do you feel (all right, alright)?
9. The sailor left the ship (altogether, all together).
10. The three men shared the costs (among, between) them.

▶ **More Practice**

Grammar Exercise Workbook
• pp. 121–122
On-line Exercise Bank
• Section 25.2
  Go on-line:
  PHSchool.com
  Enter Web Code:
  egk-1202

Common Usage Problems • **647**

3. Suggest that when differentiating between *all ready* and *already* and *all together* and *altogether*, students should say the terms aloud. If they pause slightly after *all*, then they probably need the two-word form.

Customize for
Less Advanced Students

Many usage problems arise with similar words that are different parts of speech. Have students write columns on their papers for various parts of speech. Then have them place words such as *affect* and *effect* in the appropriate columns, along with original example sentences for each. Students can add to this chart as you work through the chapter.

Customize for
ESL Students

Some students may have difficulty remembering the many subtleties among words that sound and look alike. Choose word pairs that you think students will use most often (*accept/except, all right/alright* and later, *their/there/they're* and *to/too/two*), and concentrate efforts on these. Have students first work independently, writing a brief definition plus two or three original sentences for each word in a pair. Then have them test each other: Student A can read each sentence aloud to Student B, who writes it and checks with Student A to see if it is the correct spelling, and vice versa.

Answer Key

▶ **Exercise 11**

1. hasn't	6. annoyed
2. effect	7. adapting
3. already	8. all right
4. an	9. altogether
5. accept	10. among

Critical Viewing

Distinguish Possible sentences: We are *all ready* to board. I have *already* packed my trunk.

ONGOING ASSESSMENT: Monitor and Reinforce

If students miss more than two items in Exercise 11, refer them to the following for additional practice.

In the Textbook	Print Resources	Technology
Section Review, Ex. 18–20, Section 25.2	*Grammar Exercise Workbook,* pp. 121–122	*On-Line Exercise Bank,* Section 25.2

Common Usage Problems 11–20

1. Explain that some dictionaries will list *eager* as a synonym for *anxious*; however, *anxious* has a negative connotation. It is derived from the Latin word *angere*, meaning "to choke, give pain."

2. One test that might help students distinguish between *anyone* and *any one* and *everyone* and *every one* is to say the term aloud. If they pause slightly after *any* or *every*, then they probably need the two-word form.

3. An easy way to remember not to use forms like *anywheres* and *somewheres* is to recall that these indicate place and so are adverbs. Adverbs are never plural; hence no -s should be used with them.

continued

Integrating Vocabulary

Learning New Words Study of common usage problems can easily lead to vocabulary development. As you introduce certain usage problems, look for opportunities to expand students' vocabularies. For the word *aggravate*, for instance (see page 646), tell students they can find numerous synonyms that might better fit certain contexts: *intensify*, *exacerbate*, and *foment* are just a few. For *anxious*, they can try *fearful*, *troubled*, *apprehensive*. Encourage students to use their dictionaries and a thesaurus to find new words as they work through this section.

Customize for
Logical/Mathematical Learners

Have students keep track of usage errors they hear during the course of a week or two, and tell them to track in a log the number of times they hear each. Then, have students tally the frequency of the errors they hear and prepare charts, or lists, that dramatize error frequency in some way. One suggestion might be that students compute the percentage of incorrect usage for each error (based on the total they find). Suggest publishing this information for the school. (Note: Making this assignment due toward the end of the semester provides an opportunity to review for a term exam.)

25.2

(11) anxious *Anxious* means "worried," "uneasy," or "fearful." Do not use it as a substitute for *eager*.

AMBIGUOUS: Privateers were *anxious* to make their fortune.
CLEAR: Privateers were *eager* to make their fortune.
             Privateers were always *anxious* about safety.

(12) anyone, any one, everyone, every one *Anyone* and *everyone* mean "any person" and "every person." *Any one* means "any single person (or thing)," and *every one* means "every single person (or thing)."

EXAMPLES: *Anyone* could become a pirate.
             Any one of those pirates could be a privateer.

(13) anyway, anywhere, everywhere, nowhere, somewhere These adverbs should never end in -s.

NONSTANDARD: Merchants learned that they weren't safe *anywheres* on the high seas.
CORRECT: Merchants learned that they weren't safe *anywhere* on the high seas.

(14) as Do not use this conjunction to mean "because" or "since."

LESS ACCEPTABLE: Privateering grew *as* each European country wanted control.
PREFERRED: Privateering grew *because* each European country wanted control.

(15) as to *As to* is awkward. Replace it with *about*.

NONSTANDARD: There are many theories *as to* why people turned to piracy.
CORRECT: There are many theories *about* why people turned to piracy.

(16) at Do not use *at* after *where*. Simply eliminate *at*.

NONSTANDARD: Only he knows *where* the plunder is hidden *at*.
CORRECT: Only he knows *where* the plunder is hidden.

(17) at about Avoid using *at* with *about*. Simply eliminate *at* or *about*.

LESS ACCEPTABLE: The golden age of European piracy was over *at about* the end of the 1720's.
PREFERRED: The golden age of European piracy was over *at* the end of the 1720's. (or *by*)

648 • Miscellaneous Problems in Usage

⊛ Technology Tip

Keep a list of words you sometimes misuse. When you work in a word-processing program, do a search for each word on your list. Correct any misuses. Soon, you will start to notice the problem words as you are using them and can correct yourself while drafting.

(18) awful, awfully *Awful* is used informally to mean "extremely bad." *Awfully* is used informally to mean "very." Both modifiers are overused and should be replaced with more descriptive words. In formal writing, *awful* should be used only to mean "inspiring fear."

INFORMAL:	The Spanish fleet suffered many *awful* losses to the British privateers.
BETTER:	The Spanish fleet suffered many *catastrophic* losses to the British privateers.
INFORMAL:	Pirates are depicted as *awfully* fierce.
BETTER:	Pirates are depicted as *savage* and *bloodthirsty*.
FORMAL:	Many feared the great pirates because of their *awful* reputations.

(19) awhile, a while *Awhile* is an adverb that means "for a short time." *A while* (an article and a noun) means "a period of time." The term is usually used after the preposition *for*.

ADVERB:	A sea voyage could last *awhile*.
NOUN:	The ship docked in port for *a while*.

(20) beat, win *Win* means "to achieve victory in." *Beat* means "to overcome (an opponent)." Do not use *win* in place of *beat*.

NONSTANDARD:	The captain *won* the boatswain playing checkers.
CORRECT:	The captain *beat* the boatswain playing checkers.

▶ **Exercise 12** Avoiding Usage Problems Choose the correct expression to complete each sentence.
1. Lighthouses were built (somewhere, somewheres) on the coast to guide ships around rough spots.
2. There are several theories (as to, about) the history of lighthouse use.
3. She was (eager, anxious) to take over duties as a lighthouse keeper when her father was away.
4. (Everyone, Every one) of the lighthouses sends out its own light patterns to help ships identify their locations.
5. (As, Because) the light is not visible during the day, lighthouses are painted bright colors and patterns.
6. Do you know where the lighthouse (is, is at)?
7. Most lighthouses were automated (at about, by) the 1970's.
8. A lighthouse keeper's job can be (awfully, extremely) lonely.
9. You might not see another person for (a while, awhile).
10. He (won, beat) the loneliness by listening to music.

▼ **Critical Viewing** Make two statements expressing whether or not you would like to live in a lighthouse. In the first statement, use *a while*. In the second statement, use *awhile*. **[Distinguish]**

4. Ask students to think of more descriptive words to use in place of *awful* and *awfully* (for example, *extreme, tragic, worrisome, terribly*). Have them practice using these in sentences so that they get out of the habit of overusing *awful* and *awfully*.

5. Explain that *a while* and *awhile* mean the same thing; the choice of which to use is based solely on its position in a sentence. Write on the board: *After waiting in line for a while, we lingered awhile in the store.* Have students tell why the two different spellings were used.

Answer Key

▶ **Exercise 12**

1. somewhere
2. about
3. eager
4. Every one
5. Because
6. is
7. by
8. extremely
9. a while
10. beat

Critical Viewing

Distinguish Sample response: I would like to live in a lighthouse for *a while*. My enthusiasm might last *awhile*, but then it would probably wane.

☑ **ONGOING ASSESSMENT: Monitor and Reinforce**

If students miss more than two items in Exercise 12, refer them to the following for additional practice.

In the Textbook	Print Resources	Technology
Section Review, Ex. 19–20, Section 25.2	*Grammar Exercise Workbook*, pp. 121–122	*On-Line Exercise Bank*, Section 25.2

⏱ **TIME SAVERS!**

🎞 **Answers on Transparencies** Use the *Grammar Exercises Answers on Transparencies* for Chapter 25 to facilitate correction by students.

💻 **On-Line Exercise Bank** Have students complete the exercises on computer. The Auto Check feature will grade their work for you!

Common Usage Problems 21–30

1. Explain to students that the definition of *because* is "for the reason that." Therefore, it should not be used with the word *reason* to avoid redundancy. Insert *for the reason that* in the place of *because* in the nonstandard example to demonstrate the error.

2. Point out that the expressions *being that* and *being as* are considered *colloquialisms* (forms of expression used in familiar talk). Though acceptable in certain informal speaking situations, they should not be used in writing.

3. Use the words *in* and *away* to help students remember that *bring* contains *in* and means "incoming," while *take* has an *a* like the word *away*. Then, write on the board the following: *Mary will ___ me with her to South America. She will ___ me back home again afterwards.* Ask students to supply the right words and explain how they chose.

4. Read aloud these questions that are commonly heard in the classroom: *Can I get a drink of water? Can I use the rest room? Can I have an extension on my paper?* Explain that while this usage of *can* in the sense of "have permission to" is common in speech, it should be avoided in writing.

continued

Critical Viewing

Analyze Sample response: One *reason* wearing armor might be uncomfortable is that it must get very hot inside.

25.2

(21) because Do not use *because* after *the reason*. Say "The reason is . . . that" or reword the sentence.

NONSTANDARD: *The reason* privateers disappeared is *because* the countries at war signed a treaty.

CORRECT: *The reason* privateers disappeared is *that* the countries at war signed a treaty.
Privateers disappeared *because* the countries at war signed a treaty.

(22) being as, being that Avoid using either expression. Use *because* instead.

NONSTANDARD: *Being that* (or *as*) books today are mass produced, there is no longer a need for scribes.

CORRECT: *Because* books today are mass produced, there is no longer a need for scribes.

(23) beside, besides As prepositions, these two words have different meanings and cannot be interchanged. *Beside* means "at the side of" or "close to." *Besides* means "in addition to."

EXAMPLES: Illuminations appear *beside* the text.
Besides using colored paints, illuminators also used precious metals, such as gold leaf.

(24) bring, take *Bring* means "to carry from a distant place to a nearer one." *Take* means the opposite: "to carry from a near place to a more distant place."

EXAMPLES: Would you *bring* me the illuminated book?
Take the book back to the illuminator.

(25) can, may Use *can* to mean "to have the ability to." Use *may* to mean "to have permission to" or "to be possible or likely to."

ABILITY: Economics often dictates whether buyers *can* afford illuminations in their manuscripts.
PERMISSION: You *may* borrow the book.
POSSIBILITY: They *may* decide to have the manuscript illuminated at a much later date, when fortunes allow.

(26) clipped words Avoid using clipped or shortened words, such as *gym*, *phone*, and *photo*, in formal writing.

INFORMAL: *Photos* and drawings have replaced illuminations in today's books.
FORMAL: *Photographs* and drawings have replaced illuminations in today's books.

▼ **Critical Viewing** Present one reason why it might be uncomfortable to wear armor. Use either *reason* or *because* in your explanation. **[Analyze]**

650 • Miscellaneous Problems in Usage

✎ STANDARDIZED TEST PREPARATION WORKSHOP

Grammar and Usage Many standardized tests require students to correct errors in a passage. Use the following to demonstrate.

Mrs. Harris wants us students to do more work. She don't think we done enough exercises.

What is the correct way to write the second sentence?

A She don't think we have did enough exercises.

B She doesn't think we have done enough exercises.

C She doesn't think we done enough exercises.

D Correct as is.

The correct answer is **B**. The third person singular pronoun, *she*, agrees with *doesn't* in the present, and the past participle *done* should follow a helping verb such as *have*.

(27) different from, different than *Different from* is preferred.

LESS ACCEPTABLE: Illuminations are *different than* illustrations in their techniques and materials.

PREFERRED: Illuminations are *different from* illustrations in their techniques and materials.

(28) doesn't, don't Do not use *don't* with third-person singular subjects. Use *doesn't* instead.

NONSTANDARD: A scribe *don't* need to provide illuminations.

CORRECT: A scribe *doesn't* need to provide illuminations.

(29) done *Done* is the past participle of the verb *do*. It should always follow a helping verb.

NONSTANDARD: Monastic illuminators always *done* their work in complete silence.

CORRECT: Monastic illuminators *have* always *done* their work in complete silence.

(30) due to *Due to* means "caused by" and should be used only when the words *caused by* can logically be substituted.

NONSTANDARD: The manuscript survives today *due to* its expensive illumination.

CORRECT: *Due to* the invention of the printing press, books became widely available.

▶ **Exercise 13** Recognizing Standard Usage For each pair of sentences, write the letter of the one that follows the conventions of standard English. Copy the other sentence on a separate sheet of paper, correcting the usage error.

1. (a) The first knights were not socially superior because anyone could become a knight.
   (b) The reason knighthood came to signify a noble class is because the costs of knighthood became steep.
2. (a) Beside learning the code of behavior, a knight learned how to handle small arms.
   (b) Beside the castle was a cluster of smaller buildings.
3. (a) Being as a squire was of inferior rank, he performed many tasks for the knight he served.
   (b) A squire would bring a knight his meals.
4. (a) Gaffers, or glass blowers, can make almost any shape out of glass.
   (b) Can I borrow your book?
5. (a) In the Middle Ages, the fine, thin glass of Italy was different from the heavier, darker northern glass.
   (b) Glass blowers always done their work with great care.

▶ **More Practice**

Grammar Exercise Workbook
• pp. 121–122
On-line Exercise Bank
• Section 25.2
 Go on-line:
 PHSchool.com
 Enter Web Code:
 egk-1202

Interactive Textbook

Get instant feedback! Exercise 13 is available on-line or on CD-ROM.

5. Explain that *different than* followed by an object is common in speech but should be avoided in formal writing. *Different than* is correct, however, in clauses showing comparison. Write on the board: *My answer was different from Sarah's* and point out that *Sarah's* is the object of a preposition. Then write *My answer was better than Sarah's* and point out that *than* introduces an elliptical adverb clause (*than Sarah's was*).

Customize for
Less Advanced Students

Expressions like *he don't* and *I done it* are common among speakers of nonstandard English. Provide extra practice by asking students to find and correct any errors in the following sentences. Provide additional sentences as needed.

He done all his homework before dinner. (did)

He doesn't want to stay home tonight. (correct)

Don't she know any better? (Doesn't)

Answer Key

▶ **Exercise 13**

1. (a); The reason . . . is that
2. (b); Besides learning the code
3. (b); Since a squire was
4. (a); May I borrow
5. (a); Glass blowers have always done

☑ **ONGOING ASSESSMENT: Monitor and Reinforce**

If students miss more than one item in Exercise 13, refer them to the following for additional practice.

In the Textbook	Print Resources	Technology
Section Review, Ex. 19–20, Section 25.2	*Grammar Exercise Workbook*, pp. 121–122	*On-Line Exercise Bank*, Section 25.2

🕐 **TIME SAVERS!**

Answers on Transparencies Use the *Grammar Exercises Answers on Transparencies* for Chapter 25 to facilitate correction by students.

On-Line Exercise Bank Have students complete the exercises on computer. The Auto Check feature will grade their work for you!

Common Usage Problems 31–40

1. Explain that *farther* has the root word *far* and that that is a clue for remembering that it refers only to distance. *Further* refers to extent, though sometimes in informal speech it is also used to refer to distance.

2. Using *less* for *fewer* is a common error. Give students practice recognizing items that can be counted (concrete nouns, like *feet* and *hours*) and those that cannot be (nouns that name ideas, like *courage* and *time*). Write on the board the following: *The Cowardly Lion had less courage than Dorothy, who had fewer feet than Toto.* Ask students if the words *less* and *fewer* are used correctly and why.

continued

Critical Viewing

Distinguish Students would use *fewer* in the sentence.

Integrating Viewing and Representing Skills

Have students monitor television programs for a week to detect usage errors. Ask them to write down the errors that they hear and to keep track of their frequency. When the week is up, have students report their findings to the class. Discuss why such errors are allowed to slip by in the media.

Real-World Connection

Although many of the usage items on these pages are acceptable in informal or everyday speech, remind students that they are not acceptable in formal situations. Certain jobs—teacher, editor, writer, proofreader—require thorough knowledge of grammar. Additionally, in many other professions one careless mistake in an interview, job application, or letter could reduce one's chances of getting hired. Discuss usage errors that first-time job applicants might make.

25.2

(31) each other, one another *Each other* and *one another* are usually interchangeable. At times, however, *each other* is more logically used in reference to only two; *one another*, in reference to more than two.

EXAMPLES: They must work with *each other* (or *one another*).
The scribe and the illuminator respected *each other*'s tasks.
Illuminators often shared *one another*'s exemplars for specific texts.

(32) farther, further *Farther* refers to distance. *Further* means "additional" or "to a greater degree or extent."

EXAMPLES: Illuminators discovered how to make some objects appear *farther* away than others.
They made *further* discoveries and invented new perspectives in painting.

(33) fewer, less Use *fewer* with things that can be counted. Use *less* with qualities and quantities that cannot be counted.

EXAMPLES: *fewer* commissions, *fewer* colors, *fewer* artisans
less blue paint, *less* need, *less* experience

(34) get, got, gotten These forms of the verb *get* are acceptable in standard English, but whenever possible, it is best to find a more specific word.

INFORMAL: *get* an exemplar, *got* a commission, to have *gotten* payment

BETTER: *obtain* an exemplar, *received* a commission, to have *earned* payment

(35) gone, went *Gone* is the past participle of *go* and should be used only with a helping verb. *Went* is the past tense of *go* and is never used with a helping verb.

NONSTANDARD: He *gone* to London to learn from a master illuminator.
He *could have went* to any major city.

CORRECT: He *has gone* to London to learn from a master illuminator.
He *went* to London to learn from a master illuminator.
He *could have gone* to any major city.

▲ **Critical Viewing**
If you wanted to note that not as many people can understand Latin today as in the past, would you use *fewer* or *less* in your sentence? **[Distinguish]**

⊚ **Technology Tip**

When you're in a word-processing application and want to find a more specific word to replace *get*, highlight the word and then click on the thesaurus feature.

(36) good, lovely, nice Whenever possible, replace these weak and overused words with a more specific adjective.

WEAK: *good* description, *lovely* painting, *nice* taste
BETTER: *clear* description, *exotic* painting, *refined* taste

(37) in, into *In* refers to position. *Into* suggests motion.

POSITION: How many illuminations are *in* the typical prayerbook?
MOTION: How many illuminations did an artist put *into* the typical prayerbook?

(38) irregardless Avoid this word. Use *regardless*.

(39) kind of, sort of Do not use *kind of* or *sort of* to mean "rather" or "somewhat."

(40) lay, lie *Lay* means "to put or set (something) down." Its principal parts—*lay, laying, laid,* and *laid*—are usually followed by a direct object. *Lie* means "to recline." Its principal parts—*lie, lying, lay,* and *lain*—are never followed by a direct object.

LAY: *Lay* your tools on the table.
        They *are laying* their tools down for the evening.
        He *laid* the manuscript in its carrying pouch.
        She had *laid* the book away for safe keeping.
LIE: The monks may *lie* down for their evening's rest.
        The exemplars are *lying* on the desk over there.
        The monk *lay* down after a difficult day of close handwork.
        The old manuscript has *lain* in our attic for decades.

> **Exercise 14** **Revising to Eliminate Usage Problems** Write each sentence on a separate sheet of paper. Revise to eliminate any usage problems, informal usage, or overused words. If a sentence is correct, write *correct as is.*

1. A cooper and a blacksmith must work with one another to produce barrels.
2. Barrels were needed to store a ship's provisions. They were further necessary for containing the whale oil.
3. Because the barrels were made before the voyage began, a cooper had less steps to assemble them.
4. Highwaymen got money from travelers.
5. Good stories about highwaymen survive today.
6. The character Robin Hood appeared into several movies.
7. Many people consider Robin Hood to be heroic.
8. Irregardless of his motives, he was in the eyes of the sheriff a criminal.
9. It seems as if he could never lay down and take a rest.
10. I gone to the library to find that book.

3. Ask students what each of these sentences means literally:

> *Helen walked in the ocean.* (Helen walked while she was in the water.)
>
> *Helen walked into the ocean.* (Helen moved from shore into the water.)

Have students explain the difference between *in* and *into*; then give them another pair to complete:

> *I put the cash ___ my pocket.* (into)
>
> *The cash is ___ my pocket. (in)*

Have students explain why they chose the prepositions they did.

Answer Key

> **Exercise 14**

Expect varying responses for some items.

1. must work with each other
2. correct as is
3. a cooper had fewer steps
4. Highwaymen stole money
5. Exciting stories
6. appeared in several movies
7. correct as is
8. Regardless of
9. he could never lie down
10. I went

☑ ONGOING ASSESSMENT: Monitor and Reinforce

If students miss more than two items in Exercise 14, refer them to the following for additional practice.

In the Textbook	Print Resources	Technology
Section Review, Ex. 19–20, Section 25.2	*Grammar Exercise Workbook,* pp. 121–122	*On-Line Exercise Bank,* Section 25.2

Common Usage Problems 41–50

1. To help students distinguish between *learn* and *teach*, explain that no one can "learn" anyone how to do anything.

2. Ask students to identify the part of speech of all possible uses of the word *like* (adjective, adverb, noun, preposition, verb). Point out that *like* and *as* both can be used as prepositions, but remind students that *like* is never a subordinating conjunction. This means it is not interchangeable with *as* when *as* introduces an elliptical or adverb clause.

3. Point out that *should've* sounds a lot like *should of*. However, the word *of* should never follow helping verbs. The correct replacement is *have*.

continued

25.2

(41) learn, teach *Learn* means "to acquire knowledge." *Teach* means "to give knowledge to."

EXAMPLES: It is difficult to *learn* that skill.
Originally, a master craftsman would *teach* you.

(42) leave, let *Leave* means "to allow to remain." *Let* means "to permit."

NONSTANDARD: *Leave* it go!
CORRECT: *Let* it go!

(43) like *Like* is a preposition and should not be used in place of the conjunction *as* to join two clauses.

NONSTANDARD: A smart apprentice was valued *like* a prized possession is valued.
CORRECT: A smart apprentice was valued *as* a prized possession is valued.
A smart apprentice was valued *like* a prized possession.

(44) loose, lose *Loose* is usually an adjective or part of such idioms as *cut loose*, *turn loose*, or *break loose*. *Lose* is always a verb, generally meaning "to miss from one's possession."

EXAMPLES: The ropemaker cut *loose* the excess hemp.
An artisan did not want to *lose* a good apprentice.

(45) maybe, may be *Maybe* is an adverb meaning "perhaps." *May be* is a helping verb and a verb.

ADVERB: *Maybe* this apprentice will be promoted to journeyman.
VERB: Choosing an apprentice *may be* a personal matter.

(46) of Do not use *of* after a helping verb such as *should*, *would*, *could*, or *must*. Use *have* instead. Do not use *of* after *outside*, *inside*, *off*, and *atop*. Simply eliminate it.

NONSTANDARD: By now, he should *of* known the proper steps for making a barrel.
CORRECT: By now, he should *have* known the proper steps for making a barrel.

(47) OK, O.K., okay In informal writing, *OK*, *O.K.*, and *okay* are acceptably used to mean "all right." Do not use either the abbreviations or *okay* in formal writing, however.

INFORMAL: The Romans thought gladiator competitions were *okay*.
FORMAL: The Romans thought gladiator competitions were acceptable forms of entertainment.

654 • Miscellaneous Problems in Usage

More Practice

Grammar Exercise
Workbook
• pp. 121–122
On-line Exercise Bank
• Section 25.2
Go on-line:
PHSchool.com
Enter Web Code:
egk-1202

(48) only *Only* should be placed in front of the word it logically modifies.

EXAMPLES: *Only* they used nets as weapons. (No one else used a net as a weapon.)
They used *only* nets and a small trident as weapons. (They used no other weapons.)

(49) ought Never use *ought* with *have* or *had*. Simply eliminate *have* or *had*.

NONSTANDARD: Some think that chivalry *had ought* to be practiced today.

CORRECT: Some think that chivalry *ought* to be practiced today.

(50) outside of Do not use this expression to mean "besides" or "except."

NONSTANDARD: No one remembers the names of any gladiators *outside of* Spartacus.

CORRECT: No one remembers the names of any gladiators *except* Spartacus.

> **Exercise 15** **Revising Sentences to Eliminate Usage Problems** Write each sentence on a separate sheet of paper. Revise to eliminate any usage problems, informal usage, or overused words. If a sentence is correct, write *correct as is.*
> 1. In the past, blacksmiths must of enjoyed respect.
> 2. Jim's parents think he maybe good at metalworking.
> 3. Jim was learned the skills by a master.
> 4. The shop becomes hot like a sauna.
> 5. The instructor wouldn't let Jim try to shape a horseshoe.
> 6. When he banged it with a hammer, it was so lose it fell.
> 7. The king thought the jester's performance was witty.
> 8. He only felt the jester lacked a costume.
> 9. He had ought to be better prepared.
> 10. No one outside of the jester could have spoken to the king in such a way.

▼ **Critical Viewing** Write a sentence discussing something a blacksmith ought to know. Consult usage problem 49 (ought) before you write your sentence. **[Make a Judgment]**

Common Usage Problems • 655

Common Usage Problems
51–60

1. Remind students that English is a derivative language and that words from other languages sometimes follow different rules (the rules of their source languages) in forming plurals. Have students use a dictionary to find the plurals of words like *alumnus (alumni)* and *thesis (theses)*.

2. Write on the board: *I was preceded by the guide as we proceeded deeper into the forest.* Ask students to supply definitions of the verbs *precede* and *proceed*. Point out that the prefix *pre-* means "before"; recalling the meaning of *pre-* can help students remember the definition of *precede*.

3. Explain that substituting *then* for *than* is a common writing error, usually caused by carelessness, and that students should check their written work for it. Remind them that *than* is often used if a comparison is being made.

continued

25.2

(51) plurals that do not end in -s The plurals of certain nouns from Greek and Latin are formed as they were in their original language. Words such as *criteria, media,* and *phenomena* are plural and should not be treated as if they were singular (*criterion, medium, phenomenon*).

INCORRECT: The modern *media* has romanticized the story of Spartacus.

CORRECT: The modern *media* have romanticized the story of Spartacus.

(52) precede, proceed *Precede* means "to go before." *Proceed* means "to move or go forward."

EXAMPLES: The gladiator had been trained carefully *preceding* his first fight.
His victory means that he can *proceed* to the next contest.

(53) principal, principle As an adjective, *principal* means "most important" or "chief." As a noun, it means "a person who has controlling authority." *Principle,* always a noun, means "a fundamental law."

ADJECTIVE: The *principal* goal of a gladiator was to stay alive.
NOUN: The *principal* of the gladiator school was responsible for the fighters' physical health.
NOUN: Fighting was not against the Romans' *principles.*

(54) real *Real* means "authentic." The use of *real* to mean "very" or "really" should be avoided in formal writing.

INFORMAL: The crowd was *real* disappointed with the outcome.
FORMAL: The crowd was *sorely* disappointed with the outcome.

(55) says *Says* should not be used as a substitute for *said.*

NONSTANDARD: Afterward, the emperor *says* to the crowd, "Let the games begin!"
CORRECT: Afterward, the emperor *said* to the crowd, "Let the games begin!"

(56) than, then *Than* is used in comparisons. Do not confuse it with the adverb *then,* which usually refers to time.

EXAMPLES: He is stronger *than* his opponent.
First, he learned to handle a sword; *then,* he began to compete.

 **Spelling Tip**

When trying to decide which word you need, remember this useful hint: *Principal* is spelled p-a-l; the princi*pal* of your school can be a "pal."

656 • Miscellaneous Problems in Usage

(57) that, which, who *That* and *which* refer to things; *who* refers to people.

EXAMPLES: He dropped the sword *that* was his only weapon.
Spartacus was a slave *who* incited a rebellion of gladiators.
The rebellion, *which* ended in defeat for Spartacus, lasted for two years.

(58) their, there, they're *Their*, a possessive pronoun, always modifies a noun. *There* can be used either as an expletive at the beginning of a sentence or as an adverb. *They're* is a contraction for *they are*.

PRONOUN: Spectators in the Colosseum cheered for *their* favorite gladiators.

EXPLETIVE: *There* is no doubt who is the winner.

ADVERB: *There* are the winners in that large open area.

CONTRACTION: *They're* waiting for their next competitions to begin.

(59) to, too, two *To*, a preposition, begins a prepositional phrase. It may also be connected to a verb to form an infinitive. *Too*, an adverb, modifies verbs, adjectives, or other adverbs. *Two* is a number and can be used as an adjective or a noun.

PREPOSITION: *to* the Colosseum, *to* the school

INFINITIVE: *to* fight, *to* win

ADVERB: *too* slowly, *too* sweet

NUMBER: *two* blows, *two* victories

(60) when, where Do not use *when* or *where* directly after a linking verb. Do not use *where* as a substitute for *that* or *which*.

NONSTANDARD: After his tenth victory was *when* the poets began to sing his praises.
A ludi is *where* gladiators were trained for fighting.
The museum is a place *where* we like to visit.

CORRECT: After his tenth victory, the poets began to sing his praises.
A ludi is a school *where* gladiators were trained for fighting.
The museum is a place *that* we like to visit.

4. Write *there*, *their*, and *they're* on the board. Remind students that *there* usually indicates location, as does *here*, the word found within it. When distinguishing between *their* and *they're*, recommend that students mentally substitute the uncontracted form *(they are)*. If this form does not make sense in the sentence, then they should use *their*.

5. Writing *to* for *too* is a common error that students can generally avoid if they proofread their work. Challenge students to create one sentence that correctly uses *to*, *too*, and *two*. (*I went to two movies, and Sally went, too.*) Point out that *too* derives from the word *to*; perhaps its extra *o* can help students remember its meaning, "as well; in addition to."

Integrating Writing Skills

Using Pairs Correctly Have students write a brief composition about a typical day in school, using all the word pairs on these two pages correctly. You may want to have students read their compositions aloud when they have finished and explain which spellings or forms of words they have used.

Answer Key

> **Exercise 16**

1. (b) the jester proceeded
2. (a) against his principles
3. (b) the emperor said to the jester
4. (b) a culture that was very interested
5. (b) hear poetry than stories
6. (b) was canceled because of
7. (b) Carvers who produced
8. (b) The bakery was a place that
9. (a) proud of their post office
10. (b) for the courthouse, too

> **Exercise 17**

Even before the telegraph, there was <u>already</u> one means of long-distance communication. The semaphore method, using lights or signals, <u>preceded</u> the telegraph. The telegraph, however, was more efficient, and it <u>let</u> people send longer messages over greater distances. At first, there were many speculations about the future of the telegraph. It soon became the <u>principal</u> means of sending information over great distances.

Critical Viewing

Distinguish Sample response: Public transportation is different now *than* it was in earlier times. Now we use trains and buses; *then* they used horse-drawn vehicles.

25.2

> **Exercise 16** **Recognizing Standard Usage** For each pair of sentences, write the letter of the one that follows the conventions of standard English. Revise the other sentence, correcting the usage error.

1. (a) With his timely remarks, the jester preceded to make himself one of the king's favorites.
   (b) Each joke was preceded by a jingle of bells.
2. (a) In time, Will became the king's principal advisor.
   (b) Lying is against his principals.
3. (a) After the performance, the emperor says to the jester that he did a good job.
   (b) Everyone says that he is very funny.
4. (a) She had grown up in a culture that was real interested in oral poetry.
   (b) The festival included a real *griot*—a traditional storyteller.
5. (a) She'd rather hear poetry then stories.
   (b) First, we heard stories. Then, we heard poems.
6. (a) The knights' tournament was canceled due to bad weather.
   (b) The loyal page stood valiantly beside his knight.
7. (a) Carvers that produced signposts and shop signs were essential to a town's economy.
   (b) The signs that identified places were both decorative and functional.
8. (a) The bakery was a place where a person could buy bread.
   (b) Do you know where we can buy some bread?
9. (a) Paul carved the ornate fence bordering the post office over there.
   (b) The townspeople are very proud of there post office.
10. (a) He made the statue of Justice for the courthouse, to.
   (b) Many people came to the unveiling.

> **Exercise 17** **Revising a Passage to Eliminate Usage Problems** On a separate sheet of paper, revise the following paragraph to eliminate awkward or problematic usage.

Even before the telegraph, there was all ready one means of long-distance communication. The semaphore method, using lights or signals, proceeded the telegraph. The telegraph, however, was more efficient, and it leave people send longer messages over greater distances. At first, there were many speculations about the future of the telegraph. It soon became the principle means of sending information over great distances.

▼ **Critical Viewing** Think of two sentences to describe ideas in this picture: one containing *then* and one containing *than*. Consult usage problem 56 *(than, then)* before you write. **[Distinguish]**

⏱ **TIME SAVERS!**

🖨 **Answers on Transparencies**
Use the *Grammar Exercises Answers on Transparencies* for Chapter 25 to facilitate correction by students.

💻 **On-Line Exercise Bank**
Have students complete the exercises on computer. The Auto Check feature will grade their work for you!

☑ **ONGOING ASSESSMENT: Monitor and Reinforce**

If students have difficulty with Exercise 16 or 17, refer them to the following for additional practice.

In the Textbook	Print Resources	Technology
Section Review, Ex. 19–20, Section 25.2	*Grammar Exercise Workbook,* pp. 121–122	*On-Line Exercise Bank,* Section 25.2

Section 25.2 Section Review

GRAMMAR EXERCISES 18–23

Exercise 18 Supplying the Correct Article Write each phrase on your paper, supplying *a* or *an* in the blank.

1. ___?___ archaic career
2. ___?___ useful skill
3. ___?___ honorific title
4. ___?___ old cobbler
5. ___?___ onetime matchmaker

Exercise 19 Proofreading to Correct Usage Errors Rewrite any sentence below that contains a usage error. If a sentence is correct, write *correct*.

1. Before the twentieth century, their was no refrigeration.
2. Because people didn't have fridges, they used icehouses and iceboxes to keep food cold.
3. A need for preserved food proceeded the demand for ice.
4. Previous methods of preservation were different from the process of keeping the food cold.
5. There are many theories as to what was the best method of preserving food before the use of ice became so widespread.
6. Outside of using ice, people could preserve their food by smoking, drying, salting, or canning it.
7. Some food, however, doesn't taste as fresh or appetizing after salting and drying.
8. Being that ice was in such demand, a profitable industry sprang up.
9. Icemen were hired to bring ice from frozen ponds, lakes, and rivers to towns and cities.
10. The reason they gathered ice from frozen bodies of water is because they had no means of producing their own ice yet.

Exercise 20 Revising a Paragraph to Eliminate Usage Problems Rewrite the following paragraph, correcting any errors in usage.

Since ancient times, weavers done much of the work for making cloth. Weaving is a craft that has been around for quite awhile. Almost anywheres you go, you will find examples of looms and woven cloth. The hand loom was first used in China and the Middle East, and than it was used in Europe as well. The principals of weaving haven't changed much for thousands of years. A pick is used to push the yarn against the fabric that has all ready been woven. The reason this is done is because the fabric has to be evenly knit. While weaving is still very popular, you will find less weavers around today then in the past.

Exercise 21 Find It in Your Reading Review a newspaper article to find examples of correct usage of *there, their; lose, loose; then, than;* and *fewer, less.*

Exercise 22 Find It in Your Writing Choose one piece of writing in your portfolio. Proofread it carefully for the usage problems discussed in this chapter. Identify examples of correct usage. Correct any usage errors that you find.

Exercise 23 Writing Application Use each word below in a sentence. Be sure your sentence reflects the right meaning.

1. done
2. adapt
3. gone
4. into
5. bring

Section Review • 659

ASSESS and CLOSE

Section Review

Each of these exercises correlates to the instruction on common usage problems, pages 646–657. The exercises may be used for more practice, for reteaching, or for review of the key concepts presented. Answers for all chapter exercises are available in *Grammar Exercises Answers on Transparencies* in your Teaching Resources.

Answer Key

Exercise 18

1. an
2. a
3. an
4. an
5. a

Exercise 19

1. there was no
2. didn't have refrigerators
3. preceded the demand
4. correct
5. There are many theories about the best
6. Besides using ice
7. correct
8. Because ice was
9. correct
10. from frozen bodies of water is that

Exercise 20

Since ancient times, weavers <u>have</u> done . . . for quite <u>a while</u>. Almost <u>anywhere</u> you go, . . . and <u>then</u> it was used in Europe as well. The <u>principles</u> . . . already been woven. The reason for this is <u>that</u> the fabric . . . you will find <u>fewer</u> weavers around today than in the past.

Exercise 21

Find It in Your Reading
Students should be prepared to explain why each usage they have found is correct.

Exercise 22

Find It in Your Writing
When students have finished, have them exchange papers with a partner to see if all errors have been identified.

Exercise 23

Writing Application
Students' sentences will vary. After students write their sentences, have them go back to the chapter to review the rules that apply.

☑ **ONGOING ASSESSMENT: Assess Mastery**

Use the following resources to assess student mastery of common usage problems.

In the Textbook	Technology
Chapter Review, Ex. 28–31	*On-Line Exercise Bank,* Section 25.2

Each of these exercises correlates to a section of the chapter on miscellaneous problems in usage, pages 638–659. The exercises may be used for more practice, for reteaching, or for review of the key concepts presented. Answers for all chapter exercises are available in *Grammar Exercises Answers on Transparencies* in your Teaching Resources.

Answer Key

▶ Exercise 24

1. any
2. ever
3. any
4. any
5. can

▶ Exercise 25

1. some
2. ever
3. any
4. could
5. anywhere

▶ Exercise 26

Answers may vary; samples are given.
1. Medicine is one profession that hardly ever
2. Medical research isn't ever standing still
3. Not all the changes have been
4. who didn't know anything about it
5. if there weren't any doctors anywhere nearby

▶ Exercise 27

Answers may vary slightly.
1. Transportation in not an unchanging area of technology.
2. Airplanes are not an inconvenient way to travel.
3. Airlines hire not incompetent pilots to fly their planes.
4. Pilots are hardly untrained before they are allowed to fly solo.
5. There are not just a few air-travel-related jobs a pilot can handle.

▶ Exercise 28

1. a while
2. then
3. their
4. each other
5. proceed

GRAMMAR EXERCISES 24–31

▶ **Exercise 24** Supplying Words to Correctly Form Negative Sentences
Rewrite each sentence below on your paper, filling the blank with a word that does not form a double negative.

1. Some old careers didn't last ___?___ great length of time at all.
2. Other careers will probably not ___?___ fade away.
3. Because we need food, we can't survive without ___?___ farmers.
4. A farmer 200 years ago didn't have ___?___ of the large farm machinery used today.
5. No one ___?___ deny that the methods of farming have changed.

▶ **Exercise 25** Avoiding Double Negatives Choose the word in parentheses that makes each sentence negative without creating a double negative.

1. Without technology, we wouldn't have (some, none) of the jobs we have today.
2. For example, electricians weren't (never, ever) needed until we learned how to harness electricity.
3. The world didn't have (no, any) need for electricians until the twentieth century.
4. Even after we learned how to use electricity, not everyone (could, couldn't) afford it.
5. Before long, it seemed as if there wasn't (nowhere, anywhere) in the United States that didn't have electric lights.

▶ **Exercise 26** Revising Sentences to Correct Double Negatives Rewrite each sentence on your paper, correcting the double negative.

1. Medicine is one profession that hardly

never stays the same.
2. Medical research isn't never standing still, and much progress has been made during the hundreds of years that medicine has been practiced.
3. Not all the changes haven't been of a medical nature.
4. Other advances have included preventing people from practicing medicine who didn't know nothing about it.
5. Oftentimes in the Old West, for example, if there weren't no doctors nowhere nearby, a barber might perform surgical procedures.

▶ **Exercise 27** Revising Sentences to Achieve Understatement Rewrite each sentence to achieve understatement.

1. Transportation is a changing area of technology.
2. Airplanes are a convenient way to travel.
3. Airlines hire competent pilots to fly their planes.
4. Pilots are trained before they are allowed to fly solo.
5. There are many air-travel-related jobs a pilot can handle.

▶ **Exercise 28** Avoiding Usage Problems Choose the correct expression to complete each sentence.

1. As a profession, the practice of law has been around for (awhile, a while).
2. To become a lawyer, one must first study for many years and (than, then) take a qualifying examination.
3. Attorneys and solicitors represent and act for (their, there) clients in such matters as drawing up wills, settling property, or working out details of contracts.
4. Oftentimes, two opposing counsels will

discuss the details of a particular case with (one another, each other).

5. They may come to an agreement rather than to (proceed, precede) to a trial.

Exercise 29 Proofreading to Correct Usage Problems
Rewrite each sentence, correcting the errors in usage.

1. The reason Ansel Adams is famous is because he is a great photographer.
2. His principle focus was the American West.
3. Few photographers outside of Adams have received such acclaim.
4. Some say his talent lays in him choosing the right subjects.
5. Adams had first went to Yosemite National Park in 1916, where many believe he was inspired by the beauty he saw there.
6. Perhaps what he saw was different than anything he had seen before.
7. Surely, his works have learned others about the glory of the Western landscape.
8. Sally always brings at least two cameras with her whenever she goes out.
9. She has many feelings as to what components are needed for a good picture.
10. Early evening is when the light is ideal for outdoor shots.
11. When shooting in the early evening, she must work quickly before she looses the light.
12. Her photos have appeared in numerous art exhibitions.
13. Outside of the work of Ansel Adams, we've never seen such moving nature photography.
14. Everyone of the spectators at her last show agreed with us.
15. Many people couldn't hardly believe how nice her pictures were.

Exercise 30 Revising to Eliminate Usage Problems
On a separate sheet of paper, rewrite the following paragraph. Revise to eliminate errors in usage. You may rearrange words or make other minor changes if necessary.

(1)There are many different genres of writing today, and one person can use a number of them. (2)The two principle types of fiction writers are novelists and short-story writers. (3)The to types are most obviously different than one another in length. (4)Since there are no boundaries to the imagination, fiction writers may find it difficult to invent a good plot. (5)A reporter, however, all ready has the story. (6)Once she gets the information, she only needs to write it down in an interesting and coherent form. (7)A critic, being as his job is to review recent art productions and current trends, often relies on knowledge and taste. (8)Critics hope that their opinions will effect the way consumers spend they're money. (9)Their opinions often aggravate the artist they are reviewing, especially when they write less then enthusiastic or awful comments about the work. (10)Sometimes, it is difficult to remember that one critic don't represent everyone.

Exercise 31 Writing Application
Write five pairs of sentences about jobs you may pursue in the future. In each sentence, use one of the two words correctly to illustrate the difference in meaning.

1. among, between
2. can, may
3. all ready, already
4. learn, teach
5. they're, there

Answer Key

Exercise 29
Answers may vary slightly.
1. The reason Ansel Adams is famous is that
2. His principal focus was
3. Few photographers besides Adams
4. Some say his talent lies in his choosing the right subjects.
5. Adams had first gone to the West
6. Perhaps what he saw was different from anything
7. Surely, his works have taught others
8. Sally always takes
9. She has many feelings about
10. In early evening the light is ideal
11. before she loses the light
12. Her photographs
13. Except for the work of Ansel Adams
14. Every one of the spectators
15. Many people could hardly believe how moving

Exercise 30
Answers may vary slightly.
1. . . . one person may . . .
2. The two principal types . . .
3. The two types of writing are most obviously different from one another . . .
4. Because there are . . .
5. A reporter, however, already . . .
6. Once the information is gathered, he or she needs only . . .
7. Because a critic's job is . . . he or she . . .
8. . . . their opinions will affect . . . their money.
9. . . . often annoy the artist . . . less than enthusiastic or unflattering . . .
10. . . . one critic doesn't represent . . .

Exercise 31
Writing Application
Answers will vary. Have students check each other's work for correctness.

⏱ TIME SAVERS!
Answers on Transparencies Use the *Grammar Exercises Answers on Transparencies* for Chapter 25 to facilitate correction by students.

On-Line Exercise Bank Have students complete the exercises on computer. The Auto Check feature will grade their work for you!

✓ ONGOING ASSESSMENT: Assess Mastery
Use the following resources to assess student mastery of miscellaneous problems in usage.

In the Textbook	Print Resources	Technology
Chapter Review, Ex. 24–31 Standardized Test Preparation Workshop	*Formal Assessment*, Chapter 25	*On-Line Exercise Bank*, Chapter 25

Step-by-Step Teaching Guide

Recognizing Standard English Usage

Teaching Resources: Standardized Test Preparation Workbook, pp. 49–50

1. Suggest that students read through each entire Practice passage quickly, filling in the blanks with any appropriate words that occur to them. With this general idea of the topic in mind, students can return to each numbered blank and choose a response that fits the context.

2. Point out that a response must fit into a sentence contextually as well as grammatically.

3. You might list several general areas of English usage that students could encounter on tests, such as agreement, double negatives, verb tenses, and pronouns. It may be helpful to review more specifically some special usage problems and some common areas of confusion. Some of these include *accept/except, allusion/illusion, affect/effect, bad/badly, phenomena/phenomenon, beside/besides, emigrate/immigrate, less/fewer,* and *like/as if.*

4. Go over the Sample Test Item and Practices 1 and 2. Have students explain their reasons for their response choices.

Standardized Test Preparation Workshop

Recognizing Standard English Usage

Your mastery of standard English usage is frequently evaluated on standardized tests. Some test items focus on choosing the correct word to fill in a blank; others may test your ability to avoid or correct double negatives.

The following questions will give you practice with a format that is used to assess your understanding of standard English usage.

Test Tip

When looking for the best word or group of words to complete a sentence, read the entire sentence to yourself after placing each choice in the sentence.

Sample Test Item	Answer and Explanation

Directions: Read the sentence, and choose the word or group of words that belongs in each space. Mark the letter for your answer.
 	
No one ___(1)___ Joe could answer the question about the movie.
 	
1 A accept
   B except
   C accepted
   D exception
	The correct answer is *B*. The word *except* completes the sentence according to the conventions of standard English usage and makes sense in the sentence. *Except* means "other than," whereas *accept* means "to take what is offered."

662 • Miscellaneous Problems in Usage

🖊 TEST-TAKING TIP

Remind students that context, as well as grammatical correctness, is crucial in choosing a response. Once they have determined the main idea of a test passage, they should eliminate any response choices that they know are nonstandard English. Then they can choose the correct response based on their knowledge of the sentence's context.

Practice 1 **Directions:** Read the passage, and choose the word or group of words that belongs in each space.

The movie was produced ___(1)___ the book was written. For once, the director didn't ___(2)___ change the ___(3)___ the author told the story. The main character, Jerry, is lost ___(4)___ far from his home, and he has lost his memory. During the movie, Jerry wanders ___(5)___ away from his starting point and the truth of his identity.

1 A like
   B as
   C as to
   D similar to

2 F substantially
   G but
   H hardly
   J scarcely

3 A way
   B ways
   C anyway
   D anyways

4 F anywheres
   G somewheres
   H somewhere
   J nowhere

5 A further
   B farther
   C less
   D fewer

Practice 2 **Directions:** Read the passage, and choose the word or group of words that belongs in each space.

___(1)___ being lost and losing his memory, Jerry becomes involved in a spy ring. I can't imagine what else could have ___(2)___ wrong for him! Finally, he learns about his true identity after seeing himself on a flyer posted in a store window. After he reads ___(3)___ flyer, Jerry discovers he is ___(4)___ than an hour from his home. The movie ends with Jerry embracing his wife and children. It was a great book and a great movie, ___(5)___ .

1 A Besides
   B Besides that
   C Being that
   D Beside

2 F gone
   G goed
   H go
   J went

3 A that there
   B this here
   C their
   D that

4 F fewer
   G closer
   H more
   J less

5 A to
   B too
   C two
   D there

Answer Key

▶ **Practice 1**

1. B
2. F
3. A
4. H
5. B

▶ **Practice 2**

1. A
2. F
3. D
4. J
5. B

Customize for
Less Advanced Students
Suggest that students try whisper-reading to test possible response choices in sentences. It is often easier to determine a word's correctness after hearing it used in context, as well as after reading it silently.

Customize for
AP Students
Students might want to skim the responses for an entire test item before returning to the passage. This can provide advance clues about the usage issues that are being addressed.

Each of these exercises reviews concepts taught in the chapters on usage, Chapters 20–25. The exercises may be used for more practice, for review of the key concepts presented, or for assessment of student mastery of the major concepts.

Exercise A

Answers will vary; samples are given.

1. Homer wrote the *Iliad* and the *Odyssey* to describe the interactions among the gods and mortals.
2. To appreciate the *Iliad*, the reader must understand the stories of the Trojan War.
3. The *Iliad* uses the conflict between Agamemnon and Achilles as background.
4. After Achilles leaves the battle, the Greeks suffer many setbacks at the hands of the Trojans.
5. When his friend Patroclus leads the troops in his place and is slain, Achilles turns on Hector.
6. He wanted both to express his sadness and to take revenge.
7. Achilles met with King Priam after fighting King Priam's son.
8. Similarly, Achilles and Priam had both faced a tragedy.
9. Achilles, Agamemnon, and Priam, characters in the *Iliad*, deal with emotions, face dilemmas, and fight a war.
10. The *Odyssey*, which scholars believe may have been written by a different person than Homer, has different themes.

Exercise B

1. describes, his
2. he
3. were
4. his
5. recognizes

Exercise C

1. great
2. who, highest
3. more
4. are learning
5. spends, more
6. had swum
7. they
8. more, other gods were

continued

Cumulative Review

USAGE

> **Exercise A** Writing Effective Sentences Rewrite the following sentences according to the instructions in parentheses.

1. Homer wrote the *Iliad*. The *Odyssey* was written by Homer, describing the interactions between gods and mortals. (Combine by creating a compound direct object and an infinitive phrase.)
2. To appreciate the *Iliad*, the stories of the Trojan War must be understood. (Correct the dangling modifier.)
3. Using the conflict between Agamemnon and Achilles as the background, the *Iliad*. (Correct the sentence fragment and begin with a noun.)
4. Achilles leaves the battle; the Greeks proceed to suffer many setbacks against the Trojans. (Correct the faulty coordination; start with a subordinate clause.)
5. When his friend Patroclus leads the troops in his place he is slain and Achilles turns on Hector. (Create a compound verb and correct the run-on.)
6. He both wanted to be expressing his sadness and to take revenge. (Correct the faulty parallelism.)
7. Achilles after fighting his son met with King Priam. (Correct the misplaced modifier and the ambiguous reference.)
8. They felt sad similarly. Achilles and Priam had both faced a tragedy. (Combine with a compound subject and start the sentence with an adverb.)
9. The characters in the *Iliad* deal with emotions, facing dilemmas, and they fight a war. They are Achilles, Agamemnon, and Priam. (Combine sentences with an appositive phrase and correct faulty parallelism.)
10. The *Odyssey* has different themes, which scholars believe may have been written by a person other than Homer. (Correct the misplaced modifier.)

> **Exercise B** Making Words Agree Choose the correct word or groups of words that makes each sentence correct.

1. The *Odyssey* (describe, describes) the travels of Odysseus after (his, its) time in the Trojan War.
2. Odysseus fought for the Greeks, and (he, they) is credited with the idea for the Trojan horse.
3. Some in Ithaca (was, were) courting his wife, Penelope, in his absence.
4. Each wanted her for (his, their) wife.
5. Either Penelope or the dog (recognize, recognizes) Odysseus first.

> **Exercise C** Using Pronouns, Verbs, and Modifiers Choose the correct word or group of words that makes each sentence correct.

1. The (great, greatest) importance of the mythological Greek gods is demonstrated by their presence in all stories, including Homer's epic poems.
2. Zeus is king of the gods (who, whom) lived on Mount Olympus, the (higher, highest) point in all of Greece.
3. He is (more, most) powerful than the other gods.
4. This year, we (learned, are learning) about several of the Greek gods.
5. Poseidon, who rules the sea and all its creatures, (spend, spends) (most, more) of his time in his sea kingdom than on Olympus.
6. Anyone who (had swum, had swam) in the sea honored Poseidon.
7. Poseidon ruled the Nereids and Tritons, lesser sea gods. It is (they, them) who carried out his orders.
8. Demeter was (more, most) associated with the Earth and agriculture than (any other gods, other gods were.)

9. Hestia is not as well known. However, the goddess of the hearth and the home is (she, her).
10. Homemakers in ancient Greece would have given (she, her) special honors.

Exercise D Proofreading Sentences to Correct Miscellaneous Problems in Usage

Rewrite the following sentences, correcting negative sentences and other common usage problems.

1. Athena was more important then many other goddesses in Greek mythology.
2. There wasn't hardly anything that she wasn't involved with.
3. Because she was loyal too the people of the city of Athens, they built her major temple, the Parthenon, there.
4. One of the reasons Athena was so popular is because she was Zeus' favorite child.
5. Irregardless of the other gods, Athena was a strong supporter of the Greeks during the Trojan War.
6. However, after the Greeks disregarded her wishes concerning the prophet Cassandra, Athena wasn't going to do nothing for them.
7. Then, Athena gave fewer support to Greek ships returning from that war.
8. The storms she and Poseidon sent gave the sailors a farther challenge.
9. Athena was awful useful as the goddess of wisdom, industry, and the arts.
10. Between her gifts to men were the flute and the instructions for building ships and taming animals.

Exercise E Revising a Passage to Eliminate Usage Errors

On a separate sheet of paper, copy the following paragraph. Revise to eliminate all errors. You may need to rearrange words or make other minor changes.

(1)The Graces, the three goddesses of joy, charm, and beauty, was daughters of Zeus. (2)They are most often treated as a group than as individuals. (3)They're tasks included bringing joy to both gods and mortals, and she presided over dances, dinners, and other social events. (4)In art, they are usually represented as three young maidens. (5)Together with the Muses, they sung and danced. (6)The Muses was a group of nine goddesses, also daughters of Zeus. (7)They were each associated with but one particular art. (8)Clio, for example, have been associated with history, and Melpomene with tragedy. (9)On Olympus, they sat closer to the throne of Zeus, where they sang of his greatness. (10)The Muses were kind of a group that was worshiped all over Greece, but more at Helicon and Pieria than anywhere.

Exercise F Writing Application

Write a summary of a myth or legend with which you are familiar. Make your writing interesting by varying your sentence lengths and structures. Try to avoid sentence errors and the common usage problems that you have studied. Be sure that the words in your sentences follow the rules of agreement and that your modifiers are used correctly. Then, list your verbs and verb phrases, identifying their tense. Make a list of your pronouns, and label the cases of each.

Exercise C
9. she
10. her

Exercise D
1. Athena was more important than
2. There was hardly anything
3. Because she was loyal to the people
4. One of the reasons Athena was so popular is that she was
5. Regardless of the other
6. Athena wasn't going to do anything
7. Then Athena gave less support
8. gave the sailors a further challenge
9. Athena was very useful
10. Among her gifts to men

Exercise E
1. The Graces . . . <u>were</u> daughters
2. They are <u>more</u> often treated
3. <u>Their</u> tasks included . . . and <u>they</u> presided
4. correct
5. they <u>sang</u> and danced
6. The Muses <u>were</u> a group of
7. correct
8. Clio, for example, <u>has</u>
9. On Olympus, they sat <u>close</u> to
10. The Muses <u>were</u> a group that was worshiped . . . Helicon and Pieria than anywhere <u>else</u>.

Exercise F

Writing Application
When students have finished, have them share their summaries with a partner. Partners should check to see that usage rules are followed and that verbs and pronouns are labeled correctly.

In-Depth Lesson Plan

LESSON FOCUS	PRINT AND MEDIA RESOURCES
DAY 1 — **Using Capitals for First Words and for Proper Nouns** Students learn and apply capitalization concepts covering capitals for first words, proper nouns, and geographical and place names. (pp. 668–670/Ⓗ494–496)	*Writing and Grammar* Interactive Text, Ch. 26; *On-line Exercise Bank,* Ch. 26 **Teaching Resources** *Grammar Exercise Workbook,* pp. 123–124; *Grammar Exercises Answers on Transparencies,* Ch. 26
DAY 2 — **Using Capitals for Proper Nouns (continued)** Students learn and apply concepts covering capitals for events, times, and various groups. (pp. 671–673/Ⓗ497–499)	**Teaching Resources** *Grammar Exercise Workbook,* pp. 123–124
DAY 3 — **Using Capitals for Proper Adjectives, Titles, and Letters** Students learn and apply capitalization concepts covering proper adjectives, titles, and letters and do the Hands-on Grammar activity. (pp. 674–681/Ⓗ500–507)	**Teaching Resources** *Grammar Exercise Workbook,* pp. 123–126; *Hands-on Grammar Activity Book,* Ch. 26
DAY 4 — **Review and Assess** Students review the chapter and demonstrate mastery of capitalization concepts. (pp. 682–683)	*On-line Exercise Bank,* Section 26 **Teaching Resources** *Formal Assessment,* Ch. 26

Accelerated Lesson Plan

LESSON FOCUS	PRINT AND MEDIA RESOURCES
DAY 1 — **Using Capitals for First Words and for Proper Nouns** Students cover capitalization concepts as determined by the Diagnostic Test. (pp. 668–673/Ⓗ494–499)	*Writing and Grammar* Interactive Text, Ch. 26; *On-Line Exercise Bank,* Ch. 26 **Teaching Resources** *Grammar Exercise Workbook,* pp. 123–124; *Grammar Exercises Answers on Transparencies,* Ch. 26
DAY 2 — **Using Capitals for Proper Adjectives, Titles, and Letters** Students cover capitalization concepts as determined by the Diagnostic Test. (pp. 674–681/Ⓗ500–507)	**Teaching Resources** *Grammar Exercise Workbook,* pp. 123–126
DAY 3 — **Review and Assess** Students review the chapter and demonstrate mastery of concepts. (pp. 682–683)	**Teaching Resources** *Formal Assessment,* Ch. 26

Options for Adapting Lesson Plans

HOMEWORK

Have students complete any section of the chapter for homework.

FEATURES

Extend coverage with the Standardized Test Preparation Workshop (p. 684).

TECHNOLOGY

Students can use *Writing and Grammar* Interactive Text to complete the exercises interactively on computer. They can complete additional exercises in the *On-line Exercise Bank:* The Auto Check feature will grade their work. Go on-line: PHSchool.com Use Web Code: egk-1202

Writing and Grammar Handbook Alignment

Page numbers in Step-by-Step Teaching Guides in this Teacher's Edition refer to pages from the full student text. Handbook page references, indicated with this icon 🄷, are provided in Time and Resource Manager boxes and at the bottom of each Teacher's Edition page.

INTEGRATED SKILLS COVERAGE

Writing
Find It in Your Writing, SE p. 681/🄷507
Writing Application, SE p. 683
Integrating Writing Skills, ATE p. 672

Spelling
ATE p. 672

Viewing and Representing
Critical Viewing, SE pp. 666, 669, 671, 674, 677, 678, 679, 680/🄷492, 495, 497, 500, 503, 504, 505, 506

Technology SE p. 679/🄷505

Vocabulary
ATE p. 669

Workplace Skills
ATE p. 676

Real-World Connection
ATE p. 679

ASSESSMENT SUPPORT

Standardized Test Preparation Workshop SE p. 684; ATE pp. 671, 676

Standardized Test Preparation Workbook, pp. 51–52

Formal Assessment, Ch. 26

MEETING INDIVIDUAL NEEDS

Less Advanced Students ATE pp. 668, 675, 685. See also Ongoing Assessments ATE pp. 669, 673, 675, 678.

ESL Students ATE pp. 671, 675

AP Students ATE pp. 671, 685

Musical Learners ATE p. 669

BLOCK SCHEDULING

Pacing Suggestions
For 90-minute Blocks
• Administer the Diagnostic Test to students to determine instructional coverage.
• Have students complete the necessary exercises in class. Use the Hands-on Grammar activity to provide a change of pace.

Resources for Varying Instruction
• *Writing and Grammar* Interactive Text A 90-minute block provides an ideal opportunity for students to work on the computer.

Professional Development Support
• *How to Manage Instruction in the Block* This teaching resource provides management and activity suggestions.

MEDIA AND TECHNOLOGY

For the Student
• *Writing and Grammar* Interactive Text, Ch. 26
• *On-line Exercise Bank,* Ch. 26

For the Teacher
• Teacher**EXPRESS** CD-ROM

WRITING AND GRAMMAR ON-LINE

Interactive Text (On-line or on CD-ROM)
• Easily navigable instruction with on-line supporting resources
• Self-scoring exercises and diagnostic tests

Companion Web Site PHSchool.com
• On-line Exercise Bank (use Web Code egk-1202)

See the Go On-line! feature, SE p. iii.

Lesson Objectives

1. To place capitals correctly at the beginnings of sentences and at the beginning of many lines of poetry
2. To identify and capitalize all proper nouns and proper adjectives
3. To place capitals correctly in titles and letters
4. To use the conventions of capitalization
5. To proofread for capitalization within the context of a written passage

Critical Viewing

Describe Possible answer: You would use capital letters to give the name of the waterfall, the country where it is located, and the person who discovered it.

Chapter 26 Capitalization

When you're writing an e-mail message and you want to express strong emotion or emphasize a word, you can do so by typing in capital letters. Showing emotion by using capital letters is one of the most recently developed uses of capitals. Throughout the history of the English language, many rules have been developed for using capital letters to indicate changes of thought, to highlight certain types of words, and to serve a variety of other purposes. In this chapter, you will review the rules of capitalization to help you apply them to your writing.

▲ **Critical Viewing** In what ways would you use capital letters in a written description of this waterfall? **[Describe]**

✓ ONGOING ASSESSMENT: Diagnose

If students have difficulty with any category, direct them to the relevant pages of the textbook and assign exercises for practice and review.

Capitalization	Diagnostic Test Items	Teach	Practice	Chapter Review
Skill Check A				
Recognizing Proper Nouns	A 2, 5	pp. 670–673/Ⓗ496–499	Ex. 2–4	Ex. 13–14
Recognizing Proper Adjectives	A 1, 3–4	pp. 674–675/Ⓗ500–501	Ex. 4	Ex. 11, 14
Skill Check B				
Capitalizing First Words	B 6–15	pp. 668–669/Ⓗ494–495	Ex. 1–3	Ex. 12
Capitalizing Proper Nouns	B 6–15	pp. 670–673/Ⓗ496–499	Ex. 2–4	Ex. 13–14

Diagnostic Test

Directions: Write all answers on a separate sheet of paper.

Skill Check A. Label each of the underlined words *proper noun* or *proper adjective*.

1. <u>italian</u> language
2. the state of <u>arizona</u>
3. an <u>english</u> accent
4. <u>russian</u>-born playwright
5. ex-senator <u>harris</u>

Skill Check B. Copy the following sentences. Add capitals where needed.

6. the highest uninterrupted cataract in the world is called angel falls, which is located in southeastern venezuela.
7. it was named for an american aviator, james c. angel, in 1937.
8. on the río churún, it descends around 3,000 feet from the guiana highlands.
9. another famous waterfall, victoria falls, can be found in south central africa.
10. this waterfall, on the zambezi river, straddles the border of zimbabwe and zambia.
11. the zambezi is more than a mile wide at this point and falls about 350 feet into the gorge below.
12. there is also an impressive waterfall to be found in north america, on the border of new york state and ontario, canada.
13. it is called niagara falls, and it is on the niagara river.
14. there are two branches that make up niagara falls: one located on the american side and one on the canadian side.
15. the canadian falls, also known as the horseshoe falls, carries about nine times more water than the american falls.

Skill Check C. Copy the following sentences. Add capitals where needed.

16. uncle louis was an engineer on the wisconsin central railroad until he retired on memorial day 1962.
17. on super bowl sunday, more pretzels and potato chips are eaten in the united states than anywhere else in the world.
18. when joe was a senior, he was a member of the brunswick high school chess club.
19. grandma and i took aunt martha's children to the bronx zoo to see the special exhibit of the himalayan snow leopards.
20. the allegheny and monongahela rivers come together in pittsburgh, pennsylvania, to form the ohio river.

Skill Check A

1. proper adjective
2. proper noun
3. proper adjective
4. proper adjective
5. proper noun

Skill Check B

6. The, Angel Falls, Venezuela
7. It, American, James C. Angel
8. On, Río Churún, Guiana Highlands
9. Another, Victoria Falls, South Central Africa
10. This, Zambezi River, Zimbabwe, Zambia
11. The, Zambezi
12. There, North America, New York State, Ontario, Canada
13. It, Niagara Falls, Niagara River
14. There, Niagara Falls, American, Canadian
15. The, Canadian, Horseshoe Falls, American

Skill Check C

16. Uncle Louis, Wisconsin Central Railroad, Memorial Day
17. On, Super Bowl Sunday, United States
18. When, Joe, Brunswick High School Chess Club
19. Grandma, I, Aunt Martha's, Bronx Zoo, Himalayan
20. The Allegheny, Monongahela, Pittsburgh, Pennsylvania, Ohio, River

---

☑ ONGOING ASSESSMENT: Diagnose *continued*

Capitalization	Diagnostic Test Items	Teach	Practice	Chapter Review
Capitalizing Proper Adjectives	B 7, 14–15	pp. 674–675/🅗500–501	Ex. 4	Ex. 11, 14
Skill Check C				
Capitalizing First Words	C 16–20	pp. 668–669/🅗494–495	Ex. 1–3	Ex. 12
Capitalizing Proper Nouns	C 16–20	pp. 670–673/🅗496–499	Ex. 2–4	Ex. 13–14
Capitalizing Proper Adjectives	C 19	pp. 674–675/🅗500–501	Ex. 4	Ex. 11, 14
Capitalizing Titles	C 16, 19	pp. 676–677/🅗502–503	Ex. 5, 10	Ex. 14
Cumulative Reviews and Applications			Ex. 7–9	Ex. 17–18

⏱ TIME SAVERS!

🔲 **Answers on Transparencies** Use the *Grammar Exercises Answers on Transparencies* for Chapter 26 to facilitate correction by students.

💻 **On-Line Exercise Bank** Have students complete the Diagnostic Test on computer. The Auto Check feature will grade their work for you!

PREPARE and ENGAGE

Interest GRABBER Write the following on the board:
INEARLYWRITINGONLYCAPITALLETTERSWEREUSEDITWASHARDTOSEEWHERESENTENCESSTOPPEDANDSTARTED

Have students mark off the two sentences above and indicate which words would be capitalized in today's writing (*In, It*). Explain that lowercase letters—and hence the need to decide what to capitalize—did not come into common use until near the end of the first millennium.

Activate Prior Knowledge

Ask students to listen as you say a series of common nouns such as *foreign country, mountain range,* and *state.* For each, ask students to write five proper nouns that fit in the category, and write some of their words on the board. Then, ask for volunteers to come up with as many more common noun categories as they can, and have the rest of the class name proper nouns for each category.

TEACH

Step-by-Step Teaching Guide

Capitals for First Words

1. Make sure students recognize that indirect quotations, which are usually introduced by *said that*, do not need capitalization. Make the point with these examples:

   Lou said, "The tour leaves soon."

   Lou said that the tour was leaving soon.

   continued

Customize for
Less Advanced Students

If students have trouble deciding which words to capitalize in quotations broken by *he said* or *she said*, tell them to take out the interrupting phrase and look at what remains. If a new thought follows the interrupter, it should be capitalized. Demonstrate this idea with the first two examples after the third key concept in the textbook.

Using Capitals for First Words

Capitalization signals the beginning of a sentence or points out certain words within a sentence.

▶ **KEY CONCEPT** Capitalize the first word in declarative, interrogative, imperative, and exclamatory sentences. ■

DECLARATIVE:	The mountain was tall and forbidding.
INTERROGATIVE:	Where is the highest peak in the world?
IMPERATIVE:	Take your camera with you.
EXCLAMATORY:	What a breathtaking view!

▶ **KEY CONCEPT** Capitalize the first word in interjections and incomplete questions. ■

INTERJECTIONS:	Oh! Marvelous!
INCOMPLETE QUESTIONS:	Why not? When?

▶ **KEY CONCEPT** Capitalize the first word in a quotation if the quotation is a complete sentence. ■

EXAMPLES:

"The water rushes to the edge of the falls," the tour guide said. "Its force could crush a person."

"As the water crashes to the bottom of the falls," he said, "a thick spray of mist is flung up."

After seeing the Grand Canyon, Theodore Roosevelt said that "the ages have been at work upon it and man cannot improve it."

The first example shows a quotation that consists of two sentences. Notice that the first word of each sentence is capitalized.

The second example consists of one sentence that is interrupted by a "he said/she said" expression. Only the first word of the sentence that has been interrupted is capitalized.

The last example contains a portion of a quotation that is not a complete sentence. When only a portion of a sentence is quoted, do not capitalize the first word unless it is the first word of the sentence in which it is used.

668 • Capitalization

Theme: Natural Wonders

In this section, you will learn about capitalization. The examples and exercises in this lesson are about natural wonders.

Cross-Curricular Connection: Science

⏱ TIME AND RESOURCE MANAGER

Resources
Print: *Grammar Exercise Workbook*, pp. 123–126; *Grammar Exercises Answers on Transparency*, Ch. 26
Technology: *Writing and Grammar* Interactive Text, Ch. 26; *On-Line Exercise Bank*, Ch. 26

Using the Full Student Edition	Using the Handbook🄷
• Work through all key concepts, pp. 668–678. • Assign and review Exercises 1–10. • Do the Hands-on Grammar activity, p. 681.	• Work through all key concepts, pp. 494–504. • Assign and review Exercises 1–10. • Assign the Hands-on Grammar activity, p. 507.

KEY CONCEPT Capitalize the first word after a colon if the word begins a complete sentence. ■

COMPLETE SENTENCE: In 1866, David Livingstone set out to attempt something never before accomplished: He led an expedition to discover the source of the Nile.

LIST OF WORDS OR PHRASES: Previous to this, Livingstone had explored much of Africa: the Kalahari Desert, the Zambezi River, Lake Ngami, and Victoria Falls.

Poetry should always be written as the poet intended it to be. In most poetry, the first word in each line is capitalized, even if it does not begin a new sentence.

KEY CONCEPT Capitalize the first word in each line of traditional poetry. ■

EXAMPLE:

Tyger! Tyger! burning bright,
In the forests of the night,
What immortal hand or eye
Could frame thy fearful symmetry?
—William Blake

KEY CONCEPT Capitalize the first word after a colon in a formal resolution that states the subject of debates, legislative decisions, and acts. ■

EXAMPLE: Resolved: That the Senior Class hold an exhibit of its work on natural wonders.

Exercise 1 **Capitalizing First Words** Copy each of the following items, capitalizing the appropriate words.

1. the falls at Niagara were formed about 12,000 years ago.
2. since that time, erosion has taken its toll: the waterfall has been pushed about seven miles upstream.
3. "a man who has never looked on Niagara," said Lord Macauley, "has but a faint idea of a cataract."
4. it is fortunate for humankind that more people did not listen to the poet Tennyson: "surely, surely, slumber is more sweet than toil."
5. instead, many great explorers went in search of nature's wonders among what Shakespeare called the "thorns and dangers of this world."

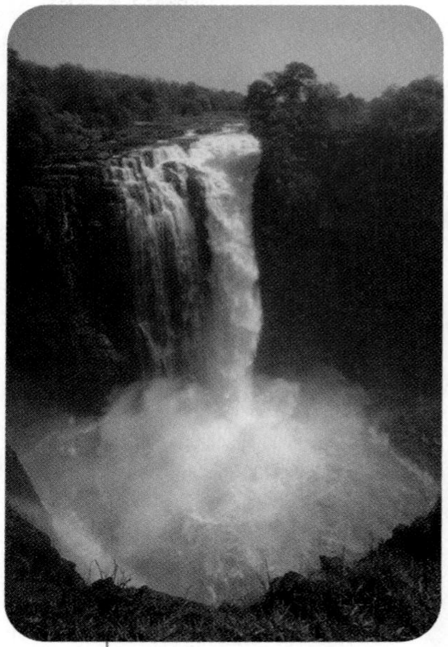

▲ Critical Viewing
How would you compare Victoria Falls (pictured here) with Niagara Falls (shown on page 666)? **[Compare and Contrast]**

More Practice

Grammar Exercise Workbook
- pp. 123–124

On-line Exercise Bank
- Chapter 26

Go on-line:
PHSchool.com
Enter Web Code:
egk-1202

ONGOING ASSESSMENT: Monitor and Reinforce

If students miss more than one item in Exercise 1, refer them to the following for additional practice.

In the Textbook	Print Resources	Technology
Chapter Review, Ex. 12	*Grammar Exercise Workbook,* pp. 123–124	*On-Line Exercise Bank,* Ch. 26

Step-by-Step Teaching Guide continued

2. Remind students that unlike sentences following colons, complete sentences following semicolons or dashes are not capitalized. Complete sentences within parentheses are capitalized only if they stand alone. Present these examples:

   Have one of these cookies before you leave; they are macaroons.

   Have one of these cookies—they are macaroons—before you leave.

   Have one of these cookies before you leave (they are macaroons).

   Have one of these cookies before you leave. (They are macaroons.)

3. Stress to students the importance of following a poet's style when copying lines of verse. Modern poets often do not begin every line with a capital letter.

Integrating Vocabulary Skills

Latin Roots Warn students not to confuse the words *capital* and *capitol*. Although they have the same root (the Latin word *caput* means "head"), *capitol* refers only to a capitol building. Ask students to think of other words that may have the same Latin root (*captain, capitalism, cape*).

Customize for *Musical Learners*

Have students write down a verse of a favorite song, observing the rules of capitalization. See if they can hum the song quietly to determine where lines begin. Point out that, as with poetry, capital letters must begin each new line.

Answer Key

Exercise 1

1. The
2. Since, The
3. "A
4. It, "Surely
5. Instead

Critical Viewing

Compare and Contrast Possible answer: Victoria Falls looks narrower than Niagara Falls.

Capitals for Proper Nouns

1. Explain to students that spellings and capitalizations of name parts other than *O'* and *St.* may vary. For example, *Mc* is sometimes spelled *Mac*, and forms like *L'* and *Vanden* may or may not be capitalized. When in doubt about a name's spelling, check with the individual.

2. Make sure students understand that words like *road*, *county*, and *sea* are common nouns and are capitalized only when part of a name. If necessary, ask for volunteers to use each word in a sentence, first as a common noun and then as a proper noun.

3. Students may have trouble understanding when to capitalize direction words. Explain that they are capitalized only when they refer to specific areas and that often a modifying word accompanies them. Present examples like *the Southwest, the Midwest, the Deep South, the Pacific Northwest, the Middle East*.

continued

Language Highlight

Many surnames have beginning letters that, in their languages of origin, mean "of" or "son of." *Mc* (or *Mac*) is a Gaelic prefix that means "son." *De*, written *de* or *D'*, is a prefix from the Romance languages, including French, Spanish, and Italian, meaning "of." (Example: *D'Artagnan* is *of the Artagnan family*.) *O'* is a prefix in Irish names that means "descendant of." *Van* is a Dutch prefix that originally indicated where a person was from. Some other last names result from other conventions: The son of Robert, for instance, would be named *Roberts* or *Robertson*.

26

Using Capitals for Proper Nouns

Nouns, as you know, name people, places, and things. They are classified as either *common* or *proper*.

COMMON NOUNS: river, mountain, prairie, lake, sea, hill, valley

Proper nouns—which name specific examples of people, places, or things—require capitalization.

▶**KEY CONCEPT** Capitalize all proper nouns. ■

PROPER NOUNS: Henry, Sir Edmund Hillary, the White House, Cincinnati, H.M.S. *Beagle, National Geographic*

As you can see from the preceding examples, there are several categories of proper nouns.

▶**KEY CONCEPT** Capitalize each part of a person's full name. ■

EXAMPLES: Roald Amundsen, T. S. Eliot, Francis Drake

Surnames sometimes consist of several parts. Capitalize both parts of surnames beginning with *Mc, O',* or *St.*

EXAMPLES: McCarthy   O'Donovan   St. James

The proper names of animals should also be capitalized.

EXAMPLES: Lassie, a dog   Velvet, a horse

Proper nouns referring to particular places must also be capitalized. Articles are not usually capitalized.

▶**KEY CONCEPT** Capitalize geographical and place names. ■

EXAMPLES: Hillside Road, Dallas, Putnam County, Arizona, British Columbia, Australia, the Alps, Kalahari Desert, Fiji Islands, the Southwest, Amazon River, Angel Falls, Coral Sea, Saturn, Halley's Comet, the Alamo, the Pentagon, the Oval Office, Room 14, Laboratory C

Note About *Capitalizing Directions:* Words indicating direction can be used in two ways: to name a section of a country and to give travel directions. These words are capitalized only when they refer to a section of a country.

EXAMPLES: Urban areas of the *Northeast* face many problems. We traveled two miles *west* and one mile *south*.

670 • Capitalization

Step-by-Step Teaching Guide
continued

▶ **KEY CONCEPT** Capitalize the names of specific events and periods of time. ■

SPECIAL EVENTS AND TIMES	
Historical Events	the Louisiana Purchase, the Battle of Waterloo, the Russian Revolution
Historic and Geographic Periods	the Renaissance, the Bronze Age, the Mesozoic Era, the Ice Age
Documents	the Magna Carta, the Declaration of Independence
Days and Months	Tuesday, Fridays, July 20, the third week in April
Holidays and Religious Days	Easter, Father's Day, Memorial Day, Hanuka, Christmas
Special Events	the World's Fair, the Super Bowl, the Montreux International Jazz Festival

Most dictionaries and encyclopedias include lists of historic events and periods that require capitalization.

Note About *the Seasons*: Do not capitalize any reference to the seasons.

EXAMPLE: The winds were so cold during the winter that we thought we were at the North Pole.

▶ **KEY CONCEPT** Capitalize abbreviations of titles before and after names. ■

EXAMPLES: Mr. Green
Mrs. Bellamy
Mr. Paige
Arthur Romano, Ph.D

Although *Miss* is not an abbreviation, it is capitalized when used with a name.

▼ **Critical Viewing**
This photograph shows the Arctic Ocean. What are some of the ways in which you would use capital letters in a research report about the Arctic region? **[Connect]**

Capitalization • 671

4. Point out that in the chart the word *the* is not capitalized when it precedes many proper nouns. Ask for volunteers to give more examples. (*the Second World War, the Fourth of July*)

5. Point out that, in addition to seasons, other words that are not capitalized are *sun* and *moon*. The word *earth* is capitalized only when it is referred to as one of the planets. In general, *earth* is not capitalized when preceded by *the*.

6. Mention that *Ms.*, capitalized and followed by a period, is the correct form to use when the marital status of a woman is unspecified. Additionally, many unmarried women prefer it to *Miss*.

continued

Customize for
ESL Students

Make sure students understand that the personal pronoun *I* is always capitalized; the corresponding personal pronoun is not capitalized in many other languages. Tell students that one reason *I* became a capitalized form was that it was hard to distinguish in written manuscripts. Ask students to write five sentences about a river, lake, or ocean that they have seen. They should use *I* in each sentence.

Critical Viewing

Connect Possible answers: To name the region, to name oceans and seas in the region, to name islands and continents that are in the region.

Customize for
AP Students

Have students research exactly how and when lowercase letters did become part of the Roman alphabet. In their research they should get information about half-uncials and Carolingian letters. Have them find examples of these forms and show them to the class.

✎ STANDARDIZED TEST PREPARATION WORKSHOP

Mechanics Many standardized tests require students to identify types of errors in a passage. Use the following example to demonstrate.

After waiting in line for three hours, we were allowed in for a tour of The White House.

What is the error in this sentence?

A Punctuation   **C** Capitalization
B Spelling   **D** No error

The correct answer is **C**. The word *the* is not capitalized when it precedes a place name unless it is formally part of the name.

Capitals for Proper Nouns
continued

1. As students read through the chart on this page, explain that terms like *pep club* or *chess club* are capitalized only when they are part of a specific name: *Tri-Cities Chess Club*.

2. Explain to students that, although usage varies, words like *army* and *air force* are generally capitalized only when used with the name of a country: *the United States Army, the Israeli Air Force*.

3. Mention that, when referring to races, the terms *white* and *black* are usually not capitalized.

continued

Integrating Spelling Skills

Acronyms Many words about computers in common use are not really words at all but abbreviations or acronyms (words formed from the initial letters of other words). Ask students what *RAM*, *ROM*, *CD*, and *DVD* stand for (random access memory, read-only memory, compact disc, digital video disc). Have students brainstorm for other computer terms and consult dictionaries to see if they are acronyms. (Examples: *WORM*: write once, read many; *BASIC*: Beginners' All-purpose Symbolic Instruction Code) Point out that acronyms such as these are written in all capital letters and without punctuation because they are considered words.

Integrating Writing

Writing With Capital Letters Ask students to look over the capitalization categories on this page. Then have them decide on a writing topic in which they could use a proper noun representative of most or all of the categories. Have them write short compositions, using different proper nouns from those in the chart.

26

▶ **KEY CONCEPT** Capitalize the names of various organizations, government bodies, political parties, races, nationalities, languages, and religious references. ■

VARIOUS GROUPS	
Clubs	Kennedy High School Stamp Club, Rotary, New York Athletic Club
Organizations	the Salvation Army, American Medical Association
Institutions	National Museum of Art, the Boston Symphony, Johns Hopkins Hospital
Schools	Adlai E. Stevenson High School, Stanford University
Businesses	Allied Chemical Corporation, Prentice-Hall Canada, Inc.
Government Bodies	the Senate, the House of Lords, Nuclear Regulatory Commission, Army of the Potomac
Political Parties	Republican party, Liberal party, the Democrats
Nationalities	American, Canadian, Mexican, German, Israeli, Chinese, Mexican
Languages	English, Spanish, Polish, Swahili
Religious References	*Christianity:* God, the Lord, the Father, the Holy Spirit, the Bible, the New Testament, the Savior *Judaism:* God, the Lord, the Prophets, the Torah, the Talmud *Islam:* Allah, the Prophets, the Koran, Mohammed, Muslims *Hinduism:* Brahma, the Bhagavad-Gita, the Vedas *Buddhism:* the Buddha, Mahayana, Hinayana

672 • Capitalization

Note About *Religious References:* When you use pronouns to refer to the Judeo-Christian deity, they should always be capitalized.

EXAMPLE: I prayed for *His* help.

When referring to ancient mythology, you should not capitalize the word *god* or *goddess*. The names of the gods and goddesses, however, are capitalized.

EXAMPLES: the *gods* of ancient Greece
the Roman *god* Mars

KEY CONCEPT Capitalize names of awards; names of specific types of air, sea, space, and land craft; and brand names. ∎

AWARDS:	Nobel Peace Prize, the Pulitzer Prize, Phi Beta Kappa, the Medal of Honor
SPECIFIC CRAFTS:	Boeing 747, the U.S.S. *Kearsarge*, *Apollo V*, Ford Mustang
BRAND NAMES:	Aunt Molly's Crackers, John's Elixir

Exercise 2 **Capitalizing Proper Nouns** Write the following sentences, adding the missing capitals.

EXAMPLE: st. louis, missouri, is subject to turbulent weather in the summer partly because of its proximity to the mississippi river and the missouri river.

St. Louis, Missouri, is subject to turbulent weather in the summer partly because of its proximity to the Mississippi River and the Missouri River.

1. i watched the knights of columbus march in the memorial day parade.
2. nat fein won the pulitzer prize for photography for his picture of babe ruth entitled *the babe bows out.*
3. the author of the declaration of independence was thomas jefferson.
4. the roman god jupiter is the equivalent of the greek god zeus.
5. lassen volcanic national park was the home of the only active volcano in the northwestern region of the united states until mount saint helens erupted in 1980.

More Practice

Grammar Exercise Workbook
• pp. 123–124
On-line Exercise Bank
• Chapter 26
Go on-line:
PHSchool.com
Enter Web Code:
egk-1202

Interactive Textbook

Get instant feedback! Exercise 2 is available on-line or on CD-ROM.

4. Remind students that all religions have different deities, scriptures, and ceremonies that are capitalized according to each religion's rules and traditions. When in doubt, students should check a dictionary.

5. Point out that unless they are part of the name of the prize, categories in which prizes are awarded are not capitalized: *the Pulitzer Prize for feature photography.*

Answer Key

Exercise 2

1. I watched the Knights of Columbus march in the Memorial Day Parade.
2. Nat Fein won the Pulitzer Prize for photography for his picture of Babe Ruth entitled *The Babe Bows Out.*
3. The author of the Declaration of Independence was Thomas Jefferson.
4. The Roman god Jupiter is the equivalent of the Greek god Zeus.
5. Lassen Volcanic National Park was the home of the only active volcano in the northwestern region of the United States until Mount Saint Helens erupted in 1980.

Capitalization • **673**

✓ ONGOING ASSESSMENT: Monitor and Reinforce

If students miss more than one item in Exercise 2, refer them to the following for additional practice.

In the Textbook	Print Resources	Technology
Chapter Review, Ex. 13	*Grammar Exercise Workbook,* pp. 123–124	*On-Line Exercise Bank,* Ch. 26

⏱ TIME SAVERS!

Answers on Transparencies Use the *Grammar Exercises Answers on Transparencies* for Chapter 26 to facilitate correction by students.

On-Line Exercise Bank Have students complete the exercises on computer. The Auto Check feature will grade their work for you!

> **Exercise 3**

1. The Colorado River flows through the Grand Canyon.
2. A particularly spectacular section of the canyon is preserved as the Grand Canyon National Park.
3. The first Europeans to see the Grand Canyon were a group of Spaniards led by Francisco Vásquez de Coronado.
4. The group left Mexico, then known as New Spain, in February of 1540.
5. Some surveys and maps were made in the 1800's, but the Civil War interrupted the work.
6. After the war, an American named John Wesley Powell . . .
7. Powell became the first person . . . of the Colorado River.
8. Though the erosion on the Grand Canyon began about six million years ago, . . .
9. There are about nine layers . . . geological periods: the Permian, Mississippian, Devonian, and Cambrian periods.
10. Oldest of all are the Precambrian Period rocks on the bottom of the Grand Canyon: They are . . .

Step-by-Step Teaching Guide

Capitals for Proper Adjectives

1. Tell students that many other proper adjectives besides those at the bottom of this page are commonly used to describe nouns. Recommend that students check a dictionary whenever they are not sure if such terms should be capitalized.

2. Make sure students can distinguish between brand names used as proper nouns and those used as proper adjectives to modify common nouns. Explain that the type of item is not usually part of the brand name and thus not capitalized: *Sneezex tissues*. Ask students for other examples.

Critical Viewing

Connect Possible answers: <u>Grand</u> Canyon vista, <u>Bright Angel</u> and <u>South</u> Kaibab trails, <u>Colorado River</u> raft trip

---

26

> **Exercise 3** Proofreading to Correct Errors in Capitalization of First Words and Proper Nouns Revise this passage, adding and eliminating capitals as necessary.

The Colorado river flows through the Grand canyon. A particularly spectacular section of the Canyon is preserved as the Grand Canyon national park.

The first europeans to see the grand canyon were a group of spaniards led by francisco vásquez de coronado. the group left mexico, then known as new spain, in february of 1540. Some surveys and maps were made in the early 1800's, but the civil war interrupted the work. After the war, an american named John Wesley Powell studied the region and wrote geology reports. Powell became the first person to travel the full length of the Colorado river.

Though the erosion of the grand canyon began about Six Million Years Ago, the rocks in its walls are older than that. there are about thirteen layers of rock deposited in different geological periods: the permian, mississippian, devonian, and cambrian periods. Oldest of all are the precambrian period rocks on the bottom of the grand canyon: they are from half a billion to two billion years old.

Using Capitals for Proper Adjectives

A proper adjective is an adjective formed from a proper noun or a proper noun used as an adjective. Most proper adjectives require capitalization.

> **KEY CONCEPT** Capitalize most proper adjectives. ■

PROPER ADJECTIVES FROM PROPER NOUNS:	American, Elizabethan, biblical, Chinese
PROPER NOUNS AS ADJECTIVES:	a Chicago accent, a March day, a Eugene O'Neill play

Some proper adjectives that once were capitalized have become such a common part of the language that they are no longer capitalized.

> **KEY CONCEPT** Do not capitalize certain frequently used proper adjectives. ■

EXAMPLES:	bowie knife, china cabinet, french toast, afghan blanket, napoleon pastry, quixotic quest

▲ Critical Viewing What proper adjectives might you use in writing about the Grand Canyon? **[Connect]**

▶ **KEY CONCEPT** Capitalize a brand name used as an adjective, but do not capitalize the common noun it modifies. ■

EXAMPLES: Everlasting refrigerator, Big Guy jeans

▶ **KEY CONCEPT** Do not capitalize a common noun used with two proper adjectives. ■

Compare the examples in the following chart. Notice in each case that a common noun used with two or more proper adjectives is not capitalized.

Compound Proper Noun	Two Proper Adjectives With Common Noun
Volstead Act	Volstead and Payne-Aldrich acts
Main Street	Main, Welch, and Macopin streets
Mississippi River	Mississippi and Missouri rivers

▶ **KEY CONCEPT** Do not capitalize prefixes attached to proper adjectives unless the prefix refers to a nationality. ■

EXAMPLES: pro-English   Franco-Prussian War

Notice that the prefix in the example on the left is not capitalized. The prefix in the example on the right is capitalized because it refers to a nationality.

▶ **KEY CONCEPT** In a hyphenated adjective, capitalize only the proper adjective. ■

EXAMPLE: Swedish-speaking immigrant

▶ **Exercise 4** Capitalizing Proper Adjectives and Nouns
Copy each of the following items, making the necessary corrections in capitalization.

1. niagara falls
2. russo-chinese border
3. house of lords
4. nile river delta
5. bay of fundy
6. the democratic party
7. lake titicaca
8. northwest new york
9. european explorers
10. anti-british protesters
11. the magna carta
12. dutch colonizers
13. henry m. stanley
14. anglo-american journalist
15. native american
16. rocky mountains
17. chitambo, zambia
18. irish accent
19. british and french Empires
20. nepalese-speaking guides

Interactive Textbook
Get instant feedback! Exercises 3 and 4 are available on-line or on CD-ROM.

▶ **More Practice**
Grammar Exercise Workbook
• pp. 123–124
On-line Exercise Bank
• Chapter 26
Go on-line:
PHSchool.com
Enter Web Code:
egk-1202

Capitalization • 675

☑ **ONGOING ASSESSMENT: Monitor and Reinforce**
If students have difficulty with Exercise 3 or 4, refer them to the following for additional practice.

In the Textbook	Print Resources	Technology
Chapter Review, Ex. 11, 13–14	*Grammar Exercise Workbook,* pp. 123–124	*On-Line Exercise Bank,* Ch. 26

Capitals for Titles

1. If necessary, review the three uses of titles—in direct address, as proper nouns, and as common nouns. Have students write three examples using the same title, or provide these examples:

   I enjoyed today's lecture, Professor. (direct address)

   I enjoyed Professor Will's lecture today. (proper noun)

   I enjoyed my professor's lecture today. (common noun)

2. Point out that words like *mom* and *grandpa* are capitalized when they are used alone (*Pick Grandpa up at the airport*). If they are preceded by a possessive pronoun (*He needs to call his mom*), they should not be capitalized.

continued

Integrating Workplace Skills

Abbreviations Students may find the need in various workplace situations to correspond in writing with persons in the medical or teaching professions. Hence, it is important to be comfortable with a variety of title abbreviations. Ask students to correctly capitalize the following abbreviations: *m.d., d.d.s., d.v.m., ph.d.* Discuss with students the meanings of these abbreviations (medical doctor, doctor of dental surgery, doctor of veterinary medicine, doctor of philosophy) and ask them to mention others. (Examples: *M.A.*: master of arts; *Ed.D.*: doctor of education; *R.N.*: registered nurse)

26

Using Capitals for Titles

Capitalize a person's title when it is used with the person's name or when it is used as a name.

▶ **KEY CONCEPT** Capitalize titles of people and titles of works. ■

WITH A PROPER NAME:	Yesterday, Governor Wilson addressed the state legislature.
AS A NAME:	Mrs. Alvarez is on the phone, Doctor.
IN A GENERAL REFERENCE:	Have you ever met the mayor of our city?

TITLES OF PEOPLE	
Commonly Used Titles	Sir, Madam, Doctor, Professor, Father, Reverend, Rabbi, Sister, Archbishop, Sergeant, Governor, Senator, Ambassador
Abbreviated Titles	*Before names:* Mr., Mrs., Dr., Prof. *After names:* Jr., Sr., Ph.D., Esq.
Compound Titles	Commander in Chief, Vice President, Secretary of Defense, Lieutenant Governor
Titles With Prefixes or Suffixes	Mayor-elect Ross, ex-Senator Norman

▶ **KEY CONCEPT** Capitalize the titles of certain high government officials even when the titles are not used with a proper name or in direct address. ■

Titles that are always capitalized include those of the current President, Vice President, and Chief Justice of the Supreme Court of the United States, as well as that of the Queen of England.

EXAMPLE: The Chief Justice was appointed by the President.

As a sign of respect, you may also capitalize other titles used without names.

STANDARDIZED TEST PREPARATION WORKSHOP

Mechanics Many standardized tests require students to identify types of errors in a passage. Use the following example to demonstrate.

"At the International Medical conference north of Geneva," said Doctor Mark Perez, "you will see my new research."

What change would you make in this sentence?

A Capitalize conference. C Capitalize you.

B Capitalize north. D Correct as is.

The correct answer is **A**. All nouns in the name of a formal event should be capitalized.

▶ **KEY CONCEPT** Capitalize titles showing family relationships when they are used with a name or as a name. ■

WITH THE PERSON'S
NAME: Aunt Liz speaks two languages.
IN DIRECT ADDRESS: I'm glad you're coming to lunch, Grandma.

REFERRING TO A
SPECIFIC PERSON: Will Grandfather come with us on our trip to Africa?

▶ **KEY CONCEPT** Capitalize the titles and subtitles of works of literature, art, and media and of various publications. ■

Capitalize the first word and all other key words in the titles of books, periodicals, poems, stories, plays, television programs, paintings, and other works of art.

BOOK: *Profiles in Courage*
MOVIE: *The Great Train Robbery*
MAGAZINE: *Life*
PLAY: *The Tragedy of Macbeth*

▶ **KEY CONCEPT** Capitalize titles of courses when they are language courses or when they are followed by a number. ■

WITH CAPITALS: Spanish, Sociology 1, English 2
WITHOUT CAPITALS: biology, zoology, home economics

▶ **Exercise 5** Capitalizing Titles of People and Things Copy the following sentences, capitalizing the titles correctly. Underline any words that should be printed in italics.
1. After his successful assault on Mount Everest, mr. Edmund Hillary was knighted by the queen of england.
2. The leader of the expedition, colonel John Hunt, was made a life peer and took the title of baron.
3. The television station the discovery channel shows many programs about nature.
4. Before his famous encounter with doctor Livingstone, mr. Stanley had gone on an expedition in the American West led by general Winfield Scott Hancock.
5. When no one had heard from dr. Livingstone for several years, mr. James Gordon Bennet, jr., told Stanley, who worked for him at the new york herald, to go to Africa to find him.

▲ **Critical Viewing**
Identify ten magazines, books, television programs, or courses in which you might find information about this type of monkey. Which titles would and would not be capitalized? **[Identify]**

▶ **More Practice**
Grammar Exercise Workbook
• pp. 125–126
On-line Exercise Bank
• Chapter 26
Go on-line:
PHSchool.com
Enter Web Code:
egk-1202

3. Explain that, besides initial words, "key words" in titles include the final word as well as all nouns, verbs, adjectives, and adverbs. Prepositions and conjunctions of four or more letters are also capitalized. Tell students to be particularly careful to capitalize *is* in titles.

4. You may want to review with students which kinds of titles need to be italicized (or underlined). These include titles of books, periodicals, plays, television series, paintings, and very long poems. Short stories, most poems, songs, chapters, and essays are put in quotation marks.

5. Mention that *magazine* is not capitalized unless it is a part of the title (*Newsweek* magazine).

Critical Viewing

Identify Answers will vary. Publications should be capitalized; general course names should not.

Answer Key

▶ **Exercise 5**

1. After his successful assault on Mount Everest, Mr. Edmund Hillary was knighted by the Queen of England.
2. The leader of the expedition, Colonel John Hunt, was made a life peer and took the title of baron.
3. The television station the Discovery Channel shows many programs about nature.
4. Before his famous encounter with Doctor Livingstone, Mr. Stanley had gone on an expedition in the American West led by General Winfield Scott Hancock.
5. When no one had heard from Dr. Livingstone for several years, Mr. James Gordon Bennet, Jr., told Stanley, who worked for him at the <u>New York Herald</u>, to go to Africa to find Livingstone.

Capitals in Letters

1. Explain that the first word and all nouns in salutations are capitalized. Use the example *My dear Sir* to make the point.

2. Point out that only the first word is capitalized in closings. Use this example: *Very truly yours.*

Answer Key

> 23 Spur Avenue
> North Salem, New York
> August 29, 20_ _

Mr. Daniel Lucey
Far Horizons Travel, Incorporated
232 Sherman Avenue
New York, NY 10063

Dear Mr. Lucey,

I am a student at State University, where I am working on my Ph.D. I have an opportunity to do some travel and research in my area of interest. I plan to travel first to Australia in the wake of Captain James Cook. While there, I wish to explore the Great Barrier Reef off the coast of Queensland. I also wish to visit Uluru National Park in the Northern Territory to examine the world's largest monolith, formerly known as Ayers Rock.

I recently read in *National Geographic* magazine that your agency specializes in the kind of adventure tour that I am seeking and that you offer flights over the Antarctic. I wish to trace the route of Sir Ernest Shackleton and his ship, the *Endurance*. I would like to see South Georgia, the Weddell Sea, the South Sandwich Islands, and Elephant Island in the South Shetlands. I am hoping that you can assist in planning my itinerary, as well as advise me on climatic conditions. I look forward to hearing your suggestions.

> Sincerely,
>
> Jerry Coughlan

Critical Viewing

Speculate Possible answer: It is clear that the student would like to visit Antarctica because he says in his letter that he wishes to trace the route of antarctic explorer Sir Ernest Shackleton.

26

Using Capitals in Letters

Capitalization is also required in parts of personal letters and business letters.

▶ **KEY CONCEPT** Capitalize the first word and all nouns in letter salutations and the first word in letter closings. ■

SALUTATIONS: Dear Eric,   Dear Sirs:
CLOSINGS: With love,   Yours truly,

▶ **Exercise 6** Using Capitals in a Business Letter Copy the following letter, adding and removing capital letters as appropriate.

> 23 spur avenue
> north Salem, New York
> august 29, 20--

mr. daniel lucey
Far Horizons Travel, incorporated
232 sherman avenue
new york, new york 10063

dear mr. lucey,

I am a Student at state university, where i am working on my ph.d. i have an opportunity to do some travel and research in my area of interest. i plan to travel first to australia in the wake of captain james cook. while there, I wish to explore the Great Barrier reef off the Coast of queensland. i also wish to visit uluru national park in the northern territory to examine the world's largest Monolith, formerly known as Ayers rock.

i recently read in national geographic magazine that your agency specializes in the kind of adventure tour that i am seeking and that you offer flights over the antarctic. i wish to trace the route of sir ernest shackleton and his ship, the endurance. i would like to see south Georgia, the weddell sea, the south Sandwich Islands, and elephant island in the south shetlands. i am hoping that you can assist in planning my itinerary, as well as advise me on climatic conditions. i look forward to hearing your suggestions.

> sincerely,
> Jerry Coughlan

▲ **Critical Viewing** Do you think that the student who wrote the letter to the left would be interested in traveling to Antarctica (shown here)? On what do you base your answer? **[Speculate]**

▶ **More Practice**

Grammar Exercise Workbook
• pp. 125–126
On-line Exercise Bank
• Chapter 26
  Go on-line:
  PHSchool.com
  Enter Web Code:
  egk-1202

☑ **ONGOING ASSESSMENT: Monitor and Reinforce**

If students have difficulty with Exercise 5, 6, 7, or 8, refer them to the following for additional practice.

In the Textbook	Print Resources	Technology
Chapter Review, Ex. 15–17	*Grammar Exercise Workbook,* pp. 125–126	*On-Line Exercise Bank,* Ch. 26

Exercise 7 Using All the Rules of Capitalization Write the words that should be capitalized, and underline anything that should be printed in italics.

1. today, the memorial to david livingstone is found near the place where he was born, by the river clyde in scotland.
2. though never finding the source of the nile river, he was among the first europeans to discover lake ngami and victoria falls.
3. the nile river is the longest river in the world.
4. its major source is lake victoria, and it flows north through uganda, the sudan, and egypt to the mediterranean sea.
5. the ruvyironza river, one of the upper branches of the kagera in tanzania, is regarded as the ultimate source of the nile.
6. different sections of the nile are known by different names: the victoria nile, the blue nile, and the white nile.
7. other explorers have written accounts of their travels: in 1895, major john wesley powell published a book entitled canyons of the colorado.
8. the grand canyon was so awe-inspiring that powell said later, "the wonders of the grand canyon cannot be adequately represented in symbols of speech, nor by speech itself."
9. natural wonders are not seen only above ground.
10. australia boasts an amazing underwater attraction called the great barrier reef.

▲ **Critical Viewing**
What capitalization rules might you use in describing this underwater scene from Australia's Great Barrier Reef? **[Describe]**

Exercise 8 Applying Capitalization Rules to Writing Write a few paragraphs describing an interesting or beautiful location you have seen or visited. Include each of the following items, correctly capitalized.

1. name of the main attraction
2. proper adjective that describes this attraction
3. name of the place where the attraction is located
4. name of someone who suggested that you visit it
5. date you saw or visited it
6. name of the person who discovered or built it
7. nationalities of other visitors
8. date it was discovered or built
9. name of the organization that administers the site
10. your first reactions to the site put into words
11. names of any famous visitors
12. name of another place you would like to see
13. language spoken in the country the site is in
14. historical event associated with the place
15. sentence that contains a colon

 Internet Tip

To learn more about natural wonders and explorers, use search words like *discovery, exploration,* and *nature.* Use proper nouns, such as *Mount Everest,* to be more specific.

Capitalization • 679

▶ **Exercise 9**

1. correct
2. They release steam . . . instead of lava and ash.
3. . . . countries: the United States, New Zealand, and Iceland.
4. A famous geyser in the United States is Old Faithful.
5. It is in Yellowstone National Park in the state of Wyoming.
6. Old Faithful erupts . . . minutes: It expels . . .
7. Four types of glaciers . . .
8. A glacier is a large mass . . .
9. Alpine glaciers, such as those found on Mount Rainier in Washington, . . . high mountain ranges.
10. The Hubbard Glacier in Alaska is . . . alpine glaciers
11. Piedmont glaciers, which result from glaciers flowing together in a valley, are particularly common in Alaska.
12. The largest piedmont glacier in the world is the Malaspina Glacier in Alaska.
13. An example of a continental glacier is the glacial blanket that covers almost the entire surface of Greenland.
14. It is similar to the one that covers the Antarctic continent, . . .
15. Icebergs are formed . . . chunks of these glaciers . . .

▶ **Exercise 10**

Student responses will vary. Suggest that students try to create a coherent composition with their sentences.

Critical Viewing

Describe Possible answers: The glacier is large, crumbling, and jagged. Uses of capitals might include the first words of sentences, the name of the glacier, and the name of the place it is located.

26

▶ **Exercise 9** Proofreading to Correct All Types of Capitalization Errors Revise these two paragraphs, adding and removing capitals as necessary.

Another natural phenomenon that erupts is a geyser. they release steam and hot water instead of Lava and ash. Most known geysers are found in only three countries: the united states, new zealand, and iceland. a famous geyser in the united states is old faithful. It is in Yellowstone national park in the state of wyoming. Old faithful erupts at intervals of 33 to 120 minutes: it expels from 3,700 to 8,400 gallons of water per eruption.

Four types of Glaciers include the alpine, piedmont, icecap, and continental. a Glacier is a large mass of ice formed where the rate of snowfall is greater than the rate of melting. alpine glaciers, such as those found on Mount rainier in washington, are found worldwide on high Mountain ranges. the hubbard Glacier in alaska is one of the longest alpine Glaciers in the world. piedmont Glaciers, which result from glaciers flowing together in a valley, are particularly common in alaska. The largest piedmont glacier in the world is the malaspina glacier in alaska. An example of a continental Glacier is the glacial blanket that covers almost the entire surface of greenland. it is similar to the one that covers the antarctic continent, which has an area of 5 million square miles. Icebergs are formed when chunks of these Glaciers break off near the sea.

▶ **Exercise 10** Writing Application Write a sentence for each numbered item that includes the type of word or words specified. Use capitals as needed.

1. name of a business
2. title
3. name of a country and city
4. language
5. quotation
6. name of a celestial body
7. specific date
8. name of a land craft, sea craft, spacecraft, or aircraft
9. street or road name
10. person's name

680 • Capitalization

▶ **More Practice**

Grammar Exercise Workbook
• pp. 123–126
On-line Exercise Bank
• Chapter 26
 Go on-line:
 PHSchool.com
 Enter Web Code:
 egk-1202

interactive **Textbook**

Get instant feedback! Exercises 9 and 10 are available on-line or on CD-ROM.

▲ Critical Viewing How would you describe this glacier? How would you use capitals in your description? [Describe]

Hands-on Grammar

Memo Mania

In the business world, there is another way in which capitalization is used: It is used in memorandums to emphasize key points. For example, to stress the importance of a looming deadline, a manager might write a sentence spelling out the implications of missing the deadline and type the entire sentence in capital letters.

Work with a group of classmates to experiment with the impact of presenting various sentences in capital letters. Type one or more imaginary memoranda about situations at a workplace. If you can't come up with any ideas, use the sample below. Then, retype the memo or memos in capital letters. Cut each of the sentences into strips.

Then, experiment with pasting the capitalized sentences over the corresponding sentences in the original memo. Discuss how emphasizing different sentences affects the overall impact of the memo. Share your findings with classmates.

TO: Development Staff
FR: Arthur Singer
Re: Schedule

I have been notified that the development schedule has slipped. However, it is essential that we meet our April deadline for product delivery. To move the process forward, all decisions about specifications must be finalized. In addition, staff members must come up with solutions for cutting time out of the schedule. Suggestions should be submitted to me no later than next Thursday. Once we have decided how to streamline the schedule, we must see to it that all interim deadlines are met. No additional slippage will be tolerated.

NO ADDITIONAL SLIPPAGE WILL BE TOLERATED.

SUGGESTIONS SHOULD BE SUBMITTED TO ME NO LATER THAN THURSDAY.

Find It in Your Reading The technique of capitalizing words and sentences for emphasis is also used in e-mail messages. For a week, track the use of capitalization in e-mail messages that you read.

Find It in Your Writing If you have any samples of business writing in your portfolio, review them to see if any sentences should be capitalized for emphasis.

Capitalization • 681

Hands-on Grammar

Teaching Resources: Hands-on Grammar Activity Book, Ch. 26

1. If you wish to do this activity in class, be prepared with tape or paste as well as scissors for the students. Give each student a copy of the Hands-on Grammar activity sheet.

2. Have students follow the directions to prepare their memos. If typewriters or computers are unavailable in your classroom, have students write out any replacement strips by hand.

3. As an alternative, have students use computers to carry out this activity. You might also assign the activity as homework, with students assigned to send e-mail messages to partners with some sentences capitalized.

4. Let students know that some e-mail users consider excessive use of capital letters the equivalent of yelling. Have students experiment with capitalizing individual words, rather than complete sentences, to create emphasis without overusing capitalization.

☑ ONGOING ASSESSMENT: Assess Mastery

Use the following resources to assess student mastery of capitalization.

In the Textbook	Print Resources	Technology
Chapter Review, Ex. 11–17 Standardized Test Preparation Workshop	*Formal Assessment,* Ch. 22	*On-Line Exercise Bank,* Ch. 26

⏱ TIME SAVERS!

✋ **Hands-on Grammar**
Use the Hands-on Grammar activity sheet for Chapter 26 to facilitate this activity.

Chapter Review

Each of these exercises correlates to a section of the chapter on capitalization, pages 668–681. The exercises may be used for more practice, for reteaching, or for review of the key concepts presented.

Answer Key

> **Exercise 11**

1. Scottish-born
2. Norwegian explorer
3. Shackleton's ship
4. anti-British
5. Siamese cat

> **Exercise 12**

1. In
2. Three
3. Many
4. After
5. In
6. In, An
7. During
8. "I, "The
9. "We
10. Though

> **Exercise 13**

1. Mount Etna, Mount Vesuvius
2. Italy, Vesuvius, Naples, Etna, Sicily
3. Stromboli, Lipari Islands, Sicily
4. Ring of Fire, Pacific Ocean
5. Vesuvius
6. Mount Saint Helens, Washington
7. Philippines, Mount Pinatubo
8. Nevada del Ruiz, Colombia
9. Indonesia, Krakatoa
10. Mount Saint Helens, Krakatoa

TIME SAVERS!

Answers on Transparencies
Use the *Grammar Exercises Answers on Transparencies* for Chapter 26 to facilitate correction by students.

On-Line Exercise Bank
Have students complete the exercises on computer. The Auto Check feature will grade their work for you!

Chapter 26 Chapter Review

GRAMMAR EXERCISES 11–18

> **Exercise 11** Capitalizing Proper Adjectives Correctly capitalize each of the following.

1. scottish-born
2. norwegian explorer
3. shackleton's ship
4. anti-british
5. siamese cat

> **Exercise 12** Capitalizing First Words On a separate sheet of paper, capitalize words in the following sentences, as needed.

1. in the 1840's, Antarctica's status as a continent was confirmed.
2. three separate expeditions sailed along enough coast to realize that Antarctica was, in fact, a continental landmass.
3. many expeditions visited Antarctica between the late nineteenth and early twentieth centuries.
4. after Robert Peary reached the North Pole, Roald Amundsen decided to go south "just as swiftly as the news had spread through the cables."
5. in 1911, he became the first man to reach the South Pole.
6. in the 1920's, people began to fly over Antarctica: an Australian became the first to fly over the Antarctic continent in 1928.
7. during the winter, Antarctica doubles in size because of all the sea ice that forms at its edges.
8. "i could not doubt now that the *Endurance* was confined for the winter," wrote Shackleton. "the seals were disappearing and the birds were leaving us."
9. "we must wait for the spring," he continued, "which may bring us better fortune."

10. though Shackleton and his men did not reach the South Pole, they all survived the loss of the *Endurance* and a long trek to South Georgia and rescue.

> **Exercise 13** Capitalizing Proper Nouns On a separate sheet of paper, write the words in the following sentences that should be capitalized.

1. Many volcanoes, such as mount etna and mount vesuvius, are born on the sea floor.
2. These volcanoes are both located in italy: vesuvius is near naples, and etna is in sicily.
3. Some volcanoes are more active than others: stromboli, in the lipari islands near sicily, has been continually active since ancient times.
4. Other constantly active volcanoes are found in an area called the ring of fire that encircles the pacific ocean.
5. Some volcanoes, like vesuvius, are moderately active and then become dormant for months or years.
6. An eruption that follows a long period of inactivity is usually violent, as was the case with mount saint helens in washington.
7. It erupted after a 123-year period of dormancy; in the philippines, mount pinatubo erupted after six quiet centuries.
8. Volcanic eruptions trigger mudflows that are extremely dangerous; the one caused by the eruption of nevada del ruiz in colombia claimed more than 25,000 lives in 1985.
9. In indonesia in 1883, the volcano krakatoa erupted with so much energy that ash was reportedly flung to a height of 17 miles.
10. The summit of mount saint helens was

blown off when it erupted in 1980, and the eruption of krakatoa destroyed most of the island on which it was located.

> **Exercise 14** Proofreading Sentences to Correct Capitalization of Proper Nouns and Adjectives Revise these sentences, adding capitals as necessary. Underline any words that should be printed in italics.

1. The motion picture industry has evolved dramatically since the days of the lumière brothers, edwin s. porter, and d. w. griffith.
2. Early films were controlled and limited by the motion picture patents company until americans and europeans formed independent production companies.
3. The star of *queen elizabeth* was sarah bernhardt, the french actress who was to achieve worldwide fame.
4. The most influential filmmaker of the early silent era was d. w. griffith, who in 1908, at the biograph studio in new york city, began to refine his craft.
5. It was griffith who trained such future stars as mary pickford, lionel barrymore, and lillian gish.

> **Exercise 15** Writing Sentences With Capitals Write a sentence about each of the following. Follow the rules for capitalization.

1. great vacation spot
2. governor of your state
3. battle of World War II
4. national park
5. piece of music
6. work of art
7. largest city in your state
8. museum you have visited
9. your birthplace
10. famous government building

> **Exercise 16** Proofreading to Correct the Use of Capitals in Letters
Copy the following letter onto a separate sheet of paper. Use capitals where needed.

1401 smith street
sanderville, texas 11101

march 26, 20--

chamber of commerce
fort lauderdale, florida

to whom it may concern:

i am preparing a brochure for my english class in which i would like to describe the attractions of the fort lauderdale area. please send me the tourism package that you distribute to travel agents. i asked for one at my local travel agency, jet travel, inc., but they have been out of brochures since the thanksgiving break. i would appreciate any materials you can send me.

with thanks,

carly meyer

> **Exercise 17** Proofreading for All Types of Errors in Capitalization Revise the following paragraph, correcting errors in capitalization.

The name of mount Everest in tibetan is *chomo lungma*, which means "goddess-mother." its name in english is in honor of sir George everest, who was surveyor-general of india from 1830 to 1843. he first recorded the location and height of the Mountain in 1841.

> **Exercise 18** Writing Application
Write a paragraph about a voyage of discovery. Include important names, dates, and places. When you are finished, underline each capitalized word. Give the reason for each capitalization.

Answer Key continued

> **Exercise 17**

The name of Mount Everest in Tibetan is *Chomo Lungma*, which means "goddess-mother." Its name in English is in honor of Sir George Everest, who was surveyor-general of India from 1830 to 1843. He first recorded the location and height of the mountain.

> **Exercise 18**

Writing Application
When students have finished, have volunteers read their papers to the class. Let class members challenge the readers about where they got their information.

Answer Key *continued*

> **Exercise 14**

1. The motion picture industry has evolved dramatically since the days of the Lumière brothers, Edwin S. Porter, and D. W. Griffith.
2. Early films were controlled and limited by the Motion Picture Patents Company until Americans and Europeans formed independent production companies.
3. The star of *Queen Elizabeth* was Sarah Bernhardt, the French actress who was to achieve worldwide fame.
4. The most influential filmmaker of the early silent era was D. W. Griffith, who in 1908, at the Biograph Studio in New York City, began to refine his craft.
5. It was Griffith who trained such future stars as Mary Pickford, Lionel Barrymore, and Lillian Gish.

> **Exercise 15**

Student responses will vary. Encourage students to include as many capitalized words in their sentences as are feasible.

> **Exercise 16**

1401 Smith Street
Sanderville, Texas 11101
March 26, 20_ _

Chamber of Commerce
Fort Lauderdale, Florida

To whom it may concern:

I am preparing a brochure for my English class in which I would like to describe the attractions of the Fort Lauderdale area. Please send me the tourism package that you distribute to travel agents. I asked for one at my local travel agency, Jet Travel, Inc., but they have been out of brochures since the Thanksgiving break. I would appreciate any materials you can send me.

With thanks,

Carly Meyer

continued

Lesson Objectives

1. To demonstrate knowledge of accurate spelling and correct use of punctuation and capitalization
2. To produce error-free writing in the final draft

Step-by-Step Teaching Guide

Proofreading

Teaching Resources: Standardized Test Preparation Workbook, pp. 51–52

Review with students some basic rules of capitalization. You might include proper nouns, abbreviations, races, religions, school subjects, words of family relationship, book and movie titles, government bodies, and historical events.

Standardized Test Preparation Workshop

Proofreading

Standardized tests will often measure your understanding of the rules of capitalization. You will be given a passage to proofread and identify the types of errors, including capitalization, spelling, and punctuation. The following sample items will help you practice proofreading for errors.

Test Tip

Remember that errors in capitalization can be words that should be capitalized but are not, as well as words that are capitalized when they shouldn't be.

Sample Test Item	Answers and Explanations
Directions: Read the passage, and decide which type of error, if any, appears in each underlined section. One of my favorite Poets is Emily Dickinson. (1) My Mother gave me a copy of her complete (2) works on my birthday.	

1 A Spelling error
   B Capitalization error
   C Punctuation error
   D No error
	The correct answer for item 1 is *B*. The common noun *poets* should not be capitalized.

2 F Spelling error
   G Capitalization error
   H Punctuation error
   J No error
	The correct answer for item 2 is *G*. Titles showing family relationships, such as *mother*, are not capitalized when they are preceded by a possessive pronoun, such as *my*.

684 • Capitalization

 TEST-TAKING TIP

Tell students to be sure to check carefully the underlined part of the passage before making a decision about a possible error. They should be aware of the possibility of unnecessary capitalization and too many commas or periods, as well as their omission.

Practice 1 **Directions:** Read the passage, and decide which type of error, if any, appears in each underlined section.

Last thursday, the entire team went out for
(1)
Italian Food after the game. Our Eagles
(2)
trounced the other Team. Next week,
(3)
maybe coach Hay will join us, but only if
(4)
we are buying!
(5)

1 **A** Spelling error
   B Capitalization error
   C Punctuation error
   D No error

2 **F** Spelling error
   G Capitalization error
   H Punctuation error
   J No error

3 **A** Spelling error
   B Capitalization error
   C Punctuation error
   D No error

4 **F** Spelling error
   G Capitalization error
   H Punctuation error
   J No error

5 **A** Spelling error
   B Capitalization error
   C Punctuation error
   D No error

Practice 2 **Directions:** Read the passage, and decide which type of error, if any, appears in the underlined section.

I was born in sewickley, Pennsylvania,
(1)
in October 1962. My Parents, Tom and
(2)   (3)
Nancy, brought me home to a brand new
(4)
three-bedroom house in Suburbia.
(5)

1 **A** Spelling error
   B Capitalization error
   C Punctuation error
   D No error

2 **F** Spelling error
   G Capitalization error
   H Punctuation error
   J No error

3 **A** Spelling error
   B Capitalization error
   C Punctuation error
   D No error

4 **F** Spelling error
   G Capitalization error
   H Punctuation error
   J No error

5 **A** Spelling error
   B Capitalization error
   C Punctuation error
   D No error

Answer Key

Practice 1

1. B
2. G
3. B
4. G
5. D

Practice 2

1. B
2. J
3. B
4. J
5. B

Customize for
Less Advanced Students

Tell students to pay special attention to the parts of the underlined sentence that contain the names of people and places. These are items that often contain capitalization errors.

Customize for
AP Students

Have students read the test passage as though they are proofreading their own work. If they wish, they should make editing marks on the test paper. Writing editing marks might speed up their decision-making process as they make response choices.

In-Depth Lesson Plan

	LESSON FOCUS	PRINT AND MEDIA RESOURCES
DAY 1	**End Marks and Commas** Students learn and apply concepts relating to periods, question marks, exclamation marks, and commas. (pp. 688–711/ Ⓗ510–533)	*Writing and Grammar* **Interactive Text,** Sections 27.1–2; *On-line Exercise Bank,* Sections 27.1–2 **Teaching Resources** *Grammar Exercise Workbook,* pp. 127–134; *Grammar Exercises Answers on Transparencies,* Ch. 27
DAY 2	**Semicolons and Colons** Students learn and apply concepts relating to semicolons and colons. (pp. 712–721/Ⓗ534–543)	*Writing and Grammar* **Interactive Text,** Section 27.3; *On-line Exercise Bank,* Section 27.3 **Teaching Resources** *Grammar Exercise Workbook,* pp. 135–136; *Hands-on Grammar Activity Book,* Ch. 27
DAY 3	**Quotation Marks and Underlining** Students learn and apply concepts relating to quotation marks, underlining, and italics. (pp. 722–735/Ⓗ544–557)	*Writing and Grammar* **Interactive Text,** Section 27.4; *On-line Exercise Bank,* Section 27.4 **Teaching Resources** *Grammar Exercise Workbook,* pp. 137–142
DAY 4	**Dashes to Apostrophes** Students learn and apply concepts relating to dashes, parentheses, brackets, hyphens, and apostrophes. (pp. 736–756/Ⓗ558–577)	*Writing and Grammar* **Interactive Text,** Sections 27.5–6; *On-line Exercise Bank,* Sections 27.5–6 **Teaching Resources** *Grammar Exercise Workbook,* pp. 143–150
DAY 5	**Review and Assess** Students review the chapter and demonstrate mastery of punctuation concepts. (pp. 757–759)	**Teaching Resources** *Formal Assessment,* Ch. 27

Accelerated Lesson Plan

	LESSON FOCUS	PRINT AND MEDIA RESOURCES
DAY 1	**End Marks and Commas** Students cover concepts relating to periods, question marks, exclamation marks, and commas as determined by their performance on the Diagnostic Test. (pp. 686–711/Ⓗ508–533)	*Writing and Grammar* **Interactive Text,** Sections 27.1–2; *On-line Exercise Bank,* Sections 27.1–2 **Teaching Resources** *Grammar Exercise Workbook,* pp. 127–134; *Grammar Exercises Answers on Transparencies,* Ch. 27
DAY 2	**Semicolons to Underlining** Students cover concepts relating to semicolons, colons, quotation marks, underlining, and italics. (pp. 712–735/Ⓗ534–557)	*Writing and Grammar* **Interactive Text,** Sections 27.3–4; *On-line Exercise Bank,* Sections 27.3–4 **Teaching Resources** *Grammar Exercise Workbook,* pp. 135–142
DAY 3	**Dashes to Apostrophes** Students cover concepts relating to dashes, parentheses, brackets, hyphens, and apostrophes. (pp. 736–756/Ⓗ558–577)	*Writing and Grammar* **Interactive Text,** Sections 27.5–6; *On-line Exercise Bank,* Sections 27.5–6 **Teaching Resources** *Grammar Exercise Workbook,* pp. 143–150; *Formal Assessment,* Ch. 27

Options for Adapting Lesson Plans

HOMEWORK

Have students complete any section of the chapter for homework.

FEATURES

Extend coverage with the Grammar in Literature features (pp. 692, 703, 727, 738, 751/Ⓗ514, 525, 549, 560, 573) and the Standardized Test Preparation Workshop (p. 760).

TECHNOLOGY

Students can use *Writing and Grammar* Interactive Text to complete the exercises interactively on computer. They can complete additional exercises in the *On-line Exercise Bank:* The Auto Check feature will grade their work. Go on-line: PH School.com Use Web Code: egk-1202

Writing and Grammar Handbook Alignment

Page numbers in Step-by-Step Teaching Guides in this Teacher's Edition refer to pages from the full student text. Handbook page references, indicated with this icon 🄷, are provided in Time and Resource Manager boxes and at the bottom of each Teacher's Edition page.

INTEGRATED SKILLS COVERAGE

Grammar in Literature SE pp. 692, 703, 727, 738, 751/
🄷514, 525, 549, 560, 573

Writing
Find It in Your Writing SE pp. 693, 711, 721, 735, 744, 756/
🄷515, 533, 543, 557, 566
Writing Application SE pp. 693, 711, 721, 735, 744, 756, 759, 763/
🄷515, 533, 543, 557, 566
Grammar and Style SE pp. 706, 713, 748, 753/🄷528, 535, 570, 575
Integrating Writing Skills ATE p. 733

Spelling Skills SE pp. 728, 743, 747/🄷550, 565, 569

Viewing and Representing Skills
Critical Viewing, SE pp. 686, 689, 696, 698, 700, 703, 705, 706,
708, 712, 713, 714, 723, 725, 726, 729, 737, 739, 741, 745, 746,
749, 750/🄷508, 511, 518, 520, 522, 525, 527, 528, 530, 534, 535,
536, 545, 547, 548, 551, 559, 561, 563, 567, 568, 571, 572

Speaking and Listening Skills ATE pp. 701, 723

Technology Skills SE pp. 691, 704, 715, 729, 736/🄷513, 526,
537, 551, 558

Vocabulary Skills ATE pp. 691, 716

Workplace Skills ATE pp. 689, 739

Real-World Connection ATE p. 750

ASSESSMENT SUPPORT

Standardized Test Preparation Workshop SE p. 760;
ATE pp. 701, 740

Standardized Test Preparation Workbook, pp. 53–54

Formal Assessment, Ch. 27

MEETING INDIVIDUAL NEEDS

Less Advanced Students ATE pp. 732, 761. See also Ongoing
Assessments ATE pp. 689, 690, 692, 695, 697, 698, 700, 703,
709, 714, 717, 724, 727, 730, 733, 739, 742, 748, 754.

AP Students ATE p. 713

Gifted and Talented Students ATE p. 705

ESL Students ATE pp. 715, 732, 751

Spatial Learners ATE pp. 697, 746, 761

Logical/Mathematical Learners ATE p. 740

BLOCK SCHEDULING

Pacing Suggestions
For 90-minute Blocks
• Administer the Diagnostic Test to students to determine instructional coverage.
• Have students complete the necessary exercises in class. Use the Hands-on Grammar activity to provide a change of pace.

Resources for Varying Instruction
• *Writing and Grammar* Interactive Text A 90-minute block provides an ideal opportunity for students to work on the computer.

Professional Development Support
• *How to Manage Instruction in the Block* This teaching resource provides management and activity suggestions.

MEDIA AND TECHNOLOGY

For the Student
• *Writing and Grammar* Interactive Text, Ch. 27
• *On-line Exercise Bank,* Sections 27.1–6

For the Teacher
• Teacher**EXPRESS** CD-ROM

WRITING AND GRAMMAR ON-LINE

Interactive Text (On-line or on CD-ROM)
• Easily navigable instruction with on-line supporting resources
• Self-scoring exercises and diagnostic tests

Companion Web Site PHSchool.com
• On-line Exercise Bank (use Web Code egk-1202)

See the Go On-line! feature, SE p. iii.

LITERATURE CONNECTIONS

Grammar in Literature selections from *Prentice Hall Literature, Penguin Edition,* The British Tradition:

from *Jane Eyre,* Charlotte Brontë, SE pp. 692, 703/🄷514

from *Hard Times,* Charles Dickens, SE pp. 727, 738/🄷549

from *Macbeth,* Act IV, William Shakespeare, SE p. 751/🄷573

Lesson Objectives

1. To use periods, question marks, and exclamation marks correctly
2. To use commas correctly
3. To use semicolons and colons correctly
4. To use quotation marks, single quotation marks, and italics correctly
5. To identify situations requiring dashes, parentheses, and brackets and to use them correctly
6. To use hyphens and apostrophes correctly
7. To produce legible work that shows correct use of the conventions of punctuation
8. To analyze the characteristics of clear texts such as conciseness, correctness, and completeness

Critical Viewing

Describe Sample response:

"This is one of the most beautiful castles I've ever seen," my friend Raphaela said.

"Should we add it to the places we want to visit?" I asked.

"Definitely!" she replied.

Chapter 27 Punctuation

Neuschwanstein Castle

Punctuation marks help to make a written work easier to understand by helping to organize and clarify the ideas in each sentence.

To understand the rules of punctuation and to punctuate your writing correctly, you must have a thorough knowledge of the elements of sentence structure. You should be able to recognize an appositive, a participial phrase, items in a series, and a complex or compound sentence. Each of these elements—and many others—is punctuated in a specific way.

In this chapter on punctuation, you will learn the major rules of punctuation that are so important to effective writing.

▲ Critical Viewing Neuschwanstein Castle in Bavaria, Germany, looks like a fairy-tale castle. Write several lines of dialogue about this castle, and punctuate them correctly. [Describe]

686 • Punctuation

☑ **ONGOING ASSESSMENT: Diagnose**

If students miss more than one item in any category, direct them to the relevant pages of the textbook and assign exercises for practice and review.

Verb Usage	Diagnostic Test Items	Teach	Practice	Section Review	Chapter Review
Skill Check A					
End Marks	A 1–5	pp. 688–692/Ⓗ510–514	Ex. 1–4	Ex. 5–8	Ex. 78
Skill Check B					
Commas	B 6–10	pp. 694–708/Ⓗ516–530	Ex. 12–22	Ex. 23–27	Ex. 79
Skill Check C					
Semicolons	C 11, 14	pp. 712–713/Ⓗ534–535	Ex. 31	Ex. 34, 36–38	Ex. 80
Colons	C 12–13, 15	pp. 715–716/Ⓗ537–538	Ex. 32–33	Ex. 35–38	Ex. 80

Diagnostic Test

Directions: Write all answers on a separate sheet of paper.

Skill Check A. Write the following sentences, using proper end marks to punctuate them.

1. Germany is a country in central Europe
2. Is France to the west of Germany
3. Yes, they share a border that has been a source of conflict
4. The Maginot line was a series of fortifications that the French built on that border for protection
5. Imagine their alarm when it proved utterly useless

Skill Check B. Use commas to punctuate these sentences.

6. Germany is large and it contains many beautiful cities.
7. Berlin Munich Bonn Frankfurt and Stuttgart are some of its principal cities.
8. The capital is Berlin which was famous for the wall that divided the city during the Cold War.
9. At that time in Germany's history Bonn served as the capital of West Germany the noncommunist nation that encompassed more than half of German territory.
10. The reunification of Germany however ended those divisions and the German economy became much stronger.

Skill Check C. Add colons and semicolons to these sentences.

11. Industry is the backbone of the German economy some of the world's largest corporations are based in that country.
12. Economic success has come with a price industrial pollution.
13. That pollution is particularly acute in Germany's major rivers the Rhine, the Danube, and the Elbe.
14. Most of Germany's woodlands have been harmed by acid rain in fact, the famed Black Forest has suffered extensive damage.
15. The largest cities in Germany are as follows Berlin, Bonn, Hamburg, and Munich.

Skill Check D. Punctuate the following sentences properly using quotation marks, underlining, dashes, and parentheses where necessary.

16. It was in Berlin that U.S. President John F. Kennedy uttered his now famous line: Ich bin ein Berliner!
17. Did you know that in some translations, that means, I am a jelly doughnut? my friend asked.
18. I responded, That shows how important it is to avoid grammatical errors; my friend nodded in agreement.
19. Germany now plays a central role along with France, Great Britain, and several other countries in the stability of Europe.
20. Few nations have had such a profound effect on the world a fact we must never forget.

Diagnostic Test

Each item in the Diagnostic Test corresponds to a specific section in the punctuation chapter, enabling you to tailor instruction to the particular needs of your students. See "Ongoing Assessment: Diagnose" below for further details.

Skill Check A

1. Europe.
2. Germany?
3. conflict.
4. protection.
5. useless! *or* .

Skill Check B

6. large, and
7. Berlin, Munich, Bonn, Frankfurt, and
8. Berlin, which
9. history, Bonn . . . West Germany, the
10. Germany, however . . . divisions, and

Skill Check C

11. economy;
12. price:
13. rivers:
14. rain;
15. follows:

Skill Check D

16. It was in Berlin that U.S President John F. Kennedy uttered his now famous line: "<u>Ich bin ein Berliner</u>!"
17. "Did you know that, in some translations, that means 'I am a jelly doughnut'?" my friend asked.
18. I responded, "That shows how important it is to avoid grammatical errors"; my friend nodded in agreement.
19. Germany now plays a central role (along with France, Great Britain, and several other countries) in the stability of Europe.
20. Few nations have had such a profound effect on the world—a fact we must never forget.

	✓ ONGOING ASSESSMENT: Diagnose *continued*				
Verb Usage	**Diagnostic Test Items**	**Teach**	**Practice**	**Section Review**	**Chapter Review**
Skill Check D					
Quotation Marks	D 16–18, 50	pp. 722–730/Ⓗ544–552	Ex. 42–45	Ex. 47–48, 50	Ex. 81
Underlining	D 16	pp. 731–733/Ⓗ553–555	Ex. 46	Ex. 49–50	Ex. 81
Skill Check E					
Dashes	D 20	pp. 736–739/Ⓗ558–561	Ex. 54–55	Ex. 58, 60	Ex. 82
Parentheses	D 19	pp. 740–743/Ⓗ562–565	Ex. 56–57	Ex. 59–60	Ex. 82
Cumulative Reviews and Applications				Ex. 9–11, 28–30, 39–41, 51–53, 61–63, 75–77	Ex. 83–86

⏱ TIME SAVERS!

📑 **Answers on Transparencies** Use the *Grammar Exercises Answers on Transparencies* for Chapter 27 to facilitate correction by students.

🖥 **On-Line Exercise Bank** Have students complete the Diagnostic Test on computer. The Auto Check feature will grade their work for you!

⚡ **Interest** Write *The team*
GRABBER *won the game* on
the board, and ask for volunteers to
read it in three different ways: as a
statement of fact, a question, and an
exclamation. Then, have students
volunteer other sentences that could
also be read to express three feelings.

Activate Prior Knowledge

Briefly review the functions of
sentences—exclamatory,
interrogative, declarative, and
imperative—as well as the kinds of
punctuation marks that usually end
each. Then have students tell how
they would punctuate the following:

*I asked him if he had ever visited
Germany (.)*

Who would like to travel there (?)

You're not excited to be going (. or ?)

Let's be sure to sign up (. or !)

TEACH

Step-by-Step Teaching Guide

Using End Marks

1. Make sure students understand
the difference between a direct
and an indirect question. Explain
that indirect questions do not use
question marks, quotation marks,
or inverted sentence order.

continued

Answer Key

▶ **Exercise 1**

Answers will vary; samples are given.

1. Germany is a vast, varied
country.
2. Look for Berlin east of the center
of Germany.
3. I wondered which German author
had recently won a Nobel Prize.
4. I think German food is delicious.
5. Learn all you can about Germany
for the social studies test!

End Marks

End marks include the period, the question mark, and the
exclamation mark. They are used mainly to conclude sentences. The period and the question mark are also used in
several special situations.

Using End Marks

To conclude sentences correctly, you must know whether to
use a period, a question mark, or an exclamation mark. First,
look at the rules governing the use of the period.

Period The period is the end mark used most often.

▶ **KEY CONCEPT** Use a period to end a declarative
sentence, a mild imperative, and an indirect question. ■

A declarative sentence is a statement of fact or opinion.
An imperative sentence gives a command or a direction.
(Imperative sentences often begin with a verb.) An indirect
question restates a question within a declarative sentence.

STATEMENT OF FACT:	Herman Hesse was a famous German writer.
STATEMENT OF OPINION:	I enjoyed many of his works.
COMMAND:	Finish your reading before you go out.
DIRECTION:	Turn left at the second traffic light.
INDIRECT QUESTION:	I asked him where he had learned to ski.

▶ **Exercise 1** Writing Declarative and Imperative Sentences
Follow each of the directions to write a declarative or imperative sentence, and punctuate it correctly.

EXAMPLE:	command about reading
ANSWER:	Read your assignment.

1. statement of fact about Germany
2. direction for finding Berlin on a map
3. indirect question about a German author
4. statement of opinion about German food
5. command about studying for a social studies test

Theme: Germany

In this section, you
will learn when to
use periods, question
marks, and exclama-
tion marks. Most of
the examples and
exercises in this
section are about
Germany.

**Cross-Curricular
Connection:
Social Studies**

▶ **More Practice**

**Grammar Exercise
Workbook**
• pp. 127–128
On-line Exercise Bank
• Section 27.1
Go on-line:
PHSchool.com
Enter Web Code:
egk-1202

⏱ TIME AND RESOURCE MANAGER

Resources
Print: *Grammar Exercise Workbook*, pp. 127–128; *Grammar Exercises Answers on Transparencies*, Ch. 27
Technology: *Writing and Grammar* Interactive Text, Section. 27.1; *On-Line Exercise Bank*, Section 27.1

Using the Full Student Edition	Using the Handbook 🄷
• Work through all key concepts, pp. 688–692.	• Work through all key concepts, pp. 510–514.
• Assign and review Exercises 1–4.	• Assign and review Exercises 1–4.
• Read and discuss Grammar in Literature, p. 692.	• Read and discuss Grammar in Literature, p. 514.

Brandenburg Gate, Germany

Question Mark Direct questions, often in inverted word order, require a question mark at the end.

▶ **KEY CONCEPT** Use a question mark to end an interrogative sentence, an incomplete question, or a statement intended as a question. ■

INTERROGATIVE SENTENCES:	Have you visited Germany? Which country will you visit next?
INCOMPLETE QUESTIONS:	Why? How much?
STATEMENTS INTENDED AS QUESTIONS:	This clock runs on batteries? We're going to have spaghetti?

Statements intended as questions should not be used too often. It is often better to rephrase them as direct questions.

STATEMENT INTENDED AS A QUESTION:	You agree?
REPHRASED AS A DIRECT QUESTION:	Do you agree?

Exclamation Mark An exclamation mark is intended for emphasis. It calls attention to an exclamatory sentence, an imperative sentence, or an interjection. Exclamation marks should be used sparingly. Reserve them for those situations in which you want to indicate strong emotion in a dramatic way.

▲ **Critical Viewing**
Write three questions about the Brandenburg Gate in Berlin, Germany. Make sure you punctuate your questions correctly. [Analyze]

End Marks • 689

ONGOING ASSESSMENT: Monitor and Reinforce

If students miss more than one item in Exercise 1, refer them to the following for additional practice.

In the Textbook	Print Resources	Technology
Section Review, Ex. 5, Section 27.1	*Grammar Exercise Workbook*, pp. 127–128	*On-Line Exercise Bank*, Section 27.1

Step-by-Step Teaching Guide continued

2. For further practice with periods and question marks, have students punctuate these examples and explain the marks they used:

   I asked Ralph where he put the car keys (.) (indirect question)

   Where did Ralph put the car keys (?) (interrogative sentence)

   Where (?) (incomplete question)

   Ralph put the car keys there (.) or (?) (statement *or* statement intended as a question)

3. Students may be unsure about punctuating interjections. Provide these examples, and have students discuss how the context dictates the choice of end mark.

   Yes? He really said yes to her question?

   Yes! I'm so happy he said yes!

   Yes, I am aware of his response to her question.

   Yes. That's all there is to say.

4. Remind students that exclamation marks are best used sparingly, especially in formal writing.

Integrating Workplace Skills

TelePrompTers™ Point out that when newscasters read from TelePrompTers™, they see only a few words at a time. At the end of each sentence, the end mark indicates how to intone the preceding sentence. Ask students to think of sentences that may be read differently than the end mark dictates because the newscaster was unable to see the entire sentence (*"The weather today will be sunny? Isn't that right, Bill?"* or *"The weather today will be sunny. That's right, Bill."*). Discuss with students cues that could help newscasters intone sentences correctly.

Critical Viewing

Analyze Sample questions: When was the Brandenburg Gate constructed? Who designed the Gate? What is the figure atop the Brandenburg Gate?

Exercise 2

1. literate.
2. degree.
3. country.
4. gymnasium.
5. Wow! program. or !

Step-by-Step Teaching Guide

Other Uses of End Marks

1. Read through the abbreviation examples with students and have volunteers clarify the meanings of any that students are unsure of.

2. Challenge students to explain why forms like *FBI* and *NASA* don't need periods (they are acronyms and are used like words). Mention that the use of periods varies with abbreviations of group and company names, and tell them to check a dictionary whenever they are not sure.

continued

Language Highlight

Scribes in Ireland during the Middle Ages are thought to be the first to consistently use spaces in between words they transcribed from Latin. They may have done so because Latin was not their native language, and separating the Latin words made it easier for them to comprehend. At this time, punctuation was not a system of formal marks. Because most writing was intended to be read aloud, punctuation marks consisted of indications for pauses. Such marks were not used consistently and often differed from region to region.

27.1

> **KEY CONCEPT** Use an exclamation mark to end an exclamatory sentence, a forceful imperative sentence, or an interjection expressing strong emotion. ■

EXCLAMATORY SENTENCES: His admission of guilt shocked us! That sunset is magnificent!

IMPERATIVE SENTENCES: Never try that trick again! Come here quickly!

An interjection can be used with either a comma or an exclamation mark. An exclamation mark increases the emphasis.

WITH A COMMA: Oh, she is usually on time.
WITH AN EXCLAMATION MARK: Oh! I am amazed!

> **Exercise 2** Using End Marks Copy each item, and punctuate it correctly.

1. Linda thinks that nearly all Germans are literate
2. Impressed with the German education system, she asked the professor where he had studied for his degree
3. He mentioned Heidelberg University, the foremost institution in the country
4. The most difficult school before the university level is called the gymnasium
5. Wow The gymnasium has an intense academic program

Other Uses of End Marks

> **KEY CONCEPT** Use a period to end most abbreviations. ■

ABBREVIATIONS FOR TITLES:	Dr. Sr. Mrs. Mr. Gov. Maj. Rev. Prof. Lt.
ABBREVIATIONS FOR PLACE NAMES:	Ave. Bldg. Blvd. Mt. Dr. Jct. St. Ter. Rd. Pk.
ABBREVIATIONS FOR TIME AND DATES:	Sun. Dec. sec. min. hr. wk. yr. mo. Sat. A.M. P.M.
ABBREVIATIONS FOR MEASUREMENTS:	in. ft. yd. mi. tsp. tbsp. gal. pt. oz. lb. F.
ABBREVIATIONS WITHOUT PERIODS:	mm cm m km mg g kg L C

---

interactive Textbook

Complete the exercise on-line! Exercise 2 is available on-line or on CD-ROM.

More Practice

Grammar Exercise Workbook
• pp. 127–128
On-line Exercise Bank
• Section 27.1
Go on-line:
PHSchool.com
Enter Web Code:
egk-1202

Learn More

For a full list of abbreviations and the words for which they stand, see pages 934–937.

☑ ONGOING ASSESSMENT: Monitor and Reinforce

If students miss more than one item in Exercise 2, refer them to the following for additional practice.

In the Textbook	Print Resources	Technology
Section Review, Ex. 5, Section 27.1	*Grammar Exercise Workbook,* pp. 127–128	*On-Line Exercise Bank,* Section 27.1

▶**KEY CONCEPT** When an abbreviation ending with a period is placed at the end of a sentence, do not add another period as an end mark. If an end mark other than a period is required, however, you must add the end mark. ■

INCORRECT:	The speaker will be Adam Martin, Jr..
CORRECT:	The speaker will be Adam Martin, Jr.
INCORRECT:	Is the speaker Adam Martin, Jr.
CORRECT:	Is the speaker Adam Martin, Jr.?

The following chart lists some abbreviations.

ABBREVIATIONS WITH AND WITHOUT END MARKS

anon.	anonymous	mgr.	manager
approx.	approximately	misc.	miscellaneous
assoc.	association	mph	miles per hour
A.W.O.L.	absent without leave	myth.	mythology or mythological
C.O.D.	cash on delivery	No.	number
dept.	department	pg.	page
doz.	dozen(s)	pkg.	package
ea.	each	poet.	poetical, poetry
EDT	Eastern Daylight Time	POW	prisoner of war
EST	Eastern Standard Time	pp.	pages
FM	frequency modulation	pub.	published, publisher
gov. or govt.	government	pvt.	private
Gr.	Greek	recd.	received
ht.	height	rpm	revolutions per minute
incl.	including	R.S.V.P.	please reply
intro.	introduction	sp.	spelling
ital	italics	SRO	standing room only
kt.	karat or carat	SST	Supersonic transport
meas.	measure	vol.	volume
mfg.	manufacturing	wt.	weight

📟 Internet Tip

When choosing a user name for the Internet, don't put any periods in the name. Periods have special significance to computers as they communicate with each other over the Internet, and a bad user name (one with periods) can cause all kinds of trouble for you, such as lost e-mail.

3. Discuss with students the rationale for not including another period after an abbreviation like *Jr.* (A double period looks funny and may be misread as part of ellipses.)

4. Have students familiarize themselves with the abbreviations in the chart. Discuss which ones, if any, would be appropriate to use in formal writing.

Integrating Vocabulary Skills

Punctuation Marks Explain that two meanings of *punctuate* are "to interrupt" and "to emphasize" and ask students how these definitions apply to punctuation marks (they interrupt the flow of a sentence to indicate a pause or emphasize an element by setting it off). Have students use their dictionaries to find the roots of *question* (Latin *quaestio,* "to ask"), *exclamation* (Latin prefix *ex-* "out" and the verb *clamare,* "to shout"), and *abbreviation* (Latin *abbrebiare,* "to shorten"). Then have them look for other words with the same roots.

Other Uses of End Marks
continued

1. Remind students that the actual items in outlines are not followed by end punctuation unless the outline is a sentence outline.

2. If you prefer that students use other outline formats, show students how to puncutate them.

Answer Key

Exercise 3

1. C.O.D.; today.
2. Prof.; philosophers.
3. Ph.D. candidate.
4. Mr.; Jr.; Dept.; U.; birth.
5. A.D. 1770.

Exercise 4

Have students read their work aloud.

Grammar in Literature

1. Have a volunteer read the dialogue aloud, using intonation to suggest the various end marks.

2. Have students discuss how the punctuation marks affect the meaning of Helen's words.

More About the Writer

Charlotte Brontë's brief, unhappy life was bound by rigid conventions and haunted by failure and loss. As children, she and her sisters, Emily and Anne, found solace in a vivid fantasy life. Later, Charlotte endured a disappointing teaching career, critical rejection, and the fatal illnesses of several family members. Not long after wedding her father's curate, Charlotte Brontë died.

Connections With Literature

More from *Jane Eyre* can be found in *Prentice Hall Literature, Penguin Edition,* The British Tradition.

27.1

▶ **KEY CONCEPT** Use a period after numbers and letters in outlines. ∎

EXAMPLE:
    I. Maintaining your pet's health
      A. Diet
        1. For a puppy
        2. For a mature dog
      B. Exercise

▶ **Exercise 3** Using End Marks in Other Situations On a separate sheet of paper, add the necessary end marks to the following.

1. A package arrived COD from Munich today
2. Prof Schmidt sent books about German philosophers
3. The names of Hegel and Kant, who are giants in that field, are familiar to any Ph D candidate
4. I checked with Mr George Frasier, Jr, in the German Studies Dept at the U of Wisconsin, in Madison, Wisconsin, but he was unsure of Hegel's date of birth
5. He suggested the year AD 1770

▶ **Exercise 4** Using End Marks Correctly in Your Own Writing Write a paragraph about a famous German writer or scientist. Correctly use each type of end mark.

GRAMMAR IN LITERATURE

from **Jane Eyre**
Charlotte Brontë

The end punctuation marks in this passage from Brontë's novel reflect the earnest and spirited tone of this conversation between Jane Eyre and her friend Helen.

"Well," I asked impatiently, "is not Mrs. Reed a hard-hearted, bad woman?"

"She has been unkind to you, no doubt; because, you see, she dislikes your cast of character, as Miss Scatcherd does mine: but how minutely you remember all she has done and said to you! What a singularly deep impression her injustice seems to have made on your heart! No ill usage so brands its record on my feelings. Would you not be happier if you tried to forget her severity, together with the passionate emotions it excited? Life appears to me too short to be spent in nursing animosity or registering wrongs."

692 • Punctuation

More Practice

Grammar Exercise Workbook
• pp. 127–128
On-line Exercise Bank
• Section 27.1
Go on-line:
PHSchool.com
Enter Web Code:
egk-1202

Get instant feedback! Exercises 3 and 4 are available on-line or on CD-ROM.

☑ **ONGOING ASSESSMENT: Monitor and Reinforce**

If students have difficulty with Exercise 3 or 4, refer them to the following for additional practice.

In the Textbook	Print Resources	Technology
Section Review, Ex. 5–6, Section 27.1	*Grammar Exercise Workbook,* pp. 127–128	*On-Line Exercise Bank,* Section 27.1

Section 27.1 Section Review

GRAMMAR EXERCISES 5–11

Exercise 5 **Using End Marks** On a separate sheet of paper, add the proper end marks to these sentences.

1. Schooling in Germany is compulsory and free for those aged 6 to 18
2. Children are given extensive tests after primary school, around the age of 10
3. What is the purpose of those tests
4. He asked if we had heard that many students are also musically talented
5. Do you know that the concert halls in Dresden attract large audiences

Exercise 6 **Using End Marks in Special Situations** On a separate sheet of paper, add end marks to these sentences.

1. I had nearly sixty dollars—$58 25, to be precise—that I wanted to convert to German marks
2. The US Treasury office in Boston, MA, gave me the shocking news: The mark effectively doesn't exist anymore
3. I asked Prof Martin, who has a PhD in economics, how that could be
4. Dr Martin explained that Germany is one of several member countries of the European Union (EU) that have agreed to use a single new currency, the euro
5. As of 12 PM today, a euro was worth $1 041, just over a dollar

Exercise 7 **Using All Types of End Marks** Rewrite the following items, adding end marks as needed.

1. Two of Germany's many music festivals are the Wagner Festival and the Bach Festival
2. Many believe that there was nothing—preludes, operas, concertos, sonatas—that Mozart could not compose or play

3. Oh I had no idea that Mozart was Austrian, not German
4. Who can top Brahms and Mendelssohn, two great composers
5. Did all these great classical composers really emerge from one country Why

Exercise 8 **Revising to Add Correct End Marks** Revise the following letter, adding or revising end marks as necessary.

(1) 45 Blazewood Dr
(2) Uniondale, NY. 11553
(3) Mon, Jan 3, 2010
(4) Dear Mr Kohl:
(5) Wow. Thanks for the tickets to Bayreuth! (6) I'm sorry about that late phone call the other night; I forgot that 7:00 PM in New York is 1:00 AM in Germany (7) At least now I know how to pronounce *Wagner* properly? (8) That's "VAHGner," right
(9) Sincerely,
(10) Lincoln Townes, Jr

Exercise 9 **Find It in Your Reading** Skim through a magazine article, and highlight at least three uses of each type of end mark. Explain each example.

Exercise 10 **Find It in Your Writing** Choose a piece of writing from your portfolio. Revise one of the paragraphs so that it includes question marks and exclamation marks as well as periods.

Exercise 11 **Writing Application** Write a letter like the one above. Use every type of end mark at least once.

Put this sentence on the board; have students speculate on its meaning:

We eat boys and girls in order to be well nourished.

After students' discussion, go back and set off *boys and girls* with commas. Have students tell what the sentence means now.

Activate Prior Knowledge

Present the following sentences and have students revise them to correct comma errors:

The bride wore a beautiful, taffeta dress but the groom showed up in blue jeans. (The bride wore a beautiful taffeta dress, but the groom showed up in blue jeans.)

David Lewis M.D. the father of the bride was furious. (David Lewis, M.D., the father of the bride, was furious.)

TEACH

Step-by-Step Teaching Guide

Commas With Compound Sentences

1. Have students discuss which coordinating conjunctions they find most often in compound sentences (probably *and, but,* and *or*). Ask for volunteers to create compound sentences using the other coordinating conjunctions and to write them correctly on the board.

2. Mention to students that they will sometimes see commas in sentences like *The couple intended to honeymoon in Las Vegas, but finally decided against it,* where the second part of the compound verb is preceded by *but*. Explain that this use is generally avoided in formal writing.

Section 27.2 Commas

This section presents the rules governing the use of commas. To use commas correctly, you must have a thorough knowledge of sentence structure. Studying this section can help you master the rules governing the use of commas and, at the same time, serve as a review of some basic elements of sentence structure.

Using Commas With Compound Sentences

A single independent clause expresses a complete thought and often stands alone as a simple sentence. Two independent clauses, correctly joined and punctuated, form a compound sentence. The conjunctions used to connect independent clauses are called *coordinating conjunctions*. The seven coordinating conjunctions are *and, but, for, nor, or, so,* and *yet*.

▶ **KEY CONCEPT** Use a comma before the conjunction to separate two or more independent clauses in a compound sentence. ■

EXAMPLES: My cousin is getting married this summer, but I won't be able to attend the wedding.

The Newport Jazz Festival draws a big crowd every year, and this year won't be any different.

Remember to use both a comma and a coordinating conjunction in a compound sentence. Using only a comma would result in a run-on sentence.

Notice also that the ideas in both independent clauses in each of the preceding examples are related. Do not construct a compound sentence from two unrelated clauses.

Finally, do not confuse a compound sentence with a simple sentence that has a compound verb.

SIMPLE SENTENCE
WITH A COMPOUND VERB: John bought them a blender and waited to have it gift wrapped.

COMPOUND SENTENCE: John bought them a blender, and he waited to have it gift wrapped.

Theme: Celebrations

In this section, you will learn about the many uses of the comma. Most of the examples and exercises in this section are about different kinds of celebrations and milestones.

Cross-Curricular Connection: Social Studies

⏱ TIME AND RESOURCE MANAGER

Resources
Print: *Grammar Exercise Workbook,* pp. 129–134; *Grammar Exercises Answers on Transparencies,* Ch. 27
Technology: *Writing and Grammar* Interactive Text, Section 27.2; *On-Line Exercise Bank,* Section 27.2

Using the Full Student Edition	Using the Handbook Ⓗ
• Work through all key concepts, pp. 694–708. • Assign and review Exercises 12–22. • Read and discuss Grammar in Literature, p. 703.	• Work through all key concepts, pp. 516–530. • Assign and review Exercises 12–22. • Read and discuss Grammar in Literature, p. 525.

Exercise 12 Using Commas to Separate Independent Clauses Copy each of the following sentences, adding commas as needed.

EXAMPLE: I wanted to go to my cousin's wedding in Denver but plane tickets cost too much.

ANSWER: I wanted to go to my cousin's wedding in Denver, but plane tickets cost too much.

1. The wedding was on January 12 and that is a popular time to go to Denver.
2. People fly into Denver and drive to ski resorts from there.
3. I enjoy going to weddings for there is always great food and good dancing music.
4. My father doesn't usually dance but at a wedding he might.
5. I was invited to the wedding so I will have to send a wedding present.
6. I don't know my cousin's bride very well so I don't know what to send.
7. Money is always a good present but it seems too impersonal for my cousin.
8. My mother usually sends towels but I don't know what color their bathroom is.
9. Art is very personal yet I think I know my cousin well enough to choose art for him.
10. I will go to the mall today and I will browse in the art store.

Exercise 13 Proofreading to Correct the Use of Commas Revise the following paragraph, adding and deleting commas as necessary.

(1) Celebrations are the familial, or communal sharing of an event. (2) Many celebrations are based on traditional customs and many of those customs involve rites of passage. (3) Birthdays and "sweet-sixteen" parties celebrate a new phase in the life of a person and new responsibilities, and attitudes are expected. (4) In many cultures, sweet-sixteen parties are elaborate and some families consider them as formal as a wedding. (5) Marriage and death are two other life phases, that are celebrated in different ways around the world.

More Practice

Grammar Exercise Workbook
• pp. 129–134
On-line Exercise Bank
• Section 27.2
Go on-line:
PHSchool.com
Enter Web Code:
egk-1202

Interactive Textbook

Get instant feedback! Exercises 12 and 13 are available on-line or on CD-ROM.

Answer Key

▶ **Exercise 12**

1. January 12, and
2. correct
3. weddings, for
4. dance, but
5. wedding, so
6. well, so
7. present, but
8. towels, but
9. personal, yet
10. today, and

▶ **Exercise 13**

1. communal,
2. customs, and
3. person, and new responsibilities and attitudes
4. elaborate, and
5. life phases that

☑ **ONGOING ASSESSMENT: Monitor and Reinforce**

If students have difficulty with Exercise 12 or 13, refer them to the following for additional practice.

In the Textbook	Print Resources	Technology
Section Review, Ex. 23, Section 27.2	*Grammar Exercise Workbook,* pp. 129–130	*On-Line Exercise Bank,* Section 27.2

Commas with Series and Adjectives

1. Write the terms *words*, *phrases*, and *subordinate clauses* on the board. Ask students to give you three examples, related in topic, of each. Then, ask them to explain how they would include the three items in a sentence and to offer complete sentences using each series.

2. Mention to students that sometimes they will see items in a series without a comma before the *and*. Explain that this style is preferred primarily in magazines and newspapers. Because it can cause confusion in reading, it is generally avoided in formal writing.

continued

Critical Viewing

Describe Sample response: I see bright colors, happy people, and a very crowded street.

27.2

Using Commas With Series and Adjectives

Series A series consists of three or more words, phrases, or subordinate clauses of a similar kind.

▶ **KEY CONCEPT** Use commas to separate three or more words, phrases, or clauses in a series. ■

WORDS IN A SERIES:	Venice, Rio, and Trinidad have notable carnivals.
	Her costume was exotic, exciting, and original.
PHRASES IN A SERIES:	The groom was fidgeting at first, then chewing his lip, and finally sweating profusely.
	It's important to drink plenty of fluids before the day arrives, during the event, and immediately afterward.
SUBORDINATE CLAUSES IN A SERIES:	The newspapers reported that the weather was flawless, that the dinner was impeccable, and that the band played remarkably well.

Notice that the number of commas in each of the preceding series is one fewer than the number of items in the series. If there are three items in a series, two commas are used; if there are four items in a series, three commas are used; and so on.

◀ **Critical Viewing** Describe what you see in this picture of the Carnival in Brazil. Use commas in a series in at least one place in your description. **[Describe]**

When conjunctions are used to separate all of the items in a series, no commas are needed.

EXAMPLE: We saw fireworks and streamers and confetti.

You should also avoid placing commas before items, such as *salt and pepper,* that are paired so often that they are thought of as one item.

EXAMPLE: The best man, bride and groom, and maid of honor sat together.

Coordinate Adjectives Sometimes, two or more adjectives are used together. Follow the rules below.

▶ **KEY CONCEPT** Use commas to separate *coordinate adjectives,* or adjectives of equal rank. ■

COORDINATE ADJECTIVES: a tasteless, boring affair
                                               a raucous, festive, thrilling occasion

An adjective is equal in rank to another if the word *and* can be inserted between them without changing the meaning of the sentence. Another way to test whether or not adjectives are coordinate is to reverse their order. If the sentence still sounds correct, they are of equal rank.

If you cannot place the word *and* between adjectives or reverse their order without changing the meaning of the sentence, they are called *cumulative adjectives.*

▶ **KEY CONCEPT** Do not use a comma between cumulative adjectives. ■

CUMULATIVE ADJECTIVES: a new dinner jacket
                                              many unusual guests

▶ **Exercise 14** Supplying Commas to Separate Items in a Series Copy each of the following sentences, inserting commas to separate items as needed.
1. The bride's mother was making up the list of invitations arranging for the delivery of flowers and making place-cards for the reception.
2. The groom's mother was arranging for the rehearsal the rehearsal dinner and accommodations for the guests.
3. The bride and groom were responsible for the dinner menu the reception the music and gifts for the bridal party.
4. They were hoping to arrange a truly tasteful lovely wedding.
5. Getting married buying a house and having children are some of the most stressful things in life.

interactive Textbook

Get instant feedback! Exercise 14 is available on-line or on CD-ROM.

▶ **More Practice**

Grammar Exercise Workbook
• pp. 129–134
On-line Exercise Bank
• Section 27.2
    Go on-line:
    PHSchool.com
    Enter Web Code:
    egk-1202

Commas • **697**

3. Ask for volunteers to write original phrases that demonstrate both coordinate and cumulative adjectives.
4. Write students' phrases on the board, and as a class check them by applying the two tests mentioned in the text. Explain that if you cannot put *and* between the adjectives or change their order, then the adjectives are cumulative.
5. Point out that the rules for comma usage with coordinate adjectives apply to all parts of speech used as adjectives.
6. Finally, challenge students to think of pairs of adjectives that are never divided by commas (stock phrases such as *pretty little, great big*).

Customize for
Spatial Learners

To help students focus on the specific elements requiring punctuation in a sentence with a series of adjectives, write only the adjective series and the noun it modifies on the board. For example, for the sentence *He was a strong healthy baby* you would write *baby strong healthy.* Draw an arrow from each of the modifiers to *baby.* Then demonstrate that (1) the order of *strong* and *healthy* can be reversed and (2) *and* can be put between them. Therefore, a comma should be put between these adjectives.

Answer Key

▶ **Exercise 14**

1. making up the list of invitations, arranging for the delivery of flowers, and
2. for the rehearsal, the rehearsal dinner, and
3. for the dinner menu, the reception, the music, and
4. a truly tasteful, lovely
5. Getting married, buying a house, and

☑ **ONGOING ASSESSMENT: Monitor and Reinforce**

If students miss more than one item in Exercise 14, refer them to the following for additional pratice.

In the Textbook	Print Resources	Technology
Section Review, Ex. 23–24, Section 27.2	*Grammar Exercise Workbook,* pp. 129–130	*On-Line Exercise Bank,* Section 27.2

Answer Key

Because of . . . common, welcome, and necessary . . . milking, feeding animals, sowing, and harvesting.

Today, parents worry whether the new baby is healthy, whether its needs are provided for, and whether . . . more confident, and . . .

For monarchs, . . . continuing the line, maintaining authority, and . . . the hoisting of castle flags, cannon or rifle salutes, and a . . .

Births are celebrated and commemorated . . . a festive, noisy party . . . to help guide, nurture, and . . . presentation ceremony, a bris, or . . .

Critical Viewing

Connect The photograph best illustrates the second paragraph. The photograph seems to have no connection to farm chores (first paragraph), the monarchy (third), or celebrations (fourth).

◄ **Critical Viewing** Which of the paragraphs in the exercise below does this photograph illustrate? Explain. [Connect]

► **Exercise 15** Proofreading to Correct Errors in the Use of Commas to Separate Items in a Series Revise the following, adding or deleting commas as necessary.

Because of the agricultural nature of previous centuries, large families were common welcome, and necessary. Children were needed for the farm chores of milking feeding animals sowing and harvesting.

Today, parents worry whether the new baby is healthy whether its needs are provided for and whether its future happiness is secure. New parents both feed and dress the baby—often nervously. As time passes, they become more confident and the tasks that once took hours are quickly performed.

For monarchs, producing children is a necessary means of continuing, the line maintaining authority and receiving the country's financial stipends. Announcements of royal births are still cause for the hoisting of castle flags cannon or rifle salutes and a national day of celebration.

Births are celebrated, and commemorated throughout the world in a variety of ways. In Denmark, families celebrate births with a festive noisy party and a traditional dance. Selecting godparents to help guide nurture and protect the child is a common practice in various countries. In most cultures, the baby is introduced to the community in a celebration such as a presentation ceremony a bris or a christening.

698 • Punctuation

☑ **ONGOING ASSESSMENT: Monitor and Reinforce**

If students have difficulty with Exercise 15, refer them to the following for additional practice.

In the Textbook	Print Resources	Technology
Section Review, Ex. 23–24, Section 27.2	*Grammar Exercise Workbook,* pp. 129–130	*On-Line Exercise Bank,* Section 27.2

Using Commas After Introductory Material

Most introductory material is set off with a comma.

▶ **KEY CONCEPT** Use a comma after an introductory word, phrase, or clause. ■

INTRODUCTORY WORDS:	Yes, we do expect to hear from them soon. No, there has been no response. Well, I was definitely surprised by her question.
NOUNS OF DIRECT ADDRESS:	Joe, will you attend?
INTRODUCTORY ADVERBS:	Hurriedly, they gathered up their equipment. Patiently, the children's mother explained it to them again.
PARTICIPIAL PHRASES:	Moving quickly, she averted a potential social disaster. Marching next to each other in the parade, we introduced ourselves and started to chat.
PREPOSITIONAL PHRASES:	In the shade of the maple tree, a family spread a picnic cloth. After the lengthy festivities, we were all exhausted.
INFINITIVE PHRASES:	To choose the right gift, I consulted the bridal registry. To finish my speech on time, I will have to cut some remarks.
ADVERBIAL CLAUSES:	When she asked for a permit for the fair, she was sure it would be denied. If you compete in marathons, you may be interested in this one.

Only one comma should be used after two prepositional phrases or a compound participial or infinitive phrase.

EXAMPLES:	In the pocket of his vest, he found the ring. Lost in the crowd and overwhelmed by the confusion, the children asked the policeman for help.

Commas • 699

Step-by-Step Teaching Guide

Commas After Introductory Material

1. Write this sentence on the board and ask students to supply words or groups of words to add to the beginning of the sentence: *I walked to school.*

2. Help students add introductory words or phrases and identify the kinds of elements these are: nouns of direct address (*Ralph,*), introductory adverbs (*Quickly,*), long prepositional phrases (*Through the steadily falling rain,*), participial phrases (*Carrying my lunch,*), infinitive phrases (*To arrive on time,*), and adverbial clauses (*After the snowstorm stopped,*).

✓ ONGOING ASSESSMENT: Prerequisite Skills

If students have difficulty with some of the constructions requiring commas, you may find it necessary to review the following to assure coverage of prerequisite knowledge.

In the Textbook	Print Resources	Technology

Phrases and Clauses,
   Sections 19.1, 19.2, 19.3
	Grammar Exercise Workbook,
	   pp. 33–44
		On-Line Exercise Bank,
		   Sections 19.1, 19.2, 19.3

Answer Key

▶ Exercise 16

1. doubt,
2. societies,
3. correct
4. Traditionally,
5. cases, *or* correct
6. training,
7. Yes,
8. merit,
9. ways, *or* correct
10. the same,

Critical Viewing

Infer Sample response: Having finished four years of study, these young people are celebrating their graduation from high school.

27.2

It is not absolutely necessary to set off short prepositional phrases. However, you may find that a comma is needed with a two- or three-word phrase in order to avoid confusion.

CLEAR: In the evening we ate dinner at the reception.
CONFUSING: In the rain drops stained the fine tablecloths.
CLEAR: In the rain, drops stained the fine tablecloths.

▶ Exercise 16 Using Commas to Set Off Introductory Material Copy each sentence that needs commas, adding them as necessary. If a sentence needs no commas, write *correct*.

1. Without a doubt entering into adulthood is one of the most difficult steps of life.
2. In many Middle Eastern, Native American, and African societies very specific ceremonies welcome teenage boys and girls into adulthood.
3. These rituals and ceremonies include being taught by selected elders.
4. Traditionally customs and beliefs held sacred by the community are taught to the young people.
5. In some cases boys and girls are secluded for months to concentrate exclusively on matters of growing up.
6. After this intensive training the young people prove their worthiness by demonstrating their maturity.
7. Yes some even undergo dangerous physical endurance tests, such as surviving a night out in the deep woods.
8. To prove their merit other young people must flawlessly recite or perform traditional oral and written works of the culture.
9. In some ways these are similar to such religious rites of passage as bar and bat mitzvahs, first communion, and confirmation.
10. Though not quite the same a secular equivalent might be high-school or college final exams.

More Practice

Grammar Exercise Workbook
• pp. 129–134
On-line Exercise Bank
• Section 27.2
Go on-line:
PHSchool.com
Enter Web Code:
egk-1202

interactive
Textbook

Complete the exercise on-line! Exercise 16 is available on-line or on CD-ROM.

▶ **Critical Viewing** Using introductory phrases, describe what the people in this picture are celebrating. **[Infer]**

☑ ONGOING ASSESSMENT: Monitor and Reinforce

If students miss more than two items in Exercise 16, refer them to the following for additional practice.

In the Textbook	Print Resources	Technology
Section Review, Ex. 23–26, Section 27.2	*Grammar Exercise Workbook,* pp. 131–132	*On-Line Exercise Bank,* Section 27.2

KEY CONCEPT Use commas to set off parenthetical expressions—words or phrases that interrupt the flow of a sentence. ■

Parenthetical expressions may come at the end of a sentence or in the middle. When a parenthetical expression appears in the middle of a sentence, two commas are needed to set it off from the rest of the sentence.

NOUNS OF DIRECT ADDRESS:	Will you have lunch with us, Ted? I wonder, Mr. Green, where they'll go for their honeymoon.
CONJUNCTIVE ADVERBS:	Someone else had already bought them a toaster, however. We could not, therefore, buy one.
COMMON EXPRESSIONS:	I listened to the teacher's explanation as carefully as anyone else, I think.
CONTRASTING EXPRESSIONS:	Tom is seventeen, not eighteen. Lisa's personality, not her beauty, won Bill's heart.

Appositives, participial phrases, and adjective clauses can be either essential or nonessential. (The terms *restrictive* and *nonrestrictive* are also used to refer to these two kinds of materials.) Essential material, which is necessary to the meaning of a sentence, is not set off with commas.

ESSENTIAL APPOSITIVE:	The singer *Diana Ross* is also an actress.
ESSENTIAL PARTICIPIAL PHRASE:	The woman *buying the tomatoes* is my mother.
ESSENTIAL ADJECTIVE CLAUSE:	The report *that the committee will consider today* was prepared by members of the first-aid squad.

The preceding examples illustrate three kinds of essential elements. In the first example, the appositive *Diana Ross* identifies the specific singer. In the next example, the participial phrase *buying the tomatoes* identifies the specific woman. In the last example, the adjective clause *that the committee will consider today* identifies the specific report. Because they limit, or restrict, identification to the person or thing described in the appositive, participial phrase, or adjective clause, these items are all essential. They cannot be removed without changing the meaning of the sentence, so they require no commas.

Commas • 701

Commas for Parenthetical Elements

1. Tell students that a common error with parenthetical expressions is to precede them with a comma but forget the comma that follows them. Suggest that they look carefully for this mistake when revising their writing.

2. Point out that certain commonly used parenthetical expressions, such as *of course, without a doubt, in fact, by the way,* and *for example,* are short prepositional phrases. Because they are parenthetical, they are set off even at the beginnings of sentences.

3. Have students read the last three examples and discuss why they do not need commas (the italicized material is essential to meaning).

Integrating Speaking and Listening Skills

Commas Dictate the following sentences to the class, and ask students to write them with the proper commas in place:

After the ballgame was over, we stood up, and I grabbed my mitt, the popcorn, and the program.

Walking toward the gate, the excited crowds were still cheering, of course, for the winning team.

The usher, Pablo, stood on his seat and supervised the exiting crowd.

Have students volunteer to read aloud their sentences, pausing where commas are used. As the other students listen to the sentences with the pauses, discuss whether the sentence has been punctuated correctly.

STANDARDIZED TEST PREPARATION WORKSHOP

Grammar and Usage Many standardized tests require students to recognize incorrect punctuation and to revise errors in a composition. Use the following example to demonstrate.

The woman who sang the national anthem before the game is a renowned star of stage and screen.

What revision, if any, is needed in this sentence?

A Place a comma after *woman*.

B Place a comma after *game*.

C Place a comma after *woman* and after *game*.

D No revision is needed.

The answer is **D**. The adjective clause *who sang the national anthem before the game* is essential to the sentence and does not need to be set off with commas.

Commas With Nonessential Elements

1. Remind students that the more specific the word being modified, the more likely the appositive, participle, or clause that modifies it will not be essential to meaning. For example, clauses following proper nouns are virtually always nonessential and need to be set off with commas.

2. For practice, have students write two sentences with basically the same meaning, one with a nonessential expression and one with an essential expression. Write one pair on the board, and have another student analyze the punctuation of the two sentences.

Answer Key

1. feasts, without a doubt,
2. careful, not haphazard,
3. festivals, in fact,
4. festivals, in most cases,
5. individuals, however,
6. correct
7. Traditions, such as . . . ago,
8. Costumes, many of them homemade,
9. originated, one would think,
10. festivals, such as the Carnival in Trinidad,

27.2

Nonessential elements also provide information, but that information is not essential to the meaning of the sentence. Because nonessential elements do not alter the meaning and are not necessary for purposes of identification, they require commas to set them off.

▶ **KEY CONCEPT** Use commas to set off nonessential expressions. ■

NONESSENTIAL APPOSITIVE:	Diana Ross, *the singer*, is also an actress.
NONESSENTIAL PARTICIPIAL PHRASE:	My mother, *buying the tomatoes*, is an excellent cook.
NONESSENTIAL ADJECTIVE CLAUSE:	The first-aid squad's report, *which the committee will consider today*, took six months to prepare.

The nonessential elements in the preceding examples are interesting, but they are not necessary to the main ideas in the sentences. *Diana Ross*, *my mother*, and *the first-aid squad's report* clearly identify the items *being discussed*. The nonessential elements, therefore, are set off with commas.

▶ **Exercise 17** Setting Off Parenthetical Expressions Copy these sentences, inserting commas to set off nonessential parenthetical expressions. If the sentence is correct as is, write *correct*.

EXAMPLE: You look best I think in bright colors.
ANSWER: You look best, I think, in bright colors.

1. Festivals and feasts without a doubt are favorite forms of celebration.
2. They are community or national celebrations involving the careful not haphazard planning of events.
3. People don't realize that festivals in fact don't just happen; they are usually organized by civic and cultural groups.
4. Feasts and festivals in most cases honor some special event that occurred in the history of the town or nation.
5. Heroic individuals however are sometimes the subject of these celebrations; Zapata is one such Mexican hero.
6. Historical and cultural aspects of a nation are celebrated.
7. Traditions such as baking bread in earthen clay ovens as practiced centuries ago are usually included in festivals.
8. Costumes many of them homemade are often the most fascinating part of festivals such as the Carnival in Venice.
9. These traditional feasts and festivals originated one would think with the ancient festivities at harvest time.
10. Some festivals such as the Carnival in Trinidad include the selection of the King and Queen of Calypso.

Interactive Textbook

Get instant feedback! Exercises 17 and 18 are available on-line or on CD-ROM.

GRAMMAR IN LITERATURE

from **The Life of Samuel Johnson**
James Boswell

Notice the abundance of nonessential expressions, set off by commas, in Boswell's sentences. These elements contribute to the stately rhythm of his prose.

Eager to take any opening to get into conversation with him, I ventured to say, "O, Sir, I cannot think Mr. Garrick would grudge such a trifle to you." "Sir," said he, with a stern look, "I have known David Garrick longer than you have done: and I know no right you have to talk to me on the subject." Perhaps I deserved this check; for it was rather presumptuous in me, an entire stranger, to express any doubt of the justice of his animadversion upon his old acquaintance and pupil. I now felt myself much mortified, and began to think that the hope which I had long indulged of obtaining his acquaintance was blasted. And, in truth, had not my ardor been uncommonly strong, and my resolution uncommonly persevering, so rough a reception might have deterred me forever from making any further attempts.

> **Exercise 18** Distinguishing Between Essential and Nonessential Material Add commas to the following sentences where necessary.

1. Festivals the world over serve many beneficial purposes.
2. The Italian navigator Christopher Columbus is credited with bringing knowledge of the Americas to Europeans.
3. The American holiday that bears his name acknowledges his contributions to exploration.
4. The Balloon Fiesta which is held in Albuquerque is widely attended.
5. Local celebrations that boost the morale of a town by honoring local successes are usually well attended.
6. Patriot's Day which is observed in Massachusetts combines the celebration of local heroes with the sponsorship of the Boston Marathon.
7. Judging which festival is best is a task that anyone would find difficult.
8. Independence celebrations which note release from control by another country build national pride.
9. In places like ancient Athens where women's freedoms were severely restricted festivals were an opportunity for female citizens to relax and to release tensions for a day.
10. These days, women like Margaret Thatcher the former British prime minister lead their governments and are celebrated in their own right.

Commas • 703

✓ ONGOING ASSESSMENT: Monitor and Reinforce

If students miss more than two items in Exercise 17 or 18, refer them to the following for additional practice.

In the Textbook	Print Resources	Technology
Section Review, Ex. 25–26, Section 27.2	*Grammar Exercise Workbook,* pp. 131–132	*On-Line Exercise Bank,* Section 27.2

Using Commas in Other Ways

1. Have students take particular note of the comma after *Texas* in the first example sentence. Point out that this final comma in a geographical name or a date is frequently forgotten in sentences. Suggest that students check their written work and correct this error if they find it.

2. Explain that when a month and year (but not the day) are written in a sentence, the comma between the two elements is optional. Thus either *February 1946* or *February, 1946* is correct.

continued

Critical Viewing

Connect Sample response: The Boston Marathon, an endurance race, commemorates the resolve that the patriots had to demonstrate.

27.2

Using Commas in Other Ways

Geographical Names Geographical names that have more than one part require commas.

▶ **KEY CONCEPT** When a geographical name is made up of two or more parts, use a comma after each item. ■

EXAMPLES: My cousin who lives in Dallas, Texas, is cutting the ribbon for the grand opening.

They're going to Kouchibouguac, New Brunswick, Canada, for their honeymoon.

Dates Dates that have more than one part require commas.

▶ **KEY CONCEPT** When a date is made up of two or more parts, use a comma after each item. ■

EXAMPLES: The wedding took place on June 16, 1985, and their son was born on June 16, 1986.

Friday, August 23, was the first day of the fair.

Titles After a Name Whenever you use a title after the name of a person or a company, add commas.

▶ **KEY CONCEPT** When a name is followed by one or more titles, use a comma after the name and after each title. ■

EXAMPLE: Susan Martini, Ph.D., announces her engagement to Bob Taormina, M.D.

● Technology Tip

If you are a writer who uses too many commas, you can use the "Find" or "Search" function under the "Edit" to find all the commas in your document. This way, you can focus solely on them and decide whether they are really required.

▼ Critical Viewing How is the Boston Marathon a fitting celebration of Patriot's Day in Massachusetts? Use nonessential elements in your response. **[Connect]**

704 • Punctuation

3. Have students note that a comma does not come between a state name and a Zip code.

Customize for
Gifted and Talented Students

Have students imagine that they will be throwing a formal dinner party. First, tell them to make a list of names and addresses of at least five guests. Then, have them write a detailed letter to the caterer giving the date of the event, describing the menu and the decorations, and listing the guests. Students might also make a menu for the guests, designed and decorated appropriately, that includes the date, locale, and occasion. Students might want to display their finished documents for the class.

Critical Viewing

Speculate Sample response: Candles are used for birthday celebrations and for some religious holidays such as Christmas and Hanukkah. Candles bring light and hope.

Addresses Commas are also necessary in addresses.

▶ **KEY CONCEPT** Use a comma after each item in an address made up of two or more parts. ■

EXAMPLE: Send an invitation to Mrs. Robert Brooks, 145 River Road, Jacksonville, Florida 32211.

Commas are placed after the name, street, and city in the preceding example. Instead of inserting a comma between the state and the ZIP Code, extra space is left between them.

Most commas in an address are unnecessary when stacked in a letter or on an envelope or package. A comma is still required, however, between the city and the state.

EXAMPLE: Mrs. Robert Brooks
             145 River Road
             Jacksonville, Florida 32211

Salutations and Closings Commas are also needed in other parts of letters.

▶ **KEY CONCEPT** Use a comma after the salutation in a personal letter and after the closing in all letters. ■

SALUTATIONS: Dear Emily, Dear Uncle Frank,   My dear Jane,
CLOSINGS: Yours truly, Sincerely, Your friend,

▲ **Critical Viewing**
For what kind of celebrations are candles used? Why do you think we use candles? Make sure you punctuate your response correctly.
[Speculate]

Commas • **705**

Step-by-Step Teaching Guide

Using Commas in Other Ways
continued

1. Mention that in addition to Zip codes, telephone numbers, and the other examples presented, Social Security numbers also do not use commas.

2. To make the point that commas are needed in elliptical sentences, have students fill in the missing words represented by the comma in the example sentence (*celebrates his birthday*). Point out that the word after the semicolon would make no sense without the comma.

continued

Critical Viewing

Infer Answers will vary. Some students will suggest that the address is in a rather posh section of a city.

Large Numbers Commas make large numbers easier to read.

▶ **KEY CONCEPT** With numbers of more than three digits, use a comma after every third digit from the right. ■

EXAMPLES: 3,823 students
205,000 gallons
2,674,970 tons

Do not use commas in ZIP Codes, telephone numbers, page numbers, serial numbers, years, or house numbers.

ZIP CODE:	07632
TELEPHONE NUMBER:	(805) 555-6224
PAGE NUMBER:	1258
SERIAL NUMBER:	602 988 6768
HOUSE NUMBER:	18436
YEAR:	2004

Elliptical Sentences In elliptical sentences, words that are understood are left out. Commas make these sentences easier to read.

▶ **KEY CONCEPT** Use a comma to indicate the words left out of an elliptical sentence. ■

EXAMPLE: Alan celebrates his birthday solemnly; Fred, casually.

The words *celebrates his birthday* have been omitted from the second clause of the elliptical sentence. The comma has been inserted in their place, however, so the meaning is still clear.

▶ **Critical Viewing** What can you conclude about the address pictured here based on the details in the photograph? **[Infer]**

🌼 Grammar and Style Tip

Elliptical sentences require parallel construction between clauses to be easily understood; if the two clauses aren't exactly the same in construction, do not use an elliptical sentence for that idea.

Direct Quotations Another use of commas is to indicate where direct quotations begin and end.

> **KEY CONCEPT** Use commas to set off a direct quotation from the rest of the sentence. ■

EXAMPLES: "You came home late," commented James's mother.

He said, "The wedding rehearsal ran longer than expected."

"I hope," James's mother said, "the best man doesn't forget the ring."

Misuses of Commas You have now seen many rules governing the use of commas. Studying these rules will help you use commas correctly. Knowing the rules will also help you avoid using unnecessary commas. Because commas appear so frequently in writing, some people are tempted to use them where no commas are required. Be sure you know the reason that you are inserting commas each time you use them.

MISUSED WITH AN ADJECTIVE AND NOUN:	After a dance, I enjoy a cool, refreshing, drink.
CORRECT:	After a dance, I enjoy a cool, refreshing drink.
MISUSED WITH A COMPOUND SUBJECT:	After the election, my friend Nancy, and her sister Julia, were invited to the inaugural ball.
CORRECT:	After the election, my friend Nancy and her sister Julia were invited to the inaugural ball.
MISUSED WITH A COMPOUND VERB:	The groom looked deep into her eyes, and spoke from his heart.
CORRECT:	The groom looked deep into her eyes and spoke from his heart.
MISUSED WITH A COMPOUND OBJECT:	She chose a dress with long sleeves, and a train.
CORRECT:	She chose a dress with long sleeves and a train.
MISUSED WITH PHRASES:	Reading the invitation, and wondering who sent it, Brian did not hear the phone ringing.
CORRECT:	Reading the invitation and wondering who sent it, Brian did not hear the phone ringing.

Commas • **707**

Step-by-Step Teaching Guide continued

3. Point out that if a statement identifying the speaker interrupts in the middle of a quotation, that interrupter, known as a *conversational tag*, is also set off with commas. Give this example:

> *"I called Great-aunt Millie," said David, "but she can't come to the wedding."*

Tell students they will learn more about the placement of commas in the section on Quotation Marks.

You might want to present students with one other common misuse of commas: between a subject and predicate, especially when the subject is rather long. Have students correct this sentence:

> *Who will catch the bouquet at the wedding, is anyone's guess.*

Customize for
Less Advanced Students

Students who are unsure about comma use sometimes tend to overuse commas. Have students work in pairs to analyze each other's most recent pieces of writing. Have the partners point out places where commas are included but should not be.

Answer Key

> **Exercise 19**

Thanksgiving . . . November 26, 1789. . . . Today, it is meant . . . Plymouth, Massachusetts. Turkey is the traditional meal, served . . .

Holiday observances . . . On November 1, Mexicans . . . Since May 30, 1868, . . . South Americans, Simon Bolívar. . . . Martin Luther King, Jr., who said, "Free . . . last," is . . .

National celebrations, such as Oktoberfest, can be fun-filled, too. Oktoberfest, which has been held in Germany since October 17, 1810, originally honored the wedding of Louis I, King of Bavaria.

Critical Viewing

Connect Sample response: The photo shows some of the typical food that is served at Thanksgiving.

MISUSED WITH CLAUSES:	He discussed what elements are crucial to a successful office party, and which caterers are most reliable.
CORRECT:	He discussed what elements are crucial to a successful office party and which caterers are most reliable.

> **Exercise 19** Using Commas in Geographical Names, Dates, Titles, Addresses, Large Numbers, Elliptical Sentences, and Direct Quotations Revise the following passage, inserting the necessary commas.

Thanksgiving was first celebrated on November 26 1789. Today it is meant to be a reenactment of the Pilgrim survival in Plymouth Massachusetts. Turkey is the traditional meal served in remembrance of the four wild turkeys that were the main source of food for the entire settlement at Plymouth in 1621.

Holiday observances not only honor survivors but also honor the dead. On November 1 Mexicans clean and decorate cemeteries in respect for those who have died. Since May 30 1868 Memorial Day has been set aside in the United States to honor war heroes. National celebrations often center on the birthdays of deceased heroes: United States citizens celebrate George Washington; South Americans Simon Bolívar. The fallen civil rights leader Martin Luther King Jr. who said "Free at last, free at last, thank God almighty, we're free at last" is honored on his birthday.

National celebrations such as Oktoberfest can be fun-filled too. Oktoberfest which has been held in Germany since October 17 1810 originally honored the wedding of Louis I King of Bavaria.

> **More Practice**

Grammar Exercise Workbook
• pp. 129–134
On-line Exercise Bank
• Section 27.2
Go on-line:
PHSchool.com
Enter Web Code:
egk-1202

Get instant feedback! Exercises 19, 20, 21, and 22 are available on-line or on CD-ROM.

▼ **Critical Viewing** How does this photograph relate to the information in the exercise above? **[Connect]**

Exercise 20 Using Commas in a Letter Add the missing information and necessary commas to complete this letter.

Your address (Make one up if you wish.)
February 12 20--
Dear Martha

   Thanks for the invitation to your wedding on August 14 2010. I am sending a gift as soon as I can to your apartment at 255 Great Lane Eden New York. Martha I forgot to tell you that I did a research paper on marriage and weddings and I read it at the club last month. Are you and Jim "the Brain" going to have an engagement party? If so are you going to have it in Chicago Illinois? I'll call you after six at the dorm on Friday June 20.

Your friend always
Your name

Exercise 21 Writing a Paragraph Using Commas for Various Purposes Write a paragraph in which you use commas for at least five of the purposes explained in this section.

Exercise 22 Using Commas Correctly in Your Writing
Write ten original sentences following each direction below.
1. Write a compound sentence about a birthday celebration.
2. Write a sentence listing four presents you received at a birthday or other celebration.
3. Write a sentence using the introductory phrase "In some cases."
4. Write a sentence using the introductory word "Yes."
5. Write a sentence using the introductory phrase "Moving quickly."
6. Write a sentence using the parenthetical phrase "in fact."
7. Write a sentence about a national holiday using the parenthetical phrase "although I tried."
8. Write a sentence describing an actor or singer at a celebration or holiday concert using "talented" and "attractive."
9. List the dates of birth of two friends. Begin with: "(Name) was born on. . . ."
10. Write a sentence about yourself. Within the sentence, show two academic or other titles that you would like to have after your name.

Answer Key

1000 Lake Drive
Milwaukee, Wisconsin 54211
February 12, 20--

Dear Martha,

Thanks for the invitation to your wedding on August 14, 2010. I am sending a gift as soon as I can to your apartment at 255 Great Lane, Eden, New York. Martha, I forgot to tell you that I did a research paper on marriage and weddings, and I read it at the club last month. Are you and Jim, "the Brain," going to have an engagement party? If so, are you going to have it in Chicago, Illinois? I'll call you after six at the dorm on Friday, June 20.

Your friend always,

Exercise 21

Ask students to write their papers on some family celebration, such as a marriage or an anniversary party. Have volunteers read their completed work aloud, while other students note where commas should be used.

Exercise 22

Answers will vary; samples are given.
1. My family always celebrates my birthday, and last year they gave me a great party.
2. At my party, I received a pair of hiking boots, a tent, a book about camping, and a can of insect repellent.
3. In some cases, people who give you presents are trying to tell you something.
4. Yes, I know my family sounds a little strange.
5. Moving quickly, I hid the can of insect repellent so no one else could use it.
6. I hid it so well, in fact, that I still can't find it.
7. Last year, although I tried, I could not get anyone to celebrate Groundhog Day with me.
8. I had even engaged a talented, attractive person to sing at the celebration.
9. Nate was born on January 2, 1985, and Ed was born on May 8, 1987.
10. I would like eventually to go to graduate school to become Ada Louis, M.S., Ph.D.

✓ ONGOING ASSESSMENT: Monitor and Reinforce

If students miss more than two items in Exercise 19, 20, 21, or 22, refer them to the following for additional practice.

In the Textbook	Print Resources	Technology
Section Review, Ex. 27, Section 27.2	*Grammar Exercise Workbook,* pp. 129–134	*On-Line Exercise Bank,* Section 27.2

531 H • 709

Section Review

Each of these exercises correlates to the instruction on commas, pages 694–708. These exercises may be used for more practice, for reteaching, or for review of the key concepts presented. Answers for all chapter exercises are available in *Grammar Exercises Answers on Transparencies* in your Teaching Resources.

Answer Key

▶ **Exercise 23**

1. times, and as a social contract, it
2. cultures, marriage
3. such as the United States, Canada, England, and Italy, an . . . bride, the families . . . other, and
4. Japan, India, and China, for example . . . matters,
5. arrangements, the right time for the wedding, and other
6. Usually, an outside
7. fertility, prosperity, and
8. cultures, . . . knot, and in some African-based wedding rituals, the
9. societies, health, fortune, and prosperity
10. culture, gifts vary widely, . . . silverware, and they

▶ **Exercise 24**

1. Today, romantic, free-will
2. However, in Middle Eastern, Asian, and African families, arranged
3. tradition, they
4. union, happy, healthy children, and family stability
5. people, and, therefore, logic, good sense, and a

▶ **Exercise 25**

1. societies, such . . . Americas, weddings . . . people, not
2. However, in . . . societies, such . . . East, weddings
3. example, traditional . . . designs, whereas
4. Throughout the world,
5. Obviously, a groom . . . time, as is . . . marriage, can

Section 27.2 Section Review

GRAMMAR EXERCISES 23–30

▶ **Exercise 23** Punctuating Simple and Compound Sentences, Introductory Elements, and Items in a Series Revise the following paragraphs, adding commas where necessary.

(1) Marriage has existed since ancient times and as a social contract it reflects the customs of its society. (2) In almost all cultures marriage is preceded by a betrothal period during which gifts are exchanged and families get to know each other. (3) In Western nations such as the United States Canada England and Italy an engagement ring is given to the prospective bride the families of the betrothed visit each other and engagement parties are held. (4) In Eastern societies—Japan India and China for example—families spend the engagement period socializing and negotiating business matters such as a dowry. (5) Families also discuss future living arrangements the right time for the wedding and other important matters that will affect the marriage. (6) Usually an outside consultant of some kind is present at the planning.

(7) Wedding ceremonies of most cultures are filled with symbols and rituals of fertility prosperity and long-lasting union. (8) In certain cultures the couple actually ties a knot and in some African-based wedding rituals the couple "jumps the broom." (9) In all societies health fortune and prosperity are wished along with the presentation of gifts to the marrying couple. (10) Depending on the culture gifts vary widely from pigs or cattle to blenders or silverware and they are given before the wedding or on the actual day of the ceremony.

▶ **Exercise 24** Punctuating Items in a Series, in Coordinate Adjectives, and After Introductory Material Revise this paragraph, adding commas as necessary.

(1) Today most marriages are romantic free-will marriages. (2) However in Middle Eastern Asian and African families arranged marriages still exist. (3) Although many arranged marriages are the result of regional tradition they also occur in aristocratic groups of all cultures as a means of maintaining societal status and financial solvency. (4) It is believed that an arranged marriage guarantees a long-lasting union happy healthy children and family stability. (5) The professional marriage arranger objectively studies the two people and therefore logic good sense and a dispassionate perspective prevail in approving the match.

▶ **Exercise 25** Setting Off Introductory Elements, Parenthetical Expressions, and Nonessential Material Revise these sentences, adding commas as necessary.

1. In Western societies such as Europe and the Americas weddings are often seen as a private matter between the two people not a public event.
2. However in non-Western societies such as Asia, Africa, and the Middle East weddings are seen as a family and community event.
3. Wedding preparations vary considerably; for example traditional East Indian brides have their hands tattooed in ornate, intricate designs whereas Western brides usually wear white.
4. Throughout the world brides are usually veiled.
5. Obviously a groom seeing his veiled bride for the first time as is sometimes the case in an arranged marriage can be in for a surprise.

Exercise 26 Punctuating Introductory and Nonessential Material
Revise these sentences, adding commas where necessary.

1. In recent times the color white which represents innocence and purity has been the color of choice for wedding dresses in the West.
2. Traditional East Indian wedding attire which is quite different from Western equivalents bursts with color.
3. Asian wedding dresses of red silk embroidered with gold thread dazzle the eye.
4. In Western weddings the bride wears a certain gown for the ceremony and changes during the reception into her "going-away" or honeymoon dress.
5. In Asian weddings the bride will occasionally disappear and then reappear each time in a stunning new outfit.

Exercise 27 Proofreading for the Correct Use of Commas
Revise these paragraphs, adding and deleting commas where necessary.

Weddings are usually at least, several hours long and often a full day from dawn to dusk consisting of ceremonial rites and feasting is typical in some cultures. Without question the reception is the most costly part of a wedding. It is a ritual in which the bride, and groom are introduced to society for the first time as man and wife. It is also a time when friends and family welcoming new members into their circle extend their best wishes and hopes for the young couple. Merriment, and a good time are the object of the reception.

Regardless of how simple, or how ornate weddings are they are the favorite celebrations of many people. The wedding celebration is seen as a time of hope for a better future.

Exercise 28 Find It in Your Reading
Read through one of your favorite magazines, and find at least one example each of ten of the rules in this section.

Exercise 29 Find It in Your Writing
Review a sample from your portfolio, finding examples of different uses of commas. Then, use commas to combine four pairs of sentences to form compound sentences.

Exercise 30 Writing Application
Write an original sentence for each of the following:

1. A compound sentence about what the perfect graduation party would be like.
2. A sentence listing some of the things you'd like to do after graduation.
3. A sentence about a famous actress, describing what awards ceremonies she might attend and in which capacity.
4. A sentence beginning, "In any case."
5. A brief letter inviting someone with an impressive title to a royal wedding.

Answer Key

Exercise 26
1. times, . . . white, which . . . purity, has
2. attire, which is . . . equivalents, bursts
3. correct
4. weddings, . . . "going away," or honeymoon,
5. weddings, . . . reappear, each time

Exercise 27
Weddings are usually at least several hours long, and often a full day, from dawn to dusk, consisting of ceremonial rites and feasting, is . . . Without question, . . . in which the bride and groom are introduced . . . when friends and family, welcoming new members into their circle, extend . . . Merriment and a good time are . . .

Regardless of how simple or how ornate weddings are, they . . .

Exercise 28
Find It in Your Reading
Have students make photocopies of the page they find and mark the comma uses, jotting down the rule each obeys.

Exercise 29
Find It in Your Writing
Have students check with a partner to make sure they have formed compounds with sentences appropriately related in meaning.

Exercise 30
Writing Application
Students' sentences will vary. You might ask volunteers to read some of their sentences aloud.

✓ ONGOING ASSESSMENT: Assess Mastery

Use the following resources to assess student mastery of commas.

In the Textbook	Technology
Chapter Review, Ex. 79	On-Line Exercise Bank, Section 27.2

⏱ TIME SAVERS!

Answers on Transparencies
Use the *Grammar Exercises Answers on Transparencies* for Chapter 27 to facilitate correction by students.

On-Line Exercise Bank
Have students complete the exercises on computer. The Auto Check feature will grade their work for you!

Write a large semicolon on the board and ask students what two punctuation marks they see in it (a period and a comma). Explain that a semicolon can work like both these punctuation marks—like a period to separate independent clauses and like a comma to separate items in a series. Then, write a colon and point out that it is two periods. Explain that in many of its uses a colon does function like a period, to conclude a clause, but that it also signals that more information follows.

Activate Prior Knowledge

Write the following sentences on the board. Have students tell which ones illustrate correct use of colons and semicolons:

Right now, it is 12:00; John's class should be ending. (correct)

Bring me two of each: apples, pears, and oranges. (correct)

They visited: Reno, Nevada, Phoenix, Arizona, and Provo, Utah. (They visited Reno, Nevada; . . . Phoenix, Arizona; . . .)

TEACH

Step-by-Step Teaching Guide

Using Semicolons

1. Emphasize that when semicolons join independent clauses, no coordinating conjunction is necessary. Also, the second clause is not capitalized.

continued

Critical Viewing

Speculate Sample response: The treasure the diver has found may be gold doubloons; on the other hand, it may be gold and silver artifacts.

Section 27.3

Semicolons and Colons

This section presents rules governing the use of semicolons (;) and colons (:). Semicolons can help you establish a relationship between independent clauses. They can also help you avoid confusion in sentences with other internal punctuation. Colons can be used as introductory devices to point ahead to additional information as well as in other special situations.

Using Semicolons

Semicolons establish relationships between independent clauses that are closely related in thought and structure.

▶ **KEY CONCEPT** Use a semicolon to join independent clauses that are not already joined by the conjunction *and, but, for, nor, or, so,* or *yet.* ■

The most common way to join independent clauses is by using a coordinate conjunction and a comma.

EXAMPLE: We explored the attic together, and we were amazed at all the useless junk we found there.

When no coordinating conjunction is used, however, closely related independent clauses can be joined with a semicolon.

EXAMPLE: We explored the attic together; we were amazed at all the useless junk we found there.

Sometimes, the second independent clause may begin with a conjunctive adverb or a transitional expression. Conjunctive adverbs include such words as *also, furthermore, accordingly, besides, consequently, however, instead, otherwise, similarly, therefore,* and *indeed.* Transitional expressions include *as a result, first, second, at this time, for instance, for example, in fact, on the other hand, that is, in conclusion,* and *finally.*

▶ **Critical Viewing** This scuba diver may be searching for treasure. Imagine and describe the treasure that can be found in the ocean. Use independent clauses and semicolons in your response. **[Speculate]**

712 • Punctuation

Theme: Treasures

In this section, you will learn about the uses of semicolons and colons. Most of the examples and exercises in this section are about the treasures of different cultures.

Cross-Curricular Connection: Social Studies

⏱ TIME AND RESOURCE MANAGER

Resources
Print: *Grammar Exercise Workbook,* pp. 135–136; *Grammar Exercises Answers on Transparencies,* Ch. 27; *Hands-on Grammar Activity Book,* Ch. 27
Technology: *Writing and Grammar* Interactive Text, Section 27.3; *On-Line Exercise Bank,* Section 27.3

Using the Full Student Edition	Using the Handbook🄷
• Work through all key concepts, pp. 712–716. • Assign and review Exercises 31–33. • Do the Hands-on Grammar activity, pp. 718–719.	• Work through all key concepts, pp. 534–538. • Assign and review Exercises 31–33. • Do the Hands-on Grammar activity, p. 540–541.

◀ Critical Viewing
What type of
discovery has this
scuba diver made?
[Speculate]

KEY CONCEPT Use a semicolon to join independent clauses separated by either a conjunctive adverb or a transitional expression. ∎

CONJUNCTIVE ADVERB: We visited curio shops in eight counties in only two days; *consequently,* we had no time for sightseeing.

TRANSITIONAL
EXPRESSION: She never found the shipwreck; *in fact,* she really had no interest in scuba diving.

In the first example, the conjunctive adverb *consequently* is set off by a semicolon and a comma. A comma follows it because it is an introductory expression.

In the second example, the transitional expression is *in fact.* It, too, is set off by a semicolon and a comma.

KEY CONCEPT Use semicolons to avoid confusion when independent clauses or items in a series already contain commas. ∎

INDEPENDENT CLAUSES: The city, supposedly filled with gold, was a fable; and the hungry, tired explorers would only find it in their dreams.

ITEMS IN A SERIES: I was convinced that we had won when I heard the music of the band playing our victory march; the jubilant players clapping and shouting; and the roar of spectators rising to their feet.

In the last example, semicolons are used instead of commas to separate the three major parts of the series. Commas are used within each of the major parts to set off nonessential participial phrases. You should also consider the use of semicolons when items in a series contain nonessential appositives or adjective clauses.

⚙ **Grammar**
⚙ and **Style Tip**

You can add more variety to your writing by alternating the use of compound sentences joined by commas and conjunctions with sentences containing independent clauses joined by a semicolon.

Semicolons and Colons • 713

---

2. Emphasize that conjunctive adverbs should be preceded by semicolons only when they join independent clauses. Point out differences in these examples:

   I think; therefore, I exist.

   I think, therefore, that he is right.

3. Mention some other types of series where semicolons are typically required, such as lists of cities and states and lists of people's names and titles. Ask students to think of others.

Customize for
AP Students

Some critics contend that semicolons are becoming "lost" punctuation marks, rarely if ever used in everyday writing. Have students do some research into the semicolon—how it originated and how its uses have changed over time. They should also do an analysis of current books and magazines to see if warnings about the semicolon's imminent demise are warranted.

Critical Viewing

Speculate Sample response: The diver may have found coins.

▶ **Exercise 31**

A treasure . . . in high value;
an antique . . . in recent years;
consequently, items . . .

Every country . . . treasures;
however, many . . . often cross
boundaries; in fact, . . . to discover a
treasure; and if the host country . . .
Cautionary measures are taken;
nevertheless, . . .

At one time, there . . .
government officials, claiming . . .
over the work; . . . art community,
trying to protect a priceless painting;
. . . restoration team, seeking . . . are
resolved; rancorous . . .

Critical Viewing

Speculate Possible answer:
Collectors are willing to pay a
premium for rare coins or coins in
good condition, so such coins
become worth more than their face
value.

27.3

▶ **Exercise 31** Using Semicolons Revise the following
paragraphs, adding semicolons where necessary.

A treasure is something held in high value an antique is a
piece of furniture or decorative object that is a hundred years
old or older. Opinions have changed in recent years consequently, items that are only fifty years old are now considered
antiques.

Every country has its antiques and treasures however,
many such objects are universally acclaimed. Treasures often
cross boundaries in fact, vigorous discussions have been held
between countries in regard to ownership of valued objects.
Conflicts can arise if a crew seeks ownership after spending
months, sometimes years, to discover a treasure and if the
host country is poor, proud, or seeks international recognition. Now, agreements are made before large amounts of time,
money, and energy have been spent on diving expeditions,
land excavations, or art restorations and before expectations
are raised unrealistically. Cautionary measures are taken
nevertheless, things aren't always smooth between host and
"discoverers."

At one time, there was a dispute over Leonardo da Vinci's
The Last Supper between Italian government officials claiming
authority over the work the international art community trying to protect a priceless painting and the restoration team
seeking greater autonomy in their efforts. Almost all of these
conflicts are resolved rancorous arguing would serve no purpose, since the objective of both parties is to preserve a treasure. In the end, most recovered treasures are preserved or
restored for people of all cultures to enjoy.

▶ **More Practice**

**Grammar Exercise
Workbook**
• pp. 135–136
On-line Exercise Bank
• Section 27.3
  Go on-line:
  PHSchool.com
  Enter Web Code:
  egk-1202

Get instant feedback!
Exercise 31 is available
on-line or on CD-ROM.

◀ **Critical Viewing**
Why do some coins
become worth more
than their "face"
value? [**Speculate**]

☑ **ONGOING ASSESSMENT: Monitor and Reinforce**

If students miss more than two items in Exercise 31, refer them to the following for additional
practice.

In the Textbook	Print Resources	Technology
Section Review, Ex. 34, Section 27.3	*Grammar Exercise Workbook,* pp. 135–136	*On-Line Exercise Bank,* Section 27.3

Using Colons

Colons are used in several situations. Primarily, colons serve as introductory devices.

> **KEY CONCEPT** Use a colon before a list of items following an independent clause. ■

EXAMPLES:　As part of our assignment, we had to interview a group of experts: an economist, a scientist, and a business manager.
His travels took him to a number of continents: Africa, Australia, Asia, and South America.

Notice that each list above follows an independent clause. If terms such as *a group of experts* or *a number of continents* were not used, colons would not be appropriate because there would no longer be independent clauses preceding the lists.

EXAMPLES:　As part of our assignment, we had to interview an economist, a scientist, and a business manager.
His travels took him to Africa, Australia, Asia, and South America.

Sometimes, an independent clause preceding a list ends in a phrase such as *the following* or *the following items.* These phrases should signal the use of a colon to introduce the list.
Colons also introduce certain kinds of quotations.

> **KEY CONCEPT** Use a colon to introduce a quotation that is formal or lengthy or a quotation that does not contain a "he said/she said" expression or tag line. ■

EXAMPLE:　Oliver Wendell Holmes, Jr., wrote this about freedom: "It is only through free debate and free exchange of ideas that government remains responsive to the will of the people and peaceful change is effected."

Dialogue or a casual remark should be introduced by a comma even if it is lengthy. Use the colon if the quotation is formal or has no tag line.
A colon may also be used to introduce a sentence that explains the sentence that precedes it.

🖳 Internet Tip

Most World Wide Web addresses (URLs) use a colon in the beginning section. Avoid colons in other parts of the URL because they could render the address unreadable by certain systems. A full Web address might read as follows:
http://www.your website.com

Using Colons

1. Some students have a tendency to misuse colons, inserting them before any series of items. Emphasize that a colon should be used only if an independent clause precedes the list; it does not precede a series of direct objects or predicate nominatives.

2. For more practice, have students decide whether colons are needed in these sentences.

   At the game I bought a program, a poster, a foam hand, and trading cards. (no colon needed)

   My lunch consisted of the following turkey sandwich, cookies, and carrot sticks. (colon needed after *following*)

3. Reiterate the three criteria for using a colon to introduce a direct quotation: the quote must be lengthy, formal, and not introduced by a conversational tag (*he said, she said*). Explain that these criteria preclude using the colon to introduce quotations in informal writing.

Customize for
ESL Students

Because many languages have different rules for punctuation and even different punctuation marks (e.g.,◇,ç, ö, ¿, ¡), methods for writing dialogue in English may be new or confusing to some students. Explain that in a written narrative, dialogue is enclosed in quotation marks and introduced by conversational tags. Point out that scripts for plays, television programs, and movies use a different method: Each new speaker is introduced by the name and a colon, and then the spoken words follow (*Girl in Red: How are you?*). Show students a photo of two or more people and ask them to write in screenplay style some lines of dialogue between the two. Encourage students to read their completed dialogues aloud.

Using Colons *continued*

1. Emphasize to students that a colon cannot be used in a compound sentence simply because the two clauses are related. The second must summarize or explain the first; otherwise, a semicolon should be used.

2. As practice, have students combine these two pairs of sentences, using the correct punctuation mark:

   I needed money to buy a book. He needed money to rent a video. (semicolon)

   We finally made a decision. We would go to the mall to get what we needed. (colon)

Integrating Vocabulary Skills

Semicolon Have students look up and define the prefix *semi-* ("half; partial"). Explain that a semicolon can be thought of as providing half the stopping force of a colon. Have students list other words using the prefix *semi-* (*semimonthly, semiprivate*) write down the words' meanings, and check a dictionary to see if any are hyphenated.

27.3

▶ **KEY CONCEPT** Use a colon to introduce a sentence that summarizes or explains the sentence before it. ∎

EXAMPLE: His explanation for being late was believable: He had had a flat tire on the way.

Notice that the complete sentence introduced by the colon starts with a capital letter.

▶ **KEY CONCEPT** Use a colon to introduce a formal appositive that follows an independent clause. ∎

EXAMPLE: I had finally decided on a career: nursing.

The colon is a stronger punctuation mark than a comma. Using the colon gives more emphasis to the appositive it introduces.

▶ **KEY CONCEPT** Use a colon in a number of special writing situations. ∎

The chart below shows colons used in special writing situations. Study the examples carefully.

SPECIAL SITUATIONS REQUIRING COLONS	
Numerals Giving the Time	1:30 A.M. 9:15 P.M.
References to Periodicals (Volume Number:Page Number)	*Scientific American* 74:12 *Sports Illustrated* 53:15
Biblical References (Chapter Number:Verse Number)	1 Corinthians 13:13
Subtitles for Books and Magazines	*A Field Guide to the Birds: Eastern Land and Water Birds*
Salutations in Business Letters	Dear Mrs. Gordon: Dear Sir:
Labels Used to Signal Important Ideas	**Danger:** High-voltage wires

Exercise 32 Using Colons Revise the following letter, adding colons where appropriate.

Dear Ms. Richards

Thank you for the information you sent me. However, instead of biochemistry, I have chosen another major archaeology. I'm fascinated by a number of things about the field travel, ancient cultures, and the strange customs of other times and places. For example, the ancient Egyptians filled tombs with gold objects and precious jewelry, which makes sense in light of their religion They believed in a rich afterlife. Especially notable was the tomb of Tutankhamen, which was described as follows "Everything was gold. Gold! Gold! Everywhere!" Stories like this, retold in *National Geographic* 181 54, offer insight as to why I find the prospect of a dig so exciting. Also, I have a personal explanation for this career choice Several of my ancestors were archaeologists. I'd love to explain further, but I have a flight to a Peruvian site at 6 15 P.M., and if I don't leave now, I'll miss the flight.

Exercise 33 Using Semicolons and Colons Revise the following paragraph, adding semicolons and colons where appropriate.

Treasures found in tombs include a variety of items amulets shaped like real animals, fanciful creatures, and plant-life brooches made of gold and silver and necklaces and head-dresses studded with precious jewels. An abundance of jewelry was made for funeral ceremonies and tombs on the other hand, the living also enjoyed displays of finery on a daily basis. This love of finery was especially true of nobility for example, Empress Theodora of Italy wore a dress that was stiff with gold and inlaid with jewels diamonds, emeralds, and rubies. To complete this show of wealth, the dress was worn with stunning jewelry a neckpiece made of emeralds set in gold. Many special jewels are world treasures the Hope diamond, the Phoenix jewel, and the Canning jewel. Intricate designs displaying fine craftsmanship clever mechanics, boxes within boxes, and exquisite jewel settings creating stunning arrangements are the hallmarks of some famous jewelry makers. Collections of jeweled treasures are in many museums the Hermitage in Russia, the British Museum in London, and the Vienna Treasury are just a few. The Smithsonian in Washington, D.C., houses an extensive collection of jewels from a variety of Asian countries, including China, Japan, and Burma. Silver and gold are employed abundantly in Asian jewelry many pieces are in filigree, lacy metalwork. Ivory ornaments are important Japanese treasures nevertheless, the most precious material in Japan is jade.

More Practice

Grammar Exercise Workbook
• pp. 135–136
On-line Exercise Bank
• Section 27.3
  Go on-line:
  PHSchool.com
  Enter Web Code:
  egk-1202

iInteractive Textbook

Get instant feedback! Exercises 32 and 33 are available on-line or on CD-ROM.

Answer Key

Exercise 32

Dear Ms. Richards:

Thank you . . . another major: archaeology. . . . things about the field: travel, . . . in the light of their religion: They . . . described as follows: "Everything . . . *National Geographic* 181:54 . . . this career choice: Several of . . . 6:15 P.M.

Exercise 33

Treasures . . . a variety of items: amulets . . . plant-life; brooches . . . silver; and necklaces . . . funeral ceremonies and tombs; on the other hand, . . . true of nobility; for example, . . . inlaid with jewels: diamonds, . . . stunning jewelry: a neckpiece . . . world treasures: the Hope diamond . . . Intricate designs . . . craftsmanship; clever mechanics; . . . within boxes; and exquisite . . . in many museums: the Hermitage . . . abundantly in Asian jewelry; many pieces . . . important Japanese treasures; nevertheless, . . .

☑ ONGOING ASSESSMENT: Monitor and Reinforce

If students miss more than two items in Exercise 32 or 33, refer them to the following for additional practice.

In the Textbook	Print Resources	Technology
Section Review, Ex. 36–38, Section 27.3	*Grammar Exercise Workbook,* pp. 135–136	*On-Line Exercise Bank,* Section 27.3

⏱ TIME SAVERS!

Answers on Transparencies
Use the *Grammar Exercises Answers on Transparencies* for Chapter 27 to facilitate correction by students.

On-Line Exercise Bank
Have students complete the exercises on computer. The Auto Check feature will grade their work for you!

Hands-on Grammar

Teaching Resources: Hands-on Grammar Activity Book, Ch. 27

1. If you wish to do this activity in class, you might bring in colored self-sticking dots for students to use. Have students enter the passage into a computer at home or in class, or enter it for them and make enough copies for the class.

2. Have students work individually or in pairs to mark up the passage. When they have finished, compare their result with those of the rest of the class.

Find It in Your Reading

Students might either find their own articles or use ones that you provide.

Find It in Your Writing

Students might trade punctuation-less compositions with partners and see if the partners agree on the marks that should be used.

continued

27.3

Hands-on Grammar

Punctuation Circles

1. On the next page is a piece of writing from which the punctuation has been removed. Photocopy the passage or retype it (without punctuation) using a word-processing program. Use a large font size—18 or 20 points. Print out the complete passage.
2. Obtain different-colored self-sticking dots at an office-supply store.
3. Read the selection aloud. Following the chart below, place the different-colored self-sticking dots in places where you feel punctuation is needed based on the sound of your reading.
4. Compare your punctuated version with those of some other students. What did you punctuate differently? Why? What did you punctuate the same? Why?

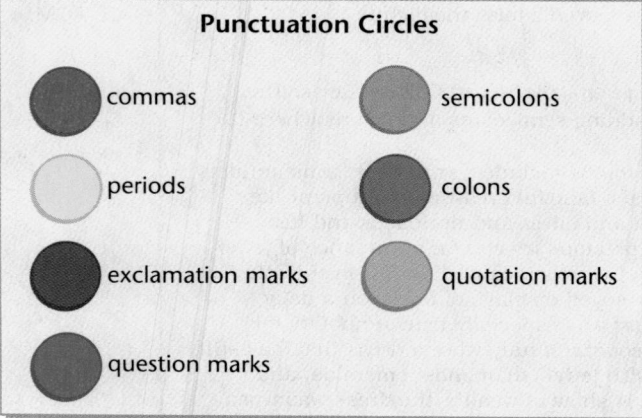

Punctuation Circles

- commas
- periods
- exclamation marks
- question marks
- semicolons
- colons
- quotation marks

Find It in Your Reading Try the above activity with a piece of writing from your portfolio. Eliminate the punctuation, and complete the steps above. How does your color-coded version compare with the original?

Find It in Your Writing Select an article from a newsmagazine. Choose a passage that especially interests you. Then, follow the steps outlined above.

718 • Punctuation

⏱ **TIME SAVERS!**

Hands-on Grammar
Use the Hands-on Grammar activity sheet for Chapter 27 to facilitate this activity.

718 • 540 Ⓗ

Hands-on Grammar

today the average American can expect to
live about 76 years only 100 years ago life
expectancy was less than 48 years in the
seventeenth century life expectancy was
about 30 to 35 years improvements in disease
prevention and treatment general medical
care diet exercise environmental conditions
and other factors have continued to increase
the length of time people can expect to live
moreover not only has the average life
expectancy increased but the average
Americans general health and the resultant
quality of life has improved as well the average American can now expect to be vigorous
and active throughout most of his or her life

Here is one possible rewrite of the passage; other versions are possible.

Today the average American can expect to live about 76 years; only 100 years ago life expectancy was less than 48 years. In the seventeenth century, life expectancy was about 30 to 35 years. Improvements in disease prevention and treatment, general medical care, diet, exercise, environmental conditions, and other factors have continued to increase the length of time people can expect to live. Moreover, not only has the average life expectancy increased, but the average American's general health and the resultant quality of life has improved as well. The average American can now expect to be vigorous and active throughout most of his or her life.

Semicolons and Colons • 719

Section Review

Each of these exercises correlates to the instruction on semicolons and colons, pages 712–716. These exercises may be used for more practice, for reteaching, or for review of the key concepts presented. Answers for all chapter exercises are available in *Grammar Exercises Answers on Transparencies* in your Teaching Resources.

Answer Key

▶ **Exercise 34**

1. jewelry; semiprecious
2. cultures; as a result
3. work; consequently
4. relics; legends
5. explorers; however
6. sun; in fact
7. shines; encrusted
8. sunlight; sport . . . nostrils; and
9. jewelry; for example
10. move; their elaborate

▶ **Exercise 35**

1. headdresses: the British
2. treasures: bronzes
3. *Treasures: Jeweled*
4. display: the Smithsonian
5. "Attention: Do not

▶ **Exercise 36**

Dear Mr. Newssance:

   Our government . . . *Relics: The Bounty* . . . won't stop there: We are also . . . artifacts you took: six vases and dozens of jewels. . . . "Warning: Trespassers . . . Our minister of culture observes: "That . . . is reprehensible; that he has . . . most apt summary to date: "There is . . . man: thief." Our is . . . spanning millennia; a proud . . . Rest assured: You will . . .

⏱ TIME SAVERS!

📄 Answers on Transparencies
Use the *Grammar Exercises Answers on Transparencies* for Chapter 27 to facilitate correction by students.

🖥 On-Line Exercise Bank
Have students complete the exercises on computer. The Auto Check feature will grade their work for you!

Section 27.3 Section Review

GRAMMAR EXERCISES 34–41

▶ **Exercise 34** Using Semicolons
Revise these sentences, adding semicolons where necessary.

1. Materials of all types are used in jewelry semiprecious stones, feathers, leather, and metal are common.
2. Rituals are a vital part of Native American cultures as a result, special jewelry was made of turquoise, shells, and silver beads for these ceremonies.
3. Masks, pendants, and feather headdresses are prevalent in Native American work consequently, the Museum of the American Indian has a large collection of these treasures.
4. Many outsiders, drawn by rumors of the native peoples' exotic treasures, tried to plunder relics legends persist—some fact-based, some fanciful—about explorers finding statuettes encrusted with rubies and emeralds.
5. These items were of monetary value to the explorers however, to the tribes they were spiritual symbols.
6. Gold represented the sun in fact, the sun is considered a god in many cultures.
7. But the sun isn't the only thing that shines encrusted in decorative metals, women in traditional East Indian garb shine as well.
8. They may wear earrings, flashing in the sunlight sport nose rings, gleaming from their nostrils and don bracelets and anklets, jangling as they move.
9. Men in ancient Persia also wore a rich array of jewelry for example, pearls and rubies adorned their turbans, sashes, and silk slippers.
10. At times, Chinese and Japanese empresses could barely move their elaborate headdresses were heavy with jewels and precious metals.

▶ **Exercise 35** Using Colons Add colons to the following sentences.

1. Museums exhibit many royal headdresses the British royal crown, tiaras, diamond-studded veils, and so on.
2. Books of African art invariably show the Benin treasures bronzes, pendants, earrings, and statuettes.
3. A book entitled *Art Treasures Jeweled Objects of the World* shows the gem-studded umbrellas of Ethiopia.
4. Nonetheless, treasures are best viewed at the museum with perhaps the greatest jewelry display the Smithsonian Institution.
5. A prominently displayed sign there warns, "Attention Do not lean on the display window!"

▶ **Exercise 36** Revising a Letter With Semicolons and Colons Revise the following letter, adding or deleting semicolons and colons where necessary.

Dear Mr. Newssance

   Our government is filing suit to stop the publication of your book *Relics The Bounty From Smuggling*. Our legal action won't stop there we are also filing to recover the artifacts you took six vases; and dozens of jewels. The sign at the excavation site reads "Warning Trespassers will be prosecuted." The damage you have done, disturbing a research project in progress, is irreparable. Our Minister of Culture observes; "That Newssance absconded with some of our greatest treasures is reprehensible that he has flaunted his crimes is astonishing." He concludes with the most apt summary to date "There is only one word for this man thief." Ours is a proud culture, spanning millennia a proud nation, standing firmly on the side of justice. Rest assured You will be brought to justice.

Exercise 37 Revising Sentences With Semicolons and Colons
Rewrite the following sentences, inserting the necessary punctuation.

1. The world is full of treasures not all of them are of the precious stone variety.
2. Literary treasures abound Herman Melville's *Moby-Dick*, Gabriel García Marquez's *Cien Años de Soledad*, and so on.
3. However, in the English language, the works of one writer are held above all others William Shakespeare.
4. Great works have been penned by other English-language writers, too from the poems of Walt Whitman to the plays of Tennessee Williams, a store of words awaits those who would explore them.
5. Other creative endeavors yield their own gems the paintings of Leonardo da Vinci and the sculptures of Michelangelo in the fine arts the operas of Verdi in the performing arts and the music of Wolfgang Amadeus Mozart and Scott Joplin.
6. In cinema, noted treasures include *Citizen Kane*, revered for its ground-breaking techniques *The Wizard of Oz*, popular for bringing a children's classic to life through the use of color film and *Schindler's List*, for its moving examination of the Holocaust.
7. Of course, not everyone agrees on what constitutes a gem *Star Wars, Episode IV A New Hope* is one movie-goer's breakthrough, another's pablum.
8. Controversy over many films still rages however, quality is more apparent with the perspective of time.
9. That may explain why television's treasures are so hard to identify the medium is still too young.

10. Other precious things exist beyond the scope of human creation the natural world offers treasures of its own.

Exercise 38 Writing Sentences With Semicolons and Colons
Complete each sentence. Then, add to or revise the sentence by following the instructions. Use colons and semicolons as needed.

1. My favorite dinner has ___?___ as its main course.
   Write a sentence with a colon pointing to a list.
2. The most annoying habit is ___?___.
   Write a sentence with a colon pointing to a formal appositive.
3. My favorite sport is ___?___.
   Write a sentence using semicolons to separate a series of items that contain internal punctuation.
4. I have a hard time studying when ___?___ is on television.
   Write a sentence containing a semicolon and a conjunctive adverb.
5. If I could see any musician perform, I would see ___?___.
   Write a sentence with a semicolon joining two contrasting clauses.

Exercise 39 Find It in Your Reading
In a newspaper, find an example of each use of semicolons and colons.

Exercise 40 Find It in Your Writing
Revise a piece of your writing to add three semicolons and two colons.

Exercise 41 Writing Application
Demonstrate your knowledge of semicolons and colons by writing a brief essay containing each of the following:
two independent clauses
items in a series
a list after an independent clause
a quotation within a quotation

Section Review • 721

✓ ONGOING ASSESSMENT: Assess Mastery

Use the following resources to assess student mastery of semicolons and colons.

In the Textbook	Technology
Chapter Review, Ex. 80	*On-Line Exercise Bank,* Section 27.3

Read aloud a portion of dialogue from a short story that includes few if any conversational tags ("The Rocking Horse Winner," in *Prentice Hall Literature, Penguin Edition,* The British Tradition, is a possible source.) When you are finished, ask students if they had trouble keeping track of who was speaking. Then discuss how writers get around this problem.

Activate Prior Knowledge

Have students write a short dialogue between two characters, using conversational tags to show who is speaking. Have them include in their dialogue the title of a book, a play, and a short poem. When students have finished, have them work in pairs to decide if all items in their dialogues are correctly punctuated.

TEACH

Step-by-Step Teaching Guide

Quotation Marks for Direct Quotations

1. Explain to students that in an indirect quotation, the quotation and conversational tag are combined into one unified sentence. Mention that the word *that* preceding what the speaker said is one clue that the quotation is indirect.

2. Point out that many other grammatical rules still apply when quotation marks are used. For example, capital letters are used for the first word of every complete sentence whether it is in or outside of quotation marks.

continued

Quotation Marks and Underlining

Theme: Horses
In this section, you will learn about the many uses of quotation marks and underlining. Most of the examples and exercises in this section are about horses.

Cross-Curricular Connection: Science

Using direct quotations in your writing can enliven short stories and other works of fiction. Direct quotations, the actual words of a character, provide readers much information about a character, both from what he or she says and from the way he or she speaks.

Direct quotations can also be used to support or refute ideas and arguments in nonfiction. You can quote an expert in a particular field to help prove a point you are trying to make.

Using Quotation Marks for Direct Quotations

There are two ways in which you can cite a person's ideas: through direct quotations and through indirect quotations.

▶ **KEY CONCEPTS** A **direct quotation** represents a person's exact speech or thoughts and is enclosed in quotation marks (" "). An **indirect quotation** reports only the general meaning of what a person said or thought and does not require quotation marks. ■

DIRECT QUOTATION:	"When I learn to ride," said the student, "I'll use the bridle path every day."
INDIRECT QUOTATION:	The student said that when she learns to ride, she plans to use the bridle path every day.

Both types of quotations are acceptable when you write. Using a direct quotation whenever possible, however, generally results in more interesting and convincing writing.

To enclose a sentence that is an uninterrupted direct quotation, place double quotation marks around the quotation.

EXAMPLE:	"One can live in the shadow of an idea without grasping it."—Elizabeth Bowen

Notice that this quotation begins with a capital letter. The same is true of every complete sentence of quoted material.

You may also quote just part of a sentence directly. When a phrase or a fragment is quoted, enclose the quoted words in quotation marks just as you would a full sentence. Capitalize the first word of the quote, however, only when it falls at the beginning of the sentence you are writing or when it is a proper noun or a proper adjective that would be capitalized in any case.

⏱ TIME AND RESOURCE MANAGER

Resources
Print: *Grammar Exercise Workbook,* pp. 137–142; *Grammar Exercises Answers on Transparencies,* Ch. 27
Technology: *Writing and Grammar* Interactive Text, Section 27.4; *On-Line Exercise Bank,* Section 27.4

Using the Full Student Edition	Using the Handbook🖽
• Work through all key concepts, pp. 722–733.	• Work through all key concepts, pp. 544–555.
• Assign and review Exercises 42–46.	• Assign and review Exercises 42–46.
• Read and discuss Grammar in Literature, p. 727.	• Read and discuss Grammar in Literature, p. 549.

EXAMPLES: In one of his essays, George Mistry calls the stables near his home "the source of an almost profound stench."
"The source of an almost profound stench" is how Mistry refers to the stables near his home.

Many direct quotations contain not only the actual words of a speaker but also words identifying the speaker. These identifying words or phrases are called conversational tags. They include such expressions as *she asked*, *they replied*, *my father explained*, and *Jenny shrieked*. Conversational tags are never enclosed in quotation marks.

Conversational tags may appear in various positions in relation to direct quotations.

KEY CONCEPT Use a comma after short introductory expressions that precede direct quotations. ■

EXAMPLE: My mother warned, "If you get a horse, you'll be responsible for taking care of it."

If the introductory conversational tag is very long or formal in tone, set it off with a colon instead of a comma.

EXAMPLES: Bert rose to his feet: "I'd like to announce the winner of the event."
At the end of the meeting, Marge spoke of her dreams: "I hope to advance the cause of women jockeys everywhere."

▶ Critical Viewing Write a brief dialogue in which the woman shown here describes riding a horse to someone who's never ridden one. **[Describe]**

3. Have students notice that in all the examples in this subsection, periods and commas come within the final quotation marks. Explain to students that this is simply a convention, not based on any inherent logic. (The practice came about when typesetters set hot type; putting a period or comma inside the quotes kept the mark from being dropped or lost.)

Integrating Speaking and Listening Skills

Dialogue Using "The Rocking Horse Winner" or another story, have a volunteer read aloud a passage of dialogue to the class. Have the reader change his or her voice enough to differentiate the characters. Ask the class to determine the number of characters involved in the dialogue. Discuss the conversational tags used and how the reader's intonation clarified the number of speakers.

Critical Viewing

Describe Possible response:
"Is horseback riding difficult?" he asked.
"There's a lot to learn, but it's really fun," she replied. "You have to be able to control the horse."
"How do you do that?"
"Mainly with the bridle," she explained, "but the way you shift your weight makes a difference, too."

Quotation Marks and Underlining • **723**

Quotation Marks for Direct Quotations *continued*

4. Point out that interrupting expressions should fall at logical places in quoted material—for instance, at natural breaks between sentences, phrases, or clauses—not at places where they might confuse a reader.

5. Direct students' attention to the final key concept and remind them that a period falls only at the very end of a sentence. If quoted material and conversational tags are included in the same sentence, other end marks (? or !) may be used, but a comma will always replace a period unless the quotation falls at the very end of the sentence.

Answer Key

▶ **Exercise 42**

During a lecture, a speaker stated that horses have existed since the Eocene epoch. She remarked, "Fossils indicate that a leaf-browsing mammal about the size of a fox was the precursor to the horse. Descendants of this species developed high-crowned teeth," she continued. "This allowed them to graze on grass instead of browsing on leaves."

She told us how this animal developed over the centuries. "The scientific name for the present-day domestic horse is *Equus caballus*," she said.

An expert on the Q & A panel chimed in: "A marked characteristic of the modern horse is one single toe on each of its four feet." He informed us that earlier species had four toes on the forefeet and three on the hind feet!

"Both male and female horses can reproduce from the age of two," another panelist explained, "but breeding is delayed until they are three."

"The gestation period for horses is about eleven months," a panelist added.

The handout from the museum suggested that we do further research on horses.

27.4

Conversational tags may also act as concluding expressions.

▶ **KEY CONCEPT** Use a comma, question mark, or exclamation mark after a direct quotation followed by a concluding expression. ■

EXAMPLE: "If you get a horse, you'll be responsible for taking care of it," my mother warned.

In addition, you may use a conversational tag to interrupt the words of a direct quotation.

▶ **KEY CONCEPT** Use a comma after part of a quoted sentence followed by an interrupting conversational tag. Use another comma after the tag. Use two sets of quotation marks to enclose the quotation. ■

EXAMPLE: "If you get a horse," my mother warned, "you'll be responsible for taking care of it."

Sometimes, a conversational tag interrupts a quotation several sentences in length.

▶ **KEY CONCEPT** Use a comma, question mark, or exclamation mark after a quoted sentence that comes before an interrupting conversational tag. Use a period after the tag. ■

EXAMPLE: "You own a horse now," warned my mother. "You are responsible for taking care of it."

▶ **Exercise 42** Revising With Quotation Marks and Capitalization Revise the following passage, breaking it into paragraphs and adding necessary punctuation and capitalization.

During a lecture, a speaker stated that horses have existed since the Eocene epoch. She remarked fossils indicate that a leaf-browsing mammal about the size of a fox was the precursor to the horse. Descendants of this species developed high-crowned teeth, she continued. This allowed them to graze on grass instead of browsing on leaves. She told us how this animal developed over the centuries. The scientific name for the present-day domestic horse is *Equus caballus*, she said. An expert on the Q & A panel chimed in A marked characteristic of the modern horse is one single toe on each of its four feet. He informed us that earlier species had four toes on the forefeet and three on the hind feet! Both male and female horses can reproduce from the age of two, another panelist explained, but breeding is delayed until they are three. The gestation period for horses is about eleven months, a panelist added. The handout from the museum suggested that we do further research on horses.

▶ **More Practice**

Grammar Exercise Workbook
• pp. 135–142
On-line Exercise Bank
• Section 27.4
Go on-line:
PHSchool.com
Enter Web Code:
egk-1202

Complete the exercise on-line! Exercise 42 is available on-line or on CD-ROM.

☑ **ONGOING ASSESSMENT: Monitor and Reinforce**

If students have difficulty with Exercise 42, refer them to the following for additional practice.

In the Textbook	Print Resources	Technology
Section Review, Ex. 47, Section 27.4	*Grammar Exercise Workbook,* pp. 137–138	*On-Line Exercise Bank,* Section 27.4

Using Other Punctuation Marks With Quotation Marks

Quotation marks are used with commas, semicolons, colons, and all the end marks. The location of the quotation marks in relation to the different punctuation marks varies. Below are rules to help you place the punctuation marks correctly.

KEY CONCEPT Always place a comma or a period inside the final quotation mark. ∎

EXAMPLES: "Secretariat was a great horse," sighed Mother.
              Marge said, "We're all ready to ride now."

The rule for the use of semicolons and colons with quotation marks is just the opposite.

KEY CONCEPT Always place a semicolon or colon outside the final quotation mark. ∎

EXAMPLES: We were just informed about his "earth-shaking discovery"; we are all pleased.
              The panelists gave her ideas their "strong endorsement": Most of them promised to spread her theory of equine development.

▼ **Critical Viewing**
Write a brief dialogue about the horses pictured here. Include both a colon and a semicolon. **[Describe]**

Quotation Marks and Underlining • 725

Step-by-Step Teaching Guide

Other Punctuation Marks With Quotation Marks

1. To help students with the position of other punctuation with quotation marks, begin with a chart like the following:

Inside	Outside	Either
periods	colons	question marks
commas	semicolons	exclamation marks

2. Recommend that with question marks and exclamation marks, students look at the meaning of the quoted material to decide where the end punctuation belongs. If the quotation is a question or an exclamation, the end mark goes inside the quotes; otherwise, it goes outside. Have students add punctuation to the following:

   Did you hear him say, "Meet at noon" (. . . noon"?)

   He said, "Do we meet at noon" (. . . noon?")

   continued

Critical Viewing

Describe Possible response:

"What a life those horses have: rolling hills, green grass, and freedom to run under the blue sky," Jim said.

"Well," Hank replied, "think about their 'freedom'; they're working horses, so they're only as free as their owner lets them be."

⏱ TIME SAVERS!

Answers on Transparencies
Use the *Grammar Exercises Answers on Transparencies* for Chapter 27 to facilitate correction by students.

On-Line Exercise Bank
Have students complete the exercises on computer. The Auto Check feature will grade their work for you!

Other Punctuation Marks with Quotation Marks *continued*

3. Write on the board: *Did he ask, "What time is it?"* Explain that the convention is that the question mark goes within the quotation marks even though it would apply to both the quoted material and the larger sentence. Repeating end marks is incorrect.

4. Have students suggest sentences that require question marks or exclamation marks to go inside the quotation marks. Then, ask for sentences that require those end marks to be outside the quotation marks.

Critical Viewing

Analyze Possible response: He lived in a warlike time; he lived at a time when steel armor gave protection against the common enemy weapons; horses were an important form of transportation.

27.4

◄ **Critical Viewing**
This is a statue of King Richard III of England. What can you tell about the time in which he lived based on the statue? [**Analyze**]

▶ **KEY CONCEPT** Place a question mark or an exclamation mark inside the final quotation mark if the end mark is part of the quotation. ■

EXAMPLES: Larry wondered, "How could such a fast stallion lose the race?"

King Richard shouted, "My kingdom for a horse!"

The question mark and exclamation mark in these examples are placed inside the final quotation mark because they apply only to the quoted portion of each sentence.

▶ **KEY CONCEPT** Place a question mark or an exclamation mark outside the final quotation mark if the end mark is not part of the quotation. ■

EXAMPLES: Did the officer say, "I'll be back soon"?

We were shocked when he said, "Yes"!

Exercise 43 Using Other Punctuation Marks Correctly With Quotations Revise this passage, adding the necessary punctuation.

My friend sounded bored when he broke the news: Horses came to the Americas by way of Egypt. He stated that Syrian invaders were able to conquer Egypt in the seventeenth century B.C. because of their new weapon: horse-drawn chariots.

These Egyptian horses were the predecessors of the highly prized, fast Arabian breed, explains a book that he lent me. The book further explains, Europeans had slower, heavier horses, but these horses were powerful. According to the book's author, an idea was born: Arabian stallions should be brought into England and France to breed with mares of the sturdier stock. He writes: Introduced into various parts of Europe, these horses, along with the purebred Arabians, were brought to the Americas by the Spanish conquistadors; in this manner, the Arabian bloodline made the leap across the Atlantic.

I asked my friend, Why did Cortés and others abandon their horses?

Who said anything about their being abandoned? my friend sighed in exasperation, adding, The men, being tired, lost, and demoralized in unknown territory, simply lost many of their horses.

I asked, Did these horses become, as my friend put it, the galloping, gorgeous wild horses of western North America?

Precisely! my friend replied.

GRAMMAR IN
LITERATURE

from **Hard Times**
Charles Dickens

The placement of end punctuation inside quotation marks in this excerpt illustrates the correct way to punctuate dialogue.

"Very well," said this gentleman, briskly smiling, and folding his arms. "That's a horse. Now, let me ask you girls and boys, Would you paper a room with representations of horses?"

After a pause, one half of the children cried in chorus, "Yes, sir!" Upon which, the other half, seeing in the gentleman's face that Yes was wrong, cried out in chorus, "No, sir!"—as the custom is, in these examinations.

More Practice

Grammar Exercise Workbook
• pp. 135–142
On-line Exercise Bank
• Section 27.4
Go on-line:
PHSchool.com
Enter Web Code:
egk-1202

interactive
Textbook

Complete the exercise on-line! Exercise 43 is available on-line or on CD-ROM.

Quotation Marks and Underlining • **727**

Answer Key

Exercise 43

1. "Horses came . . . Egypt."
2. correct
3. "These . . . breed,"
4. explains, "Europeans . . . powerful."
5. "Arabian . . . stock,"
6. "Introduced . . . conquistadors";
7. "Why did . . . horses?"
8. "Who . . . abandoned?" my friend . . . adding, "The men . . . horses."
9. "Did these . . . become," . . . "the . . . America?"
10. "Precisely!" my

Step-by-Step Teaching Guide

Grammar in Literature

1. Ask a student to read the passage aloud, emphasizing the question and the exclamations. Discuss with the class why the question mark and exclamation marks belong inside the quotation marks. (In each case, the punctuation is part of the quoted matter, not of the sentence that contains the quotation.)

2. Have students suggest sentences in which a question mark or exclamation mark would belong outside the quotation marks. (Possible responses: Did he say, "Come here"? I can't believe he said "No"!)

More About the Writer

In his masterpiece *Hard Times,* Charles Dickens exposes the brutalizing effects of rising industrialism. He himself had been forced to join the Machine Age child-labor force when his father was put in a debtors' prison. After a brief career in journalism, Dickens channeled his talent for observation into a series of successful novels. The best of these offer lively entertainment, psychological depth, and biting social criticism.

Connection With Literature

The full text of *Hard Times* can be found in *Prentice Hall Literature, Penguin Edition,* The British Tradition.

1. The rule that a new paragraph begins for each speaker is often ignored in student writing. Explain that dialogue can become very confusing to read if the rule is not followed.

2. Tell students that the lack of end quotes at the end of a paragraph is intended as a clue to the reader that the quotation continues.

continued

27.4

Using Quotation Marks in Special Situations

Dialogue and Long Quotations Dialogue—spoken words of characters—is one of the best ways to move the action forward in a story. When writing dialogue, rules must be followed so that readers can keep track of who is speaking.

KEY CONCEPT When writing dialogue, begin a new paragraph with each change of speaker. ■

Look at this example from *The Pearl* by John Steinbeck.

EXAMPLE: The wind drove off the clouds and skimmed the sky clean and drifted the sand of the country like snow.
    Then Juan Tomas, when the evening approached, talked long with his brother. "Where will you go?"
    "To the north," said Kino. "I have heard that there are cities in the north."
    "Avoid the shore," said Juan Tomas. "They are making a party to search the shore. The men in the city will look for you. Do you still have the pearl?"
    "I have it," said Kino. "And I will keep it. I might have given it as a gift, but now it is my misfortune and my life and I will keep it."

A different rule is followed when a writer uses several consecutive paragraphs of material quoted from the same person.

KEY CONCEPT For quotations longer than a paragraph, put quotation marks at the beginning of each paragraph and at the end of the final paragraph. ■

EXAMPLE: John McPhee has written an essay about a canoe trip down the St. John River in northern Maine. He introduces his readers to the river in the following way: "We have been out here four days now and rain has been falling three. The rain appears to be ending. Breaks of blue are opening in the sky. Sunlight is coming through, and a wind is rising.
    "I was not prepared for the St. John River, did not anticipate its size. I saw it as a narrow trail flowing north, twisting through the balsam and spruce—a small and intimate forest river, something like the Allagash, . . ."

Spelling Tip

When writing dialogue, you may deliberately misspell words in order to show a character's particular style of pronunciation, such as a regional accent, but be sure to use correct spelling in the rest of the work.

Ellipsis Marks and Single Quotation Marks Ellipsis marks (. . .) are used when you want to present only part of a long quotation.

▶ **KEY CONCEPT** Use three ellipsis marks in a quotation to indicate that words have been omitted. ∎

The examples below show how to use ellipsis marks at the beginning, in the middle, and at the end of a quotation.

AN ENTIRE QUOTATION:	"The Black River, which cuts a winding course through southern Missouri's rugged Ozark highlands, lends its name to an area of great natural beauty. Within this expanse are old mines and quarries to explore, fast-running waters to canoe, and wooded trails to ride." —Suzanne Charle
ELLIPSIS AT THE BEGINNING:	Suzanne Charle described the Black River area in Missouri as having ". . . old mines and quarries to explore, fast-running waters to canoe, and wooded trails to ride."
ELLIPSIS IN THE MIDDLE:	Suzanne Charle wrote, "The Black River . . . lends its name to an area of great natural beauty. Within this expanse are old mines and quarries to explore, fast-running waters to canoe, and wooded trails to ride."
ELLIPSIS AT THE END:	Suzanne Charle wrote, "The Black River, which cuts a winding course through southern Missouri's rugged Ozark highlands, lends its name to an area of great natural beauty. . . ."

Notice in the last example that when a period falls right before an omitted portion of the quotation, it is added along with the ellipsis marks to conclude the sentence.

Another special situation involving quotation marks occurs when a writer wishes to include one quotation within another.

⊛ **Technology Tip**

In some word-processing programs, you may select preferences for curved or straight quotation marks. When using curved marks, make sure your marks are curving in the correct direction—toward the type, whether they are opening or closing quotation marks.

▼ Critical Viewing
What can you conclude about Missouri's Ozark highlands based on this photograph? **[Analyze]**

Ozark Mountains, Missouri

Quotation Marks and Underlining • 729

*Step-by-Step Teaching Guide
continued*

3. Ask students where in their own writing using ellipsis marks may come in handy (quoting only certain pieces of source material in a research paper).

4. Emphasize that ellipsis marks are only a group of three periods with spaces between them, never more or less. In the final example on the page, the fourth period ends the sentence. If that sentence ended with a question mark or exclamation mark, that mark would precede the ellipsis.

Critical Viewing

Analyze Possible response: The Ozark highlands have tree-covered hills, but in many places the bedrock is visible.

Quotation Marks in Special Situations *continued*

5. Point out that quotations within quotations can be confusing—and a group of three hatch marks (' ") can appear to be an error—so, wherever possible, it is wise to rearrange sentences of this structure. To make the point, provide this example:

> I asked, "Did you decide, as the saying goes, to 'Put up or shut up'?"

Have students explain the rationale for the end punctuation (single quotes pertain to the saying; question mark and double quotes pertain to the whole quotation).

6. Use the preceding example, as well as those in the textbook, to make the point that single quotes work with other marks of punctuation in the same way that double quotes do.

Answer Key

Exercise 44

1. having " . . . large tracts . . . foreman."
2. stated, "This ranch . . . horses."
3. wrote, "The ranch . . . high standards. . . ."
4. continued, "The Wild . . . its name. . . ."
5. "I plan . . . Galway said, 'mane . . . wind,' " Alan's letter
6. "The foreman said, 'You . . . ranch,' " Alan
7. "Luck indeed!" Alan . . . adding, "I told that foreman, 'You're . . . patronage!' "
8. Alan, "Try to . . . saying: 'Don't . . . son.' "
9. reminded me, "Alan . . . puts it, 'like a . . . stallion'; . . . him?"
10. "Go West . . . West!"

Exercise 45

When students write their dialogues, remind them to start a new paragraph each time the speaker changes.

27.4

> **KEY CONCEPT** Use single quotation marks for a quotation within a quotation. ∎

> **EXAMPLES:** "I will always remember my grandmother quoting Shelley, 'If winter comes, can spring be far behind?'" Michael commented.
>
> "The doctor said, 'Good news!'" she explained.

Rephrase most sentences with one quotation within another to include the same information in a less complicated way.

Exercise 44 Punctuating With Ellipsis Marks and Single Quotation Marks Copy each of the following sentences, inserting double quotation marks or single quotation marks as required.

1. The brochure described the ranch as having . . . large tracts of land; many horses of different types, including several Shetlands; and a well-informed ranch foreman.
2. The brochure also stated, This ranch in Montana . . . is known for western hospitality and knowledge of horses.
3. In a letter to me, my friend Alan wrote, The ranch was once owned by J.R. Blackwell and has been kept up to his high standards. . . .
4. Alan continued, The Wild Horse Ranch, filled with these beautiful animals . . . truly lives up to its name. . . .
5. I plan to join you there to see, as Galway said, mane blowing free, magnificence racing in the wind, Alan's letter concluded.
6. The foreman said, You are in luck regarding your reservations at the ranch, Alan informed me.
7. Luck, indeed! Alan huffed indignantly, adding, I told that foreman, You're lucky to have our patronage!
8. I told Alan, Try to remember what your mother is always saying: Don't let your temper gallop away like a wild stallion, son.
9. My friend Beth reminded me, Alan has always had a temper, as his own mother puts it, like a wild stallion; are you sure you want to go to Montana with him?
10. But the next morning, I heeded Horace Greeley's advice: Go West, young man. Go West!

Exercise 45 Writing Original Dialogue Write one page of original dialogue between two people on a horseback ride. Include a few lines of description wherever necessary. Enclose the lines of dialogue in quotation marks. Include enough conversational tags so that there will be no confusion about the speaker.

730 • Punctuation

More Practice

Grammar Exercise Workbook
• pp. 137–142
On-line Exercise Bank
• Section 27.4
 Go on-line:
 PHSchool.com
 Enter Web Code:
 egk-1202

Get instant feedback! Exercises 44 and 45 are available on-line or on CD-ROM.

☑ ONGOING ASSESSMENT: Monitor and Reinforce

If students have difficulty with Exercise 44 or 45, refer them to the following for additional practice.

In the Textbook	Print Resources	Technology
Section Review, Ex. 48, Section 27.4	*Grammar Exercise Workbook*, pp. 139–140	*On-Line Exercise Bank*, Section 27.4

Using Underlining and Quotation Marks

Several methods are used to indicate different types of titles in various situations. These methods include italics, underlining, and quotation marks. Books, magazines, and other printed material are set in *italics*, a slanted typeface that indicates some types of titles. In handwritten or typed material, underlining would be used for those titles. Other titles require quotation marks.

> **KEY CONCEPT** Underline the titles of long written works; of publications that are published as a single work; of plays, movies, and television series; and of other works of art. ■

BOOK:	<u>To Kill a Mockingbird</u> is a modern classic.
PLAY:	He starred in <u>Long Day's Journey Into Night</u>.
MAGAZINE:	I read <u>Newsweek</u> to keep up with current events.
NEWSPAPER:	She agreed with the story in the <u>Los Angeles Times</u>.
MUSICAL:	She went to see <u>Peter Pan</u>.
PAINTING:	I saw Chagall's painting <u>The Green Violinist</u>.

The portion of a newspaper title that should be underlined will vary from newspaper to newspaper. <u>The New York Times</u> should always be fully capitalized and underlined. Other papers, however, can usually be treated in one of two ways: the <u>Los Angeles Times</u> or the Los Angeles <u>Times</u>.

> **KEY CONCEPT** Underline names of individual air, sea, space, and land craft. ■

EXAMPLE:	I wonder if Columbus had horses aboard the <u>Santa Maria</u>.

> **KEY CONCEPT** Underlining is also used for foreign words and phrases not yet accepted into English. ■

EXAMPLES:	The voyage was so rough that they suffered from <u>mal de mer</u> constantly.
	Her <u>sturm und drang</u> manner was shocking to those of us who had expected a milder response.

Underlining and Quotation Marks

1. Ask a student to explain the general principle that all the underlined examples of titles provided in the textbook adhere to (all are long works or stand-alone works).

2. Then ask the class if they know the precise title of their local paper. Does it include the word *the* in its title or is that optional? Explain that most titles are flexible but *The New York Times* in particular capitalizes and underlines (or italicizes) its *The*.

Underlining and Quotation Marks *continued*

3. Recommend that if students are uncertain whether words are "foreign" enough to require underlining that they check a dictionary.

4. Explain that one of the reasons numbers, letters, and words used as words are underlined is to make them stand out in a sentence and prevent confusion in reading. To make the point, provide these examples:

   Look for the word <u>very</u> as you read.

   Doesn't it have an <u>l</u> too many?

5. Point out that casual writing may use underlining to emphasize words, but this practice is often considered a flaw in formal writing. Too much underlining tends to make writing seem juvenile or poorly worded.

6. Discuss the logic for underlining or quoting titles. Underlined titles are long or stand-alone works, and quoted ones are shorter works that sometimes are part of these larger, underlined works (chapters, episodes, songs).

Customize for
ESL Students

Ask students to think of words from their native languages and to use them in an English sentence. (Example: My favorite meal is *arroz con pollo.*) Then have them exchange papers and check each other's words to see if they are in an English dictionary. If they are not, then explain that they should be underlined when used in an English sentence.

Customize for
Less Advanced Students

To help students decide whether to use underlining or quotation marks for titles, suggest that they prepare charts for their own personal use. Have them use the categories presented or listed on pages 731 and 732, and write an original example for each one. Students can use the information as they complete Exercise 46 and do the Integrating Writing activity on the following Teacher's Edition page.

27.4

Many foreign words and phrases are used so often by English-speaking people that they are now considered part of the language. Although these words may often retain their foreign pronunciation, they are no longer underlined or italicized.

NOT UNDERLINED: chili, amour, milieu, lasagne, plaza, gestalt, raconteur, teriyaki, andante, sauna

Consult a dictionary that includes foreign words and phrases if you are in doubt about whether a particular word or phrase should be underlined.

▶**KEY CONCEPT**   Underline numbers, symbols, letters, and words used as names for themselves. ■

EXAMPLES: Her <u>i</u>'s and her <u>l</u>'s look too much alike.
Is that an <u>8</u> or a <u>6</u>?
Avoid sprinkling your speech with <u>you know</u>.

▶**KEY CONCEPT**   Underline words that you wish to stress. ■

EXAMPLE: What a <u>ridiculous</u> situation!

In most cases, you should indicate emphasis not by underlining but by choosing and arranging your words with care. Reserve underlining for use only in special instances.

▶**KEY CONCEPT**   Use quotation marks to enclose the titles of short written works, episodes in a television series, songs, and parts of long musical compositions or collections. ■

EXAMPLES: "Edward, Edward" and "Lord Randall" are two familiar English ballads.
Winifred Welles's essay "The Attic" describes her as a child exploring her grandfather's attic.
Read Chapter 1, "Dialogue and Action," in <u>Understanding Drama</u>.
"The Tell-Tale Heart" is an effective horror tale.
One of the most loved songs of the American people is Woody Guthrie's "This Land Is Your Land."

Titles That Do Not Use Underlining or Quotation Marks

Religious works require neither underlining nor quotation marks.

KEY CONCEPT Do not underline or place in quotation marks the name of scriptures, such as the Bible, the Torah, and the Koran, or their books, divisions, or versions. ■

EXAMPLE: She recited the Twenty-third Psalm.

Other titles needing neither underlining nor quotation marks include various kinds of government documents.

KEY CONCEPT Do not underline or place in quotation marks the titles of government charters, alliances, treaties, acts, statutes, or reports. ■

EXAMPLE: The Versailles Treaty officially ended World War I.

Exercise 46 Revising for Underlining and Quotation Marks
Add the quotation marks and underlining needed in this passage.

Horse and Rider magazine, in the ranch library, lists all the equestrian activities: rodeos, harness racing, steeplechase competitions, and so on. One thing we learned from an article entitled Horsemanship 101 was never, ever mount a horse with your right foot first; if you do, you will be facing backward.

Before reaching the ranch, I explored the equestrian theme; I rented the movie National Velvet on video and read the book Black Beauty as we crossed the Atlantic aboard the Queen Elizabeth II. I also amused myself on deck by painting a portrait of a horse I call Mare of the Sea—a pun, because the English word mare refers to a female horse, although in Latin, mare means "sea."

The ranch foreman told us that he learned about a bridle bit from a series of articles in Ranch Animal. Then, in a column he read called Know Your Horse, the writer explained that there is a wide gap in the mouth of a horse between the canine and premolars, where the metal bit is designed to fit. The foreman also confessed that in those early days, he had a motorcycle, but traveling that way lacked a certain je ne sais quoi compared to horseback riding.

From Horsemanship, we learned that an ungelded male horse is called a colt until his fifth year; from then on, he is referred to as a stallion. A female horse is called a filly up to her fifth year; then she is referred to as a mare, according to Horseman's Catalog. My favorite book about horses is called Everything You Ever Wanted to Know About Horses.

More Practice

Grammar Exercise Workbook
• pp. 137–142
On-line Exercise Bank
• Section 27.4
Go on-line:
PHSchool.com
Enter Web Code:
egk-1202

Interactive Textbook

Get instant feedback! Exercise 46 is available on-line or on CD-ROM.

Titles Without Underlining or Quotation Marks

1. Work through the key concepts with students. Discuss possible reasons for these exceptions to the pattern that all titles of published works are underlined or surrounded by quotation marks. (Possible answers: Religious works are especially important; government documents, in a way, belong to everybody, not just to the person who wrote them.)

2. Emphasize that, for whatever reasons these exceptions exist, students need to remember these special cases.

Answer Key

Exercise 46

1. Horse and Rider
2. "Horsemanship 101"
3. National Velvet, Black Beauty, Queen Elizabeth II
4. Mare of the Sea, mare, mare
5. Ranch Animal
6. "Know Your Horse,"
7. je ne sais quoi
8. Horsemanship, colt, stallion
9. filly, mare, Horseman's Catalog
10. Everything You . . . Horses

Integrating Writing Skills

Have students think of four or five works of different genres that they have read throughout the year. Ask them to write a paragraph or two briefly explaining why they liked or did not like each work. Stress that they should punctuate titles correctly.

ONGOING ASSESSMENT: Monitor and Reinforce

If students have difficulty with Exercise 46, refer them to the following for additional practice.

In the Textbook	Print Resources	Technology
Section Review, Exercise 49, Section 27.4	*Grammar Exercise Workbook,* pp. 141–142	*On-Line Exercise Bank,* Section 27.4

Section Review

Each of these exercises correlates to the instruction on quotation marks and underlining, pages 722–733. These exercises may be used for more practice, for reteaching, or for review of the key concepts presented. Answers for all chapter exercises are available in *Grammar Exercises Answers on Transparencies* in your Teaching Resources.

Answer Key

▶ **Exercise 47**

1. "Every Friday . . . relax," the manager
2. me, "We . . . <u>A Funny Thing</u> . . . Forum on Broadway," he added
3. "Of course," Ashley quipped, "in the musical <u>Oklahoma!</u> . . . horse."
4. "One . . . surrey," she added
5. "The first line . . . song—'When I take you out in a surrey . . .'— sets a cheerful tone," she

▶ **Exercise 48**

1. artist, "There . . . a horse"; however,
2. "There are many portraits," he continued, "depicting . . . steeds."
3. "Any on horseback?" Hank
4. "In fact," the artist continued, "legend has it . . . the term <u>sport of kings</u> . . . language."
5. writes: " . . . Into the valley of Death rode the six hundred. . . ."

▶ **Exercise 49**

1. <u>National Geographic</u> recently wrote, "Arabian . . . regarded."
2. "Their . . . unmatched," she concluded
3. "Cavalry" . . . <u>Warfare</u>
4. racing: "I'd like . . . Stakes."
5. "I'm . . . events," Beth said, "most of . . . <u>The Horseman's Catalog</u>."
6. "Among these 'sportly champions,' as . . . them," Beth continued, "were Citation . . . Dancer."
7. <u>Towers</u>, <u>The Horseman's Catalog</u>

8. "Man O' War . . . races!" Beth
9. "There were . . . time," the foreman interjected, "such as 'Town Talk.' "

continued

Section 27.4 Section Review

GRAMMAR EXERCISES 47–53

▶ **Exercise 47** Enclosing Direct Quotations in Quotation Marks Copy each sentence, and supply the correct quotations marks or underlining if needed. If the sentence is correct, write *correct*.

1. Every Friday at the ranch, we would have some form of entertainment just to relax, the manager said.
2. Hank told me, We saw a movie starring Nathan Lane last year. He was also the lead in A Funny Thing Happened on the Way to the Forum on Broadway, he added excitedly.
3. Of course, Ashley quipped, in the musical Oklahoma!, everybody rides a horse.
4. One of the songs sung by Curly, the hero, is about a horse-drawn surrey, she added with a smile.
5. The first line he sings of that song— When I take you out in a surrey . . . — sets a cheerful tone, she volunteered teasingly.

▶ **Exercise 48** Using Other Punctuation Marks Correctly With Quotations, Dialogue, and Ellipsis Marks Copy each sentence, and supply the correct quotation marks or underlining if needed.

1. According to the visiting artist, There probably isn't a home in Britain that doesn't have a picture or a painting of a horse; however, I already knew that the English were great equestrians.
2. There are many portraits, he continued, depicting members of royal families with their beloved steeds.
3. Any on horseback? Hank muttered.
4. In fact, the artist continued, legend has it that because of Charles II of England, who was an avid horseman, the term sport of kings came into the language.
5. Tennyson writes: . . . Into the breach rode ten thousand . . . .

▶ **Exercise 49** Underlining and Quotation Marks Copy each sentence, and supply the correct quotation marks or underlining if needed.

1. A journalist from National Geographic recently wrote, Arabian horsemen are the most highly regarded.
2. Their abilities are unmatched, she concluded, commenting on their cavalrylike horsemanship.
3. At one of our Friday night shows at the ranch, we watched Cavalry, an installment of the Channel 72 series Warfare, about the fierce and destructive nature of cavalry units.
4. Mike started a conversation about horse racing: I'd like to see the big races, such as Royal Ascot in England, the Kentucky Derby, and the Belmont Stakes.
5. I'm interested in the famous horses that emerge from these events, Beth said, most of whom are discussed in The Horseman's Catalog.
6. Among these sportly champions, as the foreman calls them, Beth continued, were Citation, Secretariat, Bold Ruler, and Native Dancer.
7. However, in books from Towers (1922) to present-day editions of The Horseman's Catalog, the most revered horse is the American colt Man O' War.
8. Man O' War set track records for speed and was defeated only once in 21 races! Beth exclaimed.
9. There were many stories about Man O' War in newspaper columns of that time, the foreman interjected, such as Town Talk.

734 • Punctuation

10. Bob started reading aloud from Grayson's Encyclopedia: Racing horses are a breed unto themselves . . . called thoroughbreds.
11. The foreman told us that Native Americans have a long history with the wild horses that roam the plains.
12. Appaloosas and palominos had to be captured first and then tamed, added the foreman, before they could become part of a valuable herd.
13. Lippizaners are another example of a powerful horse; they were originally imperial carriage horses, stated a pamphlet from the local riding school.
14. The pamphlet, Horses Around the World, continued: Lippizaners are trained at the Spanish Riding School in Vienna to execute extremely intricate and difficult movements.
15. Many of these movements are done in unison with other Lippizaners, inside a covered circle, and often with a rider. I was reading that very same pamphlet just a moment ago, Beth explained after quoting verbatim.

> **Exercise 50** Applying All the Rules Governing the Use of Quotation Marks and Underlining Copy the following sentences, using quotation marks or underlining as necessary.

1. The professor began the lecture by saying, Horses belong to a group of animals called ungulates.
2. This term, he continued, comes from the Latin word ungula, meaning hoof.
3. I was shocked when the professor so matter-of-factly said, Both the horse and the elephant are ungulates!
4. According to The Audubon Field Guide to African Mammals, there are no wild horses on that continent.
5. Of course, zebras live there, Wilfredo interjected, and they're closely related; however, as my brother says, Close, but not close enough!
6. In fact, both horses and zebras belong to the same genus: Equus.

7. The zebra's well-known black-and-white stripe pattern serves to make it hard for a predator to pick a single target; in a herd of hundreds of moving zebras, the professor chuckled, a lion can get really confused!
8. Tragically, the quagga (Equus quagga) of southern Africa is extinct.
9. The New York Times reported, however, that quagga genes may exist in the gene pool of closely related zebras.
10. The professor concluded, If so, might it not one day be possible to restore that species to the Earth?

> **Exercise 51** Find It in Your Reading Find a passage in one of your favorite novels that illustrates the rules of punctuating dialogue. Write a brief explanation of each rule that the passage shows.

> **Exercise 52** Find It in Your Writing Choose one story and one research report from your portfolio. Find at least two indirect quotations in each, and rework them into direct quotations. Make sure that you follow the rules for punctuating direct quotations.

> **Exercise 53** Writing Application Write a brief passage of dialogue involving two or three people discussing their pets or some other topic about animals. Use quotation marks correctly where appropriate. Include titles of works—books, movies, art, and so on—in the conversation.

ONGOING ASSESSMENT: Assess Mastery

Use the following resources to assess student mastery of quotation marks and underlining.

In the Textbook	Technology
Chapter Review, Ex. 81	*Writing and Grammar* Interactive Text, Section 27.4 Section Review; *On-Line Exercise Bank,* Section 27.4

> **Exercise 49**
10. Grayson's Encyclopedia: "Racing . . . thoroughbreds."
11. correct
12. "Appaloosas . . . tamed," added the foreman, "before . . . herd."
13. "Lippizaners are . . . horses," stated
14. "Horses Around the World," continued: "Lippizaners . . . movements."
15. "'Many . . . a rider.' I was . . . ago," Beth explained

> **Exercise 50**
1. saying, "Horses . . . ungulates."
2. "This term," he continued, "comes . . . ungula . . . 'hoof.' "
3. said, "Both . . . ungulates"!
4. The Audubon Field Guide to African Mammals,
5. "Of course . . . there," Wilfredo interjected, "and . . . 'Close, but . . . enough!' "
6. Equus
7. "The zebra's . . . zebras," the professor chuckled, "a lion . . . confused!"
8. quagga (Equus quagga)
9. The New York Times
10. concluded, "If so . . . Earth?"

> **Exercise 51**
Find It in Your Reading
Have students share their passages and rules with partners to see whether the partners agree with what they have stated.

> **Exercise 52**
Find It in Your Writing
When students have finished, have them write a brief analysis of why they think a direct or indirect quotation is more effective in each sentence that they rewrote.

> **Exercise 53**
Writing Application
When students have finished, have them work in groups to choose one or two dialogues that they find well written. Have members of the group then read the dialogue aloud.

Dashes, Parentheses, and Brackets

Interest GRABBER Put : -) on the board and see if students know what it is called (a "smiley"). Have them tell what punctuation marks it is made of (colon, hyphen, parenthesis). Then put : —) on the board and tell them it is a smiley called "You lie like Pinocchio." Ask what the middle mark is (a dash). Have them create several original smileys using these marks and, if possible, one or more brackets [ ]. Then explain that in this section they will review more customary uses of these punctuation marks.

Activate Prior Knowledge

Put on the board these three terms: *More Emphasis, Less Emphasis, Clarification*. Tell students to list the punctuation marks *brackets*, *parentheses*, and *dashes* under the appropriate head (*More Emphasis:* dashes; *Less Emphasis:* parentheses; *Clarification:* brackets).

TEACH

Step-by-Step Teaching Guide

Dashes

1. Since most students tend to overuse dashes, suggest that they commit to memory those few proper uses of dashes mentioned in this subsection.

continued

Although they are used infrequently, you should be familiar with the use of dashes (—), parentheses (( )), and brackets ([ ]) and be able to use them when necessary.

Using Dashes

The dash is a strong, dramatic punctuation mark. It has specific uses and should not be used as a substitute for a comma, a semicolon, or parentheses. Overuse of the dash diminishes its effectiveness. Consider the proper uses of the dash in the Key Concepts below.

KEY CONCEPT Use dashes to indicate an abrupt change of thought, a dramatic interrupting idea, or a summary statement. ■

EXAMPLES: The tornado struck at dusk—to this day, survivors remember which houses were leveled.
It was a dilapidated wreck—it should have been condemned—but she bought it anyway.
The foundation, the roof, and the plumbing—every aspect of the house was in good condition.

The following chart shows the three basic uses of the dash.

USES OF THE DASH	
To indicate an abrupt change of thought	The article doesn't provide enough information on Japan—by the way, did you find it in the school library?
To set off interrupting ideas dramatically	The pagoda was built—you may find this hard to believe—in one month. The pagoda was built—where did they get the money?—in one month.
To set off a summary statement	A good scholastic record and good political connections—if you have these, you may be able to get a job in a congressional office.

Words such as *all, these, those, this*, and *that* will often be found at or near the beginning of a summary sentence preceded by a dash.

Theme: Houses

In this section, you will learn about the many uses of dashes, parentheses, and brackets. Most of the examples and exercises are about types of houses.

Cross-Curricular Connection: Social Studies

Technology Tip

Don't let your word-processing program put spaces around dashes; there should never be a space between the dash and the two phrases that it connects.

⏱ TIME AND RESOURCE MANAGER

Resources
Print: *Grammar Exercise Workbook*, pp. 143–146; *Grammar Exercises Answers on Transparencies*, Ch. 27
Technology: *Writing and Grammar* Interactive Text, Section 27.5; *On-Line Exercise Bank*, Section 27.5

Using the Full Student Edition	Using the Handbook 🄷
• Work through all key concepts, pp. 736–743.	• Work through all key concepts, pp. 558–565.
• Assign and review Exercises 54–57.	• Assign and review Exercises 54–57.
• Read and discuss Grammar in Literature, p. 738.	• Read and discuss Grammar in Literature, p. 560.

▶ **KEY CONCEPT** Use dashes to set off a nonessential appositive or modifier when it is long, when it is already punctuated, or when you want to be dramatic. ■

APPOSITIVE: The cause of the damage to the porch and the roof—a rare species of termite—went undiscovered for years.

MODIFIER: The home-improvement book editor—bored with writing about cement, joists, and grout—quit the next day.

Dashes may be used to set off one other special type of sentence interrupter—the parenthetical expression.

▶ **KEY CONCEPT** Use dashes to set off a parenthetical expression when it is long, already punctuated, or especially dramatic. ■

EXAMPLE: Yesterday we visited a castle—could you imagine living in such a place?—set on a small body of water out in the country.

▼ Critical Viewing
What types of people do you imagine would have lived in a "house" like this one? [Speculate]

Step-by-Step Teaching Guide continued

2. Discuss the final example on the page. Be sure students understand that only question marks and exclamation marks—not periods—can be included within dashes. Similarly, structures set off by dashes, even if they are complete sentences, are never capitalized.

Critical Viewing

Speculate Possible answers: There must have been many of them to build such a massive home; they must have needed to defend themselves from their neighbors; they must have been skillful builders to construct a building in a lake.

▶ **Exercise 54**

1. huts—one scarcely . . . can be—
   to elaborate
2. adversaries—these are
3. areas—the pampas . . .
   example—people
4. animals—except . . . pets—are
5. today—unless . . . small—include
6. home—is there . . . basic?—gives
7. Melanesians—gregarious . . .
   community-oriented—share
8. Americans—clustering . . .
   groups—has
9. Sudan—as well . . . tribes—build
10. States—in Queens . . .
    example—are

Step-by-Step Teaching Guide

Grammar in Literature

1. Read the passage aloud so
   students can hear the pause that
   the dash signifies.

2. Ask students to insert other
   punctuation in place of the dash.
   Discuss the impact of the change
   on the passage. (Students may
   agree that a comma makes the
   passage less dramatic or that a
   colon makes it seem too formal.)

More About the Translator

Biographical information about
Burton Raffel appears on page 418.

Connection With Literature

A longer excerpt from "Beowolf" can
be found in *Prentice Hall Literature,
Penguin Edition,* The British Tradition.

27.5

▶ **Exercise 54** Revising a Paragraph With Dashes Revise the
following paragraph, adding dashes where necessary.

  Houses range from remote tropical huts one scarcely can
believe how simple they can be to elaborate stone castles. To
serve as a dwelling place, provide shelter from weather, and provide protection from adversaries these are the three basic functions of a house. In rural areas the pampas of Argentina is a good
example people and animals once shared the same housing quarters. Now, animals except those that are pets are kept outside in
separate areas. Houses today unless the unit is very small
include areas for storage, work, rest, and entertainment. The
basic home is there really one type that can be considered
basic? gives way to endless variations among tribal groups on
every continent. Extended groups of Melanesians gregarious,
socially active, as well as community-oriented share one large
home with communal areas for cooking and relaxing. The custom of some Native Americans clustering housing in family-related
groups has largely been supplanted by urban ways. The Dogons
of Sudan as well as Zambian tribes build family dwellings so
that they join with other houses. Houses built in this way in the
United States in Queens, New York, for example are called semi-
attached houses.

GRAMMAR IN
LITERATURE

from **Beowulf**
Translated by **Burton Raffel**

The dash in this passage from Beowulf *sets off a
nonessential appositive, which not only renames a
significant object, but also elaborates on its history.*

. . . Remembering
Everything his lord and cousin had given him,
Armor and gold and the great estates
Wexstan's family enjoyed, Wiglaf's
Mind was made up; he raised his yellow
Shield and drew his sword—an ancient
Weapon that had once belonged to Onela's
Nephew, and that Wexstan had won, killing
The prince when he fled from Sweden, sought safety
With Herdred, and found death.

▶ **More Practice**

Grammar Exercise
Workbook
• pp. 143–148
On-line Exercise Bank
• Section 27.5
  Go on-line:
  PHSchool.com
  Enter Web Code:
  egk-1202

Get instant feedback!
Exercises 54 and 55 are
available on-line or on
CD-ROM.

◀ Critical Viewing
How would you describe this Victorian house?
[Describe]

▶ **Exercise 55** Revising Sentences With Dashes Revise the following sentences, adding one or two dashes where necessary.

1. Victorian houses my favorite type of house are often painted in colors such as plum or pink.
2. They often have very fancy trim work some people call it gingerbread.
3. Cape May a town filled with Victorian houses is in New Jersey.
4. There is a house in Cape May called the Pink House, which is covered with gingerbread the gingerbread is unique to that house.
5. I read somewhere I'm not sure where that gingerbread trim was different on each house.
6. Some people not me particularly prefer a Cape Cod style house.
7. A Cape Cod house my mother doesn't agree looks like a box with a pointed roof.
8. They are actually much larger inside than they look from the outside usually three bedrooms.
9. Cape Cod houses are often sided in cedar that is allowed to weather to a natural gray good if you don't like house-painting.
10. I plan to own a Victorian house someday which means I'd better learn to paint!

Dashes, Parentheses, and Brackets • **739**

Critical Viewing

Describe Possible answers: The house is ornate, highly decorated, colorful, old-fashioned, or elegant.

Answer Key

▶ **Exercise 55**

1. Victorian houses—my favorite type of house—are
2. They often have very fancy trim work—some people
3. Cape May—a town filled with Victorian Houses—is in
4. There is a house in Cape May called the Pink House, which is covered with gingerbread—the gingerbread is unique to that house.
5. I read somewhere—I'm not sure where—that gingerbread
6. Some people—not me particularly—prefer
7. A Cape Cod house—my mother doesn't agree—looks
8. They are actually much larger inside than they look from the outside—usually three bedrooms.
9. Cape Cod houses are often sided in cedar that is allowed to weather to a natural gray—good if you don't like house-painting.
10. I plan to own a Victorian house someday—which means

Integrating Workplace Skills

Using Punctuation Marks The writing required in many jobs needs to be concise because of time and space limitations. Ask students to locate or create examples of punctuation used to save space. Use these to get them started:

• Headline writers may use dashes to help them compress ideas, as in "Fire Consumes Building—Three Injured."

• Parentheses may be used in a headline when the copywriter wants to add a pun. For example, "Lady in (Hot) Water" might appear over a story about a woman caught by police as she attempted to swim away from the scene of a crime.

☑ **ONGOING ASSESSMENT: Monitor and Reinforce**

If students have difficulty with Exercise 54 or 55, refer them to the following for additional practice.

In the Textbook	Print Resources	Technology
Section Review, Ex. 58, Section 27.5	*Grammar Exercise Workbook,* pp. 143–144	*On-Line Exercise Bank,* Section 27.5

Parentheses

1. Ask students to describe the material within the parentheses in the examples (subordinate clause, independent clause) and explain how the parenthetical material relates to the main sentence (it is a modifier conveying interesting but nonessential information).

2. Be sure students understand that a parenthetical statement within a sentence is not capitalized, nor does it have end marks.

Other Punctuation Marks With Parentheses

1. Students may benefit from creating a chart showing the punctuation of parenthetical phrases and sentences.

2. Begin a chart like the following:

Within Sentences	Punctuation
Phrase	no caps or periods
Statement	no caps or periods

3. Have students add the correct information for questions and exclamations (both caps and end marks are used).

continued

Customize for
Logical/Mathematical Learners

Compare the uses of parentheses in sentences with those in mathematical equations. Explain that parentheses in equations are often used to indicate the order in which a problem should be solved. For example, in the equation $3(4-2)=X$, the parentheses tell mathematicians that $4-2$ must be computed before solving the rest of the equation. In sentences, parentheses tell readers that the items enclosed (1) may be figures or numbers showing order or (2) may add information about the rest of a sentence.

27.5

Using Parentheses

Parentheses are occasionally used to set off material within a sentence. Commas are the appropriate punctuation marks to use for this purpose in most cases, especially when the material is short and closely related in meaning to the rest of the sentence. Parentheses, on the other hand, are appropriate in some circumstances.

KEY CONCEPT Use parentheses to set off asides and explanations only when the material is not essential or when it consists of one or more sentences. ■

EXAMPLES: The task of cleaning the mansion (as she learned within the month) was far greater than she had believed.

Turn-of-the-century wealth (two of the more famous fortunes are those of the Rockefeller and Frick families) spawned estate homes of incredible opulence.

Parentheses are the strongest separators that writers can use. Although material enclosed in parentheses is not essential to the meaning of the sentence, a writer indicates that the material is important and calls attention to it by using parentheses.

Using Parentheses With Other Punctuation Marks
Four rules govern parentheses used with other marks:

KEY CONCEPT When a phrase or declarative sentence interrupts another sentence, do not use an initial capital letter or end mark inside the parentheses. ■

EXAMPLE: Bill Frazier finally sold his vacation home (we used to love to visit) to a young couple.

KEY CONCEPT When a question or exclamation interrupts another sentence, use both an initial capital letter and an end mark inside the parentheses. ■

EXAMPLES: Joseph Allen (Didn't he once star in the television show *Homes for Tomorrow*?) has had a string of personal difficulties.

Uncle Bruce (He is a fabulous decorator!) chose our window treatments.

✎ STANDARDIZED TEST PREPARATION WORKSHOP

Grammar and Usage Many standardized tests require students to revise the errors in a composition. Use the following example to demonstrate.

Harriet Beecher Stowe 1811–1896 lived long enough to see her bestseller, Uncle Tom's Cabin, *produced on stage.*

What, if anything, needs to be added to this sentence?

A Parentheses around *1811–1896*

B Dashes around *1811–1896*

C Commas after *Stowe* and *1896*

D Nothing needs to be added.

The correct answer is **A**. Parentheses set off nonessential explanations or other data in sentences.

Step-by-Step Teaching Guide continued

▶ **KEY CONCEPT** When you place a sentence in parentheses between two other sentences, use both an initial capital letter and an end mark inside the parentheses. ■

EXAMPLE: Newport is known for its incredible mansions. (See the Vanderbilt home as an example.) These wild excesses of wealth are staggering to behold.

▶ **KEY CONCEPT** In a sentence that includes parentheses, place any punctuation belonging to the main sentence after the parenthesis. ■

EXAMPLE: The town council approved the construction (after some deliberation), and they explained the new zoning laws to the public (with some doubts about how the changes would be received).

Special Uses of Parentheses Parentheses are also used to set off numerical explanations such as dates of a person's birth and death and numbers and letters marking a series.

EXAMPLES: Frank Lloyd Wright (1867–1959) was an innovative American architect.

His phone number is (303) 555-4211.

Her research will take her to (1) Portugal, (2) Canada, and (3) Romania.

▼ Critical Viewing How does this grass hut differ from most of the houses you are used to seeing? Use parentheses at least once in making your comparison. **[Compare]**

4. Continue the chart with categories for "Other Sentence Punctuation" and "Separate Sentences." Make sure students note that the period always goes outside parenthetical material that is within a sentence.

Critical Viewing

Compare Possible answers: It is smaller; it is made of natural materials; it doesn't have glass windows (to keep weather and insects out).

Answer Key

▶ Exercise 56

1. purposes (unlike the joined family dwellings of the Dogon and Zambians).
2. tradition (their devotion . . . admired) is
3. African influence endures (persisting in . . . as well).
4. village in Tobago (a small . . . chain) and find
5. families (though from disparate areas) also seem
6. geometric appearance (as can be . . . aerial photographs), like a beehive.
7. relative isolation (compared . . . Zambians). Inuit
8. Today, the Inuit (also known, less accurately, as Eskimos) live
9. long journey (for example, . . . expedition), an igloo is built.
10. These snow houses (rarely seen . . . in Alaska!) were once

---

27.5

▶ **Exercise 56** Enclosing Material in Parentheses Copy the following items, adding parentheses and capital letters where needed.

EXAMPLE: Cockroaches how I detest them! invaded our home.

ANSWER: Cockroaches (How I detest them!) invaded our home.

1. In the United States, semi-attached housing was used to bring affordable homes to a rising middle class, not for communal purposes unlike the joined family dwellings of the Dogon and Zambians.
2. Another feature of the Dogon and Zambian housing tradition their devotion to communal principles that must be admired is that homes are built close to the civic center.
3. This tradition can also be seen in places such as in the Caribbean, where a strong African influence endures persisting in other areas such as music and religion as well.
4. You can go into any village in Tobago a small Caribbean island situated to the north of Venezuela, lying at the far southern end of the Caribbean chain and find sections of about four or five houses occupied by one family unit.
5. Mediterranean and Latin American families though from disparate areas also seem to follow this tradition.
6. The Dogon-Zambian style of home building creates a fascinating geometric appearance as can be discerned in aerial photographs, like a beehive.
7. Accustomed to the solitary life of the Arctic, the Inuit can live in relative isolation, compared to the cultural traditions of the Dogon and Zambians. Inuit housing reflects that.
8. Today, the Inuit also known, less accurately, as Eskimos live in modern homes, with a walrus skin or sealskin covering used the way one might use shingles.
9. On occasions when the family must go on a long journey for example, on an ice-fishing expedition, an igloo is built.
10. These snow houses rarely seen in Greenland and unknown in Alaska! were once the permanent winter homes of the Inuit in eastern Canada.

▶ **More Practice**

Grammar Exercise Workbook
• pp. 143–148
On-line Exercise Bank
• Section 27.5
Go on-line:
PHSchool.com
Enter Web Code:
egk-1202

Get instant feedback! Exercises 56 and 57 are available on-line or on CD-ROM.

☑ **ONGOING ASSESSMENT: Monitor and Reinforce**

If students have difficulty with Exercise 56 or 57, refer them to the following for additional practice.

In the Textbook	Print Resources	Technology
Section Review, Ex. 59, Section 27.5	*Grammar Exercise Workbook,* pp. 143–146	*On-Line Exercise Bank,* Section 27.5

Using Brackets

Brackets are used to enclose a word or phrase added by a writer to the words of another.

KEY CONCEPT Use brackets to enclose words you insert in quotations when quoting someone else. ■

EXAMPLES: Cooper noted: "And with [*ET*'s] success, 'Phone home' is certain to become one of the most oft-repeated phrases of the year [1982]."

Lady Caroline Lamb wrote of Byron, "[He is] mad, bad, and dangerous to know."

The Latin expression *sic* (meaning "thus") is sometimes enclosed in brackets to show that the author of the quoted material has misspelled or mispronounced a word or phrase.

EXAMPLE: Michaelson, citing Dorothy's signature line from *The Wizard of Oz*, wrote, "Theirs [sic] no place like home."

Exercise 57 Enclosing Material in Brackets Insert brackets and *sic* where needed. Added words are underlined.

EXAMPLE: "These houses are all picture-prefect."
ANSWER: "These houses are all picture-prefect [sic]."

1. According to an expert on nomadic tribes, "Homes of nomads all have one feature in common: They must be potable."
2. "Whether they were in the plains of the American Wild West 1890's or are living today on the tranquil plains of Tibet, the ability to pack up quickly <u>if necessary</u> and efficiently is paramount," he claims.
3. A rival expert on nomadic tribes expresses a different view: "To suggest that portability is the only share characteristic of the dwelling structures of nomads is pure poppycock."
4. "The cone-shaped teepee of the Plains Indians is an example; it is made of animal hide stretched around poles <u>arranged in a tripod</u>, used as a framework," she continues.
5. "At any given moment, the pegs holding the skins securely to the ground could be removed and the entire skin structure rolled up to become a lightweigt bundle with three poles."

💇 Spelling Tip

Sic is used only when there is an error in a work from which you are quoting. You cannot use it after misspellings in your own work!

✓ ONGOING ASSESSMENT: Assess Mastery

Use the following resources to assess student mastery of dashes, parentheses, and brackets.

In the Textbook	Technology
Chapter Review, Ex. 82	*On-Line Exercise Bank,* Section 27.5

Section Review

Each of these exercises correlates to the instruction on dashes, parentheses, and brackets, pages 736–743. These exercises may be used for more practice, for reteaching, or for review of the key concepts presented. Answers for all chapter exercises are available in *Grammar Exercises Answers on Transparencies* in your Teaching Resources.

Answer Key

▶ Exercise 58

1. is—in the most literal sense—a
2. fixtures—these
3. big—have you been to the White House?—it
4. House—perhaps . . . world—is
5. House—as if . . . exciting!—are

▶ Exercise 59

1. palace (as you can imagine) is
2. the [British] royal . . . (600 in total) and . . . grounds (a well-manicured 50 acres)."
3. George III (1738–1820).
4. uses (no doubt . . . upkeep), such as
5. Spain (It is a beautiful structure!) is

▶ Exercise 60

Students may be able to provide rationales for using parentheses rather than dashes, and vice versa, in items 2, 3, and 4.
1. flats—no matter
2. that (1) was in a safe neighborhood; (2) got lots of sunlight (he's fond of his plants); and (3) wouldn't
3. tiny (it fit the bill . . . bed), but he
4. lease—you . . . head!—he
5. 'flat' [sic].

▶ Exercise 61

Find It in Your Reading
Once students have found their examples, have them explain to the class whether their usage follows the rules given in this textbook.

Section 27.5 Section Review

GRAMMAR EXERCISES 58–63

▶ **Exercise 58** Using Dashes Copy the following sentences, inserting dashes where needed.

1. Home for some people in the world is in the most literal sense a castle.
2. Manors, palaces, marbled halls, gold fixtures these are the amenities of daily life for them.
3. Sometimes, these homes are so big have you been to the White House? it takes a day to see the whole place.
4. The White House perhaps the most exclusive estate in the world is made of white sandstone from Virginia.
5. Probably the most exciting rooms at the White House as if there could be any rooms there that aren't exciting! are the state rooms where balls, receptions, and dinners are held.

▶ **Exercise 59** Enclosing Material in Parentheses and Brackets Insert parentheses or brackets as appropriate, using capital letters where necessary. Added material is underlined.

1. A palace as you can imagine is a larger and more ornate version of a mansion.
2. "Buckingham Palace, the official residence of the <u>British</u> royal family, has a vast number of rooms 600 in total and is known for its beautiful garden grounds, a well-manicured 50 acres."
3. The palace was purchased for the royal family by George III 1738–1820.
4. Many formerly residential palaces have long since been converted to other uses no doubt because of the enormous expense of their upkeep, such as ballet institutes, art museums, and libraries.
5. The Alhambra in Granada, Spain, it is a beautiful structure! is still as alive and vibrant as it was centuries ago.

▶ **Exercise 60** Using Dashes, Parentheses, and Brackets Punctuate the following sentences.

1. Studios, efficiency apartments, one-room flats no matter the euphemism, there's no concealing that affordable Manhattan apartments are small.
2. For example, Richard insisted on a home that 1 was in a safe neighborhood; 2 got lots of sunlight he's fond of his plants; and 3 wouldn't send him into bankruptcy.
3. The apartment he found was tiny it fit the bill but couldn't fit his bed but he took it anyway.
4. After he signed the lease you wouldn't believe how much of his income would be paying for the roof over his head! he felt outraged by what he was paying.
5. He wrote, "Now I know why they call these apartments a 'flat': That's the only way anything fits into them, and they leave you flat broke!"

▶ **Exercise 61** Find It in Your Reading Skim through a reference book about architecture. Find at least two examples of dashes, parentheses, or brackets.

▶ **Exercise 62** Find It in Your Writing Review a piece of research writing to find at least one place where you can use information in brackets to clarify a quotation.

▶ **Exercise 63** Writing Application Write a paragraph about your home or someone else's. Use dashes, parentheses, and brackets—each at least once.

▶ Exercise 62

Find It in Your Writing
When students have finished, have them exchange their results with partners to check whether brackets have been used correctly.

▶ Exercise 63

Writing Application
When students have finished, have them go back and label their uses of brackets, dashes, and parentheses according to the rules they follow.

Hyphens and Apostrophes

Section 27.6

As a writer, you must know the rules governing the use of hyphens and apostrophes. Although the rules are not difficult, you must carefully study them and the examples that illustrate them to avoid making mistakes.

Using Hyphens

Hyphens are used to join some words and to divide others. The hyphen (-) resembles the dash (—) but is shorter. In your handwriting, make your hyphens about half the length of your dashes. In typewriting, one hyphen mark is used for a hyphen and two hyphen marks are used for a dash.

Writers use hyphens with numbers, word parts, and words.

With Numbers Hyphens are used to join compound numbers.

KEY CONCEPT Use a hyphen when writing out the compound numbers *twenty-one* through *ninety-nine*. ■

EXAMPLES: twenty-eight ounces
fifty-five apartments

With Fractions Fractions used as adjectives are also hyphenated.

KEY CONCEPT Use a hyphen with fractions used as adjectives. A fraction used as a noun is not hyphenated. ■

EXAMPLES: seven-tenths full
three-quarters finished
One fourth of the members were present.

▶ Critical Viewing How can you determine fractions of an inch using a tape measure? **[Analyze]**

Theme: The Ordinary and the Unusual

In this section, you will learn about the many uses of hyphens and apostrophes. Most of the examples and exercises are about ordinary objects and animals as well as some unusual places, things, or ideas.

Cross-Curricular Connection: Social Studies

Hyphens and Apostrophes • 745

PREPARE and ENGAGE

Interest GRABBER Write these two categories on the board: *Separators* and *Connectors.* Have students name punctuation marks that fit in the first category (periods, question marks). Then list *hyphens* and *apostrophes* in the second category and have a volunteer explain why they belong there.

Activate Prior Knowledge

Write the following on the board:

pro French politicians

cant find the keys

in mid May

Henrys new coat

twenty two days

president elect Mitchell

Have students add hyphens and apostrophes where needed.

TEACH

Step-by-Step Teaching Guide

Hyphens

1. Discuss the differences between dashes and hyphens: In appearance, dashes are longer; in their uses, dashes signify breaks, while hyphens signify connections.

2. Make the point that the longer line—the dash—goes in the longer space between ideas, while the shorter line—the hyphen—goes in the smaller space between letters.

continued

Critical Viewing

Analyze Possible answer: The numbers on this tape measure indicate inches, the longest lines between numbers indicate one-quarter inches, and the next-longest lines show one-eighth-inch increments.

Hyphens *continued*

3. Make the point that in general, prefixes are not followed by hyphens. Review the cases in which they are.

4. Ask students to think of more examples of prefixes with proper nouns (*post-Depression, anti-Fascist*) and of words using the prefixes *all-, ex-, self-,* and *-elect* (*ex-wife, self-sufficient, all-consuming*).

5. Write these words on the board: *anti-inflammatory, semi-invalid.* Explain that in those rare cases where *anti-* and *semi-* connect to words beginning with *i*, a hyphen is used.

6. In addition to recommending that students check a dictionary for hyphenated compound words, also stress that that dictionary should be current. Many compounds start out as hyphenated and quickly evolve into single words.

continued

Customize for
Spatial Learners

Discuss the visual distinctions between dashes and hyphens, pointing out that these marks differ both in length and in function. Give students a graphic example on the board by writing the dashes noticeably longer than the hyphens:

Our class ex-president is an attentive—but not over-eager—student.

Review the difference in the uses of the two marks and then have students redo one of the exercises about dashes by also hyphenating two words per sentence as if they fell at the ends of lines. Tell students to distinguish the lengths of their dashes and hyphens as they write them.

Critical Viewing

Connect Possible answers include semi-trailer, tanker-truck, and eighteen-wheeler.

27.6

With Word Parts In some circumstances, a hyphen is used after a prefix.

 **KEY CONCEPT** Use a hyphen after a prefix that is followed by a proper noun or a proper adjective. ■

EXAMPLES: pre-Renaissance
mid-February
un-American

Prefixes that may be used before proper nouns or proper adjectives are *ante-, anti-, mid-, post-, pre-, pro-,* and *un-.*

KEY CONCEPT Use a hyphen in words with the prefixes *all-, ex-, self-,* and words with the suffix *-elect.* ■

EXAMPLES: all-powerful
ex-jockey
self-made
mayor-elect

With Compound Words Some compound words are also joined with hyphens.

KEY CONCEPT Use a hyphen to connect two or more words that are used as one word unless the dictionary gives a contrary spelling. ■

Although some compound words are written as one word and others are written as two words, many compound words are joined with hyphens. Always consult your dictionary if you are in doubt about the spelling of a compound word.

EXAMPLES: sister-in-law
tractor-trailer
six-year-old

▲ **Critical Viewing** What hyphenated word could you use to describe this truck? **[Connect]**

🔁 **Learn More**

For additional information about using hyphens, see Chapter 29: "Vocabulary and Spelling."

KEY CONCEPT Use a hyphen to connect a compound modifier that comes before a noun unless it includes a word ending in *-ly* or is a compound proper adjective or compound proper noun acting as an adjective. ■

EXAMPLES WITH HYPHENS: a well-made pair of jeans
the bright-eyed children
an up-to-date decision

EXAMPLES WITHOUT HYPHENS: widely distributed information
East European languages
Red River valley

When compound modifiers follow a noun, they generally do not require the use of hyphens.

EXAMPLE: The jeans were well made.

If your dictionary lists a word as hyphenated, however, it should always be hyphenated.

EXAMPLE: The news was up-to-date.

For Clarity Sometimes, a word or group of words might be misread if a hyphen were not used.

KEY CONCEPT Use a hyphen within a word when a combination of letters might otherwise be confusing. ■

EXAMPLES: semi-illiterate
re-press (to press again)

KEY CONCEPT Use a hyphen between words to keep readers from combining them erroneously. ■

INCORRECT: the special delivery-man
CORRECT: the special-delivery man

Dividing Words at the End of a Line Although you should try to avoid dividing a word at the end of a line, if a word must be broken, use a hyphen to show the division.

KEY CONCEPT If a word must be divided at the end of a line, always divide it between syllables. ■

EXAMPLE: The lonely children had been sending letters describing their adventures at camp.

💡 Spelling Tip

Generally, words that contain double letters are divided between the double letters, as in *run-ner*. Check a dictionary if you are unsure of where to break a word.

7. See if students can think of other words like *re-press*, where the hyphenated and nonhyphenated forms have different meanings (*recreate, relay, reform*).

8. Ask a student to explain the two different meanings of the next-to-last example on the page (*special* modifies *delivery-man* or *special-delivery* modifies the *man*).

9. Refer to the Interest Grabber on page 745. Though breaking words into syllables is in fact separating them, in what way is it also connecting them? (It signals that the word parts belong together.)

continued

Hyphens *continued*

10. Have students check a dictionary for any words that they are not sure how to syllabicate. Spaces or dots within an entry word show correct syllabication.

11. Add to the rules in this section that students should break closed compounds only at the compound (*book-keeper*, not *bookkeep-er*).

Customize for
Less Advanced Students

Students having trouble dividing words into syllables will need extra practice dividing words at the ends of lines. To keep such students from constantly consulting dictionaries, drill them orally. Read lists of multisyllabic words one at a time and have students listen for the syllables; then have them write each word as though it falls at the end of a line and needs to be hyphenated. Discuss their answers and point out any errors. Begin by using these words:

chronology (chro-nol-ogy)

fraternal (fra-ter-nal)

nationality (na-tion-al-ity)

declaration (dec-la-ra-tion)

fragmentation (frag-men-ta-tion)

responsibility (re-spon-si-bi-li-ty)

thunderclap (thunder-clap)

Answer Key

▶ Exercise 64

1. third-largest
2. mountain-rimmed
3. self-imposed
4. large-scale
5. flat-topped
6. correct
7. west-east
8. non-Chinese-speaking
9. mineral-rich
10. ten-year

▶ Exercise 65

1. enter-prise
2. Beijing
3. correct
4. popula-tion
5. correct
6. Chinese
7. cul-ture
8. correct
9. state-owned
10. correct

27.6

▶ **KEY CONCEPT** Do not divide a word so that a single letter or the letters *-ed* stand alone. ■

INCORRECT:	a-bout	scream-ed	toast-y
CORRECT:	about	screamed	toasty

▶ **KEY CONCEPT** Avoid dividing proper nouns and proper adjectives. ■

INCORRECT:	Fe-licia	Amer-ican
CORRECT:	Felicia	American

▶ **KEY CONCEPT** Divide a hyphenated word only after the hyphen. ■

INCORRECT:	We are going with my sister and my bro-ther-in-law.
CORRECT:	We are going with my sister and my brother-in-law.

▶ **Exercise 64** Using Hyphens to Join Words Add hyphens as needed. Write *correct* if none are required.

1. third largest country
2. mountain rimmed area
3. self imposed isolation
4. large scale project
5. flat topped mountains
6. estimated population
7. west east direction
8. non Chinese speaking
9. mineral rich country
10. ten year plan

▶ **Exercise 65** Using Hyphens at the Ends of Lines If a word is broken correctly, write *correct*. If not, rewrite it.

EXAMPLE:	cur-ed
ANSWER:	cured

1. enterp-rise
2. Bei-jing
3. pan-da
4. populat-ion
5. politi-cal
6. Chi-nese
7. cult-ure
8. mon-soon
9. state-own-ed
10. tour-ism

748 • Punctuation

✿ Grammar and Style Tip

When writing, avoid placing a broken or hyphenated word at the end of a page.

▶ **More Practice**

Grammar Exercise Workbook
• pp. 147–148
On-line Exercise Bank
• Section 27.6
Go on-line:
PHSchool.com
Enter Web Code:
egk-1202

interactive Textbook

Get instant feedback! Exercises 64 and 65 are available on-line or on CD-ROM.

☑ ONGOING ASSESSMENT: Monitor and Reinforce

If students miss more than two items in Exercise 64 or 65, refer them to the following for additional practice.

In the Textbook	Print Resources	Technology
Section Review, Ex. 68–69, Section 27.6	*Grammar Exercise Workbook,* pp. 147–148	*On-Line Exercise Bank,* Section 27.6

Using Apostrophes

Apostrophes are used to form possessives, contractions, and a few special plurals.

Forming Possessives The following rules tell you how to show possession with various types of nouns.

> **KEY CONCEPT** Add an apostrophe and an *-s* to show the possessive case of most singular nouns. ■

EXAMPLES: the wallet of the woman   the woman's wallet
the collar of the dog   the dog's collar
the lines of the actress   the actress's lines

For classical references ending in *-s*, only an apostrophe is used.

EXAMPLES: Confucius' teachings
Tacitus' history

The possessive case of plural nouns follows two rules:

> **KEY CONCEPT** Add an apostrophe to show the possessive case of plural nouns ending in *-s* or *-es*. ■

EXAMPLES: the barking of the dogs
the dogs' barking
the color of the leaves
the leaves' color

> **KEY CONCEPT** Add an apostrophe and an *-s* to show the possessive case of plural nouns that do not end in *-s* or *-es*. ■

EXAMPLES: the books of the women
the women's books
the grazing lands of oxen
the oxen's grazing lands

▶ Critical Viewing Write a sentence describing this photograph, using the possessive form of the word *dog*. **[Connect]**

Step-by-Step Teaching Guide

Apostrophes With Possessives

1. Many students will need careful review of the formation and use of possessives, as this is an area where errors frequently occur.

2. To form the plural possessive of single words, tell students first to form the plural of the word. Once they see the plural form, they can decide whether they need to add 's (if the plural does not end in *-s* or *-es*) or just an apostrophe (if it does end in *s*).

continued

Critical Viewing

Connect Possible answer: The dog's face has a white blaze down the center.

Hyphens and Apostrophes • 749

Apostrophes With Possessives
continued

3. Remind students that an apostrophe is never used to form the plurals of words.

4. Write on the board: *attorney general job, attorneys general job, ex-wife phone number, ex-wives phone numbers.* Have volunteers change them into possessive nouns (*attorney general's job, attorneys general's job, ex-wife's phone number, ex-wives' phone numbers*). Point out that students will need to look at the final word of the compound in deciding whether to add *'s* or just an apostrophe.

continued

Real-World Connection

Point out that apostrophes are always around us, especially in advertisements, on billboards, and on store signs (*Miller's Hardware*). Discuss places where students have noticed errors in the use of apostrophes to show possession. Discuss the many rules that need to be remembered and the confusion that possessive forms can cause.

Critical Viewing

Connect Possible answers: I can usually finish my homework in forty-five minutes' time. On average, my evening's homework takes one hour's time.

27.6

▶ **KEY CONCEPT** Add an apostrophe and an *s* (or just an apostrophe if the word is a plural ending in *s*) to the last word of a compound noun to form the possessive. ■

NAMES OF BUSINESSES AND ORGANIZATIONS:	the Salvation Army's headquarters the Department of the Interior's budget the Johnson Associates' clients
TITLES OF RULERS AND LEADERS:	Catherine the Great's victories Louis XVI's palace the chairman of the board's desk
HYPHENATED COMPOUND NOUNS USED TO DESCRIBE PEOPLE:	my sister-in-law's car the secretary-treasurer's idea the nurse-practitioner's patient

▶ **KEY CONCEPT** To form possessives involving time, amounts, or the word *sake,* use an apostrophe and an *-s* or just an apostrophe if the possessive is plural. ■

TIME:	a month's vacation three days' vacation a half-hour's time
AMOUNT:	one quarter's worth two cents' worth
SAKE:	for Marjorie's sake for goodness' sake

▶ **Critical Viewing** How much time does it take for you to do your homework on an average day? Respond using a time phrase with an apostrophe. **[Connect]**

When you make words possessive, you should also indicate the difference between something owned jointly by two or more people and something owned by individuals.

▶ **KEY CONCEPT** To show joint ownership, make the final noun possessive. To show individual ownership, make each noun possessive. ■

| JOINT OWNERSHIP: | I always enjoyed Bob and Ray's radio show. |
| INDIVIDUAL OWNERSHIP: | Liz's and Meg's coats are hanging here. |

Use the owner's complete name before the apostrophe to form the possessive case.

INCORRECT SINGULAR:	Jame's idea
CORRECT SINGULAR:	James's idea
INCORRECT PLURAL:	two girl's books
CORRECT PLURAL:	two girls' books

Forming the possessives of pronouns requires two rules:

▶ **KEY CONCEPT** Use an apostrophe and an -*s* with indefinite pronouns to show possession. ■

| EXAMPLES: | everyone's time | one another's friends |
| | somebody's umbrella | each other's homework |

Notice in two of the examples that you add an apostrophe and an -*s* only to the last word of a two-word indefinite pronoun to form the possessive.

GRAMMAR IN LITERATURE

from **Macbeth, Act IV**
William Shakespeare

This excerpt from a spell spoken by one of the witches in Macbeth illustrates the use of apostrophes in possessives.

Fillet of a fenny snake,
In the cauldron boil and bake;
Eye of newt and toe of frog,
Wool of bat and tongue of dog,
Adder's fork and blindworm's sting,
Lizard's leg and howlet's wing,
For a charm of pow'rful trouble,
Like a hell-broth boil and bubble.

Hyphens and Apostrophes • **751**

5. Use the example *James's idea* to initiate a discussion of possessives of names. Point out that this is a common area for mistakes and that the rules that apply here are slightly different from those of regular possessives. Point out that even when a name ends in -*s*, an apostrophe and an *s* are added (*Miles's, Jones's*). You might also mention that the base spelling of a name does not change in the plural (*Kellys*, not *Kellies; the Kellys' house*, not *the Kelly's house*).

6. Ask students for a definition of indefinite pronouns (pronouns used to refer to persons, places, and things, often without specifying which ones). Ask them to provide additional examples *(most, some, all)*.

continued

Customize for
ESL Students

Students may need to learn which indefinite pronouns can show possession and which cannot. Refer to the chart of indefinite pronouns on page 375. Point out that neither the plural forms nor the forms that can be either singular or plural can take the possessive in English. Neither can *little*. Give students practice by having them write short phrases using possessives with the other indefinites.

Step-by-Step Teaching Guide

Grammar in Literature

1. Ask students to list the words using apostrophes in possessives (*adder's, blindworm's, lizard's, howler's*).

2. Have students find another way that possession is shown in this excerpt (using *of*, as in *fillet of a fenny snake, eye of newt, toe of frog, wool of bat, tongue of dog*).

3. Tell students to rewrite the phrases using an apostrophe to show possession (*fenny snake's fillet, newt's eye, frog's toe, bat's wool, dog's tongue*).

More About the Writer

Biographical information about William Shakespeare appears on page 423.

Connections With Literature

A longer excerpt from Shakespeare's *Macbeth* can be found in *Prentice Hall Literature, Penguin Edition,* The British Tradition.

Apostrophes With Possessives
continued

7. Recommend that, when students have a choice between *it's* and *its*, *who's* and *whose*, and *their* and *they're*, they mentally substitute the uncontracted form (*it is, who is, they are*).

8. If this form does not make sense in the sentence, then students should use the spelling without the apostrophe.

Apostrophes With Contractions and Plurals

1. Have a student volunteer define the word *contraction* (a word contracted in size by the removal of some letter or letters and the insertion of an apostrophe to indicate the missing letters).

2. Point out the spelling of *can't*, which some students erroneously form as *cann't*.

3. Point out that in addition to personal pronouns, indefinite pronouns may also be used in contractions. Review the distinction between possessive and contraction by presenting these sentences:

    Everyone's going to the fair. (contraction of *Everyone is*)

    Everyone's family is going to the fair. (possessive indefinite pronoun)

4. Mention that both *will* and *would* can also contract with nouns in informal English. Provide these examples: *Tom'll bring the salad*; *Jane'd like to go with you*. Emphasize that these uses are informal.

continued

27.6

▶ **KEY CONCEPT** Do not use an apostrophe with the possessive forms of personal pronouns. ■

The possessive forms of personal pronouns already show ownership. Pronouns in this form should be left just as they are to show possession.

EXAMPLES: his jazz records
our house
her blue sweater
its tires
their party
whose paper

Be careful not to confuse the contractions *who's, it's,* and *they're* with possessive pronouns. They are contractions for *who is, it is* or *it has,* and *they are*. Remember also that *whose, its,* and *their* show possession.

PRONOUNS: *Whose* homework is this?
Its tires were all flat.
Their dinner is ready.

CONTRACTIONS: *Who's* at the door?
It's going to rain.
They're going to the beach.

Forming Contractions Another important use of the apostrophe is in forming contractions. One general rule covers all the different types of contractions:

▶ **KEY CONCEPT** Use an apostrophe in a contraction to indicate the position of the missing letter or letters. ■

APOSTROPHES INDICATING MISSING LETTERS				
VERB AND *NOT*:	cannot could not	can't couldn't	are not will not	aren't won't
PRONOUN AND *WILL*:	he will you will she will	he'll you'll she'll	I will we will they will	I'll we'll they'll
PRONOUN AND *WOULD*:	she would he would you would	she'd he'd you'd	I would we would they would	I'd we'd they'd
PRONOUN OR NOUN AND THE VERB *BE*:	you are she is they are	you're she's they're	I am Jane is	I'm Jane's

Notice that one of these contractions changes letters as well as drops them. *Will not* becomes *won't* in contracted form.

Contractions with verbs should be used mainly in informal writing and in dialogue. The same is true for another type of contraction, one for years.

EXAMPLES: the class of '04
             the depression of '29

Still another type of contraction is found in poetry.

EXAMPLES: e'en (for even)
             o'er (for over)

Other contractions represent the abbreviated form of *of the* and *the* as they are written in several different languages.

EXAMPLES: O'Hare   o'clock
             d'Lorenzo   *l'Abbé*

These letters are most often combined with surnames.

A final use of contractions is for representing individual speaking styles in dialogue. As noted above, you will often want to use contractions with verbs in dialogue. You may also want to approximate a regional dialect or a foreign accent, which may include unusual pronunciations of words or omitted letters.

EXAMPLES: "Hi, ol' buddy. How you been feelin'?"
             "Don' you be afoolin' me."

Avoid overusing the apostrophe with contractions even in dialogue. Overuse reduces the effectiveness of the apostrophe.

Using Apostrophes for Special Plurals The following rule presents four other situations in which apostrophes are used:

▶ **KEY CONCEPT** Use an apostrophe and an *-s* to write the plurals of numbers, symbols, letters, and words used to name themselves. ■

EXAMPLES: during the 1860's
             m's and *n*'s
             your *2*'s and *3*'s
             no *if*'s or *maybe*'s
             three *?*'s in a row

**Grammar
and Style Tip**

In formal writing, it is always best to avoid contractions. Write the words out in full.

Answer Key

▶ Exercise 66

1. the country's written language
2. who's
3. the regions' dialects
4. the government's efforts
5. its climate
6. the regions' topography
7. the minorities' languages
8. their religion
9. the fauna's and flora's diversity
10. won't
11. 15's
12. its home
13. Whose home is southeast China?
14. Confucius' importance
15. the dialects' variety
16. the Han's and non-Han people's dialects
17. 1940's
18. they're
19. China's mineral deposits
20. China's and Russia's borders

▶ Exercise 67

Challenge students to write sentences that are connected in meaning.

▶ **Exercise 66** Using Apostrophes Rewrite each of the following items, following the instructions in parentheses.

1. the written language of the country (Use the possessive case.)
2. who is (Write the contracted form.)
3. the dialects of the regions (Use the possessive case.)
4. the efforts of the government (Use the possessive case.)
5. the country's climate (Use a possessive pronoun for *country's*.)
6. the topography of the regions (Use the possessive case.)
7. the languages of the minorities (Use the possessive case.)
8. the religion of the people (Use a possessive pronoun for *people*.)
9. the diversity of the fauna and flora (Use the possessive case.)
10. will not (Write the contracted form.)
11. 15 (Write the plural form.)
12. the home of the panda (Use a possessive pronoun for *panda*.)
13. Southeast China is home to whom? (Rewrite, using a possessive pronoun instead of *to whom*.)
14. the importance of Confucius (Use the possessive case.)
15. the variety of the dialects (Use the possessive case.)
16. the dialects of the Han and non-Han people (Use the possessive case to show individual ownership.)
17. 1940 (Write the plural form.)
18. they are (Write the contracted form.)
19. the mineral deposits of China (Use the possessive case.)
20. the borders of China and Russia (Use the possessive case.)

▶ **Exercise 67** Using the Rules for Hyphens and Apostrophes in Original Sentences Choose ten different rules from this section. Then, write sentences of your own that illustrate each of the rules you have chosen.

▶ More Practice

Grammar Exercise Workbook
• pp. 149–150

On-line Exercise Bank
• Section 27.6

Go on-line:
PHSchool.com
Enter Web Code:
egk-1202

Get instant feedback! Exercises 66 and 67 are available on-line or on CD-ROM.

☑ ONGOING ASSESSMENT: Monitor and Reinforce

If students have difficulty with Exercise 66 or 67, refer them to the following for additional practice.

In the Textbook	Print Resources	Technology
Section Review, Ex. 70–74, Section 27.6	*Grammar Exercise Workbook,* pp. 149–150	*On-Line Exercise Bank,* Section 27.6

Section 27.6 Section Review

GRAMMAR EXERCISES 68–71

Exercise 68 **Using Hyphens to Join Words** If an item does not need hyphenating, write *correct*. If it does, add one.

1. pro isolationist policies
2. one fifth of the world's population
3. Sino Russian border
4. geographically diverse regions
5. life size figures
6. thirty first floor
7. ex Senator
8. well intentioned advice
9. South American history
10. pro American

Exercise 69 **Using Hyphens at the Ends of Lines** If a word is broken correctly, write *correct*. If not, rewrite it.

1. Budd-hist
2. tradit-ion
3. dy-nasty
4. nam-ed
5. communic-ation
6. sis-ter-in-law
7. partici-pation
8. Span-ish
9. excitem-ent
10. frisk-y

Exercise 70 **Using Apostrophes to Show the Possessive Case** Choose the correct word in parentheses to complete the following sentences.

1. Confucius was one of (China's, Chinas') most influential figures.
2. Despite his (families, family's) poverty, he received a fine education.
3. After mourning his (mother's, mothers) death, he began to travel and teach.
4. Confucius deplored his (societies, society's) vices and urged a return to ancient values.

5. He believed that (ruler's, rulers') lives must be exemplary if their states were to prosper.
6. He was born in the state of Lu (now Shandong), and, at age 51, was elected that (state's, states') minister of crime.
7. His (administrations', administration's) policies were successful.
8. Lu became so powerful that a neighboring ruler contrived to secure (Confucius', Confucius's) dismissal.
9. Confucius was venerated both during and after his life, and his (philosophys's, philosophy's) principles were practical and ethical.
10. His (teachings', teaching's) influence on the Chinese nation has been profound.

Exercise 71 **Using Apostrophes Correctly With Pronouns** Rewrite the following sentences, choosing the correct form from the choices in parentheses.

1. The population of China is larger than (any other country's, any other countries).
2. (It's, Its) the third largest country in the world in area.
3. (It's, Its) recorded history dates from around 3500 B.C.
4. The regional climates of China are similar to those of the United States, but (they're, their) weather patterns usually have greater contrasts.
5. The giant panda, (who's, whose) only home is southwestern China, feeds on certain bamboo shoots.
6. China was one of the first countries to enact environmental legislation, and (its, it's) chief concerns are deforestation and erosion.
7. Close to ten million people call Shanghai (they're, their) home.

ASSESS and CLOSE

Section Review

Each of these exercises correlates to the instruction on hyphens and apostrophes, pages 745–753. These exercises may be used for more practice, for reteaching, or for review of the key concepts presented. Answers are available in *Grammar Exercises Answers on Transparencies* in your Teaching Resources.

Answer Key

Exercise 68

1. pro-isolationist policies
2. correct
3. Sino-Russian border
4. correct
5. life-size figures
6. thirty-first floor
7. ex-Senator
8. well-intentioned advice
9. correct
10. pro-American

Exercise 69

1. Buddhist
2. tradi-tion
3. correct
4. named
5. communica-tion
6. sister-in-law
7. correct
8. Spanish
9. excite-ment
10. frisky

Exercise 70

1. China's
2. family's
3. mother's
4. society's
5. rulers'
6. state's
7. administration's
8. Confucius'
9. philosophy's
10. teachings'

Exercise 71

1. any other country's
2. It's
3. Its
4. their
5. whose
6. its
7. their

continued

☑ ONGOING ASSESSMENT: Assess Mastery

Use the following resources to assess student mastery of punctuation.

In the Textbook	Print Resources	Technology
Chapter Review, Ex. 82–85	*Formal Assessment,* Chapter 27	*On-Line Exercise Bank,* Chapter 27

Exercise 71

8. Education's and literacy's
9. his
10. ours

Exercise 72

1. they're
2. *B*'s
3. 1900's
4. *but*'s
5. he'd

Exercise 73

1. <u>I've</u> learned . . . now that <u>we're</u> studying <u>China's</u> history and culture, <u>I'm</u>
2. For much of <u>its</u> history
3. symbol of <u>China's</u> desire
4. China took <u>its</u> name
5. The Chinese trace <u>their</u> ancestry
6. I enjoy reading <u>Confucius'</u> teachings
7. He taught about <u>everyone's</u> duties
8. Confucius' ideas helped <u>China's</u> government . . . for <u>years</u>.
9. <u>It'd</u> take a <u>month's</u> vacation
10. My <u>sister-in-law's</u> family . . . during the <u>'60's</u>.

Exercise 74

Answers will vary. Sample answers:

1. Danny's voice is deep and resonant.
2. They like to fix up their old cars, but I don't.
3. Are these anyone's earrings?
4. Meet me at the fountain in the mall at six o'clock.
5. Bonnie's hair is light and curly, but Elisa's is dark and straight.

Exercise 75

Find It in Your Reading
When students finish, have them list the kinds of examples they found.

Exercise 76

Find It in Your Writing
When students work, tell them to look particularly for errors in plural possessives and in using apostrophes to form plurals of words.

Exercise 77

Writing Application
You might ask some students to read their paragraphs aloud while others listen for places where hyphens and apostrophes would be used.

Section Review Exercises cont'd.

8. (Education and literacy's, Education's and literacy's) growths are of primary concern to the Chinese government.
9. Confucius dedicated (his, he's) life to the betterment of the people.
10. The Chinese language is quite different from (ours, our's).

Exercise 72 Using Apostrophes in Contractions and Special Situations

Add an apostrophe to the following items to form contractions or plurals.

1. they are
2. B
3. 1900
4. but
5. he would

Exercise 73 Proofreading for All the Rules for Apostrophes

Revise the following sentences, using apostrophes to form contractions, possessive nouns, and possessive pronouns where appropriate.

1. Ive learned a lot of interesting things in my social studies class, but now that were studying Chinas history and culture, Im really interested.
2. For much of it's history, China had little to do with the rest of the world.
3. The Great Wall of China is a symbol of Chinas desire to keep the world at a distance.
4. China took it's name from the Qing dynasty.
5. The Chinese trace they're ancestry to the Han dynasty.
6. I enjoy reading Confucius's teachings.
7. He taught about everyones duties and responsibilities.
8. Confucius' ideas helped Chinas government run smoothly for year's.
9. Itd take a months vacation to tour just a small part of China.
10. My sister's-in-law's family went to China during the 60s.

Exercise 74 Writing Sentences With Possessives and Contractions

Write sentences with possessives and contractions requiring apostrophes, following the instructions.

1. Describe the speaking voice of a family member, using his or her name.
2. Tell about something they would do but you would not. Use contractions.
3. Ask a question to find out who owns the earrings you found. Use the possessive of an indefinite pronoun.
4. Write instructions for your friend to meet you at the mall at a specific time. Write out the time.
5. Compare the hairstyles of two friends. Use their names.

Exercise 75 Find It in Your Reading

Look through a section of an atlas about a country that interests you. Find examples of at least five different uses of hyphens and apostrophes.

Exercise 76 Find It in Your Writing

Proofread a piece from your portfolio one more time to correct any errors in the use of hyphens and apostrophes.

Exercise 77 Writing Application

Write a few paragraphs about a country that interests you. Use hyphens and apostrophes in at least five different ways.

Chapter

27 Chapter Review

GRAMMAR EXERCISES 78–86

> **Exercise 78**   **Using End Marks**
Copy each of the following items, correcting the punctuation where necessary.

1. The subcontinent of India was its own island continent until about 5,000 BC, though perhaps that date is incorrect
2. It is bordered by significant territories, though it is an entire peninsula unto itself
3. China lies to the north and Bangladesh to its east
4. Are you aware that India is bordered on the west by Pakistan
5. These two areas have been engaged in disagreements for many years
6. Never try to intercede in that territorial dispute
7. Go north and start on an upward trek to find the Himalayas
8. This mountain range extends 1,500 miles across India
9. The Himalayas, which include Mt Everest—the tallest mountain in the world, measuring over 29,000 ft at its highest elevation—are astonishing
10. Sir Edmund Hillary, in addition to earning a PhD degree, has also received the honor of Officer of the Order of the British Empire for his work in the Himalayas

> **Exercise 79**   **Using All the Rules for Commas**   Revise the following paragraph, inserting commas as necessary.

(1) Receiving abundant rainfall India's verdant and vast land teems with a variety of animal life. (2) Miles of impenetrable jungle create a safe haven and the hills and mountains also provide protection. (3) Tigers panthers and cheetahs inhabit many sections of the forests. (4) Other members of the cat family such as the snow leopard roam the slopes of the Himalayas. (5) Elephants can be found on the broad fertile plains though these elephants are a different species from those found in Africa. (6) It may seem strange that there are wolves in the Himalayan area. (7) A pair was seen on August 24 1997 west of the Kashi Hills Deccan Plateau. (8) Venomous reptiles including cobras saltwater snakes and vipers are widespread in India. (9) Pythons though a nuisance to small cattle and humans when hungry keep down the rodent population. (10) Crocodiles not to be confused with alligators are also prevalent in the estuaries of India's rivers.

> **Exercise 80**   **Using Colons and Semicolons**   Use colons and semicolons to punctuate the following items correctly.

1. Throughout history, India has been a prize to be won even Alexander the Great led an expedition into India.
2. The Macedonian influence on India was negligible politically in contrast, the art, sculpture, and science of Greece did have an effect on Indian culture.
3. Leaders of the Mughal Empire controlled the trade routes in fact, it was through their connection that Europeans became aware of India.
4. To European monarchs eager to expand, one thing was clear A new route to the Far East could not be overlooked.
5. India became the object of a fierce struggle between three European countries Portugal, the Netherlands, and Great Britain. To find new treasures and stake out new lands before their rivals could lay a claim, these nations sent forth men who would become the great explorers in history Christopher Columbus, Amerigo Vespucci, and Vasco da Gama.

Chapter Review • **757**

CHAPTER REVIEW

Each of these exercises correlates to a section of the chapter on punctuation, pages 686–756. The exercises may be used for more practice, for reteaching, or for review of the key concepts presented. Answers for all chapter exercises are available in *Grammar Exercises Answers on Transparencies* in your Teaching Resources.

Answer Key

> **Exercise 78**

1. B.C., incorrect.
2. itself.
3. north, and . . . east.
4. Pakistan?
5. years.
6. dispute! *or* dispute.
7. Himalayas.
8. India.
9. Mt., ft., astonishing! *or* astonishing.
10. Ph.D., Himalayas.

> **Exercise 79**

1. rainfall,
2. haven,
3. Tigers, panthers,
4. family, such . . . leopard,
5. broad, fertile plains,
6. correct
7. 24, 1997, Hills, Deccan
8. reptiles, including cobras, snakes, vipers,
9. Pythons, hungry,
10. Crocodiles, alligators,

> **Exercise 80**

1. won;
2. politically;
3. routes;
4. clear:
5. countries: history:

Exercise 81

1. "John . . . information," said
2. speaker-phone, "Bombay . . . 8,225,000!"
3. "The . . . mile," he continued
4. warned, "We'd . . . populous."
5. "That's . . . idea," Brian said,
6. . . .than the "enchanting," shimmering . . .
7. . . . the gown was "too bright."
8. "While I can . . . come with me?"
9. . . . attending the wedding might "broaden our horizons."
10. "I'd . . . attend," said Janet. "I . . . event."

Exercise 82

1. India's assets—a varied population—is
2. class—all
3. (1) Hindus; (2) Muslims; and (3) Buddhists,
4. (see . . . separatism).
5. well-intentioned social programs—there are thousands of programs in India!—are
6. adequate transportation— maintaining roads . . . can be difficult—are hindrances
7. (Smith's . . . report)
8. Mary Sanderson (1942–1992),
9. 2000—an improvement over 1944, when i [sic] was 32 years old.
10. mortality—a great tragedy in any country—is still high

Chapter Review Exercises cont'd.

Exercise 81 Using Quotations and Underlining
Use quotation marks and underlining to punctuate the following sentences. Quoted fragments are underlined.

1. John Assam lives in India, so we should call him for information, said Brian.
2. John exclaimed over the speaker-phone, Bombay has a vast population: over 8,225,000!
3. The population density is about 762 per square mile, he continued.
4. Brian's sister Janet warned, We'd better go to New Delhi, because even though it's the capital, it's not as populous.
5. That's a good idea, Brian said, hastening to add that New Delhi and Delhi are two different cities.
6. Janet was eager to see a range of saris because she regards this traditional Indian women's garb as even more gorgeous than the enchanting, shimmering gown I wore the night of the junior prom.
7. Brian, who prefers more conservative clothes, claimed the gown was too bright.
8. John was eager to cut short any sibling bickering: While I can still get a word in edgewise, I should mention I have to go to a wedding; maybe you two would like to come with me?
9. He felt that attending the wedding might broaden our horizons.
10. I'd love to attend said Janet I think we'll enjoy the event.

Exercise 82 Using Dashes, Parentheses, Brackets, Hyphens, and Apostrophes
Add the necessary punctuation to each sentence. Added material is underlined.

1. One of Indias assets a varied population is also a drawback.
2. Culture, ethnicity, religion, class all these divisions still exist in India.
3. Major religious groups in India, for example, include 1 Hindus; 2 Muslims; and 3 Buddhists, to name just a few.
4. Though many groups have assimilated and have lived together for centuries, India's leadership still has a difficult task in forming a unified country see recent articles on Sikh separatism.
5. Many well intentioned social programs there are thousands of programs in India! are unsuccessful because of language differences and social taboos.
6. Distances between villages and lack of adequate transportation maintaining roads in extreme weather conditions can be difficult are hindrances to the implementation of many programs.
7. The greatest challenges Smith's assertion is verified by a recent World Bank report are in the two areas that most affect children: health programs and education.
8. Mary Sanderson 1942–1992, like Mother Theresa, devoted her entire life to helping those in need.
9. Overall life expectancy grew to 60 years by 2000 an improvement over 1944, when i was 32 years old.
10. Sadly, infant mortality a great tragedy in any country is still high in India.

Exercise 83 Proofreading for Punctuation Revise the following passage, adding the necessary punctuation.

The most widely practiced religion in India is Hinduism which is a polytheistic religion. Central to Hindu belief is a supreme triad formed by three deities Brahma the father of the gods and humankind and the creator of the universe Vishnu the god of love and Siva or Shiva the god of the cosmic dance. An interesting contrast can be drawn between Hindu deities and Greek gods Greek gods always looked and acted more or less human albeit with some incredible tricks up their sleeves Hindu gods sometimes take on some very nonhuman attributes. For example Brahmas wife Sarasvati grew out of his side. Can you think of any similar stories from other cultures Vishnu a god of light and love and the enemy of darkness is described as having dark blue skin. The last of the triad Siva is perhaps the most complicated god of all in some myths he acts as protector but in others as destroyer. A blue throat, a third eye in his forehead, anywhere from two to who knows how many arms are just a few of the physical attributes that reflect Sivas complexity. To be sure with all those extra arms Siva can do a lot of pointing. Hindu gods and goddesses are worshiped in many forms and appear in all sorts of guises indeed the concept of gods who reincarnate through the centuries in several human forms called avatars is an important key to understanding Hinduism

Exercise 84 Proofreading Paragraphs for Punctuation Rewrite the following paragraphs, adding the necessary punctuation.

Various powers have ruled the nation of Burma in its long embattled history From 1885 Britain ruled Burma as a province of India another of its territories By the 1920's when George Orwell author of the short story Shooting an Elephant served in Burma as a police officer Burmese protests against British rule were growing stronger

In 1937 Britain granted Burma some rights to self government However in 1942 Japan occupied the country which they ruled until 1945 At the end of World War II Britain resumed control of Burma Finally in 1948 Burma gained independence

Exercise 85 Writing and Punctuating Original Sentences Choose a subject with which you are familiar. It might be a person you know, a sport you play, a restaurant you like, or a topic you're studying in one of your classes. Then, write sentences, following the directions below.

1. Describe three features of your subject using commas in a series.
2. Write something you like about your subject using your subject as a possessive noun.
3. Quote something that someone else has said about your subject inserting a remark or clarification of your own inside the quotation.
4. Complete a sentence that begins, "These two things are good (or bad) about [your subject]."
5. Describe one thing that may affect your subject in the future; add a contrary or explanatory comment in the middle or at the end of the sentence.

Exercise 86 Writing Application Write a description of one of your favorite places. Correctly use each type of punctuation at least once.

Answer Key

Exercise 83

1. Hinduism, which
2. deities: Brahma, the . . . universe; Vishnu, the god of love; and Siva, or Shiva,
3. gods: Greek . . . human (albeit . . . sleeves); Hindu . . . non-human
4. For example, Brahma's wife, Sarasvati,
5. cultures?
6. Vishnu, a . . . darkness,
7. triad, Siva, is . . . all: In some myths, he . . . protector, but in others
8. who-knows-how-many . . . Siva's
9. To be sure, . . . arms,
10. guises; indeed, the . . . forms (called avatars) is . . . Hinduism.

Exercise 84

Various powers have ruled the nation of Burma in its long, embattled history. From 1885, Britain ruled Burma as a province of India, another of its territories. By the 1920's, when George Orwell, author of the short story "Shooting an Elephant," served in Burma as a police officer, Burmese protests against British rule were growing stronger.

In 1937, Britain granted Burma some rights to self-government. However, in 1942, Japan occupied the country, which they ruled until 1945. At the end of World War II, Britain resumed control of Burma. Finally, in 1948, Burma gained independence.

Exercise 85

Answers will vary; sample answers are given.

1. Bobbie is bright, friendly, and hard working.
2. I especially like Bobbie's sense of humor and her hearty laugh.
3. Mom says, "Bobbie is just herself [that's an old family expression]."
4. These two things are good about Bobbie: her calm outlook and her grace under pressure.
5. Bobbie would make a good manager (even though she might be happier working with her lab equipment).

Exercise 86

Writing Application
Students might tell which punctuation marks seemed to be most difficult to use.

Lesson Objectives

1. To recognize work that shows accurate spelling and the correct use of the conventions of punctuation and capitalization
2. *To recognize and produce error-free writing*
3. To analyze the characteristics of clear text such as correctness and completeness

Proofreading

Teaching Resources: Standardized Test Preparation Workbook, pp. 53–54

1. Have students read the first sample test question and its explanation. Ask them to explain why the exclamation point belongs inside the quotation marks (because it is part of the quotation itself).

2. Challenge students to write a sentence in which the exclamation point belongs outside the quotation marks. (Sample answer: I was stunned when he said, "I ate the plums that you were saving for breakfast"!)

3. Have students read the second sample test question and its explanation. Ask them to explain why semicolons, rather than commas, are sometimes used to separate items in a series. (Semicolons are used to prevent confusion when the items already contain commas.)

4. Challenge students to write a sentence that demonstrates this rule. (Sample answer: Marla brought her brother's old, worn-out jacket; several thick, woolen sweaters; and two pairs of mittens, both insulated against the cold and wind.)

Standardized Test Preparation Workshop

Proofreading

Standardized tests often include items that test your knowledge of punctuation rules. Most often, this testing involves proofreading written passages for errors in punctuation.

The following sample items will give you practice with identifying punctuation errors.

Sample Test Items	Answers and Explanations
Directions: Choose the best way to write each underlined section. If the underlined section needs no change, mark the choice "Correct as is."	
(1) <u>"Look" she called, "up there"!</u>	
(2) <u>The science teacher directed the students parents and other guests to look at the migrating birds.</u>	

1   A   "Look she called, "up there."
     B   "Look," she called, "up there!"
     C   "Look"! she called "up there."
     D   Correct as is
	The correct answer for item 1 is *B*. As a part of the direct quotation, the exclamation mark belongs before the quotation mark. All other punctuation in this passage is correct.

2   F   The science teacher directed the students: parents: and other guests to look at the migrating birds.
 	
     G   The science teacher directed, the students parents and other guests, to look at the migrating birds.
 	
     H   The science teacher directed the students, parents, and other guests to look at the migrating birds.
 	
     J   Correct as is
	The correct answer for item 2 is *H*. The series *students, parents, and other guests* requires commas to separate each element.

✎ TEST-TAKING TIP

Students might want to jot down a brief checklist of common errors to consult before choosing "Correct as is." This way, they will be sure to check for a number of different errors before settling for this answer.

Remind students to use the process of elimination to narrow down the number of possible answers. For example, in question 2 on page 761, students can immediately eliminate choices G and H because *3:45* is written incorrectly. Then, if they have to guess, their odds will be much better with two choices than with four.

▶ **Practice** | **Directions:** Choose the best way to write each underlined section. If the underlined section needs no change, mark the choice "Correct as is."

(1) Last call for flight 1233 to Washington D.C announced the ticket agent, (2) "The 345 PM. flight to Washington D.C. will be leaving the gate immediately"! (3) Mr. Solomon his wife and their three children ran down the stairs to the small plane? (4) Thank goodness we made it exclaimed Dr. Solomon, (5) "I was afraid we would miss the AMA Convention in Washington." (6) Mr Solomon settled into his seat his wife reviewed her notes for her presentation at the conference

1 **A** "Last call for flight 1233 to Washington D.C" announced the ticket agent,

   B "Last call for flight 1233 to Washington D.C" announced the ticket agent.

   C "Last call for flight 1233 to Washington, D.C.," announced the ticket agent.

   D Correct as is

2 **F** "The 3:45 P.M. flight to Washington, D.C., will be leaving the gate immediately!"

   G "The 345 P.M. flight to Washington D.C. will be leaving the gate immediately"!

   H "The 345 PM flight to Washington D.C. will be leaving the gate immediately!"

   J Correct as is

3 **A** Mr. Solomon, his wife, and their three children, ran down the stairs to the small plane.

   B Mr. Solomon, his wife, and their three children ran down the stairs to the small plane.

   C Mr. Solomon; his wife; and their three children ran down the stairs to the small plane.

   D Correct as is

4 **F** "Thank goodness we made it." exclaimed Dr. Solomon,

   G "Thank goodness we made it"! exclaimed Dr. Solomon.

   H "Thank goodness we made it!" exclaimed Dr. Solomon.

   J Correct as is

5 **A** "I, was afraid we would miss the AMA Convention, in Washington."

   B "I was afraid we would miss the A.M.A. Convention in Washington."

   C I was afraid "we would miss the AMA Convention in Washington."

   D Correct as is

6 **F** Mr. Solomon settled into his seat! his wife reviewed her notes for her presentation at the conference.

   G Mr. Solomon settled into his seat; his wife reviewed her notes for her presentation at the conference.

   H Mr Solomon settled into his seat, his wife reviewed her notes for her presentation at the conference?

   J Correct as is

Customize for
Less Advanced Students

Make sure students can explain why **G** is the correct answer to question 6. Remind them that a semicolon is used to join two independent clauses that are not already joined by a comma and a coordinating conjunction.

Customize for
Spatial Learners

Students might feel overwhelmed by the number and variety of punctuation rules they have to know. Have the class decide on the ten rules they find most tricky, and ask spatial learners to make a poster that explains these rules and offers examples for each. Display the poster in your classroom so students can review the problem rules frequently.

Each of these exercises reviews concepts taught in the chapters on capitalization and punctuation. The exercises may be used for more practice, for review of the key concepts presented, or for assessment of student mastery of the major concepts.

Answer Key

> **Exercise A**

1. William Shakespeare, Stratford-upon-Avon, Warwickshire, England
2. At, Anne Hathaway
3. It, Stratford, Sir Thomas Lucy's
4. Seeking, Shakespeare, London
5. The, "Venus and Adonis," "The Rape of Lucrece," Shakespeare's
6. With, Henry Wriothesley, Earl, Southampton, Shakespeare, Renaissance
7. He, Lord Chamberlain's Men, King's Men
8. Shakespeare, Globe Theater, Blackfriars
9. His, Queen Elizabeth, King James
10. However, King Richard, Shakespeare, Elizabeth
11. After, London, Shakespeare, Stratford
12. By, New Place
13. After, Shakespeare, Stratford Church
14. His, *Julius Caesar, Romeo and Juliet, The Life of King Henry the Fifth*
15. His, English, Kings Henry, Richard

> **Exercise B**

1. A.D., writing.
2. plays: *The First Part of King Henry the Sixth, The Second Part of King Henry the Sixth, The Third Part of King Henry the Sixth,* and *The Tragedy of King Richard the Third.*
3. Seneca?
4. Yes! *or* Yes, seen, bloody, plays.
5. period, comedies; satirical.
6. first, *The Comedy of Errors,* 1592, farcical, identity.
7. Wow! style?
8. romance, society; fact, playwrights.

continued

Cumulative Review

MECHANICS

> **Exercise A** Using Capitalization

Copy all the items in the following sentences that require capitalization, adding the missing capitals.

1. william shakespeare was born in 1564 in stratford-upon-avon, warwickshire, a part of england.
2. at a young age, he was married to anne hathaway, and they had two daughters.
3. it is rumored that he was forced from stratford after he was caught hunting sir thomas lucy's deer.
4. seeking success as an actor and a playwright, shakespeare arrived in london in 1588.
5. the publication of two poems, "venus and adonis" and "the rape of lucrece," as well as a compilation of his sonnets, established shakespeare's reputation.
6. with the patronage of henry wriothesley, third earl of southampton, shakespeare continued to write in the renaissance style.
7. he had arrangements allowing him to share in the profits of his acting company, known as the lord chamberlain's men and later known as the king's men.
8. shakespeare is associated with two theaters, the globe theater and the blackfriars.
9. his plays were frequently performed for both queen elizabeth I and king james I.
10. however, a performance of his play about king richard III almost caused shakespeare to fall out of favor with elizabeth.
11. after almost twenty years in london, which is when he wrote his 38 plays, shakespeare moved back to stratford.
12. by 1608, he had moved his family to a house called new place and had become a prominent local citizen.

13. after his death in 1616, shakespeare was buried in the stratford church.
14. his many plays, from *julius caesar* to *romeo and juliet* to *the life of king henry the fifth,* have become the most widely known and highly quoted works.
15. his earliest works are about english kings henry IV and richard III.

> **Exercise B** Using End Marks, Commas, Semicolons, and Colons

Write the following sentences, inserting end marks, commas, semicolons, and colons where necessary.

1. The years up to AD 1594 form Shakespeare's first period of writing
2. This period is the time he wrote his first historical plays *The First Part of King Henry the Sixth The Second Part of King Henry the Sixth The Third Part of King Henry the Sixth* and *The Tragedy of King Richard the Third*
3. Was he influenced by the Roman playwright Seneca
4. Yes Seneca's influence can be seen particularly in the bloody tragic scenes in Shakespeare's early plays
5. During this time period Shakespeare wrote a wide range of comedies their styles vary from farcical to satirical
6. The first *The Comedy of Errors* written in 1592 imitates the farcical improbable style of classic Roman comedies by using the motif of mistaken identity
7. Wow Did you realize that *Love's Labour's Lost* was written in such a different style
8. Satirizing the noble pursuit of knowledge before romance this play is concerned with revealing the pretensions of society in fact it also mocks the writing of other contemporary playwrights

9. In particular the dialogue seems to invoke the works of one English novelist at the time John Lyly

10. Do the plays *The Taming of the Shrew The Two Gentlemen of Verona* and *Titus Andronicus* fall into this time period

▶ **Exercise C** Using All the Rules of Punctuation Write the following sentences, inserting end marks, commas, semicolons, colons, quotation marks, underlining, dashes, brackets, parentheses, hyphens, and apostrophes where necessary. Quotations are underlined.

1. The play that I saw on Apr 13 1994 Twelfth Night was one of Shakespeares most charming love stories

2. Is that the play that features the strong minded character Beatrice however Im not sure Was she in Much Ado About Nothing 1599

3. In Twelfth Night the two pairs of lovers encounter obstacles they are also confronted with an entire cast of amusing characters

4. Feste who is also known as Fool and is the jester to Olivia has a similar role to Puck in A Midsummer Night's Dream 1595 They speak to the audience

5. Festes first aside is this <u>Wit, an't be thy will, put me into good fooling</u> sic

6. Malvolio whose name literally means ill wisher in Latin reveals on lines 80 86 that he is not concerned with his mistress Olivias happiness

7. <u>But that's all one, our play is done, And we'll strive to please you every day</u> sings Feste to end Twelfth Night

8. Have you ever seen Shakespeares plays As You Like It or The Merry Wives of Windsor

9. Besides writing comedies Shakespeare wrote some tragedies The tone of the writing is so different from his comedies during this period

10. Gosh I found Romeo and Juliet very sad the family feuds and the misunderstandings are frustrating.

▶ **Exercise D** Using Capitalization and Punctuation Write the following dialogue, inserting the proper capitalization, punctuation, and indentation.

1. what plays fall into shakespeares third period of writing are those the years from 1600 1608 ken asked

2. well said emma there is othello which is about a general in the venetian army and his jealousy

3. is that the play with iago oh yes i remember his wife is desdemona

4. right emma continued have you heard of the play king lear it is about one of britains early rulers

5. ken replied yes we read that in english class it is certainly an epic tragedy another tragedy is macbeth

6. antony and cleopatra written around 1606 is another tragedy about love the roman general mark antony falls in love with the egyptian queen cleopatra

7. i have never heard of the play coriolanus is it a tragedy or a comedy

8. when i read the introduction to coriolanus in my anthology the complete works of shakespeare it said that the play is also set in ancient rome

9. emma are you going to read hamlet before we watch the movie version of the play asked ken

10. there are so many movie versions of shakespeares plays said ken

▶ **Exercise E** Writing Application

Write a brief first-person narrative that includes dialogue in which you and a friend discuss a play, movie, or show. Be sure to follow all the rules of capitalization and punctuation.

Sentence Diagraming Workshop

A pictorial representation of a sentence is called a diagram. Just as a map can help a driver understand directions, so can a diagram help you visualize a sentence's structure. This section will explain the traditional rules for diagraming the basic sentence patterns that were covered in these chapters on grammar.

Subjects, Verbs, and Modifiers

To diagram a subject and a verb, draw a horizontal line and place the subject on the left and the verb on the right of the line. Separate the two with a vertical line.

EXAMPLE: Malcolm should have volunteered.

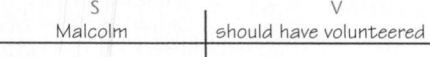

Adjectives and adverbs sit on slanted lines beneath the words they modify.

EXAMPLE: The very large bird glided surprisingly gracefully.

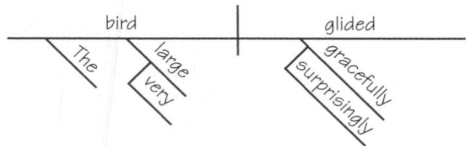

When the subject of an imperative sentence is understood to be *you*, place it in parentheses on the main line. Inverted sentences, in which the subject follows the verb, are also diagramed in the regular subject-verb order. The capital letter shows which word begins the sentence.

EXAMPLE: Call home soon.   Has Regina telephoned yet?

Rearrange a sentence beginning with *there* or *here* so that the subject comes first. Then, if *there* or *here* functions as an adverb, diagram it below the verb. If *there* functions as an expletive, place it on a horizontal line above the subject. Use the position of an expletive for interjections and nouns of direct address also. Diagrams illustrating these types of sentences are shown below.

EXAMPLE: There is a stranger here.   Hey, Diana, hurry up.

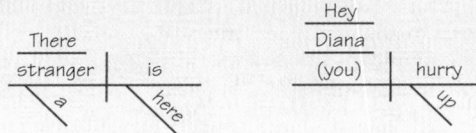

Exercise 1 Diagraming Subjects, Verbs, and Modifers
Correctly diagram each sentence.
1. The giant python slithered silently.
2. Her extremely high fever finally dropped.
3. Is my notebook here?
4. My, there goes one expensive automobile.
5. Leslie, do not dawdle.

Adding Conjunctions

Conjunctions are generally shown in a diagram on a dotted line between the words they connect. In the example presented below, conjunctions join both adjectives and adverbs.

EXAMPLE: The long and difficult report was read quickly but not easily.

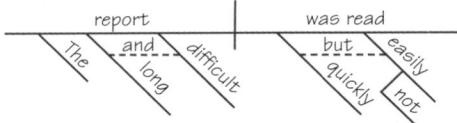

Conjunctions connecting compound subjects and compound verbs are also placed on dotted lines drawn between the words they connect. In the example on the next page, the horizontal line of the diagram is split so that each of the compound parts appears on a line of its own. Notice how correlative conjunctions and helping verbs shared by more than one verb are placed. If each part of the compound verb had its own helping verb, each helping verb would be placed on the line with its own verb.

Answer Key

Exercise 1

1.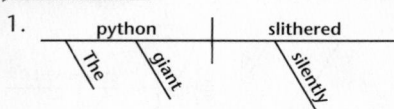

2.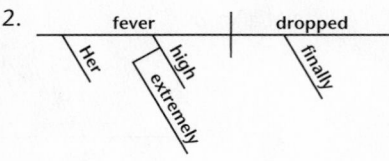

3.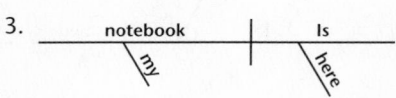

4.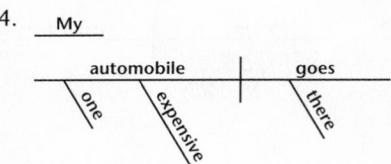

5.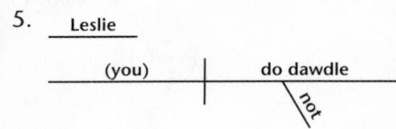

Answer Key

1.
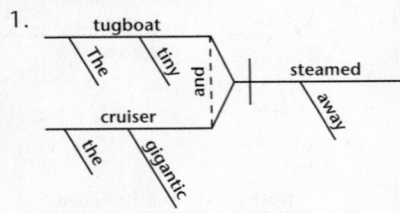

2.
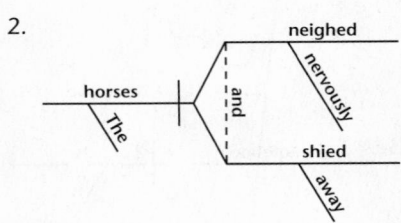

3.
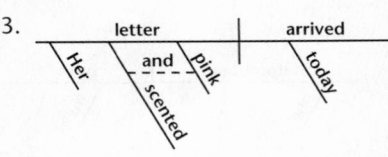

4.
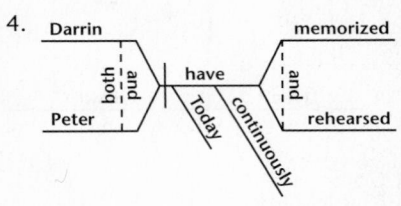

5.
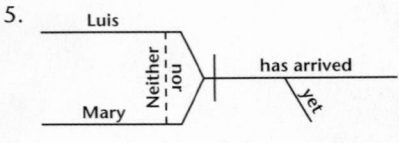

EXAMPLE: Both you and I must pack today and move tomorrow.

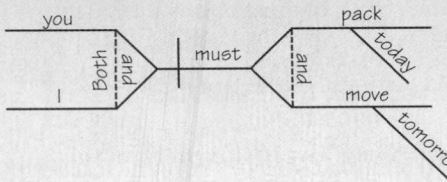

As the above example shows, modifiers in sentences that contain compound parts are carefully positioned with the individual words they modify. If a word modifies an entire compound element, as illustrated in the following example, the modifier is positioned beneath the main line of the diagram.

EXAMPLE: Yesterday, the campers and counselors swam and fished.

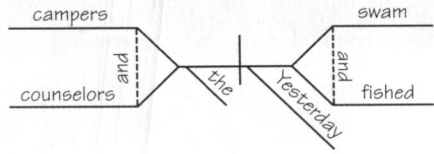

▶ **Exercise 2** Diagraming Sentences With Conjunctions

Correctly diagram each sentence.
1. The tiny tugboat and the gigantic cruiser steamed away.
2. The horses neighed nervously and shied away.
3. Her letter, scented and pink, arrived today.
4. Today, both Darrin and Peter have continuously memorized and rehearsed.
5. Neither Luis nor Mary has arrived yet.

Complements

Because complements complete the meaning of a verb, they are diagramed on the predicate side of the sentence. Direct objects sit on the same line as the subject and verb and are separated from the verb by a short vertical line. Indirect objects are placed on a horizontal line extending from a slanted line directly below the verb.

EXAMPLE: I sliced the cheese.   Dick bought us a wok.

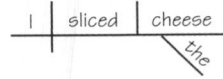   

An objective complement is placed right after a direct object. A short slanted line pointing toward the direct object separates it from the rest of the sentence.

EXAMPLE: The supervisor named Lee division manager.

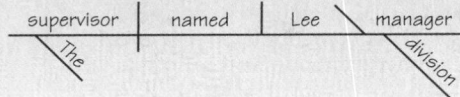

Subject complements are also placed on the main line, separated from the linking verb by a short line that slants back toward the subject and verb.

EXAMPLE: Margarita is a soprano. The dirt road is bumpy.

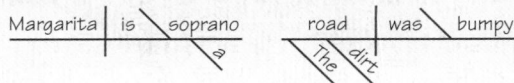

Compound complements are diagramed by splitting the lines on which they appear. Conjunctions are placed on dotted lines drawn between the words they connect.

EXAMPLE: We gave our grandmother and grandfather airplane tickets and money.

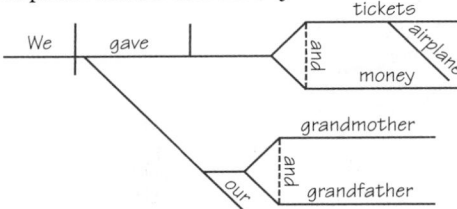

▶ **Exercise 3** Diagraming Complements Correctly diagram each sentence.
1. My old scrapbook held old snapshots and other mementos.
2. The group gave Kirk and Nat an elaborate map and some instructions.
3. His monthly salary was meager and inadequate.
4. My parents consider me an excellent driver.
5. Tammy is my sister and a good friend.

▶ **Exercise 3**

1.
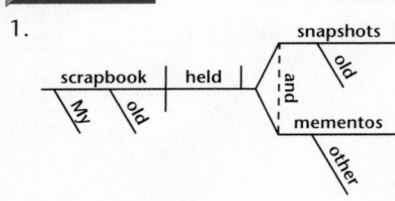

2.
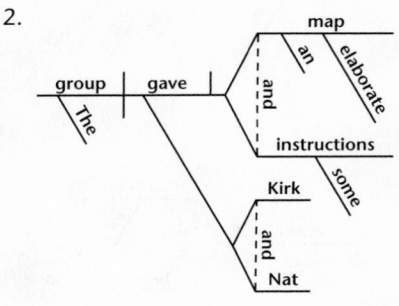

3.
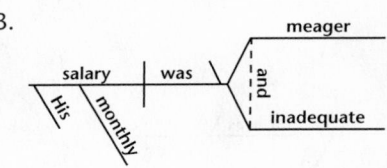

4.
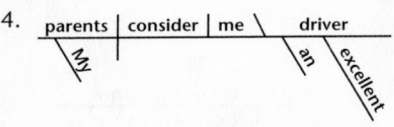

5.
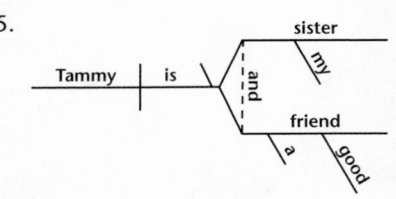

Answer Key

1.
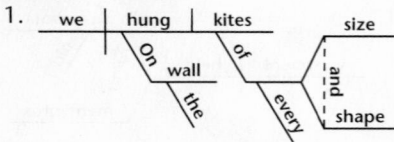

2.
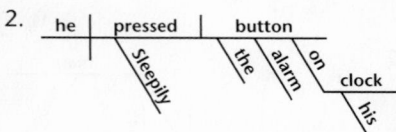

3.
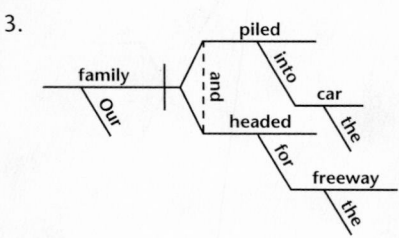

4.
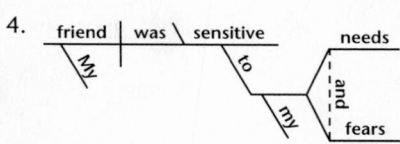

5.
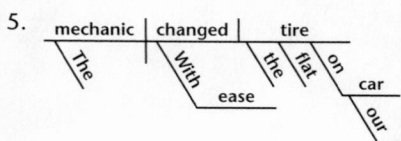

Prepositional Phrases

Diagram a prepositional phrase beneath the word it modifies. Place an adjective phrase beneath the noun or pronoun it modifies; place an adverb phrase beneath the verb, adjective, or adverb it modifies. Put the preposition on a slanted line and its object on a horizontal line. Place modifiers of the object beneath it on slanted lines. Diagram compound objects of the preposition just as you would other compound sentence parts.

EXAMPLE: The desk with the faulty leg is located in the first row or the second one.

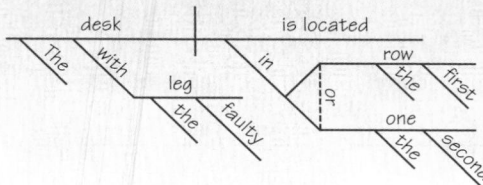

To diagram an objective phrase that modifies the object of the preposition of another prepositional phrase, study the first example below. To diagram an adverb phrase that modifies an adjective or an adverb, study the second example below.

EXAMPLES: The keys are on the table by the door.

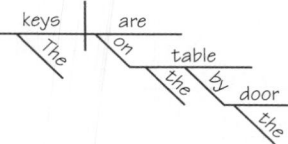

I arrived home late at night.

To diagram two prepositional phrases that modify the same word, use the following example as a guide.

EXAMPLE: I will meet you near the door or in the auditorium.

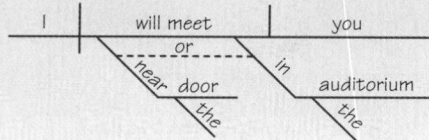

> **Exercise 4** **Diagraming Prepositional Phrases** Correctly diagram each sentence.
> 1. On the wall, we hung kites of every size and shape.
> 2. Sleepily, he pressed the alarm button on his clock.
> 3. Our family piled into the car and headed for the freeway.
> 4. My friend was sensitive to my needs and fears.
> 5. With ease, the mechanic changed the flat tire on our car.

Appositives and Appositive Phrases

Put an appositive in parentheses following the noun or pronoun it renames. Any modifiers go directly beneath it.

EXAMPLE: Mrs. Rebholtz, a friend of the family, will visit us.

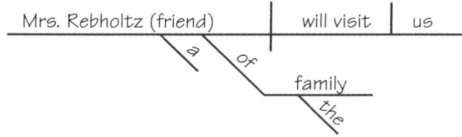

> **Exercise 5** **Diagraming Appositive Phrases** Correctly diagram each sentence.
> 1. My home, a small two-bedroom apartment, is convenient.
> 2. I gave the bride, a young woman of twenty, a handmade quilt.
> 3. The organization, a group of parents, wrote letters.
> 4. We visited Columbia, a town in Missouri.
> 5. Jurors should report to Judge Bean, a strict but fair guardian of the law.

Answer Key

> **Exercise 5**

1.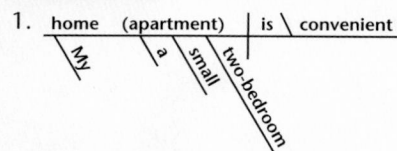

2.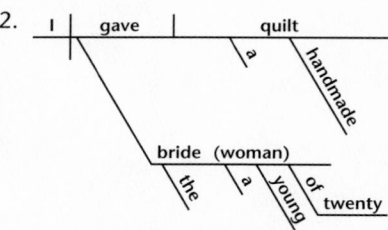

3.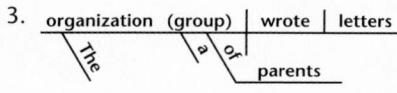

4.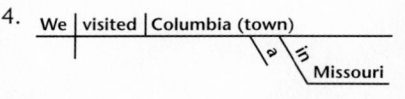

continued

Answer Key
continued

5.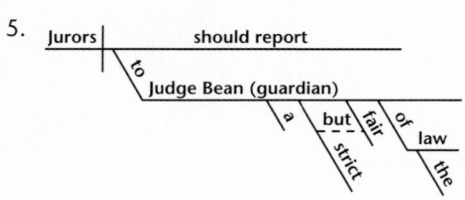

Verbals and Verbal Phrases

Verbal phrases—which are constructed with participles, gerunds, and infinitives—are never diagramed on a straight line.

Participles and Participial Phrases Because a participle functions as an adjective, it is placed partly on a slanted line and partly on a horizontal line beneath the noun or pronoun it modifies. Adverbs or adverb phrases that modify the participle are placed below it. When a participle has a complement, the complement is placed in its normal position on the horizontal line with the participle, separated from it by a short vertical line.

EXAMPLE: A child selling candy came to our house.

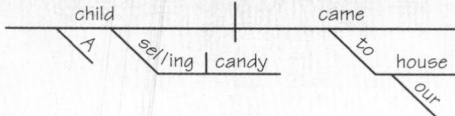

Because it is grammatically separate from the rest of the sentence, a nominative absolute is diagramed in the same way that an expletive is.

EXAMPLE: The meeting having been concluded for this month, we left.

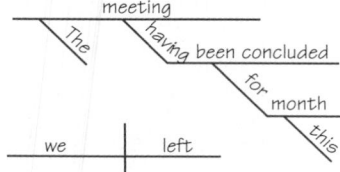

Gerunds and Gerund Phrases Gerunds can occupy any position in a diagram that a noun can. When they function as subjects, direct objects, predicate nominatives, or appositives, gerunds sit atop a pedestal on a stepped line. Modifiers and complements are diagramed in the usual way.

EXAMPLE: Fixing the garbage disposal required much time.

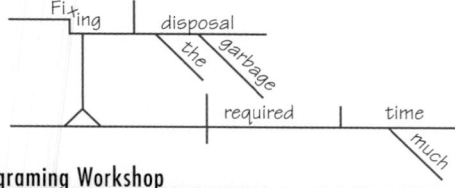

A gerund phrase functioning as an indirect object or as the object of a preposition goes on a stepped line extending from a slanted line.

EXAMPLE: We bought a small car for driving around town.

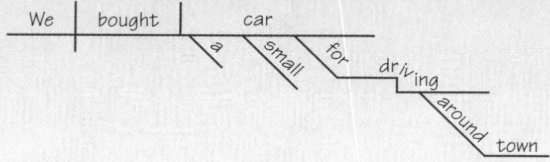

Infinitives and Infinitive Phrases An infinitive used as a noun sits on a pedestal on a line similar to, yet less complex than, the line used for a gerund. Modifiers and complements are diagramed in the usual way.

EXAMPLE: My resolution for the new year is to exercise daily.

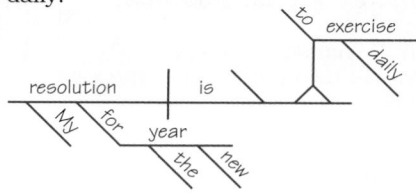

The diagram of an infinitive used as an adjective or adverb looks like the diagram of a prepositional phrase.

EXAMPLE: World War I was supposedly the war to end all wars.

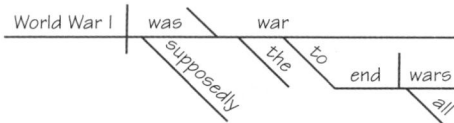

Answer Key

> **Exercise 6**

1.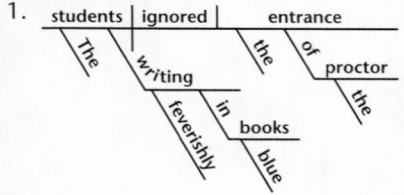

2.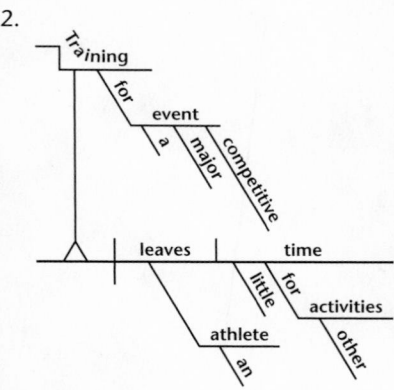

3.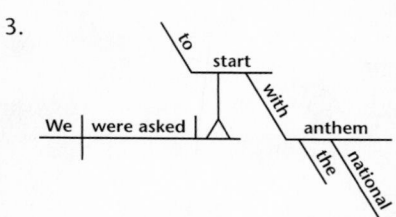

4.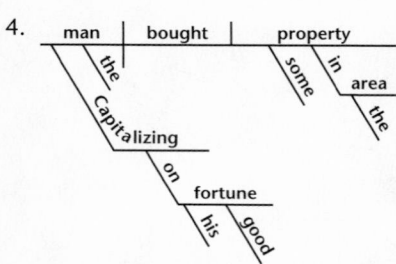

5.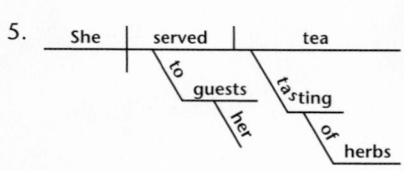

continued

When an infinitive has an understood *to*, indicate the implied word in parentheses. If the infinitive has a subject, extend the left side of the infinitive line and place the subject there.

EXAMPLE: We heard thunder rumble during the night.

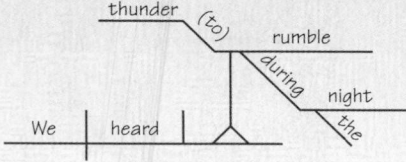

> **Exercise 6** **Diagraming Verbal Phrases** Correctly diagram each sentence.
> 1. The students writing feverishly in blue books ignored the entrance of the proctor.
> 2. Training for a major competitive event leaves an athlete little time for other activities.
> 3. We were asked to start with the national anthem.
> 4. Capitalizing on his good fortune, the man bought some property in the area.
> 5. She served tea tasting of herbs to her guests.
> 6. Help me tie this bow securely.
> 7. We had no desire to see that movie again.
> 8. Furnishing oranges and sodas was the responsibility of the team manager.
> 9. Learning to diagram sentences develops both manual and mental skills.
> 10. Her worst habit, being tardy, greatly irritated all of her teachers.

Compound, Complex, and Compound-Complex Sentences

All the sentences you have diagramed up to this point have been simple sentences. However, diagraming the other three sentence structures—compound, complex, and compound-complex—involves most of the same rules. The primary difference is that another base line is added for each additional clause.

Compound Sentences Each of the independent clauses in a compound sentence is diagramed separately. They are then joined together at the verbs by a dotted step line. The conjunction or semicolon is written on this step line.

772 • Sentence Diagraming Workshop

EXAMPLE: I drove for six hours, and he slept soundly.

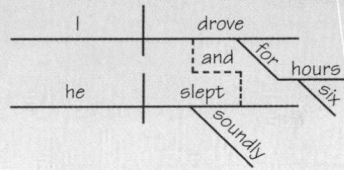

Complex Sentences Diagraming complex sentences involves knowing how to position each of the three kinds of subordinate clauses in relation to the independent clause. An adjective clause is diagramed below the main clause as if it were a separate sentence. A slanted dotted line joins the relative pronoun or relative adverb in the adjective clause to the word the clause modifies. The position of the relative pronoun varies depending on its function in the adjective clause. In the following example, the relative pronoun functions within the subordinate clause as a subject.

EXAMPLE: The car that sped around the corner had no headlights.

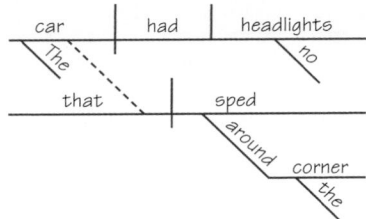

The dotted line must be bent to connect the clauses properly when a relative pronoun acts as either an object of a preposition or as an adjective. The dotted line must also be bent when a relative adverb introduces an adjective clause.

EXAMPLE: The person to whom you spoke is president of the firm.

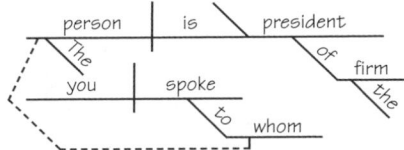

Sentence Diagraming Workshop • **773**

6.

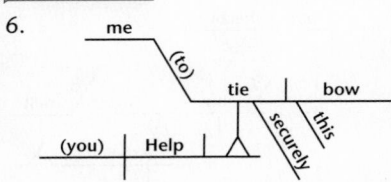

7.

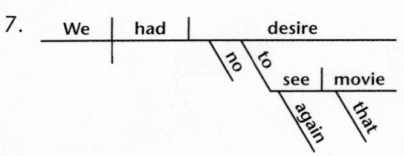

8.

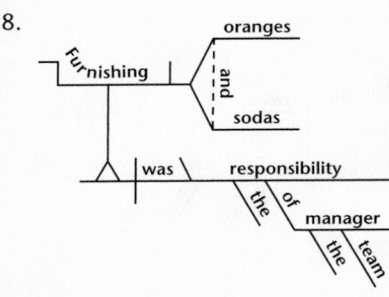

9.

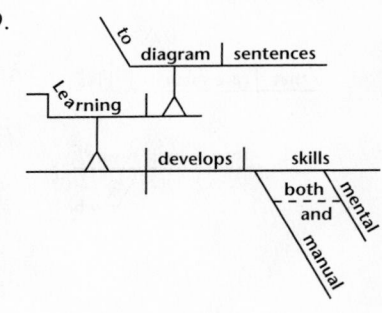

10.

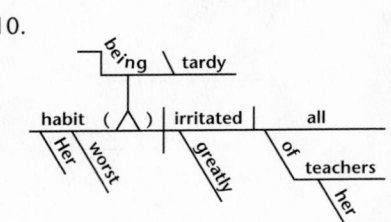

Answer Key

1.
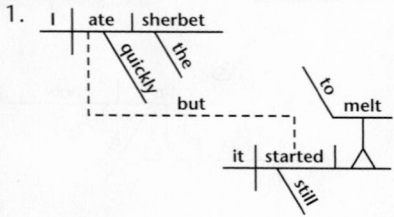

2.
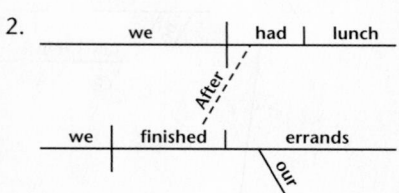

3.
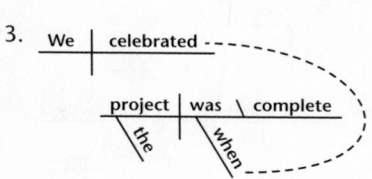

4.
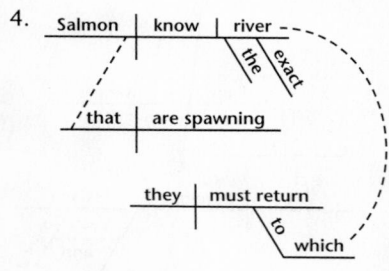

5.
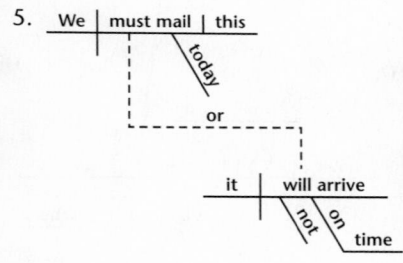

continued

An understood relative pronoun in an adjective clause should be included in parentheses in a diagram.

EXAMPLE: I wrote the letter I owed to my friend.

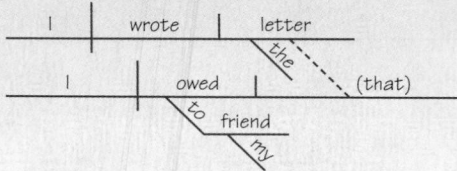

An adverb clause is diagramed with the subordinate conjunction written on the connecting line. This line should join the verb in the adverb clause to the modified verb, adjective, adverb, or verbal in the main clause.

EXAMPLE: When the speaker became ill, the lecture was canceled.

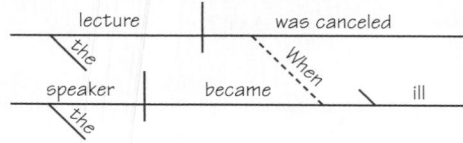

Place in parentheses any understood words in an elliptical adverb clause.

EXAMPLE: Our dog is larger than yours.

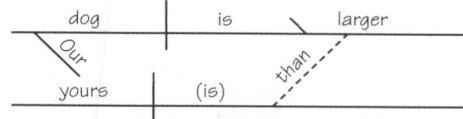

A noun clause is placed on a pedestal in the position it occupies within the sentence. The pedestal meets the noun clause at the verb. In the following example, the noun clause is acting as a direct object.

EXAMPLE: I will wear whatever is clean.

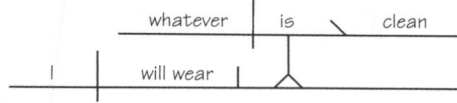

If a noun clause's introductory word has no other function than to introduce the clause, write it alongside the pedestal.

EXAMPLE: Earl said that you had a birthday.

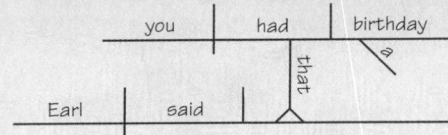

Compound-Complex Sentences To diagram compound-complex sentences, simply combine the skills you learned for diagraming compound and complex sentences.

EXAMPLE: The man who owned the shop fixed my type-writer, but he refused to charge me because the repairs were minor.

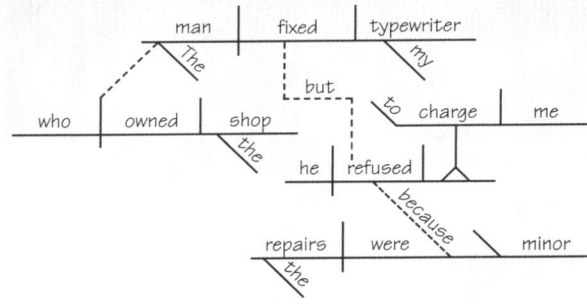

Exercise 7 Diagraming Compound, Complex, and Compound-Complex Sentences Correctly diagram each sentence.

1. I ate the sherbet quickly, but it still started to melt.
2. After we finished our errands, we had lunch.
3. We celebrated when the project was complete.
4. Salmon that are spawning know the exact river to which they must return.
5. We must mail this today, or it will not arrive on time.
6. We should stay at whatever place is cheapest; money is scarce at this time.
7. Tracy saw an automobile accident on Tuesday, and now she is driving more carefully.
8. The couple sat inside the warm house while the snow fell.
9. When he noticed a spot on his coat, he took it to the cleaners, but they were unable to remove the spot.
10. The bus that was scheduled to take us had engine problems, so the company sent us another.

Sentence Diagraming Workshop • **775**

6.
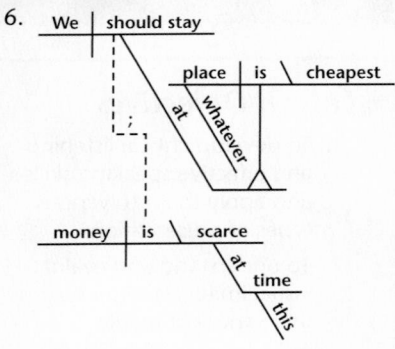

7.
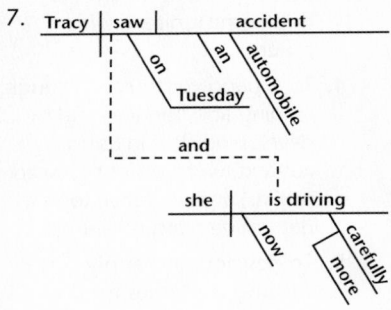

8.
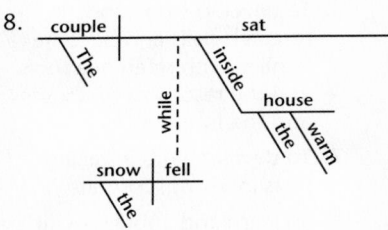

9.
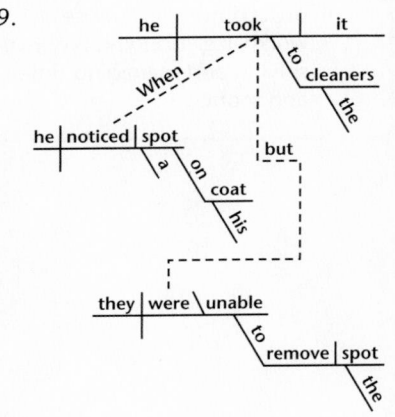

10.
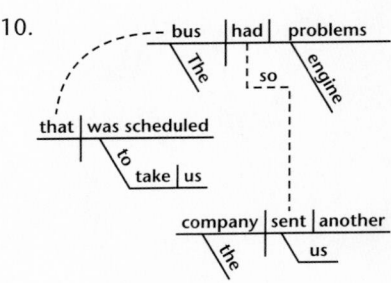

Lesson Objectives

1. To develop critical listening and effective speaking skills and apply them to various types of presentations

2. To understand and evaluate visual images and messages in a variety of media

3. To produce visual images, messages, and meanings that communicate with others

4. To expand vocabulary through reading and listening and by developing skills in using context, word structure, word origins, and reference tools to determine word meanings

5. To develop and apply reading strategies for a variety of purposes and texts

6. To develop study and research skills and become familiar with reference tools and the resources of libraries and the Internet

7. To develop skills in taking tests in various formats

8. To learn and apply specific communication and procedural skills of the workplace, including problem-solving and managing time and money

PART

3

Academic and Workplace Skills

Details of a Lost Library, Stella Waitzkin, Collection of the artist

Academic and Workplace Skills • **777**

Responding to Fine Art

Details of a Lost Library (1995)
by Stella Waitzkin

Use this work of art to start a discussion about the definition of academic and workplace skills.

1. Have students examine the image. Tell students that it is a painted wall-relief, or installation. (In the art world, an installation is any type of art designed to be set up for viewing by the public; it is often designed for a specific site.) *Details of a Lost Library* is large, 7 feet by 8 feet, and all "books" on the shelves are individually cast. You might use the following questions to prompt discussion:

   What else besides books has the artist created for her shelving? (Students may note small paintings, book ends, knickknacks, sculpture.)

   Stella Waitzkin has said that she communicates "best visually because I see more than I hear. And in this way I tell stories by combining painting and sculpture." What story do you think she tells with her installation?

2. Ask students what workplace skills might be the subjects of some of the books on Waitzkin's shelves? What skills do they feel they must improve upon to make themselves attractive to future employers?

About the Artist

New York-born Stella Waitzkin (b. 1920) is still active as an artist and produces, in addition to paintings, sculptures in materials as diverse as cast marble, sandstone, and bronze. She says that what the viewer sees in *Details of a Lost Library* are "collections of short stories and essays, novels, encyclopedias—containers of my energy."

In-Depth Lesson Plan

	LESSON FOCUS	PRINT AND MEDIA RESOURCES
DAY 1	**Speaking and Listening Skills** Students learn key elements of speaking in a group discussion, speaking in public, and preparing, presenting, and evaluating a speech. (pp. 778–782/⊞580–584)	**Teaching Resources** *Academic and Workplace Skills Activity Book,* pp. 1–2
DAY 2	**Speaking and Listening Skills** *continued* Students learn to listen critically and to ask different types of questions. (pp. 783–785/⊞585–587)	**Teaching Resources** *Academic and Workplace Skills Activity Book,* p. 3
DAY 3	**Viewing Skills** Students interpret maps and graphs and view media and fine art critically. (pp. 786–791/⊞588–593)	**Teaching Resources** *Academic and Workplace Skills Activity Book,* pp. 4–7
DAY 4	**Representing Skills** Students create graphic organizers, use formatting, work with multimedia, create a video, and learn about performing and interpreting. (pp. 792–797/⊞594–599)	**Teaching Resources** *Academic and Workplace Skills Activity Book,* pp. 8–12
DAY 5	**Review and Assess** Students review chapter and demonstrate mastery of concepts. (pp. 798–799)	**Teaching Resources** *Formal Assessment,* Ch. 28

Accelerated Lesson Plan

	LESSON FOCUS	PRINT AND MEDIA RESOURCES
DAY 1	**Speaking and Listening Skills** Students learn group discussion and public speaking skills, and strategies for listening critically and asking different types of questions. (pp. 778–785/⊞580–587)	**Teaching Resources** *Academic and Workplace Skills Activity Book,* pp. 1–3
DAY 2	**Viewing and Representing Skills** Students learn skills for viewing maps, graphs, media, and fine art critically. Students learn skills for representing, performing, and interpreting. (pp. 786–797/⊞588–599)	**Teaching Resources** *Academic and Workplace Skills Activity Book,* pp. 4–12
DAY 3	**Review and Assess** Students review chapter and demonstrate mastery of concepts. (pp. 798–799)	**Teaching Resources** *Formal Assessment,* Ch. 28

Options for Adapting Lesson Plans

HOMEWORK

Have students complete any stage of the lesson for homework.

FEATURES

Extend coverage with the Standardized Test Preparation Workshop (pp. 798–799).

Writing and Grammar Handbook Alignment

Page numbers in Step-by-Step Teaching Guides in this Teacher's Edition refer to pages from the full student text. Handbook page references, indicated with this icon Ⓗ, are provided in Time and Resource Manager boxes and at the bottom of each Teacher's Edition page.

INTEGRATED SKILLS COVERAGE

Viewing and Representing Skills
Critical Viewing, SE pp. 778, 786, 787, 788, 791, 793, 796/Ⓗ580, 588, 589, 590, 593, 595, 598; ATE p. 781

Research Skills
SE p. 791/Ⓗ593

Technology Skills
SE pp. 781, 790, 794, 795, 796/Ⓗ583, 592, 596, 597, 598

Vocabulary Skills
ATE p. 782

Workplace Skills
ATE p. 783

Real-World Connection
ATE p. 782

ASSESSMENT SUPPORT

Standardized Test Preparation Workshop, SE p. 798; ATE pp. 788, 798

Standardized Test Preparation Workbook, pp. 55–56

Formal Assessment, Ch. 28

MEETING INDIVIDUAL NEEDS

Less Advanced Students ATE pp. 780, 792. See also Ongoing Assessments ATE pp. 782, 784, 787, 790, 794, 797.

AP Students ATE pp. 793, 794, 799

Gifted and Talented Students ATE p. 789

ESL Students ATE p. 785

Spatial Learners ATE pp. 791, 799

Bodily/Kinesthetic Learners ATE p. 796

BLOCK SCHEDULING

Pacing Suggestions
For 90-minute Blocks
- Have students complete the Speaking and Listening Skills sections in a single period.
- Focus one class period on Viewing and Representing Skills. Allow an additional period for student presentations.

Resources for Varying Instruction
- *Academic and Workplace Skills Activity Book,* pp. 1–12

Professional Development Support
- *How to Manage Instruction in the Block* This teaching resource provides management and activity suggestions.

MEDIA AND TECHNOLOGY

For the Teacher
- **Teacher**EXPRESS™ CD-ROM

WRITING AND GRAMMAR ON-LINE

Interactive Text (On-line or on CD-ROM)
- Easily navigable instruction with interactive Revision Checkers
- Full use of e-rater™, the essay-scoring system (on-line only)

Companion Web Site PHSchool.com
- Scoring rubrics with models (use Web Code egk-1201)

See the Go On-line! **feature, SE p. iii.**

▶ **Lesson Objectives**

1. To communicate effectively in group discussions and public speaking situations
2. To demonstrate proficiency in critical, emphatic, appreciative, and reflective listening
3. To interpret visual presentations, including maps and graphs
4. To evaluate techniques of the information media
5. To communicate by means of a variety of visual forms and technologies
6. To create media presentations to engage specific audiences
7. To prepare and present an interpretive performance

Critical Viewing

Analyze The presence of soldiers suggests the reporter is covering some type of armed conflict. However, the small number of soldiers and the absence of heavy military equipment suggest it may be a peace-keeping mission.

Chapter 28 Speaking, Listening, Viewing, and Representing

The world is in the midst of a communications explosion. Through radio, television, print, film, and the World Wide Web, information is in constant and rapid supply. Today, more than ever before, it is essential to be a strong critical listener and viewer, and it is important to be able to communicate your ideas using the latest visual media.

This chapter focuses on the viewing and listening skills needed to sift through information and to evaluate it critically. It also delves into the speaking and representing skills necessary to communicate ideas to others in this multimedia age. It provides guidance in how to be an effective oral communicator in a wide range of speaking situations—from informal group discussions and one-on-one interviews to formal public speeches—and it explores varying approaches to presenting material visually. All of these skills will be essential in both your personal and work life as you move into the future.

▲ **Critical Viewing**
What type of event do you think this news reporter is covering? How do you know? **[Analyze]**

778 • Speaking, Listening, Viewing, and Representing

⏱ TIME AND RESOURCE MANAGER

Resources
Print: *Academic and Workplace Skills Activity Book*, pp. 1–3

Using the Full Student Edition	Using the Handbook🄷
• Cover pp. 778–785 in class. • Discuss effective speaking and listening techniques. • Allow time for students to complete Exercises 1–7. Exercise 3 will require considerable time because each student will prepare and give a speech.	• Cover pp. 580–587 in class. • Discuss effective speaking and listening techniques. • Allow time for students to complete Exercises 1–7. Exercise 3 will require considerable time because each student will prepare and give a speech.

Speaking and Listening Skills

Section 28.1

Developing your speaking skills will enable you to participate more effectively in class discussions, give formal presentations with greater confidence, and, in general, communicate your feelings and ideas to other people more easily. Improving your listening skills will enable you to focus your attention and identify important information when you hear it.

Speaking in a Group Discussion

A *group discussion* is an informal meeting at which people openly share ideas and observations. In school, group discussions enable you to compare your own interpretations of material with those of your classmates. In the workplace, group discussions are an excellent means for coming up with processes to improve working conditions and productivity.

KEY CONCEPT To benefit from group discussions, it is important to be an active participant, contributing your ideas and asking others questions about the ideas they contribute. ■

Thinking Before You Speak Sometimes, we may speak before we think about what we want to say, and sometimes we may want to take back what we've said. Avoid this problem in group discussions by taking a moment to think about what you're going to say before you say it. Make sure that you choose the right words to express yourself and that what you're saying will not offend any of the others.

Communicating Clearly and Effectively When you make a series of points, present them in a logical order. In addition, provide facts and examples to illustrate each point.

Asking Questions When you'd like to know more about something or an idea seems unclear, ask questions. Take care, however, to ask your questions in a polite and nonthreatening manner. Don't attack or ridicule the person you are addressing.

Making Relevant Contributions Contribute your ideas as frequently as you can, while making sure to allow others time to speak. However, avoid making contributions that stray from the topic being discussed.

Exercise 1 Holding a Group Discussion Hold a group discussion with a few classmates on an important current event.

PREPARE and ENGAGE

Interest GRABBER Have students rate their own speaking skills on a scale of 1 to 10. Then, have them rate their own listening skills on the same scale. Ask students which skills they rated higher: speaking or listening. Which do they feel is more difficult, and why?

Activate Prior Knowledge

Have students make a list of the qualities of a good speaker and a good listener. Discuss their ideas. As they read the chapter, have them compare their ideas with the speaking and listening skills presented.

TEACH

Step-by-Step Teaching Guide

Speaking in a Group Discussion

Teaching Resources: Academic and Workplace Skills Activity Book, p. 1

1. Have a prepared student or students read this section aloud. Define any terms unfamiliar to students.

2. Ask the following questions to promote discussion:

   During group discussions, which of the four guidelines do you find most challenging?

   What can make it difficult to follow these guidelines? (Students may mention being excited about the ideas they want to share, feeling impatient with others in the group, or feeling shy or uncertain.)

Answer Key

Exercise 1

For groups with students learning English, you may want to suggest that group members speak in an assigned order. This way, students who are hesitant to speak up will not also have to worry about finding an entry into the conversation.

Recognizing Different Kinds of Speeches

1. Explore the kinds of speeches by asking the following questions:

   Which kind of speech requires the least preparation? (extemporaneous)

   Which kind requires in-depth knowledge? (All successful speeches require knowledge of the subject.)

   Which kind of speech do you think is easiest to present? Most difficult?

2. Ask students to reflect on the kinds of speeches they have presented or heard in the past.

3. Refer students to the Learn More note referring to chapters that provide information about description, persuasion, and exposition.

Customize for
Less Advanced Students

Make Exercise 2 more structured by having students draw a four-column chart. Have them label the columns "Type of Speech," "Occasion," "Audience," and "Topic" and work with partners to fill in each column.

Answer Key

> **Exercise 2**

Have students complete this exercise in small groups. If possible, have each group bring in a short video clip of one type of speech. Have each group present its clip and discuss it with the class.

28.1

Speaking in Public

Public speaking is the presentation of ideas, information, and points of view to an audience. Often, people feel anxious or intimidated the first few times they speak before an audience. Through practice and preparation, however, you will overcome your anxiety and become a strong presenter.

Recognizing Different Kinds of Speeches There are several different types of speeches. Each type is suited to certain occasions, audiences, and topics.

> **KEY CONCEPT** Choose the kind of speech you will give by considering your topic, your audience, and the occasion on which you will give the speech. ■

- An **informative speech** explains an idea or event or provides information about the status of something. Facts are presented in a clear, organized way. Examples of informative speeches include business presentations about a company's performance, a budget overview at a town meeting, and a review of upcoming events at a school assembly.

- A **persuasive speech** tries to convince the audience to agree with the speaker's position or to take some action. Campaign speeches by politicians are a common type of persuasive speech. In these speeches, as well as in other kinds of persuasive speeches, speakers support their opinions with examples and facts and use a variety of techniques—including repetition and appeals to emotion—to sway listeners.

- An **entertaining speech** is delivered simply to provide enjoyment to the audience. It may be included in other kinds of speeches to offer variety or emphasis. Entertaining speeches are often delivered at celebrations, such as weddings and birthday parties.

- An **extemporaneous speech** can serve any of the purposes outlined above. The key feature of this type of speech is that the speaker does not rely on a prepared manuscript. Major ideas may be outlined, but the speaker uses knowledge and skills to deliver the speech. In many cases, the speaker does not even use an outline.

> **Exercise 2** Matching Types of Speeches to Occasions
Using the descriptions above of the kinds of speeches, give an example of an occasion, an audience, and a topic (other than those mentioned) that might determine when you would give each kind of speech. Explain each of your choices.

Learn More

Earlier chapters in this book (especially Chapters 6–11) provide information about writing for description, persuasion, and exposition. Apply those same concepts and skills to your speaking.

Preparing and Presenting a Speech The keys to a successful speech are thorough preparation and practice and a strong, confident delivery.

KEY CONCEPT Prepare for a speech by collecting and organizing information and practicing your delivery. ■

Gather Information Thoroughly research your topic in the library, on the Internet, or by conducting interviews.

Prepare an Outline Arrange the information you gather into an outline. Divide your outline into major points and supporting details. Arrange the information in a logical sequence.

SAMPLE OUTLINE

> **Jane Austen's**
> *Pride and Prejudice*
>
> A. Overview
>   1. Fitzwilliam Darcy is proud and rich.
>   2. Elizabeth Bennet is simple and strong-willed.
>   3. Social differences complicate their relationship.
>
> B. Aristocracy
>   1. Rigid social customs
>   2. Accept class divisions
>
> C. Pride
>   1. All people all fallible.
>   2. Some are wise enough to admit their error.

Prepare Note Cards and Visual Aids Prepare a note card for each main point on your outline. List opening points, key details, and quotations on each card. You may also want to prepare visual aids. See pages 792–793 to learn more.

Practice Your Speech Study your outline and note cards. Then, practice your speech, using the note cards to guide you.

Deliver Your Speech Use your note cards to guide you as you deliver your speech. Make eye contact with your audience.

Use Rhetorical Strategies Repeat key words and phrases to make your points stand out. Use parallelism, the repetition of grammatical structures, to emphasize key ideas.

Use Verbal and Nonverbal Strategies Vary the tone, volume, and pace of your voice to emphasize your key points. Also, use nonverbal methods, such as hand gestures, for emphasis.

⊕ **Technology Tip**

On its Web site, Toastmasters International provides more tips for honing your public-speaking skills and fending off nervousness.
http://www.toastmasters.org

Step-by-Step Teaching Guide

Preparing and Presenting a Speech

Teaching Resources: Academic and Workplace Skills Activity Book, p. 2

1. Have volunteers read the steps in preparing and presenting a speech.

2. Stress that students must begin their preparations with a clear thesis or main point. Their details must support this thesis.

3. Point out that the purpose of the speech and the intended audience will help students decide what to say and how to say it. They will want to avoid repeating what the audience already knows.

4. Remind students of the methods of organization they learned in Chapter 14. They can use the same approaches in a speech. For example, in an informative speech, they may organize main points in a logical way. In a persuasive speech, they will organize their arguments so that the strongest one is last.

Integrating Viewing and Representing Skills

Point out that effective speakers use rhetorical strategies to emphasize key points. Read these excerpts from John F. Kennedy's inaugural address:

> *"We observe today not a victory of party but a celebration of freedom, symbolizing an end as well as a beginning, signifying renewal as well as change. . . ."*

> *"Now the trumpet summons us again — not as a call to bear arms, though arms we need; not as a call to battle, though embattled we are; but a call to bear the burden of a long twilight of struggle. . . ."*

Invite students to discuss the examples of parallelism and repetition in these excerpts.

Evaluating a Speech

1. Read aloud the key concept and review the questions on the note cards.

2. Discuss with students whether what is said in a speech is more important than how it is said.

3. As students complete Exercise 4, have them forward their comments to the speaker they evaluated. Encourage speakers to give consideration to any suggestions they receive.

Answer Key

▶ **Exercise 3**

Have students work with partners to practice their speeches and evaluate the effectiveness of their visual aids.

▶ **Exercise 4**

Videotape a volunteer's speech. Play only the audio portion of the tape and have students evaluate it. Next, play both the audio and visual portions. Discuss how the speaker's gestures and facial expressions affect the speech.

Integrating Vocabulary Skills

Stress that speakers must use words their audiences will understand, or they must clearly define unfamiliar terms. What strategies have students used to evaluate their audience's level of comprehension?

Real-World Connection

Explain that public speaking skills are often important in the workplace. Ask students to think of examples of workers that might have to give speeches (for example, a coach or a town council member) and the types of speeches they might have to give (awards presentations or a budget report).

28.1

Evaluating a Speech You can use what you've learned about delivering a successful speech to evaluate speeches that others give.

▶ **KEY CONCEPT** Evaluate speeches by critically examining both content and delivery. ■

Use these questions to help guide you in making evaluations.

QUESTIONS FOR EVALUATING SPEECHES

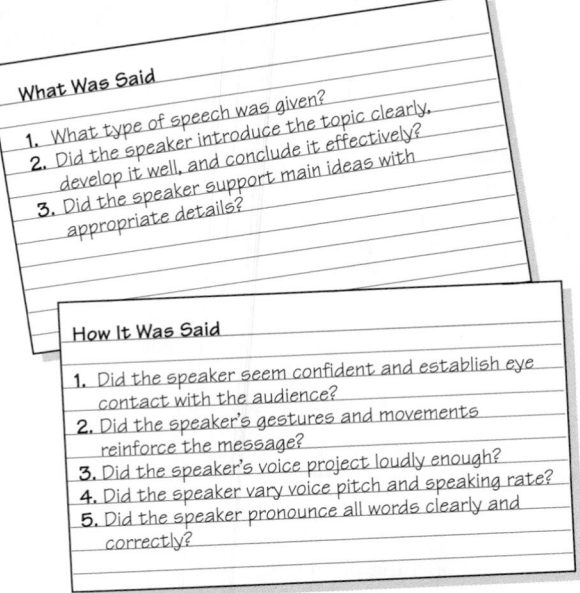

What Was Said

1. What type of speech was given?
2. Did the speaker introduce the topic clearly, develop it well, and conclude it effectively?
3. Did the speaker support main ideas with appropriate details?

How It Was Said

1. Did the speaker seem confident and establish eye contact with the audience?
2. Did the speaker's gestures and movements reinforce the message?
3. Did the speaker's voice project loudly enough?
4. Did the speaker vary voice pitch and speaking rate?
5. Did the speaker pronounce all words clearly and correctly?

▶ **Exercise 3** Preparing and Giving a Speech Prepare and deliver a speech on a current issue or topic that interests you. Follow the steps on page 781.

▶ **Exercise 4** Evaluating a Speech Using the questions above, evaluate a speech given in class. Note the speaking skills the person used effectively, and plan to use them in a speech you will give.

☑ ONGOING ASSESSMENT: Monitor and Reinforce

If students have difficulty presenting a speech in front of the class, try the following strategies.

Option 1 Before they present their speeches, assign an activity that requires small groups to make short presentations to the class. Students will get to practice addressing the class, but they will also have the comfort of not being alone.	**Option 2** Skip ahead to the section on representing skills, which starts on page 792. Have students create visual aids for their speeches. This will give the audience something else to look at, which might help the speaker feel more comfortable.

Listening Critically

In today's world, much of the information that people receive comes through television, radio, and other multimedia sources. For this reason, it is essential to develop the skills to critically evaluate what you hear.

KEY CONCEPT Critical listening involves the careful analysis of the purpose, accuracy, and thoroughness of spoken messages. ■

Learning the Listening Process Becoming a critical listener starts with simply learning to listen attentively. You can then go beyond comprehending *what* a person says and begin analyzing *how* it was said.

Focus Your Attention To be an effective listener, you must not only listen attentively but also focus your thoughts entirely on what the person is saying, ignoring any outside distractions.

Interpret the Information It won't be possible to remember everything a speaker says, so it is essential to identify the key points or main ideas of the message. Use the following suggestions to guide you:

1. Listen for words or phrases that are repeated or emphasized through the volume or tone of the speaker's voice.
2. Take careful note of words or phrases, such as *most important, it is essential,* and *my main point,* that signal that an idea following them is important.
3. Test your understanding by rephrasing the speaker's ideas in your own words.
4. If possible, take notes in which you record key ideas.
5. Watch for nonverbal signals—tone of voice, gestures, and facial expressions—that may alert you to important ideas.
6. Carefully follow the connections among ideas. Signal words and phrases—such as *in comparison, next, last but not least,* and *as a result*—can help you identify important connections.

Respond to the Speaker's Message After the speaker has finished, respond to what you've heard. Think about whether you agree or disagree with the speaker's thoughts and why. Connect the speaker's message to your own experiences, and consider what, if anything, you can learn from the message that you can apply to your life. Finally, ask questions about anything that especially interested you or was unclear.

Exercise 5 Using the Listening Process Apply the strategies on this page as you listen to a classroom lecture.

Listening Critically

Teaching Resources: Academic and Workplace Skills Activity Book, p. 3

1. Ask students to name some internal and external things that can distract listeners. (*Internal:* thinking about other topics, planning a response, fatigue. *External:* other people talking, too much noise.)

2. Show a videotape of a speech, and guide students through the listening process. Ask them to point out repeated words, signal words, nonverbal signals, and connecting phrases.

3. Have students paraphrase the speaker's points in their own words. Ask volunteers to paraphrase aloud to the class. Discuss any discrepancies among the paraphrasing.

4. Invite students to share their responses to the speaker's message.

Answer Key

> **Exercise 5**

Remind students to listen closely to the questions asked by their classmates. Often, they will learn a great deal from the answers.

Integrating Workplace Skills

Ask students for examples of instances when listening skills are important in the workplace (listening to instructions on their first day of work or listening closely so they can take the minutes at a meeting).

Using Different Types of Listening

1. Explore the types of listening by asking the following questions:

   Which types include not only listening, but also talking and asking questions? (empathic, reflective, sometimes critical)

   Which type of listening do you do most often?

   Under what conditions might you mix two types of listening? (watching a play [appreciative] and then discussing it with friends [reflective]; listening to a speaker [critical] and then disagreeing with another listener about what the speaker meant [empathic])

2. Encourage students to volunteer information about when they use each type of listening.

Asking Different Types of Questions

1. Ask volunteers to read aloud the different types of questions listed on the page. Define any unfamiliar terms.

2. Have students suggest examples of each type of question.

3. Point out that questions for clarification or support can be closed- or open-ended. Challenge students to ask both closed- and open-ended questions about the same topic and compare the information they gather. (Examples: "Did you mean . . . ?" and "What did you mean when you said . . . ?")

28.1

Using Different Types of Listening There are a number of types of listening, each appropriate for different situations. The following chart shows four types of listening and the situations for which they are most appropriate.

Types of Listening		
Type	**How to Listen**	**Situation**
Critical	Listen for facts and supporting details to understand and evaluate the speaker's message.	Informative or persuasive essays, class discussions, announcements
Empathic	Imagine yourself in the other person's position, and try to understand what he or she is thinking.	Conversations with friends or family
Appreciative	Identify and analyze aesthetic or artistic elements, such as character development, rhyme, imagery, and descriptive language.	Oral presentations of a poem or short story and dramatic performances
Reflective	Ask questions to get information, and use or reflect on the speaker's responses to form new questions.	Class or group discussions

Asking Different Types of Questions Asking questions is the best way to ensure that you have understood what a speaker has said or to delve more deeply into the speaker's topic. Following are some types of questions you might ask:

- A **question that calls for clarification** is a question that you ask to ensure that you have heard accurately what has been said. These questions might begin as follows: "What did you mean by . . . ?" or "If I understand correctly, . . . ?"

- A **question that calls for support** asks the speaker to back up his or her points with supporting facts and details. These questions might begin, "On what do you base . . . ?"

- A **closed question** leads to a *yes* or *no* response.

- An **open-ended question** does not have a specific response but can lead to further exploration of the topic.

784 • Speaking, Listening, Viewing, and Representing

☑ **ONGOING ASSESSMENT: Monitor and Reinforce**

Use the following strategy to help students see the connections between the various types of listening and questioning.

Ask students to match the types of questions to the types of listening. What types of questions would they most likely ask during critical listening (clarification, support, open-ended)? During empathic listening (clarification, open-ended)? During appreciative listening (none, as appreciative listening is usually for entertainment, not for information)? During reflective listening (clarification, support, closed, open-ended)?

Evaluating Your Listening Developing strong listening skills is an ongoing process. However, improvement occurs only if you are willing to critically evaluate your own performance as a listener and find ways to improve.

Repeat or Paraphrase Key Ideas Test your understanding of a speech by repeating or restating the speaker's main points. When you use your own words to restate what you've heard, it is called **paraphrasing.** Ideally, you should share your paraphrase with the speaker and see whether he or she agrees with it.

Compare and Contrast Interpretations If you are among a group of listeners, compare your interpretation of what you've heard with other listeners' interpretations.

Use the following questions to guide your discussion:

• What was the main point or central message?
• What was the strongest argument or example?
• Do I agree with or accept the information presented or the speaker's position? Why or why not?

Check the Accuracy of the Speaker's Points If you are unsure about a point or think it sounds inaccurate, research it on the Internet or in the library.

Exercise 6 Using the Different Types of Listening and Questioning Come up with at least two specific situations in which you would use each type of listening and two specific situations in which you would ask each type of question.

Exercise 7 Tracking Your Listening Skills For one week, keep a record of your performance in listening situations. Use each of the strategies above at least once.

Evaluating Your Listening

1. Invite a pair of volunteers to demonstrate paraphrasing. Ask one student to explain something, such as an opinion or directions to the nearest gas station. The second student will then paraphrase what he or she heard. Have the class help determine whether the paraphrasing was accurate.

2. Caution students on using the Internet when checking the accuracy of the speaker's points. Explain that anyone can set up a Web site and that no one checks the accuracy of the information offered there. Stress that not everything they read on the Internet is accurate.

Customize for
ESL Students

Encourage students to use the paraphrasing strategy when reading as well as listening. They can paraphrase material in their original language if it helps them to understand it.

Answer Key

Exercise 6

When they finish, have students share their answers. Remind them to use critical listening skills when their classmates are speaking.

Exercise 7

If students include telephone conversations in their records, ask them how this type of listening compares with face-to-face listening.

Interpreting Maps

Teaching Resources: Academic and Workplace Skills Activity Book, p. 4

1. Explain the following types of maps and show students examples, if possible.

   General reference maps give names and locations of features of the earth. **Topographic maps** concentrate on natural surface features such as plains, mountains, rivers, oceans, and lakes. **Political maps** highlight governmental units such as cities and county/state/country divisions. **Navigation maps** are intended to get people from one place to another by way of **road maps** and **street maps**.

2. Make sure students are familiar with the following map components:

   symbols for airports, railroads, schools, and other structures

   color to indicate types of terrain and bodies of water

   a **scale** to show distances

   a **compass rose** to indicate which direction is north

   stars and circles to show cities and capital cities

   solid and dotted lines of different colors to indicate boundaries

3. Ask students, working in pairs, to write five facts they learned from the map of the United States on page 786. Have pairs take turns sharing this information with the class.

Critical Viewing

Analyze This map can be used to locate the names, locations, and boundaries of the fifty states and the four regions of the United States.

Visual representation is an important and effective way to communicate. Television programs, textbooks, Web sites, and works of art are common types of media that use images to add to your view of the world. In this section, you will learn how to interpret information from visual sources.

Interpreting Maps and Graphs

Any map, graph, or photograph can be a treasure chest of information. The key to the information these representations hold is your ability to interpret them.

Maps

A map can show more than the fastest route between two cities. For example, maps can identify population clusters and movement, provide demographic information for politicians and marketers, report weather patterns, clarify battle activities in war, and illustrate the geography and topography of planets.

To interpret a map, (1) determine the type and purpose of the map; (2) examine the symbols, scale, orientation, and other pertinent data (often, maps have a key that can help you decipher symbols and scale); (3) make connections between the key details of the map to written text that accompanies it.

REGIONS OF THE UNITED STATES

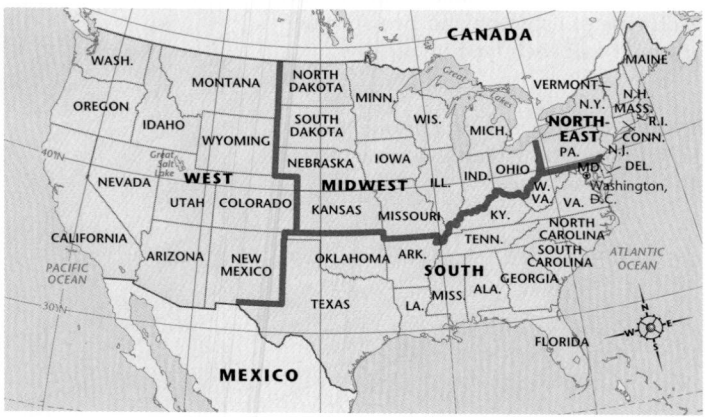

▲ Critical Viewing For what types of purposes might you use this map? Explain. [Analyze]

⏱ TIME AND RESOURCE MANAGER

Resources
Print: *Academic and Workplace Skills Activity Book*, pp. 4–7

Using the Full Student Edition	Using the Handbook🖽
• Cover pp. 786–791 in class. • Point out ways in which viewing skills are necessary at the workplace. • Provide time for students to complete Exercises 8–11. Review and discuss their answers.	• Cover pp. 588–593 in class. • Point out ways in which viewing skills are necessary at the workplace. • Provide time for students to complete Exercises 8–11. Review and discuss their answers.

Graphs

Graphs are an excellent tool for comparing pieces of related information. Following are the main types of graphs:

Bar Graph A bar graph compares and contrasts amounts by showing differing heights or lengths of the bars. To interpret a bar graph, (1) compare and contrast the bars and (2) search the text for possible causes for the similarities and differences.

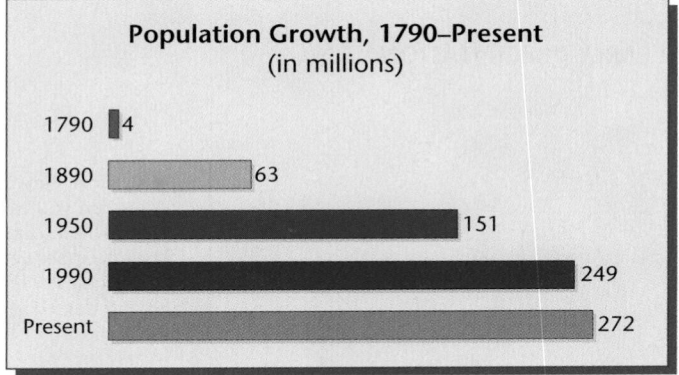

Population Growth, 1790–Present
(in millions)

1790	4
1890	63
1950	151
1990	249
Present	272

◀ **Critical Viewing**
What are some of the conclusions you can draw about population growth in the United States based on this graph?
[Analyze]

Line Graph Line graphs illustrate changes over time. A line graph is based on two scales—one vertical and one horizontal—with each point having a value on both scales. To interpret a line graph, (1) identify patterns of change and (2) search the text for reasons for the changes.

Immigration to the United States, 1940–1990

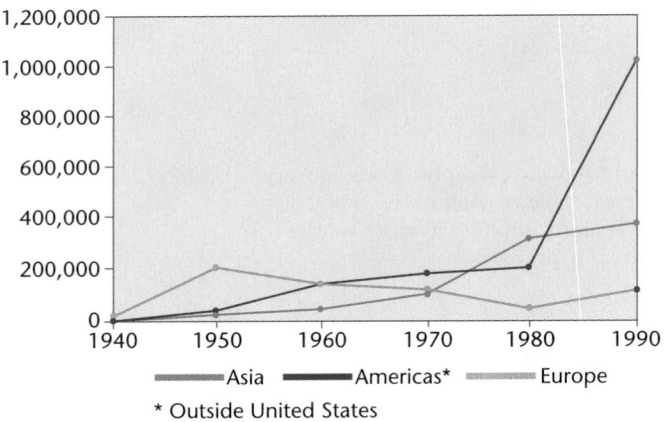

—— Asia —— Americas* —— Europe
* Outside United States

◀ **Critical Viewing**
What does this graph reveal about how immigration patterns have shifted over the last several decades? **[Analyze]**

Viewing Skills • 787

✓ ONGOING ASSESSMENT: Monitor and Reinforce

Help students hone their graph-reading skills by using the following strategies.

Option 1 Have each student write three questions about one of the graphs on this page. Have them exchange papers with partners and answer one another's questions.

Option 2 Have students explain in writing why the information on immigration was turned into a line graph rather than a bar graph. (The line graph shows growth over time. It also creates a clear visual comparison of the growth of the three groups.)

Step-by-Step Teaching Guide

Bar Graph

Teaching Resources: Academic and Workplace Skills Activity Book, p. 5

1. Help students interpret this graph by asking the following questions.

   What general trend does the graph show? (Population has grown steadily.)

   Why should a person be hesitant to declare that since 1950 there has been a dramatic drop in growth? (The graph measures 160 years before 1950, but only fifty years after it. Therefore, it does not make sense to compare these two time periods.)

2. Invite students to discuss other things they can learn from this graph.

Critical Viewing

Analyze Students might notice that between 1790 and 1890, the population grew by almost sixty million, or about six million per decade. In the decade between 1990 and today, the population grew by 26 million.

Step-by-Step Teaching Guide

Line Graph

1. Explore the line graph by asking students the following questions.

   Approximately how many people immigrated to the U.S. from the Americas in 1980? 1990? (200,000; 1,000,000)

   What general trend does the graph show? (The graph shows a gradual decrease from Europe, a gradual rise from Asia, and, after 1980, a dramatic rise from the Americas.)

2. Have students find other line graphs in their textbooks and discuss them with partners.

Critical Viewing

Analyze Students should notice that emigration from the Americas has risen dramatically since 1980; from Europe and Asia, it has risen only slightly.

Pie Graph

1. Ask students the following questions to engage them in a discussion about the pie graph.

   Based on this pie graph, what statement could you make about precipitation in Los Angeles? (It rarely rains there and it never snows.)

   What statement could you make about precipitation in Boston? (It rains or snows about a third of the year.)

2. Have students name the kind of graph they would use to show each of the following types of information. Write the following examples on the board.

   The increase in sales of home computers from 1980 to 2000 (line graph or bar graph)

   The number of grams of fat in various cereals (bar graph)

   The types of transportation used by a company's staff to get to work (pie graph)

Critical Viewing

Analyze Students should notice that there is much more precipitation in Boston than there is in Los Angeles.

Answer Key

> **Exercise 8**

Have students share and discuss their findings in small groups.

28.2

Pie Graph A pie graph shows the relationship of parts to a whole. A circle, or pie, is divided into segments, each representing a percentage of the whole. The combined segments equal 100 percent. To interpret a pie graph, (1) read the title to determine what the whole (100 percent) stands for; (2) determine what each percentage represents, and relate the percentages to each other as well as to the whole; (3) relate the graph information to the text to determine the significance and possible reasons for the percentages.

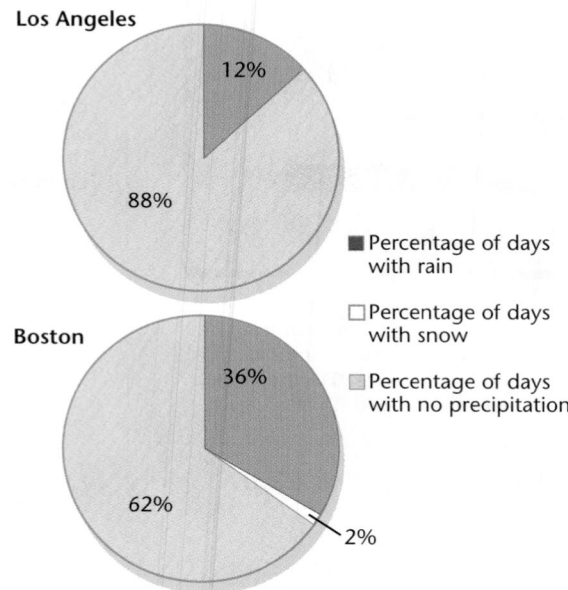

AVERAGE YEARLY PRECIPITATION

◀ **Critical Viewing** What can you tell about the differences in climate between Los Angeles and Boston based on these graphs? **[Analyze]**

> **Exercise 8** Interpreting Maps and Graphs In the library or on the Internet, find one example of each of the types of maps and graphs. Analyze each example, and write a brief explanation of the information it provides.

STANDARDIZED TEST PREPARATION WORKSHOP

Interpreting Graphs Standardized tests might require students to interpret graphs. Provide students with practice in this skill.

Based on the pie graph for Los Angeles on page 788, about how many days out of every year have no precipitation?

A 12   **C** 321
B 88   **D** 365

Students should recognize that **C** is the correct answer. Answers A and B are merely repeats of the percentage figures. Answer D is the total number of days in a year, not the total number of days without precipitation.

Viewing Information Media Critically

It is important to be a critical listener in today's media-rich world. It is perhaps even more essential to be a critical viewer. Being a critical viewer involves thinking carefully about what you see and carefully analyzing its purpose and its effectiveness. One of the first steps in becoming a critical viewer is to learn to differentiate among the various kinds of media and to understand the purposes of each.

Recognizing Kinds of Information Media In our fast-paced world, it sometimes seems that we encounter new forms of visual media almost every day. Internet Web pages, print advertisements, commercials—these are just a few of the kinds of media you'll encounter, as the chart below shows.

TODAY'S VISUAL MEDIA			
Form of Media	**Topic(s)**	**Coverage and Content**	**Point of View**
Internet Web Pages	Unlimited	Interactive content updated regularly	Can be biased
Television News Program	Current events or news	Brief summaries illustrated by video footage	Usually gives objective information; can be biased
Television Documentary	One topic of social interest	Story shown through narration and video footage	Often focuses on one side of an issue
Television Interview	Topics of social interest	Questions and answers	Sometimes presents opinions of interviewer
Print Advertisement and Television Commercial	Products, people, and ideas	Short message of images and slogans	Presents information to sell something or to persuade viewer

Viewing Information Media Critically

Teaching Resources: Academic and Workplace Skills Activity Book, p. 6

1. In their notebooks, have students draw a fifth column for the chart and label it "Example." Have them work with partners to think of an example of each form of media listed in the first column.

2. Then, have pairs choose one of their examples and write a paragraph about it. The paragraph should describe the topic, content, and point of view of the example.

3. Have students share their examples with the class. Make sure each form of media is covered at least once.

Customize for
Gifted and Talented Students

Challenge students to create their own example of a television news program. It should be three to five minutes long, and it should cover local news. Students should strive to convey an objective point of view toward the material.

Step-by-Step Teaching Guide

Evaluating Persuasive Techniques

1. Have volunteers read aloud the section. Define any unfamiliar terms.

2. Invite students to give several examples of facts and opinions relating to the same topic, such as travel destinations or movies.

3. Have students describe political advertisements they have seen that use loaded language and images.

4. Discuss the kinds of bias that students have detected in news programs. How is this bias shown? (Examples: in the selection of the topics to broadcast; in the people who are interviewed; in what is shown from those interviews)

5. Have students identify current advertising slogans. The fact that these slogans are so familiar shows that their repetition does have an impact on us.

Step-by-Step Teaching Guide

Evaluating Information From the Media

1. Have volunteers read this section aloud. Define any unfamiliar terms.

2. Help students apply the bulleted techniques to their lives by asking the following questions:

   Which of these techniques seems hardest to carry out? Why?

   Why is it more difficult to detect bias when you agree with it? (Bias seems true when it matches one's opinion.)

Answer Key

▶ Exercise 9

Students can extend the activity by noting the commercials shown throughout the broadcast. Do they follow a pattern? Do they seem to be aimed at a certain audience?

▶ Exercise 10

Students might enjoy analyzing a commercial they've seen many times in the past. What do they notice about it now that they've never noticed before?

Evaluating Persuasive Techniques Much of the material presented through visual media intends to persuade. In some cases, this is immediately apparent—in commercials, for example. In other cases, it is less obvious; a news program may include persuasive segments, for instance.

▶ **KEY CONCEPT** Learn to identify and evaluate the use of persuasion in all visual media. ■

To identify the use of persuasion and to evaluate its effectiveness, be aware of these persuasive elements and techniques:

Facts are statements that can be verified. **Opinions** are viewpoints that cannot be verified, or proved true.

Loaded language and **loaded images** are emotional words and visuals used to stir up your feelings and persuade you to think a certain way.

Bias is a tendency to think in a certain way without considering other viewpoints.

Slogans and **repetition** are other techniques used to sway your opinions.

Evaluating Information From the Media Once you've become aware of the various persuasive techniques, use the following techniques to critically evaluate what you see:

- Distinguish between facts and opinions, and determine whether opinions are supported by facts.

- Try to avoid being swayed; instead, focus on how well the position being presented has been supported.

- Check for bias by seeing whether both sides of an issue have been addressed.

- Verify questionable information in other sources that you find in the library or on the Internet.

- Don't let slogans sway you, even though they are catchy.

- View the complete program. Develop your own views about the issues, people, and information.

▶ **Exercise 9** Analyzing Information Media Complete a written analysis and evaluation of a television news program or Web site. Follow the strategies above.

▶ **Exercise 10** Evaluating Television Commercials Write an evaluation of the effectiveness of a television commercial.

⊙ Technology Tip

Several libraries and media centers offer tips for evaluating information on their Web sites. Try these:

http://www.lib.duke.edu/libguide/evaluating.html

http://www.cl.utoledo.edu/info/guides/info_eval.html

☑ ONGOING ASSESSMENT: Monitor and Reinforce

If students have trouble evaluating persuasive techniques, try the following strategies.

Option 1 Students might not know how to determine whether a statement is a fact or an opinion. Help them make a list of ways to verify information, such as using reference books in the library or relevant Web sites on the Internet, talking to experts, or investigating a situation on their own.	**Option 2** Brainstorm with students for a list of ways to recognize bias. For example, students might notice excessive praise or condemnation, or the omission of an important side of a story.

Viewing Fine Art Critically

When you look at a painting, you'll discover more than just a reproduction of a person or a scene. You may also find a mood, a movement of color, an explosion of attitude, or the drama of an event. By interpreting the elements of a work of art, you can travel on imaginative and inspirational journeys.

> **KEY CONCEPT** Interpret the elements of art to understand the devices used to enrich your appreciation of it. ■

Effect of the Sun on the Water, 1905, Andre Derain, Giraudon

◄ **Critical Viewing**
What is your first impression of this painting? Why? **[Respond]**

QUESTIONS FOR INTERPRETING ARTWORK

- What is the medium? Is the work a painting, drawing, photograph, and so on?
- What scenes, shapes, images, and colors do you see?
- Are lines thick or thin, straight or curvy, solid or broken?
- Are people and objects proportional? Do they seem ordinary in size, gigantic, or tiny?
- How does the artist use light and dark tones? How do the two tones contrast with one another?
- Which parts are clearly defined? Which parts are not?
- What is the mood of the work? How do all the individual elements work together to create a feeling or an idea?

> **Exercise 11** **Interpreting Fine Art** Interpret the painting above by asking and answering the preceding questions. Write your answers, and then share and compare them with those of your classmates.

🔲 Research Tip

Many museums offer virtual tours on their Web sites. Use the World Wide Web to enhance your appreciation of art and to hone your interpretation skills.

Viewing Fine Art Critically

Teaching Resources: Academic and Workplace Skills Activity Book, p. 7

1. Have volunteers read this page aloud. Make sure students understand all of the questions.
2. Point out that many people appreciate one artistic style more than they appreciate others. Ask students to consider how we can learn to appreciate a range of styles (by learning more about them and seeing them more often).
3. Challenge students to add to the list a question that would help viewers focus on aesthetic aspects of a piece of art. (Example: What is the artist showing about the subject that the viewer may not have considered before?)

Critical Viewing

Respond Answers will vary. Students might say the painting looks ominous because of the dark, menacing clouds.

Answer Key

> **Exercise 11**

Ask students to explain in a single sentence how Derain might describe the effect of the sun on water.

Customize for
Spatial Learners

After completing Exercise 11, have students try to duplicate Derain's technique in paintings of their own, using whatever medium they prefer.

Producing Graphic Organizers

Teaching Resources: Academic and Workplace Skills Activity Book, p. 8

1. Briefly explain the types of graphic organizers below. Have students share their experiences in creating any of them.

   Charts have two or more columns; items can be listed in different categories.

   Venn diagrams have overlapping circles, used to compare and contrast two things; the common area shows similarities.

   Word or concept webs show how things are related to each other.

   Flowcharts have arrows that lead from one box to the next, showing the steps in a process.

   Organizational charts are a series of boxes connected by lines that indicate the lines of authority in an organization.

   Timelines show when the parts of a project should be completed or are due.

2. Encourage students to analyze and limit the amount of information they include in a graphic organizer. Explain that "crowded" organizers are unclear and their meaning is often lost.

Answer Key

▶ **Exercise 12**

Encourage students to flip through their history or science textbooks for models of various types of graphic organizers.

Customize for
Less Advanced Students

For Exercise 12, choose appropriate information from a textbook for students to organize. If you wish, you might also suggest the form of the organizers and provide them with a model of each.

Section 28.3 | # *Representing Skills*

Writing is communication through words. Representing is communication through various media, such as graphic organizers, pictures, videos, and dramatic performances. As we move into the future, the ability to present your ideas through media becomes increasingly important.

Producing Graphic Organizers

Graphic organizers are useful in helping you to sort out and comprehend what you read, see, and hear; they are also a valuable tool when you present your own ideas to an audience. For instance, you may use graphic organizers in business presentations when you leave school and enter your work life.

▶ **KEY CONCEPT** When you have a lot of information or technical data to comprehend or present, consider putting the information into a graphic organizer that suits the type of information. ∎

Analyzing the Information Think carefully about the type of information with which you are dealing. If, for example, the information involves comparisons, you would probably want to consider using a Venn diagram. On the other hand, if you were dealing with events taking place over a period of time, you'd probably want to use a flowchart or a timeline.

Limiting the Amount of Information You Include Graphic organizers lose their effectiveness if they present too much information. Remember that the whole point of using a graphic organizer is to present the information visually, not through words. Limit the amount of text you include in graphic organizers. Use phrases and words rather than complete sentences to indicate main ideas or details.

▶ **Exercise 12** Producing a Graphic Organizer Produce two different graphic organizers: The first should record information from a history or science textbook. The second should present information on a subject of special interest to you. The first organizer can serve as a study aid to help you prepare for a test. The second organizer can be used in a presentation.

⏱ TIME AND RESOURCE MANAGER

Resources
Print: *Academic and Workplace Skills Activity Book*, pp. 8–12

Using the Full Student Edition	Using the Handbook🖪
• Cover pp. 792–797 in class. • Draw students' attention to ways that representing skills are used in the workplace. • Give students time to complete Exercises 12–17. Review and discuss their answers.	• Cover pp. 594–599 in class. • Draw students' attention to ways that representing skills are used in the workplace. • Give students time to complete Exercises 12–17. Review and discuss their answers.

Producing Other Visual Aids

In addition to graphic organizers, there are a variety of other visual aids that you can use in presentations.

Charts, Graphs, and Tables These are excellent tools for presenting data. For example, you might use a graph in a business presentation to show how a company's earnings have grown over time.

Maps Consider using maps in presentations discussing one or more places. For example, you might show two maps to compare and contrast the average temperatures in two different states.

Diagrams, Illustrations, and Pictures Simple line drawings, diagrams, and hand-drawn pictures can visually represent a process or specific features of something. Look at the diagram below.

▼ **Critical Viewing**
In what type of presentation might you use this diagram? Why? **[Connect]**

THE EARTH'S ORBIT AND THE SEASONS

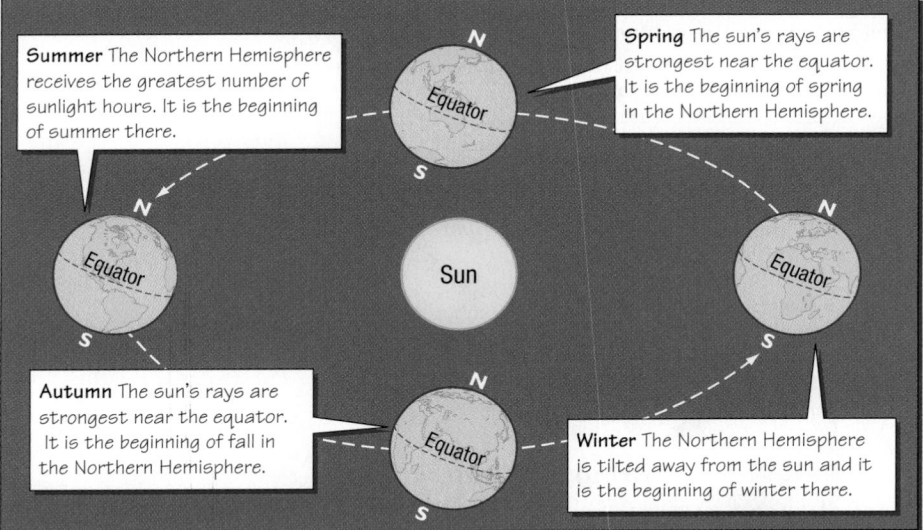

Summer The Northern Hemisphere receives the greatest number of sunlight hours. It is the beginning of summer there.

Spring The sun's rays are strongest near the equator. It is the beginning of spring in the Northern Hemisphere.

Autumn The sun's rays are strongest near the equator. It is the beginning of fall in the Northern Hemisphere.

Winter The Northern Hemisphere is tilted away from the sun and it is the beginning of winter there.

Exercise 13 Producing Visual Aids Produce two different types of visual aids listed above. Do not simply copy your examples from a book. Instead, use information gathered through research to prepare your own.

Step-by-Step Teaching Guide

Producing Other Visual Aids

1. Read and discuss the information and the chart on this page.

2. Have pairs of students think of a specific kind of information that might be represented in a visual aid and write it on a note card (the yearly rainfall for a ten-year period, the cost of living in different areas of the nation, a company's sales territories). Students don't need to list specific figures; they should simply describe the type of information.

3. Collect the cards and redistribute them. Have the recipients decide on an appropriate visual aid to show that kind of information. Have students share their decisions with the class.

Critical Viewing

Connect The diagram might be used in a presentation about how the earth's orbit determines the seasons.

Answer Key

▶ **Exercise 13**

Students might conduct a class survey on a topic that interests them, such as career goals. They can present their results in the form of a visual aid.

Customize for
AP Students

For Exercise 13, challenge students to use information from one of the visual aids to create an entirely different type of visual aid. (Examples: turn a line graph into a timeline or turn a table into a map.)

Using Formatting

Teaching Resources: Academic and Workplace Skills Activity Book, p. 9

1. Read and discuss this page. Ask students which of the formatting tools they already use and when they use them.

2. Urge students to use formatting discriminately. Explain that boldface, italics, and color lose their impact when they are overused. (Example: If all of the words are written in capitals, the important ones will not stand out.)

3. Point out that numbered or bulleted lists can help break up a page and make it more reader-friendly. This technique creates more white space, which invites readers in. Pages of dense paragraphs tend to discourage readers.

4. Ask students to select a piece of their own writing and improve its formatting. Have them share their new versions in small groups.

Answer Key

> **Exercise 14**

Remind students to keep their audience (students at their school) in mind and to choose words and graphics that will appeal to this audience.

Customize for
AP Students

For Exercise 14, have students research the effects of recycling and lack of recycling, the types of materials that can be recycled, and how the recycled materials are used again. Ask them to include some of these persuasive facts and statistics in their brochures.

28.3

Using Formatting

You can enhance any piece of writing with the basic formatting and design features of a word-processing program or a multimedia presentation program. Formatting features include type styles and sizes, fonts, capital letters, tabs, and bullets. Design features include arrangement, balance, and color.

- **Capitals** Use capital letters in heads to call out important topics and ideas.

- **Boldface and Italics** Use boldface and italic type to add emphasis and to direct the readers' eyes to key information and ideas.

- **Fonts** Use different fonts and type sizes to distinguish heads, captions, or even sections of information. Fonts also help create a mood.

- **Numbered Lists** Use numbered lists when you are providing sequential steps in a process.

- **Bulleted Lists** Use bulleted lists for items that can be presented in any order.

- **Arrangement** Arrange your information in a way that captures and directs the readers' attention.

- **Color** Use color to highlight important information and to create a particular emotional response.

Join the Chess Club
- Learn how to
  1. open with a strong move
  2. dominate the middle
  3. finish your opponent
- Watch expert games
- Compete against other clubs

Come to our organizational meeting next Wednesday at 3:30 P.M. in the library.

Bring a friend!

> **Exercise 14** Using Formatting to Design a Brochure Use the tips on formatting and design to prepare a flyer or brochure that promotes recycling. When your flyer is complete, ask a classmate to evaluate your use of various formatting and design features.

794 • Speaking, Listening, Viewing, and Representing

⊙ Technology Tip

Today's word-processing programs have many formatting features that can help you achieve many of the effects explained here. A desktop publishing program can offer you even more options.

☑ ONGOING ASSESSMENT: Monitor and Reinforce

If you observe that some students do not know how to use the formatting capabilities on a computer, use the following strategy.

Ask for volunteers with advanced computer skills to run a brief in-school tutorial on the use of a computer for formatting. You may have to set up a schedule and find available time in your school's computer lab. This is an ideal opportunity for students to use visual aids to enhance the clarity of a presentation.

Working With Multimedia

In a multimedia presentation, the presenter utilizes a combination of speech and aural and visual aids. Ideally, the different components complement each other, resulting in an interesting, engaging, multisensory experience.

KEY CONCEPT Multimedia presentations supply information through a variety of media, including text, slides, videos, music, maps, charts, and art. ∎

Tips for Preparing a Multimedia Presentation

- Choose a topic, and generate an outline of what you want to communicate.

- Choose a form of media that is suited to your topic. For example, a presentation about the first moonwalk might include photographs of the astronauts and models of the spaceship, as well as music, art, and other representations of popular culture of that era. It might also contain a dramatic reading from appropriate newscasts and editorials.

- Plan the use of media you've found and created so that it is evenly spaced throughout your presentation.

- Make sure that the media you've selected is large enough and loud enough for everyone to see and hear. Photocopy and enlarge the images of small objects, or make slides of them.

- Before the presentation, check that all of your equipment works properly.

- Always have a backup plan just in case anything goes wrong with the equipment.

- Rehearse with the equipment prior to the day of your presentation.

Exercise 15 Preparing a Multimedia Presentation

Working with two or three classmates, choose a topic of interest from science, social studies, literature, or another school subject. Write an outline of the subtopics you would like to cover in an oral report, and select three types of media that will best enhance a multimedia presentation. Using the suggestions discussed in this section, prepare, practice, and present a dynamic multimedia report.

 **Technology Tip**

There are a variety of presentation programs that can help you design multimedia presentations on a computer.

Working With Multimedia

Teaching Resources: Academic and Workplace Skills Activity Book, p. 10

1. Read and discuss the information on this page. On the board, define any unfamiliar terms.

2. Invite students to describe multimedia presentations they have seen. What media were used? What did they enjoy about the presentations? How did the combinations of media add to the overall effect? Was there anything they would have changed?

3. Ask students to suggest several possible topics for a multimedia presentation (an analysis of some aspect of television commercials, a comparison of popular singing groups, the explanation of a certain career field).

4. Choose a topic and use it to guide students through the steps on this page.

5. Ask students to consider how multimedia presentations have changed the way they receive information at school.

Answer Key

Exercise 15

You may want to invite the school's media specialist to offer advice and instruction to your class. Have students share their presentations when they finish.

Producing a Video

Teaching Resources: Academic and Workplace Skills Activity Book, p. 11

1. Have volunteers read aloud the tips for creating a video. Define any unfamiliar terms. If possible, bring a video camera to class and point out the various parts and functions.

2. Encourage students to share their experiences with filming a video. What was the purpose? What preparation did they do? How did it turn out? Who watched it? What could they have improved?

3. Invite a knowledgeable student, parent, or community member to speak to the class about shooting and editing videos.

Critical Viewing

Analyze Students are probably watching an educational video. The woman on the screen is either teaching or explaining something.

Answer Key

> **Exercise 16**

Suggest that students borrow documentaries from your school library and use them as models for their own films.

Customize for
Bodily/Kinesthetic Learners

Have students plan, write, and present a documentary even if they are not able to videotape it. They might create simple backdrops and walk from one to the other as they explain what they expect life will be like after high school. The experience will give students practice in communicating information through a combination of narration and visual aids.

28.3

Producing a Video

Video is a powerful form of communication. Using a camera lens as your eyes, you can produce an entertaining and memorable presentation that will inform, amuse, and/or entertain your audience.

▶ **KEY CONCEPT** If you have access to the necessary technology, try your hand at producing a video by following the steps below. ■

Tips for Producing a Video A video can last a few seconds or several hours. Video subjects range from the sublimely ridiculous to the unflinchingly serious. Certain production steps apply to all video making:

1. **Write a shooting script.** A shooting script contains the characters' lines and dialogue. It also contains directions about camera angles, transitions, and descriptions of sets, wardrobe, and props.
2. **Prepare a storyboard** to show a clear sequence of events. A storyboard looks like a comic strip, with each important shot mapped out. Using index cards allows you to rearrange shots easily until you find the sequence that works best.
3. **Select locations for shooting**, and get any necessary permissions to use them.
4. **Cast the roles** and/or parts, and rehearse.
5. **Write a shooting schedule** that includes *who*, *what*, *when*, and *where*. Distribute the schedule to everyone involved.
6. **Film the scenes**.
7. **Edit the video** and store it in a safe place.

▶ **Exercise 16** Producing a Video
Produce a ten-minute documentary about your goals after graduation. Follow the steps outlined above. Use the tips for filming to help you in development and production.

▶ Critical Viewing What type of video do you think these students are viewing? Why? [**Analyze**]

796 • Speaking, Listening, Viewing, and Representing

Technology Tip

This Web site gives many tips on video editing—for beginners as well as for the more experienced: http://www. videonics.com/ Articles.html

Performing and Interpreting

Performance art is one of the most effective and entertaining means of communicating.

KEY CONCEPT Performers use a variety of techniques to convey the meaning of a text. ■

Steps for Preparing an Interpretive Performance

Use the following strategies when preparing for a performance:

1. Carefully review the text. Put yourself in the place of the characters. Consider the tone of the piece, or the attitude the writer takes toward the subject.
2. Practice reading the text aloud several times. Experiment with the volume, tone, and pace of your voice to capture the mood of the piece and to emphasize key lines and ideas.
3. Memorize the text if this is called for in your presentation.
4. Add physical gestures to your performance to enhance the meaning and the mood.
5. If appropriate, find costumes, props, sets, and music to add flavor to your presentation.
6. Rehearse until you feel comfortable doing your presentation.

Exercise 17 Performing for Your Class Select an excerpt from a novel or a soliloquy from a play that you'd like to perform for your class. Think about the mood, tension, comic relief, and appeal of the piece you select. Decide the effect you'd like your performance to have. Then, offer your interpretation of the piece in a dramatic performance.

Reflecting on Your Speaking, Listening, Viewing and Representing

Review the concepts discussed in this chapter. Write a one-page reflection on your experiences, responding to the following questions:

- How might effective speaking and listening benefit me in the different areas of my life—school, work, hobbies, friends, and family?
- How can I use the speaking and listening strategies to improve my skills in these areas?
- What types of media are most effective in providing information?
- What did I learn from my experience of preparing and presenting my own media presentation or performance?

Representing Skills • **797**

Use one of the following strategies to assess mastery of speaking, listening, viewing, and representing skills.

Self-Assessment Ask students to respond to one of the reflecting questions on page 797. You may wish to have students present their responses as speeches to the class or as audio or video presentations.	**Teacher Assessment** You may wish to assign one of the exercises in the chapter as a "final exam" for the chapter. Assess both students' presentations and their skills as critical viewers of their classmates' presentations.

Performing and Interpreting

Teaching Resources: Academic and Workplace Skills Activity Book, p. 12

1. Discuss dramatic interpretations students have watched or been part of. What is the biggest challenge when preparing and performing?
2. Have students each choose an excerpt from a play they read in class. Encourage students to visualize their character or characters and complete the steps on this page.
3. Have students present their readings in small groups. This will provide an intimate, non-threatening setting.

Answer Key

Exercise 17

Remind students to consult the tips for preparing and presenting a speech on page 781.

ASSESS and CLOSE

Speaking, Listening, Viewing, and Representing

Teaching Resources: Formal Assessment, Ch. 28

1. Use one of the Assess Mastery options provided in the Ongoing Assessment Chart.
2. You may wish to use the following options:
   - Review the Standardized Test Preparation Workshop on pages 798–799 and have students complete the practice items.
   - Administer the Chapter 28 assessment to measure students' grasp of the concepts presented.

Lesson Objectives

1. To establish and adjust purpose for reading such as to understand and interpret

2. To respond to informational and aesthetic elements in texts, such as graphic aids

Step-by-Step Teaching Guide

Interpreting Graphic Aids

Teaching Resouces: Standardized Test Preparation Workbook, pp. 55–56

1. Have students read page 798 and study the graph.

2. Ask students the following questions to check that they understand the graph.

   How would you describe the growth in steel production from 1870 through 1910?
   (It rose continually in all three countries, but most rapidly after about 1890.)

   How much steel did each country produce in 1900?
   (Answers are in millions of metric tons. Great Britain: about five; United States: about seven; Germany: about ten.)

3. Ask students to write down two other things they learned from this graph. Have them take turns sharing answers with the class, trying not to duplicate any information.

Standardized Test Preparation Workshop

Interpreting Graphic Aids

Some standardized tests contain questions testing your ability to gather details and draw conclusions from the information provided in maps, charts, graphs, and other graphic aids. The following sample items will help you become familiar with these types of questions.

Test Tip

As you examine each graphic aid, ask yourself what each part of the graphic means or represents in relation to the whole.

Sample Test Items

Directions: Read the passage, study the chart, and answer the questions that follow.

Before Sir Henry Bessemer developed a process to inexpensively produce steel from pig iron (the Bessemer process), industrialized nations produced only a few thousand tons of steel a year. By the end of the 1800's, steel production was measured in the millions.

1 Which of the following lists countries in order of least steel produced to most steel produced in 1890?

   A United States, Germany, Great Britain
   B Germany, Great Britain, United States
   C Great Britain, United States, Germany
   D Germany, United States, Great Britain

2 How is the Bessemer process responsible for the statistics in the chart?

   F The process industrialized nations.
   G It allowed for an inexpensive and easy way to produce steel.
   H It helped provide steel producers with new minerals.
   J It had no influence over the statistics presented in the chart.

Answers and Explanations

Steel Production 1870–1910

Millions of Metric Tons (y-axis: 0, 5, 10, 15, 20, 25, 30)
Year (x-axis: 1870, 1880, 1890, 1900, 1910)

— Germany   — United States
— Great Britain*

* Data for British steel production in 1870 are unavailable.
Source: European Historical Statistics, 1750–1970, and Historical Statistics of the U.S.

The correct answer for item 1 is *B*. In 1890, Germany produced the least steel followed by Great Britain. The United States produced the most of the three countries.

The correct answer for item 2 is *G*. Because the Bessemer process allowed for steel to be produced cheaply and quickly, countries such as Germany, Great Britain, and the United States were able to move steel production from thousands to millions of tons per year.

798 • Speaking, Listening, Viewing, and Representing

⬦ TEST-TAKING TIP

Remind students to read the titles and other headings of all charts and graphs. For instance, in the chart on page 798, it is important to know that steel production is measured in millions, as opposed to hundreds or thousands, of metric tons.

Often, the text that accompanies a chart helps to make it clear. For example, after reading the text in the Sample Item, the students will understand the reasons for the drastic increase in steel production. Remind students to read this text carefully, and to reread it if they are having trouble understanding a graphic aid.

Practice 1 **Directions:** Read the passage, and answer the questions that follow.

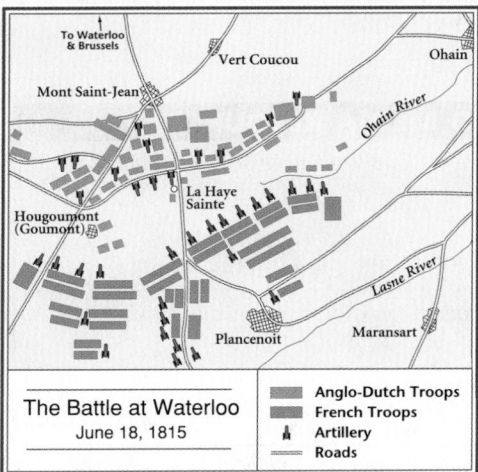

The Battle at Waterloo
June 18, 1815

Anglo-Dutch Troops
French Troops
Artillery
Roads

In 1793, France declared war on Britain. Thus began a series of wars that would go on for twenty-two years, ending only when Britain and its allies defeated Napoleon at the Battle of Waterloo in 1815. A crucial moment in that battle came when one of Napoleon's officers, Marshal Ney, captured the farmhouse of La Haye Sainte. Even so, the Duke of Wellington was still able to lead British and Prussian troops to victory.

1 The British stationed most troops—
   A in major cities
   B along riverbanks
   C around the farmhouse
   D along roads

2 Where is La Haye Sainte farmhouse located in relation to the British troops?
   F It is near the major artillery.
   G It is located at the center of the troops.
   H It is where the British leaders are residing.
   J It is located near most British troops.

3 Why would it have been to France's advantage to hold the farmhouse?
   A They could block the road from advancement and divide British troops.
   B They could disable artillery.
   C They could capture British troops.
   D It meant they won the battle.

4 Which statement about the artillery is true?
   F The British had more artillery than the French.
   G The British artillery was more effectively placed than the French artillery.
   H The French had more artillery than the British.
   J The French artillery was pointed in the wrong direction.

5 What town is at the crossroads that is cut off from the French troops?
   A Maransart
   B Ohain
   C Mont Saint-Jean
   D Plancenoit

Answer Key

▶ **Practice 1**

1. D
2. J
3. A
4. H
5. C

Customize for
Spatial Learners

Challenge students to make a map like the one of the Battle at Waterloo. They might make a map of the town and include things such as schools, parks, and major landmarks. They might have to do some research in the local interest section of your library to learn about the town's boundaries.

Customize for
AP Students

Have students do some research on the life of Napoleon or the Duke of Wellington. They might present their findings to the class in the form of a short speech with visual aids.

Time and Resource Manager

In-Depth Lesson Plan

	LESSON FOCUS	PRINT AND MEDIA RESOURCES
DAY 1	**Developing Vocabulary** Students learn strategies for developing vocabulary, such as wide reading, context clues, connotation and denotation, and analogies. (pp. 800–804/⊞600–604)	*Teaching Resources* *Academic and Workplace Skills Activity Book,* pp. 13–16
DAY 2	**Studying Words Systematically; Studying Word Parts and Origins** Students learn and apply strategies for studying vocabulary words. (pp. 805–811/⊞605–611)	*Teaching Resources* *Academic and Workplace Skills Activity Book,* pp. 17–22
DAY 3	**Improving Your Spelling** Students learn strategies for improving spelling, such as studying problem words, keeping a spelling notebook, and applying spelling rules. (pp. 812–816/⊞612–616)	*Teaching Resources* *Academic and Workplace Skills Activity Book,* pp. 23–25
DAY 4	**Improving Your Spelling** *continued* Students learn and apply strategies for improving spelling and for proofreading carefully. (pp. 816–821/⊞616–621)	*Teaching Resources* *Academic and Workplace Skills Activity Book,* pp. 26–28; *Formal Assessment,* Ch. 29

Accelerated Lesson Plan

	LESSON FOCUS	PRINT AND MEDIA RESOURCES
DAY 1	**Developing Vocabulary** Students learn and apply strategies for developing vocabulary. (pp. 800–804/⊞600–604)	*Teaching Resources* *Academic and Workplace Skills Activity Book,* pp. 13–16
DAY 2	**Studying Words Systematically; Studying Word Parts and Origins** Students learn and apply strategies for studying vocabulary words. (pp. 805–811/⊞605–611)	*Teaching Resources* *Academic and Workplace Skills Activity Book,* pp. 17–22
DAY 3	**Improving Your Spelling** Students learn and apply strategies for improving spelling and for proofreading carefully. (pp. 812–821/⊞612–621)	*Teaching Resources* *Academic and Workplace Skills Activity Book,* pp. 23–29; *Formal Assessment,* Ch. 29

Options for Adapting Lesson Plans

HOMEWORK

Have students complete any section of the chapter for homework.

FEATURES

Extend coverage with the Standardized Test Preparation Workshop (pp. 822–823).

TECHNOLOGY

Students may use the Internet to conduct independent research. Have them print out their completed work.

Writing and Grammar Handbook Alignment

Page numbers in Step-by-Step Teaching Guides in this Teacher's Edition refer to pages from the full student text. Handbook page references, indicated with this icon Ⓗ, are provided in Time and Resource Manager boxes and at the bottom of each Teacher's Edition page.

INTEGRATED SKILLS COVERAGE

Viewing and Representing Skills
Critical Viewing, SE pp. 800, 803, 805, 811, 820/Ⓗ600, 603, 605, 611, 620

Technology Skills
SE pp. 805, 810, 819/Ⓗ605, 610, 619

Reading Skills
ATE p. 803

Writing Skills
ATE p. 817

Study Skills
ATE pp. 805, 806

Research Skills
SE pp. 804, 811, 813/Ⓗ604, 611, 613

ASSESSMENT SUPPORT

Standardized Test Preparation Workshop SE p. 822; ATE p. 806
Standardized Test Preparation Workbook, pp. 57–58
Formal Assessment, Ch. 29

MEETING INDIVIDUAL NEEDS

Less Advanced Students ATE pp. 805, 809, 818, 823. See also Ongoing Assessment ATE p. 803.
AP Students ATE pp. 803, 808, 815
ESL Students ATE pp. 802, 806, 813, 815, 818, 823
Linguistic Learners ATE pp. 804, 817
Interpersonal Learners ATE p. 807

BLOCK SCHEDULING

Pacing Suggestions
For 90-minute Blocks
• Have students complete the strategies for developing vocabulary and studying words in a single period.
• Focus one class period on spelling strategies and proofreading carefully.

Professional Development Support
• *How to Manage Instruction in the Block* This teaching resource provides management and activity suggestions.

MEDIA AND TECHNOLOGY

For the Student
• *On-line Exercise Bank,* Section 17.1

For the Teacher
• Teacher**EXPRESS** CD-ROM

WRITING AND GRAMMAR ON-LINE

Interactive Text (On-line or on CD-ROM)
• Easily navigable instruction with interactive Revision Checkers
• Full use of e-rater™, the essay-scoring system (on-line only)

Companion Web Site PHSchool.com
• Scoring rubrics with models (use Web Code egk-1201)

See the Go On-line! **feature, SE p. iii.**

Lesson Objectives

1. To expand vocabulary through wide reading, listening, and discussing

2. To rely on context to determine meanings of words

3. To read and understand analogies

4. To organize and record new information in systematic ways such as notes, charts, and graphic organizers

5. To use reference material such as glossary, dictionary, thesaurus, and available technology to determine precise meanings and usage

6. To apply meanings of prefixes, roots, and suffixes in order to comprehend

7. To research word origins as an aid to understanding meanings, derivations, and spellings

Critical Viewing

Interpret Most students will say that the girl is practicing a form of written communication. Perhaps she is writing a letter or a diary entry.

Chapter 29 Vocabulary and Spelling

▲ Critical Viewing
What kind of communication is this girl practicing in this photograph? [Interpret]

Developing a good vocabulary and improving your spelling skills can help you be more successful in school and in the work world. With a good vocabulary at your command, you can express yourself clearly and communicate exactly the meaning you intend, whether you are speaking or writing. In addition, any reading that you do will be accomplished more quickly and be more enjoyable. When you utilize good spelling, your written communications will be more effective and persuasive because your readers can concentrate on your ideas and information and not be distracted by mistakes.

The keys to building vocabulary and spelling skills are extensive reading and the use of proper reference sources. In addition, use whichever memory techniques suit you best.

800 • Vocabulary and Spelling

⏱ TIME AND RESOURCE MANAGER

Resources
Print: *Academic and Workplace Skills Activity Book*, pp. 13–16

Using the Full Student Edition	Using the Handbook🔲
• Read and discuss pp. 800–804 in class. • Have students work on Exercises 1–3 in class.	• Read and discuss pp. 600–604 in class. • Have students work on Exercises 1–3 in class.

Section 29.1 Developing Vocabulary

Listening, Discussing, and Reading

Your vocabulary is a tool that you will use throughout your life. You use words to communicate: to express yourself, to impart information, to receive information, and to persuade people. The more control you have over your vocabulary, the more effective your communication will be.

Learn Through Conversation For most people, the process of learning new vocabulary starts with hearing words and using them in conversation. This a process that begins in childhood and continues throughout your life. Most of the words you learned as a toddler you heard in conversation. You learned the meanings and pronunciations of new words by listening to family members, teachers, and friends. Then, you used the words. Keep up this process throughout your life. Listen for unfamiliar words whenever you talk to teachers or other adults, people from different backgrounds, or those whose interests and ideas are different from your own. If you don't know a word you hear, think about how it is used, ask about its meaning, or look it up in a dictionary.

Learn From Works Read Aloud Have you ever listened to a book on audiocassette or CD? If you have, then you have discovered another good way to build your vocabulary. The authors or actors reading the works will introduce you to new words and demonstrate how they are pronounced. You can use context clues from the reading to help determine a new word's meaning. You can reinforce the vocabulary-building process by reading a printed copy of the work while it is being read aloud. In that way, you can see and hear new words at the same time.

Learn From Your Reading Most important of all, keep reading. The more you read, the more new words you will encounter. Meeting the same new word several different times will help you become familiar with it. In addition, try to read a variety of materials in many different subject areas. Magazine articles or Internet pages on scientific topics will introduce you to valuable new words. So will newspaper articles about politics and current events. Read from a variety of sources to encounter a wide variety of words.

When you encounter an unfamiliar word in your reading, sometimes you may not have to use a dictionary to discover what it means. You can make inferences about its meaning by looking at the surrounding words.

Developing Vocabulary • 801

PREPARE and ENGAGE

Interest GRABBER Have students meet with partners and teach one another new words. Have them work together to develop ways to remember the word, such as funny mnemonic devices or repetition. Have students share with the class their new words and their strategies for memorizing them.

Activate Prior Knowledge

Write this sentence on the board.

The ominous clouds indicate bad weather for tomorrow.

Ask students to define the underlined word (threatening, sinister). Ask them about the clues they used. Explain that these are called *context clues*. Ask students to name other methods they know for learning new words.

TEACH

Step-by-Step Teaching Guide

Developing Vocabulary

1. Ask students to recall and share the last time they learned a word through conversation.

2. Other than the three methods listed on this page, can students name other methods they use for developing their vocabulary? Students may suggest studying word lists for standardized tests such as the SAT, playing word games, or pursuing a new hobby or interest.

3. Discuss with students whether they consider it important to have a good vocabulary. Explain that a good vocabulary can help them when they read, write, speak, and listen—activities they take part in every day.

☑ ONGOING ASSESSMENT: Diagnose

Use one of the following options to diagnose students' current level of proficiency in vocabulary and spelling skills.

Option 1 Ask students to select a short piece from their portfolios. Have them read it and circle every spelling error they notice. Students who have many mistakes, or who have difficulty noticing their mistakes, will need extra support in spelling skills.	**Option 2** Ask students to explain in writing how they would go about studying for a ten-word vocabulary test at the end of this week. What specific strategies would they use? Students who have trouble with this exercise will need extra support in strategies for studying new words.

Recognizing Context Clues

Teaching Resources: Academic and Workplace Skills Activity Book, p. 13

1. Discuss the three types of context clues on p. 802.

2. Teach students a new word, such as *threnody*, which means "a song of lamentation." Working in pairs, have students write three sentences that include the word. Each sentence should contain a different type of context clue. Have students share their sentences.

3. Have students brainstorm for examples of figurative language as a context clue. (Example: It was a *sultry* day; I felt like I was in a sauna.) Ask for volunteers to share their sentences with the class.

4. Have students repeat the exercise, using idioms instead of figurative language. If necessary, brainstorm with the class for a list of idioms before they begin this exercise.

Customize for
ESL Students

Encourage students to bring in a difficult paragraph from a textbook they are reading in another class. Have them underline the unfamiliar words and then work with partners to use context clues to try to determine their meanings.

Answer Key

▶ **Exercise 1**

1. honoree; award winner
2. having to do with the branch of surgery dealing with deformities, disease, and injuries of the bone;
3. created or investigated something new
4. new methods or devices
5. artificial limbs

29.1

Using Context

Recognizing Context Clues If you look carefully at the sentence or paragraph that contains an unfamiliar word, you can sometimes figure out its meaning by using clues from the author. These are called *context clues.*

▶ **KEY CONCEPT** The **context** of a word is the group of words that surround it. ■

Figurative Language Writers often use figurative language to create "word pictures" in a reader's mind. Many times, the writers use familiar words in unfamiliar ways. You might encounter the sentence: "Janice stared at him angrily, her face a thundercloud." You know that a thundercloud comes before a storm, so you know that Janice's face is gloomy and threatening.

Idioms An idiom is an expression that takes on a special meaning different from the words in the idiom. For example, *let off steam* means to release emotion, not vapor. Use context clues to figure out the meanings of idioms. Compare unfamiliar idioms with expressions that you use to convey a similar meaning.

Technical Terms Material in your school reading, lectures, and research often includes technical words. You will find unfamiliar words and familiar words with unfamiliar meanings. For example, you know several meanings for the word *cast.* In geology, however, a *cast* is a fossil in which the space left behind in a rock by an organism has filled in, showing the same shape as the organism. Use context to determine the meaning of such words. Keep a special section of your notebook in each subject area for listing new words, along with their meanings and pronunciations. Use the glossary at the back of many textbooks to find meanings specific to a subject area.

▶ **Exercise 1** Recognizing Context Clues Use context clues to determine the meaning of each underlined word in the passage below. Check your answers in a dictionary.

Dr. Sandra Sisson, recently named Doctor of the Year, works at the Bronx Family Hospital in New York. The fifty-year-old (1) <u>laureate</u> has been chief of (2) <u>orthopedic</u> medicine for more than fifteen years. She does more than set broken bones at the hospital. The inventive doctor has (3) <u>broken new ground</u> with such (4) <u>innovations</u> as computerized (5) <u>prostheses</u>, or artificial limbs, that do more than respond to wearers' nerve impulses.

▶ **More Practice**

Academic and Workplace Skills Activity Book
• pp. 13–14

Denotation and Connotation

Denotation is the objective meaning of a word—that to which a word refers, independent of other associations the word calls to mind. Dictionaries list the denotative meanings of words. The *connotation* of a word refers to the associations that a word calls to mind in addition to its dictionary meaning.

▶ **KEY CONCEPTS** The **denotation** of a word is its literal definition. Its **connotations** include the ideas, images, and feelings that are associated with the word in people's minds. ■

For example, the words *home* and *domicile* have the same dictionary meaning. However, *home* has positive connotations of warmth and security, whereas *domicile* does not.

▶ **Exercise 2** Discriminating Between Denotation and Connotation Read each pair of sentences below. For each pair, write a sentence explaining the different connotations of the underlined words. Use a dictionary to help you.
1. We have a large stone fireplace in our <u>home</u>.
   We have a large stone fireplace in our <u>residence</u>.
2. He welcomed the <u>beggar</u> into his house.
   He welcomed the <u>panhandler</u> into his house.
3. Marsha thinks that her sister is extremely <u>stubborn</u>.
   Marsha thinks that her sister is extremely <u>headstrong</u>.
4. In order to succeed in business, you must be <u>aggressive</u>.
   In order to succeed in business, you must be <u>domineering</u>.
5. Behind the diner, the dumpster is quite <u>malodorous</u>.
   Behind the diner, the dumpster is quite <u>stinky</u>.

▶ Critical Viewing Write two sentences describing this photograph. In one, use words with a positive connotation; in the other, put a more negative slant on it. [Apply]

Developing Vocabulary • **803**

Denotation and Connotation

Teaching Resources: Academic and Workplace Skills Activity Book, p. 14

1. Point out that the context can help determine a word's meaning. The connotation can then help determine the writer's tone and aid in understanding the meaning of the whole passage.

2. Tell students that in many cases, experience and context are the only ways to determine subtle differences between words with similar meanings, but generally the dictionary will be their greatest ally, giving definitions and, sometimes, synonyms.

Customize for
AP Students

Tell students that a good source for new words is the editorial page of *The New York Times* and other well-respected newspapers. Encourage them to read these pages to learn new words and to keep up with current events.

Answer Key

▶ **Exercise 2**

Responses will vary. In item 1, *home* is more personal and positive. In items 2–4, *beggar*, *stubborn*, and *domineering* are harsher and more negative. In item 5, *malodorous* is more formal.

Integrating Reading Skills

Ask students to pick a hobby that interests them, such as computers, sailing, or fly-fishing, and read about it in the library or on the Internet. As students read, they should jot down unfamiliar vocabulary words. Have them look up the definitions and group these words into logical categories.

Critical Viewing

Apply Sample sentences: These students are working hard on their assignments. These students are slaving away at a tedious task.

☑ **ONGOING ASSESSMENT: Monitor and Reinforce**

Help students learn new words in other content areas by using one of the following options.

Option 1 If possible, meet with other teachers and ask them to give you short lists of vocabulary words your students will need to learn in their classes. Use some of these terms in vocabulary exercises and quizzes.	**Option 2** Once a week, bring in an interesting editorial from your local newspaper. Read it with the class and keep a list of new words students learn while reading it. This will help students learn words relating to politics, economics, science, and more.

Recognizing Related Words

Teaching Resources: Academic and Workplace Skills Activity Book, p. 15

1. Explain to students that it is helpful to group together words that have similar meanings. For example, have them list as many synonyms as possible for *talkative* (*garrulous, loquacious, verbose, prolix*).

2. This is a useful memory aid because students can memorize one definition and a list of words rather than many words and many definitions.

3. Give students a few other words, and have them come up with a list of synonyms for each. Have them record these lists in their vocabulary notebooks.

Analogies

Teaching Resources: Academic and Workplace Skills Activity Book, p. 16

1. Tell students that *analogy* means "a relation of similarity between one thing and another, either entirely or partially." Analogy tests require that students identify the relationship between two words and then select another pair of words that has the same relationship.

2. Remind students that they must identify the relationship between the given pair of words as precisely as possible.

3. Review the list of common analogy relationships and have students work in pairs to brainstorm for examples of each type of relationship.

Customize for
Linguistic Learners

Tell students to read aloud the original word pair in the form of a sentence. For example, in Exercise 3, they should say "*Malevolent* is to *kind* as . . ." This will remind them of the structure and purpose of the analogy form.

29.1

Recognizing Related Words

You can increase your vocabulary by recognizing related words that may be similar or opposite in meaning.

> **KEY CONCEPT** **Synonyms** are words that are similar in meaning. **Antonyms** are words that are opposite in meaning. ■

Synonyms For example, if you want to remember the meaning of *evocative*, it is easier to remember its synonym, "suggestive," than it is to memorize a long definition.

Antonyms For example, if you want to recall that *pungent* means "sharp and stimulating to the mind and senses," it would be easier to remember that its antonym is *bland*.

Finding Relationships in Analogies

Working with analogies, or word relationships, leads you to look for connections between word meanings. The way to solve analogies is to form a clear idea of the relationship between the initial pair of words. In the example below, the relationship is *part to whole*—a *rim* is a part of a *wheel*.

EXAMPLE: RIM : WHEEL ::
                     a. house : apartment   c. singer : choir
                     b. molecule : atom

The pair that expresses a similar relationship is choice *c*.

Other common analogy relationships include *synonym, antonym, type, defining characteristic, instrument used for a purpose, degree, sequence,* and *proximity*.

> **Exercise 3** **Working With Analogies** Identify the relationship of the capitalized pair in each item below. Then, choose the lettered pair that best expresses the same relationship.
>
> 1. MALEVOLENT : KIND ::
>   a. despair : sadness   c. masculine : virile
>   b. famous : unknown
> 2. HUMOR : COMEDIAN ::
>   a. finish line : runner   c. intelligence : genius
>   b. lecture : teacher
> 3. DISLIKE : LOATHE ::
>   a. agree : argue   c. tap : wallop
>   b. entire : whole
> 4. RULER : LENGTH ::
>   a. altimeter : height   c. calculator : problem
>   b. race : mile
> 5. NEARBY : ADJOINING ::
>   a. ocean : shore   c. perpendicular : parallel
>   b. noisy : stentorious

804 • Vocabulary and Spelling

> **Research Tip**

Find a standardized test-preparation book in the school library or guidance office. Practice working with the analogies included in the book.

> **More Practice**

Academic and Workplace Skills Activity Book
• pp. 15–16

Answer Key

> **Exercise 3**

1. antonym, b
2. defining characteristic, c
3. degree, c
4. instrument, a
5. synonym, b

Section 29.2

Studying Words Systematically

Remembering Vocabulary Words

This section will introduce you to several different methods for listing and studying the new words you find in your school and personal reading. Find the method that works best for you, and follow it regularly.

KEY CONCEPT A vocabulary notebook will help you to learn new words. You can use the notebook, flashcards, and a tape recorder to help you review. Study and review new words a few times each week. ■

Set Up a Vocabulary Notebook Keep a section in each of your subject's notebooks for vocabulary words. On the top of each page in the section, write the chapter or book title. Divide your page into three columns that cover the *words* you want to learn, hints or *bridge words* that help you remember their meanings, and their *definitions.*

Exercise 4 Setting Up a Vocabulary Notebook Select one of your current textbooks or a book you are reading for pleasure that contains new words or terms. As you read, jot down any unfamiliar words or expressions. When you have finished a chapter, look up unfamiliar words in a dictionary or the glossary (if you are studying a textbook). Record "bridge" words and the meanings of new words in your notebook. Then, write a sentence using each word.

◉ Technology Tip

Find a short entry in an on-line encyclopedia about an unfamiliar subject. Find several related words, and prepare a categorized table for your notebook.

▶ Critical Viewing What tools might this student be using to study vocabulary words? [Infer]

Studying Words Systematically • 805

Step-by-Step Teaching Guide

Remembering Vocabulary Words

Teaching Resources: Academic and Workplace Skills Activity Book, p. 18

1. Have students practice using *bridge words* to remember definitions. Explain that a bridge word should be a simple, vivid word that sparks the memory of the longer or more involved definition.

2. Give students the following words and definitions. Have them come up with bridge words for each.

   noisome: unwholesome or offensive (gross)

   bellicose: hostile or quarrelsome (warlike)

Customize for *Less Advanced Students*

Have students work in pairs and read a page from a textbook chapter they are working on in another class. Have them write down a list of unfamiliar words, look up their definitions, and brainstorm for a bridge word for each.

Answer Key

Exercise 4

Answers will vary. Remind students to choose bridge words that are relevant, vivid, and memorable as they set up their vocabulary notebooks.

Integrating Study Skills

Remind students to be careful to spell words correctly when they list them in their vocabulary notebooks. They will refer to this notebook often, so they will want to make sure its content is accurate.

Critical Viewing

Infer Students may mention reference books, dictionaries, glossaries, and so on.

⏱ TIME AND RESOURCE MANAGER

Resources
Print: *Academic and Workplace Skills Activity Book*, pp. 17–18

Using the Full Student Edition	Using the Handbook🄷
• Read and discuss pp. 805–807 in class.	• Read and discuss pp. 605–607 in class.
• Work on Exercises 4–5 in class.	• Work on Exercises 4–5 in class.
• Discuss the types of reference aids listed on p. 807. To reinforce the material, assign Exercise 6.	• Discuss the types of reference aids listed on p. 607. To reinforce the material, assign Exercise 6.

Studying New Words

1. Remind students that their sentences must provide information about the vocabulary word. For example, "The man was *raucous*" does not give any hints about what *raucous* might mean. "We thought the man was *raucous* because he was so loud" clearly conveys its meaning.

2. Explain to students that they will not feel comfortable with every strategy on this page. Encourage them to try them all and decide which one they find the most effective.

3. Encourage students to express their opinions about the advantages and disadvantages of each method.

Integrating Study Skills

Tell students they will have a vocabulary quiz on the words in Exercise 5 in three days. Discuss the best ways to study for this quiz. What strategy will they use?

Customize for
ESL Students

If they choose to make vocabulary flashcards, encourage students to include definitions in both English and their first language.

Answer Key

▶ **Exercise 5**

1. *crescendo*: a gradual increase in loudness
2. *scarcity*: inadequate supply; dearth
3. *innocuous*: harmless
4. *cajole*: to coax with flattery; wheedle
5. *odious*: arousing or deserving hatred
6. *valor*: bravery; courage
7. *sundry*: several; various
8. *intemperance*: lack of self-control or moderation; excess
9. *credulous*: easily deceived
10. *harbingers*: forerunners; those that announce another's arrival

---

29.2

Studying New Words

Make studying vocabulary a part of your daily activities. Set aside a regular time, such as before you begin your other assignments, to review new words. Use one or more of the following methods to review:

Using Your Notebook Use a book or your hand to cover the definition of a word, and try to remember the meaning by looking at the word and the bridge word. Then, uncover the definition and read it. You can also write sentences with your new vocabulary words. Reinforce the meaning of the word by using its definition in the sentence to give your memory an extra boost.

EXAMPLE: We thought the man was *raucous* because he was so *loud*.

Using Flashcards Use index cards to create your own vocabulary flashcards. On the front of a card, write a word you want to remember. On the back, write its definition. Flip through the cards, and try to supply the definitions, or have a friend test you. Add difficult words to your vocabulary notebook.

Using a Tape Recorder It might be easier for you to learn the definitions of new words when you hear them. If you have a tape recorder, record vocabulary words one at a time. Leave a space of about ten seconds after you record a word, and then record the definition for that word. Continue in this way with all your words. Replay the tape. Try to supply the definition of each word during the space that follows it. Repeat the exercise until you can give the definitions easily. Listen to the tape a few times each week.

Setting Goals Try to memorize new words in small groups each week, so you won't become discouraged. Take five unfamiliar words, and enter them in your notebook. Test yourself on them. Each week, add five more words.

▶ **Exercise 5** Making Flashcards or Tapes Make a set of flashcards or tapes to study the words below. Add more words from your own reading or from assigned vocabulary lists.

1. crescendo
2. scarcity
3. innocuous
4. cajole
5. odious
6. valor
7. sundry
8. intemperance
9. credulous
10. harbingers

✎ STANDARDIZED TEST PREPARATION WORKSHOP

Analogies Standardized test questions may require students to demonstrate their understanding of analogies. Provide students with the opportunity to practice this skill.

Choose the lettered pair that has the same relationship as the capitalized words.

MERCURIAL: FICKLE

A humid: arid
B electron: proton
C diligent: perfection
D elaborate: complex

Students should recognize that *mercurial* and *fickle* are synonyms and that **D** is the correct choice. Students should also recognize that A contains antonyms, and B and C both contain related terms.

Using Reference Aids

Two valuable resources available for building your vocabulary are a dictionary and a thesaurus. You may also have other printed and electronic resources available to help you.

> **KEY CONCEPT** Use a dictionary to find the meaning, spelling, pronunciation, and origin of words. Use a thesaurus to find words that more precisely express your meaning. ■

Using a Dictionary It is a good idea to keep a dictionary nearby to study the pronunciation of a word, note its part of speech, and learn its different definitions or meanings. In addition, most dictionaries provide the origins of a word. Knowing a word's history can help you make associations with other words that share the origin.

Using a Thesaurus A thesaurus provides words with meanings that are the same as, or similar to, the word you are looking up. It may also provide words that reflect subtle differences in meaning. A thesaurus is helpful when you have used the same word repeatedly in your writing and need to vary your writing. You should check the definition in a dictionary to make sure that the new word gives the exact meaning you want.

Using a Synonym Finder Many word-processing programs include on-line synonym finders. While you are writing a draft, you can highlight a word for which you want to find a synonym and use the finder to check alternative words.

Using a Glossary Many textbooks contain a glossary listing terms and definitions specific to the textbook's field of study. Locate the glossary in your textbooks, and use it to help you define the new words in each book.

Using Software Like most references, dictionaries and thesauruses are available in electronic form. Some can be purchased and loaded onto your computer's hard drive, while others are available on the Internet.

> **Exercise 6** Using Vocabulary Reference Aids Look up each of the following words in the references indicated. Compare and contrast the information found in each source.
> 1. orbit (dictionary, science textbook glossary)
> 2. society (social studies textbook glossary, dictionary)
> 3. volatile (dictionary, thesaurus)
> 4. permeate (science textbook glossary, on-line thesaurus)
> 5. precipitous (dictionary, thesaurus)

> **More Practice**
> Academic and
> Workplace Skills
> Activity Book
> • pp. 17–18

Using Reference Aids

Teaching Resources: Academic and Workplace Skills Activity Book, p. 17

1. Make sure students can explain the difference between a dictionary and a thesaurus. For a vivid illustration of the differences, have them look up a single word in both sources and compare their results.

2. Ask students how using a thesaurus might improve their writing. (It can help them convey meanings more precisely; it can help them avoid repetition.)

3. Remind students that not every synonym for a word has the same connotation. For example, *content* and *ecstatic* are both synonyms of *happy*, but they have very different connotations. Students should keep this in mind when looking for synonyms in a thesaurus.

Customize for
Interpersonal Learners

After students complete Exercise 6, organize the class into small groups to compare the information they found in each source. In each group, have interpersonal learners lead a discussion of the results. Have them summarize the main points from their groups and share them with the class.

Answer Key

> **Exercise 6**

Answers will vary. Students should note that dictionary definitions are more complete and general than those found in textbook glossaries and often include such information as etymologies and examples. A thesaurus will provide synonyms and related words but not complete definitions.

Using Roots

Teaching Resources: Academic and Workplace Skills Activity Book, p. 20

1. Ask students to explain why understanding roots is important. (Roots offer clues to the meanings of words. They can make unfamiliar words somewhat familiar.)

2. Write *aero* on the board. Explain that this Greek root means "air; of the air; of gas or gases." Write some examples on the board of words that use the root *aero* (*aerobic, aerospace, aerobatics*).

3. Have students think of additional words that contain the roots in the chart on this page.

4. Ask students to give examples of more word roots and at least two words than contain each root.

Customize for
AP Students

Ask students to research other Latin and Greek roots using a variety of sources, such as the dictionary and the Internet. Working independently or in pairs, they can create a chart showing these roots and related words.

Answer Key

▶ **Exercise 7**

1. *intercede*: to intervene
   proceed: to advance or go on
   cedere: to go
2. *legible*: readable
   logical: adhering to the principles of correct reasoning
   legere: to read, see
3. *conscious*: having a feeling or knowledge
   science: the state or fact of knowledge
   scire: to know
4. *tenant*: a person who pays rent to use a space
   retain: to hold or keep in possession
   tenere: to hold
5. *convert*: transform
   diversion: a turning aside
   vertere: to change, turn

▶ **Exercise 8**

1. d   2. e   3. c   4. a   5. b

Studying Word Parts and Origins

Using Roots

The base of a word is its *root*. By learning the meaning of a root, you will have a clue to defining a whole group of related words. For example, if you know the root *puls* (or *pel*) means "drive," you have a key to the meaning of words such as *impulse, repel, propeller, expel, appellate, expulsion,* and *propulsion.*

▶ **KEY CONCEPT** A **root** is the base of a word. Many roots come originally from Latin or Greek words. ∎

TEN COMMON ROOTS

Root and Origin	Meaning	Examples
-chron- [Gr.]	time	chronicle
-manu- [L.]	hand	manuscript
-mono- [Gr.]	single, alone	monologue
-plic- (-pli-, -ploy-) [L.]	to fold	explicate, pliant, employer, reply
-port- [L.]	to carry	transport
-quir- (-ques-, -quis-) [L.]	to ask, say	require, request, inquisition
-sens- (-sent-, -senti-) [L.]	to feel	sensible, resent, sentiment
-tend- (-tens-, -tent-) [L.]	to stretch	pretend, tense, extent
-top- [Gr.]	place	topographer
-vad- (-vas-) [L.]	to go	pervade, evasive

▶ **Exercise 7** Finding Common Roots Look up each pair of words in a dictionary, paying close attention to their roots. Then, write the basic meaning shared by each pair of words.

1. intercede, proceed
2. legible, logical
3. conscious, science
4. tenant, retain
5. convert, diversion

▶ **Exercise 8** Using Roots to Define Words Using the chart to check the italicized roots, select the definition that matches the word. Check your answers in a dictionary.

1. U*top*ia
2. *port*able
3. com*plic*ate
4. con*sens*us
5. *manu*al

a. feelings held by many people
b. operated by hand
c. to make difficult
d. an imaginary place
e. capable of being carried

808 • Vocabulary and Spelling

⏱ TIME AND RESOURCE MANAGER

Resources
Print: *Academic and Workplace Skills Activity Book*, pp. 19–22

Using the Full Student Edition	Using the Handbook⊞
• Read pp. 808–811 in class. • After reading and discussing each topic, have students complete the related exercise in class.	• Read pp. 608–611 in class. • After reading and discussing each topic, have students complete the related exercise in class.

Using Prefixes

Many prefixes used in English come from the Latin, Greek, and the Anglo-Saxon languages.

KEY CONCEPT A **prefix** is added at the beginning of a word to change its meaning or to form a new word. ∎

Learn the meanings and origins of the prefixes below. The abbreviations *L., Gr.,* and *AS.* mean *Latin, Greek,* and *Anglo-Saxon*, the languages from which the prefixes have come.

TEN COMMON PREFIXES		
Prefix and Origin	**Meaning**	**Examples**
ad- (ac-, af-, al-, ap-, as-, at-) [L.]	to, toward	*ad*here, *ac*cede, *a*spect, *at*tend
com- (co-, col-, con-, cor-) [L.]	with, together	*com*rade, *col*lapse, *con*fer, *cor*relate
epi- [Gr.]	on, upon, over	*epi*demic
hyper- [Gr.]	above, excessive	*hyper*bole
mal- [L.]	bad, wrongful	*mal*function
mis- [AS.]	wrong	*mis*trial
pre- [L.]	before	*pre*date
sub- (suc-, suf-, sup-) L.	beneath, under, below	*sub*conscious, *suc*cession, *suf*fer
syn- (syl-, sym-, sys-) [Gr.]	with, together, at the same time	*syn*thesis, *syl*lable, *sym*pathy, *sys*tem
un- [AS.]	not	*un*forgivable

Exercise 9 Defining Words With Prefixes Using your knowledge of prefixes, try to match each word on the left with its definition on the right. Check your answers in a dictionary.

1. unerring   a. foul smelling
2. synergy   b. exact or not wrong
3. subvert   c. cooperative action
4. preamble   d. introduction
5. malodorous   e. undermine

Exercise 10 Defining Prefixes and Prefix Origins Using a dictionary, write the definition of each prefix and its origin. Then, provide a word that contains each prefix. Define the words you list in a way that incorporates the meaning of the prefix.

1. *anti-*   4. *super-*
2. *in- (il-, im-, ir-)*   5. *ob- (o-, oc-, of-, op-)*
3. *over-*

More Practice

Academic and Workplace Skills Activity Book
• pp. 19–20

Step-by-Step Teaching Guide

Using Prefixes

Teaching Resources: Academic and Workplace Skills Activity Book, p. 19

1. Discuss the prefixes shown in the chart on this page. Challenge students to come up with more words that contain each prefix.

2. Have students brainstorm for examples of other common prefixes and examples of words that contain them.

Customize for
Less Advanced Students

If students do not know the meanings of any prefix in Exercise 9, have them look them up and record them in a "prefix list" in their vocabulary notebooks.

Answer Key

Exercise 9

1. b
2. c
3. e
4. d
5. a

Exercise 10

1. *anti-*: Greek prefix meaning "against or opposed to," as in *antislavery*
2. *in- (il-, im-, ir-)*: Latin prefix meaning "no, not, or without," as in *incorrect*
3. *over-*: related to the Latin prefix *super* and means "above or superior to," as in *overcooked*
4. *super-*: Latin prefix meaning "above or on top of," as in *superior*
5. *ob- (o-, oc-, of-, op-)*: Latin prefix meaning "toward, before, or in front of," as in *obtrude*

Using Suffixes

Teaching Resources: Academic and Workplace Skills Activity Book, p. 21

1. Read and discuss the suffixes listed in the chart. Have students think of words that contain each suffix.

2. Challenge students to think of more examples of commonly used suffixes. Can they think of words that contain each suffix?

Answer Key

> **Exercise 11**

1. *-esque*: from French, used to form adjectives meaning "like or in the style of," as in *Romanesque*
2. *-ism*: from Greek, used to form nouns meaning "the act, practice, or result of," as in *terrorism*
3. *-or*: from various sources (Middle English, Old French), used to form nouns meaning "a person or thing that," as in *inventor*, a person who invents
4. *-ant (-ent)*: from Latin, used to form adjectives meaning "has, shows, or does," as in *defiant*; *-ant* is also used to form nouns meaning "a person or thing that," as in *occupant*, a person that occupies
5. *-ance*: from French, used to form nouns meaning "an act or fact of ___ing," such as *utterance*, which is an act of uttering; also "a quality or state of being ___ed," such as *inheritance*, which is something being inherited.

> **Exercise 12**

1. graphology, *noun*
2. motive, *noun*
3. capture, *verb*
4. positioned, *verb*
5. laughable, *adjective*

29.3

Using Suffixes

A suffix is added to the end of a word. It often alters the part of speech: For example, if you add the suffix *-ion* to the verb *predict*, you form the noun *prediction*.

> **KEY CONCEPT** A **suffix** is a syllable or group of syllables added to the end of a root or word to form a new word. ■

The chart below lists suffixes, their forms, origins, meanings, and words containing each suffix. The abbreviations *L.*, *Gr.*, and *AS.* mean *Latin*, *Greek*, and *Anglo-Saxon*.

TEN COMMON SUFFIXES

Suffix and Origin	Meaning and Examples	Part of Speech
-ac (-ic) [Gr.]	characteristic of; relating to: *posaic*	noun or adjective
-al [L.]	like, suitable for: *comical*	adjective
-ary (-ery) [L.]	pertaining to, connected to: *surgery*	noun or adjective
-cy (-acy) Gr.	condition of: *hesitancy*	noun
-ish [AS.]	of, tending to: *stylish*	adjective
-ive [L.]	tending; a person who: *detective*	noun or adjective
-ize (-ise) [Gr.]	to make: *improvise*	verb
-ly [AS.]	in a certain way: *deliberately*	adjective or adverb
-tion (-ion, -sion, -ation, -ition) [L.]	the action or state of: *friction, motion*	noun
-ure [L.]	act or result of: *pleasure*	noun

> **Exercise 11** Defining Suffixes For each suffix, write its definition and origin, Use a dictionary to assist you. Then, write a word that contains each suffix.

1. -esque
2. -ism
3. -or
4. -ant (-ent)
5. -ance (-ence)

> **Exercise 12** Using Suffixes to Form New Words Add a suffix to each root to form a word that fits the definition given. Write each word with its part of speech. Check the spellings and meanings in a dictionary.

Root	Definition	Word/Part of Speech
1. *graph-*	study of handwriting	?
2. *mot-*	a reason for tending to	?
3. *cap-*	the act of seizing	?
4. *pos-*	the state of being placed	?
5. *laugh-*	causing laughter	?

810 • Vocabulary and Spelling

> **Technology Tip**

Search for an on-line Web site that provides more information about adding suffixes to words. Find five new words, and add them and their definitions to your vocabulary notebook.

> **More Practice**

Academic and Workplace Skills Activity Book
• pp. 21–22

Using Etymologies

Many English words have interesting histories. In fact, more than 70 percent of the words we call English are borrowed from other languages. Other English words have been added to the language in different ways. If you learn about the origins of unfamiliar words, you can determine and remember their meanings more easily. You can find a word's etymology near the beginning of its dictionary entry.

KEY CONCEPT Etymology is the study of a word's history, its origin. ■

English borrows words from other languages, primarily Greek, Latin, and French.

EXAMPLES: The word *axis* comes from Latin, and the word *gelatin* comes from French.

The English language grows by giving new meaning to old words.

EXAMPLE: The word *havoc* was once an order telling an army to begin plundering.

Words can be invented, or coined, to serve new purposes.

EXAMPLE: The word *boycott* means "refusing to have any dealings with." It was coined from a man's name, Captain C. C. Boycott.

Words can be combined.

EXAMPLE: The word *dictaphone* is a combination of *dictate* and *telephone*.

Words can be shortened.

EXAMPLE: The word *bus* is short for *omnibus*.

Exercise 13 Using a Dictionary to Learn About Etymologies Find the etymology of each word below. Write its meaning, and explain where it originated.

1. diabolical
2. culpable
3. liberty
4. chaos
5. boomerang
6. radar
7. cardigan
8. pajama
9. canyon
10. eon

Research Tip

Find five unfamiliar words in the dictionary. Look them up in an unabridged dictionary to determine their etymology. Add the new words to your notebook.

▲ **Critical Viewing**
Think of some other English words that use the suffix *tele-* and the root *phone*. **[Apply]**

Studying Word Parts and Origins • 811

Starting a Personal Spelling List

Teaching Resources: Academic and Workplace Skills Activity Book, p. 24

1. Read and discuss this page. Have students form small groups and brainstorm for examples of frequently misspelled words. Then, have them brainstorm for base words and derivatives that can help them improve spelling.

2. Next, have students list possible sources where they can find words to include in their personal spelling lists (corrected tests, essays, homework, lists in books or on the Internet of commonly misspelled words, or the "miscellaneous problems" listed in Ch. 25).

3. Point out that not pronouncing a word correctly can sometimes contribute to the difficulty of remembering its spelling. Tell students to check words they hear before they use them, because the speaker may have added syllables. A common mistake is *irregardless*; the correct term is *regardless*.

4. Encourage students to develop memory tricks that will help them remember correct spellings. For example, *complement* has two *e*'s, and so does *complete,* which defines the word.

5. Encourage students to be aware of spelling errors in signs and bulletins around town. Have them bring in examples of these errors to share with the class.

Section 29.4

Improving Your Spelling

Starting a Personal Spelling List

In addition to learning words you are required to study and words on which you will be tested, improve your spelling by starting a personal spelling list.

▶ **KEY CONCEPT** Select words for your personal spelling list, enter them in your notebook, and study them regularly. ■

Recording Frequently Misspelled Words Make it a practice to keep a list of all the words that you regularly have trouble spelling. Review corrected tests, essays, and homework to find your personal problem words. Add to the list words that sound the same or similar but have different spellings and meanings, such as *your/you're* or *affect/effect*.

Including Derivatives A derivative is a word that is formed from another word. Once you know how to spell a base word from which the others are formed, you can more easily spell its derivatives.

BASE WORDS: custom, guard
DERIVATIVES: customer, accustomed, guardian, guarded

Identifying Your Error Patterns Sometimes your spelling errors may follow a pattern, such as adding an extra syllable to a word (*athelete*, instead of *athlete*). Learn to identify the error patterns in your misspellings. The chart below lists common error patterns. Your own error patterns may be similar to or different from these:

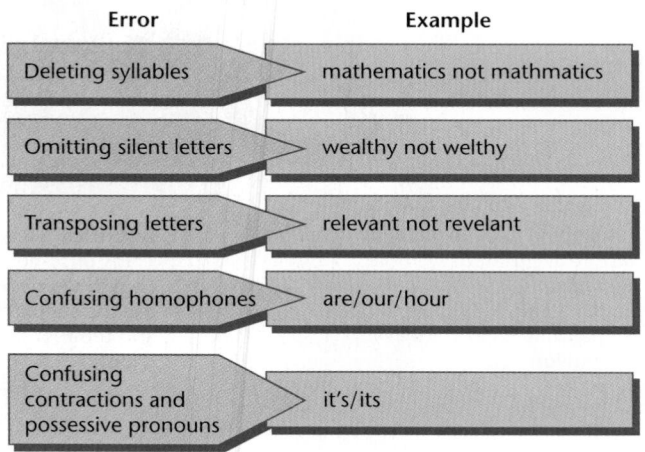

Error	Example
Deleting syllables	mathematics not mathmatics
Omitting silent letters	wealthy not welthy
Transposing letters	relevant not revelant
Confusing homophones	are/our/hour
Confusing contractions and possessive pronouns	it's/its

⏱ TIME AND RESOURCE MANAGER

Resources
Print: *Academic and Workplace Skills Activity Book,* pp. 23–29

Using the Full Student Edition	Using the Handbook🄷
• Read pp. 812–813 and help students create personal spelling lists. • Read pp. 814–821 and discuss each spelling rule. • Have students complete Exercises 14–24 in class.	• Read pp. 612–613 and help students create personal spelling lists. • Read pp. 614–621 and discuss each spelling rule. • Have students complete Exercises 14–24 in class.

Answer Key

> **Exercise 14**

1. burglar, chimney
2. Except
3. condemn
4. They're
5. knew, prescription

Customize for
ESL Students

Ask students to select something they wrote in the past two weeks. Working with a more-fluent English speaker, have them look for and circle spelling errors. Then, have them select another paper and follow the same procedure. The partners should determine whether any patterns emerge and assist students in making corrections.

Step-by-Step Teaching Guide

Studying Your Problem Words

Teaching Resources: Academic and Workplace Skills Activity Book, p. 23

1. Recommend that students choose a certain time to review their personal spelling lists. They might do this before starting their other assignments, before bed, or as they eat breakfast. Making this part of their routine will help them remember to do it.

2. Once a week, have students test one another on some of their words. Doing well on a test will give them an incentive to keep studying.

Exercise 14 Identifying Error Patterns Each sentence below contains one or more incorrect spellings. Identify the error pattern of the misspelled word, and write the correct spelling. Then, look over the writing you have done in the past two weeks. Circle misspelled words in your work, and try to identify your own error patterns.

1. A burgular climbed down the chimiiney of our house.
2. Accept for Rob, everyone was in the living room.
3. The group did not condem Rob for being late.
4. There all waiting for him now.
5. We new he went to the pharmacy to get a perscription filled.

Studying Your Problem Words

Review sessions can help you to master problem words. Whether you have trouble with everyday words or words you seldom use, you can use a study system to help you. The four steps listed in the chart below will help you.

STEPS FOR REVIEWING PROBLEM WORDS

1. *Look* at each word carefully to notice the arrangement or pattern of the letters. Try to see the word in your mind.
2. *Pronounce* each syllable of the word to yourself.
3. *Write* the word and check its spelling in the dictionary.
4. *Review* your list until you can write each word correctly.

KEY CONCEPT Review your personal spelling list several times each week. ■

Exercise 15 Using a Dictionary for Spelling Help Use a dictionary to answer each question below. Record your answers on your paper.

1. Of *affect* and *effect*, which one is usually used as a verb?
2. How is the pronunciation of *psychic* indicated?
3. Which is correct: *begginning* or *beginning*?
4. Which spelling is listed first: *catalogue* or *catalog*?
5. What is the difference in meaning between *corps* and *core*?

Exercise 16 Recording Problem Words In your notebook, record words you have misspelled in your compositions or tests. Prepare columns for misspelled words, correct spellings, and hints for remembering the correct spellings.

🖥 **Research Tip**

Choose five words from the dictionary that would be problem words for you. Add them to your spelling notebook, and enter the rules that apply to each one.

More Practice

Academic and Workplace Skills Activity Book
• pp. 23–24

Answer Key

> **Exercise 15**

1. affect
2. sī'kik
3. beginning
4. catalog
5. A *corps* is a group of people who are associated in some work under common direction. A *core* is the central part of something.

> **Exercise 16**

Answers will vary. Check students' notebooks once or twice to make sure they are keeping up with their work.

Adding Suffixes

Teaching Resources: Academic and Workplace Skills Activity Book, p. 25

1. Remind students of what they have already learned about prefixes and suffixes earlier in the chapter (pages 809–810).

2. Ask students to study carefully the three types of spelling changes that occur when adding suffixes.

3. Work through some examples of spelling changes with the class. Write the examples on the board.

4. Point out that the suffix *-ed,* shown in example 2 of words ending in *y,* makes the word past tense. Remind students that *pay* is an irregular verb, and that most irregular verbs either do not take the *–ed* suffix at all, or change like *pay.* Ask students to think of the verbs that change like *pay (lay/laid, say/said)* as well as a few samples of verbs that don't use *–ed* at all to form the past *(sing/sang, ride/rode).*

5. Encourage students to write each of the key concepts in their notebooks. Remind them to refer to these words when completing writing assignments.

29.4

Applying Spelling Rules

In addition to studying words that give you particular trouble, you should study rules that apply to groups of words. Keep a spelling rules section in your vocabulary notebook. Write down the rules you learn in this section, and keep examples of words that follow those rules. Also, keep examples of words that are exceptions to the rules. You should look for examples in your reading and in your writing.

> **Spelling Changes When Adding Suffixes to Words Ending in *e***
> **Rule:** There is no change if the suffix starts with a consonant.
> **Examples:** settlement
> **Examples From My Writing:**
> "I felt tremendously grateful that no one had done anything careless in the glass museum."
> —from "A Visit Abroad" (personal story)
> **Examples From My Reading:**
> "Turning from her own face as precipitately as she had gone to meet it, she went to the chest where the things were, unlocked it, threw up the lid, and knelt to search."
> —from "The Demon Lover" by Elizabeth Bowen

Adding Suffixes

Adding a suffix often involves making a spelling change in the original word. Here are some rules you should learn:

▶ **KEY CONCEPT** Use the following rules for spelling changes when adding suffixes to words ending in *y.* ■

1. When adding a suffix to words ending in *y* preceded by a consonant, change *y* to *i* except for suffixes beginning with *i:*

   mercy + *-ful* = merciful   whimsy + *-cal* = whimsical
   defy + *-ance* = defiance   defy + *-ing* = *defying*
   hurry + *-ing* = hurrying   dry + *-ing* = drying

2. For words ending in a *y* preceded by a vowel, make no change when adding most suffixes, with a few exceptions:

   convey + *-ance* = conveyor   employ + *-ment* = employment
   day + *-ly* = daily   pay + *-ed* = paid

KEY CONCEPT Use the following rules for spelling changes when adding suffixes to words ending in *e*. ■

1. For words ending in *e*, drop the *e* when adding a suffix beginning with a vowel. Exceptions are (1) words ending in *ce* or *ge* with suffixes beginning with *a* or *o*, (2) words ending in *ee*, and (3) a few special words:

prove + *-able* = provable   strive + *-ing* = driving
notice + *-able* = noticeable   care + *-ing* = caring
foresee + *-able* = foreseeable   hoe + *-ing* = hoeing
dye + *-ing* = dyeing   be + *-ing* = being

2. For words ending in *e*, make no change when adding a suffix beginning with a consonant, with a few exceptions:

care + *-ful* = careful   love + *-ly* = lovely
argue + *-ment* = argument   judge + *-ment* = judgment
true + *-ly* = truly

KEY CONCEPT Use these rules for cases in which a final consonant may or may not change when adding a suffix. ■

1. For words ending consonant + vowel + consonant in a stressed syllable, double the final consonant when adding a suffix beginning with a vowel. The exceptions to the rules are (1) words ending in *x* or *w* and (2) words in which the stress changes after the suffix is added:

run´ + *-y* = run´ ny   forbid´ + *-en* = forbid´ den
box + *-ed* = boxed   draw + *-ing* = drawing
refer´ + *-ence* = ref´ erence   confer´ + *-ence* = con´ ference

2. For words ending consonant + vowel + consonant in a unstressed syllable, make no change when adding a suffix beginning with a vowel. There are no major exceptions:
an´ gel + *-ic* = angel´ ic   bud´ get + *-ed* = bud´ geted

Exercise 17 Spelling Words With Suffixes Write the correct spelling for the words below. Check your answers in a dictionary.

1. propel + *-er*
2. wrap + *-ing*
3. peace + *-ful*
4. arrive + *-ing*
5. extreme + *-ity*
6. complete + *-ly*
7. marry + *-age*
8. medal + *-ion*
9. liberal + *-ize*
10. acquit + *-al*
11. confine + *-ing*
12. repeal + *-ed*
13. compel + *-ed*
14. judge + *-ment*
15. classify + *-ed*
16. whole + *-some*
17. copy + *-er*
18. shutter + *-ed*
19. chilly + *-er*
20. suspense + *-ful*

▶ **More Practice**

Academic and Workplace Skills Activity Book
• p. 25

Customize for
AP Students

Write a paragraph that contains some misspelled words, and have students underline and correct each mistake. This will give them practice identifying errors in context, which is more difficult and realistic than doing so in a spelling exercise designed for that purpose.

Customize for
ESL Students

For Exercise 17, pair students with more fluent English speakers and have them work together to complete the exercise. Suggest that students write down words they encounter in the next few days that contain the suffixes studied. Encourage them to use a dictionary to check definitions of the words they find.

Answer Key

▶ **Exercise 17**

1. propeller
2. wrapping
3. peaceful
4. arriving
5. extremity
6. completely
7. marriage
8. medallion
9. liberalize
10. acquittal
11. confining
12. repealed
13. compelled
14. judgment
15. classified
16. wholesome
17. copier
18. shuttered
19. chillier
20. suspenseful

Adding Prefixes

Teaching Resources: Academic and Workplace Skills Activity Book, p. 26

1. Encourage students to examine the word *prefix*. They should notice that it contains the prefix *pre-*, which means "before." Therefore, a prefix is a syllable or group of syllables added to the beginning of, or before, a word.

2. Emphasize that, although adding a prefix does not affect the spelling of the original word or root, many prefixes change their own spelling when joined to a root. Refer students to the chart on p. 809.

3. Review the meanings of the prefixes listed in Exercise 18. Challenge students to think of and define other examples of prefixes.

Answer Key

> **Exercise 18**

1. illiterate
2. misinterpret
3. reengineer
4. dissolve
5. unknown

Forming Regular Plurals

Teaching Resources: Academic and Workplace Skills Activity Book, p. 26

1. Read and discuss the rules for forming plurals. Challenge students to think of more examples for each rule.

2. Remind them that these are only the rules for regular plurals. Many irregular plurals exist, and if students are at all unsure about the spelling of a plural, they should look it up in the dictionary.

29.4

Adding Prefixes

> **KEY CONCEPT** When a prefix is added to a root word, the spelling of the root word remains the same. ■

EXAMPLES: *dis-* + satisfy = dissatisfy
un- + necessary = unnecessary

> **Exercise 18** Spelling Words With Prefixes Form new words by combining the prefixes and root words below.
> 1. *il-* + literate
> 2. *mis-* + interpret
> 3. *re-* + engineer
> 4. *dis-* + solve
> 5. *un-* known

Forming Plurals

The plural form of a noun means "more than one." The plural forms can be either *regular* or *irregular*.

Regular Plurals Most nouns have regular plural forms. Their plurals are formed by adding *-s* or *-es* to the singular form of the noun.

> **KEY CONCEPT** The regular plural form of most nouns is formed by adding *-s* or *-es* to the singular form. Occasionally, you may also have to change a letter or two in the word. ■

The spelling of some regular nouns changes in the plural form. Check the rules below for examples that change slightly.

1. Words ending in *s, ss, x, z, sh,* or *ch*: Add *-es* to the base word:

   business + *-es* = businesses   walrus + *-es* = walruses
   box + *-es* = boxes   church + *-es* = churches
   waltz + *-es* = waltzes   dish + *-es* = dishes

2. Words ending in *y* or *o* preceded by a vowel: Add *-s* to the base word:

   donkey + *-s* = donkeys   guy + *-s* = guys
   radio + *-s* = radios   journey + *-s* = journeys

3. Words ending in *y* preceded by a consonant: Change the *y* to *i* and add *-es*. For most words ending in *o* preceded by a consonant, add *-es*. Musical terms ending in *o* simply add *-s*:

   colony + *-ies* = colonies   fly + *-ies* = flies
   tomato + *-es* = tomatoes   soprano + *-s* = sopranos

4. For some words ending in *f* or *fe*: Change the *f* or *fe* to *v* and add *-es*. For words ending *ff*, always add *-s*:

   wolf + *-es* = wolves   dwarf + *-es* = dwarves
   life + *-es* = lives   cliff + *-s* = cliffs
   belief + *-s* = beliefs   gulf + *-s* = gulfs

816 • Vocabulary and Spelling

> **More Practice**

Academic and Workplace Skills Activity Book
• pp. 24–25

Irregular Plurals Irregular plurals are not formed according to the rules on page 816. If you are unsure how to form a plural, check a dictionary. Irregular plurals are usually listed directly after the pronunciation of the word. If no plural form is given in the dictionary, simply add -s or -es to the singular form.

> **KEY CONCEPT** Use the dictionary to look up the correct spelling of irregular plurals, and memorize them. ■

Below is a list of common irregular plurals.

IRREGULAR PLURALS		
Singular Forms	**Ways of Forming Plurals**	**Plural Forms**
ox	add -en	oxen
child	add -ren	children
tooth, mouse, woman	change one or more letters	teeth, mice, women
radius, focus, alumnus	change -us to -i	radii, foci, alumni
alumna	change -a to -ae	alumnae
crisis, emphasis	change -is to -es	crises, emphases
medium, datum, curriculum	change -um to -a	media, data, curricula
phenomenon, criterion	change -on to -a	phenomena, criteria
deer, sheep	plural form same as singular	deer, sheep
	plural form only	scissors, slacks

> **Exercise 19** Forming Plurals Write the plural for each word. Consult a dictionary if possible.

1. soprano
2. wife
3. fox
4. supply
5. lynx
6. chief
7. son-in-law
8. crisis
9. x-ray
10. tomato
11. rodeo
12. criterion
13. gratuity
14. fantasy
15. ballerina

> **More Practice**

Academic and Workplace Skills Activity Book
• p. 26

Forming Irregular Plurals

Teaching Resources: Academic and Workplace Skills Activity Book, p. 26

1. Have students review the irregular plurals on page 817. Discuss what makes these words irregular (they don't simply add -s).

2. Ask students whether they can think of other irregular plurals. Have them give both the plural and singular forms (for example, *goose/geese, fish/fish*).

3. Remind students that there are only two ways to be sure of spelling irregular plurals correctly: memorize them or look them up.

Customize for
Linguistic Learners

Suggest that students try to discover the etymologies of some of the irregular words. What are their origins, and why are they formed differently?

Integrating Writing Skills

Ask students to look through their portfolios for examples of plurals. Have them record each word in both its singular and plural forms. Then, have them write out the spelling rule they used to create the plural form. Have them correct any misspelled plurals.

Answer Key

> **Exercise 19**

1. sopranos
2. wives
3. foxes
4. supplies
5. lynxes *or* lynx
6. chiefs
7. sons-in-law
8. crises
9. x-rays
10. tomatoes
11. rodeos
12. criteria
13. gratuities
14. fantasies
15. ballerinas

Customize for
ESL Students

Working with a more-fluent English speaker, students should pronounce each word included in Exercise 20. Their partners will help them notice subtle differences in pronunciation between the singular and plural forms, like in *leaf* and *leaves*.

Answer Key

> **Exercise 20**

1. leaves	11. alumni
2. circuses	12. loaves
3. memoranda	13. jellies
4. flies	14. solos
5. waltzes	15. mice
6. pen pals	16. echoes
7. roofs	17. potatoes
8. lunches	18. salmon
9. data	19. enemies
10. radios	20. attorneys-at-law

Step-by-Step Teaching Guide

Spelling *ie* and *ei* Words and Words Ending in *-cede*, *-ceed*, and *-sede*

Teaching Resources: Academic and Workplace Skills Activity Book, p. 27

1. Have students work on memorizing the words on this list.
2. Have students begin a vocabulary list for words ending in *-cede*, *-ceed*, and *-sede*.

Customize for
Less Advanced Students

Have students write their own sentences using each of the words in the exceptions list to demonstrate their knowledge of the words' meanings.

Plurals of Compound Words Most compound nouns that are one word have regular plural forms. If the main part of the compound noun is irregular, the plural form will also be irregular.

EXAMPLE: thunderstorm, thunderstorms (regular)
              stepchild, stepchildren (irregular)

When you are forming the plural of a compound word written as two or more separate or hyphenated words, add *-s* or *-es* to the singular form of the main part—the word being modified by the other word.

EXAMPLE: bucket seat, bucket seats
              passer-by, passers-by

> **Exercise 20** Forming Plurals Write the plural for each word. Consult a dictionary if necessary, and add any difficult words to your personal spelling list.

1. leaf	11. alumnus
2. circus	12. loaf
3. memorandum	13. jelly
4. fly	14. solo
5. waltz	15. mouse
6. pen pal	16. echo
7. roof	17. potato
8. lunch	18. salmon
9. datum	19. enemy
10. radio	20. attorney-at-law

Spelling *ie* and *ei* Words and Words Ending in *-cede*, *-ceed*, and *-sede*

> **KEY CONCEPTS** For *ie* and *ei* words, use the traditional rule *i* before *e* except after *c* or when sounded like *a*, as in *neighbor* or *weigh*. Memorize the exceptions. Words that end in *-cede*, *-ceed*, and *-sede* should be memorized. ■

Exceptions for *ie* words: counterfeit, either, foreign, forfeit, heifer, height, heir, leisure, neither, seismology, seize, sheik, sleight, sovereign, their, weird

Exceptions for *ei* words: ancient, conscience, efficient, financier, sufficient

---

☑ **ONGOING ASSESSMENT SYSTEM: Prerequisite Skills**		
If students have difficulty with spelling compound nouns, you may find it helpful to refer them to the following materials to ensure coverage of prerequisite knowledge.		
In the Textbook	**Print Resources**	**Technology**
Nouns, Ch. 17	*Grammar Exercise Workbook*, pp. 1–2	*On-Line Exercise Bank*, Section 17.1

Spelling Homophones

KEY CONCEPT Homophones are words that sound alike but have different meanings and may have different spellings. ■

The following homophones sometimes cause spelling problems:

EXAMPLES:

their:	a possessive pronoun that means "belonging to them"
they're:	a contraction for "they are"
there:	a sentence starter or word meaning "in that place"
brake:	a verb meaning "slow down or stop" or a noun meaning "a device for slowing or stopping"
break:	a verb meaning "cause to come apart" or a noun meaning "a fracture"
clothes:	a plural noun meaning "wearing apparel"
close:	a verb meaning "shut"
passed:	the past tense of the verb *pass*
past:	a word meaning "time gone by" or a preposition meaning "beyond"
principal:	a noun meaning "head of a school" or an adjective meaning "main"
principle:	a noun meaning "a rule or belief"
write:	a verb meaning "put words on paper"
right:	an adjective meaning "correct"

Exercise 21 Spelling Homophones Select the correct word in parentheses. Check your answers in a dictionary. Add misspelled words to your personal spelling list, and review them.
1. I (past, passed) this car several times on the highway.
2. I put on the (break, brake) to slow down.
3. I wonder if (there, they're) planning to attend the meeting.
4. What is your (principal, principle) objection to the rule?
5. Would you please (write, right) it down for me?

Exercise 22 Writing Sentences With Homophones Write a sentence using each word in the pairs below. Check a dictionary to make sure you are using and spelling each word correctly.
1. (a) to   (b) too
2. (a) stationary   (b) stationery
3. (a) plain   (b) plane
4. (a) miner   (b) minor
5. (a) site   (b) cite

Technology Tip

Spelling checkers will not catch homophones that you have misused. Proofread all of your work, even if you have used an electronic spell checker.

More Practice
Academic and Workplace Skills Activity Book
• p. 28

Step-by-Step Teaching Guide

Spelling Homophones

1. Read and discuss the examples of homophones. Encourage students to brainstorm for other homophones. Write their responses on the board.

2. Remind students that word processing software such as spell checkers will not pick up incorrectly used homophones as long as the words are spelled correctly.

3. If students keep proofreading checklists, tell them to add "incorrect use of homophones" to the list as something to check for.

Answer Key

Exercise 21

1. passed
2. brake
3. they're
4. principal
5. write

Exercise 22

While sentences will vary, it is important to make certain that the words are used correctly. Read the definitions aloud, or have a student read them. Then, after each word pair is defined, ask volunteers to share sentences that use the words correctly. (Two or three examples for each word pair should be sufficient for illustration.) Allow students to correct their own work, or have them exchange papers with partners. If they find that any word is used incorrectly, ask students to write a new sentence using the word correctly.

Understanding the Influence of Other Languages and Cultures

1. Have students look at the examples of different letters used to spell the same sound. Have them brainstorm for additional examples. (*f*: enough, quaff, felt, phenomenal; *j*: gerund, joke, sage; *k*: cackle, kind, trick, make)

2. Have students read the examples of words containing silent letters and try to think of other examples (silent *p*: pneumatic, silent *k*: knit, silent *b*: plumber). Ask for volunteers to share their responses.

3. Encourage students learning English to provide borrowed words from their first languages as further examples.

Answer Key

> **Exercise 23**

1. silhouette, French
2. succumb, Latin
3. malign, Latin
4. wreck, Anglo-French
5. exhaust, Latin
6. trough, Old English
7. chrome, French
8. beret, French
9. leisure, Old English, Latin
10. scheme, Latin, Greek

Critical Viewing

Deduce Students may guess that the word *giraffe* comes from Africa, since this is where the animal lives. While the people who live in the same area as the giraffe have a different name for it, this animal, which lives in sub-Saharan grasslands, was well known in North Africa. The Arabic name was *Zarafah,* which became *giraffa* in Italian. It means "one who walks swiftly."

29.4

Understanding the Influence of Other Languages and Cultures

Most languages have a set of rules for spelling and pronunciation that are predictable and constant. In English, however, more than 70 percent of the words are borrowed words. Along with a borrowed word come some unique features of the spelling and pronunciation of the original language. For this reason, English uses a variety of letters to spell the same sounds.

EXAMPLE: *f* sound in puff, cough, fuel, phone
j sound in giraffe, jump, page
k sound in call, keep, pack, hike

For the same reason, English words often contain "silent letters."

EXAMPLE: silent *p* in pneumonia, psychiatrist, ptomaine
silent *k* in knowledge, knuckle, knot
silent *b* in climb, dumb, crumb

Be aware of these problem areas, and use a print or electronic dictionary to confirm the spelling of any word about which you are unsure.

> **Exercise 23** **Choosing the Correct Spelling** On your paper, write the correct word from each group. Check your answers in a dictionary. Note the language(s) from which each word originates.

1. silouette	silhouette	siluette
2. succumb	sucumm	sukkum
3. maline	malign	malin
4. reck	wrek	wreck
5. exaust	exost	exhaust
6. troff	trough	trouff
7. chrome	krome	crome
8. baray	beray	beret
9. leasure	leesure	leisure
10. scheme	skeam	skeem

▲ **Critical Viewing**
Where do you think the word *giraffe* comes from? Why? **[Deduce]**

Proofreading

It is a good idea to get into the habit of proofreading everything you write for spelling errors. By proofreading, you can eliminate misspellings caused by hasty writing, and you will begin to pinpoint words that present problems. You should also use a dictionary, electronic spell checker, and a textbook glossary to check your spelling.

KEY CONCEPT The more you proofread, the easier it will be for you to spot your errors. Use a variety or combination of strategies. ■

- Proofread your work by slowly reading it, aloud or silently, to yourself.
- Proofread only one line at a time. Use a ruler or other device to focus on the line you are proofreading.
- Read backward, from the last word to the first. This forces you to focus only on the words themselves.
- Consult a dictionary if you suspect a word is misspelled.
- Check the spelling of proper nouns.

Exercise 24 Proofreading for Spelling Errors Copy and proofread the following paragraph, correcting spelling errors.

Sometimes, large numbers of people are neglected by the
esbableshed orgens of communication. When that happens,
new media are deviced. This press of the masses might be
considered elamental and emotionel. Ordnarily, the masses
will probly prefer journelism that could be called "sensationel."
In 1620, 1833, the 1890's, and 1920, there was a waive of
sensationelizm.

> **More Practice**
> Academic and
> Workplace Skills
> Activity Book
> • p. 29

Reflecting on Your Spelling and Vocabulary

Think about what you have learned in this chapter by asking yourself the following questions:

- Which of the techniques do I find the most effective for studying spelling words?
- Which do I find the most effective for studying vocabulary words?
- What do the techniques have in common? In what ways are they different?

Improving Your Spelling • 821

Step-by-Step Teaching Guide

Proofreading

Teaching Resources: Academic and Workplace Skills Activity Book, p. 28

1. Encourage students to create individual proofreading checklists to help them remember commonly confused words or spelling exceptions or remind them of things for which they need to check.

2. Have students select a work from their portfolios. Have them proofread the selection, following the steps on their proofreading checklists.

Answer Key

> **Exercise 24**

1. established, organs
2. devised
3. elemental, emotional
4. Ordinarily, probably, journalism, sensational
5. wave, sensationalism

ASSESS and CLOSE

Step-by-Step Teaching Guide

Reflecting on Your Spelling and Vocabulary

Teaching Resources: Formal Assessment, Ch. 29

1. Give students time in class to answer the "Reflecting" questions. Encourage them to make additional notes about what they learned in this chapter.

2. Check to make sure that students have begun their spelling and vocabulary lists. Encourage them to continue adding to these lists.

3. You may also wish to administer the Chapter 29 assessment from *Formal Assessment* in Teaching Resources to measure students' grasp of concepts presented.

✓ **ONGOING ASSESSMENT: Assess Mastery**

Use one of the following options to assess students' mastery of the skills taught in this chapter.

Option 1 Ask students to use the spelling strategies they learned to proofread a selection from their portfolios. Have them correct all spelling errors and write out the rule they used to determine the correct spelling of each word.	**Option 2** Check students' vocabulary notebooks. Make sure they have been adding new words that they have encountered in their other classes and in outside reading.

Lesson Objectives

1. To rely on context to determine meanings of words and phrases

2. To apply meanings of prefixes, roots, and suffixes in order to comprehend

3. To read and understand analogies

Step-by-Step Teaching Guide

Analogies

Teaching Resources: Standardized Test Preparation Workbook, pp. 57–58

1. Review each of the listed types of relationships commonly tested in analogy tests (antonyms, part-to-whole, etc.). Ask students to give examples of each relationship.

2. Go through the sample test item and answer with students, emphasizing that choosing the correct answer depends on their knowledge of word meanings and an accurate identification of word relationships.

3. Assign the practice test and go over the answers with students.

Standardized Test Preparation Workshop

Analogies

Analogy questions on standardized tests test your vocabulary. In order to answer an analogy question correctly, you must first determine the relationship between the original pair.

When determining the relationship between words, use the parts of speech as a clue. The words in the correct answer choice will often, but not always, be the same parts of speech combination (nouns, pronouns, verbs, adjectives, or adverbs) as the original pair. Then, find a more specific relationship between the words; the following are relationship types that are most commonly tested:

- Antonyms
- Part-Whole or Whole-Part
- Definitional/Synonyms
- Cause-Effect or Effect-Cause
- Functional Relationship
- Relationship of Degrees

Test Tips

- Make sure that your choice reflects or parallels the structure in the given word pair.
- Sometimes, the relationship between two words is multiple. Always probe beneath the first relationship you recognize to see if there is a less obvious but more important secondary relationship.
- Parts of speech may be a clue. Often, but not always, the correct answer choice will be a word with the same part of speech as the given word pair.

Sample Test Item	Answer and Explanation
Directions: Each question below consists of a related pair of words, followed by five pairs of words labeled *A* through *E*. Select the pair that best expresses a relationship similar to that expressed in the original pair.	
CEASE-FIRE : HOSTILITIES:: (A) reckoning : probabilities (B) truce : belligerents (C) artillery : tanks (D) campaign : strategies (E) adjournment : proceedings	The correct answer is *(E)*. The noun *adjournment* is caused by the end of proceedings, also a noun. In the original pair, the noun *cease-fire* is caused by the end of hostilities, also a noun. Answers *(B)* and *(D)* express a similar relationship to the original pair, but neither pair expresses an end to an occurrence. For example, a *truce* is not an end to *belligerents,* and a *campaign* is not an end of *strategies.* Answers *(A)* and *(C)* do not express a cause-effect relationship.

822 • Vocabulary and Spelling

✎ TEST-TAKING TIP

Remind students to look for word relationships that reflect the same structure used in the pair of words for each item. Prefixes, suffixes, and roots may assist them in deciphering the relationships.

You might also tell them to go through the five pairs of possible answers for each item and try to "weed out" the wrong ones. For example, if students know that the related word pair is a set of synonyms, they should try to eliminate the words in the list that they know for sure are not synonym pairs.

▶ **Practice 1** **Directions:** Each question below consists of a related pair of words or phrases, followed by five pairs of word or phrases labeled *A* through *E*. Select the pair that best expresses a relationship similar to that expressed in the original pair.

1 CRAVEN : COWARDLY ::
  A liberal : conservative
  B juvenile : adult
  C genuine : fake
  D feeble : fragile
  E regal : common

2 IMPERVIOUS : ACCESSIBLE ::
  A impertinent : interfering
  B articulate : eloquent
  C parched : dry
  D priceless : invaluable
  E obstinate : pliable

3 ISOLATION : LONELINESS ::
  A gloomy : murky
  B affliction : comfort
  C explanation : comprehension
  D happiness : disaster
  E impartial : partial

4 SCIENCE : ASTRONOMY ::
  A geology : physical science
  B star : planet
  C notes : music
  D chemistry : biology
  E computer language : BASIC

5 PARSIMONY : STINGINESS ::
  A falsehood : verity
  B greed : generosity
  C extraneous : relevant
  D enthusiasm : passivity
  E candor : forthrightness

6 INSOLVENT : BANKRUPT ::
  A rich : poor
  B lethargic : sluggish
  C wealthy : fortune
  D impoverished : poverty
  E serious : humorous

7 DETERIORATE : CORROSION ::
  A rain : flood
  B lecture : lesson
  C perplex : mystery
  D musician : orchestra
  E fatigue : invigoration

8 INNOCUOUS : HARMLESS ::
  A sensitive : insensitive
  B habitual : occasional
  C joyous : pleased
  D despicable : contemptible
  E social : antisocial

9 CHALK : CHALKBOARD ::
  A pen : paper
  B needle : thread
  C eraser : mistake
  D brush : paint
  E crayon : drawing

10 CANKER : DECAY ::
  A tense : fear
  B sun : moon
  C automobile : driver
  D tragedy : grief
  E destruction : earthquake

Customize for
Less Advanced Students

You may wish to review parts of speech with students. You may also wish to cite some examples of word pairs illustrating synonyms, antonyms, and other relationships included in the test. After the practice test, discuss why the correct answers are correct.

Customize for
ESL Students

Depending on students' level of fluency, you may wish to allow them to do this exercise using a dictionary. Analogies become difficult to impossible if students do not know what any of the words mean.

In-Depth Lesson Plan

	LESSON FOCUS	PRINT AND MEDIA RESOURCES
DAY 1	**Reading Methods and Tools** Students study textbook features and learn strategies for reading textbooks. (pp. 824–830/H622–628)	**Teaching Resources** *Academic and Workplace Skills Activity Book,* pp. 30–34
DAY 2	**Reading Nonfiction Critically** Students learn strategies for reading, analyzing, and evaluating nonfiction. (pp. 831–836/H629–634)	**Teaching Resources** *Academic and Workplace Skills Activity Book,* pp. 35–38
DAY 3	**Reading Literary Writing** Students learn strategies for reading and analyzing fiction, drama, and poetry. (pp. 837–841/H635–639)	**Teaching Resources** *Academic and Workplace Skills Activity Book,* pp. 39–42
DAY 4	**Reading from Varied Sources** Students learn strategies for reading various sources such as journals, newspapers, speeches, and electronic texts. Students review the concepts presented in the chapter. (pp. 842–843/H640–641)	**Teaching Resources** *Academic and Workplace Skills Activity Book,* p. 43; *Formal Assessment,* Ch. 30

Accelerated Lesson Plan

	LESSON FOCUS	PRINT AND MEDIA RESOURCES
DAY 1	**Reading Methods and Tools; Reading Nonfiction Critically** Students learn strategies for reading and analyzing textbooks and other nonfiction materials. (pp. 824–836/H622–634)	**Teaching Resources** *Academic and Workplace Skills Activity Book,* pp. 30–38
DAY 2	**Reading Literary Writing; Reading from Varied Sources** Students learn strategies for reading literary writing and other print and electronic texts. (pp. 837–843/H635–641)	**Teaching Resources** *Academic and Workplace Skills Activity Book,* pp. 39–43; *Formal Assessment,* Ch. 30

Options for Adapting Lesson Plans

HOMEWORK
Have students complete any of the exercises for homework.

FEATURES
Extend coverage with the Standardized Test Preparation Workshop (pp. 844–845).

Writing and Grammar Handbook Alignment

Page numbers in Step-by-Step Teaching Guides in this Teacher's Edition refer to pages from the full student text. Handbook page references, indicated with this icon ⊞, are provided in Time and Resource Manager boxes and at the bottom of each Teacher's Edition page.

INTEGRATED SKILLS COVERAGE

Viewing and Representing
Critical Viewing, SE pp. 824, 832, 835, 837, 842/⊞622, 630, 633, 635, 640; ATE p. 838

Writing Skills
ATE p. 837

Speaking and Listening Skills
ATE pp. 835, 842

Real-World Connection
ATE p. 836

Research
SE pp. 825, 833, 839/⊞623, 631, 637

Technology
SE pp. 829, 831, 841/⊞627, 629, 639

Organization Skills
ATE p. 828

ASSESSMENT SUPPORT

Standardized Test Preparation Workshop, SE p. 844; ATE p. 833
Standardized Test Preparation Workbook, pp. 59–60
Formal Assessment, Ch. 30

MEETING INDIVIDUAL NEEDS

Less Advanced Students ATE pp. 826, 832, 845. See also Ongoing Assessments ATE pp. 827, 829, 835, 839, 841
AP Students ATE pp. 834, 845
ESL Students ATE pp. 837, 839
Gifted and Talented Students ATE p. 830
Spatial Learners ATE pp. 828, 841
Interpersonal Learners ATE p. 831
Bodily/Kinesthetic Learners ATE p. 840

BLOCK SCHEDULING

Pacing Suggestions
For 90-minute Blocks
• Have students review the Reading Methods and Tools section and complete Exercises 1–5 in a single period.
• Focus one class period on Reading Nonfiction Critically. Allow an additional period for Reading Literary Writing and Reading from Varied Sources.

Resources for Varying Instruction
• *Academic and Workplace Skills Activity Book,* pp. 30–43

Professional Development Support
• *How to Manage Instruction in the Block* This teaching resource provides management and activity suggestions.

MEDIA AND TECHNOLOGY

For the Teacher
• Teacher EXPRESS™ CD-ROM

WRITING AND GRAMMAR ON-LINE

Interactive Text (On-line or on CD-ROM)
• Easily navigable instruction with interactive Revision Checkers
• Full use of e-rater™, the essay-scoring system (on-line only)

Companion Web Site PHSchool.com
• Scoring rubrics with models (use Web Code egk-1201)

See the Go On-line! **feature, SE p. iii.**

Lesson Objectives

1. To establish and adjust purpose for reading
2. To use study strategies such as note taking, outlining, and using study-guide questions
3. To construct images such as graphic organizers based on text descriptions and text structures
4. To analyze text structures such as compare/contrast, cause/effect, and chronological order for how they influence understanding
5. To draw inferences and support them with textual evidence and experience
6. To evaluate the credibility of information sources, including how the writer's motivation may affect that credibility
7. To recognize logical, deceptive, and/or faulty modes of persuasion in text

Critical Viewing

Speculate The student might be doing homework or research. He is reading a textbook, and he has a pen and notebook for taking notes.

Chapter 30 Reading Skills

What does it mean to be a good reader? As you will learn in this chapter, effective reading means more than simply understanding the words you read. As you become a more mature thinker, it will become increasingly important to read critically and to develop the skills necessary to meaningfully evaluate the material you read. These important skills will serve you for years to come, in your schoolwork as well as in your personal reading.

▲ **Critical Viewing**
What type of reading do you think this student is doing? Why do you think so? **[Speculate]**

824 • Reading Skills

⏱ TIME AND RESOURCE MANAGER

Resources
Print: *Academic Workplace Skills Activity Book*, pp. 30–34

Using the Full Student Edition	Using the Handbook 🄷
• Read and discuss pp. 824–830 in class. • Give students time in class to complete Exercises 1–2. • Assign Exercise 3 for homework. Have students share their graphic organizers in class.	• Read and discuss pp. 622–628 in class. • Give students time in class to complete Exercises 1–2. • Assign Exercise 3 for homework. Have students share their graphic organizers in class.

Section 30.1 Reading Methods and Tools

You will use reading skills your whole life. In college, you will read books and textbooks. On the job, you will read materials from a variety of sources, such as manuals or handbooks. Reading successfully requires that you think critically, taking in as much important information as you can.

Using Sections of Textbooks

Textbooks are organized so that you can learn the information they contain with ease and efficiency. Textbooks are divided into segments that contain reading and study aids that help you understand and remember the information.

> **KEY CONCEPT** Use textbook reading and study aids to help you understand and remember what you read. ■

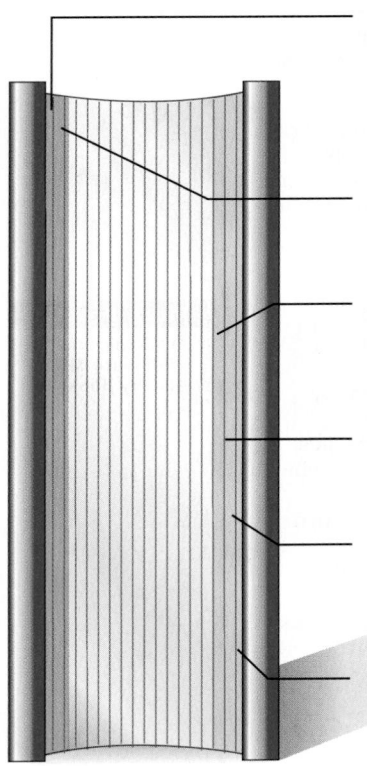

Table of Contents Provides a quick overview of the book and shows how the book is organized by listing units and chapters with their page numbers

Preface/Introduction States the author's purpose in writing the book

Index Lists alphabetically all topics covered in the book and the pages on which they can be found

Glossary Lists alphabetically and defines all specialized terms used in the book

Appendix Includes charts, lists, and other materials related to the book's subject; a general reference source

Bibliography Lists books and articles that the author has used or referred to in writing the book

🗂 Research Tip

Imagine that you will be writing a book on your favorite academic topic. Seek out books in a library or bookstore that would be most useful to you in your research. Write a bibliography, table of contents, and introduction to your imaginary book. All three of these elements should give your readers a clear sense of what the contents of your intended book will be.

PREPARE and ENGAGE

Interest GRABBER Hand out examples of material that needs to be read carefully, such as advertisements for music and book clubs, junk mail that announces "You may have already won!" and newspaper editorials. Ask students what might happen if one were to read any of these materials without due caution. (He or she might miss important words and details or mistake opinion for fact.)

Activate Prior Knowledge

By twelfth grade, students have become very familiar with textbooks. Ask them to make a list of the textbook features they find most helpful (review questions, written or visual examples of concepts, section heads, and so on). Then, have them make a list of other features they'd like to see in textbooks.

TEACH

Step-by-Step Teaching Guide

Using Sections of Textbooks

Teaching Resources: Academic and Workplace Skills Activity Book, p. 30

1. Use the following questions to prompt discussion.

   Where should you look to determine whether a textbook has the information you need? (in the table of contents)

   Where can you find the author's purpose for writing the textbook? (in the preface or introduction)

   If you want to find additional information about your subject, where can you look? (in the bibliography)

2. Give students time to locate the six features in this textbook. They might want to flag them with self-sticking notes for easy access.

✓ ONGOING ASSESSMENT: Diagnose

Use one of the following options to diagnose students' current level of proficiency with reading skills.

Option 1 Ask students to explain what they do to improve their comprehension when they encounter a difficult text. If students do not know any strategies to use on such occasions, they will need extra support in the section on reading strategies.	**Option 2** Give students a brief excerpt from a short story. Have them infer two or three things about one of the characters based on his or her actions. Students who have trouble with this exercise might need extra support in the sections on making inferences and strategies for reading fiction.

Using Features of Textbooks

Teaching Resources: Academic and Workplace Skills Activity Book, p. 31

1. Read and discuss the information on this page.

2. Ask the class to imagine they are developing a book on the history of pop music. In small groups, have them create the following features of the book:

   Book title

   Chapter titles

   2–3 sentence overview of one of the chapters

   Set of three questions for the end of that chapter

   Idea for one picture and caption in that chapter

3. Have the groups share and discuss their ideas.

Customize for
Less Advanced Students

Have students work in small groups to complete Exercise 1. As they discuss the questions, let one student write down the answers. When the group gives its report to the class, allow students to refer to these notes.

Answer Key

▶ Exercise 1

Ask students whether they noticed certain features that are particularly helpful in math or science books and others that are particularly helpful in language arts or history books.

30.1

Using Features of Textbooks

Textbooks have special features designed to help you find, organize, and review material.

▶ **KEY CONCEPT** Use the special features of your textbook to aid your reading and studying of the material. ■

Titles, Headings, and Subheadings Printed in large, heavy type and in different sizes and colors, headings give you an idea of what the material is about. They also divide the material into sections so that you can learn it more easily. Main topics usually have larger and more prominent headings; subtopics have smaller headings.

Overviews Often, a chapter or unit will begin with an overview, an outline, or a summary of what will be covered. Use the overview to preview and review the chapter or unit.

Questions and Exercises These are often located at the end of a chapter. Review questions and exercises before you read the chapter to give you an idea of the main points to look for as you read. Afterward, answer the questions and exercises to retain the information you have read.

Pictures, Captions, and Graphics A picture can make a confusing idea clearer. Usually, next to a picture there is a caption—information describing the picture. Graphics—such as maps, charts, and diagrams—present complex information in a clear format.

▶ **Exercise 1** Examining Two Textbooks Select two textbooks on different subjects, and evaluate them by answering these questions:
1. How is the table of contents in each text organized (by theme, chronologically, or by some other method)?
2. If the text contains a preface, does it explain the book's purpose and give suggestions for using the book? In which of the books is the preface more helpful?
3. Which text's chapter headings can you more easily turn into questions?
4. Are the end-of-chapter questions in each text useful for study? Are the questions in one text more helpful?
5. Does each text contain an index, a glossary, an appendix, and a bibliography? How do the elements help you to use the book's material?

▶ **More Practice**

Academic and Workplace Skills Activity Book
• pp. 31–32

Using Reading Strategies

Vary Your Reading Style

By the time you are a senior in high school, you have probably established a reading style that incorporates the important reading skills: skimming, scanning, and close reading. Understanding which skill is suitable to your purpose and material is as important as understanding your learning style or style of communication.

KEY CONCEPT Adjust your reading style whenever your purpose in reading changes. ■

Skimming involves reading a text quickly to get a general overview of its contents. You skim a book when you are previewing it or trying to get a broad idea of its meaning. Skimming is perhaps most useful to review material that you have previously read more carefully.

Scanning involves leafing through several pages at a time, paying attention to section heads and subheads and the general contents. You scan when you do research or when you are trying to locate a particular piece of information.

Close reading is just what it sounds like—reading a text closely to understand and remember its main ideas, to find relationships between ideas, and to draw conclusions. You read closely when you are studying a text and trying to make sense of and retain information.

Use Question-Answer Relationships (QARs)

Understanding how questions are written can help you answer them. There are four general types of questions. Learning to identify these types will help you answer questions more easily. You can also improve your reading skills by asking and answering these types of questions as you read:

1. **Right There** This type of question deals with answers that are right there in the text, usually in one or two sentences.

2. **Think and Search** The answer to this type of question is in the text, but you need to think about the question's answer and then search for evidence to support it.

3. **Author and You** These questions call on you to consider what the author says and connect it to what you know.

4. **On Your Own** The answers to these questions are not in the text. They require you to draw on your experiences.

Reading Methods and Tools • 827

Step-by-Step Teaching Guide

Vary Your Reading Style

Teaching Resources: Academic and Workplace Skills Activity Book, p. 32

1. After students read this section, invite them to discuss occasions when they have used each of the three reading styles.

2. Have students name which reading style they would use in the following situations:

   Looking at a library book to see whether its topics are those needed for a report (skimming)

   Studying a textbook chapter for an upcoming test (close reading)

   Gathering information from a book for a research project (scanning)

3. Have students tell about upcoming assignments for which they may need to use skimming, scanning, or close reading.

4. Challenge students to choose a reading style for their next assignment in one of their classes. After completing the assignment, have them record in a journal whether the strategy was effective, and why. Students can then report back to the class on their experiences. Perhaps some of them developed useful strategies of their own.

Step-by-Step Teaching Guide

Use Question/Answer Relationships

1. Have students read this section, and then have small groups locate examples of each type of question in another textbook.

2. Have students share these questions. As they read the questions, have the rest of the class categorize them.

3. Help students recognize the value of identifying the types of questions. Students should note that this strategy will prevent them from wasting time by looking for answers in the wrong places.

☑ ONGOING ASSESSMENT: Monitor and Reinforce

If students have difficulty distinguishing among the four types of questions, try the following strategy.

Work with students to make a list of key words and expressions they are likely to find in each of the four question types. Have them keep this list in their notebooks and refer to it when they answer textbook review questions in the future.	Examples: **Right There**: *describe, define, identify, find, cite* **Think and Search**: *summarize, compare, contrast, explain* **Author and You**: *apply, interpret, infer, generalize* **On Your Own**: *appraise, assess, evaluate*

Use the SQ4R Method

Teaching Resources: Academic and Workplace Skills Activity Book, p. 32

1. Ask students why it is helpful to preview a textbook before reading it. (This will give students a sense of the main points to come; it will help them organize the small details around the larger ideas.)

2. Have students practice using the "Question" step by turning the heading on this page into a useful question. (Possible answer: How can you use the SQ4R method to help you read and understand a textbook?)

3. Discuss the "Review" step. Ask students to explain what they think the terms *review* and *on a regular basis* mean. (Answers will vary based on learning styles and assignments.)

Integrating Organization Skills

Students might make a checklist of the SQ4R skills so they remember to use them for the next chapter they read. After they complete each strategy, they can check it off. This will ensure that they read thoroughly and actively.

Customize for
Spatial Learners

Encourage students to make a graphic organizer for the skills involved in SQ4R. Remind them to keep the progression of the skills in mind when they create the organizer. Have them draw it on a poster and display it in the classroom as a reminder.

Answer Key

▶ **Exercise 2**

When they finish, discuss the differences among the three strategies. Which strategies do students find most and least useful, and why?

30.1

Use the SQ4R Method

You can use a book's organization to your advantage by mastering the following six skills: *Survey, Question, Read, Record, Recite,* and *Review,* abbreviated as SQ4R.

▶ **KEY CONCEPT** Use the SQ4R method to guide your reading and to help you recall information later. ■

Following are explanations of each step:

Survey	Preview the material, taking note of chapter titles, headings, subheadings, introduction, summary, and questions or exercises.
Question	Turn each heading into a question to help you think about what will be covered under that heading.
Read	Search for the answers to the questions you've asked yourself in the previous step.
Record	Take notes to reinforce information, listing the main ideas and major details.
Recite	Orally or mentally recall the questions and their related answers.
Review	Review the material on a regular basis using some or all of the steps above.

▶ **Exercise 2** Using Reading Styles and Strategies Choose three nonfiction books on different topics. Use the first book to help you practice varying your reading style. Start by skimming the whole book. Note what this activity reveals about the main topics. Then, scan through to find a section that especially interests you. Complete a close reading of this section, and take detailed notes. Next, choose sections from the second and third books, and apply the QAR and SQ4R strategies, respectively. Take notes as you apply the strategies.

▶ **More Practice**

Academic and Workplace Skills Activity Book
• p. 30

828 • Reading Skills

Using Graphic Organizers

A graphic organizer is an excellent tool for summarizing and reviewing information, as well as for showing relationships between ideas. Match your choice of graphic organizer to the way in which the various parts of your subject are related.

KEY CONCEPT Use graphic organizers to help you understand relationships between ideas in a text. ■

Analyze Comparison-and-Contrast Structure

Venn diagrams are extremely useful tools for demonstrating points of similarity and differences between two or more subjects. They can be used to analyze different characters, settings, or themes. If you have two subjects to compare, use a Venn diagram with two circles; if you have three, use one with three circles. Use the illustration below as an example.

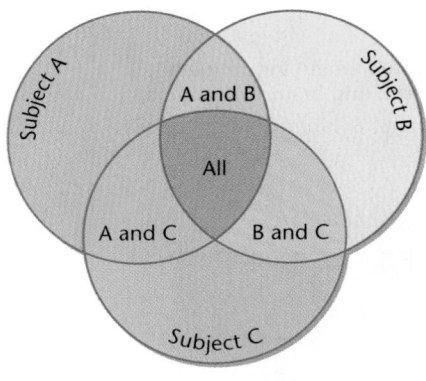

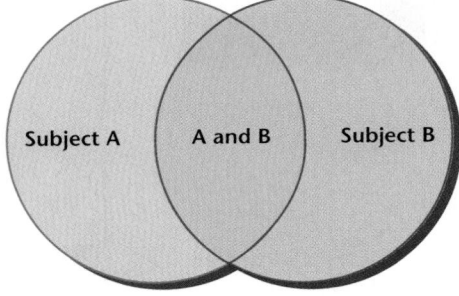

Technology Tip

Using a computer, see if you can design a graphic organizer like one of those that appear in this chapter.

Step-by-Step Teaching Guide

Using Graphic Organizers

Teaching Resources: Academic and Workplace Skills Activity Book, pp. 33–34

1. Explain that a Venn diagram is a visual representation of the points of similarity and difference between two or more items.

2. Remind students to be aware of the overlapping spaces in a three-ring Venn diagram. The space in the center shows the similarities among all three items. The other overlapping spaces show similarities between only two of the items.

3. Have students choose a story they read in class this year. Work with them to create a Venn diagram comparing and contrasting two or three characters from the story.

☑ ONGOING ASSESSMENT: Monitor and Reinforce

If students have trouble using the graphic organizers, try one of the following strategies.

Option 1 For students who have trouble with three-part Venn diagrams, have them make lists of the qualities of the three things they are comparing. Then, have them underline the qualities that appear on two lists and circle the qualities that appear on all three. They can then transfer this information into the Venn diagram.	**Option 2** For students who have trouble with the herringbone organizer on page 830, explain that the arrows show main ideas and the lines list the details that support these ideas.

Using Graphic Organizers
continued

1. Demonstrate the use of the herringbone organizers by applying it to a character from a story that the class has recently read.

2. After reviewing the context chart with students, demonstrate how it might be applied to a work of British literature. *Beowulf, Morte d'Arthur,* and *Macbeth* would be ideal choices if students have read them.

Answer Key

▶ **Exercise 3**

When they finish the exercise, have students write a short explanation of why they chose the graphic organizer they did.

Customize for
Gifted and Talented Students

Have students organize the information in a textbook chapter in two different ways by using two different graphic organizers. For example, if they choose a section about Franklin Delano Roosevelt, they might draw a timeline of his life or presidency and a Venn diagram comparing his presidency with that of Herbert Hoover before him.

30.1

Chart Main Points and Subtopics

Herringbone organizers can help you organize your main ideas and supporting details, show multiple causes of a complex event, or pinpoint areas for research. The sample below shows how you would use a herringbone organizer to analyze the actions that reveal a character's traits.

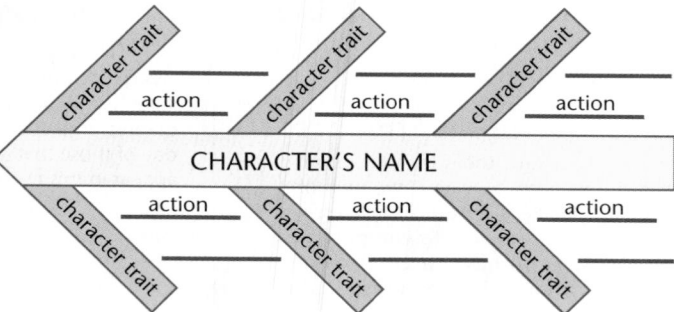

Analyze Historical Context

Context charts, like the one below, are useful for seeing a work of literature in its literary, cultural, and historical context.

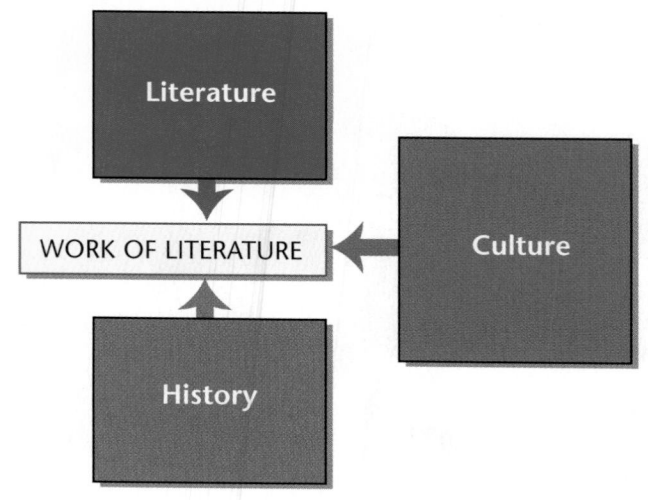

▶ **Exercise 3** Using Graphic Organizers Read a chapter from one of your textbooks or a work of fiction. Use a graphic organizer to present the information from the text.

▶ **More Practice**

Academic and Workplace Skills Activity Book
• pp. 33–34

830 • Reading Skills

Section 30.2 *Reading Nonfiction Critically*

Nonfiction is writing that has a basis in fact. Nonfiction provides a fine source for gathering information on just about any subject. However, just because information is published in a book or an article doesn't ensure that it is accurate. You need to read nonfiction critically, analyzing what the writer is saying and evaluating the credibility of the writer's points.

Analyzing and Evaluating Nonfiction

KEY CONCEPT Use critical reading strategies to analyze, evaluate, and form judgments about nonfiction. ■

Make Inferences Not every point a writer makes is stated directly. It is often left up to the reader to "read between the lines" by making inferences, or drawing conclusions, based on what the writer does provide. For example, if a writer points out the major impact of a specific battle, you might infer that the battle was an important one.

Make Generalizations When you make a generalization, you piece together a related set of facts and details on one topic to make a broad statement about that topic.

Recognize the Author's Purpose or Bias It is important to recognize that every writer wants to achieve a specific purpose through writing. Sometimes, this goal involves persuading readers or telling just one side of a story. When writing to persuade, writers usually have a bias, or point of view. Watch out for language and details that suggest a bias.

Evaluate the Writer's Points or Statements Note each of the facts, statistics, and other evidence that a writer offers in support of his or her position. Evaluate whether the examples are strong ones and whether enough are presented.

Evaluate Credibility Check to see that a writer has expertise or has done thorough research in the topic being covered.

Recognize Persuasive Techniques Don't be swayed by appeals to emotion—even if the topic is one about which you have strong opinions.

Exercise 4 Analyzing and Evaluating Nonfiction Design a six-column chart, labeled with the strategies above. Then, read a nonfiction article, and fill in the chart as you read.

◉ Technology Tip

Treat material that you find on the Internet the same way you would treat material in a book or magazine. Read critically to evaluate it, looking for purpose and bias.

Step-by-Step Teaching Guide

Analyzing and Evaluating Nonfiction

Teaching Resources: Academic and Workplace Skills Activity Book, p. 35

1. Ask students to describe inferences they have made recently while reading or having a conversation. For example, they might have inferred that a friend was unhappy based on his or her facial expressions or tone of voice.

2. Ask students for some examples of language or details that suggest a bias (details that show only one side of a story, excessive praise or condemnation, words that carry strongly emotional overtones).

3. Ask students to brainstorm for ways to evaluate a writer's statements (use library materials or the Internet, talk to experts, or investigate situations on their own).

Customize for *Interpersonal Learners*

Remind students that these strategies also apply to everyday conversations. Students should be aware that in both speaking and writing, people have various goals and motivations, such as to entertain, to instruct, or to persuade. Critical reading skills are similar to critical listening skills.

Answer Key

▶ **Exercise 4**

When they finish, have students add a seventh column labeled "Reactions" to their charts. In this column, have them explain whether each strategy was useful, how they altered it, what they learned from it, and so on.

◷ TIME AND RESOURCE MANAGER

Resources
Print: *Academic and Workplace Skills Activity Book,* pp. 35–38

Using the Full Student Edition	Using the Handbook Ⓗ
• Read and discuss pp. 831–836 in class.	• Read and discuss pp. 629–634 in class.
• Give students time to complete Exercises 4–7. Allow students to work in pairs on Exercise 6.	• Give students time to complete Exercises 4–7. Allow students to work in pairs on Exercise 6.
• Discuss their answers in class.	• Discuss their answers in class.

Distinguishing Fact From Opinion

Teaching Resources: Academic and Workplace Skills Activity Book, p. 36

1. Students should be familiar with distinguishing facts from opinions. Give them copies of two newspaper articles: a news report and a news analysis or editorial. Cover the headlines, and do not tell them which one is which.

2. Have students read the articles and try to determine which is the editorial. Have them write down three pieces of evidence from the articles that support their answer.

3. Have students share and discuss their answers. They should realize that the editorial is the article that not only reports facts, but offers analyses and opinions of them.

Answer Key

▶ **Exercise 5**

1. *fact*; verify by checking reference articles on Shakespeare's plays
2. *opinion*; could be supported with facts about costs and benefits of space-shuttle missions
3. *fact*; verify by checking biographical references on Napoleon
4. *opinion*; could be supported with comparative statistics on family life
5. *opinion*; could be supported with other opinions from professional film reviewers and film scholars

Critical Viewing

Analyze The student should realize that his opinions of colleges might differ from others' opinions based on his interests and needs. He should read the literature carefully and then form his own opinions.

Customize for
Less Advanced Students

Give students more practice by having them rewrite each opinion as a fact and each fact as an opinion. For example, they might rewrite the first sentence to say, "*Hamlet* is Shakespeare's greatest play."

30.2

Distinguishing Fact From Opinion

One of the single most essential skills in being an effective critical reader is the ability to distinguish fact from opinion.

▶ **KEY CONCEPT** As you read, separate facts from opinions, and check to see that writers back up their opinions with facts. ∎

A **fact** is the most reliable type of information because it can be verified, or proved true objectively. A fact can be verified in several ways: records searching, experimentation, and personal observation. The method you choose to determine whether or not a fact is accurate will depend on the type of statement made.

An **opinion** is a statement that cannot be proved because it is subjective; that is, influenced by personal experiences and beliefs. Opinions are most often expressed as personal feelings, judgments, or predictions. Sometimes, facts and opinions can be hard to distinguish. In persuasive writing, such as editorials and speeches, opinions are often couched in what appear to be factual statements.

When opinions are presented in a piece of nonfiction, they should be thoroughly backed up by facts. When evaluating an author's opinions, check to see that the opinions have been thoroughly supported.

▼ **Critical Viewing** Why is it important for this student to distinguish fact from opinion when he is reading magazines? **[Analyze]**

▶ **Exercise 5** Analyzing Fact and Opinion Statements

Identify each statement below as *fact* or *opinion*. For each fact, list a source or method you could use to verify it. For each opinion, tell whether it could be supported by facts.

1. *Hamlet* is Shakespeare's longest play.
2. The information gathered by space-shuttle missions does not justify the high expenditures of the program.
3. Napoleon was born on the island of Corsica.
4. Children today are subject to greater stress than those in earlier times because fewer live with both natural parents.
5. Ingrid Bergman's finest role was as Ilsa in *Casablanca*.

▶ **More Practice**

Academic and Workplace Skills Activity Book
• p. 36

Applying Modes of Reasoning

In addition to applying critical reading strategies to the nonfiction you read, it is important to use sound critical reasoning skills, such as the following:

Inductive Reasoning This strategy proceeds from specific facts to a conclusion, or generalization, based on those facts. A valid generalization is a statement supported by evidence and holds true in a large number of cases. To determine, for example, whether apples in a basket are sweet for eating or tart for cooking, you sample many of the apples. If the apples you taste are all sweet, then you might conclude that all the apples are eating apples. Of course, when you reason inductively like this, the more evidence you have, the sounder your generalization will be.

Deductive Reasoning This strategy starts with a general statement that is assumed to be true and applies that statement to a particular case, whereas induction starts with facts and proceeds to a general statement. The purpose of deduction is to determine whether a particular case fits the general rule. A deductive argument is typically stated in a three-part formula called a *syllogism*, as shown in the following example.

SYLLOGISM: All mammals are warmblooded.
(major premise)
Whales are mammals.
(minor premise)
Therefore, whales are warmblooded.
(conclusion)

If the premises of a syllogism are true and properly worded, the conclusion is sound, like the one above.

Examining a Syllogism When examining a syllogism, ask yourself the following three questions:

QUESTIONS FOR TESTING SYLLOGISMS

1. Is the major premise true? (Could it have been arrived at inductively through studying enough examples?)
2. Is the fact stated in the minor premise true?
3. Does the conclusion follow logically from each premise?

Research Tip

To understand the use of generalizations, research the published results of polls and surveys. Note the conclusions drawn from the results, and determine whether the generalizations are hasty or valid.

Step-by-Step Teaching Guide

Applying Modes of Reasoning

Teaching Resources: Academic and Workplace Skills Activity Book, p. 37

1. Have students create graphic representations of inductive and deductive reasoning. Both graphics should contain four parts: general statement, fact, fact, fact. The difference is how they are arranged. (Deductive reasoning might be an upside down triangle with "general statement" at the top; inductive reasoning might be the other way around.)

2. Work with the class to make the syllogism on this page false. For example, you might change the minor premise to "Whales are warmblooded" and the conclusion to "Therefore, whales are mammals." Make sure students can explain why this is false. (Even though whales are warmblooded mammals, this cannot be proven from the syllogism.)

3. Have students brainstorm for a list of hasty generalizations they often hear. (Examples: "All teenagers are disrespectful to their parents" or "All television shows are a waste of time.")

4. Have students come up with an example of a non sequitur. (Example: Eduardo's little sister loves to be in the kitchen. She loves to mix ingredients. She must be a good cook.)

continued

STANDARDIZED TEST PREPARATION WORKSHOP

Faulty Logic Standardized tests might require students to differentiate between sound and faulty logic.

Read the major and minor premises of the syllogism. Choose the conclusion that makes the syllogism true.

All soccer players must have a B average or better.

Nicole is on the soccer team.

A Nicole is also eligible to play softball.

B Nicole always gets good grades.

C Nicole's friends all have a B average or better.

D Nicole has a B average or better.

Students should note that the answer is **D**. If Nicole is on the soccer team, then she must have a B average or better.

5. Read and discuss page 834.

6. Ask students to give examples of real-life situations in which cause-and-effect reasoning and analogies are used. (Examples: Cause-and-effect reasoning can be used by a traffic police officer at the scene of an accident. An analogy can be used by a teacher to explain an unfamiliar concept to his or her class.)

7. Have students work in pairs to write two or three analogies that begin this way: "Trying to learn grammar is like . . ." Have students share their answers.

Customize for
AP Students

Ask students to research a historical event in which faulty reasoning was used (example: the Salem witch trials). In writing, have them summarize the event, explain how faulty reasoning played a role in it, and show what resulted from this use of faulty reasoning.

Answer Key

▶ **Exercise 6**

1. *inductive*, invalid
2. *analogy*, valid
3. *cause-and-effect*, valid
4. *cause-and-effect*, invalid
5. *deductive*, invalid

30.2

Logical Fallacies Logical fallacies are errors in logic. One type of logical fallacy is a hasty generalization, a generalization based on only a few facts or samples. Tasting only one apple and deciding that the whole basket contains sweet apples is an example of a hasty generalization.

A *non sequitur* (Latin for "it does not follow") is another type of logical fallacy in which a conclusion is drawn that does not follow from the evidence given.

NON SEQUITUR: Members of Congress are elected by the people. They make laws in Washington, D.C. They know what is best for the country.

The fact that members of Congress are elected by the people to make laws does not mean that they always know or do what is right. The conclusion does not follow from the evidence that is given.

Other Forms of Reasoning Induction and deduction are not the only forms of reasoning. There are two other forms that are used to draw valid conclusions: *cause and effect* and *analogy*.

A **cause-and-effect** sequence is one in which something is caused by one or more events that happened previously. False cause-and-effect reasoning makes a connection between two unrelated events.

An **analogy** is a comparison of two things that are alike in a number of important ways. A good analogy can promote understanding of something unfamiliar by comparing it with something familiar. A false analogy ignores obvious and important differences between the things compared.

▶ **Exercise 6** Analyzing Forms of Reasoning Identify the form of reasoning (*inductive* or *deductive, cause-and-effect, analogy*) found in each of the following statements, and explain whether it is valid or invalid.

1. It has been below freezing for three nights in a row, but the water in this pail beside the garage hasn't frozen. It must have antifreeze in it.
2. America in the 1930's was like the Roman Empire whose economic conditions brought about its collapse.
3. The Roman Empire collapsed after a period of great prosperity. We must guard against too much prosperity in this country or risk suffering a similar fate.
4. Mr. Ruiz won a million dollars in the lottery. A week later, he won two thousand dollars. His good luck the first time made him lucky again.
5. All humans are bipeds. An ostrich is a biped. An ostrich is a human.

834 • Reading Skills

More Practice

Academic and Workplace Skills Activity Book
• p. 37

Analyzing and Evaluating

Evaluate the Use of Language

Critical reading demands that you be attentive to the ways writers use language to convey their thoughts. Following are some types of language usage of which you should be aware:

Denotation and Connotation When speakers or writers have a neutral attitude toward their subject and are simply interested in conveying information, they will use language in its *denotative*, or literal, sense. Speakers or writers who want to subtly influence their audience's attitude will use more *connotative* language, or words with negative or positive associations surrounding them.

DENOTATION: The team defeated its opponent.
CONNOTATION: The team soundly thrashed its opponent.

Irony Irony refers to a contrast between perception and reality; between what is said and what is actually meant. Writers use irony to highlight key points and to create humor.

EXAMPLE: The game flew by, lasting only five hours and extending into the time of night when only the worst of insomniacs are still awake.

Understatement When an idea is played down or treated casually, it is considered to be an understatement.

Inflated Language and Jargon Inflated language refers to overly scholarly or scientific language. One type of inflated language is called jargon. Jargon is the specialized vocabulary used by people in a particular field. In its place, it is useful, but jargon is often misused to impress the reader or to conceal meaning.

Euphemism A euphemism is a word or phrase used to replace words that may be considered offensive.

Slanting Slanting is the writing of a passage so that it leans toward one point of view or presents just one side of the story. Choosing words with either positive or negative connotations is one type of slanting. Another type of slanting is presenting only one side of an issue by leaving out important facts that would support another point of view. For example, a story on the negative impact of a tax increase would be slanted if it failed to mention the benefits of the increase.

▲ **Critical Viewing**
Write a denotative and a connotative description of what is happening in this photograph.
[Interpret]

Reading Nonfiction Critically • 835

Step-by-Step Teaching Guide

Evaluate the Use of Language

Teaching Resources: Academic and Workplace Skills Activity Book, p. 38

1. After reading and discussing each use of language, have students share examples they have heard or read.

2. Have students identify the following types of language uses.

   "Your knee has edema," the medical student said.
   "That just means your knee is swollen," Mom explained. (jargon)

   "Well, you certainly managed to snatch defeat from the jaws of victory out there," the coach told the losing team. (irony)

3. Give students the following statement and have them rephrase it five ways, preserving the basic meaning but employing a different language usage each time:

   Billy earned a fifty-five percent on the math test.

Integrating Speaking and Listening Skills

Students who are having difficulty recognizing irony might benefit from hearing it aloud. In a dramatic voice, read aloud the examples of irony from this page and from the step-by-step teaching guide above. Students can often detect irony more easily from tone of voice than in their reading.

Critical Viewing

Interpret Possible responses: He caught the fly ball (denotative). He robbed the batter of a sure home run (connotative).

☑ **ONGOING ASSESSMENT: Monitor and Reinforce**

If students are having difficulty understanding the difference between connotation and denotation, use the following strategy.

Have students choose a simple word, such as *good*. Ask them to look in the thesaurus and write down a list of synonyms for the word (examples: *moral*, *friendly*, *beneficial*). Ask students whether describing something as *good* is the same as describing it as *moral* or *friendly*. They should note that although the words have the same basic meaning, they vary in tone and implication. They have similar denotations, but very different connotations.

Identify the Author's Purpose

1. Read and discuss the criteria for critical reading. Ask students whether they have any other points to add to the list. (For example, they might add something about originality in writing style or thinking.)

2. Have students apply the criteria to a selection from their portfolios. They might exchange papers with a partner to evaluate one another's work.

Answer Key

▶ Exercise 7

Students should note that the writer achieves his or her purpose: to explain the barriers to economic self-sufficiency of newcomers to Boston. The writer cites the 1990 Census, which is a trustworthy source. He or she offers credible reasons for the economic hardships and offers basic ways to begin to solve the problem.

Real-World Connection

Bring in copies of a few nonfiction book reviews from a newspaper. Have students read them and underline instances in which the reviewer uses the criteria outlined on this page. What other criteria or standards does the reviewer use? Discuss with students their opinions about the importance of book reviews. Is it important to evaluate a book review with the same criteria they would use to evaluate a book?

30.2

Identify the Author's Purpose

When you have finished reading a work of nonfiction, piece together all the information you have gathered about the author's purpose, the use of language, the presentation of facts and opinions, and the forms of reasoning that have been offered to draw your final conclusions about the work and its effectiveness. Consider these questions:

> ### Criteria For Critical Reading
>
> 1. Does the author accomplish his or her purpose? Is there an honest use of language to reveal meaning, or does the author use techniques to distort meaning?
>
> 2. Does the author have something of value to say? What are the implications of the author's ideas? How are they related to other ideas?
>
> 3. Does the author have something valuable to say to you? How do the author's ideas increase your understanding or change your way of looking at things?

▶ **Exercise 7** Making Final Judgments Apply the questions above to the following passage:

The newcomer population of Boston has grown dramatically in recent years. The 1990 Census showed 114,547 foreign-born residents living in the Boston Metro Area—the fourteenth largest concentration in the United States. These newcomers face multiple barriers to economic self-sufficiency. Many received little or no education in their countries of origin, and their English language skills are minimal. In their home countries, they were seamstresses, farmers, shopkeepers, street vendors, military personnel—backgrounds that do not translate well to the modern American workplace. While their life experience and motivation to work are impressive, improved language and literacy skills, specialized work and cultural orientation, and job placement are critical for these individuals to access even entry-level jobs.

Section 30.3 Reading Literary Writing

When reading fiction, turn your mind into a kind of theater, in which the mind is the stage, the actors, and the director all at the same time. Use this theater to find the relationship between the details the playwright presents and the meaning of the piece.

Analyzing and Evaluating Fiction

▶ **KEY CONCEPT** Use a variety of strategies to help you read and interpret fiction. ■

Identify With the Character or Situation When you identify with a situation in a novel or a short story, you live it with the character. You share the character's feelings and perceptions of the events. In this way, you may relate to experiences from your own life—or to experiences that you may never actually have had firsthand.

Draw Inferences By implying meanings without stating them directly, writers offer us a world in which the mind can stretch itself, finding connections wherever it looks. Fictional characters and situations don't come neatly labeled with "Villain" or "Danger"—you have to infer information from significant word choices, patterns of events, and other clues in order to understand what a writer is saying between the lines.

Question and Challenge the Text As you read, question what is going on in the text. It will help reveal secrets in the text if, as a reader, you pursue questions such as, What is happening? Why did he say that? Why is this character behaving in this way? You may not always find answers right away, but pieces of the story will start to collect around your questions, and a larger picture will take shape. Then, challenge the story: Are the characters and situations true? Do you accept the author's view of the world?

Draw Conclusions About What You Read Once you have understood and thought about the events and characters in a story, make judgments about the author's message. What general notions about human nature or the world does the author want you to carry away from the text?

Respond to the Story An important step in understanding a text is identifying your own reactions. Are you puzzled, thrilled, or scared? Is a character endearing? Disgusting? You may then judge whether your response was intended by the author, and you can analyze how the author evoked that reaction.

▼ **Critical Viewing** What kind of a book do you suppose this student is reading? Why do you think so? **[Speculate]**

Reading Literary Writings • 837

Reading Fiction

Teaching Resources: Academic and Workplace Skills Activity Book, p. 40

1. Draw on the board a graphic organizer similar to the one on this page.

2. Have students choose a character from a short story or novel the class read this year. In the graphic organizer, have them list his or her traits.

3. Discuss how the character's traits relate to his or her actions in the story.

4. Using the same selection, discuss the point of view used by the author. Does it stay the same throughout, or does it change? Why do students think the author chose this particular point of view? How might the story differ if it were told from another point of view?

continued

Integrating Viewing Skills

Encourage students to be aware of point of view as they watch television and movies. How might point of view affect the way certain characters or events are described? How might the story change if it were told from the point of view of a different character?

30.3

Reading Fiction

Writers of short stories and novels construct worlds that trigger our imagination and help us to learn about ourselves, other people, and the world around us. When you are familiar with the different elements of a story, you can read the story on many levels. The following reading strategies will help you peer behind the plot of a text in order to discover the ideas and messages behind the story.

Describe the Characters Being able to describe the characters in a work of fiction is an important aspect of reading. These descriptions should encompass the character's physical qualities as well as the character's personality traits. Beyond that, you should try to analyze the character's motivation—the personality traits and goals that strongly direct a character's actions. Doing this will help you understand a character more fully and possibly predict a character's behavior.

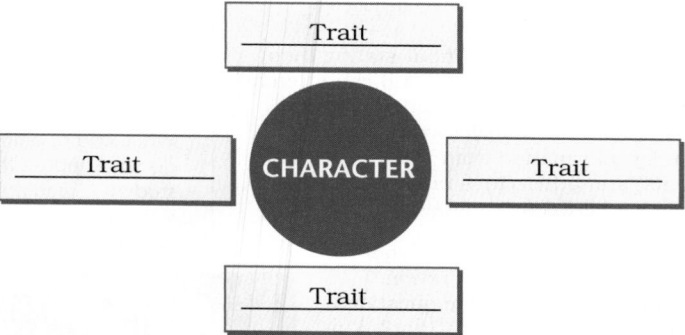

Determine the Point of View A reader must be able to answer this question: From whose vantage point is the story being told? Authors choose the point of view of a story carefully, and therefore you as the reader must pay close attention. As you begin reading, note how the story is being told: Is it a first-person narrative or is it narrated in the third-person objective? Is it limited omniscient or omniscient? Pay attention to the point of view, because it can change over the course of the novel or short story.

Unveil the Symbols Symbols are often embedded within stories. A symbol is an object, a person, a place, or some other detail that stands for something other than what it appears to be. Its literal meaning is what it appears to be in the story. Its figurative meaning is what it represents. Noticing and appreciating the symbolic meaning of an event or an object in a story shows that you are seeing beyond the plot and discovering the hidden meaning.

Analyze the Theme Understanding the theme, or main idea and truth, in a story means that you have moved from reading on a literal level to reading on a figurative one. The literal level is what happens in the story according to the plot development, and the figurative level is where the meaning lies. You can discover a story's theme by asking yourself: What does this story show me about human nature or about life? What did I learn from watching and observing these characters?

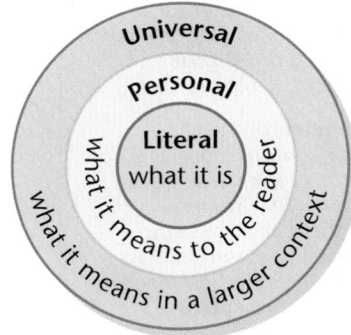

Recognize Allusions An allusion is an implied or indirect reference that is commonly found in literature. An allusion might be made to some character or situation in history or politics.

▶ **Exercise 8** Reading Short Stories and Novels Read a short story or novel. As you read, answer the following questions:
1. What are the motivations behind the behavior of the main characters?
2. What are important symbols in the story?
3. What are notable themes in the story?
4. Have you recognized any allusions? If so, describe them.

   Next time you read a short story or novel, ask these same questions.

🖱 **Research Tip**

Using books from the library, research an allusion from a work of fiction. How does what you learn about the allusion help you see its connection to the story in which you found it?

▶ **More Practice**

Academic and Workplace Skills Activity Book
• pp. 39–40

5. Work with students to make a list on the board of the symbols they see in everyday life. For example, they might note the United States flag or a varsity jacket. What ideas do these objects communicate?

6. Have students make a list of symbols and allusions they have encountered in the fictional selections they read this year.

7. Repeat the exercise in step 6, but focus on theme instead of symbol or allusion. Discuss with students why it's important to consider the theme in a piece of work. (Students should note that the theme often expresses a new understanding about life. It is the author's way of helping the reader see things in a new way. Theme in fiction can be compared to author's purpose in a nonfiction piece.)

Customize for
ESL Students

Ask students to bring in or describe an example of a common symbol from their family's country of origin. For example, they might bring in a flag or a well-known advertising symbol for a product or service.

Answer Key

▶ **Exercise 8**

Remind students that all of these questions are related. In other words, authors include details, symbols, and allusions that will clarify and emphasize larger themes.

☑ **ONGOING ASSESSMENT: Monitor and Reinforce**

If students have difficulty recognizing symbols in literary works, try one of the following strategies.

Option 1 Point out that the major symbol in a story often appears multiple times. Tell students to be aware of objects or images that appear more than once in the course of a story. These are sometimes symbols.	**Option 2** Use a well-known poem, such as Frost's "The Road Not Taken," to show an example of a symbol in literature. Students should be able to explain that the diverging roads stand for, or symbolize, a choice in the speaker's life.

Reading Drama

Teaching Resources: Academic and Workplace Skills Activity Book, p. 41

1. Ask students to describe their experiences in reading drama. How does reading drama differ from reading other forms of literature? (Students might feel that the stage directions get in the way of the narrative. They might note that it is hard to get a sense of a character through dialogue alone.)

2. Ask students to share examples of dramatic irony in plays and movies they've seen. For example, in *Hamlet*, the reader knows that Hamlet feigns madness, but the other characters do not know this. Discuss the effect this has on the reader.

Customize for
Bodily/Kinesthetic Learners

Choose a scene from a play and have the class read it. Then, have volunteers act it out. Make sure the performers pay attention to the stage directions. Afterward, have the class discuss the parts of the scene they found easier to understand after seeing it performed.

Answer Key

▶ Exercise 9

Allow students to read the assignment aloud in small groups. Dramatizing a written script often makes the characters and plot easier to follow.

30.3

Reading Drama

Plays are unique literary forms because they are written with a stage performance and an audience in mind. Unlike most works of fiction that rely heavily on narration, the story of a play is told mostly through dialogue and action and sometimes through monologues. When reading a play, you must place the text and the characters on stage.

▶ **KEY CONCEPT** Use the following strategies for reading drama. ■

Picture the Action in Your Mind As you read, try to picture in your mind how the play would look if it were being performed on stage. Use the stage directions, which appear in brackets, to help you envision the costumes, characters, setting, and action.

Connect the Play to Its Historical Context What is the time period and setting in which the play takes place? What are the manners, customs, and morals of the time? Look in the stage directions for information about when the play is set.

Summarize the Events Dramas are often broken into acts or scenes. These natural breaks give you an opportunity to review the action. After each scene or act, ask these questions: Who are the main characters? How are we supposed to feel about them? Have your feelings for them changed since the previous scene or act? Have any new conflicts arisen? As the play nears its end, evaluate whether the action has reached its climax and whether the conflicts have been resolved.

Recognize Dramatic Irony The audience sometimes knows more about the characters' situations than the characters know themselves. This is dramatic irony, and it is another way the playwright creates tension for the audience. For example, a prince may speak favorably about a king, while the audience knows that the prince is actually plotting to have the king murdered.

▶ **Exercise 9** Reading Drama Read the first act of a play. As you read, take notes on the strategies discussed above. List three details describing the play's historical context. Name five stage directions that you feel contributed to the play's action. What has happened in the first act? What are the tensions in the play? Describe an example of dramatic irony.

⟳ Learn More

Use a context chart like the one presented in this chapter to organize the historical context of a play you have read or are reading.

▶ **More Practice**

Academic and Workplace Skills Activity Book
• pp. 39–42

Reading Poetry

Written in lines and stanzas, poems are visual, but they can also be very musical when recited. When reading a poem, you must look very closely at the word choice, examine the form, and feel the rhythm. Because poetry is such a compact literary form, each word is highly significant to the overall meaning of the poem. To gain the most from poetry, use these strategies:

Read the Poem Aloud and Listen Poems were meant to be read aloud. When you read a poem, listen to its sounds and feel its rhythm. Pay attention to its tone and pace, as well as to the repetition of certain sounds. Consider how all of these attributes contribute to the mood and meaning of the poem.

Identify the Poem's Speaker Recognizing the poem's speaker will give you insight into the drama of a poem. The voice "speaking" the poem is not necessarily that of the poet, although it can be. The speaker could be a fictional character created by the poet. Using clues from the poem, decide who you think the speaker is.

Envision the Imagery Poetry often appeals to the senses. When your imagination can hear the sounds, feel the textures, and smell the aromas that are described, you will find greater enjoyment and will see how the images contribute to the poem's meaning.

Connect Structure and Meaning Poets carefully craft their poems in lines, and they often use stanzas to group their ideas. How the poet chooses to place the words in the poem often relates to the meaning in the poem. Although it may be tempting to read a poem line by line, a thought may span several lines or an entire stanza. To understand complete thoughts, read in sentences.

Paraphrase Restate the passages from the poem in your own words.

Consider the Historical Context Understanding the social, political, economic, and literary environment in which a poem was written helps you to see the poem in a more meaningful context. Research the time period in which the poem was written and the background of the poet.

> **Exercise 10** **Reading Poetry** Choose a poem from your textbook. Read the poem aloud accurately, paying close attention to the punctuation. As you read, identify the speaker, list three sensory images, and paraphrase each stanza. After you have done all of this, write a personal response to the ideas expressed in the poem.

Technology Tip

Find information on a poet and his or her works of poetry on the Internet. Type in the poet's name, and see what you can find. It's possible that you may discover a home page prepared by an enthusiast of the same poet or even by the poet. If you choose a contemporary poet, see if you can find an e-mail address where you could send the poet a letter.

Step-by-Step Teaching Guide

Reading Poetry

Teaching Resources: Academic and Workplace Skills Activity Book, p. 42

1. Give students a copy of a poem from *Prentice Hall Literature, Penguin Edition,* The British Tradition. Work with the class to use all six strategies as you read the poem.

2. Allow students to work in pairs to complete Exercise 10. Remind them to use the poem you just discussed as a model for how to employ the reading strategies.

Customize for
Spatial Learners

In addition to answering the questions in Exercise 10, have students draw a picture to show how they envision the poem's imagery. Have them share their pictures and compare the ways in which each student interpreted the imagery.

Answer Key

> **Exercise 10**

Students might be unfamiliar with writing a "personal response." Explain that this means they should explain what the poem made them think about and how it made them feel.

☑ ONGOING ASSESSMENT: Monitor and Reinforce

If students are having difficulty with the strategies for reading poetry, try one of the following options.

Option 1 For the paraphrasing strategy, have students draw a two-column chart in their notebooks. Have them label the left side "Author's Words" and the right side "My Own Words." When they read a difficult line, have them write it in the left column. In the right, have them try to translate it into everyday language.

Option 2 For the imagery strategy, have students use a sensory language chart. They can make their own charts by drawing five columns and writing one of the five senses at the top of each. As they read, have them record all language that relates to one of the five senses in the proper column.

Reading From Varied Sources

Teaching Resources: Academic and Workplace Skills Activity Book, p. 43

1. After reading page 842, have students draw a three-column chart in their notebooks. On the left, have them write the three types of texts discussed on this page (newspapers; diaries, letters, and journals; speeches). In the middle, have them explain the key features of each type. In the right, have them write two or three reading strategies to keep in mind when reading each type of text.

2. Have students meet in small groups and discuss their charts.

3. Then, give students an example of one of these types of texts. Have them read it, applying the strategies they outlined in their charts. In a journal, have them explain how and why each strategy was helpful.

Integrating Speaking Skills

Have students read a copy of a famous speech. Then, challenge them to read the speech or some section of it aloud. As they prepare, remind them of the various ways they can use their voices to emphasize certain ideas: varying pitch, altering tone, slowing down or speeding up.

Critical Viewing

Interpret The cartoonist has labeled various symbols (the tree, the axes, the nests) to make their meaning clear and unmistakable.

Section 30.4

Reading From Varied Sources

Many reading skills and strategies can be applied to just about any type of reading. However, when reading specific types of texts, such as the ones that follow, you should be aware of the key features of each. Understanding these key features will also help you understand and evaluate the works. In addition, being aware of the key features will help you to determine when it is appropriate to consult each type of text.

▲ **Critical Viewing**
What clues tell you that this cartoon communicates a message about a political conflict? **[Interpret]**

Read Newspapers

When you are looking for up-to-the-minute information on current events or when you want to know how an event was reported at the time it occurred, newspapers are probably your best source. Newspapers are one of the most objective sources of information. However, articles do at times reflect a bias or present only one side of a story—particularly feature articles. In addition, newspapers contain editorials, which by definition present a point of view on a topic.

Read Diaries, Letters, and Journals

When you are looking for a firsthand account of a historical or cultural event, you may want to consult diaries, letters, or journals. These sources let you experience what it was actually like to be a part of the events in question because they are written by people who actually lived through them. Often, you will be called on to consult these types of sources—referred to as primary sources—when you are doing research papers in school. As you read, keep in mind that each diary, letter, or journal presents events from the writer's point of view. As a result, these types of writing may reflect some bias.

Read Speeches

Like diaries, letters, and journals, speeches can provide you with a firsthand view of historical events. In addition, they are a great source for learning about the various sides of political issues. When reading a speech, keep in mind that it was originally written to be presented orally to an audience. Also, consider that a speech presents a single point of view—that of the speaker. Many speeches, such as political speeches, have a persuasive purpose. As a result, speakers often carefully choose words and details to have an intended effect.

Read Electronic Texts

Because the Internet makes them available at your fingertips, electronic texts are becoming one of the most accessible sources of information in today's world. The main type of electronic texts that you will encounter are Web pages. Some of the information on the Web is reliable and objective; some is biased or targeted toward a specific audience. When you read material on the Internet, do so with a critical eye. Determine the purpose behind the material. Often, you will discover that the material has a persuasive purpose. Look to see that any points made in a text on the Web are thoroughly supported by facts and details. Also, evaluate the credibility of the source.

> **Exercise 11** Reading Varied Sources Find examples of each of the sources listed in this section. Read each example carefully. Then, write a few paragraphs in which you compare and contrast these types of sources, and explain situations in which you think each would be most useful.

> **More Practice**
> Academic and
> Workplace Skills
> Activity Book
> • p. 43

Reflecting on Your Reading Skills

After a week of practicing your reading skills for both fiction and nonfiction works, write a paragraph about your reading skills and what you have learned about them. Focus on the areas in which you found success and on those which you need to improve. Use the following questions as guidelines for what to include in your paragraph:

- Which sections of my textbook did I find most useful?

- How has varying my reading style improved my ability to locate and remember information?

- Which steps of the SQ4R method did I find most useful? Which steps do I need to improve?

- Which graphic organizers did I use to help organize ideas?

- What materials have I recently read in which critical reading was a necessity? Which skills most helped my overall comprehension of the material?

- Which strategies for reading fiction did I find most useful? Which strategies did I find most difficult to use?

Reading From Varied Sources • 843

Step-by-Step Teaching Guide

Read Electronic Texts

1. Have students share examples of reliable and unreliable Web sites they have visited. Ask them to describe, in their own words, how they differentiate between these sites. Point out that reliable Web sites usually come from recognized institutions and contain information that can be verified.

2. Remind students that almost anyone can post information on the Internet and that it is easy to make a Web page look reliable and trustworthy. Students should double-check information they gather while doing research on the Web.

Answer Key

> **Exercise 11**

Explain that for the most thorough understanding of a certain time period or event, students should read as many of these sources as possible.

ASSESS and CLOSE

Step-by-Step Teaching Guide

Reading Skills

1. Remind students to refer to this chapter when they need strategies for reading challenging texts.

2. Use one of the Assess Mastery options below to have students reflect on what they learned in this chapter.

3. Administer the Chapter 30 assessment from *Formal Assessment* in the Teaching Resources to measure students' grasp of the concepts presented.

☑ ONGOING ASSESSMENT: Assess Mastery

Use one of the following options to assess students' mastery of the concepts presented.

Self-Assessment Ask students to answer the Reflecting on Your Reading Skills questions on this page. When they finish, discuss their answers as a class.	**Teacher Assessment** Ask students to make a list of the three most useful strategies they learned in this chapter. In writing, have them describe each strategy and explain why they find it useful. Review their answers.

Lesson Objectives

1. To draw inferences
2. To use elements of text to clarify interpretations
3. To analyze relevance of setting and time frame to text's meaning

Step-by-Step Teaching Guide

Make Inferences and Predictions

Teaching Resources: Standardized Test Preparation Workbook, pp. 59–60

1. Have students read the first sample test question on this page. Before reading the answer, have students identify and explain it in their own words.

2. Have students read the second sample question and then complete the response by writing at least two sentences. Have students share their answers.

3. Have students complete Practices 1–2 individually. Go over their answers, clearing up any problems they had.

Standardized Test Preparation Workshop

Make Inferences and Predictions

In the reading sections of standardized tests, you may be asked to make inferences, or draw logical conclusions, about the characters and story you have read or about the author's purpose or point of view. Some questions require you to make a prediction, based on the material you have read. You may be asked to read part or all of a fictional story. Several multiple-choice questions will typically be followed by one or two essay questions. The essay question will ask you to respond in writing to some specific aspect of the reading.

Sample Test Items	Answers and Explanations
Directions: Read each passage. Then, answer the questions that follow the passage. from "The Lagoon" by Joseph Conrad The short words of the paddlers reverberated loudly between the thick and somber walls of vegetation. Darkness oozed out from between the trees, through the tangled maze of the creepers, from behind the great fantastic and unstirring leaves; the darkness mysterious and invincible; the darkness scented and poisonous of impenetrable forests. 1 The author uses this description of the lagoon to — A establish setting and character B describe the water conditions C explain the story's title D create a mood of mystery and foreboding	The answer for item 1 is **D**. By repeating the word *darkness* and by using vivid words and phrases like *oozed, tangled maze, mysterious and invincible,* and *scented and poisonous,* Conrad creates a dark and ominous mood.
In "The Lagoon," Joseph Conrad tells the story of Arsat, a man who ultimately loses his brother and his wife. How does the setting emphasize Arsat's isolation? Support your answer with details and information from the story.	Your answer should include a topic sentence and details from the passage that support it. The following is part of a possible response: In "The Lagoon," Conrad uses the imagery of a tangled maze and of walls of vegetation to emphasize the theme of isolation.

844 • Reading Skills

✏ TEST-TAKING TIP

Tell students that when taking a multiple-choice test, they should skim the test questions and choices first and then go back to read the passage. For example, before reading the excerpt from "The First Seven Years," students should skim to discover that they need to make inferences about Feld and Sobel and a prediction about Miriam. As they read the passage, they can note details about these characters.

Tell students that before answering an essay question, they should make a brief outline that includes their main points and the evidence that supports each one. The outline will help them decide the best way to organize this information.

> **Practice 1** **Directions:** Read each passage. Then, answer the questions that follow the passage.

from "The First Seven Years"
by Bernard Malamud

Though the attack was very mild, he lay in bed for three weeks. Miriam spoke of going for Sobel, but sick as he was Feld rose in wrath against the idea. Yet in his heart he knew there was no other way, and the first weary day back in the shop thoroughly convinced him, so that night after supper he dragged himself to Sobel's rooming house.

He toiled up the stairs, though he knew it was bad for him, and at the top knocked at the door. Sobel opened it and the shoe-maker entered. The room was a small, poor one, with a single window facing the street. It contained a narrow cot, a low table and several stacks of books piled haphazardly around on the floor along the wall, which made him think how queer Sobel was, to be uneducated and read so much.

1 What does the author reveal about Sobel in the description of the room?

  A Sobel is a sloppy housekeeper.

  B Sobel enjoys entertaining in his room.

  C Sobel leads a simple life and reads many books.

  D Sobel is a highly educated man.

2 Which of the following words best describe Feld?

  F weary and defeated

  G dignified and gentlemanly

  H cheerful and jolly

  J simplistic and shallow

3 Because Feld struggles to reach Sobel, you can infer—

  A that Sobel and Feld have serious business to discuss

  B that the two men are strangers

  C that Sobel is delighted to see Feld at his door

  D that Sobel is afraid of Feld

4 Feld was in bed for three weeks because—

  F he was ill

  G he suffered from exhaustion

  H he wants Miriam to take care of him

  J he is depressed about his relationship with Sobel

5 Predict Miriam's reaction to her father's visit to Sobel.

  A She will be angry with Feld for visiting Sobel.

  B She will be sad that Feld visited Sobel.

  C She will not care one way or the other.

  D She will be glad that Feld visited Sobel.

> **Practice 2** **Directions:** Answer the following question. Base your answer on "The First Seven Years" by Bernard Malamud.

How does Feld feel about going to see Sobel?

> **Practice 1**

1. C
2. F
3. A
4. F
5. D

> **Practice 2**

Students should note that Feld feels reluctant about going to see Sobel. Feld is a proud man who hates to admit he needs help. He goes only when he realizes he has no other choice.

Customize for
Less Advanced Students

Emphasize that students should draw inferences and make predictions based on specific statements in a passage. For example, one can infer that Sobel's life is simple from the description of his room as a "small, poor one, with a single window." Predictions should be based on solid evidence, not on guesswork.

Customize for
AP Students

Review with students the techniques for sentence combining, and urge them to employ these techniques when answering essay questions.

In-Depth Lesson Plan

	LESSON FOCUS	PRINT AND MEDIA RESOURCES
DAY 1	**Basic Study Skills** Students develop a study plan and take notes in outline and summary form. (pp. 846–849/H642–645)	**Teaching Resources** *Academic and Workplace Skills Activity Book*, pp. 44–45
DAY 2	**Reference Skills** Students gather information using a variety of library resources, including electronic catalogs and other nonprint materials. (pp. 850–855/H646–651)	**Teaching Resources** *Academic and Workplace Skills Activity Book*, pp. 46–48
DAY 3	**Using Dictionaries** Students survey a dictionary's contents and review various types of dictionaries. (pp. 856–859/H652–655)	**Teaching Resources** *Academic and Workplace Skills Activity Book*, p. 49
DAY 4	**Using Other References** Students consult encyclopedias, atlases, and almanacs as well as electronic and media resources such as videos, CD-ROMs, and the Internet. (pp. 860–863/H656–659)	**Teaching Resources** *Academic and Workplace Skills Activity Book*, pp. 50–52
DAY 5	**Test-Taking Skills** Students learn to budget time while taking tests, and how to approach various types of questions on standardized tests such as the SAT and ACT. (pp. 864–869/H660–665)	**Teaching Resources** *Academic and Workplace Skills Activity Book*, pp. 53–54; *Formal Assessment*, Ch. 31

Accelerated Lesson Plan

	LESSON FOCUS	PRINT AND MEDIA RESOURCES
DAY 1	**Basic Study and Reference Skills** Students review the full array of library resources available to them, as well as strategies for organizing their study. (pp. 846–863/H642–659)	**Teaching Resources** *Academic and Workplace Skills Activity Book*, pp. 44–49
DAY 2	**Test-Taking Skills** Students work independently to review the use of reference tools such as videotape and the Internet, and review test-taking skills and strategies. (pp. 864–869/H660–665)	**Teaching Resources** *Academic and Workplace Skills Activity Book*, pp. 50–54; *Formal Assessment*, Ch. 31

Options for Adapting Lesson Plans

HOMEWORK

Have students conduct independent library research.

FEATURES

Extend coverage with the Standardized Test Preparation Workshop (pp. 870–871).

TECHNOLOGY

Students may use the Internet to conduct independent research. Have them print out their completed work.

Writing and Grammar Handbook Alignment

Page numbers in Step-by-Step Teaching Guides in this Teacher's Edition refer to pages from the full student text. Handbook page references, indicated with this icon ⑭, are provided in Time and Resource Manager boxes and at the bottom of each Teacher's Edition page.

INTEGRATED SKILLS COVERAGE

Research Skills
SE p. 854/⑭650

Technology
SE pp. 851, 854, 860, 861, 862, 863/⑭647, 650, 656, 657, 658, 659

Spelling
ATE pp. 853, 857

Workplace Skills
ATE p. 848

Viewing and Representing
Critical Viewing, SE pp. 846, 855, 860, 863, 866, 867, 868/⑭642, 651, 656, 659, 662, 663, 664; ATE pp. 862, 863

Test-Taking Skills
ATE p. 864

ASSESSMENT SUPPORT

Standardized Test Preparation Workshop, SE p. 870; ATE p. 852.

Standardized Test Preparation Workbook, pp. 61–62

Formal Assessment, Ch. 31

MEETING INDIVIDUAL NEEDS

Less Advanced Students ATE pp. 853, 871. See also Ongoing Assessment ATE p. 856.

AP Students ATE pp. 857, 871

ESL Students ATE pp. 856, 857, 867

Logical/Mathematical Learners ATE p. 860

Interpersonal Learners ATE pp. 849, 855

Linguistic Learners ATE pp. 859, 866

Spatial Learners ATE pp. 851, 860

BLOCK SCHEDULING

Pacing Suggestions
For 90-minute Blocks
• Have students review the extensive Reference Skills section in a single period.
• Focus one class period on Test-Taking Skills. Give students a half-hour sample ACT or SAT test.

Resources for Varying Instruction
• *Academic and Workplace Skills Activity Book,* pp. 44–54

Professional Development Support
• *How to Manage Instruction in the Block* This teaching resource provides management and activity suggestions.

MEDIA AND TECHNOLOGY

For the Teacher
• **Teacher EXPRESS** CD-ROM

WRITING AND GRAMMAR ON-LINE

Interactive Text (On-line or on CD-ROM)
• Easily navigable instruction with interactive Revision Checkers
• Full use of e-rater™, the essay-scoring system (on-line only)

Companion Web Site PHSchool.com
• Scoring rubrics with models (use Web Code egk-1201)

See the Go On-line! **feature, SE p. iii.**

Lesson Objectives

1. To use study strategies such as note taking, outlining, and using study-guide questions to better understand texts

2. To compile information from primary and secondary sources in systematic ways using available technology

3. To use writing to discover, record, review, and learn

4. To read in varied sources such as diaries, journals, textbooks, maps, newspapers, letters, speeches, memoranda, electronic texts, and other media

5. To use reference material such as glossary, dictionary, thesaurus, and available technology to determine precise meaning and usage

6. To investigate the source of a media presentation or production such as who made it and why it was made

7. To locate appropriate print and non-print information using text and technical resources, including databases and the Internet

8. To produce summaries of texts by identifying main ideas and their supporting details

9. To construct images such as graphic organizers based on text descriptions and text structures

Critical Viewing

Evaluate Students may say the student is well organized, because he is making use of various sources and taking detailed notes on them.

Chapter 31 Study, Reference, and Test-Taking Skills

▲ Critical Viewing
How well-organized for studying do you think this student is? Explain. **[Evaluate]**

In this chapter, you will assess and develop your study, reference, and test-taking skills, making improvements that can enhance your ability to perform various tasks in a wide range of areas.

The first section of this chapter teaches you how to acquire good study skills—skills that will enable you to learn information in a college or job setting more easily. The second section discusses learning how to use the library and other reference materials, as well as how to find the information you need. A final section offers practical strategies to improve your test scores, a skill that is not only important for the aspiring scholar, for whom tests are a way of life, but is also important for those who will encounter employment tests as they enter the job market.

846 • Study, Reference, and Test-Taking Skills

⏱ TIME AND RESOURCE MANAGER	
Resources **Print:** *Academic and Workplace Skills Activity Book*, pp. 44–45	
Using the Full Student Edition	**Using the Handbook**🄷
• Read and discuss pp. 846–849 in class. • Have students develop and evaluate their study plans in small groups. • Have students complete Exercises 1–2 in class.	• Read and discuss pp. 642–645 in class. • Have students develop and evaluate their study plans in small groups. • Have students complete Exercises 1–2 in class.

Section 31.1 Basic Study Skills

Acquiring good study habits can make you a more effective learner in school and at work. This section provides practice in developing a systematic approach to studying. By organizing your study time effectively, you can accomplish everything you need to do and still have leisure time.

Developing a Study Plan

The purpose of a *study plan* is to help you make the best use of the time available to you for studying and completing assignments. Your study plan should include setting up a study area, establishing a study schedule, and keeping a study notebook.

KEY CONCEPT Use a study plan to manage your time for school, study, and other activities. ■

The chart below shows the necessary steps for setting up an effective study plan and its three main parts—study area, study schedule, and study notebook.

STUDY AREA

1. Set up a well-lit area free from distractions.
2. Have available: pens, paper, ruler, dictionary, etc.

STUDY SCHEDULE

1. Block out times for fixed activities: school, job, chores, sports.
2. Plan to study 2–3 hours a day, in 30–45-minute periods.

STUDY PLAN

STUDY NOTEBOOK

1. List assignments and their due dates.
2. List long-term assignments in steps.
3. Check off assignments, or steps of longer ones, as you complete them.

Exercise 1 Using and Evaluating Your Own Study Plan
Develop and use a plan for one week. At the end of the week, identify which parts of your plan need improvement and revise your plan accordingly.

Study, Reference, and Test-Taking Skills • 847

Answer Key

Exercise 1

Have students discuss study plans and revision ideas with partners.

Taking Notes: Outlines

Teaching Resources: Academic and Workplace Skills Activity Book, p. 45

1. Ask students to describe their systems for taking notes. Explain that taking notes can help clarify information, as well as summarize and reinforce it.

2. Have students read the examples of modified and free-form outlines. Ask students to write in a coherent paragraph the content that these notes outline. (The human brain is divided into right and left hemispheres. The left brain is used for logical, organized, mathematical, and grammatical thinking, while the right brain is used for creative, artistic, poetic, and musical thinking.)

3. To practice taking notes, have students close their books. Read them the information in parentheses in Step 2 above. Ask them to take notes in one of the forms shown. After they finish, have students look back at the text to see how close they came to the original notes.

4. Ask students to compare the two types of note-taking. Explain that both forms are useful for quick note-taking from spoken or written material and for organizing ideas on essay tests. Ask which format they feel more comfortable with, and why.

Integrating Workplace Skills

Outlining Tasks In many jobs, experienced workers are asked to outline tasks for less skilled or new workers. (Example: a police officer might outline the process of responding to a burglar alarm for a new officer. The police officer's outline must be clear and easy to follow so that the rookie can act effectively.) Encourage students to brainstorm for other occupations that rely on outlining tasks. Have them write an outline to teach a new student about important procedures in your class or your school.

31.1

Taking Notes

Note-taking, if done properly, can clarify information, as well as summarize and reinforce it. For effective note-taking, keep the information you write down in a notebook that is organized, easy to follow, and up to date. Two valuable methods for taking notes are *outlines* and *summaries.*

▶ **KEY CONCEPT** Keep an organized notebook in which you take notes, in outline or summary form, while listening or reading. ∎

Modified Outlines A modified outline is most useful for quick note-taking from spoken or written material and for organizing ideas for questions on essay tests. When you take notes in a **modified outline form,** record each major topic as a heading when it is introduced. Use capitalization, underlining, or circling to emphasize the heading. Then, under each heading, list the important details using numbers, letters, or dashes.

The notes below, about the functions of the two hemispheres of the human brain, are in modified outline form. Notice the use of capitalization, underlining, and numbers to organize the information.

MODIFIED OUTLINE

Heading	(Left Brain	Right Brain)	Heading
Major topic	(1. Language	1. Synthesizing	Major topic
	People with	People with	
	damage to areas	damage to	
	of the left brain	the right	
Included Ideas	may lose the	brain may	Included Ideas
	ability to speak	have	
	coherently.	difficulty	
		recognizing	
		familiar	
		faces and	
		objects.	

☑ **ONGOING ASSESSMENT: Diagnose**

Use one of the following options to diagnose students' current level of proficiency in study, reference, and test-taking skills.

Option 1 Show students a segment from the *Writers at Work* DVD. Ask them to take notes on the segment. When they finish, collect and review their notes. Students who include too many details or omit the main ideas may need extra support with note-taking skills.

Option 2 Ask students to define a summary. Then have them summarize a short story or essay they've read in class this year. Students who have difficulty with this exercise may need extra support in writing a summary.

Free-form Outlines Use a free-form outline when you are taking notes from loosely structured material. Unlike other outline forms, the **free-form outline** is not written and organized from top to bottom. Instead, the main idea is placed in the center, with related information branching off from it. The following free-form outline shows notes about the same subject as the modified outline. Notice how the format is loose and only brief notes are taken.

FREE-FORM OUTLINE

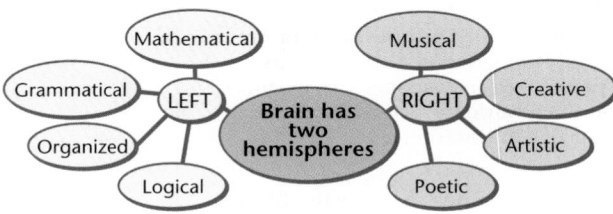

Summaries A **summary** is a brief statement or account that presents the essential information or main ideas of a reading or lecture. Writing a summary forces you to determine what the most important information is and helps you to remember this information by putting it into your own words.

Use the following suggestions to help you summarize information from your reading and listening:

• Listen or read for main ideas.

• Write main ideas in your own words.

• Shape these main ideas into sentences that express the purpose and point of view of the writer or speaker.

• Write the summary in paragraph form. The final material should be no more than one third of its original length.

Exercise 2 Making Modified and Free-form Outlines and Writing a Summary Read a section from one of your textbooks, and take notes on the important information. Use a modified outline form. Then, rewrite this outline as a free-form outline. As a final step, write a summary based on the information in your outlines.

Basic Study Skills • 849

Taking Notes: Summaries

1. Review the definition of a summary with students. Explain to students that writing a summary will help them determine the most important information. This will make it easier for them to remember it.

2. Have students list places they typically read summaries (blurbs on book covers, movie reviews, television guides). Discuss why these summaries are helpful.

3. To practice writing summaries, have students write a summary of a book they have read recently, and share it with a partner. Each summary should consist of one paragraph that describes the book's main idea. If students cannot determine the main idea from their partner's summary, encourage students to rewrite and clarify their work.

Customize for
Interpersonal Learners

Have students work in pairs to complete Exercise 2. Have them take notes on the same section of a textbook. After they finish, have them share and discuss their summaries. Did they both focus on the same main ideas? If not, how do they account for this discrepancy? Did they both include the important details? If necessary, have both students revise their summaries so that they are accurate, clear, and complete.

Answer Key

Exercise 2

Students' outlines and summaries should cover the same information that was contained in their original notes.

Using the Library Catalog

Teaching Resources: Academic and Workplace Skills Activity Book, p. 46

1. Have students review the information on the author card. Pose questions that the card answers. (Example: Is the book fiction or nonfiction? How many pages does it have? When was it published?)

2. If students will be using card catalogs, bring in sample cards for them to examine. Be sure to include author, title, and subject cards. Have students work in pairs and make short quizzes for one another like the questions asked in Step 1 above.

3. Borrow some books from your school or local library and have students create sample catalog cards for them. Make sure that each student makes at least one author card, one title card, and one subject card.

Section 31.2 # *Reference Skills*

The growth of technology in the Information Age has made it possible for you to acquire a great deal of information on your own. Almost every form of printed reference now has its electronic equivalent, either on CD-ROM or on-line or both. Many of these works, in both printed and electronic form, are available at school or in public libraries.

Using the Library: An Overview

Most school and public libraries contain some or all of the following resources: fiction and nonfiction books, audiocassettes and videocassettes, periodicals (newspapers, magazines, and scholarly journals), reference works in printed and electronic form, and computer access to the Internet.

▶ **KEY CONCEPT** Use the library catalog to find valuable information about the resources that a library contains. ■

Using the Library Catalog Whether the books you seek are for pleasure or for research, your starting point is usually the *library catalog*. The catalog will show you whether a library owns a particular book. It can also help you find books by a particular author or books on a particular subject.

The library catalog will be in one of these three forms:

Card Catalog The card catalog lists books on index cards, with each book having a separate *author card* and *title card*; if the book is nonfiction, it also has at least one *subject card*. Cards are filed alphabetically in small drawers, with author cards alphabetized by last names and title cards alphabetized by the first words of the titles, excluding *A*, *An*, and *The*.

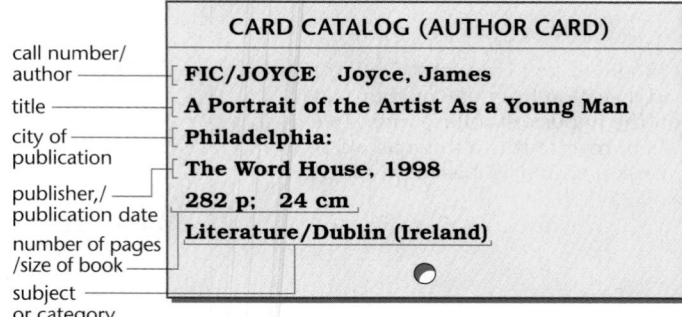

	CARD CATALOG (AUTHOR CARD)
call number/author	FIC/JOYCE Joyce, James
title	A Portrait of the Artist As a Young Man
city of publication	Philadelphia:
publisher,/publication date	The Word House, 1998
number of pages/size of book	282 p; 24 cm
subject or category	Literature/Dublin (Ireland)

⏱ TIME AND RESOURCE MANAGER

Resources
Print: *Academic and Workplace Skills Activity Book*, pp. 46–52

Using the Full Student Edition	Using the Handbook⊞
• Read and discuss pp. 850–860. Have students work on Exercises 3 and 5 in the library, and the others in class.	• Read and discuss pp. 646–656. Have students work on Exercises 3 and 5 in the library, and others in class.
• After covering technology references and the Internet (pp. 861–863), have students do Exercise 10 on computers in school.	• After covering technology references and the Internet (pp. 657–659), have students do Exercise 10 on computers in school.
• Review the exercises with the class.	• Review the exercises with the class.

Printed Catalog This catalog lists books in printed booklets, with each book listed alphabetically by author, by title, and—if nonfiction—by subject. Often there are separate booklets for author, title, and subject listings.

PRINTED CATALOG (TITLE LISTING)		
title		author
A PORTRAIT OF THE ARTIST AS A YOUNG MAN/		James Joyce
city of publication	publisher	publication date
Philadelphia	Chelsea House	1998
number of pages	size of book	
282p.	24cm.	
subject		call number
Literature/Dublin (Ireland)		FIC JOYCE

Electronic Catalog This catalog lists books on a CD-ROM or in an on-line database that you access from special computer terminals in the library. You can usually find a book's catalog entry by typing in its title, key words in the title, its author's name, or for nonfiction, an appropriate subject.

Author:	**Joyce, James.**
Title:	**A Portrait of the Artist As a Young Man.**
Published:	**Philadelphia: Chelsea House.**
Description:	**282p.; 24 cm.**
Subject:	**Literature/Dublin(Ireland).**
Call No.:	**FIC JOYCE**
Status:	**On shelf.**

Exercise 3 **Using the Library Catalog** Visit your school or local library, and use the catalog to answer these questions.
1. What kind of catalogs does the library use—card, printed, or electronic? Where are they located?
2. Who wrote *War and Peace*? Is it fiction or nonfiction?
3. What are the titles, subjects, and call numbers of the books that your library carries by author George Schaller?
4. What are the titles, authors, and call numbers of three books about Japan published since 1985?
5. What are the titles and call numbers of two nonfiction books about whales that are more than 100 pages long?

 **Technology Tip**

In electronic database searches, be sure to type carefully and spell everything correctly. One wrong letter often means inaccurate results.

Printed Catalog and Electronic Catalog

1. Ask students to compare and contrast the card catalog and the printed card catalog. Make sure that students notice that all the same information is given, but that the information is in a different order.

2. Explain how to use an electronic card catalog. If your students have used this type of catalog before, have them add to your description. If possible, bring students to the school library and demonstrate the process as you discuss it.

3. Have students generate a list of ways someone might search for the book *A Portrait of the Artist as a Young Man* with an electronic catalog. (Any words in the book title, other than very short words such as articles and conjunctions, can be used in the search.)

4. If your students will be using electronic catalogs to find books, allow them to practice on a computer.

Customize for
Spatial Learners

Have students draw a map of the school library that shows where the catalogs and reference desk are located. They can fill in the rest of the map when they learn about the location of other library materials later in the chapter. These maps can be used as reference aids for the classroom.

Answer Key

Exercise 3
1. Answers will vary.
2. Leo Tolstoy; fiction
3. Answers will vary.
4. Answers will vary.
5. Answers will vary.

Finding Books on Library Shelves

Teaching Resources: Academic and Workplace Skills Activity Book, p. 47

1. Have each student pick a fiction, nonfiction, biography, or reference book from a sample group you have collected from the library. Cover the call numbers with labels beforehand. Students may work in groups if classroom resources are limited.

2. Have students decide into what category each book falls and what classification system would appear on the book's spine. Note that nonfiction books might be classified under either the Dewey Decimal or Library of Congress system. Discuss each with the class.

3. Next, have students group the books in fiction and nonfiction categories. Ask students to decide in what order the books might appear on the library shelves. Remind students that fiction should be shelved alphabetically by author. Nonfiction and other reference books should be ordered by number according to the main classes of the Dewey Decimal System. Biographies should be alphabetized by the last name of the subject, not the author.

31.2

Finding Books on Library Shelves By using a special method of organizing books, a library ensures that people can find specific titles. A library distinguishes between two kinds of books: *fiction* (made-up stories) and *nonfiction* (factual material), which is organized according to one of two systems—the *Dewey Decimal System* or the *Library of Congress System*. Nonfiction also includes two smaller groups that are often shelved separately: *biographies* and *reference books*.

▶ **KEY CONCEPT** Fiction and nonfiction books are shelved separately in a library. Each category follows a special method of organization. ■

Fiction In most libraries, fiction books are shelved in a special section alphabetized by authors' last names. In the library catalog and on the book's spine, a work of fiction may be labeled *F* or *FIC*, followed by one or more letters of the author's last name.

Nonfiction Nonfiction books are assigned different numbers and letters. These number and letter codes, called *call numbers*, are placed on the spine of each book, and the books are arranged in number-letter order (according to the Dewey Decimal System) or letter-number order (according to the Library of Congress System) on the shelves. To find a nonfiction book, look it up in the library catalog and find out its call number; then, follow number-letter or letter-number order to locate the book on the library shelves.

The **Dewey Decimal System** can help you determine the subject of a book from its number. This classification system divides all knowledge into ten main areas numbered from 000 to 999. The chart below shows the main content areas:

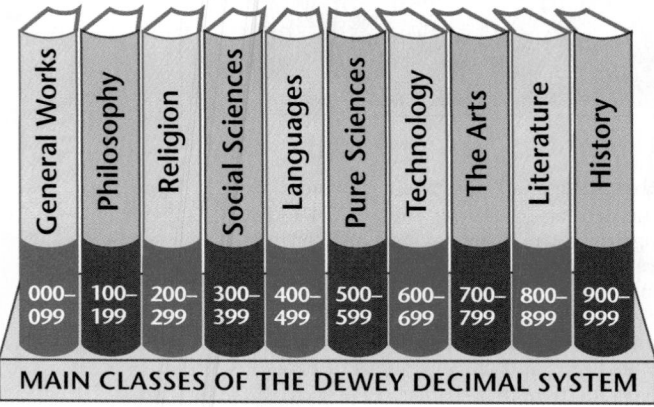

General Works	Philosophy	Religion	Social Sciences	Languages	Pure Sciences	Technology	The Arts	Literature	History
000–099	100–199	200–299	300–399	400–499	500–599	600–699	700–799	800–899	900–999

MAIN CLASSES OF THE DEWEY DECIMAL SYSTEM

852 • Study, Reference, and Test-Taking Skills

Standardized test questions may require students to demonstrate their knowledge of library and reference skills. Provide students with opportunities to learn and practice these skills.

Which phrase below describes the main function of a call number in the Dewey Decimal or Library of Congress system?

A to enable readers to locate a book

B to identify the title of each book

C to divide a library's books into categories

D to provide a reference in the library

Students should recognize that **A**, to enable readers to locate a book, is the main purpose of a call number. This system is used in almost all libraries so that readers will always know how and where to locate books.

The **Library of Congress System**, unlike the Dewey Decimal System, is organized letter-number, meaning that the call numbers begin with letters. The main classes are designated by a single letter; combinations of two letters designate subclasses. The letter designations are followed by a numerical notation from 1 to 9999, which can be further subdivided:

MAIN CLASS: H   Social Sciences
SUBCLASS: HA   Statistics
DIVISION: HA   Theory and Method
             29

Biographies are nonfiction books about real-life people. Most often, they are not assigned call numbers but are shelved in a special section alphabetized by the last names of their subjects (the people they are about). In the library catalog and on the book's spine, a biography may be labeled *B* or *BIO*, followed by one or more letters of the subject's last name: For example, *BIO Ein* may appear on a biography of Albert Einstein.

Reference books may also be shelved in their own special section of a library. Frequently, the sources in the library's reference section are labeled *R* or *REF*. If the book is nonfiction, a call number follows the abbreviation. Thus, if a book you look up in the card catalog has *REF* before its call number, go first to the library's reference section, and then use the call number to locate the book on the shelves in that section. Reference books are usually not allowed to circulate outside the library.

▶ **Exercise 4** Finding Books on Library Shelves

1. To find fiction by Graham Greene, would you look before or after fiction by Nadine Gordimer?
2. To find a nonfiction book with the call number 912.82N, would you look before or after a book with the call number 913.35F?
3. For a book with call number J438.4R, would you look in the reference, biography, or children's nonfiction section?
4. List these works of fiction in the order in which you would find them on the library shelves: *Clear Light of Day* by Anita Desai, *Emma* by Jane Austen, *Jude the Obscure* by Thomas Hardy, *Bleak House* by Charles Dickens, *Miguel Street* by V. S. Naipaul.
5. Arrange these call numbers in the order in which you would find them on the library shelves: 276.2M, 276.2J, 276.1L , 275.6R, 277.3S. What general subject matter would you expect to be the subject of these books?

Integrating Spelling Skills

Alphabetizing Explain that when students are looking for fiction or a biography, they will have to search by alphabetical order. Remind students of the rules for alphabetizing. To practice alphabetizing with the whole class, ask the students to pretend they are all the subjects of biographies. Have them arrange books about themselves on an imaginary library shelf.

Customize for
Less Advanced Students

Students may have difficulty knowing which of the strategies to apply to each question in Exercise 4. To avoid confusion, read through the questions one by one with the students. After reading each question, ask the students to decide whether it is about fiction, nonfiction, biographies, or reference books. Have students write their answers beside each question. This will help students know which book-finding strategy to apply to each question.

Answer Key

▶ **Exercise 4**

1. After
2. Before
3. children's nonfiction
4. Austen, Desai, Dickens, Hardy, Naipaul
5. 275.6R, 276.1L, 276.2J, 276.2M, 277.3S; Religion

Using Periodicals, Periodical Indexes, and the Vertical File

Teaching Resources: Academic and Workplace Skills Activity Book, p. 48

1. Although not all students will be familiar with the term *periodicals*, most students will have read them. Ask students to list newspapers and magazines that they read regularly. Explain that these are all periodicals.

2. Have students examine the sample Readers' Guide entry on page 854. Ask students to compare this entry to the information given about a book in a catalog entry. (Periodical indexes give the title of the magazine, the volume, and page number in addition to the author, title, and publication date.)

3. Have students consider when a periodical might be more useful to their research than a book. (Example: An article might have the most up-to-date information about a subject.)

4. Point out the Technology Tip and Research Tip on page 854. Students may need to get bibliographical information about a periodical from a periodical index. This is especially true if an article is downloaded by computer. The downloaded article may be text only and may not include the necessary bibliographical information.

31.2

Using Periodicals, Periodical Indexes, and the Vertical File

Periodicals are printed materials (newspapers, magazines, and journals) published daily, weekly, or at another regular interval. To search through this information, you need to use *periodical indexes* and the citations found within them. Folded maps, booklets, and pamphlets (works with a narrow focus in a small format) are found in the vertical file.

▶ **KEY CONCEPT** Use articles from periodicals for up-to-date information and use periodical indexes and citations to locate the articles. ■

Periodicals Some periodicals are of general interest, while others are devoted to specialized topics. Because of their current nature, periodicals can be a valuable research aid for information that is not available in books.

Periodical Indexes and Citations To find which periodicals contain articles on a particular subject, you need to consult a *periodical index*. Issued regularly in printed or electronic form, these indexes contain *citations* that tell where and when the article was published.

SOME COMMON PERIODICAL INDEXES

- *Readers' Guide to Periodical Literature*, often referred to as the *Readers' Guide*, covers all types of periodicals
- *Art Index, Humanities Index*
- *Business Periodicals Index*

Below is a sample entry from the *Readers' Guide*:

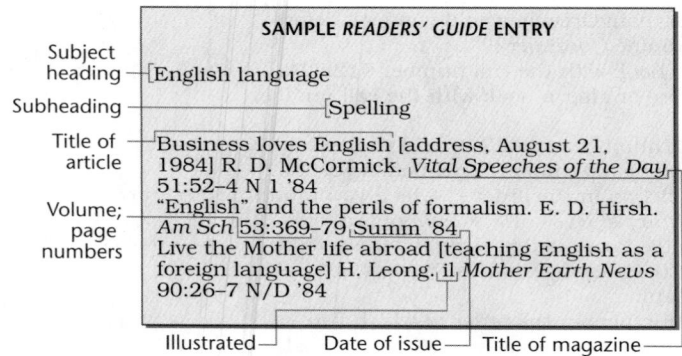

SAMPLE *READERS' GUIDE* ENTRY

Subject heading — English language
Subheading — Spelling
Title of article — Business loves English [address, August 21, 1984] R. D. McCormick. *Vital Speeches of the Day* 51:52–4 N 1 '84
Volume; page numbers — "English" and the perils of formalism. E. D. Hirsh. *Am Sch* 53:369–79 Summ '84
Live the Mother life abroad [teaching English as a foreign language] H. Leong. il *Mother Earth News* 90:26–7 N/D '84

Illustrated — Date of issue — Title of magazine

Technology Tip

If the library computer is connected to a printer, you can generally print out a list of citations or the full text of articles for a fee. It may also be possible to download information onto a diskette that you can then use on another computer.

Research Tip

The information provided in the citation is also the information you need to list the article in a bibliography.

How to Use Periodical Indexes The citations in *printed indexes* are listed alphabetically by subject and, sometimes, also by author. These citations may include *abstracts*, or brief summaries, of the articles. In *electronic indexes*, citations are contained in a database that you can usually search by entering the subject, the author's name, or a key word or phrase in the title of the article. Some electronic indexes also provide the full text of the article cited.

Vertical Files Small printed materials, unsuitable for shelving, are arranged alphabetically by subject in a special filing cabinet called a *vertical file*. These materials include pamphlets, booklets, folded maps, original newspaper and magazine clippings, and photographs. The vertical file contains material of both historic interest (newspaper clippings) and current concern (pamphlets). Do not hesitate to ask the librarian whether information on the topic of your research might be found in the vertical file.

> ### ▶ Learn More
>
> For more on how dictionaries can help improve your vocabulary, see Chapter 29.

Exercise 5 Using Periodicals, Periodical Indexes, and the Vertical File Visit your school or local library to answer these questions.

1. Which printed periodical indexes does the library have? Which electronic indexes are available?
2. Which newspapers does the library carry? Is microfilm or microfiche available for back issues of the newspapers?
3. Give the titles of two magazines about nature and conservation that the library carries. How far back do they go? In what format are they available?
4. Using the most current issue of the *Readers' Guide*, find a citation for an article on someone you admire. Read the article in a copy of the magazine in the library, and then summarize it. (Many libraries store copies of the most current magazines and newspapers for reference use until they are bound or transferred onto microfilm.)
5. What specialized maps are available in the vertical file?

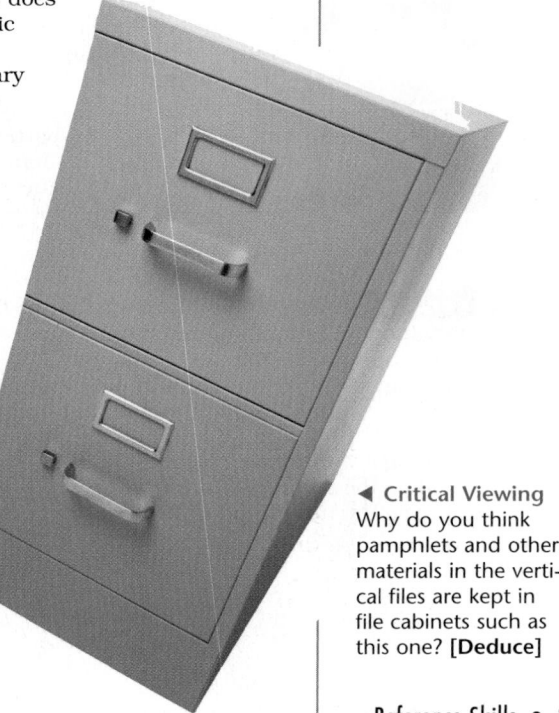

◀ Critical Viewing Why do you think pamphlets and other materials in the vertical files are kept in file cabinets such as this one? [Deduce]

Reference Skills • 855

Using Dictionaries

Teaching Resources: Academic and Workplace Skills Activity Book, p. 49

1. Review the three types of dictionaries on page 856. Have students explain why they might use each type of dictionary. (They use unabridged dictionaries to find very unusual words or words for which they need a complete definition. They use abridged dictionaries for quick references of commonly used words. They use specialized dictionaries for particular subjects such as chemistry or math.)

2. To practice finding words in dictionaries, stage a race. Give each student or group of students a dictionary. Choose a word for students to find and then time them to see how quickly they can find the word. Record students' times and see whether each student or team can beat its own score.

Customize for
AP Students

Encourage students to generate a list of specialized dictionaries and post their lists for class reference. Among the specialized dictionaries they might list are dictionaries of American slang, zoological dictionaries, dictionaries of literary terms, and rhyming dictionaries.

Customize for
ESL Students

Have students make a list of the reference materials in your school library that are helpful for English language learners. For example, they might find bilingual dictionaries, thesauruses, or English language primers. If they cannot find any helpful materials, have them talk to the librarian about obtaining some.

Answer Key

▶ **Exercise 6**

1. unabridged
2. specialized
3. abridged
4. unabridged
5. specialized

31.2

Using Dictionaries

A *dictionary*, in either printed or electronic form, is an indispensable reference tool that contains a vast amount of information about words.

▶ **KEY CONCEPT** A **dictionary** contains information about words, including spellings, definitions, pronunciations, parts of speech, and origins. ■

Distinguishing Types of Dictionaries Dictionaries are compiled for different audiences and purposes: for students to use in schoolwork, for adults to use at home or at work, and for scholars to use in research. Dictionaries may come in both printed and electronic form. The following are the three main types of dictionaries.

THREE TYPES OF DICTIONARIES	
Unabridged	Exhaustive study of the English language containing over 250,000 words
Abridged	Compact editions containing listings of 55,000 to 160,000 words
Specialized	Limited to words of a particular type or field, such as foreign languages or mathematics

▶ **Exercise 6** Choosing a Dictionary Name the kind of dictionary (*unabridged*, *abridged*, or *specialized*) that would be the most appropriate for each task:
1. finding special detailed information about a word
2. finding a comprehensive definition of a legal or medical term
3. finding a word's basic meaning
4. finding the origin of a word
5. finding the translation of a foreign word

☑ ONGOING ASSESSMENT: Monitor and Reinforce

Help students become familiar with the various parts of a dictionary by using one of the following strategies.

Option 1 Have students create a dictionary entry for a word they have learned in a foreign language class. To find the etymology of the word, they might consult a bilingual dictionary or ask their language teacher about other useful resources.	**Option 2** Have students teach a partner a word they recently learned in a class discussion, lecture, or textbook. Make sure they include all of the information in the dictionary entry in their explanations.

Finding Words in Printed Dictionaries

A word listed in a dictionary, along with all the information about it, is called an *entry*. The *entry word* is the word defined. In printed dictionaries, entry words are arranged alphabetically. To speed your search for a word, use the following aids:

Thumb Index This series of right-hand notches allows you to thumb alphabetically through a dictionary. Each notch, labeled *A, B, C,* and so on, shows the section of entries for words that start with the letter or letters on it.

Guide Words Two large or boldfaced words at the top of each dictionary page show the first and last entry words on that page. All other entry words on that page fall alphabetically between these two guide words.

The Four-Section Approach To find words quickly, use the four-section approach, following these steps:

1. Mentally divide the dictionary into the four sections:

    ABCD   MNOPQR

    EFGHIJKL   STUVWXYZ

2. When you go to look up a word, decide into which section the word falls. For example, if you want to look up *homeostasis*, you know that the word falls near the middle of the second section. If, on the other hand, you want to look up *scruple*, you know that the word falls near the beginning of the last section. Flip to that section, and then complete your search using the thumb index and guide words.

Finding Words in Electronic Dictionaries

In electronic dictionaries, you usually find a word's entry simply by typing the word and having the computer search the dictionary database. If you are unsure of a word's spelling, you can usually type in the first few letters and see a list of words that are similar in spelling.

> **Exercise 7** Working With a Dictionary Use a dictionary or your knowledge of a dictionary to answer these questions.
> 1. Which dictionary would be the most appropriate for finding detailed information of a word's history?
> 2. Which dictionary would be most appropriate for finding the translation of a word?
> 3. In your dictionary, what two guide words appear on the page with the word *declivity*?
> 4. Which entry words would appear on a page with the guide words *infective* and *infix*?
>   a. infer   b. infinite   c. inflame   d. infirmary
> 5. Which guide words would appear with the word *powder*?
>   a. powerboat/practice b. practiced/proa c. poultry/power

Integrating Spelling Skills

British-English Words Encourage students to notice how English differs from one English-speaking nation to the next. Explain to students that understanding the origin of English words is beneficial when using dictionary entries. Write the following words containing British spellings on the board. Challenge students to find the U.S.-English versions and their definitions. Then, challenge students to find more British-English words.

organisation

travelled

colour

Answer Key

> **Exercise 7**

1. unabridged
2. specialized
3. answers will vary
4. a, b, d
5. c

Customize for
ESL Students

Students whose native language does not use the Roman alphabet may need extra assistance with questions 3–5 of Exercise 6. Although these students may be able to read and understand the questions, they might benefit from a visual display of the alphabet. If necessary, have them write the alphabet on the top of their notebook paper. They can refer to it as they answer these questions.

Understanding Dictionary Entries

1. Before students read the text pages 858–859, have them generate a list of all the things a dictionary tells about a word.

2. Have students compare their lists with the list in the text.

3. Read aloud or have students take turns reading each of the dictionary entry definitions.

4. After reading each item, have students look at the definition of the word *cue*. Which of the types of information can be found in the dictionary entry for the word *cue*?

31.2

Understanding Dictionary Entries In a dictionary, a word and all the information about it are called an *entry*. The word itself is called an *entry word*.

MAIN ENTRY IN A DICTIONARY

Part of Speech

Etymology

Entry Word — **cue**[1] (kyo͞o) *n.* [< *q, Q,* used in plays in 16th &
Pronunciation — 17th c. to indicate actors' entrances; prob.
Etymology — abbrev. of some L. word (as *quando,* when, *qualis,* in what manner)] **1.** a bit of dialogue, action, or music that is a signal for an actor's entrance or speech, or for the working of
Numbered Definitions — curtains, lights, sound effects, etc. **2.** the few notes or bars of music directly preceding an instrumentalist's or vocalist's part and serving as a signal to begin that part **3.** anything serving as a signal to do something **4.** [Now
Usage Labels — Rare] the role that one is assigned to play **5.** [Archaic] frame of mind; mood; temperament
Field Label — **6.** *Psychol.* a secondary stimulus that guides behavior, often without entering
Part of Speech (2) — consciousness —*vt.* **cued, cu′ing** or **cue′ing**
Inflected Forms — to give a cue to —**cue in** to add (dialogue,
Idiom — music, etc.) at a particular point in a script

Entry Word An entry word may be a single word, a compound word (two words acting as a single word), an abbreviation, a prefix or suffix, or a person, place, or event.

Syllabification Dots, spaces, or slashes in an entry word show where that word may be divided when breaking words at the end of a line. Remember that you cannot leave a syllable of just one letter on a line by itself. Words with one syllable are never divided.

Pronunciation Appearing right after the entry word, the pronunciation uses symbols to show how to say the word and which syllable to stress. (The key to these symbols may be found along the bottom of the page or at the beginning of the dictionary.) The syllable that gets the most emphasis has a *primary stress*, usually shown by a heavy mark after the syllable. Words of more than one syllable may also have a *secondary stress*, usually shown by a shorter, lighter mark.

858 • Study, Reference, and Test-Taking Skills

Part-of-Speech Label This label, an abbreviation usually given after the pronunciation, tells how a word can be used in a sentence—whether it functions as a noun, a verb, or some other part of speech.

Plurals and Inflected Forms After the part-of-speech label, dictionaries may also show the plural forms of nouns and the inflected forms of verbs—past tense and past participle—if their spelling is irregular.

Etymology The origin and history of a word are called its *etymology*. The word's etymology usually appears in brackets, parentheses, or slashes near the beginning or end of the entry. Abbreviations for languages are explained in the dictionary's key to abbreviations.

Definition and Example The *definition* is the meaning of the word. Definitions are numbered if there is more than one. Often, they include examples illustrating the uses of meanings in phrases or sentences.

Usage Labels These labels show how the word is generally used. Words labeled *Archaic* (*Arch.*), *Obsolete* (*Obs.*), *Poetic*, or *Rare* are not widely used today. Words labeled *Informal* (*Inf.*), *Colloquial* (*Colloq.*), or *Slang* are not considered part of standard English. Words labeled *Brit.* are used mainly in Britain, not in the United States.

Field Labels These labels show whether a word is used in a special way by people in a certain occupation or activity, such as *History* (*Hist.*), *Astronomy* (*Astron.*), or *Biology* (*Biol.*).

Idioms and Derived Words The end of an entry may list and define idioms, or expressions, that contain the entry word. It may also list derived words, which are formed from the entry word, along with a part-of-speech label.

▶ **Exercise 8** Understanding Dictionary Entries Use a dictionary to answer these questions.
1. If you have to break the word *nourish* at the end of a line, where should you put the hyphen?
2. From what language does the word *indulge* originally come? What does it mean in that language?
3. Identify two meanings of the word *incident*—one as an adjective and one as a noun.
4. What does the idiom *whistle in the dark* mean?
5. Is there an adverb and a noun derived from the word *mean*? If so, what are they?

Answer Key

▶ **Exercise 8**

1. nour-ish
2. Latin. "To be kind or to yield to"
3. Adjective: "liable to happen"; Noun: "an event; occurence"
4. "To pretend confidence in the face of a threat"
5. Answers will vary.

Using Other Print References

Teaching Resources: Academic and Workplace Skills Activity Book, p. 50

1. Ask students to discuss the reference section of their public or school library. In addition to dictionaries, what books might they find in this section of the library? (encyclopedias, almanacs, thesauruses)

2. Have students look at the list of other reference works to remind them of the various types of books they will find in the reference section.

3. Read or have a student read about each type of reference work listed. After reading each entry, have students offer ideas about how and why they might use each type of reference book. Refer students to the Technology Tip.

Critical Viewing

Analyze Students may suggest encyclopedia entries on Henry James, on nineteenth century fiction, or on the history of New York City.

Customize for
Logical/Mathematical Learners

Students will enjoy the challenge of finding the answers to Exercise 9 in the fewest possible steps. Have students record the number of steps or searches it took them to find the answers. Which questions took the fewest steps? Which took the most? How can they explain these differences? What can they do to perform more efficient searches?

Answer Key

> **Exercise 9**

1. *Roderick Hudson*
2. Elizabeth Blackwell
3. Mt. Kilimanjaro
4. Lisbon
5. Answers will vary but may include *cunning, tricky, wily, crafty, slippery, shrewd, clever, deceitful,* and *subtle.*

31.2

Using Other Print References

Most libraries have a variety of useful *reference works*, resources to which you can refer for specific information.

> **KEY CONCEPT** Libraries offer a wide range of useful reference works in printed and electronic form. ∎

Encyclopedias An encyclopedia is a collection of articles providing basic information on a great many subjects.

A *general* encyclopedia contains articles providing information on a wealth of subjects. *Specialized encyclopedias*, such as an encyclopedia of literature or of animals, cover a particular subject comprehensively, featuring articles that may be more detailed than those in a general encyclopedia.

Encyclopedia articles are arranged alphabetically by subject. People are alphabetized by their last name. Printed encyclopedias usually span several volumes, with letters printed on each spine to show which subjects a particular volume contains. Not all topics have their own article, but an alphabetical index tells you in which articles particular topics are covered. *Electronic encyclopedias* offer searches by key term.

Almanacs Almanacs are annually issued handbooks that provide lists and statistics on many subjects, including government, history, geography, weather, science, technology, and entertainment. To find a subject in a *printed almanac*, use the index. In an *electronic almanac*, use the search feature.

Atlases and Gazetteers *Atlases* and *gazetteers* contain maps and geographical information based on them. Some also show statistics about population, climates, agriculture, and so on. A *gazetteer* is a dictionary or index of place names, often including populations and sizes. In *printed atlases*, you use the *index* to find out which map shows a particular place. *Electronic map collections* offer a search feature.

Thesauruses A *thesaurus* is a specialized dictionary, arranged alphabetically or thematically, that lists *synonyms*, or words with similar meanings.

> **Exercise 9** Using Other Reference Works Use printed or electronic reference works to find answers to these questions. Indicate the type of reference you used.
> 1. What was Henry James's first published novel?
> 2. Who was the first American woman to receive a medical degree?
> 3. What is the highest mountain in Africa?
> 4. What is the capital city of Portugal?
> 5. What are five synonyms for the adjective *sly*?

⊕ Technology Tip

In electronic reference works, you can find information by browsing an alphabetical list or by typing in a subject or key word and having the computer search the database.

▼ **Critical Viewing** Give the names of two encyclopedia articles in which you might expect to find information about Henry James. **[Analyze]**

Customize for
Spatial Learners

Exercise 9 may be more beneficial if these students create a chart. Have them divide their papers into four equal parts. Label these parts, "encyclopedia," "almanac," "atlas," and "thesaurus." As students read each question, have them place it in the category in which they think they will find the answer. Then, have them look in the reference works to determine whether they were correct.

Using Electronic and Media References

There are more resources for research than just books. A wide range of electronic and media resources—including video collections, CD-ROMs, the Internet, and on-line subscription services—can aid you in research.

Video References Much information can be found in video format. Consult your librarian to find out about videos such as the following:

- **News programs** offer current information and insights into how people reacted to historical events as they happened.
- **Documentaries** give in-depth information on specific topics.
- **Special-interest series** provide extended, detailed coverage of many aspects of a topic—for example, the Bill Moyers series on the history of the English language provides valuable insights into how the language evolved.

CD-ROM References Reference works may appear on CD-ROM, as well as in printed form.

- **CD-ROM encyclopedias** contain the same amount of information as a complete print encyclopedia. Many CD-ROM encyclopedias also include video and audio segments. Their search function typically enables you to find information on a topic in each place it is discussed.
- **CD-ROM atlases** take the form of a database. By entering a place name or key word, you can call up relevant maps.

Electronic Databases Electronic databases are collections of data on a specific topic. They may be available on CD-ROM or over the Internet. Databases enable you to search for specific terms. These forms of data storage do not suffer from some of the limitations of traditional forms. All of the data appear in one "place"—your computer screen—rather than being spread out in different file cabinets. Computer searches can also reduce the time spent finding specific information.

Technology Tip

Although electronic reference works are valuable resources for your research, your library probably has a limited number of computer terminals for users. Ask the librarian if there is a time when there may be less demand for the computers.

Using Electronic and Media References

Teaching Resources: Academic and Workplace Skills Activity Book, p. 51

1. Discuss informational videos that students have seen. Have them volunteer the subjects of the videos, and compile a class list. What kinds of topics seem appropriate to video coverage? (Students may cite current events, modern history, popular culture.) Which of these might make a good essay topic?

2. Encourage students to familiarize themselves with CD-ROM resources in their school or local libraries. Ask students to tell you why a CD-ROM encyclopedia may be easier to use than a printed copy. (Key words and topics may be searched for quickly and easily.)

3. Determine whether your school's library subscribes to any electronic databases. Arrange for a librarian to demonstrate how to access them and to describe the types of information they offer. Encourage students to use these databases at their earliest opportunity and report on their experiences to the class.

4. Have students compare the information offered by print and electronic maps and atlases. Which type is more complete? Which type is easier to read?

Using the Internet

Teaching Resources: Academic and Workplace Skills Activity Book, p. 52

1. Ask students to describe their experiences searching for information on the Internet. Did they find it easy or difficult to use? Could they move quickly from one topic to another? Could they tell whether one site was better than another? How?

2. Caution students that anyone can post a Web page; therefore, the quality of information on the World Wide Web varies widely. Significant information obtained from an Internet source should be cross-checked.

3. Ask students to think of ways to ensure that their research on the World Wide Web is reliable. (check a second Internet source, check a library source, talk to an expert)

Integrating Viewing and Representing Skills

Have students create a graphic representation of an Internet search. In the center of the page have students place their choice of search engine and the word or phrase that they will search for. Then, have students list the results of the search in a circle around the search engine. Finally, have students visit several of the sites and record any helpful links these sites contain. The end results should be web-like diagrams representing the interconnected information the Internet provides.

31.2

Using the Internet

As you may know, the *Internet* is a global network of computers connected by telephone and cable lines. When you go *online*, or access the Internet, you can visit (call up on screen) any Web site on the network. A huge variety of information is available on these sites. Each Web site has its own address, or URL (Universal Resource Locator). It usually consists of several pages of text, graphics, and sometimes audio or video displays. Many school and public libraries offer Internet access.

▶ **KEY CONCEPT** Use search engines to locate information on the Internet. ■

Locating Appropriate Web Sites Use these tips for searching the Web.

- If you know a reliable Web site and its address (URL), simply type the address into your Web browser.

- If you don't know of a particular Web site for a topic, you can use an Internet search engine to find the information. Use general search engines to search for a key term. Use other search engines to search by category. Use "metasearch engines" to find the top "hits" from other search engines.

▶ **KEY CONCEPT** Always evaluate the reliability of each Internet source you use. ■

Evaluating Web Sites Almost anyone can create a Web site, but not everyone will provide reliable information. Use these tips to evaluate information you find on the Internet:

- Check the sponsor of the site. Rely more on sites established by respected publishers or organizations than on those placed by a discussion group or an individual.

- Check the credentials of the source, such as experience in the field or affiliation with a recognized organization.

- Analyze the motives of the source. Some organizations or individuals may have an interest in persuading you to form a certain opinion or to buy a certain product and may be less objective than other sources.

- Check the date when the page was last updated, to determine how up to date the information is.

- Also, consult reference librarians familiar with the Internet or Internet coverage in established library journals (such as *Booklist* and the *Library Journal*) for information on useful, reliable reference Web sites.

Technology Tip

Whenever possible, copy and paste URLs from an electronic source to the location (address) line of your browser. This common editing feature allows you to transfer URLs among word-processing programs, e-mail, and the Internet. It's easier, saves time, and there is no chance that you will type one or two letters or numbers of the URL incorrectly.

862 • Study, Reference, and Test-Taking Skills

Evaluating Information on Web Sites Even a reliable Web site may contain inaccurate or misleading information. Critically examine the information you find. Look for the evidence given for important claims. As in all research, verify important information using at least one, preferably two, additional sources. Generally, print sources are preferred to electronic sources.

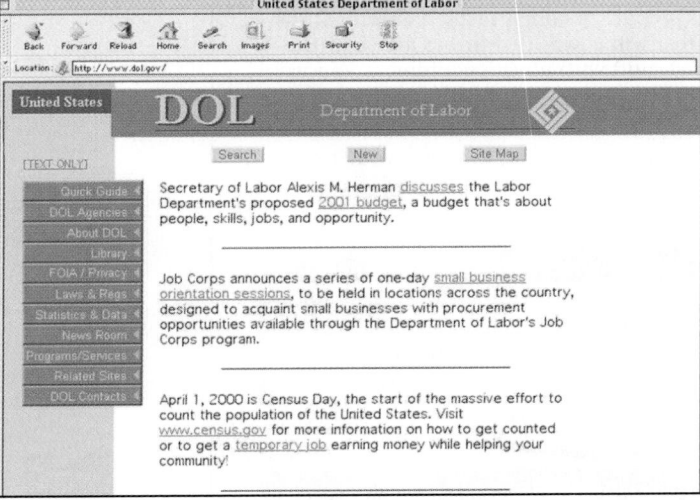

Exercise 10 Using the Internet Using a computer in your library, school computer lab, or at home, go on-line and research information to carry out the following tasks.
1. Find the ZIP Code for Anaheim, California.
2. Find the director and cast members of a contemporary film.
3. List the names and URLs of four Web sites that you think can help you write a history paper on the Roman Empire.
4. Find lyrics for a version of the ballad "John Henry." Record the name and URL of your source. Give an evaluation of the credibility of the source, explaining the reasons for your judgment.
5. From a reliable source, find five facts about tigers. Record your source information, and include an evaluation of its credibility, giving support for your evaluation.

Technology Tip

You can often print out a Web page or download it onto a diskette. On a home computer, you can also highlight and copy and paste it into a file in your word-processing program.

◄ **Critical Viewing** What can you tell about this Web site based on its Home Page? **[Analyze]**

Reference Skills • 863

Step-by-Step Teaching Guide

Evaluating Information on Web Sites

1. Discuss how the Internet affects students' lives. How would their lives change if there were suddenly no Internet? How do they expect the Internet and its uses to change by the time they are thirty years old?

2. Invite students to share the kinds of information they have gathered and the kinds of services they have received from the Internet.

3. Caution students to evaluate the credibility and biases of Internet sources before they use them. Students should ask themselves questions such as these when evaluating their sources:

   Does this site present a balanced description or argument, or is it biased in one direction?

   Does this source have a reputation for providing accurate, factual information?

   Can students discern whether the site's content provider has the expertise and experience to back up his or her statements?

   Does this source offer the most current information on this topic?

Integrating Viewing and Representing Skills

Comparing Servers A growing number of Internet Service Providers (ISPs) are available. Have students identify two or three and compare them. How do the ISPs use design, color, sound effects, organization, and other techniques to make themselves user-friendly? What are the disadvantages or limitations of each ISP? What groups of people do students think are the intended users of each ISP? Which of these ISPs do students prefer? Why?

Critical Viewing

Analyze Students may note that the Web site offers news about the Department of Labor as well as a menu of other resources.

Answer Key

▶ **Exercise 10**
1. 92801–92808
2.–5. Answers will vary.

Taking Objective Tests

Teaching Resources: Academic and Workplace Skills Activity Book, pp. 53–54

1. Ask students to discuss whether and how they budget their time during a test. After the discussion, refer students to the chart on this page. Have them compare their methods with the one described here.

2. Ask students the maximum amount of time they should spend looking over a test if the total time for the test is thirty minutes (about three minutes). One hour? (about six minutes)

3. Read aloud or have a student read the second section of the chart. Ask students the minimum amount of time they should spend answering questions on a test if the total time for the test is thirty minutes (about twenty-one minutes). One hour? (about forty-two minutes)

4. Read aloud or have a student read the third section of the chart. Ask students to discuss how this will help them with a test. (It will help them make sure they have followed all the directions and not skipped any questions.) Ask students the maximum amount of time they should spend proofreading a test if the total time for the test is thirty minutes (about six minutes). One hour? (about twelve minutes)

5. To reinforce the ideas on the chart, have students re-create it as a pie chart. Students should keep the pie charts on loose-leaf paper in the front of their notebooks so that they can refer to the chart easily when taking a test.

Integrating Test-Taking Skills

When taking objective tests, students must often transfer their answers from a test booklet to an answer sheet. In the proofreading stage, students should make sure that they have accurately transferred their answers to the correct portion of the answer sheet.

Test-Taking Skills

In this section, you will learn strategies to improve your performance on objective tests.

Taking Objective Tests

Objective tests are those in which each question has a single correct answer. To prepare for such tests, carefully study the material that the test will cover. Be sure to arrive at the test on time, well rested, and with all the equipment you were told to bring—pencils, pens, books, watch, and so on.

KEY CONCEPT When taking a test, organize your time, dividing it among three steps: previewing, answering, and proofreading. ■

LOOK OVER THE TEST (No more than 10% of time)

1. Skim the test to get an overview of the types of questions.
2. Decide how much time you want to spend on each section.
3. Plan to devote the most time to questions that are hardest or worth the most points.

ANSWER THE QUESTIONS (allow at least 70% of time)

1. Answer the easy questions first. Put a check next to harder questions, and come back to them later.
2. If permitted, use scratch paper to jot down your ideas.
3. Read each question at least twice before answering.
4. Supply the single best answer.
5. Answer all questions on the test unless you are told not to guess or that there is a penalty for wrong guesses.
6. Do not change your first answer without a good reason.

PROOFREAD ANSWERS (No more than 20% of time)

1. Check that you have followed directions completely.
2. Reread test questions and answers. Make sure that you have answered all of the questions.

⏱ TIME AND RESOURCE MANAGER

Resources
Print: *Academic and Workplace Skills Activity Book*, pp. 53–54; *Formal Assessment*, Ch. 31

Using the Full Student Edition	Using the Handbook🄷
• Read and discuss pp. 864–869 in class. • Have students complete Exercises 11–13 in class. • Have students share and discuss their answers.	• Read and discuss pp. 660–665 in class. • Have students complete Exercises 11–13 in class. • Have students share and discuss their answers.

> **Exercise 11** Taking Objective Tests Answer these questions about any objective test that you recently took.
1. Did I study enough for the test?
2. Did I budget enough time for the hardest questions?
3. Did I change an answer for no convincing reason?
4. Did I proofread carefully?
5. What could I have done to improve my performance?

Answering Objective Questions

Although the content of objective tests varies greatly, the types of questions on these tests are fairly similar. This section will provide basic information about the different types of objective-test questions and specific strategies for answering them.

KEY CONCEPT Improve your test scores by learning about the different kinds of objective-test questions and the strategies for answering them. ■

True-or-False Questions True-or-false questions ask you to identify whether or not a statement is accurate.

- If a statement seems true, be sure that the entire statement is true.
- Pay special attention to the word *not*, which often changes the whole meaning of a statement.
- Take note of the generalizing words *all*, *always*, *never*, *no*, *none*, and *only*. They often make a statement false.
- Take note of the qualifying words *generally*, *much*, *many*, *most*, *often*, *sometimes*, and *usually*. They often make a statement true.

Fill-in Questions A fill-in question asks you to supply an answer in your own words. The answer may complete a statement, or it may simply answer a question.

- Read the question or incomplete statement carefully.
- If you are completing a statement, look for context clues that may signal the answer. Pay special attention if the word *an* appears right before the missing word. This indicates that the missing word begins with a vowel sound.
- If you are answering a question using interrogative words such as *Who? What? How much?* or *What kind?* replace these words with your answer and make a statement out of the question. Check to make sure this statement makes sense.

 **Learn More**

For tips and practice in responding to essay questions, see Chapter 15, "Writing for Assessment."

Answer Key

> **Exercise 11**

Answers will vary, but students should show awareness of how they can improve their study skills.

Step-by-Step Teaching Guide

Answering Objective Questions

1. Ask students to devise true/false questions using the word *not*. (Example: Sixteen-year-olds are not required to go to school. True or False?) Then, have students remove the word *not* and notice the way it changes the meaning of the sentence.

2. Ask students to come up with true/false questions that use generalizations. (Example: All sixteen-year-olds go to school. True or False?) Have students notice that not all sixteen-year-olds in all countries go to school. Then have them replace *all* with a qualifying word, such as *most*. This word allows for some exceptions and therefore makes the statement true.

3. Read the section about fill-in questions aloud or have a student read it. Write this sentence or a similar one on the board.

   The most commonly eaten citrus fruit in America is an ___.

   Have the class note that the article "an" indicates that the answer must begin with a vowel. Therefore, the answer cannot be grapefruit or tangerine.

4. Ask students to apply the strategies for answering fill-in questions to answer the question on the board. (The correct answer is *orange*.)

Multiple-Choice and Matching Questions

1. Read and discuss the section on multiple-choice questions. Write the following multiple choice question on the board.

   Where is Uganda?

   A. *In the United States*

   B. *In East Africa, south of Sudan*

   C. *In Western Canada*

   D. *In Australia*

2. Show students how eliminating obviously incorrect answers immediately narrows the choices down and increases their odds of choosing the correct response.

3. Review the strategies for matching questions. If you wish to walk through an example, list five school events on the board, then list six dates (in random order, with one "wrong" date). Have students match items from the two lists.

Answer Key

> **Exercise 12**

Answers will vary, but students should have structured their questions correctly in each section.

Customize for
Linguistic Learners

Students might learn more from responding to Exercise 12 with written comments in addition to a numerical grade. Encourage these students to write a critique of their classmate's work. (Example: "This student did well with multiple-choice questions but needs to practice strategies for true/false questions.")

Critical Viewing

Apply A watch would enable a student to more effectively budget time during a test.

31.3

Multiple-Choice Questions This kind of question asks you to choose from four or five possible responses.

- Try answering the question before reading the choices. If your answer matches one of the choices, select that choice.
- Eliminate any obviously incorrect answers. If you are allowed to write on the test paper, cross them out.
- Change a question to a statement by inserting your answer. See whether the statement makes sense.

Matching Questions Matching questions require that you match items in one group with items in another.

- Count the items in each group to see whether any will be left over.
- Read all the items before you start matching.
- Match the items you know first, and then match the others. If you can write on the paper, cross out items as you use them.

▶ **Exercise 12** Understanding Objective Questions Using a subject you are studying in one of your classes, prepare an objective test on the material. Write five true-or-false questions, five matching questions, five multiple-choice questions, and five fill-in questions. Exchange papers with another student, and take that student's test, writing your answers on a separate sheet of paper. Exchange again and grade the test.

Analogies An *analogy* is a special type of multiple-choice question that often appears on vocabulary and reading tests. Analogy items usually provide a pair of words and ask you to choose another pair that expresses a similar relationship.

PECAN : NUT ::

a. apple : fruit

b. house : domestic

c. instrument : piano

d. orange : peel

In the preceding example, the answer is *a*. The relationship between the pairs of words is *kind*. A pecan is a *kind* of nut, and an apple is a *kind* of fruit. Notice that the sequence of the words matters: a piano is a kind of instrument, but the relationship is given in reverse order. Review the common analogy relationships in the chart:

▼ Critical Viewing
Why is wearing a watch to a test, as this student has, a good idea? [**Apply**]

Analogies

1. Review the analogy example with the class, and then discuss each element of the relationship chart on page 867. For additional instruction on analogies, see pages 804 and 822–823 in Chapter 29.

2. Tell students that success on analogy tests depends on knowledge of word meanings and an accurate identification of word relationships.

Answer Key

▶ **Exercise 13**

1. b, lack of a quality
2. a, part to whole
3. c, instrumental relations
4. a, instrumental relations
5. c, quality

Critical Viewing

Analyze Sample response: BASKETBALL : TENNIS BALL :: Sun : Earth. The relationship is one of degree.

Customize for
ESL Students

Students may have difficulty reading some English words out of context. Work with these students as a group. Have them focus on only one question at a time. Suggest that they try to use the individual words in sentences to check for understanding before they attempt to answer the analogy.

Common Analogy Relationships	
Relationship	**Example**
Quality	disturbance : riot
Lack of a quality	shyness : congeniality
Degree (greater or lesser)	shout : speak
Part to whole	leg : chair
Kind	carrot : vegetable
Sequence	student : graduate
Proximity	sidewalk : street
Instrumental relations	stethoscope : doctor

Exercise 13 Answering Analogies For each item, choose the letter of the pair of words that expresses the relationship most like the relationship expressed by the words in capital letters. Also, indicate the type of relationship.

1. IMPOVERISHED : AFFLUENT ::
   a. poor : honest
   b. depleted : enriched
   c. rich : wealth
   d. hungry : thin
2. ARCHIPELAGO : ISLAND ::
   a. constellation : star
   b. symphony : orchestra
   c. mountain : hill
   d. leaf : tree
3. GUITAR : PICK ::
   a. bow : violin
   b. clarinet : reed
   c. drum : drumsticks
   d. conductor : baton
4. ARROW : ARCHER ::
   a. needle : tailor
   b. choir : organ
   c. actor : stage
   c. dessert : chef
5. AVARICE : GREED ::
   a. extravagant : frugal
   b. valor : cowardice
   c. candor : honesty
   d. charity : piety

▲ Critical Viewing Come up with an analogy for the subject of this picture. [**Analyze**]

Test-Taking Skills • 867

663 Ⓗ • 867

Performing on Standardized Tests

1. Encourage students to develop strategies to help them relax before, during, and after a test.

2. Review the tips in the student text, and ask students what they might add to the list.

3. Remind students that exercise can help them meet challenges. A brisk walk in the morning after breakfast helps clear the mind, and helps work off test-day jitters.

4. Suggest that students practice taking a few deep breaths from time to time during a test—to help them focus, to reduce stress, and to take in extra oxygen.

5. Remind students that reading the instructions carefully can often make the difference between success and failure.

6. Encourage students to spend a little time reflecting on their experience after a test. They may want to consider how they felt about their performance, whether they budgeted their time well, and what strategies they would add to their list.

Critical Viewing

Speculate Answers will vary, but should reflect an understanding of both the tips and the test-taking process.

31.3

Performing on Standardized Tests

In addition to the tests you take for particular classes, you will also take standardized tests, often used to evaluate your readiness for the next level of education. These include state tests, high-school exit exams, and college board tests, such as the SAT and the ACT. The following tips will help you to perform well on standardized tests:

Tips for Taking Standardized Tests

1. **Get plenty of sleep the night before**.
2. **Eat a healthy meal beforehand**.
3. **Build confidence with thorough preparation.** Confidence is one of the keys to success on standardized tests. To build your confidence, begin preparing for the test weeks or even months beforehand. Use sample tests available in books, on the Internet, or from your teacher.
4. **Arrive prepared for the test.** Determine which supplies— pencils, paper, calculator, and so on—you need or are allowed to use for the test, and bring them with you.
5. **Fill in bubble sheets carefully.** If you skip an item on the test, make sure that you skip the corresponding row on the bubble sheet. To make sure you have filled in the sheet properly, check it over before you turn in your test.
6. **Budget your time.** Determine how much time you have for each section and how many questions each contains. Then, calculate how much time you can allow for each question. Skip questions you can't answer, so that you don't run out of time to complete the test.

▶ Critical Viewing
What is some advice you might offer to this student to help her on the standardized test she is taking? [Speculate]

Types of Standardized Tests

Familiarize yourself with the format of any test you are preparing to take. Following are a few important standardized tests for college-bound students:

PSAT The PSAT is the preliminary SAT (see the description below). Given nationwide, it is designed to provide students with the opportunity to practice for the SAT. PSAT results also determine which students are eligible for National Merit Scholarships. The PSAT has the same basic format as the SAT, except that it does not contain an essay.

New SAT Many colleges use an applicant's SAT score as one factor in deciding whether to admit the student. The test is given nationwide, once a month from October through June except in February. You may repeat the test in the hope of improving your score; however, results of every SAT you take will be reported to the schools to which you apply. The new SAT has a math portion, a critical reading portion, and a new writing portion.

The critical reading portion contains sentence-completion questions that test vocabulary and mechanics and contains reading comprehension questions based on short, long, and paired passages.

The writing portion of the new SAT includes a short essay and multiple-choice questions on grammar, usage, and word choice.

ACT Many colleges use ACT scores to make admissions decisions. Questions on the test—covering English, math, reading, and science reasoning—are all multiple choice. On the English portion, you must identify errors in grammar, usage, mechanics, logic, and organization. The reading portion presents four passages from different fields. You must answer questions about each passage that test your reading and reasoning skills. You can also choose to take the new ACT Plus Writing test, which includes a thirty-minute essay.

ⓛ Learn More

The Standardized Test Preparation Workshop that appears at the end of each chapter throughout this book provides instruction and practice for most of the types of items covered in these tests. The Test Preparation Handbook on pages 886–917 provides instruction and practice for the Writing Section of the new SAT, the Writing Test of the ACT, and the types of Reading Comprehension questions that appear in the reading sections of both exams.

Reflecting on Your Test-Taking Skills

Think about strategies presented in this section and how they apply to you. Use these questions to help you reflect:

- How can I budget my time better while taking tests?
- How can I apply new test-taking strategies when I take tests?

Test-Taking Skills • 869

Use one of the following options to assess students' understanding of study, reference, and test-taking skills.

Option 1 Have students choose a topic they are interested in learning more about. Then, have them go to the library and prepare a bibliography for a research report on that topic. Challenge them to find at least seven useful sources. At least two of them should be non-print materials. Review their work when they finish.	**Option 2** Have students imagine that the research paper in Option 1 must be ten pages in length and is due three weeks from today. Have them create a comprehensive plan for finishing the paper on time. When they finish, review their plans.

Step-by-Step Teaching Guide

Types of Standardized Tests

1. Assure students that SAT and ACT tests are not the only factor that helps determine whether they are admitted into a college or university. Still, encourage them to take these tests seriously, since they can help improve their chances at the school of their choice.

2. Explain that the more comfortable students become with the test process, the more likely they are to do their best. Suggest that students consider acquiring one or more of the various test-preparation guides now available for the SAT or ACT. These contain sample tests in every test area, along with detailed explanations of skills and strategies, and provide valuable practice opportunities.

ASSESS and CLOSE

Step-by-Step Teaching Guide

Test-Taking Skills

Teaching Resources: Formal Assessment, Ch. 31

1. Ask students to reflect on the material they have learned in this chapter, including the study, research, and test-taking skills. Have them share something they have learned, and how they think it might help them.

2. Encourage students to consider the Reflecting questions and make notes on how they can improve their test taking in the future.

3. You may wish to use the following assessment options:
   - review the Standardized Test Preparation Workshop on pp. 870–871 and assign the practice test.
   - administer the Chapter 31 assessment from *Formal Assessment* in the Teaching Resources to measure students' grasp of the concepts presented.

Lesson Objectives

1. To establish and adjust purpose for reading

2. To respond to informational and aesthetic elements in texts

3. To produce summaries of texts by identifying main idea and supporting detail

4. To draw inferences and support them with textual evidence and experience

Step-by-Step Teaching Guide

Constructing Meaning from Informational Texts

Teaching Resources: Standardized Test Preparation Workbook, pp. 61–62

1. Go over the bulleted points with students.

2. Have students read the passage and answer the sample question. Then check to see that students have answered correctly.

3. Have students continue with the four questions about the passage.

4. Go over students' answers, and ask students to explain why the right answer is correct.

Standardized Test Preparation Workshop

Constructing Meaning From Informational Texts

When you take a standardized test, often you must answer questions about a passage you have read. These questions test your ability to extract meaning from the information provided in the passage. When answering these types of questions, you will be required to do the following:

- Identify the main idea, stated or implied, of a section of the passage.

- Identify the best summary—a concise restating of the key points of the passage.

- Distinguish between facts and nonfacts.

- Recognize the author's point of view and purpose for writing the passage.

The following sample item will give you practice answering these types of questions. To answer the sample question, refer to the passage on the next page.

Test Tip

When answering a question about the main idea of a paragraph or the best summary of a passage, reread the entire paragraph or passage before answering.

Test Item	Answers and Explanations
Read the passage on the next page. Then, read the question below. Decide which is the best answer.	
Which of the following represents the author's main purpose in the passage?	
A. The author wishes to persuade readers that Elizabethan England was one of the best periods for theater.	The correct answer is *D*. The author's purpose is informative. The passage gives no opinions on the quality of theater in Elizabethan England (answer *A*). It focuses on facts showing the changing nature of the theater, not on amusing stories (answer *B*). While the passage mentions two kinds of theater, (answer *C*) the two kinds are not the author's main focus.
B. The author wishes to entertain readers with stories of Elizabethan theater.	
C. The author wishes to inform readers about two kinds of theater in Elizabethan England.	
D. The author wishes to inform readers about the changing nature of theater in Elizabethan England.	

◇ TEST-TAKING TIP

Tell students that after reading an informational text, they may read a multiple-choice answer that seems correct, but in fact is wrong because it does not contain enough relevant information (see 1B). Or one choice may be a statement about the feelings of historical personages, which is therefore an opinion statement (see 1D). At other times a statement may be correct but is a detail and not the main idea (see 1A).

Explain that if students encounter unfamiliar words in an informational text, they should try to get the meaning from context but not worry if they can't understand every word. Getting the main idea of each paragraph in a passage and of the passage as a whole is the key to success on a test of this type.

Answer Key

1. C
2. G
3. D
4. G

► **Practice 1** **Directions:** Read the passage. Then, read each question that follows the passage. Decide which is the best answer to each question.

Before the reign of Elizabeth I, theater companies traveled about the country putting on plays wherever they could find an audience, often performing in the open courtyards of inns. Spectators watched either from the ground or from balconies or galleries above.

When Shakespeare was just twelve years old, an actor named James Burbage built London's first theater, called simply *the theater*, just beyond the city walls in Shoreditch. James Burbage was the son of Richard Burbage—the best actor of Elizabethan times. Actors occupied a strange place in London society during Elizabeth's reign: They were frowned upon by the city fathers but were wildly popular with the common people, who clamored to see them perform in plays. Though actors were considered rogues and vagabonds by some, they were held in sufficient repute to be called on frequently to perform at court.

1 What is the main idea of the second paragraph of this passage?
  A London's first theater was built when Shakespeare was just twelve years old.
  B Actors were among the celebrities of Elizabethan England.
  C When the theater first came to London, the actors met with official disapproval and public popularity.
  D Actors in Elizabethan England were glad to leave behind their wandering life to take up quarters in Shoreditch.

2 Which of the following conclusion follows from the passage?
  F The royalty of England disapproved of the theater.
  G Shakespeare began writing his plays during a period of change in the theater in England.
  H Shakespeare was too young to have had a major impact on the changing nature of theater in Elizabethan England.
  J Theater was the only form of entertainment available to the public in Elizabethan England.

3 Which of the following is an OPINION expressed in the passage?
  A When Shakespeare was twelve years old, an actor named James Burbage built London's first theater.
  B Actors were frowned upon by the city fathers but were wildly popular with the common people.
  C Before the reign of Elizabeth I, theater companies traveled about the country putting on plays wherever they could find an audience.
  D Richard Burbage was probably the best actor of Elizabethan times.

4 Which of the following is the best summary of this passage?
  F Actors in Elizabethan England were torn between a wandering life in the countryside and official disapproval in London.
  G In Elizabethan England, theater took an important step from a wandering existence in the countryside to a settled one near the city.
  H James Burbage made an important contribution to the history of theater in England.
  J Theatergoers in Elizabethan England were enthusiastic, celebrating favorite actors and enduring less than ideal viewing conditions.

Customize for
Less Advanced Students

If students had difficulties with reading the passage, go over any words they may have had trouble with, showing them how context can help them get the meanings of the words *galleries, prominent, clamored, vagabonds,* and *sufficient.* Assure students that they can use the same strategy when taking any test.

Customize for
AP Students

Suggest that when reading informational texts independently, students practice writing summaries and statements of main idea.

Standardized Test Preparation Workshop • 871

Chapter 32 Time and Resource Manager

In-Depth Lesson Plan

	LESSON FOCUS	PRINT AND MEDIA RESOURCES
DAY 1	**Working With People** Students learn skills for successful interactions in interviews, group discussions, and meetings. (pp. 872–876/H666–670)	**Teaching Resources** *Academic and Workplace Skills Activity Book,* p. 55
DAY 2	**Moving Toward Your Goals; Solving Problems** Students learn strategies for setting and achieving goals and for problem solving. (pp. 877–879/H671–673)	**Teaching Resources** *Academic and Workplace Skills Activity Book,* pp. 56–57
DAY 3	**Managing Time and Money** Students learn strategies for managing time and money. (pp. 880–881/H674–675)	**Teaching Resources** *Academic and Workplace Skills Activity Book,* p. 58
DAY 4	**Applying Math and Computer Skills** Students learn to apply math and computer skills to real-life situations. (pp. 882–883/H676–677)	**Teaching Resources** *Academic and Workplace Skills Activity Book,* pp. 59–60; *Formal Assessment,* Ch. 32

Accelerated Lesson Plan

	LESSON FOCUS	PRINT AND MEDIA RESOURCES
DAY 1	**Working With People; Moving Toward Your Goals; Solving Problems** Students learn skills for successful interactions with others and for setting and achieving goals. (pp. 872–879/H666–673)	**Teaching Resources** *Academic and Workplace Skills Activity Book,* pp. 55–57
DAY 2	**Managing Time and Money; Applying Math and Computer Skills** Students learn strategies for managing time and money and for applying math and computer skills to real-life situations. (pp. 880–883/H674–677)	**Teaching Resources** *Academic and Workplace Skills Activity Book,* pp. 58–60; *Formal Assessment,* Ch. 32

Options for Adapting Lesson Plans

HOMEWORK

Have students complete any of the exercises for homework.

FEATURES

Extend coverage with the Standardized Test Preparation Workshop (pp. 884–885).

TECHNOLOGY

Students may use the Internet to conduct independent research. Have them print out their completed work.

Writing and Grammar Handbook Alignment

Page numbers in Step-by-Step Teaching Guides in this Teacher's Edition refer to pages from the full student text. Handbook page references, indicated with this icon 🄷, are provided in Time and Resource Manager boxes and at the bottom of each Teacher's Edition page.

INTEGRATED SKILLS COVERAGE

Research Skills
SE pp. 877, 881; ATE p. 877/🄷671, 675

Technology Skills
SE pp. 873, 874/🄷667, 668

Workplace Skills
ATE p. 876

Viewing and Representing
Critical Viewing, SE pp. 872, 875, 877, 883/🄷666, 669, 671, 677; ATE p. 881

Vocabulary
ATE p. 878

Real-World Connection
ATE p. 883

ASSESSMENT SUPPORT

Standardized Test Preparation Workshop, SE p. 884; ATE p. 879
Standardized Test Preparation Workbook, pp. 63–64
Formal Assessment, Ch. 32

MEETING INDIVIDUAL NEEDS

Less Advanced Students ATE pp. 882, 885. See also Ongoing Assessments ATE pp. 874, 881.
AP Students ATE p. 879
ESL Students ATE pp. 875, 881, 883, 885
Logical/Mathematical Learners ATE p. 882
Musical Learners ATE p. 879
Spatial Learners ATE pp. 878, 880

BLOCK SCHEDULING

Pacing Suggestions
For 90-minute Blocks
• Have students complete the Working With People and Moving Toward Your Goals sections in a single period.
• Focus one class period on Managing Time and Money and Applying Math Skills. If possible, bring students to the computer lab for the Computer Skills section.

Resources for Varying Instruction
• *Academic and Workplace Skills Activity Book,* pp. 55–60

Professional Development Support
• *How to Manage Instruction in the Block* This teaching resource provides management and activity suggestions.

MEDIA AND TECHNOLOGY

For the Teacher
• TeacherEXPRESS™ CD-ROM

WRITING AND GRAMMAR ON-LINE

Interactive Text (On-line or on CD-ROM)
• Easily navigable instruction with interactive Revision Checkers
• Full use of e-rater™, the essay-scoring system (on-line only)

Companion Web Site PHSchool.com
• Scoring rubrics with models (use Web Code egk-1201)

See the Go On-line! **feature, SE p. iii.**

▶ **Lesson Objectives**

1. To practice individual and teamwork strategies appropriate for the workplace

2. To use creative thinking strategies to generate ideas and solve problems

3. To practice making, listening to, and evaluating a variety of presentations

4. To ask clear questions for a variety of purposes and respond appropriately to the questions of others

5. To practice planning and development of personal and professional goals

6. To utilize strategies for time and money management

7. To apply math and computer skills to a range of real-life situations

Critical Viewing

Connect Students should note that the young man is well groomed and nicely dressed and that he appears to be listening intently to the other man. Also, he appears to be prepared, with a notebook that may contain résumés and will certainly enable him to take notes.

Chapter 32 Workplace Skills and Competencies

▲ **Critical Viewing** What might you learn from this photograph that you can someday apply to a job search of your own? **[Connect]**

Whether your intention is to go to college or to begin your work life right after high school, you will profit from having learned how to read and write carefully and to speak clearly. You will also benefit from knowing other skills, such as how to communicate effectively with others, how to set and achieve goals, and how to solve problems.

The material in this chapter will help you improve your abilities in these areas. It will also offer guidance on budgeting your time and money wisely as you grow more independent. You will learn how to explore career fields through internships and how to apply math and computer skills in daily life.

872 • Workplace Skills and Competencies

⏱ TIME AND RESOURCE MANAGER

Resources
Print: *Academic and Workplace Skills Activity Book*, p. 55

Using the Full Student Edition	Using the Handbook🄷
• Cover pp. 872–876 in class.	• Cover pp. 666–670 in class.
• Give students time to complete Exercises 1–5.	• Give students time to complete Exercises 1–5.
• Provide students with a list of questions in advance so they can better prepare their responses to the interview in Exercise 1.	• Provide students with a list of questions in advance so they can better prepare their responses to the interview in Exercise 1.
• Give students time to rehearse their role-playing activities in Exercise 2 so that they can perform them for the entire class.	• Give students time to rehearse their role-playing activities in Exercise 2 so that they can perform them for the entire class.

Working With People

Just as you learned to work together with teachers and students in high school, you will be expected to interact effectively with people in college and in the workplace. This section offers practical ways to hone your communication skills, working one on one and in groups.

Learn One-on-One Communication

Before you can get a job or gain admission to a college, you must impress an interviewer in a one-on-one situation. The communication skills that serve you well in an interview must then be refined as you engage a variety of other people at work or on campus.

Interviews Typically, internships, jobs, and colleges all require interviews. Learning how to make a good impression during an interview can increase your chances of success.

▶ **KEY CONCEPT** To interview successfully, you must be prepared, professional, and courteous. ■

THE INTERVIEW PROCESS		
Before the Interview	**During the Interview**	**After the Interview**
1. Find out when, where, and with whom the interview is.	1. Smile and maintain eye contact.	1. In a follow-up letter, restate your interest in the internship, job, or college and extend your thanks.
2. Gather references and prepare your résumé.	2. Ask and answer questions concisely.	2. When the deadline for a decision arrives, call to check the status.
3. Learn about your potential employer or the college to which you are applying, and prepare questions.	3. Thank the interviewer, and ask when a decision will be made.	3. If you are applying for a job, and the position has been filled, ask the company to keep your résumé on file.
4. Select a neat, appropriate outfit for the interview.		

Technology Tip

Computer software often has a built-in feature that helps you prepare a résumé. Type in the word *résumé* at the Help command to investigate this feature.

Learn More

To learn what information to include in an effective résumé and follow-up letter, see Chapter 16, "Workplace Writing."

PREPARE and ENGAGE

 **Interest GRABBER** Ask students to imagine that they are on an arts council deciding what projects or artists deserve funding. Have students speculate on what traits help influence other people, how artists should present themselves and their work, and what qualities contribute to positive group decision making.

Activate Prior Knowledge

Have students recall a time when they were in an interview situation (for employment or college application, for example). What did they say or do that helped convince someone to give them a chance? What skills might be useful in future interview situations?

TEACH

Step-by-Step Teaching Guide

Learn to Communicate One-on-One

Teaching Resources: Academic and Workplace Skills Activity Book, p. 55

1. After students read the text, ask them why making a good first impression is important (they may not get a second chance).

2. Have students identify the elements that make a good first impression, the things that continue to build on that impression, and the things that confirm the good impression (*first impression:* being on time, being appropriately dressed and well groomed; *continue:* being polite and respectful, being prepared, maintaining eye contact, listening carefully and responding as directed; *confirm:* thanking interviewer, follow-up letter).

3. Ask students why they think each element is important (being on time and being appropriately dressed establishes conscientiousness; being prepared shows high motivation and competence; a follow-up letter shows professionalism and motivation).

Successful Interaction

1. After students review the guidelines, point out that many of the items (listening carefully, finding common ground, respecting differences) are useful for communicating in any situation.

2. Discuss the principles of successful interaction by asking questions such as these:

   What are some nonverbal messages that people send, and what do they communicate? (A smile expresses friendliness, approval, or agreement. Crossed arms express sternness or defensiveness. Tapping fingers or fidgeting with hair suggests boredom or nervousness.)

   Why is using slang inappropriate with an employer or counselor? (Such language indicates lack of respect and professionalism.)

   Why is it important to avoid blaming others? (This casts a negative light on the person doing the blaming and doesn't contribute to resolution of problem.)

3. If possible, use a videotape of an interview to provide a concrete illustration of these principles.

4. Allow class time for Exercises 1 and 2. You may wish to assign preparation for Exercise 2 as homework.

Answer Key

▶ Exercise 1

After the class critiques the interviews, meet with students individually to discuss both the interviews and the critiques.

▶ Exercise 2

Have the class come up with a third role-play situation that is relevant to their own lives.

32

Successful Interaction Knowing how to interact well with different people benefits you long after high school. For example, you will find that good communication skills can relieve the tension that may result from dealings with co-workers, clients, supervisors, and classmates.

▶ **KEY CONCEPT** For successful interaction, listen closely, choose words carefully, and show respect for others. ■

Follow these suggestions for effective interaction:

KEYS TO SUCCESSFUL INTERACTION

Listen carefully.	Ask questions to clarify.
Respond to verbal and nonverbal cues.	Know when to be serious and when you may use humor.
Choose language suitable for the audience.	Don't use slang in formal situations.
Use appropriate body language.	Sit or stand with good posture. Maintain eye contact to indicate interest.
Avoid blaming others.	Look for solutions not scapegoats.

▶ **Exercise 1** Practicing Your Interviewing Skills With a teacher asking the questions, role-play an interview at a company or college. (You might arrange to be videotaped.) Afterward, have the class critique your performance.

▶ **Exercise 2** Interacting With Others in Various Situations With other students, role-play the following situations, using the tips for effective interaction noted above as a guide.
1. You must find out why a co-worker has not followed through on his or her portion of a group assignment.
2. You must convince a professor to grant you an extended deadline on a paper.

874 • Workplace Skills and Competencies

◉ Technology Tip

The skills you learn for interacting with people face to face or on the telephone can also be applied to interaction on-line.

☑ ONGOING ASSESSMENT: Monitor and Reinforce

To give students more information and experience in interviews and successful interaction, try one of the following strategies.

Option 1 Suggest that students talk to an adult who has conducted interviews. What was their best experience? Their worst? What mistakes have they seen applicants make? What things have impressed them? What advice would they offer someone going for an interview?	**Option 2** Suggest they watch interview shows on television or find a book on effective interviewing and then get together with other students and practice interviewing one another. Alternatively, they might want to ask adults to work with them.

Learn to Work as a Team

Teamwork requires more than just basic communication skills, because whether you are serving on a committee or preparing a group presentation, conflict invariably arises as you work closely together. Therefore, to interact successfully, group members must know and respect each other's roles.

Roles in Group Discussions Group discussions succeed when members understand their own and each other's roles in the pursuit of a common goal. A group is typically composed of a facilitator, a recorder, and several participants, each with distinct responsibilities.

KEY CONCEPT To realize a common goal, each member of a group must be organized, focused on the issues, and aware of his or her responsibilities. ■

Effective Participation Participants are critical to the success of a group. They must be willing to make suggestions, consider the ideas of others, give and accept criticism with grace, and help smooth tensions that arise.

KEY CONCEPT Effective participation requires a constructive exchange of ideas and a common goal. ■

Follow these suggestions for effective teamwork:

- Share your ideas, and encourage others to do so.
- Listen carefully to all points of view.
- Accept criticism; take nothing personally.
- When you disagree, focus on the idea, not on the person.
- Resolve disputes promptly.

▼ **Critical Viewing**
Based on the details in this photograph, do you think that this group is interacting effectively? Why or why not? **[Evaluate]**

Workplace Skills and Competencies • 875

Step-by-Step Teaching Guide

Roles in Group Discussions

1. Define and discuss the roles of facilitator, recorder, and participant.

2. Ask students what they think might happen if these roles are not filled in an important meeting (people get off track, not everything is covered, there is no way to distribute what was said, there is no one to contribute ideas and feedback).

3. Since it is important for each group member to be organized, ask students what can they do to prepare (gather needed information, have paper and pencil for taking notes, write down ideas and questions beforehand).

Customize for
ESL Students

When possible, include a fluent English speaker in any group discussion that involves an English-language learner. If the individual is also familiar with the learner's home language, even better. Have the more fluent student assist the other in making points and understanding what is being said.

Step-by-Step Teaching Guide

Effective Participation

1. Ask students why it is important to share ideas and encourage others to do so? (The more ideas there are, the more likely one of them will be workable.)

2. Have students discuss how one can give and receive criticism gracefully, and why it is important.

Critical Viewing

Evaluate All group members appear to be actively participating, whether they are speaking or listening.

Answer Key

For Exercise 3, you can assign student groups or invite students to form their own groups. Give groups a few minutes to get organized and select a topic. For Exercise 4, you may want to help students by making suggestions.

Integrating Workplace Skills

Mediating disputes between co-workers is an essential workplace skill. Successful conflict resolution involves acknowledging complaints and differing points of view. It also requires working with an objective third party to find a common ground that allows those who disagree to continue to work together.

Step-by-Step Teaching Guide

Meetings

1. Ask students if any have been involved in formal meetings for clubs, organizations, or student government. Have they all run smoothly, or have some gotten off track or run too long?

2. Explain that unexpected issues often arise at meetings, so it is impossible to always have a perfectly arranged and timed meeting. However, an agenda improves the chances that things will run smoothly.

3. Ask students what other types of things might appear on an agenda (reading of previous meeting's minutes, report of members present, and so on).

Answer Key

> **Exercise 5**

If a trip to a museum is an impossibility, you may want to assign or have students select another project.

32

> **Exercise 3** Holding a Group Discussion With five classmates, hold a group discussion on one of these topics: paths to take after graduation, types of volunteer work, or the impact of computer technology. Choose a facilitator and a recorder for the group, and spend fifteen minutes openly sharing your thoughts and ideas on the topic. End by working together to reach consensus about one idea to share with the class. Select one group member to present the idea.

> **Exercise 4** Critiquing a Group Effort Select an example of poor teamwork from a book or a movie. Read the passage or play the scene for the class. Point out the problems, and explain how the group could have worked better together. Refer to the tips for successful teamwork.

Meetings Discussions can be organized in several different ways. Some discussions are informal, and others are formal. A meeting is a formal group discussion; it is organized to discuss specific ideas and topics. A well-organized meeting has an **agenda** that lists the order of the topics being discussed and assigns roles, such as facilitator, note-taker, and timekeeper. If new issues or questions are raised during the meeting that cannot be solved during the meeting's time limit, all of the people involved should plan to meet again for further discussion.

> **Exercise 5** Organizing a Trip to a Local Museum Working with five or six other students, plan a trip for your entire class to a local museum. Make an agenda to decide where and when you want to go and how you will get there. Assign roles, hold the meeting, and, if necessary, plan to meet again before the trip is finalized.

AGENDA
Project Meeting
October 14

Facilitator: Malcolm
Note-taker: Leslie
Timekeeper: Bill

1. Review and amend agenda
   (All — 5 minutes)

2. Brainstorm for ideas
   (All — 10 minutes)

3. Report of project's progress/difficulties
   (Nicole — 10 minutes)

4. Discussion of project and possible solutions
   (All — 20 minutes)

876 • Workplace Skills and Competencies

Moving Toward Your Goals

Put simply, goals are dreams that you plan to achieve in a specific amount of time. They may focus on getting a raise or getting a date, on improving your SAT scores or your backstroke. They may take years to fulfill or a few days. Goals may also conflict with each other, so you must decide which ones are most important.

Personal and Professional Goals

Personal goals, such as overcoming shyness, focus on your development as a person. Professional goals, such as becoming a lieutenant in the military, focus on your career. Though they are different, personal and professional goals may affect each other. To help establish your priorities, you should outline your goals and the strategies needed to achieve them.

Set and Achieve Goals To set a goal, you must define your objective as specifically as possible. To achieve that goal, you must anticipate conflicts and map out a set time for its completion.

▶ **KEY CONCEPT** Goals require specific definition, realistic planning, and time limits. ■

Write down the goal in detail.	Set a reasonable time frame to complete each step.	Adjust the steps as needed.
	Break the goal down into specific steps.	Adjust your progress on a regular basis.

→ **G O A L**

Internships

An internship may be a goal or a means to achieving one. Internships give people the opportunity to learn about a career by working alongside professionals in the field. Employers benefit because the intern, often unpaid, provides a needed service. Interns may handle basic duties, such as answering phones and opening mail, or career-specific ones, such as compiling statistics or preparing lab experiments.

▶ **KEY CONCEPT** Internships benefit employers and students alike by providing hands-on learning experiences. ■

▲ **Critical Viewing**
What goals might the girls in this photograph set? On what do you base your answer? [Connect]

🔲 **Research Tip**

To help plan your career goals, investigate fields of interest at the career center of a local college.

Workplace Skills and Competencies • 877

Step-by-Step Teaching Guide

Personal and Professional Goals

Teaching Resources: Academic and Workplace Skills Activity Book, p. 56

1. Explain to students that setting goals and defining steps for reaching those goals is the only reliable road to achievement.

2. As students try to think of goals, suggest that they look at the want ads in the paper to identify jobs they might like, talk to school counselors about needed qualifications in fields that interest them, or think about how they would like to improve their own habits or health.

3. Have volunteers share ideas, both for goals and how they divided them into steps.

4. Discuss how an internship can help students achieve professional goals. Provide any available information on internships.

5. Help students identify which careers might benefit from, or offer, internships. Discuss alternatives, such as being a camp counselor, attending Space Camp or another theme-focused summer program, or taking career-specific classes.

Critical Viewing

Connect Students might aim to maintain peak physical condition, to perfect their footwork, and to communicate well with their teammates.

Integrate Research Skills

Have students use the library or Internet to gather information on the requirements for a career in which they are interested. Encourage them to consider educational needs and desirable personal qualities that would help them toward this career.

⏱ TIME AND RESOURCE MANAGER

Resources
Print: *Academic and Workplace Skills Activity Book*, p. 56

Using the Full Student Edition	Using the Handbook🄷
• Cover p. 877 in class, discussing the steps in setting and achieving goals. • Use Exercise 6 to help students create an action plan to get an internship.	• Cover p. 671 in class, discussing the steps in setting and achieving goals. • Use Exercise 6 to help students create an action plan to get an internship.

> **Exercise 6**

Encourage students to speak with human resources representatives at various companies about the requirements for specific internships.

Customize for
Spatial Learners

Have these students create a flow chart using the steps they need to reach their goals of obtaining an internship.

Solving Problems with Creative Thinking

Teaching Resources: Academic and Workplace Skills Activity Book, p. 56

1. Explain to students that, while one occasionally has a brilliant idea that simply resolves a problem, this is the exception. Most of the time, one needs a reliable method of solving problems. The steps given in the text are effective steps used widely by corporations as well as individuals.

2. Point out that identifying and stating the problem precisely is a key task. A vaguely-defined problem will probably generate vague and incomplete solutions.

3. Ask students to suggest other possible solutions to the example in the text (test-prep guides, math programs on television, auditing the class) and evaluate them.

Integrating Vocabulary Skills

Latin Roots Explain to students that the word *solution* comes from the Latin word *solutus*, which means "to loosen." In order to solve a problem, it is necessary to loosen and take apart the fixed ideas that we may have about it so that we might re-assemble it in a new way. Point out that by examining the etymological origins of words, we can often find an embedded or metaphorical meaning that helps us understand the word more precisely.

32

> **Exercise 6** Developing an Action Plan to Get an Internship In your notebook, develop a detailed plan on how to acquire an internship in a field of your choice. Include in your plan the steps and resources needed to achieve the goal and the estimated time each step will take. For example, what specific skills does the internship require, and how do you get those skills if you don't already have them? Share your plan with the class.

Solving Problems With Creative Thinking

While pursuing personal and professional goals, you may encounter problems. Having the skill to solve problems effectively and efficiently will help you realize your goals and make you an asset to any profession. By identifying the problem and evaluating possible options in a methodical manner, you can select the best solution. Difficult problems may require more creative thinking to generate a greater number of solutions from which to choose.

Whether you must find transportation to a new job or housing on an overcrowded campus, you will need to use an organized strategy to isolate the problem and devise a workable solution.

> **KEY CONCEPT** Solving a problem requires a thorough grasp of the challenge at hand, a variety of possible solutions, and a careful analysis of each one. ■

Solve problems by following these steps:

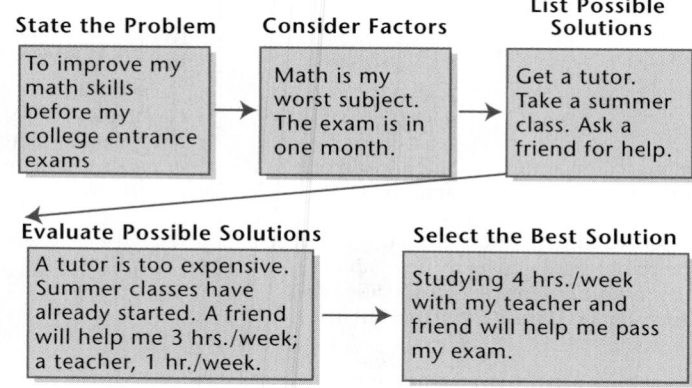

State the Problem
To improve my math skills before my college entrance exams

Consider Factors
Math is my worst subject. The exam is in one month.

List Possible Solutions
Get a tutor. Take a summer class. Ask a friend for help.

Evaluate Possible Solutions
A tutor is too expensive. Summer classes have already started. A friend will help me 3 hrs./week; a teacher, 1 hr./week.

Select the Best Solution
Studying 4 hrs./week with my teacher and friend will help me pass my exam.

⏱ TIME AND RESOURCE MANAGER

Resources
Print: *Academic and Workplace Skills Activity Book*, p. 57

Using the Full Student Edition	Using the Handbook Ⓗ
• Cover pp. 878–879 in class, discussing the steps in solving problems and creative thinking. • Give students time to complete Exercises 7–8.	• Cover pp. 672–673 in class, discussing the steps in solving problems and creative thinking. • Give students time to complete Exercises 7–8.

Use Creative Thinking Creativity is the ability to put together something new. You can find solutions to problems by thinking creatively—opening your mind to unusual ideas and drawing on the experiences of different people.

KEY CONCEPT Creative thinking requires an openness to new approaches and a wide frame of reference from which to draw ideas. ∎

Use the tips below to develop creative problem-solving skills:

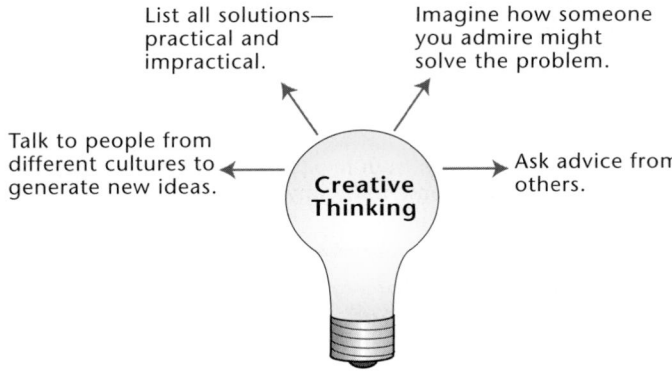

List all solutions—practical and impractical.

Imagine how someone you admire might solve the problem.

Talk to people from different cultures to generate new ideas.

Creative Thinking

Ask advice from others.

Exercise 7 Solving Problems As a class, analyze the following problems, generate three possible solutions for each, choose the best one, and explain why.
1. You inadvertently committed to baby-sitting for a neighbor's eight-year-old and to selling refreshments at a college baseball game at the same time.
2. You need a suit for an interview and are short on cash.
3. You started an internship at one company, only to be approached by another with a more interesting offer.

Exercise 8 Practicing Creative Thinking Your younger sibling or a neighbor's child is constantly following you and your friends around. With a group, brainstorm for at least five creative solutions that are positive for all parties involved. Evaluate the pros and cons of each potential solution.

Workplace Skills and Competencies • **879**

Use Creative Thinking

1. Point out to students that creative thinking involves looking at problems in new ways or recombining familiar elements using fresh styles and approaches.

2. Review the creative thinking suggestions depicted on the chart in the text. Have students offer examples of times when they have used these approaches or seen them used by others.

3. As students work on Exercise 8, encourage them to use such brainstorming techniques as freewriting. Tell them that it is alright to include humorous or unrealistic solutions in their lists. Point out that keeping an open mind often leads problem-solvers in the right direction.

Answer Key

Exercise 7

Encourage students to make a flow chart like the one on page 872 to help them think through each problem.

Exercise 8

Remind students that it is essential to explain ideas clearly, especially when the ideas are new or unconventional.

Customize for
AP Students

Encourage students to seek out further information on problem solving. There are many books available, with approaches ranging from formal logic to creative thinking games.

Customize for
Musical Learners

Encourage students to listen to music while attempting their problem solving activities in Exercises 7–8. Many behavioral psychologists believe that some recordings, such as classical music by Mozart, can enhance concentration and promote mental clarity and problem solving ability.

STANDARDIZED TEST PREPARATION WORKSHOP

Problem Solving Standardized test questions often require students to solve mathematical problems based on textual information. Provide students with opportunities to practice this skill.

Farmer Brown is building a rectangular fence around one of his fields. The longest side is 650 feet and the shortest side is 350 feet. What is the total amount of fencing he will need?

A 1,000 feet

B 2,000 feet

C 4,000 feet

D cannot be determined from the information given

Students should recognize that **B** is the correct answer. Since the perimeter of a rectangle is equal to twice the width plus twice the length, the total distance is equal to 1300 feet + 700 feet. Students should recognize that A and C are incorrect calculations and that D is false because the answer can be calculated from the information given.

Managing Time

Teaching Resources: Academic and Workplace Skills Activity Book, p. 58

1. Point out that experts say it is important to use time *effectively*, rather than merely *efficiently*. This means that one should do more complex tasks when one is fresh, and repetitive tasks, like filing papers, when one has less energy.

2. Explain that "must do" items should be added to calendars first, with "like to do" items added next.

3. Ask students how a big job such as a research paper could be made more manageable by breaking it into a series of steps (do research, drafting, editing on separate days).

4. Discuss how students might set priorities for their to-do lists (items with deadlines, with consequences, or that involve duties or a promise should get highest priority).

Answer Key

> **Exercise 9**

Remind students to include time they spend shopping, daydreaming, or socializing. Emphasize that these activities are not "bad"; they are just something to consider.

Customize for
Spatial Learners

Have students devise their own visual systems for organizing to-do lists and calendars. Point out that some people prefer to look at one-month blocks while others prefer to see only a week or a day.

32

Managing Time

Whether you choose the police academy, nursing school, or an apprenticeship with a builder, nearly all professions require the completion of duties in a certain amount of time. Therefore, you should strive to refine your time-management skills.

Proper time management—listing and prioritizing all appointments and activities—helps you accomplish projects, make time for activities, and minimize the impact of interruptions.

> **KEY CONCEPT** Proper time management requires a prioritized list of appointments, activities, and deadlines. ■

Use the following strategies to budget your time well:

- Write appointments, activities, and deadlines on a calendar that you can carry with you.
- Divide large projects into a series of steps.
- Make a to-do list with daily activities ranked from most important to least important. At the day's end, move any unfinished items to the next day.

To-Do List

1. Call Mr. Carroll about math homework.
2. Make an appointment for a haircut.
3. Return movies to video store.
4. Buy flowers for Julie.

Mon	9:30 Project meeting
Tues	
Wed	3:00–5:00 Baseball tryouts
Thur	6:00 Drive mom to airport
Fri	
Sat	10:30 Help Uncle Mike paint house
Sun	

> **Exercise 9** Analyzing Your Time-Management Skills In your notebook, write down the amount of time you spend on every activity for a week. Tally the amounts at the end of the week (for example, 15 hours on homework, 3 hours driving to activities). Observe how you spend your time, and write down where you need improvement.

880 • Workplace Skills and Competencies

⏱ TIME AND RESOURCE MANAGER

Resources
Print: *Academic and Workplace Skills Activity Book*, p. 58

Using the Full Student Edition	Using the Handbook Ⓗ
• Cover pp. 880–881 in class.	• Cover pp. 674–675 in class.
• Share examples of calendars, time organizers, and to-do lists with students. You can also find and share examples of budgets plans in books or magazine articles about personal finance.	• Share examples of calendars, time organizers, and to-do lists with students. You can also find and share examples of budget plans in books or magazine articles about personal finance.
• Give students time to complete Exercises 9–10 in class.	• Give students time to complete Exercises 9–10 in class.

Managing Money

New graduates also profit, literally and figuratively, from being wise money managers who make the most of every dollar. Proper money management—planning expenditures, paying your savings account like a bill, and spending less than you make—will

- allot money for what you really want.
- curb impulsive spending.
- provide a cushion for emergencies.

KEY CONCEPT Wise money managers live within their means, save regularly, and know their goals. ■

Following is a sample budget plan for someone who earns $350 a month, has $210 in expenses, saves at least $140 a month, and wants to buy a $580 car CD player in four months.

My Budget Plan to Buy a Car CD Player

	Monthly Income	Monthly Expenses	Monthly Savings
Part-time Job	$350.00		
Car Insurance		$100.00	
Gasoline		25.00	
Club Dues		10.00	
Gifts/Misc.		75.00	
Total	$350.00	210.00	$140.00

Exercise 10 Managing a Budget Using the figures in the sample budget provided, do four months of budgets, showing how you could manage your money to buy the CD player and still have $100 to buy CDs.

Research Tip

You can find easy-to-understand guides to managing your time and money at your local library.

Step-by-Step Teaching Guide

Managing Money

Teaching Resources: Academic and Workplace Skills Activity Book, p. 58

1. Discuss why it is wise to limit spending for non-essentials (to avoid debt, to save for emergencies or special occasions).

2. Invite students to share their experiences in saving money. What were some of the techniques and approaches they used?

3. Encourage students to make a list of expenses, identify items as essential and non-essential, and explain their choices.

4. Encourage students to create budgets for themselves.

Answer Key

Exercise 10

Point out that, without changes, the individual in the example won't save enough; the total will be twenty dollars short of what is needed. Discuss with students the changes that could be made to "find" more money. (The individual could cut back on gifts and miscellaneous spending, drive less, or do additional work.)

Integrating Viewing and Representing Skills

Encourage students to format a table to present their own budget plans. Remind them that they may want to arrange their table differently from the sample, depending on time constraints and the categories that seem most relevant to their situations.

Customize for
ESL Students

Prior to assigning Exercise 10, review the definitions of the following money terms: *savings, budget, dues, insurance, loan, monthly, weekly,* and *yearly.* Ask whether any other money-related terms are confusing.

✓ ONGOING ASSESSMENT: Monitor and Reinforce

Some students may have less experience than others with budgeting. For those students, try one of the following strategies.

Option 1 Have students discuss budgets with someone who has experience in setting a personal, household, or business budget. Before this discussion, have students prepare a list of questions that they would like to have answered.	**Option 2** At the library or bookstore, find examples of budgets or guides to budgeting that you can share with the class. Alternatively, encourage students to search out these books and bring to class sample budgets and a list of useful tips.

Applying Math Skills

Teaching Resources: Academic and Workplace Skills Activity Book, p. 59

1. Provide students with an array of real-life samples of things that require practical applications of math skills: order forms, blueprints, statistical summaries, recipes.

2. Discuss ways in which students expect to use math skills as adults. Have them talk about times they already have used math skills outside of school.

3. Ask students to find examples of statistics in a daily newspaper. Explore questions that they have about stock averages, interest rates, sports statistics, or economic graphs.

4. Review metric conversions of standard units of volume, length, and weight. You may want to provide conversion tables or formulas and support in how to use them.

Customize for
Logical/Mathematical Learners

After students complete Exercise 11, suggest that they calculate the recipe's measurements so that it might serve all the students in your class.

Customize for
Less Advanced Students

Rather than have students do the metric conversions in Exercise 11, suggest that they change the recipe by doubling it or cutting the amount in half.

Answer Key

> **Exercise 11**

Remind students to account for the different measurements of solids and liquids.

> **Exercise 12**

Remind students to clearly explain any mathematical terms that a general audience might not understand.

32

Applying Math Skills

Math and computer knowledge will help you whether your career path takes you into physics or physical education, engineering or catering. From measuring recipe ingredients or board feet to calculating gas mileage or the best buy, math has many practical applications. Computers are ideal when it comes to research and writing.

> **KEY CONCEPT** Math skills enable you to manage money properly, shop economically, calculate measurements, and evaluate certain types of information. ■

Refer to this list for common math applications:

- **Balancing Checkbooks** To keep track of expenditures and to calculate interest earned, you must know basic math.
- **Making Wise Purchases** Faced with multiple choices from stores, mail-order catalogs, and cable and on-line shopping networks, you will need to understand unit prices, credit rates, taxes, and shipping and handling charges to calculate the most economical buys.
- **Calculating Measurements** From baking to building, proper measurements are critical. Besides basic conversions, you should know how to translate metric measures into their U.S. equivalents.
- **Analyzing Statistics** Business reports and daily newspapers often use statistics to support certain points of view. Knowing how to weigh the value of those numbers helps you make informed judgments.

Writing About Math

The ability to produce written explanations of how you go about solving a math problem or keeping a budget is a key skill in both school and business. When writing about math, apply many of the skills you learned in Chapters 10 and 11—"Exposition: Cause and Effect" and "Exposition: Problem and Solution."

> **Exercise 11** Using Math Skills to Prepare a Recipe
Choose a recipe from a cookbook. Imagine that you have only metric measuring cups and spoons. Convert the recipe amounts to fit the tools you have.

> **Exercise 12** Writing About Math Prepare a concise written explanation of a problem you recently solved in math class.

882 • Workplace Skills and Competencies

⏱ TIME AND RESOURCE MANAGER

Resources
Print: *Academic and Workplace Skills Activity Book*, pp. 59–60, *Formal Assessment*, Ch. 32

Using the Full Student Edition	Using the Handbook Ⓗ
• Cover pp. 882–883 in class. • Give students time to complete Exercise 11. You may want to allow students to work collaboratively on math calculations. • Arrange for students to practice keyboarding skills on a learn-to-type keyboarding program for Exercise 13.	• Cover pp. 676–677 in class. • Give students time to complete Exercise 11. You may want to allow students to work collaboratively on math calculations. • Arrange for students to practice keyboarding skills on a learn-to-type keyboarding program for Exercise 13.

Applying Computer Skills

On the job and in the classroom, you will benefit from quick keyboarding skills, knowledge of software tools to present information accurately and attractively, and the ability to research on the Internet.

> **KEY CONCEPT** Basic computer skills entail the ability to type quickly and accurately, use formatting features, and access Internet information. ■

Use these suggestions to make the most of a computer:

- **Learn formatting techniques**. Use fonts, boldface, bullets, and other features to organize and highlight information.
- **Use spelling, grammar, and language tools.** Find just the right word or catch errors missed during proofreading.
- **Try to type 45 words per minute** or as fast as you can while retaining accuracy.
- **Learn to use the Internet**. With a teacher's guidance, discover the information available on-line.

> **Exercise 13** Practicing Your Skills Choose a passage from a book, and practice your keyboarding skills by typing it on the computer as quickly as you can. Time yourself to see how close you are to the 45-word-per-minute goal. Use the spell-check function to check accuracy.

▲ Critical Viewing How can peers help one another get the most out of using a computer? **[Apply]**

Reflecting on Your Workplace Skills and Competencies

Practice your communication and organizational skills, and write about your progress in your journal. Use the following questions to guide your response:

- What skills would I most like to improve? Why?
- What are my greatest strengths? Why?
- What exercises proved most helpful? Why?

Critical Viewing

Apply Students might suggest that computer-proficient students could assist those students who need instruction.

Step-by-Step Teaching Guide

Applying Computer Skills

Teaching Resources: Academic and Workplace Skills Activity Book, p. 60

1. Review the features of a commonly used word-processing program with students through direct demonstration or by using an instructional video.

2. Encourage students to practice formatting and other word processing techniques, allocating time in the computer lab, if possible.

3. Remind students that relying too much on spell checkers can be a bad idea, since computers don't recognize the wrong word if it's spelled correctly (for example, *there, their, they're*).

4. Have students suggest a topic for researching on the Internet, and then allow them time to do the search and compare their results.

5. Give students time to reflect on their workplace skills and competencies using the questions on this page.

Answer Key

> **Exercise 13**

Alternatively, have students practice typing their answers to Exercise 12.

Customize for
ESL Students

Show students how to make accent marks, Spanish's inverted punctuation (¡ and ¿), French quotation marks (« »), and other characters or elements useful to students who may be typing in another language (and useful for those studying other languages as well).

Real-World Connection

At nearly every job site, from restaurants to offices, computers have come to play a central role. Invite students to write brief entries of their own experiences using computers on the job or at home.

Lesson Objectives

1. To establish and adjust purpose for reading
2. To analyze text structures for how they influence understanding
3. To draw inferences and support them with textual evidence and experience

Step-by-Step Teaching Guide

Reading Informational Texts

Teaching Resources: Standardized Test Preparation Workbook, pp. 63–64

1. Assign the sample test item and the question that follows. Discuss the answer. Make sure students can explain why answer choices C and D are incorrect.

2. Have students write two more multiple-choice questions based on this announcement. Have them trade with partners and answer the questions.

3. Ask students to note the test tip. Explain that this is helpful because it will prevent them from falling for "trap" answers. These are incorrect answers that test writers predict will be appealing to the average student.

4. Tell students that the practice test requires them to study the User's Guide page shown. Assign the practice item, and then go over the answers with students.

Standardized Test Preparation Workshop

Reading Informational Texts

Some standardized tests assess your ability to read real-world texts, such as flyers, brochures, and advertisements. Often, this involves carefully following a sequence of steps or directions. Look at the example below.

Test Tip

Try to answer multiple-choice questions on your own before you look at the answers that are given.

Sample Test Items	Answer and Explanation

Directions: Read the announcement, and then answer the questions that follow.
 	
Town Meeting
Thursday, April 5 at 8 PM
Issues under discussion:
1. School budget
  • plan for new football stadium
  • increased faculty
2. July 4 celebration
  • parade
  • fireworks
3. Open Forum
 	
Attendance open to <u>all residents.</u> Meeting will begin promptly at 8 P.M. Those wishing to participate in an open forum will have five minutes each. Participation in other discussions is also welcome.	

According to the announcement, who will be allowed to participate in the discussion of the school budget? **A** all town residents who attend **B** everyone **C** any town residents **D** school board members	The correct answer is *A, all town residents who attend*. Although any town resident has the opportunity to participate in discussions of the school budget, only those who attend the meeting will be able to take advantage of this opportunity. Answer *B* is too broad, because it does not exclude those who do not live in the town.

TEST-TAKING TIP

Tell students that the key to success on a test that requires them to read informational texts is to pay attention to details in the test item and to be certain they understand what is being asked.

Tests of this type are not designed to trick the test taker but to assess one's ability to understand factual information. Remind students to be aware of key words such as *not, always, never, most likely*, and *best describes*.

Practice 1 **Directions:** Read the passage, and then answer the questions that follow.

Ron had been given the assignment of writing a literary analysis of the poetry of William Wordsworth. To help gather background for his essay, Ron used the AuthorWorks CD-ROM program, which provides extensive background, analyses, critical reviews, and more for Wordsworth and several other authors. After he had installed the software, Ron consulted the page below in the User's Guide. The page provided him with directions on how to navigate through the software.

Takes you back a step from your current position.

Takes you to the Author Directory, or Main Menu.

Gives you access to Help.

Life — Gives you access to the Scrapbook, Personal Timeline, Map, and Family History for a selected author.

Work — Gives you access to the Published Work, Reviews, Notes & Letters, and Literary Connections for a selected author.

Times — Gives you access to the Politics & Economics, Science & Technology, Arts, Daily Life, and Literary Trends sections of the program.

Moves you forward and backward through slide shows.

A highlighted speaker icon indicates that there is audio information or music to hear. Select this icon to start or stop the selection.

1 Which of the following types of information would Ron *not* be likely to find in the software?
A critical reviews
B a timeline of key dates in Wordsworth's life
C readings of Wordsworth's poetry by the poet himself
D a family history of the poet

2 What function do the two horizontal arrows serve?
F They allow the user to move back and forth through a slide show.
G They take the user to another author.
H They enable users to scroll through a timeline.
J They take users to the next feature.

3 Why did Ron consult the User's Guide?
A because the software was confusing
B because he wanted to be able to see at a glance how to navigate through the program
C because he was looking for background on Wordsworth
D because he wanted to see what support the software provides.

4 Which of the following is *not* a content feature that the program provides?
F information on daily life and literary trends during the periods in which the authors lived
G literary maps
H video performances of the writers' works
J scrapbooks for selected authors

5 Which of the following best describes how to find information on Wordsworth in the software?
A Click to access the Author Directory or the Main Menu.
B Click the Help button.
C Key in Wordsworth's name.
D Use the Menu Bar.

Answer Key

▶ **Practice 1**
1. C
2. F
3. B
4. H
5. A

Customize for
Less Advanced Students

You might give students extra practice in reading "real-world" texts by bringing flyers, brochures, announcements, advertisements, and coupons to class. Ask them to answer questions about details that require them to read closely, such as costs, restrictions, and expiration dates.

Customize for
ESL Students

Ask students to bring to class a copy of an annoucement from the school hallway, gym, or library. Have them analyze the directions on the announcement. Is the sequence clear? Have any important details been omitted? What questions do students have?

Interest GRABBER Invite students to describe the types of newspaper or magazine articles they have read and the different subjects the articles addressed. Then ask, "What was your purpose in reading these articles?" Encourage students to think about purposes for reading (to glean information, for enjoyment).

Discuss what makes an article interesting or fun to read. Ask, "What must you be able to do in order to become engrossed in an article?" Guide students to realize that they must be able to understand, or *comprehend,* what they read.

Tell students to read a newspaper or magazine article and prepare to tell a friend about it. Encourage students to convey interesting or entertaining points.

Activate Prior Knowledge

Have volunteers share brief overviews of their articles. Discuss the reading skills students have learned that allow them to understand and enjoy what they read. List each skill on the board as it is suggested (e.g., vocabulary skills, context clue skills, comparing skills, cause-and-effect skills, idiom skills, punctuation and capitalization skills, and so on). Point out to students that they have already mastered a wide variety of skills that will help them do well on the reading comprehension and other parts of the new SAT® and the ACT® tests.

Test Preparation Handbook

Preparing for the New SAT® and the ACT®

If you are applying to college, chances are you will take the new SAT®, the ACT®, or both. The new SAT® and the ACT® are standardized tests designed to help colleges compare the abilities of prospective students from all over the United States and the world.

This test preparation guide will focus on the Writing Section of the new SAT® and the Writing Test of the ACT®. A brief Reading section is also included to introduce you to the Reading Comprehension questions that appear in the reading sections of both exams.

The Writing Section of the New SAT® and the ACT®

The writing sections on both tests include a timed essay. In addition to a timed essay, the new SAT®'s Writing Section contains three types of multiple-choice questions on grammar and usage. This Test Preparation Handbook will introduce you to grammar and usage questions typical of the new SAT®. It will also be helpful to students preparing for the ACT®, because many of the same topics are addressed in the English Section of that exam.

CONTENTS

886 • Test Preparation Handbook

🖊 TEST-TAKING TIP

Ask students, "How many of you have taken a standardized test?" Most students have probably taken state assessment tests or the PSAT® tests. Some may have taken the new SAT®. Invite volunteers to describe how such tests differ from ordinary classroom tests (students may mention the test booklet, the answer sheet, how the answer sheet is filled in, and so forth). Explain that the new SAT® and the ACT® tests use a similar format, so students should have no trouble understanding what to do. Create a simple answer sheet on the board and show them how to fill in the circles next to the question number.

Reading Comprehension Questions

Both the new SAT® and the ACT® test your ability to understand what you read. Reading comprehension questions typically test three reading skills:

- **Vocabulary in Context:** These questions test your ability to understand what a word means based on the way it is used in a sentence or passage.
- **Finding Information in Text:** These questions test your ability to understand the basic information stated in a text.
- **Extended Reasoning:** These questions test your ability to infer meaning from a text. You should expect questions that ask about the passage's main idea and details, the author's logic and attitude, and the implications of the author's statements.

The following section contains one example of each type of reading passage presented on the new SAT®. These include:

Short passages	These passages can be as short as one hundred words and are followed by two questions.
Long passages	These passages can be as long as eight hundred words and are followed by as many as thirteen questions.
Paired passages	These consist of two passages and are followed by questions that ask about each passage, as well as questions that ask you to compare and contrast the paired passages.

Please note that on the new SAT®, these passages will be followed by at least two questions. In this Test Preparation Handbook, only one question for each reading passage is presented, along with suggested steps to take to answer it.

It is a good idea to practice further by completing reading comprehension questions from old tests. Your teacher can help you find books that contain practice tests. Finally, another excellent way to prepare for the Reading Comprehension section of these exams, and for college, is to read widely and often.

Lead ESL students through an overview of the handbook. Direct students to the list of sections and topics in the Contents. Write the three sections—Reading Comprehension, Grammar, and Writing—on the board.
Explain that reading comprehension skills allow students to find information, decode unfamiliar vocabulary, and infer extended meaning from the text as they read. Using the Contents on page 886, read aloud a few of the Grammar topics. Invite volunteers to write sentences on the board illustrating usage rules.
Finally, discuss the steps in writing a timed essay: planning, drafting, and proofreading. Point out that on a timed essay, students will have to fit these writing stages into the allotted time.

Customize for
Less Advanced Students

Have students work in small groups to brainstorm for a list of the types of questions they would expect to be asked on a reading comprehension test based on literature. Then, have them do the same for a reading comprehension test based on nonfiction. Groups might also discuss which of these types of questions they personally find most difficult and why. Encourage students to discuss strategies they already know to answer these types of questions.

✍ TEST-TAKING TIP

Ask, "Have you taken tests that contain multiple-choice questions?" Most likely, all students will answer yes, so reassure them that they will understand how to answer this kind of question on the new SAT® and the ACT®. Explain that this handbook will familiarize them with the kinds of questions that might be new to them, and give them a solid understanding of all the formats they will see on the new SAT® and the ACT® tests.

Step-by-Step Teaching Guide

Strategies for Making Inferences

1. Ask a volunteer to read aloud the strategy. Discuss what it means to *infer* meaning from a selection. Inform students that inferences are educated guesses made by using prior knowledge and textual clues to identify suggestions and implications in the text.

2. Guide students through the steps identified on student page 889. Read aloud step 1. Then, ask students to read the long passage silently. After a reasonable time interval, have a student read the question aloud. Ask, "What word in the sentence signals that you must make an inference?" Point out that the word *suggest* indicates that the answer is not stated in the text. Explain that this kind of question requires students to think about what a passage implies; the answer is not stated in the passage itself.

3. Invite a volunteer to read aloud step 2. Then have students reread the passage, focusing on the last two paragraphs. Have students describe Jenna's state of mind based on clues from the passage (*she reacted almost hysterically*, he says *relax, some of us are worth trusting*).

4. Explain that students must choose one of the answer choices, A–E. Ask volunteers to read each answer choice. Have students compare each choice to information in the text to decide whether or not think the choice is correct. Ask students to identify the correct answer (D). Have students refer to the text to explain why this is the correct answer.

Reading Comprehension

Long Passage

This passage is an excerpt from a story about a young woman who becomes extremely preoccupied with an invention.

 **STRATEGY** **Make Inferences:** If the answer to a question is not plainly stated in the selection, look beyond the details and information to understand the suggestions and implications of the author's words.

▶ Sample Test Question

Directions: Read the passage carefully. Then, answer the question based on the information in the passage.

A Young Inventor

Seventeen-year-old Jenna didn't want to reveal her invention to anyone. She felt anxious as she dragged her computer files into innocent-looking folders, trying desperately to make sure that her notes were secure. Next week, Jenna would make her work public.

Jenna was part of an elite group of high-school students gathered from across the country to take part in a special science program. Her friends in the Young Inventors' Workshop had worked on what might be called everyday innovations. For example, Maggie had worked on improving the look and durability of old-fashioned linoleum floors. Derek had worked on easy-to-wear water packs for quenching athletes' thirst. Eileen and Ben had wavered between projects. They had not been able to decide whether to build on someone else's innovation or hold out for a unique idea.

Jenna had gotten to work immediately. She had a preference for inventions that could help the world. To that end, she was trying to figure out a better way to store radioactive waste. She knew it could be dangerous to store high-level waste in the containers that were currently available. In fact, some believed the use of the current containers could lead to tragic results.

Jenna was almost ready to present her solution, but she feared that someone would get into her files and take credit for her ideas. Maggie and Derek thought she was being silly, but they didn't know just how important her project was. Jenna stayed awake long nights working on the details of her invention and fretting over what might happen to it. It was no wonder, then, that she reacted almost hysterically when she saw one of the workshop advisors browsing through her computer files.

"Relax, Jenna," he said. "I'm just doing a virus scan. You know, if humanity is worth saving, then at least some of us must be worth trusting."

 **TIP:** In the actual new SAT® test, the passage will be about 850 words long. As many as thirteen questions might follow a long passage. Expect to see questions that test the following skills:

- Making inferences
- Identifying details
- Inferring the meaning of words and phrases from context
- Drawing conclusions
- Following an author's logic
- Identifying a work's tone and purpose
- Making predictions

Customize for
ESL Students

Encourage students to reread the sample passage to be sure they understand the main ideas. Then have them work in small groups to orally make connections between the passage and their own experience. Use questions like these to focus discussion:

What do they know about Jenna? Have they ever encountered anyone like her in real life or in a movie or television show?
Have they ever been overly worried about something?
Making these types of connections will help students correctly infer meaning about characters in passages.

QUESTION: The workshop advisor's comments to Jenna suggest that

    A   he is furious with her.

    B   her files have a virus.

    C   she unquestioningly accepts her advisor's behavior.

    D   he thinks she needs to get some perspective.

    E   her view of radioactive waste is correct.

STEPS

1. **Read the passage carefully to be sure you understand its general meaning.** Then, read the question.

2. **Reread the passage with the question in mind.** Focus on the portion of the passage pertaining to the question. Notice that Jenna reacts *almost hysterically* when she sees the workshop advisor browsing through her computer files. This intense reaction prompts her advisor's comment that she needs to show more trust in others.

3. **Read the workshop advisor's words again.** Notice that he says *relax* and encourages Jenna to see that *some of us are worth trusting.* He is indicating that she is very tense and has lost trust in others.

4. **Review the answer choices.** Choice A is not supported by the text. Choice B reflects the advisor's comment that he is doing a virus scan on Jenna's computer. Since the advisor *states* that he is running a virus scan and does not suggest that her files have a virus, choice B is incorrect. Choice C is contradicted by the text. Choice E is not supported by the text. Choice D makes sense in the context of the passage. The detail that Jenna was *almost hysterical* and the quotation from her advisor suggest that the advisor feels she has lost perspective. Therefore, the answer to the question is choice D.

FOR REVIEW

To review reading fiction in greater depth, see Chapter 30, Section 3.

Reading Comprehension • 889

Integrating Vocabulary Skills

Tell students that the words *imply* and *infer*, and *implication* and *inference*, are often confused. Offer this sentence, and ask students to explain its meaning: "Authors imply and readers infer." Students should understand that *imply* means to make a suggestion beyond what is directly stated. By contrast, to *infer* is to determine a suggested meaning based on details in the text. Then, ask students to develop their own sentence using *implication* and *inference*.

Customize for
Less Advanced Students

Review with students what an inference is. Use simple examples, such as "I think I'll go to bed now." Ask, "What can you infer about how I am feeling?" (tired/sleepy). Point out that the answer is not stated in the sentence (or the passage) but is implied or suggested. The student must figure out what the passage or sentence implies. Write the following examples on the board and have students identify what can be inferred in each.

1. *Looking out at the darkening sky, Jeremiah sighed, "Now our game will be postponed."* (Students should infer that it will rain and Jeremiah is disappointed because of the bad weather.)

2. *Lara ran after the bus, as she did every morning. "Wait up! Please, wait!" she screamed.* (Students should infer that Lara is missing a bus and that she usually runs late.)

Customize for
Gifted/Talented Students

Ask students to make additional inferences as they read. For example, what can they infer about what kind of person Jenna is? What can they infer about her personality traits? Have students jot down their inferences, as well as the passage clues and facts on which they are based. Encourage students to create a list of adjectives to describe Jenna and then to compare their lists with those of other students.

⏱ TIME SAVERS!

On-line Exercise Bank
Have students complete the exercises on the computer. The Auto Check feature will grade their work for you.

1. To familiarize students with multiple-choice paired reading passage comprehension questions on the new SAT® and the ACT®.

2. To review how to identify the author's purpose.

3. To teach methods for identifying the author's purpose in paired passages.

Step-by-Step Teaching Guide

Strategies for Identifying the Author's Purpose

1. Review the strategy for finding the author's purpose. Remind students that an author's purpose can often be found in the topic sentence and/or the concluding sentence.

2. Read aloud the directions and sample test question. Ask, "Is the question asking you to find a way the passages are the same or a way they are different?" Encourage students to point out why the question is asking them to find a way they are the same.

3. Guide students through the steps identified on student page 891. Emphasize that when a question specifically asks about both passages, students should make sure that their answer choice is appropriate to both passages. Occasionally, a question may refer to only one passage. Then, students should refer to the specified passage to find the answer. Stress that students must always read the question carefully so they know where to look to find the correct answer.

4. Review each choice with students. Ask students to point out choices they can eliminate due to lack of support in either passage (answer choices B, C, E). Encourage students to find supporting evidence for choices A and D in the passages. Students should become aware that support for choice A is found only in passage 1. Support for choice D exists in both passages; this is the correct answer.

Reading Comprehension

Paired Passages

Passage I is an excerpt from Willa Cather's novel *O Pioneers!* Passage II is from the novel *Wuthering Heights* by Emily Brontë.

 **STRATEGY** **Identify the Author's Purpose:** Pay particular attention to the first and last sentences of a passage to determine the author's purpose.

▶ **Sample Test Question**

Directions: Read each passage carefully to be sure you understand their general meaning. Then, answer the questions based on the information in the passages.

Passage I

One January day, thirty years ago, the little town of Hanover, anchored on a windy Nebraska tableland, was trying not to be blown away. A mist of fine snowflakes was curling and eddying about the cluster of low, drab buildings huddled on the gray prairie, under a gray sky. The dwelling-houses were set about haphazardly on the tough prairie sod; some of them looked as if they had been moved in over night, and others as if they were straying off by themselves, headed straight for the open plain. None of them had any appearance of permanence, and the howling wind blew under them as well as over them.

Passage II

Wuthering Heights is the name of Mr. Healthcliff's dwelling, "wuthering" being a significant provincial adjective, descriptive of the atmospheric tumult to which its station is exposed in stormy weather. Pure, bracing ventilation they must have up there at all times, indeed. One may guess the power of the north wind blowing over the edge by the excessive slant of a few stunted firs at the end of the house, and by a range of gaunt thorns all stretching their limbs one way, as if craving alms of the sun. Happily, the architect had foresight to build it strong. The narrow windows are deeply set in the wall, and the corners defended with large jutting stones.

TIP: Paired Passages are typically followed by four questions. Two of these questions will ask you to compare and contrast the paired passages.

Integrating Writing Skills

Point out examples of vivid, precise verbs in the passages, such as *anchored, curling, eddying, huddled, straying, exposed, blowing, stretching,* and *craving.* Note also specific adjectives, such as *windy, fine, low, drab, gray, tough, open, howling, significant, stormy, excessive, stunted, gaunt,* and *jutting.* Precise words add interest to the passages and convey the images that the authors wish the reader to see. Challenge students to find colorful nouns and adverbs in the passages (nouns: *tableland, mist, cluster, sod, dwelling, tumult, ventilation, slant, firs, thorns,* *alms;* adverbs: *haphazardly, deeply*). Encourage students to incorporate such descriptive language when they write.

QUESTION: The authors of the two passages are primarily concerned with describing

A   a house that can barely stand up to fierce winds.

B   why people should not live in areas with high winds.

C   the terrible destruction caused by strong storms.

D   houses set in harsh climates.

E   how weather affects a writer's mood.

S T E P S

1. **Read the passages carefully to be sure you understand the general meaning of each passage.** As you read the second passage, think about how it is similar to, or different from, the first passage.

2. **Read the question.** The question asks about each author's purpose. Notice that the question assumes that the two authors share the same purpose.

3. **Review the answer choices.** If one answer immediately strikes you as correct, reread the passages to confirm your choice. If no answer seems correct, reread the passages to get a stronger sense of each passage.

4. **Pay particular attention to the first and last sentences of Passage I.** Notice that the first sentence is concerned with the vulnerability of a town to harsh weather and that the final sentence refers to houses set in a harsh climate.

   Now, pay close attention to the first and last sentences of Passage II. Notice that the first sentence is concerned with a house set in a harsh climate and that the final sentence refers to the same theme.

5. **Choose the answer that best defines the authors' shared purpose.** Notice that answer choice A might have been correct if you were asked about Passage I alone. Because you are asked about both passages, however, you need to select an answer that makes sense for both passages. Choices B, C, and E are all incorrect because they cannot be supported by the passages. Choice D, *houses set in harsh climates*, is the answer because it addresses the purpose of both passages.

Reading Comprehension • 891

✎ TEST-TAKING TIP

Explain that it is sometimes helpful to preview the questions on a standardized test before reading the passage(s). That way, students can focus their reading on the specific information they need rather than spending time absorbing other details. Other ways to focus reading on a standardized test include underlining or circling main ideas during reading and using the title of a passage to find clues to its general message or theme. Students should be sure they are permitted to mark the test booklet.

Lesson Objectives

1. To familiarize students with short passage reading comprehension questions on the new SAT® and the ACT®.

2. To review how to infer the meaning of unfamiliar words using context clues.

3. To teach methods for identifying and using context clues.

Step-by-Step Teaching Guide

Strategies for Vocabulary in Context

1. Review the strategy of decoding vocabulary in context. Remind students that inferences are educated guesses made by using prior knowledge to identify indirect meanings in a text. Explain that the term *context* refers to the words, phrases, and sentences that surround an unfamiliar word.

2. Have students read the question and answer choices. Point out that the question does not explicitly instruct students to use context clues. Focus students' attention on the phrase *most nearly means* in the question. This phrase tells students that they are looking for an approximate, rather than an exact, meaning. Explain that these cue words suggest using context clues.

3. Guide students through the steps identified on the student page 893. Have a volunteer read aloud the sentence containing the phrase *good breeding*.

4. Have volunteers substitute each answer choice for good breeding and read aloud the resulting sentence. Elicit that choice B is correct because it can be substituted for *good breeding* without changing the meaning of the sentence; it relates most closely to the rest of the sentence.

⏱ TIME SAVERS!

On-line Exercise Bank
Have students complete the exercises on the computer. The Auto Check feature will grade their work for you.

Reading Comprehension

Short Passage

This passage describes the beliefs and attitudes held by the people of ancient Greece regarding ancestry.

 **STRATEGY** **Vocabulary in Context:** Figure out the meaning of an unfamiliar word from the way it is used in a passage. You can make inferences about the word's meaning by looking for context clues in the surrounding words.

▶ **Sample Test Question**

Directions: Read the passage carefully. Then, answer the questions based on the information in the passage.

> 1   Before a battle, Greek soldiers would name their ancestors and call on them for help. They would proudly identify themselves with a long line of heroic warriors. Ancestry was a way of impressing—and maybe
> 5   frightening—an enemy. Aristocrats, wealthy people proud of their <u>good breeding</u>, would claim to be descended from legendary heroes, in order to show that the gods themselves were their kin.
>   The Greeks believed that ancestry affected a person's
> 10   moral character and choices in life. Therefore, ancestry had a strong influence on social standing and even on occupation and livelihood. What a person chose to do for a living was affected by family traditions and choices made by previous generations.

QUESTION: Based on the information in the passage, *good breeding* (line 6) most nearly means

A   nice parents.

B   having ancestors who were successful and heroic.

C   moral choices made in life.

D   status as a citizen of a city.

E   wealth.

A Word to the Wise
Aristocrat

The word *aristocrat* contains the suffix *-crat*, which means "a member of" or "an advocate of." Many words contain this suffix; for example, a *democrat* is a supporter of, or advocate for, democracy. The Greek word *aristos* means "best." Therefore, an *aristocrat* is a member of the *best* class of people, such as the nobility or the very rich and powerful.

Customize for
Less Advanced Students

If students need further support, write the featured sentence from the test passage on the board: "Aristocrats, wealthy people proud of their good breeding, would claim to be descended from legendary heroes in order to show that the gods themselves were their kin." Ask students to name clues from the sentence that might shed light on the term *good breeding*. Circle the clues as students name them (e.g., wealthy, descended from heroes, gods were their kin). Have students apply each answer choice to the clues you circled. Ask

students whether the choice encompasses all of the clues.

For more practice, have students use context clues in the passage to infer the meaning of the word *occupation* (clues: livelihood; meaning: what a person chose to do for a living).

STEPS

1. **Carefully read the passage to be sure you understand its general meaning.** Then, read the question. Notice that it is asking you to infer the meaning of *good breeding* from how it is used in line 6 of the passage.

2. **Carefully reread the sentence in which *good breeding* appears.** If you are still in doubt about the phrase's meaning, reread the sentences that come before and after it.

3. **Review the answer choices.** Look for the answer choice that most nearly defines what *good breeding* means in the passage. Some of the answer choices may refer to an aspect of *good breeding*. For example, choices A, *nice parents*, D, *status as a citizen of a city*, and E, *wealth*, could all be interpreted as aspects of *good breeding*. However, none of these answer choices defines the way *good breeding* is used in the passage. Choice B, *having ancestors who were successful and heroic*, best defines what *good breeding* means in this context. Therefore, choice B is the answer.

Reflecting on Reading Comprehension

Think about the various reading strategies you have studied. Decide which types of reading passages and strategies present the greatest challenge for you. Use these questions to help you reflect upon such comprehension challenges.

- What type of Reading Comprehension question do I prefer answering? Why?

- With which type of Reading Comprehension strategy do I most frequently have problems?

- What can I do to improve my performance on these types of test questions?

An excellent resource for improving your performance on Reading Comprehension questions is your teacher. Share your concerns about specific question types and reading strategies with your teacher. He or she can help you improve your skills in these areas. Remember, one of the best ways to improve your performance on reading comprehension questions is to practice by reading newspapers and news magazines. The articles in newspapers such as the *New York Times* are often of the same length as those found in short and long passages. Moreover, they contain the same academic vocabulary that appears on standardized tests.

TEST-TAKING TIP

Tell students that they can save time on a test by noting connections between similar unfamiliar words, such as *ancestors* and *ancestry*. From the context of the passage, students can infer that *ancestors* are those from whom soldiers were descended. They can then assume that *ancestry* also has to do with those from whom a person is descended.

Customize for
Gifted/Talented Students

Have students write a passage to reveal the meaning of a difficult or unfamiliar word by using context clues. Invite students to highlight the target word and then share their passages with a partner. Partners can then identify the meaning of the target word based on the context clues.

Integrating Vocabulary Skills

Tell students that if they come across an unfamiliar word in a test passage, they should pause only long enough to decide whether or not they need to know the word. If they understand the general sense of the sentence, they may skip the word and read on. If the word seems important, they should reread the word and read on to see whether the context offers help. Ask students how important it is to understand the meaning of *warriors* and *ancestry* in order to understand the passage. (They should see that the meaning of *warriors* is less necessary than *ancestry*.)

ASSESS

Ask students the following questions to help them sum up what they have learned about these three kinds of reading comprehension questions found on standardized tests:

1. **Making Inferences:** What is the difference between directly stated information and an inference? How can you tell that a test question is requiring you to make an inference?

2. **Identifying Author's Purpose:** What parts of a paragraph or passage are most likely to point to an author's purpose? What should you look for to determine an author's perspective?

3. **Vocabulary in Context:** What is meant by "context"? Why is it useful to substitute each answer choice for the target word in the sentence?

For further review, direct students to practice tests, which are available in school libraries, public libraries, and on the World Wide Web. The ExamView questions in the On-line Exercise Bank also offer practice opportunities.

⏱ TIME SAVERS!

On-line Exercise Bank
Have students complete the exercises on the computer. The Auto Check feature will grade their work for you.

1. "The team with the young players is winning."

2. "One of the teams have young players."

Students should recognize that the second sentence sounds wrong. Ask them what is wrong and how to correct it. (One of the teams has young players.)

Activate Prior Knowledge

Ask students to read the three paragraphs above the steps on student page 894 to find three singular verbs and three plural verbs. Have them identify the singular and plural subjects that agree with the verbs.

TEACH

> ### Lesson Objectives
>
> 1. To familiarize students with the format of multiple-choice, error-based grammar questions.
>
> 2. To review a systematic approach for finding errors in grammar and usage.
>
> 3. To teach techniques for identifying and correcting errors in grammar and usage.

Step-by-Step Teaching Guide

Techniques for Answering Grammar and Usage Questions

1. Stress that students should read directions, questions, and answer choices carefully.

2. Guide students through the steps identified on the student page.

3. Remind students to rely not only on what sounds wrong, but on common grammar and usage errors they have studied. Ask students to name some of these and review the rules associated with each error. Topics may cover subject-verb agreement, pronoun cases, verb tenses, word choice, and so on.

Grammar

Multiple-Choice Grammar Questions

Many students find grammar difficult. However, by focusing on the grammar and usage rules that are most often tested, you can prepare yourself to succeed on this part of the new SAT® or the ACT®. The following section of the Test Preparation Handbook introduces you to some of the most frequently tested grammar and usage topics.

Techniques for Answering Grammar and Usage Questions

Many grammar and usage questions ask you to identify an error in a sentence. Some people can spot grammar and usage errors easily. These people can spot errors because they "hear" the errors as they read. This technique does not work for everyone. If you frequently make grammar and usage errors, it is best to use a systematic approach for answering these questions.

The following steps should help you approach and answer error-based grammar and usage questions. These questions typically present a sentence with several underlined words or phrases. The direction line asks you to identify which underlined part, if any, is an error.

STEPS

1. **Read the direction line and the question carefully.**

2. **Focus on the underlined words or phrases.**

3. **Ask yourself, "Does any underlined word or phrase sound wrong?"** If one word or phrase definitely sounds wrong to you, you have probably identified the error in the sentence.

4. **If no words or phrases sound wrong to you, ask yourself, "Does any underlined word or phrase violate a grammar or usage rule that I have learned?"** If you see that one underlined word or phrase violates a grammar or usage rule, you have probably identified the error in the sentence. Try to memorize the steps above as you work through this part of the Test Preparation Handbook.

Customize for
Less Advanced Students

Review the definitions and uses of parts of speech and punctuation marks with students. Have them write clues, such as "I modify a verb and often end in -*ly*. Who am I?" Invite volunteers to read the clues to the group and invite students to solve them.

Faulty Subject-Verb Agreement

> **RULE** A singular subject must have a singular verb. A plural subject must have a plural verb.

> **Sample Test Question**

Directions: Read the sentence carefully. Identify the sentence error from the underlined options. If there is no error, select choice E.

The <u>head researcher</u> <u>among the scientists</u> in the
          A   B

laboratory <u>instruct</u> his colleagues <u>to prepare</u> a report on
            C   D

the initial test results. <u>No error</u>
                         E

QUESTION: What is the error in the sentence?

- **A** head researcher
- **B** among the scientists
- **C** instruct
- **D** to prepare
- **E** No error

S T E P S

1. **Follow the four steps presented on page 894 for identifying sentence errors.**

2. **Identify the subject of the sentence.** The subject of the sentence is *head researcher*, which is singular. The verb in the sentence must also be singular.

3. **Identify the verb in the sentence.** The verb *instruct* is plural. This is an error. In order for there to be subject-verb agreement, the verb should be singular.

4. **Review the answer choices.** The error in the sentence is *instruct*. Therefore, the answer to the question is choice C.

TIP: It is a good strategy to identify the part of speech of each underlined word or phrase in questions of this type. Knowing the part of speech will help you recognize errors of agreement in test sentences.

FOR REVIEW

To review subject-verb agreement in greater depth, see Chapter 23, Section 1.

> **TEST-TAKING TIP**

Caution students to pay special attention to forms of the verb *be,* especially *are, is, was, were.* Have students list these verbs and write a singular or plural pronoun, and a singular or plural noun before each. Remind students that if any underlined portion of a sentence contains one of these verbs, they should look for the subject of the sentence or the clause and check for agreement in number.

Language Highlight

There are several nouns in English that are the same in the singular and the plural, such as *deer, fish, sheep,* and *moose.* In addition, there are some plural forms that do not end in *s* and may not appear to be plural, such as *criteria.* Remind students to be wary of these nouns and to use the context of the sentence to determine noun-number agreement.

Lesson Objectives

1. To familiarize students with choosing from among five answers to correct a grammatical error in a sentence.

2. To review subject-verb agreement.

3. To teach approaches for identifying and correcting faulty subject-verb agreement.

> **Step-by-Step Teaching Guide**

Strategies for Identifying Faulty Subject-Verb Agreement

1. Read the rule for subject-verb agreement with srudents. Invite them to give examples of correct subject-verb agreement in a sentence.

2. Ask a volunteer to read aloud the directions. Stress that failure to read directions is a common reason students answer questions incorrectly. Remind students that they are being asked to identify an error in the sentence.

3. Read aloud the question. Explain that the underlined words or phrases in the test question are the answer choices. Point out that the letters beneath the underlined words or phrases refer to the answer choices; for example, "choice A," "choice B," and so forth.

4. Guide students through the steps identified on the student page.

5. Ask students to find the phrases that separate the subject (*head researcher*) and the verb (*instruct*). Have them identify the phrases (*among the scientists* and *in the laboratory*). Explain that when the subject and the verb are separated, it may be more difficult to recognize faulty agreement. Suggest that students identify the subject and verb, and put them together to check for correct agreement (*The head researcher… instruct*). This will make an error more apparent. Choice C is the error.

Lesson Objectives

1. To familiarize students with choosing from among five answers to correct a grammatical error in a sentence.

2. To review verb tense.

3. To teach methods for identifying and correcting faulty verb tense.

Step-by-Step Teaching Guide

Strategies for Identifying Faulty Verb Tense

1. Review the rule for verb tense with students. Remind them that verb tense must make sense within the context of the sentence.

2. Have a volunteer read aloud the directions. Explain that the question asks them to identify any error in the sample sentence.

3. Guide students through the steps identified on the student page. Ask students to identify words in the sentence that refer to time. Brainstorm for other words and phrases that indicate present or future time frames. Explain what ongoing action is, using the sentence as an example: *had been* indicates that the Corn Laws were in continuous effect for the seventeen-year period mentioned in the sentence.

4. Emphasize that a number of test questions may have "No error" as the correct answer. Explain that if students can find no error after reading and analyzing a sentence, it is possible that "No error" is the correct answer. Remind students to keep this option in mind as they analyze test sentences.

5. Point out that many sentences in test questions contain two or more verbs in different tenses, so students need to be proficient in using all six verb tenses. To extend this lesson, suggest that they read sentences in other texts and identify the tense of the verbs.

Grammar

Faulty Verb Tense

> **RULE** A tense is the form of a verb that shows the time of an action or condition. A verb's tense must fit the meaning of a sentence.

> **Sample Test Question**

Directions: Read the sentence carefully. Identify the sentence error from the underlined options. If there is no error, select choice E.

The British Corn Laws <u>had been</u> in effect for seventeen
                              A
years <u>by the time</u> they <u>were</u> finally <u>repealed</u> in 1832.
          B   C   D
<u>No error</u>
  E

QUESTION: What is the error in the sentence?

  A   had been

  B   by the time

  C   were

  D   repealed

  E   No error

STEPS

1. **Follow the four steps presented on page 894 for identifying sentence errors.**

2. **Notice that three of the four underlined words or phrases are verbs.** Check that all verbs in the sentence are in the correct tense.

3. **Look for words and phrases in the sentence that indicate the time.** From the phrases indicating time *(for seventeen years, by the time, finally, in 1832)*, we can tell that the sentence describes a condition in the past. The first verb in the sentence, *had been*, is in the past perfect progressive. This indicates an ongoing condition that took place in the past. The second verb, *were repealed*, is in the perfect tense. Both verbs are in the correct tense. The sentence has no errors. Therefore, the answer to the question is choice E.

A Word to the Wise
Tense

The word *tense* comes from the Latin word *tempus*, meaning "time." The tense of a verb tells us the time an action took place.

> **FOR REVIEW**
> To review verb tenses, see Chapter 21, Section 1.

Language Highlight

Explain that verb tense is especially challenging for some non-native speakers because the tenses vary from one language to another. For example, in Chinese languages, the verb does not change to show tense. Instead, the context of the sentence, or a word or phrase that shows time, such as *yesterday,* shows when the action takes place.

Customize for
ESL Students

Some ESL students may have difficulty with verbs and verb phrases that describe ongoing action or condition. Review this verb tense with students by having them repeat or adapt sentences you say aloud, such as "We have been studying for the SAT," "We will have studied for six months by the time we take the SAT," "I have always wanted to go to college," and so forth. On the board, write forms of the perfect and progressive verb tenses. Ask students to write and underline each in an original sentence in their notebooks.

Faulty Verb Form

> **RULE** A progressive verb form indicates an ongoing action or condition.

▶ Sample Test Question

Directions: Read the sentence carefully. Identify the sentence error from the underlined options. If there is no error, select choice E.

<u>By the time</u> Sheila gets home from school, I <u>have been</u>
　　　A　　　　　　　　　　　　　　　　　B
<u>preparing </u>for <u>tonight's</u> dinner party <u>for at least six hours</u>.
　　C　　　　　　　　　　　　　　　D

<u>No error</u>
　E

QUESTION: What is the error in the sentence?

A　by the time

B　have been preparing

C　tonight's

D　for at least six hours

E　No error

S T E P S

1. **Follow the four steps presented on page 894 for identifying sentence errors.**

2. **Notice the words that relate to the time that events happen in the sentence.** The words *by the time Sheila gets home from school* indicate that the action of the subject will begin *before* Sheila gets home from school. This is a cue that the error, if any, may relate to verb tense or form.

3. **Study the verb *have been preparing.*** It should express action that began in the past, continues in the present, and will continue in the future. The correct form of the verb should be *I will have been preparing.* This form, the future perfect progressive, indicates that the preparation will start before Sheila gets home and will continue after she is home. The error in the sentence is the verb form, *have been preparing.* Therefore, the answer to the question is choice B.

TIP: There are six progressive verb forms:

Present Progressive
Mary is sleeping.

Past Progressive
Mary was sleeping when I called.

Future Progressive
Mary will be sleeping for the rest of the evening.

Present Perfect Progressive
Mary has been sleeping more than usual lately.

Past Perfect Progressive
Mary had been sleeping when the alarm clock went off.

Future Perfect Progressive
By seven o'clock tomorrow morning, Mary will have been sleeping for ten hours.

FOR REVIEW

To review verb forms and tenses in greater depth, see Chapter 21, Section 1, Section 2.

Grammar • 897

Lesson Objectives

1. To familiarize students with choosing from among five answers to correct a grammatical error in a sentence.

2. To review the progressive verb form.

3. To teach methods for identifying and correcting faulty verb form.

Step-by-Step Teaching Guide

Strategies for Identifying Faulty Verb Form

1. Review the rule regarding the progressive verb form. Instruct students to watch for cues in a sentence to determine the time that events occur.

2. Read aloud the directions and question.

3. Guide students through the steps identified on the student page. Ask students to read choices A–E to locate the correct choice. Point out that choices A, C, and D offer cues for the time frame. Answer choice B is a verb form that does not fit with the time cues. Choice B indicates the sentence error.

4. Write sentences using progressive verb forms, expressing different time periods, on the board. Help students use the rule to explain why the verb form is correct in each of the sentences.

5. To reinforce students' knowledge, use the sample test question to review the future perfect progressive verb form, which describes action that began in the past and will continue into the future. Then, have students use this verb form (will have been) in original sentences and share these with the class.

Customize for
Less Advanced Students

Some students may have trouble with the future perfect progressive verb form. On the board, write two or three sentences that correctly use this form (you may use sentences from the textbook, Chapter 21, Sections 1 and 2). Ask volunteers to underline the full forms of the verbs and explain the time period described in each sentence. If necessary, offer clues about how they can tell that the action began in the past and will continue into the future. Invite students to write sentences in their notebooks using the future perfect progressive verb form. Have them read the sentences aloud and, if they are correct, underline the complete verb in the sentence. Encourage students to write as many sentences using this verb form as they can as a way to help them recognize it and understand how it is used.

Lesson Objectives

1. To familiarize students with choosing from among five answers to correct a grammatical error in a sentence.
2. To review the need for consistency in pronoun person in a sentence.
3. To teach ways to identify a shift in pronoun person in a sentence.

Step-by-Step Teaching Guide

Strategies for Identifying Shifts in Pronoun Person

1. Review the rule regarding pronoun person. Discuss the importance of maintaining consistent pronoun number, person, and gender in a sentence.

2. Have a volunteer read the directions. Remind students that the underlined parts of the sentence, with letters beneath, are the answer choices.

3. Guide students through the steps identified on the student page. Ask volunteers to identify the impersonal pronouns in the sentence. Note the use of two pronouns, *one* and *you*. Since *one* also appears in a part of the sentence that is not underlined, students should realize that it cannot be changed to *you* throughout the sentence. *You* can be changed since it appears only once, and is underlined in that instance. The error is therefore in choice B.

4. Reinforce that the rule requires consistency. Have students make the pronoun person *you* throughout the sentence and then read the sentence aloud.

Grammar

Shifts in Pronoun Person

> **RULE** When referring to an indefinite subject with an impersonal pronoun, such as *one* or *you*, do not switch pronoun persons in the middle of the sentence. The same pronoun should be used to refer to an antecedent throughout a sentence.

Sample Test Question

Directions: Read the sentence carefully. Identify the sentence error from the underlined options. If there is no error, select choice E.

<u>One cannot succeed</u> at any task <u>if you do not</u> make the
     A   B

effort and <u>commitment</u> to do <u>whatever it takes</u> to
          C   D

accomplish one's goal. <u>No error</u>
                   E

QUESTION: What is the error in the sentence?

A One cannot succeed

B if you do not

C commitment

D whatever it takes

E No error

S T E P S

1. **Follow the four steps presented on page 894 for identifying sentence errors.**

2. **Notice that the subject of the sentence is an impersonal pronoun *one*.** The pronoun person must not shift from the pronoun *one*, to another, such as *you*. This is an error made so frequently in conversation that most people are unaware of it. However, in writing, it is a serious error because it affects the clarity of a sentence or passage.

3. **Notice that choice B, *if you do not*, is a pronoun shift from the pronoun used for the subject of the sentence, *one*.** Therefore, the answer to the question is choice B.

A Word to the Wise
Pronoun

The word *pronoun* has the prefix *pro-,* which means "for." A pronoun is a word that stands for a noun.

FOR REVIEW

To review pronoun shifts in greater depth, see Chapter 23, Section 2.

TEST-TAKING TIP

Remind students to examine the part of speech, number, and person of the words underlined in a test question to help identify an error. Emphasize that students may need to determine these properties in both words that are underlined and those that are not. Underlined words and phrases can often be identified as errors only when they are related to other words in sentences that are not underlined.

⏱ TIME SAVERS!

 On-line Exercise Bank
Have students complete the exercises on the computer. The Auto Check feature will grade their work for you.

Faulty Pronoun Reference

RULE A pronoun must clearly refer to its antecedent.

Sample Test Question

Directions: Read the sentence carefully. Identify the sentence error from the underlined options. If there is no error, select choice E.

The trade representative <u>offered</u> <u>his foreign counterpart</u>
          A   B
a revision to the agreement when <u>he saw</u> an obstacle
             C
<u>to signing</u> the document. <u>No error</u>
  D   E

QUESTION: What is the error in the sentence?

- **A** offered
- **B** his foreign counterpart
- **C** he saw
- **D** to signing
- **E** No error

STEPS

1. **Follow the four steps presented on page 894 for identifying sentence errors.**

2. **Notice that the sentence is unclear because the reader cannot tell to whom *he saw* refers.** The sentence would make sense if *he* referred to the trade representative, but it would also make sense if *he* referred to the foreign counterpart. Therefore, the error in the sentence is the faulty, or unclear, pronoun reference in *he saw*.

3. **Review the answer choices.** There are no other errors in the sentence. Therefore, the answer to the question is choice C.

TIP: When test sentences contain pronouns, always check to make sure that the pronouns have clear antecedents. Pronouns should also agree with their antecedents in number, person, and gender.

FOR REVIEW

To review pronoun reference and usage in greater depth, see Chapter 23, Section 3.

Lesson Objectives

1. To familiarize students with choosing from among five answers to correct a grammatical error in a sentence.
2. To review pronoun referents.
3. To teach methods for identifying and correcting faulty pronoun reference.

Step-by-Step Teaching Guide

Strategies for Identifying Faulty Pronoun Reference

1. Review the rule regarding pronoun reference. Point out that if the reader cannot know with certainty to whom the pronoun refers, there is an error.

2. Invite a volunteer to read aloud the directions and sample test question.

3. Guide students through the steps identified on the student page. Have students identify the pronouns in the sentence and find the antecedent for each. Explain to students that if they cannot figure out the referent for a pronoun in an underlined part of a test sentence, then it is likely they have identified the error in the sentence.

4. Invite a volunteer to suggest how to rewrite the sentence using pronouns with clear antecedents.

5. Explain to students that if a test question contains a pronoun, they should be sure that there is a clear antecedent for that pronoun. Offer this example: *John handed Tom his pen.* To whom does the pen belong? It may belong to John or Tom so this is a faulty pronoun reference.

Customize for
Gifted/Talented Students

Invite these students to write sentences in which the pronoun referent is confusing. Have these students work one-on-one with less advanced students and ESL students to help them detect the pronoun referent errors in the sentences. Then, have the student pairs work together to write new sentences that contain clear pronoun referents.

Lesson Objectives

1. To familiarize students with choosing from among five answers to correct a grammatical error in a sentence.

2. To review pronoun-antecedent agreement.

3. To teach methods for identifying faulty pronoun antecedent agreement.

Strategies for Identifying Faulty Pronoun-Antecedent Agreement

1. Review the rule regarding pronoun-antecedent agreement.

2. Invite a volunteer to read aloud the sample test question. Have students identify each pronoun in the underlined parts of the sentence, find its antecedent, and check for agreement.

3. Guide students through the steps identified on the student page. Explain that the words separating a pronoun from its antecedent can cause confusion. Tell students to identify the pronoun and its antecedent and check that the two elements match in number, person, and gender.

4. Have students identify the sentence error and explain their reasoning. They should say that the pronoun *its* refers to *countries* and does not match in number. The pronoun *their* refers to countries; the pronoun *their* and its antecedent *countries* agree in number. The error is in choice B.

Grammar

Pronoun-Antecedent Agreement

RULE A personal pronoun must agree with its antecedent in number, person, and gender.

Sample Test Question

Directions: Read the sentence carefully. Identify the sentence error from the underlined options. If there is no error, select choice E.

Most industrialized countries <u>use</u> some of <u>its tax money</u>
                                       A   B
<u>to fund</u> elementary and secondary education
C
<u>for their citizens'</u> children. <u>No error</u>
    D   E

QUESTION: What is the error in the sentence?

  A   use

  B   its tax money

  C   to fund

  D   for their citizens'

  E   No error

S T E P S

1. **Follow the four steps presented on page 894 for identifying sentence errors.**

2. **Notice that some of the underlined sections of the sentence include pronouns.** Whenever pronouns are underlined in a test question, identify each pronoun's antecedent. Check to see that each pronoun matches its antecedent in number, person, and gender. The antecedent of *its* is *industrialized countries*, which is plural. A plural antecedent must take a plural pronoun. However, *its* is singular. This is the error in the sentence.

3. **Review the answer choices.** There are no other errors in the sentence. Therefore, the answer to the question is choice B.

A Word to the Wise
Antecedent

The word *antecedent* comes from the Latin words *ante,* which means "before," and *cedere,* which means "to go." Therefore, *antecedent* means "that which comes before." An antecedent is a noun that comes before a pronoun. The pronoun refers to the noun and must match it in number, person, and gender.

FOR REVIEW

To review pronoun-antecedent agreement in greater depth, see Chapter 23, Sections 2 and 3.

Language Highlights

Pronoun shifts occur when a speaker or writer loses sight of the antecedent that a pronoun refers to. An antecedent may be a noun or a pronoun. Collective nouns *(group, committee, audience)* pose particular problems, because the noun is usually considered singular, but it may be plural when individual members are emphasized. *(The crowd rose to its feet. The crowd waved their hats and signs.)* Singular indefinite pronouns *(everyone, nobody, one, nothing, each)* also pose a problem, because a pronoun that agrees in number can sound awkward. (example: *Everyone needs his or her ticket.*)

 TEST-TAKING TIP

Tell students to pay special attention to possessive pronouns in questions about usage. Review the possessive pronouns: *his, her, hers, its, my, mine, your, yours, our, ours, their, theirs.* Remind students that if a possessive pronoun is in an underlined part of a test question, they should check that it agrees with the noun it refers to. Clarify that apostrophes should not be used in possessive pronouns. They belong only in contractions.

Faulty Pronoun Case

RULE Case is the form of a noun or pronoun that indicates its use in a sentence. Pronouns must be in the correct case for the role they play in a sentence.

Sample Test Question

Directions: Read the sentence carefully. Identify the sentence error from the underlined options. If there is no error, select choice E.

Last Thursday after school, Sam and me had
    A   B

a great time at the county fair with our friends Anne and
    C   D

David. No error
         E

QUESTION: What is the error in the sentence?

A   Last Thursday

B   Sam and me

C   a great time

D   our friends

E   No error

S T E P S

1. **Follow the four steps presented on page 894 for identifying sentence errors.**

2. **Notice that two of the answer choices, B and D, contain pronouns.** Check that each pronoun has a clear antecedent. Since the antecedents of the pronouns are clear (both refer to the writer of the sentence, *I*), check to be certain that each pronoun is in the correct case. The pronoun *me* is part of the subject of the sentence, *Sam and me*. Because it is part of the subject, the pronoun should be in the nominative case. *Me* is in the objective case. This is the error in the sentence. The writer should have written *Sam and I* instead of *Sam and me*.

3. **Review the answer choices.** There are no other errors in the sentence. The answer to the question is choice B.

A Word to the Wise
Case

Case is the form of a noun or pronoun that indicates its use in a sentence. The three cases of nouns and pronouns are the nominative, the objective, and the possessive.

FOR REVIEW

To review pronoun case in greater depth, see Chapter 22, Section 1.

Grammar • 901

Lesson Objectives

1. To familiarize students with choosing from among five answers to correct a grammatical error in a sentence.

2. To review pronoun case.

3. To teach methods for identifying and correcting faulty pronoun case.

Step-by-Step Teaching Guide

Strategies for Identifying Faulty Pronoun Case

1. Review the rule about pronoun case. Remind students that the three cases of nouns and pronouns are the nominative, objective, and possessive.

2. Ask a volunteer to read aloud the sample test question. Have students find the pronouns in the sentence.

3. Guide students through the steps identified on the student page. Ask students to explain why the pronoun in the compound subject *Sam and me* must be in the nominative case. To make the error more obvious, reread the sentence, using only the subject pronoun and the simple predicate: *Me had a great time.* Have students read this revised sentence with the nominative case pronoun, *I.* The error is in choice B.

4. Remind students to determine the function of a pronoun in a test question. Knowing the pronoun case will help them decide if the pronoun is used correctly or if it is the sentence error.

5. Caution students to follow rules as well as their ear when identifying grammar errors. Explain that the test items are developed according to grammar rules, and not informal usage.

Customize for
Less Advanced Students

Have less advanced students create a chart in their notebooks showing pronoun forms for each case. Tell students to refer to these charts as they practice using correct pronoun forms in sentences. Then, ask students to write three sentences with each of the sentences having a pronoun in a different case. Monitor students' sentences to ensure that they are using the correct pronoun case and understand the concept of pronoun case.

⏱ TIME SAVERS!

🖥 **On-line Exercise Bank**
Have students complete the exercises on the computer. The Auto Check feature will grade their work for you.

Lesson Objectives

1. To familiarize students with choosing from among five answers to correct a grammatical error in a sentence.

2. To review comparative and superlative modifiers.

3. To teach methods for identifying errors in comparative modifiers.

Strategies for Identifying Faulty Comparisons

1. Review the rule about using modifiers to compare persons, places, or things. Explain what "comparative" and "superlative" words are, using an example of each in a sentence. Remind students that many adjectives form the comparative by adding -er, and the superlative by adding -est.

2. Read the sample test question aloud. Have students identify the comparative and superlative words that are underlined.

3. Guide students through the steps identified on the student page. Remind students to identify the types of words underlined in error-based questions. Identifying these words will help them know what types of sentence errors to look for.

4. Ask students to identify any part of the sentence that sounds wrong to them or that they know violates a grammar rule. Then, invite a student to explain why choice C, worser, is incorrect.

5. You may also wish to practice using comparatives in sentences. Write an adjective on the board, and ask students to write a set of three sentences that use the adjective and its correct comparative and superlative forms.

Grammar

Modifiers: Faulty Comparisons

> **RULE** Use the correct form of the comparative and superlative degrees to compare persons, places, or things.

Sample Test Question

Directions: Read the sentence carefully. Identify the sentence error from the underlined options. If there is no error, select choice E.

<u>Yesterday was</u> not <u>the best day</u> of my life, but today is
     A   B

even <u>worser</u>, and tomorrow will probably be <u>the worst</u> of
     C   D

all. <u>No error</u>
    E

QUESTION: What is the error in the sentence?

  A   Yesterday was
  B   the best day
  C   worser
  D   the worst
  E   No error

S T E P S

1. **Follow the four steps presented on page 894 for identifying sentence errors.**

2. **Notice that the sentence contains two adjectives in the superlative degree: *best* and *worst*.** A third adjective, *worser*, appears to be in the comparative degree because it ends in -er. It is incorrect, however. Although the comparative degree of many adjectives is formed by adding -er, the adjective *bad* is irregular. Its comparative degree is written *worse*.

3. **Review the answer choices.** There are no other errors in the sentence. Therefore, the answer choice to this question is choice C.

A Word to the Wise
Superlative

The prefix *super-* in the word *superlative* means "above" in Latin. When you use a superlative form of an adjective, you are indicating that something possesses the quality of that adjective above all others.

> **FOR REVIEW**
>
> To review faulty comparisons with modifiers in greater depth, see Chapter 24, Section 2.

✏ TEST-TAKING TIP

Remind students to look for similarities among the underlined words and phrases. Identifying these similarities—such as the repeated underlining of comparatives or superlatives—gives them clues about the error in the sentence. If they find the sentence confusing, remind students that they can make notes to help themselves identify the error. For example, in the sample sentence, students may decide that there is an error in the comparatives or superlatives, but be unable to identify it. Students may jot down a list of the comparative forms for good—*good/better/best*; and bad—*bad/worse/worst*. Referring to this list will help them identify the misuse of the comparative (*worser*) in the test question.

Misplaced Modifiers

> **RULE** When a modifier is placed too far from the word it should modify, it can appear to modify the wrong word in a sentence. This is called a *misplaced*, or *dangling, modifier*.

> **Sample Test Question**

Directions: Read the sentence carefully. Identify the sentence error from the underlined options. If there is no error, select choice E.

<u>At Sarah's birthday party</u> on Friday, <u>the magician did</u>
      A   **B**

<u>tricks</u> for <u>the children wearing a long, red cloak</u> and made
                           C

them all <u>laugh.</u> <u>No error</u>
       D   **E**

QUESTION: What is the error in the sentence?

A   At Sarah's birthday party

B   the magician did tricks

C   the children wearing a long, red cloak

D   laugh

E   No error

S T E P S

1. **Follow the four steps presented on page 894 for identifying sentence errors.**

2. **Notice that it seems odd that children would be wearing a long, red cloak.** It seems even more unlikely that a magician at a birthday party would perform for children who are wearing a long, red cloak. Nevertheless, this is exactly what the sentence means as written. Clearly, the modifying phrase *wearing a long, red cloak* is misplaced. It should be placed directly after the word *magician* in the sentence. That would make it clear that it is the magician who is wearing the long, red cloak.

3. **Review the answer choices.** The misplaced modifier is the error in the sentence. Therefore, the answer to the question is choice C.

TIP: If a sentence seems confusing even after you have carefully read it twice, the confusion is probably due to an error in the sentence.

> FOR REVIEW

To review misplaced modifiers in greater depth, see Chapter 20, Section 5.

Grammar • 903

Lesson Objectives

1. To familiarize students with choosing from among five answers to correct a grammatical error in a sentence.

2. To review correct placement of modifiers.

3. To teach the strategy of identifying parts of speech in a sentence to correct misplaced modifiers.

Step-by-Step Teaching Guide

Strategies for Identifying Misplaced Modifiers

1. Review the rule regarding placement of modifiers. Remind students that a *modifier* is a word, phrase, or clause that describes another word or group of words. Explain that *modify* means "to qualify or limit the meaning of." Discuss prepositional and adverbial phrases used as modifiers.

2. Read aloud the directions and the sample test question. Remind students that they are being asked to consider parts of a sentence to determine which has an error. Contrast this format with questions that ask students to consider a sentence in its entirety.

3. Guide students through the steps identified on the student page. Ask students to explain the literal meaning of the sample sentence. (*The children, not the magician, were wearing a long red cloak.*) Have them identify the correct choice (C).

4. Ask students to rewrite the sample sentence by correctly placing the modifier. (*At Sarah's birthday party on Friday, a magician wearing a long, red cloak did tricks for the children and made them all laugh.*)

Language Highlights

Misplaced modifiers in headlines and ads can be comical. Encourage students to look for examples, such as these: "These sneakers won't hurt your feet when you remove them." "Sit back on this couch with your feet up having an ice cream." "Friendly cat ideal for families with pleasant temperament." "Senators finally agree after months on closed beaches." Collections are available in print and online (one search term: *Humorous headlines*). Have students rewrite each example to clarify the meaning and to avoid the inadvertent comic effect.

1. To familiarize students with choosing from among five answers to correct a grammatical error in a sentence.
2. To review correct word choice.
3. To teach methods for distinguishing between frequently confused words.

Strategies for Identifying Faulty Word Choice

1. Review the rule regarding word choice. Explain that *homophones* are included in this category of easily confused words. Remind students to examine how words are spelled when they come upon commonly confused words.
2. Read aloud the directions and sample test question as students follow along.
3. Guide students through the steps identified on the student page. Then, have students identify words in the underlined answer choices that are commonly confused with other words (*adapt, affect*). Have students define each word, and then identify and define words that look similar but have a different meaning (*adopt/adept, effect*). Ask students to read the sample sentence, replacing each of these underlined words with its definition. Have students find the error (choice C) and explain their reasoning.
4. Stress that word accuracy is important on standardized tests. Remind students to read carefully to detect similar, but incorrect, words. On the board, write pairs of words that sound or look similar (e.g., *accept/except, cereal/serial, complement/compliment, canvas/canvass, then/than principal/principle, pedal/peddle, discreet/discrete, liable/libel*). Then ask students to explain the differences in meaning. Invite volunteers to use each word in a sentence.

Grammar

Faulty Word Choice

> **RULE** Words that sound alike or are spelled similarly are easily confused. Such words often have very different meanings.

> **Sample Test Question**

Directions: Read the sentence carefully. Identify the sentence error from the underlined options. If there is no error, select choice E.

<u>In the science lab</u> we are trying to <u>adapt</u> the
     A   B

instruments to our experiment, but we are unaware of the

<u>affect</u> this will have on our <u>results</u>. <u>No error</u>
 C   D   E

QUESTION: What is the error in the sentence?

A   In the science lab

B   adapt

C   affect

D   results

E   No error

S T E P S

1. **Follow the four steps presented on page 894 for identifying sentence errors.**

2. **Notice that two underlined words in the sentence are words that look and sound similar to other words:** *Adapt* is often confused with *adopt*, and *affect* is often confused with *effect*. In this sentence, *adapt* is used correctly. The word *affect*, however, is used incorrectly. As a noun, *affect* means *expression* or *countenance*. This meaning does not make sense in this sentence. The word *effect*, a noun meaning "outcome or result," would make better sense.

3. **Review the answer choices.** The use of the word *affect* is the error in the sentence. Therefore, the answer to the question is choice C.

FOR REVIEW

To review word choice in greater depth, see Chapter 29, Sections 1 and 2.

904 • Test Preparation Handbook

Customize for
Less Advanced Students

Review words that may be confused because they look and sound similar. Provide some commonly confused words from the following list of words; and ask partners to make a chart in which each word meaning is shown in words and pictures.

Commonly Confused Words: *accept/except; adapt/adopt/adept; affect/effect; angel/angle; capital/Capitol; cease/seize; command/commend, council/counsel; desert/dessert; decent/descent; device/devise; expand/expend; expect/suspect; formally/formerly; further/farther; imitate/intimate; later/latter; lose/loose; moral/morale; of/off; principle/principal; proceed/precede; quite/quit/quiet; recent/resent; then/than; there/their/they're; through/thorough/though; to/two/too.*

Encourage students to use a dictionary, as needed. Later, they may refer to their charts as they write and analyze sentences.

Improving Sentences

Introduction

Some test questions will require you to use your command of standard written English to improve the way a sentence is written. In these types of questions, all or part of a sentence is underlined. The answer choices present four different ways of rewriting the underlined material. You are asked to select the answer choice that shows the most effective revision. If the sentence is fine the way it is written, select answer choice E, no revision necessary.

Run-on Sentences

▶ **RULE** A run-on sentence is two or more complete sentences that are not properly joined or separated.

▶ **Sample Test Question**

Directions: Read the sentence carefully. Then, select the answer choice that best revises the sentence. If you think the original sentence is better than the answer choices, select answer choice E, No revision necessary.

> Albert Einstein is revered as one of the greatest scientists of all time, he changed the way people view the world and the universe.

QUESTION: Which of the following is the best revision of the sentence?

A Albert Einstein is revered as one of the greatest scientists ever, he changed the way people view the world and the universe.

B Albert Einstein is revered as one of the most great scientists ever who was changing people's view of the world and the universe.

C Albert Einstein is revered as one of the greatest scientists of all time and, he changed our view of the world and the universe.

D Albert Einstein is revered as one of the greatest scientists of all time; he changed the way people view the world and the universe.

E No revision necessary

Grammar • 905

TIP: Review the main sentence structures so that you will be able to identify how to improve different kinds of sentences easily.

A simple sentence contains a subject and a verb.

A compound sentence contains two simple sentences.

A complex sentence contains one main clause and one or more subordinate clauses.

Lesson Objectives

1. To familiarize students with choosing from among five answers to improve a sentence.
2. To define and review run-on sentences.
3. To teach methods for revising run-on sentences.

Step-by-Step Teaching Guide

Strategies for Revising Run-on Sentences

1. Review the rule that defines a run-on sentence, and have student volunteers write examples on the board.

2. Read aloud the directions. Remind students that they may pick choice E if they do not think a revision would improve the sentence.

3. Guide students through the steps identified on student page 906.

4. Have volunteers read aloud the sample test question and each of the answer choices. Ask students to identify the answer choice that best makes the test sentence clear and comprehensible. Students should explain their reasoning. Point out that a comma splice, or two sentences joined by a comma, is a common writing error.

5. Review the ways to fix a run-on sentence. Have students revise the sample sentence in all three ways (as two separate sentences, using a comma and a conjunction, and using a semicolon).

6. Using the sentences that students wrote on the board, ask volunteers to show different ways to correct them. They should demonstrate all three ways to correct run-ons.

TEST-TAKING TIP

Remind students it is important to read the directions carefully. An item with the same format (such as underlining) as a previous item may not ask the same thing as the previous item asked. Strategies for understanding directions include circling or underscoring important words, reading the directions at a slower rate than other parts of the test, and rereading directions for clarification or certainty. In this case, students should note that they are asked for the choice that *best revises* the sentence.

⏱ TIME SAVERS!

🖥 **On-line Exercise Bank** Have students complete the exercises on the computer. The Auto Check feature will grade their work for you.

1. To familiarize students with choosing from among five answers to improve a sentence.
2. To define and identify sentence fragments.
3. To teach methods for correcting sentence fragments.
4. To review using a semicolon to connect two independent clauses.
5. To teach methods for identifying the correct use of semicolons.

Step-by-Step Teaching Guide

Strategies for Revising Sentence Fragments

1. Review aloud the rule regarding sentence fragments.
2. Read aloud the directions and sample test question. Point out that all words in the sentence are underlined, so students must look at the entire sentence for the source of the error.
3. Guide students through the steps identified on student page 907. Ask students to identify the correct choice and explain in their own words why it is correct.
4. Review that a complete sentence must have a subject and a verb and must express a complete thought.
5. Write on the board a combination of complete sentences and sentence fragments. Ask students to identify the fragments and suggest how to correct them. Examples: *Clothing on the floor.* (fragment, missing a verb) *Heard an echo.* (fragment, missing a subject) *Jack called his dog.* (complete sentence) *Until the baby fell asleep.* (fragment, incomplete thought)

Language Highlights

Sentence fragments can be found easily in printed material, and they are usually correct. Careful writers who understand the rules of sentence writing may choose to write a fragment, usually for emphasis.

Grammar

STEPS

1. **Read the directions and the sentence carefully.**
2. **Decide whether the sentence needs revision.** Notice that there is something wrong with the sentence: It contains two complete sentences punctuated as if they were one sentence (*Albert Einstein is revered as one of the greatest scientists of all time* and *he changed the way people view the world and the universe*). There are three ways of correcting a run-on: Rewrite it as separate sentences, join the sentences with a comma and conjunction, or join the sentences with a semicolon.
3. **Read each answer choice to determine which revision, if any, reflects standard written English and makes the sentence clearer and more effective.** In this case, look for the choice that uses one of the solutions described in step 2. The first three choices, A, B, and C, either fail to correct the run-on or introduce other errors. Choice D uses a semicolon to connect the two sentences. Therefore, choice D is the answer to the question.

Sentence Fragments

▶ **RULE**   A sentence fragment is a group of words with end punctuation that either does not have a subject or verb or does not express a complete thought.

▶ **Sample Test Question**

Directions: Read the sentence carefully. Then, choose the best revision if you think the sentence is a fragment. If the sentence is correct as it stands, select choice E, No revision necessary.

The historical novel, which was filled with illuminating detail and vivid characters.

QUESTION: What is the best revision of the sentence?

A   The historical novel which was filled with details and vivid characters.

B   Historical novels must be illuminating and vivid.

C   The historical novel was filled with illuminating detail and vivid characters.

D   The historical novel, which had illuminating details, vivid characters, and a compelling plot.

E   No revision necessary

906 • Test Preparation Handbook

FOR REVIEW

To review sentence structure in greater depth, please see Chapter 21, Section 4.

A Word to the Wise
Fragment

The word *fragment* comes from the Latin *frangere,* which means "to break." Therefore, a sentence fragment is a broken part of a sentence, or an incomplete sentence.

Customize for
Less Advanced Students

Help students understand that a sentence with a subject and a verb may still be a sentence fragment if it does not express a complete thought. On the board, write the sentence: *The boy thought the book on the table.* Have students identify the subject (boy) and verb (thought). Help them determine why this is a sentence fragment. Point out that the sentence does not tell you what the boy "thought" about the book. Have students correct this sentence by completing it. Write other examples of sentence fragments on the board for students to complete. Examples:

When I heard the dog bark.

Sasha and Jules chose to study the same.

The coach, who was furious after we lost.

STEPS

1. **Read the directions and the sentence carefully.**

2. **Decide whether the sentence needs revision.** Notice that it is a sentence fragment. It contains a subject, and a verb, but it does not express a complete thought.

3. **Review the answer choices.** Select the revision that reflects standard written English and makes the sentence clearer. Choices A and D are sentence fragments. Choice B changes the meaning of the sentence. Choice C effectively turns a sentence fragment into a sentence by deleting the word *which*. Therefore, the answer to the question is choice C.

Punctuation: Semicolon

> **RULE**   A semicolon connects two independent clauses that are closely related in thought and structure.

▷ Sample Test Question

Directions: Read the sentence carefully. Then, select the answer choice that shows the correct way of rewriting the underlined sentence. If the sentence is correct as it stands, select choice E, No revision necessary.

Matilda was shocked to see her brother; she had never seen him before.

QUESTION: What is the correct way of writing the above sentence?

A   Matilda was shocked to see her brother, she had never seen him before.

B   Matilda was shocked to see her brother, nor had she seen him before.

C   Matilda was shocked to see her brother and she had never seen him before.

D   Matilda had never seen her brother. So she was shocked to see him.

E   No revision necessary

FOR REVIEW

To review sentence fragments in greater depth, see Chapter 18, Section 1 and Chapter 19, Section 4.

Step-by-Step Teaching Guide

Strategies for Identifying the Correct Use of Semicolons

1. Read aloud the rule regarding semicolons. Stress that a semicolon connects two complete and closely related thoughts.

2. Read aloud the directions and sample test question. Note that students are being asked to find the best revision of the sentence *without* changing the meaning.

3. Guide students through the steps identified on student page 908. Note why choices A–D are incorrect. Elicit that the sentence is correct as is.

4. Write pairs of clauses on the board and ask students if each pair could correctly be connected by a semicolon. Examples:

   Ann came from a big family. She had seven siblings. (yes)

   The Greens traveled often. It was summer vacation. (no)

   Julio loves animals. His dog's name is Lobo. (no)

   Shivani studied hard. She did four hours of homework each night. (yes)

Language Highlights

As its prefix *semi-,* which means "half," suggests, a semicolon resembles half a colon; it also has a function halfway between a comma and a period. Most independent clauses separated with a semicolon could also be written correctly as separate sentences, but they would need a conjunction if a comma replaced the semicolon. For example, the sample sentence could also be written as: *Matilda was shocked to see her brother, since she had never seen him before.*

✎ TEST-TAKING TIP

Explain that a semicolon may take the place of a comma and a conjunction in a compound sentence. Remind students that if the test sentence would also be correct with a comma and a conjunction, such as "…brother, because"—then the semicolon is used correctly. Tell students that they can use this method to help them determine if a semicolon in a test question is used correctly.

Grammar

S T E P S

1. **Read the directions and the sentence carefully.**
2. **Decide whether the sentence needs revision.** Notice that the sentence joins two independent clauses *(Matilda was shocked to see her brother* and *she had never seen him before)* with a semicolon. Because the two sentences are closely related in thought, the use of a semicolon to connect the independent clauses is correct.
3. **Review the answer choices.** Determine whether any of the revisions makes the sentence clearer and more effective. Choice A is a run-on sentence. Choice B does not make sense. Choice C does not connect the clauses with a conjunction that makes the relationship between the two clear. Choice D begins a sentence with the word *so* which is poor usage. Therefore, the answer to the question is choice E, No revision necessary.

Improving Paragraphs

Introduction

Some test questions will require you to edit and revise paragraphs. These questions may ask you:

- to revise a sentence within a paragraph so that it reflects standard written English.
- to delete or insert sentences so that a paragraph's organization is more coherent and logical.

Paragraph Coherence

▶ **RULE**   In a coherent paragraph, each sentence is essential because it either states or supports the main idea.

▷ **Sample Test Question**

Directions: Read the passage carefully. Then, answer the question on the following page.

> (1) The backhand in tennis causes players more trouble than other strokes. (2) Even though the swing is natural and free flowing, many players feel intimidated by it and try to avoid it. (3) Venus Williams, however, has a great backhand, and she often wins difficult points with it. (4) When faced with a backhand shot coming at them from across the net, some players cannot get their feet and body in the best position to hit a return shot. (5) These players tend to forget the swing altogether and lose the point. (6) The difficulties of mastering the backhand stroke keep tennis coaches busy teaching it to their clients.

908 • Test Preparation Handbook

Improving Paragraphs
Although a question may focus on a sentence in a paragraph, make sure your answer reflects an understanding of the paragraph as a whole.

A Word to the Wise
Coherence

The word *coherence* comes from the Latin *cohere*, meaning "to stick." A coherent paragraph is made up of sentences that seem to stick together.

QUESTION: Which of the following sentences could be deleted without detracting from the flow and meaning of the passage?

A   sentence (1)

B   sentence (2)

C   sentence (3)

D   sentence (4)

E   sentence (5)

S T E P S

1. **Read the paragraph quickly but carefully.** Notice any errors, unnecessary sentences, gaps in logic, or awkward expressions as you skim the paragraph.

2. **Read the question.** Then, reread the paragraph with the question in mind. In this case, the question is suggesting that a sentence can be deleted from the paragraph because it is inessential. If a sentence does not jump out to you as unnecessary, follow step 3.

3. **Consider each answer choice within the context of the paragraph.** Ask yourself: "Does this sentence contribute to the main idea of the paragraph?" In this example, sentence 3, *Venus Williams, however, has a great backhand, and she often wins difficult points with it* does not contribute to the main idea of the paragraph. Sentence (3) can be deleted from the passage without detracting from its flow or meaning. Therefore, the answer to the question is choice C.

Reflecting on Grammar Questions

Now that you have worked through the Grammar section, answer the following questions about your reading and test-taking skills:

- Which grammar and usage topics were you already familiar with?

- Which grammar and usage topics did you find challenging?

Once you have identified areas that you need to work on further, ask your teacher for help in finding materials that can help you improve your skills.

FOR REVIEW

To review paragraph unity and coherence in greater depth, see Chapter 3, Section 3, and Chapter 6, Section 4.

ASSESS

Help students summarize what they have learned about the grammar questions in standardized tests. Ask students to explain what each of the following rules means and to give an example of each:

1. A verb must agree with its subject in number.

2. Verb tenses must make sense in context.

3. A progressive verb form indicates ongoing action.

4. A pronoun must not shift in person.

5. A pronoun must clearly refer to its antecedent.

6. A pronoun must agree with its antecedent.

7. A pronoun must be in the correct case.

8. Comparisons must use the correct forms of comparative and superlative modifiers.

9. Modifiers must be placed so that what they are modifying is clear.

10. The correct word of two often confused words must be used.

11. Run-on sentences must be revised.

12. Sentence fragments must be revised.

13. A semicolon must connect two closely related independent clauses.

14. Paragraphs must be coherent; all the sentences must support one main idea.

Encourage students to complete the *Reflecting on Grammar Questions* assignments to help them direct their further study. For further review, direct students to practice tests, which are available in school libraries, public libraries, and on the World Wide Web. The ExamView questions in the On-line Exercise Bank also offer practice opportunities.

TEST-TAKING TIP

Remind students that answer sheets for the new SAT® and the ACT® are machine scored and must be filled in according to instructions. Students should not make any stray marks on the answer sheets. Students must also be sure that they completely erase any answers they wish to change. All answer spaces should be darkened completely.

Interest GRABBER Ask students to name media in which people routinely express opinions on various topics (Examples include: talk radio, television talk and interview shows, Internet postings and blogs, newspaper editorials, and opinion essays). Talk about what makes a persuasive argument effective or ineffective. Tell students that they must use effective techniques when writing to persuade. Test examiners will look for clarity, logic, and convincing arguments in essays that express an opinion or point of view.

Activate Prior Knowledge

Ask for examples of issues that concern high-schoolers. Students may name cell phones in school, changes to the legal driving age, or issues related to the World Wide Web. List several on the board, and have students make statements of opinion about each. Explain that these kinds of statements are similar to those students will write in the introductory paragraph of a persuasive or point-of-view essay.

TEACH

> ## Lesson Objectives
>
> 1. To introduce the format of a timed ACT® essay prompt.
> 2. To review elements in a persuasive essay.
> 3. To study a model essay that states and supports a point of view and creates a focused, logical argument.

Step-by-Step Teaching Guide

Studying a Model ACT® Essay

1. Review the rule that defines a persuasive essay with students. Explain that persuasive writing is tested on the new SAT® and the ACT® because it requires students to demonstrate reasoning—as well as writing—ability.

2. Read the directions line aloud. Tell students to note the amount of allotted time they will have.

continued

Writing

The ACT® Writing Test

The ACT® Writing Test is optional. It consists of an essay that you must complete in thirty minutes. You will be given a writing prompt that presents an issue. You will be asked to write a persuasive essay explaining your position on the issue.

▶ **RULE** A persuasive essay presents the writer's point of view on an issue and supports the writer's position with convincing arguments, examples, and details.

Directions: You have thirty minutes to write an essay on the topic assigned below. Think carefully about the issue presented in the following excerpt and assignment.

Sample Writing Prompt

Environmentalists have been warning for years that there is a finite supply of oil. This reality is having a significant effect on daily life in the United States. In reaction to the rising cost of gasoline, some economists are suggesting that people use public transportation, such as a bus or train, to get to work or school. They argue that this will keep down the demand for gasoline, which in turn will drive down oil prices. Environmentalists support this idea, arguing that it will be good for the environment. However, many private citizens believe that driving to work or school is essential to their daily routine and schedule. Relying on public transportation would make it hard for most citizens to carry out their busy, demanding lives.

Assignment: In your opinion, should people use public transportation to conserve energy and lower the demand for gasoline? You may defend either one of the two points of view given, or you may present a different point of view on this question. Use specific reasons and examples to support your position.

Studying a Model ACT® Essay

- **Read the prompt and the assignment carefully.** Make sure you understand the issue at hand.

- **Read the sample essay.** Decide for yourself whether the student does a good job of persuading you, the reader, that his point of view is valid and well thought out.

- **Read the call-outs.** Find out what an examiner might notice about the essay. Pay attention to the elements of the essay that are noted, such as clear and strong introductions and conclusions and the use of many types of examples. Notice especially the way the student uses a counterexample to show his ability to weigh both sides of the issue.

How to succeed on the ACT® Writing Test

1. State a clear position on the issue.
2. Focus on the topic throughout the essay.
3. Support your position with examples.
4. Show logical reasoning through a well-organized essay.
5. Use Standard English.

✏ TEST-TAKING TIP

Emphasize two critical qualities that test examiners look for in persuasive essays: organization and voice.

Using standard essay form—introductory paragraph, body of two to four paragraphs, concluding paragraph—the writer should clearly connect statements of opinion with supporting facts and examples in a logical progression of arguments.

The writer's voice should also come through in word choice and sentence variety. Point out that persuasive essays are expected to be somewhat formal. Students should use language that is natural, and respectful. As a result students should avoid using slang terms.

Model Essay

The United States is a free country. People who say that it is their right to drive their car to work or school are correct. It would be wrong and probably illegal to force people to take public transportation to work or school. Nevertheless, given the energy crisis, it would be admirable if individuals took some responsibility for not making a bad situation (the energy crisis) worse.

> A clear statement shows the student's position on the issue. In a stylish move, he places his thesis statement at the end of the first paragraph rather than at the beginning.

Citizens enjoy having rights, but rights come with responsibilities. We all have legal responsibilities to pay taxes and obey the law, but we have other responsibilities, too, responsibilities that nobody can force us to honor. One area in which these voluntary responsibilities come into play is the current energy crisis. As we read the newspapers, we cannot deny that an energy crisis is causing many problems in our country and the world. One problem it is causing is the high cost of oil. Another, even more serious problem is wars that are being fought largely because of oil. Our dependence on oil is causing grave damage to the environment. If citizens want to enjoy their rights and pass their rights on to their children, they should choose to take public transportation as much as possible.

> The student uses several examples to support his argument that the energy crisis is a problem: the high cost of oil, wars, and damage to the environment.

It is not that I am insensitive to the situation of working families and their dependence on cars. I am the son of two working parents. My mother works 50 miles from our home. She leaves the house at 6 A.M. to get to work on time. If she had to take public transportation, she would probably have to leave at 4 A.M. or even quit her job. Economists and environmentalists need to think about people like my mother when they make their recommendations. However, there are things that people like my mother could do to help ease the energy crisis. They could carpool with other people who live near them. Moreover, the government and even private companies could offer more public transportation options to make even long commutes possible by public transportation.

> The student addresses the opposite side of his argument. By discussing why some people cannot easily make use of public transportation, he shows maturity and the ability to see both sides of an issue.

> A transition word helps to make the logic clearer to readers.

Just because something is difficult does not mean we should avoid it, and just because it is our right to drive, that does not mean we should persist in driving everywhere when we know that doing so hurts the environment. In short, I believe that private citizens should spend as much time caring for their responsibilities as they spend protecting their rights. While I do not agree that everyone should take public transportation, I believe that we should all do our part to ease the energy crisis whenever we can.

> The closing statement concisely summarizes the student's point of view.

Writing • 911

Integrating Writing Skills

Have students review the essay to jot down words and phrases that show the writer's command of varied and sophisticated vocabulary. Make the point that students should try to demonstrate vocabulary knowledge but avoid "big" words that are too unfamiliar to be used appropriately.

 TIME SAVERS!

On-line Exercise Bank
Have students complete the exercises on computer. The Auto Check feature will grade their work for you.

Step-by Step Teaching Guide continued

3. Read the sample writing prompt aloud. Explain that it presents an issue about which reasonable people may disagree. Students are being asked to show their ability to weigh two sides of an issue and articulate a well-reasoned point of view.

4. Review the list of elements found in a successful persuasive essay. Use the list of current issues students generated in the *Activate Prior Knowledge* activity or brainstorm for current issues happening in the high school. Encourage students to state their point of view in a single sentence. Remind students that their opinion must be supported by examples.

5. Read the model essay aloud with students. Read the call outs and remind students that they indicate points an examiner would notice.

6. Invite students to work in small groups to make a chart or outline that identifies the arguments and possible counterexamples in the model.

Customize for
ESL Students

To help students understand a counterexample, point out that a counterexample contradicts, or expresses the opposite position, and balances the point of view. Practice designing counterarguments by providing students with statements and ask them to provide arguments against the ideas.

Teaching from the Model

Reread aloud the opening paragraph as students follow along. Have students identify the sentence that clearly states the writer's position on the issue in the test prompt. ["Nevertheless, given the energy crisis, it would be admirable if individuals took some responsibility for not making a bad situation (the energy crisis) worse."] Next, have students review the concluding paragraph. Ask them to evaluate whether the writer has successfully restated and summarized the points made in the body of the essay. Have students sum up the writer's reasons in support of her position, and ask them to identify specific examples the writer has used to support her reasons.

Lesson Objectives

1. To introduce the format of a timed ACT® essay prompt.
2. To review strategies for writing a persuasive essay.
3. To teach methods for stating and supporting a point of view and creating a focused, logical argument.

Step-by-Step Teaching Guide

Strategies for the ACT® Writing Test

1. Review and discuss persuasive essays with students. Point out that most, but not all, persuasive essays open with a statement of the writer's point of view. Explain that no single essay structure is valued over another on the ACT®, and that some writers state their position at the end or in the middle of an essay.

2. Read aloud the directions and sample writing prompt along with students.

3. Guide students through the steps identified on the student page

4. To get students started on their own essays, tell them to write a single-sentence position statement at the top of a page. Then, have them create a brief outline that lists the main arguments (one per paragraph) with supporting details. Explain that in a logical argument thoughts follow naturally and logically from one to the next. Relevant details and examples refer to the argument in the paragraph.

5. Instruct students to begin their own essays by clearly stating their position on the issue addressed in the prompt on student page 910. Stress the importance of effective introductions and conclusions, as well as the use of transition words.

6. Review the list of criteria listed in step 5 on the student page. Stress that students should keep these six points in mind as they write and proofread their essays.

Writing

Writing the ACT® Essay

STEPS

1. **Now that you have read a model essay, try out the prompt on page 910 yourself.** Give yourself thirty minutes to respond to the prompt.

2. **Determine what you are being asked to write about.** Take a moment to decide what your opinion is. Jot down arguments, examples, and details that support your opinion.

3. **Make a short outline of what you will write.** Take time to think your plan through carefully as it will drive your essay. Plan to spend five minutes creating an outline.

4. **As you draft, follow your outline to be sure you stay on task.** Allow fifteen minutes to draft your essay.

5. **Spend five minutes revising your essay.** As you revise, keep in mind that your essay will be judged against the following criteria:
   - The essay should articulate a point of view on the issue presented in the writing prompt.
   - The essay should maintain a clear focus on the stated point of view for the entire essay.
   - The essay should explain its point of view and support it with evidence.
   - The essay should be organized logically.
   - The essay should use real-life examples.
   - The essay should have few errors in grammar, punctuation, and spelling.

6. **Spend five minutes proofreading your essay.** Use the techniques on page 917 to proofread your essay in five minutes or less.

7. **Once the essay is completed, use the criteria on this page to evaluate your essay.**

Tip: The high school teachers and college professors who score the timed essays understand that the writing will not be completely polished; however, the fewer errors an essay has, the higher it will score.

FOR REVIEW

To review writing persuasive essays in greater depth, see Chapter 7.

Integrating Writing Skills

Review transitional words and phrases students might want to use in their essays, such as *moreover, therefore, in contrast, however, furthermore, finally, for example,* and *in addition.* Challenge students to identify transitional words and phrases in the model essay on student page 911. Explain that using the right transitional words in an essay makes the writing smoother, clearer, and more logical.

TEST-TAKING TIP

Tell students that although test examiners do not count the number of words in an essay, they do look for a thorough development of ideas, which usually requires about 400 words. Students may create their own target length by practicing essay writing under timed conditions. Remind them that the full development of ideas is paramount, but their handwriting must also be legible.

 New SAT PREP ACT

The New SAT® Essay

The new SAT® essay must be completed in twenty-five minutes. The writing prompt presents an issue. You must present a position on the issue and write a short essay that develops and supports your point of view.

▶ **RULE** A persuasive essay presents the writer's point of view on an issue and supports that view with convincing arguments, examples, or details.

Directions: You have twenty-five minutes to write an essay on the topic assigned below. Think carefully about the issue presented in the following excerpt and the assignment that follows.

Sample Writing Prompt

Increasingly, elementary, middle, and high schools are focusing exclusively on reading, writing, and math. In many schools, subjects such as science, social studies, art, and music have been eliminated from the curriculum. The entire emphasis of instruction is on the core language and numerical skills.

Assignment: Are schools that eliminate all but the basic educational skills shortchanging their students by providing a narrow education? Or is it prudent to focus on reading, writing, and math because if students do not gain these skills, they will not be able to learn more sophisticated skills and content. Plan and write an essay in which you develop your point of view on this issue. Support your position with reasoning and examples taken from your studies, experience, or observations.

Studying a Model Essay

- **Read the prompt and the assignment carefully.** Make sure you understand the issue at hand.

- **Read the sample essay.** Decide for yourself whether the student does a good job of persuading you, the reader, that her point of view is valid and well thought out.

- **Read the call-outs.** Find out what an examiner might notice about the essay. Pay attention to the elements of the essay that are noted, such as clear and strong introductions and conclusions and the use of many types of examples.

 New SAT PREP ACT

To address the new SAT® essay prompt successfully, your essay should

- develop a point of view on the issue.

- use logical reasoning and appropriate examples.

- be well-organized and focused.

- demonstrate good language skills and appropriate vocabulary.

- use a variety of sentences, varying sentence length.

- have relatively few errors of grammar, punctuation, or spelling.

Writing • 913

Teaching from the Model

Emphasize that the first paragraph of a persuasive essay must clearly show the writer's point of view on the issue. Tell students to reread the assignment in the sample writing prompt and the model essay's opening paragraph. Ask, "What does the writer do to show she is focusing on the assigned question?" Explain that it is fine to introduce an essay by paraphrasing or restating the question, but remind students that it is important to add related ideas to show that they are not merely copying.

✎ TEST-TAKING TIP

Tell students that it is a good idea to wear a watch. When they take the test. Explain that each part of the test is timed and, though they should not become anxious about the time, they should use their watch to pace themselves and to make sure they get to answer all questions. Tell them they should allow time to plan, write, and proofread a well-thought-out essay.

▶ Lesson Objectives

1. To introduce the format of a timed new SAT® essay prompt.

2. To review strategies for writing a persuasive essay.

3. To teach methods for stating and supporting a point of view and creating a focused, logical argument.

Step-by-Step Teaching Guide

Studying the New SAT® Essay

1. Review the rule defining persuasive essays. Explain that examples, reasons, and details can support and reinforce a point of view.

2. Read aloud the directions and sample writing prompt with students. Note that the timeframe for writing a new SAT® essay is shorter than that of the ACT®. Remind students that the prompt presents an issue that can be successfully argued from either side.

3. Read the sidebar with students. Explain that it features elements from the rubric that examiners use to determine a score. Emphasize that half of the elements focus on the strength of the argument and half focus on the quality of the writing. Review punctuation in compound, complex, and compound-complex sentences and discuss common grammar and usage errors.

4. Review the points on this page for studying a model essay. Then, ask students to read the model essay on student page 914. Discuss students' initial impressions of the essay. Point out that the call outs highlight the strengths of the essay's argument that an examiner would likely notice.

Teaching from the Model

Reread aloud the first and last sentences of the opening paragraph and the concluding paragraph. Ask students to summarize the pattern they notice. (The writer repeats the position using different language.) Then, have a volunteer read aloud the first sentence of each paragraph. Ask why each sentence is an effective introduction to the paragraph.

Customize for
ESL Students

Identify an issue that engages students. Using this frame, guide students in completing a simple statement of opinion about the issue: *I believe that ___ should ___.* Using their completed statement, offer a mix of strong and weak reasons for students to evaluate. Ask students to identify the reasons that offer good support for their statement of opinion.

Writing

Model Essay

I believe that it is necessary for schools to preserve subjects such as science, art, music, and social studies in the curriculum. Elementary, middle, and high school is where a person builds the foundation for the learning he or she will do throughout college and life. A student should be exposed to many disciplines. Schools that teach a bare-bones education—one consisting only of reading, writing, and math—will produce students with basic skills but no knowledge of how to think outside the box.

There are studies that show that creative programs, such as music and art, help students learn more quickly and easily in other subjects. Art and music classes train students to think creatively and use different kinds of logic. They also break up the school day. I know I always feel refreshed after art class because art is much more hands-on than my other classes. After art, I am able to sit at a desk and take notes with more focus and effectiveness. Some schools have added creative programs like ballroom dancing instead of cutting art and music, and these schools have seen more focus and discipline in their students as a result.

Besides creative classes, a broad range of academic classes should be offered. Students should be exposed to physical and life sciences. In my biology class this year, we did structured experiments. These experiments allowed us not only to get hands-on science experience, but also to learn important observation and trial-and-error techniques. Science taught me to use all of my senses to observe and describe something, and to follow a process when I'm experimenting. Social studies classes are just as important as science classes. They teach students how to be educated members of society. If we as students learn about other countries, we can be wise about the world. If we learn about American history, we can make voting decisions and form opinions based on events of the past and present.

I recognize that if a student is not a proficient reader, he or she cannot read the history or science book that is provided, let alone gather information from it. In addition, some schools do not have the money or resources to provide extra classes. For these reasons, some schools choose to focus on the fundamental skills in order to build a smaller, but perhaps more sound, foundation. However, this reasoning lowers the bar in education and deprives students of valuable experiences. If a school has the ability to provide science, arts, and social studies classes, it should do so. One should not assume that providing these classes detracts from the fundamentals. My cousin used to attend a school that only offered reading, writing, and math. Her grades suffered until she came to my school and started playing in the school band. She learned to play the trombone well, and this success gave her the confidence she needed to apply herself to her academic classes.

In conclusion, limiting the curriculum to reading, writing, and math produces a one-dimensional education. Students who learn many skills through varied courses are able to focus on their studies and think creatively. These students have the opportunity to build a strong educational foundation that will support them through college and life.

The student begins with a clear and strong statement of her point of view on the issue. She provides reasons for her point of view and supports them with examples.

The student presents the second part of her argument by stating that it is supported by research. She explains why this argument supports her point of view, using examples and personal experience.

The student makes a smooth transition from the second to the third paragraph. She again uses examples from personal experience and observations to support her point of view.

The student cites a counterexample and uses observations and personal experience to refute it.

The student correctly begins this final paragraph with a clear restatement of the argument.

⏱ TIME SAVERS!

💻 **On-line Exercise Bank** Have students complete the exercises on the computer. The Auto Check feature will grade their work for you.

Prewriting Tip

Remind students that if a prompt on a standardized test does not specify an audience, they should assume that they are writing for a general audience, teacher, or examiner. Remind students what this means in terms of selection of details, word choice, and other qualities of their writing. They should understand that writing should be formal and that specific jargon or ideas not understood by a novice should be explained.

Writing the SAT® Essay

S T E P S

1. **Now that you have read a model essay, try out the prompt on page 913 yourself.** Give yourself twenty-five minutes to respond to the prompt.

2. **Make a short outline of what you will write.** Take time to think your plan through carefully as it will drive your essay. This step should take no longer than five minutes.

3. **As you draft, follow your outline to be sure you stay on task.** Allow about thirteen minutes for drafting and two minutes for revising your essay.

4. **Allow for five minutes to proofread your essay.** Use the technique on page 917 to proofread your essay in five minutes or less.

5. **Once the essay is completed, use the criteria on this page to evaluate your essay.**

The essay scored 5 out of 6 on the SAT® Essay Scoring Guide because

- it effectively develops a point of view on the issue.

- it uses logical reasoning and appropriate examples.

- it is well organized and well focused.

- it demonstrates good language skills and uses appropriate vocabulary.

- it uses a variety of sentences; it varies the length of sentences.

- it has relatively few errors of grammar, punctuation, or spelling.

FOR REVIEW

To review writing persuasive essays in greater depth, see Chapter 7.

Writing • 915

Lesson Objectives

1. To introduce the format of a timed new SAT® essay prompt.

2. To review strategies for writing a persuasive essay.

3. To teach methods for stating and supporting a point of view, and creating a focused, logical argument.

Step-by-Step Teaching Guide

Strategies for Writing the New SAT® Essay

1. Review the elements of persuasive essays with students. As they reread the prompt on student page 913, tell them to note that in the last line of the assignment they are being asked to use examples from their studies, experiences, or observations to support their position.

2. Guide students through the steps identified on the student page. Remind students to take five minutes to organize an outline on which to base their essay. Each paragraph should contain a main argument and relevant supporting evidence, and there should be a logical and smooth flow of ideas from one sentence and paragraph to the next. Students should refer to their outlines as they draft their essays.

3. Encourage students to be prepared to consult a clock or watch, or to request an account of time remaining to ensure that they complete their writing within the given time limit. Students should take about fifteen minutes to write their essays after they make their outlines.

4. Stress that neat handwriting is important in the essay part of the exam. If evaluators cannot read the writing, they are more likely to give the essay a low grade.

Customize for
Less Advanced Students

Students who share a point of view on the issue in the test prompt may work together to develop an outline using this template.

1. Statement of position (first paragraph):

2. Supporting reason (second paragraph):

3. Supporting reason (third paragraph):

4. Counterexample and argument against it (fourth paragraph):

5. Restatement of position: (sixth paragraph):

Each student may then use the outline to guide the writing of his or her own essay.

Prewriting Tip

Emphasize that good organization must be determined in the outline. Students should make any organizational revisions on their outlines, not in their essays. Explain that they can make notes, cross out, and make other revisions on the outline because they do not hand it in. Making extensive changes in the essay will be more difficult. Encourage students to carefully review their outlines before they begin writing their essay.

1. To introduce five-minute essay planning.

2. To review planning, drafting, and revising a timed essay.

3. To teach test-taking strategies for planning an essay.

Step-by-Step Teaching Guide

Strategies for Planning the Persuasive Essay

1. Review the strategy for planning a persuasive essay. Point out that a thoughtful position in an essay requires the support of strong, varied examples.

2. Guide students through the steps indicated on the student page. Tell students that they can complete a PRO/CON chart and use it to create an outline for the position they choose.

3. Explain that in planning their essays, it is not important to use an elaborate outline. They should focus on organizing major arguments and related supporting evidence logically.

4. Using the writing prompt on student page 913, or another one you devise, invite a volunteer to create a sample PRO/CON chart on the board. Have students brainstorm for pro and con arguments and examples to fill in the chart. Ask the class to choose a position.

5. Remind students that a counterexample is one that contradicts their position. To illustrate this, suggest several positions related to students' experiences, such as the value of homework and good study habits, and elicit volunteers to offer counterexamples.

6. Discuss which counterexample on students would include in their essay. Stress that including a counterexample, and arguing against it, strengthens their position because it shows they have considered other view points.

7. Caution students that skipping the planning step for an essay can result in a disjointed argument.

Writing

Planning the Persuasive Essay

 **STRATEGY** Spend five minutes planning an essay before you begin to write. Make sure your outline includes at least three examples to support your argument. It should also address a counterexample.

Persuasive, or point-of-view, essays typically require you to take a position on an issue. It is important to show that you have weighed both sides of the issue. To get started thinking critically, use a graphic organizer like the one below to think through an issue.

A Word to the Wise
Counterexample

A counterexample is an example that runs against or *counter* to an argument. By discussing a counter-example, a writer shows that he or she has weighed both sides of an argument.

The Issue:		
	PRO	**CON**
Example 1		
Example 2		
Example 3		

STEPS

1. **Carefully read the essay prompt and the assignment.** Make sure you understand the issue presented. Think about where you stand on the issue. This position is the point of view that you will present in your essay.

2. **Make a chart to organize your examples.** Plan to include at least three examples that support your point of view. Notice the types of examples the assignment calls for. Try to use examples from different sources.

3. **Consider both sides of the argument.** In your essay, you should also choose a counterexample. You should acknowledge the strength of this example, but explain why it does not persuade you to change your position.

4. **Use your chart as you draft and revise your essay.** Make sure you have included at least three examples and one counterexample.

Drafting Tip

Tell students to use their five minutes of prewriting/planning time as effectively as they can to lay out the organization of their paragraphs. With just twenty-five minutes to produce a final essay, their first draft cannot be a rough one; it must be close to a final draft. However, with an outline in place, students can concentrate on developing coherent paragraphs, main idea by main idea, and avoid rambling.

⏱ TIME SAVERS!

🖥 **On-line Exercise Bank**
Have students complete the exercises on computer. The Auto Check feature will grade their work for you.

Proofreading in Five Minutes

 **STRATEGY** On a timed essay, allow five minutes for proofreading your essay. Since you do not have a lot of time, remember the acronym CUSP to proofread quickly. The letters CUSP stand for:

Capitalization: Check that every sentence begins with a capital letter and that proper nouns begin with capital letters. Make sure that no words begin with capital letters unnecessarily.

Usage: Check that your grammar and word choice is correct.

Spelling: Check that all words are correctly spelled.

Punctuation: Check that there are no missing or unnecessary punctuation marks.

Finally, check that your essay is neatly presented. If your writing is illegible, try to make it clearer. Check that any inserted words or sentences are neatly indicated.

Reflecting on Test Preparation

Now that you have reached the end of the Test Preparation Handbook, take some time to think about what aspects of test preparation were most challenging for you. Use these tips to get your ideas started.

1. Quickly flip through the pages of the Test Preparation Handbook and jot down reading, grammar, and writing topics that represent a challenge for you.

2. Once you have identified a particular problem area or areas, work through the textbook chapter on the topic. Then, review the Test Preparation Handbook so that you can learn strategies for answering questions on those topics in exams.

3. Ask your teacher for help in building your skills and accessing old standardized tests that you can use for practice.

 **TIP:** Practice writing essays in your best handwriting. When writing on the test, take care to write neatly.

Writing • 917

Lesson Objectives

1. To introduce the need to proofread a timed essay.
2. To review strategies for proofreading a persuasive essay.
3. To teach methods for successfully proofreading a point-of-view essay in five minutes.

Step-by-Step Teaching Guide

Strategies for Proofreading in Five Minutes

1. Discuss with students the need to reserve time for proofreading a timed essay. Students must track elapsed time and use only the allotted five minutes for planning and writing. Note that errors corrected in a final read-through may improve the score.

2. Explain that using an acronym such as CUSP or other form of checklist will speed up the proofreading process.

3. Discuss why it is important that the essay be neat and legible.

4. Advise students to try to proofread their work through fresh eyes, to see what they actually wrote rather than what they meant to write.

ASSESS

Ask the following questions to help students sum up what they have learned:

1. What are three important things to remember about writing a persuasive essay on a standardized test?

2. What kinds of usage errors will you need to identify and correct on standardized tests?

3. What are two strategies to use when answering questions about reading passages on standardized tests?

For further practice, direct students to practice tests, which are available in school libraries, public libraries, and on the Web. The ExamView questions in the On-line Exercise Bank also offer practice opportunities.

Proofreading Tip
Proofreading Tip

Explain that proofreading one's own writing is challenging because all writers have a tendency to see what they intended to write, instead of what is actually on the page. By checking for each kind of error methodically, rather than just rereading the whole essay, students will be more likely to find spots that need fixing. Students should also rewrite illegible words. Suggest that some students may prefer to print their essay.

Customize for
Less Advanced Students

To guide students in proofreading, read aloud one paragraph from the model essay as a dictation exercise. After each student has written the paragraph, direct students to reread carefully three times, for capitalization, spelling, and punctuation. They may then compare their proofread and corrected versions with the original.

Citing Sources and Preparing Manuscript

The presentation of your written work is important. Your work should be neat, clean, and easy to read. Follow your teacher's directions for placing your name and class, along with the title and date of your work, on the paper.

For handwritten work:

- Use cursive handwriting or manuscript printing, according to the style your teacher prefers. The penmanship reference below shows the accepted formation of letters in cursive writing.
- Write or print neatly.
- Write on one side of lined 8 $1/2$" x 11" paper with a clean edge. (Do not use pages torn from a spiral notebook.)
- Indent the first line of each paragraph.

- Leave a margin, as indicated by the guidelines on the lined paper. Write in a size appropriate for the lines provided. Do not write so large that the letters from one line bump into the ones above and below. Do not write so small that the writing is difficult to read.
- Write in blue or black ink.
- Number the pages in the upper right corner.
- You should not cross out words on your final draft. Recopy instead. If your paper is long, your teacher may allow you to make one or two small changes by neatly crossing out the text to be deleted and using a caret [^] to indicate replacement text. Alternatively, you might make one or two corrections neatly with correction fluid. If you find yourself making more than three corrections, consider recopying the work.

PENMANSHIP REFERENCE

$$Aa\ Bb\ Cc\ Dd\ Ee\ Ff$$
$$Gg\ Hh\ Ii\ Jj\ Kk\ Ll$$
$$Mm\ Nn\ Oo\ Pp\ Qq$$
$$Rr\ Ss\ Tt\ Uu\ Vv\ Ww$$
$$Xx\ Yy\ Zz\ 1234567890$$

For word-processed or typed documents:

- Choose a standard, easy-to-read font.
- Type or print on one side of unlined $8\,^{1}/_{2}$" x 11" paper.
- Set the margins for the side, top, and bottom of your paper at approximately one inch. Most word-processing programs have a default setting that is appropriate.
- Double-space the document.
- Indent the first line of each paragraph.
- Number the pages in the upper right corner. Many word-processing programs have a header feature that will do this for you automatically.

- If you discover one or two errors after you have typed or printed, use correction fluid if your teacher allows such corrections. If you have more than three errors in an electronic file, consider making the corrections to the file and reprinting the document. If you have typed a long document, your teacher may allow you to make a few corrections by hand. If you have several errors, however, consider retyping the document.

For research papers:

Follow your teacher's directions for formatting formal research papers. Most papers will have the following features:

- Title page
- Table of Contents or Outline
- Works-Cited List

Table of Contents

.... 6

.... 10

.... 12

.... 15

Cited

Sybil Luddington:
Female Paul Revere

Megan Mahoney
Language Arts
3rd Period
March 26, 20- -

Incorporating Ideas From Research

Below are three common methods of incorporating the ideas of other writers into your work. Choose the most appropriate style by analyzing your needs in each case. In all cases, you must credit your source.

- **Direct Quotation:** Use quotation marks to indicate the exact words.
- **Paraphrase:** To share ideas without a direct quotation, state the ideas in your own words. While you haven't copied word-for-word, you still need to credit your source.
- **Summary:** To provide information about a large body of work—such as a speech, an editorial, or a chapter of a book— identify the writer's main idea.

Avoiding Plagiarism

Whether you are presenting a formal research paper or an opinion paper on a current event, you must be careful to give credit for any ideas or opinions that are not your own. Presenting someone else's ideas, research, or opinion as your own—even if you have rephrased it in different words—is *plagiarism*, the equivalent of academic stealing, or fraud.

You can avoid plagiarism by synthesizing what you learn: Read from several sources and let the ideas of experts help you draw your own conclusions and form your own opinions. Ultimately, however, note your own reactions to the ideas presented.

When you choose to use someone else's ideas or work to support your view, credit the source of the material. Give bibliographic information to cite your sources of the following information:

- Statistics
- Direct quotations
- Indirectly quoted statements of opinions
- Conclusions presented by an expert
- Facts available in only one or two sources

Crediting Sources

When you credit a source, you acknowledge where you found your information and you give your readers the details necessary for locating the source themselves. Within the body of the paper, you provide a short citation, a footnote number linked to a footnote, or an endnote number linked to an endnote reference. These brief references show the page numbers on which you found the information. To make your paper more formal, prepare a reference list at the end of the paper to provide full bibliographic information on your sources. These are two common types of reference lists:

- A **bibliography** provides a listing of all the resources you consulted during your research.
- A **works-cited list** indicates the works you have referenced in your paper.

Choosing a Format for Documentation

The type of information you provide and the format in which you provide it depend on what your teacher prefers. These are the most commonly used styles:

- **Modern Language Association (MLA) Style** This is the style used for most papers at the middle-school and high-school level and for most language arts papers.
- **American Psychological Association (APA) Style** This is used for most papers in the social sciences and for most college-level papers.
- *Chicago Manual of Style* **(CMS) Style** This is preferred by some teachers.

On the following pages, you'll find sample citation formats for the most commonly cited materials. Each format calls for standard bibliographic information. The difference is in the order of the material presented in each entry and the punctuation required.

MLA Style for Listing Sources

Book with one author	Pyles, Thomas. *The Origins and Development of the English Language.* 2nd ed. New York: Harcourt Brace Jovanovich, Inc., 1971.
Book with two or three authors	McCrum, Robert, William Cran, and Robert MacNeil. *The Story of English.* New York: Penguin Books, 1987.
Book with an editor	Truth, Sojourner. *Narrative of Sojourner Truth.* Ed. Margaret Washington. New York: Vintage Books, 1993.
Book with more than three authors or editors	Donald, Robert B., et al. *Writing Clear Essays.* Upper Saddle River, NJ: Prentice-Hall, Inc., 1996.
A single work from an anthology	Hawthorne, Nathaniel. "Young Goodman Brown." *Literature: An Introduction to Reading and Writing.* Ed. Edgar V. Roberts and Henry E. Jacobs. Upper Saddle River, NJ: Prentice-Hall, Inc., 1998. 376–385. [Indicate pages for the entire selection.]
Introduction in a published edition	Washington, Margaret. Introduction. *Narrative of Sojourner Truth.* By Sojourner Truth. Ed. Washington. New York: Vintage Books, 1993. v–xi.
Signed article in a weekly magazine	Wallace, Charles. "A Vodacious Deal." *Time* 14 Feb. 2000: 63.
Signed article in a monthly magazine	Gustaitis, Joseph. "The Sticky History of Chewing Gum." *American History* Oct. 1998: 30–38.
Unsigned editorial or story	"Selective Silence." Editorial. *Wall Street Journal* 11 Feb. 2000: A14. [If the editorial or story is signed, begin with the author's name.]
Signed pamphlet	[Treat the pamphlet as though it were a book.]
Pamphlet with no author, publisher, or date	*Are You at Risk of Heart Attack?* n.p. n.d. [n.p. n.d. indicates that there is no known publisher or date]
Filmstrips, slide programs, videocassettes, DVDs, and other audiovisual media	*The Diary of Anne Frank.* Dir. George Stevens. Perf. Millie Perkins, Shelley Winters, Joseph Schildkraut, Lou Jacobi, and Richard Beymer. 1959. DVD. Twentieth Century Fox, 2004.
Radio or television program transcript	"Washington's Crossing of the Delaware." Host Liane Hansen. Guest David Hackett Fischer. *Weekend Edition Sunday.* Natl. Public Radio. WNYC, New York City. 23 Dec. 2003. Transcript.
Internet	"Fun Facts About Gum." NACGM site. National Association of Chewing Gum Manufacturers. 19 Dec. 1999. <http://www.nacgm.org/consumer/funfacts.html>. [Indicate the date of last update if known and the date you accessed the information. Content and addresses at Web sites change frequently.]
Newspaper	Thurow, Roger. "South Africans Who Fought for Sanctions Now Scrap for Investors." *Wall Street Journal* 11 Feb. 2000: A1+ [For a multipage article that does not appear on consecutive pages, write only the first page number on which it appears, followed by a plus sign.]
Personal interview	Smith, Jane. Personal interview. 10 Feb. 2000.
CD (with multiple publishers)	Simms, James, ed. *Romeo and Juliet.* By William Shakespeare. CD-ROM. Oxford: Attica Cybernetics Ltd.; London: BBC Education; London: HarperCollins Publishers, 1995.
Article from an encyclopedia	Askeland, Donald R. "Welding." *World Book Encyclopedia.* 1991 ed.

APA Style for Listing Sources

The list of citations for APA is referred to as a Reference List and not a bibliography.

Book with one author	Pyles, T. (1971). *The Origins and Development of the English Language* (2nd ed.). New York: Harcourt Brace Jovanovich, Inc.
Book with two or three authors	McCrum, R., Cran, W., & MacNeil, R. (1987). *The Story of English*. New York: Penguin Books.
Book with an editor	Truth, S. (1993). *Narrative of Sojourner Truth* (M. Washington, Ed.). New York: Vintage Books.
Book with more than three authors or editors	Donald, R. B., Morrow, B. R., Wargetz, L. G., & Werner, K. (1996). *Writing Clear Essays*. Upper Saddle River, New Jersey: Prentice-Hall, Inc. [With six or more authors, abbreviate second and following authors as "et al."]
A single work from an anthology	Hawthorne, N. (1998) Young Goodman Brown. In E. V. Roberts, & H. E. Jacobs (Eds.), *Literature: An Introduction to Reading and Writing* (pp. 376–385). Upper Saddle River, New Jersey: Prentice-Hall, Inc.
Introduction to a work included in a published edition	[No style is offered under this heading.]
Signed article in a weekly magazine	Wallace, C. (2000, February 14). A vodacious deal. *Time, 155,* 63. [The volume number appears in italics before the page number.]
Signed article in a monthly magazine	Gustaitis, J. (1998, October). The sticky history of chewing gum. *American History, 33,* 30–38.
Unsigned editorial or story	Selective Silence. (2000, February 11). *Wall Street Journal,* p. A14.
Signed pamphlet	Pearson Education. (2000). *LifeCare* (2nd ed.) [Pamphlet]. Smith, John: Author.
Pamphlet with no author, publisher, or date	[No style is offered under this heading.]
Filmstrips, slide programs, and videotape	Stevens, G. (Producer & Director). (1959). *The Diary of Anne Frank.* [Videotape]. (Available from Twentieth Century Fox) [If the producer and the director are two different people, list the producer first and then the director, with an ampersand (&) between them.]
Radio or television program transcript	Broderick, D. (1999, May 23). The First Immortal Generation. (R. Williams, Radio Host). *Ockham's Razor.* New York: National Public Radio.
Internet	National Association of Chewing Gum Manufacturers. Available: http://www.nacgm.org/consumer/funfacts.html [References to Websites should begin with the author's last name, if available. Indicate the site name and the available path or URL address.]
Newspaper	Thurow, R. (2000, February 11). South Africans who fought for sanctions now scrap for investors. *Wall Street Journal,* pp. A1, A4.
Personal interview	[APA states that, since interviews (and other personal communications) do not provide "recoverable data," they should only be cited in text.]
CD (with multiple publishers)	[No style is offered under this heading.]
Article from an encyclopedia	Askeland, D. R. (1991). Welding. In *World Book Encyclopedia*. (Vol. 21 pp. 190–191). Chicago: World Book, Inc.

CMS Style for Listing Sources

The following chart shows the CMS author-date method of documentation.

Book with one author	Pyles, Thomas. *The Origins and Development of the English Language*, 2nd ed. New York: Harcourt Brace Jovanovich, Inc., 1971.
Book with two or three authors	McCrum, Robert, William Cran, and Robert MacNeil. *The Story of English*. New York: Penguin Books, 1987.
Book with an editor	Truth, Sojourner. *Narrative of Sojourner Truth*. Edited by Margaret Washington. New York: Vintage Books, 1993.
Book with more than three authors or editors	Donald, Robert B., et al. *Writing Clear Essays*. Upper Saddle River, New Jersey: Prentice-Hall, Inc., 1996.
A single work from an anthology	Hawthorne, Nathaniel. "Young Goodman Brown." In *Literature: An Introduction to Reading and Writing*. Ed. Edgar V. Roberts and Henry E. Jacobs. 376–385. Upper Saddle River, New Jersey: Prentice-Hall, Inc., 1998.
Introduction to a work included in a published edition	Washington, Margaret. Introduction to *Narrative of Sojourner Truth*, by Sojourner Truth. New York: Vintage Books, 1993. [According to CMS style, you should avoid this type of entry unless the introduction is of special importance to the work.]
Signed article in a weekly magazine	Wallace, Charles. "A Vodacious Deal." *Time*, 14 February 2000, 63.
Signed article in a monthly magazine	Gustaitis, Joseph. "The Sticky History of Chewing Gum." *American History*, October 1998, 30–38.
Unsigned editorial or story	*Wall Street Journal*, 11 February 2000. [CMS states that items from newspapers are seldom listed in a bibliography. Instead, the name of the paper and the relevant dates are listed.]
Signed pamphlet	[No style is offered under this heading.]
Pamphlet with no author, publisher, or date	[No style is offered under this heading.]
Filmstrips, slide programs, and videotape	Stevens, George. (director). *The Diary of Anne Frank*. 170 min. Beverly Hills, California: Twentieth Century Fox, 1994.
Radio or television program transcript	[No style is offered under this heading.]
Internet	[No style is offered under this heading.]
Newspaper	*Wall Street Journal*, 11 February 2000. [CMS states that items from newspapers are seldom listed in a bibliography. Instead, the name of the paper and the relevant dates are listed.]
Personal interview	[CMS states that, since personal conversations are not available to the public, there is no reason to place them in the bibliography. However, the following format should be followed if they are listed.] Jane Smith. Conversation with author. Wooster, Ohio, 10 February 2000.
CD (with multiple publishers)	Shakespeare, William. *Romeo and Juliet*. Oxford: Attica Cybernetics Ltd.; London: BBC Education; London: HarperCollins Publishers, 1995. CD-ROM.
Article from an encyclopedia	[According to CMS style, encyclopedias are not listed in bibliographies.]

Sample Works-Cited List (MLA)

Carwardine, Mark, Erich Hoyt, R. Ewan Fordyce, and Peter Gill. *The Nature Company Guides: Whales, Dolphins, and Porpoises.* New York: Time-Life Books, 1998.

Ellis, Richard. *Men and Whales.* New York: Knopf, 1991.

Whales in Danger. "Discovering Whales." 18 Oct. 1999. <http://whales.magna.com.au/DISCOVER>

Sample Internal Citations (MLA)

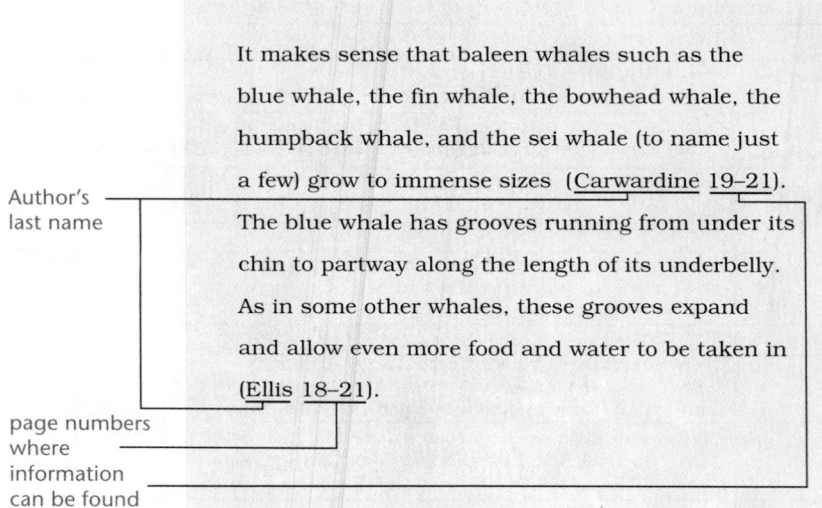

It makes sense that baleen whales such as the blue whale, the fin whale, the bowhead whale, the humpback whale, and the sei whale (to name just a few) grow to immense sizes (<u>Carwardine</u> <u>19–21</u>).

Author's last name

The blue whale has grooves running from under its chin to partway along the length of its underbelly. As in some other whales, these grooves expand and allow even more food and water to be taken in (<u>Ellis</u> <u>18–21</u>).

page numbers where information can be found

Internet Research Handbook

Introduction to the Internet

The Internet is a series of networks that are interconnected all over the world. The Internet allows users to have almost unlimited access to information stored on the networks. Dr. Berners-Lee, a physicist, created the Internet in the 1980's by writing a small computer program that allowed pages to be linked together using key words. The Internet was mostly text-based until 1992, when a computer program called the NCSA Mosaic (National Center for Supercomputing Applications at the University of Illinois) was created. This program was the first Web browser. The development of Web browsers greatly eased the ability of the user to navigate through all the pages stored on the Web. Very soon, the appearance of the Web was altered as well. More appealing visuals were added, and sound was also implemented. This change made the Web more user-friendly and more appealing to the general public.

Using the Internet for Research

Key Word Search

Before you begin a search, you should identify your specific topic. To make searching easier, narrow your subject to a key word or a group of key words. These are your search terms, and they should be as specific as possible. For example, if you are looking for the latest concert dates for your favorite musical group, you might use the band's name as a key word. However, if you were to enter the name of the group in the query box of the search engine, you might be presented with thousands of links to information about the group that is unrelated to your needs. You might locate such information as band member biographies, the group's history, fan reviews of concerts, and hundreds of sites with related names containing information that is irrelevant to your search. Because you used such a broad key word, you might need to navigate through all that information before you find a link or subheading for concert dates. In contrast, if you were to type in "Duplex Arena and [band name]" you would have a better chance of locating pages that contain this information.

How to Narrow Your Search

If you have a large group of key words and still don't know which ones to use, write out a list of all the words you are considering. Once you have completed the list, scrutinize it. Then, delete the words that are least important to your search, and highlight those that are most important.

These **key search connectors** can help you fine-tune your search:

AND: narrows a search by retrieving documents that include both terms. For example: *baseball AND playoffs*

OR: broadens a search by retrieving documents including any of the terms. For example: *playoffs OR championships*

NOT: narrows a search by excluding documents containing certain words. For example: *baseball NOT history of*

Tips for an Effective Search

1. Keep in mind that search engines can be case-sensitive. If your first attempt at searching fails, check your search terms for misspellings and try again.

2. If you are entering a group of key words, present them in order, from the most important to the least important key word.

3. Avoid opening the link to every single page in your results list. Search engines present pages in descending order of relevancy. The most useful pages will be located at the top of the list. However, read the description of each link before you open the page.

4. When you use some search engines, you can find helpful tips for specializing your search. Take the opportunity to learn more about effective searching.

Other Ways to Search

Using On-line Reference Sites *How* you search should be tailored to *what* you are hoping to find. If you are looking for data and facts, use reference sites before you jump onto a simple search engine. For example, you can find reference sites to provide definitions of words, statistics about almost any subject, biographies, maps, and concise information on many topics. Some useful on-line reference sites:

> On-line libraries
> On-line periodicals
> Almanacs
> Encyclopedias

You can find these sources using subject searches.

Conducting Subject Searches As you prepare to go on-line, consider your subject and the best way to find information to suit your needs. If you are looking for general information on a topic and you want your search results to be extensive, consider the subject search indexes on most search engines. These indexes, in the form of category and subject lists, often appear on the first page of a search engine. When you click on a specific highlighted word, you will be presented with a new screen containing subcategories of the topic you chose. In the screen shots below, the category *Sports & Recreation* provided a second index for users to focus a search even further.

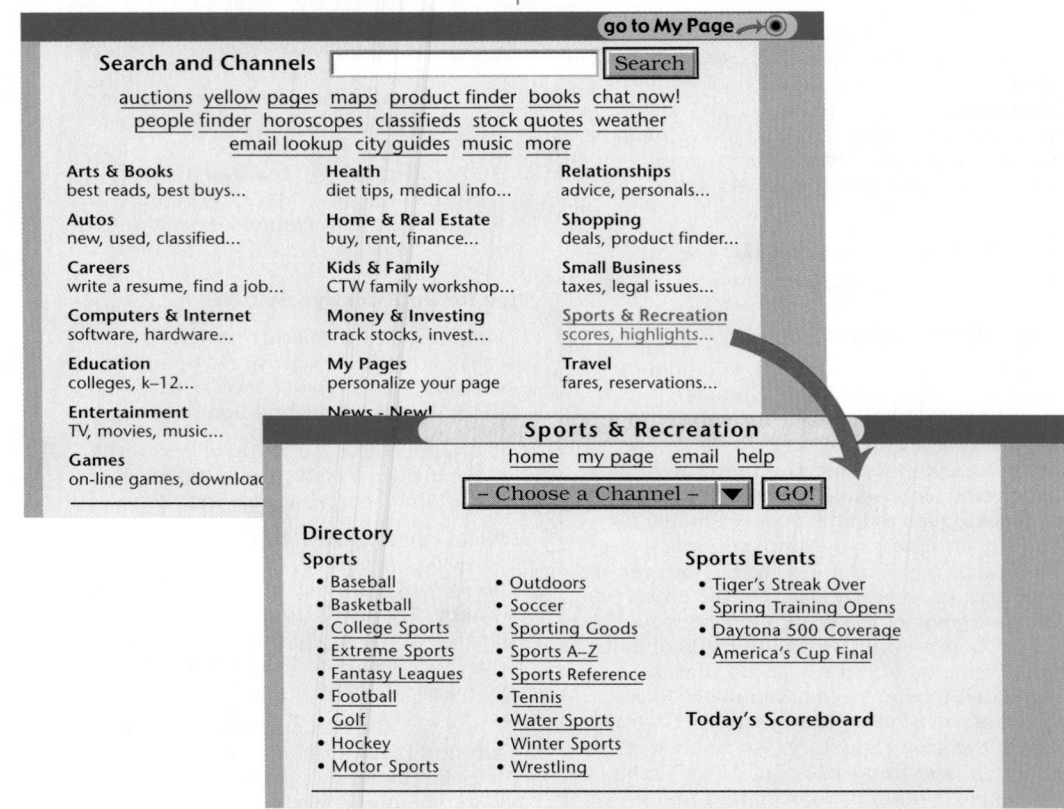

Evaluating the Reliability of Internet Resources

Just as you would evaluate the quality, bias, and validity of any other research material you locate, check the source of information you find on-line. Compare these two sites containing information on the poet and writer Langston Hughes:

Site A is a personal Web site constructed by a college student. It contains no bibliographic information or links to sites that he used. Included on the site are several poems by Langston Hughes and a student essay about the poet's use of symbolism. It has not been updated in more than six months.

Site B is a Web site constructed and maintained by the English Department of a major university. Information on Hughes is presented in a scholarly format, with a bibliography and credits for the writer. The site includes links to other sites and indicates new features that are added weekly.

For your own research, consider the information you find on Site B to be more reliable and accurate than that on Site A. Because it is maintained by experts in their field who are held accountable for their work, the university site will be a better research tool than the student-generated one.

Tips for Evaluating Internet Sources

1. Consider who constructed and who now maintains the Web page. Determine whether this author is a reputable source. Often, the URL endings indicate a source.

   - Sites ending in *.edu* are maintained by educational institutions.
   - Sites ending in *.gov* are maintained by government agencies (federal, state, or local).
   - Sites ending in *.org* are normally maintained by nonprofit organizations and agencies.
   - Sites with a *.com* ending are commercially or personally maintained.

2. Skim the official and trademarked Web pages first. It is safe to assume that the information you draw from Web pages of reputable institutions, on-line encyclopedias, on-line versions of major daily newspapers, or government-owned sites produce information as reliable as the material you would find in print. In contrast, unbranded sites or those generated by individuals tend to borrow information from other sources without providing documentation. As information travels from one source to another, the information has likely been muddled, misinterpreted, edited, or revised.

3. You can still find valuable information in the less "official" sites. Check for the writer's credentials and then consider these factors:

   - Don't let official-looking graphics or presentations fool you.
   - Make sure the information is updated enough to suit your needs. Many Web pages will indicate how recently they have been updated.
   - If the information is borrowed, see whether you can trace it back to its original source.

Respecting Copyrighted Material

Because the Internet is a relatively new and quickly growing medium, issues of copyright and ownership arise almost daily. As laws begin to govern the use and reuse of material posted on-line, they may change the way that people can access or reprint material.

Text, photographs, music, and fine art printed on-line may not be reproduced without acknowledged permission of the copyright owner.

Glossary of Internet Terms

attached file: a file containing information, such as a text document or GIF image, that is attached to an e-mail message; reports, pictures, spreadsheets, and so on transmitted to others by attaching these to messages as files

bandwidth: the amount of information, mainly compressed in bits per second (bps), that can be sent through a connection within a specific amount of time; depending on how fast your modem is, 15,000 bits (roughly one page of text) can be transferred per second

bit: a binary digit of computerized data, represented by a single digit that is either a 1 or a 0; a group of bits constitutes a byte

bookmark: a feature of your Web browser that allows you to place a "bookmark" on a Web page to which you wish to return at a later time

browser: software designed to present material accessed on the Web

bulletin-board system: a computer system that members access in order to join on-line discussion groups or to post announcements

case-sensitivity: the quality of a search engine that causes it to respond to upper- or lowercase letters in different ways

chat room: informal on-line gathering sites where people share conversations, experiences, or information on a specific topic; many chat rooms do not require users to provide their identity, so the reliability or safety of these sites is uncertain

cookie: a digitized piece of information that is sent to a Web browser by a Web server, intended to be saved on a computer; cookies gather information about the user, such as user preferences, or recent on-line purchases; a Web browser can be set to either accept or reject cookies

cyberspace: a term referring to the electronic environment connecting all computer network information with the people who use it

database: a large collection of data that have been formatted to fit a certain user-defined standard

digerati: a slang term to describe Internet experts; an offshoot of the term *literati*

download: to copy files from the Internet onto your computer

e-mail: electronic mail, or the exchange of messages via the Internet; because it is speedier than traditional mail and offers easier global access, e-mail has grown in popularity; e-mail messages can be sent to a single person or in bulk to a group of people

error message: a displayed communication or printout that reports a problem with a program or Web page

FTP site (file transfer protocol): a password-protected server on the Internet that allows the transfer of information from one computer to another

GIF (Graphic Interchange Format): a form of graphics used on the Web

graphics: information displayed as pictures or images instead of text

hits: items retrieved by a key word search; the number tracking the volume of visits to a Web site

home page: the main Web page for an individual or an organization, containing links to subpages within

HTML (HyperText Markup Language): the coding text that is the foundation for creating Web pages

interactivity: a quality of some Web pages that encourages the frequent exchange of information between user and computer

Internet: a worldwide computer network that supports services such as the World Wide Web, e-mail, and file transfer

JPEG (Joint Photo Experts Group, the developers): a file format for graphics especially suited to photographs

K: a measurement of file size or memory; short for "Kilobyte," 1,000 bytes of information (see *bit*)

key word: search term entered into the query box of a search engine to direct the results of the search

link: an icon or word on a Web page that, when clicked, transfers the user to another Web page or to a different document within the same page

login: the procedure by which users gain access to a server or a secure Web site; usually the user must enter a specific user name and password

modem: a device that transfers data to a computer through a phone line. A computer's modem connects to a server, which then sends information in the form of digital signals. The modem converts these signals into waves, for the purpose of information reception. The speed of a modem affects how quickly a computer can receive and download information

newbie: jargon used to describe Internet novices

newsgroup: an on-line discussion group, where users can post and respond to messages; the most prevalent collection of newsgroups is found on USENET

query box: the blank box in a search engine where your search terms are input

relevance ranking: the act of displaying the results of a search in the order of their relevance to the search terms

search engines: tools that help you navigate databases to locate information; search engines respond to a key word search by providing the user with a directory of multiple Web pages about the key word or containing the key word

server: a principal computer that provides services, such as storing files and providing access to the Internet, to another computer

signature: a preprogrammed section of text that is automatically added to an e-mail message

surfing: the process of reading Web pages and of moving from one Web site to another

URL (Uniform Resource Locator): a Web page's address; a URL can look like this:

http://www.phwg.phschool.com or
http://www.senate.gov/~appropriations/ labor/testimony

usenet: a worldwide system of discussion groups, or newsgroups

vanity pages: Web sites placed on-line by people to tell about themselves or their interests; vanity pages do not have any commercial or informational value

virus: a set of instructions, hidden in a computer system or transferred via e-mail or electronic files, that can cause problems with a computer's ability to perform normally

Web page: a set of information, including graphics, text, sound, and video, presented in a browser window; a Web page can be found by its URL once it is posted on the World Wide Web

Web site: a collection of Web pages that are linked together for posting on the World Wide Web

W3: a group of Internet experts, including networking professionals, academics, scientists, and corporate interests, who maintain and develop technologies and standards for the Internet

WWW (World Wide Web): a term referring to the multitude of information systems found on the Internet; this includes FTP, Gopher, telnet, and http sites

zip: the minimizing of files through compression; this function makes for easier transmittal over networks; a receiver can then open the file by "unzipping" it

Commonly Overused Words

When you write, use the most precise word for your meaning, not the word that comes to mind first. Consult this thesaurus to find alternatives for some commonly overused words. Consult a full-length thesaurus to find alternatives to words that do not appear here. Keep in mind that the choices offered in a thesaurus do not all mean exactly the same thing. Review all the options, and choose the one that best expresses your meaning.

about approximately, nearly, almost, approaching, close to

absolutely unconditionally, perfectly, completely, ideally, purely

activity action, movement, operation, labor, exertion, enterprise, project, pursuit, endeavor, job, assignment, pastime, scheme, task

add attach, affix, join, unite, append, increase, amplify

affect adjust, influence, transform, moderate, incline, motivate, prompt

amazing overwhelming, astonishing, startling, unexpected, stunning, dazzling, remarkable

awesome impressive, stupendous, fabulous, astonishing, outstanding

bad defective, inadequate, poor, unsatisfactory, disagreeable, offensive, repulsive, corrupt, wicked, naughty, harmful, injurious, unfavorable

basic essential, necessary, indispensable, vital, fundamental, elementary

beautiful attractive, appealing, alluring, exqui-

site, gorgeous, handsome, stunning

begin commence, found, initiate, introduce, launch, originate

better preferable, superior, worthier

big enormous, extensive, huge, immense, massive

boring commonplace, monotonous, tedious, tiresome

bring accompany, cause, convey, create, conduct, deliver, produce

cause origin, stimulus, inspiration, motive

certain unquestionable, incontrovertible, unmistakable, indubitable, assured, confident

change alter, transform, vary, replace, diversify

choose select, elect, nominate, prefer, identify

decent respectable, adequate, fair, suitable

definitely unquestionably, clearly, precisely, positively, inescapably

easy effortless, natural, comfortable, undemanding, pleasant, relaxed

effective powerful, successful

emphasize underscore, feature, accentuate

end limit, boundary, finish, conclusion, finale, resolution

energy vitality, vigor, force, dynamism

enjoy savor, relish, revel, benefit

entire complete, inclusive, unbroken, integral

excellent superior, remarkable, splendid, unsurpassed, superb, magnificent

exciting thrilling, stirring, rousing, dramatic

far distant, remote

fast swift, quick, fleet, hasty, instant, accelerated

fill occupy, suffuse, pervade, saturate, inflate, stock

finish complete, conclude, cease, achieve, exhaust, deplete, consume

funny comical, ludicrous, amusing, droll, entertaining, bizarre, unusual, uncommon

get obtain, receive, acquire, procure, achieve

give bestow, donate, supply, deliver, distribute, impart

go proceed, progress, advance, move

good satisfactory, serviceable, functional, competent, virtuous, striking

great tremendous, superior, remarkable, eminent, proficient, expert

happy pleased, joyous, elated, jubilant, cheerful, delighted

hard arduous, formidable, complex, complicated, rigorous, harsh

help assist, aid, support, sustain, serve

hurt injure, harm, damage, wound, impair

important significant, substantial, weighty, meaningful, critical, vital, notable

interesting absorbing, appealing, entertaining, fascinating, thought-provoking

job task, work, business, undertaking, occupation, vocation, chore, duty, assignment

keep retain, control, possess

kind type, variety, sort, form

know comprehend, understand, realize, perceive, discern

like (adj) similar, equivalent, parallel

like (verb) enjoy, relish, appreciate

main primary, foremost, dominant

make build, construct, produce, assemble, fashion, manufacture

mean plan, intend, suggest, propose, indicate

more supplementary, additional, replenishment

new recent, modern, current, novel

next subsequently, thereafter, successively

nice pleasant, satisfying, gracious, charming

old aged, mature, experienced, used, worn, former, previous

open unobstructed, accessible

part section, portion, segment, detail, element, component

perfect flawless, faultless, ideal, consummate

plan scheme, design, system, plot

pleasant agreeable, gratifying, refreshing, welcome

prove demonstrate, confirm, validate, verify, corroborate

quick brisk, prompt, responsive, rapid, nimble, hasty

really truly, genuinely, extremely, undeniably

regular standard, routine, customary, habitual

see regard, behold, witness, gaze, realize, notice

small diminutive, miniature, minor, insignificant, slight, trivial

sometimes occasionally, intermittently, sporadically, periodically

take grasp, capture, choose, select, tolerate, endure

terrific extraordinary, magnificent, marvelous

think conceive, imagine, ponder, reflect, contemplate

try attempt, endeavor, venture, test

use employ, operate, utilize

very unusually, extremely, deeply, exceedingly, profoundly

want desire, crave, yearn, long

Commonly Misspelled Words

The list on these pages presents words that cause problems for many people. Some of these words are spelled according to set rules, but others follow no specific rules. As you review this list, check to see how many of the words give you trouble in your own writing. Then, read the instruction in the "Vocabulary and Spelling" chapter in the book for strategies and suggestions for improving your own spelling habits.

abbreviate	athletic	catastrophe	curious
absence	attendance	category	cylinder
absolutely	auxiliary	ceiling	deceive
abundance	awkward	cemetery	decision
accelerate	bandage	census	deductible
accidentally	banquet	certain	defendant
accumulate	bargain	changeable	deficient
accurate	barrel	characteristic	definitely
ache	battery	chauffeur	delinquent
achievement	beautiful	chief	dependent
acquaintance	beggar	clothes	descendant
adequate	beginning	coincidence	description
admittance	behavior	colonel	desert
advertisement	believe	column	desirable
aerial	benefit	commercial	dessert
affect	bicycle	commission	deteriorate
aggravate	biscuit	commitment	dining
aggressive	bookkeeper	committee	disappointed
agreeable	bought	competitor	disastrous
aisle	boulevard	concede	discipline
all right	brief	condemn	dissatisfied
allowance	brilliant	congratulate	distinguish
aluminum	bruise	connoisseur	effect
amateur	bulletin	conscience	eighth
analysis	buoyant	conscientious	eligible
analyze	bureau	conscious	embarrass
ancient	bury	contemporary	enthusiastic
anecdote	buses	continuous	entrepreneur
anniversary	business	controversy	envelope
anonymous	cafeteria	convenience	environment
answer	calendar	coolly	equipped
anticipate	campaign	cooperate	equivalent
anxiety	canceled	cordially	especially
apologize	candidate	correspondence	exaggerate
appall	capacity	counterfeit	exceed
appearance	capital	courageous	excellent
appreciate	capitol	courteous	exercise
appropriate	captain	courtesy	exhibition
architecture	career	criticism	existence
argument	carriage	criticize	experience
associate	cashier	curiosity	explanation

extension
extraordinary
familiar
fascinating
February
fiery
financial
fluorescent
foreign
forfeit
fourth
fragile
gauge
generally
genius
genuine
government
grammar
grievance
guarantee
guard
guidance
handkerchief
harass
height
humorous
hygiene
ignorant
illegible
immediately
immigrant
independence
independent
indispensable
individual
inflammable
intelligence
interfere
irrelevant
irritable
jewelry
judgment
knowledge
laboratory
lawyer
legible
legislature
leisure
liable

library
license
lieutenant
lightning
likable
liquefy
literature
loneliness
magnificent
maintenance
marriage
mathematics
maximum
meanness
mediocre
mileage
millionaire
minimum
minuscule
miscellaneous
mischievous
misspell
mortgage
naturally
necessary
negotiate
neighbor
neutral
nickel
niece
ninety
noticeable
nuclear
nuisance
obstacle
occasion
occasionally
occur
occurred
occurrence
omitted
opinion
opportunity
optimistic
outrageous
pamphlet
parallel
paralyze
parentheses

particularly
patience
permanent
permissible
perseverance
persistent
personally
perspiration
persuade
phenomenal
phenomenon
physician
pleasant
pneumonia
possess
possession
possibility
prairie
precede
preferable
prejudice
preparation
prerogative
previous
primitive
privilege
probably
procedure
proceed
prominent
pronunciation
psychology
publicly
pursue
questionnaire
realize
really
recede
receipt
receive
recognize
recommend
reference
referred
rehearse
relevant
reminiscence
renowned
repetition

restaurant
rhythm
ridiculous
sandwich
satellite
schedule
scissors
secretary
siege
solely
sponsor
subtle
subtlety
superintendent
supersede
surveillance
susceptible
tariff
temperamental
theater
threshold
truly
unmanageable
unwieldy
usage
usually
valuable
various
vegetable
voluntary
weight
weird
whale
wield
yield

Abbreviations Guide

Abbreviations, shortened versions of words or phrases, can be valuable tools in writing if you know when and how to use them. They can be very helpful in informal writing situations, such as taking notes or writing lists. However, only a few abbreviations can be used in formal writing. They are: *Mr., Mrs., Miss, Ms., Dr., A.M., P.M., A.D., B.C., M.A, B.A., Ph.D.,* and *M.D.*

The following pages provide the conventional abbreviations for a variety of words.

Abbreviations of Common Titles

Ambassador	Amb.	Lieutenant	Lt.
Attorney	Atty.	Major	Maj.
Brigadier-General	Brig. Gen.	President	Pres.
Brother	Br.	Professor	Prof.
Captain	Capt.	Representative	Rep.
Colonel	Col.	Reverend	Rev.
Commander	Cmdr.	Secretary	Sec.
Commissioner	Com.	Senator	Sen.
Corporal	Cpl.	Sergeant	Sgt.
Doctor	Dr.	Sister	Sr.
Father	Fr.	Superintendent	Supt.
Governor	Gov.	Treasurer	Treas.
Honorable	Hon.	Vice Admiral	Vice Adm.

Abbreviations of Academic Degrees

Bachelor of Arts	B.A. (or A.B.)	Esquire (lawyer)	Esq.
Bachelor of Science	B.S. (or S.B.)	Master of Arts	M.A. (or A.M.)
Doctor of Dental Surgery	D.D.S.	Master of Business Administration	M.B.A.
Doctor of Divinity	D.D.		
Doctor of Education	Ed.D.	Master of Fine Arts	M.F.A.
Doctor of Laws	LL.D.	Master of Science	M.S. (or S.M.)
Doctor of Medicine	M.D.	Registered Nurse	R.N.
Doctor of Philosophy	Ph.D.		

Abbreviations of States

State	Traditional	Postal Service	State	Traditional	Postal Service
Alabama	Ala.	AL	Montana	Mont.	MT
Alaska	Alaska	AK	Nebraska	Nebr.	NE
Arizona	Ariz.	AZ	Nevada	Nev.	NV
Arkansas	Ark.	AR	New Hampshire	N.H.	NH
California	Calif.	CA	New Jersey	N.J.	NJ
Colorado	Colo.	CO	New Mexico	N.M.	NM
Connecticut	Conn.	CT	New York	N.Y.	NY
Delaware	Del.	DE	North Carolina	N.C.	NC
Florida	Fla.	FL	North Dakota	N.Dak.	ND
Georgia	Ga.	GA	Ohio	O.	OH
Hawaii	Hawaii	HI	Oklahoma	Okla.	OK
Idaho	Ida.	ID	Oregon	Ore.	OR
Illinois	Ill.	IL	Pennsylvania	Pa.	PA
Indiana	Ind.	IN	Rhode Island	R.I.	RI
Iowa	Iowa	IA	South Carolina	S.C.	SC
Kansas	Kans.	KS	South Dakota	S.Dak.	SD
Kentucky	Ky.	KY	Tennessee	Tenn.	TN
Louisiana	La.	LA	Texas	Tex.	TX
Maine	Me.	ME	Utah	Utah	UT
Maryland	Md.	MD	Vermont	Vt.	VT
Massachusetts	Mass.	MA	Virginia	Va.	VA
Michigan	Mich.	MI	Washington	Wash.	WA
Minnesota	Minn.	MN	West Virginia	W. Va	WV
Mississippi	Miss.	MS	Wisconsin	Wis.	WI
Missouri	Mo.	MO	Wyoming	Wyo.	WY

Common Geographical Abbreviations

Apartment	Apt.	National	Natl.
Avenue	Ave.	Park, Peak	Pk.
Block	Blk.	Peninsula	Pen.
Boulevard	Blvd.	Point	Pt.
Building	Bldg.	Province	Prov.
County	Co.	Road	Rd.
District	Dist.	Route	Rte.
Drive	Dr.	Square	Sq.
Fort	Ft.	Street	St.
Island	Is.	Territory	Terr.
Mountain	Mt.		

Abbreviations of Traditional Measurements

inch(es)	in.	ounce(s)	oz.
foot, feet	ft.	pound(s)	lb.
yard(s)	yd.	pint(s)	pt.
mile(s)	mi.	quart(s)	qt.
teaspoon(s)	tsp.	gallon(s)	gal.
tablespoon(s)	tbsp.	Fahrenheit	F.

Abbreviations of Metric Measurements

millimeter(s)	mm	liter(s)	L
centimeter(s)	cm	kiloliter(s)	kL
meter(s)	m	milligram(s)	mg
kilometer(s)	km	centigram(s)	cg
milliliter(s)	mL	gram(s)	g
centiliter(s)	cL	Celsius	C

Other Commonly Used Abbreviations

about (used with dates)	c., ca., circ.	manager	mgr.
and others	et al.	manufacturing	mfg.
anonymous	anon.	market	mkt.
approximately	approx.	measure	meas.
associate, association	assoc., assn.	merchandise	mdse.
auxiliary	aux., auxil.	miles per hour	mph
bibliography	bibliog.	miscellaneous	misc.
boxes	bx(s).	money order	M.O.
bucket	bkt.	note well; take notice	N.B.
bulletin	bull.	number	no.
bushel	bu.	package	pkg.
capital letter	cap.	page	p., pg.
cash on delivery	C.O.D.	pages	pp.
department	dept.	pair(s)	pr(s).
discount	disc.	parenthesis	paren.
dozen(s)	doz.	Patent Office	pat. off.
each	ea.	piece(s)	pc(s).
edition, editor	ed.	poetical, poetry	poet.
equivalent	equiv.	private	pvt.
established	est.	proprietor	prop.
fiction	fict.	pseudonym	pseud.
for example	e.g.	published, publisher	pub.
free of charge	grat., gratis	received	recd.
General Post Office	G.P.O.	reference, referee	ref.
government	gov., govt.	revolutions per minute	rpm
graduate, graduated	grad.	rhetorical, rhetoric	rhet.
Greek, Grecian	Gr.	right	R.
headquarters	hdqrs.	scene	sc.
height	ht.	special, specific	spec.
hospital	hosp.	spelling, species	sp.
illustrated	ill., illus.	that is	i.e.
including, inclusive	incl.	treasury, treasurer	treas.
introduction, introductory	intro.	volume	vol.
italics	ital.	weekly	wkly
karat, carat	k., kt.	weight	wt.
left	L.		

Proofreading Symbols Reference

Proofreading symbols make it easier to show where changes are needed in a paper. When proofreading your own or a classmate's work, use these standard proofreading symbols.

insert	I proofr*a*ed.
delete	I*p* proofread.
close up space	I proof read.
delete and close up space	I proofreade.
begin new paragraph	¶ I proofread.
spell out	I proofread (10) papers. (sp)
lowercase	I Proofread. (lc)
capitalize	i proofread. (cap)
transpose letters	I proofraed. (tr)
transpose words	I only proofread her paper. (tr)
period	I will proofread.
comma	I will proofread and she will help.
colon	We will proofread for the following errors
semicolon	I will proofread she will help.
single quotation marks	She said, "I enjoyed the story The Invalid."
double quotation marks	She said, I enjoyed the story.
apostrophe	Did you borrow Sylvias book?
question mark	Did you borrow Sylvia's book ?/
exclamation point	You're kidding !/
hyphen	online /=/
parentheses	William Shakespeare 1564–1616

To share your writing with a wider audience, consider submitting it to a local, state, or national publication for student writing. Following are several magazines and Web sites that accept and publish student work.

Periodicals

Merlyn's Pen merlynspen.org

Skipping Stones P.O. Box 3939, Eugene, OR 97403 http://www.skippingstones.org

Teen Ink Box 30, Newton, MA 02461 teenink.com

On-line Publications

Kid Pub http://www.kidpub.org

MidLink Magazine http://www.ncsu.edu/midlink

Contests

Annual Poetry Contest National Federation of State Poetry Societies, Contest Chair, Kathleen Pederzani, 121 Grande Boulevard, Reading, PA 19608-9680. http://www.nfsps.com

Paul A. Witty Outstanding Literature Award International Reading Association, Special Interest Group for Reading for Gifted and Creative Students, c/o Texas Christian University, P.O. Box 297900, Fort Worth, TX 76129

Seventeen Magazine Fiction Contest *Seventeen* Magazine, 1440 Broadway 13th Floor, New York, NY 10018

The Young Playwrights Festival National Playwriting Competition Young Playwrights Inc. Dept WEB, 306 West 38th Street #300, New York, NY 10018 or webmaster@youngplaywrights.org

Glossary

A

accent: the emphasis on a syllable, usually in poetry

action verb: a word that tells what action someone or something is performing (*See* linking verb.)

active voice: the voice of a verb whose subject performs an action (*See* passive voice.)

adjective: a word that modifies a noun or pronoun by telling *what kind* or *which one*

adjective clause: a subordinate clause that modifies a noun or pronoun

adjective phrase: a prepositional phrase that modifies a noun or pronoun

adverb: a word that modifies a verb, an adjective, or another adverb

adverb clause: a subordinate clause that modifies a verb, an adjective, an adverb, or a verbal by telling *where, when, in what way, to what extent, under what condition,* or *why*

adverb phrase: a prepositional phrase that modifies a verb, an adjective, or an adverb

allegory: a literary work with two or more levels of meaning—a literal level and one or more symbolic levels

alliteration: the repetition of initial consonant sounds in accented syllables

allusion: an indirect reference to a well-known person, place, event, literary work, or work of art

annotated bibliography: a research writing product that provides a list of materials on a given topic, along with publication information, summaries, or evaluations

apostrophe: a punctuation mark used to form possessive nouns and contractions

appositive: a noun or pronoun placed after another noun or pronoun to identify, rename, or explain the preceding word

appositive phrase: a noun or pronoun with its modifiers, placed next to a noun or pronoun to identify, rename, or explain the preceding word

article: one of three commonly used adjectives: *a, an,* and *the*

assonance: the repetition of vowel sounds in stressed syllables containing dissimilar consonant sounds

audience: the reader(s) a writer intends to reach

autobiographical writing: narrative writing that tells a true story about an important period, experience, or relationship in the writer's life

B

ballad: a song that tells a story (often dealing with adventure or romance) or a poem imitating such a song

bias: the attitudes or beliefs that affect a writer's ability to present a subject objectively

bibliography: a list of the sources of a research paper, including full bibliographic references for each source the writer consulted while conducting research (*See* works-cited list.)

biography: narrative writing that tells the story of an important period, experience, or relationship in a person's life, as reported by another

blueprinting: a prewriting technique in which a writer sketches a map of a home, school, neighborhood, or other meaningful place in order to spark memories or associations for further development

body paragraph: a paragraph in an essay that develops, explains, or supports the key ideas of the writing

brainstorming: a prewriting technique in which a group jots down as many ideas as possible about a given topic

C

case: the form of a noun or pronoun that indicates how it functions in a sentence

cause-and-effect writing: expository writing that examines the relationship between events, explaining how one event or situation causes another

character: a person (though not necessarily a human being) who takes part in the action of a literary work

characterization: the act of creating and developing a character through narration, description, and dialogue

citation: in formal research papers, the acknowledgment of ideas found in outside sources

classical invention: a prewriting technique in which writers gather details about a topic by analyzing the category and subcategories to which the topic belongs

clause: a group of words that has a subject and a verb

climax: the high point of interest or suspense in a literary work

coherence: a quality of written work in which all the parts flow logically from one idea to the next

colon: a punctuation mark used before an extended quotation, explanation, example, or series and after the salutation in a formal letter

comma: a punctuation mark used to separate words or groups of words

comparison-and-contrast writing: expository writing that describes the similarities and differences between two or more subjects in order to achieve a specific purpose

complement: a word or group of words that completes the meaning of a verb

compound sentence: a sentence that contains two or more independent clauses with no subordinate clauses

conclusion: the final paragraph(s) of a work of writing in which the writer may restate a main idea, summarize the points of the writing, or provide a closing remark to end the work effectively (*See* introduction, body paragraph, topical paragraph, functional paragraph.)

conflict: a struggle between opposing forces

conjugation: a list of the singular and plural forms of a verb in a particular tense

conjunction: a word used to connect other words or groups of words

connotation: the emotional associations that a word calls to mind (*See* denotation.)

consonance: the repetition of final consonant sounds in stressed syllables containing dissimilar vowel sounds

contraction: a shortened form of a word or phrase that includes an apostrophe to indicate the position of the missing letter(s)

coordinating conjunctions: words such as *and, but, nor,* and *yet* that connect similar words or groups of words

correlative conjunctions: word pairs such as *neither . . . nor, both . . . and,* and *whether . . . or* used to connect similar words or groups of words

couplet: a pair of rhyming lines written in the same meter

cubing: a prewriting technique in which a writer analyzes a subject from six specified angles: description; association; application; analysis; comparison and contrast; and evaluation

D

declarative sentence: a statement punctuated with a period

demonstrative pronouns: words such as *this, that, these,* and *those* used to single out specific people, places, or things

denotation: the objective meaning of a word; its definition independent of other associations the word calls to mind (*See* connotation.)

depth-charging: a drafting technique in which a writer elaborates on a sentence by developing a key word or idea

description: language or writing that uses sensory details to capture a subject

dialect: the form of a language spoken by people in a particular region or group

dialogue: a direct conversation between characters or people

diary: a personal record of daily events, usually written in prose

diction: a writer's word choice

direct object: a noun or a pronoun that receives the action of a transitive verb

direct quotation: a drafting technique in which writers indicate the exact words of another by enclosing them in quotation marks

documentary: nonfiction film that analyzes news events or another focused subject by combining interviews, film footage, narration, and other audio/visual components

documented essay: research writing that includes a limited number of research sources, providing full documentation parenthetically within the text

drafting: a stage of the writing process that follows prewriting and precedes revising in which a writer gets ideas on paper in a rough format

drama: a story written to be performed by actors and actresses

E

elaboration: a drafting technique in which a writer extends his or her ideas through the use of facts, examples, descriptions, details, or quotations

epic: a long narrative poem about the adventures of a god or a hero

essay: a short nonfiction work about a particular subject

etymology: the history of a word, showing where it came from and how it has evolved into its present spelling and meaning

exclamation mark: a punctuation mark used to indicate strong emotion

exclamatory sentence: a statement that conveys strong emotion and ends with an exclamation mark

exposition: writing to inform, addressing analytic purposes such as problem and solution, comparison and contrast, how-to, and cause and effect

extensive writing: writing products generated for others and from others, meant to be shared with an audience and often done for school assignments (See reflexive writing.)

F

fact: a statement that can be proved true (See opinion.)

fiction: prose writing about imaginary characters and events

figurative language: writing or speech not meant to be interpreted literally

firsthand biography: narrative writing that tells the story of an important period, experience, or relationship in a person's life, reported by a writer who knows the subject personally

five W's: a prewriting technique in which writers gather details about a topic by generating answers to the following questions: *Who? What? Where? When?* and *Why?*

fragment: an incomplete idea punctuated as a complete sentence

freewriting: a prewriting technique in which a writer quickly jots down as many ideas on a topic as possible

functional paragraph: a paragraph that performs a specific role in composition, such as to arouse or sustain interest, to indicate dialogue, to make a transition (See topical paragraph.)

G

generalization: a statement that presents a rule or idea based on particular facts

gerund: a noun formed from the present participle of a verb (ending in *-ing*)

gerund phrase: a group of words containing a gerund and its modifiers or complements that function as a noun

grammar: the study of the forms of words and the way they are arranged in phrases, clauses, and sentences

H

helping verb: a verb added to another verb to make a single verb phrase that indicates the time at which an action takes place or whether it actually happens, could happen, or should happen

hexagonal writing: a prewriting technique in

which a writer analyzes a subject from six angles: literal level, personal allusions, theme, literary devices, literary allusions, and evaluation

homophones: pairs of words that sound the same as each other yet have different meanings and different spellings, such as *hear/here*

how-to writing: expository writing that explains a process by providing step-by-step directions

humanities: forms of artistic expression including, but not limited to, fine art, photography, theater, film, music, and dance

hyperbole: a deliberate exaggeration or overstatement

hyphen: a punctuation mark used to combine numbers and word parts, to join certain compound words, and to show that a word has been broken between syllables at the end of a line

I

I-Search report: a research paper in which the writer addresses the research experience in addition to presenting the information gathered

image: a word or phrase that appeals to one or more of the senses—sight, hearing, touch, taste, or smell

imagery: the descriptive language used to recreate sensory experiences, set a tone, suggest emotions, and guide readers' reactions

imperative sentence: a statement that gives an order or a direction and ends with either a period or an exclamation mark

indefinite pronoun: a word such as *anyone*, *each*, or *many* that refers to a person, place, or thing, without specifying which one

independent clause: a group of words that contains both a subject and a verb and that can stand by itself as a complete sentence

indirect quotation: reporting only the general meaning of what a person said or thought; quotation marks are not needed

infinitive: the form of a verb that comes after the word *to* and acts as a noun, adjective, or adverb

infinitive phrase: a phrase introduced by an infinitive that may be used as a noun, an adjective, or an adverb

interjection: a word or phrase that expresses feeling or emotion and functions independently of a sentence

interrogative pronoun: a word such as *which* and *who* that introduces a question

interrogative sentence: a question that is punctuated with a question mark

interview: an information-gathering technique in which one or more people pose questions to one or more other people who provide opinions or facts on a topic

intransitive verb: an action verb that does not take a direct object (*See* transitive verb.)

introduction: the opening paragraphs of a work of writing in which the writer may capture the readers' attention and present a thesis statement to be developed in the writing (*See* body paragraph, topical paragraph, functional paragraph, conclusion.)

invisible writing: a prewriting technique in which a writer freewrites without looking at the product until the exercise is complete; this can be accomplished at a word processor with the monitor turned off or with carbon paper and an empty ballpoint pen

irony: the general name given to literary techniques that involve surprising, interesting, or amusing contradictions

itemizing: a prewriting technique in which a writer creates a second, more focused, set of ideas based on an original listing activity. (*See* listing.)

J

jargon: the specialized words and phrases unique to a specific field

journal: a notebook or other organized writing system in which daily events and personal impressions are recorded

K

key word: the word or phrase that directs an Internet or database search

L

layering: a drafting technique in which a writer elaborates on a statement by identifying and then expanding upon a central idea or word

lead: the opening sentences of a work of writing meant to grab the reader's interest, accomplished through a variety of methods, including providing an intriguing quotation, a surprising or provocative question or fact, an anecdote, or a description

learning log: a record-keeping system in which a student notes information about new ideas

legend: a widely told story about the past that may or may not be based in fact

legibility: the neatness and readability of words

linking verb: a word that expresses its subject's state of being or condition (*See* action verb.)

listing: a prewriting technique in which a writer prepares a list of ideas related to a specific topic. (*See* itemizing.)

looping: a prewriting activity in which a writer generates follow-up freewriting based on the identification of a key word or central idea in an original freewriting exercise

lyric poem: a poem expressing the observations and feelings of a single speaker

M

main clause: a group of words that has a subject and a verb and can stand alone as a complete sentence

memoir: autobiographical writing that provides an account of a writer's relationship with a person, event, or place

metaphor: a figure of speech in which one thing is spoken of as though it were something else

meter: the rhythmic pattern of a poem

monologue: a speech or performance given entirely by one person or by one character

mood: the feeling created in the reader by a literary work or passage

multimedia presentation: a technique for sharing information with an audience by enhancing narration and explanation with media, including video images, slides, audiotape recordings, music, and fine art

N

narration: writing that tells a story

narrative poem: a poem that tells a story in verse

nominative case: the form of a noun or pronoun used as the subject of a verb, as a predicate nominative, or as the pronoun in a nominative absolute (*See* objective case, possessive case.)

noun: a word that names a person, place, or thing

noun clause: a subordinate clause that acts as a noun

novel: an extended work of fiction that often has a complicated plot, many major and minor characters, a unifying theme, and several settings

O

objective case: the form of a noun or pronoun used as the object of any verb, verbal, or preposition, or as the subject of an infinitive (*See* nominative case, possessive case.)

observation: a prewriting technique involving close visual study of an object; a writing product that reports such a study

ode: a long formal lyric poem with a serious theme

onomatopoeia: words such as *buzz* and *plop* that suggest the sounds they name

open-book test: a form of assessment in which students are permitted to use books and class notes to respond to test questions

opinion: beliefs that can be supported but not proved to be true (*See* fact.)

oral tradition: the body of songs, stories, and poems preserved by being passed from generation to generation by word of mouth

outline: a prewriting or study technique that allows writers or readers to organize the presentation and order of information

oxymoron: a figure of speech that fuses two contradictory or opposing ideas, such as "freezing fire" or "happy grief"

P

parable: a short, simple story from which a moral or religious lesson can be drawn

paradox: a statement that seems to be contradictory but that actually presents a truth

paragraph: a group of sentences that share a common topic or purpose and that focus on a single main idea or thought

parallelism: the placement of equal ideas in words, phrases, or clauses of similar types

paraphrase: restating an author's idea in different words, often to share information by making the meaning clear to readers

parentheses: punctuation marks used to set off asides and explanations when the material is not essential

participial phrase: a group of words made up of a participle and its modifiers and complements that acts as an adjective

participle: a form of a verb that can act as an adjective

passive voice: the voice of a verb whose subject receives an action (*See* active voice.)

peer review: a revising technique in which writers meet with other writers to share focused feedback on a draft

pentad: a prewriting technique in which a writer analyzes a subject from five specified points: actors, acts, scenes, agencies, and purposes

period: a punctuation mark used to end a declarative sentence, an indirect question, and most abbreviations

personal pronoun: a word such as *I, me, you, we, us, he, him, she, her, they,* and *them* that refers to the person speaking; the person spoken to; or the person, place, or thing spoken about

personification a figure of speech in which a nonhuman subject is given human characteristics

persuasion: writing or speaking that attempts to convince others to accept a position on an issue of concern to the writer

phrase: a group of words without a subject and verb that functions as one part of speech

plot: the sequence of events in narrative writing

plural: the form of a word that indicates more than one item is being mentioned

poetry: a category of writing in which the final product may make deliberate use of rhythm, rhyme, and figurative language in order to express deeper feelings than those conveyed in ordinary speech (*See* prose, drama.)

point of view: the perspective, or vantage point, from which a story is told

portfolio: an organized collection of writing projects, including writing ideas, works in progress, final drafts, and the writer's reflections on the work

possessive case: the form of a noun or pronoun used to show ownership (*See* objective case, nominative case.)

prefix: one or more syllables added to the beginning of a word root (*See* root, suffix.)

preposition: a word that relates a noun or pronoun that appears with it to another word in the sentence to indicate relations of time, place, causality, responsibility, and motivation

prepositional phrase: a group of words that includes a preposition and a noun or pronoun

presenting: a stage of the writing process in which a writer shares a final draft with an audience through speaking, listening, or representing activities

prewriting: a stage of the writing process in which writers explore, choose, and narrow a topic and then gather necessary details for drafting

problem-and-solution writing: expository writing that examines a problem and provides a realistic solution

pronoun: a word that stands for a noun or for another word that takes the place of a noun

prose: a category of written language in which the end product is developed through sentences and paragraphs (*See* poetry, drama.)

publishing: a stage of the writing process in which a writer shares the written version of a final draft with an audience

punctuation: the set of symbols used to convey specific directions to the reader

purpose: the specific goal or reason a writer chooses for a writing task

Q

question mark: a punctuation mark used to end an interrogative sentence or an incomplete question

quicklist: a prewriting technique in which a writer creates an impromptu, unresearched list of ideas related to a specific topic

quotation mark: a punctuation mark used to indicate the beginning and end of a person's exact speech or thoughts

R

ratiocination: a systematic approach to the revision process that involves color-coding elements of writing for evaluation

reflective essay: autobiographical writing in which a writer shares a personal experience and then provides insight about the event

reflexive pronoun: a word that ends in *-self* or *-selves* and names the person or thing receiving an action when that person or thing is the same as the one performing the action

reflexive writing: writing generated for oneself and from oneself, not necessarily meant to be shared, in which the writer makes all decisions regarding form and purpose (*See* extensive writing.)

refrain: a regularly repeated line or group of lines in a poem or song

relative pronoun: a pronoun such as *that, which, who, whom,* or *whose* that begins a

subordinate clause and connects it to another idea in the sentence

reporter's formula: a prewriting technique in which writers gather details about a topic by generating answers to the following questions: *Who? What? Where? When?* and *Why?*

research: a prewriting technique in which writers gather information from outside sources such as library reference materials, interviews, and the Internet

research writing: expository writing that presents and interprets information gathered through an extensive study of a subject

response to literature writing: persuasive, expository, or narrative writing that presents a writer's analysis of or reactions to a published work

revising: a stage of the writing process in which a writer reworks a rough draft to improve both form and content

rhyme: the repetition of sounds at the ends of words

rhyme scheme: the regular pattern of rhyming words in a poem or stanza

rhythm: the form or pattern of words or music in which accents or beats come at certain fixed intervals

root: the base of a word (*See* prefix, suffix.)

rubric: an assessment tool, generally organized in a grid, to indicate the range of success or failure according to specific criteria

run-on sentence: two or more complete sentences punctuated incorrectly as one

S

salutation: the greeting in a formal letter

satire: writing that ridicules or holds up to contempt the faults of individuals or of groups

SEE method: an elaboration technique in which a writer presents a statement, an extension, and an elaboration to develop an idea

semicolon: a punctuation mark used to join independent clauses that are not already joined by a conjunction

sentence: a group of words with a subject and a predicate that expresses a complete thought

setting: the time and place of the action of a piece of narrative writing

short story: a brief fictional narrative told in prose

simile: a figure of speech in which *like* or *as* is used to make a comparison between two basically unrelated ideas

sonnet: a fourteen-line lyric poem with a single theme

speaker: the imaginary voice assumed by the writer of a poem

stanza: a group of lines in a poem, seen as a unit

statistics: facts presented in numerical form, such as ratios, percentages, or summaries

subject: the word or group of words in a sentence that tells whom or what the sentence is about

subordinate clause: a group of words containing both a subject and a verb that cannot stand by itself as a complete sentence

subordinating conjunction: a word used to join two complete ideas by making one of the ideas dependent on the other

suffix: one or more syllables added to the end of a word root (*See* prefix, root.)

summary: a brief statement of the main ideas and supporting details presented in a piece of writing

symbol: something that is itself and also stands for something else

T

theme: the central idea, concern, or purpose in a piece of narrative writing, poetry, or drama

thesis statement: a statement of an essay's main idea; all information in the essay supports or elaborates this idea

tone: a writer's attitude toward the readers and toward the subject

topic sentence: a sentence that states the main idea of a paragraph

topic web: a prewriting technique in which a writer generates a graphic organizer to identify categories and subcategories of a topic

topical paragraph: a paragraph that develops, explains, and supports the topic sentence related to an essay's thesis statement

transition: words, phrases, or sentences that smooth writing by indicating the relationship among ideas

transitive verb: an action verb that takes a direct object (*See* intransitive verb.)

U

unity: a quality of written work in which all the parts fit together in a complete, self-contained whole

V

verb: a word or group of words that expresses an action, a condition, or the fact that something exists while indicating the time of the action, condition, or fact

verbal: a word derived from the verb but used as a noun, adjective, or adverb (*See* gerund, infinitive, participle.)

vignette: a brief narrative characterized by precise detail

voice: the distinctive qualities of a writer's style, including diction, attitude, sentence style, and ideas

W

works-cited list: a list of the sources of a research paper, including full bibliographic references for each source named in the body of the paper (*See* bibliography.)

Index

criticizing, 302, 330
deducing, 366, 820, 955
describing, 386, 438, 490, 495,
 502, 510, 569, 570, 610, 666,
 679, 680, 686, 696, 723, 725,
 736, 739, 793
drawing conclusions, 220, 222,
 416, 426, 525
evaluating, 555, 846, 875
generalizing, 143, 267, 289,
 358
hypothesizing, 246, 248
identifying, 567, 588, 597, 605,
 677
inferring, 214, 242, 252, 290,
 382, 392, 428, 700, 706, 805
interpreting, 92, 98, 118, 140, 144,
 148, 210, 306, 341, 480, 800,
 835, 842
making a plan, 297
making connections, 12, 28,
 37, 43, 66, 115, 117, 156, 162,
 164, 170, 187, 212, 342, 348,
 377, 440, 443, 450, 453, 486,
 508, 522, 542, 549, 565, 587,
 588, 597, 600, 613, 642, 671,
 674, 698, 704, 708, 746, 749,
 750, 793, 872, 877
making distinctions, 70, 344,
 584, 647, 649, 652, 658
making generalizations, 289,
 358
making judgments, 90, 279,
 421, 655
reflecting, 100
relating, 132, 240, 251, 308,
 340, 415, 418, 423, 518, 528,
 550
responding, 24, 791
speculating, 2, 39, 221, 223,
 269, 300, 371, 400, 410, 544,
 678, 705, 712, 713, 714, 737,
 824, 837, 868
Cross-Curricular Connections
performing arts, 492
physical education, 505
science, 368, 386, 394, 402,
 412, 426, 440, 501, 548, 574,
 640, 668, 722
social studies, 379, 420, 446,
 458, 468, 480, 483, 488, 510,
 520, 532, 552, 564, 586, 600,
 608, 622, 628, 646, 688, 694,
 712, 736, 745
Cubing, **941**
analyzing by, 17
Cumulative Review
grammar, 476–477
mechanics, 762–763
sentence construction, 476–477
usage, 664–665
Cursive Writing, 918
Cyberspace, **928**

D

Dance, **8**
Dashes
in literature, 738
using, **235, 736–737**
Data, providing, 203
Database, electronic, **928**
Dates
abbreviations for, 159, 690
commas with, **704**
Declarative Sentences, **941**
function of, 480
subjects in, 420–421
Deduction, **833**, 834
Definite Articles, **387**
Definition, in dictionary, 859
Demands, expressing, 549
Demonstrative Adjectives, pronouns as, 388
Demonstrative Pronouns, 374,
 941
Denotation, **137, 803, 941**
checking for, 264
in nonfiction, 835
Depth-Charging, **941**
Derivative, **812**
Derived Words, in dictionary, 859
Description, 98–121
defined, **99, 941**
drafting, 106–107
editing and proofreading, 113
model from literature, 100–101
prewriting, 102–105
publishing and presenting, 114
revising, 108–112
rubric for self-assessment, 114
types of, 99
Descriptive Phrases, using, 111
Desktop-Publishing Software, 9
Details
deleting unnecessary, 336
descriptive, 110
in documented essay, 258
eliminating unnecessary, 259,
 336
kinds of, 335
organizing, 202
in peer review, 234
relating purpose to, 56
for supporting sentences, 35
See also Gathering Details, 110
Dewey Decimal System, 852
Diagnostic Tests
on agreement, 585
for basic sentence parts, 411
capitalization, 667
for effective sentences, 479
for parts of speech, 367
for phrases and clauses, 438
for pronoun usage, 563
punctuation, 687
usage problems, 639

using modifiers, 619
on verb usage, 519
Diagrams, as visual aids, 793
Dialect, **941**
Dialogue, **941**
adding "thought shots" to, 59
in autobiographical writing, 58
in drama, 92
in functional paragraphs, 85
punctuating, 88
quotation marks for, **728**
in short story, 77
Diaries, **941**
reading, 842
Diction, **942**
and writing style, 42
Dictionaries, **856**
electronic, 857
entry words in, 858
foreign words and phrases in,
 732
types of, **856**
understanding entries in, 858
using, 264, 492, 807
Differences, evaluating, 176
different from, **651**
Digerati, **928**
Digressions, eliminating, 317
Directions, capitalizing, **670**
Direct Objects, **426, 942**
examples of, **426–427**
gerund phrases with, 452
gerunds as, 451
infinitives as, 454
noun clauses as, 464
relative pronouns as, 460
Direct Quotations, **265, 722, 942**
Discussions
group, 209, 876
of problem-and-solution essay,
 236
and vocabulary development,
 801
Documentaries, **212, 861, 942**
making, 212
television, 789
Document-Based Writing
 Prompts, responding to, 272–
 273
Documented Essay, 246–273, **942**
defined, **247**
drafting, 257–258
editing and proofreading, 265
model from literature, 248–251
prewriting, 252–256
publishing and presenting, 266
revising, 259–264
rubric for self-assessment, 266
types of, **247**
doesn't, **651**
Dominant Impression, creating,
 108
done, **651**

Index • 959

962

Acknowledgments

Staff Credits
The people who made up the *Prentice Hall Writing and Grammar: Communication in Action* team—representing design services, editorial, editorial services, electronic publishing technology, manufacturing & inventory planning, marketing, marketing services, market research, on-line services & multimedia development, product planning, production services, project office, and publishing processes—are listed below. Bold type denotes the core team members.

Ellen Backstrom, Betsy Bostwick, Evonne Burgess, **Louise B. Capuano**, **Sarah Carroll**, **Megan Chill**, Katherine Clarke, Rhett Conklin, Martha Conway, Harold Crudup, **Harold Delmonte**, Libby Forsyth, Maggie Fritz, Ellen Goldblatt, Elaine Goldman, Jonathan Goldson, **Rebecca Graziano**, **Diana Hahn**, Rick Hickox, Kristan Hoskins, Raegan Keida, Carol Lavis, **George Lychock**, **Gregory Lynch**, William McAllister, Loretta Moser, Margaret Plotkin, Maureen Raymond, Gerry Schrenk, **Melissa Shustyk**, Annette Simmons, Robin Sullivan, Julie Tomasella, **Elizabeth Torjussen**, **Doug Utigard**

Additional Credits
Ernie Albanese, Diane Alimena, Susan Andariese, Michele Angelucci, Penny Baker, Susan Barnes, John Carle, Cynthia Clampitt, Ken Dougherty, Angelo Focaccia, Kathy Gavilanes, Beth Geschwind, Michael Goodman, Jennifer Harper, Evan Holstrom, Leanne Korszoloski, Sue Langan, Rebecca Lauth, Dave Liston, Maria Keogh, Vicki Menanteaux, Gail Meyer, Artur Mkrtchyan, LaShonda Morris, Karyl Murray, Omni-Photo Communications, Kim Ortell, Brenda Sanabria, Carolyn Sapontzis, Mildred Schulte, Slip Jig Image Research Services, Sunnyside, NY, Debi Taffet

Grateful acknowledgment is made to the following for permission to reprint copyrighted material:

Eavan Boland
Excerpt from "Meanings" by Eavan Boland. Reprinted by permission of the author.

Don Congdon Associates, Inc.
"Warding Off Wildlife" from *The Practical Gardener: A Guide to Breaking New Ground* by Roger B. Swain. Copyright © 1989 by Roger B. Swain. Reprinted by permission of Don Congdon Associates, Inc.

James Gorman
"Man, Bytes, Dog." Copyright © 1984 by James Gorman. Originally published in *The New Yorker*.

HarperCollins Publishers, Inc.
"Global Language" from *The Mother Tongue* by Bill Bryson. Copyright © 1990 by Bill Bryson. Excerpt from *An American Childhood* by Annie Dillard. Copyright © 1987 by Annie Dillard. Both selections reprinted by permission of HarperCollins Publishers, Inc.

Matthew Kachur
Excerpt from "The Debate Over Football at the Turn of the Century" from *Brutal Outrage or Healthy Exercise* by Matthew Kachur. Reprinted by permission of the author.

Pantheon Books
"The Man Who Shouted Teresa" from *Numbers in the Dark* by Italo Calvino. English translation copyright © 1995 by Tim Parks. Reprinted by permission of Pantheon Books, a division of Random House, Inc.

The Poynter Institute
"Snow Dance," Leann Goree (student model). The Poynter Institute, St. Petersburg, FL.

Viking Penguin
"Blindness," translated by Eliot Weinberger, from *Selected Non-Fictions* by Jorge Luis Borges, edited by Eliot Weinberger. Copyright © 1999 by Maria Kodama; translation copyright © 1999 by Penguin Putnam Inc. Used by permission of Viking Penguin, a division of Penguin Putnam Inc.

W. W. Norton & Company, Inc
"Miracle on Thirty-Fourth Street" from *Why Buildings Fall Down* by Matthys Levy and Mario Salvadori. Copyright © 1992 by Matthys Levy and Mario Salvadori. Used by permission of W. W. Norton & Company, Inc.

Note: Every effort has been made to locate the copyright owner of material reprinted in this book. Omissions brought to our attention will be corrected in subsequent editions.

The program authors would like to acknowledge the work of the following writers whose ideas have influenced the writing strategies presented in this series.

Brock, Paula. "Help Me, Quick." *R&E Journal 2* (1998): 14–16.

Burke, Kenneth. *A Grammar of Motives.* Berkeley: University of California Press, 1969.

Cooper, Charles R., and Lee Odell. *Evaluating Writing: Describing, Measuring, Judging.* Urbana, IL: National Council of Teachers of English, 1977.

Corbett, Edward P. J., and Robert J. Connors. *Classical Rhetoric for the Modern Student.* New York: Oxford University Press, Inc., 1998.

Cowan, Gregory, and Elizabeth Swan. *Writing.* New York: John Wiley, 1980.

Elbow, Peter. *Writing Without Teachers.* New York: Oxford University Press, 1973.

Emig, Janet. *The Composing Process of Twelfth Graders.* Urbana, IL: National Council of Teachers of English, 1971.

Lane, Barry. *After the End: Teaching and Learning Creative Revision.* Portsmouth, NH: Heinemann Educational Books, Inc., 1993.

Rico, Gabriele Lusser. *Writing the Natural Way.* Los Angeles: J. P. Tarcher, 1983.

Reif, Linda. *Seeking Diversity.* Portsmouth, NH: Heinemann Educational Books, 1992.

Stillman, Peter R. *Families Writing.* Cincinnati, OH: Writer's Digest Books, 1989.